NOTE TO STUDENTS

LEARNING AID

Make reviewing a snap! Put marketing concepts to work! A comprehensive study guide, entitled *Learning Aid for Use with Basic Marketing*, Twelfth Edition by William D. Perreault, Jr. and E. Jerome McCarthy, is available from your campus bookstore.

It's specially designed for this text and puts key chapter material at your fingertips. Sample exam questions, additional new computer-aided problems, and interesting application exercises make your study time count.

Check your campus bookstore or ask the manager to place an order today.

APPLICATIONS IN BASIC MARKETING

A free book offered in annual editions—*Applications in Basic Marketing*, by William D. Perreault, Jr. and E. Jerome McCarthy, is shrinkwrapped with all *new* texts. It features clippings from the popular business press. Separate copies may be purchased through your local campus bookstore.

About the Authors

of **Basic Marketing,** *Twelfth Edition*

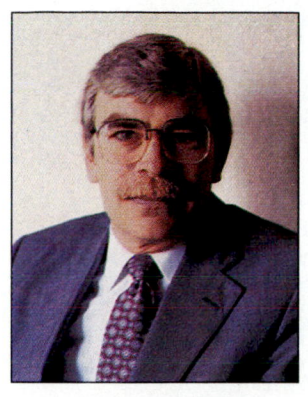

William D. Perreault, Jr., is currently Kenan Professor at the University of North Carolina Kenan-Flagler Business School and President of the American Marketing Association Academic Council. He has taught at the University of Georgia, North Carolina State University, and Stanford University. At UNC, he has twice received awards for teaching excellence. In 1987, the Decision Sciences Institute recognized him for innovations in marketing education, and *Ad Week* magazine has profiled him as one of the "10 best young marketing professors in America." In 1995, The Academy of Marketing Science recognized him with its Outstanding Educator Award.

Dr. Perreault is a well-known author, and his ideas about marketing management, marketing research, and marketing education have been published in many journals. He is a past editor of the *Journal of Marketing Research* and has served on the review board of the *Journal of Marketing* and other publications. In 1985, he received the American Marketing Association's prestigious William O'Dell Award, which recognizes long-run contributions to marketing research.

Dr. Perreault serves on the board of directors of the AMA and was previously AMA's VP-Publications. He has been chair of an advisory committee to the U.S. Bureau of the Census and a trustee of the Marketing Science Institute. He has also worked as a marketing consultant to many organizations, including IBM, GE, Whirlpool, Southwestern Bell, the Federal Trade Commission, and a variety of wholesale and retail firms. He is currently on the advisory board for Copernicus: The Marketing Investment Strategy Group. He has served as an advisor evaluating educational programs for the U.S. Department of Education, the Venezuelan Ministry of Education, and the American Assembly of Collegiate Schools of Business.

E. Jerome McCarthy received his Ph.D. from the University of Minnesota in 1958. Since then he has taught at the Universities of Oregon, Notre Dame, and Michigan State. He has been deeply involved in teaching and developing new teaching materials. Besides writing various articles and monographs, he is the author of textbooks on data processing and social issues in marketing.

Dr. McCarthy is active in making presentations to academic conferences and business meetings. He has worked with groups of teachers throughout the country and has addressed international conferences in South America, Africa, and India.

Dr. McCarthy received the American Marketing Association's Trailblazer Award in 1987, and he was voted one of the top five leaders in Marketing Thought by marketing educators. He was also a Ford Foundation Fellow in 1963–64, studying the role of marketing in global economic development. In 1959–60 he was a Ford Foundation Fellow at the Harvard Business School working on mathematical methods in marketing.

Besides his academic interests, Dr. McCarthy is involved in consulting for, and guiding the growth of, a number of businesses—both in the U.S. and overseas. He has worked with top managers from Steelcase, Dow Chemical, 3M, Bemis, Grupo Industrial Alfa, and many other large and small companies. He is also active in executive education and is a director of several organizations. His primary interests, however, are in (1) "converting" students to marketing and marketing strategy planning and (2) preparing teaching materials to help others do the same. This is why he has continued to spend a large part of his time revising and improving marketing texts. This is a continuing process, and the 12th edition of *Basic Marketing* incorporates the latest thinking in the field.

The IRWIN Series in Marketing

Twelfth Edition

Basic
Marketing

A Global-Managerial Approach

William D. Perreault, Jr., Ph.D.
University of North Carolina

E. Jerome McCarthy, Ph.D.
Michigan State University

Chicago·Bogotá·Boston·Buenos Aires·Caracas
London·Madrid·Mexico City·Sydney·Toronto

Irwin Book Team

Senior sponsoring editor: Stephen M. Patterson
Coordinating editor: Linda G. Davis
Senior developmental editor: Nancy Barbour
Marketing manager: Colleen Suljic
Project editor: Amy E. Lund
Production supervisor: Laurie Kersch
Assistant manager, desktop services: Jon Christopher
Designer: Keith McPherson
Cover illustrator: Comunigrafix, Inc.
Interior illustrator: Carlisle Communications, Ltd.
Photo separations: CR Waldman
Assistant manager, graphics: Charlene R. Breeden
Graphics supervisor: Heather D. Burbridge
Compositor: Carlisle Communications, Ltd.
Typeface: 10.5/12 Goudy
Printer: Von Hoffmann Press, Inc.

**Times Mirror
Higher Education Group**

Library of Congress Cataloging-in-Publication Data

McCarthy, E. Jerome (Edmund Jerome)
    Basic marketing : a global managerial approach / E. Jerome
McCarthy, William D. Perreault.—12th ed.
        p.   cm.—(The Irwin series in marketing)
    Includes bibliographical references and index.
    ISBN 0-256-13990-3
    1. Marketing—Management. I. Perreault, William D. II. Title.
III. Series.
HF5415.13.M369   1996
858.8—dc20   95–34965

Printed in the United States of America

1 2 3 4 5 6 7 8 9 0 VH 2 1 0 9 8 7 6 5

Preface

Basic Marketing satisfies customers' needs

Every organization needs to think about its markets and how effectively it meets its customers' or clients' needs. Organizations that don't satisfy their customers sooner or later disappear—and usually it's sooner rather than later. Conversely, organizations that find new and better ways to meet needs prosper and grow. Trust us on this: It's better to prosper than to fail and disappear.

So, there's hardly any issue that's more important than figuring out how to satisfy customers—whether old ones an organization has served in the past or new ones it hopes to attract. At its essence, that's what marketing and marketing strategy planning is all about. And, yes, it's also what this book is all about.

Further, we believe in practicing what we preach. So, you can bank on the fact that this new 12th edition of *Basic Marketing* and all of the other teaching and learning materials that accompany it will satisfy *your* needs. We're excited about this edition, and we hope that you will be as well.

In creating this edition we've made hundreds of big and small additions, changes, and improvements. We'll highlight some of those changes in this preface, but first it's useful to put this newest edition in a longer-term perspective.

Building on pioneering strengths

Basic Marketing pioneered an innovative structure—using the "four Ps" with a managerial approach—for the introductory marketing course. It quickly became one of the most widely used business textbooks ever published because it organized marketing ideas so that readers could both understand and apply them. It didn't settle for endless lists or disjointed description.

It has been 37 years since publication of the first edition of *Basic Marketing*. During that time there have been constant changes in marketing management. Some of the changes have been dramatic, and others have been subtle. Throughout all of these changes, *Basic Marketing* and the supporting materials that accompany it have been more widely used than any other teaching materials for introductory marketing. It is gratifying that the "four Ps" has proved to be an organizing structure that has worked well for *millions* of students and teachers.

Continuous innovation and improvement

Of course, this position of leadership is not the result of a single strength—or one long-lasting innovation. Rather, the text's four Ps framework, managerial orientation, and strategy planning focus have proved to be foundation pillars that are remarkably robust and powerful in supporting and encompassing new developments in the field.

Thus, with each new edition of *Basic Marketing*, we have continued to introduce innovations—and to better meet the needs of students and faculty. Our objective is to provide a flexible, high-quality text and choices from comprehensive and reliable support materials—so that instructors and students can accomplish their learning objectives. For example, included with the other innovations for this new edition are:

- Completely integrated coverage of the role of marketing in building relationships.

- A new chapter on marketing's link with other functional areas.
- Integrative video cases.
- Multimedia electronic slides and related lecture materials.
- CD-ROM technology to support multimedia teaching and learning.
- Powerful new versions of our Hypertext reference disk and computer-aided problems software.

And a symbolic change too

Another change in this edition is that we've shifted the order of the authors' names on the cover of the book. Many people who knew we planned to do that have asked why, so we'll mention it here in case other old friends and users of the text are also curious. When McCarthy wrote the first edition of *Basic Marketing*, he did it alone and when he was still in his early 20s. He was responsible for seven editions of the book before Perreault, at age 32, joined the project. Our long-term plan has always been for the "newcomer" to take over the bulk of the work of actually incorporating new innovations to the text and supplements—after we worked together very closely for a number of editions to maximize the impact of our joint efforts. As this transition has evolved, the senior partner has taken on more of a "Chairman of the Board" role—providing valuable ideas, advice, criticisms, and encouragement. Thus, the change in the masthead of the book is simply symbolic of the shift in our *current* contributions to the ongoing improvements in the book and package.

We believe in continuous quality improvement

We formed our partnership with a shared commitment to ongoing improvements, and we're both proud that we were implementing continuous quality improvements in preparing *Basic Marketing* long before the idea became popular in the world of business. Useful teaching innovations are ones that meet students' and instructors' needs well—and you can be confident that's what this innovative edition will accomplish. We work to be creative in our coverage and approaches—because creativity is at the heart of the marketing spirit. That's also why our first priority has always been—and always will be—producing quality materials that work for students and teachers as they should.

As with many other product categories, too many books come out that don't do that. It's said that the cost of poor quality is lost customers—and that's why poor quality texts routinely disappear from print. Yet, the real cost of poor quality texts is more insidious. Students only take the first marketing course once. If their only exposure is to a poor quality text, the cost is their lost learning—or worse. We see that as a totally unacceptable cost, and it's why we see it as a personal responsibility to build quality into every aspect of the text and accompanying package.

Our belief that attention to continuous quality improvement in every aspect of the text and support materials *does make a difference* is consistently reaffirmed by the enthusiastic response of students and teachers alike to each new edition.

Critically revised, updated, and rewritten

We believe that the 12th edition of *Basic Marketing* is the highest-quality teaching and learning resource ever published for the introductory marketing course. The whole text and all of the supporting materials have been critically revised, updated, and rewritten. As in past editions, clear and interesting communication has been a priority. *Basic Marketing* is designed to make it easy, interesting, and fast for students to grasp the key concepts of marketing. Careful explanations provide a crisp focus on the important "basics" of marketing strategy planning. At the same time, we have thoroughly:

- Researched and incorporated new concepts.
- Integrated hundreds of new examples that bring the concepts alive.
- Illustrated marketing ideas in a wide variety of contexts.

We have deliberately used marketing examples from a host of different contexts. Examples span profit and nonprofit organizations, large and small firms, domestic and international settings, purchases by organizations as well as by final consumers, and services and ideas or "causes" as well as physical goods, established products, and new technologies—because this variety reinforces the point that effective marketing is critical to all organizations.

Clear focus on changes in today's dynamic markets

The 12th edition focuses special attention on changes taking place in today's dynamic markets. *Throughout every chapter of the text* we have integrated discussion and examples of:

- Relationship building in marketing.
- The importance of customer satisfaction and retention.
- International perspectives.
- Ethical issues.

Similarly, we've also integrated new material on such important and fast-evolving topics as:

- Integrated marketing communications, including direct-response promotion.
- The expanding role of information technologies in all areas of marketing.
- Return on quality and quality management (with special emphasis on service quality).
- The increasing channel power of large retail chains.
- Competitor analysis.
- Marketing control, including marketing cost analysis, to name but a sampling.

Throughout the 12th edition we've continued our thrust begun in the 11th edition of focusing more attention on the importance of competitive advantage in strategy planning. You'll learn about the changing relationships among marketing partners—ranging from coordination of logistics and promotion efforts among firms to the new relationships between firms and their ad agencies and marketing research suppliers. You'll see how intense competition—both in the United States and around the world—is affecting marketing strategy planning. You'll see why rapid response in new-product development is so critical.

Some other marketing texts are attempting to describe such changes. But that's not adequate. What sets *Basic Marketing* apart is that the explanations and examples not only highlight the changes that are taking place today but also equip students to see *why* these changes are taking place—and what changes to expect in the future. That is an important distinction—because marketing is dynamic. Our objective is to equip students to analyze marketing situations and develop workable marketing strategies—not just recite an endless set of lists.

A fresh design—to make important concepts even clearer

Along with the new content, we've given the text a fresh design. The changes range from the new cover to hundreds of new photographs, ads, and illustrations. We've added new artwork and revised or updated proven pieces from past editions.

The aim of all this revising, refining, editing, and illustrating is to arrive at an overall redesign that makes important concepts and points even clearer to students. We want to make sure that each student really does get a good feel for a market-directed system and how he or she can help it—and some company—run better. We believe marketing is important and interesting—and we want every student who reads *Basic Marketing* to share our enthusiasm.

22 chapters—with an emphasis on marketing strategy planning

The emphasis of *Basic Marketing* is on marketing strategy planning. Twenty-two chapters introduce the important concepts in marketing management and help the student see marketing through the eyes of the marketing manager. The organization of the chapters and topics is carefully planned. But we took special care in writing so that:

- It is possible to rearrange and use the chapters in many different sequences—to fit different needs.
- All of the topics and chapters fit together into a clear, overall framework for marketing strategy planning.

The first two chapters deal with the nature of marketing—focusing both on its macro role in a global society and its micro role in businesses and other organizations. The first chapter stresses that the effectiveness of our macro-marketing system depends on the decisions of many producers and consumers. That sets the stage for the second chapter—and the rest of the book—which focus on how business people and, in particular, marketing managers develop marketing strategies to satisfy specific target markets.

Chapter 3 introduces a strategic planning view of how managers can find new market opportunities. The emphasis is on identifying target markets with market segmentation and positioning approaches. This strategic view alerts students to the importance of evaluating opportunities in the external environments affecting marketing—and these are discussed in Chapter 4. Chapter 5 is a contemporary view of getting information—from marketing information systems and marketing research—for marketing management planning. This chapter sets the stage for discussions in later chapters about how research and information systems can improve each area of marketing strategy planning.

The next three chapters take a closer look at *customers*—so students will better understand how to segment markets and satisfy target market needs. Chapter 6 introduces the demographic dimensions of the global consumer market, and the next two chapters study the behavioral features of the consumer market and how business and organizational customers—like manufacturers, channel members, and government purchasers—are similar to and different from final consumers.

The next group of chapters—Chapters 9 to 18—is concerned with developing a marketing mix out of the four Ps: Product, Place (involving channels of distribution, logistics, and distribution customer service), Promotion, and Price. These chapters are concerned with developing the "right" Product and making it available at the "right" Place with the "right" Promotion and the "right"

Price—to satisfy target customers and still meet the objectives of the business. These chapters are presented in an integrated, analytical way, so students' thinking about planning marketing strategies develops logically.

Chapters 9 and 10 focus on product planning for goods and services as well as new-product development and the different strategy decisions that are required at different stages of the product life cycle.

Chapters 11 through 13 focus on Place. Chapter 11 introduces channels of distribution, with special emphasis on the need for channel members to cooperate and coordinate to better meet the needs of customers. Chapter 12 focuses on the fast-changing arena of logistics and the strides that firms are making to reduce the costs of storing and transporting products while improving the distribution service they provide customers. Chapter 13 provides a clear picture of retailers, wholesalers, and their strategy planning. This new composite chapter helps students see why the big changes taking place in retailing are reshaping the channel systems for many consumer products.

Chapters 14 to 16 deal with Promotion. These chapters have been significantly reworked to build on the concept of integrated marketing communications, including direct-response promotion, which is introduced in Chapter 14. Then, Chapter 15 deals with the role of personal selling in the promotion blend, and Chapter 16 covers advertising and sales promotion.

Chapters 17 and 18 deal with Price. Chapter 17 focuses on pricing objectives and policies, including consideration of pricing in the channel and the use of discounts, allowances, and other variations from a list price. Chapter 18 covers cost-oriented and demand-oriented pricing approaches. Its careful coverage of marketing costs helps equip students to deal with the cost-conscious firms they will join.

Chapter 19 reinforces the integrative nature of marketing management and offers a specific framework for creating innovative marketing plans and programs. Chapter 20 offers completely updated coverage of marketing implementation and control and provides perspective on how new approaches are reshaping these areas now that more control-related information is available faster. The chapter also details how total quality management approaches can improve implementation, including implementation of better customer service.

Chapter 21 is a totally new chapter dealing with the link between marketing and other functional areas. The marketing concept says that people in an organization should work together to satisfy customers at a profit. No other text has a chapter that explains how to accomplish the "working together" part of that idea. Yet, it's increasingly important in the business world today, and that's what this important new chapter is designed to explore.

The final chapter considers how efficient the marketing process is. Here we evaluate the effectiveness of both micro- and macro-marketing—and consider the competitive, ethical, and social challenges facing marketing managers now and in the future. After this chapter, the student might want to look at Appendix C—which is about career opportunities in marketing.

Careful integration of special topics

Some textbooks treat "special" topics—like relationship marketing, international marketing, services marketing, marketing for nonprofit organizations, marketing ethics, and business-to-business marketing—in separate chapters. We have deliberately avoided doing that because we are convinced that treating such topics separately leads to an unfortunate compartmentalization of ideas. We think they are *too important to be isolated in that way.* Instead, they are interwoven and illustrated throughout the text to emphasize that marketing thinking is crucial in all aspects of our society and economy. Instructor examination copies of the new edition are packaged with a grid that shows, in detail, how and where specific topics are integrated throughout the text.

Students get "how-to-do-it" skill and confidence

Really understanding marketing and how to plan marketing strategies can build self-confidence—and it can help prepare a student to take an active part in the business world. To move students in this direction, we deliberately include a variety of frameworks, models, classification systems, and "how-to-do-it" techniques that should speed the development of "marketing sense"—and enable the student to analyze marketing situations in a confident and meaningful way. Taken seriously, they are practical and they work. In addition, because they are interesting and understandable, they equip students to see marketing as the challenging and rewarding area it is.

Basic Marketing motivates high-involvement learning

So students will see what is coming in each *Basic Marketing* chapter, behavioral objectives are included on the first page of each chapter. And to speed student understanding, important new terms are shown in red and defined immediately. Further, a glossary of these terms is presented at the end of the book. Within chapters, major section headings and second-level headings (placed in the margin for clarity) immediately show how the material is organized *and* summarize key points in the text. Further, we have placed annotated photos and ads near the concepts they illustrate to provide a visual reminder of the ideas—and to show vividly how they apply in the business world. All of these aids help the student understand important concepts—and speed review before exams. End-of-chapter questions and problems offer additional opportunities. They can be used to encourage students to investigate the marketing process and develop their own ways of thinking about it. They can also be used for independent study or as a basis for written assignments or class discussion.

Varied types of cases

Understanding of the text material can be deepened by analysis and discussion of specific cases. *Basic Marketing* features several different types of cases. Each chapter starts with an in-depth case study developed specifically to highlight that chapter's teaching objectives. In addition, each chapter features a special case report in a highlighted box. Each case illustrates how a particular company has developed its marketing strategy—with emphasis on topics covered in that chapter. All of these cases provide an excellent basis for critical evaluation and discussion.

In addition, there are several suggested cases at the end of each chapter. The focus of these cases is on problem solving. They encourage students to apply—and really get involved with—the concepts developed in the text. Each chapter also features a computer-aided problem. These case-based exercises stimulate a problem-solving approach to marketing strategy planning—and give students hands-on experience that shows how logical analysis of alternative strategies can lead to improved decision making. For the convenience of students and faculty alike, the cases for computer-aided problems are now incorporated in the book itself. Further, the award-winning software we developed specifically for use with these problems is provided free to instructors in two versions: the classic DOS version and a new Windows version.

New multimedia video cases are integrative

New for this edition, we've also custom developed an exciting set of video cases. Each of these combines a written case with an accompanying video. These cases are a bit longer than the text-only cases, which opens up the opportunity for students to analyze an organization's whole marketing program in more depth and with even greater integration. Marketing professors wrote the scripts for both the video and text portions of the cases—so that the videos reinforce real content while bringing a high-involvement multimedia dimension to the learning opportunity. And to ensure consistency with all of the other *Basic Marketing* materials, we've carefully edited and coordinated the whole effort. These cases deal with a variety of issues:

- Services marketing and integrated marketing communications in a hospital setting.
- The expanding role of marketing in developing export opportunities for a raw material that was previously just viewed as a commodity.
- New-product development for a major component part that is sold to producers who serve consumer markets.
- The growth strategy of a chain of franchised and company-owned restaurants in a highly competitive market.
- How a well-known company lost touch with its market and then won profits and customer loyalty by developing a marketing mix that's carefully matched to the needs of its target market.

We designed these cases so that students can analyze them before or after seeing the video, or even without seeing the video at all. They can be used in a variety of ways, either for class discussion or individual assignments. We're proud of these new video cases, and we're sure that they provide you with a valuable new way to learn about marketing.

Comprehensive, current references for independent study

Some professors and students want to follow up on text readings. Each chapter is supplemented with detailed references—to both classic articles and current readings in business publications. These can guide more detailed study of the topics covered in a chapter.

Instructor creates a system—with our P.L.U.S.

Basic Marketing can be studied and used in many ways—the *Basic Marketing* text material is only the central component of a *Professional Learning Units System* (our *P.L.U.S*) for students and teachers. Instructors (and students) can select from our units to develop their own personalized systems. Many combinations of units are possible—depending on course objectives. As a quick overview, in addition to the *Basic Marketing* text, the *P.L.U.S.* package includes several *totally new supplements*:

- *CD-ROM multimedia system*.
- *Electronic presentation slides* built with Microsoft's PowerPoint software.
- Videotapes for the video cases.
- *Windows software* for the computer-aided problems.
- A new *Multimedia Lecture Support Package*, including software.

And that's just what's totally new. In addition, we've *completely revised and updated*:

- The *Learning Aid* workbook.
- *Applications in Basic Marketing*, an annually updated book of marketing clippings from the popular press, free and shrinkwrapped with the text.
- The *Hypertext Reference Disk*, with a new interface for developing marketing plans.
- Over 200 color acetates.
- Over 200 transparency masters.
- The classic DOS version of the P.L.U.S. Computer-Aided Problems Software.
- *Instructor's Manual*.
- Author-prepared *Manual of Tests*.
- *Computest III* test-generator system (and Teletest).
- 18 new and updated *teaching videos* (and Instructor's Manual).
- A new edition of *The Marketing Game!* (and Instructor's Manual).

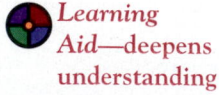 **Hypertext—a marketing knowledge navigator**

We introduced the innovative *Basic Marketing Hypertext Reference Disk* with the 11th edition of *Basic Marketing*. This easy-to-use software puts almost all of the key concepts from *Basic Marketing* at your fingertips. It features hyperlinks, which means that when you are reading about a concept on screen you can instantly jump to more detail on any topic. You simply highlight the concept or topic and click with a mouse or press the enter key. Books assemble information in some specific order—but hypertext allows you to integrate thinking on any topic or combination of topics, regardless of where it is treated in the text.

Based on suggestions from users, the new version of the software provides a clearer and easier way to search for ideas while developing a marketing plan. You can also use the software to review topics in "book order"—starting with learning objectives and then "paging" through each set of ideas.

We are convinced that this new version of the Hypertext Reference Disk is a step toward reshaping how people learn about and use marketing concepts. It brings new technology to making the concepts in *Basic Marketing* even more accessible, and no other text offers anything like it.

Free applications book—updated each year

It is a sign of the commitment of our publisher to the introductory marketing course that it will publish a new edition of *Applications in Basic Marketing* every year and provide it *free of charge* shrinkwrapped with each new copy of the 12th edition of *Basic Marketing!* This annually updated collection of marketing "clippings"—from publications such as *The Wall Street Journal*, *Advertising Age*, *Fortune*, and *Business Week*—provides convenient access to short, interesting, and current discussions of marketing issues. Each edition features about 100 articles. There are a variety of short clippings related to each chapter in *Basic Marketing*. In addition, because we revise this collection *each year*, it includes timely material that is available in no other text.

Learning Aid—deepens understanding

There are more components to P.L.U.S. A separate *Learning Aid* provides several more units and offers further opportunities to obtain a deeper understanding of the material. The *Learning Aid* can be used by the student alone or with teacher direction. Portions of the *Learning Aid* help students to review what they have studied. For example, there is a brief introduction to each chapter, a list of the important new terms (with page numbers for easy reference), true-false questions (with answers and page numbers) that cover *all* the important terms and concepts, and multiple-choice questions (with answers) that illustrate the kinds of questions that may appear in examinations. In addition, the *Learning Aid* has cases, exercises, and problems—with clear instructions and worksheets for the student to complete.

The *Learning Aid* also features computer-aided problems that build on the computer-aided cases in the text. The *Learning Aid* exercises can be used as classwork or homework—to drill on certain topics and to deepen understanding of others by motivating application and then discussion. In fact, reading *Basic Marketing* and working with the *Learning Aid* can be the basic activity of the course.

Compete and learn—with new edition of *The Marketing Game!*

Another valuable resource is *The Marketing Game! The Marketing Game!* is a microcomputer-based competitive simulation. It was developed specifically to reinforce the target marketing and marketing strategy planning ideas discussed in *Basic Marketing*. Students make marketing management decisions—blending the four Ps to compete for the business of different possible target markets. The innovative design of *The Marketing Game!* allows the instructor to increase the number of decision areas involved as students learn more about marketing. In fact, many instructors use the advanced levels of the game as the basis for a second course. *The Marketing Game!* is widely heralded as the best marketing simulation available—and the new edition widens its lead over the others available.

Author-developed instructor materials

Basic Marketing—and all of our accompanying materials—have been developed to promote student learning and get students involved in the excitement and challenges of marketing management. Additional elements of *P.L.U.S.* have been specifically developed to help an instructor offer a truly professional course that meets the objectives he or she sets for students. Complete Instructor's Manuals accompany all of the *P.L.U.S.* components.

Electronic presentation slides with many uses

With this edition we are providing instructors with a copy of innovative electronic slide presentation software based on Microsoft's popular PowerPoint program. This flexible package features PowerPoint graphics developed for every chapter in the text. An instructor can use the provided software to display the electronic slides with a computer-controlled video projector, in the order that they're provided or branching in whatever sequence is desired. Presentations can be based on composite slides, or the points on a slide can "build up" one point at a time.

Because we provide the input files, instructors can modify any slide or add other slides by using their own copy of PowerPoint. And, of course, if electronic projection equipment isn't available the instructor can print out the images to their own customized color acetates or black and white transparencies.

While the electronic slides are intended mainly for instructor use in class discussions and lectures, they are easy to use and can be placed on a school's computer network or in a computer lab as a supplement for independent review by students.

Complete multimedia lecture support

With the electronic slide software we also provide detailed lecture notes, as well as lecture outlines with miniature versions of the presentation slides that an instructor can use as handouts in class. All of these materials are packaged in a new supplement, our *Multimedia Lecture Support Package*. This supplement gives instructors a great deal of flexibility and saves time that can be spent on other teaching activities. Instructors who prefer to use materials like those that were in the past included with our *Lecture Guide* won't be disappointed either. The new package will provide that material as well—in both printed form and as word processing files (which make it easier for instructors to incorporate their own materials).

In addition, the *Multimedia Lecture Support Package* is accompanied by a high-quality selection of overhead masters and color transparencies—over 400 in all. The manual provides detailed suggestions about ways to use them.

Exciting new videos—created by marketing experts

The newly revised and expanded *Basic Marketing Videos* are also available to all schools that adopt *Basic Marketing*. Half of the video modules are completely new—based on scripts written by expert marketing scholars and carefully linked to key topics in the text. In addition, several of the most popular video modules from the previous edition—the ones instructors and students said they most wanted to keep—have been thoroughly revised and updated. These new videos are really great, but it doesn't stop there! As we noted earlier, there are also five great new videos to accompany the video cases.

CD-ROM—supports multimedia teaching and learning

New with this edition, we are also introducing the *Basic Marketing CD-ROM*, which provides exciting new opportunities for marketing faculty to take advantage of the latest advances in multimedia teaching and learning. Our CD-ROM provides easy and instantaneous access—in one convenient place—not only to the various software packages that accompany the text—but also to electronic versions of all of the instructor's manuals and much of the material in this book.

Testing that works for faculty and students

In addition, thousands of objective test questions—*written by the authors* to really work with the text—give instructors a high-quality resource. The COM-PUTEST III program for microcomputers allows the instructor to select from any of these questions, change them as desired, or add new questions—and quickly print out a finished test customized to the instructor's course.

The responsibilities of leadership

In closing, we return to a point raised at the beginning of this preface. *Basic Marketing* has been a leading textbook in marketing since its first edition. We take the responsibilities of that leadership seriously. We know that you want and deserve the very best teaching and learning materials possible. It is our commitment to bring you those materials—today with this edition and in the future with subsequent editions.

We recognize that fulfilling this commitment requires a process of continuous improvement. Improvements, changes, and development of new elements must be ongoing—because needs change. You are an important part of this evolution, of this leadership. We encourage your feedback. Thoughtful criticisms and suggestions from students and teachers alike have helped to make *Basic Marketing* what it is. We hope that you will help make it what it will be in the future.

William D. Perreault, Jr.
E. Jerome McCarthy

Acknowledgments

Planning and preparing this revision of *Basic Marketing* has been a consuming, three-year effort. The resulting text—and all of the teaching and learning materials that accompany it—represents a blending of our career-long experiences, influenced and improved by the inputs of more people than it is possible to list.

We are especially grateful to our many students who have criticized and made comments about materials in *Basic Marketing*. Indeed, in many ways, our students have been our best teachers.

We owe a special debt of gratitude to Linda G. Davis. For nearly a decade she has made contributions to every aspect of the text and package. She spent countless hours researching photos and case histories, and she critiqued thousands of manuscript pages through countless revisions of the text and all the accompanying materials. She has reviewed and edited every word we've written—and if it weren't for her the book would not be so clear (and it might have a zillion spelling errors!). Her hard work, positive attitude, and dedication to quality throughout the whole process is without match. We could not have asked for a better friend and colleague or for better support.

We've always believed that the best way to build consistency and quality into the text and all of the other *P.L.U.S.* units is to do as much as possible ourselves. With the growth of multimedia technologies it's darn hard to be an expert on them all. But we've had spectacular help in that regard.

From the very outset, Professor Phillip Niffenegger at Murray State University has been the guru of our video series. He's got a rare combination of vision about what's possible with video and also a practical sense to know what will work—and work well. With this edition, as in the past, he has done a massive amount of work not only in creating video scripts himself but also in serving as executive producer for the whole series. In that job, he has worked with Nick Childers, whose Arthur Scott Production company handles all of our video production work and editing. He also coordinates with Stephen Lovett, who prepares the computer graphics for the videos. But an even bigger job is working with us, the companies, and all of the marketing professors who contribute scripts for videos.

It has been an honor for us to work with the talented group of professors who have been involved in developing our video series. Too much of the video footage used at all levels of education is full of glitz but devoid of content—because the people who produce it too often don't understand the content. We've been able to conquer that challenge, but only because of the participation of outstanding colleagues who have converted their marketing insights to the video medium. More specifically, we express respect for and deep appreciation to:

Gary R. Brockway,
 Murray State
 University
Martha O. Cooper,
 Ohio State
 University
Carolyn Costley,
 University of Miami

Elizabeth A.
 Klompmaker,
 Sara Lee
Gene R. Lazniak,
 Marquette University
Charles S. Madden,
 Baylor University

W. Glynn Mangold,
 Murray State
 University
Michael R. Mullen,
 Florida Atlantic
 University

Thomas G. Ponzurick, West Virginia University
Roger C. Shoenfeldt, Murray State University

Jeanne M. Simmons, Marquette University
Rollie O. Tillman, University of North Carolina at Chapel Hill

Poh-Lin Yeou, University of South Carolina

We're also indebted to Lewis Hershey for his work on the new electronic presentation slides for this edition. It's rare to find a world-class multimedia technologist who is also an experienced marketing professor, but he's it.

Many improvements in the current edition were stimulated by feedback from a number of colleagues around the country. Their feedback took many forms. We received valuable insights—and hundreds of detailed suggestions—from professors who kept class-by-class diaries while teaching from *Basic Marketing*. Participants in focus group interviews shared their in-depth ideas about ways to improve teaching and materials used in the first marketing course. Professors who provided comprehensive comparative reviews helped us see ways to build on our strengths and identify where improvements would be most helpful to students and faculty. And responses to detailed surveys gave us ideas and insights for ways to update and improve not only the text but also the whole set of teaching and learning materials that accompany it. Further, some of the ideas stimulated by thorough reviewers and survey respondents for the 11th edition were more fully implemented in this edition. For all of these suggestions and criticisms we are most appreciative. In particular, we would like to recognize the helpful contributions of:

L. McTier Anderson, Francis Marion University
Raj Arora, University of Missouri–Kansas City
Ramon A. Avila, Ball State University
Harold W. Babb, University of Richmond
Thomas J. Babb, West Liberty State College
Barry J. Babin, University of Southern Mississippi
Angelos C. Ballas, West Chester University
Jeffrey Baum, SUNY–Oneonta
Stephen Bell, New York University
Dan Bello, Georgia State University

Ashok Bennett, University of Illinois at Chicago
E. Edward Blevins, DeVry Institution of Technology
Jocelyn C. Bojack, University of Central Florida
Michael Bolin, Abilene Christian University
Betsy Boze, University of Alaska–Anchorage
Carl S. Bozman, Gonzaga University
Carter Broach, University of Delaware
Wendy Bryce, Western Washington University
Jim Burley, Central Michigan University

C. R. Busch, Lee College
James R. Butts, The American University
David Campbell, Valdosta State University
Phyllis Campbell, Bethel College
Charles R. Canedy, III, University of Hartford
Kit Carman, Golden Gate University
Lawrence J. Chase, Tompkins Cortland Community College
Pravat K. Choudhury, Howard University
Gene Conyers, North Georgia College
Robert L. Cook, Central Michigan University

James H. Cox,
Jefferson Community
College
Noel Craven,
El Camino College
Susan Cremins,
Iona College
John Dailey,
St. Edward's College
William D. Danko,
SUNY–Albany
Sayeste Daser, Wake
Forest University
Hugh Daubek, Purdue
University–Calumet
Linda M. Delene,
Western Michigan
University
Preyas Desai, Purdue
University
John R. Doneth, Ferris
State University
Lawrence D. Downs,
Nichols College
Drew M. Ehrlich,
Siena College
Maurice Elliard,
Albany State
College
John M. Erickson,
Central Missouri
State University
Gary Ernst, North
Central College
Randall Ewing, Ohio
Northern University
P. Everett Fergenson,
Iona College
Sundar W. Fleming,
North Carolina
Central University
Charles W. Ford,
Arkansas State
University
Frank Franzak, Virginia
Commonwealth
University
Randy L. Frye, Saint
Francis College
Donald Fuller,
University of Central
Florida

S. J. Garner,
Eastern Kentucky
University
C. Josef Ghosn,
Atlantic Union
College
David W. Glascoff,
East Carolina
University
Marc H. Goldberg,
Portland State
University
Edward Golden,
Central Washington
University
David J. Good,
Central Missouri
State University
James S. Gould,
Pace University
Robert F. Gwinner,
Arizona State
University
Larry A. Haase,
Central Missouri
State University
Gil Harrell,
Michigan State
University
Susan E. Heckler,
University of
Arizona
Thomas J. Hickey,
SUNY–Oswego
William Hickman,
Utica College
Ross R. Higa,
Leeward Community
College
Thomas Hitzelberger,
Southern Oregon
State College
Craig A. Hollingshead,
Marshall University
Kristen B. Hovsepian,
Ashland University
G. Gregory Hughes,
Vermont Technical
College
Vaughan C. Judd,
Auburn University at
Montgomery

L. Lynn Judd,
California State
University–San
Bernardino
James J. Kellaris,
University of
Cincinnati
James M. Kenderdine,
University of
Oklahoma
Wayne Kirklin,
Heidelberg College
Judith Kizzie, Clinton
Community College
Margaret A. Klayton,
Mary Washington
College
Brenda Konrad,
University of San
Diego
Pradeep Korgaonkar,
Florida Atlantic
University
Kathleen A. Krentner,
San Diego State
University
William F. Krumske,
Jr., Illinois Institute
of Technology
Rosemary Lagace,
University of South
Florida
Richard Lancioni,
Temple University
Frederick W. Langrehr,
Valparaiso University
J. Ford Laumer, Jr.,
Auburn University
William F. Leahy,
St. Joseph's
University
Deborah H. Lester,
Kennesaw State
College
Robert Letovsky,
St. Michael's College
Thomas W. Lloyd,
Westmoreland
County Community
College

Daultram Lund,
University of Nevada
Frank M. Marion,
Christian Brothers
University
Kimball P. Marshall,
Aurora University
Ed J. Mayo, Western
Michigan University
Michael A. Mayo,
Kent State University
Jim McAlexander,
Oregon State
University
L. McKinley-Floyd,
Clark Atlanta
University
Candace Bancroft
McKinniss, Franklin
Pierce College
Ahmed F. Mekky,
Ferris State
University
Eliseo Melendez,
SUNY–Maritime
John Milewicz,
Jacksonville State
University
M. Alan Miller,
Tennessee State
University
Chip E. Miller, Pacific
Lutheran University
Laura M. Milner,
University of
Alaska–Fairbanks
Alma Minutu-Wimsatt,
East Texas State
University
Edward M. Mosher,
Laramie County
Community College
Gordon G. Mosley,
University of Maine
at Machias
Robert Munday, St.
Edward's University
Tony Muscia, Western
International
University

Margaret C. Nelson,
SUNY–Albany
Esther S. Page-Wood,
Western Michigan
University
John H. Parker,
Manchester
Community/
Technical College
Gordon L. Patzer,
University of
Northern Iowa
Karen M. Petersen,
Augustana College
Robert Harmon,
Portland State
University
Eric R. Pratt,
New Mexico
State University
Thomas K. Pritchett,
Kennesaw State
College
Tom Quirk,
Webster University
Nabil Y. Razzouk,
California State
University
Charles Restivo,
Miss Wade's Fashion
Merchandise College
Gary K. Rhoads,
Brigham Young
University
Robert G. Roe,
University of
Wyoming
Stephen R. Rose,
Nassau Community
College
Marin Roth,
Boston College
Phillip Schary, Oregon
State University
John A. Schibrowsky,
University of
Nevada–Las Vegas
Kenneth K. Shanley,
Sinclair Community
College

F. Kelly Shuptrine,
University of South
Carolina
Richard Sjolander,
The University of
West Florida
Lewis F. Small,
York College of
Pennsylvania
Carol S. Sorros,
North Carolina
State University
Vernon Stauble,
California State
Polytechnic
University–Pomona
Gail L. Stautamoyer,
Western Michigan
University
Susan Stone,
Shippensburg
University
Karen Stone,
New Hampshire
College
Robert A. Swerdlow,
Lamar University
Robert Tangsrud,
University of North
Dakota
Jack L. Taylor,
Portland State
University
Raymond E. Taylor,
Louisiana State
University of
Shreveport
Harold Teer,
James Madison
University
Ray Tewell,
American River
College
Dannie J. Tindle,
LeTourneau
University
Dillard Tinsley,
Stephen F. Austin
State University

Hale N. Tongren,
George Mason
University
Thomas A. Tully,
Clarke College
David J. Urban,
Virginia Common-
wealth University
Sandra T. Vernon,
Fayetteville Technical
Community College
R. Vish Viswanathan,
University of
Northern Colorado

S. Stephen Vitucci,
University of Central
Texas
Rockney Walters,
Indiana University
Steve Warfield,
University of
Southern Colorado
J. Donald Weinrauch,
Tennessee Technical
University
D. Joel Whalen,
De Paul University

Edward W. Wheatley,
East Carolina
University
William F. Whitbeck,
Old Dominion
University
Tim Wilson,
Clarion University
Linda Withrow, St.
Ambrose University
William Wynd,
Eastern Washington
University

Kent Pinney's insights on the challenges of international marketing had a profound effect on the integration of these topics throughout the 11th edition, and he has had an impact on this edition. Similarly, thought-provoking reviews of earlier editions provided by William R. George and Barbara A. McCuen have had an ongoing influence in shaping this edition.

Faculty and students at our current and past academic institutions—Michigan State University, University of North Carolina, Notre Dame, University of Georgia, Northwestern University, University of Oregon, University of Minnesota, and Stanford University—have significantly shaped the book. Faculty at Notre Dame had a profound effect when the first editions of the book were developed. Professor Yusaku Furuhashi had a continuing impact on the multinational emphasis over many editions. Similarly, Professor Andrew A. Brogowicz of Western Michigan University contributed many fine ideas. Carl Zeithaml's thinking about the strategy implications of cross-functional links was an important stimulus in preparing Chapter 21 for this edition. More generally, Charlotte Mason, Michele Hunt, John Workman, and Nicholas Didow have provided a constant flow of helpful suggestions. And David Robinson again helped in preparing the computer files for the hypertext reference disk.

We are also grateful to the colleagues with whom we collaborate to produce international adaptations of the text. In particular, Stan Shapiro, Pascale G. Quester, John W. Wilkinson, and K. Y. Lee have all had an impact on the way we look at marketing.

The designers, artists, editors, and production people at Richard D. Irwin, Inc., who worked with us on this edition warrant special recognition. All of them have shared our commitment to excellence and brought their own individual creativity to the project. Without Amy Lund's can-do leadership and creative problem-solving skills, we could not have succeeded with a rapid-response production schedule—which is exactly what it takes to be certain that teachers and students get the most current information possible. Ethel Shiell's good nature and command of all the details involved in assembling the whole project make a zero-defects goal achievable. Without her, we'd have given up on annual editions of *Applications in Basic Marketing* long ago; she's retiring, and we'll sorely miss her. Keith McPherson took the creative lead in designing an attractive cover and inside for the book; what a talent, and what patience! Similarly, Mike Hruby again tracked down photos and ads we wanted to illustrate important ideas. Jeff Sund, Rob Zwettler, and John Black found time in their busy executive schedules to share their publishing insights and experience—and also gave us crucial top-management support for our objective of continuous improvement. Nina McGuffin and Jerry Saykes provided good-natured prods and great advice (along with occasional therapy!). Nancy Barbour's contributions as developmental editor have been exemplary—and her warm support and friendship have made all the work fun. Without Steve Patterson's energy, vision, and dedication as senior sponsoring editor, this edition would not be as good as it is. For that, we'll forever be grateful. While he's sometimes a tough taskmaster for us, it is because he cares about the quality of every decision that might affect how well the book and supporting materials work for students and teachers alike—and that includes getting it out on time.

Our families have been patient and consistent supporters through all phases in developing *Basic Marketing*. The support has been direct and substantive. Pam Perreault and Joanne McCarthy have provided invaluable editorial assistance—and more encouragement than you could imagine—through many editions of the text. Carol McCarthy helped research and reorient the "Career Planning in Marketing" appendix—reflecting her needs and experiences as a college student looking for a career in advertising. And Will and Suzanne Perreault were patient and supportive while their Dad spent time that was rightfully theirs meeting a never-ending set of deadlines.

We are indebted to all the firms that allowed us to reproduce their proprietary materials here. Similarly, we are grateful to associates from our business experiences who have shared their perspectives and feedback and enhanced our sensitivity to the key challenges of marketing management.

A textbook must capsulize existing knowledge while bringing new perspectives and organization to enhance it. Our thinking has been shaped by the writings of literally thousands of marketing scholars and practitioners. In some cases it is impossible to give unique credit for a particular idea or concept because so many people have played important roles in anticipating, suggesting, shaping, and developing it. We gratefully acknowledge these contributors—from the early thought-leaders to contemporary authors—who have shared their creative ideas. We respect their impact on the development of marketing and more specifically this book.

To all of these persons—and to the many publishers who graciously granted permission to use their materials—we are deeply grateful. Responsibility for any errors or omissions is certainly ours, but the book would not have been possible without the assistance of many others. Our sincere appreciation goes to everyone who helped in their own special way.

William D. Perreault, Jr.
E. Jerome McCarthy

Contents

Twelfth Edition

Basic Marketing

A Global-Managerial Approach

1

Marketing's Role in the Global Economy

When You Finish This Chapter, You Should

1. Know what marketing is and why you should learn about it.

2. Understand the difference between micro-marketing and macro-marketing.

3. Know why and how macro-marketing systems develop.

4. Understand why marketing is crucial to economic development and our global economy.

5. Know why marketing specialists— including middlemen and facilitators—develop.

6. Know the marketing functions and who performs them.

7. Understand the important new terms (shown in red).

When it's time to roll out of bed in the morning, does your General Electric alarm wake you with a buzzer—or by playing your favorite radio station? Is the station playing rock, classical, or country music—or perhaps a Red Cross ad asking you to contribute blood? Will you slip into your Levi's jeans, your shirt from L.L. Bean, and your athletic team jacket, or does the day call for your Brooks Brothers suit? Will breakfast be Lender's Bagels with cream cheese or Kellogg's Frosted Flakes—made with grain from America's heartland—or some extra-large eggs and Oscar Mayer bacon cooked in a Panasonic microwave oven imported from Japan? Will you drink decaffeinated Maxwell House coffee—grown in Colombia—or some Tang instant juice? Will you eat at home or is this a day to meet a friend at a local restaurant—where you'll pay someone else to serve your breakfast? After breakfast, will you head off to school or work in a Hyundai car, on a Huffy bike, or on the bus that the city bought from General Motors?

When you think about it, you can't get very far into a day without bumping into marketing—and what the whole marketing system does for you. It affects every aspect of our lives—often in ways we don't even consider.

In other parts of the world, people wake up each day to different kinds of experiences. A family in China may have little choice about what food they will eat or where their clothing will come from. A farmer in the mountains of Jamaica may awake in a barren hut with little more than the hope of raising enough to survive. A businessperson in a large city like Tokyo may have many choices but not be familiar with products that have names like Maxwell House, General Motors, and Oscar Mayer.

What explains these differences, and what do they have to do with marketing? In this chapter, we'll answer questions like these. You'll see what marketing is all about and why it's important to you. We'll also explore how marketing affects the quality of life in different societies and why it is so crucial to economic development and our global economy.

MARKETING—WHAT'S IT ALL ABOUT?

Marketing is more than selling or advertising

If forced to define marketing, most people, including some business managers, say that marketing means "selling" or "advertising." It's true that these are parts of marketing. But *marketing is much more than selling and advertising*.

How did all those tennis rackets get here?

To illustrate some of the other important things that are included in marketing, think about all the tennis rackets being swung with varying degrees of accuracy by tennis players around the world. Most of us weren't born with a tennis racket in our hand. Nor do we make our own tennis rackets. Instead, they are made by firms like Prince, Dunlop, Kennex, Head, and Yonex.

Most tennis rackets are intended to do the same thing—hit the ball over the net. But a tennis player can choose from a wide assortment of rackets. There are different shapes, materials, weights, handle sizes, and types of strings. You can buy a prestrung racket for less than $15. Or you can spend more than $250 just for a frame!

This variety in sizes and materials complicates the production and sale of tennis rackets. The following list shows some of the many things a firm should do before and after it decides to produce tennis rackets.

1. Analyze the needs of people who play tennis and decide if consumers want more or different tennis rackets.
2. Predict what types of rackets—handle sizes, shapes, weights, and materials—different players will want and decide which of these people the firm will try to satisfy.
3. Estimate how many of these people will be playing tennis over the next several years and how many rackets they'll buy.
4. Predict exactly when these players will want to buy tennis rackets.
5. Determine where in the world these tennis players will be—and how to get the firm's rackets to them.

All tennis rackets can hit the ball over the net—but there are many variations to meet the needs of different people.

6. Estimate what price they are willing to pay for their rackets—and if the firm can make a profit selling at that price.

7. Decide which kinds of promotion should be used to tell potential customers about the firm's tennis rackets.

8. Estimate how many competing companies will be making tennis rackets, how many rackets they'll produce, what kind, and at what prices.

The above activities are not part of **production**—actually making goods or performing services. Rather, they are part of a larger process—called *marketing*—that provides needed direction for production and helps make sure that the right goods and services are produced and find their way to consumers.

Our tennis racket example shows that marketing includes much more than selling or advertising. We'll describe marketing activities in the next chapter. And you'll learn much more about them before you finish this book. For now, it's enough to see that marketing plays an essential role in providing consumers with need-satisfying goods and services.

HOW MARKETING RELATES TO PRODUCTION

Production is a very important economic activity. Whether for lack of skill and resources or just lack of time, most people don't make most of the products they use. Picture yourself, for example, building a 10-speed bicycle, a compact disc player, or a digital watch—starting from scratch! We also turn to others to produce services—like health care, air transportation, and entertainment. Clearly, the high standard of living that most people in advanced economies enjoy is made possible by specialized production.

Tennis rackets, like mousetraps, don't sell themselves

Although production is a necessary economic activity, some people overrate its importance in relation to marketing. Their attitude is reflected in the old saying: "Make a better mousetrap and the world will beat a path to your door." In other words, they think that if you just have a good product, your business will be a success.

The "better mousetrap" idea probably wasn't true in Grandpa's time, and it certainly isn't true today. In modern economies, the grass grows high on the path to the Better Mousetrap Factory—if the new mousetrap is not properly marketed. We have already seen, for example, that there's a lot more to marketing tennis rackets than just making them. This is true for most goods and services.

The point is that production and marketing are both important parts of a total business system aimed at providing consumers with need-satisfying goods and services. Together, production and marketing supply five kinds of economic utility—form, task, time, place, and possession utility—that are needed to provide consumer satisfaction. Here, **utility** means the power to satisfy human needs. See Exhibit 1–1.

Tennis rackets do not automatically provide utility

Form utility is provided when someone produces something tangible—for instance, a tennis racket. **Task utility** is provided when someone performs a task for someone else—for instance, when a bank handles financial transactions. But just producing tennis rackets or handling bank accounts doesn't result in consumer satisfaction. The product must be something that consumers want or there is no need to be satisfied—and no utility.

EXHIBIT 1–1   Types of Utility and How They Are Provided

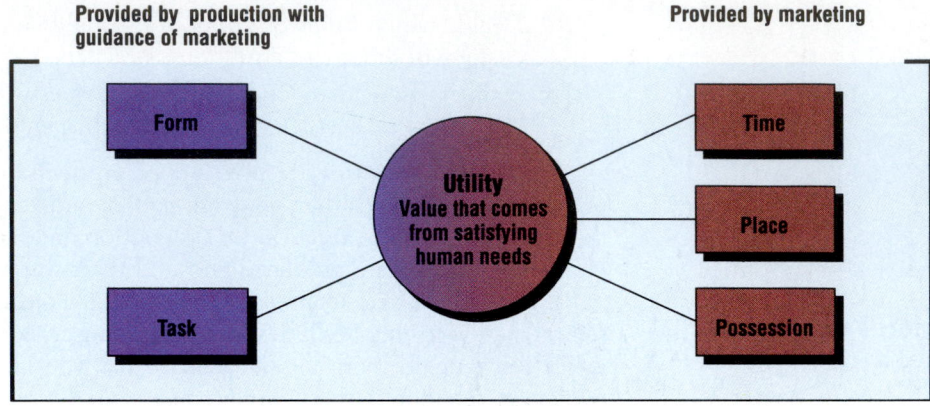

This is how marketing thinking guides the production side of business. Marketing decisions focus on the customer and include decisions about what goods and services to produce. It doesn't make sense to provide goods and services consumers don't want when there are so many things they do want or need. Let's take our "mousetrap" example a step further. Some customers don't want *any kind* of mousetrap. They may want someone else to produce a service and exterminate the mice for them, or they may live where mice are not a problem. Marketing is concerned with what customers want, and it should guide what is produced and offered. This is an important idea that we will develop more completely later.

Even when marketing and production combine to provide form or task utility, consumers won't be satisfied until possession, time, and place utility are also provided. **Possession utility** means obtaining a good or service and having the right to use or consume it. Customers usually exchange money or something else of value for possession utility.

Time utility means having the product available *when* the customer wants it. And **place utility** means having the product available *where* the customer wants it. Tennis rackets that stay at a factory don't do anyone any good. Time and place utility are very important for services too. For example, neighborhood emergency care health clinics have recently become very popular. People just walk in as soon as they feel sick, not a day later when their doctor can schedule an appointment.

Stated simply, marketing provides time, place, and possession utility. It should also guide decisions about what goods and services should be produced to provide form utility and task utility. We'll look at how marketing does this later in this chapter. First, we want to discuss why you should study marketing, and then we'll define marketing.

MARKETING IS IMPORTANT TO YOU

Marketing is important to every consumer

One reason for studying marketing is that you—as a consumer—pay for the cost of marketing activities. In advanced economies, marketing costs about 50 cents of each consumer dollar. For some goods and services, the percentage is much higher.

Marketing people at Ford research consumer interests and needs—before the firm designs and produces a new model—to be certain that a car will be what consumers want.

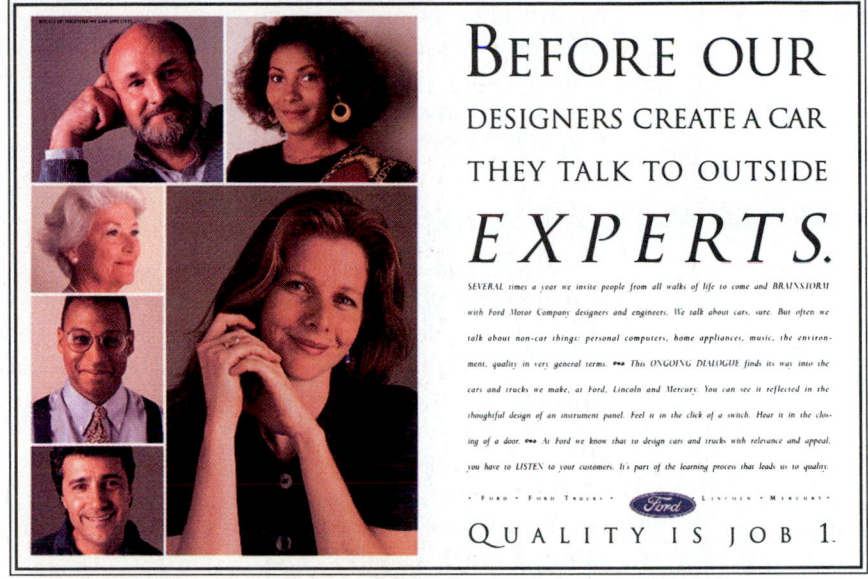

Another important reason for learning about marketing is that marketing affects almost every aspect of your daily life. All the goods and services you buy, the stores where you shop, and the radio and TV programs paid for by advertising are there because of marketing. Even your job resume is part of a marketing campaign to sell yourself to some employer! Some courses are interesting when you take them but never relevant again once they're over. Not so with marketing—you'll be a consumer dealing with marketing for the rest of your life.

Marketing will be important to your job

Still another reason for studying marketing is that there are many exciting and rewarding career opportunities in marketing. Marketing is often the route to the top. Throughout this book you will find information about opportunities in different areas of marketing—in sales, advertising, product management, marketing research, distribution, and other areas. And Appendix C is all about career planning in marketing.

Even if you're aiming for a nonmarketing job, you'll be working with marketing people. Knowing something about marketing will help you understand them better. It will also help you do your own job better. Throughout the book, we'll discuss ways that marketing relates to other functional areas—and Chapter 21 focuses on those issues. Further, remember that marketing is important to the success of every organization. A company that can't successfully sell its products doesn't need accountants, financial managers, production managers, personnel managers, computer programmers, or credit managers.

Marketing Manager for Consumer Electronics

We've got a new opportunity that should help our business grow into the next century. Put your college degree and experience in marketing consumer durables to work. Come help us analyze our markets and plan our marketing mix in a logical, creative, and enthusiastic way. This job offers income above industry standards, dynamic colleagues, relocation to desirable midwest suburb, and fast-track upward mobility. Reply in confidence, with a copy of your resume, to Box 4953.

Even if you're not planning a business career, marketing concepts and techniques apply to nonprofit organizations too. Many nonprofit organizations have a marketing manager. And the same basic principles used to sell soap are also used to "sell" ideas, politicians, mass transportation, health care services, conservation, museums, and even colleges. Think about the school where you take this course. If you didn't know about its offerings—or if they didn't interest you—you would simply pick some other school.[1]

Marketing affects economic growth

An even more basic reason for studying marketing is that marketing plays a big part in economic growth and development. Marketing stimulates research and new ideas—resulting in new goods and services. Marketing gives customers a choice among products. If these products satisfy customers, fuller employment, higher incomes, and a higher standard of living can result. An effective marketing system is important to the future of all nations.[2]

HOW SHOULD WE DEFINE MARKETING?

As we said earlier, some people think of marketing too narrowly as "selling and advertising." On the other hand, one author defined marketing as the "creation and delivery of a standard of living."[3] That definition is too broad.

An important difference between the two definitions may be less obvious. The first definition is a *micro*-level definition. It focuses on activities performed by an individual organization. The second is a *macro*-level definition. It focuses on the economic welfare of a whole society.

Micro- or macro-marketing?

Which view is correct? Is marketing a set of activities done by individual firms or organizations? Or is it a social process?

To answer this question, let's go back to our tennis racket example. We saw that a producer of tennis rackets has to perform many customer-related activities besides just making rackets. The same is true for an insurance company, an art museum, or a family-service agency. This supports the idea of marketing as a set of activities done by individual organizations.

On the other hand, people can't live on tennis rackets and art museums alone! In advanced economies, it takes thousands of goods and services to satisfy the many needs of society. For example, a typical Wal-Mart store carries 75,000 different items. A society needs some sort of marketing system to organize the efforts of all the producers and middlemen needed to satisfy the varied needs of all its citizens. So marketing is also an important social process.

The answer to our question is that *marketing is both a set of activities performed by organizations and a social process.* In other words, marketing exists at both the micro and macro levels. Therefore, we will use two definitions of marketing—one for micro-marketing and another for macro-marketing. Micro-marketing looks at customers and the organizations that serve them. Macro-marketing takes a broad view of our whole production–distribution system.

MICRO-MARKETING DEFINED

Micro-marketing is the performance of activities that seek to accomplish an organization's objectives by anticipating customer or client needs and directing a flow of need-satisfying goods and services from producer to customer or client.

Let's look at this definition.[4]

Applies to profit and nonprofit organizations

To begin with, this definition applies to both profit and nonprofit organizations. Profit is the objective for most business firms. But other types of organizations may seek more members—or acceptance of an idea. Customers or clients may be individual consumers, business firms, nonprofit organizations, government agencies, or even foreign nations. While most customers and clients pay for the goods and services they receive, others may receive them free of charge or at a reduced cost through private or government support.

The aim of marketing is to identify customers' needs—and to meet those needs so well that the product almost sells itself.

More than just persuading customers

You already know that micro-marketing isn't just selling and advertising. Unfortunately, many executives still think it is. They feel that the job of marketing is to "get rid of" whatever the company happens to produce. In fact, the aim of marketing is to identify customers' needs—and meet those needs so well that the product almost "sells itself." This is true whether the product is a physical good, a service, or even an idea. If the whole marketing job has been done well, customers don't need much persuading. They should be ready to buy. And after they do buy, they'll be satisfied and ready to buy the same way again the next time.

Begins with customer needs

Marketing should begin with potential customer needs—not with the production process. Marketing should try to anticipate needs. And then marketing, rather than production, should determine what goods and services are to be developed—including decisions about product design and packaging; prices or fees; credit and collection policies; use of middlemen; transporting and storing policies; advertising and sales policies; and, after the sale, installation, customer service, warranty, and perhaps even disposal policies.

Does not do it alone

This does not mean that marketing should try to take over production, accounting, and financial activities. Rather, it means that marketing—by interpreting customers' needs—should provide direction for these activities and try to coordinate them. After all, the purpose of a business or nonprofit organization is to satisfy customer or client needs. It is not to supply goods and services that are convenient to produce and *might* sell or be accepted free.

Builds a relationship with the customer

When marketing helps everyone in a firm really meet the needs of a customer both before and after a purchase, the firm doesn't just get a single sale. Rather, it has a sale and an ongoing *relationship* with the customer. Then, in the future, when the customer has the same need again—or some other need that the firm can meet—other sales will follow. That's why we emphasize that marketing concerns a *flow* of need-satisfying goods and services to the customer. Often, that flow is not just for a single transaction but rather is part of building a long-lasting relationship that is beneficial to both the firm and the customer.

THE FOCUS OF THIS TEXT—MANAGEMENT-ORIENTED MICRO-MARKETING

Since most of you are preparing for a career in management, the main focus of this text will be on micro-marketing. We will see marketing through the eyes of the marketing manager.

It is important to keep in mind that the micro-marketing ideas and decision areas we will be discussing throughout this text apply to a wide variety of marketing management situations. They are important not only for large and small business firms but also for all types of public sector and nonprofit organizations. They apply to new ventures started by a single entrepreneur as well as to ongoing efforts by teams of people in corporations. They are useful in domestic markets and international markets and regardless of whether the organization focuses on marketing physical goods, services, or an idea or cause. They are equally critical whether the relevant customers or clients are individual consumers, businesses, or some other type of organization. In short, every organization needs to think about its markets and how effectively it meets its customers' or clients' needs. For editorial convenience, and to reflect the fact that most readers will work in business settings, when we discuss marketing concepts we will sometimes use the term *firm* as a shorthand way of referring to any type of organization, whether it is a political party, a religious organization, a government agency, or the like. However, to reinforce the point that the ideas apply to all types of organizations, throughout the book we will illustrate marketing management concepts with examples that represent a wide variety of marketing situations.

Although micro-marketing is the primary focus of the text, marketing managers must remember that their organizations are just small parts of a larger macro-marketing system. Therefore, the rest of this chapter will look at the macro view of marketing. Let's begin by defining macro-marketing and reviewing some basic ideas. Then, in Chapter 2, we'll explain the marketing management decision areas we will be discussing in the rest of the book.

MACRO-MARKETING DEFINED

Macro-marketing is a social process that directs an economy's flow of goods and services from producers to consumers in a way that effectively matches supply and demand and accomplishes the objectives of society.

Emphasis is on whole system

Like micro-marketing, macro-marketing is concerned with the flow of need-satisfying goods and services from producer to consumer. However, the emphasis with macro-marketing is not on the activities of individual organizations. Instead, the emphasis is on *how the whole marketing system works*. This includes looking at how marketing affects society, and vice versa.

Every society needs a macro-marketing system to help match supply and demand. Different producers in a society have different objectives, resources, and skills. Likewise, not all consumers share the same needs, preferences, and wealth. In other words, within every society there are both heterogeneous (highly varied) supply capabilities and heterogeneous demands for goods and services. The role of a macro-marketing system is to effectively match this heterogeneous supply and demand *and* at the same time accomplish society's objectives.

Is it effective and fair?

The effectiveness and fairness of a particular macro-marketing system must be evaluated in terms of that society's objectives. Obviously, all nations don't share the same objectives. For example, Swedish citizens receive many "free" services—like health care and retirement benefits. Goods and services are fairly evenly distributed among the Swedish population. By contrast, Iraq places little emphasis on producing goods and services for individual consumers—and more on military spending. In India, the distribution of goods and services is very uneven—with a big gap between the "have-nots" and the elite "haves." Whether each of these systems is judged "fair" or "effective" depends on the objectives of the society.

Let's look more closely at macro-marketing.[5] And to make this more meaningful to you, consider (1) what kind of a macro-marketing system you have and (2) how effective and fair it is.

EVERY SOCIETY NEEDS AN ECONOMIC SYSTEM

All societies must provide for the needs of their members. Therefore, every society needs some sort of **economic system**—the way an economy organizes to use scarce resources to produce goods and services and distribute them for consumption by various people and groups in the society.

How an economic system operates depends on a society's objectives and the nature of its political institutions.[6] But regardless of what form these take, all economic systems must develop some method—along with appropriate economic institutions—to decide what and how much is to be produced and distributed by whom, when, to whom, and why. How these decisions are made may vary from nation to nation. But the macro-level objectives are basically similar: to create goods and services and make them available when and where they are needed—to maintain or improve each nation's standard of living or other socially defined objective.

HOW ECONOMIC DECISIONS ARE MADE

There are two basic kinds of economic systems: planned systems and market-directed systems. Actually, no economy is entirely planned or market-directed. Most are a mixture of the two extremes.

Government planners may make the decisions

In a **planned economic system**, government planners decide what and how much is to be produced and distributed by whom, when, to whom, and why. Producers generally have little choice about what goods and services to produce. Their main task is to meet their assigned production quotas. Prices are set by government planners and tend to be very rigid—not changing according to supply and demand. Consumers usually have some freedom of choice—it's impossible to control every single detail! But the assortment of goods and services may be quite limited. Activities such as market research, branding, and advertising usually are neglected. Sometimes they aren't done at all.

Government planning may work fairly well as long as an economy is simple and the variety of goods and services is small. It may even be necessary under certain conditions—during wartime, drought, or political instability, for example. However, as economies become more complex, government planning becomes

A few years ago, consumers in Moscow had to wait in a three-hour line to buy a rare delicacy—a Chiquita banana; now bananas are more available but still very expensive. Things are easier for most consumers in the U.S., Canada, and Western Europe.

more difficult. It may even break down. Planners may be overwhelmed by too many complex decisions. And consumers may lose patience if the planners don't respond to their needs. The collapse of communism in Eastern Europe dramatically illustrates this. Citizens of what was the Soviet Union were not satisfied with the government's plan—because products consumers wanted and needed were not available. To try to reduce consumer dissatisfaction, government planners tried to put more emphasis on making consumer goods available, but they were not able to produce the results consumers wanted. In short, it was consumer dissatisfaction with decisions made by government planners that brought about a revolution— one that is leading to the development of market-directed economies in the new, independent republics of Eastern Europe.[7]

Countries such as China, North Korea, and Cuba still rely primarily on planned economic systems. Even so, around the world there is a broad move toward market-directed economic systems—because they are more effective in meeting consumer needs.

A market-directed economy adjusts itself

In a **market-directed economic system**, the individual decisions of the many producers and consumers make the macro-level decisions for the whole economy. In a pure market-directed economy, consumers make a society's production decisions when they make their choices in the marketplace. They decide what is to be produced and by whom—through their dollar "votes."

Price is a measure of value

Prices in the marketplace are a rough measure of how society values particular goods and services. If consumers are willing to pay the market prices, then apparently they feel they are getting at least their money's worth. Similarly, the cost of labor and materials is a rough measure of the value of the resources used in

Lever is developing packages that can be recycled, so that individual consumers get the convenience they want at the same time that society's environmental needs are addressed.

the production of goods and services to meet these needs. New consumer needs that can be served profitably—not just the needs of the majority—will probably be met by some profit-minded businesses.

In summary, in a market-directed economic system the prices in both the production sector (for resources) and the consumption sector (for goods and services) vary to allocate resources and distribute income according to consumer preferences. Over time, the result is a balance of supply and demand and the coordination of the economic activity of many individuals and institutions.

Greatest freedom of choice

Consumers in a market-directed economy enjoy great freedom of choice. They are not forced to buy any goods or services, except those that must be provided for the good of society—things such as national defense, schools, police and fire protection, highway systems, and public-health services. These are provided by the community—and the citizens are taxed to pay for them.

Similarly, producers are free to do whatever they wish—provided that they stay within the rules of the game set by government *and* receive enough dollar "votes" from consumers. If they do their job well, they earn a profit and stay in business. But profit, survival, and growth are not guaranteed.

Conflicts can result

Producers and consumers making free choices can cause conflicts and difficulties. This is called the **micro–macro dilemma**: What is "good" for some producers and consumers may not be good for society as a whole.

Gun control in the U.S. is an example. Each year, thousands of people are killed with handguns. Yet there are producers who make and sell handguns at a profit. And there are many consumers who feel strongly about their right to own guns. But others argue that handguns are a threat to society. They want handgun sales banned and sales of all weapons limited—as is the case in many countries. Should gun producers be allowed to sell guns to consumers who want them?

Decisions don't have to involve life and death issues to be important. Many Americans want the convenience of disposable products and products in easy-to-use, small-serving packages. But these same "convenient" products and packages often lead to pollution of the environment and inefficient use of natural resources. Should future generations be left to pay the consequences of pollution that is the result of "free choice" by today's consumers?

Questions like these are not easy to answer. The basic reason is that many different people may have a stake in the outcomes—and social consequences— of the choices made by individual managers *and* consumers in a market-directed system. As you read this book and learn more about marketing, you will also learn more about social responsibility in marketing—and why it must be taken seriously.

The role of government

The American economy and most other Western economies are mainly market-directed—but not completely. Society assigns supervision of the system to the government. For example, besides setting and enforcing the "rules of the game," government agencies control interest rates and the supply of money. They also set import and export rules that affect international competition, regulate radio and TV broadcasting, sometimes control wages and prices, and so on. Government also tries to be sure that property is protected, contracts are enforced, individuals are not exploited, no group unfairly monopolizes markets, and producers deliver the kinds and quality of goods and services they claim to be offering.

You can see that we need some of these government activities to make sure the economy runs smoothly. However, some people worry that too much government "guidance" threatens the survival of a market-directed system—and the economic and political freedom that goes with it. For example, in the past decade the U.S. government has done much less "interfering"—especially in markets for services such as banking, transportation, and communications. The vigorous competition among airlines is a good example of what follows. A few years ago, a government agency controlled airline prices and routes. Now that agency doesn't exist, and these decisions are made by marketing managers—and consumers. By contrast, recently there have been proposals in Congress that focus on a much more active government role in planning and controlling health care. Some consumers might benefit by such changes, yet more government control would reduce consumer choice.[8]

ALL ECONOMIES NEED MACRO-MARKETING SYSTEMS

At this point, you may be saying to yourself: All this sounds like economics— where does marketing fit in? Studying a *macro*-marketing system is a lot like studying an economic system except we give more detailed attention to the "marketing" components of the system—including consumers and other customers, wholesalers and retailers, and other marketing specialists. We focus on the activities they perform—and how the interaction of the components affects the effectiveness and fairness of a particular system.

In general, we can say that no economic system—whether centrally planned, market-directed, or a mix of the two—can achieve its objectives without an effective macro-marketing system. To see why this is true, we will look at the role of marketing in primitive societies. Then we will see how macro-marketing tends to become more and more complex in advanced economic systems.

Marketing involves exchange

In a **pure subsistence economy**, each family unit produces everything it consumes. There is no need to exchange goods and services. Each producer–consumer unit is totally self-sufficient, although usually its standard of living is relatively low. No marketing takes place because *marketing doesn't occur unless two or more parties are willing to exchange something for something else.*

What is a market?

The term *marketing* comes from the word **market**, which is a group of potential customers with similar needs who are willing to exchange something of value with sellers offering various goods and/or services—that is, ways of satisfying those needs. Of course, some negotiation may be needed. This can be done face-to-face at some physical location (for example, a farmers' market). Or it can be done indirectly—through a complex network of middlemen who link buyers and sellers living far apart.

In primitive economies, exchanges tend to occur in central markets. **Central markets** are convenient places where buyers and sellers can meet one-on-one to exchange goods and services. We can understand macro-marketing better by seeing how and why central markets develop. We'll start with a very simple case, but thinking about it will clarify what happens when a more complex system is involved.

Central markets help exchange

Imagine a small village of five families—each with a special skill for producing some need-satisfying product. After meeting basic needs, each family decides to specialize. It's easier for one family to make two pots and another to make two baskets than for each one to make one pot and one basket. Specialization makes labor more efficient and more productive. It can increase the total amount of form utility created. Specialization also can increase the task utility in producing services, but for the moment we'll focus on products that are physical goods.

If these five families each specialize in one product, they will have to trade with each other. As Exhibit 1–2A shows, it will take the five families 10 separate exchanges to obtain some of each of the products. If the families live near each other, the exchange process is relatively simple. But if they are far apart, travel back and forth will take time. Who will do the traveling—and when?

Faced with this problem, the families may agree to come to a central market and trade on a certain day. Then each family makes only one trip to the market to trade with all the others. This reduces the total number of trips to five, which makes exchange easier, leaves more time for producing and consuming, and also provides for social gatherings.

A money system simplifies trading

While a central meeting place simplifies exchange, the individual bartering transactions still take a lot of time. Bartering only works when someone else wants what you have, and vice versa. Each trader must find others who have

EXHIBIT 1–2

A. **Ten exchanges are required when a central market is not used**

B. **Only five exchanges are required when a middleman (intermediary) in a central market is used**

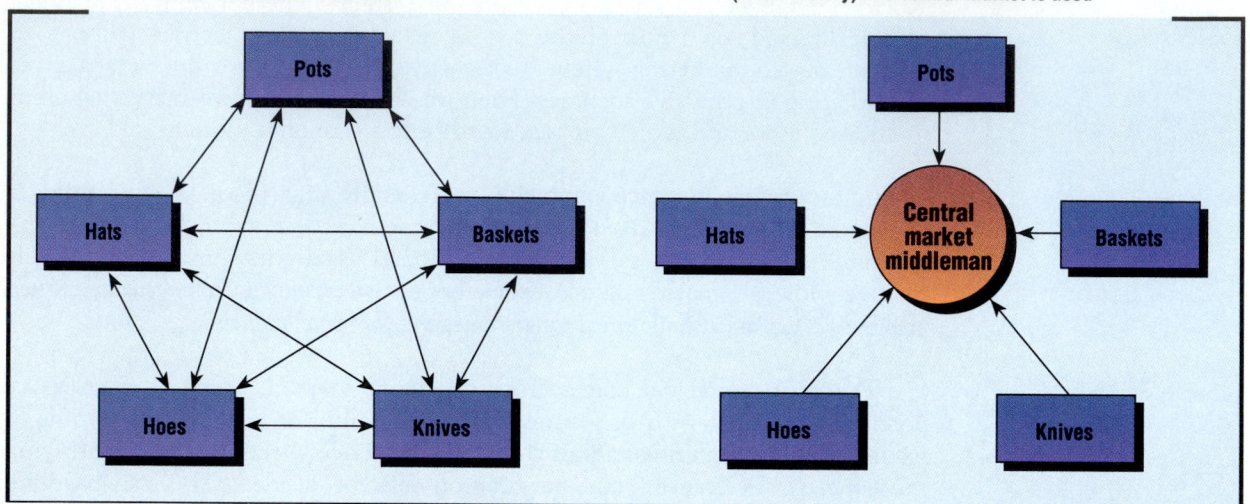

products of about equal value. After trading with one group, a family may find itself with extra baskets, knives, and pots. Then it has to find others willing to trade for these products.

A common money system changes all this. Sellers only have to find buyers who want their products and agree on the price. Then sellers are free to spend this income to buy whatever they want. (If some buyers and sellers use *different* money systems—some use dollars and others use yen—they must also agree on the rate at which the money will be exchanged.)

Middlemen intermediaries help exchange even more

The development of a central market and a money system simplifies the exchange process among the five families in our imaginary village. But the families still need to make 10 separate transactions. So it still takes a lot of time and effort for the five families to exchange goods.

This clumsy exchange process is made much simpler by a **middleman** (or **intermediary**)—someone who specializes in trade rather than production. A middleman is willing to buy each family's goods and then sell each family whatever it needs. The middleman intermediary charges for this service, of course. But this charge may be more than offset by savings in time and effort.

In our simple example, using an intermediary at a central market reduces the necessary number of exchanges for all five families from 10 to 5. See Exhibit 1–2B. Each family has more time for production, consumption, and leisure. Also, each family can specialize in producing what it produces best—creating more form and task utility. Meanwhile, by specializing in trade, the intermediary provides additional time, place, and possession utility. In total, all the villagers may enjoy greater economic utility—and greater consumer satisfaction—by using an intermediary in the central market.

Note that the reduction in transactions that results from using an intermediary in a central market becomes more important as the number of families increases. For example, if the population of our imaginary village increases from 5 to 10 families, 45 transactions are needed without an intermediary. Using an intermediary requires only one transaction for each family.

In advanced economies, a complex network of wholesalers, retailers, and other marketing specialists brings goods and services to consumers; in developing economies like Vietnam, central markets are often more basic.

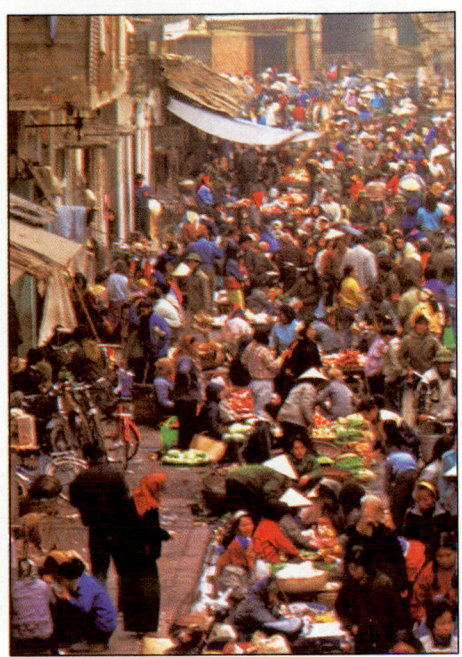

Today such intermediaries—offering permanent trading facilities—are known as *wholesalers* and *retailers*. The advantages of working with intermediaries increase with increases in the number of producers and consumers, their distance from or difficulties in communicating with each other, and the number and variety of competing products. That is why there are so many wholesalers and retailers in modern economies.

THE ROLE OF MARKETING IN ECONOMIC DEVELOPMENT

Most modern economies have advanced well beyond the five-family village, but the same ideas still apply. The main purpose of markets and market intermediaries is to make exchange easier and allow greater time for production, consumption, and other activities—including leisure.

Effective marketing system is necessary

Although it is tempting to conclude that more effective macro-marketing systems are the result of greater economic development, just the opposite is true. *An effective macro-marketing system is necessary for economic development.* Improved marketing is often the key to growth in less-developed nations.

Breaking the vicious circle of poverty

Without an effective macro-marketing system, many people in less-developed nations are not able to leave their subsistence way of life. They can't produce for the market because there are no buyers. And there are no buyers because everyone else is producing for their own needs. As a result, distribution systems and intermediaries do not develop.

Breaking this "vicious circle of poverty" may require major changes in the inefficient micro- and macro-marketing systems that are typical in less-developed nations. At the least, more market-oriented middlemen are needed to move surplus output to markets—including foreign markets—where there is more demand.[9] You can see how this works, and why links between the macro-marketing systems of different countries are so important, by considering the differences in markets that are typical at different stages of economic development.

STAGES OF ECONOMIC DEVELOPMENT

Some markets are more advanced and/or growing more rapidly than others. And some countries—or parts of a country—are at different stages of economic development. This means their demands—and their marketing systems—vary.

To get some idea of the many possible differences in potential markets, we'll discuss six stages of economic development. These stages are helpful, but they greatly oversimplify the real world for two reasons. First, different parts of the same country may be at different stages of development—so it isn't possible to identify a single country or region with only one stage. Second, some countries skip one or two stages due to investments by foreign firms or investments by their own eager governments. For example, the building of uneconomical steel mills to boost national pride—or the arrival of multinational car producers—might lead to a big jump in stages. This "stage-jumping" does not destroy the six-stage process—it just explains why more rapid movements take place in some situations.

Stage 1—Self-supporting agriculture

In this stage, most people are subsistence farmers. A simple marketing system may exist, but most of the people are not part of a money economy. Some parts of Africa and New Guinea are in this stage. In a practical sense, these people are not a market because they have no money to buy products.

Stage 2—Preindustrial or commercial

Some countries in sub-Saharan Africa and the Middle East are in this second stage. During this stage, we see more market-oriented activity. Raw materials such as oil, tin, and copper are extracted and exported. Agricultural and forest crops such as sugar, rubber, and timber are grown and exported. Often this is done with the help of foreign technical skills and capital. A commercial economy may develop along with—but unrelated to—the subsistence economy. These activities may require the beginnings of a transportation system to tie the extracting or growing areas to shipping points. A money economy operates in this stage.

Such countries import industrial machinery and equipment—and component materials and supplies for huge construction projects. They also need imports—including luxury products—to meet the living standards of technical and supervisory people.

The few large landowners—and those who benefit by this new business activity—may develop expensive tastes. The few natives employed by these larger firms—and the small business managers who serve them—may form a small, middle-income class. But most of the population has no money. For practical purposes, they are not in the market. The total market in Stage 2 may be so small that local importers can easily handle the demand. There is little reason for local producers to even try.

Stage 3—Primary manufacturing

In this third stage, a country may do some processing of metal ores or agricultural products it once exported in raw form. Sugar and rubber, for example, are both produced and processed in Indonesia. Companies based elsewhere in the world may set up factories to take advantage of low-cost labor. Most of the output

MIDDLE-CLASS POLISH CONSUMERS BECOME A DRIVING FORCE

In communist Poland, Marek Kwiatowski earned only about $100 a month working for the state-owned radio factory. He and his wife and child lived in a single room in a house shared with relatives. For 40 years, government planners had failed to spur economic development. Kwiatowski and other consumers didn't have much and had little hope things would get better. In the post-communist era, that's changing. Now, Kwiatowski is a foreman for a U.S.-based company that's assembling Japanese TVs in his hometown near Warsaw. With a salary of about $6,000 a year, he dreams of building a new home.

Kwiatowski is not alone. There is a swelling middle class in Poland with income for purchases and dreams of the future. Valhalla Custom Homes has even been developing subdivisions with rows of prefab wood homes shipped in from Canada. And foreign consumer products firms are grabbing new customers for products like Colgate toothpaste and Ajax cleanser.

The first Poles with new wealth were the international traders and tiny manufacturers who were freed to flourish by the new order. Managers of state companies that went private, and the lawyers, accountants, and advisors who landed jobs with foreign investors, also flourished. Slowly but surely, others are joining them. In 1991, 20 percent of working Poles who did not have jobs on small farms had found jobs in the private economy, but by 1992 that figure doubled and has continued to climb. With this growth has come a market for middle-class purchases—like homes and cars.

Not all of these people are poised to buy a new home or car, but now they're hoping and looking. Many consumers who had no car, or had always bought old, used cars, are now moving up, perhaps to buy a Ford Fiesta or a German-made GM Opel. Yet, there are fat import duties on cars, and it's hard to get a car loan. So it takes almost as much cash to buy a car as a house. Even so, more Poles are buying cars than ever before. And now they have more choice. As one pleased consumer remarked after buying a new red Toyota, "It's the first time I've paid attention to color."[10]

---

from these factories is exported, but the income earned by the workers stimulates economic development. In addition, a growing group of professionals and technicians is needed to run the developing agricultural–industrial complex.

The demands of this group—and the growing number of wealthy natives—differ dramatically from the needs of the lower class and the emerging middle class. Even though the local market expands in this third stage, a large part of the population continues to be almost entirely outside the money economy—and local producers are likely to have trouble finding enough demand to keep them in business.

Stage 4—Nondurable and semidurable consumer products manufacturing

At this stage, small local manufacturing begins—especially in those lines that need only a small investment to get started. Often, these industries grow from the small firms that supplied the processors dominating the last stage. For example, plants making explosives for extracting minerals might expand into soap manufacturing. Multinational firms speed development of countries in this stage by investing in promising opportunities.

Paint, drug, food and beverage, and textile industries develop in this stage. Because clothing is a necessity, the textile industry is usually one of the first to develop. This early emphasis on the textile industry in developing nations is one reason the world textile market is so competitive.

As some of the small producers become members of the middle- or even upper-income class, they help to expand the demand for imported products. As this market grows, local businesses begin to see enough volume to operate

International trade has been a major factor in the very rapid economic development of Taiwan.

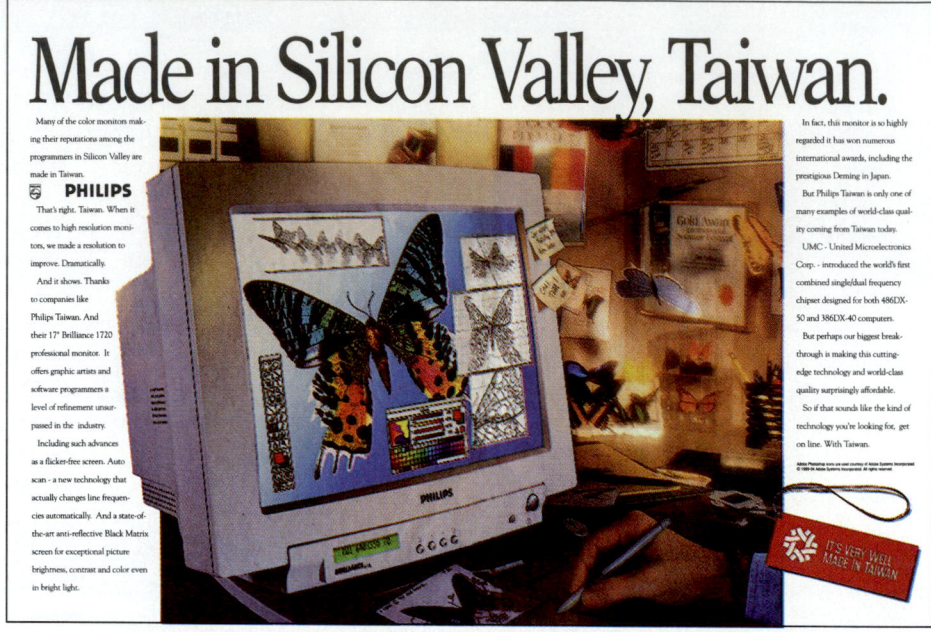

Made in Silicon Valley, Taiwan.

Many of the color monitors making their reputations among the programmers in Silicon Valley are made in Taiwan.

PHILIPS

That's right. Taiwan. When it comes to high resolution monitors, we made a resolution to improve. Dramatically.

And it shows. Thanks to companies like Philips Taiwan. And their 17" Brilliance 1720 professional monitor. It offers graphic artists and software programmers a level of refinement unsurpassed in the industry.

Including such advances as a flicker-free screen. Auto scan - a new technology that actually changes line frequencies automatically. And a state-of-the-art anti-reflective Black Matrix screen for exceptional picture brightness, contrast and color even in bright light.

In fact, this monitor is so highly regarded it has won numerous international awards, including the prestigious Deming in Japan.

But Philips Taiwan is only one of many examples of world-class quality coming from Taiwan today.

UMC - United Microelectronics Corp. - introduced the world's first combined single/dual frequency chipset designed for both 486DX-50 and 386DX-40 computers.

But perhaps our biggest breakthrough is making this cutting-edge technology and world-class quality surprisingly affordable.

So if that sounds like the kind of technology you're looking for, get on line. With Taiwan.

IT'S VERY WELL MADE IN TAIWAN

profitably, so there is less need for imports to supply nondurable and semidurable products. But most consumer durables and capital equipment are still imported.

Stage 5—Capital equipment and consumer durable products manufacturing

In this stage, the production of capital equipment and consumer durable products begins—including cars, refrigerators, and machinery for local industries. Such manufacturing creates other demands—raw materials for the local factories, and food and clothing for the rural population entering the industrial labor force.

Industrialization begins, but the economy still depends on exports of raw materials—either wholly unprocessed or slightly processed.

The country may still have to import special heavy machinery and equipment in this stage, and imports of consumer durables may still compete with local products.

Stage 6—Exporting manufactured products

Countries that haven't gone beyond the fifth stage are mainly exporters of raw materials. They import manufactured products to build their industrial base. In the sixth stage, countries begin exporting manufactured products. Countries often specialize in certain types of manufactured products—iron and steel, watches, cameras, electronic equipment, and processed food.

These countries have grown richer. They have needs—and the purchasing power—for a wide variety of products. In fact, countries in this stage often carry on a great deal of trade with each other. Each trades those products in which it has production advantages. In this stage, almost all consumers are in the money economy. And there may be a large middle-income class. The United States, most of the Western European countries, and Japan are at this last stage.[11]

It is important to see that it is not necessary to label a whole country or geographic region as being in one stage. In fact, even in the most advanced countries—like the U.S. and Canada, those in Western Europe, and Japan— different regions have developed differently and are in different stages.

NATIONS' MACRO-MARKETING SYSTEMS ARE CONNECTED

As a nation grows, its international trade grows

All countries trade to some extent—we live in an interdependent world. We saw above how trade expands as a country develops and industrializes. In fact, the largest changes in world trade are usually seen in rapidly developing economies. Over the last decade, for example, exports from Hong Kong, Taiwan, and Singapore have risen dramatically.

Even so, the largest traders are highly developed nations. For example, the top industrial nations—the U.S., Japan, Canada, and the countries of the European Community, account for about two-thirds of total world exports. These same countries account for about 63 percent of world imports. Of course, the specific percentage varies from country to country. For example, 46 percent of U.S. exports go to countries that are not among the top industrial nations; and 44 percent of U.S. imports come from countries that are not among the top industrial nations.[12]

Because trade among nations is so important in economic development, most countries—whether highly developed or not—are eager to be able to sell their goods and services in foreign markets. Yet at the same time they often don't want their local customers to spend cash on foreign-made products. They want the money—and the opportunities for jobs and economic growth—to stay in the local economy.

Tariffs and quotas may reduce trade

Taxes and restrictions at national or regional borders greatly reduce the free flow of goods and services between the macro-marketing systems of different countries. **Tariffs**—taxes on imported products—vary, depending on whether a country is trying to raise revenue or limit trade. Restrictive tariffs often block all movement. But even revenue-producing tariffs cause red tape, discourage free movement of products, and increase the prices consumers pay.

Quotas act like restrictive tariffs. **Quotas** set the specific quantities of products that can move into or out of a country. Great market opportunities may exist in the markets of a unified Europe, for example, but import quotas (or export controls applied against a specific country) may discourage outsiders from entering.

The impact of such restrictions can be seen in the Russian market. It appeared that with the fall of Communism, the Russian market would be more open to foreign automobile producers. And in a way it was. Sales of Mercedes, for example, spurted to 3,500 in 1993 versus only about 70 a year earlier. However, a Mercedes that sold for $60,000 in nearby Germany, where it was produced, cost $112,000 in Russia. The price difference was due mainly to big Russian import tariffs and taxes. And the resulting high price severely limited the number of Russians who were willing or able to pay that much for a car.

Trade restrictions can be a potential source of conflict between nations. For example, the U.S. government has charged Japan with "unfair" trading practices that restricted opportunities for U.S. firms. Of course, the United States has also worked to control Japan's export of cars into the country. (Otherwise, even more Japanese cars would have entered the U.S. market!)[13]

Markets may rely on international countertrade

To overcome the problems of trade restrictions, many firms have turned to **countertrade**—a special type of bartering in which products from one country are traded for products from another country. For example, McDonnell Douglas

Helicopter turned to countertrade when the Ugandan government wanted to buy 18 helicopters to help stamp out illegal elephant hunting. Uganda didn't have $25 million to pay for the helicopters, so a countertrade specialist for the helicopter company set up local projects to generate the money. One Ugandan factory now turns local pineapples and passion fruit into concentrated juice. The concentrate is sold to European buyers identified by the countertrade specialist. Similarly, soft drink bottlers in Mexico trade locally grown broccoli for Pepsi concentrate; then Pepsi finds a market for the broccoli in the U.S.

Distribution systems and middlemen intermediaries have not yet developed in these countries to handle this sort of exchange. So, in pursuing their own opportunities, companies like Pepsi and McDonnell Douglas are stimulating economic development. While deals such as this may seem unusual, that is not the case. Countertrade is becoming an extremely important part of foreign trade for both large and small companies. In fact, experts say that the use of countertrade has doubled in the past decade and that 20 percent of all U.S. exports now rely on countertrade. That's over $100 billion in goods and services![14]

Global trade is increasing

There are still many obstacles to free trade among nations. And trade "wars" among nations are likely to continue. Even so, the trend shows a slow movement toward fewer restrictions on trade among different countries. Perhaps the most visible evidence of this trend is the evolution of the **General Agreement on Tariffs and Trade (GATT)**—a set of rules governing restrictions on world trade and agreed to by most of the nations of the world. Fifty-three nations signed the first GATT agreement in 1947. Since then, there have been seven rounds of GATT agreements. In general, each successive round of talks has involved more countries and focused on further reducing tariffs and other nontariff trade barriers such as quotas and phony "standards" a product needs to meet to be sold in a country. Because each rule affects different countries in different ways, reaching agreement is a slow and complicated process. And some people feel that there has been more talk than change. Even so, as progress is slowly being made, global trade is becoming an even more important factor in economic development—and a more important source of opportunity for individual firms.[15]

CAN MASS PRODUCTION SATISFY A SOCIETY'S CONSUMPTION NEEDS?

Urbanization brings together large numbers of people. They must depend on others to produce most of the goods and services they need to satisfy their basic needs. Also, in advanced economies, many consumers have higher discretionary incomes. They can afford to satisfy higher-level needs as well. A modern economy faces a real challenge to satisfy all these needs.

Economies of scale mean lower cost

Fortunately, advanced economies can often take advantage of mass production with its **economies of scale**—which means that as a company produces larger numbers of a particular product, the cost for each of these products goes down. You can see that a one-of-a-kind, custom-built car would cost much more than a mass-produced standard model.

Of course, even in advanced societies, not all goods and services can be produced by mass production—or with economies of scale. Consider medical care. It's difficult to get productivity gains in labor-intensive medical services—like brain surgery. Nevertheless, from a macro-marketing perspective, it is clear that we are able to devote resources to meeting these "quality-of-life" needs because we are achieving efficiency in other areas.

Thus, modern production skills can help provide great quantities of goods and services to satisfy large numbers of consumers. But mass production alone does not solve the problem of satisfying consumers' needs. We also need effective marketing.

Effective marketing is needed to link producers and consumers

Effective marketing means delivering the goods and services that consumers want and need. It means getting products to them at the right time, in the right place, and at a price they're willing to pay. It means keeping consumers satisfied after the sale, and bringing them back to purchase again when they are ready. That's not an easy job—especially if you think about the variety of goods and services a highly developed economy can produce and the many kinds of goods and services consumers want.

Effective marketing in an advanced economy is more difficult because producers and consumers are often separated in several ways. As Exhibit 1–3 shows, exchange between producers and consumers is hampered by spatial separation, separation in time, separation of information and values, and separation of ownership. "Discrepancies of quantity" and "discrepancies of assortment" further complicate exchange between producers and consumers. That is, each

EXHIBIT 1–3 Marketing Facilitates Production and Consumption

Most consumers who drink tea live far from where it is grown. To overcome this spatial separation, someone must first perform a variety of marketing functions, like standardizing and grading the tea leaves, transporting and storing them, and buying and selling them.

(Tea-Java) Simply, Pure Tea From Java

producer specializes in producing and selling large amounts of a narrow assortment of goods and services, but each consumer wants only small quantities of a wide assortment of goods and services.[16]

Marketing functions help narrow the gap

The purpose of a macro-marketing system is to overcome these separations and discrepancies. The "universal functions of marketing" help do this.

The **universal functions of marketing** are: buying, selling, transporting, storing, standardization and grading, financing, risk taking, and market information. They must be performed in all macro-marketing systems. *How* these functions are performed—and *by whom*—may differ among nations and economic systems. But they are needed in any macro-marketing system. Let's take a closer look at them now.

Exchange usually involves buying and selling. The **buying function** means looking for and evaluating goods and services. The **selling function** involves promoting the product. It includes the use of personal selling, advertising, and other direct and mass selling methods. This is probably the most visible function of marketing.

The **transporting function** means the movement of goods from one place to another. The **storing function** involves holding goods until customers need them.

Standardization and grading involve sorting products according to size and quality. This makes buying and selling easier because it reduces the need for inspection and sampling. **Financing** provides the necessary cash and credit to produce, transport, store, promote, sell, and buy products. **Risk taking** involves bearing the uncertainties that are part of the marketing process. A firm can never be sure that customers will want to buy its products. Products can also be damaged, stolen, or outdated. The **market information function** involves the collection, analysis, and distribution of all the information needed to plan, carry out, and control marketing activities, whether in the firm's own neighborhood or in a market overseas.

WHO PERFORMS MARKETING FUNCTIONS?

Producers, consumers, and marketing specialists

From a macro-level viewpoint, these marketing functions are all part of the marketing process—and must be done by someone. None of them can be eliminated. In a planned economy, some of the functions may be performed by

Facilitators—including delivery firms like DHL and marketing research specialists like Claritas—may help a marketing manager with one or more of the marketing functions.

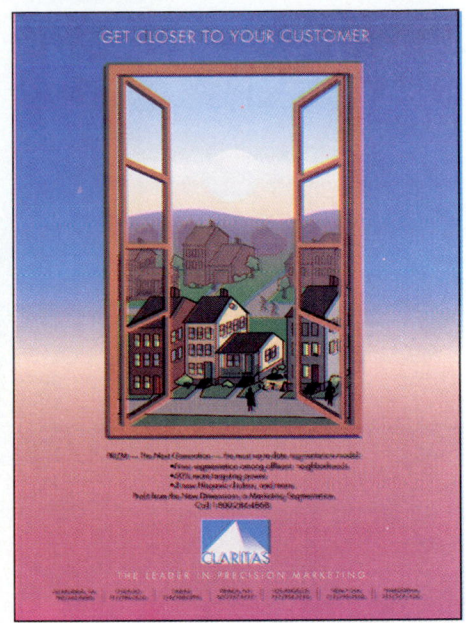

government agencies. Others may be left to individual producers and consumers. In a market-directed system, marketing functions are performed by producers, consumers, and a variety of marketing specialists (see Exhibit 1–4 on page 26). Regardless of who performs the marketing functions, in general they must be performed effectively or the performance of the whole macro-marketing system will suffer.

Keep in mind that the macro-marketing systems for different nations may interact. For example, producers based in one nation may serve consumers in another country, perhaps with help from intermediaries and other specialists from both countries. What happened to food distribution in East Germany after the fall of the Berlin Wall illustrates this point. With the reunification of Germany, the political limits on trade were gone. Yet consumers still faced problems getting the food they wanted. Eastern Germany had no efficient wholesalers to supply the chain of 170 Konsum retail stores, which were previously state-owned. And it was expensive for producers in the West who wanted to reach the market in the East to do it without help. However, the Tegut grocery chain in the West saw the opportunity and quickly did something about it. Tegut established an automated warehouse in the East to supply the Konsum stores. The warehouse made it economical to assemble needed assortments of products from many different producers. Further, Tegut set up a computer network to provide timely reordering from the warehouse, on-line management of inventories and distribution, and even payment control. With the help of middlemen like Tegut, both local and foreign producers are better able to meet consumer needs.[17]

Specialists perform some functions

Earlier in the chapter you saw how producers and consumers can benefit when a middleman takes over some buying and selling. The Tegut example shows that producers and consumers also benefit when marketing specialists perform the other marketing functions. In fact, we find marketing functions being performed not only by middlemen but also by a variety of other **facilitators**—firms that

EXHIBIT 1–4   Model of a Market-Directed Macro-Marketing System

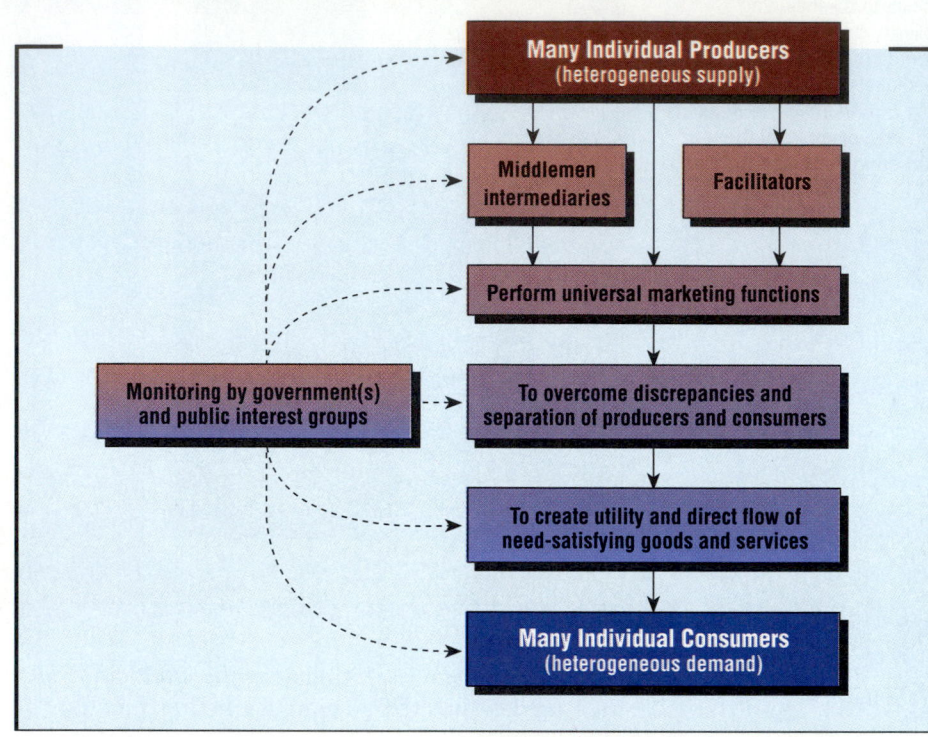

provide one or more of the marketing functions other than buying or selling. These include advertising agencies, marketing research firms, independent product-testing laboratories, public warehouses, transporting firms, communications companies, and financial institutions (including banks). Through specialization or economies of scale, marketing intermediaries and facilitators are often able to perform the marketing functions better—and at a lower cost—than producers or consumers can. This allows producers and consumers to spend more time on production and consumption.

Functions can be shifted and shared

From a macro viewpoint, all of the marketing functions must be performed by someone. But *from a micro viewpoint, not every firm must perform all of the functions. Further, not all goods and services require all the functions at every level of their production.* "Pure services"—like a plane ride—don't need storing, for example. But storing is required in the production of the plane and while the plane is not in service.

Some marketing specialists perform all the functions. Others specialize in only one or two. Marketing research firms, for example, specialize only in the market information function. The important point to remember is this: *Responsibility for performing the marketing functions can be shifted and shared in a variety of ways, but no function can be completely eliminated.*

HOW WELL DOES OUR MACRO-MARKETING SYSTEM WORK?

It connects remote producers and consumers

A macro-marketing system does more than just deliver goods and services to consumers—it allows mass production with its economies of scale. Also, mass communication, information systems, and mass transportation allow products to be shipped where they're needed. Oranges from California are found in Minnesota stores—even in December—and electronic parts made in Taiwan are used in making products all over the world.[18]

It encourages growth and new ideas

In addition to making mass production possible, a market-directed, macro-marketing system encourages **innovation**—the development and spread of new ideas and products. Competition for consumers' money forces firms to think of new and better ways of satisfying consumer needs. And the competition that marketing fosters drives down prices and gives consumers more choices and a higher standard of living.

It has its critics

In explaining marketing's role in society, we described some of the benefits of a market-directed macro-marketing system. We can see this in the macro-marketing system of the United States. It provides—at least in material terms—one of the highest standards of living in the world. It seems to be "effective" and "fair" in many ways.

We must admit, however, that marketing—as it exists in the United States and other developed societies—has many critics! Marketing activity is especially open to criticism because it is the part of business most visible to the public. There is nothing like a pocketbook issue for getting consumers excited!

Typical complaints about marketing include:

Advertising is too often annoying, misleading, and wasteful.

Products are not safe—or the quality is poor.

Marketing makes people too materialistic—it motivates them toward "things" instead of social needs.

Easy consumer credit makes people buy things they don't need and really can't afford.

Packaging and labeling are often confusing and deceptive.

Middlemen add to the cost of distribution—and raise prices without providing anything in return.

Marketing creates interest in products that pollute the environment.

Too many unnecessary products are offered.

Marketing serves the rich and exploits the poor.

Such complaints cannot and should not be taken lightly. They show that many people aren't happy with some parts of the marketing system. Certainly, the strong public support for consumer protection laws proves that not all consumers feel they are being treated like royalty.

As you consider the various criticisms of marketing, keep in mind that some of them deal with the marketing practices of specific firms and are micro-marketing oriented. Others are really criticisms of the whole macro-marketing system. This is an important distinction.

⚫ Is it an ethical issue?

Certainly some complaints about marketing arise because some individual firm or manager was intentionally unethical and cheated the market. But at other times, problems and criticism may arise because a manager did not fully consider the ethical implications of a decision. In either case, there is no excuse for sloppiness when it comes to **marketing ethics**—the moral standards that guide marketing decisions and actions. Each individual develops moral standards based on his or her own values. That helps explain why opinions about what is right or wrong often vary from one person to another, from one society to another, and among different groups within a society. It is sometimes difficult to say whose opinions are "correct." Even so, such opinions may have a very real influence on whether an individual's (or a firm's) marketing decisions and actions are accepted or rejected. So marketing ethics are not only a philosophical issue—they are also a pragmatic concern. Throughout the text we will be discussing the types of ethical issues individual marketing managers face. In fact, these issues are so important that we will highlight them with the special symbol used in the heading for this section. But we won't be moralizing and trying to tell you how you should think on any given issue. Rather, by the end of the course we hope that *you* will have some firm personal opinions about what is and is not ethical in micro-marketing activities.[19]

Keep in mind, however, that not all criticisms of marketing focus on ethical issues; fortunately, the "prevailing practice" of most businesspeople is to be fair and honest. Moreover, not all criticisms are specific to the micro-marketing activities of individual firms. Some of the complaints about marketing really focus on the basic idea of a market-directed macro-marketing system—and these criticisms often occur because people don't understand what marketing is—or how it works. As you go through this book, we'll discuss some of these criticisms. Then in our final chapter, we will return to a more complete appraisal of marketing in our consumer-oriented society.

CONCLUSION

In this chapter, we defined two levels of marketing: micro-marketing and macro-marketing. Macro-marketing is concerned with the way the whole global economy works. Micro-marketing focuses on the activities of individual firms. We discussed the role of marketing in economic development—and the functions of marketing and who performs them. We ended by raising some of the criticisms of marketing—both of the whole macro system and of the way individual firms work.

We emphasized macro-marketing in this chapter, but the major thrust of this book is on micro-marketing. By learning more about market-oriented decision making, you will be able to make more efficient and socially responsible decisions.

This will help improve the performance of individual firms and organizations (your employers). And eventually, it will help our macro-marketing system work better.

We'll see marketing through the eyes of the marketing manager—maybe *you* in the near future. And we will show how you can contribute to the marketing process. Along the way, we'll discuss the impact of micro-level decisions on society, and the ethical issues that marketing managers face. Then in Chapter 22—after you have had time to understand how and why producers and consumers think and behave the way they do—we will evaluate how well both micro-marketing and macro-marketing perform in a market-directed economic system.

QUESTIONS AND PROBLEMS

1. List your activities for the first two hours after you woke up this morning. Briefly indicate how marketing affected your activities.

2. It is fairly easy to see why people do not beat a path to a mousetrap manufacturer's door, but

would they be similarly indifferent if some food processor developed a revolutionary new food product that would provide all necessary nutrients in small pills for about $100 per year per person?

3. Distinguish between macro- and micro-marketing. Then explain how they are inter-related, if they are.

4. Distinguish between how economic decisions are made in a planned economic system and how they are made in a market-directed economy.

5. A committee of the American Marketing Association defined marketing as "the process of planning and executing the conception, pricing, promotion, and distribution of ideas, goods, and services to create exchanges that satisfy individual and organizational objectives." Does this definition consider macro-marketing? Explain your answer.

6. Identify a "central market" in your city and explain how it facilitates exchange.

7. Explain why tariffs and quotas affect international marketing opportunities.

8. Discuss the prospects for a group of Latin American entrepreneurs who are considering building a factory to produce machines that make cans for the food industry. Their country is in Stage 4—the nondurable and semidurable consumer products manufacturing stage. The country's population is approximately 20 million, and there is some possibility of establishing sales contacts in a few nearby countries.

9. Discuss the nature of marketing in a socialist economy. Would the functions that must be provided and the development of wholesaling and retailing systems be any different than in a market-directed economy?

10. Discuss how the micro–macro dilemma relates to each of the following products: high-powered engines in cars, nuclear power, bank credit cards, and pesticides that improve farm production.

11. Describe a recent purchase you made. Indicate why that particular product was available at a store and, in particular, at the store where you bought it.

12. Refer to Exhibit 1–3, and give an example of a purchase you recently made that involved separation of information and separation in time between you and the producer. Briefly explain how these separations were overcome.

13. Recently, on-line computer shopping services—like those available on CompuServe, Prodigy, and the Internet—are making it possible for individual consumers to get direct information from hundreds of companies they would not otherwise know about. In many cases, consumers can use the computer to place an order for a purchase that is then shipped to them directly. Will growth of these services ultimately eliminate the need for retailers and wholesalers? Explain your thinking, giving specific attention to what marketing functions are involved in these "electronic purchases" and who performs them.

14. Define the functions of marketing in your own words. Using an example, explain how they can be shifted and shared.

15. Explain, in your own words, why this text emphasizes micro-marketing.

16. Explain why a small producer might want a marketing research firm to take over some of its information-gathering activities.

17. Explain why a market-directed macro-marketing system encourages innovation. Give an example.

SUGGESTED CASES

1. McDonald's "Seniors" Restaurant

4. Galloway Carpet Service, Inc.

COMPUTER-AIDED PROBLEM

1. **Revenue, Cost, and Profit Relationships**

This problem introduces you to the computer-aided problem software—the PLUS computer program—and gets you started with the use of spreadsheet analysis for marketing decision making. This problem is simple. In fact, you could work it without the PLUS software. But by starting with a simple problem, you will learn how to use the program more quickly and see how it will help you with more complicated problems. Complete instructions for the PLUS software are available at the end of this text. However, while you are working with the software, you can press the H key to get help on-screen whenever you need it.

Sue Cline, the business manager at Magna University Student Bookstore, is developing plans for the next academic year. The bookstore is one of the university's nonprofit activities, but any "surplus" (profit) it earns is used to support the student activities center.

Two popular products at the bookstore are the student academic calendar and notebooks with the school name. Sue Cline thinks that she can sell calendars to 90 percent of Magna's 3,000 students, so she has had 2,700 printed. The total cost, including artwork and printing, is $11,500. Last year the calendar sold for $5.00, but Sue is considering changing the price this year.

Sue thinks that the bookstore will be able to sell 6,000 notebooks if they are priced right. But she knows that many students will buy similar notebooks (without the school name) from stores in town if the bookstore price is too high.

Sue has entered the information about selling price, quantity, and costs for calendars and notebooks in the spreadsheet program so that it is easy to evaluate the effect of different decisions. The spreadsheet is also set up to calculate revenue and profit, based on

$$\text{Revenue} = (\text{Selling price}) \times (\text{Quantity sold})$$

$$\text{Profit} = (\text{Revenue}) - (\text{Total cost})$$

Use the program to answer the questions below. Remember, you can press the H key to get help whenever you need it. Record your answers on a separate sheet of paper.

a. From the Spreadsheet Screen, how much revenue does Sue expect from calendars? How much revenue from notebooks? How much profit will the store earn from calendars? From notebooks?

b. If Sue increases the price of her calendars to $6.00 and still sells the same quantity, what is the expected revenue? The expected profit? (Note: Change the price from $5.00 to $6.00 on the spreadsheet and the program will recompute revenue and profit.) On your sheet of paper, show the calculations that confirm that the program has given you the correct values.

c. Sue is interested in getting an overview of how a change in the price of notebooks would affect revenue and profit, assuming that she sells all 6,000 notebooks she is thinking of ordering. Prepare a table—on your sheet of paper—with column headings for three variables: selling price, revenue, and profit. Show the value for revenue and profit for different possible selling prices for a notebook—starting at a minimum price of $1.60 and adding 8 cents to the price until you reach a maximum of $2.40. At what price will selling 6,000 notebooks contribute $5,400.00 to profit? At what price would notebook sales contribute only $1,080.00? (Hint: Use the What If analysis to compute the new values. Start by selecting "selling price" for notebooks as the value to change, with a minimum value of $1.60 and a maximum value of $2.40. Select the revenue and profit for notebooks as the values to display.)

For additional questions related to this problem, see Exercise 1–4 in the *Learning Aid for Use with Basic Marketing*, 12th edition.

2

Marketing's Role within the Firm or Nonprofit Organization

When You Finish This Chapter, You Should

1. Know what the marketing concept is—and how it should affect strategy planning in a firm or nonprofit organization.

2. Understand what a marketing manager does.

3. Know what marketing strategy planning is—and why it will be the focus of this book.

4. Understand target marketing.

5. Be familiar with the four Ps in a marketing mix.

6. Know the difference between a marketing strategy, a marketing plan, and a marketing program.

7. Understand the important new terms (shown in red).

Marketing and marketing management are important in our society—and in business firms and nonprofit organizations. As you saw in Chapter 1, marketing is concerned with anticipating needs and directing the flow of goods and services from producers to consumers. This is done to satisfy the needs of consumers and achieve the objectives of the firm (the micro view) and of society as a whole (the macro view).

To get a better understanding of marketing, we are going to look at things from the viewpoint of the marketing manager—the one who makes an organization's important marketing decisions. To get you thinking about the ideas we will be developing in this chapter and the rest of the book, let's consider a few decisions recently made by marketing managers.

In the winter of 1995, marketing managers in the power tool division at Black & Decker (B&D) were looking forward to improved profits because of the successful marketing program they had developed. The overall program was the result of the careful blending of detailed plans for several different marketing strategies.

Black & Decker tools were well known among consumers and dominated many segments of the do-it-yourself market. However, in 1993 they were capturing only about 10 percent of the sales to professionals who bought power tools for commercial work. There was a good opportunity for profitable growth with these customers, but B&D needed a special marketing effort targeted at their needs. Makita (a Japanese producer) already had a strong reputation with these customers. And other competitors—including Sears (with its Craftsman brand), Snap-On, and producers from Japan and Germany—were also joining the battle for this business. To come out on top in these "saw wars," B&D's managers had to make many decisions.

B&D marketing managers spent three months visiting more than 200 tool stores and job sites to get feedback from professionals about their interests and needs. Some of the details were simple but useful: "paint it yellow to make it easy to see and to signify safety." Other concerns also surfaced. For example, the well-regarded Black & Decker brand name did not have as favorable an image with these professionals as it did with consumers. The professionals thought of it as a good "consumer brand" that had no particular advantage for their needs. They wanted rugged, heavy-duty tools—ones that would stand up to their demanding applications.

Working with people in research and development and manufacturing, B&D marketing managers developed a special line of 33 tools for this target market. Tests showed that all but two of the tools would satisfy professional customers better than competing products from Makita; the two that didn't were redesigned. Going even further to meet the target customers' reliability needs, B&D set up 117 service centers and offered a 48-hour repair guarantee. To further cement its relationship with customers, B&D even promised a free loaner tool during the repair. Marketing managers also decided that it would be better to use the firm's less widely known DeWalt brand name rather than try to change the target customers' beliefs about the Black & Decker brand. Marketing research showed that the professional target market already respected the DeWalt name.

Marketing managers also had to decide the best way to reach the target market. Should they start in some introductory regions or distribute the new products in as many countries as possible all at once? Should they focus on retailers who had sold their other products in the past? Or should they put special emphasis on working closely with big chains, like Home Depot, that already had a strong relationship with the professional target market?

B&D also had to decide how to promote the new line of DeWalt tools. Marketing managers had to decide how many salespeople would be needed to work with wholesalers and retailers. They also had to develop plans for advertising to the target customers—including deciding on an advertising theme and determining how much to spend and where to spend it.

They had other decisions to make. The price on their consumer products had been set low to attract price-sensitive buyers. Should they stick with a low beat-the-competition price on the DeWalt line, or would a premium price be more profitable with professionals, who were more concerned about long-term reliability? Should they offer introductory price rebates to help attract customers from Makita and other brands? Should they offer middlemen intermediaries special discounts for large orders?

The marketing plan for the DeWalt line has proved to be successful, but it is only part of B&D's overall marketing program. For example, another newly developed marketing strategy focuses on a different target market, the serious do-it-yourselfers who routinely take on big home improvement projects. Research showed that these consumers had different needs from both the professionals and the typical power tool consumer. These consumers wanted tools with special features, like a power saw with a dust collection system. To meet these needs, B&D managers developed a line of 18 Quantum brand power tools. As with the DeWalt line, the Quantum tool line was supported with a comprehensive marketing plan that was designed to build an ongoing relationship with target customers. For example, consumers who buy Quantum tools get access to a toll-free telephone line for advice on home improvement projects. They also get a free subscription to *Shop Talk*, a newsletter with workshop tips. Quantum customers are interested in reading the information in the newsletter; so, it's an ideal place for B&D managers to promote new Quantum tools.[1]

We've mentioned only a few of many decisions Black & Decker marketing managers had to make in developing a marketing program, but you can see that each of these decisions affects the others. Making marketing decisions is never easy. But knowing what basic decision areas have to be considered helps you to plan a better, more successful strategy. This chapter will get you started by giving you a framework for thinking about all the marketing management decision areas—which is what the rest of this book is all about.

MARKETING'S ROLE HAS CHANGED A LOT OVER THE YEARS

From our Black & Decker example, it's clear that marketing decisions are very important to a firm's success. But marketing hasn't always been so complicated. In fact, it's only in the last 35 years or so that an increasing number of producers, wholesalers, retailers, and nonprofit organizations have adopted modern marketing thinking. Instead of just focusing on producing or selling *products,* these organizations focus on *customers*—and try to integrate an organizationwide effort to satisfy them on an ongoing basis.

We will discuss five stages in marketing evolution: (1) the simple trade era, (2) the production era, (3) the sales era, (4) the marketing department era, and (5) the marketing company era. We'll talk about these eras as if they applied generally to all firms—but keep in mind that *some managers still have not made it to the final stages.* They are stuck in the past with old ways of thinking.

Specialization permitted trade—and middlemen met the need

When societies first moved toward some specialization of production and away from a subsistence economy where each family raised and consumed everything it produced, traders played an important role. Early "producers for the market" made products that were needed by themselves and their neighbors. (Recall the five-family example in Chapter 1.) As bartering became more difficult, societies moved into the **simple trade era**—a time when families traded or sold their "surplus" output to local middlemen. These specialists resold the goods to other consumers or distant middlemen. This was the early role of marketing—and it is still the focus of marketing in many of the less-developed areas of the world. In fact, even in the United States, the United Kingdom, and other more advanced economies, marketing didn't change much until the Industrial Revolution brought larger factories a little over a hundred years ago.

From the production to the sales era

From the Industrial Revolution until the 1920s, most companies were in the production era. The **production era** is a time when a company focuses on production of a few specific products—perhaps because few of these products are available in the market. "If we can make it, it will sell" is management thinking characteristic of the production era. Because of product shortages, many nations—including many of the newly independent republics of Eastern Europe—continue to operate with production era approaches.

By about 1930, most companies in the industrialized Western nations had more production capability than ever before. Now the problem wasn't just to produce—but to beat the competition and win customers. This led many firms to enter the sales era. The **sales era** is a time when a company emphasizes selling because of increased competition.

To the marketing department era

For most firms in advanced economies, the sales era continued until at least 1950. By then, sales were growing rapidly in most areas of the economy. The problem was deciding where to put the company's effort. Someone was needed to tie together the efforts of research, purchasing, production, shipping, and sales. As this situation became more common, the sales era was replaced by the marketing department era. The **marketing department era** is a time when all marketing activities are brought under the control of one department to improve short-run policy planning and to try to integrate the firm's activities.

In 1899, a firm could easily sell all the sewing machines it could produce because there were few available in the market.

To the marketing company era

Since 1960, most firms have developed at least some staff with a marketing management outlook. Many of these firms have even graduated from the marketing department era into the marketing company era. The **marketing company era** is a time when, in addition to short-run marketing planning, marketing people develop long-range plans—sometimes 10 or more years ahead—and the whole company effort is guided by the marketing concept.

WHAT DOES THE MARKETING CONCEPT MEAN?

The **marketing concept** means that an organization aims *all* its efforts at satisfying its *customers*—at a profit. The marketing concept is a simple but very important idea. See Exhibit 2–1.

The marketing concept is not really a new idea—it's been around for a long time. But some managers act as if they are stuck at the beginning of the production era—when there were shortages of most products. They show little interest in customers' needs. These managers still have a **production orientation**—making whatever products are easy to produce and *then* trying to sell them. They think of customers existing to buy the firm's output rather than of firms existing to serve customers and—more broadly—the needs of society.

Well-managed firms have replaced this production orientation with a marketing orientation. A **marketing orientation** means trying to carry out the marketing concept. Instead of just trying to get customers to buy what the firm has produced, a marketing-oriented firm tries to offer customers what they need.

Three basic ideas are included in the definition of the marketing concept: (1) customer satisfaction, (2) a total company effort, and (3) profit—not just sales—as an objective. These ideas deserve more discussion.

EXHIBIT 2–1　Organizations with a Marketing Orientation Carry Out the Marketing Concept

Customer satisfaction guides the whole system

"Give the customers what they need" seems so obvious that it may be hard for you to see why the marketing concept requires special attention. However, people don't always do the logical and obvious—especially when it means changing what they've done in the past. In a typical company 35 years ago, production managers thought mainly about getting out the product. Accountants were interested only in balancing the books. Financial people looked after the company's cash position. And salespeople were mainly concerned with getting orders for whatever product was in the warehouse. Each department thought of its own activity as the center of the business—with others working around "the edges." No one was concerned with the whole system. As long as the company made a profit, each department went merrily on—doing its own thing. Unfortunately, this is still true in many companies today.

Work together to do a better job

Ideally, all managers should work together as a team because the output from one department may be the input to another. And every department may directly or indirectly impact short-term and long-term customer satisfaction. But some managers tend to build "fences" around their own departments, as seen in Exhibit 2–2A. There may be meetings to try to get them to work together—but they come and go from the meetings worried only about protecting their own turf.

We use the term *production orientation* as a shorthand way to refer to this kind of narrow thinking—and lack of a central focus—in a business firm. But keep in mind that this problem may be seen in sales-oriented sales representatives, advertising-oriented agency people, finance-oriented finance people, directors of nonprofit organizations, and so on. It is not just a criticism of people who manage production. They aren't necessarily any more guilty of narrow thinking than anyone else.

EXHIBIT 2–2

A.   **A business as a box**
     (most departments have high fences)

B.   **Total system view of a business**
     (implementing marketing concept; still have
     departments but all guided by what customers want)

The "fences" come down in an organization that has accepted the marketing concept. There are still departments, of course, because specialization often makes sense. But the total system's effort is guided by what customers want—instead of what each department would like to do.

In such a firm, it is more realistic to view the business as a box with both internal and external activities, as shown in Exhibit 2–2B. Some departments—like production, accounting, and research and development (R&D)—are mainly concerned with affairs inside the firm. The external departments are concerned with outsiders—sales, advertising, and sales promotion. Finally, some departments—warehousing, shipping, purchasing, finance, and personnel—work with both insiders and outsiders.

In Chapter 21, we'll go into more detail on the relationship between marketing and other functions. Here, however, you should see that the marketing concept provides a guiding focus that *all* departments adopt. It should be a philosophy of the whole organization, not just an idea that applies to the marketing department. It helps the organization work as a total "system" rather than a lot of separate parts. The marketing concept, however, is more complete than many systems-oriented ideas. It actually specifies a high-level objective—customer satisfaction—that is logical for each and every part of the system. It also specifies a profit objective, which is necessary for the system's survival.

Survival and success require a profit

Firms must satisfy customers, or the customers won't continue to "vote" for the firm's survival and success with their money. But firms must also keep in mind that sales revenue from customers comes at a cost. It may cost more to satisfy some needs than any customers are willing to pay. Or, it may be much more costly to try to attract new customers than it is to build a strong relationship with—and repeat purchases from—existing customers. So profit—the difference between a firm's revenue and its total costs—is the bottom-line measure of the firm's success and ability to survive. It is the balancing point that helps the firm determine what needs it will try to satisfy with its total (sometimes costly!) effort.

ADOPTION OF THE MARKETING CONCEPT HAS NOT BEEN EASY OR UNIVERSAL

The marketing concept seems so logical that you would think most firms would quickly adopt it. But this isn't the case. Many firms are still production-oriented. In fact, the majority are either production-oriented—or regularly slip back that way—and must consciously refocus their planning on customers' interests.

The marketing concept was first accepted by consumer products companies such as General Electric and Procter & Gamble. Competition was intense in some of their markets—and trying to satisfy customers' needs more fully was a way to win in this competition. Widespread publicity about the success of the marketing concept at companies like General Electric and Procter & Gamble helped spread the message to other firms.[2]

Producers of industrial commodities—steel, coal, paper, glass, and chemicals—have accepted the marketing concept slowly if at all. Similarly, many traditional retailers have been slow to accept the marketing concept—in part because they are so close to final consumers that they think they really know their customers.

Service industries are catching up

Service industries—including airlines, banks, investment firms, lawyers, physicians, accountants, and insurance companies—were slow to adopt the marketing concept too. But this has changed dramatically in the last decade, partly due to government regulation changes that forced many of these businesses to be more competitive.[3]

Many service businesses, including Continental Bank, which is now part of the Bank of America, have begun to apply the marketing concept and are working harder to develop long-run relationships with their customers.

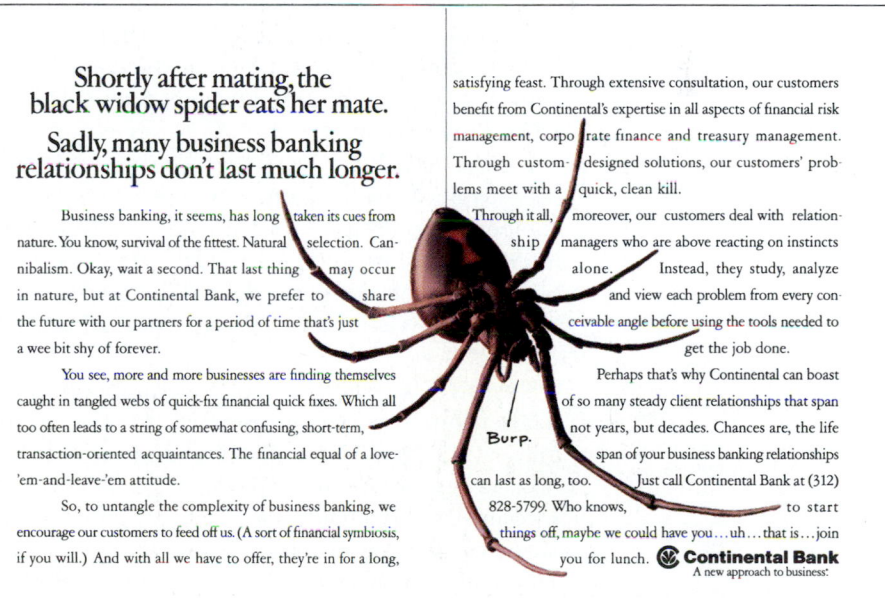

Shortly after mating, the black widow spider eats her mate.
Sadly, many business banking relationships don't last much longer.

Business banking, it seems, has long taken its cues from nature. You know, survival of the fittest. Natural selection. Cannibalism. Okay, wait a second. That last thing may occur in nature, but at Continental Bank, we prefer to share the future with our partners for a period of time that's just a wee bit shy of forever.

You see, more and more businesses are finding themselves caught in tangled webs of quick-fix financial quick fixes. Which all too often leads to a string of somewhat confusing, short-term, transaction-oriented acquaintances. The financial equal of a love-'em-and-leave-'em attitude.

So, to untangle the complexity of business banking, we encourage our customers to feed off us. (A sort of financial symbiosis, if you will.) And with all we have to offer, they're in for a long, satisfying feast. Through extensive consultation, our customers benefit from Continental's expertise in all aspects of financial risk management, corporate finance and treasury management. Through custom-designed solutions, our customers' problems meet with a quick, clean kill.

Through it all, moreover, our customers deal with relationship managers who are above reacting on instincts alone. Instead, they study, analyze and view each problem from every conceivable angle before using the tools needed to get the job done.

Perhaps that's why Continental can boast of so many steady client relationships that span not years, but decades. Chances are, the life span of your business banking relationships can last as long, too. Just call Continental Bank at (312) 828-5799. Who knows, to start things off, maybe we could have you...uh...that is...join you for lunch.

Burp.

Continental Bank
A new approach to business.

Banks used to be open for limited hours that were convenient for bankers—not customers. Many closed during lunch hour! But now financial services are less regulated, and banks compete with companies like Merrill Lynch or American Express for checking accounts and retirement investments. Innovative banks are opening branches in grocery stores and other places that are more convenient for customers. They stay open longer, often during evenings and on Saturdays. They also offer more services for their customers—automated teller machines that take credit cards or a "personal banker" to give financial advice. Most banks now aggressively advertise their special services and even interest rates so customers can compare bank offerings.

It's easy to slip into a production orientation

The marketing concept may seem obvious, but it's very easy to slip into a production-oriented way of thinking. For example, a retailer might prefer only weekday hours—avoiding nights, Saturdays, and Sundays when many customers would prefer to shop. Or a company might rush to produce a clever new product developed in its lab—rather than first finding out if it will fill an unsatisfied need. Many firms in high-technology businesses fall into this trap. They think that technology is the source of their success, rather than realizing that technology is only a means to meet customer needs.

Take a look at Exhibit 2–3. It shows some differences in outlook between adopters of the marketing concept and typical production-oriented managers. As the exhibit suggests, the marketing concept—if taken seriously—is really very powerful. It forces the company to think through what it is doing—and why. And it motivates the company to develop plans for accomplishing its objectives.

Where does competition fit?

Some critics say that the marketing concept doesn't go far enough in today's highly competitive markets. They think of marketing as "warfare" for customers—and argue that a marketing manager should focus on competitors, not customers. That viewpoint, however, misses the point. The marketing concept idea isn't just to satisfy customers—but to do it at a profit through an integrated, whole-company effort. All three must be considered simultaneously. Profit opportunities depend not only on outdoing some other firm—but also on doing the right thing. In fact, often the best way to beat the competition is to be first to find and satisfy a need that others have not even considered. The competition between Pepsi and Coke illustrates this.

Coke and Pepsi were spending millions of dollars on promotion—fighting head-to-head for the same cola customers. They put so much emphasis on the competitor that they missed opportunities. Then, Pepsi recognized consumer interest in a potential new product idea: a soft drink based on fruit juice. Pepsi's Slice brand soft drink was first on the market, and that helped Slice win space on retailers' shelves—and loyal consumers who would make repeat purchases.

Build relationships with customers

Firms that embrace the marketing concept seek ways to build a long-term relationship with each customer. This is an important idea. Even the most innovative firms—ones that find new ways to satisfy consumers—face competition sooner or later. And trying to get new customers by taking them away from a competitor is usually more costly than retaining current customers by really satisfying their needs. Equally important, happy customers buy again and again. This makes their buying job easier, and it also increases the firm's profits.

EXHIBIT 2–3   Some Differences in Outlook between Adopters of the Marketing Concept and the Typical Production-Oriented Managers

Topic	Marketing Orientation	Production Orientation
Attitudes toward Customers	Customer needs determine company plans.	They should be glad we exist, trying to cut costs and bringing out better products.
Product Offering	Company makes what it can sell.	Company sells what it can make.
Role of Marketing Research	To determine customer needs and how well company is satisfying them.	To determine customer reaction, if used at all.
Interest in Innovation	Focus on locating new opportunities.	Focus is on technology and cost cutting.
Importance of Profit	A critical objective.	A residual, what's left after all costs are covered.
Role of Customer Credit	Seen as a customer service.	Seen as a necessary evil.
Role of Packaging	Designed for customer convenience and as a selling tool.	Seen merely as protection for the product.
Inventory Levels	Set with customer requirements and costs in mind.	Set to make production more convenient.
Transportation Arrangements	Seen as a customer service.	Seen as an extension of production and storage activities, with emphasis on cost minimization.
Focus of Advertising	Need-satisfying benefits of products and services.	Product features and how products are made.
Role of Sales Force	Help the customer to buy if the product fits customer's needs, while coordinating with rest of firm.	Sell the customer, don't worry about coordination with other promotion efforts or rest of firm.
Relationship with Customer	Customer satisfaction before and after sale leads to a profitable long-run relationship.	Relationship is seen as short term—ends when a sale is made.

Building mutually beneficial relationships with customers requires that everyone in an organization work together to achieve customer satisfaction before *and after* each purchase. If there is a problem with a customer's bill, the accounting people can't just leave it to the salesperson to straighten it out or, even worse, act like it's "the customer's problem." Rather, it's the firm's problem. The long-term relationship with the customer—and the lifetime value of the customer's future purchases—is threatened if the accountant, the salesperson, and anyone else who might be involved don't work together quickly to make things right for the customer. Similarly, the firm's advertising people can't just develop ads that try to convince a customer to buy once. If the firm doesn't deliver on the benefits promised in its ads, the customer is likely to go elsewhere the next time the need arises. And the same ideas apply whether the issue is meeting promised delivery dates, resolving warranty problems, giving a customer help on how to use a product, or even making it easy for the customer to return a purchase made in error.

L.L. Bean is a good example of a firm that has been able to build enduring relationships with its customers by really implementing the marketing concept. Bean focuses on consumers who are interested in enjoying the outdoors. To build a relationship with these consumers, Bean offers quality products that are well suited to a wide variety of outdoor needs—whether it's clothing or equipment for fishing, camping, or kayaking. Bean field-tests every product it plans to sell—to be certain that products live up to the firm's "100% satisfaction" guarantee. Although Bean operates a retail store in Freeport, Maine, it uses a catalog to reach customers all over the world. By using computers to track what each customer is buying, Bean can mail new catalogs directly to the people who are most interested. To make ordering convenient, customers can call toll-free 24 hours a day—and they get whatever advice they need because all of the salespeople in every department are real experts on what they sell. To ensure that orders reach the customer's place fast, Bean uses UPS to ship most items directly from its own warehouse. Bean also makes it easy for consumers to return a product, and encourages them to complain about any problem. That way, Bean can do whatever it takes to solve a problem before it disrupts the relationship. Although Bean's pricing is basically competitive with other outdoor sporting specialty stores, customers are loyal repeat buyers because they like the benefits of the relationship with the company.[4]

THE MARKETING CONCEPT APPLIES IN NONPROFIT ORGANIZATIONS

Newcomers to marketing thinking

The marketing concept is as important for nonprofit organizations as it is for business firms. However, prior to 1970 few people paid attention to the role of

Everyone who works at L.L. Bean is part of a team effort to satisfy customers' needs before and after each sale, and that has helped it build profitable long-run relationships with its loyal customers.

marketing in facilitating the types of exchanges and relationships that are typical of nonprofits. Now marketing is widely recognized as applicable to all sorts of public and private nonprofit organizations—ranging from government agencies, health care organizations, educational institutions, and religious groups to charities, political parties, and fine arts organizations.

Some nonprofit organizations operate just like a business. For example, there may be no practical difference between the gift shop at a museum and a for-profit shop located across the street. On the other hand, some nonprofits differ from business firms in a variety of ways.

Support may not come from satisfied "customers"

As with any business firm, a nonprofit organization needs resources and support to survive and achieve its objectives. Yet support often does not come directly from those who receive the benefits the organization produces. For example, the World Wildlife Fund protects animals. If supporters of the World Wildlife Fund are not satisfied with its efforts—don't think the benefits are worth what it costs to provide them—they will, and should, put their time and money elsewhere.

Just as most firms face competition for customers, most nonprofits face competition for the resources and support they need. A sorority will falter if potential members join other organizations. A shelter for the homeless may fail if supporters decide to focus on some other cause, such as AIDS education. A community theater group that decides to do a play that the actors and the director like—never stopping to consider what the audience might want to see—may find that the theater is empty and the audience is at home watching a video.

What is the "bottom line"?

As with a business, a nonprofit must take in as much money as it spends or it won't survive. However, a nonprofit organization does not measure "profit" in the same way as a firm. And its key measures of long-term success are also different. The YMCA, colleges, symphony orchestras, and the post office, for example, all seek to achieve different objectives—and need different measures of success.

Profit guides business decisions because it reflects both the costs and benefits of different activities. In a nonprofit organization, it is sometimes more difficult to be objective in evaluating the benefits of different activities relative to what they cost. However, if everyone in an organization agrees to *some*

Marketing is being more widely accepted by nonprofit organizations.

measure of long-run success, it helps serve as a guide to where the organization should focus its efforts.

May not be organized for marketing

Some nonprofits face other challenges in organizing to adopt the marketing concept. Often no one has overall responsibility for marketing activities. A treasurer or accountant may keep the books, and someone may be in charge of "operations"—but marketing may somehow seem less crucial, especially if no one understands what marketing is all about. Even when some leaders do the marketing thinking, they may have trouble getting unpaid volunteers with many different interests to all agree with the marketing strategy. Volunteers tend to do what they feel like doing!

The marketing concept provides focus

We have been discussing some of the differences between nonprofit and business organizations. However, the marketing concept is helpful in *any* type of organization. Success is unlikely if everyone doesn't pull together to strive for common objectives that can be achieved with the available resources. Adopting the marketing concept helps to bring this kind of focus. After all, each organization is trying to satisfy some group of consumers in some way.[5]

Nonprofits achieve objectives by satisfying needs

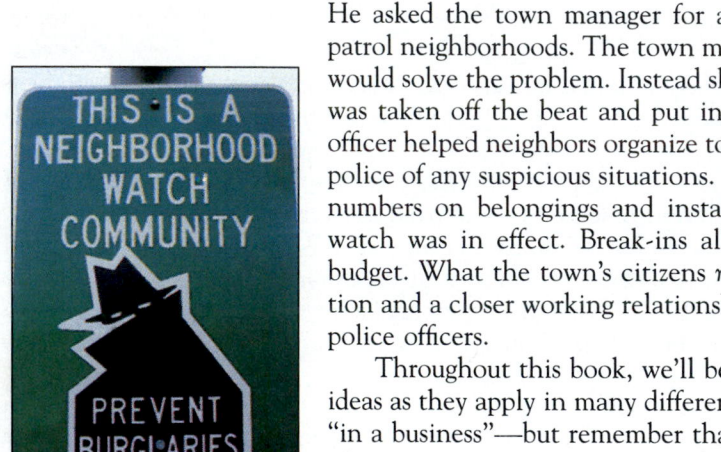

A simple example shows how marketing concept thinking helped one nonprofit service organization do a better job of achieving its objectives. A police chief in a small town was trying to fight increased robberies in residential areas. He asked the town manager for a larger budget—for more officers and cars to patrol neighborhoods. The town manager wasn't convinced a bigger police budget would solve the problem. Instead she tried a different approach. One police officer was taken off the beat and put in charge of a community watch program. This officer helped neighbors organize to look after each others' property and notify the police of any suspicious situations. The officer also set up a program to engrave ID numbers on belongings and installed signs warning thieves that a community watch was in effect. Break-ins all but stopped—without increasing the police budget. What the town's citizens *really* needed was more effective crime prevention and a closer working relationship with the police department—not just more police officers.

Throughout this book, we'll be discussing the marketing concept and related ideas as they apply in many different settings. Often we'll simply say "in a firm" or "in a business"—but remember that most of the ideas can be applied in *any* type of organization.

THE MARKETING CONCEPT, SOCIAL RESPONSIBILITY, AND MARKETING ETHICS

Society's needs must be considered

The marketing concept is so logical that it's hard to argue with it. Yet when a firm focuses its efforts on satisfying some consumers—to achieve its objectives—there may be negative effects on society. (Remember that we discussed this micro-macro dilemma in Chapter 1.) This means that marketing managers should be concerned with **social responsibility**—a firm's obligation to improve its positive effects on society and reduce its negative effects. Being socially responsible sometimes requires difficult trade-offs.

Consider, for example, the environmental problems created by CFCs, chemicals used in hundreds of critical products including fire extinguishers, refrigerators, cooling systems for skyscrapers, insulation, and electronic circuit boards. We now know that CFCs deplete the earth's ozone layer. The result is a possible "global warming" and exposure to cancer-causing ultraviolet radiation. Yet it is not possible to immediately stop producing and using all CFCs. For many products critical to society, there is no feasible short-term substitute for CFCs. Du Pont and other producers of CFCs are working hard to balance these conflicting demands. Yet you can see that there are no easy answers for how these conflicts should be resolved.[6]

The issue of social responsibility in marketing also raises other important questions—for which there are no easy answers.

Should all consumer needs be satisfied?

Some consumers want products that may not be safe or good for them in the long run. Some critics argue that businesses should not offer cigarettes, high-heeled shoes, alcoholic beverages, sugar-coated cereals, soft drinks, and many processed foods because they aren't "good" for consumers in the long run.

Similarly, bicycles are one of the most dangerous products identified by the Consumer Product Safety Commission. Should Schwinn stop production? What about skis, mopeds, and scuba equipment? Who should decide if these products will be offered to consumers? Is this a micro-marketing issue or a macro-marketing issue?

What if it cuts into profits?

Being more socially conscious often seems to lead to positive customer response. For example, Gerber had great success when it improved the nutritional quality of its baby food. And many consumers have been eager to buy products that are friendly to the environment (even at a higher price).

Yet as the examples above show, there are times when being socially responsible conflicts with a firm's profit objective. Concerns about such conflicts have prompted critics to raise the basic question: Is the marketing concept really desirable?

Many marketing managers and socially conscious marketing companies are trying to resolve this problem. Their definition of customer satisfaction includes long-range effects—as well as immediate customer satisfaction. They try to balance consumer, company, *and* social interests.

You too will have to make choices that balance these social concerns—either in your role as a consumer or as a manager in a business firm. So throughout the text we will be discussing many of the social issues faced by marketing management.

The marketing concept guides marketing ethics

Organizations that have adopted the marketing concept are concerned about marketing ethics as well as broader issues of social responsibility. It is simply not possible for a firm to be truly consumer-oriented and at the same time intentionally unethical in decisions or actions that affect customers.

Individual managers in an organization may have different values. As a result, problems may arise when someone does not share the same marketing ethics as others in the organization. One person operating alone can damage a firm's reputation and even survival. Because the marketing concept involves a companywide focus, it is a foundation for marketing ethics common to everyone in a firm—and helps to avoid such problems.

To be certain that standards for marketing ethics are as clear as possible, many organizations have developed their own written codes of ethics. Consistent with the marketing concept, these codes usually state—at least at a general level—the ethical standards that everyone in the firm should follow in dealing with customers and other people. Many professional societies have also adopted such codes. For example, the American Marketing Association's code of ethics—see Exhibit 2–4—sets specific ethical standards for many aspects of the management job in marketing.[7]

THE MANAGEMENT JOB IN MARKETING

Now that you know about the marketing concept—a philosophy to guide the whole firm—let's look more closely at how a marketing manager helps a firm to achieve its objectives. The marketing manager is a manager, so let's look at the marketing management process.

The **marketing management process** is the process of (1) *planning* marketing activities, (2) directing the *implementation* of the plans, and (3) *controlling* these plans. Planning, implementation, and control are basic jobs of all managers—but here we will emphasize what they mean to marketing managers.

Exhibit 2–5 shows the relationships among the three jobs in the marketing management process. The jobs are all connected to show that the marketing management process is continuous. In the planning job, managers set guidelines for the implementing job—and specify expected results. They use these expected results in the control job—to determine if everything has worked out as planned. The link from the control job to the planning job is especially important. This feedback often leads to changes in the plans—or to new plans.

Marketing managers should seek new opportunities

Exhibit 2–5 shows that marketing managers must seek attractive new opportunities—as customers' needs change or as the organization's ability to meet customers' needs changes. In the next two chapters, we will discuss how marketing managers seek and evaluate opportunities. For now, however, note that marketing managers cannot be satisfied just planning present activities. Markets are dynamic. Consumers' needs, competitors, and the environment keep changing.

Consider Parker Brothers, a company that seemed to have a "Monopoly" in family games. While it continued selling board games, firms like Sega and Nintendo zoomed in with video game competition. Of course, not every opportunity is good for every company. Really attractive opportunities are those that fit with what the whole company wants—and is able to do.

Strategic management planning concerns the whole firm

The job of planning strategies to guide a whole company is called **strategic (management) planning**—the managerial process of developing and maintaining a match between an organization's resources and its market opportunities. This is a top-management job that includes planning not only for marketing activities but also for production, finance, research and development, and other functional areas. We'll touch on some of these issues in Chapter 21 as we consider the relationship between marketing and other functional areas. Yet, the focus of this text is not on whole-company planning, and you need to understand that marketing department plans are not whole-company plans.

EXHIBIT 2–4   Code of Ethics, American Marketing Association

CODE OF ETHICS

Members of the American Marketing Association (AMA) are committed to ethical professional conduct. They have joined together in subscribing to this Code of Ethics embracing the following topics:

Responsibilities of the Marketer

Marketers must accept responsibility for the consequences of their activities and make every effort to ensure that their decisions, recommendations, and actions function to identify, serve, and satisfy all relevant publics: customers, organizations and society.

Marketers' professional conduct must be guided by:

1. The basic rule of professional ethics: not knowingly to do harm;
2. The adherence to all applicable laws and regulations;
3. The accurate representation of their education, training and experience; and
4. The active support, practice and promotion of this Code of Ethics.

Honesty and Fairness

Marketers shall uphold and advance the integrity, honor, and dignity of the marketing profession by:

1. Being honest in serving consumers, clients, employees, suppliers, distributors and the public;
2. Not knowingly participating in conflict of interest without prior notice to all parties involved; and
3. Establishing equitable fee schedules including the payment or receipt of usual, customary and/or legal compensation for marketing exchanges.

Rights and Duties of Parties in the Marketing Exchange Process

Participants in the marketing exchange process should be able to expect that:

1. Products and services offered are safe and fit for their intended uses;
2. Communications about offered products and services are not deceptive;
3. All parties intend to discharge their obligations, financial and otherwise, in good faith; and
4. Appropriate internal methods exist for equitable adjustment and/or redress of grievances concerning purchases.

It is understood that the above would include, *but is not limited to,* the following responsibilities of the marketer:

In the area of product development and management,

- disclosure of all substantial risks associated with product or service usage;

- identification of any product component substitution that might materially change the product or impact on the buyer's purchase decision;
- identification of extra-cost added features.

In the area of promotions,

- avoidance of false and misleading advertising;
- rejection of high pressure manipulations, or misleading sales tactics;
- avoidance of sales promotions that use deception or manipulation.

In the area of distribution,

- not manipulating the availability of a product for purpose of exploitation;
- not using coercion in the marketing channel;
- not exerting undue influence over the reseller's choice to handle a product.

In the area of pricing,

- not engaging in price fixing;
- not practicing predatory pricing;
- disclosing the full price associated with any purchase.

In the area of marketing research,

- prohibiting selling or fund raising under the guise of conducting research;
- maintaining research integrity by avoiding misrepresentation and omission of pertinent research data;
- treating outside clients and suppliers fairly.

Organizational Relationships

Marketers should be aware of how their behavior may influence or impact on the behavior of others in organizational relationships. They should not demand, encourage or apply coercion to obtain unethical behavior in their relationships with others, such as employees, suppliers or customers.

1. Apply confidentiality and anonymity in professional relationships with regard to privileged information;
2. Meet their obligations and responsibilities in contracts and mutual agreements in a timely manner;
3. Avoid taking the work of others, in whole, or in part, and represent this work as their own or directly benefit from it without compensation or consent of the originator or owner;
4. Avoid manipulation to take advantage of situations to maximize personal welfare in a way that unfairly deprives or damages the organization of others.

Any AMA members found to be in violation of any provision of this Code of Ethics may have his or her Association membership suspended or revoked.

EXHIBIT 2–5 The Marketing Management Process

On the other hand, company plans should be market-oriented. And the marketing manager's plans can set the tone and direction for the whole company. So we will use *strategy planning* and *marketing strategy planning* to mean the same thing.[8]

WHAT IS MARKETING STRATEGY PLANNING?

Marketing strategy planning means finding attractive opportunities and developing profitable marketing strategies. But what is a "marketing strategy"? We have used these words rather casually so far. Now let's see what they really mean.

What is a marketing strategy?

A **marketing strategy** specifies a target market and a related marketing mix. It is a "big picture" of what a firm will do in some market. Two interrelated parts are needed:

EXHIBIT 2–6
A Marketing Strategy

1. A **target market**—a fairly homogeneous (similar) group of customers to whom a company wishes to appeal.
2. A **marketing mix**—the controllable variables the company puts together to satisfy this target group.

The importance of target customers in this process can be seen in Exhibit 2–6, where the customer—the "C"—is at the center of the diagram. The customer is surrounded by the controllable variables that we call the "marketing mix." A typical marketing mix includes some product, offered at a price, with some promotion to tell potential customers about the product, and a way to reach the customer's place.

Brøderbund Software's marketing strategy aims at a specific group of target customers—young parents who have a computer at home and want their kids to learn while playing. Brøderbund's strategy calls for a variety of educational software products—ranging from its popular *Print Shop* to *Where in the World Is Carmen Sandiego?* Brøderbund designs all of its software with entertaining graphics and sound, and it tests the software on kids before it's released to be certain that it is easy to use. To make it convenient for target customers to buy the software, Brøderbund works with retailers like EggHead and Babbages. Retailers are happy to give new Brøderbund products shelf space because they know that Brøderbund's promotion will help bring customers into the store. For example, when Brøderbund released *Where in Time Is Carmen Sandiego?* it not only placed ads in kids' magazines and family-oriented computer magazines but also sent direct-mail flyers to its database of registered customers. Other software publishers sell less-expensive games for kids, but parents are loyal to Brøderbund because it consistently does a better job of catering to their needs.[9]

SELECTING A MARKET-ORIENTED STRATEGY IS TARGET MARKETING

Target marketing is not mass marketing

Note that a marketing strategy specifies some *particular* target customers. This approach is called "target marketing" to distinguish it from "mass marketing." **Target marketing** says that a marketing mix is tailored to fit some specific target customers. In contrast, **mass marketing**—the typical production-oriented approach—vaguely aims at "everyone" with the same marketing mix. Mass marketing assumes that everyone is the same—and considers everyone a potential customer. It may help to think of target marketing as the "rifle approach" and mass marketing as the "shotgun approach."

Mass marketers may do target marketing

Commonly used terms can be confusing here. The terms *mass marketing* and *mass marketers* do not mean the same thing. Far from it! *Mass marketing* means trying to sell to "everyone," as we explained above. *Mass marketers* like General Foods and Wal-Mart are aiming at clearly defined target markets. The confusion with mass marketing occurs because their target markets usually are large and spread out.

Target marketing can mean big markets and profits

Target marketing is not limited to small market segments—only to fairly homogeneous ones. A very large market—even what is sometimes called the "mass market"—may be fairly homogeneous, and a target marketer will deliberately aim at it. For example, a very large group of parents of young children are homogeneous on many dimensions—including their attitudes about changing baby diapers. In the United States alone, this group spends about $3.5 billion a year on disposable diapers—so it should be no surprise that it is a major target market for companies like Kimberly-Clark (Huggies) and Procter & Gamble (Pampers). These days, so many customers in this target market buy disposable diapers that the challenge isn't just offering them a product they want but finding an ecologically sound way to dispose of it!

The basic reason for a marketing manager to focus on some specific target customers is to gain a competitive advantage—by developing a more satisfying marketing mix that should also be more profitable for the firm. Toshiba, for example, established a competitive advantage with traveling business computer users by being first to offer a powerful laptop computer. Tianguis, a three-store grocery chain in Southern California, attracts Hispanic customers with special product lines and Spanish-speaking employees. Charles Schwab, the discount stock brokerage firm, targets knowledgeable investors who want a convenient, low-cost way to buy and sell stocks by phone without a lot of advice (or pressure) from a salesperson. All of these firms have developed specific offerings that result in an ongoing relationship with the target market.

DEVELOPING MARKETING MIXES FOR TARGET MARKETS

There are many marketing mix decisions

There are many possible ways to satisfy the needs of target customers. A product can have many different features and quality levels. Service levels can be adjusted. The package can be of various sizes, colors, or materials. The brand name and warranty can be changed. Various advertising media—newspapers, magazines, radio, television, billboards—may be used. A company's own sales force or other sales specialists can be used. Different prices can be charged. Price discounts may be given, and so on. With so many possible variables, is there any way to help organize all these decisions and simplify the selection of marketing mixes? The answer is yes.

The four "Ps" make up a marketing mix

It is useful to reduce all the variables in the marketing mix to four basic ones:

Product.

Place.

Promotion.

Price.

It helps to think of the four major parts of a marketing mix as the "four Ps." Exhibit 2–7 emphasizes their relationship and their common focus on the customer—"C."

EXHIBIT 2–7
A Marketing Strategy— Showing the Four Ps of a Marketing Mix

Customer is not part of the marketing mix

The customer is shown surrounded by the four Ps in Exhibit 2–7. Some students assume that the customer is part of the marketing mix—but this is not so. The customer should be the *target* of all marketing efforts. The customer is placed in the center of the diagram to show this. The C stands for some specific customers—the target market.

Exhibit 2–8 shows some of the strategy decision variables organized by the four Ps. These will be discussed in later chapters. For now, let's just describe each P briefly.

Product—the good or service for the target's needs

The Product area is concerned with developing the right "product" for the target market. This offering may involve a physical good, a service, or a blend of both. Keep in mind that Product is not limited to "physical goods." For example, the Product of H & R Block is a completed tax form. The Product of a political party is the set of causes it will work to achieve. The important thing to remember is that your good and/or service should satisfy some customers' needs.

Along with other Product-area decisions shown in Exhibit 2–8, we will talk about developing and managing new products and whole product lines. We'll also discuss the characteristics of various kinds of products so that you will be able to make generalizations about product classes. This will help you to develop whole marketing mixes more quickly.

Place—reaching the target

Place is concerned with all the decisions involved in getting the "right" product to the target market's Place. A product isn't much good to a customer if it isn't available when and where it's wanted.

EXHIBIT 2–8   Strategy Decision Areas Organized by the Four Ps

Product	Place	Promotion	Price
Physical good	Objectives	Objectives	Objectives
Service	Channel type	Promotion blend	Flexibility
Features	Market exposure	Salespeople	Level over
Quality level	Kinds of	Kind	product life
Accessories	middlemen	Number	cycle
Installation	Kinds and	Selection	Geographic terms
Instructions	locations of	Training	Discounts
Warranty	stores	Motivation	Allowances
Product lines	How to handle	Advertising	
Packaging	transporting	Targets	
Branding	and storing	Kinds of ads	
	Service levels	Media type	
	Recruiting	Copy thrust	
	middlemen	Prepared by	
	Managing	whom	
	channels	Sales promotion	
		Publicity	

A product reaches customers through a channel of distribution. A **channel of distribution** is any series of firms (or individuals) from producer to final user or consumer.

Sometimes a channel system is quite short. It may run directly from a producer to a final user or consumer. This is especially common in business markets and in the marketing of services. Often the system is more complex—involving many different kinds of intermediaries and specialists. See Exhibit 2–9 for some examples. And if a marketing manager has several different target markets, several different channels of distribution might be needed.

A firm's product may involve a physical good (like a Dramamine tablet for motion sickness), a service (like flying and eating on British Airways), or a combination of both.

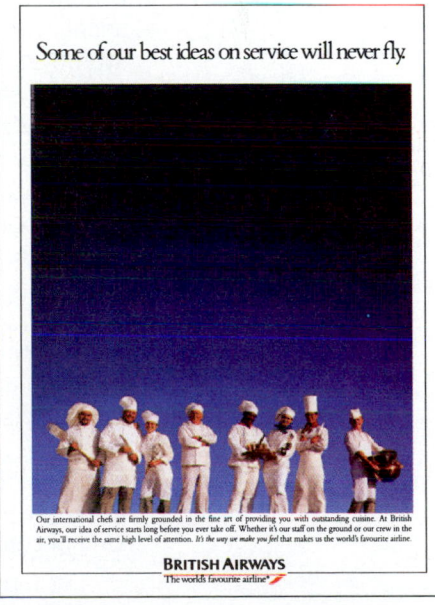

EXHIBIT 2–9 Four Examples of Basic Channels of Distribution for Consumer Products

We will also see how physical distribution service levels and decisions concerning logistics (transporting and storing) relate to the other Place decisions and the rest of the marketing mix.

Promotion—telling and selling the customer

The third P—Promotion—is concerned with telling the target market about the "right" product. Promotion includes personal selling, mass selling, and sales promotion. It is the marketing manager's job to blend these methods.

Personal selling involves direct communication between sellers and potential customers. Personal selling usually happens face-to-face, but sometimes the communication occurs over the telephone. Personal selling lets the salesperson adapt the firm's marketing mix to each potential customer. But this individual attention comes at a price; personal selling can be very expensive. Often this personal effort has to be blended with mass selling and sales promotion.

Mass selling is communicating with large numbers of customers at the same time. The main form of mass selling is **advertising**—any *paid* form of nonpersonal presentation of ideas, goods, or services by an identified sponsor. **Publicity**—any *unpaid* form of nonpersonal presentation of ideas, goods, or services—is another important form of mass selling.

Sales promotion refers to those promotion activities—other than advertising, publicity, and personal selling—that stimulate interest, trial, or purchase by final customers or others in the channel. This can involve use of coupons, point-of-purchase materials, samples, signs, catalogs, novelties, and circulars. Sales promotion specialists work with the personal selling and mass selling people.

Price—making it right

In addition to developing the right Product, Place, and Promotion, marketing managers must also decide the right Price. In setting a price, they must consider the kind of competition in the target market—and the cost of the whole marketing mix.

HOSPITALS BUILD A HEALTHY RELATIONSHIP WITH PATIENTS

Most of us think about a hospital when we're sick—really sick. But in the fast-changing market for health care services, more hospitals are putting a new emphasis on patient "wellness." They're opening fitness centers, offering jogging programs, courses in t'ai chi, and even belly dancing classes. Each day, Riverside Walter Reed Hospital has five times as many people involved with its health club programs as it has in its acute care facilities. Hundreds of other hospitals are promoting such "wellness centers." Many even have a sales force to call on local businesses; the salespeople sign up firms to pay for wellness programs for their employees.

Health care competition is changing, and focusing on wellness is part of the change. For hospitals, it's one good way to capture new customers. When they do get sick, they are more likely to go to the hospital with which they already have a relationship. Further, the price patients pay for fitness programs is often $50 or more a month; that money contributes to hospital profit or supports other activities. Moreover, just as health maintenance organizations (HMOs) and traditional insurance companies offer health services for a lump-sum fee or premium, many experts feel that more hospitals will move in that direction in the future. And, of course, it's less costly to serve patients who are generally healthy and fit than those who are not. Finally, the free "health risk" screening tests that hospitals offer before people sign up for a fitness program sometimes reveal problems that might have gone undetected.

For all of these reasons, it makes sense for hospitals to target customers who are interested in wellness, and to offer them a whole mix of health care services that meet their needs. And, of course, the hospitals' new focus on wellness turns out to be a healthy idea for patients too.[10]

They must also try to estimate customer reaction to possible prices. Besides this, they also must know current practices as to markups, discounts, and other terms of sale. Further, they must be aware of legal restrictions on pricing.

If customers won't accept the Price, all of the planning effort will be wasted. So you can see that Price is an important area for a marketing manager.

Each of the four Ps contributes to the whole

All four Ps are needed in a marketing mix. In fact, they should all be tied together. But is any one more important than the others? Generally speaking, the answer is no—all contribute to one whole. When a marketing mix is being developed, all (final) decisions about the Ps should be made at the same time. That's why the four Ps are arranged around the customer (C) in a circle—to show that they all are equally important.

Let's sum up our discussion of marketing mix planning thus far. We develop a *Product* to satisfy the target customers. We find a way to reach our target customers' *Place*. We use *Promotion* to tell the target customers (and intermediaries in the channel) about the product that has been designed for them. And we set a *Price* after estimating expected customer reaction to the total offering and the costs of getting it to them.

Strategy jobs must be done together

It is important to stress—it cannot be overemphasized—that selecting a target market *and* developing a marketing mix are interrelated. Both parts of a marketing strategy must be decided together. It is *strategies* that must be evaluated against the company's objectives—not alternative target markets or alternative marketing mixes.

Toddler University's marketing strategy has been successful because it realizes that the needs of a target market virtually determine the nature of an appropriate marketing mix.

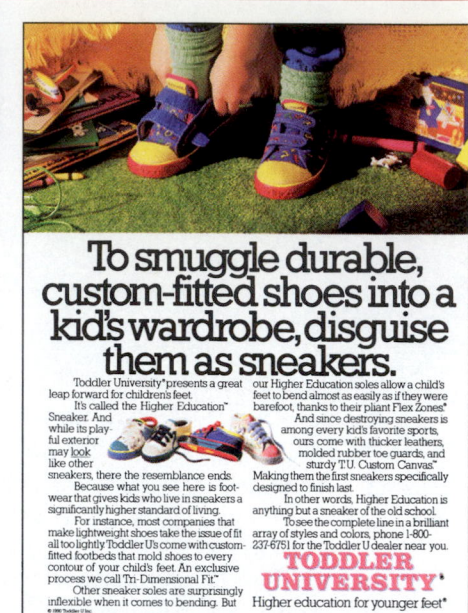

Understanding target markets leads to good strategies

The needs of a target market virtually determine the nature of an appropriate marketing mix. So marketers must analyze their potential target markets with great care. This book will explore ways of identifying attractive market opportunities and developing appropriate strategies.

These ideas can be seen more clearly with an example in the children's fashion market.

Market-oriented strategy planning at Toddler University

The case of Toddler University (TU), Inc., a shoe company, illustrates the strategy planning process—and how strategy decisions guide how the plan will be carried out. It has only been a few years since 24-year-old Jeff Silverman started TU, but the company's shoes for children have been a huge success.

During high school and college, Silverman worked as a salesperson at local shoe stores. He also gained valuable experience during a year working for Nike. From these jobs he learned a lot about customers' needs and interests—and he realized that there were some parents whose needs were not being satisfied when it came to finding shoes for their preschool children.

By combining several kinds of customer needs and information about customer characteristics, Silverman came up with a view of this market. Exhibit 2–10 summarizes his key ideas.

As shown in the middle of Exhibit 2–10, there turned out to be a large (but hard to describe) "Mass market" for general-purpose baby shoes—perhaps 60 or 70 percent of the potential for all kinds of baby shoes. Silverman did not focus on this market because it didn't make sense for his small company to compete head on with many other firms where he had no particular advantage. The other four markets—the Traditionalists, Fashion Conscious, Economy Oriented, and Attentive Parents—are placed in the four corners of the market diagram to show that they are different. In the following description of these markets, note that useful marketing mixes come to mind immediately.

EXHIBIT 2–10   The Children's Fashion Market (baby footwear area) in the United States and Europe

The *Traditionalists* seemed to be satisfied with a well-manufactured shoe that was available from "quality" stores where they could seek help in selecting the right size and fit. They didn't mind if the design was old-fashioned and didn't change. They wanted a well-known brand that had a reputation for quality, even if it was a bit more expensive.

Many of the *Economy Oriented* parents were in the lower income group. They wanted a basic shoe at a low price. They saw baby shoes as all pretty much the same—so a "name" brand didn't have much appeal. They were willing to shop around to see what was on sale at local discount, department, or shoe stores.

The *Fashion Conscious* were interested in dressing up baby in shoes that looked like smaller versions of the latest styles that they bought for themselves. Fit was important, but beyond that a colorful design is what got their attention. They were more likely to look for baby-size shoes at the shop where they bought their own athletic shoes.

The *Attentive Parents* wanted shoes that met a variety of needs. They wanted shoes to be fun and fashionable and functional. They didn't want just a good fit but also design and materials that were really right for baby play and learning to walk. These well-informed, upscale shoppers were likely to buy from a store that specialized in baby items. They were willing to pay a premium price if they found the right product.

Silverman thought that Stride Rite Corp. and Wohl Shoe Co. (makers of the Buster Brown brand) were meeting the needs of the Traditionalists quite well, and that the Economy Oriented and Fashion Conscious customers were satisfied with shoes from a variety of other companies, including Nike. But Silverman saw a way to get a toe up on the competition by targeting the Attentive Parents with a marketing mix that combined, in his words, "fit and function with fun and fashion." He developed a detailed marketing plan that attracted financial backers, and his company came to life.

TU didn't have its own production facilities, so Silverman contracted with a producer in Taiwan to make shoes with his brand name and to his specs. And his specs were different—they improved the product for his target market. Unlike most rigid high-topped infant shoes, he designed softer shoes with more comfortable rubber soles. The shoes last longer because they are stitched rather than glued. An extrawide opening makes fitting easier on squirming feet. He also patented a special insert so parents could adjust the width. This change also helped win support from other channel members. Since there are 11 sizes of children's shoes—and five widths—retailers usually need to stock 55 pairs of each model. TU's adjustable width helps relieve this stocking problem—and makes it more profitable for retailers to sell the line. It also makes it possible for TU to resupply sold-out inventory faster than competitors—within a week. These advantages helped TU recruit the big Kids "R" Us apparel chain and other retailers that reach his target market. Silverman's Product and Place decisions worked together well to give him a competitive advantage.

For promotion, Silverman developed print ads with close-up photos of babies wearing his shoes and informative details about their special benefits. Creative packaging also helps promote the shoe and attract customers in the store. For example, one athletic-style shoe comes in a box that looks like a gray gym locker (complete with a plastic Gatorade squeeze bottle). Silverman also provides the stores with "shoe rides"—electric-powered rocking replicas of its shoes. The rides not only attract kids to the shoe department, but since they are coin-operated, they pay for themselves in a year.

TU prices most of its shoes at $35 to $40 a pair. This is a premium price, but with today's smaller families, the Attentive Parents are willing to spend more on each child.

In just four years, TU's sales jumped from $100,000 to over $40 million. To keep growth going, Silverman expanded distribution to reach new markets in Europe. To take advantage of TU's relationship with its satisfied target customers, he also added shoes for older kids to the Toddler University product assortment. Recently Silverman made his biggest sale of all: He sold his company to Genesco, one of the biggest firms in the footwear business.[11]

THE MARKETING PLAN IS A GUIDE TO IMPLEMENTATION AND CONTROL

Now that the key ideas of marketing strategy planning have been introduced, we can return to our overview of the marketing management process. You will see how a marketing strategy leads to a marketing plan and ultimately to implementation and control (see Exhibit 2–5).

Marketing plan fills out marketing strategy

A marketing strategy sets a target market and a marketing mix. It is a "big picture" of what a firm will do in some market. A marketing plan goes farther. A **marketing plan** is a written statement of a marketing strategy *and* the time-related details for carrying out the strategy. It should spell out the following in detail: (1) what marketing mix will be offered, to whom (that is, the target market), and for how long; (2) what company resources (shown as costs) will be needed at what rate (month by month perhaps); and (3) what results are expected (sales and profits perhaps monthly or quarterly, customer satisfaction levels, and the like). The plan should also include some control procedures—so that whoever is to carry out the plan will know if things are going wrong. This might be something as simple as comparing actual sales against expected sales—with a warning flag to be raised whenever total sales fall below a certain level.

Implementation puts plans into operation

After a marketing plan is developed, a marketing manager knows *what* needs to be done. Then the manager is concerned with **implementation**—putting marketing plans into operation.

Strategies work out as planned only when they are effectively implemented. Many **operational decisions**—short-run decisions to help implement strategies— may be needed.

Managers should make operational decisions within the guidelines set down during strategy planning. They develop product policies, place policies, and so on as part of strategy planning. Then operational decisions within these policies probably will be necessary—while carrying out the basic strategy. Note, however, that as long as these operational decisions stay within the policy guidelines, managers are making no change in the basic strategy. If the controls show that operational decisions are not producing the desired results, however, the managers may have to reevaluate the whole strategy—rather than just working harder at implementing it.

It's easier to see the difference between strategy decisions and operational decisions if we illustrate these ideas using our Toddler University example. Possible four-P or basic strategy policies are shown in the left-hand column in Exhibit 2–11, and examples of operational decisions are shown in the right-hand column.

It should be clear that some operational decisions are made regularly—even daily—and such decisions should not be confused with planning strategy. Certainly, a great deal of effort can be involved in these operational decisions. They might take a good part of the sales or advertising manager's time. But they are not the strategy decisions that will be our primary concern.

Our focus has been—and will continue to be—on developing marketing strategies. But it is also important to see that eventually marketing managers must develop, implement, and control marketing plans. We discuss this more fully in Chapters 19 and 20.[12]

Several plans make a whole marketing program

Most companies implement more than one marketing strategy—and related marketing plan—at the same time. They may have several products—some of them quite different—that are aimed at different target markets. The other

EXHIBIT 2–11 Relation of Strategy Policies to Operational Decisions for Baby Shoe Company

Marketing Mix Decision Area	Strategy Policies	Likely Operational Decisions
Product	Carry as limited a line of colors, styles, and sizes as will satisfy the target market.	Add, change, or drop colors, styles, and/or sizes as customer tastes dictate.
Place	Distribute through selected "baby-products" retailers who will carry the full line and provide good in-store sales support and promotion.	In market areas where sales potential is not achieved, add new retail outlets and/or drop retailers whose performance is poor.
Promotion	Promote the benefits and value of the special design and how it meets customer needs.	When a retailer hires a new salesperson, send current training package with details on product line; increase use of local newspaper print ads during peak demand periods (before holidays, etc.).
Price	Maintain a "premium" price, but encourage retailers to make large-volume orders by offering discounts on quantity purchases.	Offer short-term introductory price "deals" to retailers when a new style is first introduced.

EXHIBIT 2–12   Elements of a Firm's Marketing Program

elements of the marketing mix may vary too. Gillette's Right Guard deodorant, its Atra Plus razor blades, and its Liquid Paper correction fluid all have different marketing mixes. Yet the strategies for each must be implemented at the same time.[13]

A **marketing program** blends all of the firm's marketing plans into one "big" plan. See Exhibit 2–12. This program, then, is the responsibility of the whole company. Typically, the whole *marketing program* is an integrated part of the whole-company strategic plan we discussed earlier.

Ultimately, marketing managers plan and implement a whole marketing program. In this text, however, we will emphasize planning one marketing strategy at a time, rather than planning—or implementing—a whole marketing program. This is practical because it is important to plan each strategy carefully. Too many marketing managers fall into sloppy thinking. They try to develop too many strategies all at once—and don't develop any very carefully. Good plans are the building blocks of marketing management. We'll talk about merging plans into a marketing program in Chapter 19.

Control is analyzing and correcting what you've done

The control job provides the feedback that leads managers to modify their marketing strategies. To maintain control, a marketing manager uses a number of tools—like computer sales analysis, marketing research surveys, and accounting analysis of expenses and profits. A section of Chapter 20 is devoted to the important topic of controlling marketing plans and programs.

In addition, as we talk about each of the marketing decision areas, we will discuss some of the control problems. This will help you understand how control keeps the firm on course—or shows the need to plan a new course.

All marketing jobs require planning and control

At first, it might appear that only high-level management or really large companies need be concerned with planning and control. This is not true. Every organization needs planning—and without control it's impossible to know if the plans are working.

This means that marketing strategy planning may be very important to you soon—maybe in your present job or college activities. In Appendix C on marketing careers, we present some strategy planning ideas for getting a marketing job.

Many different products are included in the marketing program for the Clorox Company, but the marketing plan for each individual product includes useful literature designed to improve customer satisfaction by helping consumers get better results with the product.

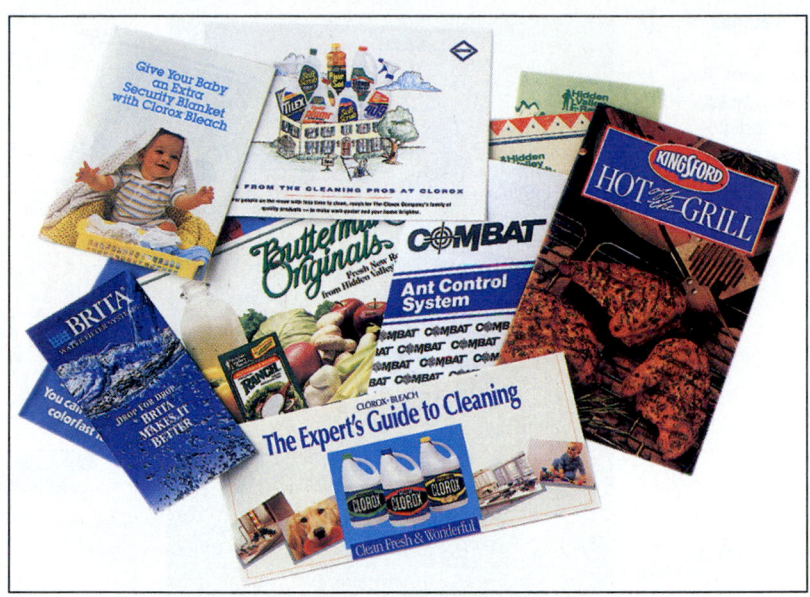

THE IMPORTANCE OF MARKETING STRATEGY PLANNING

We emphasize the planning part of the marketing manager's job for a good reason. The "one-time" strategy decisions—the decisions that decide what business the company is in and the strategies it will follow—usually determine success—or failure. An extremely good plan might be carried out badly and still be profitable, while a poor but well-implemented plan can lose money. The case history that follows shows the importance of planning—and why we emphasize marketing strategy planning throughout this text.

Time for new strategies in the watch industry

The conventional watch makers—both domestic and foreign—had always aimed at customers who thought of watches as high-priced, high-quality symbols to mark special events—like graduations or retirement. Advertising was concentrated around Christmas and graduation time and stressed a watch's symbolic appeal. Expensive jewelry stores were the main retail outlets.

This commonly accepted strategy of the major watch companies ignored people in the target market that just wanted to tell the time—and were interested in a reliable, low-priced watch. So the U.S. Time Company developed a successful strategy around its Timex watches—and became the world's largest watch company. Timex completely upset the watch industry—both foreign and domestic—not only by offering a good product (with a one-year repair or replace guarantee) at a lower price, but also by using new, lower-cost channels of distribution. Its watches were widely available in drugstores, discount houses, and nearly any other retail stores that would carry them.

Marketing managers at Timex soon faced a new challenge. Texas Instruments, a new competitor in the watch market, took the industry by storm with its low-cost but very accurate electronic watches—using the same channels Timex had originally developed. But other firms quickly developed a watch that used a more stylish liquid crystal display for the digital readout. Texas Instruments could

The market for watches is dynamic and highly competitive, but Timex has used new technology to develop a line of Indiglo watches that do a better job of meeting the needs of some target customers.

not change quickly enough to keep up, and the other companies took away its customers. The competition became so intense that Texas Instruments stopped marketing watches altogether.

While Timex and others were focusing on lower-priced watches, Japan's Seiko captured a commanding share of the high-priced gift market for its stylish and accurate quartz watches by obtaining strong distribution. All of this forced many traditional watch makers—like some of the once-famous Swiss brands—to close their factories.

In 1983, Switzerland's Swatch launched its colorful, affordable plastic watches—and changed what consumers see when they look at their watches. Swatch promoted its watches as fashion accessories and set them apart from those of other firms, whose ads squabbled about whose watches were most accurate and dependable. Swatch was also able to attract new retailers by focusing its distribution on upscale fashion and department stores. The marketing mix Swatch developed around its fashion watch idea was so successful it didn't just increase Swatch's share of the market. The total size of the watch market increased because many consumers bought several watches to match different fashions.

Swatch's success prompted Timex, Seiko, and others to pay more attention to consumer fashion preferences. For example, Timex developed its fashionable Watercolors line targeted at teens. Timex has also emphasized better styling to compete in the higher-priced market—and broadened its offering to defend its position in the low- to mid-priced segment.

The economic downturn in the early 90s brought more changes. Sales of fashion watches leveled off, so Swatch is now targeting segments with other needs. For example, in 1990 it introduced a $45 scuba watch guaranteed to keep ticking at depths of 600 feet. Consumers have become more cost conscious—and less interested in expensive watches like those made by Rolex that were the "in" status symbol a few years earlier. The reemergence of value-seeking customers prompted Timex to return to its famous advertising tagline of the 1960s: "it takes a licking and keeps on ticking." Its position as the inexpensive-but-durable choice has helped it strengthen its distribution in department stores, sporting goods stores, and other channels, and given it a leg up in getting shelf space for new products, such as its Indiglo line of watches. However, just as the new Indiglo technology allowed Timex to develop new watches, other firms are looking for ways to use technology to open new markets and attract customers with unmet needs. For example, Casio has introduced a watch that includes a remote control for TVs and VCRs. With such changes constantly under way, marketing strategies must constantly be updated and revised.[14]

Creative strategy planning needed for survival

Dramatic shifts in strategy—like those described above—may surprise conventional, production-oriented managers. But such changes are becoming much more common—and should be expected. Industries or firms that have accepted the marketing concept realize that they cannot define their line of business in terms of the products they currently produce or sell. Rather they have to think about the basic consumer needs they serve—and how those needs may change in the future. If they are too nearsighted, they may fail to see what's coming until too late.

Creative strategy planning is becoming even more important because firms can no longer win profits just by spending more money on plant and equipment. Moreover, domestic and foreign competition threatens those who can't create more satisfying goods and services and find ways to build stronger relationships with their customers. New markets, new customers, and new ways of doing things must be found if companies are to operate profitably in the future—and contribute to the macro-marketing system.

STRATEGY PLANNING DOESN'T TAKE PLACE IN A VACUUM

Strategy planning takes place within a framework

Our examples show that a marketing manager's strategy planning cannot take place in a vacuum. Instead, the manager works with controllable variables within a framework involving many variables that must be considered even though the manager can't control them. Exhibit 2–13 illustrates this framework and shows that the typical marketing manager must be concerned about the competitive environment, economic and technological environment, political and legal environment, cultural and social environment, and the firm's resources and objectives. We discuss these marketing environment variables in more detail in the next two chapters. But clearly, the environment in which the marketing manager operates affects strategy planning.

MARKET-ORIENTED STRATEGY PLANNING HELPS NONMARKETING PEOPLE TOO

While market-oriented strategy planning is helpful to marketers, it is also needed by accountants, production and personnel people, and all other specialists. A market-oriented plan lets everybody in the firm know what "ballpark" they are playing in—and what they are trying to accomplish. In other words, it gives direction to the whole business effort. An accountant can't set budgets without a plan, except perhaps by mechanically projecting last year's budget. Similarly, a financial manager can't project cash needs without some idea of expected sales to target customers—and the costs of satisfying them.

EXHIBIT 2–13 Marketing Manager's Framework

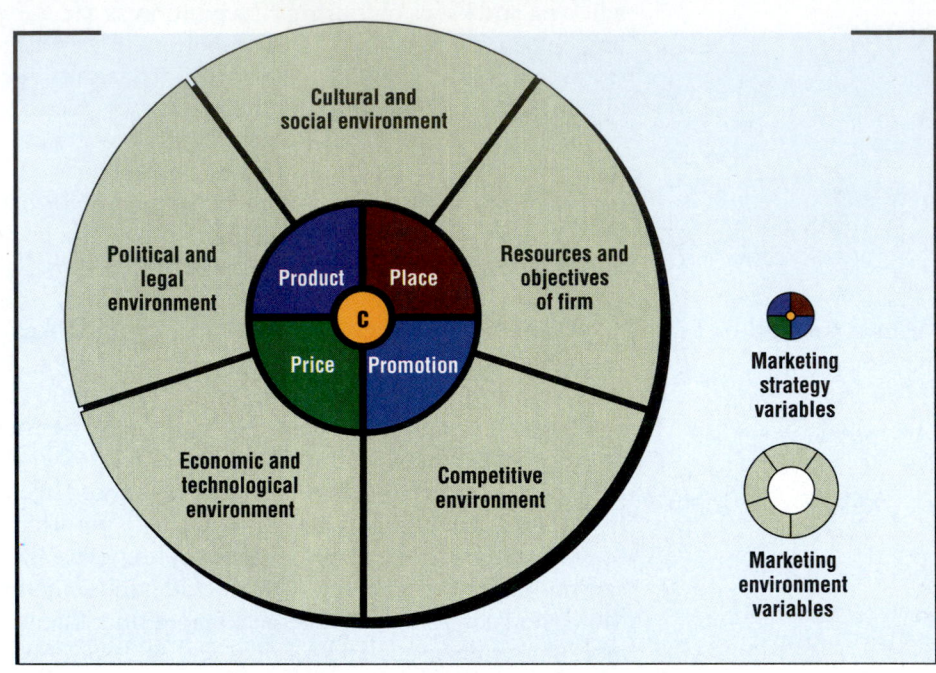

We will use the term *marketing manager* for editorial convenience, but really, when we talk about marketing strategy planning, we are talking about the planning that a market-oriented manager should do when developing a firm's strategic plans. This kind of thinking should be done—or at least understood—by everyone in the organization who is responsible for planning. And this means even the entry-level salesperson, production supervisor, retail buyer, or personnel counselor.

CONCLUSION

Marketing's role within a marketing-oriented firm is to provide direction for a firm. The marketing concept stresses that the company's efforts should focus on satisfying some target customers—at a profit. Production-oriented firms tend to forget this. Often the various departments within a production-oriented firm let their natural conflicts of interest lead them to building fences.

The job of marketing management is one of continuous planning, implementing, and control. The marketing manager must constantly study the environment—seeking attractive opportunities and planning new strategies. Possible target markets must be matched with marketing mixes the firm can

offer. Then, attractive strategies—really, whole marketing plans—are chosen for implementation. Controls are needed to be sure that the plans are carried out successfully. If anything goes wrong along the way, continual feedback should cause the process to be started over again—with the marketing manager planning more attractive marketing strategies.

A marketing mix has four variables: the four Ps—Product, Place, Promotion, and Price. Most of this text is concerned with developing profitable marketing mixes for clearly defined target markets. So after several chapters on analyzing target markets, we will discuss each of the four Ps in greater detail.

QUESTIONS AND PROBLEMS

1. Define the marketing concept in your own words and then explain why the notion of profit is usually included in this definition.

2. Define the marketing concept in your own words and then suggest how acceptance of this concept might affect the organization and operation of your college.

3. Distinguish between production orientation and marketing orientation, illustrating with local examples.

4. Explain why a firm should view its internal activities as part of a total system. Illustrate your answer for (*a*) a large grocery products producer, (*b*) a plumbing wholesaler, and (*c*) a department store chain.

5. Give an example of a recent purchase you made where the purchase wasn't just a single transaction but rather part of an ongoing relationship with the seller. Discuss what the seller has done (or could do better) to strengthen the relationship and increase the odds of your being a loyal customer in the future.

6. Distinguish clearly between a marketing strategy and a marketing mix. Use an example.

7. Distinguish clearly between mass marketing and target marketing. Use an example.

8. Why is the customer placed in the center of the four Ps in the text diagram of a marketing strategy (Exhibit 2–7)? Explain, using a specific example from your own experience.

9. Explain, in your own words, what each of the four Ps involves.

10. Evaluate the text's statement, "A marketing strategy sets the details of implementation."

11. Distinguish between strategy decisions and operational decisions, illustrating for a local retailer.

12. Distinguish between a strategy, a marketing plan, and a marketing program, illustrating for a local retailer.

13. Outline a marketing strategy for each of the following new products: (*a*) a radically new design for a toothbrush, (*b*) a new fishing reel, (*c*) a new wonder drug, and (*d*) a new industrial stapling machine.

14. Provide a specific illustration of why marketing strategy planning is important for all business people, not just for those in the marketing department.

SUGGESTED CASES

COMPUTER-AIDED PROBLEM

2. Target Marketing

Marko, Inc.'s managers are comparing the profitability of a target marketing strategy with a mass marketing "strategy." The spreadsheet gives information about both approaches.

The mass marketing strategy is aiming at a much bigger market. But a smaller percent of the consumers in the market will actually buy this product—because not everyone needs or can afford it. Moreover, because this marketing mix is not tailored to specific needs, Marko will get a smaller share of the business from those who do buy than it would with a more targeted marketing mix.

Just trying to reach the mass market will take more promotion and require more retail outlets in more locations—so promotion costs and distribution costs are higher than with the target marketing strategy. On the other hand, the cost of producing each unit is higher with the target marketing strategy—to build in a more satisfying set of features. But, because the more targeted marketing mix is trying to satisfy the needs of a specific target market, those customers will be willing to pay a higher price.

In the spreadsheet, "quantity sold" (by the firm) is equal to the number of people in the market who will actually buy one each of the product—multiplied by the share of those purchases won by the firm's marketing mix. Thus, a change in the size of the market, the percent of people who purchase, or the share captured by the firm will affect quantity sold. And a change in quantity sold will affect total revenue, total cost, and profit.

   a. *On a piece of paper, show the calculations that prove that the spreadsheet "total profit" value for the target marketing strategy is correct. (Hint: Remember to multiply unit production cost and unit distribution cost by the quantity sold.) Which approach seems better—target marketing or mass marketing? Why?*

   b. *If the target marketer could find a way to reduce distribution cost per unit by $.25, how much would profit increase?*

   c. *If Marko, Inc., decided to use the target marketing strategy and better marketing mix decisions increased its share of purchases from 50 to 60 percent—without increasing costs—what would happen to total profit? What does this analysis suggest about the importance of marketing managers knowing enough about their target markets to be effective target marketers?*

For additional questions related to this problem, see Exercise 2–4 in the *Learning Aid for Use with Basic Marketing*, 12th edition.

Economics Fundamentals

When You Finish This Appendix, You Should

1. Understand the "law of diminishing demand."

2. Understand demand and supply curves—and how they set the size of a market and its price level.

3. Know about elasticity of demand and supply.

4. Know why demand elasticity can be affected by availability of substitutes.

5. Know the different kinds of competitive situations and understand why they are important to marketing managers.

6. Recognize the important new terms (shown in red).

A good marketing manager should be an expert on markets—and the nature of competition in markets. The economist's traditional analysis of demand and supply is a useful tool for analyzing markets. In particular, you should master the concepts of a demand curve and demand elasticity. A firm's demand curve shows how the target customers view the firm's Product—really its whole marketing mix. And the interaction of demand and supply curves helps set the size of a market—and the market price. The interaction of supply and demand also determines the nature of the competitive environment, which has an important effect on strategy planning. These ideas are discussed more fully in the following sections.

PRODUCTS AND MARKETS AS SEEN BY CUSTOMERS AND POTENTIAL CUSTOMERS

Economists provide useful insights

How potential customers (not the firm) see a firm's product (marketing mix) affects how much they are willing to pay for it, where it should be made available, and how eager they are for it—if they want it at all. In other words, their view has a very direct bearing on marketing strategy planning.

Economists have been concerned with market behavior for years. Their analytical tools can be quite helpful in summarizing how customers view products and how markets behave.

Economists see individual customers choosing among alternatives

Economics is sometimes called the dismal science—because it says that most customers have a limited income and simply cannot buy everything they want. They must balance their needs and the prices of various products.

Economists usually assume that customers have a fairly definite set of preferences—and that they evaluate alternatives in terms of whether the alternatives will make them feel better (or worse) or in some way improve (or change) their situation.

But what exactly is the nature of a customer's desire for a particular product?

Usually economists answer this question in terms of the extra utility the customer can obtain by buying more of a particular product—or how much utility would be lost if the customer had less of the product. (Students who wish further discussion of this approach should refer to indifference curve analysis in any standard economics text.)

It is easier to understand the idea of utility if we look at what happens when the price of one of the customer's usual purchases changes.

The law of diminishing demand

Suppose that consumers buy potatoes in 10-pound bags at the same time they buy other foods such as bread and rice. If the consumers are mainly interested in buying a certain amount of food and the price of the potatoes drops, it seems reasonable to expect that they will switch some of their food money to potatoes and away from some other foods. But if the price of potatoes rises, you expect our consumers to buy fewer potatoes and more of other foods.

The general relationship between price and quantity demanded illustrated by this food example is called the **law of diminishing demand**—which says that if the price of a product is raised, a smaller quantity will be demanded and if the price of a product is lowered, a greater quantity will be demanded. Experience supports this relationship between prices and total demand in a market, especially for broad product categories or commodities such as potatoes.

EXHIBIT A–1 Demand Schedule for Potatoes (10-pound bags)

Point	(1) Price of Potatoes per Bag (P)	(2) Quantity Demanded (bags per month) (Q)	(3) Total Revenue per Month (P × Q = TR)
A	$1.60	8,000,000	$12,800,000
B	1.30	9,000,000	_____
C	1.00	11,000,000	11,000,000
D	0.70	14,000,000	_____
E	0.40	19,000,000	_____

The relationship between price and quantity demanded in a market is what economists call a "demand schedule." An example is shown in Exhibit A–1. For each row in the table, Column 2 shows the quantity consumers will want (demand) if they have to pay the price given in Column 1. The third column shows that the total revenue (sales) in the potato market is equal to the quantity demanded at a given price times that price. Note that as prices drop, the total unit quantity increases, yet the total revenue decreases. Fill in the blank lines in the third column and observe the behavior of total revenue—an important number for the marketing manager. We will explain what you should have noticed—and why—a little later.

The demand curve—usually down-sloping

If your only interest is seeing at which price the company will earn the greatest total revenue, the demand schedule may be adequate. But a demand curve shows more. A **demand curve** is a graph of the relationship between price and quantity demanded in a market—assuming that all other things stay the same. Exhibit A–2 shows the demand curve for potatoes—really just a plotting of the demand schedule in Exhibit A–1. It shows how many potatoes potential customers will demand at various possible prices. This is a "down-sloping demand curve."

Most demand curves are down-sloping. This just means that if prices are decreased, the quantity customers demand will increase.

Demand curves always show the price on the vertical axis and the quantity demanded on the horizontal axis. In Exhibit A–2, we have shown the price in dollars. For consistency, we will use dollars in other examples. However, keep in mind that these same ideas hold regardless of what money unit (dollars, yen, francs, pounds, etc.) is used to represent price. Even at this early point, you should keep in mind that markets are not necessarily limited by national boundaries—or by one type of money.

Note that the demand curve shows only how customers will react to various possible prices. In a market, we see only one price at a time—not all of these prices. The curve, however, shows what quantities will be demanded—depending on what price is set. You probably think that most business people would like to set a price that would result in a large sales revenue. Before discussing this, however, we should consider the demand schedule and curve for another product to get a more complete picture of demand-curve analysis.

EXHIBIT A–2   Demand Curve for Potatoes (10-pound bags)

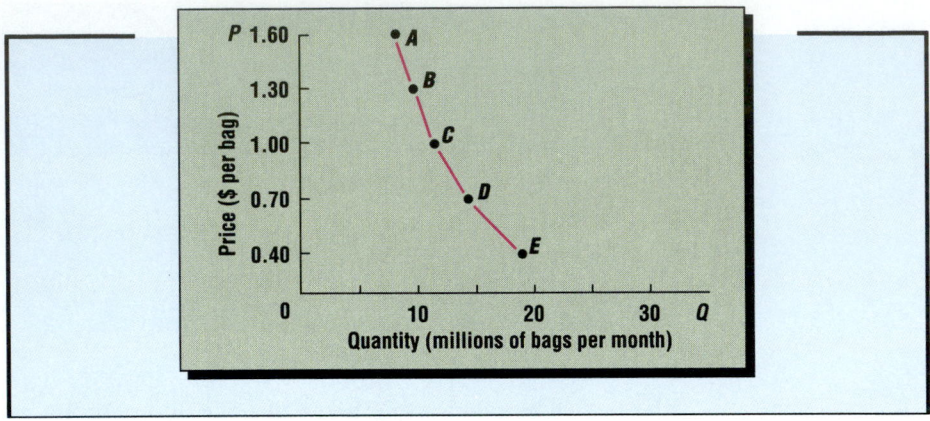

Microwave oven demand curve looks different

A different demand schedule is the one for standard 1-cubic-foot microwave ovens shown in Exhibit A–3. Column (3) shows the total revenue that will be obtained at various possible prices and quantities. Again, as the price goes down, the quantity demanded goes up. But here, unlike the potato example, total revenue increases as prices go down—at least until the price drops to $150.

Every market has a demand curve—for some time period

These general demand relationships are typical for all products. But each product has its own demand schedule and curve in each potential market—no matter how small the market. In other words, a particular demand curve has meaning only for a particular market. We can think of demand curves for individuals, groups of individuals who form a target market, regions, and even countries. And the time period covered really should be specified—although this is often neglected because we usually think of monthly or yearly periods.

The difference between elastic and inelastic

The demand curve for microwave ovens (see Exhibit A–4) is down-sloping—but note that it is flatter than the curve for potatoes. It is important to understand what this flatness means.

EXHIBIT A–3   Demand Schedule for 1-Cubic-Foot Microwave Ovens

Point	(1) Price per Microwave Oven (P)	(2) Quantity Demanded per Year (Q)	(3) Total Revenue (TR) per Year ($P \times Q = TR$)
A	$300	20,000	$ 6,000,000
B	250	70,000	15,500,000
C	200	130,000	26,000,000
D	150	210,000	31,500,000
E	100	310,000	31,000,000

EXHIBIT A–4   Demand Curve for 1-Cubic-Foot Microwave Ovens

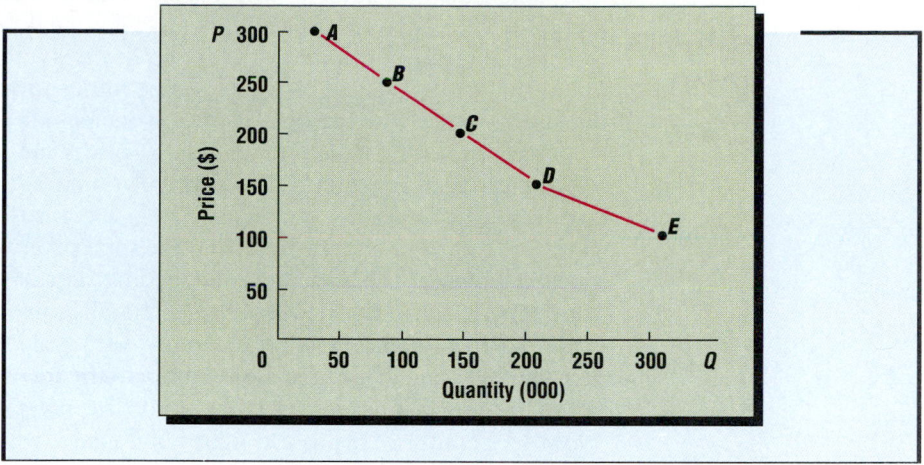

We will consider the flatness in terms of total revenue—since this is what interests business managers.*

When you filled in the total revenue column for potatoes, you should have noticed that total revenue drops continually if the price is reduced. This looks undesirable for sellers—and illustrates inelastic demand. **Inelastic demand** means that although the quantity demanded increases if the price is decreased, the quantity demanded will not "stretch" enough—that is, it is not elastic enough—to avoid a decrease in total revenue.

In contrast, **elastic demand** means that if prices are dropped, the quantity demanded will stretch (increase) enough to increase total revenue. The upper part of the microwave oven demand curve is an example of elastic demand.

But note that if the microwave oven price is dropped from $150 to $100, total revenue will decrease. We can say, therefore, that between $150 and $100, demand is inelastic—that is, total revenue will decrease if price is lowered from $150 to $100.

Thus, elasticity can be defined in terms of changes in total revenue. *If total revenue will increase if price is lowered, then demand is elastic. If total revenue will decrease if price is lowered, then demand is inelastic.* (Note: A special case known as "unitary elasticity of demand" occurs if total revenue stays the same when prices change.)

Total revenue may increase if price is raised

A point often missed in discussions of demand is what happens when prices are raised instead of lowered. With elastic demand, total revenue will *decrease* if the price is *raised*. With inelastic demand, however, total revenue will *increase* if the price is *raised*.

---

*Strictly speaking, two curves should not be compared for flatness if the graph scales are different, but for our purposes now, we will do so to illustrate the idea of "elasticity of demand." Actually, it would be more correct to compare two curves for one product—on the same graph. Then both the shape of the demand curve and its position on the graph would be important.

The possibility of raising price and increasing dollar sales (total revenue) at the same time is attractive to managers. This occurs only if the demand curve is inelastic. Here total revenue will increase if price is raised, but total costs probably will not increase—and may actually go down—with smaller quantities. Keep in mind that profit is equal to total revenue minus total costs. So—when demand is inelastic—profit will increase as price is increased!

The ways total revenue changes as prices are raised are shown in Exhibit A–5. Here total revenue is the rectangular area formed by a price and its related quantity. The larger the rectangular area, the greater the total revenue.

P_1 is the original price here, and the total potential revenue with this original price is shown by the area with blue shading. The area with red shading shows the total revenue with the new price, P_2. There is some overlap in the total revenue areas, so the important areas are those with only one color. Note that in the left-hand figure—where demand is elastic—the revenue added (the red-only area) when the price is increased is less than the revenue lost (the blue-only area). Now, let's contrast this to the right-hand figure, when demand is inelastic. Only a small blue revenue area is given up for a much larger (red) one when price is raised.

An entire curve is not elastic or inelastic

It is important to see that it is *wrong to refer to a whole demand curve as elastic or inelastic*. Rather, elasticity for a particular demand curve refers to the change in total revenue between two points on the curve—not along the whole curve. You saw the change from elastic to inelastic in the microwave oven example.

EXHIBIT A–5   Changes in Total Revenue as Prices Increase

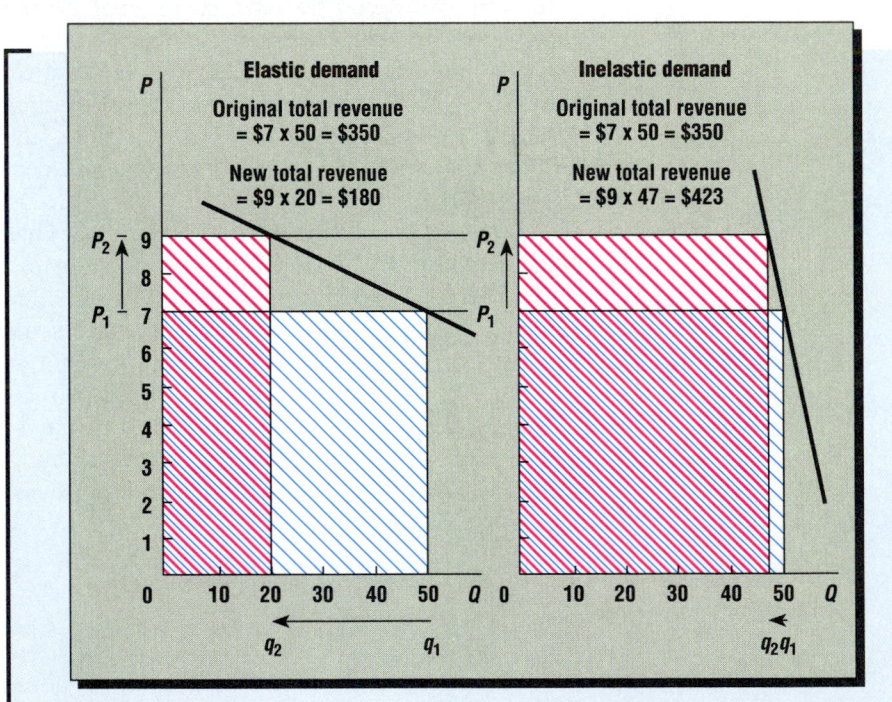

Generally, however, nearby points are either elastic or inelastic—so it is common to refer to a whole curve by the degree of elasticity in the price range that normally is of interest—the *relevant range*.

Demand elasticities affected by availability of substitutes and urgency of need

At first, it may be difficult to see why one product has an elastic demand and another an inelastic demand. Many factors affect elasticity—such as the availability of substitutes, the importance of the item in the customer's budget, and the urgency of the customer's need and its relation to other needs. By looking more closely at one of these factors—the availability of substitutes—you will better understand why demand elasticities vary.

Substitutes are products that offer the buyer a choice. For example, many consumers see grapefruit as a substitute for oranges and hot dogs as a substitute for hamburgers. The greater the number of "good" substitutes available, the greater will be the elasticity of demand. From the consumer's perspective, products are "good" substitutes if they are very similar (homogeneous). If consumers see products as extremely different—or heterogeneous—then a particular need cannot easily be satisfied by substitutes. And the demand for the most satisfactory product may be quite inelastic.

As an example, if the price of hamburger is lowered (and other prices stay the same), the quantity demanded will increase a lot—as will total revenue. The reason is that not only will regular hamburger users buy more hamburger, but some consumers who formerly bought hot dogs or steaks probably will buy hamburger too. But if the price of hamburger is raised, the quantity demanded will decrease—perhaps sharply. Still consumers will buy some hamburger—depending on how much the price has risen, their individual tastes, and what their guests expect (see Exhibit A–6).

In contrast to a product with many "substitutes"—such as hamburger—consider a product with few or no substitutes. Its demand curve will tend to be inelastic. Motor oil is a good example. Motor oil is needed to keep cars running. Yet no one person or family uses great quantities of motor oil. So it is not likely that the quantity of motor oil purchased will change much as long as price changes are *within a reasonable range*. Of course, if the price is raised to a staggering figure, many people will buy less oil (change their oil less frequently). If the price is dropped to an extremely low level, manufacturers may buy

EXHIBIT A–6 Demand Curve for Hamburger (a product with many substitutes)

EXHIBIT A–7   Demand Curve for Motor Oil (a product with few substitutes)

more—say, as a lower-cost substitute for other chemicals typically used in making plastic (Exhibit A–7). But these extremes are outside the relevant range.

Demand curves are introduced here because the degree of elasticity of demand shows how potential customers feel about a product—and especially whether they see substitutes for the product. But to get a better understanding of markets, we must extend this economic analysis.

MARKETS AS SEEN BY SUPPLIERS

Customers may want some product—but if suppliers are not willing to supply it, then there is no market. So we'll study the economist's analysis of supply. And then we'll bring supply and demand together for a more complete understanding of markets.

Economists often use the kind of analysis we are discussing here to explain pricing in the marketplace. But that is not our intention. Here we are interested in how and why markets work—and the interaction of customers and potential suppliers. Later in this appendix we will review how competition affects prices, but our full discussion of how individual firms set prices—or should set prices—will come in Chapters 17 and 18.

Supply curves reflect supplier thinking

Generally speaking, suppliers' costs affect the quantity of products they are willing to offer in a market during any period. In other words, their costs affect their supply schedules and supply curves. While a demand curve shows the quantity of products customers will be willing to buy at various prices, a **supply curve** shows the quantity of products that will be supplied at various possible prices. Eventually, only one quantity will be offered and purchased. So a supply curve is really a hypothetical (what-if) description of what will be offered at various prices. It is, however, a very important curve. Together with a demand curve, it summarizes the attitudes and probable behavior of buyers and sellers about a particular product in a particular market—that is, in a product-market.

Some supply curves are vertical

We usually assume that supply curves tend to slope upward—that is, suppliers will be willing to offer greater quantities at higher prices. If a product's market price is very high, it seems only reasonable that producers will be anxious to produce more of the product—and even put workers on overtime or perhaps hire

EXHIBIT A–8   Supply Schedule for Potatoes (10-pound bags)

Point	Possible Market Price per 10-lb. Bag	Number of Bags Sellers Will Supply per Month at Each Possible Market Price
A	$1.60	17,000,000
B	1.30	14,000,000
C	1.00	11,000,000
D	0.70	8,000,000
E	0.40	3,000,000

Note: This supply curve is for a month to emphasize that farmers might have some control over when they deliver their potatoes. There would be a different curve for each month.

more workers to increase the quantity they can offer. Going further, it seems likely that producers of other products will switch their resources (farms, factories, labor, or retail facilities) to the product that is in great demand.

On the other hand, if consumers are willing to pay only a very low price for a particular product, it's reasonable to expect that producers will switch to other products—thus reducing supply. A supply schedule (Exhibit A–8) and a supply curve (Exhibit A–9) for potatoes illustrate these ideas. This supply curve shows how many potatoes would be produced and offered for sale at each possible market price in a given month.

In the very short run (say, over a few hours, a day, or a week), a supplier may not be able to change the supply at all. In this situation, we would see a vertical supply curve. This situation is often relevant in the market for fresh produce. Fresh strawberries, for example, continue to ripen, and a supplier wants to sell them quickly—preferably at a higher price—but in any case, they must be sold.

If the product is a service, it may not be easy to expand the supply in the short run. Additional barbers or medical doctors are not quickly trained and licensed, and they only have so much time to give each day. Further, the prospect of much higher prices in the near future cannot easily expand the supply of many services. For example, a hit play or an "in" restaurant or nightclub is limited in the amount of "product" it can offer at a particular time.

EXHIBIT A–9   Supply Curve for Potatoes (10-pound bags)

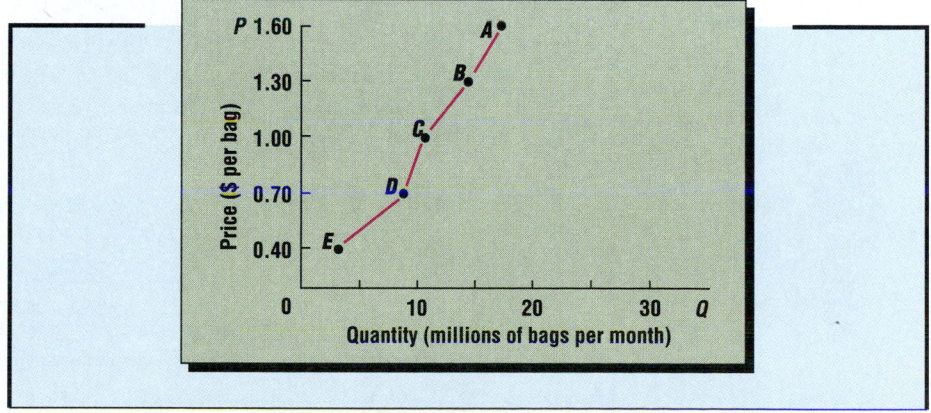

Elasticity of supply

The term *elasticity* also is used to describe supply curves. An extremely steep or almost vertical supply curve—often found in the short run—is called **inelastic supply** because the quantity supplied does not stretch much (if at all) if the price is raised. A flatter curve is called **elastic supply** because the quantity supplied does stretch more if the price is raised. A slightly up-sloping supply curve is typical in longer-run market situations. Given more time, suppliers have a chance to adjust their offerings, and competitors may enter or leave the market.

DEMAND AND SUPPLY INTERACT TO DETERMINE THE SIZE OF THE MARKET AND PRICE LEVEL

We have treated market demand and supply forces separately. Now we must bring them together to show their interaction. The *intersection* of these two forces determines the size of the market and the market price—at which point (price and quantity) the market is said to be in *equilibrium*.

The intersection of demand and supply is shown for the potato data discussed above. In Exhibit A–10, the demand curve for potatoes is now graphed against the supply curve in Exhibit A–9.

In this potato market, demand is inelastic—the total revenue of all the potato producers would be greater at higher prices. But the market price is at the **equilibrium point**—where the quantity and the price sellers are willing to offer are equal to the quantity and price that buyers are willing to accept. The $1 equilibrium price for potatoes yields a smaller *total revenue* to potato producers than a higher price would. This lower equilibrium price comes about because the many producers are willing to supply enough potatoes at the lower price. *Demand is not the only determiner of price level. Cost also must be considered—via the supply curve.*

Some consumers get a surplus

Presumably, a sale takes place only if both buyer and seller feel they will be better off after the sale. But sometimes the price a consumer pays in a sales transaction is less than what he or she would be willing to pay.

The reason for this is that demand curves are typically down-sloping, and some of the demand curve is above the equilibrium price. This is simply another

EXHIBIT A–10   Equilibrium of Supply and Demand for Potatoes (10-pound bags)

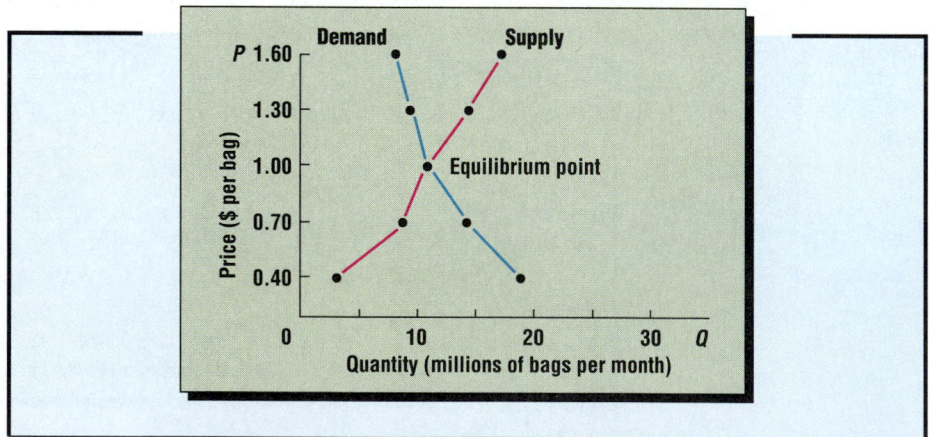

way of showing that some customers would have been willing to pay more than the equilibrium price—if they had to. In effect, some of them are getting a bargain by being able to buy at the equilibrium price. Economists have traditionally called these bargains the **consumer surplus**—that is, the difference to consumers between the value of a purchase and the price they pay.

Some business critics assume that consumers do badly in any business transaction. In fact, sales take place only if consumers feel they are at least getting their money's worth. As we can see here, some are willing to pay much more than the market price.

DEMAND AND SUPPLY HELP US UNDERSTAND THE NATURE OF COMPETITION

The elasticity of demand and supply curves—and their interaction—help predict the nature of competition a marketing manager is likely to face. For example, an extremely inelastic demand curve means that the manager will have much choice in strategy planning—and especially price setting. Apparently customers like the product and see few substitutes. They are willing to pay higher prices before cutting back much on their purchases.

Clearly, the elasticity of a firm's demand curves makes a big difference in strategy planning, but other factors also affect the nature of competition. Among these are the number and size of competitors and the uniqueness of each firm's marketing mix. Understanding these market situations is important because the freedom of a marketing manager—especially control over price—is greatly reduced in some situations.

A marketing manager operates in one of four kinds of market situations. We'll discuss three kinds: pure competition, oligopoly, and monopolistic competition. The fourth kind, monopoly, isn't found very often and is like monopolistic competition. The important dimensions of these situations are shown in Exhibit A–11.

When competition is pure

Many competitors offer about the same thing

Pure competition is a market situation that develops when a market has:

1. Homogeneous (similar) products.
2. Many buyers and sellers who have full knowledge of the market.
3. Ease of entry for buyers and sellers; that is, new firms have little difficulty starting in business—and new customers can easily come into the market.

More or less pure competition is found in many agricultural markets. In the potato market, for example, there are thousands of small producers—and they are in pure competition. Let's look more closely at these producers.

Although the potato market as a whole has a down-sloping demand curve, each of the many small producers in the industry is in pure competition, and each of them faces a flat demand curve at the equilibrium price. This is shown in Exhibit A–12.

As shown at the right of Exhibit A–12, an individual producer can sell as many bags of potatoes as he chooses at $1—the market equilibrium price. The equilibrium price is determined by the quantity that all producers choose to sell given the demand curve they face.

EXHIBIT A–11 Some Important Dimensions Regarding Market Situations

Important dimensions	Types of situations			
	Pure competition	Oligopoly	Monopolistic competition	Monopoly
Uniqueness of each firm's product	None	None	Some	Unique
Number of competitors	Many	Few	Few to many	None
Size of competitors (compared to size of market)	Small	Large	Large to small	None
Elasticity of demand facing firm	Completely elastic	Kinked demand curve (elastic and inelastic)	Either	Either
Elasticity of industry demand	Either	Inelastic	Either	Either
Control of price by firm	None	Some (with care)	Some	Complete

But a small producer has little effect on overall supply (or on the equilibrium price). If this individual farmer raises 1/10,000th of the quantity offered in the market, for example, you can see that there will be little effect if the farmer goes out of business—or doubles production.

The reason an individual producer's demand curve is flat is that the farmer probably couldn't sell any potatoes above the market price. And there is no point in selling below the market price! So, in effect, the individual producer has no control over price.

EXHIBIT A–12 Interaction of Demand and Supply in the Potato Industry and the Resulting Demand Curve Facing Individual Potato Producers

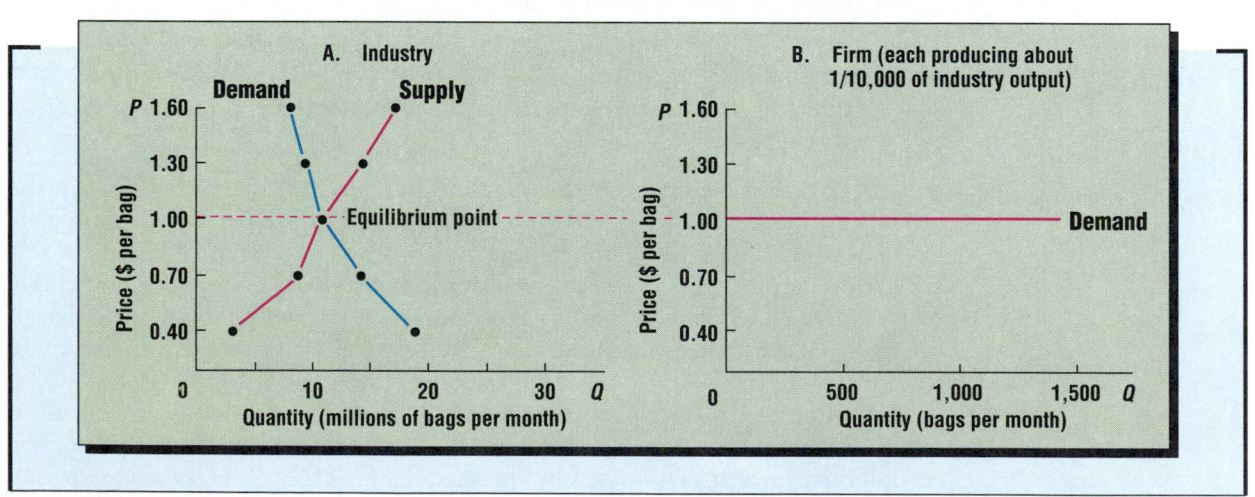

Markets tend to become more competitive

Not many markets are *purely* competitive. But many are close enough so we can talk about "almost" pure competition situations—those in which the marketing manager has to accept the going price.

Such highly competitive situations aren't limited to agriculture. Wherever *many* competitors sell *homogeneous* products—such as textiles, lumber, coal, printing, and laundry services—the demand curve seen by *each producer* tends to be flat.

Markets tend to become more competitive, moving toward pure competition (except in oligopolies—see below). On the way to pure competition, prices and profits are pushed down until some competitors are forced out of business. Eventually, in long-run equilibrium, the price level is only high enough to keep the survivors in business. No one makes any profit—they just cover costs. It's tough to be a marketing manager in this situation!

When competition is oligopolistic

A few competitors offer similar things

Not all markets move toward pure competition. Some become oligopolies.

Oligopoly situations are special market situations that develop when a market has:

1. Essentially homogeneous products—such as basic industrial chemicals or gasoline.
2. Relatively few sellers—or a few large firms and many smaller ones who follow the lead of the larger ones.
3. Fairly inelastic industry demand curves.

The demand curve facing each firm is unusual in an oligopoly situation. Although the industry demand curve is inelastic throughout the relevant range, the demand curve facing each competitor looks "kinked." See Exhibit A–13. The current market price is at the kink.

There is a market price because the competing firms watch each other carefully—and know it's wise to be at the kink. Each firm must expect that raising its own price above the market price will cause a big loss in sales. Few, if any,

EXHIBIT A–13 Oligopoly—Kinked Demand Curve—Situation

competitors will follow the price increase. So the firm's demand curve is relatively flat above the market price. If the firm lowers its price, it must expect competitors to follow. Given inelastic industry demand, the firm's own demand curve is inelastic at lower prices—assuming it keeps "its share" of this market at lower prices. Since lowering prices along such a curve will drop total revenue, the firm should leave its price at the kink—the market price.

Actually, however, there are price fluctuations in oligopolistic markets. Sometimes this is caused by firms that don't understand the market situation and cut their prices to get business. In other cases, big increases in demand or supply change the basic nature of the situation and lead to price-cutting. Price cuts can be drastic—such as Du Pont's price cut of 25 percent for Dacron. This happened when Du Pont decided that industry production capacity already exceeded demand, and more plants were due to start production.

It's important to keep in mind that oligopoly situations don't just apply to whole industries and national markets. Competitors who are focusing on the same local target market often face oligopoly situations. A suburban community might have several gas stations—all of which provide essentially the same product. In this case, the "industry" consists of the gas stations competing with each other in the local product-market.

As in pure competition, oligopolists face a long-run trend toward an equilibrium level—with profits driven toward zero. This may not happen immediately—and a marketing manager may try to delay price competition by relying more on other elements in the marketing mix.

When competition is monopolistic

A price must be set

You can see why marketing managers want to avoid pure competition or oligopoly situations. They prefer a market in which they have more control. **Monopolistic competition** is a market situation that develops when a market has:

1. Different (heterogeneous) products—in the eyes of some customers.
2. Sellers who feel they do have some competition in this market.

The word *monopolistic* means that each firm is trying to get control in its own little market. But the word *competition* means that there are still substitutes. The vigorous competition of a purely competitive market is reduced. Each firm has its own down-sloping demand curve. But the shape of the curve depends on the similarity of competitors' products and marketing mixes. Each monopolistic competitor has freedom—but not complete freedom—in its own market.

Judging elasticity will help set the price

Since a firm in monopolistic competition has its own down-sloping demand curve, it must make a decision about price level as part of its marketing strategy planning. Here, estimating the elasticity of the firm's own demand curve is helpful. If it is highly inelastic, the firm may decide to raise prices to increase total revenue. But if demand is highly elastic, this may mean many competitors with acceptable substitutes. Then the price may have to be set near that of the competition. And the marketing manager probably should try to develop a better marketing mix.

CONCLUSION

The economist's traditional demand and supply analysis provides a useful tool for analyzing the nature of demand and competition. It is especially important that you master the concepts of a demand curve and demand elasticity. How demand and supply interact helps determine the size of a market—and its price level. The interaction of supply and demand also helps explain the nature of competition in different market situations. We discuss three competitive situations: pure competition, oligopoly, and monopolistic competition. The fourth kind, monopoly, isn't found very often and is like monopolistic competition.

The nature of supply and demand—and competition—is very important in marketing strategy planning. We will return to these topics in Chapters 3 and 4—and then build on them throughout the text. So careful study of this appendix will build a good foundation for later work.

QUESTIONS AND PROBLEMS

1. Explain in your own words how economists look at markets and arrive at the "law of diminishing demand."

2. Explain what a demand curve is and why it is usually down-sloping. Then, give an example of a product for which the demand curve might not be down-sloping over some possible price ranges. Explain the reason for your choice.

3. What is the length of life of the typical demand curve? Illustrate your answer.

4. If the general market demand for men's shoes is fairly elastic, how does the demand for men's dress shoes compare to it? How does the demand curve for women's shoes compare to the demand curve for men's shoes?

5. If the demand for perfume is inelastic above and below the present price, should the price be raised? Why or why not?

6. If the demand for shrimp is highly elastic below the present price, should the price be lowered?

7. Discuss what factors lead to inelastic demand and supply curves. Are they likely to be found together in the same situation?

8. Why would a marketing manager prefer to sell a product that has no close substitutes? Are "high profits" almost guaranteed?

9. If a manufacturer's well-known product is sold at the same price by many retailers in the same community, is this an example of pure competition? When a community has many small grocery stores, are they in pure competition? What characteristics are needed to have a purely competitive market?

10. List three products that are sold in purely competitive markets and three that are sold in monopolistically competitive markets. Do any of these products have anything in common? Can any generalizations be made about competitive situations and marketing mix planning?

11. Cite a local example of an oligopoly—explaining why it is an oligopoly.

3

Finding Target Market Opportunities with Market Segmentation

When You Finish This Chapter, You Should

1. Understand how to find marketing opportunities.

2. Know about the different kinds of marketing opportunities.

3. Understand why opportunities in international markets should be considered.

4. Know about defining generic markets and product-markets.

5. Know what market segmentation is and how to segment product-markets into submarkets.

6. Know three approaches to market-oriented strategy planning.

7. Know dimensions that may be useful for segmenting markets.

8. Know a seven-step approach to market segmentation that you can do yourself.

9. Know what positioning is—and why it is useful.

10. Understand the important new terms (shown in red).

You've probably never heard of Acucobol. The users of this company's products are not final consumers; they're the computer specialists who program information systems for business firms. Although Acucobol is a new company, its growth has been fast and profitable.

Pamela Coker, the entrepreneur who started Acucobol, is a key to this success. She realized that a change in the marketing environment left a large group of potential customers with unmet needs. Then she was creative in developing products—actually whole marketing mixes—to serve the needs of her target market.

In the 1970s, businesses all around the world bought IBM mainframe computers to speed up tasks like payroll processing and invoicing. Firms also invested millions of dollars to develop specialized computer programs to do these jobs. Many of these programs were written in COBOL, the mainframe programming language pushed by IBM. Unfortunately, when firms wanted to replace their mainframes, it was very difficult to modify their COBOL programs for use on desktop computers. IBM was slow to offer its customers a good solution to this problem, perhaps because of fear that mainframe sales would erode even faster.

Coker saw this situation as an opportunity. Her firm developed new software products to make it fast and easy for programmers to modernize the old COBOL programs. Acucobol listened to programmers' preferences and designed software with color screens and simple commands that work with the Windows operating system. Coker started Acucobol on a shoestring, so she initially focused on a segment of the market that she felt would respond to a low-cost market mix, specifically targeting the many local software houses that develop programs for other businesses. She was able to contact these customers at computer trade shows or with direct-mail promotions, and then she followed up to close sales with telephone selling. Those early sales provided the money to pursue opportunities to sell Acucobol products to new target markets, including overseas customers.

Reaching new target markets required changes in the marketing mix. In Germany, for example, Coker started by placing ads in trade publications; they were an efficient way to introduce Acucobol to many potential customers. The ads also paved the way for the personal selling effort, which was handled by a German sales agent who already had relationships with some potential customers. As in the U.S., much of the personal selling was done by telephone. This was unusual in Europe, but it helped hold down costs—and the price. The low price in turn stimulated increased sales and healthy profits. Next Coker targeted large corporations like Saab in Brazil and Daimler-Benz in Germany. Purchase decisions in these multinational firms involve more people, are more complicated, and take longer. In addition, much more service is needed to keep the relationship strong. Coker realized that relying on middlemen was not the best way to deal with these challenges. Thus, Acucobol is putting more emphasis on building its own direct sales force as it expands distribution into new countries.[1]

WHAT ARE ATTRACTIVE OPPORTUNITIES?

This book focuses primarily on marketing strategy planning—an important part of which involves finding attractive target markets. But how do you identify a target market and decide if it offers good opportunities?

In this chapter and the next, you will learn how to find possible market opportunities and choose the ones to turn into strategies and plans. We will look first at how to identify attractive target markets. Exhibit 3–1 overviews the key topics we will be considering.

We will evaluate possible opportunities against various screening criteria. We will be covering screening criteria in more detail in the next chapter. For now, however, you should see in Exhibit 3–1 that these criteria grow out of analysis of the company's resources, trends in the external environments the firm faces, and the objectives of top management.

Attractive opportunities for a particular firm are those that the firm has some chance of doing something about—given its resources and objectives. Marketing

EXHIBIT 3–1   Finding and Evaluating Marketing Opportunities

Attractive opportunities are often fairly close to markets the firm already knows.

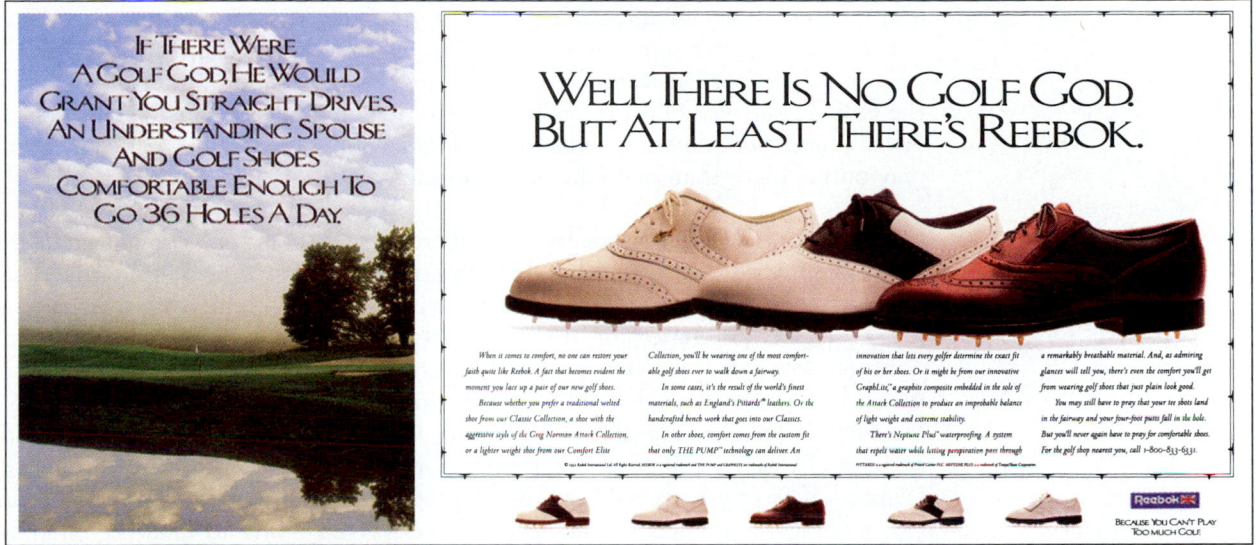

strategy planning tries to match opportunities to the firm's resources (what it can do) and its objectives (what it wants to do).

How many opportunities a firm "sees" depends on the thinking of top management—and the objectives of the firm. Some want to be innovators and eagerly search out new opportunities. Others are willing to be creative imitators or risk-avoiding "me-too" marketers.

Breakthrough opportunities are best

Throughout this book, we will emphasize finding **breakthrough opportunities**—opportunities that help innovators develop hard-to-copy marketing strategies that will be very profitable for a long time. Finding breakthrough opportunities is important because imitators are always waiting to "share" the profits—if they can.

Competitive advantage is needed—at least

Even if a firm can't find a breakthrough opportunity, it should try to obtain a competitive advantage to increase its chances for profit or survival. **Competitive advantage** means that a firm has a marketing mix that the target market sees as better than a competitor's mix. A competitive advantage may result from efforts in different areas of the firm—cost cutting in production, innovative R&D, more effective purchasing of needed components, or financing for a new distribution facility. Whatever the source, an advantage only succeeds if it allows the firm to satisfy customers better than some competitor.

Sometimes a firm can achieve breakthrough opportunities and competitive advantage by simply fine-tuning its marketing mix(es) or developing closer relationships with its customers. Sometimes it may need new facilities, new people in new parts of the world, and totally new ways of solving problems. But every firm needs some competitive advantage—so the promotion people have something unique to sell and success doesn't just hinge on offering lower and lower prices.[2]

TYPES OF OPPORTUNITIES TO PURSUE

Most people have unsatisfied needs—and alert marketers who see these needs find opportunities all around them. Unfortunately, some opportunities seem "obvious" only after someone else identifies them. Marketers need a framework for thinking about the kinds of opportunities they may find. Exhibit 3–2 shows the four broad possibilities: market penetration, market development, product development, and diversification. We will look at these separately, but some firms may pursue more than one type of opportunity at the same time.

Market penetration

Market penetration means trying to increase sales of a firm's present products in its present markets—probably through a more aggressive marketing mix. The firm may try to strengthen its relationship with customers to increase their rate of use or repeat purchases, or try to attract competitors' customers or current nonusers. For example, Visa increased advertising to encourage customers to use its card when they travel—and to switch from using American Express.

New promotion appeals alone may not be effective. A firm may need to add more stores in present areas for greater convenience. Short-term price cuts or coupon offers may help. MCI increased advertising and offered special discounts to encourage consumers to choose MCI over AT&T—and to urge the "friends and family" that they call to do the same.

Obviously, to do effective analysis and planning, marketers need to really understand why some people are buying now and what will motivate them to buy more, begin or resume buying, or change brands.

Market development

Market development means trying to increase sales by selling present products in new markets. Firms may try advertising in different media to reach new target customers. Or they may add channels of distribution or new stores in new areas, including overseas. For example, to reach new customers, McDonald's opens outlets in airports, office buildings, zoos, casinos, hospitals, and military bases. And it's rapidly expanding into international markets with outlets in places like Russia, Brazil, Hong Kong, Mexico, and Australia.

Market development may also involve searching for new uses for a product, as when Lipton provides recipes showing how to use its dry soup mixes for chip dip.

Product development

Product development means offering new or improved products for present markets. By knowing the present market's needs, a firm may see ways to add or modify product features, create several quality levels, or add more types or sizes to

EXHIBIT 3–2   Four Basic Types of Opportunities

	Present products	**New products**
Present markets	Market penetration	Product development
New markets	Market development	Diversification

better satisfy customers. Computer software firms like Microsoft boost sales by introducing new versions of popular programs. Microsoft also develops other types of new products for its customers. It now sells computer books (some in the new CD-ROM format) and even computer hardware. Similarly, many ski resorts have developed trails for hiking and mountain bikes, to bring their ski customers back in the summer when the snow is gone and the lodge would otherwise be empty. Blockbuster is expanding the ways that it can appeal to its home entertainment customers by selling audio CDs and cassettes in addition to renting videotapes and laserdiscs.

Diversification

Diversification means moving into totally different lines of business—perhaps entirely unfamiliar products, markets, or even levels in the production-marketing system. Until recently, the Coleman name has been nearly synonymous with lanterns and other camping gear. Now, however, Coleman has added a line of air compressors that are used to drive power tools ranging from paint sprayers to nail drivers. The compressors will be of interest primarily to building contractors and tradespeople rather than the outdoor enthusiasts market with which Coleman has been so successful in the past. Coleman is also considering other hardware-related products for European markets that may take it even further from its traditional business.

Diversification presents the most challenging opportunities. Diversification involves both new products *and* new markets. The further the opportunity from what the firm is already doing, the more attractive it may look to the optimists—and the harder it will be to evaluate. Opportunities very different from a firm's current experiences involve higher risks. The landscape is littered with failed efforts at diversification. For example, Holiday Corporation learned fast that making mattresses (like the ones used in its Holiday Inn motels) was *not* one of its strengths.

Which opportunities come first?

Usually firms find attractive opportunities fairly close to markets they already know. This may allow them to capitalize on changes in their present markets—or more basic changes in the external environment. Moreover, many firms are finding that the easiest way to increase profits is to do a better job of hanging onto the customers that they've already won—by meeting their needs so well that they wouldn't consider switching to another firm.

Most firms think first of greater market penetration. They want to increase profits where they already have experience and strengths. Marketers who understand their present markets well may also see opportunities in product development—especially because they already have a relationship with their present customers and a way to reach them. But a firm that already has as big a share as it can get in its present markets should consider market development—finding new markets for its present products—including expanding regionally, nationally, or internationally.[3]

INTERNATIONAL OPPORTUNITIES SHOULD BE CONSIDERED

It's easy for a marketing manager to fall into the trap of ignoring international markets, especially when the firm's domestic market is prosperous. Why go to the trouble of looking elsewhere for opportunities?

The world is getting smaller

International trade is increasing all around the world, and trade barriers are coming down. In addition, advances in communications and transportation are making it easier and cheaper for even small firms to reach international customers. Around the world, potential customers have needs and money to spend. Ignoring these customers doesn't make any more sense than ignoring potential customers in the same town. The real question is whether a firm can effectively use its resources to meet these customers' needs at a profit.

Develop a competitive advantage at home and abroad

If customers in other countries are interested in the products a firm offers—or could offer—serving them may result in even more economies of scale. Lower costs (and prices) may give a firm a competitive advantage both in its home markets *and* abroad. This sort of competitive pressure may actually *force* a marketing manager to expand into international markets. Marketing managers who are only interested in the "convenient" customers in their own backyards may be rudely surprised to find that an aggressive, low-cost foreign producer is willing to pursue those customers—even if doing it is not convenient. Many companies that thought they could avoid the struggles of international competition have learned this lesson the hard way.

Get an early start in a new market

A marketing manager looking for development opportunities in international markets often finds them. Different countries are at different stages of economic and technological development, and their consumers have different needs at different times.

A company facing tough competition, thin profit margins, and slow sales growth at home may get a fresh start in another country where demand for its product is just beginning to grow. A marketing manager may be able to "transfer" marketing know-how—or some other competitive advantage—the firm has already developed. Consider Cybex, a small company that sells exercise equipment, including some high-tech units that hook up to computers to analyze muscle injuries. In the U.S., Cybex faces slow market growth and intense competition. But in many overseas countries, demand is still growing because consumer interest in fitness started later. To develop these markets, Cybex added a director of international marketing, international salespeople, and new international middlemen. Now Cybex sells its specialized $40,000 products in markets like Japan where customers had never before paid more than $3,000 for fitness equipment. These export sales to 30 foreign markets are a key to Cybex's profits.[4]

Many firms are finding that there are attractive opportunities in foreign markets.

**Find better trends
in variables**

Unfavorable trends in the marketing environment at home—or favorable trends in other countries—may make international marketing particularly attractive. For example, population growth in the United States has slowed and income is leveling off. In other places in the world, population and income are increasing rapidly. Marketing managers for U.S. firms can no longer rely on the constant market growth that drove increased domestic sales during the last 30 years. For many firms, growth—and perhaps even survival—will come only by aiming at more distant customers.

Our point here is basic. In today's world, it doesn't make sense to ignore international markets and casually assume that all of the best opportunities exist "at home."

SEARCH FOR OPPORTUNITIES CAN BEGIN BY UNDERSTANDING MARKETS

**Breakthrough
opportunities from
understanding target
markets**

When marketing managers really understand their target markets, they may see breakthrough opportunities. But a target market's real needs—and the breakthrough opportunities that can come from identifying and serving those needs—are not always obvious. So let's look at some ways to better understand a company's target markets.

**What is a company's
market?**

Identifying a company's market is an important but sticky issue. In general, a **market** is a group of potential customers with similar needs who are willing to exchange something of value with sellers offering various goods and/or services—that is, ways of satisfying those needs.

Market-oriented managers develop marketing mixes for *specific* target markets. Getting the firm to focus on specific target markets is vital. As shown in Exhibit 3–3, target marketing requires a "narrowing-down" process—to get

EXHIBIT 3–3   Narrowing Down to Target Markets

beyond production-oriented mass market thinking. But firms often misunderstand this narrowing-down process.

Don't just focus on the product

Some production-oriented managers ignore the tough part of defining markets. To make the narrowing-down process easier, they just describe their markets in terms of *products* they sell. For example, producers and retailers of greeting cards might define their market as the "greeting-card" market. But this production-oriented approach ignores customers—and customers make a market! This also leads to missed opportunities. Hallmark isn't missing these opportunities. Instead, Hallmark aims at the "personal-expression" market. It offers all kinds of products that can be sent as "memory makers"—to express one person's feelings toward another. Hallmark has expanded far beyond holiday and birthday cards—the major greeting card days—to jewelry, gift wrap, plaques, candles, and puzzles as well as to all-occasion and humorous cards.[5]

From generic markets to product-markets

It's useful to think of two basic types of markets. A **generic market** is a market with *broadly* similar needs—and sellers offering various—*often diverse*—ways of satisfying those needs. In contrast, a **product-market** is a market with *very* similar needs and sellers offering various *close substitute* ways of satisfying those needs.[6]

A generic market description looks at markets broadly and from a customer's viewpoint. Entertainment seekers, for example, have several very different ways to satisfy their needs. An entertainment seeker might buy a new RCA satellite receiving system for a TV, sign up for a Lindblad tour, or reserve season tickets for the symphony. Any one of these *very different* products may satisfy this entertainment need. Sellers in this generic entertainment seeker market have to focus on the need(s) the customers want satisfied—not on how one seller's product (satellite disk, vacation, or live music) is better than that of another producer.

Different fax companies may compete with each other in the same product-market— and with overnight carriers in a broader generic market. Reynolds Wrap aluminum foil competes with other aluminum foils in its product-market—and with plastic zipper bags and Tupperware sandwich containers in a broader generic market.

It is sometimes hard to understand and define generic markets because *quite different product types may compete with each other*. For example, free-lance journalists often need a fast, worry-free way to get articles to their editors. Sanyo's fax machines, FedEx's overnight service, and Microsoft's electronic mail network may all compete to serve our journalists' needs. If customers see all these products as substitutes—as competitors in the same generic market—then marketers must deal with this complication.

Suppose, however, that one of our journalists decides to satisfy this need with a fax machine. Then—in this product-market—Ricoh, Hewlett-Packard, Samsung, and many other brands may compete with each other for the customer's dollars. In this *product*-market concerned with fax machines *and* needs to reduce worry, consumers compare similar products to satisfy their communication needs.

Most companies quickly narrow their focus to specific product-markets because of the firm's past experience, resources, or management preferences. And we will usually be thinking of product-markets when we refer to markets. But when looking for opportunities—especially new opportunities—a marketing manager should consider a broader generic market view.

Broaden market definitions to find opportunities

Broader market definitions—including both generic market definitions and product-market definitions—can help firms find opportunities. But deciding *how* broad to go isn't easy. Too narrow a definition limits a firm's opportunities—but too broad a definition makes the company's efforts and resources seem insignificant.

Our strategy planning process helps define relevant markets. Here we try to match opportunities to a firm's resources and objectives. So the *relevant market for finding opportunities* should be bigger than the firm's present product-market—but not so big that the firm couldn't expand and be an important competitor. A small manufacturer of screwdrivers in Mexico, for example, shouldn't define its market as broadly as "the worldwide tool users market" or as narrowly as "our present screwdriver customers." But it may have the production and/or marketing potential to consider "the handyman's hand-tool market in North America." Carefully naming your product-market can help you see possible opportunities.

NAMING PRODUCT-MARKETS AND GENERIC MARKETS

Product-related terms do not—by themselves—adequately describe a market. A complete product-market definition includes a four-part description.

What:	1. **Product type (type of good and type of service)**
To meet what:	2. **Customer (user) needs**
For whom:	3. **Customer types**
Where:	4. **Geographic area**

In other words, a product-market description must include customer-related terms—not just product-related terms. We refer to these four-part descriptions as product-market "names" because most managers label their markets when they think, write, or talk about them. Such a four-part definition can be clumsy, however, so we often use a nickname—as long as everyone understands the underlying four-part terms. And the nickname should refer to people—not products—because, as we emphasize, people make markets!

Lever 2000 deodorant bar soap and Neutrogena's liquid pump soap may compete in the same broad product-market, but each may appeal to a different submarket of customers with different needs.

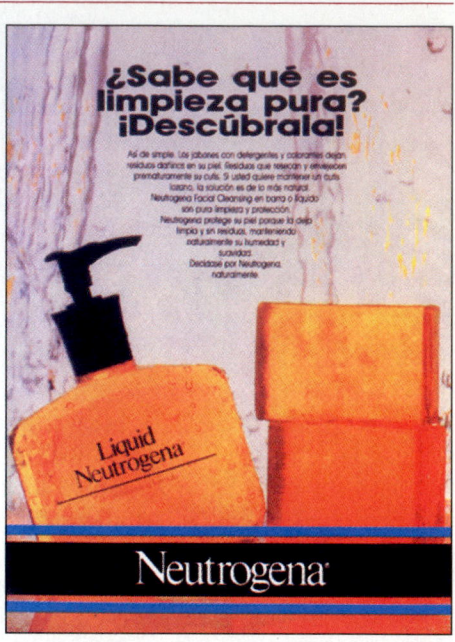

Product type should meet customer needs

Product type describes the goods and/or services that customers want. Sometimes the product type is strictly a physical good or strictly a service. But marketing managers who ignore the possibility that *both* are important to meeting customer needs can miss opportunities. For example, a marketing manager at a videocassette firm may think carefully about all of the benefits customers want from a VCR—but fail to see that many customers would also like a convenient way to ask *a person* a question about how to use it. A toll-free telephone helpline might make a big difference in whether customers buy the product in the first place and also help to build customer satisfaction and a stronger relationship after the purchase.

Customer (user) needs refer to the needs the product type satisfies for the customer. At a very basic level, product types usually provide functional benefits such as nourishing, protecting, warming, cooling, transporting, cleaning, holding, saving time, and so forth. Although we need to identify such "basic" needs first, in advanced economies, we must go beyond basic needs to emotional needs—such as needs for fun, excitement, pleasing appearance, or status. Correctly defining the need(s) relevant to a market is crucial and requires a good understanding of customers. We discuss these topics more fully in Chapters 7 and 8.

Customer type refers to the final consumer or user of a product type. Here we want to choose a name that describes all present (possible) types of customers. To define customer type, marketers should identify the final consumer or user of the product type, rather than the buyer—if they are different. For instance, producers should avoid treating middlemen as a customer type—unless middlemen actually use the product in their own business.

The *geographic area* is where a firm competes—or plans to compete—for customers. Naming the geographic area may seem trivial, but understanding geographic boundaries of a market can suggest new opportunities. Supermarkets in London, or Los Angeles, or Toronto don't cater to all consumers in these areas.

EXHIBIT 3–4 Relationship between Generic and Product-Market Definitions

There may be opportunities to serve unsatisfied customers in the same areas. Similarly, a firm aiming only at the U.S. market may want to expand into Canada, Mexico, or other world markets.

No product type in generic market names

A generic market description *doesn't include any product-type terms*. It consists of only three parts of the product-market definition—without the product type. This emphasizes that any product type that satisfies the customer's needs can compete in a generic market. Recall that in our "entertainment seeker" market example, very different product types were competitors. Exhibit 3–4 shows the relationship between generic market and product-market definitions.

Creativity is needed in naming markets

By creatively analyzing the needs and attitudes of present and potential target markets—in relation to the benefits offered by a firm and its competitors—you can see new opportunities. Later we'll study the many possible dimensions for segmenting markets. But for now you should see that defining markets only in terms of current products is not the best way to find new opportunities—or plan marketing strategies.

MARKET SEGMENTATION DEFINES POSSIBLE TARGET MARKETS

Market segmentation is a two-step process

Market segmentation is a two-step process of: (1) *naming* broad product-markets and (2) *segmenting* these broad product-markets in order to select target markets and develop suitable marketing mixes.

This two-step process isn't well understood. First-time market segmentation efforts often fail because beginners start with the whole mass market and try to find one or two demographic characteristics to segment this market. Customer behavior is usually too complex to be explained in terms of just one or two demographic characteristics. For example, not all old men—or all young women—buy the same products or brands. Other dimensions usually must be considered—starting with customer needs.

**Naming broad
product-markets is
disaggregating**

The first step in effective market segmentation involves naming a broad product-market of interest to the firm. Marketers must "break apart"—disaggregate—all possible needs into some generic markets and broad product-markets in which the firm may be able to operate profitably. See Exhibit 3–3. No one firm can satisfy everyone's needs. So the naming—disaggregating—step involves "brainstorming" about very different solutions to various generic needs and selecting some broad areas—broad product-markets—where the firm has some resources and experience. This means that a car manufacturer would probably ignore all the possible opportunities in food and clothing markets and focus on the generic market, "transporting people in the world," and probably on the broad product-market, "cars and trucks for transporting people in the world."

Disaggregating, a practical rough-and-ready approach, tries to narrow down the marketing focus to product-market areas where the firm is more likely to have a competitive advantage—or even to find breakthrough opportunities. It looks easy, but disaggregating actually requires a lot of thought and judgment about what the firm may be able to do for some consumers—do better than some or all competitors—so it will have a competitive advantage.

**Market grid is a
visual aid to market
segmentation**

Assuming that any broad product-market (or generic market) may consist of submarkets, picture a market as a rectangle with boxes that represent the smaller, more homogeneous product-markets.

Exhibit 3–5, for example, represents the broad product-market of bicycle riders. The boxes show different submarkets. One submarket might focus on people who want basic transportation, another on people who want exercise, and so on. Alternatively, in the generic "transporting market" discussed above, we might see different product-markets of customers for bicycles, motorcycles, cars, airplanes, ships, buses, and "others."

**Segmenting is an
aggregating process**

Marketing-oriented managers think of **segmenting** as an aggregating process—clustering people with similar needs into a "market segment." A **market segment** is a (relatively) homogeneous group of customers who will respond to a marketing mix in a similar way.

EXHIBIT 3–5   A Market Grid Diagram with Submarkets

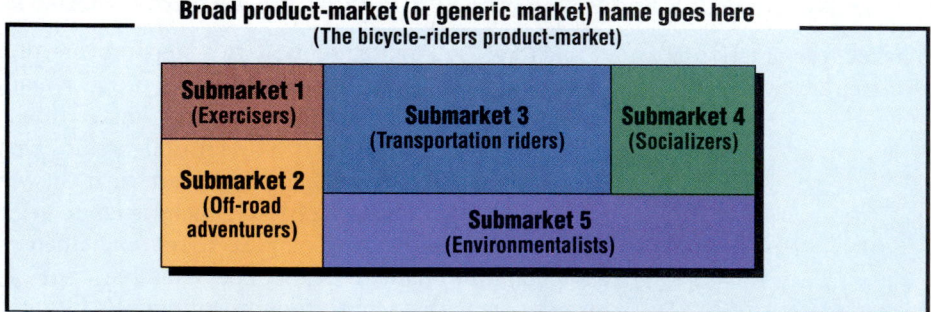

This part of the market segmentation process (see Exhibit 3–3) takes a different approach from the naming part. Here we look for similarities rather than basic differences in needs. Segmenters start with the idea that each person is one of a kind but that it may be possible to aggregate some similar people into a product-market.

Segmenters see each of these one-of-a-kind people as having a unique set of dimensions. Consider a product-market in which customers' needs differ on two important segmenting dimensions: need for status and need for dependability. In Exhibit 3–6A, each dot shows a person's position on the two dimensions. While each person's position is unique, many of these people are similar in terms of how much status and dependability they want. So a segmenter may aggregate them into three (an arbitrary number) relatively homogeneous submarkets—A, B, and C. Group A might be called "status-oriented" and Group C "dependability-oriented." Members of Group B want both and might be called the "demanders."

How far should the aggregating go?

The segmenter wants to aggregate individual customers into some workable number of relatively homogeneous target markets—and then treat each target market differently.

Look again at Exhibit 3–6A. Remember we talked about three segments. But this was an arbitrary number. As Exhibit 3–6B shows, there may really be six segments. What do you think—does this broad product-market consist of three segments or six?

Another difficulty with segmenting is that some potential customers just don't fit neatly into market segments. For example, not everyone in Exhibit 3–6B was put into one of the groups. Forcing them into one of the groups would have made these segments more heterogeneous—and harder to please. Further, forming additional segments for them probably wouldn't be profitable. They are too few and not very similar in terms of the two dimensions. These people are simply too unique to be catered to and may have to be ignored—unless they are willing to pay a high price for special treatment.

EXHIBIT 3–6   Every Individual Has His or Her Own Unique Position in a Market—Those with Similar Positions Can Be Aggregated into Potential Target Markets

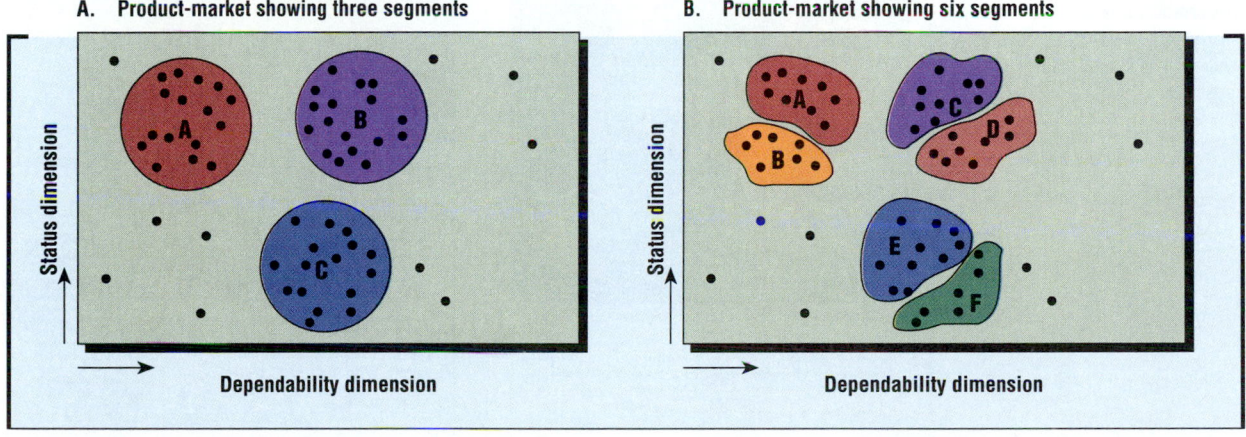

A. **Product-market showing three segments**

B. **Product-market showing six segments**

The number of segments that should be formed depends more on judgment than on some scientific rule. But the following guidelines can help.

Criteria for segmenting a broad product-market

Ideally, "good" market segments meet the following criteria:

1. *Homogeneous (similar) within*—the customers in a market segment should be as similar as possible with respect to their likely responses to marketing mix variables *and* their segmenting dimensions.
2. *Heterogeneous (different) between*—the customers in different segments should be as different as possible with respect to their likely responses to marketing mix variables *and* their segmenting dimensions.
3. *Substantial*—the segment should be big enough to be profitable.
4. *Operational*—the segmenting dimensions should be useful for identifying customers and deciding on marketing mix variables.

It is especially important that segments be *operational*. This leads marketers to include demographic dimensions such as age, income, location, and family size. Information on these dimensions, usually readily available, can be very useful in determining the size of markets and planning marketing mixes. In fact, it is difficult to make some Place and Promotion decisions without such information.

Avoid segmenting dimensions that have no practical operational use. For example, you may find a personality trait such as moodiness among the traits of heavy buyers of a product, but how could you use this fact? Salespeople can't give a personality test to each buyer. Similarly, advertising media buyers or copywriters couldn't make much use of this information. So although moodiness might be related in some way to previous purchases, it would not be a useful dimension for segmenting.

USAir uses a multiple target market approach; its supporting services, promotions, and even prices for business customers who plan group meetings and conventions are quite different from what it offers families that travel with their kids.

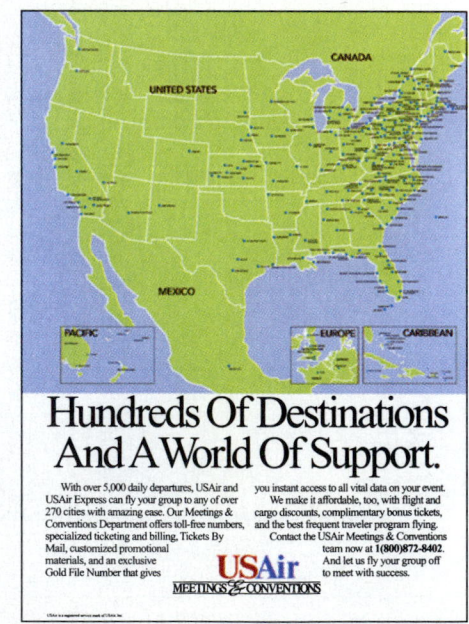

Target marketers aim at specific targets

Once you accept the idea that broad product-markets may have submarkets, you can see that target marketers usually have a choice among many possible target markets.

There are three basic ways to develop market-oriented strategies in a broad product-market.

1. The **single target market approach**—segmenting the market and picking one of the homogeneous segments as the firm's target market.

2. The **multiple target market approach**—segmenting the market and choosing two or more segments, then treating each as a separate target market needing a different marketing mix.

3. The **combined target market approach**—combining two or more submarkets into one larger target market as a basis for one strategy.

Note that all three approaches involve target marketing. They all aim at specific, clearly defined target markets. See Exhibit 3–7. For convenience, we call people who follow the first two approaches the "segmenters" and people who use the third approach the "combiners."

Combiners try to satisfy "pretty well"

Combiners try to increase the size of their target markets by combining two or more segments. Combiners look at various submarkets for similarities rather than differences. Then they try to extend or modify their basic offering to appeal to these "combined" customers with just one marketing mix. See Exhibit 3–7. For example, combiners may try a new package, more service, a new brand, or new flavors. But even if they make product or other marketing mix changes, they don't

EXHIBIT 3–7 Target Marketers Have Specific Aims

EXHIBIT 3–8   There May Be Different Demand Curves in Different
Market Segments

try to satisfy unique smaller submarkets. Instead, combiners try to improve the general appeal of their marketing mix to appeal to a bigger "combined" target market.

A combined target market approach may help achieve some economies of scale. It may also require less investment than developing different marketing mixes for different segments—making it especially attractive for firms with limited resources. These potential benefits may be very appealing and make combining seem less risky.

Too much combining is risky

It is tempting to aim at larger combined markets instead of using different marketing mixes for smaller segmented markets. But combiners must be careful not to aggregate too far. As they enlarge the target market, it becomes less homogeneous—and individual differences within each submarket may begin to outweigh the similarities. This makes it harder to develop marketing mixes that can effectively reach and satisfy potential customers within each of the submarkets.

A combiner faces the continual risk of innovative segmenters "chipping away" at the various segments of the combined target market—by offering more attractive marketing mixes to more homogeneous submarkets. IBM saw this happen very quickly when it came out with personal computers. Apple took the segment that wanted an easy-to-use computer. Toshiba took travelers who wanted laptop convenience. Compaq got those who wanted the fastest machines. Dell attracted customers who wanted reliability at a low price.

Segmenters try to satisfy "very well"

Segmenters aim at one or more homogeneous segments and try to develop a different marketing mix for each segment. Segmenters usually adjust their marketing mixes for each target market—perhaps making basic changes in the product itself—because they want to satisfy each segment very well.

Instead of assuming that the whole market consists of a fairly similar set of customers (like the mass marketer does) or merging various submarkets together (like the combiner), a segmenter sees submarkets with their own demand curves—as shown in Exhibit 3–8. Segmenters believe that aiming at one—or

KAEPA, INC., EARNS CHEERS FROM CUSTOMERS

During the 1980s, interest in fitness resulted in exploding demand for athletic shoes. Most producers took advantage of the growth with a multiple target market approach. They developed innovative products, expanded distribution, and aimed their promotion at specific needs—like jogging, aerobics, cross-training, and walking. Nike, for example, pumped interest in its air technology basketball shoes with help from high-flying celebrities like Michael Jordan. Similarly, Reebok successfully positioned its appeal for fashion-conscious consumers.

As other firms won customers, sales of the all-purpose sneakers produced by Kaepa, Inc., plummeted. Kaepa shoes were still popular in Japan, but by 1990 Kaepa's sales in the U.S. all but disappeared. Now, however, Kaepa is turning things around by focusing its efforts on a specific target market—cheerleaders. Cheerleaders are a bigger market than you might think. They spend about $35

million a year on shoes. And millions of other teens follow their lead.

Kaepa has a competitive edge with this segment because it has fine tuned its marketing for their needs. Cheerleading squads can order Kaepa shoes with custom team logos and colors. The soles of the shoes feature finger grooves that make it easier for cheerleaders to build human pyramids. Kaepa also carefully targets its market research and promotion. Kaepa salespeople attend the cheerleading camps that each summer draw 40,000 enthusiasts. Kaepa also builds interest in its brand by placing ads in magazines—like *Teen* and *Seventeen*—that are popular with its target market. Kaepa even arranges for the high-profile cheering teams it sponsors to do demonstrations at retail stores. Because this generates free publicity and pulls in customers, retailers are willing to put more emphasis on the Kaepa line. With all this attention, it's no wonder that cheerleaders are jumping away from other brands to Kaepa shoes.[7]

some—of these smaller markets will satisfy the target customers better and provide greater profit potential for the firm.

Segmenting may produce bigger sales

Note that segmenters are not settling for a smaller sales potential. Instead, they hope to increase sales by getting a much larger share of the business in the market(s) they target. A segmenter who really satisfies the target market can often build such a close relationship with customers that it faces no real competition.

AFG Industries, a company that manufactures glass, had a small market share when it was trying to sell glass in the construction market. Then AFG's marketing managers focused on the special needs of firms that used tempered and colored glass in their own production. AFG used a multiple target market approach and planned marketing mixes for "niche" segments that didn't get attention from the bigger producers. Because of careful segmenting and close relationships with the customers it serves, AFG now sells 70 percent of the glass for microwave oven doors and 75 percent of the glass for shower enclosures and patio tabletops. AFG also earns the best profit margins in its industry.[8]

Should you segment or combine?

Which approach should a firm use? This depends on the firm's resources, the nature of competition, and—most important—the similarity of customer needs, attitudes, and buying behavior.

In general, it's usually safer to be a segmenter—that is, to try to satisfy some customers *very* well instead of many just *fairly* well. That's why many firms use the single or multiple target market approach instead of the combined target market approach. Procter & Gamble, for example, offers many products that seem to compete directly with each other (e.g., Tide versus Cheer or Crest versus Gleem). However, P&G offers "tailor-made" marketing mixes to each submarket large— and profitable—enough to deserve a separate marketing mix. Though extremely effective, this approach may not be possible for a smaller firm with more limited resources. A smaller firm may have to use the single target market approach— aiming all its efforts at the one submarket niche where it sees the best opportunity.[9]

Profit is the balancing point

Target marketers develop and implement whole strategies—they don't just segment markets. In practice, cost considerations probably encourage more aggregating—to obtain economies of scale—while demand considerations suggest less aggregating—to satisfy needs more exactly.

Profit is the balancing point. It determines how unique a marketing mix the firm can afford to offer to a particular group.

WHAT DIMENSIONS ARE USED TO SEGMENT MARKETS?

Segmenting dimensions guide marketing mix planning

Market segmentation forces a marketing manager to decide which product-market dimensions might be useful for planning marketing strategies. The dimensions should help guide marketing mix planning. Exhibit 3–9 shows the basic kinds of dimensions we'll be talking about in Chapters 6 through 8—and their probable effect on the four Ps. Ideally, we want to describe any potential product-market in terms of all three types of customer-related dimensions—plus a product type description—because these dimensions help us develop better marketing mixes.

EXHIBIT 3–9   Relation of Potential Target Market Dimensions to Marketing Strategy Decision Areas

Potential Target Market Dimensions	Effects on Strategy Decision Areas
1. Behavioral needs, attitudes, and how present and potential goods and services fit into customers' consumption patterns.	Affects *Product* (features, packaging, product line assortment, branding) and *Promotion* (what potential customers need and want to know about the firm's offering, and what appeals should be used).
2. Urgency to get need satisfied and desire and willingness to seek information, compare, and shop.	Affects *Place* (how directly products are distributed from producer to customer, how extensively they are made available, and the level of service needed) and *Price* (how much potential customers are willing to pay).
3. Geographic location and other demographic characteristics of potential customers.	Affects size of *Target Markets* (economic potential), *Place* (where products should be made available), and *Promotion* (where and to whom to target advertising and personal selling).

Many segmenting dimensions may be considered

Customers can be described by many specific dimensions. Exhibit 3–10 shows some dimensions useful for segmenting consumer markets. A few are behavioral dimensions, others are geographic and demographic. Exhibit 3–11 shows some additional dimensions for segmenting markets when the customers are businesses, government agencies, or other types of organizations. Regardless of whether customers are final consumers or organizations, segmenting a broad product-market may require using several different dimensions at the same time. Which ones are most important depends on the specific product-market.[10]

With so many possible segmenting dimensions—and knowing that several dimensions may be needed to show what is really important in specific product-markets—how should we proceed?

EXHIBIT 3–10 Possible Segmenting Dimensions and Typical Breakdowns for Consumer Markets

Behavioral

Needs	Economic, functional, physiological, psychological, social, and more detailed needs.
Benefits sought	Situation specific, but to satisfy specific or general needs.
Thoughts	Favorable or unfavorable attitudes, interests, opinions, beliefs.
Rate of use	Heavy, medium, light, nonusers.
Purchase relationship	Positive and ongoing; intermittent, no relationship, bad relationship.
Brand familiarity	Insistence, preference, recognition, nonrecognition, rejection.
Kind of shopping	Convenience, comparison shopping, specialty, none (unsought product).
Type of problem-solving	Routinized response, limited, extensive.
Information required	Low, medium, high.

Geographic

Region of world, country	North America (United States, Canada), Europe (France, Italy, Germany), and so on.
Region in country	(Examples in United States): Pacific, Mountain, West North Central, West South Central, East North Central, East South Central, South Atlantic, Middle Atlantic, New England.
Size of city	No city; population under 5,000; 5,000–19,999; 20,000–49,999; 50,000–99,999; 100,000–249,999; 250,000–499,999; 500,000–999,999; 1,000,000–3,999,999; 4,000,000 or over.

Demographic

Income	Under $5,000; $5,000–$9,999; $10,000–$14,999; $15,000–$19,999; $20,000–29,999; $30,000–$39,999; $40,000–$59,999; $60,000 and over.
Sex	Male, female.
Age	Infant, under 6; 6–11, 12–17; 18–24; 25–34; 35–49; 50–64; 65 or over.
Family size	1, 2, 3–4, 5 or more.
Family life cycle	Young, single; young, married, no children; young, married, youngest child under 6; young, married, youngest child over 6; older, married, with children; older, married, no children under 18; older, single; other variations for single parents, divorced, etc.
Occupation	Professional and technical; managers, officials, and proprietors; clerical sales; craftspeople, foremen; operatives; farmers; retired; students; housewives; unemployed.
Education	Grade school or less, some high school, high school graduate, some college, college graduate.
Race	White, black, Asian, and so on.
Social class	Lower-lower, upper-lower, lower-middle, upper-middle, lower-upper, upper-upper.

Note: Terms used in this table are explained in detail later in the text.

EXHIBIT 3–11   Possible Segmenting Dimensions for Business/Organizational Markets

Kind of relationship	Weak loyalty → strong loyalty to vendor Single source → multiple vendors "Arm's length" dealings → close partnership No reciprocity → complete reciprocity
Type of customer	Manufacturer, service producer, government agency, military, nonprofit, wholesaler or retailer (when end user), and so on.
Demographics	Geographic location (region of world, country, region within country, urban → rural) Size (number of employees, sales volume) Primary business or industry (Standard Industrial Classification) Number of facilities
How customer will use product	Installations, components, accessories, raw materials, supplies, professional services
Type of buying situation	Decentralized → centralized Buyer → multiple buying influence Straight rebuy → modified rebuy → new-task buying
Purchasing methods	Vendor analysis, inspection buying, sampling buying, specification buying, competitive bids, negotiated contracts, long-term contracts

Note: Terms used in this table are explained in detail later in the text.

What are the qualifying and determining dimensions?

To select the important segmenting dimensions, think about two different types of dimensions. **Qualifying dimensions** are those relevant to including a customer type in a product-market. **Determining dimensions** are those that actually affect the customer's purchase of a specific product or brand in a product-market.

A prospective car buyer, for example, has to have enough money—or credit—to buy a car and insure it. Our buyer also needs a driver's license. This still doesn't guarantee a purchase. He or she must have a real need—like a job that requires "wheels" or kids that have to be carpooled. This need may motivate the purchase of *some* car. But these qualifying dimensions don't determine what specific brand or model car the person might buy. That depends on more specific interests—such as the kind of safety, performance, or appearance the customer wants. Determining dimensions related to these needs affect the specific car the customer purchases. If safety is a determining dimension for a customer, a Volvo that offers side impact protection and air bags might be the customer's first choice.

Determining dimensions may be very specific

How specific the determining dimensions are depends on whether you are concerned with a general product type or a specific brand. See Exhibit 3–12. The more specific you want to be, the more particular the determining dimensions may be. In a particular case, the determining dimensions may seem minor. But

EXHIBIT 3–12   Finding the Relevant Segmenting Dimensions

they are important because they *are* the determining dimensions. In the car status-seekers market, for example, paint colors or brand name may determine which cars people buy.

Qualifying dimensions are important too

The qualifying dimensions help identify the "core features" that must be offered to everyone in a product-market. Qualifying and determining dimensions work together in marketing strategy planning.

Segmenting dimensions should be useful for identifying customers and deciding on marketing mix variables.

Different dimensions needed for different submarkets

Note that each different submarket within a broad product-market may be motivated by a different set of dimensions. In the snack food market, for example, health food enthusiasts are interested in nutrition, dieters worry about calories, and economical shoppers with lots of kids may want volume to "fill them up." The related submarkets might be called: health-conscious snack food market, dieters' snack food market, and kids' snack food market. They would be in different boxes in a market grid diagram for snack food customers.

Ethical issues in selecting segmenting dimensions

Marketing managers sometimes face ethical decisions when selecting segmenting dimensions. Problems may arise if a firm targets customers who are somehow at a disadvantage in dealing with the firm or who are unlikely to see the negative effects of their own choices. For example, some people criticize makers of malt liquor for marketing mixes that appeal to inner-city youths, especially those below the drinking age. Others pinpoint shoe companies for targeting poor, inner-city kids who see expensive athletic shoes as an important status symbol. Many firms, including producers of infant formula, have been criticized for targeting consumers in less-developed nations. Encyclopedia publishers have been criticized for aggressive selling to less-educated parents who want their children to have better opportunities but who don't seem to understand that the "pennies a day" credit terms add up to more than they can really afford. Some nutritionists criticize firms that market soft drinks, candy, and snack foods to children.

Sometimes a marketing manager must decide whether a firm should serve customers it really doesn't want to serve. For example, some hospitals only want to serve patients who have health insurance; others discourage parents from bringing sick children to the emergency room in the middle of the night. Banks sometimes offer marketing mixes that are attractive to wealthy customers but that basically drive off low-income consumers.

People often differ about what segmenting dimensions are ethical in a given situation. A marketing manager needs to consider not only his or her own views but also the views of other groups in society. Even when there is no clear "right" answer, negative publicity may be very damaging.[11]

A SEVEN-STEP APPROACH TO SEGMENTING PRODUCT-MARKETS

Now let's go on to a logical, seven-step approach to market segmentation. Chapter 5 discusses how marketing research could help fine tune some of the decisions made with this approach. But even without additional research *this approach works*—and has led to successful strategies. It is especially useful for finding the determining dimensions for product types. However, when you want to find dimensions for specific brands—especially when there are several competing brands—you may need more sophisticated techniques.

To be sure you understand this approach, we will review each step separately, explain its importance, and use an ongoing example to show how each step works. The example concerns people who need a place to stay—in particular, the market for motel guests in a big urban area.

1. Name the broad product-market

First, decide what broad product-market the firm wants to be in. This may be stated in the firm's objectives. Or if the firm is already successful in some product-market, its current position might be a good starting point. Try to build on the firm's strengths and avoid its weaknesses—and competitors' strengths. Available resources, both human and financial, will limit the possibilities—especially if the firm is just getting started.

Example: A firm has been building small motels around the edges of a large city and renting rooms to travelers. A narrow view—considering only the firm's current products and markets—might lead the firm to think only of more small motels. A bigger view might see such motels as only a small part of the total motel market or even the total "overnight lodging needs" market in the firm's geographic area. Taking an even bigger view, the firm could consider expanding to other geographic areas—or moving into other kinds of products (like apartment buildings or restaurants).

There has to be some balance between naming the product-market too narrowly (same old product, same old market) and naming it too broadly (the whole world and all its needs). Here the firm decides on the whole market of motel users in one city—because this is where the firm has some experience.

2. List potential customers' needs

Write down as many relevant needs as you can—considering all of the potential customers in the broad product-market. This is a brainstorming step. The list doesn't have to be complete yet but should provide enough input to help stimulate your thinking in the next steps. To see possible needs, think about *why* some people buy the present offerings in this broad product-market.

Example: In the broad motel guest market, you can easily list some possible needs: a private room and furnishings, safety and security, convenience (to something), parking, food and beverages, entertainment, space for recreation, attractive interiors, and good maintenance and service to ensure trouble-free and comfortable stays.

3. Form "homogeneous" submarkets—that is, "narrow" product-markets

Assuming that some people have different needs from others, form different submarkets based on each submarket's needs. Start by forming one submarket around some typical type of customer (perhaps even yourself) and then aggregate similar people into this segment as long as they can be satisfied by the same marketing mix. Write down the important need dimensions and customer-related characteristics (including demographic characteristics) of each submarket to help you decide whether each new customer type should be included in the first segment. This will also help later—when you name the submarkets.

For example, if the people in one market are young families looking for a good place to stay on vacation, this will help you understand what they want and why—and will help you name the market (perhaps as "family vacationers").

Put people who are not homogeneous—who don't fit in the first segment—in a new submarket. List their different need dimensions on another line. Continue this classifying until three or more submarkets emerge.

Example: A young family on a vacation probably wants a motel to provide a clean room large enough for adults and children, convenient parking, a location near tourist attractions, a pool for recreation with a lifeguard for safety, entertainment in the room (a TV and video movies), and perhaps a refrigerator or vending machine for snacks. A traveling executive, on the other hand, has quite different interests—a room with a desk, but *also* a nice restaurant, fast transportation to and from an airport, more services (room-service, dry-cleaning, a way to send and receive a fax, and fast check-in)—without distracting noise from children.

4. Identify the determining dimensions

Review the list of need dimensions for each possible segment and identify the determining dimensions (perhaps by putting an asterisk beside them). Although the qualifying dimensions are important—perhaps reflecting "core needs" that should be satisfied—they are not the *determining* dimensions we are seeking now.

To help identify the determining dimensions, think carefully about the needs and attitudes of the people in each possible segment. They may not seem very different from market to market, but if they are determining to those people then they *are* determining!

Example: With our motel customers, basic comfort needs (heating and cooling, a good bed, a clean bathroom), a telephone for communicating, and safety and security are probably not determining. Everyone has these qualifying needs. Looking beyond these common needs helps you see the determining dimensions—such as different needs with respect to recreation, restaurant facilities, services, and so on. See Exhibit 3–13.

5. Name (nickname) the possible product-markets

Review the determining dimensions—market by market—and name (nickname) each one based on the relative importance of the determining dimensions (and aided by your description of the customer types). A market grid is a good way to help visualize this broad product-market and its narrow product-markets.

Draw the market grid as a rectangle with boxes inside representing smaller, more homogeneous segments. See Exhibit 3–13. Think of the whole rectangle as representing the broad product-market with its name on top. Now think of each of the boxes as narrow product-markets. Since the markets within a broad product-market usually require very different dimensions, don't try to use the same two dimensions to name the markets—or to label the sides of the market grid boxes. Rather, just think of the grid as showing the relative sizes of product-market segments. Then label each segment with its nickname.

Example: We can identify the following overnight guest submarkets: Family vacationers, upscale executives, budget-oriented travelers, resort seekers, event-centered visitors, and long-stay guests. See Exhibit 3–13. Note that each segment has a different set of determining dimensions (benefits sought) that follows directly from customer type and needs.

6. Evaluate why product-market segments behave as they do

After naming the markets as we did in Step 5, think about what else you know about each segment to see how and why these markets behave the way they do. Different segments may have similar—but slightly different—needs. This may explain why some competitive offerings are more successful than others. It can also mean you have to split and rename some segments.

Example: The resort seekers might have been treated as family vacationers in Step 5 because the "family" characteristic did not seem important. But with more thought, we see that while some of the resort seekers are interested in the same sort of fun and recreation as the family vacationers, resort seekers focus on adult fun—not activities with children. For them, getting away from the family vacationers' children may be part of the escape they want. Further, although the resort seekers are a higher income group who are similar to the upscale executives, they have different needs from the executives and probably should be treated as a separate market. The point is that you might discover these market differences only in Step 6. At this step you would name the "resort seekers" market—and create a related row to describe the new segment.

7. Make a rough estimate of the size of each product-market segment

Remember, we are looking for *profitable* opportunities. So now we must try to tie our product-markets to demographic data—or other customer-related characteristics—to make it easier to estimate the size of these markets. We aren't trying to estimate our likely sales yet. Sales depend on the competition as well as

EXHIBIT 3–13 Segmenting the Broad Market for Motel Guests in a Metropolitan Area

	Need dimensions (benefits sought)	Customer-related characteristics	Nickname of product-market
1	Comfort, security, privacy, *family fun, recreation (playground, pool), entertainment (game room, movies), child care, and snacks.*	Couples and single parents with children who want a fun family experience; young, active, and energetic.	**Family vaca-tioners**
2	Comfort, security, privacy, *distinctive furnishings, attentive staff, prestige, status, easy access to airport and business meetings, express check-in and check-out, quality dining.*	Senior business executives with a big expense account who want to be "pampered" with "very important person" service and accommodations.	**Upscale executives**
3	Comfort, security, privacy, *economy (no "extras" to increase cost), convenience (to low-cost restaurants, highways), free parking.*	Young people, retired couples, and salespeople who travel by car, pay their own expenses, and want a simple place to stay for one night—before moving on.	**Budget-oriented travelers**
4	Comfort, security, privacy, *home-like amenities (kitchenette, separate living room), laundry and exercise facilities, pleasant grounds, entertainment.*	Business people, out-of-town visitors, and others who stay in the same motel for a week or more; want many of the comforts they have at home.	**Long-stay guests**
5	Comfort, security, privacy, *socializing (lounges and public spaces), conference facilities (including catering for group meals), message and transportation services.*	Individuals who are attending events scheduled at the motel (a business meeting or conference, family reunion, etc.), often for several days.	**Event-centered visitors**
6	Comfort, security, privacy, *relaxation (golf), pleasure (fine dining, whirlpool bath), attractive views (elaborate landscaping), fun, variety (information/arrangements for theater).*	Sophisticated couples with leisure time to relax and have "adult" fun; they want to show their individuality and have discretionary income to spend.	**Resort seekers**

Upscale executives	Resort seekers	Event-centered visitors
Long-stay guests	**Family vacationers**	**Budget-oriented travelers**

the particulars of the marketing mix. Now we only want to provide a basis for later forecasting and marketing mix planning. The more we know about possible target markets, the easier those jobs are.

Fortunately, we can obtain a lot of data on the size of markets—especially demographic data. And bringing in demographics adds a note of economic reality. Some possible product-markets may have almost no market potential. Without hard facts, we risk aiming at such markets.

To refine the market grid, redraw the inside boxes so that they give a better idea of the size of the various segments. This will help highlight the larger—and perhaps more attractive—opportunities. Remember, the relative sizes of the markets might vary depending on what geographic areas you consider. The market sizes might vary from city to city—or from one country to another.

Example: We can tie the family vacationers to demographic data. Most of them are between 21 and 45. The U.S. Census Bureau publishes detailed data by age, family size, and related information. Moreover, a state tourist bureau or city Chamber of Commerce might be able to provide estimates of how many families vacation in a specific city during a year and how long they stay. Given this information, it's easy to estimate the total number of nights family vacationers will need motel rooms in a certain city.

Market dimensions suggest a good mix

Once we follow all seven steps, we should be able to outline the kinds of marketing mixes that would appeal to the various markets. For example, based on the determining dimensions (benefits sought) in Exhibit 3–13, a motel designed to appeal to the upscale executives might offer rooms with quality furniture (including a desk and chair for reading), a high-quality restaurant with all-hours room service, special secretarial services (copying, dictation, and fax) on an extra-cost basis, limousine pickup at the airport, someone to help with travel problems, and precleared check-in and check-out. The motel might also provide a quiet bar and exercise room and extras such as thick bath towels and a valet service for free shoe shines. It might also offer a business library for after-hours reading and a free copy of *The Wall Street Journal* delivered every morning. Of course, the price could be high to pay for this special treatment. It's also useful to think about what the executives would not want: facilities shared by families with young children!

While the discussion above focuses on the upscale executives, profitable marketing mixes can be developed for the other segments as well. For example, Motel 6 has done very well by targeting the budget-oriented travelers. Similarly, Residence Inns developed a competitive advantage by catering to the needs of the long-stay guests—those who stay at the motel for a week or more. Residence Inns feature fully equipped kitchens and grocery shopping services, fireplaces, and convenient recreation areas. Courtyard by Marriott has been successful with facilities designed for event-centered visitors. During the week many customers are there for business conferences, but on the weekend the focus often shifts to family events—such as meals and receptions related to a wedding or family reunion.[12]

Improve the marketing mix for current customers

Our motel example highlights using the seven-step approach to identify new target market and marketing mix opportunities. Of course, the same approaches provide a basis for identifying new ways to serve existing customers and strengthen the relationship with them. Too often firms let their strategies get stagnant after they've established a base of customers and a set of marketing mix decisions. For example, special business services related to the determining needs of upscale executives might initially help a motel win this business. However, the motel will lose its competitive edge if other motels start to offer the same benefits. Then, the determining dimensions change. To avoid this problem and retain the base of customers it has built, the motel needs to find new and better ways to meet the executives' needs. Reevaluating the need dimensions and customer-related characteristics, perhaps in greater detail, may point to new opportunities. For example, the motel might make it easier for traveling executives to get messages by providing a phonemail system—or perhaps by loaning them pagers—for use during their stay.

SEVEN-STEP APPROACH APPLIES IN BUSINESS MARKETS TOO

We can use a similar seven-step approach for markets where the customers (or final users) are business organizations rather than individual consumers. The major change is in the first step—selecting the broad product-market. Business markets, especially in industrial settings, often have different needs.

Business organizations usually make purchases to meet basic functional needs. Their demands derive from final consumer demands—so the business (or non-profit organization) market makes purchases that help it produce finished goods or services. The functions these customers are concerned about include but are not limited to: forming, bending, grading, digging, cutting, heating, cooling, conducting, transmitting, containing, filling, cleaning, analyzing, sorting, training, and insuring. They may buy physical goods and do the work themselves, or they may pay someone else to provide the service.

By defining the relevant broad product-market using both geographic dimensions and basic functional needs, we can usually ensure that our focus is broad enough—that is, not exclusively on the product now being supplied to present customers. But it also keeps us from expanding our focus to "all the business needs in the world."

As with consumer markets, it is better to focus on needs satisfied by products, *not* product characteristics themselves. We may find new ways of satisfying a need—and completely surprise and upset current producers—if we don't define the product-market too narrowly. For example, desktop computers and printers now compete in what some producers thought was the "typewriter market." And telephone calls and fax machines replace letters, further reducing the need for typing. Perhaps this broad product-market is concerned with "thought processing and transmitting." Certainly, the typewriter view is too narrow. Market-oriented strategy planners try to avoid surprises that result from such tunnel vision.

After the first step in the seven-step approach, the other steps are similar to segmenting consumer markets. The main difference is that we use segmenting dimensions like those shown in Exhibit 3–11 and discussed in Chapter 8.[13]

INTERNATIONAL MARKETING REQUIRES EVEN MORE SEGMENTING

Success in international marketing requires even more attention to segmenting. There are over 228 nations with their own unique cultures! And they differ greatly in language, customs (including business ethics), beliefs, religions, race, and income distribution patterns. (We'll discuss some of these differences in Chapters 6 and 7.) These additional differences can complicate the segmenting process. Even worse, critical data are often less available—and less dependable—as firms move into international markets. The number of variables increases, but the quantity and quality of data decrease. This is one reason why some firms insist that local operations and decisions be handled by natives. They, at least, have a "feel" for their markets.

EXHIBIT 3–14   Segmenting in International Markets

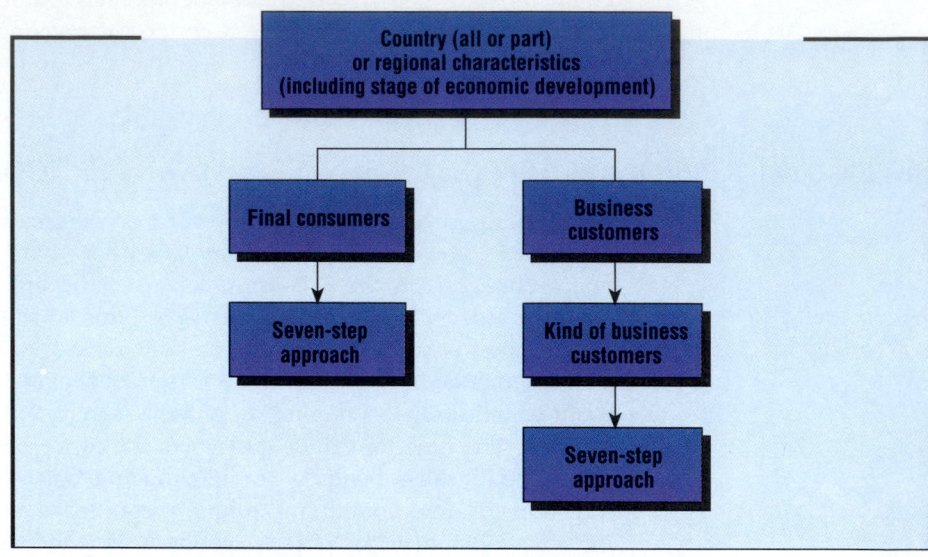

Segmenting international markets may require more dimensions. But one practical method adds just one step to the seven-step approach discussed above. See Exhibit 3–14. First, marketers segment by country or region—looking at demographic, cultural, and other characteristics, including stage of economic development. This may help them find regional or national submarkets that are fairly similar. Then—depending on whether the firm is aiming at final consumers or business markets—they apply the seven-step approach discussed earlier.

MORE SOPHISTICATED TECHNIQUES MAY HELP IN SEGMENTING

The seven-step approach is inexpensive, logical, practical—*and it works*. But computer-aided methods can help too. A detailed review of the possibilities is beyond the scope of this book. But a brief discussion of some approaches will give you a flavor of how computer-aided methods work.

Clustering usually
requires a computer

Clustering techniques try to find similar patterns within sets of data. Clustering groups customers who are similar on their segmenting dimensions into homogeneous segments. Clustering approaches use computers to do what previously was done with much intuition and judgment.

The data to be clustered might include such dimensions as demographic characteristics, the importance of different needs, attitudes toward the product, and past buying behavior. The computer searches all the data for homogeneous groups of people. When it finds them, marketers study the dimensions of the people in the groups to see why the computer clustered them together. The results sometimes suggest new, or at least better, marketing strategies.[14]

A cluster analysis of the toothpaste market, for example, might show that some people buy toothpaste because it tastes good (the sensory segment), while others are concerned with the effect of clean teeth and fresh breath on their social image (the sociables). Still others worry about decay or tartar (the worriers), and some are just interested in the best value for their money (the value seekers). Each of these market segments calls for a different marketing mix—although some of the four Ps may be similar.

Finally, a marketing manager has to decide which one (or more) of these segments will be the firm's target market(s).

You can see that clustering techniques only *aid* managers. Managers still need judgment to develop an original list of possible dimensions—and to name the resulting clusters.

Trade-off analysis helps develop the marketing mix

Another computer-based approach often used in segmenting markets is **trade-off analysis** (sometimes called **conjoint analysis**)—a technique that helps marketing managers determine how important certain elements of the firm's marketing mix are to target customers. It shows how much money (in terms of a higher price) a customer would "trade off" for a particular product feature.

Marketing managers for Marriott Courtyard motels used trade-off analysis to evaluate customers' reactions to various features Marriott considered offering. For example, the analysis revealed that customers viewed elaborate landscaping as worth about 50 cents a night more than they were willing to pay for a motel with minimal landscaping. Rooms with an enclosed central hall were worth about 65 cents a night more than rooms with outside stairs and walkways. Customers saw a motel with an indoor pool as worth about 85 cents a night more than one with no pool.[15]

POSITIONING HELPS IDENTIFY PRODUCT-MARKET OPPORTUNITIES

As we've emphasized throughout, the reason for focusing on a specific target market—by using marketing segmentation approaches or tools such as cluster analysis and trade-off analysis—is so that you can fine tune the whole marketing

Firms often use promotion to help "position" how a product meets a target market's specific needs.

mix to appeal to some group of potential customers better than competitors. By *differentiating* the marketing mix to do a better job meeting customers' needs, the firm builds a competitive advantage. In other words, target customers will view the firm's position in the market as uniquely suited to their preferences and needs. Further, because everyone in the firm is clear about what position it wants to achieve with customers, Product, Promotion, and other marketing mix decisions can be blended better to achieve the desired objectives.

Although the marketing manager may want customers to see the firm's offering as unique, that is not always possible. Me-too imitators may come along and copy the firm's strategy. Further, even if a firm's marketing mix is different, busy consumers don't always recognize it. Thus, in looking for opportunities, it's important for the marketing manager to know how customers *do* view the firm's offering. That's where another important approach—*positioning*—comes in.

Positioning shows how customers locate proposed and/or present brands in a market. Like cluster analysis and trade-off analysis, it requires some formal marketing research but may be helpful when competitive offerings are quite similar. The results are usually plotted on graphs to help show how consumers view the competing products. Usually, the products' positions are related to two or three product features that are important to the target customers.

Assuming the picture is reasonably accurate, managers then decide whether they want to leave their product (and marketing mix) alone or reposition it. This may mean *physical changes* in the product or simply *image changes based on promotion*. For example, most beer drinkers can't pick out their favorite brand in a blind test—so physical changes might not be necessary (and might not even work) to reposition a beer brand.

Managers make the graphs for positioning decisions by asking product users to make judgments about different brands—including their "ideal" brand—and then use computer programs to summarize the ratings and plot the results. The details of positioning techniques—sometimes called "perceptual mapping"—are beyond the scope of this text. But Exhibit 3–15 shows the possibilities.[16]

Exhibit 3–15 shows the "product space" for different brands of bar soap using two dimensions—the extent to which consumers think the soaps moisturize and deodorize their skin. For example, consumers see Dial as quite low on moisturizing but high on deodorizing. Lifebuoy and Dial are close together—implying that consumers think of them as similar on these characteristics. Dove is viewed as different and is further away on the graph. Remember that positioning maps are based on *customers' perceptions*—the actual characteristics of the products (as determined by a chemical test) might be different!

The circles in Exhibit 3–15 show different sets (submarkets) of consumers clustered near their ideal soap preferences. Groups of respondents with a similar ideal product are circled to show apparent customer concentrations. In this graph, the size of the circles suggests the size of the segments for the different ideals.

Ideal clusters 1 and 2 are the largest and are close to two popular brands—Dial and Lever 2000. It appears that customers in cluster 1 want more moisturizing than they see in Dial and Lifebuoy. However, exactly what these brands should do about this isn't clear. Perhaps both of these brands should leave their physical products alone—but emphasize moisturizing more in their promotion to make a stronger appeal to those who want moisturizers. A marketing manager talking about this approach might simply refer to it as "positioning the brand as a good moisturizer." Of course, whether the effort is successful depends on whether the whole marketing mix delivers on the promise of the positioning communication.

EXHIBIT 3–15 "Product Space" Representing Consumers' Perceptions for Different Brands of Bar Soap

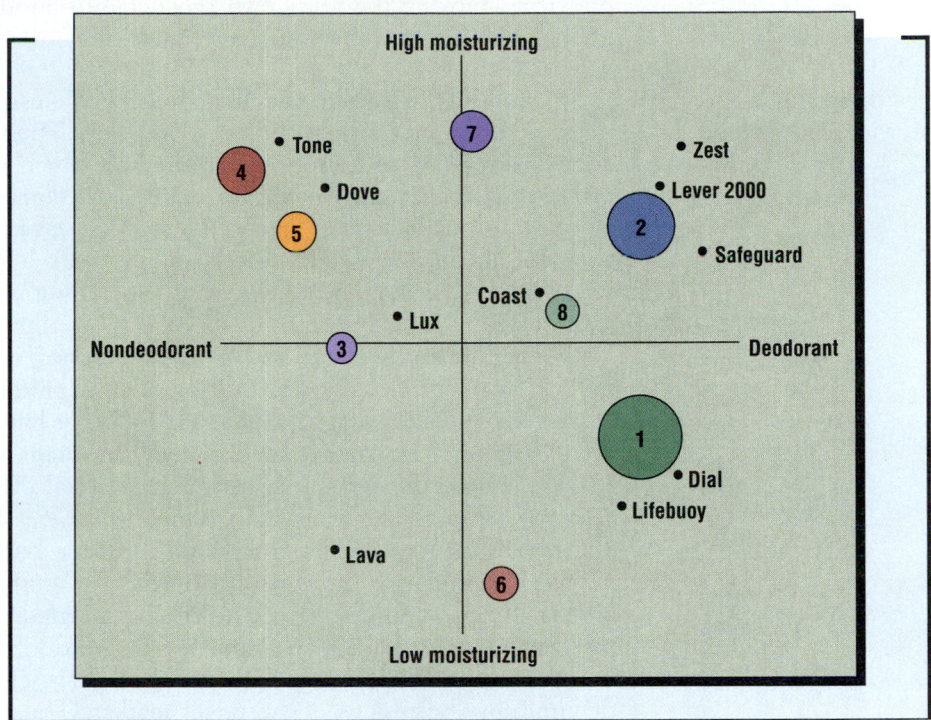

This perceptual map suggests that Lava doesn't seem to satisfy any of the ideal clusters very well. Therefore, some attempt might be made to reposition Lava—either through physical or image changes. However, Lava is distinctive because it offers strong cleaning power for really dirty hands, which isn't one of the dimensions considered in the analysis. If cleaning power is really important to some consumers at some times, Lava might use promotion to encourage consumers to think more about this feature—and to favorably position Lava with the cleaning benefit. While promotion may help to call consumer attention to a product feature and link a particular brand to the benefits offered by that feature, changing consumer attitudes usually isn't easy. However, it does work in some situations. For example, 7UP used this approach to position itself as different from the colas—as the "uncola" for people who wanted a different taste and who *didn't* want caffeine in their soft drinks.

Note that ideal cluster 7 is not near any of the present brands. This may suggest an opportunity for introducing a new product—a strong moisturizer with some deodorizers. A firm that chooses to follow this approach would be making a segmenting effort.

Combining versus segmenting

Positioning analysis may lead a firm to combining—rather than segmenting—if managers think they can make several general appeals to different parts of a "combined" market. For example, by varying its promotion, Coast might try to appeal to segments 8, 1, and 2 with one product. These segments are all quite similar (close together) in what they want in an ideal brand. On the other hand, there may be clearly defined submarkets—and some parts of the market may be "owned" by one product or brand. In this case, segmenting efforts may be practical—moving the firm's own product into another segment of the general market area where competition is weaker.

Positioning as part of broader analysis

Positioning helps managers understand how customers see their market. It is a visual aid to understanding a product-market. The first time such an analysis is done, managers may be shocked to see how much customers' perceptions of a market differ from their own. For this reason alone, positioning is useful. But positioning usually focuses on specific product features and brands that are close competitors in the product-market. Thus, it is a product-oriented approach. Important *customer*-related dimensions—including needs and attitudes—may be overlooked.

Premature emphasis on product features is dangerous in other ways as well. As our bar soap example shows, starting with a product-oriented definition of a market and how bar soaps compete against other bar soaps can make a firm miss more basic shifts in markets. For example, bars might be losing popularity to liquid soaps. Or other products, like bath oils or facial cleansers, may be part of the relevant competition. Managers wouldn't see these shifts if they looked only at alternative bar soap brands—the focus is just too narrow.

As we emphasize throughout the text, you must understand potential needs and attitudes when planning marketing strategies. If customers treat different products as substitutes, then a firm has to position itself against those products too. It can't just focus on a few product characteristics or benefits if they aren't the determining dimensions of the target market. Thus, it's usually best to rely on positioning approaches when they are part of a broader analysis—which in turn helps to ensure that the whole marketing mix is positioned for competitive advantage.

CONCLUSION

Firms need creative strategy planning to survive in our increasingly competitive markets. In this chapter, we discussed how to find attractive target market opportunities. We started by considering four basic types of opportunities—market penetration, market development, product development, and diversification—with special emphasis on opportunities in international markets. We also saw that carefully defining generic markets and product-markets can help find new opportunities. We stressed the shortcomings of a too narrow, product-oriented view of markets.

We also discussed market segmentation—the process of naming and then segmenting broad product-markets to find potentially attractive target markets. Some people try to segment markets by starting with the mass market and then dividing it into smaller submarkets based on a few dimensions. But this can lead to poor results. Instead, market segmentation should first focus on a broad product-market and then group similar customers into homogeneous submarkets. The more similar the potential customers are, the larger the submarkets can be. Four criteria for evaluating possible product-market segments were presented.

Once a broad product-market is segmented, marketing managers can use one of three approaches to market-oriented strategy planning: (1) the single target market approach, (2) the multiple target market approach, and (3) the combined target market approach. In general, we encouraged marketers to be segmenters rather than combiners.

We discussed a practical—rough-and-ready—seven-step approach to market segmentation that works for both consumer and business markets and, with minor additions, for international markets as well. We also discussed some computer-aided segmenting approaches—clustering techniques, trade-off analysis, and positioning.

In summary, good marketers should be experts on markets and likely segmenting dimensions. By creatively segmenting markets, they may spot opportunities—even breakthrough opportunities— and help their firms succeed against aggressive competitors offering similar products. Segmenting is basic to target marketing. And the more you practice segmenting, the more meaningful market segments you will see.

QUESTIONS AND PROBLEMS

1. Distinguish between an attractive opportunity and a breakthrough opportunity. Give an example.

2. Explain how new opportunities may be seen by defining a firm's markets more precisely. Illustrate for a situation where you feel there is an opportunity—namely, an unsatisfied market segment—even if it is not very large.

3. Distinguish between a generic market and a product-market. Illustrate your answer.

4. Explain the major differences among the four basic types of opportunities discussed in the text and cite examples for two of these types of opportunities.

5. Explain why a firm may want to pursue a market penetration opportunity before pursuing one involving product development or diversification.

6. In your own words, explain several reasons why marketing managers should consider international markets when evaluating possible opportunities.

7. Give an example of a foreign-made product (other than an automobile) that you personally have purchased. Give some reasons why you purchased that product. Do you think that there was a good opportunity for a domestic firm to get your business? Explain why or why not.

8. Explain what market segmentation is.

9. List the types of potential segmenting dimensions and explain which you would try to apply first, second, and third in a particular situation. If the nature of the situation would affect your answer, explain how.

10. Explain why segmentation efforts based on attempts to divide the mass market using a few demographic dimensions may be very disappointing.

11. Illustrate the concept that segmenting is an aggregating process by referring to the admissions policies of your own college and a nearby college or university.

12. (a) Evaluate how "good" the six submarkets identified in the market for motels are (Exhibit 3–13) with respect to the four criteria for selecting good market segments. (b) Same as (a) but evaluate the four corner markets in the Toddler University baby footwear market (Exhibit 2–10).

13. Review the types of segmenting dimensions listed in Exhibits 3–10 and 3–11, and select the ones you think should be combined to fully explain the market segment you personally would be in if you were planning to buy a new watch today. List several dimensions and try to develop a shorthand name, like "fashion-oriented," to describe your own personal market segment. Then try to estimate what proportion of the total watch market would be accounted for by your market segment. Next, explain if there are any offerings that come close to meeting the needs of your market. If not, what sort of a marketing mix is needed? Would it be economically attractive for anyone to try to satisfy your market segment? Why or why not?

14. Identify the determining dimension or dimensions that explain why you bought the specific brand you did in your most recent purchase of a (a) soft drink, (b) shampoo, (c) shirt or blouse,

and (*d*) larger, more expensive item, such as a bicycle, camera, or boat. Try to express the determining dimension(s) in terms of your own personal characteristics rather than the product's characteristics. Estimate what share of the market would probably be motivated by the same determining dimension(s).

15. Apply the seven-step approach to segmenting consumer markets to the market for off-campus apartments in your city. Then evaluate how well the needs in these market segments are being met in your geographic area. Is there an obvious breakthrough opportunity waiting for someone?

16. Explain how the first step in the seven-step approach to segmenting markets would have to be changed to apply it in business markets. Illustrate your answer.

17. Explain how positioning can help a marketing manager identify target market opportunities.

SUGGESTED CASES

3. Gerber Products Company
7. Pillsbury's Häagen-Dazs

29. Castings Supply, Inc.

COMPUTER-AIDED PROBLEM

3. Segmenting Customers

The marketing manager for Micro Software Company is seeking new market opportunities. He is focusing on the word processing market and has narrowed it down to three segments: the Fearful Typists, the Power Users, and the Specialists. The Fearful Typists don't know much about computers—they just want a fast way to type letters and simple reports without errors. They don't need a lot of special features. They want simple instructions and a program that's easy to learn. The Power Users know a lot about computers, use them often, and want a word processing program with many special features. All computer programs seem easy to them—so they aren't worried about learning to use the various features. The Specialists have jobs that require a lot of writing. They don't know much about computers but are willing to learn. They want special features needed for their work—but only if they aren't too hard to learn and use.

The marketing manager prepared a table summarizing the importance of each of three key needs in the three segments.

Micro's sales staff conducted interviews with seven potential customers who were asked to rate how important each of these three needs was in their work. The manager prepared a spreadsheet to help him cluster (aggregate) each person into one of the segments—along

Market Segment	Importance of Need (1=not important; 10=very important)		
	Features	**Easy to Use**	**Easy to Learn**
Fearful Typists	3	8	9
Power Users	9	2	2
Professional Specialists	7	5	6

with other similar people. Each person's ratings are entered in the spreadsheet, and the clustering procedure computes a similarity score that indicates how similar (a low score) or dissimilar (a high score) the person is to the typical person in each of the segments. The manager can then "aggregate" potential customers into the segment that is most similar (that is, the one with the *lowest* similarity score).

a. *The ratings for a potential customer appear on the first spreadsheet. Into which segment would you aggregate this person?*

b. *The responses for seven potential customers who were interviewed are listed in the table on the next page.*

Potential Customer	Importance of Need (1=not important; 10=very important)			Type of Computer
	Features	Easy to Use	Easy to Learn	
A.	8	1	2	Dell
B.	6	6	5	IBM
C.	4	9	8	Macintosh
D.	2	6	7	Macintosh
E.	5	6	5	IBM
F.	8	3	1	Dell
G.	4	6	8	Macintosh

Enter the ratings for a customer in the spreadsheet and then write down the similarity score for each segment. Repeat the process for each customer. Based on your analysis, indicate the segment into which you would aggregate each customer. Indicate the size (number of customers) of each segment.

c. *In the interview, each potential customer was also asked what type of computer he or she would be using. The responses are shown in the table along with the ratings. Group the responses based on the customer's segment. If you were targeting the Fearful Typists segment, what type of computer would you focus on when developing your software?*

d. *Based on your analysis, which customer would you say is least like any of the segments? Briefly explain the reason for your choice.*

For additional questions related to this problem, see Exercise 3–4 in the *Learning Aid for Use with Basic Marketing*, 12th edition.

4

Evaluating Opportunities in the Changing Marketing Environment

When You Finish This Chapter, You Should

1. Know the variables that shape the environment of marketing strategy planning.

2. Understand why company objectives are important in guiding marketing strategy planning.

3. See how the resources of a firm affect the search for opportunities.

4. Know how the different kinds of competitive situations affect strategy planning.

5. Understand how the economic and technological environment can affect strategy planning.

6. Know why you might be sent to prison if you ignore the political and legal environment.

7. Understand how to screen and evaluate marketing strategy opportunities.

8. Understand the important new terms (shown in red).

arketing managers do not plan strategies in a vacuum. When choosing target markets and developing the four Ps, they must work with many variables in the broad marketing environment. Marketing planning at Rubbermaid shows why this is important.

Wolfgang Schmidt, the new top executive at Rubbermaid, set ambitious profit and sales objectives for the firm. To continue the growth the company had achieved every year for more than a decade, he also declared that one-third of Rubbermaid revenues should come from new products.

Rubbermaid's marketing managers had built a respected brand name in plastic kitchenware—but they knew that just working harder at that market would not be enough to achieve Schmidt's objectives. The target market for kitchenware was no longer growing in the United States, so sales growth was slipping. A sluggish economy made the problem worse. Faced with increased competition, Rubbermaid had to cut prices to retailers to stimulate in-store promotions and sales, but the lower prices reduced Rubbermaid's profit margin.

These changes did not take Rubbermaid's marketing managers by surprise. For a number of years, they had been studying the changing environment and looking for opportunities in new product-markets.

For example, in the late 1980s they saw an opportunity to develop a new marketing mix for consumers interested in plastic toys. Rubbermaid had the money to move quickly. It acquired Little Tikes Co.—a small firm that was already making sturdy plastic toys—and immediately expanded its old product assortment. Marketing managers also then took advantage of Rubbermaid's strong relationships with retailers to get scarce shelf space for the new toys—and they developed new ads to stimulate consumer interest. Unlike many toy companies, Rubbermaid was sensitive to parents' concerns about TV ads targeted at children. It aimed its cost-effective print ads at parents. This approach helped to speed Rubbermaid's entry in the market—and Little Tikes toys proved to be very profitable.

Although production capacity limited additional short-term growth from toys, marketing managers had identified many other new opportunities—ranging from a litterless school lunch box to garden sheds to playground equipment for day care centers. For example, day care centers were a growing market because of the cultural trend toward more dual-career and single-parent families. So Little Tikes designed a durable $3,000 PlayCenter targeted at day care centers. The outside of the PlayCenter is colorful plastic that is safe and appealing to young kids. It can also be installed quickly and easily. These benefits give the PlayCenter a big advantage over competing all-steel units that cost three times as much.

While Rubbermaid marketing managers were developing markets for new types of products, they were also pursuing sales growth for the firm's products in the newly unified European market. This posed new challenges. Rubbermaid was less well known there, it did not have strong relationships with retailers, and the political, legal, and cultural environment was very different. So Rubbermaid formed a partnership with a Dutch firm that already knew the European market, and it worked with wholesalers who could help build strong new distribution channels. By successfully adapting its strategies to these environments, Rubbermaid should be able to achieve another of Schmidt's objectives: By the year 2000, he wants 25 percent of the firm's revenues to come from markets outside the U.S.[1]

THE MARKETING ENVIRONMENT

You saw in the last chapter that finding target market opportunities takes a real understanding of what makes customers tick. The Rubbermaid case shows that understanding the marketing environment is also important in planning marketing strategy and evaluating opportunities.

The marketing environment falls into five basic areas:

1. Objectives and resources of the firm.
2. Competitive environment.
3. Economic and technological environment.
4. Political and legal environment.
5. Cultural and social environment.

A marketing manager controls the choice of marketing strategy variables within the framework of the broader marketing environment and how it is changing (see Exhibit 2–13). In the short run the marketing manager doesn't control environmental variables. That's why it's sometimes useful to think of them as uncontrollable variables. Although the marketing manager may not be able to control these environmental variables directly, they must be considered carefully when evaluating opportunities and selecting marketing strategies. In this chapter, we'll see how these variables shape opportunities—limiting some possibilities and making others more attractive. Exhibit 3–1 shows how Chapters 3 and 4 fit together.

OBJECTIVES SHOULD SET FIRM'S COURSE

A company must decide where it's going, or it may fall into the trap expressed so well by the quotation: "Having lost sight of our objective, we redoubled our efforts." Company objectives should shape the direction and operation of the whole business. So we will treat this matter in some depth—discussing its effect on both finding attractive opportunities and developing marketing strategies.

It is difficult to set objectives that really guide the present and future development of a company. The process forces top management to look at the whole business, relate its present objectives and resources to the external environment, and then decide what the firm wants to accomplish in the future.

One specific British Airways objective is to increase its share of air travel between London and New York. The promotion objective of this particular billboard, which appears at only one much-viewed site between New York City's major airports, is to remind business travelers that the airline's Concorde is the fastest bridge between the two countries.

It would be convenient if a company could set one objective—such as making a profit—and let that serve as the guide. Actually, however, setting objectives is much more complicated, which helps explain why it's often done poorly—or not done at all.

Three basic objectives provide guidelines

The following three objectives provide a useful starting point for setting a firm's objectives. They should be sought *together* because—in the long run—a failure in even one of the three areas can lead to total failure of the business. A business should:

1. Engage in specific activities that will perform a socially and economically useful function.
2. Develop an organization to carry on the business and implement its strategies.
3. Earn enough profit to survive.[2]

Should be socially useful

The first objective says that the company should do something useful for society. This isn't just a "do-gooder" objective. Businesses can't exist without the approval of consumers. If a firm's activities appear to be contrary to the consumer "good," the firm can be wiped out almost overnight by political or legal action—or consumers' own negative responses.

The first objective also implies that a firm should try to satisfy customer needs. This is why the marketing manager should be heard when the company is setting objectives. But setting whole-company objectives—within resource limits—is ultimately the responsibility of top management. In this sense, whole-company objectives are usually outside the marketing manager's "control."

A firm should define its objectives broadly—setting need-satisfying objectives rather than production-oriented objectives. Because customer needs change, too narrow a view may lead the company into a product-market in which the product itself will soon be obsolete.[3]

Should organize to innovate

In a macro-marketing sense, consumers in market-directed economies have granted businesses the right to operate—and to make a profit if they can. With this right comes the responsibility for businesses to be dynamic agents of change, adjusting their offerings to meet new needs. Competition is supposed to encourage innovation and efficiency. A business firm should develop an organization that ensures these consumer-assigned tasks are carried out effectively—and that the firm itself continues to prosper.

Should earn some profit

In the long run a firm must make a profit to survive. But just saying that a firm should try to make a profit isn't enough. Management must specify the time period involved since many plans that maximize profit in the long run lose money during the first few years. On the other hand, seeking only short-term profits may steer the firm from opportunities that would offer larger long-run profits.

Further, trying to maximize profit won't necessarily lead to big profits. Competition in a particular industry may be so fierce as to almost guarantee failure. For example, Greyhound Corp. struggled to maximize profits selling long-distance bus travel, but low airfares attracted much of the business. Even the maximum possible profit was disappointing. In a situation like this, it might be better to set a *target* rate of profit that will lead the firm into areas with more promising possibilities.

Objectives should be explicit

Our three general objectives provide guidelines, but a firm should develop its own *specific* objectives. This is important, but top executives often don't state their objectives explicitly. Too often, they say what their objectives were after the fact! If objectives aren't clear and specific from the start, different managers may hold unspoken and conflicting objectives—a common problem in large companies and in nonprofit organizations.

The whole firm must work toward the same objectives

Objectives chosen by top management should be compatible—or frustrations and even failure may result. For example, top management may set a 25 percent annual return on investment as one objective, while at the same time specifying that current plant and equipment be used as fully as possible. In such a case, competition may make it impossible to use resources fully *and* achieve the target return. Efficient U.S. papermakers like Weyerhaeuser set the objective of operating at nearly full capacity so that they can keep their costs low—and keep foreign competitors out of the market. This does not mean, however, that executives can expect marketing managers to find a way to earn a 25 percent return on investment. To earn that high a profit in the short term, Weyerhaeuser would have to set prices too high—so high that they would attract competitors into the market. Soon sales lost to competitors would prevent Weyerhaeuser from running its plant and equipment at full capacity. In a situation like this, conflicting objectives can lead to disaster. Managers may try to achieve the return on investment objective during the year and then, at year end, find it impossible to keep running at full capacity. The two objectives are impossible to achieve together![4]

Top-management myopia may straitjacket marketing

We are assuming that it is the marketing manager's job to work within the framework of objectives provided by top management. But some of these objectives may limit marketing strategies—and perhaps damage the whole business. This is another reason why it is desirable for the marketing manager to help shape the company's objectives.

EXHIBIT 4–1   A Hierarchy of Objectives

Some top managements want a large sales volume or a large market share because they feel this ensures greater profitability. But many large firms with big market shares have gone bankrupt. Eastern Airlines went under and so did International Harvester. These firms sought large market shares—but earned little profit. Increasingly, companies are shifting their objectives toward *profitable* sales growth rather than just larger market share—as they realize that the two don't necessarily go together.[5]

Company objectives should lead to marketing objectives

You can see why the marketing manager should be involved in setting company objectives. Company objectives guide managers as they search for and evaluate opportunities—and later plan marketing strategies. Particular *marketing* objectives should be set within the framework of larger, company objectives. As shown in Exhibit 4–1, firms need a hierarchy of objectives—moving from company objectives to marketing department objectives. For each marketing strategy, firms also need objectives for each of the four Ps—as well as more detailed objectives. For example, in the Promotion area, we need objectives for mass selling, sales promotion, *and* personal selling.

Xerox provides a good example of this thinking. One of its corporate objectives is to achieve higher customer satisfaction than any other supplier in every market in which it competes. To achieve that objective, the R&D people know they must design every piece of equipment to meet specific reliability objectives. Similarly, the production people work toward very specific objectives to improve quality and eliminate manufacturing defects. The marketing department, in turn, sets specific customer satisfaction objectives for every product and every market segment. That leads to specific promotion objectives to ensure that the sales and advertising people don't promise customers more than the company can deliver. Service people, in turn, work toward specific objectives—such as responding to a certain percentage of all service calls within four hours.

Managers at Xerox set all of the specific objectives very carefully. That is relevant to another key point. Both company objectives and marketing objectives should be realistic and achievable. Overly ambitious objectives are useless if the firm lacks the resources to achieve them.

COMPANY RESOURCES MAY LIMIT SEARCH FOR OPPORTUNITIES

Every firm has some resources—hopefully some unique ones—that set it apart from other firms. Breakthrough opportunities—or at least some competitive advantage—come from making use of these strengths while avoiding direct competition with firms having similar strengths.

To find its strengths, a firm must evaluate its functional areas (production, research and engineering, marketing, general management, and finance) as well as its present products and markets. By analyzing successes or failures in relation to the firm's resources, management can discover why the firm was successful—or why it failed—in the past.

Harley-Davidson's motorcycle business was on the ropes, and it was losing customers to Japanese competitors. Competitors' prices were so low that Harley initially thought the Japanese were "dumping"—selling in the United States at prices below cost. However, careful analysis revealed that superior manufacturing techniques kept Japanese companies' operating costs 30 percent lower than Harley's. Studying the Japanese firms helped Harley identify ways to use its resources more efficiently and improve the quality of its products. With these resource-use problems resolved, new opportunities opened up—and Harley was again on the road to achieving its objectives.[6]

The pressure of competition focused Harley's attention on manufacturing resources. Other resources that should be considered—as part of an evaluation of strengths and weaknesses—are discussed in the following sections.

Financial strength

Some opportunities require large amounts of capital just to get started. Money may be required for R&D, production facilities, marketing research, or advertising—before a firm makes its first sale. And even a really good opportunity may not be profitable for years. So lack of financial strength is often a barrier to entry into an otherwise attractive market.

Producing capability and flexibility

In many businesses, the cost of producing each unit decreases as the quantity produced increases. Therefore, smaller producers can be at a great cost disadvantage if they try to win business from larger competitors.

On the other hand, new—or smaller—firms sometimes have the advantage of flexibility. They are not handicapped with large, special-purpose facilities that are obsolete or poorly located. U.S. Steel (USX), Bethlehem, and other large steel producers once enjoyed economies of scale. But today they have trouble competing with producers using smaller, more flexible plants. Similarly, poorly located or obsolete retail or wholesale facilities can severely limit marketing strategy planning.

Firms that own or have assured sources of supply have an important advantage—especially in times of short supply. Big firms often control their own sources of supply. Companies that don't have guaranteed supply sources may have difficulty meeting demand—or even staying in business.

Marketing managers for the Lincoln Continental recently had to deal with this problem. They had developed a new model and a strategy that focused on special safety features, including antilock brakes and dual air bags. Advertising touted these advantages—and safety-oriented luxury car buyers were buying every Continental produced. However, sales suffered and the whole strategy had to be changed after a fire at the air bag supplier's factory. Lincoln could no longer equip

A familiar brand name—and other marketing strengths—can be an advantage in seeking new opportunities.

More than 100 million Americans play sports. Nine out of ten know and trust Spalding. They'll buy 200 million Spalding products this year.

SPALDING.
The ultimate edge in 40 lines of high-performance products worldwide.

every car with dual air bags as standard equipment. By the time Lincoln finally got an adequate supply of air bags, several competitors had similar offerings—and Continental had lost its competitive advantage.[7]

Marketing strengths

Our marketing strategy framework helps in analyzing current marketing resources. In the product area, for example, a familiar brand can be a big strength or a new idea or process may be protected by a *patent*. A patent owner has a 17-year monopoly to develop and use its new product, process, or material. If one firm has a strong patent, competitors may be limited to second-rate offerings—and their efforts may be doomed to failure.

Good relations with established middlemen—or control of good locations—can be important resources in reaching some target markets. When marketing managers decided to introduce the Crest Precision toothbrush, Crest toothpaste had already proved profitable to drugstores, grocery stores, and other retailers who could reach the target market. So these retailers were willing to give Crest shelf space for the toothbrush.

Promotion and price resources must be considered too. Westinghouse already has a skilled sales force. Marketing managers know these sales reps can handle new products and customers. And low-cost facilities may enable a firm to undercut competitors' prices.

Finally, thorough understanding of a target market can give a company an edge. Many companies fail in new product-markets because they don't really understand the needs of the new customers—or the new competitive environment.

THE COMPETITIVE ENVIRONMENT

Choose opportunities that avoid head-on competition

The **competitive environment** affects the number and types of competitors the marketing manager must face—and how they may behave. Although marketing managers usually can't control these factors, they can choose strategies that avoid head-on competition. And, where competition is inevitable, they can plan for it.

Illycaffe would like to avoid head-on competition from other coffee brands, but that is difficult if potential customers view the products as essentially similar.

Variazioni sul tema.   *Tema.*

illy presenta illy collection. Sei tazzine d'autore per gustare in bellezza   un caffè squisito. Le vedrete nei bar migliori. *illy. Il caffè perfettamente espresso.*

Economists describe four basic kinds of market (competitive) situations: pure competition, oligopoly, monopolistic competition, and monopoly. Understanding the differences among these market situations is helpful in analyzing the competitive environment, and our discussion assumes some familiarity with these concepts. (For a review, see Exhibit A–11 and the related discussion in Appendix A, which follows Chapter 2.)

The economist's traditional view is that most product-markets head toward pure competition—or oligopoly—over the long run. In these situations, a marketing manager competes for customers against competitors who are offering very similar products. Because customers see the different available products (marketing mixes) as close substitutes, competing firms must compete with lower and lower prices, especially in pure competition where there are likely to be large numbers of competitors. Profit margins shrink until they are just high enough to keep the most efficient firms in business. Avoiding pure competition is sensible— and certainly fits with our emphasis on target marketing.

Effective target marketing is fundamentally different from effective decision making in other areas of business. Accounting, production, and financial managers for competing firms can learn about and use the same standardized approaches—and they will work well in each case. By contrast, marketing managers can't just learn about and adopt the same "good" marketing strategy being used by other firms. That just leads to head-on competition—and a downward spiral in prices and profits. So target marketers try to offer customers a marketing mix better suited to their needs than competitors' offerings.

Competition-free environments are rare

Most marketing managers would like to have such a strong marketing mix that customers see it as uniquely able to meet their needs. This competition-free ideal guides the search for breakthrough opportunities. Yet monopoly situations, in which one firm completely controls a broad product-market, are rare in market-directed economies. Further, governments commonly regulate monopolies. For example, in most parts of the world prices set by utility companies must be approved by a government agency. Although most marketing managers can't expect to operate with complete control in an unregulated monopoly, they can move away from head-on competition.

Monopolistic competition is typical— and a challenge

In monopolistic competition, a number of different firms offer marketing mixes that at least some customers see as different. Each competitor tries to get control (a monopoly) in its "own" target market. But competition still exists because some customers see the various alternatives as substitutes. A subset of these firms may even compete head-on for the same customers with similar marketing mixes. With monopolistic competition, each firm has its own down-sloping demand curve. But the shape of the demand curve—and elasticity of demand—depends on how similar competitors' products and marketing mixes are. Most marketing managers in developed economies face monopolistic competition.

In monopolistic competition, marketing managers sometimes try to differentiate very similar products by relying on other elements of the marketing mix. For example, Clorox Bleach uses the same basic chemicals as other bleaches. But marketing managers for Clorox may help to set it apart from other bleaches by offering an improved pouring spout, by producing ads that demonstrate its stain-killing power, or by getting it better shelf positions in supermarkets. Yet such approaches may not work, especially if competitors can easily imitate the new ideas. Efforts to promote real—but subtle—differences may not do any good either. If potential customers view the different offerings as essentially similar, the market will become more and more competitive—and firms will have to rely on lower costs to obtain a competitive advantage.

Analyze competitors to find a competitive advantage

The best way for a marketing manager to avoid head-on competition is to find new or better ways to satisfy customers' needs. The search for a breakthrough opportunity—or some sort of competitive advantage—requires an understanding not only of customers but also of competitors. That's why marketing managers turn to **competitor analysis**—an organized approach for evaluating the strengths and weaknesses of current or potential competitors' marketing strategies. A complete discussion of the possible approaches for competitor analysis is beyond the scope of the first marketing course. But we will briefly cover an approach that works well in many different market situations.

The approach we will discuss is a logical extension of the marketing strategy planning framework that is the focus of this book. The basic idea is simple. You compare the strengths and weaknesses of your current (or planned) target market and marketing mix with what competitors are currently doing or are likely to do in response to your strategy.

The initial step in competitor analysis is to identify potential competitors. It's useful to start broadly—and from the viewpoint of target customers. Companies may offer quite different products to meet the same needs, but they are competitors if customers see them as offering close substitutes. For example, disposable diapers, cloth diapers, and diaper rental services all compete in the same generic market concerned with baby care. Identifying a broad set of potential competitors helps marketing managers understand the different ways customers are currently meeting needs—and sometimes points to new opportunities. For example, even parents who usually prefer the economy of cloth diapers may be interested in the convenience of disposables when they travel.

Usually, however, marketing managers quickly narrow the focus of their analysis to the set of **competitive rivals**—firms that will be the closest competitors. Rivals offering similar products are usually easy to identify. However, with a really new and different product concept, there may not be a current competitor with a similar product. In that case, the closest competitor may be a firm that is currently serving similar needs with a different product. Although such firms may not appear to be close competitors, they are likely to fight back—perhaps with a directly competitive product—if another firm starts to take away customers.

Anticipate competition that will come

Even if no specific competitors can be identified, marketing managers must consider how long it might take for potential competitors to appear and what they might do. It's easy to make the mistake of assuming that there won't be competition in the future—or of discounting how aggressive competition may become. But a successful strategy attracts others who are eager to jump in for a share of the profit—even if profits only hold up for a short time. That is why it is important for firms to find opportunities where they can sustain a competitive advantage over the longer run.

Finding a sustainable competitive advantage requires special attention to competitor strengths and weaknesses. For example, it is very difficult to dislodge a competitor who is already a market leader simply by attacking with a strategy that has similar strengths. An established leader can usually defend its position by quickly copying the best parts of what a new competitor is trying to do. On the other hand, an established competitor may not be able to defend quickly if it is attacked where it is weak. For example, Right Guard deodorant built its strong position with an aerosol spray dispenser. But many consumers don't like the messy aerosol cloud—or have become concerned about the effect of aerosols on the environment. That weakness provided Old Spice with a competitive opportunity for a deodorant in a pump dispenser. Right Guard did not quickly fight back with its own pump. The company thought that promoting a pump could hurt sales of its established product—and might even help Old Spice build interest in *its* pump.[8]

Watch for competitive barriers

In a competitor analysis, you also consider **competitive barriers**—the conditions that may make it difficult, or even impossible, for a firm to compete in a market. Such barriers may limit your own plans or, alternatively, block competitors' responses to an innovative strategy.

For example, Exhibit 4–2 summarizes a competitor analysis in the Japanese market for disposable diapers. P&G was about to replace its original Pampers, which were selling poorly, with a new version that offered improved fit and better absorbency. Kao and Uni-Charm, the two leading Japanese producers, both had better distribution networks. Because most Japanese grocery stores and drugstores are very small—about 150 square feet—shelf space is limited and frequent restocking by wholesalers is critical. So, getting cooperation in the channel was a potential competitive barrier for P&G. Uni-Charm further reduced P&G's access to customers when it took advantage of its relationship with retailers to introduce

EXHIBIT 4–2 Competitor Analysis (summary): Disposable Diaper Competition in Japan

	P&G's Current and Planned Strategy	*Kao's Strengths (+) and Weaknesses (-)*	*Uni-Charm's Strengths (+) and Weaknesses (-)*
Target Market(s)	Upscale, modern parents who can afford disposable diapers	Same as for P&G	Same as for P&G, but also budget-conscious segment that includes cloth diaper users (+)
Product	Improved fit and absorbency (+); brand name imagery weak in Japan (-)	Brand familiarity (+), but no longer the best performance (-)	Two brands—for different market segments—and more convenient package with handles (+)
Place	Distribution through independent wholesalers to both food and drugstores (+), but handled by fewer retailers (-)	Close relations with and control over wholesalers who carry only Kao products (+); computerized inventory reorder system (+)	Distribution through 80% of food stores in best locations (+); shelf space for two brands (+)
Promotion	Heaviest spending on daytime TV, heavy sales promotion, including free samples (+); small sales force (-)	Large efficient sales force (+); lowest advertising spending (-) and out-of-date ad claims (-)	Advertising spending high (+); effective ads that appeal to Japanese mothers (+)
Price	High retail price (-), but lower unit price for larger quantities (+)	Highest retail price (-), but also best margins for wholesalers and retailers (+)	Lowest available retail price (+); price of premium brand comparable to P&G (-)
(Potential) Competitive Barriers	Patent protection (+), limits in access to retail shelf space (-)	Inferior product (-), excellent logistics support system (+)	Economies of scale and lower costs (+); loyal customers (+)
Likely Response(s)	Improve wholesaler and retailer margins; faster deliveries in channel; change package to require less shelf space	Press retailers to increase in-store promotion; change advertising and/or improve product	Increase short-term sales promotions; but if P&G takes customers, cut price on premium brand

a second, lower-priced brand. To help overcome resistance in the channel, P&G offered wholesalers and retailers better markups and changed to packaging that took less shelf space.[9]

Seek information about competitors

A marketing manager should actively seek information about current or potential competitors. Although most firms try to keep the specifics of their plans secret, much public information may be available. For example, many firms routinely monitor competitors' local newspapers. In one such case, an article discussed a change in the competitor's sales organization. An alert marketing manager realized that the change was made to strengthen the competitor's ability to take business from one of her firm's key target markets. This early warning provided time to make adjustments. Other sources of competitor information include trade publications, alert sales reps, middlemen, and other industry experts. In business markets, customers may be quick to explain what competing suppliers are offering.

Ethical issues may arise

The search for information about competitors sometimes raises ethical issues. For example, it's not unusual for people to change jobs and move to a competing firm in the same industry. Such people may have a great deal of information about the competitor, but is it ethical for them to use it? Similarly, some firms have been criticized for going too far—like waiting at a landfill for competitors' trash to find copies of confidential company reports.

Beyond the moral issues, stepping over the line of ethical behavior can prove to be very costly. Spying on competitors to obtain trade secrets is illegal, and damage awards can be huge. For example, the courts ordered Keebler Co., Nabisco Brands, and Frito-Lay to pay Procter & Gamble about $125 million in damages for stealing secrets about its Duncan Hines soft cookies. Nabisco had obtained Duncan Hines' recipe by entering a restricted area. Keebler had gone so far as to hire an airplane to take aerial photographs of a Duncan Hines manufacturing facility that was under construction. A Frito-Lay employee posed as a potential customer to attend a confidential sales presentation.[10]

The competition may vary from country to country

A firm that faces very stiff competition may find that the competitive environment—and the opportunities—are much better in another region or country.

Twenty years ago, when many small American companies were content to build their businesses in the huge U.S. market, marketing managers at H. B. Fuller Co. saw international markets as an opportunity—and a matter of survival. It was hard for their small firm, a producer of paints, adhesives, and industrial coatings, to compete against giant suppliers like Du Pont and Dow Chemical for a larger share of the U.S. market. Fuller's marketing managers didn't want to diversify into some other business, so they decided to go where the competition wasn't. They quickly found that developing a competitive advantage with overseas customers required constant sales and service contacts. So instead of exporting from the United States, Fuller now produces customized products in plants run by local people in 27 countries across Latin America, Europe, and Asia. That allows the company to be close to its customers and to deliver products quickly. Fuller's move to new competitive environments has been worth the effort. Foreign business now accounts for half of its profit.[11]

Direct competition cannot always be avoided

Despite the desire to avoid highly competitive situations—especially pure competition—a firm may find that it can't. Some firms are already in an industry before it becomes intensely competitive. Then as competitors fail, new firms enter the market, possibly because they don't have more attractive alternatives and can at least earn a living. In less-developed economies, this is a common pattern with small retailers and wholesalers. New entrants may not even know how competitive the market is—but they stick it out until they run out of money. Production-oriented firms are more likely to make such a mistake.

THE ECONOMIC ENVIRONMENT

The **economic and technological environment** affects the way firms—and the whole economy—use resources. We will treat the economic and technological environments separately to emphasize that the technological environment provides a *base* for the economic environment. Technical skills and equipment affect the way companies convert an economy's resources into output. The economic environment, on the other hand, is affected by the way all of the parts of a macro-economic system interact. This then affects such things as national income, economic growth, and inflation. The economic environment may vary from one country to another, but economies around the world are linked.

Economic conditions change rapidly

The economic environment can—and does—change quite rapidly. The effects can be far-reaching—and require changes in marketing strategy.

Even a well-planned marketing strategy may fail if the country goes through a rapid business decline. As consumers' incomes drop, they must shift their spending patterns. They may simply have to do without some products. A weak economy, like the one in the United States and many other parts of the world in the early 90s, also undermines consumer confidence, even among families whose income is not affected. When consumer confidence is low, people delay purchasing—especially big ticket items. Similarly, firms cut back on their own purchases. Many companies aren't strong enough to survive such bad times.

Interest rates and inflation affect buying

Changes in the economy are often accompanied by changes in the interest rate—the charge for borrowing money. Interest rates directly affect the total price borrowers must pay for products. So the interest rate affects when—and if—they will buy. This is an especially important factor in some business markets. But it also affects consumer purchases of homes, cars, furniture, and other items usually bought on credit.

Changes in interest rates may also have indirect effects on noncredit purchases. For example, when interest rates dropped significantly in 1991, many families refinanced their homes at the lower rate. Then they used the extra money from lower loan payments for purchases, like clothing, that they had postponed.

Interest rates usually increase during periods of inflation, and inflation is a fact of life in many economies. In some Latin American countries, inflation has exceeded 400 percent a year in recent years. In contrast, recent U.S. levels—3 to 20 percent—seem "low." Still, inflation must be considered in strategy planning. When costs are rising rapidly and there are no more cost-cutting measures to take, a marketing manager may have to increase prices. But the decisions of individual marketing managers to raise prices add to macro-level inflation. That can lead to government policies that reduce income, employment, *and* consumer spending.

The global economy is connected

In the past, marketing managers often focused their attention on the economy of their home country. It's no longer that simple. The economies of the world are connected—and at an increasing pace changes in one economy affect others. One reason for this is that the amount of international trade is increasing—and it is affected by changes in and between economies.

Changes in the *exchange rate*—how much one country's money is worth in another country's money—have an important effect on international trade. When the dollar is strong, it's worth more in foreign countries. This sounds good—but it makes U.S. products more expensive overseas and foreign products cheaper in the United States. Companies like Caterpillar (tractors) lose foreign customers to producers from other countries.

A marketing manager isn't safe from the forces of changing exchange rates just because his or her firm is not involved in foreign trade. New competition arises in domestic markets as foreign products gain a competitive edge with lower prices. Many companies find themselves helpless during such economic change. In fact, a country's whole economic system can change as the balance of imports and exports shifts—affecting jobs, consumer income, and national productivity.

You can see that the marketing manager must watch the economic environment carefully. In contrast to the cultural and social environment, economic conditions change continuously. And they can move rapidly—up or down—requiring immediate strategy changes.[12]

THE TECHNOLOGICAL ENVIRONMENT

The technological base affects opportunities

Underlying any economic environment is its **technological base**—the technical skills and equipment that affect the way an economy's resources are converted to output. Technological developments affect marketing in two basic ways: with new products and with new processes (ways of doing things). Many argue, for example, that we are moving from an industrial society to an information society. Advances in electronic communications make it possible for people in different parts of the world to communicate face-to-face with satellite video-conferencing and to transmit faxes—including complex design drawings—by regular telephone lines. Computers allow more sophisticated planning and control. These process changes are accompanied by an exciting explosion of high-tech products—from robots in factories to skin patches that dispense medicines to genetically engineered tomatoes that taste great year-round.

New technologies have created important industries that didn't even exist a few years ago. In 1981 Microsoft was a tiny company. Now the largest software company in the world, it is worth more than General Motors. Similarly, as interest in personal computers grew, Michael Dell saw a new opportunity to sell computers by mail, and he quickly became a multimillionaire. With such big opportunities at stake, you can also see why there is such rapid transfer of technology from one part of the world to another. But technology transfer is not automatic. Someone—perhaps you—has to see the opportunity.

As you move through this text, you should see that many of the big advances in business have come from early recognition of new ways to do things. Marketers should help their firms see such opportunities by trying to understand the "why" of present markets—and what is keeping their firms from being more successful. Then, as new technological developments come along, the marketers will be alert to possible uses of those technologies—and see how opportunities can be turned into profits.

Technology also poses challenges

The rapid pace of technological change opens up new opportunities, but it also poses challenges for marketers. For many firms, success hinges on how quickly new ideas can be brought to market. It's easy for a firm to slip into a production orientation in the flush of excitement that follows a new discovery in a research and development lab. That makes it more important than ever for marketing thinking to guide the production process—starting at the beginning with decisions about where basic R&D effort will be focused.

❓ Technology and ethical issues

Marketers must also help their firms decide what technical developments are ethically acceptable. For example, many firms have now installed a system to identify the telephone number of an incoming telephone call. When linked with a computer, this makes it possible for a firm to know what customer is calling even

The R. R. Donnelley & Sons Co. sells a service that takes advantage of new developments in information technology and communications to help other firms be more successful in entering overseas markets.

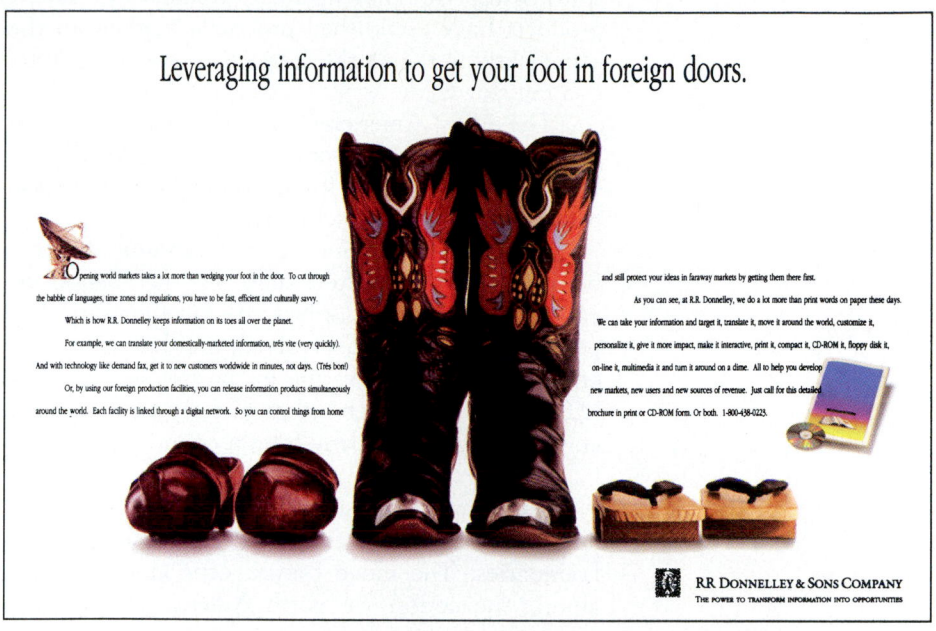

before the customer says the first word. It also makes instantly available detailed information about what a customer has purchased in the past. This is a very powerful technology, but many people feel that this sort of automatic number identification system is an invasion of privacy.

Similarly, with the growing concern about environmental pollution and the quality of life, some attractive technological developments may be rejected because of their long-run effects on the environment. Aseptic drink boxes, for example, are very convenient but difficult to recycle. In a case like this, what's good for the firm and some customers may not be good for the cultural and social environment—or acceptable in the political and legal environment. Being close to the market should give marketers a better feel for current trends—and help firms avoid serious mistakes.[13]

THE POLITICAL ENVIRONMENT

The attitudes and reactions of people, social critics, and governments all affect the political environment. Consumers in the same country usually share a common political environment, but the political environment can also have a dramatic effect on opportunities at a local or international level. Some business managers have become very successful by studying the political environment and developing strategies that take advantage of opportunities related to changing political dimensions.

Nationalism can be limiting in international markets

Strong sentiments of **nationalism**—an emphasis on a country's interests before everything else—affect how macro-marketing systems work. They can affect how marketing managers work as well. Nationalistic feelings can reduce sales—or even block all marketing activity—in some international markets. For many years, Japan has made it difficult for outside firms to do business there—in spite of the fact that Japanese producers of cars, color TVs, VCRs, and other products have established profitable markets in the United States, Europe, and other parts of the world. Japan is under pressure to change, but the changes are coming slowly.

The "Buy American" policy in many government contracts and business purchases reflects this same attitude in the U.S., as does support for protecting U.S. producers from foreign competition—especially producers of footwear, textiles, production machinery, and cars.[14]

Nationalistic feelings can determine whether a firm can enter markets because businesses often must get permission to operate. In some political environments, this is only a routine formality. In others, a lot of red tape and personal influence are involved, and bribes are sometimes expected. This raises ethical issues for marketing managers—and legal issues too—since it's illegal for U.S. firms to offer such bribes. Clearly, that can make it difficult for a U.S. firm to compete with a company from a country that doesn't have similar laws.

Regional groupings are becoming more important

Important dimensions of the political environment are likely to be similar among nations that have banded together to have common regional economic boundaries. The move toward economic unification of Europe and free trade among the nations of North America are outstanding examples of this sort of regional grouping.

The unification of European markets

In the past, each of the countries of the European Union (EU) had its own trade rules and regulations. These differences made it difficult and expensive to move products from one country to the others. Now, these countries are abandoning old political squabbles and nationalistic prejudices in favor of cooperative efforts to reduce taxes and other barriers commonly applied at national boundaries. This unification has eliminated over 300 separate barriers to inter-European trade. Trucks loaded with products spill across the European continent and Britain. The increased efficiency is reducing costs—and the prices European consumers pay—and creating millions of new jobs. These changes make Europe the largest unified market in the world, and more changes are coming. By the year 2000 the EC may expand to include at least 25 countries and 450 million people.

These changes have dramatically altered opportunities available to marketing managers both in Europe and in other parts of the world. The international competition fostered by the unification of Europe has also provided impetus for the U.S., Mexico, and Canada to develop more cooperative trade agreements.

NAFTA is building trade cooperation

The **North American Free Trade Agreement (NAFTA)** lays out a plan to reshape the rules of trade among the U.S., Canada, and Mexico. NAFTA enlarges the free-trade pact that had already knocked down most barriers to U.S.–Canada trade, and over a 15-year period will eliminate most such barriers with Mexico. It also establishes a forum for resolving future trade disputes.

NAFTA is a long-term proposition, and so far its overall economic impact has not been that great. However, tariffs that have already dropped are having a significant impact on specific businesses. For example, Raychem Corp., a small producer of telecommunications equipment, no longer faces a 25 percent tariff on exports to Mexico. That is leveling its competitive playing field and creating new opportunities. More generally, NAFTA is creating a free-trade region that

The North American Free Trade Agreement will result in increased demand for business communications between Mexico and the U.S. To capture that business, AT&T is offering a new service that makes it easier to call the U.S. from Mexico.

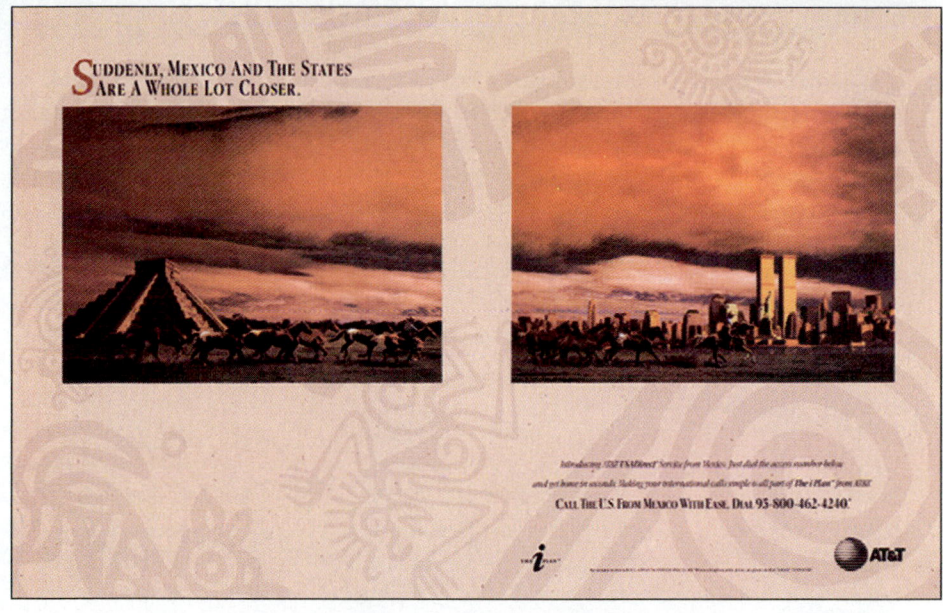

encompasses 376 million people and three economies that produce $7 trillion worth of goods and services annually. Thus, the changes that result from NAFTA may ultimately be as significant as those involved in the unification of Europe.

Of course, removal of some economic and political barriers— whether across North America or Europe—will not eliminate the need to adjust strategies to reach submarkets of consumers. Centuries of cultural differences will not disappear overnight—they may never disappear. Yet these cooperative arrangements will give firms operating in regions easier access to larger markets, and the countries involved will have a more powerful voice in protecting their own interests.[15]

Some dramatic changes in the political environment—like the fall of communism in Eastern Europe—happen fast and are hard to predict. Yet, many important political changes—both within and across nations—evolve more gradually. The development of consumerism is a good example.

Consumerism is here—and basic

Consumerism is a social movement that seeks to increase the rights and powers of consumers. In the last 30 years, consumerism has emerged as a major political force. Although the consumer movement has spread to many different countries, it was born in America.

The basic goals of modern consumerism haven't changed much since 1962, when President Kennedy's "Consumer Bill of Rights" affirmed consumers' rights to safety, to be informed, to choose, and to be heard.

Twenty-five years ago, U.S. consumerism was much more visible. Consumers staged frequent boycotts and protest marches and attracted much media attention. Today, consumer groups provide information and work on special projects like product safety standards. Publications like *Consumer Reports* provide product comparisons and information on other consumer concerns.

ARTAIS FLIES HIGH IN INTERNATIONAL MARKETS

Artais Weather Check, Inc., is a small company that produces automated weather-observing systems for small airports. Its high-tech equipment records runway wind speed and temperature and converts the data into a voice message that is broadcast to pilots. Although Artais is one of only three suppliers certified by the Federal Aviation Agency, economic conditions in the U.S. have limited sales potential to about 75 systems a year. So, to support its growth objectives, Artais is targeting airports in other countries.

The Artais name was largely unknown in places such as China and Egypt. Even so, it is winning customers from big firms like Raytheon and Westinghouse because of its strengths in technology and cost control as well as its flexibility in responding to customers. For example, to win an account in Egypt,

it expanded its training programs and adapted its system to give weather reports in Arabic as well as English. Still, dealing with foreign political environments has sometimes been difficult. For example, Artais lost a contract with a Romanian airport. A German producer got the contract, perhaps because the Romanian government—in its bid to join the European Union—wanted to win favor with Germany.

Artais' sales increased by about 60 percent—to $5.5 million—from 1993 to 1994, and most of that growth was in foreign markets. That's a big jump, but Artais is not alone in finding such success. A survey estimates that now about half of all manufacturers with revenues below $100 million export their products, and that's a big increase from 36 percent in 1990.[16]

Business is responding to public expectations

Many companies have responded to the spirit of consumerism. For example, Chrysler adopted a consumer bill of rights, and Ford set up a consumer board to help resolve customer complaints. Many firms have established a consumer affairs position to directly represent consumer interests within the company.

Clearly, top management—and marketing managers—must continue to pay attention to consumer concerns. The old, production-oriented ways of doing things are no longer acceptable.[17]

THE LEGAL ENVIRONMENT

Changes in the political environment often lead to changes in the legal environment—and in the way existing laws are enforced. It's hard for marketing managers to know all the relevant laws, but it's important that they do because the legal environment sets the basic rules for how a business can operate in society. The legal environment may severely limit some choices, but changes in laws and how they are interpreted also create new opportunities. To illustrate the effects of the legal environment, we will discuss how it has evolved in the United States. However, keep in mind that laws often vary from one geographic market to another—especially when different countries are involved.

Trying to encourage competition

American economic and legislative thinking is based on the idea that competition among many small firms helps the economy. Therefore, attempts by business to limit competition are considered contrary to the public interest.

As industries grew larger after the Civil War, some became monopolies controlled by wealthy businessmen—the robber barons. Smaller producers had trouble surviving. A movement grew—especially among Midwestern farmers—to control monopolists.

The government regulates marketing of many goods and services. Prescription drugs, for example, are controlled by the Food, Drug, and Cosmetic Act and must be preapproved by the FDA.

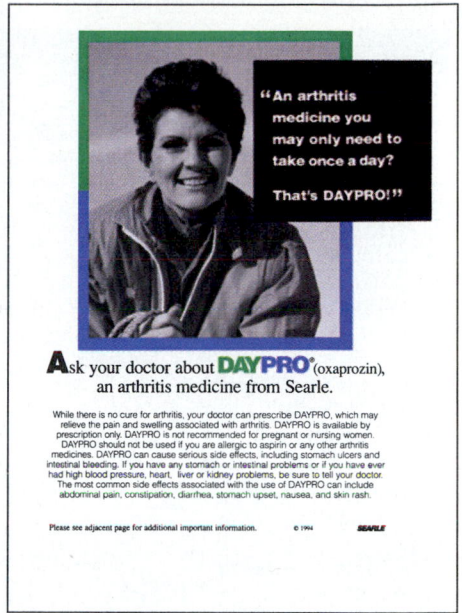

Starting in 1890, Congress passed a series of antimonopoly laws. Exhibit 4–3 shows the names and dates of these laws. Although the specific focus of each law is different, in general they are all intended to encourage competition.

Antimonopoly law and marketing mix planning

In later chapters, we will specifically apply antimonopoly law to the four Ps. For now you should know what kind of proof the government must have to get a conviction under each of the major laws. You should also know which of the four Ps are most affected by each law. Exhibit 4–3 provides such a summary—with a phrase following each law to show what the government must prove to get a conviction.

Prosecution is serious— you can go to jail

Businesses and *business managers* are subject to both criminal and civil laws. Penalties for breaking civil laws are limited to blocking or forcing certain actions—along with fines. Where criminal law applies, jail sentences can be imposed. For example, several managers at Beech-Nut Nutrition Company were recently fined $100,000 each and sentenced to a year in jail. In spite of unfair ads claiming that Beech-Nut's apple juice was 100 percent natural, they tried to bolster profits by secretly using low-cost artificial juices. The individuals responsible paid a personal price for their criminal behavior, but it cost the firm as well. Bad publicity from the incident resulted in a big drop in Beech-Nut sales.[18]

Consumer protection laws are not new

Although antimonopoly laws focus on protecting competition, the wording of the laws in Exhibit 4–3 has, over time, moved toward protecting consumers. Some consumer protections are also built into the English and U.S. common law systems. A seller has to tell the truth (if asked a direct question), meet contracts, and stand behind the firm's product (to some reasonable extent). Beyond this, it is expected that vigorous competition in the marketplace will protect consumers—*so long as they are careful.*

EXHIBIT 4–3 Focus (mostly prohibitions) of Federal Antimonopoly Laws on the Four Ps

Law	Product	Place	Promotion	Price
Sherman Act (1890) Monopoly or conspiracy in restraint of trade	Monopoly or conspiracy to control a product	Monopoly or conspiracy to control distribution channels		Monopoly or conspiracy to fix or control prices
Clayton Act (1914) Substantially lessens competition	Forcing sale of some products with others—tying contracts	Exclusive dealing contracts (limiting buyers' sources of supply)		Price discrimination by manufacturers
Federal Trade Commission Act (1914) Unfair methods of competition		Unfair policies	Deceptive ads or selling practices	Deceptive pricing
Robinson-Patman Act (1936) Tends to injure competition		Prohibits paying allowances to "direct" buyers in lieu of middlemen costs (brokerage charges)	Prohibits "fake" advertising allowances or discrimination in help offered	Prohibits price discrimination on goods of "like grade and quality" without cost justification, and limits quantity discounts
Wheeler-Lea Amendment (1938) Unfair or deceptive practices	Deceptive packaging or branding		Deceptive ads or selling claims	Deceptive pricing
Antimerger Act (1950) Lessens competition	Buying competitors	Buying producers or distributors		
Magnuson-Moss Act (1975) Unreasonable practices	Product warranties			

Yet focusing only on competition didn't protect consumers very well in some areas. So the government found it necessary to pass other laws. For example, various laws regulate packaging and labels, credit practices, and environmental issues. Usually, however, the laws focus on specific types of products.

Foods and drugs are controlled

Consumer protection laws in the United States go back to 1906, when Congress passed the Pure Food and Drug Act. Unsanitary meat-packing practices in the Chicago stockyards stirred consumer support for this act. After much debate, Congress decided to pass a general law to control the quality and labeling of food and drugs in interstate commerce. This was a major victory for consumer protection. Before the law, it was assumed that common law and the old warning "let the buyer beware" would take care of consumers.

Later acts corrected some loopholes in the law. The law now bans the shipment of unsanitary and poisonous products and requires much testing of drugs. The Food and Drug Administration (FDA) attempts to control manufacturers of these products. It can seize products that violate its rules—including regulations on branding and labeling.

In general, the FDA has done a good job. But there have been some problems. For example, the FDA was heavily criticized after it was revealed that many of the firms selling generic (unbranded) versions of popular prescription drugs were not meeting standards the FDA should have been enforcing. In other cases, critics complain about too much regulation. FDA rules for testing new drugs are much more demanding than the rules in many other countries, so many drugs are slower coming to market.

Product safety is controlled

The Consumer Product Safety Act (of 1972), another important consumer protection law, set up the Consumer Product Safety Commission. This group has broad power to set safety standards and can impose penalties for failure to meet these standards. Again, there is some question as to how much safety consumers really want—the commission found the bicycle the most hazardous product under its control!

But given that the commission has the power to *force* a product off the market—or require expensive recalls to correct problems—it is obvious that safety must be considered in product design. And safety must be treated seriously by marketing managers.[19]

State and local laws vary

Besides federal legislation—which affects interstate commerce—marketers must be aware of state and local laws. There are state and city laws regulating minimum prices and the setting of prices, regulations for starting up a business (licenses, examinations, and even tax payments), and in some communities, regulations prohibiting certain activities—such as door-to-door selling or selling on Sundays or during evenings.

Know the laws— follow the courts and federal agencies

Often laws are vaguely phrased—to convey intent but not specific detail. Then it's up to the courts and government agencies to spell out the details. As a result, a law may be interpreted and enforced differently over time. For example, during the late 1970s and 1980s, many U.S. government agencies regulated businesses less zealously and instead focused more on encouraging competition. Attention to regulation is swinging the other way in the 1990s—in part to correct abuses such as those that occurred in the savings and loan industry.

Because legislation must be interpreted by federal agencies and the courts, marketing managers need to study both legislative developments and the thinking of the courts and agencies. See Exhibit 4–4 for a description of some important federal regulatory agencies that should be considered in marketing strategy planning.

EXHIBIT 4–4 Some Important U.S. Federal Regulatory Agencies

Agencies	Responsibilities
Federal Trade Commission (FTC)	Enforces laws and develops guidelines regarding unfair business practices
Food and Drug Administration (FDA)	Enforces laws and develops regulations to prevent distribution and sale of adulterated or misbranded foods, drugs, cosmetics, and hazardous consumer products
Consumer Product Safety Commission (CPSC)	Enforces the Consumer Product Safety Act—which covers any consumer product not assigned to other regulatory agencies
Interstate Commerce Commission (ICC)	Regulates interstate rail, bus, truck, and water carriers
Federal Communications Commission (FCC)	Regulates interstate wire, radio, and television
Environmental Protection Agency (EPA)	Develops and enforces environmental protection standards
Office of Consumer Affairs (OCA)	Handles consumers' complaints

Consumerists and the law say, "Let the seller beware"

The old rule about buyer–seller relations—*let the buyer beware*—has changed to *let the seller beware*. The current shift to proconsumer laws and court decisions suggests that lawmakers are more interested in protecting consumers. This may upset production-oriented managers. But times have changed—and managers must adapt to this new political and legal environment. After all, it is the consumers—through their government representatives—who determine the kind of economic system they want.[20]

THE CULTURAL AND SOCIAL ENVIRONMENT

The **cultural and social environment** affects how and why people live and behave as they do—which affects customer buying behavior and eventually the economic, political, and legal environment. Many variables make up the cultural and social environment. Some examples are the languages people speak, the type of education they have, their religious beliefs, what type of food they eat, the style of clothing and housing they have, and how they view marriage and family. Because the cultural and social environment has such broad effects, most people don't stop to think about it, or how it may be changing, or how it may differ for other people.

A marketing manager can't afford to take the cultural and social environment for granted. Although changes tend to come slowly, they can have far-reaching effects. A marketing manager who sees the changes early may be able to identify big opportunities. Further, within any broad society, different subgroups of people may be affected by the cultural and social environment in different ways. In most countries, the trend toward multiculturalism is making such differences even more important to marketers. They require special attention when segmenting markets. In fact, dealing with these differences is often one of the greatest challenges managers face when planning strategies, especially for international markets.

Twenty-five years ago, United Airlines' ads attracted flight attendants by bragging that most of its "girls" found a husband within a few years of taking the job. The ad explains that the woman shown is viewed as an old maid because she's been on the job three years and isn't yet married. Today, because of shifts in the cultural environment, such an ad would not only be ineffective but also viewed as sexist.

Since we will discuss details of how the cultural and social environment relates to buying behavior in Chapters 6 through 8, here we will just use an example to illustrate its impact on marketing strategy planning.

Changing women's roles

The shifting roles of women in society illustrate the importance of the cultural and social environment on marketing strategy planning. Forty years ago, most people in the United States felt that a woman's role was in the home—first and foremost as a wife and mother. Women had less opportunity for higher education and were completely shut out of many of the most interesting jobs. Obviously, there have been big changes in that stereotyped thinking. With better job opportunities, more women are delaying marriage, and once married they are likely to stay in the workforce and have fewer children. For example, in 1950, only 24 percent of wives worked outside the home. This figure rose to more than 55 percent in the 80s and now is about 60 percent. Among women in the 35–44 age group, the percentage is already over 70.

The flood of women into the job market boosted economic growth and changed U.S. society in many other ways. Many in-home jobs that used to be done primarily by women—ranging from family shopping to preparing meals to doing volunteer work—still need to be done by someone. Husbands and children now do some of these jobs, a situation that has changed the target market for many products. Or a working woman may face a crushing "poverty of time" and look for help elsewhere, creating opportunities for producers of frozen meals, child care centers, dry cleaners, financial services, and the like.

Although there is still a big wage gap between men and women, the income working women generate gives them new independence and purchasing power. For example, women now purchase about half of all cars. Not long ago, many car dealers insulted a woman shopper by ignoring her or suggesting that she come back with her husband. Now car companies have realized that women are important customers. It's interesting that Japanese car dealers, especially Mazda and Toyota, were the first to really pay attention to women customers. In Japan, fewer women have jobs or buy cars—the Japanese society is still very much male-oriented. Perhaps it was the extreme contrast with Japanese society that prompted these firms to pay more attention to women buyers in the United States.[21]

Women's changing role has created opportunities for marketing but also complications. A marketing mix targeted at women, for example, may require a real balancing act. Advertising showing a woman at the office may attract some customers but alienate housewives who feel that their job doesn't command as much status as it should. Conversely, an ad that shows a woman doing housework might be criticized for encouraging stereotypes.

Changes come slowly

Most changes in basic cultural values and social attitudes come slowly. An individual firm can't hope to encourage big changes in the short run. Instead, it should identify current attitudes and work within these constraints—as it seeks new and better opportunities.[22]

HOW TO EVALUATE OPPORTUNITIES

A progressive firm constantly looks for new opportunities. Once the opportunities are identified, the firm must screen and evaluate them. Usually, a firm can't pursue all available opportunities, so it must try to match its opportunities to its resources and objectives. First, management must quickly screen out obvious mismatches so other opportunities can be analyzed more carefully. Let's look at some approaches for screening and evaluating opportunities.

Developing and applying screening criteria

After you analyze the firm's resources (for strengths and weaknesses), the environmental trends the firm faces, and the objectives of top management, you merge them all into a set of product-market screening criteria. These criteria should include both quantitative and qualitative components. The quantitative components summarize the firm's objectives: sales, profit, and return on investment (ROI) targets. (Note: ROI analysis is discussed briefly in Appendix B, which follows Chapter 17.) The qualitative components summarize what kinds of businesses the firm wants to be in, what businesses it wants to exclude, what weaknesses it should avoid, and what resources (strengths) and trends it should build on.[23]

Developing screening criteria is difficult—but worth the effort. They summarize in one place what the firm wants to accomplish—in quantitative terms—as well as roughly how and where it wants to accomplish it. The criteria should be realistic—that is, they should be achievable. Opportunities that pass the screen should be able to be turned into strategies that the firm can implement with the resources it has.

EXHIBIT 4–5   An Example of Product-Market Screening Criteria for a Small Retail and Wholesale Distributor ($5 million annual sales)

1. **Quantitative criteria**
   a. Increase sales by $750,000 per year for the next five years.
   b. Earn ROI of at least 25 percent before taxes on new ventures.
   c. Break even within one year on new ventures.
   d. Opportunity must be large enough to justify interest (to help meet objectives) but small enough so company can handle with the resources available.
   e. Several opportunities should be pursued to reach the objectives—to spread the risks.

2. **Qualitative criteria**
   a. Nature of business preferred.
      (1) New goods and services for present customers to strengthen relationships.
      (2) "Quality" products that do not cannibalize sales of current products.
      (3) Competition should be weak and opportunity should be hard to copy for several years.
      (4) Should build on our strong sales skills.
      (5) There should be strongly felt (even unsatisfied) needs—to reduce promotion costs and permit "high" prices.
   b. Constraints.
      (1) Nature of businesses to exclude.
         (a) Manufacturing.
         (b) Any requiring large fixed capital investments.
         (c) Any requiring many support people who must be "good" all the time and would require much supervision.
      (2) Geographic.
         (a) United States, Mexico, and Canada only.
      (3) General.
         (a) Make use of current strengths.
         (b) Attractiveness of market should be reinforced by more than one of the following basic trends: technological, demographic, social, economic, political.
         (c) Market should not be bucking any basic trends.

Exhibit 4–5 illustrates the product-market screening criteria for a small retail and wholesale distributor. These criteria help the firm's managers eliminate unsuitable opportunities—and find attractive ones to turn into strategies and plans.

Whole plans should be evaluated

You need to forecast the probable results of implementing a marketing strategy to apply the quantitative part of the screening criteria because only implemented plans generate sales, profits, and return on investment (ROI). For a rough screening, you only need to estimate the likely results of implementing each opportunity over a logical planning period. If a product's life is likely to be three years, for example, a good strategy may not produce profitable results for 6 to 12 months. But evaluated over the projected three-year life, the product may look like a winner. When evaluating the potential of possible opportunities (product-market strategies), it is important to evaluate similar things—that is, *whole* plans.

Opportunities that pass the screen—or all opportunities if you don't use screening criteria—should be evaluated in more detail before being accepted as *the* product-market strategic plans for implementation. Usually, a firm has more opportunities than resources and has to choose among them—to match its opportunities to its resources and objectives. The following approaches help firms select among possible plans.

EXHIBIT 4–6 Expected Sales and Cost Curves of Two Strategies over Five-Year Planning Periods

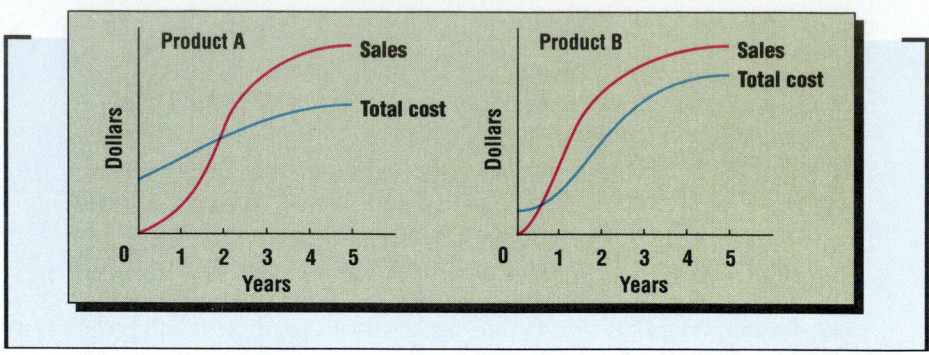

Total profit approach can help evaluate possible plans

In the total profit approach, management forecasts potential sales and costs during the life of the plan to estimate likely profitability.

Managers may evaluate the prospects for each plan over a five-year planning period, using monthly and/or annual sales and cost estimates. This is shown graphically in Exhibit 4–6.

Note that managers can evaluate different marketing plans at the same time. Exhibit 4–6 compares a much-improved product and product concept (Product A) with a "me-too" product (Product B) for the same target market. In the short run, the me-too product will make a profit sooner and might look like the better choice—if managers consider only one year's results. The improved product, on the other hand, will take a good deal of pioneering—but over its five-year life will be much more profitable.

Return-on-investment (ROI) approach can help evaluate possible plans too

Besides evaluating the profit potential of possible plans, firms may also calculate the return on investment (ROI) of resources needed to implement plans. One plan may require a heavy investment in advertising and channel development, for example, while another relies primarily on lower price.

ROI analyses can be useful for selecting among possible plans because equally profitable plans may require vastly different resources and offer different rates of return on investment. Some firms are very concerned with ROI, especially those that borrow money for working capital. There is little point in borrowing to implement strategies that won't return enough to meet the cost of borrowing.

PLANNING GRIDS HELP EVALUATE A PORTFOLIO OF OPPORTUNITIES

When a firm has many possibilities to evaluate, it usually has to compare quite different ones. This problem is easier to handle with graphical approaches—such as the nine-box strategic planning grid developed by General Electric and used by many other companies. Such grids can help evaluate a firm's whole portfolio of strategic plans or businesses.

General Electric looks for green positions

General Electric's strategic planning grid—see Exhibit 4–7—forces company managers to make three-part judgments (high, medium, and low) about the business strengths and industry attractiveness of all proposed or existing product-

EXHIBIT 4–7   General Electric's Strategic Planning Grid

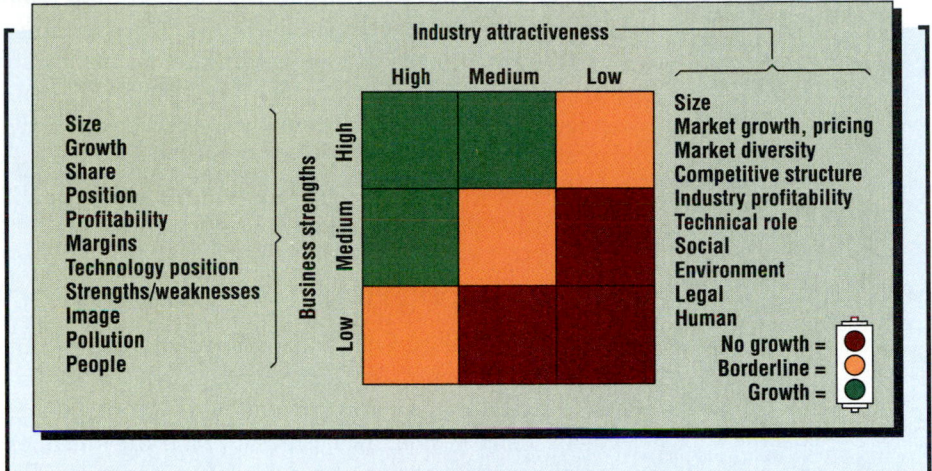

market plans. As you can see from Exhibit 4–7, this approach helps a manager organize information about the company's marketing environments (discussed earlier in this chapter) along with information about its strategy.

The industry attractiveness dimension helps managers answer the question: "Does this product-market plan look like a good idea?" To answer that question, managers have to judge such factors as the size of the market and its growth rate, the nature of competition, the plan's potential environmental or social impact, and how laws might affect it. Note that an opportunity may be attractive for *some* company—but not well suited to the strengths (and weaknesses) of a particular firm. That is why the GE grid also considers the business strengths dimension.

The business strengths dimension focuses on the ability of the company to pursue a product-market plan effectively. To make judgments along this dimension, a manager evaluates whether the firm has people with the right talents and skills to implement the plan, whether the plan is consistent with the firm's image and profit objectives, and whether the firm could establish a profitable market share given its technical capability, costs, and size.

GE feels opportunities that fall into the green boxes in the upper left-hand corner of the grid are its best growth opportunities. Managers give these opportunities high marks on both industry attractiveness and business strengths. The red boxes in the lower right-hand corner of the grid, on the other hand, suggest a no-growth policy. Existing red businesses may continue to generate earnings, but they no longer deserve much investment. Yellow businesses are borderline cases—they can go either way. GE may continue to support an existing yellow business but will probably reject a proposal for a new one.

GE's "stoplight" evaluation method is a very subjective, multiple-factor approach. It avoids the traps and possible errors of trying to use oversimplified, single-number criteria—like ROI or market share. Instead, top managers review detailed written summaries of many factors that help them make summary judgments. Then they can make a collective judgment. This approach generally leads to agreement. It also helps everyone understand why the company supports some new opportunities and not others.[24]

Factors can change to reflect objectives

General Electric considers various business strength and industry attractiveness factors that reflect its objectives. Another firm might modify the evaluation to emphasize other factors—depending on its objectives and the type of product-market plans it is considering. For example, a small firm with only one product might consider a similar grid—with different criteria—to evaluate new product or market opportunities. While different firms focus on different factors, using many factors helps ensure that managers consider all the company's concerns when evaluating alternative opportunities.

MULTIPRODUCT FIRMS HAVE A DIFFICULT STRATEGY PLANNING JOB

Multiproduct firms—like General Electric—obviously have a more difficult strategic planning job than firms with only a few products or product lines aimed at the same or similar target markets. Multiproduct firms have to develop strategic plans for very different businesses. And they have to balance plans and resources so the whole company reaches its objectives. This means they must analyze alternatives using approaches similar to the General Electric strategic planning grid and only approve plans that make sense for the whole company—even if it means getting needed resources by "milking" some businesses and eliminating others.

Details on how to manage a complicated multiproduct firm are beyond our scope. But you should be aware (1) that there are such firms and (2) that the principles in this text are applicable—they just have to be extended. For example, some firms use strategic business units (SBUs), and some use portfolio management.

Strategic business units may help

Some multiproduct firms try to improve their operations by forming strategic business units. A **strategic business unit (SBU)** is an organizational unit (within a larger company) that focuses on some product-markets and is treated as a separate profit center. By forming SBUs, a company formally acknowledges its very different activities. One SBU of Sara Lee, for example, produces baked goods for consumers and restaurants—another produces and markets Hanes brand T-shirts and underwear.

Some SBUs grow rapidly and require a great deal of attention and resources. Others produce only average profits and should be "milked"—that is, allowed to generate cash for the businesses with more potential. Product lines with poor market position, low profits, and poor growth prospects should be dropped or sold.

Companies that set up strategic business units usually do change their attitudes and methods of operation. They rate managers in terms of achieving strategic plans—rather than short-term profits or sales increases. With SBUs, the emphasis is on developing plans; those accepted are implemented aggressively. Under this concept, companies reward some managers for successfully phasing out product lines, while others are rewarded for expanding sales in other markets.

Each manager carries out a market-oriented strategic plan approved by top management. The manager's job is to help develop effective plans and then implement them—to ensure that the company's resources are used effectively and that the firm accomplishes its objectives.

Some firms use portfolio management

Some top managements handle strategic planning for a multiproduct firm with an approach called **portfolio management**—which treats alternative products, divisions, or strategic business units (SBUs) as though they were stock

Large multiproduct firms, like Philip Morris, evaluate and pursue a portfolio of strategic opportunities all around the world.

investments, to be bought and sold using financial criteria. Such managers make trade-offs among very different opportunities. They treat the various alternatives as investments that should be supported, milked, or sold off—depending on profitability and return on investment (ROI). In effect, they evaluate each alternative just like a stock market trader evaluates a stock.[25]

This approach makes some sense if alternatives are really quite different. Top managers feel they can't become very familiar with the prospects for all of their alternatives. So they fall back on the easy-to-compare quantitative criteria. And because the short run is much clearer than the long run, they place heavy emphasis on *current* profitability and return on investment. This puts great pressure on the operating managers to "deliver" *in the short run*—perhaps even neglecting the long run.

Neglecting the long run is risky—and this is the main weakness of the portfolio approach. This weakness can be overcome by enhancing the portfolio management approach with market-oriented strategic plans. They make it possible for managers to more accurately evaluate the alternatives' short-run and long-run prospects.

EVALUATING OPPORTUNITIES IN INTERNATIONAL MARKETS

Evaluate the risks

The approaches we've discussed so far apply to international markets just as they do to domestic ones. But in international markets it is often harder to fully understand the marketing environment variables. This may make it harder to see the risks involved in particular opportunities. Some countries are politically unstable; their governments and constitutions come and go. An investment safe under one government might become a takeover target under another. Further, the possibility of foreign exchange controls—and tax rate changes—can reduce the chance of getting profits and capital back to the home country.

Some products, like Unisys information systems, are used the same way all over the world. Other products, like anchovy paste, are more sensitive to different cultures.

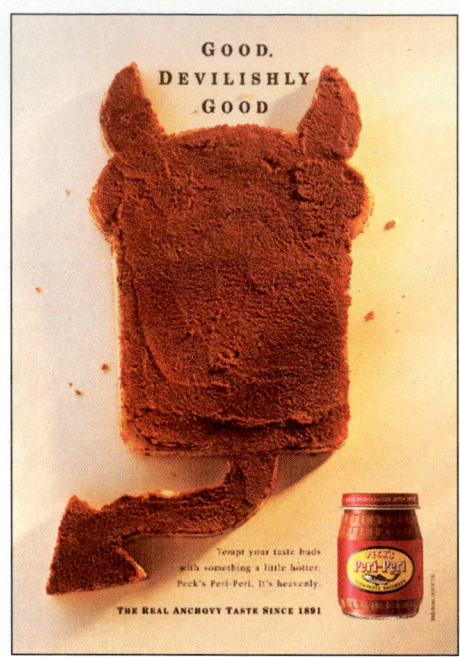

To reduce the risk of missing some basic variable that may help screen out a risky opportunity, marketing managers sometimes need a detailed analysis of the market environment they are considering entering. Such an analysis can reveal facts about an unfamiliar market that a manager in a distant country might otherwise overlook. Further, a local citizen who knows the marketing environment may be able to identify an "obvious" problem ignored even in a careful analysis. Thus, it is very useful for the analysis to include inputs from locals—perhaps cooperative middlemen.[26]

Risks vary with environmental sensitivity

The farther you go from familiar territory, the greater the risk of making big mistakes. But not all products—or marketing mixes—involve the same risk. Think of the risks as running along a "continuum of environmental sensitivity." See Exhibit 4–8.

Some products are relatively insensitive to the economic and cultural environment they're placed in. These products may be accepted as is—or may require just a little adaptation to make them suitable for local use. Most industrial products are near the insensitive end of this continuum.

At the other end of the continuum, we find highly sensitive products that may be difficult or impossible to adapt to all international situations. Consumer products closely linked to other social or cultural variables are at this end. For example, some of the scanty women's clothing popular in Western countries would be totally inappropriate in Arab countries where women are expected to cover even their faces. Similarly, some cultures view dieting as unhealthy; that explains why products like Diet Pepsi that are popular in the United States have done poorly there. "Faddy" type consumer products are also at this end of the

EXHIBIT 4–8   Continuum of Environmental Sensitivity

Insensitive		Sensitive
Industrial products	Basic commodity-type consumer products	Consumer products that are linked to cultural variables

continuum. It's sometimes difficult to understand why such products are well accepted in a home market. This, in turn, makes it even more difficult to predict how they might be received in a different environment.

This continuum helps explain why many of the early successes in international marketing were basic commodities such as gasoline, soap, transportation vehicles, mining equipment, and agricultural machinery. It also helps explain why some consumer products firms have been successful with basically the same promotion and products in different parts of the globe.

Yet some managers don't understand the reason for these successes. They think they can develop a global marketing mix for just about *any* product. They fail to see that firms producing and/or selling products near the sensitive end of the continuum should carefully analyze how their products will be seen and used in new environments—and plan their strategies accordingly. American-made blue jeans, for example, have been status symbols in Western Europe and Latin America—and producers have been able to sell them at premium prices through the best middlemen.[27]

What if risks are still hard to judge?

If the risks of an international opportunity are hard to judge, it may be wise to look first for opportunities that involve exporting. This gives managers a chance to build experience, know-how, and confidence over time. Then the firm will be in a better position to judge the prospects and risks of taking further steps.

CONCLUSION

Businesses need innovative strategy planning to survive in our increasingly competitive markets. In this chapter, we discussed the variables that shape the environment of marketing strategy planning—and how they may affect opportunities. First we looked at how the firm's own resources and objectives may help guide or limit the search for opportunities. Then, we went on to look at the external environments. They are important because changes in these environments present new opportunities—as well as problems—that a marketing manager must deal with in marketing strategy planning.

A manager must study the competitive environment. How well established are competitors? Are there competitive barriers, and what effect will they have? How will competitors respond to a plan?

The economic environment—including chances of recessions or inflation—also affects the choice of strategies. And the marketer must try to anticipate, understand, and deal with these changes—as well as changes in the technological base underlying the economic environment.

The marketing manager must also be aware of legal restrictions—and be sensitive to changing political climates. The acceptance of consumerism has already forced many changes.

The social and cultural environment affects how people behave and what marketing strategies will be successful.

Developing good marketing strategies within all these environments isn't easy. You can see that marketing management is a challenging job that requires integration of information from many disciplines.

Eventually, managers need procedures for screening and evaluating opportunities. We ex-

plained an approach for developing screening criteria—from an analysis of the strengths and weaknesses of the company's resources, the environmental trends it faces, and top management's objectives. We also considered some quantitative techniques for evaluating opportunities. And we discussed ways for evaluating and managing quite different opportunities—using the GE strategic planning grid, SBUs, and portfolio management.

Now we can go on—in the rest of the book—to discuss how to turn opportunities into profitable marketing plans and programs.

QUESTIONS AND PROBLEMS

1. Explain how a firm's objectives may affect its search for opportunities.

2. Specifically, how would various company objectives affect the development of a marketing mix for a new type of baby shoe? If this company were just being formed by a former shoemaker with limited financial resources, list the objectives the shoemaker might have. Then discuss how they would affect the development of the shoemaker's marketing strategy.

3. Explain how a firm's resources may limit its search for opportunities. Cite a specific example for a specific resource.

4. Discuss how a company's financial strength may have a bearing on the kinds of products it produces. Will it have an impact on the other three Ps as well? If so, how? Use an example in your answer.

5. In your own words, explain how a marketing manager might use a competitor analysis to avoid situations that involve head-on competition.

6. The owner of a small grocery store—the only one in a medium-sized town in the mountains—has just learned that a large chain plans to open a new store nearby. How difficult will it be for the owner to plan for this new competitive threat? Explain your answer.

7. Discuss the probable impact on your hometown if a major breakthrough in air transportation allowed foreign producers to ship into any U.S.

market for about the same transportation cost that domestic producers incur.

8. Will the elimination of trade barriers between countries in Europe eliminate the need to consider submarkets of European consumers? Why or why not?

9. Which way does the U.S. political and legal environment seem to be moving (with respect to business-related affairs)?

10. Why is it necessary to have so many laws regulating business? Why hasn't Congress just passed one set of laws for business problems?

11. What and whom is the U.S. government attempting to protect in its effort to preserve and regulate competition?

12. For each of the *major* laws discussed in the text, indicate whether in the long run the law will promote or restrict competition (see Exhibit 4–3). As a consumer without any financial interest in business, what is your reaction to each of these laws?

13. Are consumer protection laws really new? Discuss the evolution of consumer protection. Is more such legislation likely?

14. Explain the components of product-market screening criteria that can be used to evaluate opportunities.

15. Explain the differences between the total profit approach and the return-on-investment approach to evaluating alternative plans.

16. Explain General Electric's strategic planning grid approach to evaluating opportunities.

17. Distinguish between the operation of a strategic business unit and a firm that only pays lip service to adopting the marketing concept.

SUGGESTED CASES

2. Agricom, Inc.

6. Inland Steel Company

COMPUTER-AIDED PROBLEM

4. Competitor Analysis

Mediquip, Inc., produces medical equipment and uses its own sales force to sell the equipment to hospitals. Recently, several hospitals have asked Mediquip to develop a laser-beam "scalpel" for eye surgery. Mediquip has the needed resources, and 200 hospitals will probably buy the equipment. But Mediquip managers have heard that Laser Technologies—another quality producer—is thinking of competing for the same business. Mediquip has other good opportunities it could pursue—so it wants to see if it would have a competitive advantage over Laser Tech.

Mediquip and Laser Tech are similar in many ways, but there are important differences. Laser Technologies already produces key parts that are needed for the new laser product—so its production costs would be lower. It would cost Mediquip more to design the product—and getting parts from outside suppliers would result in higher production costs.

On the other hand, Mediquip has marketing strengths. It already has a good reputation with hospitals—and its sales force calls only on hospitals. Mediquip thinks that each of its current sales reps could spend some time selling the new product—and that it could adjust sales territories so only four more sales reps would be needed for good coverage in the market. In contrast, Laser Tech's sales reps call on only industrial customers, so it would have to add 14 reps to cover the hospitals.

Hospitals have budget pressures—so the supplier with the lowest price is likely to get a larger share of the business. But Mediquip knows that either supplier's price will be set high enough to cover the added costs of designing, producing, and selling the new product—and leave something for profit.

Mediquip gathers information about its own likely costs and can estimate Laser Tech's costs from industry studies and Laser Tech's annual report. Mediquip has set up a spreadsheet to evaluate the proposed new product.

a. The initial spreadsheet results are based on the assumption that Mediquip and Laser Tech will split the business 50/50. If Mediquip can win at least 50 percent of the market, does Mediquip have a competitive advantage over Laser Tech? Explain.

b. Because of economies of scale, both suppliers' average cost per machine will vary depending on the quantity sold. If Mediquip had only 45 percent of the market and Laser Tech 55 percent, how would their costs (average total cost per machine) compare? What if Mediquip had 55 percent of the market and Laser Tech only 45 percent? What conclusion do you draw from these analyses?

c. It is possible that Laser Tech may not enter the market. If Mediquip has 100 percent of the market, and quantity purchases from its suppliers will reduce the cost of producing one unit to $6,500, what price would cover all its costs and contribute $1,125 to profit for every machine sold? What does this suggest about the desirability of finding your own unsatisfied target markets? Explain.

For additional questions related to this problem, see Exercise 4–4 in the *Learning Aid for Use with Basic Marketing*, 12th edition.

5

Getting Information for Marketing Decisions

When You Finish This Chapter, You Should

1. Know about marketing information systems.

2. Understand a scientific approach to marketing research.

3. Know how to define and solve marketing problems.

4. Know about getting secondary and primary data.

5. Understand the role of observing, questioning, and using experimental methods in marketing research.

6. Understand the important new terms (shown in red).

LensCrafters has quickly become one of the largest chains of eyewear stores in the United States and Canada, and now it's developing new stores in the United Kingdom. A key to LensCrafters' success is that its managers use marketing research to better understand target market needs.

When LensCrafters was first evaluating the eye care market, a situation analysis revealed that there was a big opportunity. For example, library research revealed that 57 percent of people aged 18 or older wear eyeglasses, contact lenses, or both. Similarly, government statistics showed that demographic trends were favorable to long-run growth in the $10 billion a year eye care market.

Subsequent LensCrafters research provided guidance for turning this opportunity into a marketing strategy. Focus group interviews and consumer surveys confirmed that most consumers viewed shopping for glasses as very inconvenient. Frame selections were too small, opticians' shops were typically closed when customers were off work and had time to shop, and the whole process usually required long waits and repeat trips. So LensCrafters put the labs that make the glasses right in its stores and kept the stores open nights and weekends. Ads tout LensCrafters' high-quality, one-hour service.

To be sure that service quality lives up to the advertising promises, LensCrafters sends a cus-

tomer satisfaction survey to every customer. Surveys are analyzed by store and used to find out what's going on where. LensCrafters even ties satisfaction results to employee bonuses.

To make it convenient for more consumers to shop at LensCrafters, the chain has been aggressively opening up new stores. Because the size and the growth rate of various age groups in a geographic market drive demand for vision products, LensCrafters analyzes demographic data to locate new stores where profit potential is greatest. And each store carries a very large selection of frame styles tailored to the age, gender, and ethnic makeup of the local market.

Managers at LensCrafters also routinely analyze sales data that is available in the firm's marketing information system. By breaking down sales by product, store, and time period, they can spot buying trends early and plan for them.

Research also guides promotion decisions. For example, ad media that work well in Toronto are not used in Atlanta, where other media are better. Similarly, guided by research results, LensCrafters uses direct-mail advertising targeted to customers in segments where interest in its convenient eyeglass service is highest.

LensCrafters is doing well. Of course, you'd probably expect that from a firm that wisely uses marketing research to get a clear view of its market.[1]

Specialized computer software and hardware are available to make it easier for companies to gather and analyze marketing information.

MARKETING MANAGERS NEED INFORMATION

This example shows that successful planning of marketing strategies requires information—information about potential target markets and their likely responses to marketing mixes as well as about competition and other marketing environment variables. Information is also needed for implementation and control. Without good marketing information, managers have to use intuition or guesses—and in today's fast-changing and competitive markets, this invites failure.

Yet managers seldom have all the information they need to make the best decision. Both customers and competitors can be unpredictable. Getting more information may cost too much or take too long. For example, data on international markets is often incomplete, outdated, or difficult to obtain. So managers often must decide if they need more information and—if so—how to get it. In this chapter, we'll talk about how marketing managers can get the information they need to plan successful strategies.

MARKETING INFORMATION SYSTEMS CAN HELP

Marketing managers for some companies make decisions based almost totally on their own judgment—with very little hard data. When it's time to make a decision, they may wish they had more information. But by then it's too late to do anything about it, so they do without.

MIS makes available data accessible

There is a difference between information that is *available* and information that is readily *accessible*. Some information—such as the details of competitors' plans—is just not available. Some information is available but not without time-consuming collection. Such information is not really accessible. For example, a company may have records of customer purchases, what was sold by sales reps last month, or what is in the warehouse. But, if a manager can't get this information when it's needed, it isn't useful.

EXHIBIT 5–1   Elements of a Complete Marketing Information System

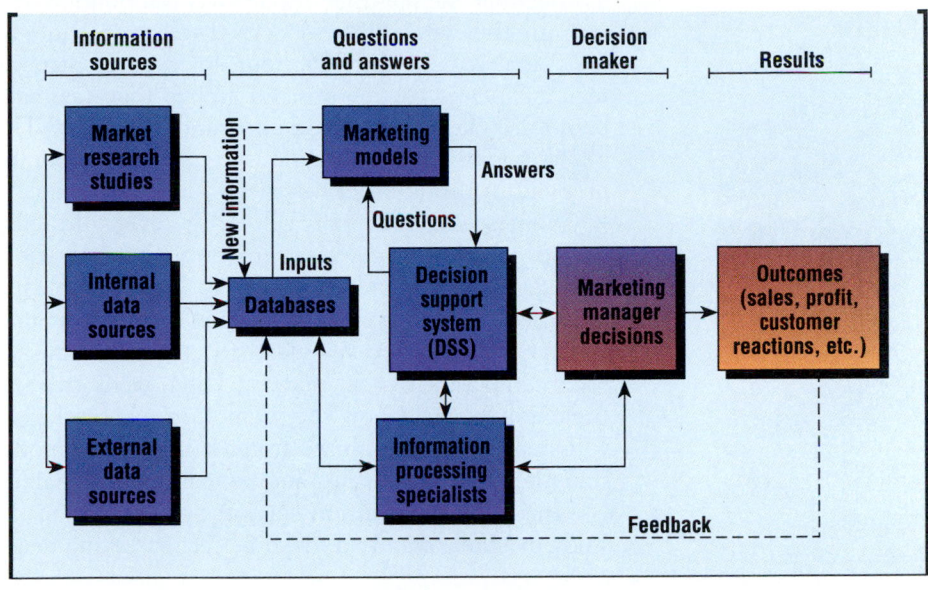

Some firms like LensCrafters have realized that it doesn't pay to wait until they have important questions they can't answer. They are working to develop a *continual flow of information*—and to make it more accessible to managers whenever they need it.

A **marketing information system (MIS)** is an organized way of continually gathering and analyzing data to provide marketing managers with information they need to make decisions. In some companies, an MIS is set up by marketing specialists. In other companies, it is set up by a group that provides *all* departments in the firm with information.

The technical details of setting up and running an MIS are beyond the scope of this course. But you should understand what an MIS is so you know some of the possibilities. Exhibit 5–1 shows the elements of a complete MIS.

Marketing managers must help develop an MIS

Marketing managers often don't know in advance exactly what questions they will have—or when. But they do know what data they've routinely used or needed in the past. They can also foresee what types of data might be useful. They should communicate these needs to the MIS manager so the information will be there when they want it.

Decision support systems put managers "on-line"

An MIS system organizes incoming data in a database so that it is available when needed. Most firms with an MIS have information processing specialists who help managers get standard reports and output from the database.

To get better decisions, some MIS systems provide marketing managers with a decision support system. A **decision support system (DSS)** is a computer program that makes it easy for a marketing manager to get and use information *as he or she is making decisions.* Typically the DSS helps change raw data—like product sales for the previous day—into more *useful information.* For example, it may draw graphs to show relationships in data—perhaps comparing yesterday's sales to the sales on the same day in the last four weeks. The MIS that managers at Frito-Lay use illustrates the possibilities.

All of Frito-Lay's salespeople are equipped with hand-held computers. Throughout the day they input sales information at the stores they visit. In the evening they send all the data over telephone lines to a central computer, where it is analyzed. Within 24 hours marketing managers at headquarters and in regional offices get reports and graphs that summarize how sales went the day before—broken down by brands and locations. The information system even allows a manager on a computer terminal to zoom in and take a closer look at a problem in Peoria or a sales success in Sacramento.[2]

Some decision support systems go even further. They allow the manager to see how answers to questions might change in various situations. For example, a manager at Kraft Foods may want to estimate how much sales will increase if the firm uses a certain type of promotion in a specific market area. The DSS will ask the manager for a *personal* judgment about how much business could be won from each competitor in that market. Then, using this input and drawing on data in the database about how the promotion had worked in other markets, the system will make a sales estimate using a marketing model. A **marketing model** is a statement of relationships among marketing variables.

In short, the decision support system puts managers "on-line" so they can study available data and make better marketing decisions—faster.[3]

Information makes managers greedy for more

Once marketing managers see how a functioning MIS—and perhaps a DSS—can help their decision making, they are eager for more information. They realize that they can improve all aspects of their planning—blending individual Ps, combining the four Ps into mixes, and developing and selecting plans. Further, they can monitor the implementation of current plans, comparing results against plans and making necessary changes more quickly. (Note: The sales and cost analysis techniques discussed in Chapter 20 are often used in an MIS.) Marketing information systems will become more widespread as managers become more sensitive to the possibilities and computer costs continue to drop.

Many firms are not there yet

Of course, not every firm has a complete MIS system. And in some firms that do, managers don't know how to use the system properly. A major problem is that many managers are used to doing it the old way—and they don't think through what information they need.

One sales manager thought he was progressive when he asked his assistant for an MIS report listing each sales rep's sales for the previous month and the current month. The assistant provided the report—but later was surprised to see the sales manager working on the list with a calculator. He was figuring the percentage change in sales for the month and ranking the reps from largest increase in sales to smallest. The computer could have done all of that—quickly—but the sales manager got what he *asked for*, not what he really needed. An MIS can provide information—but only the marketing manager knows what problem needs solving. It's the job of the manager—not the computer or the MIS specialist—to ask for the right information in the right form.

MIS use is growing rapidly

Marketing information systems will become even more widespread as marketing people become more sensitive to the possibilities. Some people think that only large firms can develop an effective MIS. Not so! In fact, just the opposite may be true. Low-cost microcomputers make a powerful MIS affordable—even for small firms. Further, big firms with complicated marketing programs often face a challenge trying to develop an MIS from scratch. Small firms can get started with a simple system and then expand it as needs expand. There is a lot of opportunity in this area for students who are able and willing to apply quantitative techniques to solve real marketing problems.[4]

New questions require new answers

MIS systems tend to focus on recurring information needs. Routinely analyzing such information can be valuable to marketing managers. But it shouldn't be their only source of information for decision making. They must try to satisfy ever changing needs in dynamic markets. So marketing research must be used—to supplement data already available in the MIS.

WHAT IS MARKETING RESEARCH?

Research provides a bridge to customers

The marketing concept says that marketing managers should meet the needs of customers. Yet today, many marketing managers are isolated in company offices—far from potential customers. It is just not possible for managers to keep up with all of the changes taking place in their markets.

This means marketing managers have to rely on help from **marketing research**—procedures to develop and analyze new information to help marketing managers make decisions. One of the important jobs of a marketing researcher is to get the "facts" that are not currently available in the MIS.

Continued improvements in research methods are making marketing research information more dependable. This has encouraged firms to put more money and trust in research. Managers in some consumer product companies don't make any major decisions without the support—and sometimes even the official approval—of the marketing research department. As a result, some marketing research directors rise to high levels in the organization.

Who does the work?

Most large companies have a separate marketing research department to plan and carry out research projects. These departments often use outside specialists—including interviewing and tabulating services—to handle technical assignments. Further, they may call in specialized marketing consultants and marketing research organizations to take charge of a research project.

Small companies (those with less than $4 or $5 million in sales) usually don't have separate marketing research departments. They often depend on their salespeople or managers to conduct what research they do.

Some nonprofit organizations have begun to use marketing research—usually with the help of outside specialists. For example, many politicians rely on research firms to conduct surveys of voter attitudes.[5]

❓ Ethical issues in marketing research

The basic reason for doing marketing research is to get information that people can trust in making decisions. But, as you will see in this chapter, research often involves many hidden details. A person who wants to misuse marketing research to pursue a personal agenda can often do so.

Perhaps the most common ethical issues concern decisions to withhold certain information about the research. For example, a manager might selectively share only those results that support his or her viewpoint. Others involved in a decision might never know that they are getting only partial truths. Or, during a set of interviews, a researcher may discover that consumers are interpreting a poorly worded question many different ways. If the researcher doesn't admit the problem, an unknowing manager may rely on meaningless results.

Another problem involves more blatant abuses. It is unethical for a firm to contact consumers under the pretense of doing research when the real purpose is to sell something. For example, some political organizations have been criticized for surveying consumers to find out their attitudes about various political candidates and issues. Then, armed with that information, someone else calls back to solicit donations. Legitimate marketing researchers are very concerned about such abuses. If the problem were to become widespread, consumers might not be willing to participate in any research.

The relationship between the researcher and the manager sometimes creates an ethical conflict, especially when the research is done by an outside firm. Managers must be careful not to send a signal that the only acceptable results from a research project are ones that confirm their existing viewpoints. Researchers are supposed to be objective, but that objectivity may be swayed if future jobs depend on getting the "right" results.

Effective research usually requires cooperation

Good marketing research requires much more than just technical tools. It requires cooperation between researchers and marketing managers. Good marketing researchers must keep both marketing research *and* marketing management in mind to be sure their research focuses on real problems.

Marketing managers must be involved in marketing research too. Many marketing research details can be handled by company or outside experts. But marketing managers must be able to explain what their problems are—and what kinds of information they need. They should be able to communicate with specialists in the specialists' language. Marketing managers may only be "consumers" of research. But they should be informed consumers—able to explain exactly what they want from the research. They should also know about some of the basic decisions made during the research process so they know the limitations of the findings.

For this reason, our discussion of marketing research won't emphasize mechanics—but rather how to plan and evaluate the work of marketing researchers.[6]

THE SCIENTIFIC METHOD AND MARKETING RESEARCH

The scientific method—combined with the strategy planning framework we discussed in Chapter 2—can help marketing managers make better decisions.

The **scientific method** is a decision-making approach that focuses on being objective and orderly in *testing* ideas before accepting them. With the scientific method, managers don't just *assume* that their intuition is correct. Instead, they use their intuition and observations to develop **hypotheses**—educated guesses about the relationships between things or about what will happen in the future. Then they test their hypotheses before making final decisions.

A manager who relies only on intuition might introduce a new product without testing consumer response. But a manager who uses the scientific method might say, "I think (hypothesize) that consumers currently using the most popular brand will prefer our new product. Let's run some consumer tests. If at least 60 percent of the consumers prefer our product, we can introduce it in a regional test market. If it doesn't pass the consumer test there, we can make some changes and try again."

EXHIBIT 5–2   Five-Step Scientific Approach to Marketing Research Process

The scientific method forces an orderly research process. Some managers don't carefully specify what information they need. They blindly move ahead—hoping that research will provide "the answer." Other managers may have a clearly defined problem or question but lose their way after that. These hit-or-miss approaches waste both time and money.

FIVE-STEP APPROACH TO MARKETING RESEARCH

The **marketing research process** is a five-step application of the scientific method that includes:

1. Defining the problem.
2. Analyzing the situation.
3. Getting problem-specific data.
4. Interpreting the data.
5. Solving the problem.

Exhibit 5–2 shows the five steps in the process. Note that the process may lead to a solution before all of the steps are completed. Or, as the feedback arrows show, researchers may return to an earlier step if needed. For example, the interpreting step may point to a new question—or reveal the need for additional information—before a final decision can be made.

DEFINING THE PROBLEM—STEP 1

Defining the problem is the most important—and often the most difficult—step in the marketing research process. Sometimes it takes over half the total time spent on a research project. But it's time well spent if the objectives of the research are clearly defined. The best research job on the wrong problem is wasted effort.

Finding the right problem level almost solves the problem

The strategy planning framework introduced in Chapter 2 can be useful here. It can help the researcher identify the real problem area—and what information is needed. Do we really know enough about our target markets to work out all of the four Ps? Do we know enough to decide what celebrity to use in an ad—or how to handle a price war in New York City or Tokyo? If not, we may want to do research rather than rely on intuition.

The importance of understanding the problem—and then trying to solve it—can be seen in the introduction of Fab One Shot, a laundry product developed to clean, soften, and reduce static cling all in one step. Marketing managers were sure that Fab One Shot was going to appeal to heavy users—especially working women with large families. As one manager summarized the situation, "Our research showed that while over 50 percent of women were going back to work, 70 percent were still responsible for the family wash . . . and 80 percent use three different laundry products. These women are looking for convenience."

When marketing managers found that other firms were testing similar products, they rushed Fab One Shot into distribution. To encourage first-time purchases, they offered introductory price discounts, coupons, and rebates. And they supported the sales promotion with heavy advertising on TV programs that research showed the heavy users watched.

However, research never addressed the problem of how the heavy user target market would react. After the introductory price-off deals were dropped, sales dropped off too. While the product was convenient, heavy users weren't willing to pay the price—about 25 cents for each washload. For the heavy users, price was a qualifying dimension. And these consumers didn't like Fab's premeasured packets because they had no control over how much detergent they could put in. The competing firms recognized these problems at the research stage—and decided not to introduce their products.

After the fact, it was clear that Fab One Shot was most popular with college students, singles, and people living in small apartments. They didn't use much—so the convenience benefit offset the high price. But the company never targeted those segments. It just assumed that it would be profitable to target the big market of heavy users.[7]

The moral of this story is that our strategy planning framework is useful for guiding the problem definition step—as well as the whole marketing research process. First, a marketing manager should understand the target market—and what needs the firm can satisfy. Then the manager can focus on lower-level problems—namely, how sensitive the target market is to a change in one or more of the marketing mix ingredients. Without such a framework, marketing researchers can waste time—and money—working on the wrong problem.

Don't confuse problems with symptoms

The problem definition step sounds simple—and that's the danger. It's easy to confuse symptoms with the problem. Suppose a firm's MIS shows that the company's sales are decreasing in certain territories while expenses are remaining the same—resulting in a decline in profits. Will it help to define the problem by asking: How can we stop the sales decline? Probably not. This would be like fitting a hearing-impaired patient with a hearing aid without first trying to find out *why* the patient was having trouble hearing.

It's easy to fall into the trap of mistaking symptoms for the problem. When this happens, the research objectives are not clear, and researchers may ignore relevant questions—while analyzing unimportant questions in expensive detail.

Setting research objectives may require more understanding

Sometimes the research objectives are very clear. A manager wants to know if the targeted households have tried a new product and what percent of them bought it a second time. But research objectives aren't always so simple. The manager might also want to know *why* some didn't buy—or whether they had even heard of the product. Companies rarely have enough time and money to study everything. Managers must narrow their research objectives. One good way is to develop a list of research questions that includes all the possible problem areas. Then managers can consider the items on the list more completely—in the situation analysis step—before they narrow down to final research objectives.

ANALYZING THE SITUATION—STEP 2

What information do we already have?

When the marketing manager thinks the real problem has begun to surface, a situation analysis is useful. A **situation analysis** is an informal study of what information is already available in the problem area. It can help define the problem and specify what additional information—if any—is needed.

Pick the brains around you

The situation analysis usually involves informal talks with informed people. Informed people can be others in the firm, a few good middlemen who have close contact with customers, or others knowledgeable about the industry. In industrial markets—where relationships with customers are close—researchers may even call the customers themselves. Informed customers may have already worked on the same problem—or know about a source of helpful information. Their inputs can help to sharpen the problem definition too.

Situation analysis helps educate a researcher

The situation analysis is especially important if the researcher is a research specialist who doesn't know much about the management decisions to be made—or if the marketing manager is dealing with unfamiliar areas. They both must be sure they understand the problem area—including the nature of the target market, the marketing mix, competition, and other external factors. Otherwise, the researcher may rush ahead and make costly mistakes—or simply discover facts that management already knows. The following case illustrates this danger.

A marketing manager at the home office of a large retail chain hired a research firm to do in-store interviews to learn what customers liked most—and least—about some of its stores in other cities. Interviewers diligently filled out their questionnaires. When the results came in, it was apparent that neither the marketing manager nor the researcher had done the required homework. No one had even talked with the local store managers! Several of the stores were in the middle of some messy remodeling—so all the customers' responses concerned the noise and dust from the construction. The research was a waste of money. You can imagine why this retailer—one of the largest in the country—doesn't want to be named! But the point is: Even big companies make marketing research mistakes if they don't take the situation analysis seriously.

Secondary data may provide the answers— or some background

The situation analysis should also find relevant **secondary data**—information that has been collected or published already. Later, in Step 3, we will cover **primary data**—information specifically collected to solve a current problem. Too often researchers rush to gather primary data when much relevant secondary information is already available—at little or no cost! See Exhibit 5–3.

EXHIBIT 5-3 Sources of Secondary and Primary Data

Much secondary data is available

Ideally, much secondary data is already available from the firm's MIS. Data that has not been organized in an MIS may be available from the company's files and reports. Secondary data also is available from libraries, trade associations, government agencies, and private research organizations.

One of the first places a researcher should look for secondary data—after looking within the firm—is a good library. The *Index of Business Periodicals* helps identify published references to a topic.

Many computerized database and index services are available through libraries and private firms. Lockheed's DIALOGUE system, for example, allows a distant researcher to access a computer and get summaries of articles written on a specific subject. Similarly, ABI Inform is an on-line service that indexes approximately 800 Canadian and U.S. business periodicals. A computerized search can be a big time saver and help the researcher cover all the bases.

Government data is inexpensive

Federal and state governments publish data on many subjects. Government data is often useful in estimating the size of markets. In the next chapter—and throughout the book—you will get a feel for what types of data are available. Almost all government data is available in inexpensive publications. Much of it is also available in computer form ready for further analysis.

Sometimes it's more practical to use summary publications for leads to more detailed documents. For the U.S. market, one of the most useful summaries is the *Statistical Abstract of the United States*. Like an almanac, it is issued each year and gives 1,500 summary tables from more than 200 published sources. Detailed footnotes guide readers to more specific information on a topic. Similarly, the *United Nations Statistical Yearbook* is one of the finest summaries of worldwide data.

Secondary data is very limited on some international markets. However, most countries with advanced economies have government agencies that help researchers get the data they need. For example, Statistics Canada compiles a great deal of information on the Canadian market. Eurostat, the statistical office for the European Community countries, and the Organization for Economic Cooperation (in Paris) offer many publications packed with data on Europe. In the United States, the Department of Commerce distributes statistics compiled by all other federal departments. Commerce Department branch and field offices in many major cities provide assistance in locating specific data. Some city and state governments have similar agencies for local data. For example, if a swimming pool company wants leads on new prospects and knows that a building permit is needed to build a new home, the company could check the county's building permit list and call the owners—before the homes are finished.

Private sources are useful too

Many private research organizations—as well as advertising agencies, newspapers, and magazines—regularly compile and publish data. A good business library is valuable for sources such as *Sales & Marketing Management*, *Advertising Age*, *Journal of Global Marketing*, and the publications of the National Industrial Conference Board. Some information is available inexpensively as a customer service to clients of advertising agencies or buyers of advertising space or time. Often a company's suppliers can provide useful information.

The *Encyclopedia of Associations* lists 75,000 U.S. and international trade and professional associations that can be good sources of information. For example, the American Marketing Association has an information center with many marketing publications; most other developed nations have a similar association for marketing professions.

Most trade associations compile data from and for their members. Some also publish magazines that focus on important topics in the industry. *Chain Store Age,* for example, has much information on retailing.

Standard & Poor's Industry Surveys is another source of information on whole industries. And the local telephone company or your library usually has copies of the Yellow Pages for many cities. Similarly, a number of firms sell computer CD-ROM discs that include all of the businesses in the country. Resources such as these may be a big help in estimating the amount of competition in certain lines of business—and where it is located.[8]

Situation analysis yields a lot—for very little

The virtue of a good situation analysis is that it can be very informative but takes little time. And it's inexpensive compared with more formal research efforts—like a large-scale survey. Situation analysis can help focus further research—or even eliminate the need for it entirely. The situation analyst is really trying to determine the exact nature of the situation—and the problem. Too-hasty researchers may try to skip this step in their rush to get out questionnaires. Often these researchers find the real problem only when the questionnaires come back—and they must start over. One marketing expert put it this way: "Some people never have time to do research right the first time, but they seem to have time to do it over again."

Determine what else is needed

At the end of the situation analysis, you can see which research questions—from the list developed during the problem definition step—remain unanswered. Then you have to decide exactly what information you need to answer those questions—and how to get it.

This may require discussion between technical experts and the marketing manager. Often companies use a written **research proposal**—a plan that specifies what information will be obtained and how—to be sure no misunderstandings occur later. The research plan may include information about costs, what data will be collected, how it will be collected, who will analyze it and how, and how long the process will take. Then the marketing manager must decide if it makes sense to go ahead—if the time and costs involved seem worthwhile. It's foolish to pay $100,000 for information to solve a $50,000 problem! When the decision is not clear-cut, marketing managers should know more about the next steps in the marketing research process.

GETTING PROBLEM-SPECIFIC DATA—STEP 3

<table>
<tr><td>Gathering primary data</td><td>The next step is to plan a formal research project to gather primary data. There are different methods for collecting primary data. Which approach to use depends on the nature of the problem and how much time and money are available.

In most primary data collection, the researcher tries to learn what customers think about some topic—or how they behave under some conditions. There are two basic methods for obtaining information about customers: *questioning* and *observing*. Questioning can range from qualitative to quantitative research. And many kinds of observing are possible.</td></tr>
<tr><td>Qualitative questioning—open-ended with a hidden purpose</td><td>**Qualitative research** seeks in-depth, open-ended responses, not yes or no answers. The researcher tries to get people to share their thoughts on a topic—without giving them many directions or guidelines about what to say.

A researcher might ask different consumers, "What do you think about when you decide where to shop for food?" One person may talk about convenient location, another about service, and others about the quality of the fresh produce. The real advantage of this approach is *depth*. Each person can be asked follow-up questions so the researcher really understands what *that* respondent is thinking. The depth of the qualitative approach gets at the details—even if the researcher needs a lot of judgment to summarize it all.

Some types of qualitative research don't use specific questions. For example, a cartoon may show a situation—such as a woman and a man buying coffee in a supermarket. The respondent may be asked to explain what the woman is saying to the man. Or the consumer might simply be shown a product or an ad and asked to comment.</td></tr>
</table>

Focus groups stimulate discussion

The most widely used form of qualitative questioning in marketing research is the **focus group interview**, which involves interviewing 6 to 10 people in an informal group setting. The focus group also uses open-ended questions, but here the interviewer wants to get group interaction—to stimulate thinking and get immediate reactions.

A skilled focus group leader can learn a lot from this approach. A typical session may last an hour, so participants can cover a lot of ground. Sessions are often videotaped (or broadcast by satellite) so different managers can form their own impressions of what happened.[9] However, conclusions reached from watching a focus group session vary depending on who watches it! A typical

Renfro Corporation, a producer of socks, strengthens its relationships with retailers by sharing market research information, including competitive shopping analyses, consumer preference studies, and focus group results. Its MIS also allows it to custom-tailor the product mix for a particular retailer and provide faster deliveries.

problem—and serious limitation—with qualitative research is that it's hard to measure the results objectively. The results seem to depend so much on the viewpoint of the researcher. In addition, people willing to participate in a focus group—especially those who talk the most—may not be representative of the broader target market.

Focus groups can be conducted quickly and at relatively low cost—an average of about $3,500 each. This is part of their appeal. But focus groups are probably being overused. It's easy to fall into the trap of treating an idea arising from a focus group as a "fact" that applies to a broad target market.

To avoid this trap, some researchers use qualitative research to prepare for quantitative research. For example, the Jacksonville Symphony Orchestra wanted to broaden its base of support and increase ticket sales. It hired a marketing research firm to conduct focus group interviews with small groups of current subscribers, former subscribers, and qualified prospects. These interviews helped the marketing managers refine their ideas about what these target "customers" liked and did not like about the orchestra—and what kinds of music future audiences might want. The ideas were then tested with a larger, more representative sample. Interviewers telephoned 500 people and asked them how interested they would be in various orchestra programs, event locations, and guest artists. Then they planned their promotion and the orchestra's program for the year based on the research. The result? Subscription ticket sales nearly doubled from the previous year.[10]

As this example suggests, qualitative research can provide good ideas—hypotheses. But we need other approaches—perhaps based on more representative samples and objective measures—to *test* the hypotheses.

A skilled leader can learn a lot from a focus group, like this one in which the group is reacting to different brands of toothpaste.

Structured questioning gives more objective results

When researchers use identical questions and response alternatives, they can summarize the information quantitatively. Samples can be larger and more representative, and various statistics can be used to draw conclusions. For these reasons, most survey research is **quantitative research**—which seeks structured responses that can be summarized in numbers, like percentages, averages, or other statistics. For example, a marketing researcher might calculate what percentage of respondents have tried a new product—and then figure an average "score" for how satisfied they were.

Fixed responses speed answering and analysis

Survey questionnaires usually provide fixed responses to questions to simplify analysis of the replies. This multiple-choice approach also makes it easier and faster for respondents to reply. Simple fill-in-a-number questions are also widely used in quantitative research. A questionnaire might ask an industrial buyer, "From approximately how many suppliers do you currently purchase electronic parts?" Fixed responses are also more convenient for computer analysis, which is how most surveys are analyzed.

Quantitative measures of attitudes too

One common approach to measuring consumers' attitudes and opinions is to have respondents indicate how much they agree or disagree with a questionnaire statement. A researcher interested in what target consumers think about frozen pizzas, for example, might include statements like those at the top of Exhibit 5–4.

Another approach is to have respondents *rate* a product, feature, or store. Exhibit 5–4 shows commonly used rating "scales." Sometimes rating scales are labeled with adjectives like *excellent, good, fair,* and *poor.*

EXHIBIT 5–4 Sample Questioning Methods to Measure Attitudes and Opinions

A. Please check your level of agreement with each of the following statements.

	Strongly Agree	Agree	Uncertain	Disagree	Strongly Disagree
1. I add extra toppings when I prepare a frozen pizza.	___	___	___	___	___
2. A frozen pizza dinner is more expensive than eating at a fast-food restaurant.	___	___	___	___	___

B. Please rate how important each of the following is to you in selecting a brand of frozen pizza:

	Not at all Important					Very Important
1. Price per serving	___	___	___	___	___	___
2. Toppings available	___	___	___	___	___	___
3. Amount of cheese	___	___	___	___	___	___
4. Cooking time	___	___	___	___	___	___

C. Please check the rating that best describes your feelings about the last frozen pizza you prepared.

	Poor	Fair	Good	Excellent
1. Price per serving	___	___	___	___
2. Toppings available	___	___	___	___
3. Amount of cheese	___	___	___	___
4. Cooking time	___	___	___	___

Surveys by mail, phone, or in person

Decisions about what specific questions to ask—and how to ask them—are usually related to how respondents will be contacted—by mail, on the phone, or in person.

Mail surveys are the most common and convenient

The mail questionnaire is useful when extensive questioning is necessary. With a mail questionnaire, respondents can complete the questions at their convenience. They may be more willing to fill in personal or family characteristics—since a mail questionnaire can be returned anonymously. But the questions must be simple and easy to follow since no interviewer is there to help.

A big problem with mail questionnaires is that many people don't complete or return them. The **response rate**—the percent of people contacted who complete the questionnaire—is often only around 25 percent in consumer surveys. And it can be even lower. Also, respondents may not be representative. People who are most interested in the questionnaire topic may respond—but answers from this group may be very different from the answers of a typical "don't care" group.[11]

Mail surveys are economical if a large number of people respond. But they may be quite expensive if the response rate is low. Further, it can take a month or more to get the data—too slow for some decisions. Moreover, it is difficult to get respondents to expand on particular points. In markets where illiteracy is a problem, it may not be possible to get any response. In spite of these limitations, the convenience and economy of mail surveys make them popular for collecting primary data.

Telephone surveys—fast and effective

Telephone interviews are growing in popularity. They are effective for getting quick answers to simple questions. Telephone interviews allow the interviewer to probe and really learn what the respondent is thinking. On the other hand, some consumers find calls intrusive—and about a third refuse to answer any questions. Moreover, the telephone is usually not a very good contact method if the interviewer is trying to get confidential personal information—such as details of family income. Respondents are not certain who is calling or how such personal information might be used.

Research firms—with up to 50 interviewers calling at the same time on long-distance lines—can complete 1,000 or more interviews in one evening. In addition, with computer-aided telephone interviewing, answers are immediately recorded on a computer, resulting in fast data analysis. The popularity of telephone surveys is partly due to their speed and high response rates.[12]

Personal interview surveys—can be in-depth

A personal interview survey is usually much more expensive per interview than a mail or telephone survey. But it's easier to get and keep the respondent's attention when the interviewer is right there. The interviewer can also help explain complicated directions—and perhaps get better responses. For these reasons, personal interviews are commonly used for research on business customers. To reduce the cost of locating consumer respondents, interviews are sometimes done at a store or shopping mall. This is called a mall intercept interview because the interviewer stops a shopper and asks for responses to the survey.

Researchers have to be careful that having an interviewer involved doesn't affect the respondent's answers. Sometimes people won't give an answer they consider embarrassing. Or they may try to impress or please the interviewer. Further, in some cultures people don't want to give any information. For example, many people in Africa, Latin America, and Eastern Europe are reluctant to be interviewed. This is also a problem in many low-income, inner-city areas in the United States; even Census Bureau interviewers have trouble getting cooperation.

Sometimes questioning has limitations. Then observing may be more accurate or economical.

Observing—what you see is what you get

Observing—as a method of collecting data—focuses on a well-defined problem. Here we are not talking about the casual observations that may stimulate ideas in the early steps of a research project. With the observation method, researchers try to see or record what the subject does naturally. They don't want the observing to *influence* the subject's behavior.

A museum director wanted to know which of the many exhibits was most popular. A survey didn't help. Visitors seemed to want to please the interviewer—and usually said that all of the exhibits were interesting. Putting observers near

After extensive research with French consumers, including mall intercept interviews like the one shown here, Colgate-France improved the marketing mix for its Plax mouthwash, which is now the number one mouthwash outside the U.S.

exhibits—to record how long visitors spent at each one—didn't help either. The curious visitors stood around to see what the observer was recording, and that messed up the measures. Finally, the museum floors were waxed to a glossy shine. Several weeks later, the floors around the exhibits were inspected. It was easy to tell which exhibits were most popular—based on how much wax had worn off the floor!

In some situations, consumers are recorded on videotape. Later, researchers can study the tape by running the film at very slow speed or actually analyzing each frame. Researchers use this technique to study the routes consumers follow through a grocery store—or how they select products in a department store.

Similarly, many franchise companies use the observation method— to check how well a franchisee is performing. KFC hires people to go to different KFC stores and act like normal customers. Then, they report back to KFC on how they were treated, the quality of the service and food, and the cleanliness of the store.

Observation data can be plotted on graphs or maps. A shopping center developer wondered if one of its shopping centers was attracting customers from all the surrounding areas. The developer hired a firm to record the license plate numbers of cars in the parking lot. Using registration information, the firm obtained the addresses of all license holders and plotted them on a map. Very few customers were coming from one large area. The developer aimed direct-mail advertising at that area and generated a lot of new business.

Observing is common in advertising research

Observation methods are common in advertising research. For example, A.C. Nielsen Company has developed a device called the "people meter" that adapts the observation method to television audience research. This machine is attached to the TV set in the homes of selected families. It records when the set is on and what station is tuned in. Nielsen uses the results to rate the popularity of TV

WHIRLPOOL HEATS UP SALES WITH MARKETING RESEARCH

Marketing managers at Whirlpool want to build a profitable, long-lasting relationship with the customers that they serve—and to bring new consumers into the fold. Each year the firm mails an appliance satisfaction survey to 180,000 households. Respondents rate all of their appliances on dozens of dimensions. When a competing product scores higher, Whirlpool engineers take it apart to see why and build the best ideas into their new models. However, they don't just wait for competitors to figure things out first.

A new oven, one of Whirlpool's hottest sellers, illustrates their approach. A survey showed that consumers wanted an oven with easy-to-clean controls. That didn't seem consistent with previous sales patterns; the firm's MIS showed that models with knobs consistently outsold models with easier-to-clean push buttons. Rather than disregard the survey, Whirlpool designed a range with touch pad controls

by listening to consumers at every step along the way. Consumers who played with computer simulations of the touch pad explained what they liked and didn't. Videotapes of consumers who tried prototype models in mall intercept interviews provided ideas to further refine the design. The result is a touch pad control that is easy to clean and so easy to use that consumers don't even need to read the manual.

Consumer research has been an even more important factor in Whirlpool's growth overseas. For example, until recently only about one-third of European households had a microwave oven. Whirlpool researchers learned that more people would buy a microwave oven if it could crisp food as it heated the food. Whirlpool designed a microwave with a broiler coil and other innovations. The result is an oven that is popular in Britain for frying bacon and eggs and in Italy for crisping pizza crusts.[13]

---

shows. Some claim that once families get used to the meter, it no longer influences their behavior. Note, however, that the meter only records what channel is on—not whether anyone is watching.

Checkout scanners see a lot

Computerized scanners at retail checkout counters, a major breakthrough in observing, help researchers collect very specific—and useful—information. Often this type of data feeds directly into a firm's MIS. Managers of a big department store can see exactly what products have sold each day—and how much money each department earned. But the scanner also has wider applications for marketing research.

Information Resources, Inc., and A.C. Nielsen use **consumer panels**—a group of consumers who provide information on a continuing basis. Whenever a panel member shops for groceries, he or she gives an ID number to the clerk, who keys in the number. Then the scanner records every purchase—including brands, sizes, prices, and any coupons used. For a fee, clients can evaluate actual customer purchase patterns—and answer questions about the effectiveness of their discount coupons. Did the coupons draw new customers, or did current customers simply use them to stock up? If consumers switched from another brand, did they go back to their old brand the next time? The answers to such questions are important in planning marketing strategies—and scanners can help marketing managers get the answers.

Some members of the consumer panel are also tied into a special TV cable system. With this system, a company can direct advertisements to some houses and not others. Then researchers can evaluate the effect of the ads by comparing the purchases of consumers who saw the ads with those who didn't.

Data from electronic scanners helps retailers decide what brands they will sell and helps their suppliers plan so that products arrive at the store in time to prevent stock-outs.

The use of scanners to "observe" what customers actually do is changing consumer research methods. Companies can turn to firms like Information Resources as a *single source* of complete information about customers' attitudes, shopping behavior, and media habits.

Data captured by electronic scanners is equally important in business-to-business markets. Increasingly, firms mark their shipping cartons and packages with computer-readable bar codes that make it fast and easy to track inventory, shipments, orders, and the like. As information about product sales or shipments becomes available, it is instantly included in the MIS. That way, a manager can access any detailed piece of information or do an analysis to summarize trends and patterns. Here, as with scanner data on consumers, the information available is so detailed that the possibilities are limited more by imagination—and money—than by technology.[14]

Experimental method controls conditions

A marketing manager can get a different kind of information—with either questioning or observing—using the experimental method. With the **experimental method**, researchers compare the responses of two (or more) groups that are similar except on the characteristic being tested. Researchers want to learn if the specific characteristic—which varies among groups—*causes* differences in some response among the groups. For example, a researcher might be interested in comparing responses of consumers who had seen an ad for a new product with consumers who had not seen the ad. The "response" might be an observed behavior—like the purchase of a product—or the answer to a specific question—like "How interested are you in this new product?"

Marketing managers for Mars—the company that makes Snickers candy bars—used the experimental method to help solve a problem. Other candy and snack foods were taking customers. But why? Surveys showed that many consumers thought candy bars were becoming too small. But they also didn't want to pay more for a larger bar. Mars' managers wanted to know if making their candy bar bigger would increase sales enough to offset the higher cost. To decide, they conducted a marketing experiment.

Simmons' ad agency used an experiment to improve a new print ad for the Beautyrest mattress. Groups of consumers saw two different ads. The ads were the same, except that one featured a father holding a baby and the other featured a mother. The ad with the father earned higher recall scores.

The company carefully varied the size of candy bars sold in *different* markets. Otherwise, the marketing mix stayed the same. Then researchers tracked sales in each market area to see the effect of the different sizes. They saw a difference—a big difference—immediately. It was clear that added sales would more than offset the cost of a bigger candy bar. So marketing managers at Mars made a decision that took them in the opposite direction from other candy companies. And, yes, it proved to be a sweet success.

Test-marketing of new products is another type of marketing experiment. In a typical approach, a company tries variations on its planned marketing mix in a few geographic market areas. The results of the tests help to identify problems or refine the marketing mix—before deciding to go to broader distribution. However, alert competitors may disrupt such tests—perhaps by increasing promotion or offering retailers extra discounts. To avoid these problems, some small firms conduct some of their tests in foreign markets. For example, Carewell, producer of Dentax toothbrushes, tested its new line and various in-store promotions in Singapore and Malta before trying to enter the very competitive U.S. market. Similarly, the firm that makes Pudgies baby wipes did its test-market experiments in the United Kingdom.

Researchers don't use the experimental method as often as surveys and focus groups because it's hard to set up controlled situations where only one marketing variable is different. But there are probably other reasons too. Many managers don't understand the valuable information they can get from this method. Further, they don't like the idea of some researcher "experimenting" with their business.[15]

Syndicated research shares data collection costs

Some private research firms specialize in collecting data and supplying it to managers in many different client firms. Often the marketing manager subscribes to the research service and gets regular updates.

The producers of Dentax toothbrushes and Pudgies baby wipes did test-market experiments in overseas markets—where competitors were less likely to disrupt the results.

Marketing managers from many different firms may have to make the same kinds of decisions—and need the same type of data. The most economical approach in a situation like this is for one specialist firm to collect the data and distribute it to the different users, who share the cost. This is how Information Resources, Inc., and A.C. Nielsen operate.

Many other firms collect and distribute specialized types of data. For example, Market Facts sells access to its surveys on home appliances and electronics, retail banking and insurance, and other product categories. Simmons Market Research Bureau does extensive research on consumer media habits and then sells its data to many advertising agencies and producers of consumer products who want to find out about their particular target markets. Many different auto producers use J. D. Power's surveys of customer satisfaction—often as the basis for advertising claims. Subscription data services are available for numerous different industries—ranging from food service to prescription drugs to micro-electronic devices.[16]

INTERPRETING THE DATA—STEP 4

What does it really mean?

After someone collects the data, it has to be analyzed to decide what it all means. In quantitative research, this step usually involves statistics. **Statistical packages**—easy-to-use computer programs that analyze data—have made this step easier. As we noted earlier, some firms provide *decision support systems* so managers can use a statistical package to interpret data themselves. More often, however, technical specialists are involved at the interpretation step.

Cross-tabulation is one of the most frequently used approaches for analyzing and interpreting marketing research data. It shows the relationship of answers to two different questions. Exhibit 5–5 is an example. In this case, a telephone company was interested in learning more about customers who had adopted its Touch-Tone dialing service. With a survey, the firm asked customers if they had moved in the last year. The survey also asked if they had adopted the Touch-Tone service. Then, the answers to the two questions were cross-tabulated. The results of the analysis showed that customers who had moved in the last year were much

SPSS and STATGRAPHICS are statistical packages that make it easy to summarize and graph marketing research data.

more likely than nonmovers to have adopted the Touch-Tone service. So the researchers concluded that people who had just moved were a prime target market for the service.

Cross-tabulation is popular because the results are usually easy to interpret. But there are many other approaches for statistical analysis—the best one depends on the situation. The details of statistical analysis are beyond the scope of this book. But a good manager should know enough (and be able to ask enough good questions) to understand what a research project can—and can't—do.[17]

Is your sample really representative?

It's usually impossible for marketing managers to collect all the information they want about everyone in a **population**—the total group they are interested in. Marketing researchers typically study only a **sample**, a part of the relevant population. How well a sample *represents* the total population affects the results. Results from a sample that is not representative may not give a true picture.

The manager of a retail store might want a phone survey to learn what consumers think about the store's hours. If interviewers make all of the calls during the day, the sample will not be representative. Consumers who work outside the home during the day won't have an equal chance of being included. Those interviewed might say the limited store hours are "satisfactory." Yet it would be a mistake to assume that *all* consumers are satisfied. Marketing managers must be aware of how representative a sample really is.

Random samples tend to be representative

You can see that getting a representative sample is very important. One method of doing so is **random sampling**, where each member of the population has the same chance of being included in the sample. Great care must be used to ensure that sampling is really random—not just haphazard.

EXHIBIT 5–5 Cross-Tabulation Breakdown of Responses to a Phone Company Consumer Survey

		Have You Moved in the Last Year?		
	Answers:	No	Yes	Total
Do You Have Touch-Tone Dialing at Your Home?	**Yes**	10.2%	23.4%	15.5%
	No	89.8	76.6	84.5
	Total	100.0%	100.0%	100.0%

Interpretation: 15.5 percent of people in the survey said that they had Touch-Tone Dialing in their homes. However, the percentage was much higher (23.4%) among people who had moved in the last year, and lower (10.2%) among people who had not moved.

If a random sample is chosen from a population, it will tend to have the same characteristics and be representative of the population. "Tend to" is important because it is only a tendency—the sample is not exactly the same as the population.

Much marketing research is based on nonrandom sampling because of the high cost and difficulty of obtaining a truly random sample. Sometimes nonrandom samples give very good results—especially in industrial markets where the number of customers may be relatively small and fairly similar. But results from nonrandom samples must be interpreted—and used—with care.

Research results are not exact

An estimate from a sample—even a representative one—usually varies somewhat from the true value for a total population. Managers sometimes forget this. They assume that survey results are exact. Instead, when interpreting sample estimates, managers should think of them as *suggesting* the approximate value.

If random selection is used to develop the sample, researchers can use various methods to help determine the likely accuracy of the sample value. This is done in terms of **confidence intervals**—the range on either side of an estimate that is likely to contain the true value for the whole population. Some managers are surprised to learn how wide that range can be.

Consider a wholesaler who has 1,000 retail customers and wants to learn how many of these retailers carry a product from a competing supplier. If the wholesaler randomly samples 100 retailers and 20 say yes, then the sample estimate is 20 percent. But with that information the wholesaler can only be 95 percent confident that the percentage of all retailers is in the confidence interval between 12 and 28 percent.[18]

The larger the sample size, the greater the accuracy of estimates from a random sample. With a larger sample, a few unusual responses are less likely to make a big difference.

You can see that the nature of the sample—and how it is selected—make a big difference in how the results of a study can be interpreted. Managers must consider this factor when planning data collection—to make sure that the final results can be interpreted with enough confidence to be useful in marketing strategy planning.

Validity problems can destroy research

Even if the sampling is carefully planned, it is also important to evaluate the quality of the research data itself.

Survey Sampling, Inc., helps marketing researchers develop samples that are really representative of the target market; Donnelley Marketing Information Services provides shared cost data on special markets, including the Hispanic market.

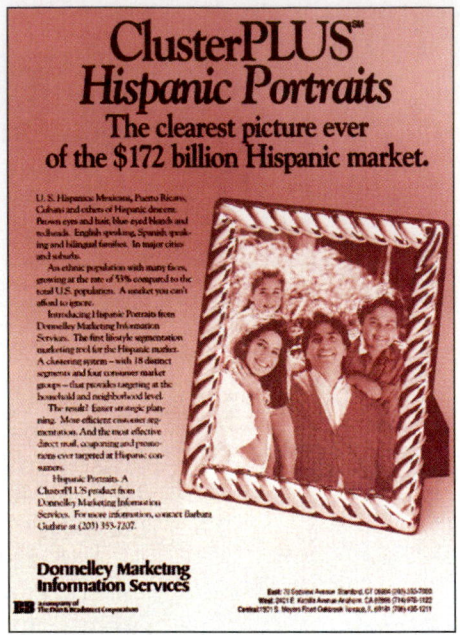

Managers and researchers should be sure that research data really measures what it is supposed to measure. Many of the variables marketing managers are interested in are difficult to measure accurately. Questionnaires may let us assign numbers to consumer responses, but that still doesn't mean that the result is precise. An interviewer might ask, "How much did you spend on soft drinks last week?" A respondent may be perfectly willing to cooperate—and be part of the representative sample—but just not be able to remember.

Validity concerns the extent to which data measures what it is intended to measure. Validity problems are important in marketing research because most people want to help and will try to answer—even when they don't know what they're talking about. Further, a poorly worded question can mean different things to different people—and invalidate the results. Often, one or more pretests of a research project are required to evaluate the quality of the questions and measures and to ensure that potential problems have been identified. Managers must be sure that they only pay for research results that are representative—and valid.

Poor interpretation can destroy research

Besides sampling and validity problems, a marketing manager must consider whether the analysis of the data supports the *conclusions* drawn in the interpretation step. Sometimes technical specialists pick the right statistical procedure—their calculations are exact—but they misinterpret the data because they don't understand the management problem. In one survey, car buyers were asked to rank five cars in order from "most preferred" to "least preferred." One car was ranked first by slightly more respondents than any other car so the researcher reported it as the "most liked car." That interpretation, however, ignored the fact that 70 percent of the respondents ranked the car *last*!

Interpretation problems like this can be subtle but crucial. Some people draw misleading conclusions—on purpose—to get the results they want. Marketing managers must decide whether *all* of the results support the interpretation—and are relevant to their problem.

Marketing manager and researcher should work together

Marketing research involves some technical details. But you can see that the marketing researcher and the marketing manager must work together to be sure that they really do solve the problem facing the firm. If the whole research process has been a joint effort, then the interpretation step can move quickly to decision making—and solving the problem.

SOLVING THE PROBLEM—STEP 5

The last step is solving the problem

In the problem solution step, managers use the research results to make marketing decisions.

Some researchers—and some managers—are fascinated by the interesting tidbits of information that come from the research process. They are excited if the research reveals something they didn't know before. But if research doesn't have action implications, it has little value—and suggests poor planning by the researcher and the manager.

When the research process is finished, the marketing manager should be able to apply the findings in marketing strategy planning—the choice of a target market or the mix of the four Ps. If the research doesn't provide information to help guide these decisions, the company has wasted research time and money.

We emphasize this step because it is the reason for and logical conclusion to the whole research process. This final step must be anticipated at each of the earlier steps.

INTERNATIONAL MARKETING RESEARCH

Research contributes to international success

Marketing research on overseas markets is often a major contributor toward international marketing success. Conversely, export failures are often due to a lack of home-office management expertise concerning customer interests, needs, and other segmenting dimensions as well as environmental factors such as competitors' prices and products. Effective marketing research can help to overcome these problems.

Avoid mistakes with local researchers

Whether a firm is small and entering overseas markets for the first time or already large and well established internationally, there are often advantages to working with local market research firms. These research suppliers know the local situation and are less likely to make mistakes based on misunderstanding the customs, language, or circumstances of the customers they study.

As we've emphasized, however, it's still important for a marketing manager to work closely with the researchers to be certain that they're not just "doing their own thing" with research that doesn't solve the manager's problem. Just because researchers are experts on doing research in their local settings doesn't mean that they are experts on the specific marketing problems the manager needs to solve. Finding a research supplier with relevant experience helps to reduce the likelihood of problems. Many large research firms have a network of local offices around the world to help with such efforts. Similarly, multinational or local advertising agencies and middlemen can often provide leads on identifying the best research suppliers.

Some coordination and standardization makes sense

When a firm is doing similar research projects in different markets around the world, it makes sense for the marketing manager to coordinate the efforts. If the manager doesn't establish some basic guidelines at the outset, the different research projects may all vary so much that the results can't be compared from one market area to another. When key questions and issues are studied in similar ways, comparisons across markets are possible. Such comparisons give a home-office manager a much better chance of understanding how the markets are similar and how they differ. This can be a key to knowing if it is appropriate for marketing strategies to be standardized across markets, or alternatively what customized approaches are necessary.

Multinational companies with operations in various countries often attempt to centralize some market research functions. One reason is to reduce costs or achieve research economies of scale. The centralized approach also improves the firm's ability to transfer experience and know-how from one market area or project to another.

The African, Asian, and Australian unit of Eastman Kodak's International Photographic Division recognized the value of coordinating its marketing re-search activities. It appointed one or more market research specialists in each subsidiary company throughout the region. The specialists report to local marketing managers but also receive research direction from expert research managers in the head office in the U.S. Head office control ensures a high standard of research quality worldwide. For example, the head office coordinates the marketing research training that is handled on a regional basis. Centralized coordination also ensures that research findings in any particular country can be meaningfully compared with those from other countries.

There is even greater opportunity and need to standardize and coordinate elements of a marketing information system in an international marketing operation. A custom market research survey designed to obtain primary data may only be used one time and may need to focus on specifics of the local situation. Yet, by their very nature, computer databases and information systems are most useful when they are designed to include the same variables organized consistently over time. Without this, it is impossible for the manager to go into much depth in comparing and contrasting data from different markets.[19]

HOW MUCH INFORMATION DO YOU NEED?

Information is costly— but reduces risk

We have been talking about the benefits of good marketing information, but dependable information can be expensive. A big company may spend millions developing an information system. A large-scale survey can cost from $20,000 to $100,000—or even more. The continuing research available from companies such as Information Resources, Inc., can cost a company well over $100,000 a year. And a market test for 6 to 12 months may cost $200,000 to $500,000 per test-market!

Companies that are willing and able to pay the cost often find that marketing information pays for itself. They are more likely to select the right target market and marketing mix—or see a potential problem before it becomes a costly crisis.

What is the value of information?

The high cost of good information must be balanced against its probable value to management. Managers never get all the information they would like to have. Very detailed surveys or experiments may be "too good" or "too expensive" or "too late" if all the company needs is a rough sampling of retailer attitudes toward a new pricing plan—by tomorrow. Money is wasted if research shows that a manager's guesses are wrong—and the manager ignores the facts. For example, GM faced an expensive disaster with its 1986 Riviera, which was released even after extensive research predicted a flop.[20]

Marketing managers must take risks because of incomplete information. That's part of their job and always will be. But they must weigh the cost of getting more data against its likely value. If the risk is not too great, the cost of getting more information may be greater than the potential loss from a poor decision. A decision to expand into a new territory with the present marketing mix, for example, might be made with more confidence after a $25,000 survey. But just sending a sales rep into the territory for a few weeks to try to sell potential customers would be a lot cheaper. And, if successful, the answer is in and so are some sales.

Faced with many risky decisions, the marketing manager should only seek help from research for problems where the risk can be reduced at a reasonable cost.[21]

CONCLUSION

Marketing managers face difficult decisions in selecting target markets and managing marketing mixes. And managers rarely have all the information they would like to have. This problem is usually worse for managers who work with international markets. But they don't have to rely only on intuition. They can usually obtain good information to improve the quality of their decisions.

Computers are helping marketing managers become full-fledged members of the information age. Both large and small firms are setting up marketing information systems (MIS)—to be certain that routinely needed data is available and accessible quickly.

Marketing managers deal with rapidly changing environments. Available data is not always adequate to answer the detailed questions that arise. Then a marketing research project may be required to gather new information.

Marketing research should be guided by the scientific method. The scientific approach to solving marketing problems involves five steps: defining the problem, analyzing the situation, obtaining data, interpreting data, and solving the problem. This objective and organized approach helps to keep research on target—reducing the risk of doing costly research that isn't necessary or doesn't solve the problem.

Our strategy planning framework can be helpful in finding the real problem. By finding and focusing on the real problem, the researcher and marketing manager may be able to move quickly to a useful solution—without the cost and risks of gathering primary data in a formal research project. With imagination, they may even be able to find the "answers" in their MIS or in other readily available secondary data.

QUESTIONS AND PROBLEMS

1. Discuss the concept of a marketing information system and why it is important for marketing managers to be involved in planning the system.

2. In your own words, explain why a decision support system (DSS) can add to the value of a marketing information system. Give an example of how a decision support system might help.

3. Discuss how output from a marketing information system (MIS) might differ from the output of a typical marketing research department.

4. Discuss some of the likely problems facing the marketer in a small firm that has just purchased an inexpensive personal computer to help develop a marketing information system.

5. Explain the key characteristics of the scientific method and show why these are important to managers concerned with research.

6. How is the situation analysis different from the data collection step? Can both these steps be done at the same time to obtain answers sooner? Is this wise?

7. Distinguish between primary data and secondary data and illustrate your answer.

8. If a firm were interested in estimating the distribution of income in the state of California, how could it proceed? Be specific.

9. If a firm were interested in estimating sand and clay production in Georgia, how could it proceed? Be specific.

10. Go to the library and find (in some government publication) three marketing-oriented "facts" on international markets that you did not know existed or were available. Record on one page and show sources.

11. Explain why a company might want to do focus group interviews rather than individual interviews with the same people.

12. Distinguish between qualitative and quantitative approaches to research—and give some of the key advantages and limitations of each approach.

13. Define response rate and discuss why a marketing manager might be concerned about the response rate achieved in a particular survey. Give an example.

14. Prepare a table that summarizes some of the key advantages and limitations of mail, telephone, and personal interview approaches for administering questionnaires.

15. Would a firm want to subscribe to a shared cost data service if the same data were to be available to competitors? Discuss your reasoning.

16. Explain how you might use different types of research (focus groups, observation, survey, and experiment) to forecast market reaction to a new kind of disposable baby diaper, which is to receive no promotion other than what the retailer will give it. Further, assume that the new diaper's name will not be associated with other known products. The product will be offered at competitive prices.

17. Marketing research involves expense—sometimes considerable expense. Why does the text recommend the use of marketing research even though a highly experienced marketing executive is available?

18. A marketing manager is considering opportunities to export her firm's current consumer products to several different countries. She is interested in getting secondary data that will help her narrow down choices to countries that offer the best potential. The manager then plans to do more detailed primary research with consumers in those markets. What suggestions would you give her about how to proceed?

19. Discuss the concept that some information may be too expensive to obtain in relation to its value. Illustrate.

SUGGESTED CASES

8. Maria's Place

9. Mountain View Lodge

COMPUTER-AIDED PROBLEM

5. Marketing Research

Texmac, Inc., has an idea for a new type of weaving machine that could replace the machines now used by many textile manufacturers. Texmac has done a telephone survey to estimate how many of the old-style machines are now in use. Respondents using the present machines were also asked if they would buy the improved machine at a price of $10,000.

Texmac researchers identified a population of about 5,000 textile factories as potential customers. A sample of these were surveyed, and Texmac received 500 responses. Researchers think the total potential market is about 10 times larger than the sample of respondents. Two hundred twenty of the respondents indicated that their firms used old machines like the one the new machine was intended to replace. Forty percent of those firms said that they would be interested in buying the new Texmac machine.

Texmac thinks the sample respondents are representative of the total population, but the marketing manager realizes that estimates based on a sample may not be exact when applied to the whole population. He wants to see how sampling "error" would affect profit estimates. Data for this problem appears in the spreadsheet. Quantity estimates for the whole market are computed from the sample estimates. These quantity estimates are used in computing likely sales, costs, and profit contribution.

a. *An article in a trade magazine reports that there are about 5,200 textile factories that use the old-style machine. If the total market is really 5,200 customers—not 5,000 as Texmac originally thought—how does that affect the total quantity estimate, expected revenue, and profit contribution?*

b. *Some of the people who responded to the survey didn't know much about different types of machines. If the actual number of old machines in the market is really 200 per 500 firms—not 220 as estimated from survey responses—how much would this affect the expected profit contribution (for 5,200 factories)?*

c. *The marketing manager knows that the percentage of textile factories that would actually buy the new machine might be different from the 40 percent who said they would in the survey. He estimates that the proportion that will replace the old machine might be as low as 36 and as high as 44 percent—depending on business conditions. Use the What If analysis to prepare a table that shows how expected quantity and profit contribution change when the sample percent varies between a minimum of 36 and a maximum of 44 percent. What does this analysis suggest about the use of estimates from marketing research samples? (Note: Use 5,200 for the number of potential customers and use 220 as the estimate of the number of old machines in the sample.)*

For additional questions related to this problem, see Exercise 5–3 in the *Learning Aid for Use with Basic Marketing*, 12th edition.

6

Demographic Dimensions of Global Consumer Markets

When You Finish This Chapter, You Should

1. Know about population and income trends in global markets—and how they affect marketers.

2. Understand how population growth is shifting in different areas and for different age groups.

3. Know about the distribution of income in the United States.

4. Know how consumer spending is related to family life cycle and other demographic dimensions.

5. Know how to estimate likely consumer purchases for broad classes of products.

6. Know why ethnic markets are important—and why increasingly they are the focus of multicultural marketing strategies.

7. Understand the important new terms (shown in red).

As export sales of Taiwan's computers and other high-tech products expanded, so did the income of Taiwan's workers. And with more money in the hands of more consumers, local demand is growing for goods and services that were out of reach just a few years ago. The economic boom in Taiwan is also taking place in many other Asian countries. Even ignoring Japan and China, more than 10 million Asian consumers earn at least $30,000 a year—and that number could triple by the turn of the century as Asian economies rapidly mature.

These changes explain why Citibank is seeking new opportunities in these growing markets. For example, Taiwanese consumers traditionally paid for homes by borrowing from family or tapping into lifetime savings. But home prices soared as more young people entered the market. Without financing, it was impossible to buy. So Citibank became a pioneer in making home mortgage loans in Taiwan. Although local banks followed, Citibank is still one of Taiwan's leading mortgage lenders.

In India, per capita income is much lower than in Taiwan. Seventy-five percent of the population lives in rural areas at barely a subsistence level. Even in cities, the growing middle class still rides to work on mopeds. But Citibank is betting that within a decade more Indian consumers will be buying cars. To be in position when that happens, Citibank now offers loans for moped purchases.

Local regulations in Citibank's Asian–Pacific market region often limit the number of branches it can open. However, Citibank has been innovative and turned necessity into a virtue. For example, in Australia it established a relationship with a drugstore chain and trained the chain's checkout clerks to accept deposits. Similarly, Citibank also saw an opportunity for demographic segmentation with its Citigold service. Citigold targets high-income consumers, whose deposits are over $100,000, with separate tellers, fast personal service, and custom investment options.[1]

Like many other large and small U.S. firms, Citibank looks to international markets for growth. One reason is that U.S. population and income are growing slower than they did in the past. But that doesn't mean some markets aren't growing. Consider the teenage market. After years of decline, the teen group is growing again—at twice the pace of the overall population. And, with teens spending more money, they are a target for many firms. For example, MCI is making teens a big target for its new 1-800-COLLECT service and MasterCard is targeting teens with its credit card promotions. Similarly, Bausch & Lomb's contact lens sales hit record levels when the firm refocused its marketing efforts on teens. Even Oil of Olay, which for years has told older women it will help them stay young, is now running ads in teen magazines.[2]

TARGET MARKETERS FOCUS ON THE CUSTOMER

Target marketers believe that the *customer* should be the focus of all business and marketing activity. These marketers hope to develop unique marketing strategies by finding unsatisfied customers and offering them more attractive marketing mixes. They want to work in less-competitive markets with more inelastic demand curves. Finding these attractive opportunities takes real knowledge of potential customers and what they want. This means finding those market dimensions that make a difference—in terms of population, income, needs, attitudes, and buying behavior.

Marketers need to answer three important questions about any potential market:

1. What are its relevant segmenting dimensions?
2. How big is it?
3. Where is it?

The first question is basic. Management judgment—perhaps aided by analysis of existing data and new findings from marketing research—is needed to pick the right dimensions.

To help build your judgment regarding buying behavior, this chapter and the next two will discuss what we know about various kinds of customers and their buying behavior. Keep in mind that we aren't trying to make generalizations about average customers or how the mass market behaves—but rather how *some* people in *some* markets behave. You should expect to find differences.

In this chapter, we focus on demographic dimensions. Demographic dimensions provide marketing managers with critical information about the size, location, and characteristics of target markets. Marketing managers must also be alert to demographic trends. They often provide an early warning about new opportunities—or the need to adjust existing strategies.

Get the facts straight—for good marketing decisions

Everybody "knows" that the income of Japanese consumers has grown rapidly in the last decade, that there is a vast and largely untapped market in China, and that many people in Ethiopia live in desperate poverty. It's also clear that demographic dimensions vary within countries: lots of retired people live in Florida, many Californians speak Spanish, and the population in the Sun Belt states is growing fast. Generalities like these may be partly true—but "partly true" isn't good enough when it comes to making marketing strategy decisions.

Fortunately, much useful information is available on the demographic dimensions of consumer markets around the world. Most of it is free because it has been collected by government agencies. With valid data available, managers have no excuse for basing their decisions on guesses. Look at the data in the next few chapters in terms of selecting relevant market dimensions—and estimating the potential in different market segments. Also, check your own assumptions against this data. Now is a good time to get your facts straight!

PEOPLE WITH MONEY MAKE MARKETS

Markets consist of people with money to spend. So it makes sense to start with a broad view of how population, income, and other key demographic dimensions vary for different countries around the world. This will help you to see

Whirlpool is pursuing the growing market in Bangkok, but there its refrigerators must be smaller and available in more colors because consumers often put them in their living rooms.

why so many firms pursue opportunities in international markets. And our examples will illustrate why companies can't depend on half-truths in increasingly competitive international markets.

Marketers search for growing markets

Some marketing managers never consider opportunities outside of their own country. That may make sense in some cases, but it may also lead to missed opportunities. For example, crowded cities in the U.S. may seem to offer great potential, but the U.S. population makes up less than 5 percent of the total world population—which is over 5.6 billion and will top 6 billion by the year 2000.

Although a country's current population is important, it provides only a snapshot of the market. The population trend is also important. Exhibit 6–1 shows where long-term world population growth will come from. Notice the expected growth of countries in the Middle and Far East. India (with a population of about 920 million) and China (with a population of almost 1.2 billion) are getting even larger. You can see why so many firms from all over the world want to reach consumers in these countries now that trade barriers are relaxing. Although many of the countries in South America and Africa have much smaller populations, they too are growing at a rapid rate.[3]

Exhibit 6–1 shows that, over the long term, population growth is expected in most countries. But how rapidly? And will output increase faster than population? These are important questions for marketers. The answers affect how rapidly a country moves to higher stages of development—and becomes a new market for different kinds of products.

Population, income, and other demographic dimensions help to answer these questions. Exhibit 6–2 summarizes current data for representative countries from different regions around the world. Note that population growth varies dramatically from country to country. In general, less-developed countries experience the fastest rate of growth. The populations of Mexico, Pakistan, Kenya, and Egypt are

EXHIBIT 6–1 Population Added between 1994 and 2020

![red]	10.0 to 19.9	
![blue]	20.0 or above	

Inset B

185

EXHIBIT 6–2   Demographic Dimensions for Representative Countries

Country	1994 Population (000s)	1994 Percent Annual Population Growth	1992 Years for Population to Double	1994 Population Density (people per square mile)	1992 Percent Population in Urban Areas	1991 GNP (millions of $ U.S.)	1991 GNP per Capita	1991 Percent Annual GNP Growth	1992 Literacy Percent
Afghanistan	16,903	2.5	17	68	18	3,154	192	0.0	29
Algeria	27,895	2.3	31	30	48	56,351	2,166	3.0	50
Argentina	33,913	1.1	66	32	86	68,368	2,093	-0.3	95
Australia	18,077	1.4	50	6	85	257,376	14,888	3.1	100
Bangladesh	125,149	2.3	33	2,421	14	21,373	183	3.6	35
Brazil	158,739	1.3	42	49	75	401,090	2,582	3.4	81
Cameroon	13,132	2.9	29	72	42	13,201	1,159	6.4	54
Canada	28,114	1.2	66	8	77	534,938	19,934	3.4	99
Chile	13,951	1.5	50	48	84	23,649	1,780	1.6	93
China	1,190,431	1.1	47	331	26	479,870	417	10.5	73
Colombia	35,578	1.8	36	89	68	40,958	1,213	3.0	87
Cuba	11,064	1.0	73	258	73	26,384	2,458	-1.0	94
Czech Republic	10,408	0.2	350	215	75	88,116	8,482	1.4	n/a
Ecuador	10,677	2.0	33	100	55	11,143	1,036	1.7	86
Egypt	60.765	2.2	33	158	45	36,243	666	5.6	46
Ethiopia	58,710	3.4	26	138	12	6,085	114	1.1	62
Finland	5,069	0.3	234	43	62	116,838	23,410	3.2	100
France	57,840	0.5	177	275	73	1,035,185	18,291	1.7	99
Germany	81,088	0.4	177	600	90	1,418,577	18,625	1.7	99
Ghana	17,225	3.1	25	194	32	5,725	367	2.0	60
Greece	10,565	0.8	350	209	58	54,271	5,404	0.6	93
Haiti	6,491	1.6	33	610	28	2,541	404	-0.3	53
Iceland	264	0.9	73	7	90	5,677	21,835	3.0	100
India	919,903	1.8	40	801	27	319,864	369	5.5	48
Indonesia	200,410	1.6	42	284	31	94,746	489	3.8	77
Iran	65,615	3.5	23	104	54	94,437	1,599	0.5	54
Iraq	19,890	3.7	21	119	73	44,872	2,298	5.0	60
Israel	5,051	2.2	50	643	90	47,001	10,498	3.2	92
Italy	58,138	0.2	350	512	72	907,182	15,703	2.0	97
Jamaica	2,555	1.0	80	611	51	2,969	1,193	-0.7	98
Japan	125,107	0.3	177	821	77	3,158,607	25,469	4.0	99
Kenya	28,241	3.1	23	128	22	9,484	376	3.9	69
Kuwait	1,819	5.2	23	264	100	34,216	15,525	1.7	74
Libya	5,057	3.7	26	7	70	20,323	4,671	-6.0	64
Madagascar	13,428	3.2	25	60	23	2,528	207	-0.3	80
Malaysia	19,283	2.3	32	152	35	40,025	2,226	4.0	78
Mexico	92,202	1.9	35	124	71	172,442	1,916	0.7	87
Morocco	28,559	2.1	36	166	46	23,641	903	3.5	50
Mozambique	17,346	5.9	18	57	23	1,077	71	-5.0	33
Nepal	21,042	2.4	32	398	7	3,514	179	4.7	26
Netherlands	15,368	0.6	119	1,173	89	245,073	16,314	1.6	99
Nicaragua	4,097	2.7	28	88	57	2,830	754	-1.4	57
Nigeria	98,091	3.1	26	279	16	27,751	314	-1.0	51
North Korea	23,067	1.8	40	496	64	21,218	973	3.0	90
Norway	4,315	0.4	142	36	71	99,804	23,357	4.1	99
Pakistan	128,856	2.9	31	429	28	45,350	386	6.3	35
Panama	2,630	1.9	36	90	52	4,398	1,776	2.2	88
Peru	23,651	1.9	38	48	69	23,471	1,050	1.0	85
Philippines	69,809	1.9	36	606	42	42,754	650	0.0	90
Poland	38,655	0.4	697	329	62	70,365	1,862	2.5	98
Romania	23,181	0.1	142	261	54	81,579	3,487	1.1	96
Russia	149,609	0.2	102	23	74	882,501	5,988	1.4	98
Saudi Arabia	18,197	3.2	20	22	73	86,070	4,816	-2.2	62
Singapore	2,859	1.1	57	11,867	100	32,124	11,656	7.0	88

continued

EXHIBIT 6–2 *Continued*

Country	1994 Population (000s)	1994 Percent Annual Population Growth	1992 Years for Population to Double	1994 Population Density (people per square mile)	1992 Percent Population in Urban Areas	1991 GNP (millions of $ U.S.)	1991 GNP per Capita	1991 Percent Annual GNP Growth	1992 Literacy Percent
Somalia	6,667	3.2	24	28	35	1,047	156	0.6	24
South Africa	43,931	2.6	29	93	58	88,629	2,183	1.5	76
South Korea	45,083	1.0	90	1,189	71	222,355	5,155	9.2	96
Spain	39,303	0.3	234	204	91	377,229	9,578	2.6	95
Sri Lanka	18,130	1.1	61	725	22	7,906	454	4.3	86
Sudan	29,420	2.4	26	32	20	7,759	285	−1.3	27
Sweden	8,778	0.5	177	55	83	191,673	22,381	2.0	99
Switzerland	7,040	0.7	119	458	60	205,579	30,304	1.9	99
Syria	14,887	3.7	22	209	50	12,544	967	0.4	64
Taiwan	21,299	1.0	66	1,710	71	146,005	7,067	7.9	91
Tanzania	27,986	2.5	24	82	20	3,216	120	2.2	46
Thailand	59,510	1.3	53	301	18	72,128	1,270	5.8	93
Turkey	62,154	2.0	35	209	60	83,020	1,471	5.4	81
Uganda	19,859	2.6	22	248	10	4,305	230	0.6	48
Ukraine	51,847	0.0	234	222	67	250,160	4,838	1.4	98
United Kingdom	58,135	0.3	234	623	87	884,967	15,387	3.0	99
United States	260,714	1.0	90	74	74	5,567,478	22,049	3.1	97
Venezuela	20,562	2.2	32	60	83	47,447	2,350	0.3	88
Vietnam	73,104	1.8	36	582	20	16,563	245	8.0	88
Zaire	42,684	3.2	24	49	40	9,001	238	0.9	72

expected to double in 35 years or less. It will take about twice as long for the populations of the U.S. and Canada to double. Population growth is even slower in Japan and the European countries.[4]

Population is becoming more concentrated

The population in some countries is spread over a very large area. Population density is important to marketers. If the population is very spread out, as it is in many of the African countries, it is difficult and expensive for marketers to adjust time and place discrepancies between producers and consumers. This is especially a problem in countries without efficient highway and rail systems. Similarly, a widely spread population may make promotion more difficult, especially if there are language differences or communication systems are poor. Of course, even in countries with low population density, major cities may be packed with people.

The extent to which a country's population is clustered around urban areas varies a lot. In the U.S., Venezuela, Australia, Israel, and Singapore, for example, a high percentage of people live in urban areas. See Exhibit 6–2. By contrast, in Thailand, Nigeria, and Afghanistan less than 18 percent of the people live in major urban areas.

People everywhere are moving off the farm and into industrial and urban areas. Shifts in population—combined with already dense populations—have led to extreme crowding in some parts of the world. And the crowding is likely to get worse.

The worldwide trend toward urbanization has prompted increased interest in international markets. For many firms, the concentration of people in major cities simplifies Place and Promotion strategy decisions—especially for major cities in

While many consumers in India still live in poverty and can afford only the most simple clothing, upscale shoppers in Bombay's modern malls are more like wealthy consumers in the major urban areas of the U.S. or Europe.

the wealthiest nations. Affluent, big-city consumers often have similar lifestyles and needs. Thus, many of the products successful in Toronto, New York City, or Paris are likely to be successful in Caracas and Tokyo.

However, keep in mind that many of the world's consumers—whether crowded in cities or widely spread in rural areas—live in deplorable conditions. These people have little hope of escaping the crush of poverty. They certainly have needs—but they don't have the income to do anything about the needs.

There's no market when there's no income

Profitable markets require income—as well as people. The amount of money people can spend affects the products they are likely to buy. When considering international markets, income is often one of the most important demographic dimensions.

The best available measure of total income in most countries is **gross national product (GNP)**—the total market value of goods and services produced in an economy in a year. Unfortunately, GNP measures are not ideal for comparing very different cultures and economies. For instance, do-it-yourself activities, household services, and the growing of produce or meat by family members for their own use are not usually figured as part of GNP. Since the activities of self-sufficient family units are not included, GNP can give a false picture of economic well-being in less-developed countries. At the other extreme, GNP may not do a good job of measuring service-oriented output in highly developed economies.

GNP also has limits when comparing countries with different patterns of international investment. A country's GNP does not include income earned by foreigners who own resources located in that country. For example, the profit earned by Toyota's U.S. operations is not included in the U.S. GNP. On the other hand, that income would be included in Japan's GNP.

But gross national product *is* useful—and sometimes it's the only available measure of market potential. Exhibit 6–2 gives a GNP estimate for each country listed. You can see that the more developed industrial nations—including the

U.S., Japan, and Germany—have the biggest share of the world's GNP. This is why so much trade takes place between these countries—and why many firms see them as the more important markets.[5]

Income growth expands markets

However, the fastest *growth* in GNP is not, in general, occurring in the nations with the largest GNPs. For example, total U.S. GNP in 1991 was close to $5.57 trillion; it has increased approximately 3 percent a year since 1880. This means that GNP doubled—on the average—every 20 years. Recently, this growth slowed—and even declined for a while.

Declines in GNP may not just be due to temporarily bad economic conditions. GNP is related to the output of employees. When the population growth rate slows, there are fewer young workers and more retired people. This may become a serious political problem—everyone expects the economy to deliver more, while fewer young people are available to support the older ones. Many other developed economies face this problem too. However, no one knows for certain what will happen in the future. While many firms are downsizing, they're also using technology to help workers be more productive. They're also reengineering—that is, finding totally new ways of doing what they do. These efforts by individual firms may help improve long-run productivity in economies around the world, but only time will tell.

GNP tells us about the income of a whole nation, but in a country with a large population that income must be spread over more people. GNP per person is a useful figure because it gives some idea of the income level of people in a country. Exhibit 6–2 shows, for example, that GNP per capita in the U.S. is quite high—about $22,000. Japan, Canada, Switzerland, and Germany are among those with the highest GNP per capita. In general, markets like these offer the best potential for products that are targeted at consumers with higher income levels.

Many managers, however, see great potential—and less competition—where GNP per capita is low. For example, Mars is making a big push to promote its candy in the countries of Eastern Europe. As with many other firms, it hopes to establish a relationship with consumers now, and then turn strong brand loyalty into profitable growth as consumer incomes increase.

A business and a human opportunity

The large number of countries with low GNP per capita is a stark reminder that much of the world's population lives in extreme poverty. Even among countries with the largest overall GNPs, you see some sign of this. In India, for example, GNP per person is only $369 a year. Many countries are in the early stages of economic development. Most of their people work on farms—and live barely within the money economy. At the extreme, in Mozambique GNP per person per year is only about $71 (in U.S. dollars).

These people, however, have needs, and many are eager to improve themselves. But they may not be able to raise their living standards without outside help. This presents a challenge and an opportunity to the developed nations—and to their business firms.

Some companies—including American firms—are trying to help the people of less-developed countries. Corporations such as Pillsbury, Corn Products, Monsanto, and Coca-Cola have developed nutritious foods that can be sold cheaply—but still profitably—in poorer countries. One firm sells a milk-based drink (Samson)—with 10 grams of protein per serving—to the Middle East and the Caribbean areas. Such a drink can make an important addition to diets. Poor people in less-developed lands usually get only 8 to 12 grams of protein per day in their normal diet (45 to 55 grams per day are considered necessary for an adult).[6]

What do Third World consumers really need?

Marketing managers from developed nations sometimes face an ethical dilemma about whether their products help or hurt consumers in less-developed nations. For example, a United Nations report criticized Coke and Pepsi for expanding their soft-drink sales in the Philippines. The study concluded that consumers had shifted to soft drinks from local beverages—such as a mixture of lime juice and coconut water—that provided needed vitamins.

In another much publicized case, producers of infant formula were criticized for giving free samples to hospitals. Nestlé and American Home Products (AHP) Corp., two of the biggest suppliers in this market, say that they only gave the free samples to children who were in need—and at the request of hospitals. But critics argued that the practice encouraged new mothers to give up breast-feeding. Away from the hospital, mothers could not understand the directions for using the formula or would rely on unsanitary water supplies. Improper use of the formula could lead to malnutrition, diarrhea, and other illnesses. In 1991, Nestlé and AHP pledged to stop giving away free samples. Although that step will stop misuse, the formula won't be available to many people who really need it.

In cases like these, a marketing manager may need to weigh the benefits and risks of trying to serve Third World markets. For example, in the U.S. Quicksilver Enterprises sells its 250-pound aluminum and fiberglass "ultralight" airplanes—that look like go-carts with wings—to wealthy hobbyists. However, Quicksilver found a growing market for ultralights in developing nations, where farmers use them for crop dusting. They help farmers increase production of much needed foods. So what's the problem? In the U.S., the government bans ultralights as not being safe enough for crop dusting. Some critics argue that a firm shouldn't sell its products in foreign markets if they are illegal in the U.S. But ultimately, the marketing manager often must decide what to do.[7]

Reading, writing, and marketing problems

The ability of a country's people to read and write has a direct influence on the development of its economy—and on marketing strategy planning. The degree of literacy affects the way information is delivered—which in marketing means promotion. Unfortunately, only about two-thirds of the world's population can read and write. Data on literacy rates are inexact because different countries use different measures. Even so, you may be surprised by the low literacy rates for some of the countries in Exhibit 6–2.

Low literacy sometimes causes difficulties with product labels and instructions—for which we normally use words. This was one issue in the infant formula conflict. In an even more extreme case, some producers of baby food found that consumers misinterpreted a baby's picture on their packages. Illiterate natives believed that the product was just that—a ground-up baby! Many companies meet this lack of literacy with instructions that use pictures instead of words. Singer used this approach with its sewing machines.

Even in Latin America—with generally higher literacy rates than Africa or Asia—a large number of people cannot read or write. Marketers have to use symbols, colors, and other nonverbal communication to reach the masses.[8]

Much segmenting may be required

Marketers can learn a great deal about possible opportunities in different countries by studying available demographic data and trends. The examples we considered here give you a feel, but keep in mind that much useful data is available. For example, an easy-to-use computer program called *Maps 'N' Facts* provides extensive data on every country in the world.

After finding some countries or regions of possible interest (and eliminating unattractive ones), much more segmenting may be required. To illustrate how useful demographic dimensions can be in this effort, we will consider specific characteristics of the U.S. market in some detail. Similar ideas apply to other markets around the world.

POPULATION TRENDS IN THE U.S. CONSUMER MARKET

Where does your state stand?

Exhibit 6–3 is a map of the U.S. showing the relative population for each state. The "high areas" on this map emphasize the concentration of population in different geographic regions. Note that California is the most populated state, with Texas a distant second. New York, which recently dropped a notch to third place, still has almost as large a population as Texas, but Texas' population is

EXHIBIT 6–3 Map of United States Showing Population by State (all figures in thousands)

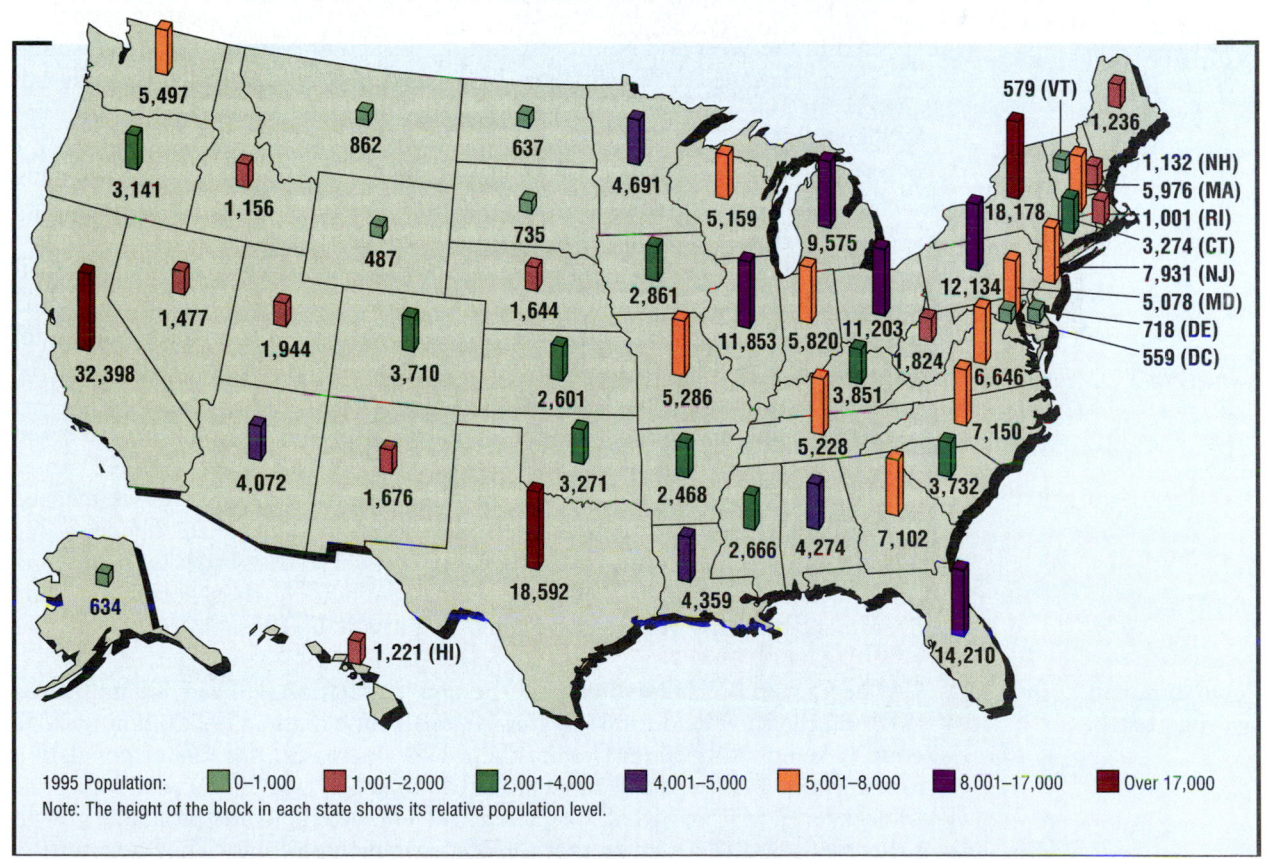

1995 Population: 0–1,000 | 1,001–2,000 | 2,001–4,000 | 4,001–5,000 | 5,001–8,000 | 8,001–17,000 | Over 17,000

Note: The height of the block in each state shows its relative population level.

much more spread out. More generally, the heavy concentration of people in the Northeast makes this market more than a quarter larger than the whole West Coast.

As is the case in many countries, the most populated U.S. areas developed near inexpensive water transportation—on ocean harbors (East and West Coasts), along major rivers (like the Mississippi), or in the Great Lakes region. Obviously, these markets are attractive to many marketers. But this can also mean tough competition—as in the big urban East and West Coast markets.

Marketers anxious to avoid the extremely competitive East and West Coast markets often view the midwestern and southern states as unique target markets. Note, too, the few people in the plains and mountain states, which explains why some national marketers pay less attention to these areas. Yet these states can provide an opportunity for an alert marketer looking for less competitive markets.

Where are the people today and tomorrow?

Population figures for a single year don't show the dynamic aspects of markets. The U.S. population has been growing continuously since the founding of the country—more than doubling from 1930 to 1995—until it reached about 263 million. But—and this is important to marketers—the population did *not* double everywhere. Marketers always look for fast-growing markets. They want to know where growth has occurred recently—and where growth is likely to occur in the future.

Exhibit 6–4 shows the percentage growth in population in different regions of the country. The states with the green shading are growing at the fastest rate. The gold states are just holding their own. Note that the greatest growth is expected in the West and Northwest—in states such as Nevada, Idaho, Washington, Utah, Hawaii, Alaska, Arizona, New Mexico, and California. Growth will continue in the Sun Belt states of the South, but not at as fast a pace as for the last few decades.

Notice that some of the most populated areas in Exhibit 6–3 are not growing the fastest. The populations of Massachusetts and New York, for example, are expected to grow less than 1 percent during the next decade.

These different rates of growth are especially important to marketers. Sudden growth in one area may create a demand for many new shopping centers—while retailers in declining areas face tougher competition for a smaller number of customers. In growing areas, demand may increase so rapidly that profits may be good even in poorly planned facilities.

These maps summarize state-level data to give the big picture. However, much more detailed population data is available. You can obtain detailed census data—or updated estimates—for very small geographic areas. Just as we mapped population changes at the state level, a local marketer can divide a big metropolitan area into many smaller areas to see where the action is. By the end of the decade, census data may be outdated—but by then local and state government planning groups may be able to provide updates.

Population will keep growing, but . . .

The Census Bureau predicts that the U.S. population will top 300 million by 2010, and that it will continue to grow to an all-time high of 392 million by 2050 before it begins to decline. Despite these large increases, the *rate* of population growth in the U.S. has slowed dramatically—to about 1 percent a year during the last decade. In fact, many U.S. marketers who enjoyed rapid and profitable growth in the 1960s and 1970s know that the domestic picnic is over. They now turn to international markets where population—and sales revenues—continue to grow.

EXHIBIT 6–4   Percent Change in Population by State, 1995–2005

Percent change in population:
Decreasing–3.9%   4.0–6.9%   7.0–9.9%   10.0–15.9%   16–24.9%

In the U.S., most of our future growth is expected to come from immigration. In fact, even now the total U.S. population would start to decline if immigration stopped. Let's look at some of these trends—and what they mean to marketing managers.[9]

Birthrate—boom or bust?

The U.S. **birthrate**—the number of babies born per 1,000 people—fluctuated greatly in the last 50 years. Exhibit 6–5 shows a clear pattern. A post–World War II baby boom began as returning soldiers started families, and it lasted about 15 years into the early 1960s. In the 1970s the situation changed to a "baby bust" as more women stayed in the workforce and couples waited longer to have children. When you see the dip in the birthrate—and think about the declining market for baby products—you can understand why Johnson & Johnson promotes its baby shampoo to adults who want a gentle product. You can also understand why Johnson & Johnson looks for opportunities in Asia and Latin America where the birthrate is higher.

The U.S. birthrate hit a low in 1976 and then rose again—but only slightly. From 1980 to 1990, the birthrate ranged from 15 to 17. It is starting to drop again now, and this trend should continue—with an estimated birthrate of about 14.2 around the year 2000. These shifts are easy to explain. As the baby boom generation entered its child-bearing years, there were more women to have babies. However, as the boomers aged this baby "boomlet" passed and turned to what some have called a "baby bust." In addition, American couples are having fewer children. There may be less need for big family homes and large, family-sized food packages—and more demand for small apartments, out-of-home entertainment, travel, and smaller food packages.

With fewer children, parents can spend more money on each child. For example, expensive bikes, home video games, and designer clothes for children have all sold well in recent years because parents can indulge one or two children more easily than a house full.[10]

EXHIBIT 6-5   Changes in the U.S. Birthrate, 1935–2005

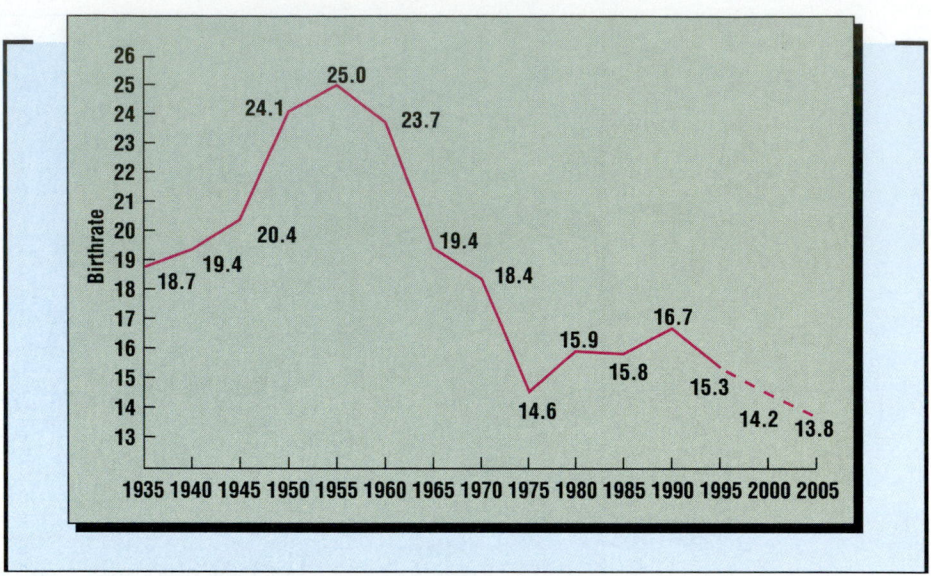

The graying of America

Because our population is growing slowly, the average age is rising. In 1970, the average age of the population was 28—but, by the year 2000, the average age will jump to about 36.

Stated another way, the percentage of the population in different age groups is changing. Exhibit 6–6 shows the number of people in different age groups in 1980 and 1990—and how the size of these groups will look in 2000. Note the big increases in the 25–44 age group from 1980 to 1990—and how that growth is carrying over to the 45–64 age group from 1990 until 2000.

The major reason for the changing age distribution is that the post–World War II baby boom produced about one-fourth of the present U.S. population. This large group crowded into the schools in the 1950s and 60s—and then into the job market in the 1970s. In the 1980s, they swelled the middle-aged group. And early in the 21st century, they will reach retirement—still a dominant group in the total population. According to one population expert, "It's like a goat passing through a boa constrictor."

Some of the effects of this big market are very apparent. For example, recording industry sales exploded—to the beat of rock and roll music and the Beatles—as the baby boom group moved into their record-buying teens. Soon after, colleges added facilities and faculty to handle the surge—then had to cope with excess capacity and loss of revenue when the student-age population dwindled. To relieve financial strain many colleges now add special courses and programs for adults to attract the now-aging baby boom students. On the other hand, the fitness industry and food producers who offer low-calorie foods are reaping the benefit of a middle-aged "bulge" in the population.

Medical advances help people live longer and are also adding to the proportion of the population in the senior citizen group. Note from Exhibit 6–6 that the over-65 age group grew by 23 percent during the 1980s—and will grow another 12 percent before the turn of the century. These dramatic changes create new opportunities for such industries as tourism, health care, and financial services.

EXHIBIT 6–6 Population Distribution by Age Groups for the Years 1980, 1990, and 2000

Age Group:	Under 5	5–17	18–24	25–44	45–64	65+
Year 2000				83,360		
		52,358			59,860	
			25,911			35,322
Population estimate (000)	19,431					
Percent of population in this age group	7.0%	18.9%	9.4%	30.1%	21.7%	12.8%
1990				81,555		
		45,629			46,842	
	18,408		25,897			31,559
	7.4%	18.2%	10.4%	32.6%	18.7%	12.6%
1980				63,494		
		47,237	30,350		44,156	
	16,458					25,704
	7.2%	20.8%	13.3%	27.9%	19.6%	11.3%
Percent change in age group: 1980–1990	11.8	-3.4	-14.7	28.4	6.1	22.8
1990–2000	5.6	14.7	.05	2.2	27.8	11.9

The teen cycle is starting again

While society—and many marketers—have been fixated on the aging baby boomers, the ranks of teenagers have started to grow again. This is in part reflected in the 14.7 percent growth of the 5–17 age group during this decade (see Exhibit 6–6). But, the coming changes are even bigger than this suggests. For 15 years, there was a steady decline in the number of teenagers. Ever since that decline turned around in 1992, however, the growth rate for this group has been picking up. Between 1995 and 2005, the teenage group will grow at close to twice the rate of the overall population. As a result, by the time this new group of teens reaches its peak in 2010, it will top the baby boom–fueled teen explosion of the 1960s and 1970s in both size and duration. At that point, there will be over 30 million teens—and along the way a new teen-oriented culture will shape society and markets. However, marketers who simultaneously try to appeal to aging boomers and to the bulge of teens who will shape future markets may find themselves right in the middle of a real clash of cultures.[11]

Household composition is changing

Many people incorrectly think of the "typical" American household as a married couple with two children—living in the suburbs. This never was true and is even less true now. Couples with no children under 18 at home now account for more than half of all households. Although almost all Americans marry, they are marrying later, delaying child bearing, and having fewer children.

And couples don't stay together as long as they used to. The U.S. has the highest divorce rate in the world—about 50 percent of marriages end in divorce. But divorce does not seem to deter people from marrying again. Over 80 percent

Specialized media, like *Modern Maturity*, help advertisers reach older consumers. Many firms, including cereal producers, are paying more attention to this target market now that the size and income of this group is increasing.

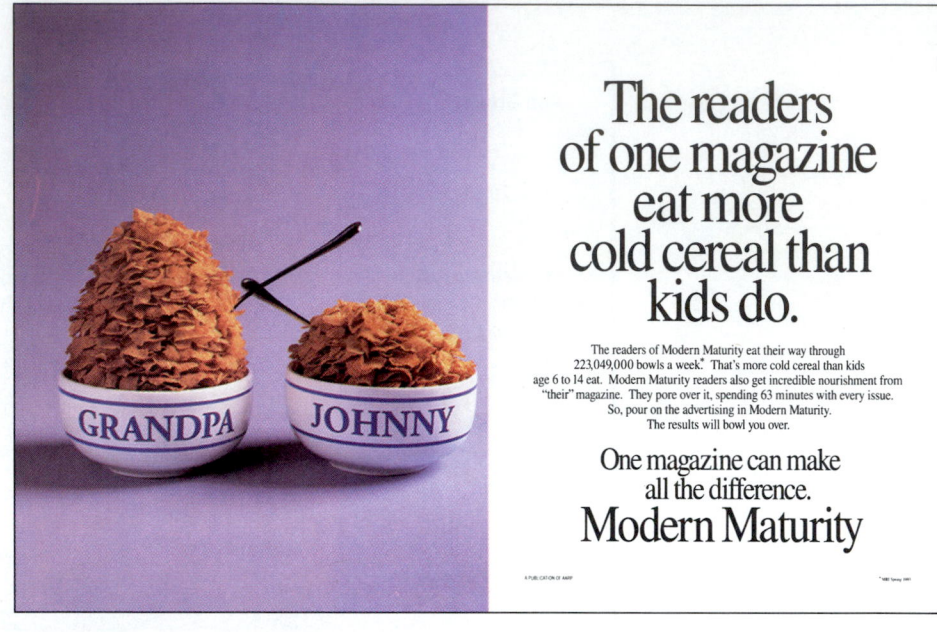

The readers of one magazine eat more cold cereal than kids do.

The readers of Modern Maturity eat their way through 223,049,000 bowls a week.* That's more cold cereal than kids age 6 to 14 eat. Modern Maturity readers also get incredible nourishment from "their" magazine. They pore over it, spending 63 minutes with every issue. So, pour on the advertising in Modern Maturity. The results will bowl you over.

One magazine can make all the difference.
Modern Maturity

of divorced people remarry in what is described as "the triumph of hope over experience." Still, even with all this shifting around, about two-thirds of all adults are married.

Nonfamily households are increasing

Many households are not families in the traditional sense. *Single-adult households* account for about one-fourth of all households—almost 24 million people! These households include young adults who leave home when they finish school, as well as separated, divorced, or widowed people who live alone.

In some big cities, the percentage of single-person households is even higher—around 30 percent in New York City and Washington, D.C. These people need smaller apartments, smaller cars, smaller food packages, and, in some cases, less-expensive household furnishings because many singles don't have much money. Other singles have ample discretionary income and are attractive markets for top-of-the-line stereos and clothing, status cars, travel, nice restaurants, and trendy bars.

And several million unmarried people live together—some in groups but most as couples. Some of these arrangements are temporary—as in college towns or in large cities where recent graduates go for their first "real" job. But the majority are older couples who choose not to get married.

The number of these nontraditional households is still relatively small. But marketers should pay special attention to them because they are growing at a much higher rate than the traditional family households. In fact, since 1970 their number has quadrupled. And they have different needs and attitudes than the stereotypical American family. To reach this market, some banks changed their policies about loans to unmarried couples for homes, cars, and other major purchases. And some insurance companies designed coverage for unmarried couples.[12]

Computerized maps that show detailed demographic data for small geographic areas are very helpful in retail site location.

The shift to urban and suburban areas

Migration from rural to urban areas has been continuous in the U.S. since 1800. In 1920, about half the population lived in rural areas. By 1950, the number living on farms dropped to 15 percent—and now it is less than 2 percent. We have become an urban and suburban society.[13]

Since World War II, there has been a continuous flight to the suburbs by middle-income consumers. By 1970, more people lived in the suburbs than in the central cities. Retailers moved too—following their customers. Lower-income consumers—often with varied ethnic backgrounds—moved into the city, changing the nature of markets in the center of the city.

Industries too have been fleeing the cities, moving many jobs closer to the suburbs. Today's urban economic system is not as dependent on central cities. A growing population must go somewhere—and the suburbs can combine pleasant neighborhoods with easy transportation to higher-paying jobs nearby or in the city.

Purchase patterns are different in the suburbs. For example, a big city resident may not need or own a car. But with no mass transportation, living carless in the suburbs is difficult. And in some areas, it almost seems that a minivan—to carpool kids and haul lawn supplies or pets—is a necessity.

Local political boundaries don't define market areas

These continuing shifts—to and from urban and suburban areas—mean that the usual practice of reporting population by city and county boundaries can result in misleading descriptions of markets. Marketers are more interested in the size of homogeneous *marketing* areas than in the number of people within political boundaries. To meet this need, the U.S. Census Bureau has developed a separate population classification based on metropolitan statistical areas. Much data is reported on the characteristics of people in these areas. The technical definition of these areas has changed over time. But basically a **Metropolitan Statistical Area (MSA)** is an integrated economic and social unit with a large population nucleus. Generally, an MSA centers on one city or urbanized area of 50,000 or more inhabitants and includes bordering urban areas.

The largest MSAs—basically those with a population of more than a million—are called Consolidated Metropolitan Statistical Areas. Almost 40 percent of all Americans live in the 18 largest CMSAs. More detailed data are available for areas within these sprawling, giant urban areas.

Big targets are attractive—but very competitive

Some national marketers sell only in these metro areas because of the large, concentrated population. They know that having so many customers packed into a small area can simplify the marketing effort. They can use fewer middlemen and still offer products conveniently. One or two local advertising media—a city newspaper or TV station—can reach most residents. If a sales force is needed, it will incur less travel time and expense because people are closer together.

Metro areas are also attractive markets because they offer greater sales potential than their large population alone suggests. Consumers in these areas have more money to spend because wages tend to be higher. In addition, professionals—with higher salaries—are concentrated there. But, remember that competition for consumer dollars is usually stiff in an MSA.[14]

The mobile ones are an attractive market

Of course, none of these population shifts is necessarily permanent. People move, stay awhile, and then move again. In fact, about 18 percent of Americans move each year. Although about 6 out of 10 moves are within the same county, both the local and long-distance mobiles are important market segments.

Often people who move in the same city trade up to a bigger or better house or neighborhood. They tend to be younger and better educated people on the way up in their careers. Their income is rising—and they have money to spend. Buying a new house may spark many other purchases too. The old sofa may look shabby in the new house. And the bigger yard may require a new lawn mower—or even a yard service.

Many market-oriented decisions have to be made fairly quickly after moves. People must find new sources of food, clothing, medical and dental care, and household products. Once they make these basic buying decisions, they may not change for a long time. Alert marketers try to locate these potential customers early—to inform them of offerings before they make their purchase decisions. Retail chains, "national" brands, and franchised services available in different areas have a competitive advantage with mobiles. The customer who moves to a new town may find the familiar Kroger grocery store sign down the street and never even try its local competitors.[15]

INCOME DIMENSIONS OF THE U.S. MARKET

So far, we have been concerned mainly with the *number* of different types of people—and *where* they live.

More people are in middle- and upper-income levels

Earlier in this chapter you saw how GNP figures can be helpful in analyzing markets. But GNP figures are more meaningful to marketing managers when converted to family or household income—and its distribution. Family incomes in the U.S. generally increased with GNP. But even more important to marketers, the *distribution* of income changed drastically over time.

Fifty years ago, the U.S. income distribution looked something like a pyramid. Most families were bunched together at the low end of the income scale—just over a subsistence level—to form the base of the income pyramid.

EXHIBIT 6–7   Median Family Income, 1960–1993 (in 1993 dollars)

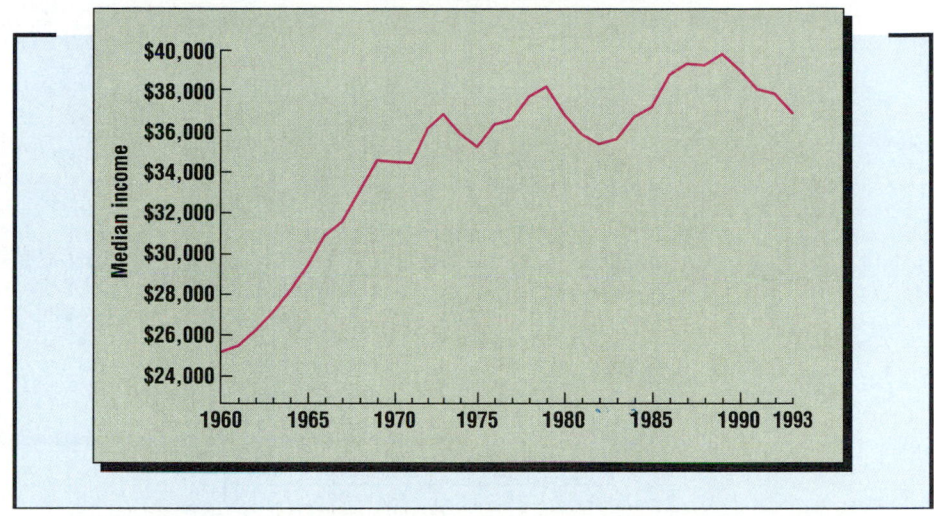

There were many fewer families in the middle range, and a relative handful formed an elite market at the top. This pattern still exists in many nations.

By the 1970s, real income (buying power) in the U.S. had risen so much that most families—even those near the bottom of the income distribution—could afford a comfortable standard of living. And the proportion of people with middle incomes was much larger. Such middle-income people enjoyed real choices in the marketplace.

This revolution broadened markets and drastically changed the U.S. marketing system. Products viewed as luxuries in most parts of the world sell to "mass" markets in the U.S. And these large markets lead to economies of scale, which boost our standard of living even more. Similar situations exist in Canada, many Western European countries, Australia, New Zealand, and Japan.

Real income growth has dropped—but for how long?

Trends in median family income from 1960 to 1990 reflect this upward shift in the income distribution—and the increased number of families with more money to spend. See Exhibit 6–7. Note, though, that (real) median income stopped its continuous rise during the inflation-ridden 1970s—and then actually dropped some. After 1981, it started to increase again. But it dropped again after 1987.

There is heated debate about what will happen to consumer incomes—and income distribution—in the future. Some business analysts feel that the lack of income growth signals worse things to come. They think that a decline in the manufacturing sector of the economy threatens America's middle-class standard of living. These analysts argue that in industries with traditionally high wages, firms are replacing workers with machines—to be able to compete with low-cost foreign producers. At the same time, new jobs are coming from growth of the lower-paying service industries. But other analysts are not so pessimistic. They agree that the percentage of the workforce earning middle-income wages has declined recently—but they think this is a temporary shift, not a long-term trend.

What happens to income levels will be critical to you—and to American consumers in general. It is easy for both consumers and marketing managers to be

EXHIBIT 6–8   Percent of Total Income Going to Different Income Groups in 1993

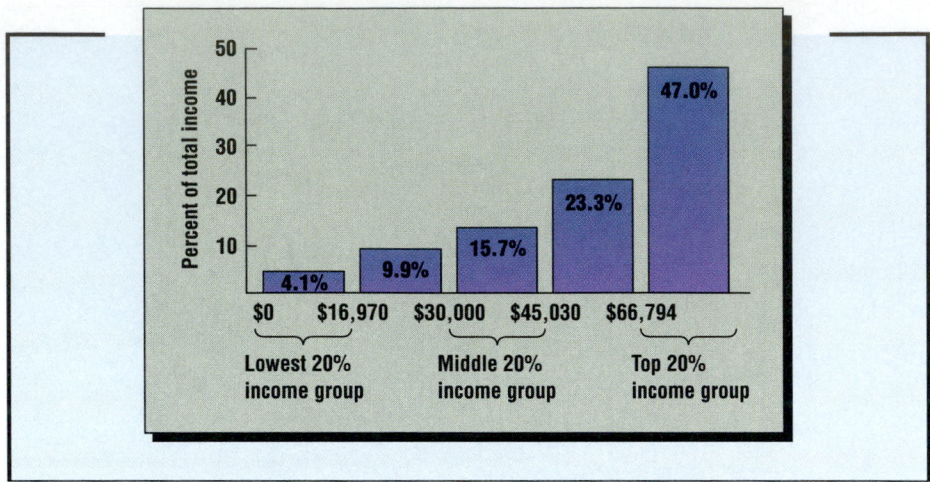

lulled by the promise of a constantly increasing standard of living. Both consumer thinking—and marketing strategy—will have to adjust if growth does not resume.

The higher-income groups receive a big share

Higher-income groups in the U.S. receive a very large share of total income as you can see in Exhibit 6–8, which divides all families into five equal-sized groups—from lowest income to highest. Note that although the median income of U.S. families in 1993 was about $36,960, the top 20 percent of the families—those with incomes over $66,794—received 47 percent of the total income. This gave them extra buying power, especially for luxury items like cellular phones, memberships in country clubs, and yachts. Well-to-do families with incomes over $113,182—the top 5 percent nationally—got more than 20 percent of the total income.

At the lower end of the scale, over 13.7 million families had less than $16,970 income. They account for 20 percent of all families but receive only 4.1 percent of total income. Even this low-income group is an attractive market for some basic commodities, especially food and clothing—even though over half of them live below the poverty level of $14,763 for a family of four. These consumers may receive food stamps, Medicare, and public housing, which increases their buying power. Some marketers target this group, usually with a lower-price marketing mix.

How much income is "enough"?

We can't stress the importance of income distribution too much. Many companies make serious marketing strategy errors by overestimating the amount of income in various target markets. Marketers can easily make such errors because of the natural tendency for people to associate with others like themselves—and to assume that almost everyone lives as they do.

The 1993 median family income of about $36,960 is a useful reference point because some college graduates start near this level. And a young working couple together can easily go way over this figure. This may seem like a lot of money at first—but it is surprising how soon needs and expenses rise and adjust to available income. America's middle-income consumers have been hit hard by the spiraling

NEON SAYS "HI" TO RECEPTIVE TARGET MARKET

Chrysler's Neon, the new model designed to woo buyers back from the small imports, is off to a strong start. Its success is partly due to good timing. A weak economy had forced low-income buyers to delay purchases, and Neon hit dealer lots just as these buyers were shopping again. Further, Chrysler did a good job designing out costs; a basic Neon, priced at about $8,000, is within the budget limits of its under-30, college-educated target market. Buyers with more discretionary income could get a loaded model for $12,000.

Neon's promotion also hit the mark. Groups of young people having fun—and the whimsical "Hi" positioned over the car at the start of each ad—helped to position Neon as approachable and afford-

able. Some Neon ads—like one featuring singer Lena Horne and a young black woman—specifically targeted African-Americans. Disproportionate numbers of black consumers have been buying the small imports. Further, Honda and Toyota dealers profited from good relations with these buyers when they were ready to trade up.

In Mexico, the Neon's target market has a different demographic profile. Mexican-made Neons are priced higher—$15,000 to $18,000—and out of reach for most entry-level buyers. So, Neon's ads in Mexico appeal to middle-aged professionals who are wealthier than average. Ads portray the Neon as a status symbol that offers superior handling and safety.[16]

costs of health care, housing, cars, taxes, and tuition bills. More than ever, these consumers look for purchases that offer good value for the money spent. Some high-living marketers may not understand that these consumers *need* to pinch their pennies, but that practical reality now explains much of the buying behavior of lower- and middle-income markets in the U.S.[17]

Can low-income consumers protect themselves?

In market-directed economies, consumers are free to make choices in the marketplace. But with little income, education, or opportunity to become informed, many consumers in the lowest income groups have few real choices. Some marketing managers struggle over whether to serve these markets. A credit company, for example, may find customers willing to pay a high finance charge to borrow money. And the high rate may be needed to cover the risk of unpaid loans. But is it exploitation to charge a higher rate to those who can least afford it and who really have no other choice?[18]

CONSUMER SPENDING PATTERNS ARE RELATED TO INCOME

We've been using the term *family income* because consumer budget studies show that most consumers spend their incomes as part of family or household units. They usually pool their incomes when planning major expenditures. So, most of our discussion will concern how families or households spend their income.

Disposable income is what you get to spend

Families don't get to spend all of their income. **Disposable income** is what is left after taxes. Out of this disposable income—together with gifts, pensions, cash savings, or other assets—the family makes its expenditures. Some families don't spend all their disposable income—they save part of it. Therefore, when trying to estimate potential sales in target markets, we should distinguish among income, disposable income, and what consumers actually spend.

Purchases of luxury items—including high-quality designer furnishings—come from discretionary income.

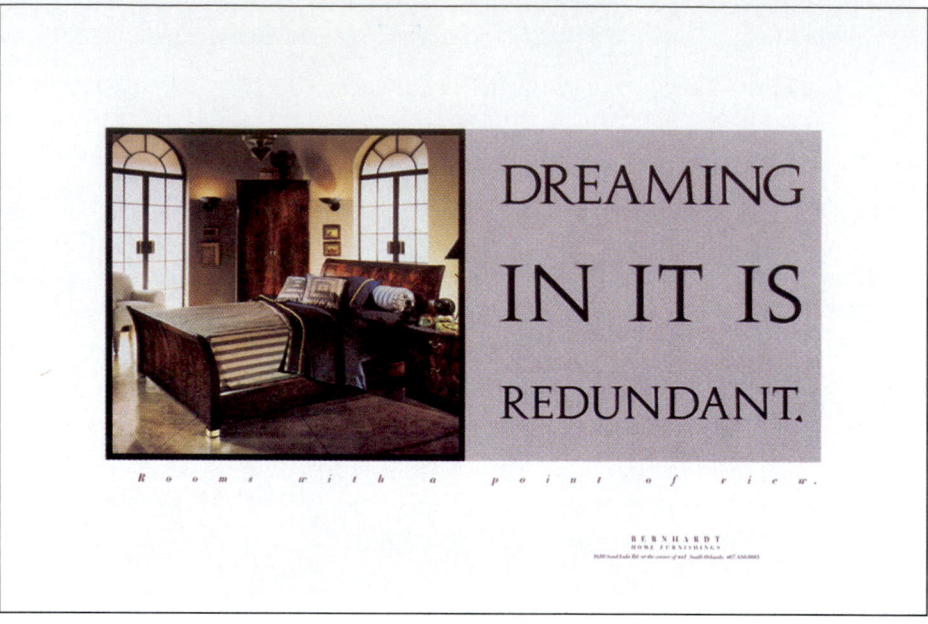

Discretionary income is elusive

Most families spend a good portion of their income on such "necessities" as food, rent or house payments, car and home furnishings payments, and insurance. A family's purchase of "luxuries" comes from **discretionary income**—what is left of disposable income after paying for necessities.

Discretionary income is an elusive concept because the definition of necessities varies from family to family and over time. It depends on what they think is necessary for their lifestyle. A color TV might be purchased out of discretionary income by a lower-income family but be considered a necessity by a higher-income family. But if many people in a lower-income neighborhood buy color TVs, they might become a "necessity" for the others—and severely reduce the discretionary income available for other purchases.

The majority of U.S. families do not have enough discretionary income to afford the lifestyles they see on TV and in other mass media. On the other hand, some young adults and older people without family responsibilities have a lot of discretionary income. They may be especially attractive markets for stereos, cameras, new cars, foreign travel, and various kinds of recreation—tennis, skiing, boating, concerts, and fine restaurants.

Expenditure data tells how target markets spend

Obviously, wealthy families spend more money than poor ones—and on different things. But how families spend—and how spending varies for different target markets—is important to marketers.

Currently the Bureau of Labor Statistics (BLS) and the U.S. Census Bureau publish the most comprehensive and easily available data on family spending. This data can serve as reference points—and should keep you from making wild guesses based only on your own experience. For example, Exhibit 6–9 shows the annual spending by urban families for several family income levels and for major categories of expenditures. The amount spent on major categories—such as food,

EXHIBIT 6–9 Family Spending for Several Family Income Levels (in 1993 dollars)

Spending Category	$15,000–$19,999 $	%	$20,000–$29,999 $	%	$30,000–$39,999 $	%
Food	3,505	16.7		15.6	4,706	14.5
Housing	6,721	31.9		31.3	9,513	29.3
Clothing	1,194	5.7		5.5	1,778	5.5
Transportation	3,850	18.3		17.7	6,361	19.6
Health care	1,803	8.6		6.8	1,881	5.8
Personal care	322	1.5		1.2	460	1.4
Education	239	1.1		1.0	305	1.0
Reading	112	0.5		0.6	183	0.6
Alcohol	175	0.8		0.9	275	0.9
Tobacco	247	1.2		1.3	329	1.0
Insurance and pensions	1,080	5.1		7.6	3,291	10.1
Contributions	470	2.2		3.2	918	2.8
Miscellaneous	435	2.1		2.6	852	2.6
Total spending	21,067	100.0		100.0	32,454	100.0

housing, clothing, transportation, and so on—does vary by income level. And the relationships are logical when you realize that many of the purchases in these categories are "necessities."[19]

Data such as that in Exhibit 6–9 can help you understand how potential target customers spend their money. Let's make this more concrete. Suppose you are a marketing manager for a swimming pool producer. You're considering a mail advertisement directed to consumers in an urban neighborhood of families with an average annual income of $25,000 a year. Looking at the center column of Exhibit 6–9, you can see how families at this income level spend their money. For example, the exhibit shows that—after paying for housing, transportation, food, clothing, and health care—families at this income level have less than $6,000 a year left for entertainment, education, personal care, and other expenditures. If a swimming pool costs at least $2,000 a year—including maintenance and depreciation—the average family in this income category would have to make a big change in lifestyle to buy a pool.

Data like this won't tell you whether a specific family will buy a pool. But it does supply useful input to help make a sound decision. If you need more information—perhaps about the strength of the target market's attitudes toward recreation products—you may have to do some marketing research. For example, you might want to see a budget study on consumers who already have a pool to see how they adjusted their spending patterns—and how they felt before and after the purchase.

SPENDING VARIES WITH OTHER DEMOGRAPHIC DIMENSIONS

Spending varies over the family life cycle

Income has a direct bearing on spending patterns, but many other demographic dimensions are also useful in understanding consumer buying. Marital status, age, and the age of any children in the family have an especially important

The fast-growing teen market is the target of promotion for a wide variety of products—ranging from MasterCard to Sears.

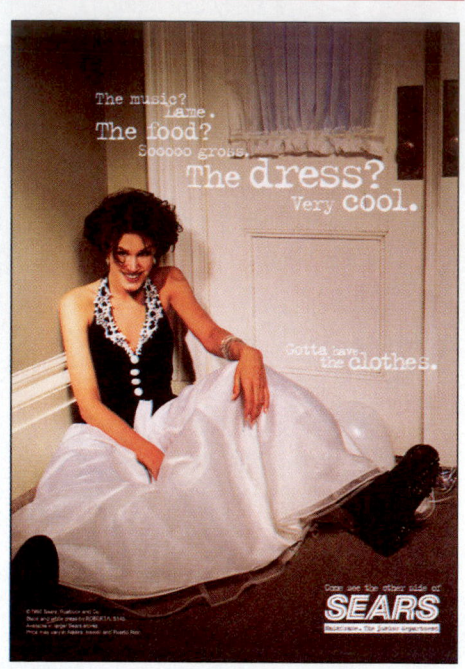

affect on how people spend their income. Put together, these dimensions tell us about the life cycle stage of a family. Exhibit 6–10 shows a summary of stages in the family life cycle. In our discussion, we will focus on the traditional flow from one stage to the next—as shown in the middle of the diagram. However, as shown at the top and bottom of the exhibit, divorce does interrupt the flow for many people; after a divorce, they may recycle through earlier stages.[20]

Young people and families accept new ideas

Singles and young couples seem to be more willing to try new products and brands—and they are careful, price-conscious shoppers. Younger people often earn less than older consumers, but they spend a greater proportion of their income on discretionary items because they don't have the major expenses of home ownership, education, and family rearing. Although many young people are waiting longer to marry, most do tie the knot eventually. These younger families—especially those with no children—are still accumulating durable goods, such as automobiles and home furnishings. They spend less on food. Only as children arrive and grow does family spending shift to soft goods and services, such as education, medical, and personal care. This usually happens when the family head reaches the 35–44 age group. To meet expenses, people in this age group often make more purchases on credit, and they save less of their income.

Divorce—increasingly a fact of American life—disrupts the family life-cycle pattern. Divorced parents don't spend like other singles. The mother usually has custody of the children, and the father may pay child support. The mother and children typically have much less income than two-parent families. Such families spend a larger percent of their income on housing, child care, and other necessities—with little left for discretionary purchases. If a single parent remarries, the family life cycle may start over again.[21]

EXHIBIT 6–10 Stages in Modern Family Life Cycles

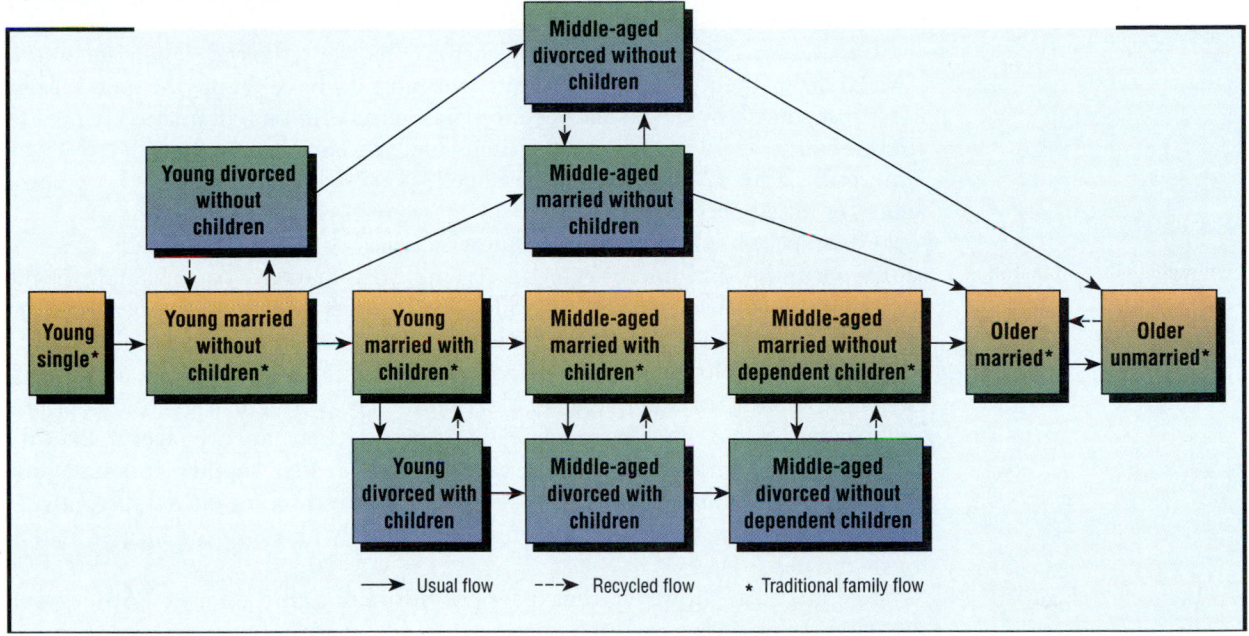

Reallocation for teenagers

Once children become teenagers, further shifts in spending occur. Teenagers eat more, want to wear expensive clothes, and develop recreation and education needs that are hard on the family budget. The parents—or, increasingly the single parent—may be forced to reallocate expenditures to cover these expenses—spending less on durable goods such as appliances, automobiles, household goods, and housing. The fast-rising expense of sending a son or daughter to college can create a major financial crisis.

For many firms, teens are an important and attractive market. The amount of money involved may surprise you. America's teens currently spend about $89 billion a year—$57 billion from their own earnings and another $32 billion from allowances. Further, in today's families with a single parent or with two wage-earners, teens play an increasingly important role in shopping and shaping family purchases. By some estimates, teens influence more than $200 billion in purchases.[22]

Selling to the empty nesters

Another important category is the **empty nesters**—people whose children are grown and who are now able to spend their money in other ways. Usually these people are in the 50–64 age group. But this is an elusive group because some people marry later and are still raising a family at this age.

Empty nesters are an attractive market for many items. They have paid for their homes, and the big expenses of raising a family are behind them. They are more interested in travel, small sports cars, and other things they couldn't afford before. Much depends on their income, of course. But this is a high-income period for many workers—especially white-collar workers.

Senior citizens are a big market

Finally, marketers should not neglect the **senior citizens**—people over 65. The number of people over 65 is increasing rapidly because of modern medicine, improved sanitary conditions, and better nutrition. This group now makes up almost 13 percent of the population—and by the year 2030 it will swell to 20 percent of the population.

Our senior citizens are more prosperous than ever before. Their income is lower than in their peak earning years, but most do have money to spend. They don't just squeak by on Social Security. Such prosperity is a dramatic change. In 1960, about a third of all senior citizens had incomes below the poverty level. Now, only about 12 percent are considered "poor"—lower than the 15.1 percent figure for all adults.

Older people also have very different needs. Many firms already cater to senior citizens—and more will be serving this market. For example, some companies developed housing and "life care" centers designed to appeal to older people. Casio makes a calculator with large, easy-to-read numbers. Publix Super Markets, a big Florida chain, trains employees to cater to older customers. Checkout clerks, for example, give older customers two light bags instead of one heavier one. Some travel agents find that senior citizens are an eager market for expensive tours and cruises. Other companies offer diet supplements and drug products—often in special easy-to-open packages. And senior citizen discounts at drugstores are more than just a courtesy—the elderly make up the biggest market for medicines.

Keep in mind, however, that older people are not all the same. With a group this large, generalities and stereotypes can be dangerous. Different senior citizen target markets have different needs—and require different marketing strategies.[23]

ETHNIC DIMENSIONS OF THE U.S. MARKET

Do ethnic groups buy differently?

America may be called the melting pot, but ethnic groups deserve special attention when analyzing markets. One basic reason is that people from different ethnic groups may be influenced by very different cultural variables. They may have quite different needs and their own ways of thinking. Moreover, Americans are beginning to recognize the value of multicultural diversity. The U.S. is becoming a multicultural market. As a result, rather than disappearing in a melting pot, some important cultural and ethnic dimensions are being preserved and highlighted. This creates both opportunities and challenges for marketers.

Some important ethnic differences are obvious. For example, more than 1 out of 10 families in the U.S. speaks a language other than English at home. Some areas have a much higher rate. In Miami and San Antonio, for example, about one out of three families speaks Spanish. This obviously affects promotion planning. Similarly, brand preferences vary for some ethnic groups. For example, cosmetic companies offer products tailored to different skin tones. But, ethnic groups don't just differ in the color of their skin. Differences in attitudes, experiences, and values, as well as where they shop and what advertising appeals they attend to, come together to shape differences in buying behavior.

Stereotypes are common—and misleading

A marketer needs to study ethnic dimensions very carefully because they can be subtle and fast changing. This is also an area where stereotyped thinking is the most common—and misleading. Many firms make the mistake of treating all consumers in a particular ethnic group as homogeneous. For example, some marketing managers treat all 32 million African-American consumers as "the black market," ignoring the great variability among African-American households on other segmenting dimensions. Income variability is a good example.

Many firms, including Chrysler's Cirrus, are paying more attention to the special needs of African-American consumers.

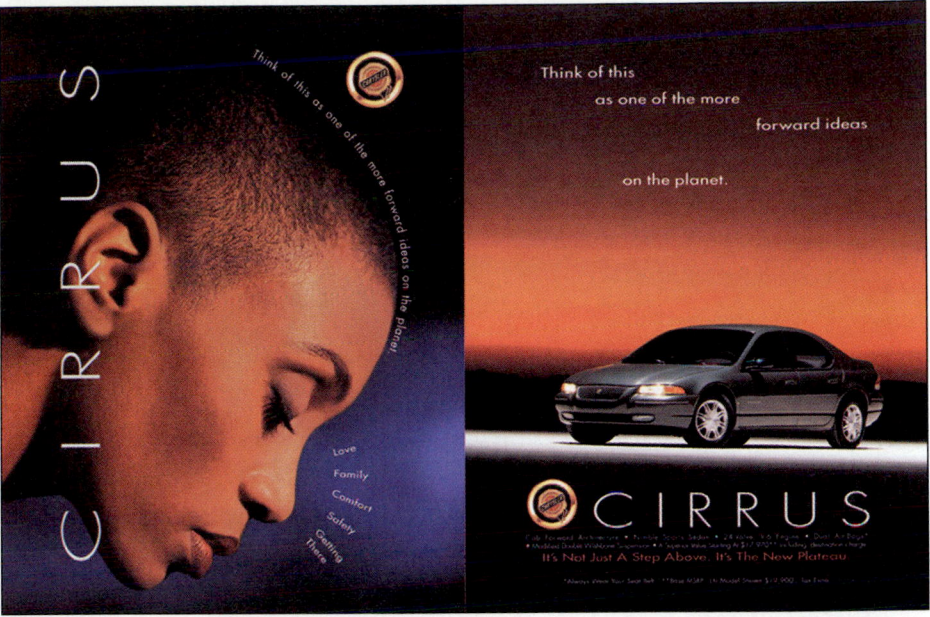

While the median income of black families is still much lower than for the whole population, that is changing. Today about 16 percent of black families have an income of at least $50,000—and about a third of those have an income of $75,000 or more. These affluent consumers are also a relatively youthful market, and a larger percentage (compared with white consumers) are in earlier stages of the life cycle and therefore a better market for certain products—especially durable goods like cars, furniture, home appliances, and electronic equipment.

Ethnic markets are becoming more important

More marketers pay attention to ethnic groups now because the number of ethnic consumers is growing at a much faster rate than the overall society. Much of this growth results from immigration. In addition, however, the median age of Asian-Americans, African-Americans, and Hispanics is much lower than that of whites—and the birthrate is higher.

In combination, these factors have a significant effect. For example, the Asian-American population, now about 7.9 million, more than doubled from 1980 to 1990 and should grow an additional 40 percent by 2000. Similarly, the number of Hispanic consumers more than doubled from about 9 million in 1970 to about 24 million now. To put this in perspective, there are as many Hispanics in the U.S. as there are Canadians in Canada. Moreover, by 2010 the U.S. Hispanic population is expected to reach 39 million, which will make it about the same size as the black population. At that point, more than one-third of American children will be black, Hispanic, or Asian; by 2030, about 40 percent of the U.S. population will be nonwhite.

The buying power of ethnic submarkets is also increasing rapidly. African-American consumers now spend over $250 billion a year—and Hispanics more than $160 billion a year. Moreover, much of this buying power is concentrated in certain cities and states. For example, 70 percent of the Hispanics in the U.S. live in California, Texas, New York, and Florida. Over 20 percent of San Francisco's residents are Asians.

As illustrated by this storyboard for a Southwestern Bell TV ad, many firms are developing new strategies to appeal to fast-growing ethnic markets.

Southwestern Bell
Telephone

INVENTIVA

"Checking on Mom"
:30 TV

DAUGHTER: Me daban nervios por no saber como seguía mamá.
DAUGHTER: I was always nervous because I couldn't check on how mom was doing.

DAUGHTER: Ella vive en otro barrio,
DAUGHTER: She lives in another neighborhood,

DAUGHTER: y no teníamos teléfono.
DAUGHTER: and we just didn't have a phone.

DAUGHTER: Ella sí, pero nosotros...
DAUGHTER: She did, but we...

DAUGHTER: Pensábamos que era muy caro.
DAUGHTER: We thought it was too expensive.

DAUGHTER: ¡Ay que equivocados!
DAUGHTER: Boy, we were wrong.

ANNCR: Usted puede tener servicio telefónico básico por sólo $17 al mes.
ANNCR: You can have basic phone service for only $17 a month.

ANNCR: La instalación es menos de $53.
ANNCR: Installation? It's less than $53.

ANNCR: Llame a Southwestern Bell Telephone
ANNCR: Call Southwestern Bell Telephone

ANNCR: al 1-800-559-0050 y ordene su servicio hoy.
ANNCR: at 1-800-559-0050 and order your service today.

ANNCR: Hablamos español.
ANNCR: We speak Spanish.
DAUGHTER: ¿Mama?
DAUGHTER: Mom?

MOM: ¡Mija!
MOM: Mija!

▲TRI-ADS™, Burbank, CA

Strategy changes may be needed

Companies may need separate strategies for these ethnically or racially defined markets. Many of these strategies may require only changes in Place and Promotion. But sometimes companies may have more difficulty developing strategies and segmenting ethnic submarkets. For example, Asian-Americans emigrated from China, Japan, the Philippines, India, Korea, Vietnam, Laos, and Cambodia. Many come from very different backgrounds, with no common language, religion, or culture. That adds to the marketing challenge; it means marketers must really understand the basic needs that motivate specific target markets to think and act as they do. This is important with any consumer market—regardless of people's ethnic or racial background or where in the world they live. We'll deal with that important issue in more detail in the next chapter.[24]

CONCLUSION

In this chapter, we studied population, income, and other demographic dimensions of consumer markets. Getting the facts straight on how over 5 billion people are spread over the world is important to marketing managers. We learned that the potential of a given market cannot be determined by population figures alone. Geographic location, income, stage in life cycle, ethnic background, and other factors are important too. We talked about some of the ways these dimensions—and changes in them—affect marketing strategy planning.

We also noted the growth of urban areas in countries around the world. The high concentration of population and spending power in large metropolitan areas of the U.S. has already made them attractive target markets. However, competition in these markets is often tough.

One of the outstanding characteristics of U.S. consumers is their mobility. Managers must pay attention to changes in markets. High mobility makes even relatively new data suspect. Data can only aid a manager's judgment—not replace it.

U.S. consumers are among the most affluent in the world. They have more discretionary income and can afford a wide variety of products that people in other parts of the world view as luxuries. However, in the U.S., as in most other societies, income is distributed unevenly among different groups. Consumers at the top income levels have a disproportionately large share of the total buying power.

The kind of data discussed in this chapter can be very useful for estimating the market potential within possible target markets. But, unfortunately, it is not very helpful in explaining specific customer behavior—why people buy *specific* products and *specific* brands. Yet such detailed forecasts are important to marketing managers. Better forecasts can come from a better understanding of consumer behavior—the subject of the next chapter.

QUESTIONS AND PROBLEMS

1. Drawing on data in Exhibit 6–2, do you think that Peru would be an attractive market for a firm that produces home appliances? What about Finland? Discuss your reasons.

2. Discuss the value of gross national product and gross national product per capita as measures of market potential in international consumer markets. Refer to specific data in your answer.

3. Discuss how the worldwide trend toward urbanization is affecting opportunities for international marketing.

4. Discuss how slower population growth will affect businesses in your local community.

5. Discuss the impact of the aging culture on marketing strategy planning in the U.S.

6. Name three specific examples of firms that developed a marketing mix to appeal to the baby boomers. Name three examples of firms that developed a marketing mix to appeal to teenagers.

7. Some demographic characteristics are more important than others in determining market potential. For each of the following characteristics, identify two products for which this characteristic is *most* important: (*a*) size of geographic area, (*b*) population, (*c*) income, and (*d*) stage of life cycle.

8. Name three specific examples (specific products or brands—not just product categories) and explain how demand for them in the U.S. will differ by geographic location *and* urban–rural location.

9. Explain how the continuing mobility of U.S. consumers—as well as the development of big metropolitan areas—should affect marketing strategy planning in the future. Be sure to consider the impact on the four Ps.

10. Explain how the redistribution of income in the U.S. has affected marketing planning thus far—and its likely impact in the future.

11. Explain why the concept of the Metropolitan Statistical Area was developed. Is it the most useful breakdown for retailers?

12. Explain why mobile consumers can be an attractive market.

13. Why are marketing managers paying more attention to ethnic dimensions of consumer markets in the U.S.?

SUGGESTED CASES

8. Maria's Place
10. Fulton's Ice Arena

30. Deluxe Foods, Ltd.

COMPUTER-AIDED PROBLEM

6. Demographic Analysis

Stylco, Inc., is a producer of specialty clothing. To differentiate its designs and appeal to its African-American target market, Stylco uses authentic African prints. Originally, it just focused on designs targeted at younger adults in the 25–34 age range. However, in the early 1990s, when sales to younger adults started to level off, Stylco added a more conservative line of clothes for older consumers. Most buyers of the conservative styles are in the 35–54 age group.

Stylco has focused on distributing its products through select fashion boutiques in metropolitan market areas with the highest concentrations of African-American consumers. This approach has reduced Stylco's personal selling expense; as a result, however, only a percentage of the total black population is served by current Stylco retailers. For example, about half of the

consumers in the 35–54 age group are in the market areas served by Stylco retailers.

Naomi Davis, Stylco's marketing manager, recently read an article about the "graying of America." She is wondering how shifts in the age distribution might affect her market and sales.

To get a long-run view of these trends, she looked at 1995 Census data on black consumers by age group. She also looked up estimates of the expected percent rate of change in the size of each group through the year 2000. By multiplying these rates by the size of her 1995 target markets, she can estimate how large they are likely to be in the year 2000. Further, from analysis of past sales data, she knows that the number of units the firm sells is directly proportional to the size of each age group. Specifically, the ratio of units sold to target market size has been about 5 units per 1,000 people (that is, a ratio of

.005). Finally, she determined the firm's average unit profit for each of the lines. To see how changes in population are likely to affect Stylco units sold and future profits from each line, Davis programmed all of these data, and the relationships discussed above, into a spreadsheet.

a. *Briefly compare the profit data for 1995 and estimated profit for 2000 as it appears on the initial spreadsheet. What is the basic reason for the expected shift? What are the implications of these and other data in the spreadsheet for Stylco's marketing strategy planning?*

b. *The rate of growth or decline for different age groups tends to vary from one geographic region to another. Davis thinks that in the market areas that Stylco serves the size of the 25–34 age group may decrease by as much as 10 to 12 percent by 2000. However, the Census Bureau estimates that the decline of the black 25–34 age group for the whole country will only be about −1.1 percent. If the decline in the target market size for Davis' market areas turns out to be −1.1 percent rather than the −10.1 she has assumed, what is the potential effect on profits from the young adult line? On overall profits?*

c. *Because more firms are paying attention to fast-growing ethnic markets, Davis thinks competition may increase in lines targeted at affluent African-Americans in the 35–54 age group. Because of price competition, the line targeted at this group already earns a lower average profit per unit. Further, as more firms compete for this business she thinks that her "ratio of units sold to market size" may decrease. Use the What If analysis to prepare a table showing how profits and percent of profit from this group, as well as total profit, might change as the ratio of units sold to market size varies between a minimum of .001 and a maximum of .010. Explain the implications to the firm.*

For additional questions related to this problem, see Exercise 6–4 in the *Learning Aid for Use with Basic Marketing*, 12th edition.

7

Behavioral Dimensions of the Consumer Market

When You Finish This Chapter, You Should

1. Understand the economic-buyer model of buyer behavior.

2. Understand how psychological variables affect an individual's buying behavior.

3. Understand how social influences affect an individual's and a household's buying behavior.

4. See why the purchase situation has an effect on consumer behavior.

5. Know how consumers use problem-solving processes.

6. Have some feel for how a consumer handles all the behavioral variables and incoming stimuli.

7. Understand the important new terms (shown in red).

In January of 1995, marketing managers at Harley-Davidson faced an unusual—but pleasant—situation. Advance orders were already in for all of the motorcycles that Harley could produce for the rest of the year—and it looked as if the firm's 60 percent market share would continue to grow. That's quite a change from a decade earlier when the famous motorcycle maker was at the edge of bankruptcy. Harley's success was the result of the marketing strategy it had developed in response to changes in consumer buying behavior.

In 1960, most consumers saw Harley motorcycles as "in" with only one group—leather-clad Hell's Angels—and in total only about 60,000 motorcycles were sold in the U.S. During the next decade, perceptions of motorcycles changed as Japanese producers promoted smaller models that had broad market appeal. Motorcycle sales grew rapidly as the number of young adults increased, and Harley shared in the growth. However, by 1980 when total U.S. motorcycle sales peaked at about 655,000 units, Harley sales had plummeted. Consumers were basing their buying decisions on economic needs. The Japanese cycles were less expensive to buy and maintain. They were also much more reliable. As the youth market disappeared, Harley sales continued to fall until 1985 when the firm was sold to new owners.

The new team of marketing managers knew they needed a new strategy to regain profitability. They decided to target upscale, middle-aged professionals. These customers didn't need economical transportation—they wanted fun, freedom, and relaxation. They wanted a weekend escape from the pressures of work and an excuse to get together with other people who had similar interests. To meet these needs and respond to a new type of buying behavior, Harley's marketing managers changed the firm's marketing mix. They didn't just offer customers a good motorcycle; instead, they promoted the whole Harley lifestyle, including a relationship with the company and other Harley owners.

First, they improved the quality and reliability of their bikes, designed quieter engines, and added fancy options like stereo systems. They also focused on big cycles, and left competitors to fight for share in the shrinking market for smaller bikes. Harley also told its dealers to clean up their stores—many of which had been dark and menacing—and encouraged them to carry the new lines of Harley-brand jewelry and clothing. More inviting dealerships bring in more customers—both men and women. And taking a trial ride is a high-involvement experience. Prospects often buy a high-ticket bike on the spot.

But that's just the start. To keep its relationship with customers, Harley set up the Harley

Owners Group (HOG). HOG is run through local dealers, so it gives a new rider instant companionship for organized rides and rallies. The rallies also give Harley marketers a chance to mix with customers and better understand their attitudes about HOG events, expectations of the company, and satisfaction with their motorcycles. To keep in touch with Harley owners, the company even publishes its own magazine. All this attention builds a lot of loyalty. When Harley owners are ready to trade up, many just routinely buy another Harley.

In recent years, Harley has set its sights on expanding the Harley following overseas. That's requiring some adjustments—ranging from publishing the Harley magazine in different languages to adapting HOG social events and ads to local cultures. The effort is off to a promising start. In Japan, the Australian outback, the roads winding through Germany's Black Forest, and Mexico City's crowded streets, hundreds of riders are discovering the thrill of hopping on a Harley.[1]

CONSUMER BEHAVIOR—WHY DO THEY BUY WHAT THEY BUY?

In the last chapter, we discussed basic data on population, income, and consumer spending patterns. This information can help marketers predict basic *trends* in consumer spending patterns. Unfortunately, when many firms sell similar products, demographic analysis isn't much help in predicting which specific products and brands consumers will purchase—and why. Our Harley-Davidson example shows that many other variables can influence consumers and their buying behavior.

To better understand why consumers buy as they do, many marketers turn to the behavioral sciences for help. In this chapter, we'll explore some of the thinking from economics, psychology, sociology, and the other behavioral disciplines.

Economic needs affect many buying decisions, but for some purchases the behavioral influences on a consumer are more important.

For dine-in, carryout or delivery, enjoy genuine Pizza Hut® pizza.
Check your local yellow pages for the Pizza Hut® nearest you.

Grandchildren not required.

Specific consumer behaviors vary a great deal for different products and from one target market to the next. In today's global markets, the variations are countless. That makes it impractical to try to catalog all the detailed possibilities for every different market situation. For example, how and why a given consumer buys a specific brand of shampoo may be very different from how that same consumer buys motor oil; and different customers in different parts of the world may have very different reactions to either product. But there are *general* behavioral principles—frameworks—that marketing managers can apply to learn more about their specific target markets. Our approach focuses on developing your skill in working with these frameworks.

THE BEHAVIORAL SCIENCES HELP YOU UNDERSTAND BUYING PROCESS

Economic needs affect most buying decisions

Most economists assume that consumers are **economic buyers**—people who know all the facts and logically compare choices in terms of cost and value received to get the greatest satisfaction from spending their time and money. A logical extension of the economic-buyer theory led us to look at consumer spending patterns. This approach is valuable because consumers must at least have income to be in a market. Further, most consumers don't have enough income to buy everything they want. So most consumers want their money to stretch as far as it can.

This view assumes that economic needs guide most consumer behavior. **Economic needs** are concerned with making the best use of a consumer's time and money—as the consumer judges it. Some consumers look for the lowest price. Others will pay extra for convenience. And others may weigh price and quality for the best value. Some economic needs are:

1. Economy of purchase or use.
2. Convenience.
3. Efficiency in operation or use.
4. Dependability in use.
5. Improvement of earnings.

Clearly, marketing managers must be alert to new ways to appeal to economic needs. Most consumers appreciate firms that offer them improved value for the money they spend. But improved value does not just mean offering lower and lower prices. Many consumers face a "poverty of time." Carefully planned place decisions can make it easier and faster for customers to make a purchase. Products can be designed to work better, require less service, or last longer. Promotion can inform consumers about their choices—or explain product benefits in terms of measurable factors like operating costs or the length of the guarantee.

The "economic value" that a purchase offers a customer is an important factor in many purchase decisions. But most marketing managers think that buyer behavior is not as simple as the economic-buyer model suggests. A product that one person sees as a good value—and is eager to buy—is of no interest to someone else. So we can't expect to understand buying behavior without taking a broader view.

How we will view consumer behavior

Many behavioral dimensions influence consumers. Let's try to combine these dimensions into a model of how consumers make decisions. Exhibit 7–1 shows that psychological variables, social influences, and the purchase situation all affect

EXHIBIT 7–1   A Model of Buyer Behavior

a person's buying behavior. We'll discuss these topics in the next few pages. Then we'll expand the model to include the consumer problem-solving process.

PSYCHOLOGICAL INFLUENCES WITHIN AN INDIVIDUAL

Here we will discuss some variables of special interest to marketers—including motivation, perception, learning, attitudes, and lifestyle. Much of what we know about these *psychological (intrapersonal) variables* draws from ideas originally developed in the field of psychology.

Needs motivate consumers

Everybody is motivated by needs and wants. **Needs** are the basic forces that motivate a person to do something. Some needs involve a person's physical well-being, others the individual's self-view and relationship with others. Needs are more basic than wants. **Wants** are "needs" that are learned during a person's life. For example, everyone needs water or some kind of liquid, but some people also have learned to want Clearly Canadian's raspberry-flavored sparkling water on the rocks.

When a need is not satisfied, it may lead to a drive. The need for liquid, for example, leads to a thirst drive. A **drive** is a strong stimulus that encourages action to reduce a need. Drives are internal—they are the reasons behind certain behavior patterns. In marketing, a product purchase results from a drive to satisfy some need.

Some critics imply that marketers can somehow manipulate consumers to buy products against their will. But marketing managers can't create internal drives. Most marketing managers realize that trying to get consumers to act against their will is a waste of time. Instead, a good marketing manager studies what consumer drives, needs, and wants already exist and how they can be satisfied better.

Consumers seek benefits to meet needs

We're all a bundle of needs and wants. Exhibit 7–2 lists some important needs that might motivate a person to some action. This list, of course, is not

EXHIBIT 7–2   Possible Needs Motivating a Person to Some Action

Types of Needs	Specific Examples			
Physiological needs	Hunger Sex Rest	Thirst Body elimination	Activity Self-preservation	Sleep Warmth/coolness
Psychological needs	Aggression Family preservation Nurturing Playing-relaxing Self-identification	Curiosity Imitation Order Power Tenderness	Being responsible Independence Personal fulfillment Pride	Dominance Love Playing-competition Self-expression
Desire for . . .	Acceptance Affiliation Comfort Esteem Knowledge Respect Status	Achievement Appreciation Fun Fame Prestige Retaliation Sympathy	Acquisition Beauty Distance—"space" Happiness Pleasure Self-satisfaction Variety	Affection Companionship Distinctiveness Identification Recognition Sociability
Freedom from . .	Fear Pain Harm	Depression Imitation Ridicule	Discomfort Loss Sadness	Anxiety Illness Pressure

complete. But thinking about such needs can help you see what *benefits* consumers might seek from a marketing mix.

When a marketing manager defines a product-market, the needs may be quite specific. For example, the food need might be as specific as wanting a thick-crust pepperoni pizza—delivered to your door hot and ready to eat.

Several needs at the same time

Some psychologists argue that a person may have several reasons for buying—at the same time. Maslow is well known for his five-level hierarchy of needs. We will discuss a similar four-level hierarchy that is easier to apply to consumer behavior. Exhibit 7–3 illustrates the four levels along with an advertising slogan showing how a company has tried to appeal to each need. The lowest-level needs are physiological. Then come safety, social, and personal needs. As a study aid, think of the PSSP needs.[2]

Physiological needs are concerned with biological needs—food, drink, rest, and sex. **Safety needs** are concerned with protection and physical well-being (perhaps involving health, food, medicine, and exercise). **Social needs** are concerned with love, friendship, status, and esteem—things that involve a person's interaction with others. **Personal needs**, on the other hand, are concerned with an individual's need for personal satisfaction—unrelated to what others think or do. Examples include self-esteem, accomplishment, fun, freedom, and relaxation.

Motivation theory suggests that we never reach a state of complete satisfaction. As soon as we get our lower-level needs reasonably satisfied, those at higher levels become more dominant. This explains why marketing efforts targeted at affluent consumers in advanced economies often focus on higher-level needs. It also explains why these approaches may be useless in parts of the world where consumers' basic needs are not being met.

EXHIBIT 7–3   The PSSP Hierarchy of Needs

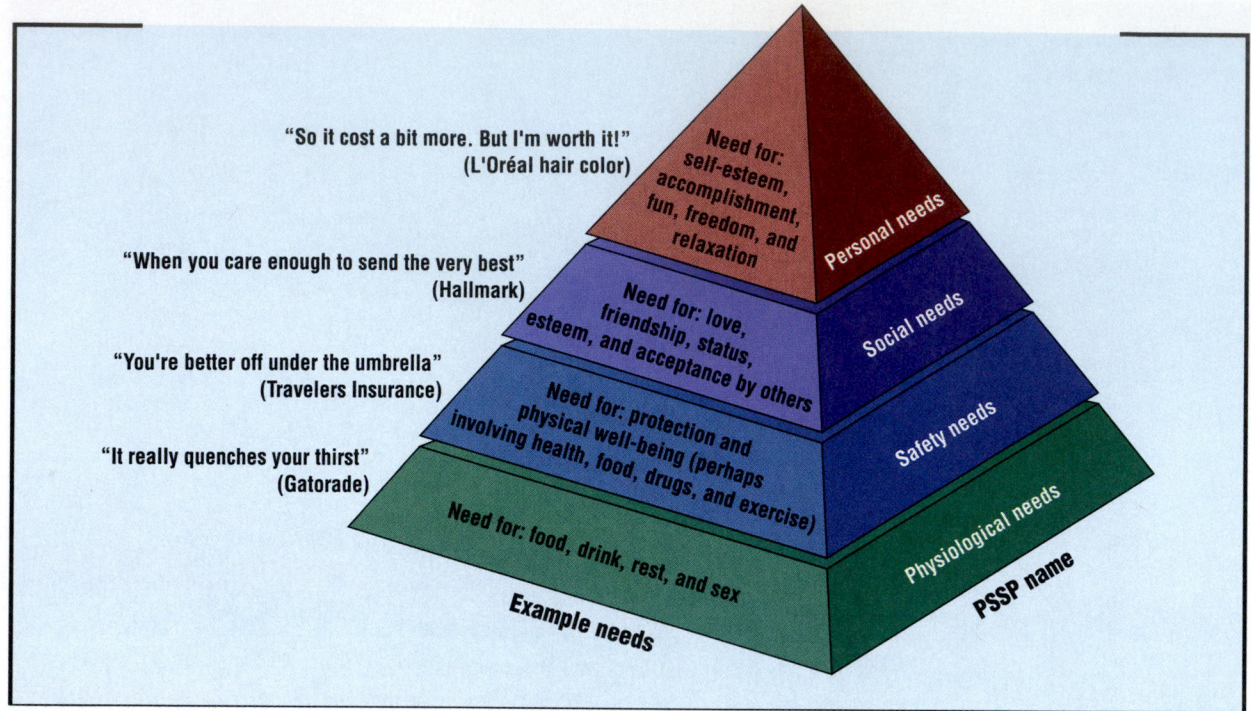

It is important to see, however, that a particular product may satisfy more than one need at the same time. In fact, most consumers try to fill a *set* of needs rather than just one need or another in sequence.

Obviously marketers should try to satisfy different needs. Yet discovering these specific consumer needs may require careful analysis. Consider, for example, the lowly vegetable peeler. Marketing managers for OXO International realized that many people, especially young children and senior citizens, have trouble gripping the handle of a typical peeler. OXO redesigned the peeler with a bigger handle that addressed this physical need. OXO also coated the handle with dishwasher-safe rubber. This makes cleanup more convenient—and the sharp peeler is safer to use when the grip is wet. The attractively designed grip also appeals to consumers who get personal satisfaction from cooking—and who want to impress their guests. Even though OXO priced the peeler much higher than most kitchen utensils, it has sold very well because it appeals to people with a variety of needs.[3]

Perception determines what consumers see and feel

Consumers select varying ways to meet their needs sometimes because of differences in **perception**—how we gather and interpret information from the world around us.

We are constantly bombarded by stimuli—ads, products, stores—yet we may not hear or see anything. This is because we apply the following selective processes:

1. **Selective exposure**—our eyes and minds seek out and notice only information that interests us.

Many needs are culturally learned.

sure · UNsure

NEW SURE® ROLL-ON KEEPS YOU DRIER THAN THE LEADING ROLL-ON. NOW   WORRYING ABOUT DRYNESS IS ANCIENT HISTORY. **BE SURE TO BE DRIER.**

2. **Selective perception**—we screen out or modify ideas, messages, and information that conflict with previously learned attitudes and beliefs.

3. **Selective retention**—we remember only what we want to remember.

These selective processes help explain why some people are not affected by some advertising—even offensive advertising. They just don't see or remember it! Even if they do, they may dismiss it immediately. Some consumers are skeptical about any advertising message.

Our needs affect these selective processes. And current needs receive more attention. For example, Michelin tire retailers advertise some sale in the newspaper almost weekly. Most of the time we don't even notice these ads—until we need new tires. Only then do we tune in to Michelin's ads.

Marketers are interested in these selective processes because they affect how target consumers get and retain information. This is also why marketers are interested in how consumers *learn*.

Learning determines what response is likely

Learning is a change in a person's thought processes caused by prior experience. Learning is often based on direct experience: a little girl tastes her first cone of Ben & Jerry's Cherry Garcia ice cream, and learning occurs! Learning may also be based on indirect experience or associations. If you watch an ad that shows other people enjoying Ben and Jerry's low-fat frozen yogurt, you might conclude that you'd like it too. Consumer learning may result from things that marketers do, or it may result from stimuli that have nothing to do with marketing. Either way, almost all consumer behavior is learned.[4]

Experts describe a number of steps in the learning process. We've already discussed the idea of a drive as a strong stimulus that encourages action. Depending on the **cues**—products, signs, ads, and other stimuli in the environment—an individual chooses some specific response. A **response** is an effort

Consumer perceptions of an ad for Scotchgard Fabric Protector might depend on whether or not they see fabric stains as a big problem.

THERE'S NO SUCH THING AS A LITTLE STAIN.

It may be just a little stain but it sure stands out on your sofa. It could spell ruin.

But professionally-applied, locked-on Scotchgard™ Fabric Protector keeps most seri-

ous spills from becoming stains. Most spills wipe right up. Protects against soiling too.

Scotchgard™ Protectors keep all kinds of things new looking longer. Things like carpeting,

children's clothing, bedspreads, drapes, wooden tabletops, outerwear, car interiors. There's even a Scotchgard™ Protector for leather.

So whenever you shop, always look for

the Scotchgard™ label. Because even a little stain is too much.

Scotchgard

Innovation working for you™ **3M**

to satisfy a drive. The specific response chosen depends on the cues and the person's past experience.

Reinforcement of the learning process occurs when the response is followed by satisfaction—that is, reduction in the drive. Reinforcement strengthens the relationship between the cue and the response. And it may lead to a similar response the next time the drive occurs. Repeated reinforcement leads to development of a habit—making the individual's decision process routine. Exhibit 7–4 shows the relationships of the important variables in the learning process.

The learning process can be illustrated by a thirsty person. The thirst *drive* could be satisfied in a variety of ways. But if the person happened to walk past a vending machine and saw a 7UP sign—a *cue*—then he might satisfy the drive with a *response*—buying a 7UP. If the experience is satisfactory, positive *reinforcement* will occur, and our friend may be quicker to satisfy this drive in the same way in the future. This emphasizes the importance of developing good products that live up to the promises of the firm's advertising. People can learn to like or dislike 7UP—reinforcement and learning work both ways. Unless marketers satisfy their customers, they must constantly try to attract new ones to replace the dissatisfied ones who don't come back.

Good experiences can lead to positive attitudes about a firm's product. Bad experiences can lead to negative attitudes that even good promotion won't be able to change. In fact, the subject of attitudes, an extremely important one to marketers, is discussed more fully in a later section.

EXHIBIT 7–4
The Learning Process

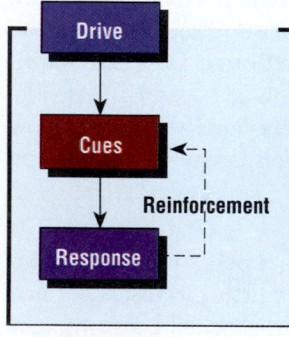

Positive cues help a marketing mix

Sometimes marketers try to identify cues or images that have positive associations from some other situation and relate them to their marketing mix. Many people associate the smell of lemons with a fresh, natural cleanliness. So companies often add lemon scent to household cleaning products—Joy dishwashing detergent and Pledge furniture polish, for example—because it has these associations. Similarly, some shampoos and deodorants are formulated to be clear and packaged in clear bottles because some consumers associate that look with being natural and pure. Similarly, many firms use ads suggesting that people who use their products have more appeal to the opposite sex.

Many needs are culturally learned

Many needs are culturally (or socially) learned. The need for food, for instance, may lead to many specific food wants. Many Japanese enjoy sushi (raw fish), and their children learn to like it. Few Americans, however, have learned to enjoy it.

Some critics argue that marketing efforts encourage people to spend money on learned wants totally unrelated to any basic need. For example, Europeans are less concerned about body odor, and few buy or use a deodorant. Yet Americans spend millions of dollars on such products. Advertising says that using Ban deodorant "takes the worry out of being close." But is marketing activity the cause of the difference in the two cultures? Most research says that advertising can't convince buyers of something contrary to their basic attitudes.

Attitudes relate to buying

An **attitude** is a person's point of view toward something. The "something" may be a product, an advertisement, a salesperson, a firm, or an idea. Attitudes are an important topic for marketers because attitudes affect the selective processes, learning, and eventually the buying decisions people make.

Because attitudes are usually thought of as involving liking or disliking, they have some action implications. Beliefs are not so action-oriented. A **belief** is a person's opinion about something. Beliefs may help shape a consumer's attitudes but don't necessarily involve any liking or disliking. It is possible to have a belief—say, that Listerine has a medicinal taste—without really caring what it tastes like. On the other hand, beliefs about a product may have a positive or negative effect in shaping consumers' attitudes. For example, a person with a headache is unlikely to switch to a new pain medicine unless she believes it will be more effective than what she used in the past.

In an attempt to relate attitude more closely to purchase behavior, some marketers stretched the attitude concept to include consumer "preferences" or "intention to buy." Managers who must forecast how much of their brand customers will buy are particularly interested in the intention to buy. Forecasts would be easier if attitudes were good predictors of intentions to buy. Unfortunately, the relationships usually are not that simple. A person may have positive attitudes toward Jacuzzi whirlpool bathtubs but no intention of buying one.

Try to understand attitudes and beliefs

Research on consumer attitudes and beliefs can sometimes help a marketing manager get a better picture of markets. For example, consumers with very positive attitudes toward a new product idea might prove a good opportunity—especially if they have negative attitudes about competitors' offerings. Or they may have beliefs that would discourage them from buying a product.

Marketing managers for Bristol-Myers's Nuprin faced this challenge. Research showed that their Nuprin brand relieved pain better than Tylenol, the most popular brand. But consumers didn't pay much attention to Nuprin ads that tried to convey that message. Most consumers believed that one pain killer was about as good as another. So Nuprin tried a different approach. Its managers developed ads focusing on a superficial product difference, its yellow color, and pitched

This ad's copy states, "51% of Swedes are prejudiced against fish-balls. You too?" In Sweden, fish-balls are a traditional dish, but most consumers think the canned variety are tasteless and boring. This ad attempts to change these attitudes by showing an attractive way to serve the product—but overcoming negative attitudes is a difficult job.

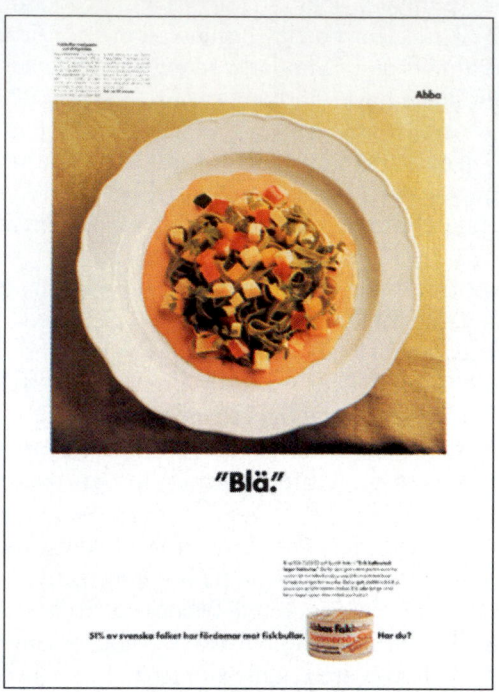

Nuprin as "little, yellow, different, better." Black-and-white TV ads showed people giving testimonials that Nuprin relieved their worst pains—toothaches, back pain, headaches. Only the yellow Nuprin tablets were shown in color. The ads resulted in more favorable attitudes toward Nuprin, and by the end of the year Nuprin's sales were growing faster than sales of any other brand. One advertising specialist explained the success this way: "You have to convince consumers that the product is different before they will believe the product is better. That Nuprin is yellow is superficial to the product's superiority, yet it opens people's minds that this product is different." Consumer beliefs—right or wrong—can have a significant impact on whether a strategy succeeds.[5]

Most marketers work with existing attitudes

Marketers generally try to understand the attitudes of their potential customers and work with them. We'll discuss this idea again when we review the way consumers evaluate product alternatives. For now, we want to emphasize that it's more economical to work with consumer attitudes than to try to change them. Attitudes tend to be enduring. Changing present attitudes—especially negative ones—is sometimes necessary. But that's probably the most difficult job marketers face.[6]

Ethical issues may arise

Part of the marketing job is to inform and persuade consumers about a firm's offering. An ethical issue sometimes arises, however, if consumers have *inaccurate* beliefs. For example, many consumers are confused about what foods are really healthy. Marketers for a number of food companies have been criticized for packaging and promotion that take advantage of inaccurate consumer perceptions about the meaning of the words *lite* or *low-fat*. A firm's lite donuts may have less fat or fewer calories than its other donuts—but that doesn't mean that the donut is *low* in fat or calories. Similarly, promotion of a "children's cold

BRITISH CONSUMERS ARE COOL ABOUT ICED TEA

No one ever declared that tea was the national drink in England. Yet, it's long been a basic ingredient of the British culture. Taking a break for a cup of tea isn't just for nourishment; it's a social moment with family or friends. And British consumers have learned to love their tea hot—very hot.

In striking contrast, most British consumers are decidedly cool about iced tea. Iced tea makers would like to change that. They look at the 330 million gallons of iced tea routinely purchased by Americans each year and ask, "Why not in Britain?" But they know that they face tough odds. When one firm test-marketed an iced tea called Coolbrew in 1989, most consumers didn't like it enough to buy it again. A basic problem is that many British consumers associate iced tea with the dregs left in the bottom of the teapot after it's cooled off. Iced tea sales are not likely to pick up much until that perception changes.

That has not kept Lipton and Snapple Beverage Corp. from trying again. This time they've changed the taste, hoping that will change how consumers think about the product. Liptonice, for example, is carbonated like a cola, and Snapple's tea is flavored like its fruit drinks. So far, sales of fizzy, fruity tea are weak. Perhaps marketing managers for the Nestea brand have the best approach: they're focusing on other European markets where getting trial and adoption doesn't depend on first overcoming negative consumer attitudes.[7]

formula" may play off of parents' fears that adult medicines are too strong—even though the basic ingredients in the children's formula are the same and only the dosage is different.

Marketers must also be careful about promotion that might encourage false beliefs, even if the advertising is not explicitly misleading. For example, ads for Ultra Slim-Fast low-fat beverage don't claim that anyone who buys the product will lose all the weight they want—or look like Brooke Shields who appears in the ads—but some critics argue that the advertising gives that impression.[8]

Meeting expectations is important

Attitudes and beliefs sometimes combine to form an **expectation**—an outcome or event that a person anticipates or looks forward to. Consumer expectations often focus on the benefits or value that the consumer expects from a firm's marketing mix. This is an important issue for marketers because a consumer is likely to be dissatisfied if his or her expectations are not met. For example, a hungry consumer who stops at a fast-food restaurant for a hamburger is likely to be dissatisfied if the service is slow, even if the burger tastes great.

A key point here is that consumers may evaluate a product not just on how well it performs but on how it performs *relative to their expectations*. A product that otherwise might get high marks from a satisfied consumer may be a disappointment if there's a gap between what the consumer gets and what the consumer expects. Promotion that overpromises what the rest of the marketing mix can really deliver leads to problems in this area. Finding the right balance, however, can be difficult. Consider the challenge faced by marketing managers for Van Heusen shirts. In 1994, Van Heusen came up with a new way to treat its shirts so that they look better when they come out of the wash than previous wash-and-wear shirts. Van Heusen promotes these shirts as "wrinkle-free" and the label shows an iron stuffed in a garbage can. Most people agree that the new shirt is an improvement. Even so, consumers who buy a shirt expecting it to look as crisp as if it had just been ironed are disappointed. For them, the improvement is not enough.[9]

EXHIBIT 7– 5   Lifestyle Dimensions (and some related demographic dimensions)

Dimension	Examples		
Activities	Work	Vacation	Community
	Hobbies	Entertainment	Shopping
	Social events	Club membership	Sports
Interests	Family	Community	Food
	Home	Recreation	Media
	Job	Fashion	Achievements
Opinions	Themselves	Business	Products
	Social issues	Economics	Future
	Politics	Education	Culture
Demographics	Income	Geographic area	Occupation
	Age	City size	Family size
	Family life cycle	Dwelling	Education

Personality affects how people see things

Many researchers study how personality affects people's behavior, but the results have generally been disappointing to marketers. A trait like neatness can be associated with users of certain types of products—like cleaning materials. But marketing managers have not found a way to use personality in marketing strategy planning.[10] As a result, they've stopped focusing on personality measures borrowed from psychologists and instead developed lifestyle analysis.

Psychographics focus on activities, interests, and opinions

Psychographics or **lifestyle analysis** is the analysis of a person's day-to-day pattern of living as expressed in that person's Activities, Interests, and Opinions—sometimes referred to as AIOs. Exhibit 7–5 shows a number of variables for each of the AIO dimensions—along with some demographics used to add detail to the lifestyle profile of a target market.

Lifestyle analysis assumes that marketers can plan more effective strategies if they know more about their target markets. Understanding the lifestyle of target customers has been especially helpful in providing ideas for advertising themes. Let's see how it adds to a typical demographic description. It may not help Mercury marketing managers much to know that an average member of the target market for a Sable station wagon is 34.8 years old, married, lives in a three-bedroom home, and has 2.3 children. Lifestyles help marketers paint a more human portrait of the target market. For example, lifestyle analysis might show that the 34.8-year-old is also a community-oriented consumer with traditional values who especially enjoys spectator sports and spends much time in other family activities. An ad might show the Sable being used by a happy family at a ball game so the target market could really identify with the ad. And the ad might be placed in a magazine like *Sports Illustrated* whose readers match the target lifestyle profile.[11]

Marketing managers for consumer products firms who are interested in learning more about the lifestyle of a target market sometimes turn to outside specialists for help. For example, SRI International, a research firm, offers a service called VALS 2 (an abbreviation for values, attitudes, and lifestyles). SRI describes a firm's target market in terms of a set of typical VALS lifestyle groups (segments). An advantage of this approach is that SRI has developed very detailed information about the various VALS groups. For example, the VALS approach has been used to profile consumers in the United Kingdom, Germany, Japan, and Canada as well as the United States. However, the disadvantage of VALS 2—and other similar approaches—is that it may not be very specific to the marketing manager's target market.[12]

SOCIAL INFLUENCES AFFECT CONSUMER BEHAVIOR

We've been discussing some of the ways needs, attitudes, and other psychological variables influence the buying process. Now we'll see that these variables—and the buying process—are usually affected by relations with other people too. We'll look at how the individual interacts with family, social class, and other groups who may have influence.

Who is the real decision maker in family purchases?

Relationships with other family members influence many aspects of consumer behavior. We saw specific examples of this in Chapter 6 when we considered the effects of the family life cycle on family spending patterns. Family members may also share many attitudes and values, consider each other's opinions, and divide various buying tasks. Historically, most marketers in the United States targeted the wife as the family purchasing agent. Now, with more women in the workforce and with night and weekend shopping becoming more popular, men and older children do more shopping and decision making. In other countries, family roles vary. For example, in Norway women do most of the family shopping.

Although only one family member may go to the store and make a specific purchase, when planning marketing strategy it's important to know who else may be involved. Other family members may have influenced the decision or really decided what to buy. Still others may use the product.

You don't have to watch much Saturday morning TV to see that Kellogg's and General Mills know this. Cartoon characters like Cap'n Crunch and Tony the Tiger tell kids about the goodies found in certain cereal packages—and urge them to remind Dad or Mom to pick up that brand on their next trip to the store. But kids also influence grown-up purchases—to the tune of $200 billion a year. Surveys show that kids often have a big say in a family's choice of products such as apparel, cars, electronics, and health and beauty aids.

Family considerations may overwhelm personal ones

A husband and wife may jointly agree on many important purchases, but sometimes they may have strong personal preferences. However, such individual preferences may change if the other spouse has different priorities. One might want to take a family vacation to Disneyland—when the other wants a new RCA video recorder and Sony large-screen TV. The actual outcome in such a situation is unpredictable. The preferences of one spouse might change because of affection for the other—or because of the other's power and influence.

Buying responsibility and influence vary greatly depending on the product and the family. A marketer trying to plan a strategy will find it helpful to research the specific target market. Remember, many buying decisions are made jointly, and thinking only about who actually buys the product can misdirect the marketing strategy.[13]

Social class affects attitudes, values, and buying

Up to now, we've been concerned with individuals and their family relationships. Now let's consider how society looks at an individual and perhaps the family—in terms of social class. A **social class** is a group of people who have approximately equal social position as viewed by others in the society.

Almost every society has some social class structure. In most countries social class is closely related to a person's occupation, but it may also be influenced by education, community participation, where a person lives, income, possessions, social skills, and other factors—including what family a person is born into.

In most countries—including the United States—there is *some* general relationship between income level and social class. But the income level of people within the same social class can vary greatly, and people with the same income level may be in different social classes. So income by itself is usually not a good measure of social class. And people in different social classes may spend, save, and borrow money in very different ways. For example, spending for clothing, housing, home furnishings, and leisure activities, as well as choices of where and how to shop, often vary with social class.

The U.S. class system is far less rigid than those in most countries. Children start out in the same social class as their parents—but they can move to a different social class depending on their educational levels or the jobs they hold. By contrast, India's social structure is much more rigid, and individuals can't easily move up in the class system.

Marketers want to know what buyers in various social classes are like. In the United States, simple approaches for measuring social class groupings are based on a person's *occupation*, *education*, and *type and location of housing*. By using marketing research surveys or available census data, marketers can get a feel for the social class of a target market. Exhibit 7–6 illustrates a multilevel social class structure for the United States. Note the relative sizes of the groupings and how they differ.

Although the exhibit uses traditional technical terms like *upper*, *middle*, and *lower*, a word of warning is in order. These terms may seem to imply "superior" and "inferior." But, in sociological and marketing usage, no value judgment is intended. We cannot say that any one class is "better" or "happier" than another.

What do these classes mean?

Social class studies suggest that the old saying—"A rich man is simply a poor man with more money"—is not true. Given the same income as middle-class consumers, people belonging to the lower class handle themselves and their money very differently. Many people think of America as a middle-class society, but in many marketing situations the social class groups are distinct. Various classes shop at different stores. They prefer different treatment from salespeople. They buy different brands of products—even though prices are about the same. And they have different spending–saving attitudes.

Reference groups are relevant too

A **reference group** is the people to whom an individual looks when forming attitudes about a particular topic. People normally have several reference groups for different topics. Some they meet face-to-face. Others they just wish to imitate. In either case, they may take values from these reference groups and make buying decisions based on what the group might accept.

We're always making comparisons between ourselves and others. So reference groups are more important when others will be able to "see" which product or brand we're using. Influence is stronger for products that relate to status in the group. For one group, owning an expensive fur coat may be a sign of "having arrived." A group of animal lovers might view it as a sign of bad judgment. In either case, a consumer's decision to buy or not buy a fur coat might depend on the opinions of others in that consumer's reference group.[14]

EXHIBIT 7–6 Characteristics and Relative Size of Different Social Class Groups in the United States

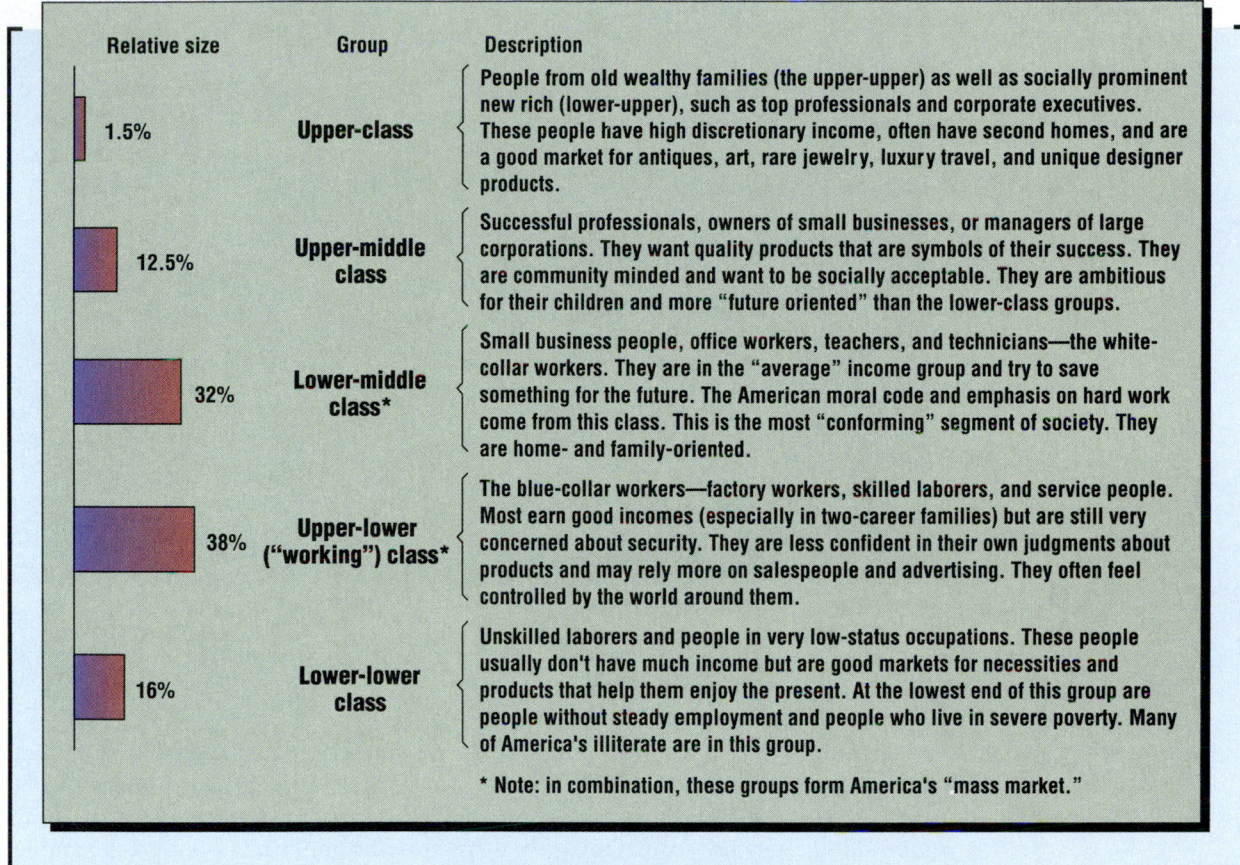

Relative size	Group	Description
1.5%	**Upper-class**	People from old wealthy families (the upper-upper) as well as socially prominent new rich (lower-upper), such as top professionals and corporate executives. These people have high discretionary income, often have second homes, and are a good market for antiques, art, rare jewelry, luxury travel, and unique designer products.
12.5%	**Upper-middle class**	Successful professionals, owners of small businesses, or managers of large corporations. They want quality products that are symbols of their success. They are community minded and want to be socially acceptable. They are ambitious for their children and more "future oriented" than the lower-class groups.
32%	**Lower-middle class***	Small business people, office workers, teachers, and technicians—the white-collar workers. They are in the "average" income group and try to save something for the future. The American moral code and emphasis on hard work come from this class. This is the most "conforming" segment of society. They are home- and family-oriented.
38%	**Upper-lower ("working") class***	The blue-collar workers—factory workers, skilled laborers, and service people. Most earn good incomes (especially in two-career families) but are still very concerned about security. They are less confident in their own judgments about products and may rely more on salespeople and advertising. They often feel controlled by the world around them.
16%	**Lower-lower class**	Unskilled laborers and people in very low-status occupations. These people usually don't have much income but are good markets for necessities and products that help them enjoy the present. At the lowest end of this group are people without steady employment and people who live in severe poverty. Many of America's illiterate are in this group.

* Note: in combination, these groups form America's "mass market."

Reaching the opinion leaders who are buyers

An **opinion leader** is a person who influences others. Opinion leaders aren't necessarily wealthier or better educated. And opinion leaders on one subject aren't necessarily opinion leaders on another. Capable homemakers with large families may be consulted for advice on family budgeting. Young women may be opinion leaders for new clothing styles and cosmetics. Each social class tends to have its own opinion leaders. Some marketing mixes aim especially at these people since their opinions affect others and research shows that they are involved in many product-related discussions with "followers." Favorable word-of-mouth publicity from opinion leaders can really help a marketing mix. But the opposite is also true. If opinion leaders aren't satisfied, they're likely to talk about it and influence others.[15]

Culture surrounds the other influences

Culture is the whole set of beliefs, attitudes, and ways of doing things of a reasonably homogeneous set of people. In Chapters 4 and 6, we looked at the broad impact of culture.

We can think of the American culture, the French culture, or the Latin American culture. People within these cultural groupings tend to be more similar in outlook and behavior. But sometimes it is useful to think of subcultures within such groupings. For example, within the American culture, there are various

Reference group influence is likely to be more important when others will be able to see which product a consumer is using, especially if the product is relevant to status in the group.

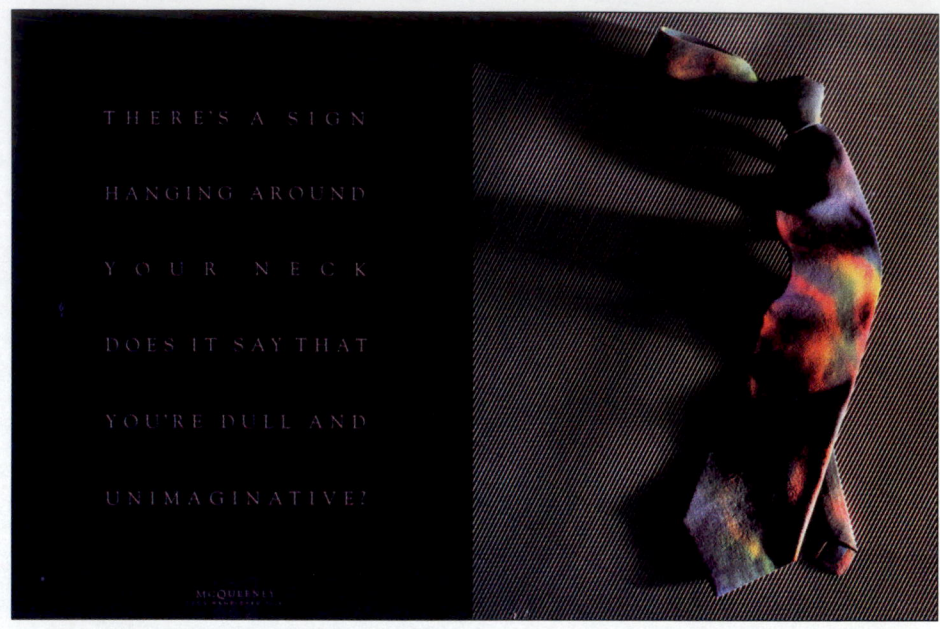

THERE'S A SIGN

HANGING AROUND

YOUR NECK

DOES IT SAY THAT

YOU'RE DULL AND

UNIMAGINATIVE?

McQUEENS

religious and ethnic subcultures; also different cultural forces tend to prevail in different regions of the country.

Culture varies in international markets

Planning strategies that consider cultural differences in international markets can be even harder—and such cultures usually vary more. Each foreign market may need to be treated as a separate market with its own submarkets. Ignoring cultural differences—or assuming that they are not important—almost guarantees failure in international markets.

For example, when marketing managers for Procter & Gamble first tried to sell the U.S. version of Cheer to Japanese consumers they promoted it as an effective all-temperature laundry detergent. But many Japanese wash clothes in cold tap water or leftover bath water—so they don't care about all-temperature washing. In addition, Cheer didn't make suds when it was used with the fabric softeners popular with Japanese consumers. When P&G's marketing managers discovered these problems, they changed Cheer so it wouldn't be affected by the fabric softeners. They also changed Cheer ads to promise superior cleaning *in cold water*. Now Cheer has become one of P&G's best-selling products in Japan.[16]

From a target marketing point of view, a marketing manager probably wants to aim at people within one culture or subculture. A firm developing strategies for two cultures often needs two different marketing plans.[17]

The attitudes and beliefs that we usually associate with culture tend to change slowly. So once marketers develop a good understanding of the culture they are planning for, they should concentrate on the more dynamic variables discussed above.

INDIVIDUALS ARE AFFECTED BY THE PURCHASE SITUATION

Purchase reason can vary

Why a consumer makes a purchase can affect buying behavior. For example, a student buying a pen to take notes might pick up an inexpensive Bic. But the same student might choose a Cross pen as a gift for a friend.

The purchase situation may have a major impact on consumer behavior. As these ads highlight—in quite different ways—how consumers shop for a gift may be different from how they would shop for themselves.

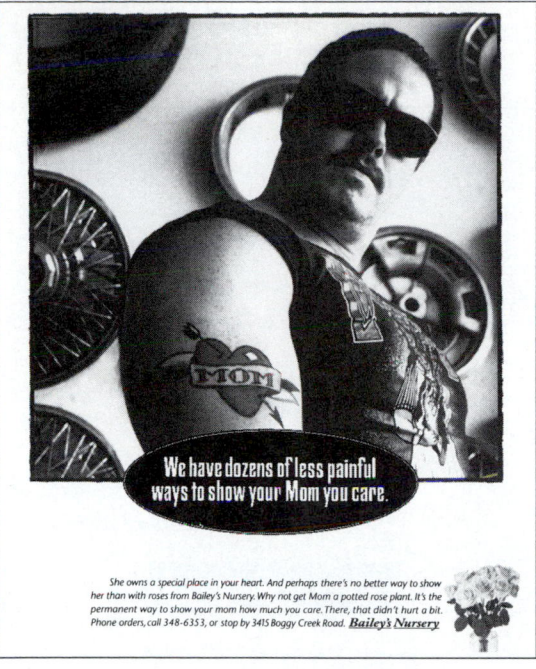

We have dozens of less painful ways to show your Mom you care.

She owns a special place in your heart. And perhaps there's no better way to show her than with roses from Bailey's Nursery. Why not get Mom a potted rose plant. It's the permanent way to show your mom how much you care. There, that didn't hurt a bit. Phone orders, call 348-6353, or stop by 3415 Boggy Creek Road. **Bailey's Nursery**

The Unconventional Gift Registry

For him and for her, Ace is the place!

Call for the participating Ace Hardware Dealer nearest you:
1-800-622-8345
Enter Code #0246

ACE Hardware

Time affects what happens

Time influences a purchase situation. *When* consumers make a purchase—and the time they have available for shopping—will influence their behavior. A leisurely dinner induces different behavior than grabbing a quick cup of 7-Eleven coffee on the way to work.

Surroundings affect buying too

Surroundings can affect buying behavior. The excitement of an auction may stimulate impulse buying. Surroundings may discourage buying too. For example, some people don't like to stand in a checkout line where others can see what they're buying—even if the other shoppers are complete strangers.

Needs, benefits sought, attitudes, motivation, and even how a consumer selects certain products all vary depending on the purchase situation. So different purchase situations may require different marketing mixes—even when the same target market is involved.[18]

CONSUMERS USE PROBLEM-SOLVING PROCESSES

The variables discussed affect *what* products a consumer finally decides to purchase. Marketing managers also need to understand *how* buyers *use* a problem-solving process to select particular products.

Most consumers seem to use the following five-step problem-solving process:

1. Becoming aware of—or interested in—the problem.
2. Recalling and gathering information about possible solutions.
3. Evaluating alternative solutions—perhaps trying some out.
4. Deciding on the appropriate solution.
5. Evaluating the decision.[19]

EXHIBIT 7–7 An Expanded Model of the Consumer Problem-Solving Process

Exhibit 7–7 presents an expanded version of the buyer behavior model shown in Exhibit 7–1. Note that this exhibit integrates the problem-solving process with the whole set of variables we've been reviewing.

When consumers evaluate information about purchase alternatives, they may weigh not only a product type in relation to other types of products, but also differences in brands within a product type *and* the stores where the products may be available. This can be a very complicated evaluation procedure, and, depending on their choice of criteria, consumers may make seemingly irrational decisions. If convenient service is crucial, for example, a buyer might pay list price for an unexciting car from a very convenient dealer. Marketers need a way to analyze these decisions.

EXHIBIT 7-8   Grid of Evaluative Criteria for Three Car Brands

Brands	Common features			
	Gas mileage	Ease of service	Comfortable interior	Styling
Nissan	–	+	+	–
Saab	+	–	+	+
Toyota	+	+	+	–

Note: Pluses and minuses indicate a consumer's evaluation of a feature for a brand.

Grid of evaluative criteria helps

Based on studies of how consumers seek out and evaluate product information, researchers suggest that marketing managers use an evaluative grid showing features common to different products (or marketing mixes). For example, Exhibit 7-8 shows some of the features common to three different cars a consumer might consider.

The grid encourages marketing managers to view each product as a bundle of features or attributes. The pluses and minuses in Exhibit 7-8 indicate one consumer's attitude toward each feature of each car. If members of the target market don't rate a feature of the marketing manager's brand with pluses, it may indicate a problem. The manager might want to change the product to improve that feature—or perhaps use more promotion to emphasize an already acceptable feature. The consumer in Exhibit 7-8 has a minus under gas mileage for the Nissan. If the Nissan really gets better gas mileage than the other cars, promotion might focus on mileage to improve consumer attitudes toward this feature and toward the whole product.

Some consumers will reject a product if they see *one* feature as substandard—regardless of how favorably they regard the product's other features. The consumer in Exhibit 7-8 might avoid the Saab, which he saw as less than satisfactory on ease of service, even if it were superior in all other aspects. In other instances, a consumer's overall attitude toward the product might be such that a few good features could make up for some shortcomings. The comfortable interior of the Toyota (Exhibit 7-8) might make up for less exciting styling—especially if the consumer viewed comfort as really important.

Of course, consumers don't use a grid like this. However, constructing such a grid helps managers think about what evaluative criteria target consumers consider really important, what consumers' attitudes are toward their product (or marketing mix) on each criteria, and how consumers combine the criteria to reach a final decision. Having a better understanding of the process should help a manager develop a better marketing mix.[20]

Three levels of problem solving are useful

The basic problem-solving process shows the steps consumers may go through trying to find a way to satisfy their needs—but it doesn't show how long this

EXHIBIT 7–9   Problem-Solving Continuum

Low involvement Frequently purchased Inexpensive Little risk Little information needed	**Routinized response behavior**	**Limited problem solving**	**Extensive problem solving**	High involvement Infrequently purchased Expensive High risk Much information desired

process will take or how much thought a consumer will give to each step. Individuals who have had a lot of experience solving certain problems can move quickly through some of the steps or almost directly to a decision.

It is helpful, therefore, to recognize three levels of problem solving: extensive problem solving, limited problem solving, and routinized response behavior. See Exhibit 7–9. These problem-solving approaches are used for any kind of product. Consumers use **extensive problem solving** for a completely new or important need—when they put much effort into deciding how to satisfy it. For example, a music lover who wants higher-quality sound might decide to buy a CD player—but not have any idea what to buy. After talking with friends to find out about good places to buy a player, she might visit several stores to find out about different brands and their features. After thinking about her needs some more, she might buy a portable Sony unit—so she could use it in her apartment and in her car.

For most consumers, selecting a new computer system would involve extensive problem solving—but selecting a frequently purchased consumer packaged good often involves routinized response behavior.

Consumers use **limited problem solving** when they're willing to put *some* effort into deciding the best way to satisfy a need. Limited problem solving is typical when a consumer has some previous experience in solving a problem but isn't certain which choice is best at the current time. If our music lover wanted some new compact discs for her player, she would already know what type of music she enjoys. She might go to a familiar store and evaluate what compact discs they had in stock for her favorite types of music.

Consumers use **routinized response behavior** when they regularly select a particular way of satisfying a need when it occurs. Routinized response behavior is typical when a consumer has considerable experience in how to meet a need and has no need for additional information. For example, our music lover might routinely buy the latest recording by her favorite band as soon as it's available.

Most marketing managers would like their target consumers to buy their products in this routinized way. Some firms provide special services for frequent buyers, encourage repeat business with discounts, or do other things to build a good relationship so that the customer purchases from them in a routinized way.

Routinized response behavior is also typical for **low-involvement purchases**—purchases that have little importance or relevance for the customer. Let's face it, buying a box of salt is probably not one of the burning issues in your life.[21]

Problem solving is a learning process

The reason problem solving becomes simpler with time is that people learn from experience—both positive and negative things. As consumers approach the problem-solving process, they bring attitudes formed by previous experiences and social training. Each new problem-solving process may then contribute to or modify this attitude set.

New concepts require an adoption process

When consumers face a really new concept, their previous experience may not be relevant. These situations involve the **adoption process**—the steps individuals go through on the way to accepting or rejecting a new idea. Although the adoption process is similar to the problem-solving process, learning plays a clearer role and promotion's contribution to a marketing mix is more visible.

In the adoption process, an individual moves through some fairly definite steps:

1. Awareness—the potential customer comes to know about the product but lacks details. The consumer may not even know how it works or what it will do.
2. Interest—*if* the consumer becomes interested, he or she will gather general information and facts about the product.
3. Evaluation—a consumer begins to give the product a mental trial, applying it to his or her personal situation.
4. Trial—the consumer may buy the product to experiment with it in use. A product that is either too expensive to try or isn't available for trial may never be adopted.
5. Decision—the consumer decides on either adoption or rejection. A satisfactory evaluation and trial may lead to adoption of the product and regular use. According to psychological learning theory, reinforcement leads to adoption.
6. Confirmation—the adopter continues to rethink the decision and searches for support for the decision—that is, further reinforcement.[22]

Marketers often want to make it easier for consumers to adopt a product. Pittsburgh Paints' Accuvision video system helps customers see how their paint choices will look. Nabisco offers free samples to encourage consumers to try the product.

Marketing managers for 3M, the company that makes Scotch tape, worked with the adoption process when they introduced Post-it note pads. Test-market ads increased awareness—they explained how Post-it notes could be applied to a surface and then easily removed. But test-market sales were slow because most consumers were not interested. They didn't see the benefit. To encourage trial, 3M distributed free samples. By using the samples, consumers confirmed the benefit—and when they used the samples up they started buying Post-its. As Post-it distribution expanded to other market areas, 3M used samples to speed consumers through the trial stage and the rest of the adoption process.[23]

Dissonance may set in after the decision

A buyer may have second thoughts after making a purchase decision. The buyer may have chosen from among several attractive alternatives—weighing the pros and cons and finally making a decision. Later doubts, however, may lead to **dissonance**—tension caused by uncertainty about the rightness of a decision. Dissonance may lead a buyer to search for additional information to confirm the wisdom of the decision and so reduce tension. Without this confirmation, the adopter might buy something else next time—or not comment positively about the product to others.[24]

SEVERAL PROCESSES ARE RELATED AND RELEVANT TO STRATEGY PLANNING

Exhibit 7–10 shows the interrelation of the problem-solving process, the adoption process, and learning. It is important to see this interrelation—and to understand that promotion can modify or accelerate it. Also note that the potential buyers' problem-solving behavior should affect how firms design their physical distribution systems. If customers aren't willing to travel far to shop, a firm may need more outlets to get their business. Similarly, customers' attitudes help determine what price to charge. Knowing how target markets handle these processes helps companies with their marketing strategy planning.

EXHIBIT 7–10   Relation of Problem-Solving Process, Adoption Process, and Learning (given a problem)

Problem-solving steps	Adoption process steps	Learning steps
1. Becoming aware of or interested in the problem	Awareness and interest	**Drive**
2. Gathering information about possible solutions	Interest and evaluation	**Cues**
3. Evaluating alternative solutions, perhaps trying some out	Evaluation, maybe trial	Reinforcement
4. Deciding on the appropriate solution	Decision	**Response**
5. Evaluating the decision	Confirmation	

CONSUMER BEHAVIOR IN INTERNATIONAL MARKETS

All the influences interact—often in subtle ways

You're a consumer, so you probably have very good intuition about the many influences on consumer behavior that we've been discussing. For many different purchase situations you also intuitively know—from experience—which variables are most important. That's good, but it's also a potential trap—especially when developing marketing mixes for consumers in international markets. The less a marketing manager knows about the *specific* social and intrapersonal variables that shape the behavior of target customers, the more likely it is that relying on intuition will be misleading. We all have a tendency to try to explain things we don't understand by generalizing from what we do know. Yet, when it comes to consumer behavior, many of the specifics do not generalize from one culture to another.

Cadbury's effort to develop a Japanese market for its Dairy Milk Chocolate candy bar illustrates the point. Cadbury marketing managers conducted marketing research to find out more about candy preferences among Japanese consumers. The consumers said that they didn't like the high milk-fat content of Cadbury's bar. Cadbury's managers, however, reasoned that this reaction must be from lack of opportunity to become accustomed to the candy. After all, in most other countries it's the rich taste of the candy that turns consumers into "chocoholics." When Cadbury introduced the bar in Japan, it was a real flop. Taste preferences in other countries simply didn't generalize to Japan. It also wasn't just a matter of opportunity. The whole diet in Japan is different enough that eating the candy was unpleasant. By contrast, Dannon was successful because it took similar research findings to heart and dramatically modified its yogurt dairy desserts until they satisfied Japanese tastes.

Cultural influences on consumers usually differ from one country to another, but there may also be a number of subcultures within a single country.

Sometimes important influences on consumer behavior are more subtle. When P&G first introduced disposable diapers in Japan, interest was limited. Research suggested that price and health concerns were a sticking point, as was product fit. The diapers leaked because the design was too large for most Japanese babies. From the Western vantage point, these were reasonable problems to work on. However, another powerful cultural force was also at work. At that time, most Japanese mothers were expected to dedicate themselves to caring for their babies. Many women who could afford the convenience of disposable diapers felt guilty using them. Further, it was often a woman's mother-in-law who aggressively kept that guilt burning. Although fathers were typically uninvolved in caring for babies, it was the Japanese mother-in-laws' traditional role to oversee how the mother cared for the grandchild. And, by tradition, caring mothers always sacrificed their own convenience for the baby's. Japanese firms that entered the market later used promotion to emphasize that disposables were best *for the baby*. That appeal relieved the mother's guilt and also helped with the mother-in-law problem. Even so, it took time for basic attitudes to change.

Watch out for stereotypes, and change

Our diaper example can also serve as a reminder to watch out for oversimplifying stereotypes. Consumers in a foreign culture may be bound by some similar cultural forces, but that doesn't mean that they are all the same. Further, changes in the underlying social forces may make outdated views irrelevant.

Many Westerners believe that the typical Japanese executive works very long hours and devotes very little time to family life. That stereotype has been highlighted in the Western media—and also in our diaper example! It's still partly true. Yet, the diaper example is, quite intentionally, dated. In today's Japan, many young Japanese executives want a more balanced family life; they don't want to continue the almost total dedication to business accepted by the previous generation. A marketer who didn't recognize this change probably wouldn't fully understand these people, their needs, or buying behavior in their families.

Developing a marketing mix that really satisfies the needs of a target market takes a real understanding of consumer behavior—and the varied forces that shape it. That holds whether the target market is local or half way around the world. So, when planning strategies for international markets, it's best to involve locals who have a better chance of understanding the experience, attitudes, and interests of your customers. Many companies, even very sophisticated ones, have faltered because they failed to heed that simple advice.[25]

CONCLUSION

In this chapter, we analyzed the individual consumer as a problem solver who is influenced by psychological variables, social influences, and the purchase situation. All of these variables are related, and our model of buyer behavior helps integrate them into one process. Marketing strategy planning requires a good grasp of this material.

Assuming that everyone behaves the way you do—or even like your family or friends do—can lead to expensive marketing errors.

Consumer buying behavior results from the consumer's efforts to satisfy needs and wants. We discussed some reasons why consumers buy and saw that consumer behavior can't be fully explained by only a list of needs.

We also saw that most societies are divided into social classes, a fact that helps explain some consumer behavior. And we discussed the impact of reference groups and opinion leaders.

We presented a buyer behavior model to help you interpret and integrate the present findings—as well as any new data you might get from marketing research. As of now, the behavioral sciences can only offer insights and theories, which the marketing manager must blend with intuition and judgment to develop marketing strategies.

Companies may have to use marketing research to answer specific questions. But if a firm has neither the money nor the time for research, then marketing managers have to rely on available descriptions of present behavior and guesstimates about future behavior. Popular magazines and leading newspapers often reflect the public's shifting attitudes. And many studies of the changing consumer are published regularly in the business and trade press. This material—coupled with the information in these last two chapters—will help your marketing strategy planning.

Remember that consumers—with all their needs and attitudes—may be elusive, but they aren't invisible. Research has provided more data and understanding of consumer behavior than business managers generally use. Applying this information may help you find your breakthrough opportunity.

QUESTIONS AND PROBLEMS

1. In your own words, explain economic needs and how they relate to the economic-buyer model of consumer behavior. Give an example of a purchase you recently made that is consistent with the economic-buyer model. Give another that is not explained by the economic-buyer model. Explain your thinking.

2. Explain what is meant by a hierarchy of needs and provide examples of one or more products that enable you to satisfy each of the four levels of need.

3. Cut out (or copy) two recent advertisements: one full-page color ad from a magazine and one large display from a newspaper. In each case, indicate which needs the ads are appealing to.

4. Explain how an understanding of consumers' learning processes might affect marketing strategy planning. Give an example.

5. Briefly describe your own *beliefs* about the potential value of wearing automobile seat belts, your *attitude* toward seat belts, and your *intention* about using a seat belt the next time you're in a car.

6. Give an example of a recent purchase experience in which you were dissatisfied because a firm's

marketing mix did not meet your expectations. Indicate how the purchase fell short of your expectations—and also explain whether your expectations were formed based on the firm's promotion or on something else.

7. Explain psychographics and lifestyle analysis. Explain how they might be useful for planning marketing strategies to reach college students, as opposed to average consumers.

8. A supermarket chain is planning to open a number of new stores to appeal to Hispanics in southern California. Give some examples that indicate how the four Ps might be adjusted to appeal to the Hispanic subculture.

9. How should the social class structure affect the planning of a new restaurant in a large city? How might the four Ps be adjusted?

10. What social class would you associate with each of the following phrases or items? In each case, choose one class if you can. If you can't choose one class but rather feel that several classes are equally likely, then so indicate. In those cases where you feel that all classes are equally interested or characterized by a particular item, choose all five classes.

    a. A gun rack in a pickup truck.
    b. The *National Enquirer*.
    c. *New Yorker* magazine.
    d. *Working Woman* magazine.
    e. People watching soap operas.
    f. TV golf tournaments.
    g. Men who drink beer after dinner.
    h. Families who vacation at a Disney theme park.
    i. Families who distrust banks (keep money in socks or mattresses).
    j. Owners of pit bulls.

11. Illustrate how the reference group concept may apply in practice by explaining how you personally are influenced by some reference group for some product. What are the implications of such behavior for marketing managers?

12. Give two examples of recent purchases where the specific purchase situation influenced your purchase decision. Briefly explain how your decision was affected.

13. Give an example of a recent purchase in which you used extensive problem solving. What sources of information did you use in making the decision?

14. On the basis of the data and analysis presented in Chapters 6 and 7, what kind of buying behavior would you expect to find for the following products: (*a*) a haircut, (*b*) a dishwasher detergent, (*c*) a printer for a personal computer, (*d*) a tennis racket, (*e*) a dress belt, (*f*) a telephone answering machine, (*g*) life insurance, (*h*) an ice cream cone, and (*i*) a new checking account? Set up a chart for your answer with products along the left-hand margin as the row headings and the following factors as headings for the columns: (*a*) how consumers would shop for these products, (*b*) how far they would travel to buy the product, (*c*) whether they would buy by brand, (*d*) whether they would compare with other products, and (*e*) any other factors they should consider. Insert short answers—words or phrases are satisfactory—in the various boxes. Be prepared to discuss how the answers you put in the chart would affect each product's marketing mix.

SUGGESTED CASES

1. McDonald's "Seniors" Restaurant
9. Mountain View Lodge

11. Runners World

COMPUTER-AIDED PROBLEM

7. Selective Processes

Submag, Inc., uses direct-mail promotion to sell magazine subscriptions. Magazine publishers pay Submag $3.12 for each new subscription. Submag's costs include the expenses of printing, addressing, and mailing each direct-mail advertisement plus the cost of using a mailing list.

There are many suppliers of mailing lists, and the cost and quality of different lists vary.

Submag's marketing manager, Shandra Debose, is trying to choose between two possible mailing lists. One list has been generated from phone directories. It is less expensive than the other list, but the supplier acknowledges that about 10 percent of the names are out-of-date (addresses where people have moved away). A competing supplier offers a list of active members of professional associations. This list costs 4 cents per name more than the phone list, but only 8 percent of the addresses are out-of-date.

In addition to concerns about out-of-date names, not every consumer who receives a mailing buys a subscription. For example, *selective exposure* is a problem. Some target customers never see the offer—they just toss out junk mail without even opening the envelope. Industry studies show that this wastes about 10 percent of each mailing—although the precise percentage varies from one mailing list to another.

Selective perception influences some consumers who do open the mailing. Some are simply not interested. Others don't want to deal with a subscription service. Although the price is good, these consumers worry that they'll never get the magazines. Submag's previous experience is that selective perception causes more than half of those who read the offer to reject it.

Of those who perceive the message as intended, many are interested. But *selective retention* can be a problem. Some people set the information aside and then forget to send in the subscription order.

Submag can mail about 25,000 pieces per week. Shandra Debose has set up a spreadsheet to help her study effects of the various relationships discussed above—and to choose between the two mailing lists.

a. *If you were Debose, which of the two lists would you buy based on the initial spreadsheet? Why?*

b. *For the most profitable list, what is the minimum number of items that Submag will have to mail to earn a profit of at least $3,500?*

c. *For an additional cost of $.01 per mailing, Submag can include a reply card that will reduce the percent of consumers who forget to send in an order (Percent Lost—Selective Retention) to 45 percent. If Submag mails 25,000 items, is it worth the additional cost to include the reply card? Explain your logic.*

For additional questions related to this problem, see Exercise 7–3 in the *Learning Aid for Use with Basic Marketing,* 12th edition.

8

Business and Organizational Customers and Their Buying Behavior

In 1978, Shahid Kahn used $13,000 in savings and a $50,000 loan to start Bumper Works, a small company that produces lightweight bumpers for pickup trucks. Bumper Works grew to employ over a hundred people, and its customer list includes major automakers like Isuzu and Toyota. But success did not come overnight.

Kahn started to make sales calls on Toyota's purchasing department in 1980, but it was 1985 before he got his first order. And the first order wasn't a big contract. Toyota had a reputation for quality with U.S. consumers. Parts buyers at Toyota didn't want to risk tarnishing that reputation by relying too heavily on a new, unproven supplier.

In 1987, Toyota decided to improve the bumpers on its trucks so they would be more durable than the ones on competing pickups. That meant designing a new bumper and rethinking who would provide it. Toyota engineers developed the specifications for the new bumper, and Toyota buyers selected three potential suppliers—including Bumper Works—to compete for the business. This gave Bumper Works a chance to get business that routinely went to other suppliers. Kahn developed an economical design that met the specs and won the contract. The contract involved supplying

the rear bumpers Toyota needed at several of its U.S. facilities.

Although Kahn won the contract, he still faced challenges. Toyota's quality control people were not satisfied with the number of minor defects in Kahn's bumpers. Further, Bumper Works' deliveries were not as dependable as Toyota's production people were requiring. Kahn knew that he would lose the Toyota account if he couldn't meet the demands of these people—and also keep the price low enough to satisfy Toyota's objective of lowering parts costs.

Toyota's purchasing people concluded that Bumper Works wouldn't be able to resolve these problems unless Kahn could make big improvements in his production process. Kahn was stuck because he didn't know what else he could do. However, rather than end the relationship and shift the business to another supplier, Toyota sent a team of experts to show Bumper Works how to build better bumpers faster and cheaper.

Following the advice of Toyota experts, Kahn reorganized all the equipment in his factory to make it more efficient. He also had to retrain all his employees to do their jobs in new ways. The changes were so complicated that two of Kahn's six production supervisors quit in frustration.

But the trouble was worth the effort. Within a year after the changes, productivity at Bumper Works went up 60 percent, and the number of defects dropped by 80 percent. The improvements also helped Bumper Works get a big new contract with Isuzu.

Of course, Toyota didn't go to all of its effort just to be friendly. It wanted a committed supplier that could meet its standards. In exchange for all its help, Toyota got a big price reduction from Bumper Works.[1]

BUSINESS AND ORGANIZATIONAL CUSTOMERS—A BIG OPPORTUNITY

Most of us think about individual final consumers when we hear the term *customer*. But many marketing managers aim at customers who are not final consumers. In fact, more purchases are made by businesses and other organizations than by final consumers. As the Bumper Works/Toyota case illustrates, the buying behavior of these customers can be very different from the buying behavior of final consumers. Developing marketing strategies for these markets requires a solid understanding of who these customers are and how they buy. That is the focus of this chapter.

What types of customers are involved?

Business and organizational customers are any buyers who buy for resale or to produce other goods and services. Exhibit 8–1 shows the different types of customers in these markets. They include industrial manufacturers, producers of services, middlemen, and various nonprofit organizations, including government agencies. There are great marketing opportunities in serving these customers, and a student heading toward a business career has a good chance of working in this area.

These varied customers do many different jobs. Yet, many of the segmenting dimensions a marketing manager needs to describe their buying behavior tend to be common across the different types of organizations. There is a reason for this. Industrial firms originally developed many of the basic approaches for organizational buying. Other types of organizations then adopted the best ideas. So many characteristics of buying behavior are common across different types of organizations. That's why the different kinds of organizational buyers are often loosely referred to as "industrial buyers" or "intermediate buyers." As we discuss organizational buying, we will intermix examples of buying by many different types of organizations. Later in the chapter, however, we will highlight some of the specific characteristics of the different customer groups.

ORGANIZATIONAL CUSTOMERS ARE DIFFERENT

Organizations buy for a basic purpose

Like final consumers, organizations make purchases to satisfy needs. But it's often easier to understand an organization's needs because most organizations make purchases for the same basic reason. They buy goods and services that will help them meet the demand for the goods and services that they in turn supply to their markets. In other words, their basic need is to satisfy their own customers and clients. A manufacturer buys because it wants to earn a profit by making and selling goods. A wholesaler or retailer buys products it can profitably resell to its customers. A town government wants to meet its legal and social obligations to citizens. Similarly, a country club wants to help its members enjoy their leisure time.

EXHIBIT 8–1   Examples of Different Types of Business and Organizational Customers

Basic purchasing needs
are economic

Organizational buyers typically focus on economic factors when they make purchase decisions. They are usually less emotional in their buying than final consumers.

Buyers try to consider the total cost of selecting a supplier and a particular product, not just the initial price of the product. For example, a hospital that needs a new type of X-ray equipment might look at both the original cost and ongoing costs, how it would affect doctor productivity, and of course the quality of the images it produces. The hospital might also consider the seller's reliability and general cooperativeness; the ability to provide speedy maintenance and repair, steady supply under all conditions, and reliable and fast delivery; and any past and present relationships (including previous favors and cooperation in meeting special requests).

Business customers usually focus on economic needs when they make purchase decisions.

We'll Make The Toppings While You Make The Dough.

Hormel Pepperoni, the #1 pizza topping in the industry, has been the main ingredient in the success of many pizza operations. But just as our pepperoni has kept many businesses cooking, so can our Performance Pizza Toppings. Our flavorful line features some of the finest chunk and crumble meat toppings in the industry and is available in beef, pork and Italian sausage varieties. As for our Canadian bacon, bacon pieces and ham slices, they're second to none. And since all our toppings are made from the finest ingredients and cooked to perfection, you'll make great tasting pizza every time. And customers always come back for a great tasting pizza. Again and again. No matter how you slice it, Performance Pizza Toppings will help you make a much better pizza. And a much better profit. Which, in the pizza business, is the best kind of dough to make.

THERE'S A NAME FOR FOOD THIS GOOD™

Hormel
Foodservice

The matter of dependability deserves further emphasis. An organization may not be able to function if purchases don't arrive when they're expected. For example, there's nothing worse to a manufacturer than shutting down a production line because sellers haven't delivered the goods. Dependable product quality is important too. The cost of a small item may have little to do with its importance. For example, a short piece of wire with faulty insulation might cause a large piece of equipment to break down, and the costs of finding and correcting the problem could be completely out of proportion to the cost of the wire.

Even small differences are important

Different types of customers may buy for the same basic purpose, but there are many variations in how they buy and why they pick specific suppliers. Understanding how the buying behavior of a particular organization differs from others can be very important. Organizational customers often make large purchases, and competition for their business is often rugged. Even "trivial" differences in buying behavior may be important because success often hinges on fine-tuning the marketing mix to precisely meet the target customer's needs.

Sellers often approach each organizational customer directly, usually through a sales representative. This gives the seller more chance to adjust the marketing mix for each individual customer. A seller may even develop a unique strategy for each individual customer. This approach carries target marketing to its extreme. But sellers often need unique strategies to compete for large-volume purchases.

In such situations, the individual sales rep takes much responsibility for strategy planning. The sales rep often coordinates the whole relationship between the supplier and the customer. That may involve working with many people—including top management—in both firms. This is relevant to your career planning since these interesting jobs are very challenging—and they pay well too.

Hercules, an international supplier of ingredients to food producers, offers its customers expert help in dealing with the differences in tastes in different parts of the world.

Serving customers in international markets

Many marketers discover that there are good opportunities to serve business customers in different countries around the world. Specific business customs do vary from one country to another—and the differences can be important. For example, a salesperson working in Japan must know how to handle a customer's business card with respect. Japanese think of a business card as a symbolic extension of the person who presents it. Thus, they consider it rude to write notes on the back of a card or put it in a wallet while the person who presented it is still in the room. While such cultural differences can be very important, the basic approaches marketers use to deal with business customers in different parts of the world are much less varied than those required to reach individual consumers.

This is probably why the shift to a global economy has been so rapid for many firms. Their business customers in different countries buy in similar ways and can be reached with similar marketing mixes. Moreover, business customers, more so than final consumers, are often willing to work with a distant supplier who has developed a superior marketing mix.

To keep the discussion specific, we will focus on organizational customers in the United States. But most of the ideas apply to international markets in general.

MANY DIFFERENT PEOPLE MAY INFLUENCE A DECISION

Purchasing managers are specialists

Many organizations, especially large ones, rely on specialists to ensure that purchases of all goods and services are handled carefully and sensibly. These specialists have different titles in different firms (such as purchasing agent, procurement officer, or buyer), but basically they are all **purchasing managers**—buying specialists for their employers. In large organizations, they usually specialize by product area and are real experts. And modern purchasing managers are serious and well educated.

Some business managers just think of purchasing as an activity handled by ink-stained clerks who sit in basement cubicles and do the paperwork required to place an order. That view is out-of-date. In today's competitive world, firms are constantly looking for ways to cut costs and at the same time improve what they do. That can't happen unless the buying function is taken seriously—goods and services that an organization buys are often among its biggest expenses. So, most firms look to their purchasing departments to help cut costs and provide competitive advantage. In this environment, purchasing people have a lot of clout. And there are good job opportunities in purchasing for business students who really understand the marketing concept. A purchasing manager must satisfy the varied needs of the different departments in the firm so that everyone in the firm is working together to satisfy the firm's own customers.

Salespeople usually have to see a purchasing manager first—before they contact any other employee. These buyers hold important positions and take a dim view of sales reps who try to go around them. Rather than being "sold," these buyers want salespeople to provide accurate information that will help them buy wisely. They like information on new goods and services, and tips on potential price changes, supply shortages, and other changes in market conditions.

Although purchasing managers usually coordinate relationships with suppliers and their salespeople, a number of other people may play important roles in influencing the actual purchase decision.[2]

Multiple buying influence in a buying center

Multiple buying influence means that several people—perhaps even top management—share in making a purchase decision. Possible buying influences include:

1. *Users*—perhaps production line workers or their supervisors.
2. *Influencers*—perhaps engineering or R&D people who help write specifications or supply information for evaluating alternatives.
3. *Buyers*—the purchasing managers who have the responsibility for working with suppliers and arranging the terms of the sale.
4. *Deciders*—the people in the organization who have the power to select or approve the supplier—usually a purchasing agent for small items but perhaps top management for larger purchases.
5. *Gatekeepers*—people who control the flow of information within the organization—perhaps a purchasing manager who shields users or other deciders. Gatekeepers can also include receptionists, secretaries, research assistants, and others who influence the flow of information about potential purchases.

An example shows how the different buying influences work.

Suppose Electrolux, the Swedish firm that produces vacuum cleaners, wants to buy a machine to stamp out the various metal parts it needs. Different vendors are eager for the business. Several people (influencers) help to evaluate the choices. A finance manager worries about the high cost and suggests leasing the machine. The quality control people want a machine that will do a more accurate job—although it's more expensive. The production manager is interested in speed of operation. The production line workers and their supervisors want the machine that is easiest to use so workers can continue to rotate jobs.

The company president asks the purchasing department to assemble all the information but retains the power to select and approve the supplier (the

A person who works on a utility firm's high-power wires needs safe, durable climbing gear. A number of different people may influence the decision about which gear the firm should buy.

decider). The purchasing manager's assistant (a gatekeeper) has been deciding what information to pass on to higher-ups as well as scheduling visits for salespeople. After all these buying influences are considered, one of the purchasing agents for the firm will be responsible for making recommendations and arranging the terms of the sale (the buyer).

It is helpful to think of a **buying center** as all the people who participate in or influence a purchase. Different people may make up a buying center from one decision to the next. This makes the marketing job difficult.

The salesperson must study each case carefully. Just learning who to talk with may be hard, but thinking about the various roles in the buying center can help. See Exhibit 8–2.

The salesperson may have to talk to every member of the buying center—stressing different topics for each. This not only complicates the promotion job but also lengthens it. Approval of a routine order may take anywhere from a day to several months. On very important purchases—a new computer system, a new building, or major equipment—the selling period may stretch out to a year or more.[3]

Vendor analysis considers all of the influences

Considering all of the economic factors and influences relevant to a purchase decision is sometimes complex. A supplier or product that is best in one way may not be best in others. To try to deal with these situations, many firms use **vendor analysis**—a formal rating of suppliers on all relevant areas of performance. The purpose isn't just to get a low price from the supplier on a given part or service. Rather, the goal is to lower the *total costs* associated with purchases. Analysis might show that the best vendor is the one that helps the customer reduce costs of excess inventory or labor time, retooling of equipment, and correcting problems caused by some defective parts. By evaluating suppliers on all aspects of how they are working out, buyers can make better decisions.[4]

EXHIBIT 8–2   Multiple Influence and Roles in the Buying Center

Behavioral needs are relevant too

Vendor analysis tries to focus on economic factors, but purchasing in organizations may also involve many of the same behavioral dimensions we discussed in Chapter 7. Purchasing managers and others involved in buying decisions are human—and they want friendly relationships with suppliers. The people in some firms are eager to imitate progressive competitors—or even to be the first to try new products. Such "innovators" deserve special attention when new products are being introduced.

The different people involved in purchase decisions are also human with respect to protecting their own interests—and their own position in the company. That's one reason people from different departments may have different priorities in trying to influence what is purchased. Similarly, purchasing managers may want to avoid taking risks that might reflect badly on their decisions. They have to buy a wide variety of products from many sources and make decisions involving many factors beyond their control. If a new source delivers late or product quality is poor, you can guess who will be blamed. Marketers who can help the buyer avoid taking risks have a definite appeal. In fact, this may make the difference between a successful and unsuccessful marketing mix.

A seller's marketing mix should satisfy *both* the needs of the customer company as well as the needs of individuals who influence the purchase. Therefore, sellers need to find an overlapping area where both can be satisfied. See Exhibit 8–3 for a summary of this idea.

Ethical conflicts may arise

Although organizational buyers are influenced by their own needs, most are real professionals who are careful to avoid a conflict between their own self-interest and company outcomes. Marketers must be careful here. A salesperson who offers one of his company pens to a prospect may view the giveaway as part of the promotion effort—but the customer firm may have a policy against any employee accepting *any* gift from a supplier.

Most organizational buyers do their work ethically—and expect marketers to work the same way. Yet there have been highly publicized abuses. For example, NYNEX (the telephone company that serves New York and New England) found out that many of its buyers were giving contracts to suppliers who offered them

EXHIBIT 8–3 Overlapping Needs of Individual Influencers and the Customer Organization

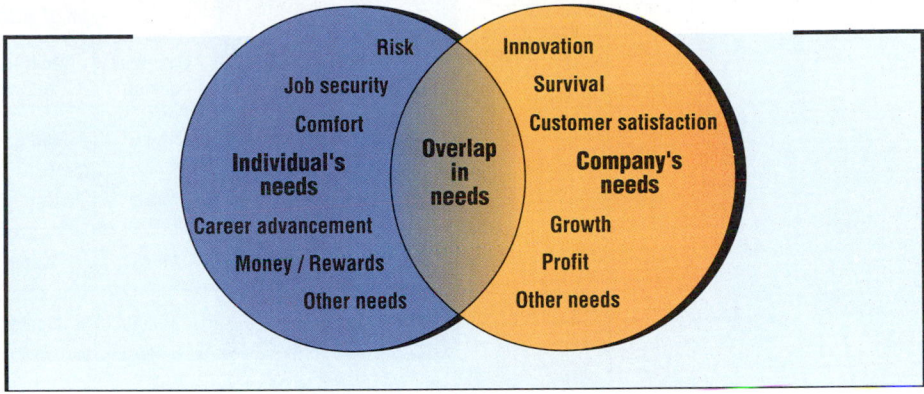

vacation trips and other personal favors. Abuses of this sort have prompted many organizations, including NYNEX, to set up policies that prohibit a buyer from accepting anything from a potential supplier.[5]

Marketers need to take concerns about conflict of interest very seriously. Part of the promotion job in marketing is to identify and persuade different individuals who may influence an organization's purchase decision. Yet the whole marketing effort may be tainted if it even *appears* that a marketer has encouraged a person who influences a decision to put personal gain ahead of company interest.

Purchasing may be centralized

If a large organization has facilities at many locations, much of the purchasing work may be done at a central location. By centralizing purchases, a firm can leverage its buying power and get the best prices from suppliers. For example, U.S. Gypsum, one of the largest building materials manufacturers, does most of the buying for over 50 plants from its Chicago offices. Similarly, Wal-Mart handles most of the purchase decisions for stores in its retail chain from its headquarters in Arkansas. Many purchasing decisions for agencies of the U.S. government are handled in Washington, D.C.

With centralized buying, a sales rep may be able to sell to facilities all over a country—or even across several countries—without leaving a base city. This makes selling easier for competitors too, so the market may be extremely competitive. The importance of such big buyers has led some companies to set up "national account" sales forces specially trained to cater to these needs. A geographically bound salesperson can be at a real disadvantage against such competitors.

ORGANIZATIONAL BUYERS ARE PROBLEM SOLVERS

Three kinds of buying processes are useful

In Chapter 7, we discussed problem solving by consumers and how it might vary from extensive problem solving to routine buying. In organizational markets, we can adapt these concepts slightly and work with three similar buying processes: a new-task buying process, a modified rebuy process, or a straight rebuy.[6] See Exhibit 8–4.

EXHIBIT 8–4 Organizational Buying Processes

Characteristics	Type of process		
	New-task buying	Modified rebuy	Straight rebuy
Time required	Much	Medium	Little
Multiple influence	Much	Some	Little
Review of suppliers	Much	Some	None
Information needed	Much	Some	Little

New-task buying occurs when an organization has a new need and the customer wants a great deal of information. New-task buying can involve setting product specifications, evaluating sources of supply, and establishing an order routine that can be followed in the future if results are satisfactory. Multiple buying influence is typical in new-task buying.

A **straight rebuy** is a routine repurchase that may have been made many times before. Buyers probably don't bother looking for new information or new sources of supply. Most of a company's small or recurring purchases are of this type—but they take only a small part of an organized buyer's time.

The **modified rebuy** is the in-between process where some review of the buying situation is done—though not as much as in new-task buying. Sometimes a competitor will get lazy enjoying a straight rebuy situation. An alert marketer can turn these situations into opportunities by providing more information or a better marketing mix.

Most firms routinize straight rebuys

To save effort and expense, most firms try to routinize the purchase process whenever they can. When some person or unit wants to buy something, a **requisition**—a request to buy something—is filled out. After approval by some supervisor, the requisition is forwarded to the purchasing department for placement with the "best" seller.

Approved requisitions are converted to purchase orders as quickly as possible. Buyers usually make straight rebuys the day they receive the requisition without consulting anyone else; new-task and modified rebuys take longer. If time is important, the buyer may place the order by telephone, fax, or computer.

Computer buying is becoming common

Many buyers now delegate a large portion of their routine order placing to computers. They program decision rules that tell the computer how to order and leave the details of following through to the machine. When economic conditions change, buyers modify the computer instructions. When nothing unusual happens, however, the computer system continues to routinely rebuy as needs develop—printing out new purchase orders or electronically sending them to the regular suppliers.

Obviously, it's a big sale to be selected as a major supplier and routinely called up in the buyer's computer program. It's also obvious that such a buyer will be more impressed by an attractive marketing mix for a whole *line* of products than just a lower price for a particular order. It may be too expensive and too much trouble to change the whole buying system just because somebody is offering a low price on a particular day.[7]

It pays to have an ongoing relationship

In routine order situations, it's very important to be one of the regular sources of supply. For straight rebuys, the buyer (or computer) may place an order without even considering other potential sources. Sellers' sales reps regularly call on these buyers—but *not* to sell a particular item. Rather, they want to maintain relations, become a preferred source, and/or point out new developments that might cause the buyer to reevaluate the present straight rebuy procedure and give more business to the sales rep's company.

New-task buying requires information

Customers in a new-task buying situation are likely to seek information from a variety of sources. See Exhibit 8–5. How much information a customer collects also depends on the importance of the purchase and the level of uncertainty about what choice might be best. The time and expense of searching for and analyzing a lot of information may not be justified for a minor purchase. But a major purchase often involves real detective work. After all, the consequences of a mistake can be very important.

Note that a particular product may be bought in any of the three ways. The marketing job may be quite different depending on the buying process. A new-task buy takes much longer than a straight rebuy—and the seller's promotion has much more chance to have an impact.[8]

BASIC METHODS IN ORGANIZATIONAL BUYING

Should you inspect, sample, describe, or negotiate?

Organizational buyers (really, buyers of all types, including final consumers) use four basic approaches to evaluating and buying products: (1) inspection, (2) sampling, (3) description, and (4) negotiated contracts. Understanding the differences in these buying methods is important in strategy planning, so let's look at each approach.

Inspection looks at everything

Inspection buying means looking at every item. It's used for products that are not standardized and require examination. Here each product is different—as in the case of livestock or used equipment. Such products are often sold in open markets—or at auction if there are several potential buyers. Buyers inspect the goods and either haggle with the seller or bid against competing buyers.

Sampling looks at some

Sampling buying means looking at only part of a potential purchase. As products become more standardized—perhaps because of careful grading or quality control—buying by sample becomes possible. For example, a power company might buy miles of heavy electric cable. A sample section might be heated to the melting point to be certain the cable is safe.

Prices may be based on a sample. Although demand and supply forces may set the general price level, actual price may vary depending on the quality of a specific sample. For example, grain markets use this kind of buying. The actual price is based on a sample withdrawn from a carload of grain and analyzed.

People in less-developed economies do a lot of buying by inspection or sampling—regardless of the product. The reason is skepticism about quality—or lack of faith in the seller.

EXHIBIT 8–5   Major Sources of Information Used by Organizational Buyers

	Marketing sources	Nonmarketing sources
Personal sources	• Salespeople • Others from supplier firms • Trade shows	• Buying center members • Outside business associates • Consultants and outside experts
Impersonal sources	• Advertising in trade publications • Sales literature • Sales catalogs	• Rating services • Trade associations • News publications • Product directories

Specifications describe the need

Description (specification) buying means buying from a written (or verbal) description of the product. Most manufactured items and many agricultural commodities are bought this way—often without inspection. When quality can almost be guaranteed, buying by description—grade, brand, or specification—may be satisfactory, especially when there is mutual trust between buyers and sellers. Because this method reduces the cost of buying, buyers use it whenever practical.

Services are usually purchased by description. Since a service is usually not performed until after it's purchased, buyers have nothing to inspect ahead of time.

Once the purchase needs are specified, it's the buyer's job to get the best deal possible. If several suppliers want the business, the buyer will often request competitive bids. **Competitive bids** are the terms of sale offered by different suppliers in response to the buyer's purchase specifications. If different suppliers' quality, dependability, and delivery schedules all meet the specs, the buyer will select the low-price bid. But a creative marketer needs to look carefully at the purchaser's specs—and the need—to see if other elements of the marketing mix could provide a competitive advantage.

Negotiated contracts handle relationships

Negotiated contract buying means agreeing to a contract that allows for changes in the purchase arrangements.

Sometimes the buyer knows roughly what the company needs but can't fix all the details in advance. Specifications or total requirements may change over time. This situation is common, for example, in research and development work and in the building of special-purpose machinery or buildings. In such cases, the general project is described, and a basic price may be agreed on—perhaps even based on competitive bids—but with provision for changes and price adjustments up or down. Or a supplier may be willing to accept a contract that provides some type of incentive—such as full coverage of costs plus a fixed fee or full costs plus a profit percentage tied to costs. The whole contract may even be subject to renegotiation as the work proceeds.

While the marketing job varies depending on which buying process and methods a firm uses to make a particular purchase, the type of relationship a supplier has with the customer firm is sometimes an even more important consideration.

Buyers may only inspect a portion of a potential fruit purchase, but the quality of the sample may affect the price or acceptability of the whole order. Most manufactured items, including spools of nylon, are bought based on written specifications.

BUYER-SELLER RELATIONSHIPS IN BUSINESS MARKETS

Build relationships—for mutual benefits

In business markets, there are often significant benefits of a close working relationship between a supplier and a customer firm. And such relationships are becoming more common. Many firms are reducing the number of suppliers with whom they work—expecting more in return from the select suppliers that remain. The best relationships involve real partnerships—where there's mutual trust and respect.

For both the customer and supplier the basic benefit of a close relationship is improved profits through cooperation that reduces total costs. Closely tied firms can often share tasks at lower total cost than would be possible working at arm's length. Costs are sometimes reduced simply by reducing uncertainty and risk. A supplier is often willing and able to reduce its selling price significantly if a customer commits to large orders or orders over a longer period of time. With a larger sales volume the supplier may capture savings through economies of scale and reduced selling costs.

The customer not only benefits from getting needed parts or services at lower cost but also is assured a dependable source of supply. Firms that work closely with fewer suppliers can focus their effort on working with suppliers to resolve joint problems. For example, it may cost both the supplier and the customer more to resolve the problems of a defective product after it is delivered than it would have cost to prevent the problem in the first place. But without the customer's help it may be impossible for the supplier to identify a solution to the problem. As the head of purchasing at Motorola puts it, "Every time we make an error it takes people at both ends to correct it."

A buyer for a multinational firm with plants in many countries might prefer to build a close relationship with a supplier that offers the same consistent quality all over the world.

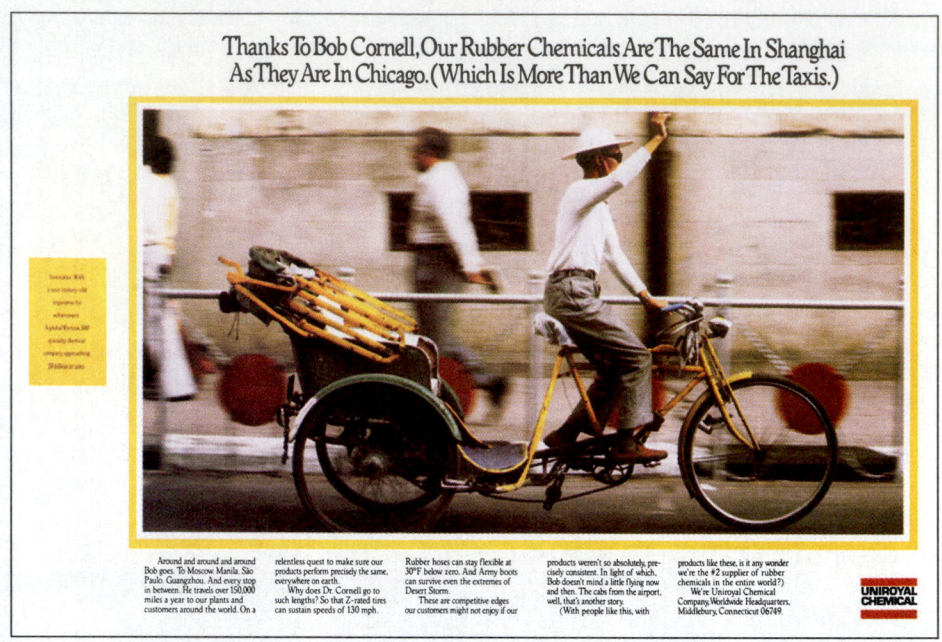

Thanks To Bob Cornell, Our Rubber Chemicals Are The Same In Shanghai As They Are In Chicago. (Which Is More Than We Can Say For The Taxis.)

Relationships may reduce flexibility

Although close relationships can produce benefits, they are not always effective. Making a long-term commitment to a partner—any partner—may result in a loss of flexibility. In many markets, the forces of competition drive down costs and spur innovative marketing mixes; then, the customer may be better off simply letting suppliers compete for the business. It may not be worth the customer's investment of time and energy to build a relationship with a supplier for purchases that are not particularly important or made that frequently.

It may at first appear that a seller would *always* prefer to have a closer relationship with a customer, but that is not so. In situations where a customer doesn't want a relationship, trying to build one is likely to cost more than it's worth. Further, just because a customer is interested in a relationship doesn't mean that it always makes sense for the supplier. Many small suppliers have made the mistake of relying too heavily on relationships with too few customers. One failed relationship may bankrupt the business![9]

Relationships have many dimensions

We've been discussing relationships almost as if they were "all or nothing" arrangements. In practice, however, there are many different aspects of buyer-seller relationships. Firms may have a close buyer-seller relationship in some ways and not be related at all in others. Thus, it's useful to know about five key dimensions that help characterize most buyer-seller relationships: cooperation, information sharing, operational linkages, legal bonds, and relationship-specific adaptations. Purchasing managers for the buying firm and salespeople for the supplier usually coordinate the different dimensions of a relationship. However, as shown in Exhibit 8–6, close relationships often involve direct contacts between a number of people from other areas in both firms. We'll discuss each of these dimensions separately, but keep in mind that a given relationship might be high on some dimensions and low on others.[10]

EXHIBIT 8–6 Key Dimensions of Relationships in Business Markets

Information sharing

Operational linkages

Cooperation

R&D
Quality
Salesperson
Supplier
Accounting
Marketing
Production

Relationship

Finance
Quality
Purchasing manager
R&D
Customer
Accounting
Production
Engineering

Legal bonds

Relationship-specific adaptations

Cooperation treats problems as joint responsibilities

In cooperative relationships, the buyer and seller work together to jointly achieve both mutual and individual objectives. This doesn't mean that the buyer (or seller) will always do what the other wants but rather that people in the two firms treat any problems that may arise as a joint responsibility. Low cooperation occurs when each firm focuses on working independently to achieve its own goals. Some buyers still see little need for cooperation. If one supplier can't satisfy their objectives, they have others who can.

Through cooperation, National Semiconductor (NS) and Siltec—one of its major suppliers of silicon wafers—have found clever ways to cut costs in spite of big increases in the cost of basic silicon. For example, workers at the NS plant used to throw away the expensive plastic cassettes that Siltec uses to ship the silicon wafers. Now Siltec and NS cooperate to recycle the cassettes. As NS' workers unpack the silicon they toss the empty cassettes into a shipping box—and when the box is full, UPS delivers it back to Siltec. This helps the environment and also saves more that $300,000 a year, most of which Siltec passes along to NS as lower prices.[11]

Shared information is useful but may be risky

Some relationships involve open sharing of information, even important propriety information, that is useful to both the buyer and seller. This might include the exchange of cost data, discussion of demand forecasts, and joint work on new product designs. Information might be shared personally or electronically through information systems.

Information sharing can lead to better decisions, reduced uncertainty about the future, and better planning. However, sometimes firms don't want to share information, especially if there is a risk that a partner might misuse it. For example, some suppliers claim that General Motors' former purchasing chief showed blueprints of their latest technology to competing suppliers. Information sharing usually requires trust in the partner. And violations of trust in a relationship are an ethical matter and should be taken seriously. However, as a practical matter, it makes sense for a firm—regardless of whether it's a supplier or customer—to know its partner well before revealing all.

In today's business markets, suppliers of both goods and services are working to build closer relationships with their business customers —to meet needs better and create a competitive advantage.

Operational linkages share functions between firms

Operational linkages are direct ties between the internal operations of the buyer and seller firms. These linkages usually involve formal arrangements and ongoing coordination of activities between the firms. Shared activities are especially important when neither firm, working on its own, can perform a function as well as the two firms can working together. For example, operational linkages are often required to reduce total inventory costs. Business customers want to maintain an adequate inventory—certainly enough to prevent stock-outs or keep production lines moving. On the other hand, keeping too much inventory is expensive. Providing a customer with inventory when it's needed may require that a supplier be able to provide **just-in-time delivery**—reliably getting products there *just* before the customer needs them. We'll discuss just-in-time systems in more detail in Chapter 12. For now, it's enough to see that just-in-time relationships between buyers and sellers usually require operational linkages (as well as information sharing). For example, an automobile producer may want a supplier of automobile seats to load the delivery truck so seats are arranged in the color and style of the cars on the assembly line. This reduces the buyer's costs because the seats only need to be handled one time when they arrive. However, it means that the supplier's production of seats and systems for loading them on the truck must be closely linked to the customer's production line.

Most buyers realize they can't just push costs of operational linkages back onto their suppliers without giving them something in return. Often what they give is a longer-term contract that shares both the costs and benefits of the working partnership.

ALLIED SIGNAL BETS ON RELATIONSHIP WITH SOLE SUPPLIER

Allied Signal is a big company that produces auto parts and aerospace electronics. It's good at what it does, partly because it's figured out the benefits of close relationships with suppliers who know what they're doing. Consider its relationship with Betz Laboratories, a smaller firm that makes industrial water-treatment chemicals. A while back, Betz was just one of several suppliers that sold Allied chemicals to keep the water in its plants from gunking up pipes and rusting machinery. But Betz didn't stop at selling commodity powders. It works to reduce all of the costs related to water use in Allied's plants.

High-level teams of Betz experts and engineers from Allied study water as it flows through a plant.

They ask if it's as safe as possible for the equipment and the environment, or if it's being wasted. In less than a year, a team in one plant found $2.5 million in potential cost reductions. The ideas included using filtered river water instead of buying city water, and recycling water instead of paying high sewer charges to dump it. By adding a few valves to recycle the water in a cooling tower, Betz was able to save 300 gallons of water a minute, which results in savings of over $100,000 a year.

Because of cost-saving ideas like this, Allied's overall use of water treatment chemicals will decrease. However, don't worry about how that affects Betz. Betz is now Allied's sole supplier, and its sales will double.[12]

Operational linkages may also involve the routinized activities of individuals. This might include design engineers, salespeople, and service representatives who closely integrate themselves into a buying organization. They may participate in developing solutions to ongoing problems, conduct regular maintenance checks on equipment, or monitor inventory and coordinate orders. These people become almost part of the customer's operations. At the Chrysler design center, for example, 30 offices are set aside for full-time use by people employed by suppliers.

Linkages may be customized to a particular relationship, or they may be standardized and operate the same way across many exchange partners. For example, in the channel of distribution for grocery products many different producers are standardizing their distribution procedures and coordinating with retail chains to make it faster and cheaper to replenish grocery store shelves.

When a customer's production line or other internal operations are dependent on those of a supplier, it may be difficult or expensive to switch to another supplier. Many buyers would rather avoid a relationship that increases their "switching costs," but there's incentive when the benefits of a relationship with a specific supplier more than offset the loss of flexibility.

Contracts spell out obligations

Many of the purchases in business markets are straightforward. The seller's basic responsibility in a transaction is to transfer title to goods or perform services, and the buyer's basic responsibility is to pay the agreed price. However, in some buyer-seller relationships the responsibilities of the parties are spelled out in a detailed legal agreement. An agreement may apply only for a short period, but long-term contracts are also common.

For example, a customer might ask a supplier to guarantee a 6 percent price reduction for a particular part for each of the next three years and pledge to virtually eliminate defects. In return, the customer might offer to double its orders and help the supplier boost productivity. This might sound attractive to the supplier but also require new people or facilities. The supplier may not be willing to make these long-term commitments unless the buyer is willing to sign a contract for promised purchases. The contract might spell out what would happen if deliveries are late or if quality is below specification. The contract might even cover what would happen if the supplier's factory burned down.

When a contract provides a formal plan for the future of a relationship, some types of risk are reduced. But a firm may not want to be legally "locked in" when it's unclear how the future might affect the relationship. Alternatively, some companies figure that even a detailed contract isn't a good substitute for regular, good faith reviews to make sure that the terms of a deal keep pace with changing business conditions—so neither party gets hurt by something that is unforeseen.

Harley-Davidson decided to use this approach. When Harley moved toward closer relationships with a smaller number of suppliers, its lawyers drafted a detailed, 40-page contract. But purchasing executives tossed it out the window and replaced it with a short statement of principles that should guide relationships between Harley and its suppliers. This "operate on a handshake" approach is typical of relationships with Japanese firms like Honda, and many other firms are now adopting it. It's great when it works, and a disaster when it doesn't.

Specific adaptations invest in the relationship

Relationship-specific adaptations involve changes in a firm's product or procedures that are unique to the needs or capabilities of a relationship partner. Industrial suppliers often custom design a new product for just one customer; this may require investments in R&D or new manufacturing technologies. Donnelly Corp. is an extreme example. It had been supplying Honda with mirrors for the interiors of its cars. Honda's purchasing people liked Donnelly's collaborative style, so they urged Donnelly to supply its exterior mirrors as well. Donnelly had never been in that business—so it had to build a factory to get started. But it did, and from first year sales of $5 million the partnership is expected to grow to $60 million by 1997.

Buying firms may also adapt to a particular supplier; a computer maker may design around Intel's memory chip, and independent photo processors say, "We use Kodak paper for the good look," in their advertising. However, buyers are often hesitant about making big investments that increase dependence on a specific supplier. Typically, they do it only when there isn't a good alternative—perhaps because only one or a few suppliers are available to meet a need—or if the benefits of the investment are clear before it's made. On the other hand, sometimes a buyer will invest in a relationship because the seller has already demonstrated a willingness to do so.

The relationships between Boeing, the giant airplane manufacturer, and one of its suppliers involves relationship-specific adaptation. Boeing is a big customer for machine tools—the equipment it uses to make airplane parts. Like many other manufacturers, Boeing usually designed parts for its planes first and then the supplier whose machines met Boeing's specs at the lowest price got the order. With that approach, neither firm did much adapting to the other. However, it didn't always produce a good result. Boeing had better success when it invited a small set of qualified suppliers to study its operations and recommend how a new landing-gear part could be designed so that the machines to produce them would be more efficient. One supplier, Ingersol, worked with Boeing to design the landing gear so that the total cost of both the parts and the machine to produce them would be lower. The design also helped Boeing speed up its production process. Ingersol put in all this work not knowing if it would win Boeing's business. The investment paid off with an $8 million contract.[13]

A seller may have more incentive to propose new ideas that save the customer money when the firms have a mutual investment in a long-term relationship. The customer firm usually rewards the seller with more orders or a larger share of its business, and this encourages future suggestions and loyalty by the supplier. In contrast, buyers who use a competitive bid system exclusively—either by choice or necessity, as in some government and institutional purchasing—may not be offered much beyond basic goods and services. They are interested primarily in price.

Powerful customer may control the relationship

Although a marketing manager may want to work in a cooperative partnership, that may be impossible with large customers who have the power to dictate how the relationship will work. For example, Duall/Wind, a plastics producer, was a supplier of small parts for Polaroid instant cameras. But when Duall/Wind wanted to raise its prices to cover increasing costs, Polaroid balked. Polaroid's purchasing manager demanded that Duall/Wind show a breakdown of all its costs, from materials to labor to profit. As Duall/Wind's president said, "I had a tough time getting through my head that Polaroid wanted to come right in here and have us divulge all that." But Polaroid is a big account and it got the information it wanted. Polaroid buyers agreed to a price increase only after they were confident that Duall/Wind was doing everything possible to control costs.[14]

Buyers may still use several sources to spread their risk

Even if a marketing manager develops the best marketing mix possible and cultivates a close relationship with the customer, the customer may not give *all* of its business to one supplier. Buyers often look for several dependable sources of supply to protect themselves from unpredictable events such as strikes, fires, or floods in one of their suppliers' plants. A good marketing mix is still likely to win a larger share of the total business—which can prove to be very important. Moving from a 20 percent to a 30 percent share may not seem like much from a buyer's point of view, but for the seller it's a 50 percent increase in sales![15]

Although most customers still want the safety net provided by using several suppliers, an increasing number of firms are relying on sole-sourcing arrangements. This business goes to suppliers who really have developed a superior marketing mix and who relentlessly show the customer that they care about customer satisfaction.

Reciprocity may influence relationship

We've emphasized that most buyer-seller relationships are based on reducing the customer's total procurement costs. However, for completeness we should mention that some relationships are based on reciprocity. **Reciprocity** means trading sales for sales—that is, "if you buy from me, I'll buy from you." If a company's customers also can supply products that the firm buys, then the sales departments of both buyer and seller may try to trade sales for sales. Purchasing managers generally resist reciprocity but often face pressure from their sales departments.

When prices and quality are otherwise competitive, an outside supplier seldom can break a reciprocity relationship. The supplier can only hope to become an alternate source of supply—and wait for the competitor to let its quality slip or prices rise.

In the past, the U.S. Justice Department tried to block reciprocal buying on the grounds that it was an attempt to monopolize—that is, to restrict the normal operation of the free market. However, in recent years the government has been more lenient in this area. Even so, reciprocity is often a bigger factor in other

Many firms, including large retailers like J.C. Penney and Sears, realize that they will do a better job of serving their multicultural customers if they build closer relationships with minority-owned suppliers.

countries than it is in the United States. In Japan, for example, reciprocity is very common.[16]

Variations in buying by customer type

We've been discussing dimensions of relationships and frameworks that marketing managers often use to analyze buying behavior in many different types of customer organizations—in both the United States and internationally. However, it's also useful to have more detail about specific types of customers.

MANUFACTURERS ARE IMPORTANT CUSTOMERS

There are not many big ones

One of the most striking facts about manufacturers is how few there are compared to final consumers. This is true in every country. In the United States, for example, there are about 386,000 factories. Exhibit 8–7 shows that the majority of these are quite small—over half have less than 10 workers. But these small firms account for less than 4 percent of manufacturing activity. In small plants, the owners often do the buying. And they buy less formally than buyers in the relatively few large manufacturing plants—which employ most of the workers and produce a large share of the value added by manufacturing. For example, plants with 250 or more employees make up less than 4 percent of the total—yet they employ over half of the production employees and produce over 61 percent of the value added by manufacturers.

In other countries, the size distribution of manufacturers varies. But across different countries, the same general conclusion holds: It is often desirable to segment industrial markets on the basis of customer size because large plants do so much of the buying.

EXHIBIT 8–7 Size Distribution of Manufacturing Establishments

Number of employees (firm size)	Percentage of total firms in each size group	Percentage of total dollar value added by each size group	Percentage of all employed people by each size group
(small) 1–9	52.0%	2.4%	3.8%
10–19	15.7%	3.1%	4.6%
20–49	15.3%	7.5%	10.2%
50–249	13.5%	25.9%	30.7%
(large) 250 or more	3.5%	61.1%	50.7%

Percent scale: 0 8 16 24 32 40 48 56 64

Customers cluster in geographic areas

In addition to concentration by company size, industrial markets are concentrated in certain geographic areas. Internationally, industrial customers are concentrated in countries that are at the more advanced stages of economic development. Within a country, there is often further concentration in specific areas. In the United States, for example, many factories are concentrated in big metropolitan areas—especially in New York, Pennsylvania, Ohio, Illinois, Texas, and California.[17]

There is also concentration by industry. In Germany, the steel industry is concentrated in the Ruhr Valley. In the United States, it's heavily concentrated in the Pittsburgh, Birmingham (Alabama), and Chicago areas. Similarly, U.S. manufacturers of advanced electronics systems are concentrated in California's famous Silicon Valley near San Francisco and along Boston's Route 128.

Much data is available on industrial markets by SIC codes

The products an industrial customer needs to buy depend on the business it is in. Because of this, sales of a product are often concentrated among customers in similar businesses. For example, apparel manufacturers are the main customers for buttons. Marketing managers who can relate their own sales to their customers' type of business can focus their efforts.

Detailed information is often available to help a marketing manager learn more about customers in different lines of business. The U.S. government regularly collects and publishes data by **Standard Industrial Classification (SIC) codes**—groups of firms in similar lines of business. The number of establishments, sales volumes, and number of employees—broken down by geographic areas—are given for each SIC code. A number of other countries collect similar data, and some of them try to coordinate their efforts with an international variation of the SIC system. However, in many countries data on business customers is incomplete or inaccurate.

In the United States, SIC code breakdowns start with broad industry categories such as food and related products (code 20), tobacco products (code 21),

A firm like Lukens Steel is likely to find that the majority of its customers are concentrated within a few industries that it can identify by SIC number.

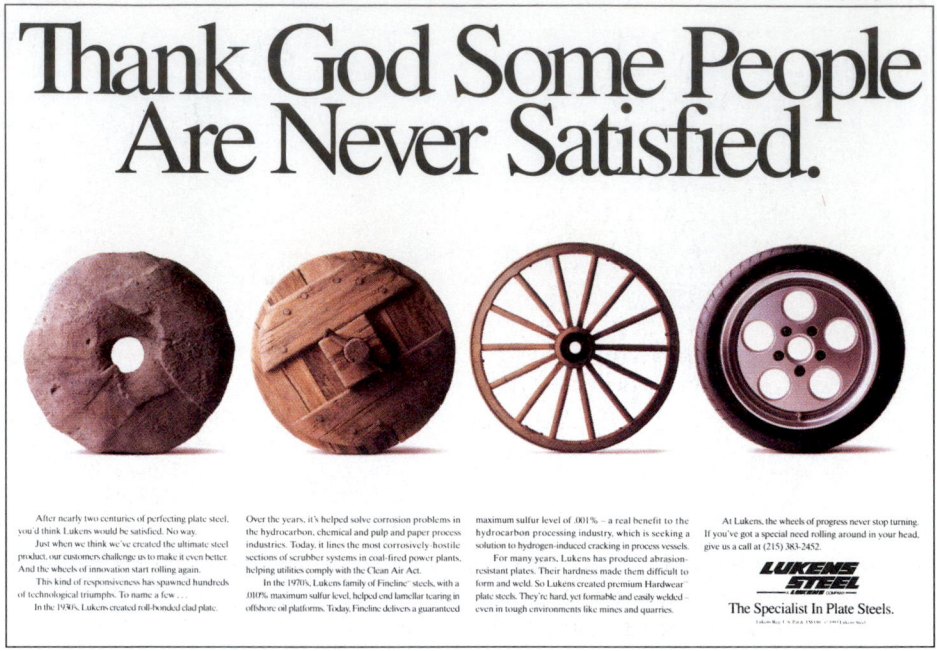

textile mill products (code 22), apparel (code 23), and so on. Within each two-digit industry breakdown, much more detailed data may be available for three-digit and four-digit industries (that is, subindustries of the two- or three-digit industries). Exhibit 8–8 gives an example of more detailed breakdowns within the apparel industry. Four-digit detail isn't available for all industries in every geographic area because the government does not provide data when only one or two plants are located in an area.

Many firms find their *current* customers' SIC codes and then look at SIC-coded lists for similar companies that may need the same goods and services. Other companies look at which SIC categories are growing or declining to discover new opportunities. If companies aiming at business target markets in the United States know exactly whom they are aiming at, readily available data organized by SIC codes can be valuable. Most trade associations and private organizations that gather data on business markets also use SIC codes.

SIC codes are not perfect. Some companies have sales in several categories but are listed in only one—the code with the largest sales. In addition, some newer businesses don't fit any of the categories very well. So although a lot of good information is available, the codes must be used carefully.[18]

PRODUCERS OF SERVICES—SMALLER AND MORE SPREAD OUT

Marketing managers need to keep in mind that the service side of the U.S. economy is large and has been growing fast. Service operations are also growing in some other countries. There may be good opportunities in providing these companies with the products they need to support their operations. But there are also challenges.

EXHIBIT 8–8 Illustrative SIC Breakdown for Apparel Industries

Less detail (fewer digits for SIC)		More detail (more digits for SIC)
20 Food	**231** Male suits, coats, and overcoats	**2321** Shirts, except workshirts
21 Tobacco	**232** Male furnishings, work clothing, and allied garments	**2322** Underwear and nightwear
23 Apparel	**233** Women's, misses', and juniors' outerwear	**2323** Neckwear
Other industries	**234** Female and infant under-garments	**2325** Separate trousers and slacks
	235 Hats, caps, and millinery	**2326** Work clothing
	236 Girls', children's, and infants' outerwear	**2329** Not elsewhere classified
	237 Fur goods	
	238 Miscellaneous apparel and accessories	
	239 Miscellaneous fabricated textile products	

The United States has about 2 million service firms—about 6 times as many as it has manufacturers. Some of these are big companies with international operations. Examples include AT&T, Hilton Hotels, Prudential Insurance, Citibank, and EDS (Electronic Data Systems). These firms have purchasing departments that are like those in large manufacturing organizations. But, as you might guess given the large number of service firms, most of them are small. They're also more spread out around the country than manufacturing concerns. Factories often locate where transportation facilities are good, raw materials are available, and it is less costly to produce goods in quantity. Service operations, in contrast, usually have to be close to their customers.

Buying may not be as formal

Purchases by small service firms are often handled by whoever is in charge. This may be a doctor, lawyer, owner of a local insurance agency, or manager of a hotel. Suppliers who usually deal with purchasing specialists in large organizations may have trouble adjusting to this market. Personal selling is still an important part of promotion, but reaching these customers in the first place often requires more advertising. And small service firms may need much more help in buying than a large corporation.

One Japanese company, Canon, capitalized on such needs. Canon knew that Xerox, the familiar name in office copiers, was very successful selling to larger accounts. But Xerox's sales force was not as good at serving the needs of smaller service firms like law offices. Canon seized this opportunity. It developed promotion materials to help first-time buyers understand differences in copiers. It emphasized that its machines were easy to use and maintain. And Canon also used retail channels to make the copiers available in smaller areas where there wasn't enough business to justify using a sales rep. As a result, Canon has been very successful in this market.[19]

SIC data is coming

The U.S. SIC system was set up when America was primarily a manufacturing economy—with less emphasis on services. In 1987, the SIC codes were updated. The new SIC system provides better information on service firms, but it may be some time before the services-oriented data will be as detailed and useful as it is for manufacturers. For example, without historical data it is difficult to tell which SIC categories are growing or shrinking in different areas of the country.

RETAILERS AND WHOLESALERS BUY FOR THEIR CUSTOMERS

Most retail and wholesale buyers see themselves as purchasing agents for their target customers—remembering the old saying that "Goods well bought are half sold." Typically, retailers do *not* see themselves as sales agents for particular manufacturers. They buy what they think they can profitably sell. And wholesalers buy what they think their retailers can sell. They don't try to make value judgments about the desirability or worth of what they're selling. Rather, they focus on the needs and attitudes of *their* target customers. For example, Super Valu—a $12 billion a year food wholesaler—calls itself "the retail support company." As a top manager at Super Valu put it, "Our mandate is to try to satisfy our retailer customers with *whatever it takes*."[20]

Committee buying is impersonal

Some buyers—especially those who work for big retail chains—are annoyed by the number of wholesalers' and manufacturers' representatives who call on them. Space in their stores is limited and they simply are not interested in carrying every product that some salesperson wants them to sell. Consider the problem facing grocery chains. In an average week, 150 to 250 new items are offered to the buying offices of a large chain like Safeway. If the chain accepted all of them, it would add 10,000 new items during a single year! Obviously, these firms need a way to deal with this overload.[21]

Because of situations like this, in some firms the major decisions to add or drop lines or change buying policies may be handled by a *buying committee*. The seller still calls on and gives a pitch to a buyer—but the buyer does not have final responsibility. Instead, the buyer prepares forms summarizing proposals for new products and passes them on to the committee for evaluation. The seller may not get to present her story to the buying committee in person. This rational, almost cold-blooded approach reduces the impact of a persuasive salesperson.

Wholesalers' and manufacturers' marketing managers must develop good marketing mixes when buying becomes this sophisticated and competitive. And such situations are more common now that so many retailers use computers to improve sales analysis and inventory control.

The founder of Soft Sheen Products, the most successful marketer of hair care products for African-Americans, calls on a buyer for the Walgreen retail chain. The buyer is a real expert who has helped many suppliers establish new products targeted at ethnic consumers.

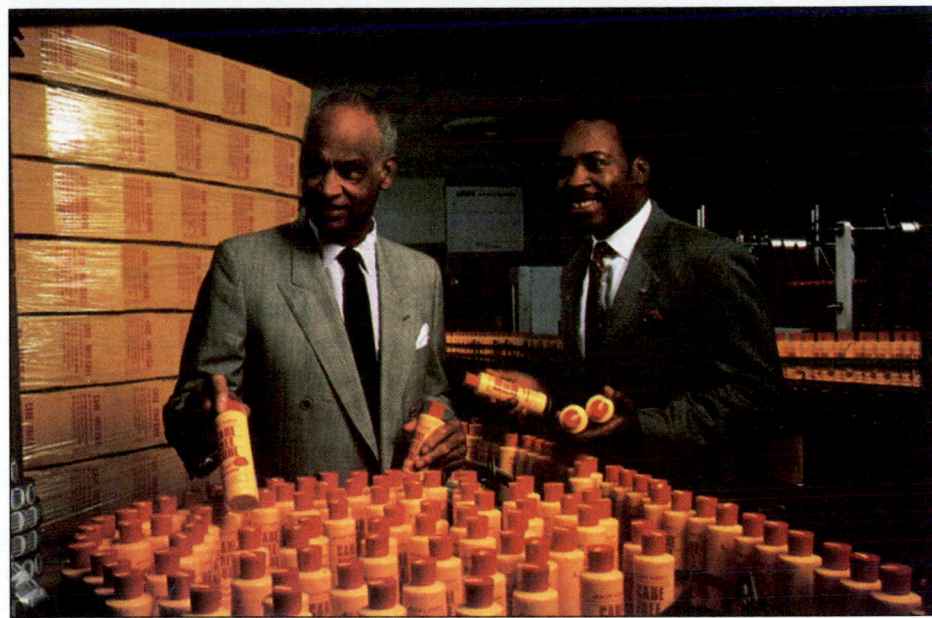

Buyers watch computer output closely

Most larger firms now use sophisticated computerized inventory control systems. Scanners at retail checkout counters keep track of what goes out the door—and computers use this data to update the records. Even small retailers and wholesalers use automated control systems that can print daily unit control reports showing sales of every product on their shelves. This is important to marketing managers selling to such firms because buyers with this kind of information know, in detail, the profitability of the different competing products. If a manufacturer's product isn't moving, the retailer isn't likely to be impressed by a salesperson's request for more in-store attention or added shelf space.

Reorders are straight rebuys

Retailers and wholesalers usually carry a large number of products. A drug wholesaler, for example, may carry up to 125,000 products. Because they deal with so many products, most middlemen buy their products on a routine, automatic reorder basis—straight rebuys—once they make the initial decision to stock specific items. Sellers to these markets must understand the size of the buyer's job and have something useful to say and do when they call. For example, they might try to save the middleman time by taking inventory, setting up displays, or arranging shelves—while trying to get a chance to talk about specific products and maintain the relationship.

Automatic computer ordering is a natural outgrowth of computerized checkout systems. McKesson Corporation—a large wholesaler of drug products—gave computers to drugstores so the stores could keep track of inventory and place orders directly into McKesson's computer. Once a retailer started using the service, McKesson's share of that store's business usually doubled or tripled.[22]

Some are not "open to buy"

Retail buyers are sometimes controlled by a miniature profit and loss statement for each department or merchandise line. In an effort to make a profit, the buyer tries to forecast sales, merchandise costs, and expenses. The figure for "cost of merchandise" is the amount buyers have budgeted to spend over the budget period. If the money has not yet been spent, buyers are **open to buy**—that is, the buyers have budgeted funds that can be spent during the current period. However, if the budget has been spent, they are no longer in the market and no amount of special promotion or price-cutting is likely to induce them to buy.[23]

Buying and selling are closely related

In wholesale and retail firms, there is usually a very close relationship between buying and selling. Buyers are often in close contact with their firm's salespeople and with customers. The housewares buyer for a local department store, for example, may even supervise the salespeople who sell housewares. Salespeople are quick to tell the buyer if a customer wants a product that is not available—especially if the salespeople work on commission. A buyer may even buy some items to satisfy the preferences of salespeople. Therefore, salespeople should not be neglected in the promotion effort.

Resident buyers may help a firm's buyers

Resident buyers are independent buying agents who work in central markets (New York City, Paris, Rome, Hong Kong, Chicago, Los Angeles, etc.) for several retailer or wholesaler customers based in outlying areas or other countries. They buy new styles and fashions and fill-in items as their customers run out of stock during the year. Some resident buyers have hundreds of employees—and buy more than $1 billion worth of goods a year.

Resident buying organizations fill a need. They help small channel members (producers and middlemen) reach each other inexpensively. Resident buyers usually are paid an annual fee based on their purchases.

THE GOVERNMENT MARKET

Size and diversity

Some marketers ignore the government market because they think that government red tape is more trouble than it's worth. They probably don't realize how big the government market really is. Government is the largest customer group in many countries—including the United States. Over 20 percent of the U.S. gross national product is spent by various government units; the figure is much higher in some economies. Different government units in the United States spend about $1,483,000,000,000 (think about it!) a year to buy almost every kind of product. They run not only schools, police departments, and military organizations, but also supermarkets, public utilities, research laboratories, offices, hospitals, and even liquor stores. These huge government expenditures cannot be ignored by an aggressive marketing manager.

Competitive bids may be required

Government buyers in the United States are expected to spend money wisely—in the public interest—so their purchases are usually subject to much public review. To avoid charges of favoritism, most government customers buy by specification using a mandatory bidding procedure. Often the government buyer must accept the lowest bid that meets the specifications. You can see how important it is for the buyer to write precise and complete specifications. Otherwise, sellers may submit a bid that fits the specs but doesn't really match what is needed. By law, a government unit might have to accept the lowest bid—even for an unwanted product.

Writing specifications is not easy—and buyers usually appreciate the help of well-informed salespeople. Salespeople *want* to have input on the specifications so

Government agencies are important customers for a wide variety of products—ranging from playground equipment for schools to earth-moving equipment for highways.

their product can be considered or even have an advantage. One company may get the business—even with a bid that is not the lowest—because the lower bids don't meet minimum specifications.

Rigged specs are an ethical concern

At the extreme, a government customer who wants a specific brand or supplier may try to write the description so that no other supplier can meet all the specs. The buyer may have good reasons for such preferences—a more reliable product, prompt delivery, or better service after the sale. This kind of loyalty sounds great, but marketers must be sensitive to the ethical issues involved. Laws that require government customers to get bids are intended to increase competition among suppliers, not reduce it. Specs that are written primarily to defeat the purpose of these laws may be viewed as illegal bid rigging.

The approved supplier list

Specification and bidding difficulties aren't problems in all government orders. Some items that are bought frequently—or for which there are widely accepted standards—are purchased routinely. The government unit simply places an order at a previously approved price. To share in this business, a supplier must be on the list of approved suppliers. The list is updated occasionally, sometimes by a bid procedure. Government units buy school supplies, construction materials, and gasoline this way. Buyers and sellers agree on a price that will stay the same for a specific period—perhaps a year.

Negotiated contracts are common too

Contracts may be negotiated for items that are not branded or easily described, for products that require research and development, or in cases where there is no effective competition. Depending on the government unit involved, the contract may be subject to audit and renegotiation, especially if the contractor makes a larger profit than expected.

Negotiation is often necessary when there are many intangible factors. Unfortunately, this is exactly where favoritism and influence can slip in. And such influence is not unknown—especially in city and state government. Nevertheless, negotiation is an important buying method in government sales—so a marketing mix should emphasize more than just low price.[24]

Learning what government wants

In the United States, there are more than 86,000 local government units (school districts, cities, counties, and states) as well as many federal agencies that make purchases. Keeping on top of all of them is nearly impossible. Potential suppliers should focus on the government units they want to cater to and learn the bidding methods of those units. Then it's easier to stay informed since most government contracts are advertised. Target marketing can make a big contribution here—making sure the marketing mixes are well matched with the different bidding procedures.

A marketer can learn a lot about potential government target markets from various government publications. In the United States, the federal government's *Commerce Business Daily* lists most current purchase bid requests. The Small Business Administration's *U.S. Purchasing, Specifications, and Sales Directory* explains government procedures to encourage competition for such business. Various state and local governments also offer guidance—as do government units in many other countries. And trade magazines and trade associations provide information on how to reach schools, hospitals, highway departments, park departments, and so on. These are unique target markets and must be treated as such when developing marketing strategies.

Dealing with foreign governments

Government agencies around the world spend a great deal of money, and they are important target customers for some firms. But selling to government units in foreign countries can be a real challenge. In many cases, a firm must get permission from the government in its own country to sell to a foreign government. Moreover, most government contracts favor domestic suppliers if they are available. Even if such favoritism is not explicit, public sentiment may make it very difficult for a foreign competitor to get a contract. Or the government bureaucracy may simply bury a foreign supplier in so much red tape that there's no way to win.

 Is it unethical to "buy help"?

In some countries, government officials expect small payments (grease money) just to speed up processing of routine paperwork, inspections, or decisions from the local bureaucracy. Outright influence peddling—where government officials or their friends request bribe money to sway a purchase decision—is common in some markets. In the past, marketers from some countries have looked at such bribes as a cost of doing business. However, the **Foreign Corrupt Practices Act**, passed by the U.S. Congress in 1977, prohibits U.S. firms from paying bribes to foreign officials. A person who pays bribes—or authorizes an agent to pay them—can face stiff penalties. However, the law was amended in 1988 to allow small grease money payments if they are customary in a local culture. Further, a manager isn't held responsible if an agent in the foreign country secretly pays bribes. An ethical dilemma may arise if a marketing manager *thinks* that money paid to a foreign agent might be used, in part, to bribe a government official. However, most U.S. businesses have learned to live with this law—and in general they comply with its intent.[25]

CONCLUSION

In this chapter, we considered the number, size, location, and buying behavior of various types of organizational customers—to try to identify logical dimensions for segmenting markets and developing marketing mixes. We looked at who makes and influences organizational buying decisions and how multiple influence may make the marketing job more difficult. We also saw that the nature of the buyer and the buying situation are relevant and that the problem-solving models of buyer behavior introduced in Chapter 7 apply here—with modifications.

Buying behavior—and marketing opportunities—may change when there's a close relationship between a supplier and a customer. However, close relationships are not an all-or-nothing thing. There are different ways that a supplier can build a closer relationship with its customers. We identified key dimensions of relationships and their benefits and limitations.

The chapter focuses on aspects of buying behavior that often apply to different types of organizational customers. However, we discussed some key differences in the manufacturer, middleman, and government markets.

A clear understanding of organizational buying habits, needs, and attitudes can aid marketing strategy planning. And since there are fewer organizational customers than final consumers, it may even be possible for some marketing managers (and their salespeople) to develop a unique strategy for each potential customer.

This chapter offers some general principles that are useful in strategy planning—but the nature of the products being offered may require adjustments in the plans. Different product classes are discussed in Chapter 9. Variations by product may provide additional segmenting dimensions to help a marketing manager fine tune a marketing strategy.

QUESTIONS AND PROBLEMS

1. In your own words, explain how buying behavior of business customers in different countries may have been a factor in speeding the spread of international marketing.

2. Compare and contrast the buying behavior of final consumers and organizational buyers. In what ways are they most similar and in what ways are they most different?

3. Briefly discuss why a marketing manager should think about who is likely to be involved in the buying center for a particular purchase. Is the buying center idea useful in consumer buying? Explain your answer.

4. If a nonprofit hospital were planning to buy expensive MRI scanning equipment (to detect tumors), who might be involved in the buying center? Explain your answer and describe the types of influence that different people might have.

5. Describe the situations that would lead to the use of the three different buying processes for a particular product—lightweight bumpers for a pickup truck.

6. Why would an organizational buyer want to get competitive bids? What are some of the situations when competitive bidding can't be used?

7. How likely would each of the following be to use competitive bids: (a) a small town that needed a road resurfaced, (b) a scouting organization that needed a printer to print its scouting handbook, (c) a hardware retailer that wants to add a new lawn mower line, (d) a grocery store that wants to install a new checkout scanner, and (e) a sorority that wants to buy a computer to keep track of member dues? Explain your answers.

8. Discuss the advantages and disadvantages of just-in-time supply relationships from an organizational buyer's point of view. Are the advantages and disadvantages merely reversed from the seller's point of view?

9. Explain why a customer might be willing to work more cooperatively with a small number of suppliers rather than pitting suppliers in a competition against each other. Give an example that illustrates your points.

10. Would a tool manufacturer need a different marketing strategy for a big retail chain like Home Depot than for a single hardware store run by its owner? Discuss your answer.

11. How do you think a furniture manufacturer's buying habits and practices would be affected by the specific type of product to be purchased? Consider fabric for upholstered furniture, a lathe for the production line, cardboard for shipping cartons, and lubricants for production machinery.

12. Discuss the importance of target marketing when analyzing organizational markets. How easy is it to isolate homogeneous market segments in these markets?

13. Explain how SIC codes might be helpful in evaluating and understanding business markets. Give an example.

14. Considering the nature of retail buying, outline the basic ingredients of promotion to retail buyers. Does it make any difference what kinds of products are involved? Are any other factors relevant?

15. The government market is obviously an extremely large one, yet it is often slighted or even ignored by many firms. Red tape is certainly one reason, but there are others. Discuss the situation and be sure to include the possibility of segmenting in your analysis.

16. Some critics argue that the Foreign Corrupt Practices Act puts U.S. businesses at a disadvantage when competing in foreign markets with suppliers from other countries that do not have similar laws. Do you think that this is a reasonable criticism? Explain your answer.

SUGGESTED CASES

5. Union Chemical Company

6. Inland Steel Company

COMPUTER-AIDED PROBLEM

8. Vendor Analysis

CompuTech, Inc., makes circuit boards for microcomputers. It is evaluating two possible suppliers of electronic memory chips.

The chips do the same job. Although manufacturing quality has been improving, some chips are always defective. Both suppliers will replace defective chips. But the only practical way to test for a defective chip is to assemble a circuit board and "burn it in"—run it and see if it works. When one chip on a board is defective at that point, it costs $2.00 for the extra labor time to replace it. Supplier 1 guarantees a chip failure rate of not more than 1 per 100 (that is, a defect rate of 1 percent). The second supplier's 2 percent defective rate is higher, but its price is lower.

Supplier 1 has been able to improve its quality because it uses a heavier plastic case to hold the chip. The only disadvantage of the heavier case is that it requires CompuTech to use a connector that is somewhat more expensive.

Transportation costs are added to the price quoted by either supplier, but Supplier 2 is further away so transportation costs are higher. And because of the distance,

delays in supplies reaching CompuTech are sometimes a problem. To ensure that a sufficient supply is on hand to keep production going, CompuTech must maintain a backup inventory—and this increases inventory costs. CompuTech figures inventory costs—the expenses of finance and storage—as a percentage of the total order cost.

To make its vendor analysis easier, CompuTech's purchasing agent has entered data about the two suppliers on a spreadsheet. He based his estimates on the quantity he thinks he will need over a full year.

a. *Based on the results shown in the initial spreadsheet, which supplier do you think CompuTech should select? Why?*

b. *CompuTech estimates it will need 100,000 chips a year if sales go as expected. But if sales are slow, fewer chips will be needed. This isn't an issue with Supplier 2; its price is the same at any quantity. However, Supplier 1's price per chip will be $1.95 if CompuTech buys less than 90,000 during the year. If CompuTech only needs 84,500 chips, which supplier would be more economical? Why?*

c. *If the actual purchase quantity will be 84,500 and Supplier 1's price is $1.95, what is the highest price at which Supplier 2 will still be the lower-cost vendor for CompuTech? (Hint: You can enter various prices for Supplier 2 in the spreadsheet—or use the What If analysis to vary Supplier 2's price and display the total costs for both vendors.)*

For additional questions related to this problem, see Exercise 8–3 in the *Learning Aid for Use with Basic Marketing*, 12th edition.

9

Elements of Product Planning for Goods and Services

When You Finish This Chapter, You Should

1. Understand what "Product" really means.

2. Know the key differences between goods and services.

3. Know the differences among the various consumer and business product classes.

4. Understand how the product classes can help a marketing manager plan marketing strategies.

5. Understand what branding is and how to use it in strategy planning.

6. Understand the importance of packaging in strategy planning.

7. Understand the role of warranties in strategy planning.

8. Understand the important new terms (shown in red).

Just about every snack bar, convenience store, supermarket, and mass-merchandise retailer in the U.S. sells chocolate candy. Usually it's sold by the checkout counter—where consumers with a sweet tooth can buy on an impulse. And there is no shortage of choices, either. Companies like Hershey, Cadbury, Mars, and Nestlé each have a line of bars to appeal to different tastes and preferences. Mars,

for example, offers up variety with familiar brand names Snickers, Milky Way, M&Ms, and Twix.

It's hard for new products to take loyal customers away from these venerable old brands—perhaps because it's even harder for new entrants to get retailers to allocate more shelf space. But that hasn't kept some firms from trying—or even succeeding. Marketing managers for Hershey's have been especially successful in developing new products. Hershey Hugs, for example, proved to be a simple but popular extension of the Hershey's Kisses idea.

Of course, the market for chocolate candy isn't so competitive everywhere. Marketing managers for Mars, for example, got a fresh start—with less competition and greater prospects for future growth—when they decided to go into the Russian market after the breakup of the Soviet Union.

Without subsidies from the government, Russian candy factories didn't have hard currency to buy the imported cocoa and sugar they needed to produce high-quality chocolate. By 1992, there was virtually no locally produced chocolate in Russia. Some Turkish chocolate was available, but consumers rejected it because poor packaging allowed it to get stale even before it arrived at the store. Years earlier, when Mars had introduced Snickers candy bars in England, marketing managers changed the brand name to Marathon. They were concerned that Snickers sounded too much like knickers, a British term for women's underwear. Later, however, they changed back to Snickers so that they could promote the same brand name throughout all of Europe. Even though Russia uses a different alphabet from Western Europe, Mars stuck with the one-name policy. That meant that TV ads had to teach consumers to recognize and pronounce the name. However, TV ads in Russia cost about $12,000 a minute—only a fraction of the cost in the U.S. And the Russian ads worked unusually well. Within a year, 82 percent of Russians recognized the Snickers name.

Now, many of Russia's 150 million consumers insist on Snickers as their candy of choice. At about 300 rubles (25 cents), Snickers is one of the most affordable Western status symbols. At that price, Mars isn't yet making a big profit.

However, as the market leader, Mars is building strong distribution channels and consumer loyalty. As incomes in Russia grow, sales and profits will as well. And now that the Snickers name is established in Russia, perhaps it won't be long before consumers there will be eagerly trying Snickers brand ice cream bars.[1]

THE PRODUCT AREA INVOLVES MANY STRATEGY DECISIONS

The Snickers case highlights some important topics we'll discuss in this chapter and the next. In this chapter, we'll cover the many different elements of product planning. In Chapter 10, we'll focus on the important role of new products and how to develop them.

Here we'll start by looking at how customers see a firm's product. Then we'll talk about product classes to help you better understand marketing strategy planning. We'll also talk about branding and packaging. Most goods need some packaging, and both goods and services should be branded. A successful marketer wants to be sure that satisfied customers know what to ask for the next time.

In summary, we will cover the strategy planning of producers—and middlemen—who make these Product decisions. Keep in mind that there are many decisions related to the Product area, as shown in Exhibit 9–1.

WHAT IS A PRODUCT?

Customers buy satisfaction, not parts

First, we have to define what we mean by a "product."

When Toyota sells a new Avalon, is it just selling a certain number of nuts and bolts, some sheet metal, an engine, and four wheels?

EXHIBIT 9–1   Strategy Planning for Product

A marketing manager needs to think about how the firm's offering will satisfy a customer's needs—and having more features may not be what the customer wants or needs.

This cellular phone I got lets the guys at the office keep in touch with me no matter where I am. Of course, there are lots of good things about it, too.

Muratec CT-50 Cellular Phone
Call 1-800-543-4636 for more information.

muratec

Faxes, phones and whatever we think of next.

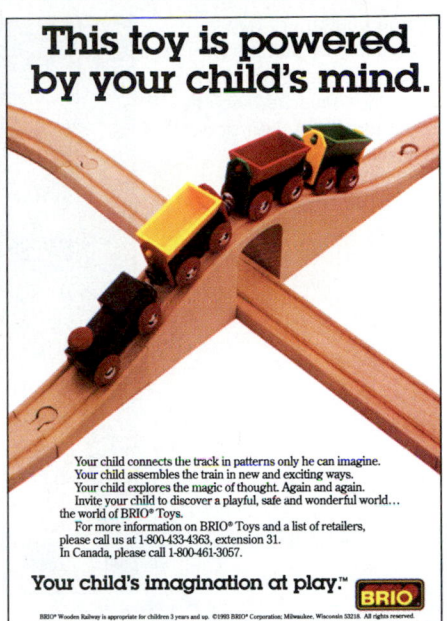

This toy is powered by your child's mind.

Your child connects the track in patterns only he can imagine.
Your child assembles the train in new and exciting ways.
Your child explores the magic of thought. Again and again.
Invite your child to discover a playful, safe and wonderful world…
the world of BRIO® Toys.
For more information on BRIO® Toys and a list of retailers,
please call us at 1-800-433-4363, extension 31.
In Canada, please call 1-800-461-3057.

Your child's imagination at play.™ **BRIO**

When Sherwin-Williams sells a can of exterior paint, is it just selling a can of chemicals?

When Air Jamaica sells a ticket for a flight to the Caribbean, is it just selling so much wear and tear on an airplane and so much pilot fatigue?

The answer to all these questions is *no*. Instead, what these companies are really selling is the satisfaction, use, or benefit the customer wants.

All customers care about is that their cars look good and keep running. They want to protect their homes with paint—not analyze it. And when they take a trip on Air Jamaica, they really don't care how hard it is on the plane or the crew. They just want a safe, comfortable trip.

In the same way, when producers and middlemen buy a product, they're interested in the profit they can make from its purchase—through use or resale—not how the product was made.

Product means the need-satisfying offering of a firm. The idea of "Product" as potential customer satisfaction or benefits is very important. Many business managers—trained in the production side of business—get wrapped up in the technical details. They think of Product in terms of physical components like transistors and screws. These are important to *them*, but components have little effect on the way most customers view the product. Most customers think about products in terms of the total satisfaction they provide. Providing satisfaction may require a "total" Product offering that is really a complex combination, perhaps including the right kind of service, a physical good with the right features, useful instructions, a convenient package, a trustworthy warranty, and perhaps even a familiar name that cuts shopping risk by identifying a product that has satisfied the consumer in the past.

Product quality and customer needs

Because consumers buy satisfaction, not just parts, marketing managers must be constantly concerned with product quality. This may seem obvious, but the obvious is sometimes easy to overlook. In the 1980s, many U.S. firms learned this

Because customers buy satisfaction, not just parts, marketing managers must be constantly concerned with the product quality of their goods and services.

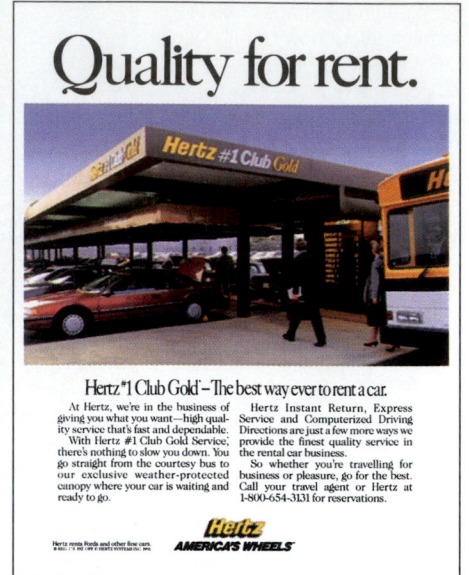

lesson the hard way when Japanese and European competitors stole market share by offering customers higher-quality products. But what does "high quality" mean? Companies focus on better quality control in production—so that products work as they should and consumers really get what they think they're buying. But quality means more than that.

From a marketing perspective, **quality** means a product's ability to satisfy a customer's needs or requirements. This definition focuses on the customer—and how the customer thinks a product will fit some purpose. For example, the "best" credit card may not be the one with the highest credit limit but the one that's accepted where a consumer wants to use it. Similarly, the best quality clothing for casual wear on campus may be a pair of jeans—not a pair of dress slacks made of a higher-grade fabric.

Among different types of jeans, the one with the strongest stitching and the most comfortable or durable fabric might be thought of as having the highest grade or *relative quality* for its product type. Marketing managers often focus on relative quality when comparing their products to competitors' offerings. However, a product with more features—or even better features—is not a high-quality product if the features aren't what the target market wants or needs.

Quality and satisfaction depend on the total Product offering. If potato chips get stale on the shelf because of poor packaging, the consumer will be dissatisfied. A broken button on a shirt will disappoint the customer—even if the laundry did a nice job cleaning and pressing the collar. A very fast and powerful computer is a poor-quality product if it makes occasional errors when doing arithmetic. A full-featured stereo VCR is a poor-quality product if it's hard for a consumer to program a recording session—or if the seller doesn't answer the phone to respond to the customer's question.[2]

Goods and/or services are the Product

You already know that a product may be a physical *good* or a *service* or a *blend* of both. You need to understand this view thoroughly. It's too easy to slip into a limited, physical-product point of view. We want to think of a Product in terms of

EXHIBIT 9–2   Examples of Possible Blends of Physical Goods and Services in a Product

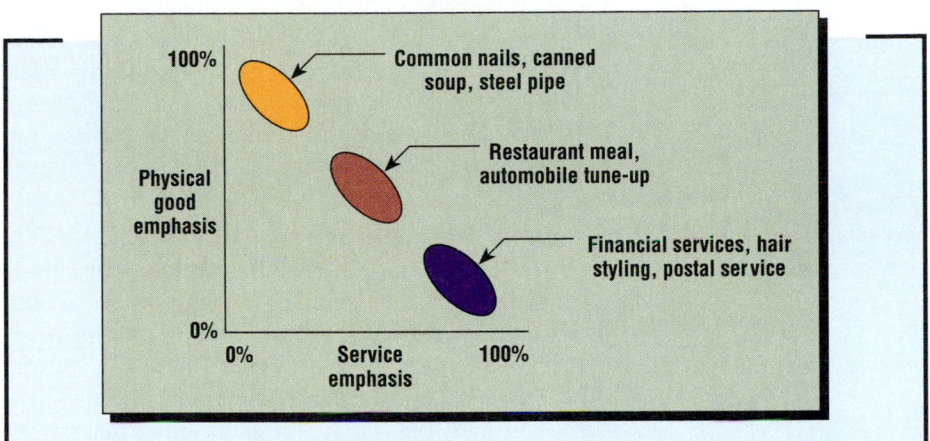

the needs it satisfies. If a firm's objective is to satisfy customer needs, service can be part of its Product—or service alone may *be* the Product—and must be provided as part of a total marketing mix.

Exhibit 9–2 shows this bigger view of Product. It shows that a product can range from a 100 percent emphasis on physical goods—for commodities like common nails—to a 100 percent emphasis on service, like advice from a lawyer. Regardless of the emphasis involved, the marketing manager must consider most of the same elements in planning products and marketing mixes. Given this, we usually won't make a distinction between goods and services but will call all of them *Products*. Sometimes, however, understanding the differences in goods and services can help fine tune marketing strategy planning. So let's look at some of these differences next.

DIFFERENCES IN GOODS AND SERVICES

How tangible is the Product?

Because a good is a physical thing, it can be seen and touched. You can try on a Benetton shirt, thumb through the latest issue of *People* magazine, or smell Colombian coffee as it brews. A good is a *tangible* item. When you buy it, you own it. And it's usually pretty easy to see exactly what you'll get.

On the other hand, a **service** is a deed performed by one party for another. When you provide a customer with a service, the customer can't keep it. Rather, a service is experienced, used, or consumed. You go see a Touchstone Studios movie, but afterwards all you have is a memory. You ride on a ski lift in the Alps, but you don't own the equipment. Services are not physical—they are *intangible*. You can't "hold" a service. And it may be hard to know exactly what you'll get when you buy it.

Most products are a combination of tangible and intangible elements. BP gas and the credit card to buy it are tangible—the credit the card grants is not. A Domino's pizza is tangible, but the fast home delivery is not.

Is the product produced before it's sold?

Goods are usually produced in a factory and then sold. A Sony TV may be stored in a warehouse or store waiting for a buyer. By contrast, services are often sold first, then produced. And they're produced and consumed in the same time frame. You can't perform a deed and then put it on the shelf. Thus, goods producers may be far away from the customer, but service providers often work in the customer's presence.

A worker in a Sony TV factory can be in a bad mood—and customers will never know. And a faulty TV can be caught by a quality control inspector. But a rude bank teller can drive customers away. The growing use of computers and machines in service businesses is partly an attempt to avoid this problem. An automated teller machine can't do everything, but it's never rude.

Services can't be stored or transported

Services are perishable—they can't be stored. This makes it harder to balance supply and demand. An example explains the problem.

MCI is a major supplier of long-distance telephone services. Even when demand is high—during peak business hours or on Mother's Day—customers expect the service to be available. They don't want to hear, "Sorry, all lines are busy." So MCI must have enough equipment and employees to deal with peak demand times. But when customers aren't making many calls, MCI's facilities are idle. MCI might be able to save money with less capacity (equipment and people), but then it would sometimes have to face dissatisfied customers.

It's often difficult to have economies of scale when the product emphasis is on service. If a firm is serving a large group of customers, it may be able to justify adding more or better equipment, facilities, or people to do a better job. But services can't be produced in large, economical quantities and then transported to customers. In addition, *services often have to be produced in the presence of the customer.* So service suppliers often need duplicate equipment and staff at places where the service is actually provided. Merrill Lynch sells investment advice along with financial products worldwide. That advice could, perhaps, be produced more economically in a single building in New York City. But Merrill Lynch uses

A service is a deed performed by one party for another, but providing consistent service quality can be a challenge because services are usually produced in the presence of the customer.

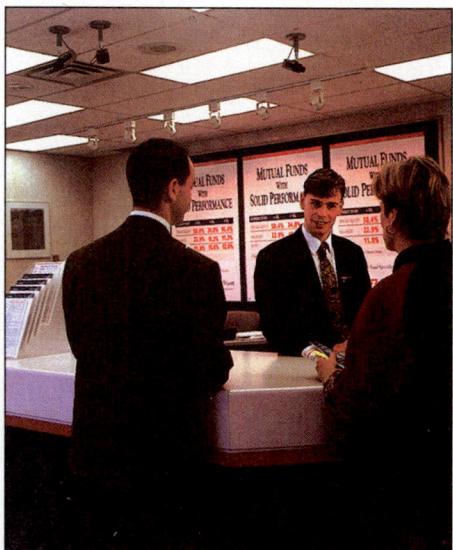

small facilities all over the United States and other countries—to be conveniently available. Customers want a personal touch from the stockbroker telling them how to invest their money.[3]

Think about the whole Product

Providing the right Product—when and where and how the customer wants it—is a challenge. This is true whether the Product is primarily a service, primarily a good, or, as is usually the case, a blend of both. Marketing managers must think about the "whole" Product they provide, and then make sure that all of the elements fit together—and work with the rest of the marketing strategy. Sometimes a single product isn't enough to meet the needs of target customers. Then, assortments of different products may be required.

WHOLE PRODUCT LINES MUST BE DEVELOPED TOO

A **product assortment** is the set of all product lines and individual products that a firm sells. A **product line** is a set of individual products that are closely related. The seller may see them as related because they're produced and/or operate in a similar way, sold to the same target market, sold through the same types of outlets, or priced at about the same level. Sara Lee, for example, has many product lines in its product assortment—including coffee, tea, luncheon meats, desserts, snacks, hosiery, sportswear, lingerie, and shoe polish. But Avis has one product line—different types of cars to rent. An **individual product** is a particular product within a product line. It usually is differentiated by brand, level of service offered, price, or some other characteristic. For example, each size of a brand of soap is an individual product. Middlemen usually think of each separate product as a stock-keeping unit (sku) and assign it a unique sku number.

Many items in CPC International's line of food products sell as both consumer and business products, and different marketing mixes are required to reach the different target markets.

EXHIBIT 9–3   Product Classes

Each individual product and target market may require a separate strategy. For example, Sara Lee's strategy for selling tea in England is different from its strategy for selling men's underwear in the United States. We'll focus mainly on developing one marketing strategy at a time. But remember that a marketing manager may have to plan *several* strategies to develop an effective marketing program for a whole company.

PRODUCT CLASSES HELP PLAN MARKETING STRATEGIES

You don't have to treat *every* product as unique when planning strategies. Some product classes require similar marketing mixes. These product classes are a useful starting point for developing marketing mixes for new products—and evaluating present mixes. Exhibit 9–3 summarizes the product classes.

Product classes start with type of customer

All products fit into one of two broad groups—based on the type of customer that will use them. **Consumer products** are products meant for the final consumer. **Business products** are products meant for use in producing other products. The same product—like Mazola Corn Oil— *might* be in both groups. Consumers buy it to use in their own kitchens, but food processing companies and restaurants buy it in large quantities as an ingredient in the products they sell. But selling the same product to both final consumers and business customers requires (at least) two different strategies.

There are product classes within each group. Consumer product classes are based on *how consumers think about and shop for products*. Business product classes are based on *how buyers think about products and how they'll be used*.

We'll talk about consumer product classes first.

EXHIBIT 9–4 Consumer Product Classes and Marketing Mix Planning

Consumer Product Class	Marketing Mix Considerations	Consumer Behavior
Convenience Products		
Staples	Maximum exposure with widespread, low-cost distribution; mass selling by producer; usually low price; branding is important.	Routinized (habitual), low effort, frequent purchases; low involvement.
Impulse	Widespread distribution with display at point of purchase.	Unplanned purchases bought quickly.
Emergency	Need widespread distribution near probable point of need; price sensitivity low.	Purchase made with time pressure when a need is great.
Shopping Products		
Homogeneous	Need enough exposure to facilitate price comparison; price sensitivity high.	Customers see little difference among alternatives, seek lowest price.
Heterogeneous	Need distribution near similar products; promotion (including personal selling) to highlight product advantages; less price sensitivity.	Extensive problem solving; consumer may need help in making a decision.
Specialty Products	Price sensitivity is likely to be low; limited distribution may be acceptable, but should be treated as a convenience or shopping product (in whichever category product would typically be included) to reach persons not yet sold on its specialty product status.	Willing to expend effort to get specific product, even if not necessary; strong preferences make it an important purchase.
Unsought Products		
New unsought	Must be available in places where similar (or related) products are sought; needs attention-getting promotion.	Need for product not strongly felt; unaware of benefits or not yet gone through adoption process.
Regularly unsought	Requires very aggressive promotion, usually personal selling.	Aware of product but not interested; attitude toward product may even be negative.

CONSUMER PRODUCT CLASSES

Consumer product classes divide into four groups: (1) convenience, (2) shopping, (3) specialty, and (4) unsought. Each class is based on the way people buy products. See Exhibit 9–4 for a summary of how these product classes relate to marketing mixes.[4]

CONVENIENCE PRODUCTS—PURCHASED QUICKLY WITH LITTLE EFFORT

Convenience products are products a consumer needs but isn't willing to spend much time or effort shopping for. These products are bought often, require little service or selling, don't cost much, and may even be bought by habit.

The three types of convenience products—staples, impulse products, and emergency products—are again based on *how customers think about products,* not the features of the products themselves.

Staples—purchased regularly by habit

Staples are products that are bought often, routinely, and without much thought—like breakfast cereal, canned soup, and most other packaged foods used almost every day in almost every household. Staples are usually sold in convenient places like food stores, discount stores, or vending machines. Branding is important with staples. It helps customers cut shopping effort and encourages repeat buying of satisfying brands.

Impulse products—bought immediately on sight

Impulse products are products that are bought quickly—as *unplanned* purchases—because of a strongly felt need. True impulse products are items that the customer hadn't planned to buy, decides to buy on sight, may have bought the same way many times before, and wants right now. An ice-cream seller at a beach sells impulse products. If sun bathers don't buy an ice-cream bar when he rings his bell, the need goes away, and the purchase won't be made later.

This buying behavior is important because it affects Place—and the whole marketing mix—for impulse products. If the buyer doesn't see an impulse product at the right time, the sale may be lost. That's why retailers put impulse products where they'll be seen and bought—near checkout counters or in other heavy traffic areas of a store. Grocery stores sell gum, candy bars, and magazines this way. And life insurance is sold in airports at convenient booths or vending machines.[5]

Emergency products—purchased only when urgently needed

Emergency products are products that are purchased immediately when the need is great. The customer doesn't have time to shop around when a traffic accident occurs, a thunderstorm begins, or an impromptu party starts. The price of the ambulance service, raincoat, or ice cubes won't be important.

Meeting customers' emergency needs may require a different marketing mix—especially regarding Place. Some small neighborhood stores carry "emergency" products to meet these needs—staying open 7 til 11 and stocking fill-in items like milk or bread. A towing service for cars is available 24 hours a day. Banks put their automated teller machines in airports. Customers don't mind the higher prices charged for these purchases because they think of them as emergencies.

SHOPPING PRODUCTS—ARE COMPARED

Shopping products are products that a customer feels are worth the time and effort to compare with competing products.

Shopping products can be divided into two types—depending on what customers are comparing: (1) homogeneous and (2) heterogeneous shopping products.

Homogeneous shopping products—the price must be right

Homogeneous shopping products are shopping products the customer sees as basically the same—and wants at the lowest price. Some consumers feel that certain sizes and types of refrigerators, television sets, washing machines, and even cars are very similar. So they shop for the best price.

Firms may try to emphasize and promote their product differences to avoid head-to-head price competition. For example, Wachovia bank in the Southeast offers customers a personal banker who provides information and advice. But if consumers don't think the differences are real or important, they'll just look at price.

Even some inexpensive products like butter or coffee may be considered homogeneous shopping products. *Some* people carefully read food store ads for the lowest prices—and then go from store to store for bargains. They don't do this for staples.

Heterogeneous shopping products—the product must be right

Heterogeneous shopping products are shopping products the customer sees as different—and wants to inspect for quality and suitability. Furniture, clothing, dishes, and some cameras are good examples. Quality and style matter more than price.

It's harder—but less important—to compare prices of nonstandardized items. Once the customer has found the right product, price may not matter—as long as it's reasonable. This is also true when service is a major part of the product, as in a visit to a dentist or car repair service. You may have asked a friend to recommend a dentist who gives pain-free treatments—without even asking what the dentist charges.

Branding may be less important for heterogeneous shopping products. The more consumers compare price and quality, the less they rely on brand names or labels. Some retailers carry competing brands so consumers won't go to a competitor to compare items.

Often the buyer of heterogeneous shopping products not only wants—but expects—some kind of help in buying. And if the product is expensive, the buyer may want *personalized* services—such as alteration of clothing or installation of appliances.

SPECIALTY PRODUCTS—NO SUBSTITUTES PLEASE!

Specialty products are consumer products that the customer really wants—and makes a special effort to find. Shopping for a specialty product doesn't mean comparing—the buyer wants that special product and is willing to search for it. It's the customer's *willingness to search*—not the extent of searching—that makes it a specialty product.

Specialty products don't have to be expensive, once-in-a-lifetime purchases. Think of your last perfect haircut—and how long you waited for the barber or hairdresser you wanted. *Any* branded product that consumers insist on by name is a specialty product. People have been observed asking for a drug product by its brand name and—when offered a chemically identical substitute—actually leaving the store in anger.

Marketing managers want customers to see their products as specialty products and ask for them over and over again. Building that kind of relationship between the customer and the firm's offering isn't easy. It means satisfying the customer every time. However, that's easier and a lot less costly than trying to win back dissatisfied customers or attract new customers who may not be seeking the product at all.

UNSOUGHT PRODUCTS—NEED PROMOTION

Unsought products are products that potential customers don't yet want or know they can buy. So they don't search for them at all. In fact, consumers probably won't buy these products if they see them—unless Promotion can show their value.

There are two types of unsought products. **New unsought products** are products offering really new ideas that potential customers don't know about yet. Informative promotion can help convince customers to accept or even seek out the product—ending their unsought status. Dannon's yogurt, Litton's microwave ovens, Sony's videotape recorders, and California Cooler's wine coolers are all popular items now, but initially they were new unsought products because they were innovations—consumers didn't know what benefits they offered.

Regularly unsought products are products—like gravestones, life insurance, and encyclopedias—that stay unsought but not unbought forever. There may be a need, but potential customers aren't motivated to satisfy it. And there's little hope that gravestones will move out of the unsought class. For this kind of product, personal selling is *very* important.

Many nonprofit organizations try to "sell" their unsought products. For example, the Red Cross supplies blood to disaster victims. Few of us see donating blood as a big need. So the Red Cross regularly holds blood drives to remind prospective donors of how important it is to give blood.

ONE PRODUCT MAY BE SEEN AS SEVERAL CONSUMER PRODUCTS

We've been looking at product classes one at a time. But the same product might be seen in different ways by different target markets—at the same time. Each of these markets might need a different marketing mix.

A tale of four motels

Motels are a good example of a service that can be seen as four different kinds of consumer products. Some tired motorists are satisfied with the first motel they come to—a convenience product. Others shop for basic facilities at the lowest price—a homogeneous shopping product. Some shop for the kind of place they want at a fair price—a heterogeneous shopping product. And others study tourist guides, talk with traveling friends, and phone ahead to reserve a place in a recommended motel—a specialty product.

Perhaps one motel could satisfy *all* potential customers. But it would be hard to produce a marketing mix attractive to everyone—easy access for convenience, good facilities at the right price for shopping product buyers, and qualities special enough to attract specialty product travelers. That's why very different kinds of motels may at first seem to be competing with each other. But they're really aiming at different markets.

Product class is likely to vary by country

The consumer product classes are based on how consumers see products—and how they shop for them. It's important to keep in mind that consumers in different countries are likely to vary significantly on these dimensions.

For example, a product viewed as a staple by most consumers in the United States, Canada, or some similar affluent country might be seen as a heterogeneous shopping product by consumers in another country. The price might be much higher when considered as a proportion of the consumer's budget, and the available choices might be very different. Similarly, a convenient place to shop often means very different things in different countries. In Japan, for example, retail stores tend to be much smaller and carry smaller selections of products.

The product class idea works in different countries, but marketers must look at the products from the viewpoint of the target customers, not from the marketer's.

Of course, marketing strategy planners need to know more about potential customers than how they buy specific products. But these classes are a good place to start strategy planning.

BUSINESS PRODUCTS ARE DIFFERENT

Business product classes are useful for developing marketing mixes too—since business firms use a system of buying related to these product classes.

Before looking at business product differences, however, we'll note some important similarities that affect marketing strategy planning.

One demand derived from another

The big difference in the business products market is **derived demand**—the demand for business products derives from the demand for final consumer products. For example, car manufacturers buy about one-fifth of all steel products. Even a steel company with a good marketing mix will lose sales to car manufacturers if demand for cars drops.[6]

Price increases might not reduce quantity purchased

The fact that demand for most business products is derived means that total *industry* demand for such products is fairly inelastic. To satisfy their customers' needs, business firms buy what they need to produce their own products—almost regardless of price. Even if the cost of basic silicon doubles, for example, Intel needs it to make computer chips. The increased cost of the silicon won't have much effect on the price of the final computer—or on the number of computers consumers demand.

But suppliers may face almost pure competition

Although the total industry demand for business products may be inelastic, the demand facing *individual sellers* may be extremely elastic—if competitive products are similar and there are many sellers. And to buy as economically as possible, sharp business buyers quickly tell suppliers that competitors are offering lower prices.

Tax treatment affects buying too

How a firm's accountants—and the tax laws—treat a purchase is also important to business customers. A **capital item** is a long-lasting product that can be used and depreciated for many years. Often it's very expensive. Customers pay for the capital item when they buy it, but for tax purposes the cost is spread over a number of years. This may increase current profits—and taxes—as well as reducing the cash available for other purchases.

An **expense item** is a product whose total cost is treated as a business expense in the year it's purchased. This reduces current profits and taxes. It doesn't affect long-run profits. Business managers think about a decision's impact on taxes and profits—and this affects the way they look at the products they buy.

BUSINESS PRODUCT CLASSES—HOW THEY ARE DEFINED

Business product classes are based on how buyers see products—and how the products will be used. Firms treat capital items and expense items differently. Products that become part of a firm's own product are seen differently from those that only aid production. And the relative size of a particular purchase can make a difference. A band saw might be a major purchase for a small cabinet shop—but not for a large furniture manufacturer like Drexel.

EXHIBIT 9–5 Business Product Classes and Marketing Mix Planning

Business Product Classes	Marketing Mix Considerations	Buying Behavior
Installations	Usually requires skillful personal selling by producer, including technical contacts, and/or understanding of applications; leasing and specialized support services may be required.	Multiple buying influence (including top management) and new-task buying are common; infrequent purchase, long decision period, and boom-or-bust demand are typical.
Accessory Equipment	Need fairly widespread distribution and numerous contacts by experienced and sometimes technically trained personnel; price competition is often intense, but quality is important.	Purchasing and operating personnel typically make decisions; shorter decision period than for installations.
Raw Materials	Grading is important, and transportation and storing can be crucial because of seasonal production and/or perishable products; markets tend to be very competitive.	Long-term contracts may be required to ensure supply.
Component Parts and Materials	Product quality and delivery reliability are usually extremely important; negotiation and technical setting typical on less-standardized items; replacement after market may require different strategies.	Multiple buying influence is common; competitive bids used to encourage competitive pricing.
Maintenance, Repair, and Operating (MRO) Supplies	Typically require widespread distribution or fast delivery (repair items); arrangements with appropriate middlemen may be crucial.	Often handled as straight rebuys, except important operating supplies may be treated much more seriously and involve multiple buying influence.
Professional Services	Services customized to buyer's need; personal selling very important; inelastic demand often supports high prices.	Customer may compare outside service with what internal people could provide; needs may be very specialized.

The classes of business products are: (1) installations, (2) accessories, (3) raw materials, (4) components, (5) supplies, and (6) professional services. Exhibit 9–5 relates these product classes to marketing mix planning.

INSTALLATIONS—MAJOR CAPITAL ITEMS

Installations—such as buildings, land rights, and major equipment—are important capital items. One-of-a-kind installations—like office buildings and custom-made equipment—generally require special negotiations for each sale. Standard major equipment is more homogeneous—and is treated more routinely. Even so, negotiations for installations involve top management—and can stretch over months or even years.

Business customers often prefer to lease installations.

Small number of customers at any one time

Installations are long-lasting products—so they aren't bought very often. The number of potential buyers *at any particular time* is usually small. Custom-made machines may have only a half-dozen potential customers—compared to a thousand or more for standard machines.

Installations, a boom-or-bust business

Installations are a boom-or-bust business. When sales are high, businesses want to expand capacity rapidly. And if the potential return on a new investment is very attractive, firms may accept any reasonable price. But during a downswing, buyers have little or no need for new installations and sales fall off sharply. Even during good times, buyers of installations may be able to request bids and buy in a very competitive market.

May have to be leased or rented

Since installations are relatively expensive, some target markets prefer to lease or rent. Leasing makes it easier for a firm to keep up with advancing technologies. Many firms lease computers so they can expand to bigger systems or incorporate new capabilities as they grow. Leasing also shifts a capital item to an expense item.[7]

Specialized services are needed as part of the product

To increase an installation's efficiency—and the expected return on the buyer's investment—suppliers sometimes include special services at no extra cost. Installing the machine in the buyer's plant, training employees in its use, and supplying repair services are good examples of services that can become part of the final product. A firm that sells equipment to dentists, for example, may help the dentist learn to use new equipment—and even provide plans for an office building to hold the equipment.

ACCESSORIES—IMPORTANT BUT SHORT-LIVED CAPITAL ITEMS

Accessories are short-lived capital items—tools and equipment used in production or office activities—like Canon's small copy machines, Sharp's fax machines, Rockwell's portable drills, Clark's electric lift trucks, Olivetti's electronic typewriters, and Steelcase's filing cabinets.

Since these products cost less—and last a shorter time—than installations, multiple buying influence is less important. Operating people and purchasing agents—rather than top managers—may make the purchase decision. As with installations, some customers may wish to lease or rent—to expense the cost.

More target markets requiring different marketing mixes

Accessories are more standardized than installations. And they're usually needed by more customers. For example, IBM sells its robotics systems, which can cost over $1 million, as custom installations to large manufacturers. But IBM's Thinkpad computers are accessory equipment for just about every type of modern business all around the world. And these different types of customers are spread out geographically. The larger number of different kinds of customers—and increased competition—means that accessories need different marketing mixes than installations.

Special services may be attractive

Ordinarily, engineering services or special advice is less important for simpler accessory equipment. Yet some companies manage to add attractive services to their accessories—such as office furniture suppliers who offer decorating services and advice on office layout or computer sellers who help customers set up their software.

RAW MATERIALS—FARM AND NATURAL PRODUCTS ARE EXPENSE ITEMS

They become part of a physical good

Raw materials are unprocessed expense items—such as logs, iron ore, wheat, and cotton—that are moved to the next production process with little handling. Unlike installations and accessories, *raw materials become part of a physical good—and are expense items*.

We can break raw materials into two types: (1) farm products and (2) natural products. **Farm products** are grown by farmers—examples are oranges, wheat, sugar cane, cattle, poultry, eggs, and milk. **Natural products** are products that occur in nature—such as fish and game, timber and maple syrup, and copper, zinc, iron ore, oil, and coal.

Raw materials involve grading, storing, and transporting

The need for grading is one of the important differences between raw materials and other business products. Nature produces what it will—and someone must sort and grade raw materials to satisfy various market segments. Top-graded fruits and vegetables may find their way into the consumer products market. Lower grades—which are treated as business products—are used in juices, sauces, and soups.

Raw materials are usually produced in specific geographic areas—in the United States, wheat in the Midwest, timber in the Northwest, coal in West Virginia. Globally, wheat is produced in Canada and France, timber in Russia, and coal in Germany. And many raw materials—like oranges and shrimp—are produced seasonally. Yet the demand for raw materials is geographically spread out and fairly constant all year. As a result, storing and transporting are important.

Large buyers may want long-term contracts

Most buyers of raw materials want ample supplies in the right grades for specific uses—fresh vegetables for Birds Eye's production lines or logs for International Paper's paper mills. To ensure steady quantities, raw materials customers often sign long-term contracts—sometimes at guaranteed prices—for a supplier's output. Another way to ensure supply is to buy producers of raw materials. This makes it difficult or impossible for independent producers—like family farmers or small coal mines—to compete.

Farm products markets are more competitive

Individual producers of farm products usually face tougher competition than suppliers of natural products. There are many farmers—and nearly pure competition may exist. They have to take the market price.

Natural products are usually produced by fewer and larger companies who can adjust supply to maintain stable prices. For example, the amount of iron ore mined in any one year can be adjusted up or down—at least within limits. And most natural products aren't perishable—so they can be easily stored to wait for better market conditions.

COMPONENT PARTS AND MATERIALS—IMPORTANT EXPENSE ITEMS

The whole is no better than . . .

Components are processed expense items that become part of a finished product. They need more processing than raw materials and require different marketing mixes from raw materials—even though they both become part of a finished product.

Component *parts* include items that are (1) finished and ready for assembly or (2) nearly finished—requiring only minor processing (such as grinding or polishing) before being assembled into the final product. CD-ROM drives included in personal computers, air bags in cars, and motors for appliances are examples.

Component *materials* are items such as wire, paper, textiles, or cement. They have already been processed—but must be processed further before becoming part of the final product.

Components must meet specifications

Some components are custom made. Much teamwork between the engineering staffs of both buyer and seller may be necessary to arrive at the right specifications. Top management may be involved in negotiating the price, especially if the price of the item is high or it is extremely important to the final product.

Other components are produced in quantity to accepted standards or specifications. Production people in the buying firm may specify quality—but the purchasing manager who does the buying often wants several dependable sources of supply.

Since components become part of the firm's own product, quality is extremely important. The buyer's own name and whole marketing mix are at stake—so a buyer tries to buy from sources that help ensure a good product. In such a situation, a buyer may even find it attractive to develop a close partnership with a single supplier who is dedicated to the same objectives as the buyer.

Profitable replacement markets may develop

Since component parts go into finished products, a replacement market often develops. This *after market* can be both large and very profitable. Car tires and batteries are two examples of components originally sold in the *OEM* (*original equipment market*) that become consumer products in the after market. The target markets are different—and different marketing mixes are usually necessary.[8]

SUPPLIES—SUPPORT MAINTENANCE, REPAIR, AND OPERATIONS

Supplies are expense items that do not become part of a finished product. Buyers may treat these items less seriously. When a firm cuts its budget, orders for supplies may be the first to go.

They are called MRO supplies

Supplies can be divided into three types: (1) maintenance, (2) repair, and (3) operating supplies—giving them their common name: MRO supplies.

Maintenance supplies include products such as paint, lightbulbs, and sweeping compounds. *Repair supplies* are parts—like filters, bearings, and gears—needed to fix worn or broken equipment. *Operating supplies* include lubricating oils and greases, grinding compounds, typing paper, paper clips, coal or electricity, and insurance.[9]

Important operating supplies

If operating supplies are needed regularly—and in large amounts—they receive special treatment from buyers. Many companies buy coal and fuel oil in railroad-car quantities. Usually there are several sources for such homogeneous products—and large volumes may be purchased in highly competitive international markets. Or contracts may be negotiated—perhaps by top-level executives—to ensure lower prices and a continuing supply.

Maintenance and small operating supplies

These products are like convenience products. They're so numerous that a purchasing agent can't possibly be an expert in buying all of them.

Each requisition for maintenance and small operating supplies may be for relatively few items. Although a purchase order may amount to only $1 or $2,

---

Businesses buy the goods and services they need to produce products for their own customers, so the demand for business products is derived from the demand for final consumer products.

handling it may cost $25 to $30. The item will be ordered because it is needed—but buyers won't spend much time on it.

Branding may become important for such products because it makes product identification and buying easier for such "nuisance" purchases. Breadth of assortment and the seller's dependability are also important when buying supplies. Middlemen usually handle the many supply items.

Repair supplies   The original supplier of installations or accessory equipment may be the only source for repair needs. But compared to the cost of a production breakdown, the cost of repairs may be so small that buyers are willing to pay whatever the supplier charges. However, rather than buying or stocking repair supplies, a customer might prefer to pay someone else to provide both the parts *and* the repair service.

PROFESSIONAL SERVICES—PAY TO GET IT DONE

Professional services are specialized services that support a firm's operations. They are usually expense items. Engineering or management consulting services can improve the plant layout—or the company's efficiency. Computer services can process data. Design services can supply designs for a physical plant, products, and promotion materials. Advertising agencies can help promote the firm's products—and food services can improve morale.

Here the *service* part of the product is emphasized. Goods may be supplied—as coffee and doughnuts are with food service—but the customer is primarily interested in the service.

Managers compare the cost of buying professional services outside the firm to the cost of having company people do them. For special skills needed only occasionally, an outsider can be the best source. Further, during the last decade, many firms have tried to cut costs by downsizing the number of people that they employ; in many cases, work that was previously done by an employee is now provided as a service by an independent supplier. Clearly, the number of service specialists is growing in our complex economy.

BRANDING NEEDS A STRATEGY DECISION TOO

There are so many brands—and we're so used to seeing them—that we take them for granted. In the grocery products area alone, there are more than 70,000 brands. Brands are of great importance to their owners. They help identify the company's marketing mix—and help customers recognize the firm's products and advertising. Branding is an important decision area that many business people ignore, so we will treat it in some detail.

What is branding?   **Branding** means the use of a name, term, symbol, or design—or a combination of these—to identify a product. It includes the use of brand names, trademarks, and practically all other means of product identification.

Brand name has a narrower meaning. A **brand name** is a word, letter, or a group of words or letters. Examples include Blockbuster Video, WD-40, 3M Post-its, and IBM ValuePoint computers.

Trademark is a legal term. A **trademark** includes only those words, symbols, or marks that are legally registered for use by a single company. A **service mark** is the same as a trademark except that it refers to a service offering.

EXHIBIT 9-6 Recognized Trademarks and Symbols Help in Promotion

The word *Buick* can be used to explain these differences. The Buick car is branded under the brand name Buick (whether it's spoken or printed in any manner). When "Buick" is printed in a certain kind of script, however, it becomes a trademark. A trademark need not be attached to the product. It need not even be a word—it can be a symbol. Exhibit 9–6 shows some common trademarks.

These differences may seem technical. But they are very important to business firms that spend a lot of money to protect and promote their brands.

BRANDING—WHY IT DEVELOPED

Brands provide identification

Branding started during the Middle Ages—when craft guilds (similar to labor unions) and merchant guilds formed to control the quantity and quality of production. Each producer had to mark his goods so output could be cut back when necessary. This also meant that poor quality—which might reflect unfavorably on other guild products and discourage future trade—could be traced back to the guilty producer. Early trademarks also protected the buyer, who could then know the source of the product.

More recently, brands have been used mainly for identification. The earliest and most aggressive brand promoters in America were the patent medicine companies. They were joined by the food manufacturers, who grew in size after the Civil War. Some of the brands started in the 1860s and 1870s (and still going strong) are Borden's Condensed Milk, Quaker Oats, Pillsbury's Best Flour, and Ivory Soap. Today, familiar brands exist for most product categories, ranging from crayons (Crayola) to real estate services (Century 21). However, what brand is familiar often varies from one country to another.

Brands make consumers' shopping easier

Well-recognized brands make shopping easier. Think of trying to buy groceries, for example, if you had to evaluate the advantages and disadvantages of each of 20,000 items every time you went to a supermarket.

Many customers are willing to buy new things—but having gambled and won, they like to buy a sure thing the next time. Even on infrequent purchases, consumers often rely on well-known brands as an indication of quality.

And if consumers try a brand and don't like it, they know what to avoid in future purchases.

Branding helps branders too

Brand promotion has advantages for branders as well as customers. A good brand speeds up shopping for the customer—and thus reduces the marketer's selling time and effort. And, when customers repeatedly purchase by brand, the brander is protected against competition from other firms. Sometimes a firm's brand name is the only element in its marketing mix that a competitor can't copy.

Good brands can improve the company's image—speeding acceptance of new products marketed under the same name. For example, many consumers quickly tried Kellogg's Rice Krispies Treats Cereal when it was introduced because they already knew they liked Rice Krispies. From a financial perspective, the money that Kellogg spent over the years to promote the original brand paid off again when consumers tried the new product. The majority of new products introduced in recent years have followed the approach of extending a successful brand name.[10]

CONDITIONS FAVORABLE TO BRANDING

Most firms, especially firms that sell consumer products, work hard to establish respected brands. On the other hand, some product categories have fewer well-known brands. For example, can you recall a brand name for file folders, bed frames, electric extension cords, or nails? As these examples suggest, it's not always easy to establish a respected brand.

The following conditions are favorable to successful branding:

1. The product is easy to identify by brand or trademark.
2. The product quality is the best value for the price. And the quality is easy to maintain.
3. Dependable and widespread availability is possible. When customers start using a brand, they want to be able to continue using it.
4. The demand for the general product class is large.
5. The demand is strong enough so that the market price can be high enough to make the branding effort profitable.
6. There are economies of scale. If the branding is really successful, costs should drop and profits should increase.
7. Favorable shelf locations or display space in stores will help. This is something retailers can control when they brand their own products. Producers must use aggressive salespeople to get favorable positions.

In general, these conditions are less common in less-developed economies, and that may explain why efforts to build brands in less-developed nations often fail.

ACHIEVING BRAND FAMILIARITY IS NOT EASY

Brand acceptance must be earned with a good product and regular promotion. **Brand familiarity** means how well customers recognize and accept a company's brand. The degree of brand familiarity affects the planning for the rest of the marketing mix—especially where the product should be offered and what promotion is needed.

Five levels of brand familiarity

Five levels of brand familiarity are useful for strategy planning: (1) rejection, (2) nonrecognition, (3) recognition, (4) preference, and (5) insistence.

Hellmann's would like Chilean consumers to insist on the Hellmann's brand when they want mayonnaise to go with avocado and other vegetables. This headline asks "Avocado Mayo?"—and then describes Hellmann's as the "real one."

Some brands have been tried and found wanting. **Brand rejection** means that potential customers won't buy a brand unless its image is changed. Rejection may suggest a change in the product—or perhaps only a shift to target customers who have a better image of the brand. Overcoming a negative image is difficult—and can be very expensive.

Brand rejection is a big concern for service-oriented businesses because it's hard to control the quality of service. A business traveler who gets a dirty room in a Hilton Hotel in Caracas, Venezuela, might not return to any Hilton anywhere. Yet it's difficult for Hilton to ensure that every maid does a good job every time.

Some products are seen as basically the same. **Brand nonrecognition** means final consumers don't recognize a brand at all—even though middlemen may use the brand name for identification and inventory control. Examples include school supplies, pencils, and inexpensive dinnerware.

Brand recognition means that customers remember the brand. This can be a big advantage if there are many "nothing" brands on the market. Even if consumers can't recall the brand without help, they may be reminded when they see it in a store among other less familiar brands.

Most branders would like to win **brand preference**—which means that target customers usually choose the brand over other brands, perhaps because of habit or favorable past experience.

Brand insistence means customers insist on a firm's branded product and are willing to search for it. This is an objective of many target marketers. Here the firm may enjoy a very inelastic demand curve.

The right brand name can help

A good brand name can help build brand familiarity. It can help tell something important about the company or its product. Exhibit 9–7 lists some

EXHIBIT 9–7   Characteristics of a Good Brand Name

• Short and simple	• Suggestive of product benefits
• Easy to spell and read	• Adaptable to packaging/labeling needs
• Easy to recognize and remember	• No undesirable imagery
• Easy to pronounce	• Always timely (does not get out-of-date)
• Can be pronounced in only one way	• Adaptable to any advertising medium
• Can be pronounced in all languages (for international markets)	• Legally available for use (not in use by another firm)

characteristics of a good brand name. Some successful brand names seem to break all these rules, but many of them got started when there was less competition.

Companies that compete in international markets face a special problem in selecting brand names. A name that conveys a positive image in one language may be meaningless in another. Or, worse, it may have unintended meanings. GM's Nova automobile is a classic example. GM stuck with the Nova name when it introduced the car in South America; it seemed like a sensible decision because Nova is the Spanish word for star. However, Nova also sounds the same as the Spanish words for "no go." Consumers weren't interested in a no-go car and sales didn't pick up until GM changed the name.[11]

A respected name builds brand equity

Because it's difficult and expensive to build brand recognition, some firms prefer to buy established brands rather than try to build their own. The value of a brand to its current owner or to a firm that wants to buy it is sometimes called **brand equity**—the value of a brand's overall strength in the market. For example, brand equity is likely to be higher if many satisfied customers insist on buying the brand and if retailers are eager to stock it. That almost guarantees ongoing profits from the brand and increases the brand's value.

Keeping customers satisfied and loyal is what builds brand equity. Concern about brand equity is another reason that there is increasing attention to building closer relationships with customers. However, traditional financial statements don't show the future profit potential of having a large base of satisfied customers. Perhaps they should. Having that information would prompt a lot of narrow-thinking finance managers to view marketing efforts as an investment, not just as an expense that drains profits.

PROTECTING BRAND NAMES AND TRADEMARKS

U.S. common law and civil law protect the rights of trademark and brand name owners. The **Lanham Act** of 1946 spells out what kinds of marks (including brand names) can be protected and the exact method of protecting them. The law applies to goods shipped in interstate or foreign commerce.

The Lanham Act does not force registration. But registering under the Lanham Act is often a first step toward protecting a trademark to be used in international markets. That's because some nations require that a trademark be registered in its home country before they will register or protect it.

Until recently, U.S. firms had to actually introduce a product to the market before they could register its trademark or brand name. Most other countries, however, allowed their firms to register names for products that had not been introduced. Now, U.S. rules have been changed to make them more similar to those of other countries.

You must protect your own

A brand can be a real asset to a company. Each firm should try to see that its brand doesn't become a common descriptive term for its kind of product. When this happens, the brand name or trademark becomes public property—and the owner loses all rights to it. This happened with the names cellophane, aspirin, shredded wheat, and kerosene. There has been concern that Teflon, Scotch transparent tape, and Xerox might become public property. And Miller Brewing Company tried—unsuccessfully—to protect its Lite beer by suing other brewers who wanted to use the word *light*.[12]

❓ Counterfeiting is accepted in some cultures

Even when products are properly registered, counterfeiters may make unauthorized copies. Many well-known brands—ranging from Levi's jeans to Rolex watches to Zantax ulcer medicine to Mickey Mouse T-shirts—face this problem. Counterfeiting is especially common in developing nations. For example, counterfeit copies of software programs like WordPerfect are available in hundreds of outlets in Taiwan—often selling for a dollar or two each. In China, most videotapes and CDs are "bootleg" copies. Multinational efforts are under way to stop such counterfeiting, but they may meet with limited success. Counterfeiting is big business in some countries, and their government agencies don't want to deal with the problem. There are also differences in cultural values. In South Korea, for example, many people don't see counterfeiting as unethical.[13]

WHAT KIND OF BRAND TO USE?

Keep it in the family

Branders of more than one product must decide whether they are going to use a **family brand**—the same brand name for several products—or individual brands for each product. Examples of family brands are Keebler snack food products and Sears' Craftsman tools and Kenmore appliances.

The use of the same brand for many products makes sense if all are similar in type and quality. The main benefit is that the goodwill attached to one or two products may help the others. Money spent to promote the brand name benefits more than one product—which cuts promotion costs for each product. Using a family brand makes it easier, faster, and less expensive to introduce new products. This can be an important competitive advantage, and it explains why many firms are expanding the number of products sold under family brand names.

A special kind of family brand is a **licensed brand**—a well-known brand that sellers pay a fee to use. For example, the familiar Sunkist brand name is owned by Sunkist Growers, a farmers' cooperative. But the Sunkist brand name has been licensed to many companies for use on more than 400 products in 30 countries. Licensees usually pay royalties ranging from 4 to 8.5 percent of the wholesale sales. In this case, many different companies are in the "family."[14]

Individual brands for outside and inside competition

A company uses **individual brands**—separate brand names for each product—when it's important for the products to each have a separate identity, as when products vary in quality or type.

If the products are really different, such as Elmer's glue and Borden's ice cream, individual brands can avoid confusion. Some firms use individual brands with similar products to make segmentation and positioning efforts easier.

Sara Lee has a number of very different products in its overall product assortment, so it uses individual brands to avoid confusion.

Unilever, for example, markets Aim, Close-Up, and Pepsodent toothpastes, but each involves different positioning efforts.

Sometimes firms use individual brands to encourage competition within the company. Each brand is managed by a different group within the firm. Some managers think that internal competition keeps everyone alert. They argue that if anyone is going to take business away from their firm, it ought to be their own brand.

Despite such reasoning, many firms that once used this approach have reorganized. Faced with slower market growth, they found they had plenty of competitive pressure from other firms. The internal competition just made it more difficult to coordinate different marketing strategies. For example, Procter & Gamble has a number of different brands of bar soap—including Ivory, Zest, and Spirit. A few years ago the managers for the individual brands were fighting it out—often going after the same target market with similar marketing mixes. Now one manager has responsibility for developing a coordinated marketing plan for all products in the bar soap category. The result is a better-integrated effort.[15]

Generic "brands"

Products that some consumers see as commodities may be difficult or expensive to brand. Some manufacturers and middlemen have responded to this problem with **generic products**—products that have no brand at all other than identification of their contents and the manufacturer or middleman. Generic products are usually offered in plain packages at lower prices. They are quite common in less-developed nations.

A decade ago, some target markets in the United States were interested in buying generic products. But price cuts by branded competitors narrowed the price gap—and won back many customers. Now generics account for only about 1.5 percent of grocery store sales in the United States—and in many product categories they've disappeared altogether. However, generics still capture significant market share in a few product categories—especially prescription drugs.[16]

WHO SHOULD DO THE BRANDING?

Manufacturer brands
versus dealer brands

Manufacturer brands are brands created by producers. These are sometimes called "national brands" because the brand is promoted all across the country or in large regions. Note, however, that this term became popular before international markets became so important; many manufacturer brands are now distributed globally. Such brands include Kellogg's, Stokely, Whirlpool, Ford, and IBM. Many creators of service-oriented firms—like McDonald's, Orkin Pest Control, and Midas Muffler—spend a lot of money promoting their brands in the same way other producers do.

Dealer brands, also called **private brands**, are brands created by middlemen. Examples of dealer brands include the brands of Kroger, Ace Hardware, and Sears. Some of these are advertised and distributed more widely than many national brands.

From the middleman's perspective, the major advantage of selling a popular manufacturer brand is that the product is already presold to some target customers. Such products may bring in new customers and can encourage higher turnover with reduced selling cost. The major disadvantage is that manufacturers normally offer lower gross margins than the middleman might be able to earn with a dealer brand. In addition, the manufacturer maintains control of the brand and may withdraw it from a middleman at any time. Customers, loyal to the brand rather than to the retailer or wholesaler, may go elsewhere if the brand is not available.

Dealer branders take on more responsibility. They must promote their own product. They must be able to arrange a dependable source of supply and usually have to buy in fairly large quantities. This increases their risk and cost of carrying inventory. However, these problems are easier to overcome if the middleman deals in a large sales volume, as is the case with many large retail chains.

Who's winning the battle
of the brands?

The **battle of the brands**, the competition between dealer brands and manufacturer brands, is just a question of whose brands will be more popular—and who will be in control.

At one time, manufacturer brands were much more popular than dealer brands. But manufacturer brands may be losing the battle. Now sales of both kinds of brands are about equal—but sales of dealer brands are expected to continue growing. Middlemen have some advantages in this battle. The number of large wholesalers and retail chains is growing. They are better able to arrange reliable sources of supply at low cost. They can also control the point of sale and give the dealer brand special shelf position or promotion. Further, the lower prices possible with dealer brands attract price-sensitive consumers.

Consumers benefit from the battle. Competition has already narrowed price differences between manufacturer brands and well-known dealer brands.[17]

THE STRATEGIC IMPORTANCE OF PACKAGING

Packaging involves promoting and protecting the product. Packaging can be important to both sellers and customers. Packaging can make a product more convenient to use or store. It can prevent spoiling or damage. Good packaging makes products easier to identify and promotes the brand at the point of purchase and even in use.

PERT SHAMPOO GETS IN CONDITION TO COMPETE

Many consumers are fickle when it's time to buy shampoo. They just pick up a brand that's conveniently available where they shop. And with a thousand brands on the market, they usually have lots of choices! This is the plight that marketing managers for Pert Shampoo faced when they were struggling to increase their 2 percent market share. Efforts to get help from retailers were futile. They wouldn't give more space to a brand with a small share. In fact, some retailers pushed Pert off their shelves to make room for their own dealer-brand shampoos.

Pert's marketing managers knew that many consumers needed to shampoo *and* condition their hair but disliked the hassle of dealing with two bottles. Focusing on this need, Pert's R&D group found a way to combine cleaning and conditioning in a single product.

To really highlight this breakthrough called for a new brand name. Yet the firm wanted to take advantage of the money spent over many years to promote the Pert name in the U.S. For that reason, extending the name and calling the product Pert Plus seemed sensible. However, in some countries the Pert Plus name sounded too similar to names already being used for other products, or it violated trademarks. So, the Pert Plus name was used for the introduction in the United States, Canada, and Latin America and when distribution expanded to other countries different names were used: Rejoy in Japan; Rejoice in Singapore and Hong Kong; Sassoon Wash & Go in Europe; and Pert 2-in-1 in Australia.

Introductory ads featured the new package design—including the convenient flip-top dispenser— so consumers would recognize the product on store shelves. Concerns about safety and the environment called for a package made of plastic that could be recycled.

Competitors from several countries quickly imitated Pert's 2-in-1 concept—and many consumers are still fickle about shampoo. But now more consumers are insisting on Pert Plus when they shop—and it's become the top brand of shampoo in the world. More generally, with the growth of shampoos that include conditioner, sales of "shampoo-only" products have started to decline.[18]

Packaging can make the difference

A new package can make *the* important difference in a new marketing strategy—by meeting customers' needs better. A better box, wrapper, can, or bottle may help create a "new" product—or a new market. For example, Crest toothpaste is available in a neat squeeze-pump dispenser that makes less mess and leaves less waste. Quaker State oil comes with a twist-off top and pouring spout to make it more convenient for customers of self-service gas stations, and popcorn for microwave ovens is sold in easy-open bags.

Sometimes a new package improves a product by making it easier or safer to use. Kodak increased sales of its light-sensitive X-ray film by packing each sheet in a separate foil pack—making the film easier to handle. Many drug and food products now have special seals to prevent product tampering. Tylenol caplets, for example, come in a tamper-resistant package.

Packaging sends a message—even for services

Packaging can tie the product to the rest of the marketing strategy. Packaging for Eveready batteries features the pink bunny seen in attention-getting TV ads—and reminds consumers that the batteries are durable. Expensive perfume may come in a crystal bottle, adding to the prestige image.

In a way, the appearance of service providers or the area where a service is provided is a form of packaging. Disney sends the message that its parks are a good place for family vacations by keeping them spotless. Lawyers put their awards and diplomas on the wall so that clients know they provide a high-quality product. In addition, some firms try to "package" their services so that there is a tangible reminder of the product. For example, the American Express Gold Card sends a signal that is understood worldwide.

Packaging may lower distribution and promotion costs

Better protective packaging is very important to manufacturers and wholesalers. They sometimes have to pay the cost of goods damaged in shipment, and goods damaged in shipment also may delay production—or cause lost sales.

Retailers need good packaging too. Protective packaging can reduce storing costs by cutting breakage, spoilage, and theft. Packages that are easier to handle can cut costs by speeding price marking, improving handling and display, and saving space.

A good package sometimes gives a firm more promotion effect than it could possibly afford with advertising. Customers see the package in stores—when they're actually buying. For example, a recent study found that 81 percent of consumers' purchase decisions on groceries are made at the store. The package may be seen by many more potential customers than the company's advertising. An attractive package may speed turnover enough to reduce total costs as a percentage of sales.

Or it may raise total costs

In other cases, costs (and prices) may rise because of packaging. But customers may be more satisfied because the packaging improves the product by offering much greater convenience or reducing waste.

Packaging costs as a percentage of a manufacturer's selling price vary widely—ranging from 1 to 70 percent. When sugar producers like Domino sell sugar in 100-pound bags, the cost of packaging is only 1 percent of the selling price. In 2- and 5-pound cartons, it's 25 to 30 percent. And for individual serving packages, it's 50 percent. But consumers don't want to haul a 100-pound bag home. They're quite willing to pay more for convenient sizes. Restaurants use one-serving envelopes of sugar to eliminate the cost of filling and washing sugar bowls—and because customers prefer the sanitary little packages.[19]

WHAT IS SOCIALLY RESPONSIBLE PACKAGING?

Some consumers say that some package designs are misleading—perhaps on purpose. Who hasn't been surprised by a candy bar half the size of the package? Others feel that the great variety of packages makes it hard to compare values. And all of us should be concerned about whether the packages are degradable or can be recycled.

Laws reduce confusion— and clutter

In the United States, consumer criticism finally led to the passage of the **Federal Fair Packaging and Labeling Act** (of 1966)—which requires that consumer goods be clearly labeled in easy-to-understand terms—to give consumers more information. The law also calls on government agencies and industry to try to reduce the number of package sizes and make labels more useful. Since then there have been further guidelines. The most far-reaching are based on the Nutrition Labeling and Education Act of 1990. It requires food manufacturers to use a uniform format and disclose what is in their products.

New food label requirements will help some consumers make healthier purchases, but it is not yet clear how many consumers will really understand and use the information.

You've seen this new format and probably know that the idea is to allow consumers to compare the nutritional value of different products. That could be a plus, and may even lead to healthier diets. However, the Food and Drug Administration estimates that the total cost to change 250,000 food labels in the U.S. marketplace will end up being between $1.4 billion and $2.4 billion. Ultimately, all consumers will share the cost of those changes—whether they use the information or not.[20]

Current laws also offer more guidance on environmental issues. Some states require a consumer to pay a deposit on bottles and cans until they're returned. These laws mean well, but they can cause problems. Channels of distribution are usually set up to distribute products, not return empty packages. Some supermarkets have installed efficient handling systems, and Reynolds Aluminum works with communities to set up centers to buy and recycle cans. But can and bottle returns add new marketing costs.[21]

Ethical decisions remain

Although various laws provide guidance on many packaging issues, many areas still require marketing managers to make ethical choices.

For example, some firms have been criticized for designing packages that conceal a downsized product, giving consumers less for the money. Similarly, some retailers have been criticized for designing packages and labels for their private-label products that look just like—and are easily confused with—manufacturer brands. Furthermore, some producers quickly put their lawyers and engineers to work so they can copy a competitor's popular packaging innovation without violating the patent. Are efforts such as these unethical, or are they simply an attempt to make packaging a more effective part of a marketing mix? Different people will answer differently.

Some marketing managers have been criticized for promoting environmentally friendly packaging on some products, while simultaneously increasing the use of problematic packages on others. Empty packages now litter our streets, and some plastic packages will lie in a city dump for decades. Empty aerosol cans may explode, and empty bottles often become broken glass. But some consumers like the convenience that accompanies these problems. Is it unethical for a marketing manager to give consumers with different preferences a choice and to develop different marketing mixes to reach different target markets? Some critics argue that it is. But others praise firms that are taking steps to give consumers a choice.

Many critics feel that labeling information is too often incomplete or misleading. Do consumers really understand the nutritional information required by law? Further, some consumers want information that is difficult—perhaps even impossible—to provide. For example, how can a label accurately describe a product's taste or texture? But the ethical issues usually focus on how far a marketing manager should go in putting potentially negative information on a package. For example, should Häagen-Dazs affix a label that says "This product will clog your arteries"? That sounds extreme, but what type of information *is* appropriate?[22]

Unit-pricing is a possible help

Some retailers—especially large supermarket chains—make it easier for consumers to compare packages with different weights or volumes. They use **unit-pricing**—which involves placing the price per ounce (or some other standard measure) on or near the product. This makes price comparison easier.[23]

Universal product codes allow more information

To speed handling of fast-selling products, government and industry representatives have developed a **universal product code (UPC)** that identifies each product with marks readable by electronic scanners. A computer then matches each code to the product and its price. Supermarkets and other high-volume retailers have been eager to use these codes. They reduce the need to mark the price on every item. They also reduce errors by cashiers—and make it easy to control inventory and track sales of specific products. Exhibit 9–8 shows a universal product code mark.

EXHIBIT 9–8 Illustration of a Universal Product Code

The codes help consumers too because they speed the checkout process. Also, most systems now include a printed receipt showing the name, size, and price of each product bought. These codes will become even more widely used in the future because they do lower operating costs.[24]

WARRANTY POLICIES ARE A PART OF STRATEGY PLANNING

Warranty puts promises in writing

A **warranty** explains what the seller promises about its product. Deciding on warranty policies is part of strategy planning. A marketing manager should decide whether to offer a specific warranty, and if so what the warranty will cover and how it will be communicated to target customers. This is an area where the legal environment—as well as customer needs and competitive offerings—must be considered.

U.S. common law says that producers must stand behind their products—even if they don't offer a specific warranty. A written warranty provided by the seller may promise more than the common law provides; however, it may actually *reduce* the responsibility a producer would have under common law.

The federal **Magnuson-Moss Act** (of 1975) says that producers must provide a clearly written warranty if they choose to offer any warranty. The warranty does not have to be strong. However, Federal Trade Commission (FTC) guidelines try to ensure that warranties are clear and definite—and not deceptive or unfair. A warranty must also be available for inspection before the purchase.

In a competitive market, a product warranty is often a very important part of the marketing mix.

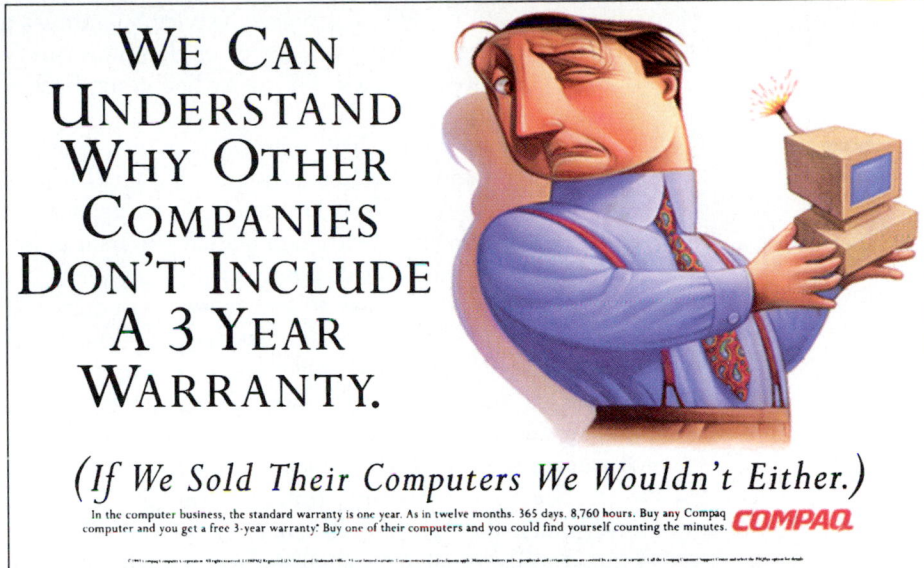

Some firms used to say their products were fully warranted or absolutely guaranteed. However, they didn't state the time period or spell out the meaning of the warranty. Now a company has to make clear whether it's offering a full or limited warranty—and the law defines what full means. Most firms offer a limited warranty—if they offer one at all.

Warranty may improve the marketing mix

Some firms use warranties to improve the appeal of their marketing mix. They design more quality into their goods or services and offer refunds or replacement—not just repair—if there is a problem. Xerox Corp. uses this approach with its copy machines. Its three-year warranty says that a customer who is not satisfied with a copier—for *any* reason—can trade it for another model. This type of warranty sends a strong signal. A buyer doesn't have to worry about whether or not the copier will work as expected, service calls will be prompt, or even that the Xerox salesperson or dealer has recommended the appropriate model.

Service guarantees

Customer service guarantees are becoming more common as a way to attract—and keep—customers. Pizza Hut guarantees a luncheon pizza in five minutes or it's free. General Motors set up a fast oil change guarantee to compete with fast-lube specialists who were taking customers away from dealers. If the dealer doesn't get the job done in 29 minutes or less, the next oil change is free. Delta Dental, an insurance company, has a guarantee that includes one month's free premium if it doesn't provide a new customer with a smooth transition from a previous insurer. The Hampton Inn motel chain guarantees "100% satisfaction"; all employees—even the cleaning crews—are empowered to offer an unhappy customer a discount or refund on the spot.

There's more risk in offering a service guarantee than a warranty on a physical product. An apathetic employee or a service breakdown can create a big expense. However, without the guarantee, dissatisfied customers may just go away mad without ever complaining. When customers collect on a guarantee, the company can clearly identify the problem. Then the problem can be addressed so it doesn't happen again to other customers. Service guarantees also seem to be effective in creating repeat customers. A survey of Hampton Inn customers who had collected on its guarantee revealed that many had come back for another stay.

Warranty support can be costly

Customers might like a strong warranty, but providing one can be expensive—even economically impossible—for small firms. Backing up warranties can be a problem too. Some customers abuse products and then demand a lot of service on warranties. Although manufacturers may be responsible, they may have to depend on reluctant or poorly trained middlemen to do the job. For example, when energy prices began to rise, many consumers bought chain saws to cut their own firewood. To reach this target market, Homelite began to distribute its chain saws through retail chains like Kmart to reach homeowners in the suburbs. But Homelite had to set up its own service centers because the retail chains had no repair facilities. In situations like this, it's hard for a small firm to compete with larger firms with many service centers.

The cost of warranty support ultimately must be covered by the price that consumers pay. This has led some firms to offer warranty choices. The basic price for a product may include a warranty that covers a short time period or that covers parts but not labor. Consumers who want more or better protection pay extra for an extended warranty or a service contract.[25]

CONCLUSION

In this chapter, we looked at Product very broadly. A product may not be a physical good at all. It may be a service, or it may be some combination of goods and services—like a meal at a restaurant. Most important, we saw that a firm's Product is *what satisfies the needs of its target market.*

We introduced consumer product and business product classes and showed their effect on planning marketing mixes. Consumer product classes are based on consumers' buying behavior. Business product classes are based on how buyers see the products and how they are used. Knowing these product classes—and learning how marketers handle specific products within these classes—will help you develop your marketing sense.

The fact that different people may see the same product in different product classes helps explain why seeming competitors may succeed with very different marketing mixes.

Branding and packaging can create new and more satisfying products. Packaging offers special opportunities to promote the product and inform customers. Variations in packaging can make a product attractive to different target markets. A specific package may have to be developed for each strategy.

Customers see brands as a guarantee of quality, and this leads to repeat purchasing. For marketers, such routine buying means lower promotion costs and higher sales.

Should companies stress branding? The decision depends on whether the costs of brand promotion and honoring the brand guarantee can be more than covered by a higher price or more rapid turnover—or both. The cost of branding may reduce pressure on the other three Ps.

Branding gives marketing managers a choice. They can add brands and use individual or family brands. In the end, however, customers express their approval or disapproval of the whole Product (including the brand). The degree of brand familiarity is a measure of the marketing manager's ability to carve out a separate market. And brand familiarity affects Place, Price, and Promotion decisions.

Warranties are also important in strategy planning. A warranty need not be strong—it just has to be clearly stated. But some customers find strong warranties attractive.

Product is concerned with much more than physical goods and service. To succeed in our increasingly competitive markets, the marketing manager must also be concerned about packaging, branding, and warranties.

QUESTIONS AND PROBLEMS

1. Define, in your own words, what a Product is.

2. Discuss several ways in which physical goods are different from pure services. Give an example of a good and then an example of a service that illustrates each of the differences.

3. What products are being offered by a shop that specializes in bicycles? By a travel agent? By a supermarket? By a new car dealer?

4. What kinds of consumer products are the following: (a) watches, (b) automobiles, and (c) toothpastes? Explain your reasoning.

5. Consumer services tend to be intangible, and goods tend to be tangible. Use an example to explain how the lack of a physical good in a pure service might affect efforts to promote the service.

6. How would the marketing mix for a staple convenience product differ from the one for a homogeneous shopping product? How would the mix for a specialty product differ from the mix for a heterogeneous shopping product? Use examples.

7. Give an example of a product that is a *new* unsought product for most people. Briefly explain why it is an unsought product.

8. In what types of stores would you expect to find: (a) convenience products, (b) shopping products, (c) specialty products, and (d) unsought products?

9. Cite two examples of business products that require a substantial amount of service in order to be useful.

10. Explain why a new law office might want to lease furniture rather than buy it.

11. Would you expect to find any wholesalers selling the various types of business products? Are retail stores required (or something like retail stores)?

12. What kinds of business products are the following: (a) lubricating oil, (b) electric motors, and (c) a firm that provides landscaping and grass mowing for an apartment complex? Explain your reasoning.

13. How do raw materials differ from other business products? Do the differences have any impact on their marketing mixes? If so, what specifically.

14. For the kinds of business products described in this chapter, complete the following table (use one or a few well-chosen words).

1. *Kind of distribution facility(ies) needed and functions they will provide.*
2. *Caliber of salespeople required.*
3. *Kind of advertising required.*

Products	1	2	3
Installations			
Buildings and land rights			
Major equipment			
Standard			
Custom-made			
Accessories			
Raw materials			
Farm products			
Natural products			
Components			
Supplies			
Maintenance and small operating supplies			
Operating supplies			
Professional services			

15. Is there any difference between a brand name and a trademark? If so, why is this difference important?

16. Is a well-known brand valuable only to the owner of the brand?

17. Suggest an example of a product and a competitive situation where it would *not* be profitable for a firm to spend large sums of money to establish a brand.

18. List five brand names and indicate what product is associated with the brand name. Evaluate the strengths and weaknesses of the brand name.

19. Explain family brands. Should Toys "R" Us develop its own dealer brands to compete with some of the popular manufacturer brands it carries? Explain your reasons.

20. In the past, Sears emphasized its own dealer brands. Now it is carrying more well-known manufacturer brands. What are the benefits to Sears of carrying more manufacturer brands?

21. What does the degree of brand familiarity imply about previous and future promotion efforts? How does the degree of brand familiarity affect the Place and Price variables?

22. You operate a small hardware store with emphasis on manufacturer brands and have barely been breaking even. Evaluate the proposal of a large wholesaler who offers a full line of dealer-branded hardware items at substantially lower prices. Specify any assumptions necessary to obtain a definite answer.

23. Give an example where packaging costs probably: (*a*) lower total distribution costs, and (*b*) raise total distribution costs.

24. Is it more difficult to support a warranty for a service than for a physical good? Explain your reasons.

SUGGESTED CASES

1. McDonald's "Seniors" Restaurant

13. Paper Products Corporation

COMPUTER-AIDED PROBLEM

9. Branding Decision

Wholesteen Dairy, Inc., produces and sells Wholesteen brand condensed milk to grocery retailers. The overall market for condensed milk is fairly flat, and there's sharp competition among dairies for retailers' business. Wholesteen's regular price to retailers is $8.88 a case (24 cans). FoodWorld—a fast-growing supermarket chain and Wholesteen's largest customer—buys 20,000 cases of Wholesteen's condensed milk a year. That's 20 percent of Wholesteen's total sales volume of 100,000 cases per year.

FoodWorld is proposing that Wholesteen produce private-label condensed milk to be sold with the Food-World brand name. FoodWorld proposes to buy the same total quantity as it does now, but it wants half (10,000 cases) with the Wholesteen brand and half with the FoodWorld brand. FoodWorld wants its brand in cans that cost $.01 less than Wholesteen pays for a can now. But FoodWorld will provide preprinted labels with its brand name—which will save Wholesteen an additional $.02 a can.

Wholesteen spends $70,000 a year on promotion to increase familiarity with the Wholesteen brand. In addition, Wholesteen gives retailers an allowance of $.25 per case for their local advertising, which features the Wholesteen brand. FoodWorld has agreed to give up the advertising allowance for its own brand, but it is only willing to pay $7.40 a case for the milk that will be sold with the FoodWorld brand name. It will continue under the old terms for the rest of its purchases.

Sue Glick, Wholesteen's marketing manager, is considering the FoodWorld proposal. She has entered cost and revenue data on a spreadsheet—so she can see more clearly how the proposal might affect revenue and profits.

a. *Based on the data in the initial spreadsheet, how will Wholesteen profits be affected if Glick accepts the FoodWorld proposal?*

b. *Glick is worried that FoodWorld will find another producer for the FoodWorld private-label milk if Wholesteen rejects the proposal. This would immedi-*

ately reduce Wholesteen's annual sales by 10,000 cases. FoodWorld might even stop buying from Wholesteen altogether. What would happen to profits in these two situations?

c. FoodWorld is rapidly opening new stores—and sells milk in every store. The FoodWorld buyer says that next year's purchases could be up to 25,000 cases of Wholesteen's condensed milk. But Sue Glick knows that FoodWorld may stop buying the Wholesteen brand and want all 25,000 cases to carry the FoodWorld private-label brand. How will this affect profit? (Hint: Enter the new quantities in the "proposal" column of the spreadsheet.)

d. What should Wholesteen do? Why?

For additional questions related to this problem, see Exercise 9–5 in the *Learning Aid for Use with Basic Marketing,* 12th edition.

10

Product Management and New-Product Development

When You Finish This Chapter, You Should

1. Understand how product life cycles affect strategy planning.

2. Know what is involved in designing new products and what "new products" really are.

3. Understand the new-product development process.

4. See why product liability must be considered in screening new products.

5. Understand the need for product or brand managers.

6. Understand the important new terms (shown in red).

For a hundred years, Kodak has been making it simple for people to "capture the moment" in pictures. Kodak is one of the best-known brand names in the world, and who doesn't recognize its famous yellow packages? Its photography-related product assortment includes everything from films and cameras to chemicals, paper, and processing equipment.

In spite of its dominant market share, Kodak's profits are not any better than they were a decade ago. Growth has slowed in most of Kodak's traditional markets. Further, competition of all sorts has increased. Fuji is a global competitor for its best films. Retail chains now push their own dealer brands. Similarly, Japanese firms dominate the popular 35 mm camera market, and Polaroid's patents have locked up much of instant photography. Price competition is increasing and profit margins are shrinking.

Kodak's chemistry-based photographic business is also facing new challenges from digital imaging products. The growth of handheld camcorders has left Kodak's home-movie cameras and film obsolete, and that is just the beginning. All kinds of film are being replaced by electronic gadgets that use microprocessors to read light and images. Once in digital form, a picture can be stored on an optical disk, sent over phone lines, and displayed on a television or computer

screen. Computer software makes it easy to include images in finished documents and print them on color printers. In this setting, Kodak must develop innovative new imaging products or its profits will slowly but surely erode. On the other hand, Kodak's marketing managers must carefully manage the current line of products to be certain that they are as profitable as possible. Kodak is now making changes to address these challenges. It is focusing its new-product development in the digital imaging area. It is introducing new products like the Photo CD that can store about a hundred images and display them on a TV or computer. Yet bringing new product concepts to market is both costly and risky. Already, Kodak has had to revise its Photo CD concept to better target it for computer users. And reaching that target market requires additional investment in promotion to attract customers and build channels.

To avoid costly new-product failures, Kodak is improving its new-product development process. It is working to make certain that it isn't just doing "development work," but rather is focusing R&D on product concepts where there is real market potential. It is reducing development cycle time to move the best product concepts to market faster. These efforts are already leading to successes. Its new CopyPrint Station combines a digital scanner, PC, and thermal printer that allow a consumer to make high-quality copies or enlargements from ordinary prints. The system is in hundreds of stores, and stores that have put it in have seen big gains in sales. Of course, as digital imaging develops, the market will continue to change. Totally new needs may develop. And sooner or later products like the Photo CD and the CopyPrint Station will be replaced by new generations of products that meet customers' needs better or at lower cost.[1]

MANAGING PRODUCTS OVER THEIR LIFE CYCLES

The life and death cycle seen in our Kodak case is being repeated over and over again in product-markets worldwide. Cellular phones are replacing short-wave radios and CBs and also making it possible for people to communicate from places where it was previously impossible. Cassette tapes replaced vinyl records, and now CDs and digital audiotape are challenged by new formats. Switchboard operators in many firms were replaced with answering machines, and now answering machines are losing ground as phone companies offer new voice mail services.

These innovations show that products, markets, and competition change over time. This makes marketing management an exciting challenge. Developing new products and managing existing products to meet changing conditions is important to the success of every firm. In this chapter, we will look at some important ideas in these areas.

Products—like consumers—go through life cycles. So product planning and marketing mix planning are important. Competitors are always developing and copying new ideas and products—making existing products out-of-date more quickly than ever.

Product life cycle has four major stages

The **product life cycle** describes the stages a new product idea goes through from beginning to end. The product life cycle is divided into four major stages: (1) market introduction, (2) market growth, (3) market maturity, and (4) sales decline.

EXHIBIT 10–1 Life Cycle of a Typical Product

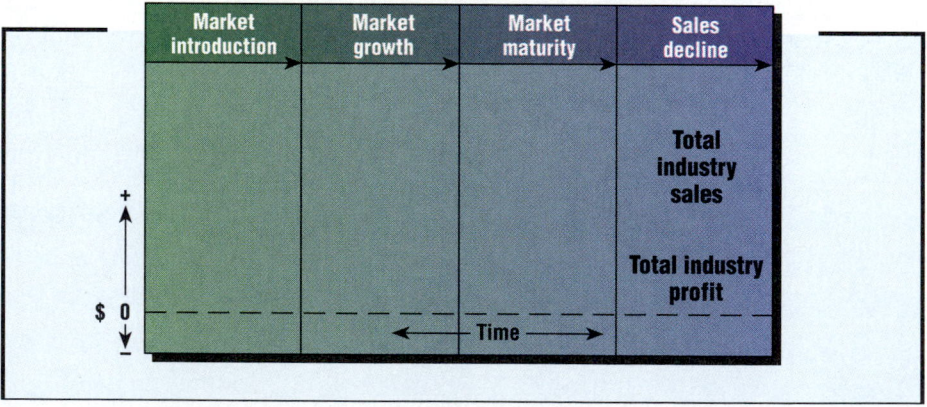

A particular firm's marketing mix usually must change during the product life cycle. There are several reasons why. Customers' attitudes and needs may change over the product life cycle. The product may be aimed at entirely different target markets at different stages. And the nature of competition moves toward pure competition or oligopoly.

Further, total sales of the product—by all competitors in the industry—vary in each of its four stages. They move from very low in the market introduction stage to high at market maturity and then back to low in the sales decline stage. More important, the profit picture changes too. These general relationships can be seen in Exhibit 10–1. Note that sales and profits do not move together over time. *Industry profits decline while industry sales are still rising.*[2]

Market introduction— investing in the future

In the **market introduction** stage, sales are low as a new idea is first introduced to a market. Customers aren't looking for the product. They don't even know about it. Informative promotion is needed to tell potential customers about the advantages and uses of the new product concept.

Even though a firm promotes its new product, it takes time for customers to learn that the product is available. Most companies experience losses during the introduction stage because they spend so much money for Promotion, Product, and Place development. Of course, they invest the money in the hope of future profits.

Market growth—profits go up and down

In the **market growth** stage, industry sales grow fast—but industry profits rise and then start falling. The innovator begins to make big profits as more and more customers buy. But competitors see the opportunity and enter the market. Some just copy the most successful product or try to improve it to compete better. Others try to refine their offerings to do a better job of appealing to some target markets. The new entries result in much product variety. So monopolistic competition— with down-sloping demand curves—is typical of the market growth stage.

This is the time of biggest profits *for the industry. But it is also when industry profits begin to decline* as competition increases. See Exhibit 10–1.

Sony's Data Discman will need informative promotion during the market introduction stage of the product life cycle—so customers will know about its benefits and uses.

Some firms make big strategy planning mistakes at this stage by not understanding the product life cycle. They see the big sales and profit opportunities of the early market growth stage but ignore the competition that will soon follow. When they realize their mistake, it may be too late. Marketing managers who pay attention to competitor analysis are less likely to encounter this problem.

Market maturity—sales level off, profits continue down

The **market maturity** stage occurs when industry sales level off—and competition gets tougher. Many aggressive competitors have entered the race for profits—except in oligopoly situations. Industry profits go down throughout the market maturity stage because promotion costs rise and some competitors cut prices to attract business. Less efficient firms can't compete with this pressure—and they drop out of the market. Even in oligopoly situations, there is a long-run downward pressure on prices.

New firms may still enter the market at this stage—increasing competition even more. Note that late entries skip the early life-cycle stages, including the profitable market growth stage. And they must try to take a share of the saturated market from established firms, which is difficult and expensive. The market leaders have a lot at stake, so they usually will fight hard to defend their market share and revenue stream. Satisfied customers who are happy with their current relationship typically won't be interested in switching to a new brand.

Persuasive promotion becomes more important during the market maturity stage. Products may differ only slightly if at all. Most competitors have discovered the most effective appeals—or quickly copied the leaders. Although each firm may still have its own demand curve, the curves become increasingly elastic as the various products become almost the same in the minds of potential consumers.

In the United States, the markets for most cars, boats, television sets, and many household appliances are in market maturity.[3] This stage may continue for many years—until a basically new product idea comes along—even though individual brands or models come and go.

Sales decline—a time of replacement

During the **sales decline** stage, new products replace the old. Price competition from dying products becomes more vigorous—but firms with strong brands may make profits until the end. These firms have down-sloping demand curves because they successfully differentiated their products.

As the new products go through their introduction stage, the old ones may keep some sales by appealing to the most loyal customers or those who are slow to try new ideas. These conservative buyers might switch later—smoothing the sales decline.

PRODUCT LIFE CYCLES SHOULD BE RELATED TO SPECIFIC MARKETS

Remember that product life cycles describe industry sales and profits for a *product idea* within a particular product-market. The sales and profits of an individual product or brand may not—and often do not—follow the life-cycle pattern. They may vary up and down throughout the life cycle—sometimes moving in the opposite direction of industry sales and profits. Further, a product idea may be in a different life-cycle stage in different markets.

Individual brands may not follow the pattern

A given firm may introduce or withdraw a specific product during any stage of the product life cycle. A "me-too" brand introduced during the market growth

New products that do a better job of meeting the needs of specific target customers are more likely to move quickly and successfully through the introductory stage of the product life cycle.

WE INVENTED A THERMOMETER THAT WORKS WITHIN THE ATTENTION SPAN OF THE AVERAGE FIVE-YEAR-OLD. *(ONE SECOND.)*

THERMOSCAN
INSTANT THERMOMETER

stage, for example, may never get any sales at all and suffer a quick death. Or it may reach its peak and start to decline even before the market maturity stage begins. Market leaders may enjoy high profits during the market maturity stage—even though industry profits are declining. Weaker products, on the other hand, may not earn a profit during any stage of the product life cycle. Sometimes the innovator brand loses so much in the introduction stage that it has to drop out just as others are reaping big profits in the growth stage.

Strategy planners who naively expect sales of an individual product to follow the general product life-cycle pattern are likely to be rudely surprised. In fact, it might be more sensible to think in terms of "product-market life cycles" rather than product life cycles—but we will use the term *product life cycle* because it is commonly accepted and widely used.

Each market should be carefully defined

How we see product life cycles depends on how broadly we define a product-market. For example, almost 80 percent of all U.S. households own microwave ovens. Although microwave ovens appear to be at the market maturity stage here, in many other countries they're still early in the growth stage. Even in European countries like Switzerland, Denmark, Italy, and Spain, fewer than 15 percent of all households own microwave ovens.[4] As this example suggests, a firm with a mature product can sometimes turn back the clock by focusing on new growth opportunities in international markets.

How broadly we define the needs of customers in a product-market also affects how we view product life cycles—and who the competitors are. For example, consider the set of consumer needs related to storing and preparing foods. Wax paper sales in the United States started to decline when Dow introduced Saran Wrap. Then, in the early 1970s, sales of Saran Wrap (and other similar products) fell sharply when small plastic storage bags became popular. However, sales picked up again by the end of the decade. The product didn't change, but customers' needs did. Saran Wrap filled a new need—a wrap that would work well in microwave cooking.

If a market is defined broadly, there may be many competitors—and the market may appear to be in market maturity. On the other hand, if we focus on a narrow submarket—and a particular way of satisfying specific needs—then we may see much shorter product life cycles as improved product ideas come along to replace the old.

PRODUCT LIFE CYCLES VARY IN LENGTH

How long a whole product life cycle takes—and the length of each stage—vary a lot across products. The cycle may vary from 90 days—in the case of toys like the Ghostbusters line—to possibly 100 years for gas-powered cars.

The product life cycle concept does not tell a manager precisely *how long* the cycle will last. But a manager can often make a good guess based on the life cycle for similar products. Sometimes marketing research can help too. However, it is more important to expect and plan for the different stages than to know the precise length of each cycle.

Some products move fast

A new product idea will move through the early stages of the life cycle more quickly when it has certain characteristics. For example, the greater the *comparative advantage* of a new product over those already on the market, the more rapidly its sales will grow. Sales growth is also faster when the product is *easy to use* and if its advantages are *easy to communicate*. If the product *can be tried* on a limited basis—without a lot of risk to the customer—it can usually be introduced more quickly. Finally, if the product is *compatible* with the values and experiences of target customers, they are likely to buy it more quickly.

The fast adoption of NutraSweet low-calorie sweetener in the U.S. market is a good example. NutraSweet offered real benefits—fewer calories compared to sugar without the bitter aftertaste of existing diet sweeteners. Free samples of NutraSweet chewing gum made it easy for consumers to try the product. And NutraSweet worked well in many products—like diet soft drinks—that were already a part of consumers' lifestyles. However, in less-developed countries where malnutrition, not dieting, is the problem, NutraSweet does not have the same comparative advantages.[5]

Product life cycles are getting shorter

Although the life of different products varies, in general product life cycles are getting shorter. This is partly due to rapidly changing technology. One new invention may make possible many new products that replace old ones. Tiny electronic microchips led to hundreds of new products—from Texas Instruments' calculators and Pulsar digital watches in the early days to microchip-controlled heart valves and fax machines now. Fax machines can transmit a letter or illustration anywhere in the world over standard phone lines—in just minutes. They're not only changing how companies communicate, they're also taking business and profits away from overnight delivery services like Federal Express and Express Mail.

Some markets move quickly to market maturity—if there are fast copiers. In the highly competitive grocery products industry, cycles are down to 12 to 18 months for really new ideas. Simple variations of a new idea may have even shorter life cycles. Competitors sometimes copy flavor or packaging changes in a matter of weeks or months.

Patents for a new product may not be much protection in slowing down competitors. Competitors can often find ways to copy the product idea without violating a specific patent. Worse, some firms find out that an unethical competitor simply disregarded the patent protection. Patent violations by foreign competitors are very common. A product's life may be over before a case can get through patent-court bottlenecks. By then, the copycat competitor may even be out of business. These problems are even more severe in international cases because different governments, rules, and court systems are involved. The patent system, in the United States and internationally, needs significant improvement if it is to really protect firms that develop innovative ideas.[6]

Although life cycles are moving faster in the advanced economies, keep in mind that many advances bypass most consumers in less-developed economies. These consumers struggle at the subsistence level, without an effective macro-marketing system to stimulate innovation. However, some of the innovations and economies of scale made possible in the advanced societies do trickle down to benefit these consumers. Inexpensive antibiotics and drought-resistant plants, for example, are making a life-or-death difference.

The early bird usually makes the profits

The increasing speed of the product life cycle means that firms must be developing new products all the time. Further, they must try to have marketing mixes that will make the most of the market growth stage—when profits are highest.

During the growth stage, competitors are likely to introduce product improvements. Fast changes in marketing strategy may be required here because profits don't necessarily go to the innovator. Sometimes fast copiers of the basic idea will share in the market growth stage. Sony, a pioneer in developing videocassette recorders, was one of the first firms to put VCRs on the market. Other firms quickly followed—and the competition drove down prices and increased demand. As sales of VCRs continued to grow, Sony doggedly stuck to its Beta format VCRs in spite of the fact that most consumers were buying VHS-format machines offered by competitors. Not until a decade later did Sony finally "surrender" and offer a VHS-format machine. However, by then the booming growth in VCR sales had ebbed, and competitors controlled 90 percent of the market. Although Sony was slow to see its mistake, its lost opportunities were minor compared to American producers who sat on the sidelines and watched as foreign producers captured the whole VCR market. Copiers can be even faster than the innovator in adapting to the market's needs. Marketers must be flexible, *but also* they must fully understand the needs and attitudes of their target markets.[7]

The short happy life of fashions and fads

The sales of some products are influenced by **fashion**—the currently accepted or popular style. Fashion-related products tend to have short life cycles. What is currently popular can shift rapidly. A certain color or style of clothing—bell-bottom jeans, miniskirts, or four-inch-wide ties—may be in fashion one season and outdated the next. Marketing managers who work with fashions often have to make really fast product changes.

How fast is fast enough? The Limited, a retail chain that specializes in women's fashions, tracks consumer preferences every day through point-of-sale computers. Based on what's selling, new product designs are sent by satellite to suppliers around the United States and in Hong Kong, South Korea, and Singapore. Within days, clothing from those distant points begins to collect in Hong Kong. About four times a week, a chartered jet brings it to the Limited's distribution center in Ohio, where items are priced and then shipped to stores within 48 hours. In spite of the speed of this system, a top manager at the Limited has commented that it's "not fast enough" for the 1990s.[8]

It's not really clear why a particular fashion becomes popular. Most present fashions are adaptations or revivals of previously popular styles. Designers are always looking for styles that will satisfy fashion innovators who crave distinc-

A certain color or style may be in fashion one season and outdated the next.

tiveness. And lower-cost copies of the popular items may catch on with other groups and survive for a while. Yet the speed of change increases the cost of producing and marketing products. Companies sustain losses due to trial and error in finding acceptable styles, then producing them on a limited basis because of uncertainty about the length of the cycle. These increased costs are not always charged directly to the consumer since some firms lose their investment and go out of business. But in total, fashion changes cost consumers money. Fashion changes are a luxury that most people in less-developed countries simply can't afford.

A **fad** is an idea that is fashionable only to certain groups who are enthusiastic about it. But these groups are so fickle that a fad is even more short lived than a regular fashion. Many toys—like the Mighty Morphin Power Rangers figures—are fads but do well during a short-lived cycle. Some teenagers' music tastes are fads. Exhibit 10–2 summarizes the shape of typical life cycles for fashions, fads, and styles. Note that the pattern for a style may go up and down as it comes back into fashion over time.[9]

PLANNING FOR DIFFERENT STAGES OF THE PRODUCT LIFE CYCLE

Length of cycle affects strategy planning

Where a product is in its life cycle—and how fast it's moving to the next stage—should affect marketing strategy planning. Marketing managers must make realistic plans for the later stages. Exhibit 10–3 on page 318 shows the relationship of the product life cycle to the marketing mix variables. The technical terms in this figure are discussed later in the book.

Introducing new products

Exhibit 10–3 shows that a marketing manager has to do a lot of work to introduce a really new product—and this should be reflected in the strategy

EXHIBIT 10−2   Patterns of Fashion, Fad, and Style Cycles for Fashion Products

planning. Money must be spent designing and developing the new product. Even if the product is unique, this doesn't mean that everyone will immediately come running to the producer's door. The firm will have to build channels of distribution—perhaps offering special incentives to win cooperation. Promotion is needed to build demand *for the whole idea*—not just to sell a specific brand. Because all this is expensive, it may lead the marketing manager to try to "skim" the market—charging a relatively high price to help pay for the introductory costs.

The correct strategy, however, depends on how fast the product life cycle is likely to move—that is, how quickly the new idea will be accepted by customers—and how quickly competitors will follow with their own versions of the product. When the early stages of the cycle will be fast, a low initial (penetration) price may make sense to help develop loyal customers early and keep competitors out.

Of course, not all new product ideas catch on. Customers may conclude that the marketing mix doesn't satisfy their needs, or other new products may meet the same need better. But the success that eludes a firm with its initial strategy can sometimes be achieved by modifying the strategy. Videodisc players illustrate this point. They were a flop during their initial introduction in the home-entertainment market. Consumers didn't see any advantage over cheaper video-tape players. But now new opportunities are developing. For example, a new generation of video games uses laser videodiscs to store sounds and images. These games are really just a special application of multimedia computer systems that link videodisc players with a personal computer. The business market for these systems is also growing. Many firms are buying these systems as a selling aid.

EXHIBIT 10–3 Typical Changes in Marketing Variables over the Product Life Cycle

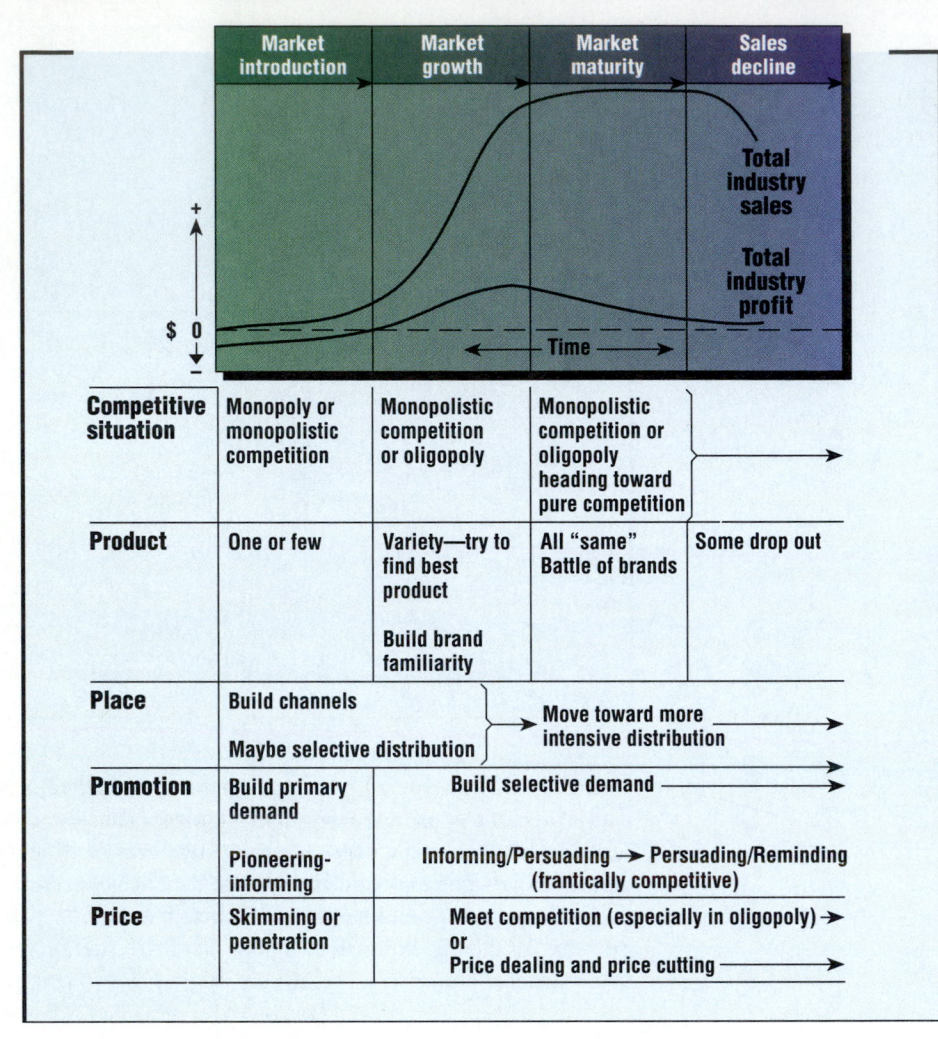

	Market introduction	Market growth	Market maturity	Sales decline
Competitive situation	Monopoly or monopolistic competition	Monopolistic competition or oligopoly	Monopolistic competition or oligopoly heading toward pure competition	→
Product	One or few	Variety—try to find best product Build brand familiarity	All "same" Battle of brands	Some drop out
Place	Build channels Maybe selective distribution	Move toward more intensive distribution →		
Promotion	Build primary demand Pioneering-informing	Build selective demand ——————→ Informing/Persuading → Persuading/Reminding (frantically competitive)		
Price	Skimming or penetration	Meet competition (especially in oligopoly) → or Price dealing and price cutting ——————→		

Salespeople use them to make presentations, and they are also used for in-store selling. Customers can shop for products by viewing pictures on a computer video screen.[10]

Also relevant is how quickly the firm can change its strategy as the life cycle moves on. Some firms are very flexible. They can compete effectively with larger, less adaptable competitors by adjusting their strategies more frequently.

Managing maturing products

It's important for a firm to have some competitive advantage as it moves into market maturity. Even a small advantage can make a big difference—and some firms do very well by carefully managing their maturing products. They are able to capitalize on a slightly better product—or perhaps lower production and/or marketing costs. Or they are simply more successful at promotion—allowing them to differentiate their more or less homogeneous product from competitors. For example, graham crackers were competing in a mature market and sales were flat. Nabisco used the same ingredients to create bite-sized Teddy Grahams and then

Faced with mature markets in the U.S., Nabisco varied products to make them more appealing to customers seeking reduced fat—while looking for new growth opportunities in the Russian market.

promoted them heavily. These changes captured new sales and profits for Nabisco. However, competing firms quickly copied this idea with their own brands.[11]

The important point here is that industry profits are declining in market maturity. Top management must see this, or it will continue to expect the attractive profits of the market growth stage—profits that are no longer possible. If top managers don't understand the situation, they may place impossible burdens on the marketing department—causing marketing managers to think about collusion with competitors, deceptive advertising, or some other desperate attempt to reach impossible objectives.

Product life cycles keep moving. But that doesn't mean a firm should just sit by as its sales decline. There are other choices. A firm can improve its product or develop an innovative new product for the same market. Or it can develop a strategy for its product (perhaps with modifications) targeted at a new market. For example, it might find a market in a country where the life cycle is not so far along, or it might try to serve a new need. Or the firm can withdraw the product before it completes the cycle—and refocus on better opportunities. See Exhibit 10–4.

Improve the product or develop a new one

When a firm's product has won loyal customers, it can be successful for a long time—even in a mature or declining market. However, continued improvements may be needed to keep customers satisfied, especially if their needs shift. An outstanding example is Procter & Gamble's Tide. Introduced in 1947, this powdered detergent gave consumers a much cleaner wash than they were able to get before because it did away with soap film. Tide led to a whole new generation of powdered laundry products that cleaned better with fewer suds. The demands on Tide continued to change because of new washing machines and fabrics—so the powdered Tide sold today is much different from the one sold in 1947. In fact, powdered Tide has had at least 55 (sometimes subtle) modifications.

Do product modifications—like those made with powdered Tide—create a wholly new product that should have its own product life cycle? Or are they

EXHIBIT 10–4 Examples of Three Marketing Strategy Choices for a Firm in a Mature Product-Market

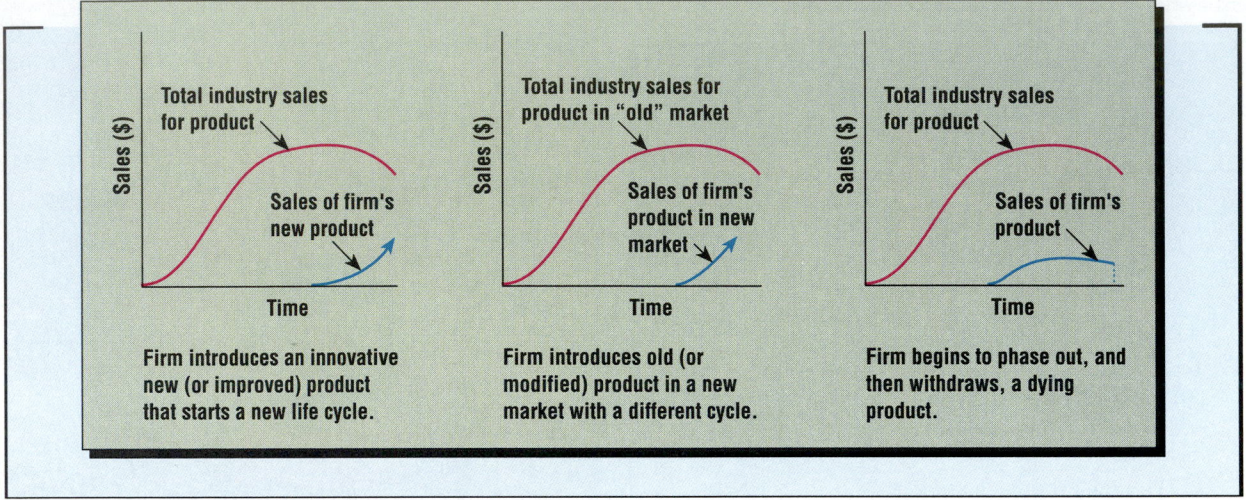

technical adjustments of the original product idea? We will take the latter position—focusing on the product idea rather than changes in features. This means that some of these Tide changes were made in the market maturity stage. But this type of product improvement can help to extend the product life cycle.

On the other hand, a firm that develops an innovative new product may move to a new product life cycle. For example, by 1985 new liquid detergents like Wisk were moving into the growth stage, and sales of powdered detergents were declining. To share in the growth-stage profits for liquid detergents and to offset the loss of customers from powdered Tide, Procter & Gamble introduced Liquid Tide. Although P&G used the familiar Tide brand name, Liquid Tide appears to be a different product concept that competes in a different product-market.

Even though powdered detergents in general appear to be in the decline stage, powdered Tide continues to sell well because it still does the job for some consumers. But sales growth is likely to come from liquid detergents.[12]

Develop new strategies for different markets

We already highlighted the fact that the same product may be in different life cycle stages in different markets. That means that a firm may have to pursue very different strategies for a product, at the same time, in different markets.

In a mature market, a firm may be fighting to keep or increase its market share. But if the firm finds a new use for the product, it may need to try to stimulate overall demand. Du Pont's Teflon fluorocarbon resin is a good example. It was developed more than 50 years ago and has enjoyed sales growth as a nonstick coating for cookware, as an insulation for aircraft wiring, and as a lining for chemically resistant equipment. But marketing managers for Teflon are not waiting to be stuck with declining profits in those mature markets. They are constantly developing strategies for new markets where Teflon will meet needs. For example, Teflon is now selling well as a special coating for the wires used in high-speed communications between computers.[13]

Phasing out dying products

Not all strategies have to be exciting growth strategies. If prospects are poor in some product-market, a phase-out strategy may be needed. The need for

Du Pont continued to improve its popular nonstick coatings for cookware, and as a result it enjoys consumer loyalty in a mature, highly competitive market.

phasing out becomes more obvious as the sales decline stage arrives. But even in market maturity, it may be clear that a particular product is not going to be profitable enough to reach the company's objectives using the current strategy. Then, the wisest move may be to develop a strategy that helps the firm phase out of the product-market—perhaps over several years.

Marketing plans are implemented as ongoing strategies. Salespeople make calls, inventory moves in the channel, advertising is scheduled for several months into the future, and so on. So the firm usually experiences losses if managers end a plan too abruptly. Because of this, it's sometimes better to phase out the product gradually. Managers order materials more selectively so production can end with a minimum of unused inventory, and they shift salespeople to other jobs. They may cancel advertising and other promotion efforts more quickly since there's no point in promoting for the long run. These various actions obviously affect morale within the company—and they may cause middlemen to pull back too. So the company may have to offer price inducements in the channels. Employees should be told that a phase-out strategy is being implemented—and hopefully shifted to other jobs as the plan is completed.

Obviously, there are some difficult implementation problems here. But phase-out is also a *strategy*—and it must be market-oriented to cut losses. In fact, it is possible to milk a dying product for some time if competitors move out more quickly. This situation occurs when there is still ongoing (though declining) demand—and some customers are willing to pay attractive prices to get their old favorite.

NEW-PRODUCT PLANNING

Competition is strong and dynamic in most markets. So it is essential for a firm to keep developing new products—as well as modifying its current products—to meet changing customer needs and competitors' actions. Not having an active new-product development process means that consciously—or subconsciously—the firm has decided to milk its current products and go out of business. New-product planning is not an optional matter. It has to be done just to survive in today's dynamic markets.

What is a new product?

In discussing the introductory stage of product life cycles, we focused on the type of product innovations that tend to disrupt old ways of doing things. However, each year firms introduce many products that are basically refinements of existing products. So a **new product** is one that is new *in any way* for the company concerned.

A product can become "new" in many ways. A fresh idea can be turned into a new product—and start a new product life cycle. For example, Alza Corporation's time-release skin patches are replacing pills and injections for some medications.

Variations on an existing product idea can also make a product new. Oral B changed its conventional toothbrush to include a strip of colored bristles that fade as you brush; that way you know when it's time for a new brush. Even small changes in an existing product can make it new.[14]

FTC says product is "new" only six months

A firm can call its product new for only a limited time. Six months is the limit according to the **Federal Trade Commission (FTC)**—the federal government agency that polices antimonopoly laws. To be called new—says the FTC—a product must be entirely new or changed in a "functionally significant or substantial respect." While six months may seem a very short time for production-oriented managers, it may be reasonable, given the fast pace of change for many products.

❓ Ethical issues in new-product planning

New product decisions—and decisions to abandon old products—often involve ethical considerations. For example, some firms (including the firm that develops drugs used in treating AIDS) have been criticized for holding back important new product innovations until patents run out—or sales slow down—on their existing products. At the same time, others have been criticized for "planned obsolescence"—releasing new products that the company plans to soon replace with improved new versions. Similarly, wholesalers and middlemen complain that producers too often keep their new-product introduction plans a secret and leave middlemen with dated inventory that they can sell only at a loss.

Companies also face ethical dilemmas when they decide to stop supplying a product—or the service and replacement parts to keep it useful. An old model of a Cuisinart food processor, for example, might be in perfect shape except for a crack in the plastic mixing bowl. It's sensible for the company to improve the design if the crack is a frequent problem, but if consumers can't get a replacement part for the model they already own, they're left holding the bag.

Criticisms are also leveled at firms that constantly release minor variations of products that already saturate markets. Consider what's happening with disposable diapers. Marketing managers may feel that they're serving some customers' needs better when they offer diapers in boys' and girls' versions and in a variety of sizes, shapes, and colors. But many retailers feel that the new products are simply a ploy to get more shelf space. Further, some consumers complain that the bewildering array of choices makes it impossible to make an informed choice.

Different marketing managers might have very different reactions to such criticisms. However, the fact remains that product management decisions often have a significant effect, one way or another, on customers and middlemen. A marketing manager who is not sensitive to this may find that a too casual decision leads to a negative backlash that affects the firm's strategy or reputation.[15]

AN ORGANIZED NEW-PRODUCT DEVELOPMENT PROCESS IS CRITICAL

Identifying and developing new-product ideas—and effective strategies to go with them—is often the key to a firm's success and survival. But this isn't easy. New-product development demands effort, time, and talent—and still the risks and costs of failure are high. Experts estimate that consumer packaged-goods companies spend at least $20 million to introduce a new brand—and 70 to 80 percent of these new brands flop. In the service sector, the front-end cost of a failed effort may not be as high, but it can have a devastating long-term effect if dissatisfied consumers turn elsewhere for help.[16]

A new product may fail for many reasons. Most often, companies fail to offer a unique benefit or underestimate the competition. Sometimes the idea is good but the company has design problems—or the product costs much more to produce than was expected. Some companies rush to get a product on the market without developing a complete marketing plan.[17]

But moving too slowly can be a problem too. With the fast pace of change for many products, speedy entry into the market can be a key to competitive advantage. A few years ago, marketing managers at Xerox were alarmed that Japanese competitors were taking market share with innovative new models of copiers. It turned out that the competitors were developing new models twice as fast as Xerox and at half the cost. For Xerox to compete, it had to slash its five-year product development cycle. Many other companies—ranging from Chrysler Corporation to Hewlett-Packard to Motorola—are working to speed up the new-product development process.[18]

Generating innovative and profitable new products requires creativity—and an organized new-product development process.

To move quickly and also avoid expensive new-product failures, many companies follow an organized new-product development process. The following pages describe such a process, which moves logically through five steps: (1) idea generation, (2) screening, (3) idea evaluation, (4) development (of product and marketing mix), and (5) commercialization.[19] See Exhibit 10–5.

The general process is similar for both consumer and business markets—and for both goods and services. There are some significant differences, but we will emphasize the similarities in the following discussion.

Process tries to kill new ideas—economically

An important element in this new-product development process is continued evaluation of a new idea's likely profitability and return on investment. In fact, the hypothesis-testing approach discussed in Chapter 5 works well for new-product development. The hypothesis tested is that the new idea will *not* be profitable. This puts the burden on the new idea—to prove itself or be rejected. Such a process may seem harsh, but experience shows that most new ideas have some flaw that can lead to problems—and even substantial losses. Marketers try to discover those flaws early, and either find a remedy or reject the idea completely. Applying this process requires much analysis of the idea—both within and outside the firm—*before* the company spends money to develop and market a product. This is a major departure from the usual production-oriented approach—in which a company develops a product first and then asks sales to "get rid of it."

Of course, the actual new-product success rate varies among industries and companies. But many companies *are* improving the way they develop new products. It's important to see that if a firm doesn't use an organized process like this, it may bring many bad or weak ideas to market—at a big loss.

Step 1. Idea generation

New ideas can come from a company's own sales or production staff, middlemen, competitors, consumer surveys, or other sources such as trade associations, advertising agencies, or government agencies. By analyzing new and different views of the company's markets and studying present consumer behavior, a marketing manager can spot opportunities that have not yet occurred to competitors—or even to potential customers. For example, ideas for new service concepts may come directly from analysis of consumer complaints.

EXHIBIT 10–5 New-Product Development Process

No one firm can always be first with the best new ideas. So in their search for ideas, companies should pay attention to what current or potential competitors are doing. For example, new-product specialists at Ford Motor Company buy other firms' cars as soon as they're available. Then they take the cars apart to see what the other firms are doing in the way of new ideas or improvements. British Airways talks to travel agents to learn about new services offered by competitors. Many other companies use similar approaches.[20]

Many firms now "shop" in international markets for new ideas. Jamaica Broilers, a poultry producer in the Caribbean, moved into fish farming; it learned that many of the techniques it was using to breed chickens were also successful on fish farms in Israel. In the same vein, food companies in the United States and Europe are now experimenting with an innovation recently introduced in Japan—a clear, odorless, natural film for wrapping food. Consumers don't have to unwrap it; when they put a product in boiling water or a microwave, the wrapper vanishes.[21]

Research shows that many new ideas in business markets come from customers who identify a need they have. Then they approach a supplier with the idea—and perhaps even with a particular design or specification. These customers become the lead users of the product, but the supplier can pursue the opportunity in other markets.[22]

But finding new product ideas can't be left to chance. Companies need a formal procedure for seeking new ideas. The checkpoints discussed below, as well as the hierarchy of needs and other behavioral elements discussed earlier, should be reviewed regularly to ensure a continual flow of new—and sound—ideas. And companies do need a continual flow so they can spot an opportunity early—while there's still time to do something about it. Although later steps eliminate many ideas, a company must have some that succeed.

Adopting the marketing concept should lead to the development of safe products.

EXHIBIT 10–6   Types of New-Product Opportunities

Step 2. Screening

Screening involves evaluating the new ideas with the product-market screening criteria described in Chapter 4. Recall that these criteria include the combined output of a resource (strengths and weaknesses) analysis, a long-run trends analysis, and a thorough understanding of the company's objectives. See Exhibit 3–1. Further, a "good" new idea should eventually lead to a product (and marketing mix) that will give the firm a competitive advantage—hopefully a lasting one.

Opportunities with better growth potential are likely to be more attractive. We discussed this idea earlier when we introduced the GE planning grid (see Exhibit 4–7). Now, however, you know that the life-cycle stage at which a firm's new product enters the market has a direct bearing on its prospects for growth. Clearly, screening should consider how the strategy for a new product will hold up over the whole product life cycle. In other words, screening should consider how attractive the new product will be both in the short and long term.

Some companies screen based on consumer welfare

Screening should also consider how a new product will affect consumers over time. Ideally, the product should increase consumer welfare—not just satisfy a whim. Exhibit 10–6 shows different kinds of new-product opportunities. Obviously, a socially responsible firm tries to find desirable opportunities rather than deficient ones. This may not be as easy as it sounds, however. Some consumers want pleasing products instead of desirable ones. They emphasize immediate satisfaction and give little thought to their own long-term welfare. And some competitors willingly offer what consumers want in the short run. Generating socially responsible new-product ideas is a challenge for new-product planners, but consumer groups are helping firms to become more aware.

Safety must be considered

Real acceptance of the marketing concept certainly leads to safe products. But consumers still buy some risky products for the thrills and excitement they provide—for example, bicycles, skis, hang gliders, and bungee jumps. Even so, companies can usually add safety features—and some potential customers want them.

The U.S. **Consumer Product Safety Act** (of 1972) set up the Consumer Product Safety Commission to encourage safety in product design and better quality control. The commission has a great deal of power. It can set safety standards for products. It can order costly repairs or return of unsafe products. And it can back up its orders with fines and jail sentences. The Food and Drug Administration has similar powers for food and drugs.

Product safety complicates strategy planning because not all customers—even those who want better safety features—are willing to pay more for safer products. Some features cost a lot to add and increase prices considerably. These safety concerns must be considered at the screening step because a firm can later be held liable for unsafe products.

Products can turn to liabilities

Product liability means the legal obligation of sellers to pay damages to individuals who are injured by defective or unsafe products. Product liability is a serious matter. Liability settlements may exceed not only a company's insurance coverage but its total assets!

Relative to most other countries, U.S. courts enforce a very strict product liability standard. Producers may be held responsible for injuries related to their products no matter how the items are used or how well they're designed. Riddell—whose football helmets protect the pros—was hit with a $12 million judgment for a high school football player who broke his neck. The jury concluded that Riddell should have put a sticker on the helmet to warn players of the danger of butting into opponents!

Cases and settlements like this are common. In the United States, companies pay over $100 billion a year to lawyers and consumers. Some critics argue that the U.S. rules are so tough that they discourage innovation and economic growth. For example, one U.S. firm decided not to introduce its new radio transmission towers in the U.S. and instead is going to England, where liability risks are much lower. The contrast between the United States and Japan is even greater. Japan's system discourages consumers from filing complaints because they are required to pay a percentage of any damages they seek as court costs—regardless of whether they win or lose.

Product liability is a serious ethical and legal matter. Many countries are attempting to change their laws so that they will be fair to both firms and consumers. But until product liability questions are resolved, marketing managers must be even more sensitive when screening new-product ideas.[23]

ROI *is a crucial screening criterion*

Getting by the initial screening criteria doesn't guarantee success for the new idea. But it does show that at least the new idea is in the right ballpark *for this firm*. If many ideas pass the screening criteria, a firm must set priorities to determine which ones go on to the next step in the process. This can be done by comparing the ROI (return on investment) for each idea—assuming the firm is ROI oriented. The most attractive alternatives are pursued first.

Step 3. Idea evaluation

When an idea moves past the screening step, it is evaluated more carefully. Note that an actual product has not yet been developed—and this can handicap the firm in getting feedback from customers. For help in idea evaluation, firms use **concept testing**—getting reactions from customers about how well a new product idea fits their needs. Concept testing uses market research—ranging from informal focus groups to formal surveys of potential customers.

Companies can often estimate likely costs, revenue, and profitability at this stage. And market research can help identify the size of potential markets. Even informal focus groups are useful—especially if they show that potential users are not excited about the new idea. If results are discouraging, it may be best to kill the idea at this stage. Remember, in this hypothesis-testing process, we're looking for any evidence that an idea is *not* a good opportunity for this firm—and should be rejected.

Product planners must think about wholesaler and retailer customers as well as final consumers. Middlemen may have special concerns about handling a proposed product. A Utah ice cream maker was considering a new line of ice cream novelty products—and he had visions of a hot market in California. But he had to drop his idea when he learned that grocery store chains wanted payments of $20,000 each just to stock his frozen novelties in their freezers. Without the payment, they didn't want to risk using profitable freezer space on an unproven product. This is not an unusual case. At the idea evaluation stage, companies often find that other members of the distribution channel won't cooperate.[24]

Idea evaluation is often more precise in business markets. Potential customers are more informed—and their needs focus on the economic reasons for buying rather than emotional factors. Further, given the derived nature of demand in business markets, most needs are already being satisfied in some way. So new products just substitute for existing ones. This means that product planners can compare the cost advantages and limitations of a new product with those currently being used. And by interviewing well-informed people, they can determine the range of product requirements—and decide whether there is an opportunity.

For example, in 1990 GE was developing a special lightbulb for automobile headlights. GE's marketing managers knew that auto designers would like the smaller, low-heat bulb because it would allow sleeker styling and thus better gas mileage, as well as better night visibility. By working with engineers at Ford, GE was able to determine that the switch to the new bulb and headlight assembly would add about $200 to the price of a car. That meant that the bulb was initially limited to luxury cars—until economies of scale brought down the costs.[25]

Whatever research methods are used, the idea evaluation step should gather enough information to help decide whether there is an opportunity, whether it fits with the firm's resources, *and* whether there is a basis for developing a competitive advantage. With such information, the firm can estimate likely ROI in the various market segments and decide whether to continue the new-product development process.[26]

Step 4. Development

Product ideas that survive the screening and idea evaluation steps must now be analyzed further. Usually, this involves some research and development (R&D) and engineering to design and develop the physical part of the product. In the case of a new service offering, the firm will work out the details of what training, equipment, staff, and so on will be needed to deliver on the idea. Input from the earlier efforts helps guide this technical work.

New computer-aided design (CAD) systems are sparking a revolution in design work. Designers can develop lifelike 3-D color drawings of packages and products. Then the computer allows the manager to look at the product from different angles and views, just as with a real product. Changes can be made almost instantly. And once the designs are finalized they feed directly into computer-controlled manufacturing systems. Companies like Motorola and Timex have found that these systems cut their new-product development time in half—giving them a leg up on foreign competitors.

Even so, it is still good to test models and early versions of the product in the market. This process may have several cycles. A manufacturer may build a model

A sales rep who sells Timken bearings and a product designer for a transmission company use computer-aided design software to improve their communications and speed up the new-product development process.

of a physical product or produce limited quantities; a service firm may try to train a small group of service providers. Product tests with customers may lead to revisions—*before* the firm commits to full-scale efforts to produce the good or service.

With actual goods or services, potential customers can react to how well the product meets their needs. Using small focus groups, panels, and larger surveys, marketers can get reactions to specific features and to the whole product idea. Sometimes that reaction kills the idea. For example, Coca-Cola Foods believed it had a great idea with Minute Maid Squeeze-Fresh, frozen orange juice concentrate in a squeeze bottle. Coca-Cola thought consumers would prefer to mix one glass at a time rather than find space for another half-gallon jug in the refrigerator. When actually tested, however, Squeeze-Fresh bombed. Consumers loved the idea but hated the product. It was messy to use, and no one knew how much concentrate to squeeze in the glass.[27]

In other cases, testing can lead to revision of product specifications for different markets. For example, AMR Corporation had plans for a new reservation system to help travel agents, hotels, and airlines provide better customer service. But tests revealed too many problems, and plans for the service had to be revised. Sometimes a complex series of revisions may be required. Months or even years of research may be necessary to focus on precisely what different market segments will find acceptable. For example, Gillette's Sensor razor took 13 years and over $300 million dollars to develop.[28]

Firms often use full-scale market testing to get reactions in real market conditions or to test product variations and variations in the marketing mix. For example, a firm may test alternative brands, prices, or advertising copy in different test cities. Note that the firm is testing the whole marketing mix, not just the

Firms often take apart competitors' products to look for ideas that they can apply or adapt in their own products.

Porsche 968: The next evolution.

product. For example, a hotel chain might test a new service offering at one location to see how it goes over.

Test-marketing can be risky because it may give information to competitors. In fact, a company in Chicago—Marketing Intelligence Services—monitors products in test markets and then sells the information to competing firms. Similar firms monitor markets in other countries.

But *not* testing is dangerous too. Frito-Lay was so sure it understood consumers' snack preferences that it introduced a three-item cracker line without market testing. Even with network TV ad support, MaxSnax met with overwhelming consumer indifference. By the time Frito-Lay pulled the product from store shelves, it had lost $52 million. Market tests can be very expensive. Yet they can uncover problems that otherwise might go undetected—and destroy the whole strategy.[29]

If a company follows the new-product development process carefully, the market test will provide a lot more information to the firm than to its competitors. Of course, the company must test specific variables—rather than just vaguely testing whether a new idea will "sell." After the market test, the firm can estimate likely ROI for various strategies to determine whether the idea moves on to commercialization.

Some companies don't do market tests because they just aren't practical. In fashion markets, for example, speed is extremely important, and products are usually just tried in market. And durable products—which have high fixed production costs and long production lead times—may have to go directly to market. In these cases, it is especially important that the early steps be done carefully to reduce the chances for failure.[30]

Step 5. Commercialization

A product idea that survives this far can finally be placed on the market. First, the new-product people decide exactly which product form or line to sell. Then they complete the marketing mix—really a whole strategic plan. And top management has to approve an ROI estimate for the plan before it is implemented. Finally, the product idea emerges from the new-product development process—but success requires the cooperation of the whole company.

Putting a product on the market is expensive. Manufacturing or service facilities have to be set up. Goods have to be produced to fill the channels of distribution, or people must be hired and trained to provide services. Further, introductory promotion is costly—especially if the company is entering a very competitive market.

Because of the size of the job, some firms introduce their products city by city or region by region—in a gradual "roll out"—until they have complete market coverage. Roll outs also permit more market testing—although that is not their purpose. Rather, the purpose is to do a good job implementing the marketing plan. But marketing managers also need to pay close attention to control—to ensure that the implementation effort is working and that the strategy is on target.

NEW-PRODUCT DEVELOPMENT: A TOTAL COMPANY EFFORT

Top-level support is vital

Companies that are particularly successful at developing new goods and services seem to have one trait in common—enthusiastic top-management support for new-product development. New products tend to upset old routines that managers of established products often try in subtle but effective ways to maintain. So someone with top-level support—and authority to get things done—needs to be responsible for new-product development.[31]

Put someone in charge

In addition, rather than leaving new-product development to anyone who happens to be interested (perhaps in engineering, R&D, or sales), successful companies put someone in charge—a person, department, or team.

A new-product development department or team (committee) from different departments may help ensure that new ideas are carefully evaluated—and profitable ones quickly brought to market. It's important to choose the right people for the job. Overly conservative managers may kill too many—or even all—new ideas. Or committees may create bureaucratic delays leading to late introduction and giving competitors a head start. A delay of even a few months can make the difference between a product's success or failure.

Market needs guide R&D effort

Many new-product ideas come from scientific discoveries and new technologies. That is why firms often assign specialists to study the technological environment in search of new ways to meet customers' needs. Many firms have their own R&D group that works on developing new products and new-product ideas. Even service firms have technical specialists who help in development work. For example, a bank thinking about offering customers a new set of investment alternatives must be certain that it can deliver on its promises. We've touched on this earlier, but the relationship between marketing and R&D warrants special emphasis.

The R&D effort is usually handled by scientists, engineers, and other specialists who have technical training and skills. Their work can make an important contribution to a firm's competitive advantage—especially if it competes in high-tech markets. However, technical creativity by itself is not enough. The R&D effort must be guided by the type of new-product development process we've been discussing.

3M CLEANS UP WITH MARKET INNOVATIONS

Minnesota Mining & Manufacturing (3M) spins out successful new products faster than just about any other company. This doesn't just happen by chance: 3M's top executive set an objective that 30 percent of 3M sales should come from products that did not exist four years ago. 3M also motivates innovation by staying close to customers, rewarding new-product champions, and sharing ideas among divisions. Teams from R&D and marketing screen new product concepts for the ones with the highest profit potential; then everyone works to bring them to market fast. 3M's new Scotch-Brite Never Rust Wool Soap Pads show how this approach can succeed.

Consumers told 3M marketing researchers that they wanted an improved soap pad. Ordinary scouring pads, like Brillo and S.O.S., are made of steel wool that leaves rust stains on sinks and tiny metal splinters in dishpan hands. Because 3M screens new products for their environmental impact, the R&D people developed a new, patented pad from recycled plastic bottles. And experts from 3M's abrasives division helped figure out how to coat the pad's plastic fibers with fine abrasives and biodegradable soap. Further marketing research helped refine the size and shape of the product, and test markets evaluated details of the marketing plan. For example, the tests confirmed that consumers would pay more for the Never Rust pads than they did for Brillo, and that they liked the colorful package (made from recycled paper).

About half of 3M's total sales come from international markets, so it's no surprise that the marketing plan for Never Rust pads was varied for different countries. For example, there were two different objectives: to capture share in mature markets such as the U.S. and Brazil—where steel wool pads already have a large consumer base—and to attract new customers and pioneer the market in places such as Japan where steel wool is not commonly used. How well have the pads done? In a firm renowned for innovation, the new product launch of Never Rust pads is one of 3M's most successful ever.[32]

From the idea generation stage to the commercialization stage, the R&D specialists, the operations people, and the marketing people must work together to evaluate the feasibility of new ideas. It isn't sensible for a marketing manager to develop elaborate marketing plans for goods or services that the firm simply can't produce—or produce profitably. It also doesn't make sense for R&D people to develop a technology or product that does not have potential for the firm and its markets. Clearly, a balancing act is involved here. But the critical point is the basic one we've been emphasizing throughout the whole book: Marketing-oriented firms seek to satisfy customer needs at a profit with an integrated, whole-company effort.

A complicated, integrated effort is needed

Developing new products should be a total company effort. The whole process—involving people in management, research, production, promotion, packaging, and branding—must move in steps from early exploration of ideas to development of the product and marketing mix. Even with a careful development process, many new products do fail—usually because a company skips some steps in the process. Because speed can be important, it's always tempting to skip needed steps when some part of the process seems to indicate that the company has a "really good idea." But the process moves in steps—gathering different kinds of information along the way. By skipping steps, a firm may miss an important aspect that could make a whole strategy less profitable—or actually cause it to fail.

Eventually, the new product is no longer new—and it becomes just another product. In some firms, at this point the new-product people turn the product over to the regular operating people—and go on to developing other new ideas. In other firms, the person who was the new-product champion continues with the new product, perhaps taking on the broader responsbility for turning it into a successful business.

NEED FOR PRODUCT MANAGERS

Product variety leads to product managers

When a firm has only one or a few related products, everyone is interested in them. But when many new products are being developed, someone should be put in charge of new-product planning to be sure it is not neglected. Similarly, when a firm has products in several different product categories, management may decide to put someone in charge of each category—or each brand—to be sure that attention to these products is not lost in the rush of everyday business. **Product managers** or **brand managers** manage specific products—often taking over the jobs formerly handled by an advertising manager. That gives a clue to what is often their major responsibility—Promotion—since the products have already been developed by the new-product people. However, some brand managers start at the new-product development stage and carry on from there.

Product managers are especially common in large companies that produce many kinds of products. Several product managers may serve under a marketing manager. Sometimes these product managers are responsible for the profitable operation of a particular product's whole marketing effort. Then they have to coordinate their efforts with others—including the sales manager, advertising agencies, production and research people, and even channel members. This is likely to lead to difficulties if product managers have no control over the marketing strategy for other related brands—or authority over other functional areas whose efforts they are expected to direct and coordinate!

To avoid these problems, in some companies the product manager serves mainly as a "product champion"—concerned with planning and getting the promotion effort implemented. A higher-level marketing manager with more authority coordinates the efforts and integrates the marketing strategies for different products into an overall plan.

Firms as diverse as Mattel (toys) and Hershey (candy) are seeking ways to speed up the new-product development cycle—without increasing the risk of new-product failure.

The activities of product managers vary a lot depending on their experience and aggressiveness—and the company's organizational philosophy. Today companies are emphasizing marketing *experience*—because this important job takes more than academic training and enthusiasm. But it is clear that someone must be responsible for developing and implementing product-related plans—especially when a company has many products.[33]

CONCLUSION

New-product planning is an increasingly important activity in a modern economy because it is no longer very profitable to just sell me-too products in highly competitive markets. Markets, competition, and product life cycles are changing at a fast pace.

The product life cycle concept is especially important to marketing strategy planning. It shows that a firm needs different marketing mixes—and even strategies—as a product moves through its cycle. This is an important point because profits change during the life cycle—with most of the profits going to the innovators or fast copiers.

We pointed out that a product is new to a firm if it is new in any way—or to any target market. But the Federal Trade Commission takes a narrower view of what you can call "new."

New products are so important to business survival that firms need some organized process for developing them. We discuss such a process—and emphasize that it requires a total company effort to be successful.

The failure rate of new products is high—but it is lower for better-managed firms that recognize product development and management as vital processes. Some firms appoint product managers to manage individual products and new-product teams in order to ensure that the process is carried out successfully.

QUESTIONS AND PROBLEMS

1. Explain how industry sales and industry profits behave over the product life cycle.

2. Cite two examples of products you feel are currently in each of the product life-cycle stages. Consider services as well as physical goods.

3. Explain how you might reach different conclusions about the correct product life-cycle stage(s) in the worldwide automobile market.

4. Explain why individual brands may not follow the product life-cycle pattern. Give an example of a new brand that is not entering the life cycle at the market introduction stage.

5. Discuss the life cycle of a product in terms of its probable impact on a manufacturer's marketing mix. Illustrate using personal computers.

6. What characteristics of a new product will help it to move through the early stages of the product life cycle more quickly? Briefly discuss each characteristic—illustrating with a product of your choice. Indicate how each characteristic might be viewed in some other country.

7. What is a new product? Illustrate your answer.

8. Explain the importance of an organized new-product development process and illustrate how it might be used for (*a*) a new hair care product, (*b*) a new children's toy, and (*c*) a new subscribers-only cable television channel.

9. Discuss how you might use the new-product development process if you were thinking about offering some kind of summer service to residents in a beach resort town.

10. Explain the role of product or brand managers. When would it make sense for one of a company's current brand managers to be in charge of the new-product development process? Explain your thinking.

11. If a firm offers one of its brands in a number of different countries, would it make sense for one brand manager to be in charge, or would each country require its own brand manager? Explain your thinking.

12. Discuss the social value of new-product development activities that seem to encourage people to discard products that are not all worn out. Is this an economic waste? How worn out is all worn out? Must a shirt have holes in it? How big?

SUGGESTED CASES

7. Pillsbury's Häagen-Dazs
12. Dow

19. Leisure World, Inc.

COMPUTER-AIDED PROBLEM

10. Growth Stage Competition

AgriChem, Inc., has introduced an innovative new product—a combination fertilizer, weed killer, and insecticide that makes it much easier for soybean farmers to produce a profitable crop. The product introduction was quite successful with 1 million units sold in the year of introduction. And AgriChem's profits are increasing. Total market demand is expected to grow at a rate of 200,000 units a year for the next five years. Even so, AgriChem's marketing managers are concerned about what will happen to sales and profits during this period.

Based on past experience with similar situations, they expect one new competitor to enter the market during each of the next five years. They think this competitive pressure will drive prices down about 6 percent a year. Further, although the total market is growing, they know that new competitors will chip away at AgriChem's market share—even with the 10 percent a year increase planned for the promotion budget. In spite of the competitive pressure, the marketing managers are sure that familiarity with AgriChem's brand will help it hold a large share of the total market—and give Agri-Chem greater economies of scale than competitors. In fact, they expect that the ratio of profit to dollar sales for AgriChem should be about 10 percent higher than for competitors.

AgriChem's marketing managers have decided the best way to get a handle on the situation is to organize the data in a spreadsheet. They have set up the spreadsheet so they can change the "years in the future" value and see what is likely to happen to AgriChem and the rest of the industry. The starting spreadsheet shows the current situation with data from the first full year of production.

a. Compare AgriChem's market share and profit for this year with what is expected next year—given the marketing managers' current assumptions. What are they expecting? (Hint: Set number of years in the future to 1.)

b. Prepare a table showing AgriChem's expected profit, and the expected industry revenue and profit, for the current year and the next five years. Briefly explain what happens to industry sales and profits and why. (Hint: Use the What If analysis to vary the number of years in the future value in the spreadsheet from a minimum of 0—the current year—to a maximum of 5. Display the three values requested.)

c. If market demand grows faster than expected—say, at 280,000 units a year—what will happen to AgriChem's profits and the expected industry revenues and profits over the next five years? What are the implications of this analysis?

For additional questions related to this problem, see Exercise 10–3 in the *Learning Aid for Use with Basic Marketing*, 12th edition.

11

Place and Development of Channel Systems

When You Finish This Chapter, You Should

1. Understand what product classes suggest about Place objectives.

2. Understand why some firms use direct channel systems while others rely on intermediaries and indirect systems.

3. Understand how and why marketing specialists develop to make channel systems more effective.

4. Understand how to develop cooperative relationships—and avoid conflict—in channel systems.

5. Know how channel members in vertical marketing systems shift and share functions—to meet customer needs.

6. Understand the differences between intensive, selective, and exclusive distribution.

7. Understand the important new terms (shown in red).

The Goodyear blimp is a familiar symbol of one of the world's leading tire producers. But a few years ago Goodyear wasn't flying so high. It had lost money for the first time in its history. Its marketing program wasn't working, and the independent tire dealers in its channel were losing market share. New marketing strategies—including distribution changes to reach new target markets—were crucial to Goodyear's quick recovery from these problems.

The problems faced by Goodyear and its dealers were in part the result of big changes in international competition among tire producers. Goodyear sales and profits plummeted after France's Michelin and Japan's Bridgestone aggressively expanded distribution in the North American market. For example, Bridgestone moved quickly by taking over Firestone and all its outlets. Both Michelin and Bridgestone were willing to "buy" market share with low prices in North America because they reap most of their profits from sales in their home markets.

Goodyear's direct sales to Detroit automakers held up. But the company was having trouble competing in the retail market for replacement tires. One reason for the trouble was that Goodyear simply wasn't putting its tires where shoppers would buy them. Goodyear sold its brands almost exclusively through its own autocenters and 2,500 independent dealers loyal to Goodyear. These stores attracted customers who came in for specific high-performance tires, like Goodyear Eagles, and quality service. But many other consumers didn't see a difference in the tires or the service—they just wanted a low price. Moreover, an increasing number were buying tires at discount outlets and warehouse clubs that carried several brands.

Goodyear's marketing managers realized they needed to add new distribution channels and change their strategies to reach these different target markets. One of their first changes was to sell Goodyear-brand tires to Sears, which in turn marketed them at its 850 autocenters. Many consumers went to Sears for tires without even considering a Goodyear dealer—and Sears sold 10 percent of all replacement tires in the U.S. market. Further, Sears agreed to devote about 20 percent of the tire inventory at each autocenter to Goodyear tires.

To better reach the price-oriented discount shoppers, Goodyear is converting many of its company-owned autocenters to no-frills, quick-serve stores operated under the Just Tires name. Goodyear also produces private-label tires and other lower-priced lines that are sold at Wal-Mart and other big chains.

Goodyear's marketing managers knew that these changes might cause conflict with Goodyear's independent dealers. In fact, hundreds of dealers initially responded by taking on other lines of tires. However, Goodyear's plan included ideas on how to rebuild the relationship with dealers. It quickly introduced new lines of premium tires—like the innovative Aquatred line and specialized lines for sports cars and

4-wheel drive vehicles. These were tires that appealed to the dealers' customers. Goodyear also increased advertising and promotion support to pull more customers into the dealers' stores. Because of this channel leadership, dealer sales of Goodyear tires increased too. In fact, demand was so strong that both Goodyear and its dealers lost some sales because Goodyear couldn't produce some of the most popular sizes fast enough to replenish dealer inventories.[1]

PLACE DECISIONS ARE AN IMPORTANT PART OF MARKETING STRATEGY

As this example shows, offering customers a good product at a reasonable price is important to a successful marketing strategy. But it's not the whole story. Managers must also think about **Place**—making goods and services available in the right quantities and locations—when customers want them. And when different target markets have different needs, a number of Place variations may be required.

In the next three chapters, we'll deal with the many important strategy decisions that a marketing manager must make concerning Place. Exhibit 11–1 gives an overview. We'll start in this chapter with a discussion of the type of channel that's needed to meet customers' needs. We'll show why specialists are often involved and how they come together to form a **channel of distribution**— any series of firms or individuals who participate in the flow of products from producer to final user or consumer. We'll also consider how to manage relations among channel members to reduce conflict and improve cooperation.

In Chapter 12, we'll expand our coverage of Place to include decisions that marketing managers make to decide what level of distribution service to offer—and why they must coordinate storing and transporting activities to provide the desired service at a reasonable cost. Then in Chapter 13, we'll take a

EXHIBIT 11–1   Strategy Decision Areas in Place

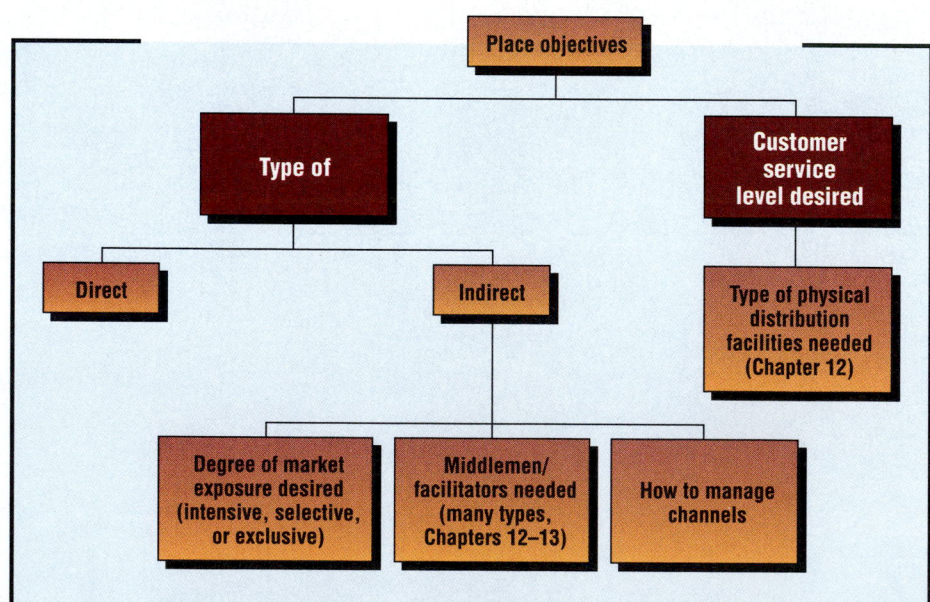

closer look at the many different types of retailing and wholesaling firms. We'll consider their role in channels as well as the strategy decisions they make to satisfy their own customers.

PLACE DECISIONS ARE GUIDED BY "IDEAL" PLACE OBJECTIVES

All marketing managers want to be sure that their goods and services are available in the right quantities and locations—when customers want them. But customers may have different needs with respect to time, place, and possession utility as they make different purchases.

Product classes suggest place objectives

You've already seen this with the product classes—which summarize consumers' urgency to have needs satisfied and willingness to seek information, shop, and compare. Now you should be able to use the product classes to handle Place decisions.

Exhibit 9–4 shows the relationship between consumer product classes and ideal Place objectives. Similarly, Exhibit 9–5 shows the business product classes and how they relate to customer needs. Study these exhibits carefully. They set the framework for making Place decisions. In particular, the product classes help us decide how much market exposure we'll need in each geographic area.

Place system is not automatic

As the Goodyear case shows, a product may be sold to both final consumers and business customers, and each type of customer may want to purchase in different ways. Further, several different product classes may be involved if different market segments view a product in different ways. Thus, just as there is no automatic classification for a specific product, we can't automatically decide the one best Place arrangement.

To more quickly reach its place objectives in the Japanese market and achieve widespread, low-cost distribution, GE agreed to form a joint venture with Hitachi. The joint venture distributes 75 different types of lightbulbs through a network of 100 wholesalers who serve 10,000 established Hitachi retail outlets.

However, people in a particular target market should have similar attitudes and therefore should be satisfied with the same Place system. If different target segments view a product in different ways, marketing managers may need to develop several strategies, each with its own Place arrangements.

Place decisions have long-run effects

The marketing manager must also consider Place objectives in relation to the product life cycle; see Exhibit 10–3. Place decisions have long-run effects. They're usually harder to change than Product, Price, and Promotion decisions. It can take years and a great deal of money to develop effective working relationships with others in the channel. Legal contracts with channel partners may also limit changes. And it's hard to move retail stores and wholesale facilities once leases are signed and customer shopping patterns are settled. Yet as products mature, they typically need broader distribution to reach different target customers.

The distribution of premium pet foods followed this pattern. Most pet food producers reached consumers through supermarkets. Yet, supermarkets weren't willing to put much emphasis on specialized pet foods because there wasn't much demand. Marketing managers for Hill's Science Diet products concentrated on establishing distribution through nongrocery outlets, primarily pet shops and veterinary offices. These pet professionals have a lot of influence on what pet owners buy, and they were reaching Science Diet's target market. By 1991, pet owners were spending over $1 billion a year for premium-priced food from pet stores and vets, where Science Diet is the leading brand. What's more, the profit margins on the specialty foods are much higher than on traditional fare. Seeing that this market was growing, Purina, Kal Kan, and other producers developed new products and worked with their supermarket channels to set up special "nutrition centers" on the pet food aisle. An executive at Science Diet concedes that the new competition from the grocery channel was inevitable. But Science Diet plans to stick with its current channels—which have been competing very well. In fact, Hill's is using the same approach for expanding distribution into 28 other countries. In pet stores across Japan, for example, Science Diet is attracting new customers with special displays featuring samples and free literature.[2]

CHANNEL SYSTEM MAY BE DIRECT OR INDIRECT

One of the most basic Place decisions producers must make is whether to handle the whole distribution themselves—or use wholesalers, retailers, and other specialists (see Exhibit 11–1). Middlemen, in turn, must select the producers they'll work with.

Why a firm might want to use direct distribution

Many firms prefer to distribute direct to the final customer or consumer. One reason is that they want complete control over the marketing job. They may think that they can serve target customers at a lower cost or do the work more effectively than middlemen. Further, working with independent middlemen with different objectives can be troublesome.

Some managers don't have a sensible reason to go direct—they just want to be in charge of a large organization. In any case, there often *are* great advantages in selling direct to the final user or consumer.

Direct contact with customers

If a firm is in direct contact with its customers, it is more aware of changes in customer attitudes. It is in a better position to adjust its marketing mix quickly because there is no need to convince other channel members to help. If a product needs an aggressive selling effort or special technical service, the marketing manager can ensure that the sales force receives the necessary training and motivation. In contrast, middlemen often carry products of several competing producers. So they aren't willing to give any one item the special emphasis its producer wants.

Suitable middlemen are not available

A firm may have to go direct if suitable middlemen are not available—or will not cooperate. This sometimes occurs with new products. Middlemen who have the best contacts with the target market may be hesitant to add unproven products, especially really new products that don't fit well with their current business. Many new products die because the producer can't find willing middlemen and doesn't have the financial resources to handle direct distribution.

In the United States, the Census Bureau publishes detailed data concerning wholesalers and retailers, including breakdowns by kind of business, product line, and geographic territory. Similar information is available for Canada and many other countries, including most of those in the European Union. This kind of data is valuable in strategy planning—especially to learn whether potential channel members are serving a target market. You can also learn what sales volume current middlemen are achieving.

Common with business customers and services

Many business products are sold direct-to-customer. Rolm, for example, sells its computerized voice mail systems direct. And Honda sells its motors direct to lawn mower producers. This is understandable since in business markets there are fewer transactions and orders are larger. In addition, customers may be concentrated in a small geographic area, making distribution easier.

Many service firms also use direct channels. If the service must be produced in the presence of customers, there may be little need for middlemen. An accounting firm like Arthur Andersen, for example, must deal directly with its customers. However, many firms that produce physical goods turn to middlemen specialists to help provide the services customers expect as part of the product. Maytag may hope that its authorized dealers don't get many repair calls, but the service is available when customers need it. Here the middleman produces the service.[3]

Some consumer products are sold direct

Of course, some consumer products are sold direct too. Tupperware, Avon cosmetics, Electrolux vacuum cleaners, Amway household products, and Fuller Brush products are examples. Most of these firms rely on direct selling, which involves personal sales contact between a representative of the company and an individual consumer. However, most of these "salespeople" are *not* company employees. Rather, they usually work as independent middlemen, and the companies that they sell for refer to them as dealers, distributors, agents, or some similar term. So, in a strict technical sense, this is not really direct producer-to-consumer distribution.[4]

Don't be confused by the term *direct marketing*

An increasing number of firms now rely on **direct marketing**—direct communication between a seller and an individual customer using a promotion method other than face-to-face personal selling. Sometimes direct marketing promotion is coupled with direct distribution from a producer to consumers. Park Seed Company, for example, sells the seeds it grows direct to consumers with a mail catalog. However, many firms that use direct marketing promotion distribute their products through middlemen. So the term *direct marketing* is primarily concerned with the Promotion area, not Place decisions. We'll talk about direct marketing promotion in more detail in Chapter 14.[5]

When indirect channels are best

Even if a producer wants to handle the whole distribution job, sometimes it's simply not possible. Customers often have established buying patterns. For example, Square D, a producer of electrical supplies, might want to sell directly to big electrical contractors. But if contractors like to make all of their purchases in one convenient stop—at a local electrical wholesaler—the only practical way to reach them is through a wholesaler.

Similarly, consumers are spread throughout many geographic areas and often prefer to shop for certain products at specific places. We saw this in the Goodyear case: some consumers see Sears as *the* place to shop for tires, so they'll only buy the brands that Sears carries. Similarly, a consumer may see a Walgreen drugstore as *the* place to shop for emergency items—because it's conveniently located in the neighborhood. Moreover, if retailers who serve target customers make most of their purchases from specific wholesalers, the producer may have to work with these wholesalers. This is one reason why most firms that produce consumer products use indirect channels (see Exhibit 2–9).[6]

Direct distribution usually requires a significant investment in facilities and people. A new company, one that has limited financial resources, or one that wants to retain flexibility, may want to avoid that investment by working with established middlemen. Middlemen may further reduce a producer's investment and need for working capital by buying the producer's output and carrying it in inventory until it's sold.

Some middlemen play a critical role by providing credit to customers at the end of the channel. This financing function may be very important to small business customers; it provides their working capital. Even if the producer could afford to provide credit, a middleman who knows local customers can help reduce credit risks.

As these examples suggest, there may be a number of very specific reasons why a producer might want to work with a specific wholesaler or retailer. However, the most important reason for using indirect channels of distribution is that middlemen intermediaries can often help producers serve customer needs better and at lower cost. Remember that we discussed this briefly in Chapter 1 (see Exhibit 1–3). Now we'll go into more detail so you'll be able to plan different kinds of distribution channels.

DISCREPANCIES AND SEPARATIONS REQUIRE CHANNEL SPECIALISTS

The assortment and quantity of products customers want may be different from the assortment and quantity of products companies produce. Producers are often located far from their customers and may not know how best to reach them. Customers in turn may not know about their choices. Specialists develop to adjust these discrepancies and separations.[7]

Middlemen supply needed information

Economists often assume that customers have "perfect information" about all producers—and that producers know which customers need what product, where, when, and at what price. But this assumption is rarely true. Specialists develop to help provide information to bring buyers and sellers together.

Bruno's, a large supermarket chain, accumulates products from many producers at its distribution center and then breaks bulk to provide the convenient assortments that consumers expect to find at individual Bruno's stores.

For example, most consumers don't know much about the wide variety of home and auto insurance policies available from many different insurance companies. A local independent insurance agent may help them decide which policy—and which insurance company—best fits their needs. In the same vein, a furniture retailer can help a customer find a producer who has a certain style chair with just the right combination of fabric and finish.

Middlemen who are close to their customers are often in a better position to anticipate customer needs and forecast demand more accurately. This information can help reduce inventory costs in the whole channel—and may help the producer smooth out production.

Most producers seek help from specialists when they first enter international markets. Specialists can provide crucial information about customer needs and insights into differences in the marketing environment.

Discrepancies of quantity and assortment

Discrepancy of quantity means the difference between the quantity of products it is economical for a producer to make and the quantity final users or consumers normally want. For example, most manufacturers of golf balls produce large quantities—perhaps 200,000 to 500,000 in a given time period. The average golfer, however, wants only a few balls at a time. Adjusting for this discrepancy usually requires middlemen—wholesalers and retailers.

Producers typically specialize by product—and therefore another discrepancy develops. **Discrepancy of assortment** means the difference between the lines a typical producer makes and the assortment final consumers or users want. Most golfers, for example, need more than golf balls. They want golf shoes, gloves, clubs, a bag, and—of course—a golf course to play on. And they usually don't want to shop for each item separately. So, again, there is a need for wholesalers and retailers to adjust these discrepancies.

In actual practice, bringing products to customers isn't as simple as the golf example. Specializing only in golfing products may not achieve all the economies possible in a channel of distribution. Retailers who specialize in sports products usually carry even wider assortments. And they buy from a variety of wholesalers who specialize by product line. Some of these wholesalers supply other wholesalers. These complications will be discussed later. The important thing to remember is that discrepancies in quantity and assortment cause distribution problems for producers—and explain why many specialists develop.

INTERMEDIARIES HELP SMALL PRODUCERS FIND BIG INTERNATIONAL MARKETS

Hamilton Manufacturing Corporation is a small firm that makes machines that exchange coins for paper currency. James Nesmith, the president of the company, wanted to break into international markets. He knew his company could develop bill changers for foreign money. Yet, after taking a course on international trade, he concluded that his company didn't have the people or expertise to target international markets with direct distribution. Instead, Nesmith developed a channel relationship with International Projects, Inc. (IPI), an export-management company in Toledo, Ohio, that serves as an international intermediary for a number of different producers.

IPI employs only six people, but it generates $8 million in annual sales for an assortment of products that range from pleasure boats and hospital supplies to air conditioner repair equipment and stationery.

IPI's president credits much of his company's growth to advances in communication technology—especially faxes and computers. This isn't unusual. Established trade intermediaries with large offices in major port cities are finding that their new competition is coming from hundreds of small firms like IPI. And there are now about 2,500 international intermediaries based in the U.S. These entrepreneurial middlemen with worldwide contacts are growing in popularity because they can help small manufacturers quickly build their international sales. However, trade intermediaries know that there is some risk of doing their job too well. For example, ITM Corporation, an intermediary, built a multimillion dollar international market for an orthopedic-products manufacturer. However, with that much volume the manufacturer decided it would be better to drop the middleman and sell direct.[8]

Channel specialists adjust discrepancies with regrouping activities

Regrouping activities adjust the quantities and/or assortments of products handled at each level in a channel of distribution.

There are four regrouping activities: accumulating, bulk-breaking, sorting, and assorting. When one or more of these activities is needed, a marketing specialist may develop to fill this need.

Adjusting quantity discrepancies by accumulating and bulk-breaking

Accumulating involves collecting products from many small producers. Much of the coffee that comes from Colombia is grown on small farms in the mountains. Accumulating the small crops into larger quantities is a way of getting the lowest transporting rate—and making it more convenient for distant food processing companies to buy and handle it. Accumulating is especially important in less-developed countries and in other situations, like agricultural markets, where there are many small producers.

Accumulating is also important with professional services because they often involve the combined work of a number of individuals, each of whom is a specialized producer. A hospital makes it easier for patients by accumulating the services of a number of health care specialists, many of whom may not actually work for the hospital.

Bulk-breaking involves dividing larger quantities into smaller quantities as products get closer to the final market. Sometimes this even starts at the producer's level. A golf ball producer may need 25 wholesalers to help sell its output. And the bulk-breaking may involve several levels of middlemen. Wholesalers may sell smaller quantities to other wholesalers—or directly to retailers. Retailers continue breaking bulk as they sell individual items to their customers.

Adjusting assortment discrepancies by sorting and assorting

Different types of specialists adjust assortment discrepancies. They perform two types of regrouping activities: sorting and assorting.

Sorting means separating products into grades and qualities desired by different target markets. For example, an investment firm might offer its customers a chance to buy shares in a mutual fund made up only of stocks for certain types of companies—high-growth firms, ones that pay regular dividends, or ones that have good environmental track records. Similarly, a wholesaler that specializes in serving convenience stores may focus on smaller packages of frequently used products, whereas a wholesaler working with restaurants and hotels might handle only very large institutional sizes.

Sorting is also a very important process for raw materials. Nature produces what it will—and then the products must be sorted to meet the needs of different target markets.

Assorting means putting together a variety of products to give a target market what it wants. This usually is done by those closest to the final consumer or user—retailers or wholesalers who try to supply a wide assortment of products for the convenience of their customers. A grocery store is a good example. But some assortments involve very different products. A wholesaler selling Yazoo tractors and mowers to golf courses might also carry Pennington grass seed, Scott fertilizer, and even golf ball washers or irrigation systems—for its customers' convenience.

Watch for changes

Sometimes these discrepancies are adjusted badly—especially when consumer wants and attitudes shift rapidly. When videotapes became popular, an opportunity developed for a new specialist. Large numbers of consumers were suddenly interested in having an assortment of movies and other tapes available—in one convenient place. Electronics stores focused only on selling the tape players and blank tapes. Videotape rental stores, like Blockbuster, emerged to meet the new need. However, movie studios lowered the prices for tapes—so more customers are buying rather than renting them. Because of that change, many types of retail stores now sell videos.[9]

Specialists should develop to adjust discrepancies *if they must be adjusted*. But there is no point in having middlemen just because that's the way it's always been done. Sometimes a breakthrough opportunity can come from finding a better way to reduce discrepancies—perhaps eliminating some steps in the channel. For example, Dell Computer in Austin, Texas, found that it could sell computers direct to customers—at very low prices—by advertising in computer magazines and taking orders by mail or phone. With such an approach, Dell not only bypassed retail stores and the wholesalers who served them, it also avoided the expense of a large field sales force. This cost advantage let Dell offer low prices and a marketing mix that appealed to some target segments.[10]

CHANNEL RELATIONSHIP MUST BE MANAGED

Marketing manager must choose type of channel relationship

Middlemen specialists can help make a channel more efficient. But there may be problems getting the different firms in a channel to work together well. How well they work together depends on the type of relationship they have. This should be carefully considered since marketing managers usually have choices about what type of channel system to join—or develop.

Glen Raven Mills, the company that produces Sunbrella brand acrylic fabrics, gets cooperation from many independent wholesale distributors and their producer-customers because it develops marketing strategies that help the whole channel compete more effectively.

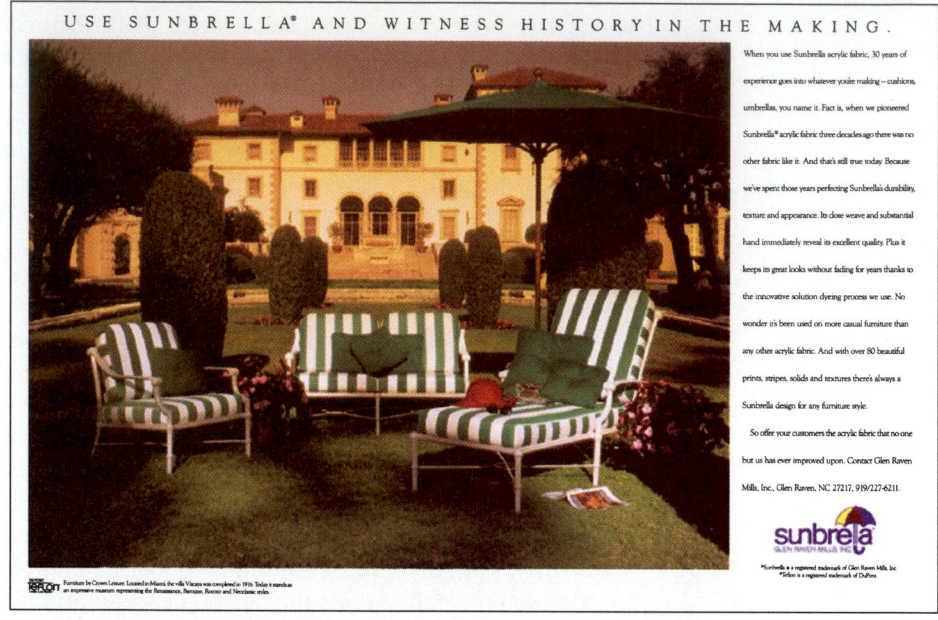

The whole channel should have a product-market commitment

Ideally, all of the members of a channel system should have a shared *product-market commitment*—with all members focusing on the same target market at the end of the channel and sharing the various marketing functions in appropriate ways. When members of a channel do this, they are better able to compete effectively for the customer's business.

This simple idea is very important. Unfortunately, many marketing managers overlook it because it's not the way their firms have traditionally handled relationships with others in the channel.

Traditional channel systems involve weak relationships

In **traditional channel systems**, the various channel members make little or no effort to cooperate with each other. They buy and sell from each other—and that's the extent of their relationship. Each channel member does only what it considers to be in its own best interest; it doesn't worry much about the effect of its policies on other members of the channel. This is shortsighted, but it's easy to see how it can happen. The objectives of the various channel members may be different. For example, General Electric wants a wholesaler of electrical building supplies to sell GE products. But an independent wholesaler who carries an assortment of products from different producers may not care whose products get sold. The wholesaler just wants happy customers and a good profit margin.

Conflict gets in the way

Specialization has the potential to make a channel more efficient—but not if the specialists are so independent that the channel doesn't work smoothly. Because members of traditional channel systems often have different objectives—and different ideas about how things should be done—conflict is common.

There are two basic types of conflict in channels of distribution. Vertical conflicts occur between firms at different levels of the channel of distribution. For example, a producer and a retailer may disagree about how much shelf space or promotion effort the retailer should give the producer's product. Or conflict may arise if a producer that wants to reduce its excess inventory pushes a wholesaler to carry more inventory than the wholesaler really needs.

Recently there's been vertical conflict between big recording companies—like Sony, Warner Music, and Capitol-EMI—and their retail outlets that want to sell used CDs as well as new releases. Retailers have found that consumers like the low cost of used CDs, but the recording companies argue that the used CDs eat into their sales and deprive artists of royalties. When Wherehouse Entertainment (one of the nation's largest retail music chains) started to sell used CDs—at about half the price of new ones—several recording companies said that they would halt cooperative advertising payments to any retailer that sold used CDs. Garth Brooks, who was the best-selling artist at the time, underscored the conflict—and the recording companies' point of view—when he announced that he would not release his new CDs to any stores that were selling used CDs.

Horizontal conflicts occur between firms at the same level in the channel of distribution. For example, a furniture store that keeps a complete line of furniture on display isn't happy to find out that a store down the street is offering customers lower prices on special orders of the same items. The discounter is getting a free ride from the competing store's investment in inventory. And nothing gets an independent retailer more charged up than finding out that a chain store is selling some product for less than the wholesale price the independent pays.

Traditional channel systems are still typical—and very important—in some industries. The members of these channels have their independence, but they may pay for it too. As we will see, such channels are declining in importance—with good reason.[11]

Cooperative relationships share common objectives

Potential channel conflicts should be anticipated and, if possible, resolved. Usually the best way to do that is to get everyone in the channel working together in a cooperative relationship that is focused on the same basic objective—satisfying the customer at the end of the channel. This leads us away from traditional channels to cooperative channel relationships and the channel captain concept.

Channel captain can guide channel relationships

Each channel system should act as a unit, where each member of the channel collaborates to serve customers at the end of the channel. In this view, cooperation is everyone's responsibility. However, some firms are in a better position to take the lead in the relationship and in coordinating the whole channel effort. This situation calls for a **channel captain**—a manager who helps direct the activities of a whole channel and tries to avoid—or solve—channel conflicts.

The concept of a single channel captain is logical. But some channels—including most traditional ones—don't have a recognized captain. The various firms don't act as a system. The reason may be lack of leadership or the fact that members of the system don't understand their interrelationship. Many managers—more concerned with individual firms immediately above and below them—seem unaware that they are part of a channel.

But, like it or not, firms are interrelated—even if poorly—by their policies. So it makes sense to try to avoid channel conflicts by planning for channel relations. The channel captain arranges for the necessary functions to be performed in the most effective way.

EXHIBIT 11–2   How Channel Functions May Be Shifted and Shared in Different Channel Systems

A. How strategy decisions are handled in a producer-led channel

Producer's part of the job — Product, Price

Middleman's part of the job — Place, Promotion

Customers

B. How strategy decisions are handled in a retailer-led channel

Producer's part of the job — Product, Price

Middleman's part of the job — Place, Promotion

Customers

Some producers lead their channels

In the United States, producers frequently take the lead in channel relations. Middlemen often wait to see what the producer intends to do—and wants them to do. After marketing managers for L'eggs set Price, Promotion, and Place policies, wholesalers and retailers decide whether their roles will be profitable—and whether they want to join in the channel effort.

Exhibit 11–2A shows this type of producer-led channel system. Here the producer has selected the target market and developed the Product, set the Price structure, done some consumer and channel Promotion, and developed the Place setup. Middlemen are then expected to finish the Promotion job in their respective places. Of course, in a retailer-dominated channel system, the marketing jobs would be handled in a different way.

Some middlemen are channel captains

Some large or well-located wholesalers or retailers do take the lead. These middlemen analyze the types of products their customers want and then seek out producers—perhaps small ones—who can provide these products at reasonable prices. This is becoming more common in the United States—and it is already typical in many foreign markets. In Japan, for example, very large wholesalers (trading companies) are often the channel captains.

Channel captains who are middlemen often develop their own dealer brands. Large retailers like Sears or Kmart—and wholesalers like Ace Hardware—in effect act like producers. They specify the whole marketing mix for a product and merely delegate production to a factory. Exhibit 11–2B shows how marketing strategy might be handled in this sort of retailer-led channel system.

Some strong middlemen use their power to control channel relationships. Wal-Mart, the largest retail chain, is constantly looking for ways to cut its own costs—and sometimes that means cutting costs in the channel. Buyers for Wal-Mart look at the value added by a wholesaler. If they think Wal-Mart can be more efficient without the wholesaler, then they tell the producer that the chain will only buy direct—usually at a lower price than was paid to the wholesaler.

The growing number of retailer-led channel systems is prompting growth of private label dealer brands in a wide variety of product categories.

Middlemen are closer to the final user or consumer and are in an ideal position to assume the channel captain role. Middlemen—especially large retailers—may even dominate the marketing systems of the future.[12]

Many marketing managers accept the view that a coordinated channel system can help everyone in the channel. These managers are moving their firms away from traditional channel systems and instead developing or joining vertical market systems.

VERTICAL MARKETING SYSTEMS FOCUS ON FINAL CUSTOMERS

In contrast to traditional channel systems are **vertical marketing systems**—channel systems in which the whole channel focuses on the same target market at the end of the channel. Such systems make sense—and are growing—because if the final customer doesn't buy the product, the whole channel suffers. There are three types of vertical marketing systems—corporate, administered, and contractual. Exhibit 11–3 summarizes some characteristics of these systems and compares them with traditional systems.

Corporate channel systems shorten channels

Some corporations develop their own vertical marketing systems by internal expansion and/or by buying other firms. With **corporate channel systems**—corporate ownership all along the channel—we might say the firm is going "direct." But actually the firm may be handling manufacturing, wholesaling, *and* retailing—so it's more accurate to think of the firm as a vertical marketing system.

Corporate channel systems develop by vertical integration

Corporate channel systems often develop by **vertical integration**—acquiring firms at different levels of channel activity. Bridgestone, for example, has rubber

EXHIBIT 11–3   Characteristics of Traditional and Vertical Marketing Systems

Characteristics	Type of channel			
	Traditional	Vertical marketing systems		
		Administered	Contractual	Corporate
Amount of cooperation	Little or none	Some to good	Fairly good to good	Complete
Control maintained by	None	Economic power and leadership	Contracts	Ownership by one company
Examples	Typical channel of "independents"	General Electric, Miller Beer, O.M. Scott & Sons (lawn products)	McDonald's, Holiday Inn, IGA, Ace Hardware, Super Valu, Coca-Cola, Chevrolet	Florsheim Shoes, Sherwin-Williams

plantations in Liberia, tire plants in Ohio, and wholesale and retail outlets all over the world. Sherwin-Williams produces paint, but it also operates 2,000 retail outlets.

Corporate channel systems are not always started by producers. A retailer might integrate into wholesaling—and perhaps even manufacturing. For example, A&P owns fish-canning plants, Genesco and Florsheim make their own shoes, and J.C. Penney controls textile plants.

Vertical integration has many possible advantages—stability of operations, assurance of materials and supplies, better control of distribution, better quality control, larger research facilities, greater buying power, and lower executive overhead. The economies of vertical integration benefit consumers through lower prices and better products.

Provided that the discrepancies of quantity and assortment are not too great at each level in a channel—that is, that the firms fit together well—vertical integration can be extremely efficient and profitable.

Administered and contractual systems may work well

Firms can often gain the advantages of vertical integration without building an expensive corporate channel. A firm can develop administered or contractual channel systems instead. In **administered channel systems,** the channel members informally agree to cooperate with each other. They can agree to routinize ordering, standardize accounting, and coordinate promotion efforts. In **contractual channel systems,** the channel members agree by contract to cooperate with each other. With both of these systems, the members achieve some of the advantages of corporate integration while retaining some of the flexibility of a traditional channel system.

An appliance producer, for example, developed an informal arrangement with the independent wholesalers in its administered channel system. It agrees to keep production and inventory levels in the system balanced—using sales data from the wholesalers. Every week, its managers do a thorough analysis of up to 130,000

Most pet food companies focus on distribution through grocery stores, but Science Diet brand premium pet foods reach consumers in the U.S. and Japan through a different channel—veterinary offices and pet stores. Because Science Diet has developed cooperative relationships with other members of this channel, Science Diet products often get special promotion support at the point of purchase.

major appliances located in the many warehouses operated by its 87 wholesalers. Because of this analysis, both the producer and the wholesalers can be sure that they have enough inventory but not the expense of too much. And the producer has better information to plan its manufacturing and marketing efforts.

Middlemen in the grocery, hardware, and drug industries develop and coordinate similar systems. Computerized checkout systems track sales. The information is sent to the wholesaler's computer, which enters orders automatically when needed. This reduces buying and selling costs, inventory investment, and customer frustration with out-of-stock items throughout the channel.

Vertical marketing systems—new wave in the marketplace

Smoothly operating channel systems are more efficient and successful. In the consumer products field, corporate chains that are at least partially vertically integrated account for about 25 percent of total retail sales. Other vertical systems account for an additional 37.5 percent. Thus, vertical systems in the consumer products area have a healthy majority of retail sales and should continue to increase their share in the future. Vertical marketing systems are becoming the major competitive units in the U.S. distribution system—and they are growing rapidly in other parts of the world as well.[13]

THE BEST CHANNEL SYSTEM SHOULD ACHIEVE IDEAL MARKET EXPOSURE

You may think that all marketing managers want their products to have maximum exposure to potential customers. This isn't true. Some product classes require much less market exposure than others. **Ideal market exposure** makes a product available widely enough to satisfy target customers' needs but not exceed them. Too much exposure only increases the total cost of marketing.

Libbey seeks intensive distribution for its casual glassware, but Oneida uses exclusive distribution for its upscale crystal.

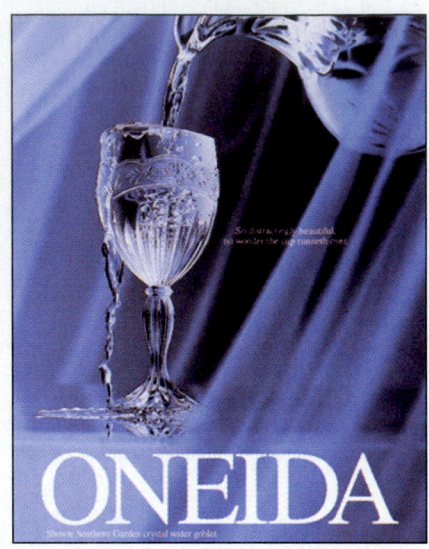

Ideal exposure may be intensive, selective, or exclusive

Intensive distribution is selling a product through all responsible and suitable wholesalers or retailers who will stock and/or sell the product. **Selective distribution** is selling through only those middlemen who will give the product special attention. **Exclusive distribution** is selling through only one middleman in a particular geographic area. As we move from intensive to exclusive distribution, we give up exposure in return for some other advantage—including, but not limited to, lower cost.

In practice, this means that Wrigley's chewing gum is handled—through intensive distribution—by about a million U.S. outlets. Rolls Royces are handled—through exclusive distribution—by only a limited number of middlemen across the country.

Intensive distribution—sell it where they buy it

Intensive distribution is commonly needed for convenience products and business supplies—such as pencils, paper clips, and typing paper—used by all plants and offices. Customers want such products nearby.

The seller's intent is important here. Intensive distribution refers to the *desire* to sell through *all* responsible and suitable outlets. What this means depends on customer habits and preferences. If target customers normally buy a certain product at a certain type of outlet, ideally, you would specify this type of outlet in your Place policies. If customers prefer to buy Sharp portable TVs only at TV stores, you would try to sell all TV stores to achieve intensive distribution. Today, however, many customers buy small portable TVs at a variety of convenient outlets—including Eckerd drugstores, a local Kmart, or over the phone from the Sharper Image catalog. This means that an intensive distribution policy requires use of all these outlets—and more than one channel—to reach one target market.

Selective distribution—sell it where it sells best

Selective distribution covers the broad area of market exposure between intensive and exclusive distribution. It may be suitable for all categories of products. Only the better middlemen are used here. Companies usually use selective distribution to gain some of the advantages of exclusive distribution—while still achieving fairly widespread market coverage.

A selective policy might be used to avoid selling to wholesalers or retailers who (1) have a poor credit rating, (2) have a reputation for making too many returns or requesting too much service, (3) place orders that are too small to justify making calls or providing service, or (4) are not in a position to do a satisfactory job.

Selective distribution is becoming more popular than intensive distribution as firms see that they don't need 100 percent coverage of a market to justify or support national advertising. Often the majority of sales come from relatively few customers—and the others buy too little compared to the cost of working with them. That is, they are unprofitable to serve. This is called the 80/20 rule—80 percent of a company's sales often come from only 20 percent of its customers *until it becomes more selective in choosing customers.*

Esprit—a producer of colorful, trendy clothing—was selling through about 4,000 department stores and specialty shops nationwide. But Esprit found that about half of the stores generated most of the sales. Sales analysis also showed that sales in Esprit's own stores were about 400 percent better than sales in other sales outlets. As a result, Esprit cut back to about 2,000 outlets and opened more of its own stores—and profits increased.[14]

Selective distribution can produce greater profits not only for the producer but for all channel members—because of the closer cooperation among them. Transactions become more routine, requiring less negotiation in the buying and selling process. Wholesalers and retailers are more willing to promote products aggressively if they know they're going to obtain the majority of sales through their own efforts. They may carry more stock and wider lines, do more promotion, and provide more service—all of which lead to more sales.

Selective distribution makes sense for shopping and specialty products and for those business products that need special efforts from channel members. It reduces competition between different channels and gives each middleman a greater opportunity for profit.

When producers use selective distribution, fewer sales contacts have to be made—and fewer wholesalers are needed. A producer may be able to contact selected retailers directly. Hanes sells men's underwear this way.

In the early part of the life cycle of a new unsought good, a producer's marketing manager may have to use selective distribution to encourage enough middlemen to handle the product. The manager wants to get the product out of the unsought category as soon as possible—but can't if it lacks distribution. Well-known middlemen may have the power to get such a product introduced but sometimes on their own terms—which often include limiting the number of competing wholesalers and retailers. The producer may be happy with such an arrangement at first but dislike it later when more retailers want to carry the product.

Exclusive distribution sometimes makes sense

Exclusive distribution is just an extreme case of selective distribution—the firm selects only one middleman in each geographic area. Besides the various advantages of selective distribution, producers may want to use exclusive distribution to help control prices and the service offered in a channel.

Retailers of shopping products and specialty products often try to get exclusive distribution rights in their territories. Fast-food franchises often have exclusive distribution—and that's one reason they're popular. Owners of

McDonald's franchises willingly pay a share of sales and follow McDonald's strategy to keep the exclusive right to a market.

Unlike selective distribution, exclusive distribution usually involves a verbal or written agreement stating that channel members will buy all or most of a given product from the seller. In return, these middlemen are granted the exclusive rights to that product in their territories. Some middlemen are so anxious to get a producer's exclusive franchise that they will do practically anything to satisfy the producer's demands. Marketing managers for Acura, the luxury car division of Honda Motor Co., decided to set up new channels of distribution to introduce the car to U.S. consumers. In return for the right to sell the car, each new dealer agreed to focus exclusively on Acura and its target market. Acura also required its dealers to build expensive new showrooms. At first, the strategy seemed to be a big success. Acura lured buyers away from competitors and surveys showed that Acura owners were more satisfied than buyers of other luxury cars. However, after three years, nearly half of Acura's dealers were still losing money or making only a small profit. Although sales were steady, they often didn't offset the big investment in new facilities. Most other car dealers were earning profits from more than one line of cars. Further, the new and reliable Acuras simply didn't keep the service department busy—and service usually produces a large share of a car dealer's profit. Acura realized that long-run success would depend on having strong channel partners. To help its troubled dealers pull in more customers, Acura increased its advertising and developed new models. And Acura worked with dealers to identify ways to earn more profit from service and used cars.[15]

Is limiting market exposure legal?

Exclusive distribution is a vague area in U.S. antimonopoly laws. Courts currently focus on whether an exclusive distribution arrangement hurts competition.

Horizontal arrangements among competitors are illegal

Horizontal arrangements—among *competing* retailers, wholesalers, or producers—to limit sales by customer or territory have consistently been ruled illegal by the U.S. Supreme Court. Courts consider such arrangements obvious collusion that reduces competition and harms customers.

Vertical arrangements may or may not be legal

The legality of vertical arrangements—between producers and middlemen—is not as clear-cut. A 1977 Supreme Court decision (involving Sylvania and the distribution of TV sets) reversed an earlier ruling that it was always illegal to set up vertical relationships limiting territories or customers. Now courts can weigh the possible good effects against the possible restrictions on competition. They look at competition between whole channels—rather than just focusing on competition at one level of distribution.

With a very small share of the overall market for television sets, Sylvania couldn't compete on price with bigger producers who sold through self-service stores. So Sylvania decided to target customers who saw TVs as a heterogeneous shopping product. These people preferred stores that specialized in TVs, had a good selection on hand, and provided advice before the purchase—and repair service afterwards. Such retailers faced added costs to provide these services. They didn't want customers to inspect their TV sets, get information at their stores, and then be able to buy the same sets somewhere else—at a lower price. In other words, they didn't want other retailers to get a free ride on their investment in inventory and higher-paid sales help. Even though this approach tends to reduce competition at the retail level, Sylvania argued that it needed such exclusive sales territories to compete with other producers. The Supreme Court basically agreed.

The Sylvania decision does *not* mean that all vertical arrangements are legal. Rather, it says that a firm has to be able to legally justify any exclusive arrangements.[16]

Caution is suggested

In spite of the 1977 Supreme Court ruling, firms should be extremely cautious about entering into *any* exclusive distribution arrangement. The antimonopoly rules still apply. The courts can force a change in expensively developed relationships. And—even worse—the courts can award triple damages if they rule that competition has been hurt.

The same cautions apply to selective distribution. Here, however, less formal arrangements are typical—and the possible impact on competition is more remote. It is now more acceptable to carefully select channel members when building a channel system. Refusing to sell to some middlemen, however, should be part of a logical plan with long-term benefits to consumers.

CHANNEL SYSTEMS CAN BE COMPLEX

Trying to achieve the desired degree of market exposure can lead to complex channels of distribution. Firms may need different channels to reach different segments of a broad product-market—or to be sure they reach each segment. Sometimes this results in competition between different channels.

Exhibit 11–4 shows the many channels used by a company that produces roofing shingles. It also shows (roughly) what percent of the sales go to different channel members. Shingles are both consumer products (sold to do-it-yourselfers) and business products (sold to building contractors and roofing contractors). This helps explain why some channels develop. But note that the shingles go through different wholesalers and retailers—independent and chain lumberyards, hardware stores, and mass-merchandisers. This can cause problems because different wholesalers and retailers want different markups. It also increases competition—including price competition. And the competition among different middlemen may result in conflicts between the middlemen and the producer.

Dual distribution systems may be needed

Dual distribution occurs when a producer uses several competing channels to reach the same target market—perhaps using several middlemen in addition to selling directly. Dual distribution is becoming more common. Big retail chains want to deal directly with producers. They want large quantities—and low prices. The producer sells directly to retail chains and relies on wholesalers to sell to smaller accounts. Some established middlemen resent this because they don't appreciate *any* competition—especially price competition set up by their own suppliers.

Other times, producers are forced to use dual distribution because their present channels are doing a poor job or aren't reaching some potential customers. For example, Reebok International had been relying on local sporting goods stores to sell its shoes to high school and college athletic teams. But Reebok wasn't getting much of the business. When it set up its own team-sales department to sell direct to the schools, it got a 30,000 unit increase in sales. Of course, some of the stores weren't happy about their supplier also selling to their potential customers. However, they did get the message that Reebok wanted *someone* to reach that target market.[17]

EXHIBIT 11–4   Roofing Shingles Are Sold through Many Kinds of Wholesalers and Retailers

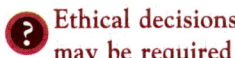

A shared product-market commitment guides cooperative relationships among channel members as long as the channel system is competitive. However, if customers' place requirements change, the current channel system may not be effective. The changes required to serve customer needs may hurt one or more members of the channel. The most difficult ethical dilemmas in the channels area arise in situations like this—because not everyone can win.

For example, wholesalers and the independent retailers that they serve in a channel of distribution may trust a producer channel captain to develop marketing strategies that will work for the whole channel. However, the producer may conclude that everyone in the channel will ultimately fail if it continues exclusive distribution. It might decide that consumers—and its own business—are best served by a change (say, dropping current middlemen and selling direct to big retail chains). A move of this sort—if implemented immediately—may not give current middlemen-partners a chance to make adjustments of their own. The more dependent they are on the producer, the more severe the impact is likely to be. It's not easy to determine the best or most ethical solution in these situations. However, marketing managers must think carefully about the implications of strategy changes in the Place area—because they can have very severe consequences for other channel members. In channels, as in any business dealing, relationships of trust must be treated with care.[18]

Ethical decisions may be required

Recognizing the growing
influence of national retail
chains that sell building
products to "do-it-yourself"
consumers, Owens-Corning
set up a new distribution
service organization that
seeks to strengthen
relationships in this channel
by providing the best
distribution customer service
and support in the industry.
To help these channel
partners compete better with
other channels, Owens-
Corning also introduced
PINKPLUS—insulation
encased in a special wrapper
that makes it easier for
do-it-yourself customers to
install.

**Reverse channels
should be planned**

Most firms focus on getting products to their customers. But some marketing managers must also plan for **reverse channels**—channels used to retrieve products that customers no longer want. The need for reverse channels may arise in a variety of different situations. Toy companies, automobile firms, drug companies, and others sometimes have to recall products because of safety problems. A producer that makes an error in completing an order may have to take returns from middlemen or other business customers. If a Panasonic computer monitor breaks while it's still under warranty, someone needs to get it to the authorized repair center. Soft-drink companies may need to recycle empty bottles. And, of course, at some point or other, most consumers buy something in error and want to return it.

When marketing managers don't plan for reverse channels, the firm's customers may be left to solve "their" problem. That usually doesn't make sense. So a complete plan for Place may need to consider an efficient way to return products—with policies that different channel members agree on. It may also require specialists who were not involved in getting the product to the consumer. But if that's what it takes to satisfy customers, it should be part of marketing strategy planning.[19]

CONCLUSION

In this chapter, we discussed the role of Place and noted that Place decisions are especially important because they may be difficult and expensive to change.

Marketing specialists—and channel systems—develop to adjust discrepancies of quantity and assortment. Their regrouping activities are basic in any economic system. And adjusting discrepancies provides opportunities for creative marketers.

Channel planning requires firms to decide on the degree of market exposure they want. The ideal level of exposure may be intensive, selective, or exclusive. They also need to consider the legality of limiting market exposure to avoid having to undo an expensively developed channel system or face steep fines.

The importance of planning channel systems was discussed—along with the role of a channel captain. We stressed that channel systems compete with each other—and that vertical marketing systems seem to be winning.

In this broader context, the "battle of the brands" is only a skirmish in the battle between various channel systems. And we emphasized that producers aren't necessarily the channel captains. Often middlemen control or even dominate channels of distribution.

QUESTIONS AND PROBLEMS

1. Review the Goodyear case at the beginning of the chapter and discuss how Goodyear's Place decisions relate to the product class concept. Explain your thinking.

2. Give two examples of service firms that work with other channel specialists to sell their products to final consumers. What marketing functions is the specialist providing in each case?

3. Discuss some reasons why a firm that produces installations might use direct distribution in its domestic market but use middlemen to reach overseas customers.

4. Explain discrepancies of quantity and assortment using the clothing business as an example. How does the application of these concepts change when selling steel to the automobile industry? What impact does this have on the number and kinds of marketing specialists required?

5. Explain the four regrouping activities with an example from the building supply industry (nails, paint, flooring, plumbing fixtures, etc.). Do you think that many specialists develop in this industry, or do producers handle the job themselves? What kinds of marketing channels would you expect to find in this industry, and what functions would various channel members provide?

6. Insurance agents are middlemen who help other members of the channel by providing information and handling the selling function. Does it make sense for an insurance agent to specialize and work exclusively with one insurance provider? Why or why not?

7. Discuss the Place objectives and distribution arrangements that are appropriate for the following products (indicate any special assumptions you have to make to obtain an answer):

   a. A postal scale for products weighing up to two pounds.
   b. Children's toys: (1) radio-controlled model airplanes costing $80 or more, (2) small rubber balls.
   c. Heavy-duty, rechargeable, battery-powered nut tighteners for factory production lines.
   d. Fiberglass fabric used in making roofing shingles.

8. Give an example of a producer that uses two or more different channels of distribution. Briefly discuss what problems this might cause.

9. Explain how a channel captain can help traditional independent firms compete with a corporate (integrated) channel system.

10. Find an example of vertical integration within your city. Are there any particular advantages to this vertical integration? If so, what are they? If there are no such advantages, how do you explain the integration?

11. What would happen if retailer-organized channels (either formally integrated or administered) dominated consumer product marketing?

12. How does the nature of the product relate to the degree of market exposure desired?

13. Why would middlemen want to be exclusive distributors for a product? Why would producers want exclusive distribution? Would middlemen be equally anxious to get exclusive distribution for any type of product? Why or why not? Explain with reference to the following products: candy bars, batteries, golf clubs, golf balls, steak knives, televisions, and industrial woodworking machinery.

14. Explain the present legal status of exclusive distribution. Describe a situation where exclu-

sive distribution is almost sure to be legal. Describe the nature and size of competitors and the industry, as well as the nature of the exclusive arrangement. Would this exclusive arrangement be of any value to the producer or middleman?

15. Discuss the promotion a new grocery products producer would need in order to develop appropriate channels and move products through those channels. Would the nature of this job change for a new producer of dresses? How about for a new, small producer of installations?

SUGGESTED CASES

COMPUTER-AIDED PROBLEM

11. **Intensive versus Selective Distribution**

Hydropump, Inc., produces and sells high-quality pumps to business customers. Its marketing research shows a growing market for a similar type of pump aimed at final consumers—for use with Jacuzzi-style tubs in home remodeling jobs. Hydropump will have to develop new channels of distribution to reach this target market because most consumers rely on a retailer for advice about the combination of tub, pump, heater, and related plumbing fixtures they need. Hydropump's marketing manager, Robert Black, is trying to decide between intensive and selective distribution. With intensive distribution, he would try to sell through all the plumbing supply, bathroom fixture, and hot-tub retailers who will carry the pump. He estimates that about 5,600 suitable retailers would be willing to carry a new pump. With selective distribution, he would focus on about 280 of the best hot-tub dealers (two or three in the hundred largest metropolitan areas).

Intensive distribution would require Hydropump to do more mass selling—primarily advertising in home renovation magazines—to help stimulate consumer familiarity with the brand and convince retailers that Hydropump equipment will sell. The price to the retailer might have to be lower too (to permit a bigger markup) so they will be motivated to sell Hydropump rather than some other brand offering a smaller markup.

With intensive distribution, each Hydropump sales rep could probably handle about 300 retailers effectively. With selective distribution, each sales rep could handle

only about 70 retailers because more merchandising help would be necessary. Managing the smaller sales force and fewer retailers—with the selective approach—would require less manager overhead cost.

Going to all suitable and available retailers would make the pump available through about 20 times as many retailers and have the potential of reaching more customers. However, many customers shop at more than one retailer before making a final choice—so selective distribution would reach almost as many potential customers. Further, if Hydropump is using selective distribution, it would get more in-store sales attention for its pump—and a larger share of pump purchases—at each retailer.

Black has decided to use a spreadsheet to analyze the benefits and costs of intensive versus selective distribution.

a. *Based on the initial spreadsheet, which approach seems to be the most sensible for Hydropump? Why?*

b. *A consultant points out that even selective distribution needs national promotion. If Black has to increase advertising and spend a total of $100,000 on mass selling to be able to recruit the retailers he wants for selective distribution, would selective or intensive distribution be more profitable?*

c. *With intensive distribution, how large a share (percent) of the retailers' total unit sales would Hydropump have to capture to sell enough pumps to earn $200,000 profit?*

For additional questions related to this problem, see Exercise 11–3 in the *Learning Aid for Use with Basic Marketing*, 12th edition.

12

Logistics and Distribution Customer Service

When You Finish This Chapter, You Should

1. Understand why physical distribution (logistics) is such an important part of Place *and* marketing strategy planning.

2. Understand why the physical distribution customer service level is a key marketing strategy variable.

3. Understand the physical distribution concept and why it requires coordination of storing, transporting, and related activities.

4. Know about the advantages and disadvantages of the various transporting methods.

5. Know how inventory decisions and storing affect marketing strategy.

6. Understand the distribution center concept.

7. See how computers help improve coordination of physical distribution in channel systems.

8. Understand the important new terms (shown in red).

If you want a Coca-Cola, there's usually one close by—no matter where you might be in the world. And that's no accident. The top marketing executive for the best-known brand name in the world states the objective simply: "To make Coca-Cola available within arm's reach of desire."

In order to meet that objective, Coke works with many and various channels of distribution. But that is merely the start. Think about what it takes for a bottle, can, or cup of Coke to be there whenever you're ready. In warehouses and distribution centers, on trucks, and at retail outlets, Coke handles, stores, and transports over 200 billion servings of soft drink a year. Getting all of that product to consumers could be a logistical nightmare, but Coke does it effectively and at a low cost. As a point of comparison: A can of Coke at the store costs about the same as it costs you to have the post office deliver a letter.

Fast information about what the market needs helps keep Coke's distribution on target. In the United States, computer systems show Coke managers exactly what's selling in each market; that allows Coke to plan inventories and deliveries. Coke also operates a 24-hour-a-day communications center to respond to the 2 million requests it gets from channel members each year. Orders are processed instantly—so sales to consumers at the end of the channel aren't lost because of stock-outs. And Coke products move efficiently through the channel. In Cincinnati, for example, Coke has the beverage industry's first fully automated distribution center. Forklifts were replaced with automatically guided vehicles which speed up the product flow and reduce labor costs.

Coke's strategies in international markets rely on many of the ideas that have worked very well in the United States. But the stage of market development varies in different countries, so Coke's emphasis varies as well. To increase sales in France, for example, Coke must first make more product available at retail stores; so Coke is installing thousands of soft drink coolers in French supermarkets. In Great Britain, Coke wants to have more inventory even closer to the point of consumption—in consumers' homes. So Coke is urging retailers to carry multipacks and larger packages. In Japan, by contrast, single-unit vending machine sales are very important—so Coke uses a small army of truck drivers to constantly restock its 750,000 vending machines, more per capita than anywhere else in the world. In less-developed areas, the Place system is not always so sophisticated. In the Philippines, for example, it's difficult for delivery trucks to reach some small shops in crowded areas. Instead, riders on bicycles equipped with sidecars make deliveries.

Coke is also working to increase fountain drink sales in international markets. As part of that effort, Coke equips restaurants and food outlets with Coke dispensers. Once a Coke dispenser is installed, the retailer usually doesn't have room for a competitor's dispenser. And when a consumer wants a fountain drink, Coke isn't just "the real thing," it's the only thing. That's why Coke has been installing 1,500

fountain dispensers a year in Taiwan—and why its fountain drink sales there are growing 60 percent a year.

Some people think Pepsi is beating Coke in the "cola wars" because Pepsi's ads get so much attention. But as this case suggests, who wins the competition will depend on whole marketing strategies—including Place—not just promotion.[1]

PHYSICAL DISTRIBUTION GETS IT TO CUSTOMERS

Choosing the right channel of distribution is crucial in getting products to the target market's Place. But as the Coke case shows, that alone is usually not enough to ensure that products are available at the right time and in the right quantities. Whenever the product includes a physical good, Place requires physical distribution (PD) decisions. **Physical distribution (PD)** is the transporting and storing of goods to match target customers' needs with a firm's marketing mix—both within individual firms and along a channel of distribution. **Logistics** is another common name for physical distribution.

PD provides time and place utility and makes possession utility possible. A marketing manager may have to make many decisions to ensure that the physical distribution system provides utility—and meets customers' needs with an acceptable service level and cost.

PD costs are very important to both firms and consumers. PD costs vary from firm to firm and, from a macro-marketing perspective, from country to country. However, for many physical goods, firms spend half or more of their total marketing dollars on physical distribution activities. The total amount of money involved is so large that even small improvements in this area can have a big effect on a whole macro-marketing system—and consumers' quality of life. And there's room for improvement. For example, many supermarket chains and the producers that supply them are collaborating to work toward a system, called Efficient Consumer Response (ECR), that may ultimately cut grocers' costs—and prices—by more than 11 percent. That would translate to savings of $30 *billion* a year for U.S. consumers! The basic idea of ECR involves paperless, computerized links between grocers and their suppliers, which would in turn lead to more effective merchandise assortments and eventually a continuous replenishment of shelves based on what actually sold each day. Obviously, this kind of innovation doesn't happen overnight, but you can see that more effective approaches in the distribution area have the potential to save firms—and their customers— massive amounts of money.[2]

PHYSICAL DISTRIBUTION CUSTOMER SERVICE

From the beginning, we've emphasized that marketing strategy planning is based on meeting customers' needs. Planning for physical distribution and Place is no exception. So let's start by looking at PD through a customer's eyes.

The physical distribution customer service level—including fast and reliable delivery—is critical to many business customers.

Customers want products—not excuses

Customers don't care how a product was moved or stored—or what some channel member had to do to provide it. Rather, customers think in terms of the physical distribution **customer service level**—how rapidly and dependably a firm can deliver what they—the customers—want. Marketing managers need to understand the customer's point of view.

What does this really mean? It means that Toyota wants to have enough windshields delivered to make cars *that* day—not late so production stops *or* early so there are a lot of extras to move around or store. It means that business executives who rent cars from Hertz want them to be ready when they get off their planes. It means you want your Lay's potato chips to be whole when you buy a bag at the snack bar—not crushed into crumbs from rough handling in a warehouse.

Physical distribution is invisible to most consumers

PD is—and should be—a part of marketing that is "invisible" to most consumers. It only gets their attention when something goes wrong. At that point, it may be too late to do anything that will keep them happy.

In countries where physical distribution systems are inefficient, consumers face shortages and inconvenient waits for the products they need. By contrast, most consumers in the United States and Canada don't think much about physical distribution. This probably means that these market-directed macro-marketing systems work pretty well—that a lot of individual marketing managers have made good decisions in this area. But it doesn't mean that the decisions are always clear-cut or simple. In fact, many trade-offs may be required.

Trade-offs of costs, service, and sales

Most customers would prefer very good service at a very low price. But that combination is hard to provide because it usually costs more to provide higher levels of service. So most physical distribution decisions involve trade-offs between costs, the customer service level, and sales.

If you want a new Compaq computer and the computer store where you would like to buy it doesn't have it on hand, you're likely to buy it elsewhere; or if that model Compaq is hard to get you might just switch to some other brand.

EXHIBIT 12–1   Trade-Offs among Physical Distribution Costs, Customer Service Level, and Sales

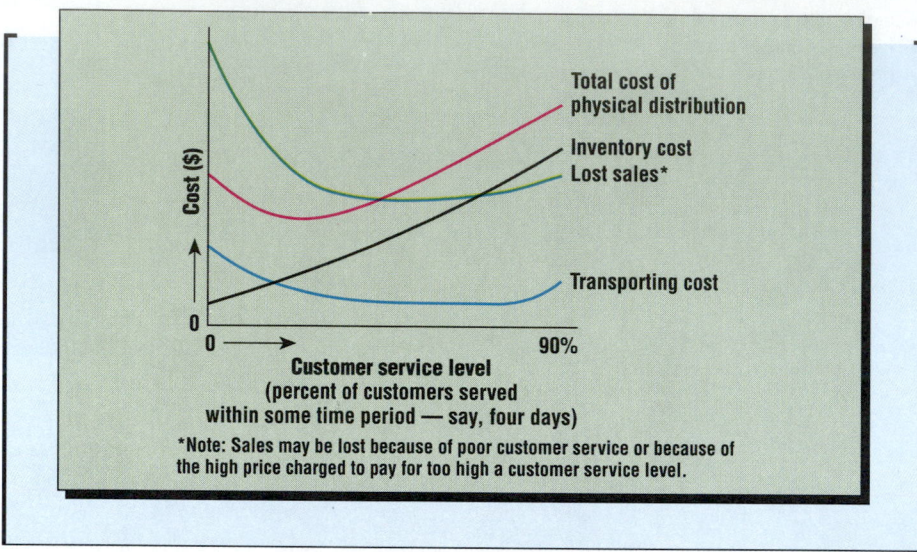

Perhaps the first store could keep your business by guaranteeing two-day delivery of your computer—by using special airfreight delivery from the factory. In this case, the manager is trading the cost of storing a large inventory for the extra cost of speedy delivery—assuming that the computer is available in inventory *somewhere* in the channel. In this example, missing one sale may not seem that important, but it all adds up. In fact, Compaq Computer, which recently became the number one producer of PCs, estimates that it lost between $500 million and $1 billion in sales in 1994 because its computers weren't available when and where customers were ready to buy them. With lost sales like that, you can see why Compaq is working hard to reevaluate the trade-offs it's been making.

Exhibit 12–1 illustrates trade-off relationships like those highlighted in the Compaq example. For example, faster—but more expensive—transportation may reduce the need for a costly inventory of computers. There is also a trade-off between the service level and sales. If the service level is too low—if products are not available on a timely and dependable basis—customers will buy elsewhere, and sales will be lost. Alternatively, the supplier may hope that a higher service level will attract more customers or motivate them to pay a higher price. But if the service level is higher than customers want or are willing to pay for, sales will be lost.

The important point is that many trade-offs must be made in the PD area. The trade-offs can be complicated. The lowest-cost approach may not be best—if customers aren't satisfied. A higher service level may make a better strategy. Further, if different channel members or target markets want different customer service levels, several different strategies may be needed.[3]

PHYSICAL DISTRIBUTION CONCEPT FOCUSES ON THE WHOLE DISTRIBUTION SYSTEM

The physical distribution concept

The **physical distribution (PD) concept** says that all transporting and storing activities of a business and a channel system should be coordinated as one system,

EXHIBIT 12–2   Examples of Factors That Affect PD Service Level

• Advance information on product availability	• Advance information on delays
• Time to enter and process orders	• Time needed to deliver an order
• Backorder procedures	• Reliability in meeting delivery date
• Where inventory is stored	• Complying with customer's instructions
• Accuracy in filling orders	• Defect-free deliveries
• Damage in shipping, storing, and handling	• How needed adjustments are handled
• Order status information	• Procedures for handling returns

which should seek to minimize the cost of distribution for a given customer service level. It may be hard to see this as a startling development. But until just a few years ago, even the most progressive companies treated PD functions as separate and unrelated activities.

Firms spread the responsibility for different distribution activities among various departments—production, shipping, sales, warehousing, and others. No one person was responsible for coordinating storing and shipping decisions—or seeing how they related to customer service levels. Some firms even failed to calculate the costs for these activities so they never knew the *total* cost of physical distribution.[4]

Unfortunately, in too many firms old-fashioned ways persist—with a focus on individual functional activities rather than the whole physical distribution system. Focusing on individual functional activities may actually increase total distribution costs for the firm—and even for the whole channel. It may also lead to the wrong customer service level. Well-run firms now avoid these problems by paying attention to the physical distribution concept.

Decide what service level to offer

With the physical distribution concept, firms decide what aspects of service are most important to their customers—and what specific service level to provide. Then they focus on finding the least expensive way to achieve the target level of service.

Exhibit 12–2 shows a variety of factors that may influence the customer service level. The most important aspects of customer service depend on target market needs. Xerox might focus on how long it takes to deliver copy machine repair parts once it receives an order. When a copier breaks down, customers want the repair "yesterday." The service level might be stated as "we will deliver 90 percent of all emergency repair parts within 8 business hours, and the remainder within 24 hours." Such a service level might require that almost all such parts be kept in inventory, that the most commonly needed parts be available on the service truck, that order processing be very fast and accurate, and that parts not available locally be sent by airfreight. Obviously, supplying this service level will affect the total cost of the PD system. But it may also beat competitors who don't provide this service level.

Increasing service levels may be very profitable in highly competitive situations where the firm has little else to differentiate its marketing mix. Dow sells homogeneous basic chemicals that are also sold by many other suppliers. Increasing the service level—perhaps through faster delivery or wider stocks—might allow Dow to make headway in a market without changing Product, Price, or Promotion. Competitors might not realize what has happened—or that Dow's improved customer service level makes its marketing mix better.[5]

EXHIBIT 12–3   Comparative Costs of Airplane versus Rail and Warehouse

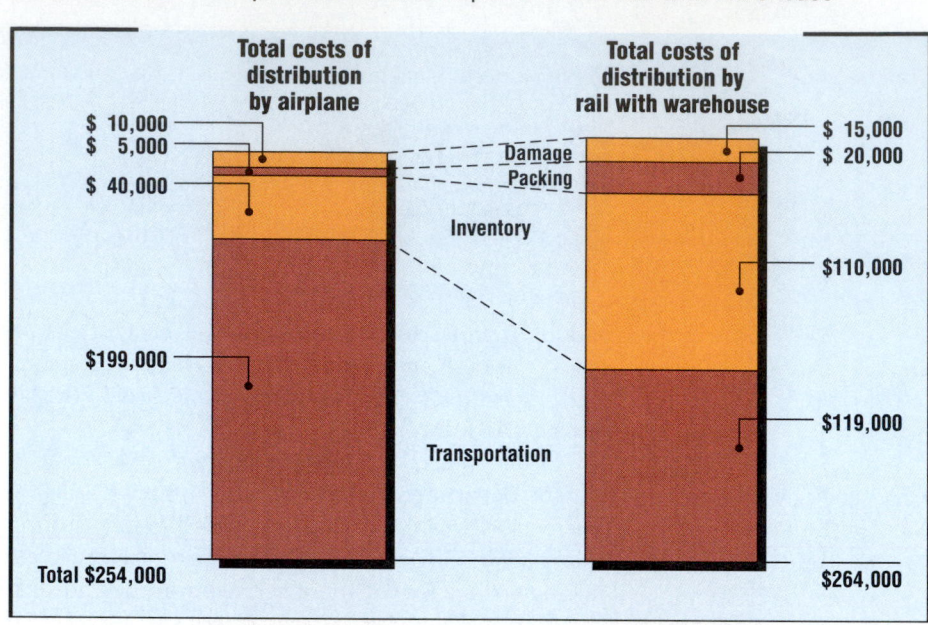

Find the lowest total cost for the right service level

In selecting a PD system, the **total cost approach** involves evaluating each possible PD system—and identifying *all* of the costs of each alternative. This approach uses the tools of cost accounting and economics. Costs that otherwise might be ignored—like inventory carrying costs—are considered. The possible costs of lost sales due to a lower customer service level may also be considered. The following example shows why the total cost approach is useful.

A cost comparison of alternative systems

The Good Earth Vegetable Company was shipping produce to distant markets by train. The cost of shipping a ton of vegetables by train averaged less than half the cost of airfreight so the company assumed that rail was the best method. But then Good Earth managers did a more complete analysis. To their surprise, they found the airfreight system was faster and cheaper.

Exhibit 12–3 compares the costs for the two distribution systems—airplane and railroad. Because shipping by train was slow, Good Earth had to keep a large inventory in a warehouse to fill orders on time. And the company was also surprised at the extra cost of carrying the inventory in transit. Good Earth's managers also found that the cost of spoiled vegetables during shipment and storage in the warehouse was much higher when they used rail shipping.

In this case, total cost analyses showed that unconventional physical distribution methods provided service as good as or better than conventional means—and at a lower cost. The case also illustrates why it is important to get beyond a focus on individual functional elements of PD and instead consider the costs and service level of a whole physical distribution system. This broader focus should consider how the whole channel operates, not just individual firms.

Careful application of the total cost approach often identifies ways to both cut costs and improve service at the same time. After two years of work with the total cost approach, National Semiconductor cut its standard delivery time in half, reduced distribution costs 2.5 percent, and increased sales by 34 percent. In the process, it shut down six warehouses around the globe and started to airfreight microchips to its worldwide customers from a new 125,000-square-foot distribution center in Singapore.

Functions can be shifted and shared in the channel

As a marketing manager develops the Place part of a strategy, it is important to decide how physical distribution functions can and should be divided within the channel. Who will store, handle, and transport the goods—and who will pay for these services? Who will coordinate all of the PD activities?

Just deciding to use certain types of wholesalers or retailers doesn't automatically—or completely—answer these questions. A wholesaler may use its own trucks to haul goods from a producer to its warehouse and from there to retailers—but only because the manufacturer gives a transportation allowance. Another wholesaler may want the goods delivered.

There is no right sharing arrangement. Physical distribution can be varied endlessly in a marketing mix and in a channel system. And competitors may share these functions in different ways—with different costs and results.

How PD is shared affects the rest of a strategy

How the PD functions are shared affects the other three Ps—especially Price. The sharing arrangement can also make (or break) a strategy. Consider Channel Master, a firm that wanted to take advantage of the growing market for the dishlike antennas used by motels and other businesses to receive TV signals from satellites. The product looked like it could be a big success, but the small company didn't have the money to invest in a large inventory. So Channel Master decided to work only with wholesalers who were willing to buy (and pay for) several units—to be used for demonstrations and to ensure that buyers got immediate delivery.

In the first few months Channel Master earned $2 million in revenues—just by providing inventory for the channel. And the wholesalers paid the interest cost of carrying inventory—over $300,000 the first year. Here the wholesalers helped share the risk of the new venture—but it was a good decision for them too. They won many sales from a competing channel whose customers had to wait several months for delivery. And by getting off to a strong start, Channel Master became a market leader.

Identifying all the alternatives is sometimes difficult

It's important for firms to compare the costs and benefits of all practical PD alternatives, including how functions can be shared in the channel. Sometimes, however, there are so many possible combinations that it is difficult to study each one completely. For example, there may be hundreds of possible locations for a warehouse. And each location might require different combinations of transporting and storing costs.

Some companies use computer simulation to compare the many possible alternatives.[6] But typically, the straightforward total cost analysis discussed above is practical—and will show whether there is need for a more sophisticated analytical approach.

Now that you see why the physical distribution concept is important, let's take a closer look at some of the PD decision areas.

THE TRANSPORTING FUNCTION ADDS VALUE TO A MARKETING STRATEGY

Transporting aids economic development and exchange

Transporting is the marketing function of moving goods. Transportation provides time and place utilities—at a cost. But the cost is less than the value added to products by moving them or there is little reason to ship in the first place.

The cost of transportation adds little to the total cost of products—like pharmaceuticals—that are already valuable relative to their size and weight. But transporting costs can be a large part of the total cost for heavy products that are low in value, like sheet aluminium.

Transporting can help achieve economies of scale in production. If production costs can be reduced by producing larger quantities in one location, these savings may more than offset the added cost of transporting the finished products to customers. Without low-cost transportation, both within countries and internationally, there would be no mass distribution as we know it today.

Transporting can be costly

Transporting costs may limit the target markets a marketing manager can consider. Shipping costs increase delivered cost—and that's what really interests customers. Transport costs add little to the cost of products that are already valuable relative to their size and weight. But transporting costs can be a large part of the total cost for heavy products of low value—like many minerals and raw materials. This is illustrated in Exhibit 12–4, which shows transporting costs as a percent of total sales dollars for several products.[7]

Governments may influence transportation

Government often plays an important role in the development of a country's transportation system—including its roads, harbors, railroads, and airports. And different countries regulate transportation differently—although regulation has in general been decreasing.

Until the 1980s, for example, the U.S. government had a lot of control over transporting. Government agencies approved routes, what services could be provided, and rates. Because rates were regulated, carriers typically did not compete on Price. And some carriers were approved to carry some products but not others.

All of this caused higher prices and much waste. For example, the rules required a carrier that took Cummins diesel engines from the Midwest to California to use an extra-long route going out—and to make the return trip

EXHIBIT 12–4   Transporting Costs as a Percent of Selling Price for Different Products

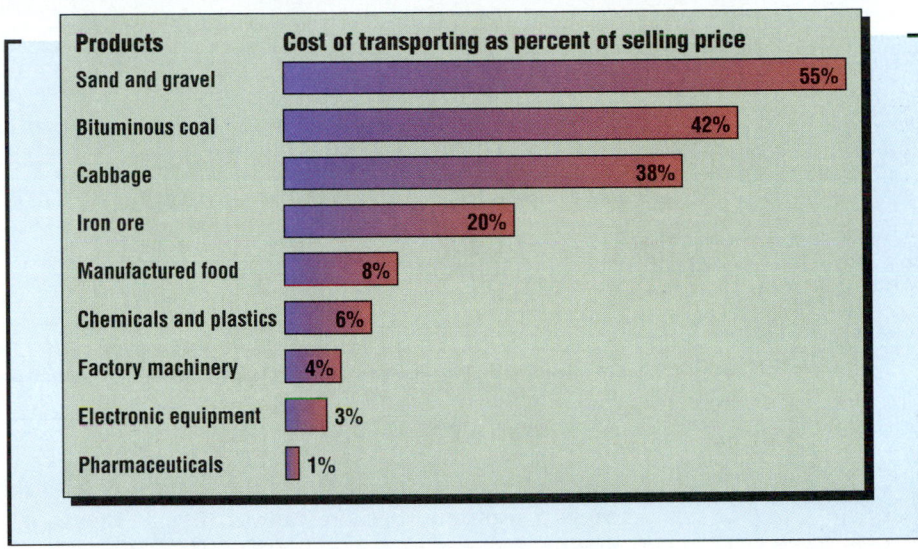

Products	Cost of transporting as percent of selling price
Sand and gravel	55%
Bituminous coal	42%
Cabbage	38%
Iron ore	20%
Manufactured food	8%
Chemicals and plastics	6%
Factory machinery	4%
Electronic equipment	3%
Pharmaceuticals	1%

empty. Other carriers took California vegetables to the Midwest—and they too went home empty.

Now you have more transporting choices

Today, most of the rules in the United States—and in many other countries— have been relaxed. For example, as part of their move toward unification, most European countries are reducing their transporting regulations. The construction of the tunnel under the English Channel is a dramatic example of the changes taking place. The "chunnel" allows trains to speed between England and the rest of Europe.

As regulations decreased, competition in the transportation industry increased. As a result, a marketing manager generally has many carriers in one or more modes competing for the firm's transporting business. Or a firm can do its own transporting. So knowing about the different modes is important.[8]

WHICH TRANSPORTING ALTERNATIVE IS BEST?

Transporting function must fit the whole strategy

The transporting function should fit into the whole marketing strategy. But picking the best transporting alternative can be difficult. The "best" alternative depends on the product, other physical distribution decisions, and what service level the company wants to offer. The best alternative should not only be as low-cost as possible but also provide the level of service (for example, speed and dependability) required. Exhibit 12–5 shows that different modes of transportation have different strengths and weaknesses.[9] Low transporting cost is *not* the only criterion for selecting the best mode.

Railroads—large loads moved at low cost

Railroads are the workhorse of the U.S. transportation system. They carry more freight over more miles than any other mode. In the United States, as in other countries, they carry heavy and bulky goods—such as raw materials, steel, chemicals, cars, canned goods, and machines—over long distances. By handling large quantities, the railroads are able to transport at relatively low cost. For

EXHIBIT 12–5   Benefits and Limitations of Different Transport Modes

Mode	Transporting Features					
	Cost	Delivery speed	Number of locations served	Ability to handle a variety of goods	Frequency of scheduled shipments	Dependability in meeting schedules
Rail	Medium	Average	Extensive	High	Low	Medium
Water	Very low	Very slow	Limited	Very high	Very low	Medium
Truck	High	Fast	Very extensive	High	High	High
Air	Very high	Very fast	Extensive	Limited	High	High
Pipeline	Low	Slow	Very limited	Very limited	Medium	High

example, in the United States the average cost to ship by rail runs about 3 to 4 cents a ton-mile. Because railroad freight moves more slowly than truck shipments, it is not as well suited for perishable items or those in urgent demand. Railroads are most efficient at handling full carloads of goods. Less-than-carload (LCL) shipments take a lot of handling and rehandling, which means they usually move more slowly and at a higher price per pound than carload shipments.

Competition has forced railroads to innovate

Railroads earned low profits for many years—in part because trucks took a large share of the most profitable business. Now railroads are cutting costs and improving services—to improve profits. Reduced government regulation helped. Many railroads merged to reduce overlap in equipment and routes. Others increased prices where competition from truck and water transport was weak.

Railroads now cater to the needs of new target customers with a variety of specially designed railcars and services—ranging from double-decker railcars to computerized freight-tracking systems.[10]

To offset the shortcomings of low speed and high cost—and still get business from small shippers—some railroads encourage **pool car service**, which allows groups of shippers to pool their shipments of like goods into a full car. Sometimes local retailers buying from a single area like Los Angeles combine their shipments in single cars. Local truckers then deliver the goods when they arrive.

Another example of a special railroad service is **diversion in transit**, which allows redirection of carloads already in transit. A Florida grower can ship a carload of oranges toward the Northeast as soon as they're ripe. While they head north, the grower can find a buyer or identify the market with the best price. Then—for a small fee—the railroad will reroute the car to this destination.

Trucks are more expensive, but flexible and essential

The flexibility of trucks makes them better at moving small quantities of goods for shorter distances. They can travel on almost any road. They go where the rails can't. That's why at least 75 percent of U.S. consumer products travel at least part of the way from producer to consumer by truck. And in countries with good highway systems, trucks can give extremely fast service. Truckers also compete with railroads for high-value items. This is reflected in their rates, which average about 13 cents per ton-mile in the United States.

Water transportation is slow—but it's very important for international shipments.

Critics complain that trucks congest traffic and damage highways. But trucks are essential to our present macro-marketing system.[11]

Ship it overseas— but slowly

Water transportation is the slowest shipping mode—but usually the lowest-cost way of shipping heavy freight. Water transportation is very important for international shipments and often the only practical approach. This explains why port cities like Boston, New York, Rotterdam, Osaka, and Singapore are important centers for international trade.

Inland waterways are important too

Inland waterways (such as the Mississippi River and Great Lakes in the United States and the Rhine and Danube in Europe) are also important, especially for bulky, nonperishable products such as iron ore, grain, steel, petroleum products, cement, gravel, sand, and coal. However, when winter ice closes freshwater harbors, alternate transportation must be used. Some shippers—such as those moving iron ore—ship their total annual supply during the summer months and store it near their production facilities for winter use. Here low-cost transporting combined with storing reduces *total* cost.

Pipelines move oil and gas

Pipelines are used primarily by the petroleum industry to move oil and natural gas. So pipelines are important both in the oil-producing and oil-consuming countries. Only a few major cities in the United States, Canada, Mexico, and Latin America are more than 200 miles from a major pipeline system. Of course, the majority of the pipelines in the United States are located in the Southwest—connecting the oil fields and refineries. From there, the more flexible railroads, trucks, and ships usually take over—bringing refined and graded products to customers.

Airfreight is expensive but fast and growing

The most expensive cargo transporting mode is airplane—but it is fast! Airfreight rates normally are at least twice as high as trucking rates—but the

The growth of airfreight has made it easier and faster for firms to serve customers in foreign markets.

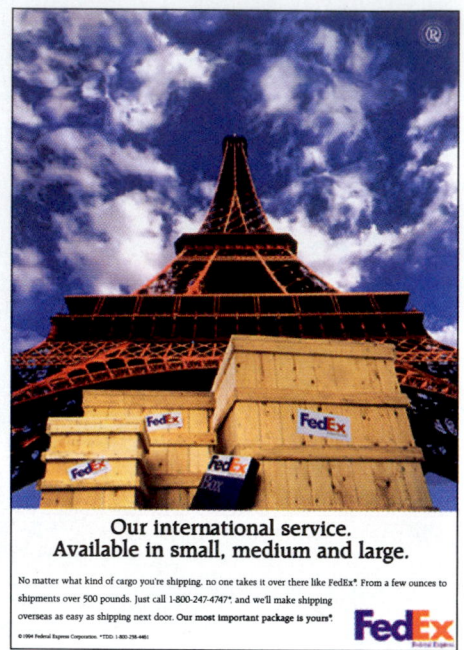

Our international service.
Available in small, medium and large.

No matter what kind of cargo you're shipping, no one takes it over there like FedEx®. From a few ounces to shipments over 500 pounds. Just call 1-800-247-4747*, and we'll make shipping overseas as easy as shipping next door. Our most important package is yours®.

FedEx

greater speed may offset the added cost. Trucks took the cream of the railroads' traffic. Now airplanes are taking the cream of the cream.

High-value, low-weight goods—like high-fashion clothing and parts for the electronics and metal-working industries—are often shipped by air. Airfreight is also creating new transporting business. Perishable products that previously could not be shipped are now being flown across continents and oceans. Flowers and bulbs from Holland, for example, now are jet-flown to points all over the world. And airfreight is also becoming very important for small emergency deliveries— like repair parts, special orders, and business documents that must be somewhere the next day.

But airplanes may cut the total cost of distribution

An important advantage of using planes is that the cost of packing, unpacking, and preparing the goods for sale may be reduced or eliminated. Planes may help a firm reduce inventory costs by eliminating outlying warehouses. Valuable by-products of airfreight's speed are less spoilage, theft, and damage. Although the *transporting* cost of air shipments may be higher, the *total* cost of distribution may be lower. As more firms realize this, airfreight firms—like DHL Worldwide Express, Federal Express, Airborne, and Emery Air Freight—are enjoying rapid growth.

These firms play an especially important role in the growth of international business. While the bulk of international cargo moves on ships, the speed of airfreight opens up global markets for many businesses that previously had only domestic opportunities. For example, DHL Worldwide Express offers 24-hour delivery service from Tokyo to Los Angeles, New York City to Rome, and London to Chicago. For a firm whose products are valuable relative to their weight and size, the cost of air deliveries may seem trivial when compared to the sales potential of competing in new markets.[12]

Put it in a container—
and move between
modes easily

We've described the modes separately, but products often move by several different modes and carriers during their journey. This is especially common for international shipments. Japanese firms—like Sony—ship stereos to the United States, Canada, and Europe by boat. When they arrive at the dock, they are loaded on trains and sent across the country. Then, the units are delivered to a wholesaler by truck or rail.

Loading and unloading goods several times used to be a real problem. Parts of a shipment would become separated, damaged, or even stolen. And handling the goods—perhaps many times—raised costs and slowed delivery. Many of these problems are reduced with **containerization**—grouping individual items into an economical shipping quantity and sealing them in protective containers for transit to the final destination. This protects the products and simplifies handling during shipping. Some containers are as large as truck bodies.

Piggyback—a ride on
two or more modes

Piggyback service means loading truck trailers—or flatbed trailers carrying containers—on railcars to provide both speed and flexibility. Railroads now pick up truck trailers at the producer's location, load them onto specially designed rail flatcars, and haul them as close to the customer as rail lines run. The trailers are then hooked up to a truck tractor and delivered to the buyer's door. Similar services are offered on ocean-going ships—allowing door-to-door service between cities around the world.

To better coordinate the flow of products between modes, transportation companies like CSX now offer customers a complete choice of different transportation modes. Then CSX, not the customer, figures out the best and lowest-cost way to shift and share transporting functions between the modes.[13]

ECONOMIES OF SCALE IN TRANSPORTING

Most transporting rates—the prices charged for transporting—are based on the idea that large quantities of a good can be shipped at a lower transport cost per pound than small quantities. Whether a furniture producer sends a truck to deliver one sofa or a full carload, the company still has to pay for the driver, the truck, the gas, and other expenses like insurance.

Transporters often give much lower rates for quantities that make efficient use of their transport facilities. Thus, transport costs per pound for less-than-full carloads or truckloads are often twice as high as for full loads. These quantity rate differences are one important reason for the development of some wholesalers. They buy in large quantities to get the advantage of economies of scale in transporting. Then they sell in the smaller quantities their customers need.

Freight forwarders
accumulate economical
shipping quantities

Freight forwarders combine the small shipments of many shippers into more economical shipping quantities. Freight forwarders do not own their own transporting facilities—except perhaps for delivery trucks. Rather, they wholesale air, ship, rail, and truck space. They accumulate small shipments from many shippers and reship in larger quantities to obtain lower transporting rates.

Freight forwarders are especially useful in arranging international shipping. They handle 75 percent of the general cargo shipped from U.S. ports to foreign countries. They are also very helpful for handling international airfreight. For example, Air Express International specializes in helping marketing managers find the most efficient air cargo firm to speed deliveries around the world.[14]

Many firms have their own truck fleets, but Saturn decided it was better to develop a close relationship with Ryder, a supplier of transportation services. Ryder helped design Saturn's state-of-the-art system for just-in-time delivery of components to the assembly line—and it also transports finished cars to dealers.

Should you do it yourself?

To cut transporting costs, some marketing managers do their own transporting rather than buy from specialists. Large producers, like Levi Strauss, often buy or lease their own truck fleets. Shell Oil and other large petroleum, iron ore, and gypsum rock producers have their own ships. Some firms now buy their own planes for airfreight.[15]

THE STORING FUNCTION AND MARKETING STRATEGY

Store it and smooth out sales, increase profits and consumer satisfaction

Storing is the marketing function of holding goods. It provides time utility. **Inventory** is the amount of goods being stored.

Having products on hand when customers want them may make the difference between a satisfied customer and a lost sale. Yet, deciding on the right inventory level is difficult when it's hard to forecast likely demand. Even so, a firm that is stocked out when its customers are ready to buy may not only lose the sale but also create a dissatisfied customer and damage the relationship and the possibility of future sales. Kmart ran into this problem. A number of consumers decided it was no longer a convenient place to shop when stores repeatedly ran out of basic staples that consumers expected to find.

Storing is necessary when production of goods doesn't match consumption. This is common with mass production. Nippon Steel, for example, might produce thousands of steel bars of one size before changing the machines to produce another size. Changing the production line can be costly and time consuming. It's often cheaper to produce large quantities of one size—and store the unsold quantity—than to have shorter production runs. Thus, storing goods allows the producer to achieve economies of scale in production.

Storing helps keep prices steady

Some products—such as agricultural commodities—can only be produced seasonally although they are in demand year-round. If crops could not be stored when they mature, all of the crop would be thrown onto the market—and prices might drop sharply. Consumers might benefit temporarily from this surplus. But later in the year—when supplies were scarce and prices high—they would suffer. Storing thus helps stabilize prices during the consumption period—although prices usually do rise slightly over time to cover storing costs.

Some buyers purchase in large quantities to get quantity discounts from the producer or transporter. Then the extra goods must be stored until there is demand. And goods are sometimes stored as a hedge against future price rises, strikes, shipping interruptions, and other disruptions.

Storing varies the channel system

Storing allows producers and middlemen to keep stocks at convenient locations—ready to meet customers' needs. In fact, storing is one of the major activities of some middlemen.

Most channel members provide the storing function for some length of time. Even final consumers store some things for their future needs. Since storing can be provided anywhere along the channel, the storing function offers several ways to vary a firm's marketing mix—and its channel system—by (1) adjusting the time goods are held, (2) sharing the storing costs, and (3) delegating the job to a specialized storing facility. This latter variation would mean adding another member to the distribution channel.

Which channel members store the product—and for how long—affects the behavior of all channel members. For example, the producer of Snapper lawn mowers tries to get wholesalers to inventory a wide selection of its machines. That way, retailers can carry smaller inventories since they can be sure of dependable local supplies. And they might decide to sell Snapper—rather than Toro or some other brand that they would have to store at their own expense.

If final customers "store" the product, more of it may be used or consumed. You saw this in the Coke case that introduces this chapter. Coke wants customers to buy six-packs and 2-liter bottles. Then consumers have an "inventory" in the refrigerator when thirst hits. Of course, consumers aren't always willing or able to hold the inventory. In China, for example, Coke had little success until it gave up on pushing 2-liter bottles and switched to single-serving 75 ml bottles. Only 1 out of 10 Chinese families has a refrigerator—so they didn't have a good way to store a bottle once it was open.

Goods are stored at a cost

Storing can increase the value of goods—and make them more available when customers want them. But a manager must remember that *storing always involves costs* too. Car dealers, for example, must store cars on their lots—waiting for the right customer. The interest expense of money tied up in the inventory is a major cost. In addition, if a new car on the lot is dented or scratched, there is a repair cost. If a car isn't sold before the new models come out, its value drops. There is also a risk of fire or theft—so the retailer must carry insurance. And, of course, dealers incur the cost of leasing or owning the display lot where they store the cars.

In today's competitive markets, most firms watch their inventories closely. Taken in total, the direct and indirect costs of unnecessary inventory can make the difference between a profitable strategy and a loser. On the other hand, a marketing manager must be very careful in making the distinction between unnecessary inventory and inventory that may be needed to provide the kind of distribution service customers expect.[16]

SPECIALIZED STORING FACILITIES CAN BE VERY HELPFUL

New cars can be stored outside on the dealer's lot. Fuel oil can be stored in a specially designed tank. Coal and other raw materials can be stored in open pits. But most products must be stored inside protective buildings. Often, firms can choose among different types of specialized storing facilities. The right choice may reduce costs—and serve customers better.

Private warehouses are common

Private warehouses are storing facilities owned or leased by companies for their own use. Most manufacturers, wholesalers, and retailers have some storing facilities either in their main buildings or in a warehouse district. A sales manager often is responsible for managing a manufacturer's finished-goods warehouse—especially if sales branches aren't near the factory. In retailing, storing is so closely tied to selling and available shelf space that the buyers may control this function.

Firms use private warehouses when a large volume of goods must be stored regularly. Private warehouses can be expensive, however. If the need changes, the extra space may be hard—or impossible—to rent to others.

Public warehouses fill special needs

Public warehouses are independent storing facilities. They can provide all the services that a company's own warehouse can provide. A company might choose a public warehouse if it doesn't have a regular need for space. For example, Tonka Toys uses public warehouses because its business is seasonal. Tonka pays for the space only when it is used. Public warehouses are also useful for manufacturers who must maintain stocks in many locations—including foreign countries.

In most countries, public warehouses are located in all major metropolitan areas and many smaller cities. Many rural towns also have public warehouses for locally produced agricultural commodities. See Exhibit 12–6 for a comparison of private and public warehouses.[17]

Warehousing facilities have modernized

The cost of physical handling is a major storing cost. Goods must be handled once when put into storage—and again when removed to be sold. Further, especially in the typical old downtown warehouse districts, traffic congestion, crowded storage areas, and slow elevators delay the process—and increase the costs.

Today, modern one-story buildings away from downtown traffic are replacing the old multistory warehouses. They eliminate the need for elevators—and permit the use of power-operated lift trucks, battery-operated motor scooters, roller-skating order pickers, electric hoists for heavy items, and hydraulic ramps to speed loading and unloading. Most of these new warehouses use lift trucks and pallets (wooden trays that carry many cases) for vertical storage and better use of space. Computers monitor inventory, order needed stock, and track storing and shipping costs. Some warehouses even have computer-controlled order picking systems that speed the process of locating and assembling the assortment required to fill an order.[18]

THE DISTRIBUTION CENTER—A DIFFERENT KIND OF WAREHOUSE

Is storing really needed?

Discrepancies of assortment or quantity between one channel level and another are often adjusted at the place where goods are stored. It reduces handling costs to regroup and store at the same place—*if both functions are required.* But sometimes regrouping is required when storing isn't.

EXHIBIT 12–6   A Comparison of Private Warehouses and Public Warehouses

Characteristics	Type of warehouse	
	Private	**Public**
Fixed investment	Very high	No fixed investment
Unit cost	High if volume is low Very low if volume is very high	Low: charges are made only for space needed
Control	High	Low managerial control
Adequacy for product line	Highly adequate	May not be convenient
Flexibility	Low: fixed costs have already been committed	High: easy to end arrangement

Don't store it, distribute it

A **distribution center** is a special kind of warehouse designed to speed the flow of goods and avoid unnecessary storing costs. Anchor Hocking moves over a million pounds of its housewares products through its distribution center each day. Faster inventory turnover and easier bulk-breaking reduce the cost of carrying inventory. This is important. These costs may run as high as 35 percent of the value of the average inventory a year. The lower costs and faster turnover lead to bigger profits.

Today, the distribution center concept is widely used by firms at all channel levels. Many products buzz through a distribution center without ever tarrying on a shelf; workers and equipment immediately sort the products and move them to a new loading dock and the vehicle that will take them to their next stop. While these "cross-docking" approaches have become more efficient, the basic benefits of the distribution center approach are still the same as they were over 25 years ago when the idea was pioneered. In fact, a good way to see how the distribution center works is to consider an early application.

Pillsbury's distribution system was overwhelmed by expanding product lines and sales

Pillsbury—the manufacturer of baking products—used to ship in carload quantities directly from its factories to large middlemen. Initially, plants were as close to customers as possible, and each plant produced the whole Pillsbury line. As lines expanded, however, no single plant could produce all the various products. When customers began to ask for mixed carload shipments and faster delivery, Pillsbury added warehouse space—and started hauling goods from plant to plant. Over time, Pillsbury set up 100 branch warehouses—controlled by 33 sales offices. Accounting, credit, and other processing operations were duplicated in each sales office. PD costs were high, but the customer service level was still a problem. It took Pillsbury a week just to process an order. And the company had no effective control over its inventories. Pillsbury needed a change to distribution centers.

The distribution center brings it all together

Pillsbury first specialized production at each plant to a few product lines. Then Pillsbury sent carload shipments directly to the distribution centers—almost

Mattel's new, computerized distribution center in Germany makes it possible to efficiently consolidate, route, and deliver orders to retailers throughout Europe.

eliminating storing at the factories. The distribution centers were controlled by four regional data processing centers, which quickly determined where and when goods were to be shipped. Centralized accounting got invoices to customers faster—resulting in quicker payment. Because each distribution center always had adequate inventory, it could ship orders the most economical way. And because the field sales organization no longer handled physical distribution or inventory, it could focus on sales. Pillsbury could guarantee customers delivery within three days.

There are many variations of the distribution center. The Pillsbury example shows it within an integrated operation. But public warehouses offer similar services.

PHYSICAL DISTRIBUTION CHALLENGES AND OPPORTUNITIES

Coordinating PD activities among firms

PD decisions interact with other Place decisions, the rest of the marketing mix, and the whole marketing strategy. As a result, if firms in the channel do not plan and coordinate how they will share PD activities, PD is likely to be a source of conflict rather than a basis for competitive advantage. Holly Farms' problems in introducing a new product illustrate this point.

Marketers at Holly Farms were encouraged when preroasted chicken performed well in a market test. But channel conflict surfaced when they moved to broader distribution. As with other perishable food products, the Holly Farm label indicated a date by which the chicken should be sold. Many grocers refused to buy the roast chicken because they worried that they had only a few days after it was delivered to sell it. They didn't want it to spoil—at their expense—on the shelf. Shelf life had not been a problem with Holly Farms' raw chicken. It sold in higher volume and moved off shelves more quickly.

The source of the problem was that it took nine days to ship the roast chicken from the plant to distant stores. Coupled with slow turnover, that didn't leave grocers enough selling time. To address the problem, Holly Farms changed its transportation arrangements. It also developed new packaging that allowed grocers to store the chicken longer. Holly Farms also shifted its promotion budget

McKesson is a leading distributor of drugs, and effective use of technology has been a key reason for its success. The space-age gizmo on this man's arm combines a scanner, computer, and two-way radio—to speed up order assembly and delivery from McKesson's distribution center.

to put more emphasis on in-store promotions to speed up sales once the chicken arrived. With these changes, Holly Farms was able to win cooperation in the channel and establish its product in the market.[19]

JIT requires a close, cooperative relationship

We introduced the concept of just-in-time (JIT) delivery in Chapter 8. Now that you know more about PD alternatives, it's useful to consider some of the marketing strategy implications of this approach.

A key advantage of JIT for business customers is that it reduces their PD costs—especially storing and handling costs. However, if the customer doesn't have any backup inventory, there's no "security blanket" if something goes wrong. If a supplier's delivery truck gets stuck in traffic, if there's an error in what's shipped, or if there are any quality problems when the products arrive, the customer's business stops. Thus, a JIT system requires that a supplier have extremely high quality control in production and in every PD activity, including its PD service.

For example, to control the risk of transportation problems, JIT suppliers often locate their facilities close to important customers. Trucks may make smaller and more frequent deliveries—perhaps even several times a day. As this suggests, a JIT system usually requires a supplier to be able to respond to very short order lead times. In fact, a supplier's production often needs to be based on the customer's production schedule. However, if that isn't possible, the supplier must have adequate inventory to meet the customer's needs.

You can see that the JIT system shifts greater responsibility for PD activities backward in the channel—to suppliers. If the supplier can be more efficient than the customer could be in controlling PD costs—and still provide the customer with the service level required—this approach can work well for everyone in the channel. However, it should be clear that JIT is not always the lowest cost—or

CLOROX COMPANY'S SPOTLESS CUSTOMER SERVICE BUILDS RELATIONSHIPS

Marketing managers at Clorox Company face a daunting task making good on their objective of "maintaining the highest standards for customer service" in all the product markets they serve. But they must do so to develop and keep strong partnerships with Clorox middlemen (supermarket chains, convenience stores, mass-merchandisers, warehouse clubs, wholesalers) and other business customers (ranging from white tablecloth restaurants to the fast-service chains). Clorox deals with more than 100,000 business customers worldwide.

Information shared between Clorox and the firms that buy its products help make the partnership work. For example, when the bleach buyer for a major retail chain went on vacation, the fill-in person was not familiar with the reorder procedures. As a result, the chain's central distribution center almost ran out of Clorox liquid bleach. But Clorox's distribution people identified the problem themselves—because of a computer system that allowed Clorox to access the chain's inventory records and sales data for Clorox products. Clorox got a shipment out fast enough to prevent the chain—and Clorox—from losing sales at individual stores. In the future when some other bleach supplier tries to tell buyers for the chain that "bleach is bleach," they will more than likely remember the distribution service Clorox provides.

Good information is not the only thing that Clorox needs to build long-lasting, competition-beating partnerships with middlemen. For example, to be able to fill unexpected orders, Clorox sets up its production facilities so they can quickly shift from one product or size to another. This helped when a northern California supermarket chain decided to promote 40-pound twin packs of Clorox's Kingsford brand charcoal. At the height of the barbecue season, Kingsford plants were already working hard to keep up with demand for the popular 10-pound bags. Filling the unexpected order for the bigger packages required changing production setups and packaging and extending crew shifts. But because Kingsford was poised to meet the chain's need, Kingsford was able to ship 140 *tons* of twin packs to the chain in less than a week—while keeping pace with the needs of other middlemen.

Meeting the distribution customer service needs of business customers can be even more demanding than working with final consumers. Building and keeping cooperative relationships with business customers takes constant attention to the quality of distribution customer service, not just quality goods. But organizational buyers know that the success of their own firms' marketing strategies depends on such service—so they reward reliable suppliers with their orders.[20]

---

best—approach. It may be better for a supplier to produce and ship in larger, more economical quantities—if the savings offset the distribution system's total inventory and handling costs.

While not every firm can—or should—use a just-in-time approach, it is an important idea. It focuses attention on the need to coordinate the PD system throughout the channel. It also highlights the value of close working relationships—and effective communication—between marketers and their customers. Whether or not a firm uses the JIT approach, good information is often the key to coordinating PD activities.[21]

Better information helps coordinate PD

Coordinating all of the elements of PD has always been a challenge—even in a single firm. Trying to coordinate PD in the whole channel is even tougher. Keeping track of inventory levels, when to order, and where goods are when they move is difficult. Even so, marketing managers for some firms are finding solutions to these challenges—with help from computers.

Many firms now continuously update their marketing information systems—so they can immediately find out what products have sold, the level of the current inventory, and when goods being transported will arrive. And coordination of physical distribution decisions throughout channels of distribution continues to improve as more firms are able to have their computers "talk to each other" directly.

Electronic data interchange sets a standard

Until recently, differences in computer systems from one firm to another hampered the flow of information. Many firms now attack this problem by adopting **electronic data interchange (EDI)**—an approach that puts information in a standardized format easily shared between different computer systems. Purchase orders, shipping reports, and other paper documents are now being replaced with computerized EDI. With EDI, a customer transmits its order information directly to the supplier's computer. The supplier's computer immediately processes the order—and schedules production, order assembly, and transportation. Inventory information is automatically updated, and status reports are available instantly. The supplier might then use EDI to send the updated information to the transportation provider's computer. This type of system is becoming very common. In fact, almost all international transportation firms rely on EDI links with their customers.[22]

This improved information flow and coordination affects other PD activities too. Instantaneous computer-to-computer order processing, for example, can have the same effect on the customer service level as faster, more expensive transportation. And knowing what a customer has in stock can improve a supplier's own inventory planning—and reduce costs in the whole channel.

Better coordination of PD activities is a key reason for the success of Pepperidge Farm's line of premium cookies. A few years ago, the company was spending a lot of money making the wrong products and delivering them—too slowly—to the wrong market. Poor information was the problem. Delivery truck drivers took orders from retailers, assembled them manually at regional offices, and then mailed them to Pepperidge Farm's bakeries. Now the company has an almost instantaneous EDI link between sales, delivery, inventory, and production. Many of the company's 2,200 drivers use hand-held computers to record the inventory at each stop along their routes. They phone the information into a computer at the bakeries—so that cookies in short supply will be produced. The right assortment of fresh cookies is quickly shipped to local markets, and delivery trucks are loaded with what retailers need that day. Pepperidge Farm now moves cookies from its bakeries to store shelves in about three days; most cookie producers take about 10 days. That means fresher cookies for consumers—and helps to support Pepperidge Farm's high-quality positioning and premium price.[23]

In summary, using computers to coordinate information is helping some firms and channels compete successfully for customers—and increase their own profits.

Ethical issues may arise

Most of the ethical issues that arise in the PD area concern communications about product availability. For example, some critics say that marketers too often take orders for products that are not available or which they cannot deliver as quickly as customers expect. Yet a marketing manager can't always know precisely how long it will take before a product will be available. It doesn't make sense for the marketer to lose a customer if it appears that he or she can satisfy the customer's needs. But the customer may be inconvenienced or face added cost if the marketer's best guess isn't accurate. Similarly, some critics say that stores too often run out of products that they promote to attract consumers to the store. Yet it may not be possible for the marketer to predict demand, or to know when placing an ad that deliveries won't arrive. Different people have different views about how a firm should handle such situations.

Some suppliers criticize customers for abusing efforts to coordinate PD activities in the channel. For example, some retailers hedge against uncertain demand by telling suppliers that they plan to place an order, but then they don't *confirm* the order until the last minute. They want to be able to say that it wasn't an order in the first place—if sales in the store are slow. This shifts the uncertainty to the supplier and reduces the retailer's inventory costs. Is this unethical? Some think it is. However, a marketing manager should realize that the firm's order policies can reduce such problems—if the cost of providing the service customers want is higher than what they will pay. In other words, this may simply be another trade-off that the marketer must consider in setting up the PD system.[24]

Transportation choices affect the environment

Marketing managers must be sensitive to the environmental effects of transportation decisions. Some say trucks cause air pollution in already crowded cities. People who live near airports suffer the consequences of noise pollution. A damaged pipeline can spew thousands of gallons of oil before it can be repaired. The Exxon *Valdez* oil spill in Alaska is a dramatic example of the kind of environmental disaster that can happen when a transportation accident occurs.

Many firms are taking steps to reduce these problems. For example, Conoco, a subsidiary of Du Pont, is building ships with double hulls to reduce the risk of leaks. Some trucking and railroad firms establish elaborate safety procedures for dealing with toxic cargo. Today, the public *expects* companies to manufacture, transport, sell, and dispose of products in an environmentally sound manner. If companies are environmentally unsafe, consumers will show their dissatisfaction through their market choices. However, these environmental efforts increase the cost of distribution. Improved technology may help to make trade-offs between cost and environment less difficult. But ultimately, the people in a society must decide whether to bear the consequences of pollution or pay for higher distribution costs.

The transportation choices a firm makes also affect how much fuel is used. Many critics argue that we are carelessly depleting our nonrenewable energy resources. In addition, the cost of fuel has fluctuated drastically in the last 25 years. Fuel costs directly affect transporting costs. Lower fuel costs might lead to new market opportunities. And if fuel costs increase, truck and air transport will be less attractive, and rails will be more appealing. Lower speed limits for trucks may make railroads look even better. Another energy crisis might force even more radical changes—such as limiting the use of private cars and stimulating mass transportation.

Such shifts could affect where people live and work, what they produce and consume, and where and how they buy. In other words, these changes could affect our future macro-marketing system. An alert marketing manager should try to anticipate and plan for this future.[25]

Look for more changes

Deregulation caused drastic changes in transporting. Many transporting firms—including some big ones—went out of business. But deregulation has given market-oriented managers new opportunities. Some firms are meeting the challenge of change and earning bigger profits while serving their customers better. Similarly, changes in technology—such as EDI and computer-controlled warehouses—are creating new opportunities to simultaneously reduce distribution costs and improve service.

A marketing manager must be sensitive to the environmental effects of transportation decisions.

Although more competitive markets and improved technology are bringing big improvements to the PD area, the biggest challenges may be more basic. As we've emphasized here, physical distribution activities transcend departmental, corporate, and even national boundaries. So seeing and taking advantage of the opportunities for improvements often requires cooperation all along the channel system. Too often, such cooperation doesn't exist—and changing ingrained ways of doing things is hard. But marketing managers who push for innovations in these areas are likely to win customers away from firms and whole channel systems that are stuck on doing things in the old ways.[26]

CONCLUSION

This chapter deals with physical distribution activities—and how they provide *time* and *place* utility. We looked at the PD customer service level and why it is important.

We emphasized the relation between customer service level, transporting, and storing. The physical distribution concept focuses on coordinating all the storing and transporting activities into a smoothly working system—to deliver the desired service level at the lowest cost.

Marketing managers often want to improve service and may select a higher-cost alternative to improve their marketing mix. The total cost approach might reveal that it is possible *both* to reduce

costs and to improve service—perhaps by identifying creative new distribution alternatives.

We discussed various modes of transporting and their advantages and disadvantages. We also discussed the ways to manage inventory needs and costs. We explained why distribution centers have become an important way to cut storing and handling costs, and we explained how computerized information links—within firms and among firms in the channel—are increasingly important in blending all of the activities into a smooth-running system.

Effective marketing managers make important strategy decisions about physical distribution. But many firms have not really accepted the physical distribution concept. Creative marketing managers may be able to cut their PD costs while maintaining or improving their customer service levels. And production-oriented competitors may not even understand what is happening.

QUESTIONS AND PROBLEMS

1. Explain how adjusting the customer service level could improve a marketing mix. Illustrate.

2. Briefly explain which aspects of customer service you think would be most important for a producer that sells fabric to a firm that manufactures furniture.

3. Briefly describe a purchase you made where the customer service level had an effect on the product you selected or where you purchased it.

4. Discuss the types of trade-offs involved in PD costs, service levels, and sales.

5. Explain the total cost approach and why it may be controversial in some firms. Give examples of how conflicts might occur between different departments.

6. Discuss the relative advantages and disadvantages of railroads, trucks, and airlines as transporting methods.

7. Discuss why economies of scale in transportation might encourage a producer to include a regional merchant wholesaler in the channel of distribution for its consumer product.

8. Discuss some of the ways that air transportation can change other aspects of a Place system.

9. Explain which transportation mode would probably be most suitable for shipping the following goods to a large Chicago department store:

    a. 300 pounds of Alaskan crab.
    b. 15 pounds of screwdrivers from New York.
    c. Three dining room tables from High Point, North Carolina.
    d. 500 high-fashion dresses from the garment district in New York City.
    e. A 10,000-pound shipment of machines from England.
    f. 600,000 pounds of various appliances from Evansville, Indiana.

    How would your answers change if this department store were the only one in a large factory town in Ohio?

10. Indicate the nearest location where you would expect to find large storage facilities. What kinds of products would be stored there? Why are they stored there instead of some other place?

11. When would a producer or middleman find it desirable to use a public warehouse rather than a private warehouse? Illustrate, using a specific product or situation.

12. Discuss the distribution center concept. Is this likely to eliminate the storing function of conventional wholesalers? Is it applicable to all products? If not, cite several examples.

13. Clearly differentiate between a warehouse and a distribution center. Explain how a specific product would be handled differently by each.

14. Discuss some of the ways computers are being used to improve PD decisions.

15. Explain why a just-in-time delivery system would require a supplier to pay attention to quality control. Give an example to illustrate your points.

16. Discuss the problems a supplier might encounter in using a just-in-time delivery system with a customer in a foreign country.

SUGGESTED CASES

16. Blackburn Company

26. Valley Packers, Inc.

COMPUTER-AIDED PROBLEM

12. Total Distribution Cost

Proto Company has been producing various items made of plastic. It recently added a line of plain plastic cards that other firms (such as banks and retail stores) will imprint to produce credit cards. Proto offers its customers the plastic cards in different colors, but they all sell for $40 per box of 1,000. Tom Phillips, Proto's product manager for this line, is considering two possible physical distribution systems. He estimates that if Proto uses airfreight, transportation costs will be $7.50 a box, and its cost of carrying inventory will be 5 percent of total annual sales dollars. Alternatively, Proto could ship by rail for $2 a box. But rail transport will require renting space at four regional warehouses—at $26,000 a year each. Inventory carrying cost with this system will be 10 percent of total annual sales dollars. Phillips prepared a spreadsheet to compare the cost of the two alternative physical distribution systems.

a. If Proto Company expects to sell 20,000 boxes a year, what are the total physical distribution costs for each of the systems?

b. If Phillips can negotiate cheaper warehouse space for the rail option so that each warehouse costs only $20,000 per year, which physical distribution system has the lowest overall cost?

c. Proto's finance manager predicts that interest rates are likely to be lower during the next marketing plan year and suggests that Tom Phillips use inventory carrying costs of 4 percent for airfreight and 7.5 percent for railroads (with warehouse cost at $20,000 each). If interest rates are in fact lower, which alternative would you suggest? Why?

For additional questions related to this problem, see Exercise 12–3 in the *Learning Aid for Use with Basic Marketing*, 12th edition.

13

Retailers, Wholesalers, and Their Strategy Planning

When You Finish This Chapter, You Should

1. Understand how retailers plan their marketing strategies.

2. Know about the many kinds of retailers that work with producers and wholesalers as members of channel systems.

3. Understand the differences among the conventional and nonconventional retailers—including those who accept the mass-merchandising concept.

4. Understand scrambled merchandising and the "wheel of retailing."

5. See why size or belonging to a chain can be important to a retailer.

6. Know the various kinds of merchant wholesalers and agent middlemen and the strategies that they use.

7. Know what progressive wholesalers are doing to modernize their operations and marketing strategies.

8. Understand why retailing and wholesaling have developed in different ways in different countries.

9. Understand the important new terms (shown in red).

Karen Caplan is president of Frieda's, Inc., a wholesale firm that each year supplies supermarkets with $22 million worth of exotic fruits and vegetables. The firm—which was originally called Produce Specialties—was started in 1962 by Karen's mother, Frieda Caplan. It is a sign of the firm's success that kiwifruit, artichokes, alfalfa sprouts, spaghetti squash, pearl onions, and mushrooms no longer seem very exotic. All of these crops were once viewed as unusual. Few farmers grew them, and consumers didn't know about them. Supermarkets and traditional produce wholesalers didn't want to handle them because they had a limited market. Frieda's helped to change all that.

Caplan realized that some supermarkets wanted to put more emphasis on their produce departments. These retailers were targeting consumers who wanted more choices in the hard-to-manage produce department. Serving this target market called for a different strategy from one that might be used with big chains that just want to compete with low prices. Caplan looked for products that would help her retailer-customers meet this need. For example, the funny looking, egg-shaped kiwifruit with its fuzzy brown skin was popular in New Zealand but virtually unknown to consumers in other parts of the world. Caplan worked with a number of small farmer-producers to ensure that she could provide her retailer-customers with an adequate supply. She packaged kiwi with interesting recipes and promoted kiwi *and* her brand name to consumers. Because of her efforts, many supermarkets now carry kiwi—which has become a $40 million crop for California farmers.

Since the demand for kiwi has grown, other large wholesalers are now handling them—and they are found in most supermarkets. But that doesn't bother Caplan. When one of her specialty items passes the point on the growth curve where it becomes a commodity with low profit margins, she replaces it with another new and novel item. And her purple "Frieda's Finest" label is on 300 products—like Asian pears, kiwano melons (from New Zealand), sun-dried yellow tomatoes, and hot Asian chiles. She also continues to have an advantage with many supermarkets because she offers many special services. She was the first to routinely use airfreight for orders, and her firm sends a weekly "hot sheet" to produce managers that tells what's selling. The Caplans even hold seminars to inform produce buyers how to improve their sales—and they know what they're talking about because they have a database with detailed information about preferences and buying habits of 100,000 consumers. These consumers responded to the invitation on Frieda's label to write the company.[1]

WHOLESALERS AND RETAILERS PLAN THEIR OWN STRATEGIES

This example shows that wholesalers are often a vital link in a channel system—and in the whole marketing process—helping both their suppliers and customers. It also shows that retailers and wholesalers—like other businesses—must select their target markets and marketing mixes carefully.

In Chapter 11, we discussed the functions that wholesalers and retailers perform as intermediaries in channel systems. In this chapter, we'll focus on the major decision areas that retailers and wholesalers consider in developing their own strategies.

We'll start with the strategies used by different types of retailers and how they are evolving. It's important to understand this evolution because the pace of change in retailing is accelerating. Understanding how and why retailing changes will help you know what to expect in the future. Then, we'll consider the different types of wholesalers and how they adjust their strategies to do a better job meeting the needs of both their suppliers and customers.

THE NATURE OF RETAILING

Retailing covers all of the activities involved in the sale of products to final consumers. Retailers range from large, sophisticated chains of specialized stores—like Toys "R" Us—to individual merchants like the woman who sells baskets from an open stall in the central market in Ibadan, Nigeria. Because they serve individual consumers, even the largest retailers face the challenge of handling small transactions. And the total number of transactions with consumers is much greater than at other channel levels.

Retailing is crucial to consumers in every macro-marketing system. For example, consumers spend $2.2 *trillion* (that's $2,200,000,000,000!) a year buying goods and services from U.S. retailers. If the retailing effort isn't effective, everyone in the channel suffers—and some products aren't sold at all.

The nature of retailing—and its rate of change—are generally related to the stage and speed of a country's economic development. In the United States, retailing tends to be more varied—and more mature—than in most other countries. By studying the U.S. system—and how it is changing—you will better understand how retailing is evolving in other parts of the world.

PLANNING A RETAILER'S STRATEGY

Retailers interact directly with final consumers—so strategy planning is critical to their survival. If a retailer loses a customer to a competitor, the retailer is the one who suffers. Producers and wholesalers still make *their* sale regardless of which retailer sells the product. Retailers must be guided by the old maxim "Goods well bought are half sold."

Most retailers in developed nations sell more than one kind of product. The assortment of products they handle can be critical to their success. Yet, it is best to think of the retailer's *whole offering*—assortment of goods and services, advice from salesclerks, convenience, and the like—as its "Product."

In the case of service retailing—dry cleaning, fast food, tourist attractions, or one-hour photo processing, for example—the retailer is also the producer. Now let's look at why customers choose particular retailers.

It's best to think of a retailer's Product as its *whole offering*—including its assortment of goods and services, advice from salespeople, and the convenience of its hours and location.

Consumers have reasons for buying from particular retailers

Different consumers prefer different kinds of retailers. But many retailers either don't know or don't care why. All too often, beginning retailers just rent a store and assume customers will show up. As a result, in the U.S. about three-fourths of new retailing ventures fail during the first year. To avoid this fate, a new retailer—or one trying to adjust to changing conditions—should carefully identify possible target markets and try to understand why these people buy where they do.[2]

Emotional and social needs may affect the choice

Our discussion of consumer behavior and needs in Chapter 7 applies here. For example, some people get an ego boost from shopping in a store with a prestige image. Others just want to shop in a store where they don't feel out of place. This kind of social influence can be subtle, but different stores do seem to attract customers from different social classes and cultural backgrounds. Most people like to shop where salespeople and other customers are similar to themselves. Dollar General—a chain of 1,300 general merchandise stores—succeeds with a "budget" image that appeals to lower-class customers. Tiffany's, on the other hand, works at its upper-class image.

The atmosphere at a retail store may also have an important emotional effect on how consumers view a retailer. How merchandise is displayed, what decorations, colors, and finishes are used, and even the temperature, sounds, and smell of a store all contribute to its "atmospherics" and store image. The right combination of these factors may attract more target customers and encourage them to spend more. But interesting surroundings are usually costly, and the money is well spent only when the shopping atmosphere is consistent with the needs of the target market the retailer is trying to attract. Ultimately, the prices that consumers pay must cover the cost of the facilities where they shop. And a store's image may be a plus or a minus depending on the target market.

There is no one right answer as to whom a retailer should appeal to. However, as in other businesses, segmentation and positioning decisions are important to retailers. And ignoring emotional and social dimensions in those decisions can lead to serious errors in a retailer's strategy planning.[3]

Economic needs—which store has the best value?

Whatever the effect of other consumer needs, factors related to economic needs are usually very important when a consumer selects a retailer. Some of the most important factors include:

- *Price* (value offered, credit, special discounts).
- *Location* (convenience, parking, safety).
- *Product selection* (width and depth of assortment, quality).
- *Special services* (home delivery, special orders, gift wrap).
- *Helpful salespeople* (courteous, knowledgeable, fast checkout).
- *Fairness in dealings* (honesty, return privileges).

Retailers should consciously make decisions that set policies on all of these factors. After all, it is the combination of these factors that differentiates one retailer's offering and strategy from another. (In later chapters we'll go into more detail on the promotion and price strategy decisions that all firms—including retailers and wholesalers—make.)

Different types of retailers emphasize different strategies

Retailers have an almost unlimited number of ways in which to alter their offerings—their marketing mixes—to appeal to a target market. Because of all the variations, it's oversimplified to classify retailers and their strategies based on a single

The store on the left is part of a new chain of 50 Little Tikes retail outlets in Korea. In spite of consumer interest in Western products and new retailing formats, most retailing in Asia is still handled by small limited-line stores, like the independently owned Japanese store on the right.

characteristic—such as merchandise, services, or store size. But a good place to start is by considering basic types of retailers—and some differences in their strategies.

Let's look first at conventional retailers—and then see how others successfully modify conventional offerings to better meet the needs of *some* consumers. Think about *why* the changes take place. That will help you identify opportunities and plan better marketing strategies.

CONVENTIONAL RETAILERS—TRY TO AVOID PRICE COMPETITION

Single-line, limited-line retailers specialize by product

A hundred and fifty years ago, **general stores**—which carried anything they could sell in reasonable volume—were the main retailers in the United States. But with the growing number of consumer products after the Civil War, general stores couldn't offer enough variety in all their traditional lines. So some stores began specializing in dry goods, apparel, furniture, or groceries.

Now most conventional retailers are **single-line** or **limited-line stores**—stores that specialize in certain lines of related products rather than a wide assortment. Many stores specialize not only in a single line—such as clothing—but also in a *limited-line* within the broader line. For example, within the clothing line, a store might carry *only* shoes, formal wear, men's casual wear, or even neckties—but offer depth in that limited line.

Single-line, limited-line stores are being squeezed

The main advantage of such stores is that they can satisfy some target markets better. By adjusting to suit specific customers, they may even build a long-term relationship with their customers and earn a position as *the* place to shop for a certain type of product. But single-line and limited-line stores face the costly problem of having to stock some slow-moving items in order to satisfy the store's target market. Many of these stores are small—with high expenses relative to sales. They try to avoid competition on identical products so they can keep prices up.

Conventional retailers like this have been around for a long time and are still found in every community. They are a durable lot and clearly satisfy some people's needs. In fact, in most countries conventional retailers still handle the vast majority of all retailing sales.

However, this situation is changing fast. Nowhere is the change clearer than in the United States. Conventional retailers are being squeezed by retailers who

Single-line mass-merchandisers, like Blockbuster, offer selections and prices that make it difficult for traditional retailers to compete.

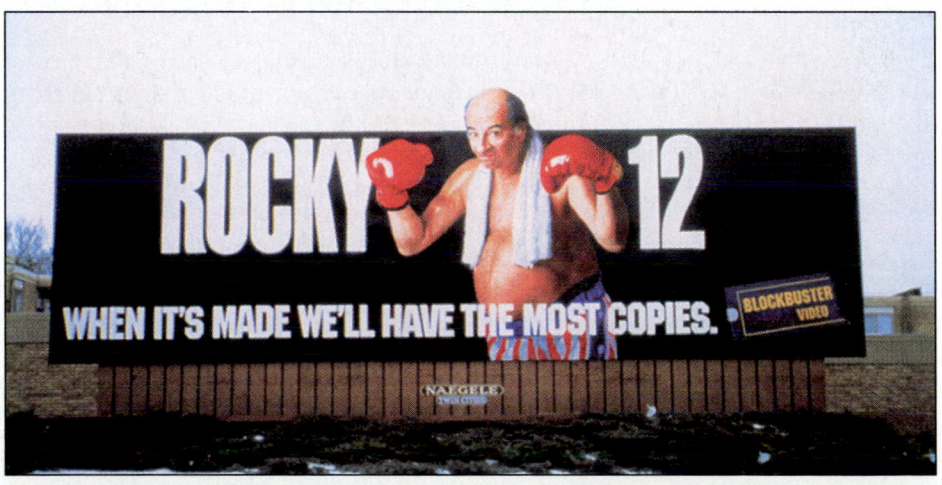

EXHIBIT 13–1 Types of Retailers and the Nature of Their Offerings

modify their mixes in the various ways suggested in Exhibit 13–1. Let's look closer at some of these other types of retailers.

EXPAND ASSORTMENT AND SERVICE—TO COMPETE AT A HIGH PRICE

Specialty shops usually sell shopping products

A **specialty shop**—a type of conventional limited-line store—is usually small and has a distinct "personality." Specialty shops often sell special types of shopping products—such as high-quality sporting goods, exclusive clothing, cameras, or even microwave ovens. They aim at a carefully defined target market by offering a unique product assortment, knowledgeable salesclerks, and better service.

The specialty shop's major advantage is that it caters to certain types of customers whom the management and salespeople come to know well. This simplifies buying, speeds turnover, and cuts costs due to obsolescence and style changes. Specialty shops probably will continue to be a part of the retailing scene as long as customers have varied tastes—and the money to satisfy them.[4]

Department stores combine many limited-line stores and specialty shops

Department stores are larger stores that are organized into many separate departments and offer many product lines. Each department is like a separate limited-line store and handles a wide variety of shopping products—such as men's wear or housewares.

Even though department stores account for less than 2 percent of the total number of retail stores, they make almost 10 percent of total retail sales. They also lead in customer services—including credit, merchandise return, and delivery. Even today, U.S. department stores average about $22 million in annual sales—compared to about $1.4 million for the average retail store.[5] But their share of retail business has declined continuously since the 1970s. Well-run limited-line stores compete with good service—and often carry the same brands. In the United States and many other countries, mass-merchandising retailers pose an even bigger threat.[6] We'll discuss them next.

EVOLUTION OF MASS-MERCHANDISING RETAILERS

Mass-merchandising is different from conventional retailing

So far we've been describing retailers primarily in terms of their product *assortment*. This reflects traditional thinking about retailing. We could talk about supermarkets and discount houses in these terms too. But then we would miss some important differences—just as some conventional retailers did when mass-merchandising retailers first appeared.

Conventional retailers think that demand in their area is fixed—and they have a "buy low and sell high" philosophy. Many modern retailers reject these ideas. They accept the **mass-merchandising concept**—which says that retailers should offer low prices to get faster turnover and greater sales volumes—by appealing to larger markets. To understand mass-merchandising better, let's look at its evolution from the development of supermarkets and discounters to modern mass-merchandisers, like Kmart and Wal-Mart in the United States and Tesco in the United Kingdom.

Supermarkets started the move to mass-merchandising

From a world view, most food stores are relatively small single- or limited-line operations, a situation that makes shopping for food inconvenient and expensive. Many Italians, for example, still go to one shop for pasta, another for meat, and yet another for milk. Although this seems outdated, keep in mind that many of the world's consumers don't have access to **supermarkets**—large stores specializing in groceries with self-service and wide assortments.

The basic idea for supermarkets developed in the United States during the early Depression years. Some innovators felt they could increase sales by charging lower prices. They also introduced self-service and provided a broad product assortment in large stores. Success and profits came from large-volume sales—not from high traditional markups.[7]

Newer supermarkets carry 30,000 product items and stores average around 40,000 square feet. The 23,000 supermarkets average about $11 million a year in sales. Today, supermarkets have reached the saturation level in the United States, but in many countries they are just becoming a force.[8]

Modern supermarkets are planned for maximum efficiency. Scanners at checkout counters make it possible to carefully analyze the sales and profit of each item—and allocate more shelf space to faster-moving and higher-profit items. This helps sell more products—faster. It also reduces the investment in inventory, makes stocking easier, and minimizes the cost of handling products. *Survival* depends on such efficiency. Net profits in supermarkets usually run a thin 1 percent of sales—*or less!*

To increase sales volume and turnover, some supermarket operators open "super warehouse" stores. These 50,000- to 100,000-square-foot stores carry more items than supermarkets, but they usually put less emphasis on perishable items like produce or meat. These efficiently run, bare-bones facilities sell groceries at about 25 percent off the typical supermarket price.[9]

Catalog showroom retailers preceded discount houses

Catalog showroom retailers sell several lines out of a catalog and display showroom—with backup inventories. Before 1940, catalog sellers were usually wholesalers who also sold at discounted prices to friends and members of groups—such as labor unions or church groups. In the 1970s, however, these operations expanded rapidly by aiming at final consumers and offering attractive catalogs and improved facilities. Catalog showroom retailers—like Service

Merchandise, Consumers Distributing, and Best—offer price savings and deliver almost all the items in their catalogs from backroom warehouses. They emphasize well-known manufacturer brands of jewelry, gifts, luggage, and small appliances but offer few services.[10]

Early catalog retailers didn't bother conventional retailers because they weren't well publicized and accounted for only a small portion of total retail sales. If those catalog retailers had moved ahead aggressively, the current retailing scene might be different. But instead, discount houses developed.

Discount houses upset some conventional retailers

Right after World War II, some retailers moved beyond offering discounts to selected customers. These **discount houses** offered "hard goods" (cameras, TVs, appliances)—at substantial price cuts—to customers who would go to the discounter's low-rent store, pay cash, and take care of any service or repair problems themselves. These retailers sold at 20 to 30 percent off the list price being charged by conventional retailers.

In the early 1950s—with war shortages finally over—manufacturer brands became more available. The discount houses were able to get any brands they wanted—and to offer wider assortments. At this stage, many discounters turned respectable—moving to better locations and offering more services and guarantees. They began to act more like regular retailers. But they kept their prices lower than conventional retailers to keep turnover high. It was from these origins that today's mass-merchandisers developed.

Mass-merchandisers are more than discounters

Mass-merchandisers are large, self-service stores with many departments that emphasize "soft goods" (housewares, clothing, and fabrics) and staples (like health and beauty aids) but still follow the discount house's emphasis on lower margins to get faster turnover. Mass-merchandisers—like Kmart and Wal-Mart—have checkout counters in the front of the store and little sales help on the floor. The average mass-merchandiser has nearly 60,000 square feet of floor space, but many new stores are 100,000 square feet or more.

Mass-merchandisers grew rapidly—and they've become the primary nonfood place to shop for many frequently purchased consumer products. In fact, they've expanded so rapidly in many areas that they're no longer taking customers from conventional retailers—but instead are locked in head-to-head competition with each other.[11]

Superstores meet all routine needs

Some supermarkets and mass-merchandisers have moved toward becoming **superstores (hypermarkets)**—very large stores that try to carry not only foods, but all goods and services that the consumer purchases *routinely*. Such a store may look like a mass-merchandiser, but it's different in concept. A superstore is trying to meet *all* the customer's routine needs—at a low price.

Superstores carry about 50,000 items. In addition to foods, a superstore carries personal care products, medicine, some apparel, toys, some lawn and garden products, gasoline—and services such as dry cleaning, travel reservations, bill paying, and banking. Some superstores are very large—over 200,000 square feet.[12]

New mass-merchandising formats keep coming

The warehouse club is another retailing format gaining in popularity. Sam's Club and Price/Costco are two of the largest. Consumers usually pay an annual membership fee to shop in these large, bare-bones facilities. Among the 3,500 items per store, they carry food, appliances, yard tools, tires, and other items that many consumers see as homogeneous shopping items—and want at the lowest

TOYS "R" US IS SERIOUS ABOUT RETAILING

Although toy sales in the United States have been flat for a number of years, sales for the Toys "R" Us chain have grown very rapidly. Moreover, about 20 cents of every dollar U.S. consumers spend on toys is now spent at a Toys "R" Us. Yet, Toys "R" Us didn't always enjoy this lofty success. In 1978, it nearly went bankrupt! At that time, most toys were distributed through thousands of small, independent toy stores—although mass-merchandisers like Kmart drew some customers by offering the fastest-selling toys at low prices. In this highly competitive market, Toys "R" Us pioneered a new retailing format—and it was a real success.

Each store—now almost 900 of them worldwide—is conveniently located, and each offers low prices on a mind-boggling selection of over 20,000 toys. The company's buying clout helps it to get low prices from toy producers. In addition, it uses computers in each store to spot fast-selling toys before they're hits. This allows the firm to buy early and avoid stock-outs that trouble other toy retailers.

Toys "R" Us is also aggressively opening stores in overseas markets—such as the United Kingdom, Hong Kong, and Japan. In these countries, small shops and department stores still dominated toy distribution before Toys "R" Us entered the market.

To understand how Toys "R" Us is affecting these markets, let's look at what happened when Toys "R" Us opened its first German store in 1987. Small toy retailers pressed local governments to keep the chain out. They criticized the Toys "R" Us self-service approach and argued that there would be no expert to warn parents about dangerous toys. German toymakers were also hostile—and many initially refused to sell to the chain. They feared that its hard-nosed buying would eat into their profits. Consumers, however, liked Toys "R" Us, and sales grew fast. As other German retailers began to copy the Toys "R" Us approach, overall toy sales rose by 50 percent. Toys "R" Us got one-fourth of that increase, but competitors got more business too—and consumers got much better selections and prices.[13]

possible price. The rapid growth of these clubs has also been fueled by sales to business customers, primarily small businesses. That's why some people call these outlets wholesale clubs. However, when half or more of a firm's sales are to final consumers, it is classified as a retailer, not a wholesaler.[14]

Single-line mass-merchandisers are coming on strong

Since 1980 some retailers—focusing on single product lines—have adopted the mass-merchandisers' approach with great success. Toys "R" Us pioneered this trend. Similarly, Payless Drugstores, B. Dalton Books, Ikea (furniture), Home Depot (home improvements), Circuit City (electronics), and Sports Unlimited attract large numbers of customers with their large assortment and low prices in a specific product category. These stores are called category killers because it's so hard for less specialized retailers to compete.[15]

SOME RETAILERS FOCUS ON ADDED CONVENIENCE

Supermarkets, discounters, and mass-merchandisers provide many different products at low prices under one roof. But sometimes consumers want more convenience even if the price is higher. Let's look at some retailers who meet this need.

Convenience (food) stores must have the right assortment

Convenience (food) stores are a convenience-oriented variation of the conventional limited-line food stores. Instead of expanding their assortment, however, convenience stores limit their stock to pickup or fill-in items like bread, milk, beer, and eat-on-the-go snacks. Stores such as 7-Eleven, Majik Market, and Stop-N-Go aim to fill consumers' needs between major shopping trips to a supermarket. They offer convenience—not assortment—and often charge prices 10 to 20 percent higher than nearby supermarkets. However, as many gas stations have been converted to convenience stores and other retailers have expanded their hours, intense competition is driving down convenience store prices and profits.[16]

Vending machines are convenient

Automatic vending is selling and delivering products through vending machines. Although the growth in vending machine sales is impressive, such sales account for only about 1.5 percent of total U.S. retail sales. Yet, for some target markets this retailing method can't be ignored.

The major disadvantage to automatic vending is high cost. The machines are expensive to buy, stock, and repair relative to the volume they sell. Marketers of similar nonvended products can operate profitably on a margin of about 20 percent. The vending industry requires about 41 percent to cover costs—so they must charge higher prices.[17]

Shop at home—with telephone, TV, and direct-mail retailing

In-home shopping is becoming more popular—especially among time-pressured dual career families. **Telephone and direct-mail retailing** allow consumers to shop at home—usually placing orders by mail or a toll-free long-distance telephone call—and charging the purchase to a credit card. Typically, catalogs and ads on TV let customers see the offerings, and purchases are delivered by United Parcel Service (UPS). Some consumers really like the convenience of this type of retailing—especially for products not available in local stores.

This approach reduces costs with computer mailing lists to help target specific customers and by using warehouse-type buildings and limited sales help. And shoplifting—a big expense for most retailers—isn't a problem. After-tax profits for successful mail-order retailers average about 7 percent of sales—more than twice the profit margins for most other types of retailers. However, with increasing competition and slower sales growth, these margins are eroding.[18]

Put the catalog on cable TV or computer

QVC, Home Shopping Network, and others are succeeding by devoting cable TV channels to home shopping. Most experts think that the coming explosion in the number of available cable channels—and interactive cable services—will make sales from this approach grow even faster.[19]

A number of marketers are trying to offer electronic shopping, which allows consumers to connect their personal computers or a push-button phone to central computer systems. Most of the early efforts in this area fizzled because they proved too complicated for most consumers. Now, however, dial-up systems such as Prodigy—a joint venture between Sears and IBM—seem to be making headway. Further, technology is fast catching up with the idea. Graphical software interfaces and multimedia computers—which can display pictures and full-motion video with CD quality sound—are becoming more commonplace and should be the impetus for growth of "networked" retailers. The electronic retailing revolution won't be immediate, but many believe that it *will* come.[20]

Door-to-door retailers—try to give personal attention

Door-to-door selling means going directly to the consumer's home. It accounts for less than 1 percent of retail sales—but meets some consumers' needs for convenience and personal attention. Door-to-door selling can also be useful

Some retailers reach consumers where it's convenient for them to buy—without going to a store.

with unsought products—like encyclopedias. But with more adults working outside the home, it's getting harder to find someone at home during the day.

RETAILING TYPES ARE EXPLAINED BY CONSUMER NEEDS FILLED

We've talked about many different types of retailers and how they evolved. Earlier, we noted that no single characteristic provided a good basis for classifying all retailers. Now it helps to see the three-dimensional view of retailing presented in Exhibit 13–2. It positions different types of retailers in terms of three consumer-oriented dimensions: (1) width of assortment desired, (2) depth of assortment desired, and (3) a price/service combination. Price and service are combined because they are often indirectly related. Services are costly to provide. So a retailer that wants to emphasize low prices usually has to cut some services—and stores with a lot of service must charge prices that cover the added costs.

We can position most existing retailers within this three-dimensional market diagram. Exhibit 13–2, for example, suggests the *why* of vending machines. Some people—in the front upper left-hand corner—have a strong need for a specific item and are not interested in width of assortment, depth of assortment, or price.

WHY RETAILERS EVOLVE AND CHANGE

Exhibit 13–2 compares different types of *existing* stores. Now we'll look at some ways that retailing is changing.

The wheel of retailing keeps rolling

The **wheel of retailing theory** says that new types of retailers enter the market as low-status, low-margin, low-price operators and then—if successful—evolve into more conventional retailers offering more services with higher operating

EXHIBIT 13–2 A Three-Dimensional View of the Market for Retail Facilities and the Probable Position of Some Present Offerings

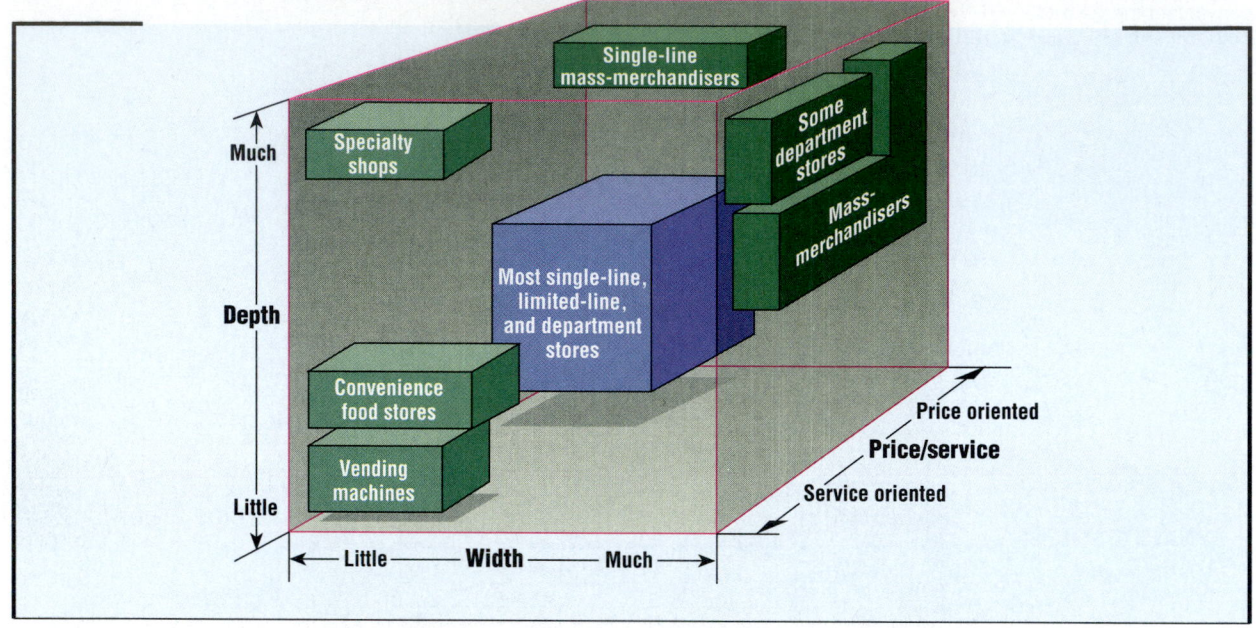

costs and higher prices. Then they're threatened by new low-status, low-margin, low-price retailers—and the wheel turns again. Department stores, supermarkets, and mass-merchandisers went through this cycle.

The wheel of retailing theory, however, doesn't explain all major retailing developments. Vending machines entered as high-cost, high-margin operations. Convenience food stores are high-priced. Suburban shopping centers don't emphasize low price.

Scrambled merchandising— mixing product lines for higher profits

Conventional retailers tend to specialize by product line. But most modern retailers are moving toward **scrambled merchandising**—carrying any product lines they think they can sell profitably. Supermarkets and drugstores sell anything they can move in volume—panty hose, magazines, one-hour photo processing, antifreeze and motor oil, potted plants, and videotapes. Mass-merchandisers don't just sell everyday items but also cameras, jewelry, and even fax machines.[21]

Product life-cycle concept applies to retailer types too

We've seen that consumers' needs help explain why different kinds of retailers developed. But we have to apply the product life-cycle concept to understand this process better. A retailer with a new idea may have big profits—for a while. But if it's a really good idea, the retailer can count on speedy imitation—and a squeeze on profits. Other retailers will copy the new format or "scramble" their product mix to sell products that offer them higher margins or faster turnover.

The cycle is illustrated by what happened with video movies. As the popularity of VCRs grew, video stores cropped up everywhere. The first ones charged $5 a night for a tape. As more competitors entered, however, they drove prices (and profits) down. Competition heated up even more as supermarkets and other stores started to rent the most popular tapes—sometimes for as little as 99

Many retailers scramble their merchandise lines to earn higher profits.

cents a night. Other specialists, like Blockbuster, increased the assortment to appeal to more consumers. In this heated competition, many video stores couldn't cover their costs and went out of business.

Although the cycle for video stores moved very quickly, it can be much slower. But cycles do exist, and some conventional retailers are far along in their life cycles and may be declining. Recent innovators are still in the market growth stage. See Exhibit 13–3. Some retailing formats that are mature in the United States are only now beginning to grow in other countries.

EXHIBIT 13–3 Retailer Life-Cycles—Timing and Years to Market Maturity

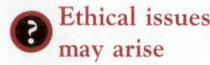

Ethical issues may arise

Most retailers face intense competitive pressure. The desperation that comes with such pressure has pushed some retailers toward questionable marketing practices.

Critics argue, for example, that retailers too often advertise special sale items to bring price-sensitive shoppers into the store but then don't stock enough to meet demand. Other stores are criticized for pushing consumers to trade up to more expensive items. What is ethical and unethical in situations like these, however, is subject to debate. Retailers can't always anticipate demand perfectly, and deliveries may not arrive on time. Similarly, trading up may be a sensible part of a strategy—if it's done honestly.

In retailing, as in other types of business, the marketing concept should guide firms away from unethical treatment of customers. However, a retailer on the edge of going out of business may lose perspective on the need to satisfy customers in both the short and the long term.[22]

RETAILER SIZE AND PROFITS

A few big retailers do most of the business

The large number of retailers (1,564,000) might suggest that retailing is a field of small businesses. To some extent this is true. As shown in Exhibit 13–4, about 60 percent of all the retail stores in the United States had annual sales of less than $500,000 (when the last census of retailers was published). But that's only part of the story. Those same retailers accounted for only about 11 cents of every $1 in retail sales!

The larger retail stores—such as supermarkets and other stores selling more than $2.5 million annually—do most of the business. Only about 7 percent of the retail stores are this big, yet they account for about 60 percent of all retail sales.

On the other hand, the many small retailers can't be ignored. They do reach many consumers—and often are valuable channel members. But their large number—and relatively small sales volume—make working with them expensive. They often require separate marketing mixes.[23]

Big chains are building market clout

One way for a retailer to achieve economies of scale is with a corporate chain. A **(corporate) chain store** is one of several stores owned and managed by the same firm. Chains now account for about half of all retail sales. Most chains use central buying for different stores. This allows them to take advantage of quantity discounts or opportunities for vertical integration—including developing their own efficient distribution centers. They can use EDI and other computer links to control inventory costs and stock-outs. They may also spread promotion and management costs to many stores. Retail chains also have their own dealer brands. Many of these chains are becoming powerful members—or channel captains—in their channel systems. In fact, the most successful of these big chains—like Home Depot, Wal-Mart, and Toys "R" Us—control access to so many consumers that they have the clout to dictate almost every detail of relationships with their suppliers.[24]

Independents form chains too

Competitive pressure from corporate chains encouraged the development of both cooperative chains and voluntary chains.

Cooperative chains are retailer-sponsored groups—formed by independent retailers—that run their own buying organizations and conduct joint promotion efforts. Sales of cooperative chains are rising as they learn how to compete with

EXHIBIT 13–4   Distribution of Stores by Size and Share of Total U.S. Retail Sales

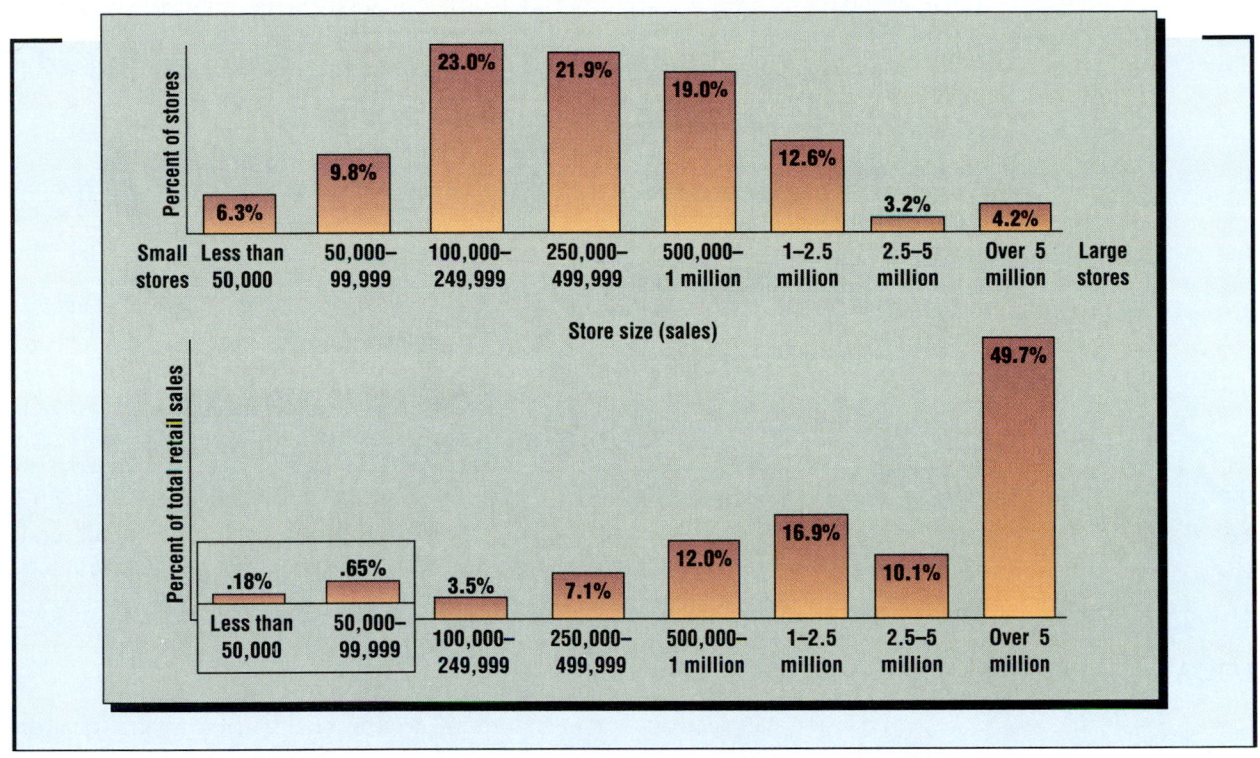

corporate chains. Examples include Associated Grocers, Certified Grocers, and True Value Hardware.

Voluntary chains are wholesaler-sponsored groups that work with "independent" retailers. Some are linked by contracts stating common operating procedures—and requiring the use of common storefront designs, store names, and joint promotion efforts. Examples include IGA and SuperValu in groceries, and Ace in hardware.

Franchisors form chains too

In a **franchise operation**, the franchisor develops a good marketing strategy, and the retail franchise holders carry out the strategy in their own units. Exhibit 13–5 shows examples of well-known franchise operations.

The franchisor acts like a voluntary chain operator—or a producer. Each franchise holder benefits from its relationship with the larger company and its experience, buying power, and image. In return, the franchise holder usually signs a contract to pay fees and commission—and to strictly follow franchise rules designed to continue the successful strategy. Relationships in some franchise channels are strong, but recently overcrowding and fights over contract terms have been a growing source of conflict for franchise operators.

Voluntary chains tend to work with existing retailers, while some franchisors like to work with—and train—newcomers. For newcomers, a franchise often reduces the risk of starting a new business. Only about 5 percent of new franchise operations fail in the first few years—compared to about 70 percent for other new retailers.

EXHIBIT 13–5   Examples of Some Well-Known Franchise Operations

Franchise holders' sales are growing fast and account for about half of all retail sales. One reason is that franchising is especially popular with service retailers, one of the fastest-growing sectors of the economy.[25]

LOCATION OF RETAIL FACILITIES

Location can spell success or failure for a retail facility. But a good location depends on target markets, competitors, and costs. Let's review some of the ideas a retailer should consider in selecting a location.

Downtown and shopping strips evolve without a plan

Most cities have a central business district with many retail stores. At first, it may seem that such a district developed according to some plan. Actually, the location of individual stores is more an accident of time—and available spaces.

As cities grow, shopping strips of convenience stores develop along major roads. Generally, they emphasize convenience products. But a variety of single-line and limited-line stores may enter too, adding shopping products to the mix. Some retailers dress up the stores in these unplanned strips. The expense of remodeling is small compared to the higher rents at big shopping centers. Even so, strips aren't the planned shopping centers that developed in the last 30 years.

Planned shopping centers—not just a group of stores

A **planned shopping center** is a set of stores planned as a unit to satisfy some market needs. The stores sometimes act together for promotion purposes—and they usually provide free parking.

Neighborhood shopping centers consist of several convenience stores. These centers usually include a supermarket, drugstore, hardware store, hairstyling salon, laundry, dry cleaner, gas station, and perhaps others—such as a bakery or video store. They normally serve 7,500 to 40,000 people living within a 6- to 10-minute driving distance. They make one-stop shopping more convenient.

Community shopping centers are larger and offer some shopping stores as well as the convenience stores found in neighborhood shopping centers. They usually include a small department store that carries shopping products (clothing and home furnishings). But most sales in these centers are convenience products. These centers serve 40,000 to 150,000 people within a radius of 5 to 6 miles.

Regional shopping centers are the largest centers and emphasize shopping stores and shopping products. Most of these are enclosed malls, making shopping easier in bad weather. They are usually "anchored" by one or more large department stores and include as many as 200 smaller stores. Stores that feature convenience products are often located at the edge of the center—so they won't get in the way of customers primarily interested in shopping.

Regional centers usually serve 150,000 or more people and are typically found near populated suburban areas. They draw customers from a radius of 7 to 10 miles—or even farther from rural areas where shopping facilities are poor. Regional shopping centers being built now often cover 2 million square feet—as large as 40 football fields![26]

DIFFERENCES IN RETAILING IN DIFFERENT NATIONS

New ideas spread across countries

New retailing approaches that succeed in one part of the world are often quickly adapted to other countries. Self-service approaches that started with supermarkets in the United States are now found in many retail operations around the world. Similarly, mass-merchandising approaches are popular in many countries. In 1969, for example, Kmart entered into a joint venture with Australia's largest department store chain to pioneer mass-merchandising there. The superstore concept, on the other hand, initially developed in Europe.

Mass-merchandising requires mass markets

The low prices, selections, and efficient operations offered by mass-merchandisers and other large chains might be attractive to consumers everywhere. But consumers in less developed nations often don't have the income to support mass distribution. The small shops that survive in these economies sell in very small quantities, often to a small number of consumers.

Some countries block change

The political and legal environment severely limits the evolution of retailing in some nations. Japan is a prime example. For years its Large Store Law—aimed at protecting the country's politically powerful small shopkeepers—has been a real barrier to retail change. The law restricts development of large stores by requiring special permits, which are routinely denied.

Japan says that it is taking steps to change the Large Store Law; in fact, that is why Toys "R" Us was able to enter the Japanese market. Even so, most experts believe that it will be many years before Japan moves away from its system of small, limited-line shops. To put this in perspective, a typical "Ma and Pa" grocery store in Japan is only about 250 square feet. The inefficiency of that retail distribution system is an important reason why Japanese consumers pay very high prices for consumer products. Many countries in other parts of Asia, Europe, and South America impose similar restrictions.

Consumer cooperatives are popular in some countries ·

Retailing in the United States is more diverse than in most other countries. Even so, some retailing formats, notably consumer cooperatives, are more prominent in other countries. Switzerland's Migros is perhaps the most successful example. Migros runs a variety of different types of stores, ranging from supermarkets to appliance and electronics centers.

Migros accounts for about 22 percent of food sales in Switzerland and nearly 16 percent of all retail sales. Consumer cooperatives probably won't become popular in markets where other types of retailers are already established and meeting customers' needs. However, some experts think consumer cooperatives like Migros could become a dominant form of retailing in central and eastern Europe.[27]

WHAT DOES THE FUTURE OF RETAILING LOOK LIKE?

Retailing changed rapidly in the last 30 years—and the changes are expected to continue.

Customers will always have needs. But retail *stores* aren't necessarily the only way to satisfy them. Sales by electronic retailing are expected to grow. For example, Compusave Corporation now has an electronic catalog order system. A videodisc player hooked to a TV-like screen allows the consumer to see pictures and descriptions of thousands of products. The product assortment is similar to that at a catalog store—and the prices are even lower. The consumer makes a selection and inserts a credit card; the computer places the order and routes it to the consumer's home. These machines, being installed in shopping centers around the country, are popular with hurried, cost-conscious consumers.[28]

Many consumers simply don't have as much time to shop as they once did—and a growing number are willing to pay for convenience. Stores will probably continue to make shopping more convenient by staying open later, carrying assortments that make one-stop shopping possible, and being sure stocks don't run out. This interest in convenience and time savings should also lead to the growth of in-home shopping, including interactive shopping using the new generation of cable-TV and computer network services.

We will continue to see growth in retail chains, franchises, and other cooperative arrangements. Such arrangements can help retailers serve their customers better—and also give the retailer more power in the channel. Similarly, changes in technology will continue to make some retailers more powerful and

Supermarkets in the future will rely on even more self-service, including fully automated checkout counters like the one illustrated here in a special store that is used to test new retailing ideas.

efficient. Managers for stores like Wal-Mart are showing that computer data can help master distribution costs—while ensuring that a store is never out of stock.

One thing is certain—change in retailing is inevitable. The future doesn't look too bright for retailers who can't—or won't—change.[29]

WHAT IS A WHOLESALER?

It's hard to define what a wholesaler is because there are so many different wholesalers doing different jobs. Some of their activities may even seem like manufacturing. As a result, some wholesalers describe themselves as "manufacturer and dealer." Some like to identify themselves with such general terms as *merchant, jobber, dealer,* or *distributor.* And others just take the name commonly used in their trade—without really thinking about what it means.

To avoid a long technical discussion on the nature of wholesaling, we'll use the U.S. Bureau of the Census definition:

Wholesaling is concerned with the *activities* of those persons or establishments which sell to retailers and other merchants, and/or to industrial, institutional, and commercial users, but who do not sell in large amounts to final consumers.

So **wholesalers** are firms whose main function is providing wholesaling activities. Wholesalers sell to all of the different types of organizational customers shown in Exhibit 8-1.

DIFFERENT KINDS OF WHOLESALERS HAVE DIFFERENT COSTS AND BENEFITS

You can understand wholesalers—and their strategies—better if you look at them as members of channels. We discussed the general functions that a channel intermediary might provide in Chapter 11 (when we explained why a producer might use an indirect channel of distribution). Moreover, wholesaling functions are just variations on the basic marketing functions—buying, selling, grading, storing, transporting, financing, risk taking and information gathering—we discussed in Chapter 1. Now we'll develop these ideas in more detail. Different types of wholesalers perform different functions for their suppliers and customers.

EXHIBIT 13–6 U.S. Wholesale Trade by Type of Wholesale Operation

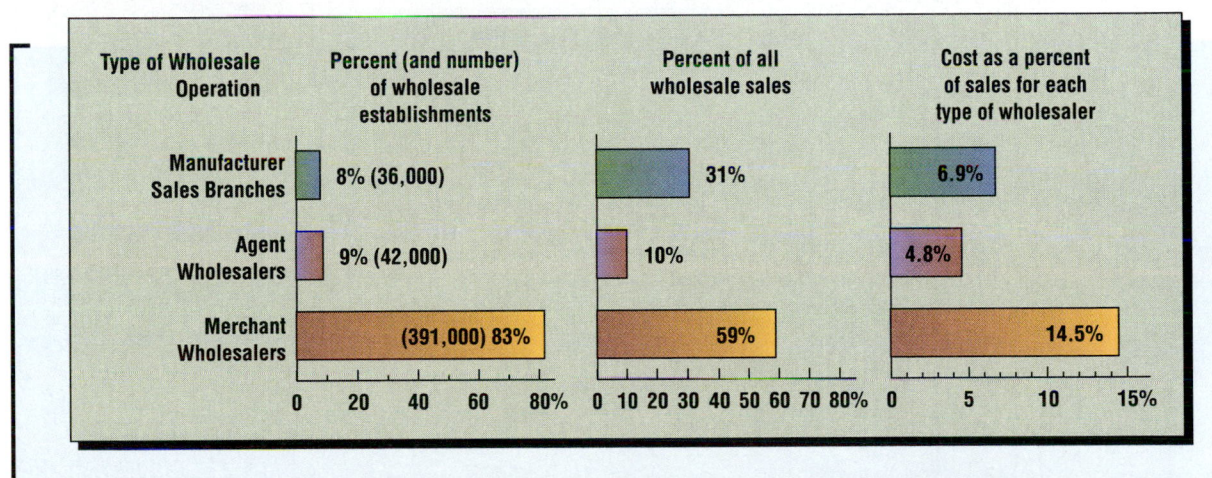

Exhibit 13–6 compares the number, sales volume, and operating expenses of some major types of wholesalers. The differences in operating expenses suggest that each of these types performs—or does not perform—certain wholesaling functions. But which ones and why? And why do manufacturers use merchant wholesalers—costing 14.5 percent of sales—when agent middlemen cost only 4.8 percent?

To answer these questions, we must understand what these wholesalers do—and don't do. Exhibit 13–7 gives a big-picture view of the wholesalers described in more detail below. Note that a major difference between merchant and agent wholesalers is whether they *own* the products they sell. Before discussing these wholesalers, we'll briefly consider producers who handle their own wholesaling activities.

Manufacturers' sales branches are considered wholesalers

Manufacturers who just take over some wholesaling activities are not considered wholesalers. However, when they set up **manufacturers' sales branches**—warehouses that producers set up at separate locations away from their factories—these establishments basically operate as wholesalers. In fact, they're classified as wholesalers by the U.S. Census Bureau and by government agencies in many other countries.

In the United States, these manufacturer-owned branch operations account for about 8 percent of wholesale facilities—but they handle 31 percent of total wholesale sales. One reason sales per branch are so high is that the branches are usually placed in the best market areas. This also helps explain why their operating costs—as a percent of sales—are often lower.[30]

EXHIBIT 13–7   Types of Wholesalers

MERCHANT WHOLESALERS ARE THE MOST NUMEROUS

Merchant wholesalers own (take title to) the products they sell. They often specialize by certain types of products or customers. For example, Fastenal is a wholesaler that specializes in distributing threaded fasteners used by a variety of manufacturers. It owns (takes title to) the fasteners for some period before selling to its customers. In Exhibit 13–6, we can see that about four out of five wholesaling establishments in the United States are merchant wholesalers—and they handle about 59 percent of wholesale sales. Merchant wholesalers are even more common in other countries. Japan is an extreme example. In its unusual multitiered distribution system, products are often bought and sold by a series of merchant wholesalers on their way to the business user or retailer.[31]

Service wholesalers provide all the functions

Service wholesalers are merchant wholesalers who provide all the wholesaling functions. Within this basic group are three types: (1) general merchandise, (2) single-line, and (3) specialty.

General merchandise wholesalers are service wholesalers who carry a wide variety of nonperishable items such as hardware, electrical supplies, plumbing supplies, furniture, drugs, cosmetics, and automobile equipment. With their broad line of convenience and shopping products, they serve hardware stores, drugstores, and small department stores. *Mill supply houses* operate in a similar way, but they carry a broad variety of accessories and supplies to serve the needs of manufacturers.

Single-line (or general-line) wholesalers are service wholesalers who carry a narrower line of merchandise than general merchandise wholesalers. For example, they might carry only food, wearing apparel, or certain types of industrial tools or supplies. In consumer products, they serve the single- and limited-line stores. In business products, they cover a wider geographic area and offer more specialized service.

Specialty wholesalers are service wholesalers who carry a very narrow range of products—and offer more information and service than other service whole-

Merchant wholesalers in Asia are often smaller, carry narrower product lines, and deal with fewer customers than their counterparts in North America.

3M produces 1,600 products that are used by auto body repair shops in the U.S., Europe, Japan, and other countries. To reach this target market, 3M works with hundreds of specialty wholesalers.

salers. A consumer products specialty wholesaler might carry only health foods or oriental foods instead of a full line of groceries.

A specialty wholesaler of business products might limit itself to fields requiring special technical knowledge or service. Richardson Electronics is an interesting example. It specializes in distributing replacement parts, such as electron tubes, for old equipment that many manufacturers still use on the factory floor. Richardson describes itself as "on the trailing edge of technology," but its unique products, expertise, and service are valuable to its target customers, many of whom operate in countries where new technologies are not yet common.[32]

Limited-function wholesalers provide some functions

Limited-function wholesalers provide only *some* wholesaling functions. Exhibit 13–8 shows the functions typically provided—and not provided. In the following paragraphs, we will discuss the main features of these wholesalers. Although less numerous in some countries, these wholesalers are very important for some products.

Cash-and-carry wholesalers want cash

Cash-and-carry wholesalers operate like service wholesalers—except that the customer must pay cash.

Some retailers, such as small auto repair shops, are too small to be served profitably by a service wholesaler. So service wholesalers set a minimum charge—or just refuse to grant credit to a small business that may have trouble paying its bills. The cash-and-carry wholesaler can operate at lower cost because the retailers take over many wholesaling functions. These cash-and-carry operators are especially common in less-developed nations where very small retailers handle the bulk of retail transactions. In the U.S., big warehouse clubs are taking some of this business.

Drop-shippers do not handle the products

Drop-shippers own (take title to) the products they sell—but they do *not* actually handle, stock, or deliver them. These wholesalers are mainly involved in

EXHIBIT 13–8   Functions Provided by Different Types of Limited-Function Merchant Wholesalers

Functions	Cash-and-Carry	Drop-Shipper	Truck	Mail-Order	Cooperatives	Rack Jobbers
For customers						
Anticipates needs	X		X	X	X	X
"Regroups" products (one or more of four steps)	X		X	X	X	X
Carries stocks	X		X	X	X	X
Delivers products			X		X	X
Grants credit		X	Maybe	Maybe	Maybe	Consignment (in some cases)
Provides information and advisory services		X	Some	Some	X	
Provides buying function		X	X	X	Some	X
Owns and transfers title to products	X	X	X	X	X	X
For producers						
Provides producers' selling function	X	X	X	X	X	X
Stores inventory	X		X	X	X	X
Helps finance by owning stocks	X		X	X	X	X
Reduces credit risk	X	X	X	X	X	X
Provides market information	X	X	Some	X	X	Some

selling. They get orders and pass them on to producers. Then the producer ships the order directly to the customer. Drop-shippers commonly sell bulky products (like lumber) for which additional handling would be expensive and possibly damaging.

Truck wholesalers deliver—at a cost

Truck wholesalers specialize in delivering products that they stock in their own trucks. By handling perishable products in general demand—tobacco, candy, potato chips, and salad dressings—truck wholesalers may provide almost the same functions as full-service wholesalers. Their big advantage is that they promptly deliver perishable products that regular wholesalers prefer not to carry. A 7-Eleven store that runs out of potato chips on a busy Friday night doesn't want to be out of stock all weekend!

Mail-order wholesalers reach outlying areas

Mail-order wholesalers sell out of catalogs that may be distributed widely to smaller industrial customers or retailers who might not be called on by other middlemen. These wholesalers operate in the hardware, jewelry, sporting goods, and general merchandise lines. For example, Inmac uses a catalog to sell a complete line of computer accessories. Inmac's catalogs are printed in six languages and distributed to business customers in the United States, Canada, and Europe. Many of these customers don't have a local wholesaler.[33]

Mail-order wholesalers sell out of catalogs—usually to distant customers who don't have easy access to a local wholesaler.

Producers' cooperatives do sorting

Producers' cooperatives operate almost as full-service wholesalers—with the profits going to the cooperative's customer-members. Cooperatives develop in agricultural markets where there are many small producers. Cooperatives usually emphasize sorting—to improve the quality of farm products offered to the market. Some also brand these improved products—and then promote the brands. Examples of such organizations are Sunkist (citrus fruits), Sunmaid Raisin Growers Association, and Land O' Lakes Creameries, Inc.[34]

Rack jobbers sell hard-to-handle assortments

Rack jobbers specialize in hard-to-handle assortments of products that a retailer doesn't want to manage—and rack jobbers usually display the products on their own wire racks. For example, a grocery store or mass-merchandiser might rely on a rack jobber to decide which paperback books or magazines it sells. The wholesaler knows which titles sell in the local area—and applies that knowledge in many stores. Rack jobbers are usually paid cash for what is sold or delivered.

AGENT MIDDLEMEN ARE STRONG ON SELLING

They don't own the products

Agent middlemen are wholesalers who do not own the products they sell. Their main purpose is to help in buying and selling. They usually provide even fewer functions than the limited-function wholesalers, so they may operate at relatively low cost—sometimes 2 to 6 percent of their selling price.

They are important in international trade

Agent middlemen are common in international trade. Many markets have only a few well-financed merchant wholesalers. The best many producers can do is get local representation through agents—and then arrange financing through banks that specialize in international trade.

Agent middlemen are usually experts on local business customs and rules concerning imported products in their respective countries. Sometimes a marketing manager can't work through a foreign government's red tape without the help of a local agent.

EXHIBIT 13–9   Functions Provided by Different Types of Agent Middlemen

Functions	Manufacturers' Agents	Brokers	Commission Merchants	Selling Agents	Auction Companies
For customers					
Anticipates needs	Sometimes	Some			
"Regroups" products (one or more of four steps)	Some		X		X
Carries stocks	Sometimes		X		Sometimes
Delivers products	Sometimes		X		
Grants credit			Sometimes	X	Some
Provides information and advisory services	X	X	X	X	
Provides buying function	X	Some	X	X	X
Owns and transfers title to products		Transfers only	Transfers only		
For producers					
Provides selling function	X	Some	X	X	X
Stores inventory	Sometimes		X		X
Helps finance by owning stocks					
Reduces credit risk				X	Some
Provides market information	X	X	X	X	

They are usually specialists

Agent middlemen—like merchant wholesalers—normally specialize by customer type and by product or product line. So it's important to determine exactly what each one does. In the following paragraphs, we'll mention only the most important points about each type. Study Exhibit 13–9 for details on the functions provided by each.

Manufacturers' agents— free-wheeling sales reps

A **manufacturers' agent** sells similar products for several noncompeting producers—for a commission on what is actually sold. Such agents work almost as members of each company's sales force—but they're really independent middlemen. More than half of all agent middlemen are manufacturers' agents.

Their big plus is that they already call on some customers and can add another product line at relatively low cost—and at no cost to the producer until something sells! If an area's sales potential is low, a company may use a manufacturers' agent because the agent can do the job at low cost. Small producers often use agents everywhere because their sales volume is too small to justify their own sales force.

Agents can be especially useful for introducing new products. For this service, they may earn 10 to 15 percent commission. (In contrast, their commission on large-volume established products may be quite low—perhaps only 2 percent.) A 10 to 15 percent commission rate may seem small for a new product with low sales. Once a product sells well, however, a producer may think the rate is high and begin using its own sales reps. Agents are well aware of this possibility. That's why most try to work for many producers and avoid being dependent on only one line.

Manufacturers' agents are very useful in fields where there are many small manufacturers who need to contact customers. They may cover a very narrow geographic area, such as a city or state. However, they are also important in international marketing, and an agent may take on responsibility for a whole country.

Import and export agents specialize in international trade

While manufacturers' agents operate in every country, **export or import agents** are basically manufacturers' agents who specialize in international trade.

These agent middlemen help international firms adjust to unfamiliar market conditions in foreign markets.[35]

Brokers provide information

Brokers bring buyers and sellers together. Brokers usually have a *temporary* relationship with the buyer and seller while a particular deal is negotiated. They are especially useful when buyers and sellers don't come into the market very often. The broker's product is information about what buyers need—and what supplies are available. They may also aid in buyer–seller negotiation. If the transaction is completed, they earn a commission from whichever party hired them. **Export and import brokers** operate like other brokers, but they specialize in bringing together buyers and sellers from different countries.

Selling agents—almost marketing managers

Selling agents take over the whole marketing job of producers—not just the selling function. A selling agent may handle the entire output of one or more producers—even competing producers—with almost complete control of pricing, selling, and advertising. In effect, the agent becomes each producer's marketing manager.

Financial trouble is one of the main reasons a producer calls in a selling agent. The selling agent may provide working capital but may also take over the affairs of the business.

A **combination export manager** is a blend of manufacturers' agent and selling agent—handling the entire export function for several producers of similar but noncompeting lines.

Commission merchants handle and sell products in distant markets

Commission merchants and **export or import commission houses** handle products shipped to them by sellers, complete the sale, and send the money—minus their commission—to each seller.

Commission agents are common in agricultural markets where farmers must ship to big-city central markets. They need someone to handle the products there—as well as sell them—since the farmer can't go with each shipment. Commission agents are sometimes used in other trades—such as textiles. Here many small producers want to reach buyers in a central market, perhaps one in a distant country, without having to maintain their own sales force.

Auction companies— speed up the sale

Auction companies provide a place where buyers and sellers can come together and complete a transaction. There aren't many auction companies, but they are important in certain lines—such as livestock, fur, tobacco, and used cars. For these products, demand and supply conditions change rapidly—and the product must be seen to be evaluated. The auction company brings buyers and sellers together. Buyers inspect the products—then demand and supply interact to determine the price.

COMEBACK AND FUTURE OF WHOLESALERS

In earlier days, wholesalers dominated distribution channels in the United States and most other countries. The many small producers and small retailers needed their services. This situation still exists in many countries, especially those with less-developed economies. However, in the developed nations, as producers became larger some bypassed the wholesalers. Similarly, large retail chains often took control of functions that had been handled by wholesalers. In light of these changes, many people predicted a gloomy future for wholesalers.

Producing profits, not chasing orders

Yet partly due to new management and new strategies, wholesalers have held their own, and many are enjoying significant growth. To be sure, many still operate in the old ways—and wholesaling changes less rapidly than retailing. But progressive wholesalers are becoming more concerned with their customers—and with channel systems. Some offer more services. Others develop voluntary chains that bind them more closely to their customers.

Modern wholesalers no longer require all customers to pay for all the services they offer simply because certain customers use them. Now some wholesalers offer basic service at minimum cost—then charge additional fees for any special services required.

Most modern wholesalers streamlined their operations to cut unnecessary costs and improve profits. To cut costs, they use computers to keep track of inventory—and to order new stock only when it's really needed. Computerized sales analysis helps them identify and drop unprofitable products. Wholesalers are also more selective in picking customers. They use a selective distribution policy—when cost analysis shows that many of their smaller customers are unprofitable. With these less desirable customers gone, wholesalers give more attention to more profitable customers.

Many modern wholesalers are using new technologies—like bar code readers and warehouse management software systems—to constantly update inventory information.

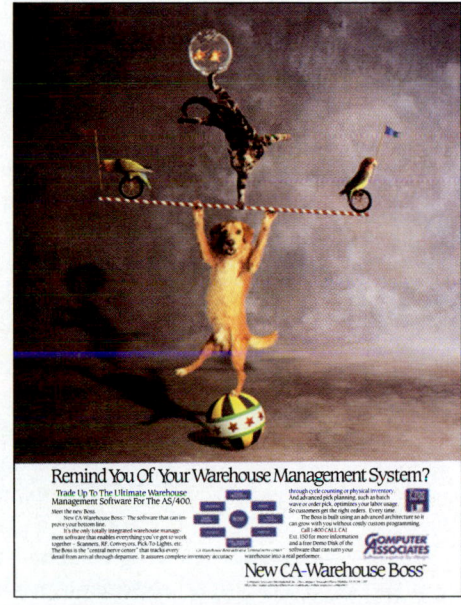

SuperValu is a wholesale supplier to retail supermarkets, but it also runs its own chain of supermarkets. Its experience with retailing helps it do a better job of serving the needs of its retailer-customers.

Progress—or fail

Many wholesalers are also modernizing their warehouses and physical handling facilities. They mark products with bar codes that can be read with hand-held scanners—so inventory, shipping, and sales records can be easily and instantly updated. Computerized order-picking systems speed the job of assembling orders. New storing facilities are carefully located to minimize the costs of both incoming freight and deliveries. Delivery vehicles travel to customers in a computer-selected sequence that reduces the number of miles traveled. And wholesalers who serve manufacturers are rising to the challenge of just-in-time delivery systems and making renewed efforts to add value in the distribution channel.

Perhaps good-bye to some

Not all wholesalers are progressive, and some of the smaller, less efficient ones may fail. Efficiency and low cost, however, are not all that's needed for success. Some wholesalers will disappear as the functions they provided in the past are shifted and shared in different ways in the channel. Cost-conscious buyers for Wal-Mart, Lowe's, and other chains are refusing to deal with some of the middlemen who represent small producers. They want to negotiate directly with the producer—not just accept the price traditionally available from a wholesaler. Similarly, more producers see advantages in having closer direct relationships with fewer suppliers—and they're paring the vendor roles to exclude wholesalers who do a poor job of meeting their needs. Efficient delivery services like UPS and Federal Express are also making it easy and inexpensive for many producers to ship directly to their customers—even ones in foreign markets.[36]

? Is it an ethical issue?

There's no doubt that some wholesalers are being squeezed out of business. Some critics—including many of the wholesalers affected by these changes— argue that it's unethical for powerful suppliers or customers to simply cut out wholesalers who spend money and time—perhaps decades—developing markets. Contracts between channel members and laws sometimes define what changes are or are not legal. But in some cases, the ethical issues are more ambiguous.

For example, as part of a broader effort to improve profits, Amana recently notified Cooper Distributing Co. that it intended to cancel their distribution agreement—in 10 days. Cooper had been handling Amana appliances for 30 years, and Amana products represented 85 percent of Cooper's sales. Amana's explanation to Cooper? "It's not because you're doing a bad job: We just think we can do it better."

Situations like this arise often. They may be cold-hearted, but are they unethical? Many argue that it isn't fair for Amana to cut off the relationship with such short notice. But most wholesalers realize that their business is always at risk—if they don't perform channel functions better or cheaper than what their suppliers or customers can do themselves.[37]

Survivors will need effective strategies

To survive, each wholesaler must develop a good marketing strategy. Profit margins are not large in wholesaling—typically ranging from less than 1 percent to 2 percent. And they've declined in recent years as the competitive squeeze tightened.

The wholesalers who do survive will need to be efficient, but that doesn't mean they'll all have low costs. Some wholesalers' higher operating expenses result from the strategies they select—including the special services they offer to *some* customers.

Wholesaling will last—but weaker, less progressive wholesalers may not.

CONCLUSION

Modern retailing is scrambled—and we'll probably see more changes in the future. In such a dynamic environment, a producer's marketing manager must choose very carefully among the available kinds of retailers. And retailers must plan their marketing mixes with their target customers' needs in mind—while at the same time becoming part of an effective channel system.

We described many types of retailers—and we saw that each has its advantages and disadvantages. We also saw that modern retailers have discarded conventional practices. The old "buy low and sell high" philosophy is no longer a safe guide. Lower margins with faster turnover is the modern philosophy as more retailers move into mass-merchandising. But even this is no guarantee of success as retailers' life cycles move on.

Scrambled merchandising will continue as retailing evolves to meet changing consumer demands. But important breakthroughs are still possible because consumers probably will continue to move away from conventional retailers. Some combination of telephone-order and electronic ordering might make a larger assortment of products available to more people—to better meet their particular needs.

Wholesalers can provide functions for those both above and below them in a channel of distribution. These services are closely related to the basic marketing functions. There are many types of wholesalers. Some provide all the wholesaling functions—while others specialize in only a few. Eliminating wholesalers would not eliminate the need for the functions they provide. And we cannot assume that direct channels are more efficient.

Merchant wholesalers are the most numerous and account for the majority of wholesale sales. Their distinguishing characteristic is that they take title to (own) products. Agent middlemen, on the other hand, act more like sales representatives for sellers or buyers—and they do not take title.

Despite various predictions, wholesalers continue to exist. The more progressive ones adapt to a changing environment. Wholesaling hasn't experienced the revolutions we saw in retailing, and none seem likely. But some smaller—and less progressive—wholesalers will probably fail, while larger, more efficient, and more market-oriented wholesalers will continue to provide these necessary functions.

QUESTIONS AND PROBLEMS

1. What sort of a "product" are specialty shops offering? What are the prospects for organizing a chain of specialty shops?

2. Distinguish among discount houses, price-cutting by conventional retailers, and mass-

merchandising. Forecast the future of low-price selling in food, clothing, and appliances.

3. Discuss a few changes in the marketing environment that you think help to explain why telephone and mail-order retailing have been growing so rapidly.

4. Apply the wheel of retailing theory to your local community. What changes seem likely? Will established retailers see the need for change, or will entirely new firms have to develop?

5. What advantages does a retail chain have over a retailer who operates with a single store? Does a small retailer have any advantages in competing against a chain? Explain your answer.

6. Discuss the kinds of markets served by the three types of shopping centers. Are they directly competitive? Do they contain the same kinds of stores? Is the long-run outlook for all of them similar?

7. Many producers are now seeking new opportunities in international markets. Are the opportunities for international expansion equally good for retailers? Explain your answer.

8. What risks do merchant wholesalers assume by taking title to goods? Is the size of this risk about constant for all merchant wholesalers?

9. Why would a manufacturer set up its own sales branches if established wholesalers were already available?

10. What is an agent middleman's marketing mix? Why do you think that many merchant middlemen handle competing products from different producers, while manufacturers' agents usually handle only noncompeting products from different producers?

11. Discuss the future growth and nature of wholesaling if low-margin retail chains and scrambled merchandising continue to become more important. How will wholesalers have to adjust their mixes? Will wholesalers be eliminated? If not, what wholesaling functions will be most important? Are there any particular lines of trade where wholesalers may have increasing difficulty?

12. What alternatives does a producer have if it is trying to expand distribution in a foreign market and finds that the best existing merchant middlemen won't handle imported products?

13. Discuss how computer systems affect wholesalers' and retailers' operations.

14. Discuss the evolution of wholesaling in relation to the evolution of retailing.

15. Do wholesalers and retailers need to worry about new-product planning just as a producer needs to have an organized new-product development process? Explain your answer.

SUGGESTED CASES

COMPUTER-AIDED PROBLEM

13. Selecting Channel Intermediaries

Art Glass Productions, a producer of decorative glass gift items, wants to expand into a new territory. Managers at Art Glass know that unit sales in the new territory will be affected by consumer response to the products. But sales will also be affected by which combination of wholesalers and retailers Art Glass selects. There is a choice between two wholesalers. One wholesaler, Gift-

ware Distributing, is a merchant wholesaler that specializes in gift items; it sells to gift shops, department stores, and some mass-merchandisers. The other wholesaler, Margaret Degan & Associates, is a manufacturers' agent that calls on many of the gift shops in the territory.

Art Glass makes a variety of glass items, but the cost of making an item is usually about the same—$5.20 a unit. The items would sell to Giftware Distributing at

$12.00 each—and in turn the merchant wholesaler's price to retailers would be $14.00—leaving Giftware with a $2.00 markup to cover costs and profit. Giftware Distributing is the only reputable merchant wholesaler in the territory, and it has agreed to carry the line only if Art Glass is willing to advertise in a trade magazine aimed at retail buyers for gift items. These ads will cost $8,000 a year.

As a manufacturers' agent, Margaret Degan would cover all of her own expenses and would earn 8 percent of the $14.00 price per unit charged the gift shops. Individual orders would be shipped directly to the retail gift shops by Art Glass—using United Parcel Service (UPS). Art Glass would pay the UPS charges at an average cost of $2.00 per item. In contrast, Giftware Distributing would anticipate demand and place larger orders in advance. This would reduce the shipping costs, which Art Glass would pay, to about $.60 a unit.

Art Glass' marketing manager thinks that Degan would only be able to sell about 75 percent as many items as Giftware Distributing—since she doesn't have time to call on all of the smaller shops and doesn't call on any department stores. On the other hand, the merchant wholesaler's demand for $8,000 worth of supporting advertising requires a significant outlay.

The marketing manager at Art Glass decided to use a spreadsheet to determine how large sales would have to be to make it more profitable to work with Giftware and to see how the different channel arrangements would contribute to profits at different sales levels.

  a. Given the estimated unit sales and other values shown on the initial spreadsheet, which type of wholesaler would contribute the most profit to Art Glass Productions?
  b. If sales in the new territory are slower than expected, so that the merchant wholesaler was able to sell only 3,000 units—or the agent 2,250 units—which wholesaler would contribute the most to Art Glass' profits? (Note: Assume that the merchant wholesaler only buys what it can sell—that is, it doesn't carry extra inventory beyond what is needed to meet demand.)
  c. Prepare a table showing how the two wholesalers' contributions to profit compare as the quantity sold varies from 3,500 units to 4,500 units for the merchant wholesaler and 75 percent of these numbers for the manufacturers' agent. Discuss these results. (Note: Use the What If analysis to vary the quantity sold by the merchant wholesaler, and the program will compute 75 percent of that quantity as the estimate of what the agent will sell.)

For additional questions related to this problem, see Exercise 13–4 in the *Learning Aid for Use with Basic Marketing*, 12th edition.

14

Promotion— Introduction to Integrated Marketing Communications

When You Finish This Chapter, You Should

1. Know the advantages and disadvantages of the promotion methods a marketing manager can use in strategy planning.

2. Understand the integrated marketing communications concept and why most firms use a blend of different promotion methods.

3. Understand the importance of promotion objectives.

4. Know how the communication process should affect promotion planning.

5. Know how the adoption processes can guide promotion planning.

6. Know how typical promotion plans are blended to get an extra push from middlemen and help from customers in pulling products through the channel.

7. Understand how direct-response promotion is helping marketers develop more targeted promotion blends.

8. Understand how to determine how much to spend on promotion efforts.

9. Understand the important new terms (shown in red).

Tom O'Flaherty, marketing manager for Modatech Systems in Vancouver, Canada, faced a challenge developing his 1994 marketing plan. Modatech's contact-management software program, *Maximizer for Windows*, made it easy for users—ranging from executives to journalists to marriage brokers—to keep track of every meeting attended, letter sent, note taken, or response promised. Modatech was already successful in Canada, but O'Flaherty's objective was to grow in the U.S. market. He was starting from scratch—with no sales, no distribution, and no brand recognition. Worse, a competitor's program had already attracted a half-million buyers; many of them were eagerly waiting for its newest version.

O'Flaherty knew that this market situation required a targeted, cost-effective promotion blend. His $700,000 promotion budget was limited, so he targeted the early adopters of contact-management software—salespeople and entrepreneurs. He needed to inform them—and potential channel members—about his product. To generate sales, he also needed to persuade them that his offering was superior.

O'Flaherty first turned to mass selling. He selected the Rizzuto Marketing and Media Group to develop attention-getting 90-second radio ads. These unusually long direct-response ads promised a specific, targeted benefit: that Maximizer software would help "close sale after sale." And to make the message credible, the ad guaranteed a full refund if the customer didn't have the best sales year ever. The agency scheduled many of the ads on Rush Limbaugh's radio talk show, which reaches Modatech's target customers, many of whom pay close attention to the show while driving to their next sales call. The agency also created ads for airline in-flight magazines. These followed the same theme as the radio ads and included a toll-free telephone number to prompt direct-response inquiries and orders. A telephone salesperson responded to questions, added the caller to the firm's database, and sent more detailed promotional brochures. To get free publicity, Modatech sent samples of the software to computer-magazine writers. Many of these opinion leaders wrote favorable reviews.

Another step was to make the product conveniently available at retail stores where salespeople could answer questions, provide demos, and close sales. To help with this objective, the agency placed ads in trade magazines read by software retailers and wholesalers. These ads touted Modatech's consumer promotion plans, encouraged middlemen to place orders in time to meet demand, and explained how to place an order.

The buyers for some big software dealers, such as Egghead Software, thought Maximizer and its promotion would pull in customers. So, they stocked it and promoted it in their own ads. Their salespeople were also ready to give an in-store promotion push.

Within months, Maximizer was the best-selling contact manager in the U.S. Now Moda-tech is developing a new version. It can build on relationships its promotion has already developed, by using its database to target new direct-mail promotions.[1]

SEVERAL PROMOTION METHODS ARE AVAILABLE

Promotion is communicating information between seller and potential buyer or others in the channel to influence attitudes and behavior. The marketing manager's main promotion job is to tell target customers that the right Product is available at the right Place at the right Price.

What the marketing manager communicates is determined by target customers' needs and attitudes. *How* the messages are delivered depends on what blend of the various promotion methods the marketing manager chooses.

As the Modatech example shows, a marketing manager can choose from several promotion methods—personal selling, mass selling, and sales promotion (see Exhibit 14–1). Further, because the different promotion methods have different strengths and limitations, a marketing manager usually uses them in combination. And, as with other marketing mix decisions, it is critical that the marketer manage and coordinate the different promotion methods as an integrated "whole"—not as separate and unrelated parts.

Personal selling—flexibility is its strength

Personal selling involves direct spoken communication between sellers and potential customers. Face-to-face selling provides immediate feedback—which helps salespeople to adapt. Although salespeople are included in most marketing mixes, personal selling can be very expensive. So it's often desirable to combine personal selling with mass selling and sales promotion.

EXHIBIT 14–1   Basic Promotion Methods and Strategy Planning

Mass selling involves advertising and publicity

Mass selling is communicating with large numbers of potential customers at the same time. It's less flexible than personal selling, but when the target market is large and scattered, mass selling can be less expensive.

Advertising is the main form of mass selling. **Advertising** is any *paid* form of nonpersonal presentation of ideas, goods, or services by an identified sponsor. It includes the use of such media as magazines, newspapers, radio and TV, signs, and direct mail. While advertising must be paid for, another form of mass selling—publicity—is "free."

Publicity avoids media costs

Publicity is any *unpaid* form of nonpersonal presentation of ideas, goods, or services. Of course, publicity people are paid. But they try to attract attention to the firm and its offerings *without having to pay media costs*. For example, book publishers try to get authors on TV talk shows because this generates a lot of interest—and book sales—without the publisher paying for TV time.

Coleco's publicity to introduce its Cabbage Patch dolls is a classic example. It held press parties for reporters and their children. A number of reporters wrote human interest stories about their kids "adopting" the cute dolls. Those stories prompted more media attention—and a very successful product introduction—without Coleco doing any introductory advertising.[2]

If a firm has a really new message, publicity may be more effective than advertising. Trade magazines, for example, may carry articles featuring the newsworthy products of regular advertisers—in part because they *are* regular advertisers. The firm's publicity people write the basic copy and then try to convince magazine editors to print it. Each year, magazines print photos and stories about new cars—and often the source of the information is the auto producers. A consumer might not pay any attention to an ad but might carefully read a long magazine story with the same information.

Some companies prepare videotapes designed to get free publicity for their products on TV news shows. For example, one video—distributed to TV stations at Halloween—discussed a government recommendation that parents use makeup rather than masks for young children. The story was effectively tied to a new makeup product for children made by PAAS Products.[3]

Sales promotion tries to spark immediate interest

Sales promotion refers to promotion activities—other than advertising, publicity, and personal selling—that stimulate interest, trial, or purchase by final cus-

Kellogg's marketing managers plan mass selling to communicate with final consumers, but most of their communication with retailers is handled by salespeople.

EXHIBIT 14–2   Example of Sales Promotion Activities

Aimed at final consumers or users	Aimed at middlemen	Aimed at company's own sales force
Contests	Price deals	Contests
Coupons	Promotion allowances	Bonuses
Aisle displays	Sales contests	Meetings
Samples	Calendars	Portfolios
Trade shows	Gifts	Displays
Point-of-purchase materials	Trade shows	Sales aids
Banners and streamers	Meetings	Training materials
Trading stamps	Catalogs	
Sponsored events	Merchandising aids	

tomers or others in the channel. Sales promotion may be aimed at consumers, at middlemen, or even at a firm's own employees. Examples are listed in Exhibit 14–2.

Relative to other promotion methods, sales promotion can usually be implemented quickly and get results sooner. In fact, most sales promotion efforts are designed to produce immediate results.

Less is spent on advertising than on personal selling or sales promotion

Many people think that promotion money gets spent primarily on advertising—because advertising is all around them. The many ads you see in magazines and newspapers and on TV are impressive—and costly. But all the special sales promotions—coupons, sweepstakes, trade shows, sporting events sponsored by firms, and the like—add up to even more money. Similarly, salesclerks complete most retail sales. And behind the scenes, much personal selling goes on in the channels and in other business markets. In total, firms spend less money on advertising than on personal selling or sales promotion.

However, the amount of emphasis on each promotion method usually varies with each specific marketing strategy—depending on the target market and other elements of the marketing mix. The reason is that different promotion methods have different strengths and limitations. Because the different promotion methods complement each other, some communication tasks can be handled better or more economically with one method than another. To get the whole promotion job done most firms use a blend of the three promotion methods.

We'll talk about individual promotion methods in more detail in the next two chapters. First, however, you need to understand the role of the whole promotion blend—personal selling, mass selling, and sales promotion combined—so you can see how promotion fits into the rest of the marketing mix.

SOMEONE MUST PLAN, INTEGRATE, AND MANAGE THE PROMOTION BLEND

Each promotion method has its own strengths and weaknesses—and in combination they provide a comprehensive set of tools for marketing communications. Yet, each method involves its own distinct activities and requires different types of expertise. As a result, it's usually the responsibility of specialists—such as sales managers, advertising managers, and promotion managers—to develop and implement the detailed plans for the various parts of the overall promotion blend.

Promotion in the channel and promotion to final consumers should be coordinated and consistent.

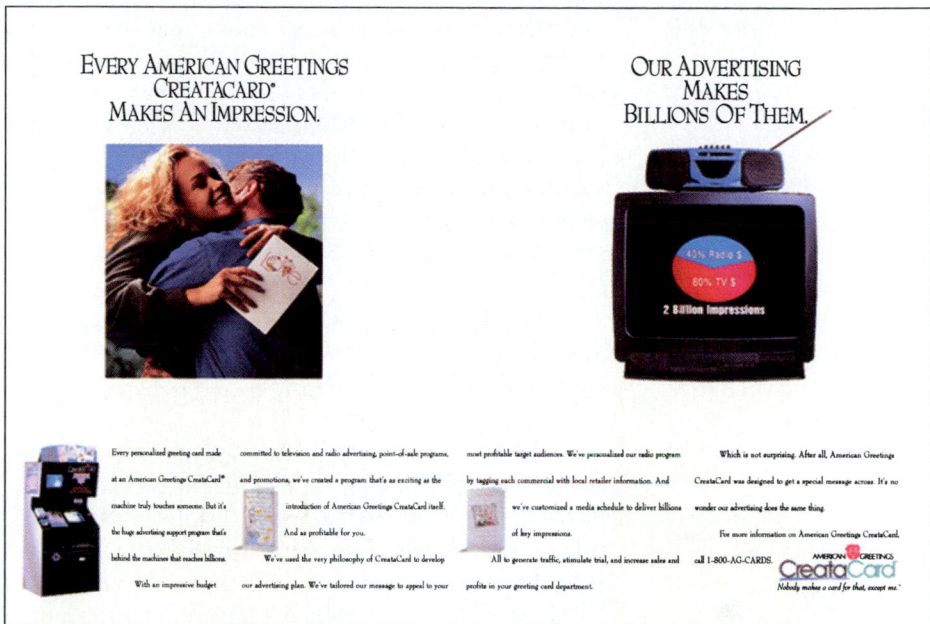

Sales managers manage salespeople

Sales managers are concerned with managing personal selling. Often the sales manager is responsible for building good distribution channels and implementing Place policies. In smaller companies, the sales manager may also act as the marketing manager—and be responsible for advertising and sales promotion.

Advertising managers work with ads and agencies

Advertising managers manage their company's mass selling effort—in television, newspapers, magazines, and other media. Their job is choosing the right media and developing the ads. Advertising departments within their own firms may help in these efforts—or they may use outside advertising agencies. The advertising manager may handle publicity too. Or it may be handled by an outside agency or by whoever handles **public relations**—communication with noncustomers, including labor, public interest groups, stockholders, and the government.

Sales promotion managers need many talents

Sales promotion managers manage their company's sales promotion effort. In some companies, a sales promotion manager has independent status and reports directly to the marketing manager. If a firm's sales promotion spending is substantial, it probably *should* have a specific sales promotion manager. Sometimes, however, the sales or advertising departments handle sales promotion efforts—or sales promotion is left as a responsibility of individual brand managers. Regardless of who the manager is, sales promotion activities vary so much that many firms use both inside and outside specialists.

Marketing manager talks to all, blends all

Although many specialists may be involved in planning for and implementing specific promotion methods, determining the blend of promotion methods is a strategy decision—and the responsibility of the marketing manager.

The various promotion specialists tend to focus on what they know best and their own areas of responsibility. A creative advertising copy writer in New York City—even a very good one—may have no idea what a salesperson does during a call on a wholesale distributor. In addition, because of differences in outlook and experience, the advertising, sales, and sales promotion managers often have trouble working with each other as partners or equals. Too often they just view other promotion methods as using up budget money they want.

The marketing manager must weigh the pros and cons of the various promotion methods, then devise an effective promotion blend—fitting in the various departments and personalities and coordinating their efforts. Then, the advertising, sales, and sales promotion managers should develop the details consistent with what the marketing manager wants to accomplish.

Send a consistent and complete message with integrated marketing communications

An effective blending of all of the firm's promotion efforts should produce **integrated marketing communications**—the intentional coordination of every communication from a firm to a target customer to convey a consistent and complete message.

The Modatech case at the start of this chapter is a good example of integrated marketing communications. Different promotion methods handle different parts of Modatech's overall communication job, but they are coordinated so that the sum is greater than the parts. Although the separate messages are complementary, they are also consistent.

It seems obvious that a firm's different communications to a target market should be consistent. However, when a number of different people are working on different promotion elements, they are likely to see the same big picture only if a marketing manager ensures that it happens. The challenge of consistency is usually greater when different aspects of the promotion effort are handled by different firms at different levels in the distribution channel. As we've discussed, different channel members may have conflicting objectives—especially if they don't have a common focus on the consumer or business user at the end of the channel.

As a starting point, to get effective coordination and consistency everyone involved with the promotion effort must clearly understand the plan for the overall marketing strategy. They all need to understand the role of each of the different promotion methods and how they will work together to achieve specific promotion objectives.

EXHIBIT 14–3   Promotion Seeks to Shift the Demand Curve

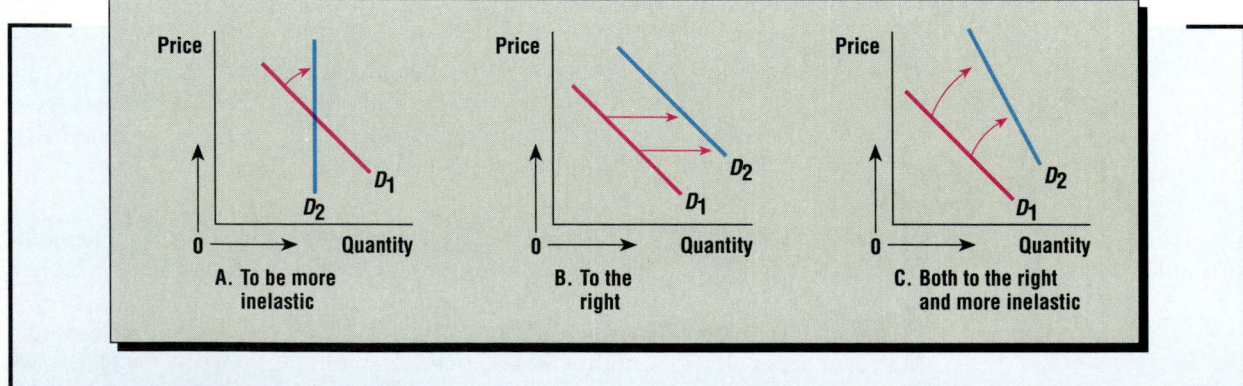

WHICH METHODS TO USE DEPENDS ON PROMOTION OBJECTIVES

Overall objective is to affect behavior

The different promotion methods are all different forms of communication. But good marketing managers aren't interested in just communicating. They want to communicate information that will encourage customers to choose a *specific* product. They know that if they have a better offering, informed customers are more likely to buy. Therefore, they're interested in (1) reinforcing present attitudes or relationships that might lead to favorable behavior or (2) actually changing the attitudes and behavior of the firm's target market.

In terms of demand curves, promotion may help the firm make its present demand curve more inelastic, or shift the demand curve to the right, or both. These possibilities are shown in Exhibit 14–3. The buyer behavior model introduced in Chapter 7 showed the many influences on buying behavior. You saw there that affecting buyer behavior is a tough job—but that is exactly the objective of Promotion.

Informing, persuading, and reminding are basic promotion objectives

For a firm's promotion to be effective, its promotion objectives must be clearly defined—because the right promotion blend depends on what the firm wants to accomplish. It's helpful to think of three basic promotion objectives: *informing, persuading,* and *reminding* target customers about the company and its marketing mix. All try to affect buyer behavior by providing more information.

Even more useful is a more specific set of promotion objectives that states *exactly who* you want to inform, persuade, or remind, and *why.* This is unique to each company's strategy—and specific objectives vary by promotion method. We'll talk about more specific promotion objectives in the next two chapters. Here we'll limit ourselves to the three basic promotion objectives—and how you can reach them.

Informing is educating

Potential customers must know something about a product if they are to buy at all. A firm with a really new product may not have to do anything but inform consumers about it—and show that it meets consumer needs better than other products. When Oldsmobile introduced its Aurora luxury sedan, the unique styling of the car simplified the promotion job. Excitement about the product also generated a lot of free publicity in car magazines and newspapers. Eager customers signed up on waiting lists to buy an Aurora—even before cars arrived at dealer lots.

When a firm introduces a new product, a basic promotion objective is to inform consumers that the product is available.

Persuading usually becomes necessary

When competitors offer similar products, the firm must not only inform customers that its product is available but also persuade them to buy it. A *persuading* objective means the firm will try to develop a favorable set of attitudes so customers will buy—and keep buying—its product. Promotion with a persuading objective often focuses on reasons why one brand is better than competing brands. To help convince consumers to buy Tylenol rather than some other firm's brand, Johnson & Johnson's ads tout Tylenol as the safe pain relief medicine most often used in hospitals.

Reminding may be enough, sometimes

If target customers already have positive attitudes about a firm's marketing mix—or a good relationship with a firm—a *reminding* objective might be suitable. This objective can be extremely important in some cases. Even though customers have been attracted and sold once, they are still targets for competitors' appeals. Reminding them of their past satisfaction may keep them from shifting to a competitor. Campbell's realizes that most people know about its soup—so much of its advertising is intended to remind.

PROMOTION REQUIRES EFFECTIVE COMMUNICATION

Communication can break down

Promotion is wasted if it doesn't communicate effectively. But there are many reasons why a promotion message can be misunderstood—or not heard at all. To understand this, it's useful to think about a whole **communication process**—which means a source trying to reach a receiver with a message. Exhibit 14–4 shows the elements of the communication process. Here we see that a **source**—the sender of a message—is trying to deliver a message to a **receiver**—a potential customer. Research shows that customers evaluate not only the message but also the source of the message in terms of trustworthiness and credibility. For example, American Dental Association (ADA) studies show that Listerine mouthwash helps reduce plaque buildup on teeth. Listerine mentions the ADA endorsement in its promotion to help make the promotion message credible.

A source can use many message channels to deliver a message. The salesperson does it in person with voice and action. Advertising must do it with magazines, newspapers, radio, TV, and other media.

A major advantage of personal selling is that the source—the seller—can get immediate feedback from the receiver. It's easier to judge how the message is being received—and change it if necessary. Mass sellers usually must depend on

EXHIBIT 14–4 The Communication Process

marketing research or total sales figures for feedback—and that can take too long. As we'll discuss later in this chapter, this has prompted some marketers to include toll-free telephone numbers and other ways of building direct-response feedback from consumers into their mass selling efforts.

The **noise**—shown in Exhibit 14–4—is any distraction that reduces the effectiveness of the communication process. Conversations and snack-getting during TV ads are noise. The clutter of competing ads in a newspaper is noise. Advertisers planning messages must recognize that many possible distractions—noise—can interfere with communications.

Encoding and decoding depend on a common frame of reference

The basic difficulty in the communication process occurs during encoding and decoding. **Encoding** is the source deciding what it wants to say and translating it into words or symbols that will have the same meaning to the receiver. **Decoding** is the receiver translating the message. This process can be very tricky. The meanings of various words and symbols may differ depending on the attitudes and experiences of the two groups. People need a common frame of reference to communicate effectively. See Exhibit 14–5. Maidenform encountered this problem with its promotion aimed at working women. The company ran a series of ads depicting women stockbrokers and doctors wearing Maidenform lingerie. The men in the ads were fully dressed. Maidenform was trying to show women in positions of authority, but some women felt the ad presented them as sex objects. In this case, the promotion people who encoded the message didn't understand the attitudes of the target market—and how they would decode the message.[4]

The same message may be interpreted differently

Different audiences may see the same message in different ways—or interpret the same words differently. Such differences are common in international marketing when cultural differences or translation are problems. Coors encouraged its English-speaking customers to "turn it loose," but in Spanish the phrase meant "to suffer from diarrhea." When Frank Perdue said, "It takes a tough man to make a tender chicken," Spanish speakers heard, "It takes a sexually stimulated man to make a chicken affectionate." Many firms run into problems like this.[5]

Problems occur even without translation difficulties. For example, a new children's cough syrup was advertised as extra strength. The advertising people thought they were assuring parents that the product worked well. But cautious Moms and Dads avoided the product because they feared that it might be too strong for their children.

Message channel is important too

The communication process is complicated even more because the receiver knows the message is not only coming from a source but also through some **message channel**—the carrier of the message. A particular message channel may enhance or detract from a message. A TV ad, for example, can *show* that Dawn dishwashing detergent "takes the grease away"; the same claim in a newspaper ad might not be very convincing. On the other hand, a receiver may attach value to a product if the message comes in a well-respected newspaper or magazine. Some consumers buy products advertised in *Good Housekeeping* magazine, for example, because they have faith in its seal of approval.

❓ Ethical issues in marketing communications

Promotion is one of the most often criticized areas of marketing, and many of the criticisms focus on whether communications are honest and fair. Marketers must sometimes make ethical judgments in considering these charges and in planning their promotion.

EXHIBIT 14–5 This same message may be interpreted differently

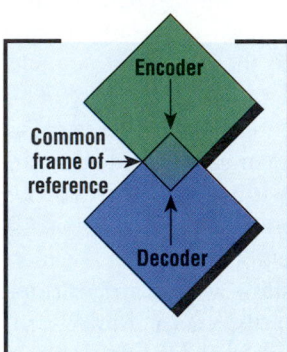

Video publicity releases provide an interesting example. When a TV news program broadcasts a video publicity release, consumers don't know it was prepared to achieve marketing objectives; they think the news staff is the source. That may make the message more credible, but is it fair? Many say yes—as long as the publicity information is truthful. But gray areas still remain. Consider, for example, SmithKline Beecham's video about its new prescription heart attack drug. An estimated 27 million consumers saw the video on various TV news programs. The video included a laundry list of possible side effects and other warnings, just as is required for normal drug advertising. But there's never any guarantee that the warnings won't be edited out by local TV stations.

Critics raise similar concerns about the use of celebrities in advertisements. A person who plays the role of an honest and trustworthy person on a popular TV series may be a credible message source in an ad, but is using such a person misleading to consumers? Some critics believe it is. Others argue that consumers recognize advertising when they see it and know celebrities are paid for their endorsements.

The most common criticisms of promotion relate to promotional messages that make exaggerated claims. What does it mean for an ad or a salesperson to claim that a product is the "best available"? Is that the personal opinion of people in the firm, or should every statement—even very general ones—be backed up by objective proof? What type of proof should be required? Some promotional messages do misrepresent the benefits of a product. However, most marketing managers want to develop ongoing relationships with—and repeat purchases from—their customers. They realize that customers won't come back if the marketing mix doesn't deliver what the promotion promises. Further, consumers are becoming more skeptical about all the claims they hear and see. As a result, most marketing managers work to make promotion claims specific and believable.[6]

Canon's color scanner is a technical product, but Canon recognizes that its promotion must be effective in communicating with target customers who don't know or like a lot of technical jargon.

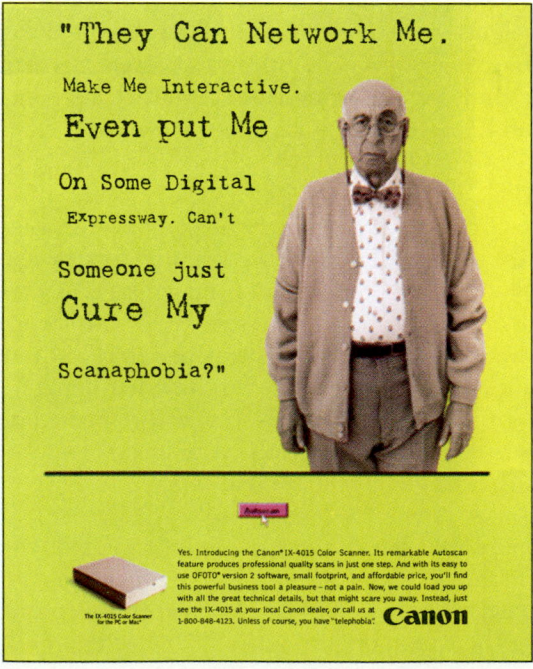

EXHIBIT 14–6   Relation of Promotion Objectives, Adoption Process, and AIDA Model

Promotion Objectives	Adoption Process (Chapter 7)	AIDA Model
Informing	Awareness Interest Evaluation Trial	Attention Interest Desire
Persuading		
Reminding	Decision Confirmation	Action

ADOPTION PROCESSES CAN GUIDE PROMOTION PLANNING

The adoption process discussed in Chapter 7 is related to effective communication and promotion planning. You learned the six steps in that adoption process: awareness, interest, evaluation, trial, decision, and confirmation. We saw consumer buying as a problem-solving process in which buyers go through these six steps on the way to adopting (or rejecting) an idea or product.

Now we see that the three basic promotion objectives relate to these six steps. See Exhibit 14–6. *Informing* and *persuading* may be needed to affect the potential customer's knowledge and attitudes about a product—and then bring about its adoption. Later promotion can simply *remind* the customer about that favorable experience—and confirm the adoption decision.

The AIDA model is a practical approach

The basic adoption process fits very neatly with another action-oriented model—called AIDA—that we will use in this and the next two chapters to guide some of our discussion.

The **AIDA model** consists of four promotion jobs—(1) to get *Attention*, (2) to hold *Interest*, (3) to arouse *Desire*, and (4) to obtain *Action*. (As a memory aid, note that the first letters of the four key words spell AIDA—the well-known opera.)

Exhibit 14–6 shows the relationship of the adoption process to the AIDA jobs. Getting attention is necessary to make consumers aware of the company's offering. Holding interest gives the communication a chance to build the consumer's interest in the product. Arousing desire affects the evaluation process—perhaps building preference. And obtaining action includes gaining trial, which may lead to a purchase decision. Continuing promotion is needed to confirm the decision—and encourage an ongoing relationship and additional purchases.

The AIDA and adoption processes look at individuals. This emphasis on individuals helps us understand how people behave. But it's also useful to look at markets as a whole. Different segments of customers within a market may behave differently—with some taking the lead in trying new products and, in turn, influencing others.

Promotion must vary for different adopter groups

Research on how markets accept new ideas has led to the adoption curve model. The **adoption curve** shows when different groups accept ideas. It shows the need to change the promotion effort as time passes. It also emphasizes the relations among groups—and shows that some groups act as leaders in accepting a new idea.

Exhibit 14–7 shows the adoption curve for a typical successful product. Some of the important characteristics of each of these customer groups are discussed below. Which one are you?

EXHIBIT 14–7   The Adoption Curve

Innovators don't mind taking some risks

The **innovators** are the first to adopt. They are eager to try a new idea—and willing to take risks. Innovators tend to be young and well educated. They are likely to be mobile and have many contacts outside their local social group and community. Business firms in the innovator group usually are large and rather specialized, but aggressive small companies with an entrepreneurial view are often willing to take the risk of doing something new and different.

An important characteristic of innovators is that they rely on impersonal and scientific information sources—or other innovators—rather than salespeople. They often search for information. For example, they might read articles in technical publications or informative ads in special-interest magazines or newspapers.

Early adopters are often opinion leaders

Early adopters are well respected by their peers—and often are opinion leaders. They tend to be younger, more mobile, and more creative than later adopters. But unlike innovators, they have fewer contacts outside their own social group or community. Business firms in this category also tend to be specialized.

Of all the groups, this one tends to have the greatest contact with salespeople. Mass media are important information sources too. Marketers should be very concerned with attracting and selling the early adopter group. Their acceptance is really important in reaching the next group because the early majority look to the early adopters for guidance. The early adopters can help the promotion effort by spreading *word-of-mouth* information and advice among other consumers.

Opinion leaders help spread the word

Marketers know the importance of personal conversations and recommendations by opinion leaders. If early groups reject the product, it may never get off the ground. For example, some moviegoers are the first to see new movies. If they

Roland's electronic keyboards can make many different sounds. Roland's ad gets musicians to stop and think about that feature and builds interest in it—because the ad makes the point in an attention-getting way.

think a movie is dull, they quickly tell their friends not to waste their time and money. Consumers are even more likely to talk about a negative experience than a positive experience.

But if opinion leaders accept a product, what they say about it can be very important. Such word-of-mouth publicity may do the real selling job—long before the customer ever walks into the retail store. Some companies try to target promotion to encourage opinion leadership. When Canon introduced a new high-quality automatic 35 mm camera, it prepared special ads designed to help opinion leaders explain to others how the camera worked. Other firms take a simpler approach. Their ads just say "tell your friends."[7]

Early majority group is deliberate

The **early majority** avoid risk and wait to consider a new idea after many early adopters have tried it—and liked it. Average-sized business firms that are less specialized often fit in this category. If successful companies in their industry adopt the new idea, they will too.

The early majority have a great deal of contact with mass media, salespeople, and early adopter opinion leaders. Members usually aren't opinion leaders themselves.

Late majority is cautious

The **late majority** are cautious about new ideas. Often they are older than the early majority group—and more set in their ways. So they are less likely to follow opinion leaders and early adopters. In fact, strong social pressure from their own peer group may be needed before they adopt a new product. Business firms in this group tend to be conservative, smaller-sized firms with little specialization.

The late majority make little use of marketing sources of information—mass media and salespeople. They tend to be oriented more toward other late adopters rather than outside sources they don't trust.

Laggards or nonadopters
hang onto tradition

Laggards or **nonadopters** prefer to do things the way they've been done in the past and are very suspicious of new ideas. They tend to be older and less well educated. They may also be low in social status and income. The smallest businesses with the least specialization often fit this category. They cling to the status quo and think it's the safe way.

The main source of information for laggards is other laggards. This certainly is bad news for marketers who are trying to reach a whole market quickly—or who want to use only one promotion method. In fact, it may not pay to bother with this group.[8]

HOW TYPICAL PROMOTION PLANS ARE BLENDED AND INTEGRATED

There is no one
right blend

We've said that most marketing managers try to integrate and blend the three different promotion methods because some promotion jobs can be done more economically one way than another. But what blend is right in a particular situation?

There is no one *right* promotion blend for all situations. Each one must be developed as part of a marketing mix—and should be designed to achieve the firm's promotion objectives in each marketing strategy. For example, if the channel of distribution for a firm's product involves middlemen, the marketing manager must consider the promotion blend that is appropriate in the channel as well as what type of promotion should be targeted at customers at the end of the channel. Similarly, the emphasis among the three types of promotion typically varies depending on whether the customers at the end of the channel are business users or final consumers. Let's take a closer look at typical promotion blends in these different situations.

A complete promotion blend may need to consider a firm's own employees and channel members as well as customers at the end of the channel.

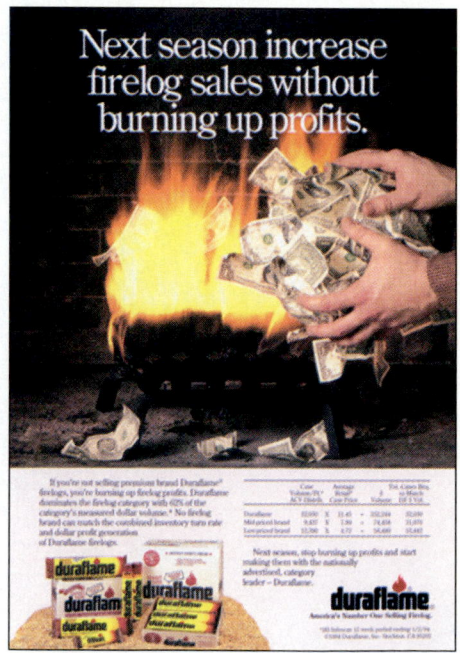

Get a push in the channel with promotion to middlemen

When a channel of distribution involves middlemen, their cooperation can be crucial to the success of the overall marketing strategy. **Pushing** (a product through a channel) means using normal promotion effort—personal selling, advertising, and sales promotion—to help sell the whole marketing mix to possible channel members. This approach emphasizes the importance of building a channel and securing the wholehearted cooperation of channel members to push the product down the channel to the final user.

Producers usually take on much of the responsibility for the pushing effort in the channel. However, most wholesalers also handle at least some of the promotion to retailers or other wholesalers further down the channel. Similarly, retailers often handle at least some of the promotion in their local markets. When different firms in the channel handle different aspects of communicating to final consumers or business users, the overall promotion effort is most likely to be effective when all of the individual messages are carefully integrated—that is, coordinated, consistent, and complete.

Promotion to middlemen emphasizes personal selling

Salespeople handle most of the important communication with middlemen. Middlemen don't want empty promises. They want to know what they can expect in return for their cooperation and help. A salesperson can answer questions about what promotion will be directed toward the final consumer, each channel member's part in marketing the product, and important details on pricing, markups, promotion assistance, and allowances.

A salesperson can help the firm determine when it should adjust its marketing mix from one middleman to another. In highly competitive urban areas, for example, mixes may emphasize price.

When a number of suppliers offer similar products and compete for attention and shelf space, the wholesaler or retailer usually pays attention to the one with the best profit potential. In these situations, the sales rep must convince the middleman that demand for the product exists—and that making a profit will be easy. A firm can make the sales rep's job easier by targeting special sales promotion at middlemen too.

Sales promotions targeted at middlemen usually focus on short-term arrangements that will improve the middleman's profits. For example, a soft-drink bottler might offer a convenience store a free case of drinks with each two cases it buys. The free case improves the store's profit margin on the whole purchase. Or a supplier might offer a price discount if the retailer uses a special point-of-purchase display. Other types of sales promotions—such as contests that offer vacation trips for high-volume middlemen—are also common.

Firms run ads in trade magazines to recruit new middlemen or to inform channel members about a new offering. Trade ads usually encourage middlemen to contact the supplier for more information, and then a salesperson takes over.

Push within a firm— with promotion to employees

Some firms emphasize promotion to their own employees—especially salespeople or others in contact with customers. This type of *internal marketing* effort is basically a variation on the pushing approach. One objective is to inform employees about important elements of the marketing strategy—so they'll work together as a team to implement it. Some firms use promotion to motivate employees to work harder at specific jobs—such as providing customer service or achieving higher sales. For example, many firms use sales contests and award free trips to big sellers.

Du Pont wants retailers to know that there is already consumer demand for its pillows and that the retailer will be able to sell them easily without a big promotional push.

Some companies design the ads they target at customers so the ads also communicate to employees—and boost the employees' image. This is typical in service-oriented industries where the quality of the employees' efforts is a big part of the product. Some of Delta Airlines' ads, for example, use the theme "we like to fly, and it shows." Although the ads communicate primarily to customers, they remind Delta's employees that the service they provide is crucial to the marketing strategy—and to customer satisfaction.

Pulling policy—customer demand pulls the product through the channel

Regardless of what promotion a firm uses to get help from channel members or employees in pushing a product, most producers focus a significant amount of promotion on customers at the end of the channel. This helps to stimulate demand for the firm's offering and can help pull the product through the channel of distribution. **Pulling** means getting customers to ask middlemen for the product.

Pulling and pushing are usually used in combination. See Exhibit 14–8. However, if middlemen won't work with a producer—perhaps because they're already carrying a competing brand—a producer may try to use a pulling approach by itself. This involves highly aggressive and expensive promotion to final consumers or users—perhaps using coupons or samples—temporarily bypassing middlemen. If the promotion works, the middlemen are forced to carry the product to satisfy customer requests. However, this approach is risky. Companies can waste an expensive promotion effort if customers lose interest before reluctant middlemen make the product available. At minimum, middlemen should be told about the planned pulling effort—so they can be ready if the promotion succeeds.

Who handles promotion to final customers at the end of the channel varies in different channel systems—depending on the mix of pushing and pulling. Further, the promotion blend typically varies depending on whether customers are final consumers or business users.[9]

Promotion to final consumers

The large number of consumers almost forces producers of consumer products and retailers to emphasize mass selling and sales promotion. Sales promotion—

EXHIBIT 14–8 Promotion May Encourage Pushing in the Channel, Pulling by Customers, or Both

such as contests or free samples—may build consumer interest and short-term sales of a product. Effective mass selling may build enough brand familiarity so that little personal selling is needed—as in self-service and discount operations.

If a product has already won brand preference or insistence—perhaps after years of satisfactory service—aggressive personal selling may not be needed. Reminder-type advertising may be all that's necessary to maintain a positive relationship. Hershey's Chocolate long prided itself on not having to do any advertising in the United States! However, Hershey's had to start advertising when competitors entered the market and took away customers. In Canada—where Hershey's is not well established—the company always advertised aggressively.[10]

Personal selling can be effective too. Some retailers—specialty shops in particular—rely heavily on well-informed salespeople. Technical products (like camcorders or computers) and personal services (like health care and estate planning) may also require personal selling. Direct selling firms like Avon and Amway also rely on personal selling. But aggressive personal selling to final consumers usually is found in relatively expensive channel systems, such as those for fashionable clothing, furniture, consumer electronics, and automobiles.

Promotion to business customers

Producers and wholesalers who target business customers usually emphasize personal selling. This is practical because these customers are much less numerous than final consumers and their purchases are typically larger.

Moreover, business customers may have technical questions or need adjustments in the marketing mix. An extremely technical business product may require a heavy emphasis on personal selling—using technically trained salespeople. This is the only sure way to make the product understood and get feedback on how customers use it. The technical sales rep meets with engineers, production managers, purchasing agents, and top managers—and can adjust the sales message to the needs of these various influences.

THE ABC'S OF PROMOTION TO SCHOOL KIDS

Schools are a targeted place for youth-oriented marketers to promote their products to the U.S.' 45 million elementary and secondary students. Coke and Pepsi are eager to contribute scoreboards (or is that billboards?) for high school sports fields. In school cafeterias, which serve 30 million meals a day, Kellogg's cereal and Dannon's yogurt sponsor programs to motivate learning (and increase consumption). One school district in Colorado is even selling local businesses advertising space on the sides of its school buses.

To be more effective in reaching students, some consumer products firms turn to promotion specialists, like Sampling Corporation of America (SCA). For example, every Halloween SCA provides schools with safety literature wrapped around product samples or coupons provided by sponsor companies. About 70 percent of all schools participate in SCA programs; in 1994 SCA distributed about 110 million product samples.

In-school promotion is not a new idea. The National Dairy Council has distributed information about nutrition—and why students should consume dairy products—since 1915. However, today's promotions are taking some innovative twists. Dole Food Co.'s third-grade nutrition curriculum, for example, centers on a multimedia CD-ROM featuring 30 animated fruits and vegetables. To better integrate the effort with promotion in its channels, Dole encourages supermarket produce managers to contact their local schools to arrange special tours. So far, 750,000 elementary school students have taken in-store produce tours.

Some educators feel that company-sponsored teaching materials make a positive contribution to budget-strapped schools. However, not everyone is happy about marketers targeting promotion at students—even if the schools get something in exchange. For example, ever since the launch of the Channel One television network with special programming for high schools, many parents and teachers have criticized its advertising as a crass attempt to exploit captive students. Yet, some of these critics are enthusiastic about participating in other promotions, such as one in which schools received a cash contribution of 10 cents for each pound of Jif peanut butter bought by students and their families.

Some in-school promotion efforts do provide budget-strapped educators with added resources, including useful teaching materials. Yet promotions targeted at students also raise sensitive issues of educational standards, ethics, and taste. Marketers who are not sensitive to these issues can provoke a hostile public backlash—including a host of new regulations.[11]

Sales reps can be more flexible in adjusting their companies' appeals to suit each customer—and personal contact is usually required to close a sale. A salesperson is also able to call back later to follow up with additional information, resolve any problems, and nurture the relationship with the customer.

While personal selling dominates in business markets, mass selling is necessary too. A typical sales call on a business customer costs $200.[12] That's because salespeople spend less than half their time actually selling. The rest is consumed by such tasks as traveling, paperwork, sales meetings, and strictly service calls. So it's seldom practical for salespeople to carry the whole promotion load. A firm invests too much in its salespeople to use their time and skill for jobs that could be handled in less costly ways.

Ads in trade magazines, for instance, can inform potential customers that a product is available; and most trade ads give a toll-free telephone or fax number to stimulate direct inquiries. Domestic and international trade shows also help identify prospects. Even so, sellers who target business customers usually spend only a small percentage of their promotion budget on mass selling and sales promotion.

Each market segment may need a unique blend

Knowing what type of promotion is typically emphasized with different targets is useful in planning the promotion blend. But each unique market segment may need a separate marketing mix—and different promotion blend. Some mass-selling specialists miss this point. They think mainly in mass marketing—rather than target marketing—terms. Aiming at large markets may be desirable in some situations, but promotion aimed at everyone can end up hitting no one. In developing the promotion blend, you should be careful not to slip into a shotgun approach when what you really need is a rifle approach—with a more careful aim.

INTEGRATED DIRECT-RESPONSE PROMOTION IS VERY TARGETED

The challenge of developing promotions that reach specific target customers has prompted many firms to turn to direct marketing—direct communication between a seller and an individual customer using a promotion method other than face-to-face personal selling. Most direct marketing communications are designed to prompt immediate feedback—a direct response—by customers. That's why this type of communication is often called *direct-response promotion.*

Early efforts in the direct-response area focused on direct-mail advertising. A carefully selected mailing list—from the many available—allowed advertisers to reach a specific target audience with specific interests. And direct-mail advertising proved to be very effective when the objective was to get a direct response by the customer.

Now it's more than direct-mail advertising

Achieving a measurable, direct response from specific target customers is still the heart of direct marketing. But the promotion medium is evolving to include not just mail but telephone, print, computer networks, broadcast, and even interactive video. The customer's response may be a purchase (or donation), a question, or a request for more information. More often than not, the customer responds by calling a toll-free telephone number, or—in the case of business markets—by sending a fax. A knowledgeable salesperson talks with the customer on the phone and follows up. That might involve filling an order and having it shipped to the customer or putting an interested prospect in touch with a salesperson who makes a personal visit. There are, however, many variations on this approach. For example, some firms route incoming information-request calls to a computerized answering system. The caller indicates what information is required by pushing a few buttons on the telephone keypad, and then the computer instantly sends requested information to the caller's fax machine.

Direct-response promotion is often an important component of integrated marketing communications programs and is closely tied to other elements of the marketing mix. However, what distinguishes this general approach is that the marketer targets more of its promotion effort at specific individuals who respond directly.

A promotion campaign marketing managers developed for Ryder Systems' move-it-yourself rental trucks illustrates these ideas. Ryder's marketing strategy focused on quality trucks and service rather than bargain-basement prices. Ryder's objective was to increase truck rentals and sales of supplies while maintaining its premium prices. Most other rental firms were competing with lower prices—hoping for gains in market share to offset a market that was shrinking because of a weak economy.

To reach the target market—consumers who were considering a move—Ryder placed 60-second ads on popular TV shows whose audience demographics matched Ryder's target market. The ads touted Ryder quality and also offered consumers a free home-moving guide and planning kit. All the consumer had to do to get the promotional brochure was call a toll-free telephone number. The brochure provided useful information about moving—including details on how Ryder's comfortable trucks and helpful services could make the move easier. It also included a discount coupon for Ryder supplies—like furniture pads and locks— that consumers could redeem at any Ryder dealer. Equally important, the computerized mailing list (database) of people who called for the brochure served as a targeted list of prospects for Ryder's telemarketing salespeople. When one of them identified a good prospect, the final personal selling job was turned over to a local Ryder dealer. The dealer's personal attention helped to resolve consumer questions and get rental contracts. Further, because the whole promotion effort was consistent in differentiating Ryder's quality services, the dealers were able to charge a higher price than competitors.[13]

Target customer directly with a database

As the Ryder case suggests, direct-response promotion usually relies on a customer (or prospect) database to target specific individuals. The computerized database includes customers' names and addresses (or telephone numbers) as well as past purchases and other segmenting characteristics. Individuals (or segments) who respond to direct promotion are the target for additional promotion. For example, a customer who buys lingerie from a catalog once is a good candidate for a follow-up. The follow-up might extend to other types of clothing. Greenpeace and the Cousteau Society send mail advertisements to people interested in environmental issues. They ask for donations or other types of support.

BMW and other car companies found that videotapes are a good way to provide consumers with a lot of information about a new model. However, it's too expensive to send tapes to everyone. To target the mailing, BMW first sends likely car buyers (high-income consumers who own a BMW or competing brand) personalized direct-mail ads that offer a free videotape. Interested consumers send back a return card. Then BMW sends the advertising videotape and updates its database so a dealer will know to call the consumer.

Direct-response methods raise ethical concerns

Direct-response promotion and database targeting have become an important part of many marketing mixes—and more and more customers find it very convenient. But not everyone is enthusiastic. Some critics argue that thousands of acres of trees are consumed each week—just to make the paper for direct response "junk mail" that consumers don't want. Other critics worry about privacy issues related to how a direct-response database might be used, especially if it includes detailed information about a consumer's purchases. Similarly, many consumers don't like getting direct promotion telephone solicitations at any time, but especially in the evening and at meal times when they seem to be particularly frequent. Most states have passed laws prohibiting automatic calling systems that use prerecorded messages rather than a live salesperson. Most firms who use direct-response promotion are very sensitive to these concerns—and take steps to address them.[14]

PROMOTION BLENDS VARY OVER THE LIFE CYCLE

The particular promotion blend a firm selects depends on the target of the promotion, but it may be influenced by many other factors—including the stage in the product life cycle and the nature of competition. Although promotion can be blended in many ways, to round out our discussion let's take a closer look at some typical ways firms spread their promotion budgets across the three promotion methods in these different situations.

Stage of product in its life cycle

A new product seldom becomes a spectacular success overnight. The adoption curve helps explain why. Further, the product must go through the product life-cycle stages described in Chapter 10—market introduction, market growth, market maturity, and sales decline. During these stages, promotion blends may have to change to achieve different promotion objectives.

Market introduction stage—"this new idea is good"

During market introduction, the basic promotion objective is informing. If the product is a really new idea, the promotion must build **primary demand**—demand for the general product idea—not just for the company's own brand. Multimedia computers, personal information managers (like Apple's Newton), and electric cars are good examples of product concepts where primary demand is just beginning to grow. There may be few potential innovators during the introduction stage, and personal selling can help find them. Firms also need salespeople to find good channel members and persuade them to carry the new product. Sales promotion may be targeted at salespeople or channel members to get them interested in selling the new product. And sales promotion may also encourage customers to try it.

Market growth stage—"our brand is best"

In the market growth stage, more competitors enter the market, and promotion emphasis shifts from building primary demand to stimulating **selective demand**—demand for a company's own brand. The main job is to persuade customers to buy—and keep buying—the company's product.

Now that more potential customers are trying and adopting the product, mass selling may become more economical. But salespeople and personal selling must still work in the channels—expanding the number of outlets and cementing relationships with current channel members.

Most kids want some kind of portable video game; Sega wants to stimulate selective demand for its brand, which is different because it has a color screen.

Market maturity stage—"our brand is better, really"

In the market maturity stage, even more competitors have entered the market. Promotion becomes more persuasive. At this stage, mass selling and sales promotion may dominate the promotion blends of consumer products firms. Business products may require more aggressive personal selling—perhaps supplemented by more advertising. The total dollars allocated to promotion may rise as competition increases.

If a firm already has high sales—relative to competitors—it may have a real advantage in promotion at this stage. If, for example, Nabisco has twice the sales for a certain type of cookie as Keebler, its smaller competitor, and they both spend the same *percentage* of total sales on promotion—Nabisco will be spending twice as much and will probably communicate to more people. Nabisco may get even more than twice as much promotion because of economies of scale.

Firms that have strong brands can use reminder-type advertising at this stage to be sure customers remember the product name. Similarly, many firms turn to various types of frequent-buyer promotions or newsletters and other communications targeted at current customers to strengthen the buyer-seller relationship and keep customers loyal. This may be much less expensive—and more effective—than persuasive efforts to win customers away from competitors in a stagnant market.

Sales decline stage—"let's tell those who still want our product"

During the sales decline stage, the total amount spent on promotion usually decreases as firms try to cut costs to remain profitable. Since some people may still want the product, firms need more targeted promotion to reach these customers.

On the other hand, some firms may increase promotion to try to slow the cycle—at least temporarily. Crayola had almost all of the market for children's crayons, but sales were slowly declining as new kinds of markers came along. Crayola slowed the cycle with more promotion spending—and a message to parents to buy their kids a "fresh box."

Nature of competition requires different promotion

Firms in monopolistic competition may favor mass selling because they have differentiated their marketing mixes and have something to talk about. As a market tends toward pure competition—or oligopoly—it is difficult to predict what will happen. Competitors in some markets try to outpromote each other. The only way for a competitor to stay in this kind of market is to match rivals' promotion efforts—unless the whole marketing mix can be improved in some other way. We see a lot of such competitive advertising in our daily newspapers—and in cents-off coupons at grocery store checkout counters.

In markets that are drifting toward pure competition, some companies resort to price-cutting. Lower prices may be offered to middlemen, customers, or both. This *may* increase the number of units sold—temporarily—but it may also reduce total revenue and the amount available for promotion *per unit*. And competitive retaliation—perhaps in the form of short-term sales promotions—may reduce the temporary sales gains and drag price levels down faster. The cash flowing into the business may decline, and promotion spending may have to be cut back.

We've focused here on promotion. But changes in the product life cycle and competitive situation may require new marketing objectives, target markets, and marketing mixes. And all of the strategy decisions—including those related to promotion spending and the promotion blend—should work together to achieve the objectives.[15]

Potato sales have been declining as pasta and rice have become more popular. To try to fight this trend, the National Potato Board has developed promotion that it hopes will rekindle primary demand for potatoes.

The thing about Chris is he doesn't like food that he has to chase around his plate. He's funny that way. Things to eat that are excessively small or cute bother him. Chris likes to sink his fork into his dinner without going for his reading glasses to see what he's getting.

Nobody likes food that's too weird or hard to get in your mouth.

Potatoes are steady. They're reliable. And they're good for you because they're a fresh vegetable. And they won't slide around just when you really need to eat them. Because when Chris comes home from a long hard day the last thing he wants is to have to wrestle his dinner off his own plate. *Potatoes*

THEY'RE AT HOME ANYWHERE!

SETTING THE PROMOTION BUDGET

Size of promotion budget affects promotion efficiency and blend

There are some economies of scale in promotion. An ad on national TV might cost less *per person* reached than an ad on local TV. Similarly, citywide radio, TV, and newspapers may be cheaper than neighborhood newspapers or direct personal contact. But the *total cost* for some mass media may force small firms—or those with small promotion budgets—to use promotion alternatives that are more expensive per contact. For example, a small retailer might want to use local television but find that there is only enough money for an ad in the Yellow Pages—and an occasional newspaper ad.

Smaller producers and firms that offer relatively undifferentiated consumer products emphasize personal selling first and rely mainly on sales promotion for the balance. The objective is to build good channel relations and encourage channel members to recommend and push the product. Note that here we are referring to percentages in the promotion blend—not the level of expenditures. Setting the overall level of promotion spending—and how much to spend on each type of promotion—is an important but difficult decision.

Budgeting for promotion—50 percent, 30 percent, or 10 percent is better than nothing

The most common method of budgeting for promotion expenditures is to compute a percentage of either past sales or sales expected in the future. The virtue of this method is its simplicity. A similar percentage can be used automatically each year—eliminating the need to keep evaluating the kind and amount of promotion effort needed and its probable cost. It allows executives who aren't too tuned into the marketing concept to write off a certain percentage or number of dollars—while controlling the total amount spent. When a company's top managers have this attitude, they often get what they deserve—something less than the best results.

This Danish ad for the Yellow Pages tries to get the consumer more involved in the message. The headline covering this woman's eyes indicates what's on her mind—a new wedding dress. The copy says, "Did he say yes? Find it in the Yellow Pages."

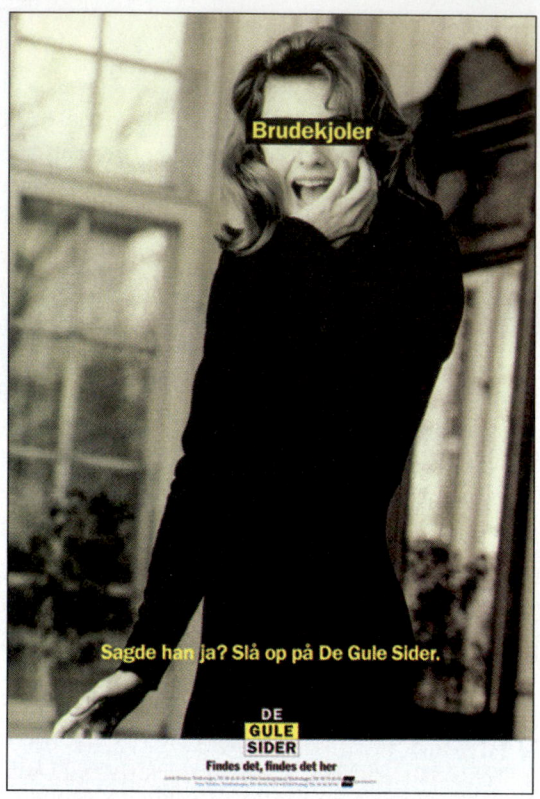

Find the task, budget for it

Just because budgeting a certain percentage of past or forecast sales is common doesn't mean that it's smart. This mechanical approach leads to expanding marketing expenditures when business is good and cutting back when business is poor. It may be desirable to increase marketing expenditures when business is good. But when business is poor, this approach may just make the problem worse—if weak promotion is the reason for declining sales. The most sensible approach may be to be *more*, not less, aggressive!

Other methods of budgeting for marketing expenditures are:

1. Match expenditures with competitors.
2. Set the budget as a certain number of cents or dollars per sales unit (by case, by thousand, or by ton) using the past year or estimated year ahead as a base.
3. Base the budget on any uncommitted revenue, perhaps including budgeted profits. Companies with limited resources may use this approach. Or a firm may be willing to sacrifice some or all of its current profits for future sales—that is, it looks at promotion spending as an *investment* in future growth.
4. Base the budget on the job to be done. For example, the spending level might be based on the number of new customers desired and the percentage of current customers that the firm must retain to leverage investments in already established relationships. This is called the **task method**—basing the budget on the job to be done.

Task method can lead to budgeting without agony

In the light of our continuing discussion about planning marketing strategies to reach objectives, the most sensible approach to budgeting promotion expenditures is the task method. In fact, this approach makes sense for *any* marketing expenditure, but here we'll focus on promotion.

A practical approach is to determine which promotion objectives are most important—to the overall strategy—and which promotion methods are most economical and effective for the communication tasks relevant to each objective. There's never enough money to do all of the promotion that you might want to do. However, this approach helps you to set priorities so that the money you spend produces specific results.

The amount budgeted using the task method can be stated as a percentage of sales. But you should see that calculating the right amount is much more involved than picking up a past percentage. It requires careful review of the specific promotion (and marketing) tasks to be accomplished and how each task fits with others to achieve the overall objectives. The costs of these tasks are then totaled—to determine how much should be budgeted for promotion (just as money is allocated for other marketing activities required by the strategy). In other words, the firm can assemble its total promotion budget directly from detailed plans—rather than by simply relying on historical patterns or ratios.

This method also helps to eliminate budget fights between different promotion areas. Such conflicts may occur if managers and specialists responsible for different promotion methods see themselves as pitted against each other for limited budget dollars. However, the task method of budgeting encourages everyone—the marketing manager and the specialists—to focus on the overall strategy and what promotion objectives need to be achieved. The specialists may still make their own proposals and suggestions about how best to perform tasks and achieve the objectives. But then the budget allocations are based on the most effective ways of getting things done—not on what the firm did last year, what some competitor does, or even on internal "politics." With this approach, different promotion specialists are also more likely to recognize that different tasks and objectives are best served with different methods—and that they must all work together to achieve truly integrated marketing communications.[16]

In this chapter our focus has been on blending the different promotion methods into an integrated whole. We've emphasized that different methods—publicity, personal selling, advertising, and sales promotion—are complementary. In different situations they must be combined in different ways to achieve an effective and integrated overall promotion blend. The concepts we've been discussing apply to all types of marketing communications. Yet, to be more skilled in matching specific promotion methods to specific tasks and objectives, it will help to know more about the strategy decisions involved in managing the major promotion areas. So, that's the focus of the next two chapters.

CONCLUSION

Promotion is an important part of any marketing mix. Most consumers and intermediate customers can choose from among many products. To be successful, a producer must not only offer a good product at a reasonable price but also inform potential customers about the product and where they can buy it. Further, producers must tell wholesalers and retailers in the channel about their product and their marketing mix. These middlemen, in turn, must use promotion to reach their customers.

The promotion blend should fit logically into the strategy being developed to satisfy a particular target market. Strategy planning needs to state *what* should be communicated to them—and *how*. The overall promotion objective is to affect buying behavior, but the basic promotion objectives are informing, persuading, and reminding.

Three basic promotion methods can be used to reach these objectives. Behavioral science findings can help firms combine various promotion methods for effective communication. In particular, what we know about the communication process and how individuals and groups adopt new products is important in planning promotion blends.

An action-oriented framework called AIDA can help marketing managers plan promotion blends. But the marketing manager has the final responsibility for combining the promotion methods into one integrated promotion blend for each marketing mix.

In this chapter, we considered some basic concepts that apply to all areas of promotion. In the next two chapters, we'll discuss personal selling, advertising, and sales promotion in more detail.

QUESTIONS AND PROBLEMS

1. Briefly explain the nature of the three basic promotion methods available to a marketing manager. What are the main strengths and limitations of each?

2. In your own words, discuss the integrated marketing communications concept. Explain what its emphasis on "consistent" and "complete" messages implies with respect to promotion blends.

3. Relate the three basic promotion objectives to the four jobs (AIDA) of promotion using a specific example.

4. Discuss the communication process in relation to a producer's promotion of an accessory product—say, a new electronic security system businesses use to limit access to areas where they store confidential records.

5. If a company wants its promotion to appeal to a new group of target customers in a foreign country, how can it protect against its communications being misinterpreted?

6. Explain how an understanding of the adoption process would help you develop a promotion blend for digital tape recorders, a new consumer electronics product that produces high-quality recordings. Explain why you might change the promotion blend during the course of the adoption process.

7. Explain how opinion leaders affect a firm's promotion planning.

8. Discuss how the adoption curve should be used to plan the promotion blend(s) for a new automobile accessory—an electronic radar system that alerts a driver if he or she is about to change lanes into the path of a car that is passing through a "blind spot" in the driver's mirrors.

9. A small company has developed an innovative new spray-on glass cleaner that prevents the buildup of electrostatic dust on computer screens and TVs. Give examples of some low-cost ways the firm might effectively promote its product. Be certain to consider both push and pull approaches.

10. Promotion has been the target of considerable criticism. What specific types of promotion are probably the object of this criticism? Give a specific example that illustrates your thinking.

11. With direct-response promotion, customers provide feedback to marketing communications. How can a marketing manager use this feedback to improve the effectiveness of the overall promotion blend?

12. Would promotion be successful in expanding the general demand for: (*a*) raisins, (*b*) air travel, (*c*) tennis rackets, (*d*) athletic shoes, (*e*) high-octane unleaded gasoline, (*f*) single-serving, frozen gourmet dinners, (*g*) cement? Explain why or why not in each case.

13. What promotion blend would be most appropriate for producers of the following established products? Assume average- to large-sized firms in each case and support your answer.
   a. Chewing gum.
   b. Panty hose.
   c. Castings for car engines.
   d. Car tires.

e. A special computer used by manufacturers for computer-aided design of new products.

f. Inexpensive plastic raincoats.

g. A camcorder that has achieved specialty-product status.

14. If a marketing manager uses the task method to budget for marketing promotions, are competitors' promotion spending levels ignored? Explain your thinking and give an example that supports your point of view.

15. Discuss the potential conflict among the various promotion managers. How could this be reduced?

SUGGESTED CASES

18. Ledges State Bank

19. Leisure World, Inc.

COMPUTER-AIDED PROBLEM

14. Selecting a Communications Channel

Helen Troy, owner of three Sound Haus stereo equipment stores, is deciding what message channel (advertising medium) to use to promote her newest store. Her current promotion blend includes direct-mail ads that are effective for reaching her current customers. She also has knowledgeable salespeople who work well with consumers once they're in the store. However, a key objective in opening a new store is to attract new customers. Her best prospects are professionals in the 25–44 age range with incomes over $38,000 a year. But only some of the people in this group are audiophiles who want the top-of-the-line brands she carries. Troy has decided to use local advertising to reach new customers.

Troy has narrowed her choice to two advertising media: an FM radio station and a biweekly magazine that focuses on entertainment in her city. Many of the magazine's readers are out-of-town visitors interested in concerts, plays, and restaurants. They usually buy stereo equipment at home. But the magazine's audience research shows that many local professionals do subscribe to the magazine. Troy doesn't think that the objective can be achieved with a single ad. However, she believes that ads in six issues will generate good local awareness with her target market. In addition, the magazine's color format will let her present the prestige image she wants to convey in an ad. She thinks that will help convert aware prospects to buyers. Specialists at a local advertising agency will prepare a high-impact ad for $2,000, and then Troy will pay for the magazine space.

The FM radio station targets an audience similar to Troy's own target market. She knows repeated ads will be needed to be sure that most of her target audience is exposed to her ads. Troy thinks it will take daily ads for several months to create adequate awareness among her target market. The FM station will provide an announcer and prepare a tape of Troy's ad for a one-time fee of $200. All she has to do is tell the station what the message content for the ad should say.

Both the radio station and the magazine have given Troy reports summarizing recent audience research. She decides that comparing the two media in a spreadsheet will help her make a better decision.

a. *Based on the data displayed on the initial spreadsheet, which message channel (advertising medium) would you recommend to Troy? Why?*

b. *The agency that offered to prepare Troy's magazine ad will prepare a fully produced radio ad—including a musical jingle—for $2,500. The agency claims that its musical ad will have much more impact than the ad the radio station will create. The agency says its ad should produce the same results as the station ad with 20 percent fewer insertions. If the agency claim is correct, would it be wise for Troy to pay the agency to produce the ad?*

c. *The agency will not guarantee that its custom-produced radio ad will reach Troy's objective—making 80 percent of the prospects aware of the new store. Troy wants to see how lower levels of awareness—between 50 percent and 70 percent—would affect the advertising cost per buyer and the cost per aware prospect. Use the What If analysis to vary the percent of prospects who become aware. Prepare a table showing the effect on the two kinds of costs. What are the implications of your analysis?*

For additional questions related to this problem, see Exercise 14–3 in the *Learning Aid for Use with Basic Marketing*, 12th edition.

15

Personal Selling

When You Finish This Chapter, You Should

1. Understand the importance and nature of personal selling.

2. Know the three basic sales tasks and what the various kinds of salespeople can be expected to do.

3. Know what the sales manager must do—including selecting, training, and organizing salespeople—to carry out the personal selling job.

4. Understand how the right compensation plan can help motivate and control salespeople.

5. Understand when and where to use the three types of sales presentations.

6. Understand the important new terms (shown in red).

Alcoa is a major supplier of sheet aluminum and special metal alloys to manufacturers who make a wide variety of products—ranging from soft-drink cans to airplanes, like Boeing's new 777 jet. To do a better job of meeting its customers' needs, Alcoa has made a companywide commitment to constantly improve the quality of its offerings. Alcoa knows understanding and meeting

customer requirements is what quality is all about. As the cover of its recent annual report states: "Customer satisfaction comes from listening, learning, understanding customer needs and continuously improving the value we provide. Our best customer relationships become long-term partnerships."

Alcoa's salespeople are at the heart of that listening, learning, and understanding process. To make the partnership a profitable success, both for Alcoa and for the customer, they perform many sales tasks. For example, with a customer like Boeing, a salesperson must work closely with engineers, purchasing people, production people, and the other purchase influences to understand their needs—and to help

find solutions to those needs. Specialists help resolve the technical challenges. But the salespeople need real skill to get the order and close the deal. That's just the start. An Alcoa salesperson is there all along the way to provide technical support after the sale, ensure that all orders meet Boeing's exact quality specifications, and promptly resolve any problems if they arise. To be certain that these challenging jobs are done well, Alcoa recruits good people and then provides the sales training to make them even better. New people may need training to build professional problem-solving and sales presentation skills. Even experienced sales reps need ongoing training. For example, Alcoa gives its salespeople training in the firm's new quality programs and how they relate to customer needs.

Different salespeople have different skills and experience. So Alcoa must carefully match them to particular territories, customers, and product lines. And to be sure that each salesperson is highly motivated, Alcoa's sales managers must make certain that sales compensation arrangements motivate and reward salespeople for producing needed results.[1]

THE IMPORTANCE AND ROLE OF PERSONAL SELLING

Salespeople are communicators who build relationships

Promotion is communicating with potential customers. As the Alcoa case suggests, personal selling is often the best way to do it. Almost every company can benefit from personal selling. While face-to-face with prospects, salespeople can get more attention than an advertisement or a display. They can adjust what they say or do to take into consideration culture and other behavioral influences on the customer. They can ask questions to find out about a customer's specific interests. They can also stay in tune with the prospect's feedback and adjust the presentation as they move along. If—and when—the prospect is ready to buy, the salesperson is there to ask for the order. And afterwards, the salesperson is there to be certain that the customer is satisfied and that the relationship between the customer and firm continues to be mutually beneficial.

Personal selling requires strategy decisions

Marketing managers must decide how much—and what kind of—personal selling effort each marketing mix needs. Specifically, as part of their strategy planning, they must decide: (1) how many salespeople they need, (2) what kind of salespeople they need, (3) what kind of sales presentation to use, (4) how to select and train salespeople, and (5) how to supervise and motivate them. The sales manager provides inputs into these strategy decisions. Once made, it's the sales manager's job to implement the personal selling part of a marketing strategy.

In this chapter, we'll discuss the importance and nature of personal selling so you'll understand the strategy decisions sales and marketing managers face. These strategy decisions are shown in Exhibit 15–1.

We'll also discuss a number of frameworks and how-to approaches that guide these strategy decisions. Because these approaches apply equally to domestic and international markets, we won't emphasize that distinction in this chapter. This does not mean, however, that personal selling techniques don't vary from one country to another. To the contrary, in dealing with *any* customer, the salesperson must be very sensitive to cultural influences and other factors that might affect the communication process. For example, a Japanese customer and an Arab customer might respond differently to subtle aspects of a salesperson's behavior. The Arab customer might expect to be very close to a salesperson, perhaps only two feet away, while they talk. The Japanese customer might consider that distance rude. Similarly, what topics of discussion are considered sensitive, how messages are interpreted, and which negotiating styles are used vary from one country to another. A salesperson must know how to communicate effectively with each customer—wherever and whoever that customer is—but those details are beyond the strategy planning focus of this text.[2]

Personal selling is important

We've already seen that personal selling is important in some promotion blends—and absolutely essential in others. Some feel that personal selling is the dynamic element that keeps our economy going. You would better appreciate the importance of personal selling if you regularly had to meet payrolls and somehow—almost miraculously—your salespeople kept coming in with orders just in time to keep the business from closing.

Personal selling is often a company's largest single operating expense. This is another reason why it is important to understand the decisions in this area. Bad sales management decisions can be costly not only in lost sales but also in actual out-of-pocket expenses.

EXHIBIT 15–1   Strategy Planning for Personal Selling

Every economy needs and uses many salespeople. In the United States, 1 person out of every 10 in the total labor force is involved in sales work. By comparison, that's about 20 times more people than are employed in advertising. Any activity that employs so many people—and is so important to the economy—deserves study. Looking at what salespeople do is a good way to start.

Helping customers is good selling

Good salespeople don't just try to *sell* the customer. Rather, they try to *help the customer buy*—by understanding the customer's needs and presenting the advantages and disadvantages of their products. Such helpfulness results in satisfied customers—and long-term relationships. And strong relationships often form the basis for a competitive advantage, especially for firms that target business markets.

You may think of personal selling in terms of an old-time stereotype of a salesperson: a bag of wind with no more to offer than a funny story, a big expense account, and an engaging grin. But that isn't true any more. Old-time salespeople are being replaced by real professionals—problem solvers—who have something definite to contribute to their employers *and* their customers.

Salespeople represent the whole company—and customers too

Increasingly, the salesperson is seen as a representative of the whole company—responsible for explaining its total effort to target customers rather than just pushing products. The salesperson may provide information about products, explain and interpret company policies, and even negotiate prices or diagnose technical problems when a product doesn't work well.

The sales rep is often the only link between the firm and its customers—especially if customers are far away. When a number of people from the firm are involved with the customer organization—which is increasingly common as more suppliers and customers form closer relationships—it is usually the sales rep who coordinates the relationship for his or her firm. See Exhibit 8–6.

While face-to-face with prospects, salespeople can adjust what they say or do to take into consideration culture and other behavioral influences.

As this suggests, salespeople also represent their *customers* back inside their own firm too. Recall that feedback is an essential part of both the communication process *and* the basic management process of planning, implementing, and control. For example, the sales rep is the likely one to explain to the production manager why a customer is unhappy with product performance or quality—or to the physical distribution manager why slow shipments are causing problems.

As evidence of these changing responsibilities, some companies give their salespeople such titles as field manager, sales consultant, market specialist, account representative, or sales engineer.

Sales force aids in market information function as well

The sales force can aid in the marketing information function too. The sales rep may be the first to hear about a new competitor or a competitor's new product or strategy. And, as the following example shows, sales reps who are well attuned to customers' needs can be a key source of ideas for new products.

Ballard Medical Products is a small producer that competes with international giants in the hospital supply business. A key factor in Ballard's success is that its salespeople have the right products to offer when they make a sales call. But that's not just luck. The salespeople all have a lot of say in what products the company produces and how they are designed. Ballard salespeople are trained as information specialists who seek and report on customer feedback. At each hospital, they work closely with the doctor and nurse specialists who use Ballard products. And when one of them says, "We need a product that would solve this problem," the Ballard sales rep is right there to follow up with questions and invite suggestions. The rep quickly relays the customer's needs back to Ballard's new product group.[3]

Salespeople can be strategy planners too

Some salespeople are expected to be marketing managers in their own territories. And some become marketing managers by default because top management hasn't provided detailed strategy guidelines. Either way, salespeople may take the initiative to fill the gap. They may develop their own marketing mixes or even their own strategies. Some firms fail to give their sales reps a clear idea of who their target customers should be. Although the sales reps are assigned a territory, they may have to start from scratch with strategy planning. The salesperson may have choices about (1) what target customers to aim at, (2) which particular products to emphasize, (3) which middlemen to call on or to work with the hardest, (4) how to use promotion money, and (5) how to adjust prices.

A salesperson who can put together profitable strategies—and implement them well—can rise very rapidly. The opportunity is there for those prepared and willing to work.

Even a starting job may offer great opportunities. Some beginning salespeople—especially those working for producers or wholesalers—are responsible for larger sales volumes than many small companies. This is a serious responsibility—and the person must be prepared for it.

Further, sales jobs are often viewed as entry-level positions and used to evaluate candidates for promotion. Success in this job can lead to rapid promotion to higher-level sales and marketing jobs—and more money and security.[4]

WHAT KINDS OF PERSONAL SELLING ARE NEEDED?

If a firm has too few salespeople—or the wrong kind—some important personal selling tasks may not be completed. And having too many salespeople—or the wrong kind—wastes money. A sales manager needs to find a good balance—the right number and the right kind of salespeople. This balance may change over time with other changes in strategy or the market environment; that's why many firms have been restructuring their sales forces.

One of the difficulties of determining the right number and kind of salespeople is that every sales job is different. While an engineer or accountant can look forward to fairly specific duties, the salesperson's job changes constantly. However, there are three basic types of sales tasks. This gives us a starting point for understanding what selling tasks need to be done—and how many people are needed to do them.

Personal selling is divided into three tasks

The three **basic sales tasks** are order-getting, order-taking, and supporting. For convenience, we'll describe salespeople by these terms—referring to their primary task—*although one person may do all three tasks in some situations.*

As the names imply, order getters and order takers obtain orders for their company. Every marketing mix must have someone or some way to obtain orders. In contrast, supporting salespeople are not directly interested in orders. Their function is to help the order-oriented salespeople. With this variety, you can see that there is a place in personal selling for nearly everyone.

ORDER GETTERS—DEVELOP NEW BUSINESS RELATIONSHIPS

Order getters are concerned with establishing relationships with new customers and developing new business. **Order-getting** means seeking possible buyers with a well-organized sales presentation designed to sell a product, service, or idea. The emphasis here is on getting results—orders—not on style, however. A good order getter may appear very low key if that's what the target customer seems to want.

Order getters must know what they're talking about—not just be personal contacts. Order-getting salespeople work for producers, wholesalers, and retailers. They normally are well paid—many earn more than $80,000 a year.

Consumers who are
interested in shopping
products often want help from
a well-informed salesperson.

Producers' order getters—find new opportunities

Producers of all kinds of products—especially business products—have a great need for order getters. They use order getters to locate new prospects, open new accounts, see new opportunities, and help establish and build channel relationships.

High-caliber order getters are essential to sell installations and accessory equipment where large sums are involved and where top-level management participates in the buying decision.

Top-level customers are more interested in ways to save or make more money than in technical details. Good order getters cater to this interest. They help the customer identify ways to solve problems, and then sell concepts and ideas—not just physical products. The goods and services they supply are merely the means of achieving the customer's end.

For example, Circadian, Inc., sells high-tech medical equipment. Changes in Medicare rules mean that doctors can no longer routinely order expensive tests in hospitals because the costs can't be recovered easily. But the doctors *can* be paid for tests done in their offices—if they have the right equipment. When Circadian order getters call on doctors, they show how the firm's testing equipment can improve patient care—and office profits. Reps can often get a $20,000 order on the spot because they can show that the equipment will pay for itself in the first year. The doctors don't care about technical details as long as the machines are accurate and easy to use.[5]

Order getters are also necessary to sell raw materials, components, supplies, and services—but mainly for initial contacts. Since many competitors offer nearly the same product, the order getter's crucial selling job is to establish the relationship and get the company's name on the approved suppliers list. Keeping it there requires constant attention to the customer's needs, and doing whatever is necessary to maintain a mutually beneficial relationship between the supplier and customer firms.

Order getters for professional services—and other products where service is a crucial element of the marketing mix—face a special challenge. The customer usually can't inspect a service before deciding to buy. The order getter's communication and relationship with the customer may be the only basis on which to evaluate the quality of the supplier.

An order getter in business markets needs the know-how to help solve customers' problems. Often the order getter needs to understand a customer's whole business as well as technical details about the product and its applications. This is especially important for salespeople whose customers are producers. To have technically competent order getters, firms often give special training to business-trained college graduates. Such salespeople can then work intelligently with their specialist customers. In fact, they may be more technically competent in their narrow specialty than anyone they encounter—so they provide a unique service. For example, a salesperson for automated manufacturing equipment must understand everything about a prospect's production process as well as the technical details of converting to computer-controlled equipment.

Wholesalers' order getters—almost hand it to the customer

Progressive merchant wholesaler sales reps are developing into consultants and store advisors rather than just order takers. Such order getters may become retailers' partners in the job of moving goods from the wholesale warehouse through the retail store to consumers. These order getters almost become a part of the retailer's staff—helping to check stock, write orders, conduct demonstrations—and plan advertising, special promotions, and other retailing activities.

Agent middlemen often are order getters—particularly the more aggressive manufacturers' agents and brokers. They face the same tasks as producers' order getters. But, unfortunately for them, once the order-getting is done and the customers become established and loyal, producers may try to eliminate the agents and save money with their own order takers.

Retail order getters influence consumer behavior

Convincing consumers about the value of products they haven't seriously considered takes a high level of personal selling ability. Order getters for unsought products must help customers see how a new product can satisfy needs now being filled by something else. Early order getters for microwave ovens, for example, faced a tough job. They had to convince skeptical customers that this new kind of cooking was safe and that it would be more convenient than traditional approaches—once the customer got used to it. Without order getters, many of the products we now rely on—ranging from mutual funds to air conditioners—might have died in the market introduction stage. The order getter helps bring products out of the introduction stage into the market growth stage. Without sales and profits in the early stages, the product may fail—and never be offered again.

Order getters are helpful for selling *heterogeneous* shopping products. Consumers shop for many of these items on the basis of price and quality. They welcome useful information. Cars, furniture and furnishings, cameras, jewelry, and fashion items can be sold effectively by an aggressive, helpful order getter. Thoughtful advice—based on an understanding of the consumer and thorough knowledge of the product and its alternatives—may really help consumers and bring profits to the salesperson and retailer.

ORDER TAKERS—NURTURE RELATIONSHIPS TO KEEP THE BUSINESS COMING

Order takers sell to the regular or established customers, complete most sales transactions, and maintain relationships with their customers. After a customer becomes interested in a firm's products through an order getter or supporting salesperson or through advertising or sales promotion—an order taker usually answers any final questions and completes the sale. **Order-taking** is the routine completion of sales made regularly to the target customers. The routine completion of sales usually requires ongoing follow-up with the customer, to make certain that the customer is totally satisfied and to be certain that the relationship will continue in the future.

Sometimes sales managers or customers use the term *order taker* as a put-down when referring to salespeople who don't take any initiative. While a particular salesperson may perform poorly enough to justify criticism, it's a mistake to downgrade the function of order-taking. Order-taking is extremely important. Many firms lose sales just because no one ever asks for the order—and closes the sale. Moreover, the order taker's job is not just limited to placing orders. Even in business markets where customers place routine orders with computerized order systems and EDI, order takers do a variety of important jobs that are essential to the business relationship.

Producers' order takers—train, explain, and collaborate

Once industrial, wholesale, or retail accounts are established, regular follow-up is necessary. Order takers work on improving the whole relationship with the customer, not just on completing a single transaction. Even if computers handle routine reorders, someone has to explain details, make adjustments, handle complaints, explain or negotiate new prices and terms, place sales promotion materials, and keep customers informed of new developments. Some-one may have to train customers' employees to use machines or products. In sales to middlemen, someone may have to train wholesalers' or retailers' salespeople. All these activities are part of the order taker's job. And a failure in meeting a customer's expectations on any of these activities might jeopardize the relation-ship and future sales.

Producers' order takers often have a regular route with many calls. To handle these calls well, they must have energy, persistence, enthusiasm, and a friendly personality that wears well over time. They sometimes have to take the heat when something goes wrong with some other element of the marketing mix.

Firms sometimes use order-taking jobs to train potential order getters and managers. Such jobs give them an opportunity to meet key customers and to better understand their needs. And frequently, they run into some order-getting opportunities.

Order takers who are alert to order-getting opportunities can make the big difference in generating new sales. NationsBank recognizes the opportunities. At most banks, tellers are basically order takers and service providers. When a customer comes in to make a deposit or cash a check, the teller provides the needed service and that's it. In contrast, NationsBank encourages its tellers to help get new business. NationsBank tellers are trained to ask customers if they have ever considered investing in one of NationsBank's certificates of deposit or if they would like to learn more about NationsBank home equity loans. They give the interested customers sales literature about NationsBank's various financial services and ask if the customer would like to speak with a customer service

A good retail order taker helps to build good relations with customers.

representative. With thousands of tellers all helping out as order getters, it's no wonder that NationsBank has grown rapidly from a small regional bank to the seventh largest bank in the U.S.[6]

Wholesalers' order takers—not getting orders but keeping them

While producers' order takers usually handle relatively few items—and sometimes even a single item—wholesalers' order takers may sell 125,000 items or more. Most wholesale order takers just sell out of their catalog. They have so many items that they can't possibly give aggressive sales effort to many—except perhaps newer or more profitable items. There are just too many items to single any out for special attention. The order taker's strength is a wide assortment—rather than detailed knowledge of individual products.

The wholesale order taker's main job is to maintain close contact with customers—perhaps once a week—and fill any needs that develop. Sometimes such order takers almost become part of the organization of the producer or retailer customers they serve. Some retailers leave it to the salesperson to take inventory—and then write up the order. Obviously, this relationship of trust cannot be abused. After writing up the order, the order taker normally checks to be sure the company fills the order promptly and accurately. The order taker also handles any adjustments or complaints and generally acts as a liaison between the company and its customers.

Such salespeople are usually the low-pressure type—friendly and easygoing. Usually these jobs aren't as high paying as the order-getting variety—but they attract many because they aren't as taxing. They require relatively little traveling, and there is little or no pressure to get new accounts. There can be a social aspect too. The salesperson sometimes becomes good friends with customers.

Retail order takers—often they are poor salesclerks

Order-taking may be almost mechanical at the retail level—for example, at the supermarket checkout counter. Even so, retail order takers play a vital role in a retailer's marketing mix. Customers expect prompt and friendly service. They will find a new place to shop—or to do their banking or have their car serviced—rather than deal with a salesclerk who is rude or acts annoyed by having to complete a sale.

Some retail clerks are poor order takers because they aren't paid much—often only the minimum wage. But they may be paid little because they do little. In any case, order-taking at the retail level appears to be declining in quality. And there will probably be far fewer such jobs in the future as more marketers make adjustments in their mixes and turn to self-service selling. Checkout counters now have automated electronic scanning equipment that reads price codes directly from packages. Some supermarkets are even experimenting with systems where customers do their own scanning and the clerk simply accepts the money.

SUPPORTING SALES FORCE—INFORMS AND PROMOTES IN THE CHANNEL

Supporting salespeople help the order-oriented salespeople—but they don't try to get orders themselves. Their activities are aimed at enhancing the relationship with the customer and getting sales in the long run. For the short run, however, they are ambassadors of goodwill who may provide specialized services and information. Almost all supporting salespeople work for producers or middlemen who do this supporting work for producers. There are two types of supporting salespeople: missionary salespeople and technical specialists.

Missionary salespeople can increase sales

Missionary salespeople are supporting salespeople who work for producers—calling on their middlemen and their customers. They try to develop goodwill and stimulate demand, help the middlemen train their salespeople, and often take orders for delivery by the middlemen. Missionary salespeople are sometimes called *merchandisers* or *detailers*.

Producers who rely on merchant wholesalers to obtain widespread distribution often use missionary salespeople. The sales rep can give a promotion boost to a product that otherwise wouldn't get much attention from the middlemen because it's just one of many they sell. A missionary salesperson for Vicks' cold remedy products, for example, might visit druggists during the cold season and encourage them to use a special end-of-aisle display for Vicks' cough syrup—and then help set it up. The wholesaler that supplies the drugstore would benefit from any increased sales, but might not take the time to urge use of the special display.

An imaginative missionary salesperson can double or triple sales. Naturally, this doesn't go unnoticed. Missionary sales jobs are often a route to order-oriented jobs. In fact, this position is often used as a training ground for new salespeople. Recent college grads are often recruited for these positions.

Technical specialists are experts who know product applications

Technical specialists are supporting salespeople who provide technical assistance to order-oriented salespeople. Technical specialists usually are science or engineering graduates with the know-how to understand the customer's applications and explain the advantages of the company's product. They are usually more skilled in showing the technical details of their product than in trying to persuade customers to buy it. Before the specialist's visit, an order getter probably has stimulated interest. The technical specialist provides the details. The order getter usually completes the sale—but only after the customer's technical people give at least tentative approval.

Today many of the decision makers who influence organizational purchases have more technical knowledge than they did in the past. As a result, firms need more technical specialists. Many companies train their technical specialists in

This Hewlett-Packard ad makes it clear that HP salespeople, like Debbie Warden who is shown in the ad, are there to solve customers' problems, not just to try to sell more Hewlett-Packard computers or software.

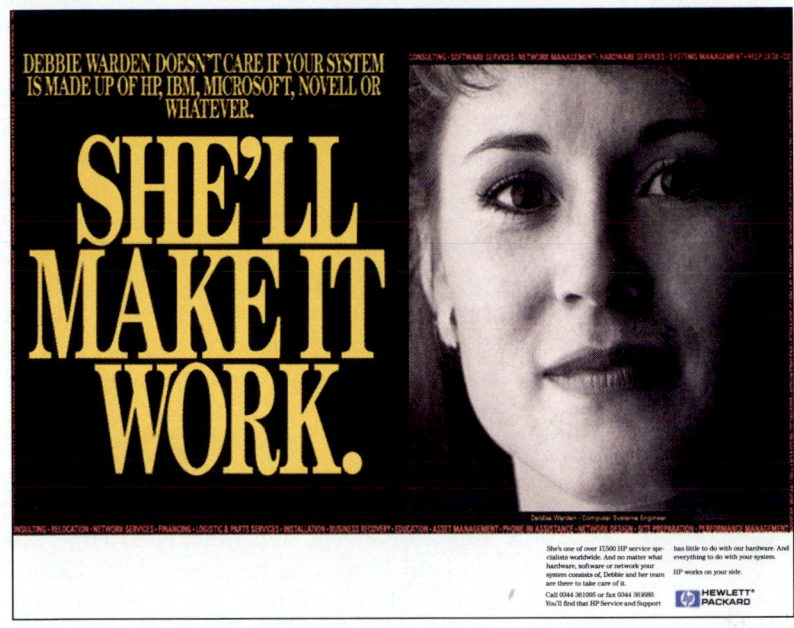

presentation skills to help them be not only technically accurate but also persuasive. Technical specialists who are also good communicators often become highly paid order getters.

Three tasks may have to be blended

We have described three sales tasks—order-getting, order-taking, and supporting. However, a particular salesperson might be given two—or all three—of these tasks. Ten percent of a particular job may be order-getting, 80 percent order-taking, and the additional 10 percent supporting. Another company might have many different people handling the different sales tasks. This can lead to **team selling**—when different sales reps work together on a specific account. Sometimes one or more of the "sales reps" on a team may not be from the sales department at all. If improving the relationship with the customer calls for technical support from the quality control manager, then that person becomes a part of the team, at least temporarily.

Producers of high-ticket items often use team selling. AT&T uses team selling to sell office communications systems for a whole business. Different specialists handle different parts of the job—but the whole team coordinates its efforts to achieve the desired result.[7]

Strategy planners need to specify what types of selling tasks the sales force will handle. Once the tasks are specified, the sales manager needs to assign responsibility for individual sales jobs so that the tasks are completed and the personal selling objectives achieved.

THE RIGHT STRUCTURE HELPS ASSIGN RESPONSIBILITY

A sales manager must organize the sales force so that all the necessary tasks are done well. A large organization might have different salespeople specializing by different selling tasks *and* by the target markets they serve.

Different target markets need different selling tasks

Sales managers often divide sales force responsibilities based on the type of customer involved. For example, Bigelow—a company that makes quality carpet for homes and office buildings—divided its sales force into two groups of specialists. Some Bigelow salespeople call only on architects to help them choose the best type of carpet for new office buildings. These reps know all the technical details, such as how well a certain carpet fiber will wear or its effectiveness in reducing noise from office equipment. Often no selling is involved because the architect only suggests specifications and doesn't actually buy the carpet.

Other Bigelow salespeople call on retail carpet stores. These reps identify stores that don't carry Bigelow carpets—and work to establish a relationship and get that crucial first order. Once a store is sold, these reps encourage the store manager to keep a variety of Bigelow carpets in stock. They also take orders, help train the store's salespeople, and try to solve any problems that occur.

Big accounts get special treatment

Very large customers often require special selling effort—and relationships with them are treated differently. Moen, a maker of plumbing fixtures, has a regular sales force to call on building material wholesalers and an elite **major accounts sales force** that sells directly to large accounts—like Lowe's or other major retail chain stores that carry plumbing fixtures.

You can see why this sort of special attention is justified when you consider Procter & Gamble's relationship with Wal-Mart. Although P&G is an international powerhouse, its total sales in every country except the U.S. and Germany add up to less than its sales to Wal-Mart. That's why the P&G sales team that calls on Wal-Mart lives in Bentonville, Arkansas, where Wal-Mart is based.[8]

Some salespeople specialize in telephone selling

Some firms have a group of salespeople who specialize in **telemarketing**—using the telephone to "call" on customers or prospects. A phone call has many of the benefits of a personal visit—including the ability to modify the message as feedback is received. The big advantage of telemarketing is that it saves time and money. Telemarketing is especially useful when customers are small or in hard-to-reach places. Many firms are finding that a telemarketing sales force can build profitable relationships with customers it might otherwise have to ignore altogether. Telemarketing is also important when many prospects have to be contacted to reach one actually interested in buying. In these situations, telemarketing may be the only economical approach.

Telemarketing is rapidly growing in popularity. Large and small firms alike find that it allows them to extend their personal selling efforts to new target markets. Telemarketing increases the frequency of contact between the firm and its customers. Convenient incoming toll-free telephone lines also make it fast and easy for customers to place orders or get assistance.[9]

Sales tasks are done in sales territories

Often companies organize selling tasks on the basis of a **sales territory**—a geographic area that is the responsibility of one salesperson or several working together. A territory might be a region of a country, a state, or part of a city—depending on the market potential. Companies like Lockheed Aircraft Corporation often consider a whole country as *part* of a sales territory for one salesperson.

Carefully set territories can reduce travel time and the cost of sales calls. Assigning territories can also help reduce confusion about who has responsibility for a set of selling tasks. Consider the case of the Hyatt Hotel chain. Until recently, each hotel had its own salespeople to get bookings for big conferences

Raychem uses telemarketing salespeople to qualify prospects and sales leads generated by advertisements, direct mail, and trade shows. By contrast, Shell Oil's technical specialists usually must meet with the customer in person.

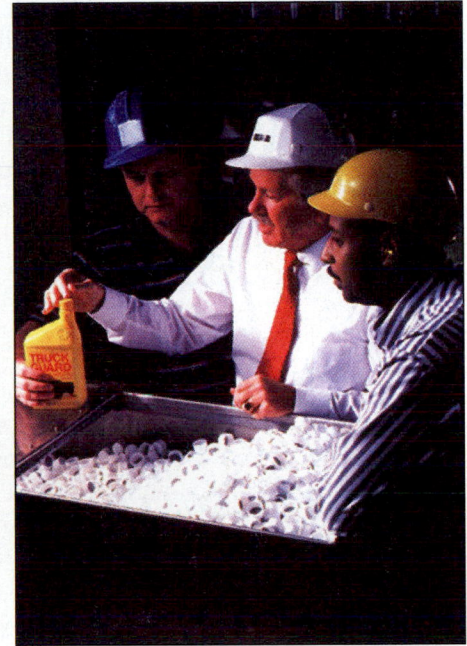

and business meetings. That meant that professional associations and other prospects who had responsibility for selecting meeting locations might be called on by sales reps from 20 or 30 different Hyatt hotels in different parts of the world. Now, the Hyatt central office divides up responsibility for working with specific accounts; one rep calls on an account and then tries to sell space in the Hyatt facility that best meets the customer's needs.

Sometimes simple geographic division isn't easy. A company may have different products that require very different knowledge or selling skills—even if products sell in the same territory or to the same customer. For example, Du Pont makes special films for hospital X-ray departments as well as chemicals used in laboratory blood tests. But a salesperson who can talk to a radiologist about the best film for a complex X ray probably can't be expected to know everything about blood chemistry!

Size of sales force depends on workload

Once the important selling tasks are specified—and the responsibilities divided—the sales manager must decide how many salespeople are needed. The first step is estimating how much work can be done by one person in some time period. Then the sales manager can make an educated guess about how many people are required in total, as the following example shows.

For many years, the Parker Jewelry Company was very successful selling its silver jewelry to department and jewelry stores in the southwestern region of the United States. But top managers wanted to expand into the big urban markets in the northeastern states. They realized that most of the work for the first few years would require order getters. They felt that a salesperson would need to call on each account at least once a month to get a share of this competitive business. They estimated that a salesperson could make only five calls a day on prospective buyers and still allow time for travel, waiting, and follow-up on orders that came in. This meant that a sales rep who made calls 20 days a month could handle about 100 stores (5 a day × 20 days).

The managers used a personal computer and a CD-ROM database that included all of the telephone Yellow Pages listings for the country. This allowed them to quickly list and get a count of the total number of jewelry departments and stores in their target market. Then they simply divided the total number of stores by 100 to estimate the number of salespeople needed. This also helped them set up territories—by defining areas that included about 100 stores for each salesperson. Obviously, managers might want to fine tune this estimate for differences in territories—such as travel time. But the basic approach can be adapted and applied to many different situations.[10]

When a company is starting a new sales force, managers are concerned about its size. But many established firms ignore this problem. Some managers forget that over time the right number of salespeople may change—as selling tasks change. Then, when a problem becomes obvious, they try to change everything in a hurry—a big mistake. Consideration of what type of salespeople and how many should be ongoing. If the sales force needs to be reduced, it doesn't make sense to let a lot of people go all at once—especially when that could be avoided with some planning. Conversely, finding and training effective salespeople takes time—and it too is an ongoing job.

SOUND SELECTION AND TRAINING TO BUILD A SALES FORCE

Selecting good salespeople takes judgment, plus

It is important to hire *good, well-qualified* salespeople. But the selection in many companies is a hit-or-miss affair—done without serious thought about exactly what kind of person the firm needs. Managers may hire friends and relations—or whoever is available—because they feel that the only qualifications for sales jobs are a friendly personality and nice appearance. This approach leads to poor sales—and costly sales force turnover.

Progressive companies are more careful. They constantly update a list of possible job candidates. They schedule candidates for multiple interviews with various executives, do thorough background checks, and even use psychological tests. Unfortunately, such techniques can't guarantee success. But a systematic approach based on several different inputs results in a better sales force.

One problem in selecting salespeople is that two different sales jobs with identical titles may involve very different selling tasks—and require different skills. A carefully prepared job description helps avoid this problem.

Job descriptions should be in writing and specific

A **job description** is a written statement of what a salesperson is expected to do. It might list 10 to 20 specific tasks—as well as routine prospecting and sales report writing. Each company must write its own job specifications. And it should provide clear guidelines about what selling tasks the job involves. This is critical to determine the kind of salespeople who should be selected—and later it provides a basis for seeing how they should be trained, how well they are performing, and how they should be paid.

Good salespeople are trained, not born

The idea that good salespeople are born may have some truth—but it isn't the whole story. A *born* salesperson—if that term refers to an outgoing, aggressive kind of individual—may not do nearly as well when the going gets rough as a less extroverted co-worker who has had solid, specialized training.

La-Z-Boy operates a sales training institute to help furniture retailers train their salespeople, and Learning International offers training programs that firms can use to ensure that their salespeople have strong professional selling skills.

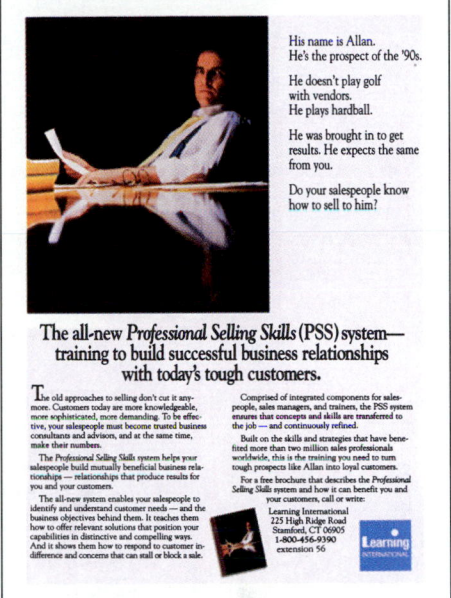

A salesperson needs to be taught—about the company and its products, about giving effective sales presentations, and about building strong relationships with the firm's customers. But this isn't always done. Many salespeople fail—or do a poor job—because they haven't had good training. Firms often hire new salespeople and immediately send them out on the road—or the retail selling floor—with no grounding in the basic selling steps and no information about the product or the customer. They just get a price list and a pat on the back. This isn't enough!

All salespeople need some training

It's up to sales and marketing management to be sure that the salespeople know what they're supposed to do—and how to do it. A job description is helpful in telling salespeople what they are expected to do. But showing them how to get the job done is harder—because people may be hired with different backgrounds, skills, and levels of intelligence. Some trainees are hired with no knowledge of the company or its products—and little knowledge of selling. Others may come in with a lot of industry knowledge and much selling experience—but some bad habits developed at another company. Saturn car dealers faced this problem. They wanted customer-oriented salespeople who would satisfy customers' needs—not just aggressively "push iron." Yet many salespeople who had been selling for other car companies found it hard to adjust to Saturn's philosophy. Saturn's training program helped to overcome these problems and now Saturn salespeople earn some of the highest customer satisfaction ratings in the automobile industry.

In other situations, salespeople may have some relevant selling experience but need to know more about the firm's customers and their needs. Even a firm's own sales veterans may get set in their ways and profit greatly by—and often welcome the chance for—additional training.

The kind of initial sales training should be modified based on the experience and skills of the group involved. But the company's sales training program should cover at least the following areas: (1) company policies and practices, (2) product information, (3) building relationships with customer firms, and (4) professional selling skills.

Selling skills can be learned

Many companies spend the bulk of their training time on product information and company policy. They neglect training in selling techniques because they think selling is something anyone can do. More progressive companies know that training in selling skills can pay off. For example, training can help salespeople learn how to be more effective in cold calls on new prospects, in listening carefully to identify a customer's real objections, and in closing the sale. Training can also help a salesperson better analyze why present customers buy from the company, why former customers now buy from competitors, and why some prospects remain only prospects. Later in this chapter, we'll talk about some key ideas in this area—especially those related to different kinds of sales presentations.

Training on selling techniques often starts in the classroom with lectures, case studies, and videotaped trial presentations and demonstrations. But a complete training program adds on-the-job observation of effective salespeople and coaching from sales supervisors.

Training is ongoing

How long the initial training period should last depends on how hard the job is—as shown in the job description. Some training programs go on for many months. For example, some new IBM sales reps don't call on an account by themselves for the first six months or more. Some form of sales training should go on indefinitely. Many companies use weekly sales meetings or work sessions, annual or semiannual conventions or conferences, and regular weekly or biweekly newsletters—as well as normal sales supervision—to keep salespeople up-to-date.[11]

COMPENSATING AND MOTIVATING SALESPEOPLE

To recruit—and keep—good salespeople, a firm has to develop an attractive compensation plan designed to motivate. Ideally, sales reps should be paid in such a way that what they want to do—for personal interest and gain—is in the company's interest too. Most companies focus on financial motivation—but public recognition, sales contests, and simple personal recognition for a job well done can be highly effective in encouraging greater sales effort.[12] Our main emphasis here, however, will be on financial motivation.[13]

Two basic decisions must be made in developing a compensation plan: (1) the level of compensation and (2) the method of payment.

Compensation varies with job and needed skills

To attract good salespeople, a company must pay at least the going market wage for different kinds of salespeople. Order getters are paid more than order takers, for example.

The job description explains the salesperson's role in the marketing mix. It should show whether the salesperson needs any special skills or has any special responsibilities that require higher pay levels. To be sure it can afford a specific type of salesperson, the company should estimate—when the job description is written—how valuable such a salesperson will be. A good order getter may be worth $50,000 to $100,000 to one company but only $15,000 to $25,000 to

Salespeople are using portable computers to save time and improve their communications with both customers and their own companies.

another—just because the second firm doesn't have enough to sell! In such a case, the second company should rethink its job specifications—or completely change its promotion plans—because the going rate for order getters is much higher than $15,000 a year.

If a job requires extensive travel, aggressive pioneering, or contacts with difficult customers, the pay may have to be higher. But the salesperson's compensation level should compare—at least roughly—with the pay scale of the rest of the firm. Normally, salespeople earn more than the office or production force but less than top management.

Payment methods vary

Once a firm decides on the general level of compensation, it has to set the method of payment. There are three basic methods of payment: (1) *straight salary*, (2) *straight commission*, or (3) a *combination plan*. Straight salary normally supplies the most security for the salesperson—and straight commission the most incentive. These two represent extremes. Most companies want to offer their salespeople some balance between incentive and security, so the most popular method of payment is a combination plan that includes some salary and some commission. Bonuses, profit sharing, pensions, stock plans, insurance, and other fringe benefits may be included too. Still, some blend of salary and commission provides the basis for most combination plans.

What determines the choice of the pay plan? Four standards should be applied: control, incentive, flexibility, and simplicity.

Salary gives control—if there is close supervision

The proportion of a salesperson's compensation paid as salary affects how much *control* the sales manager has. It also affects how much supervision is required. A salesperson on straight salary earns the same amount regardless of how he or she spends time. So the salaried salesperson is expected to do what the sales manager asks—whether it is order-taking, supporting sales activities, solving customer problems, or completing sales call reports. However, the sales manager maintains control *only* by close supervision. As a result, straight salary or a large salary element in the compensation plan increases the amount of sales supervision needed.

If such personal supervision would be difficult, a firm may get better control with a compensation plan that includes some commission—or even a straight commission plan with built-in direction. For example, if a company wants its salespeople to devote more time to developing new accounts, it can pay higher commissions for first orders from a new customer. However, a salesperson on a straight commission tends to be his or her own boss. The sales manager is less likely to get help on sales activities that won't increase the salesperson's earnings.

Incentives can be direct or indirect

An *incentive* plan can range anywhere from an indirect incentive (a modest sharing of company profits) to a very direct incentive—where a salesperson's income is strictly commission on sales. The incentive should be large only if there is a direct relationship between the salesperson's effort and results. The relationship is less direct if a number of people are involved in the sale—engineers, top management, or supporting salespeople. In this case, each one's contribution is less obvious—and greater emphasis on salary may make more sense.

When a company wants to expand sales rapidly, it usually offers strong incentives to order-getting salespeople. Strong incentives may also be sensible when the company's objectives are shifting or varied. In this way, the salesperson's activities and efforts can be directed and shifted as needed. One trucking company, for example, has a sales incentive plan that pays higher commissions on business needed to balance freight movements—depending on how heavily traffic has been moving in one direction or another.

An incentive compensation plan can help motivate salespeople, but you have to be certain that the incentives are really aligned with the firm's objectives. For example, some critics believe that IBM's sales commission plan resulted in IBM salespeople pushing customers to buy computers they didn't need; the sales reps got the sale and income, but then customers who were dissatisfied with what they'd purchased broke off their relationship with IBM and turned to other suppliers. Now, IBM is trying to more carefully align its incentive plan with a customer orientation. For example, most IBM sales reps receive incentive pay that is in part based on customer satisfaction ratings they earn from their customers and in part based on the profitability of the sales they get. Finding the right balance between these two criteria isn't easy. But many other firms use variations of this approach—because incentives that just focus on short-term or first-time sales may not be what is best to motivate sales reps to develop long-term, need-satisfying relationships with their customers.

Flexibility is desirable— but difficult to achieve

Flexibility is probably the most difficult aspect to achieve. One major reason that combination plans have become more popular is that they offer a way to meet varying situations. We'll consider four major kinds of flexibility.

Flexibility in selling costs is especially important for most small companies. With limited working capital and uncertain markets, small companies like straight commission—or combination plans with a large commission element. When sales drop off, costs do too. Such flexibility is similar to using manufacturers' agents who get paid only if they deliver sales. This advantage often dominates in selecting a sales compensation method. Exhibit 15–2 shows the general

EXHIBIT 15–2   Relation between Personal Selling Expenses and Sales Volume—for Three Basic Personal Selling Compensation Alternatives

relation between personal selling expense and sales volume for each of the basic compensation alternatives.

Sales potential usually differs from one sales territory to another, so it is desirable for a compensation plan to offer *flexibility among territories*. Unless the pay plan allows for territory differences, the salesperson in a growing territory might have rapidly increasing earnings—while the sales rep in a poor area will have little to show for the same amount of work. Such a situation isn't fair—and it can lead to high turnover and much dissatisfaction. A sales manager can take such differences into consideration when setting a salesperson's **sales quota**—the specific sales or profit objective a salesperson is expected to achieve.

Flexibility among people is important because most companies' salespeople vary in their stage of professional development. Trainees and new salespeople usually require a special pay plan with emphasis on salary. This provides at least some stability of earnings.

Flexibility among products is desirable because most companies sell several different products with different profit potentials. Unless firms recognize this fact, the salespeople may push the products that sell best—ignoring overall company profit. A flexible commission system can more easily adjust to changing profit potentials.

Simplicity

A final consideration is the need for *simplicity*. Complicated plans are hard for salespeople to understand. Salespeople become dissatisfied if they can't see a direct relationship between their effort and their income.

Simplicity is best achieved with straight salary. But in practice, it's usually better to sacrifice some simplicity to gain some incentive, flexibility, and control. The best combination of these factors depends on the job description and the company's objectives.

Sales managers must plan, implement, and control

There are no easy answers to the compensation problem. It is up to the sales manager—together with the marketing manager—to develop a good compensation plan. The sales manager's efforts must be coordinated with the whole marketing mix because personal selling objectives can be accomplished only if enough money is allocated for this job. Further, managers must regularly evaluate each salesperson's performance—and be certain that all the needed tasks are

SALESPEOPLE WORK SMARTER—WITH THEIR FINGERTIPS

Laptop computers help more salespeople work smarter, not just harder. Salespeople use computers in many different ways.

Without a laptop, it was impossible for a wholesaler's salespeople to master Cincinnati Milacron's product line. Now a computer asks a series of questions and then helps the salesperson figure out which of 65,000 grinding wheels and hundreds of cutting fluids to sell to each metal shop. After adding this system, Milacron doubled its market share—without adding new salespeople.

Laptops help keep salespeople for London Fog clothing up-to-date when they're on the road calling on accounts. Early each morning before leaving the hotel, the sales reps call into the company's central computer. It downloads to the laptops all the latest information about product availability, prices, customers' accounts, and the like. Later in the day, when a customer has a question about product delivery, the sales rep can answer it instantly—without scheduling another appointment or even calling the home office.

Salespeople for Metropolitan Life Insurance company use laptops to help customers analyze the financial implications of different investments. For example, when the manager of a pension fund wanted to see what would happen if she switched money from one investment to another, the salesperson used spreadsheet software on the laptop to do the analysis—on the spot. The customer was convinced, and the sales rep closed a $633,000 sale.

When Hewlett-Packard equipped a group of salespeople with laptops, the machines helped to improve communications and reduced the amount of time in meetings at the home office. As a result, salespeople were able to spend 27 percent more time with customers—and sales rose by 10 percent.

Results like these explain why the number of companies equipping their salespeople with laptops is growing so rapidly. New laptops that include built-in cellular phones that can send and receive faxes are attracting even more companies.[14]

being done well. The compensation plan may have to be changed if the pay and work are out of line. And by evaluating performance, firms can also identify areas that need more attention—by the salesperson or management.[15] In Chapter 20, we'll talk more about controlling marketing activities.

PERSONAL SELLING TECHNIQUES—PROSPECTING AND PRESENTING

When we discussed the need for sales training programs, we stressed the importance of training in selling techniques. Now let's discuss these ideas in more detail so you understand the basic steps each salesperson should follow—including prospecting and selecting target customers, planning sales presentations, making sales presentations, and following up after the sale. Exhibit 15–3 shows the steps we'll consider. You can see that the salesperson is just carrying out a planned communication process—as we discussed in Chapter 14.[16]

Prospecting—narrowing down to the right target

Although a marketing strategy should specify the segmenting dimensions for a target market, that doesn't mean that each target customer is individually identified! Narrowing the personal selling effort down to the right target requires constant, detailed analysis of markets and much prospecting. Basically, **prospecting** involves following all the leads in the target market to identify potential customers.

Finding live prospects who will help make the buying decision isn't as easy as it sounds. In business markets, for example, the salesperson may need to do some

EXHIBIT 15–3 Key Steps in the Personal Selling Process

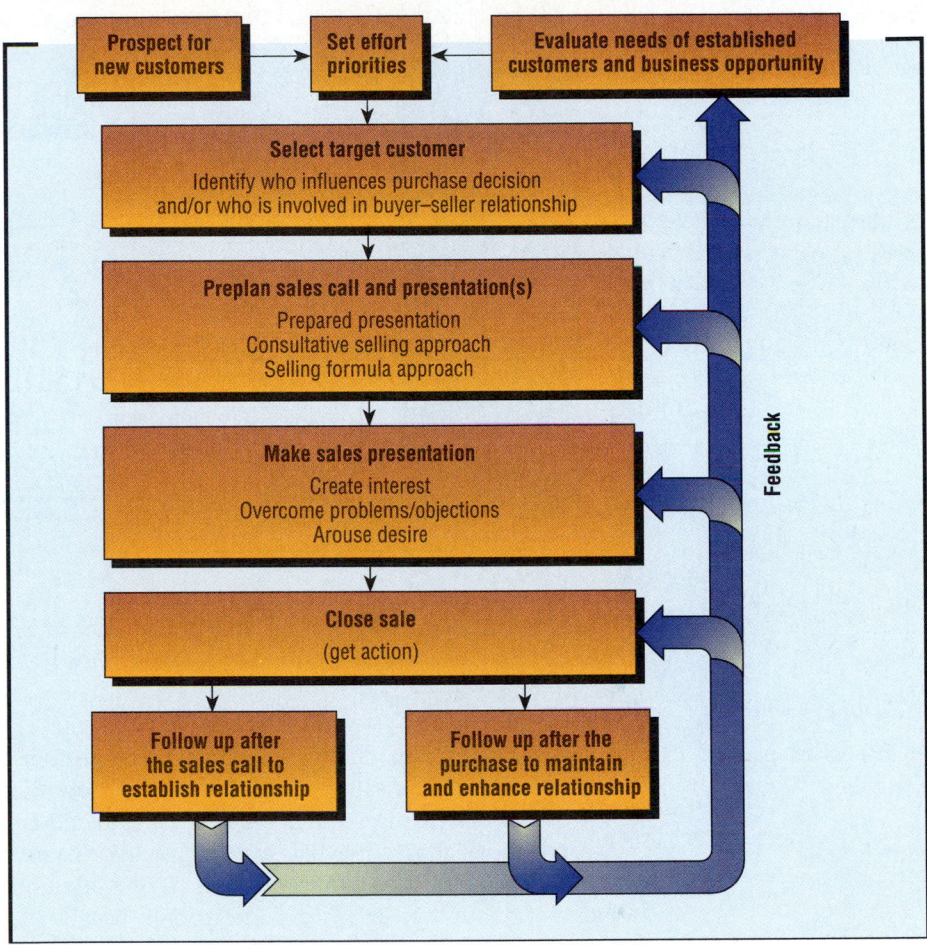

hard detective work to find the real purchase decision makers. Multiple buying influence is common, and companies regularly rearrange their organization structures and buying responsibilities.

Most salespeople use the telephone for much of their detective work. A phone call often saves the wasted expense of personal visits to prospects who are not interested—or it can provide much useful information for planning a follow-up sales visit. Some hot prospects can even be sold on the phone.

Some companies provide prospect lists to make this part of the selling job easier. For example, one insurance company checks the local newspaper for marriage announcements—then a salesperson calls to see if the new couple is interested in finding out more about life insurance.

All customers are not equal

While prospecting focuses on identifying new customers, established customers require attention too. It's often time-consuming and expensive to establish a relationship with a customer, so once established it makes sense to keep the relationship healthy. That requires the rep to routinely review active accounts, rethink customers' needs, and reevaluate each customer's long-term business potential. Some small accounts may have the potential to become big accounts,

Both Zenith and SPC
offer products that help
salespeople enhance their
sales presentations.

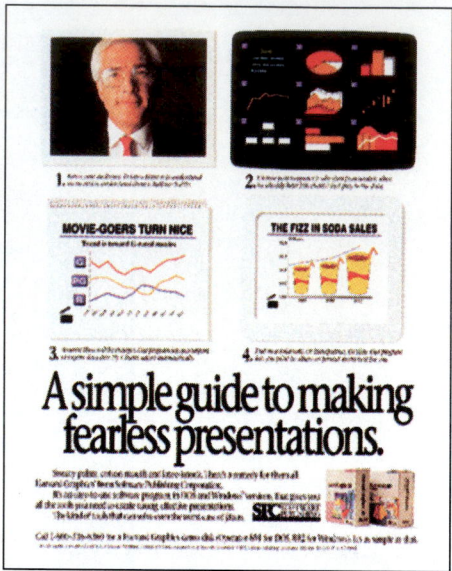

and some accounts that previously required a lot of costly attention may no longer
warrant it. So a sales rep may need to set priorities for both new prospects and
existing customers.

**How long to spend
with whom?**

Once a set of possible prospects—and customers who need attention—have
been identified, the salesperson must decide how much time to spend with each
one. A sales rep must qualify prospects and existing accounts—to see if they
deserve more effort. The salesperson usually makes these decisions by weighing
the potential sales volume—as well as the likelihood of a sale. This requires
judgment. But well-organized salespeople usually develop some system because
they have too many demands on their time. They can't wine and dine every
prospect or customer.[17]

Some firms provide their reps with personal computers—and specially
developed computer programs—to help with this process. Most of them use some
grading scheme. A sales rep might estimate how much each prospect or customer
is likely to purchase—and the probability of getting and keeping the business
given the competition. The computer then combines this information and grades
each prospect. Attractive accounts may be labeled A—and the salesperson may
plan to call on them weekly until the sale is made, the relationship is in good
shape, or the customer is moved into a lower category. B customers might offer
somewhat lower potential—and be called on monthly. C accounts might be called
on only once a year—unless they happen to contact the salesperson. And D
accounts might be transferred to a telemarketing group or even ignored—unless
the customer takes the initiative.[18]

**Three kinds of sales
presentations may
be useful**

Once the salesperson selects a target customer, it's necessary to plan for the
sales call. This precall planning usually involves preparing a **sales presentation**—a salesperson's effort to make a sale or address a customer's problem. But
someone has to plan what kind of sales presentation to make. This is a strategy
decision. The kind of presentation should be set before the sales rep goes calling.

EXHIBIT 15–4
Prepared Approach
to Sales Presentation

EXHIBIT 15–5
Consultative Selling
Approach to
Sales Presentation

EXHIBIT 15–6
Selling Formula
Approach to
Sales Presentation

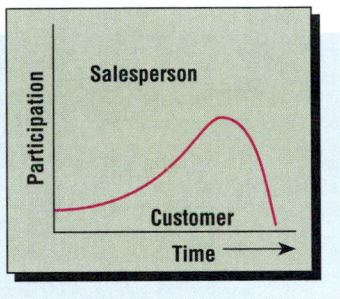

And in situations where the customer comes to the salesperson—in a retail store, for instance—planners have to make sure that prospects and customers are brought together with salespeople.

A marketing manager can choose two basically different approaches to making sales presentations: the prepared approach or the consultative selling approach. Another approach—the selling formula approach—is a combination of the two. Each of these has its place.

The prepared sales presentation

The **prepared sales presentation** approach uses a memorized presentation that is not adapted to each individual customer. A prepared (canned) presentation builds on the stimulus–response ideas discussed in Chapter 7. This model says that a customer faced with a particular stimulus will give the desired response—in this case, a yes answer to the salesperson's prepared statement, which includes a **close**, the salesperson's request for an order.

If one trial close doesn't work, the sales rep tries another prepared presentation—and attempts another closing. This can go on for some time—until the salesperson runs out of material or the customer either buys or decides to leave. Exhibit 15–4 shows the relative participation of the salesperson and customer in the prepared approach. Note that the salesperson does most of the talking.

In modern selling, firms commonly use the canned approach when the prospective sale is low in value and only a short presentation is practical. It's also sensible when salespeople aren't very skilled. The company can control what they say—and in what order. For example, a sales rep for *Time* magazine can call a prospect—perhaps a person whose subscription is about to run out—and basically read the prepared presentation. The caller needs little training or ability.

But a canned approach has a weakness. It treats all potential customers alike. It may work for some and not for others—and the salespeople probably won't know why or learn from experience. A prepared approach may be suitable for simple order-taking—but it is no longer considered good selling for complicated situations.

Consultative selling—builds on the marketing concept

The **consultative selling approach** involves developing a good understanding of the individual customer's needs before trying to close the sale. This name is used because the salesperson is almost acting as a consultant to help identify and solve the customer's problem. With this approach, the sales rep makes some general benefit statements to get the customer's attention and interest. Then the salesperson asks questions and *listens carefully* to understand the customer's needs. The customer does most of the talking at this stage. Once they agree on needs, the seller tries to show the customer how the product fills those needs—and to close the sale. This is a problem-solving approach—in which the customer and salesperson work together to satisfy the customer's needs. That's why it's sometimes called the need-satisfaction approach. Exhibit 15–5 shows the participation of the customer and the salesperson during such a sales presentation.

The consultative selling approach is most useful if there are many subtle differences among the customers in one target market. In the extreme, each customer may be thought of as a separate target market—with the salesperson trying to adapt to each one's needs and attitudes. This kind of selling takes more skill—and time. The salesperson must be able to analyze what motivates a particular customer—and show how the company's offering would help the customer satisfy those needs. The sales rep may even conclude that the customer's problem is really better solved with someone else's product. That might result in one lost sale, but it also is likely to build real trust and more sales opportunities over the life of the relationship with the customer. As you might expect, this is the kind of selling that is typical in business markets when a salesperson already has established a close relationship with a customer.

Selling formula approach—some of both

The **selling formula approach** starts with a prepared presentation outline—much like the prepared approach—and leads the customer through some logical steps to a final close. The prepared steps are logical because we assume that we know something about the target customer's needs and attitudes.

Exhibit 15–6 shows the selling formula approach. The salesperson does most of the talking at the beginning of the presentation—to communicate key points early. This part of the presentation may even have been prepared as part of the marketing strategy. As the sales presentation moves along, however, the salesperson brings the customer into the discussion to help clarify just what needs this customer has. The salesperson's job is to discover the needs of a particular customer to know how to proceed. Once it is clear what kind of customer this is, the salesperson comes back to show how the product satisfies this specific customer's needs—and to close the sale.

This approach can be useful for both order-getting and order-taking situations—where potential customers are similar and firms must use relatively untrained salespeople. Some office equipment and computer producers use this approach. They know the kinds of situations their salespeople meet—and roughly what they want them to say. Using this approach speeds training and makes the sales force productive sooner.

AIDA helps plan sales presentations

AIDA—Attention, Interest, Desire, Action: Each sales presentation—except for some very simple canned types—follows this AIDA sequence. The how-to-do-it might even be set as part of the marketing strategy. The time a sales rep spends on each of the steps might vary depending on the situation and the selling approach being used. But it is still necessary to begin a presentation by getting the prospect's *attention*, and hopefully, to move the customer to *action* through a close.[19]

Each sales manager—and salesperson—needs to think about this sequence in deciding what sales approach to use and in evaluating a possible presentation. Does the presentation get the prospect's attention quickly? Will the presentation be interesting? Will the benefits be clear so that the prospect is moved to buy the product? Does the presentation consider likely objections—and anticipate problems—so the sales rep can act to close the sale when the time is right? These may seem like simple things. But too frequently they aren't done at all—and a sale is lost.

Ethical issues may arise

As in every other area of marketing communications, ethical issues arise in the personal selling area. The most basic issue, plain and simple, is whether a salesperson's presentation is honest and truthful. But addressing that issue is a no-brainer. No company is served well by a salesperson who lies or manipulates customers to get their business.

On the other hand, most sales reps sooner or later face a sales situation in which they must make more difficult ethical decisions about how to balance company interests, customer interests, and personal interests. Conflicts are less likely to arise if the firm's marketing mix really meets the needs of its target market. Similarly, they are less likely to arise when the firm sees the value of developing a longer-term relationship with the customer. Then, the salesperson is arranging a happy marriage. By contrast, ethical conflicts are more likely when the sales rep's personal outcomes (such as commission income) or the selling firm's profits hinge on making sales to customers whose needs are only partially met by the firm's offering. But how close must the fit be between the firm's products and the customer's needs before it is appropriate for the salesperson to push for a sale?

Ideally, companies can avoid the whole problem by supporting their salespeople with a marketing mix that really offers target customers unique benefits. However, marketing managers and salespeople alike should recognize that the ideal may not exist in every sales call. Top executives, marketing managers, and sales managers set the tone for the ethical climate in which a salesperson operates. If they set impossible goals or project a "do-what-you-need-to-do" attitude, a desperate salesperson may yield to the pressure of the moment. When a firm clearly advocates ethical selling behavior and makes it clear that manipulative selling techniques are not acceptable, the salesperson is not left trying to swim "against the flow."[20]

CONCLUSION

In this chapter, we discussed the importance and nature of personal selling. Selling is much more than just getting rid of the product. In fact, a salesperson who is not given strategy guidelines may have to become the strategy planner for the market he or she serves. Ideally, however, the sales manager and marketing manager work together to set some strategy guidelines: the kind and number of salespersons needed, the kind of sales presentation desired, and selection, training, and motivation approaches.

We discussed the three basic sales tasks: (1) order-getting, (2) order-taking, and (3) supporting. Most sales jobs combine at least two of these three tasks. Once a firm specifies the important tasks, it can decide on the structure of its sales organization and the number of salespeople it needs. The nature of the job—and the level and method of compensation—also depend on the blend of these tasks. Firms should develop a job description for each sales job. This, in turn, provides guidelines for selecting, training, and compensating salespeople.

Once the marketing manager agrees to the basic plan and sets the budget, the sales manager must implement the plan—including directing and controlling the sales force. This includes assigning sales territories and controlling performance. You can see that the sales manager has more to do than jet around the country sipping martinis and entertaining customers. A sales manager is deeply involved with the basic management tasks of planning and control—as well as ongoing implementation of the personal selling effort.

We also reviewed some basic selling techniques and identified three kinds of sales presentations. Each has its place—but the consultative selling approach seems best for higher-level sales jobs. In these kinds of jobs, personal selling is achieving a new, professional status because of the competence and level of personal responsibility required of the salesperson. The day of the old-time glad-hander is passing in favor of the specialist who is creative, industrious, persuasive, knowledgeable, highly trained—and therefore able to help the buyer. This type of salesperson always has been—and probably always will be—in short supply. And the demand for high-level salespeople is growing.

QUESTIONS AND PROBLEMS

1. What strategy decisions are needed in the personal selling area? Why should the marketing manager make these strategy decisions?

2. What kind of salesperson (or what blend of the basic sales tasks) is required to sell the following products? If there are several selling jobs in the channel for each product, indicate the kinds of salespeople required. Specify any assumptions necessary to give definite answers.

   a. Laundry detergent.
   b. Costume jewelry.
   c. Office furniture.
   d. Men's underwear.
   e. Mattresses.
   f. Corn.
   g. Life insurance.

3. Distinguish among the jobs of producers', wholesalers', and retailers' order-getting salespeople. If one order getter is needed, must all the salespeople in a channel be order getters? Illustrate.

4. Discuss the role of the manufacturers' agent in a marketing manager's promotion plans. What kind of salesperson is a manufacturers' agent? What type of compensation plan is used for a manufacturers' agent?

5. Discuss the future of the specialty shop if producers place greater emphasis on mass selling because of the inadequacy of retail order-taking.

6. Compare and contrast missionary salespeople and technical specialists.

7. How would a straight commission plan provide flexibility in the sale of a line of women's clothing products that continually vary in profitability?

8. Explain how a compensation plan could be developed to provide incentives for experienced salespeople and yet make some provision for trainees who have not yet learned the job.

9. Cite an actual local example of each of the three kinds of sales presentations discussed in the chapter. Explain for each situation whether a different type of presentation would have been better.

10. Describe a consultative selling sales presentation that you experienced recently. How could it have been improved by fuller use of the AIDA framework?

11. How would our economy operate if personal salespeople were outlawed? Could the economy work? If so, how? If not, what is the minimum personal selling effort necessary? Could this minimum personal selling effort be controlled by law?

SUGGESTED CASES

COMPUTER-AIDED PROBLEM

15. Sales Compensation

Franco Welles, sales manager for Nanek, Inc., is trying to decide whether to pay a sales rep for a new territory with straight commission or a combination plan. He wants to evaluate possible plans—to compare the compensation costs and profitability of each. Welles knows that sales reps in similar jobs at other firms make about $36,000 a year.

The sales rep will sell two products. Welles is planning a higher commission for Product B—because he wants it to get extra effort. From experience with similar products, he has some rough estimates of expected sales volume under the different plans—and various ideas about commission rates. The details are found in the spreadsheet. The program computes compensation—and how much the sales rep will contribute to profit. "Profit contribution" is equal to the total revenue generated by the sales rep minus sales compensation costs and the costs of producing the units.

a. *For the initial values shown in the spreadsheet, which plan—commission or combination—would give the rep the highest compensation, and which plan would give the greatest profit contribution to Nanek, Inc.?*

b. *Welles thinks a sales rep might be motivated to work harder and sell 1,100 units of Product B if the commission rate (under the commission plan) were increased to 10 percent. If Welles is right (and everything else stays the same), would the higher commission rate be a good deal for Nanek? Explain your thinking.*

c. *A sales rep interested in the job is worried about making payments on her new car. She asks if Welles would consider paying her with a combination plan but with more guaranteed income (an $18,000 base salary) in return for taking a 3 percent commission on Products B and A. If this arrangement results in the same unit sales as Welles originally estimated for the combination plan, would Nanek, Inc., be better off or worse off under this arrangement?*

d. *Do you think the rep's proposal will meet Welles' goals for Product B? Explain your thinking.*

For additional questions related to this problem, see Exercise 15–3 in the *Learning Aid for Use with Basic Marketing*, 12th edition.

16

Advertising and Sales Promotion

The marketing manager for Grey Poupon mustard knew that his 1995 marketing plan couldn't just be a business-as-usual update of past plans. Changes in the market environment called for a new strategy—especially new promotion.

For seventeen years, witty ads showed stuffy aristocrats passing Grey Poupon out through the windows of their Rolls-Royces, in

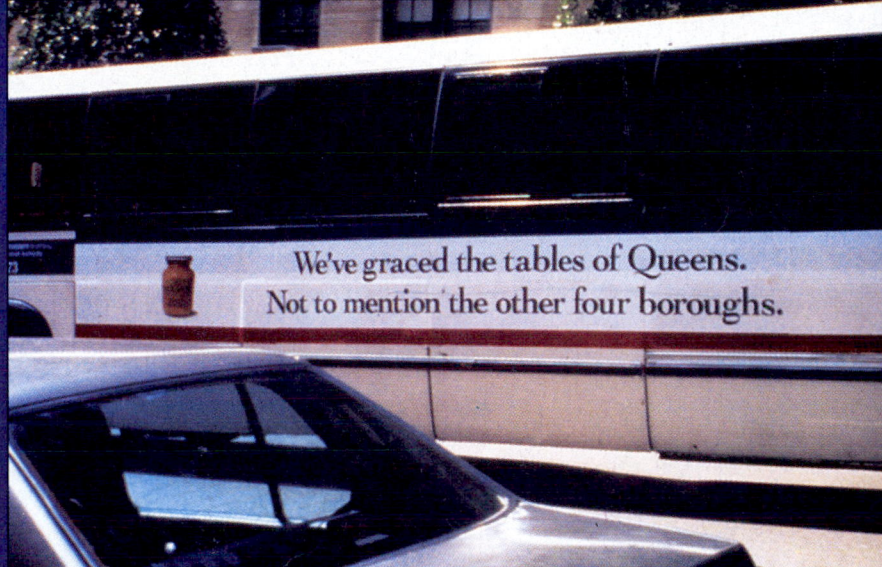

response to "Pardon me, would you have any Grey Poupon?" The ads positioned Grey Poupon as a premium product, but also sent the message that anybody could live the affluent life when it comes to mustard. Over time, the ad campaign built consumer interest in the brand and helped the sales force get strong retail distribution. Similarly, coupons, end-of-aisle displays, and other sales promotions prompted consumers to try the product—and most became repeat purchasers.

By 1994, Grey Poupon had nearly 18 percent of the market. Yet, with simpler consumer lifestyles in vogue, Grey Poupon's message didn't mean as much as it once did. In some ways it even backfired. While most consumers had Grey Poupon in the refrigerator, they didn't use it very often. They viewed it as a product mainly for special occasions—like parties and holidays. It also didn't help that fat-wary consumers were eating more turkey sandwiches and less bologna. Mustard didn't go as well with tur-

key. And Hellmann's popular new Dijonnaise—a creamy blend of mustard and mayonnaise—eroded mustard sales even further.

In a mature market, firms often turn to sales promotion to increase market share. But getting extra push from middlemen or trying to get a consumer to buy sooner won't help when the product is already in the consumer's refrigerator. Rather, in order to increase sales, the marketing challenge was to get current customers to use Grey Poupon more often. That wasn't likely unless more of them thought about using it for everyday purposes. So, the marketing manager turned to advertising—and the ad agency—for help in changing the way consumers viewed the product.

The agency responded with a new ad campaign that focused on using Poupon more often. Recognizing that network TV wasn't the best or cheapest way to convey the message, the agency emphasized other media. For example, new magazine ads urged consumers to "Poupon the potato salad" and "class up the cold cuts." The agency's creative director also targeted reminder ads at specific markets by using local media. For example, she came up with a simple but clever ad message to appear beside a picture of the Poupon package on the sides of New York City buses. The message reads: "We've graced the tables of Queens. Not to mention the other four boroughs." The play-on-words reference to New York City's Queens area helped get attention from busy New York City shoppers. Of course, one local ad won't have a big impact on Grey Poupon's total sales. However, the overall ad campaign will help change how consumers view the brand—and that may be the key to increased use and long-term sales growth.[1]

ADVERTISING, SALES PROMOTION, AND MARKETING STRATEGY DECISIONS

Mass selling makes widespread distribution possible. Although a marketing manager might prefer to use personal selling to communicate with customers, it can be expensive on a per-contact or per-sale basis. Advertising is a way around this problem. Although not as flexible as personal selling, it can often reach large numbers of potential customers at the same time. It can inform and persuade customers—and help position a firm's marketing mix as the one that meets customers' needs. Similar sales promotion aimed at final customers, channel members, or a firm's own employees is often important in swaying the target to immediate action. In the past decade, spending on sales promotion has grown at a rapid rate—especially in mature consumer-products markets where marketing managers rely heavily on sales promotion to get more attention from middlemen and to battle with rival firms for a larger share of consumers' purchases. Today, most promotion blends contain advertising and sales promotion as well as personal selling and publicity.

Advertising contacts vary in cost and results. This means marketing managers—and the advertising managers who work with them—have important strategy decisions to make. As the Grey Poupon case illustrates, they must decide: (1) who their target audience is, (2) what kind of advertising to use, (3) how to reach customers (via which types of media), (4) what to say to them (the copy

Colgate's ad in a railroad station in Warsaw stands out because there isn't yet a lot of advertising in Poland. But Colgate is careful not to do too much advertising—because many Polish consumers think that ad blitzes smack of propaganda.

EXHIBIT 16–1   Strategy Planning for Advertising

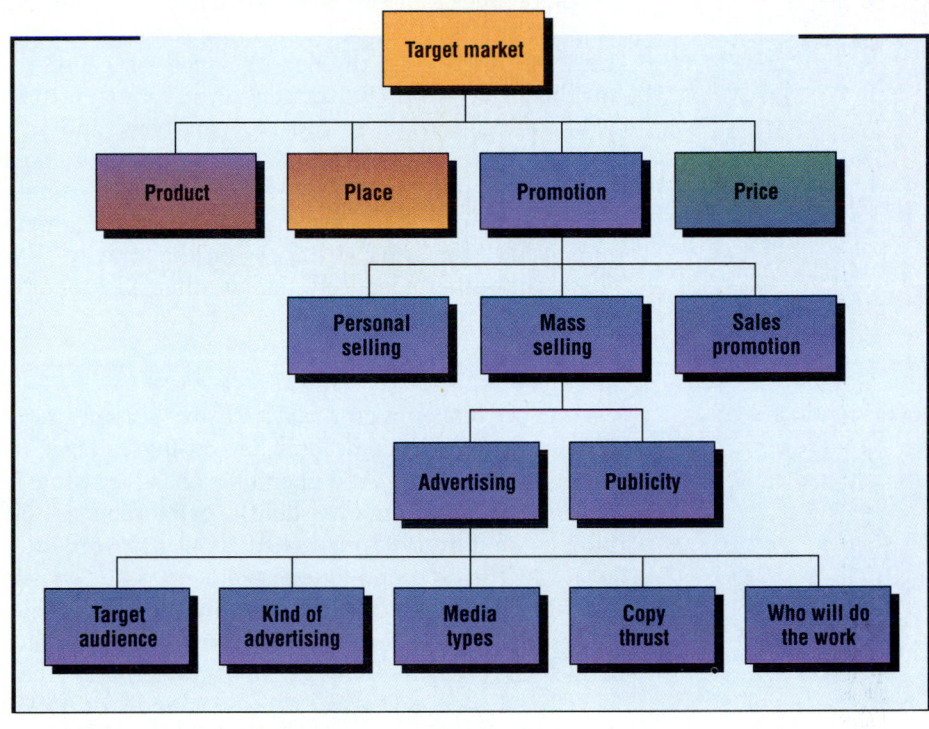

thrust), and (5) who will do the work—the firm's own advertising department or outside agencies. See Exhibit 16–1. We'll talk about these decisions in this chapter. We'll also consider how to measure advertising effectiveness—and legal limits on advertising—in an increasingly competitive environment.

After we discuss advertising, we'll go into more detail on sales promotion. We discuss the great variety of sales promotion approaches, how they typically vary for different target markets, and their basic benefits and limitations.

International dimensions are important

The basic strategy planning decisions for advertising and sales promotion are the same regardless of where in the world the target market is located. From the outset, however, remember that the choices available to a marketing manager within each of the decision areas may vary dramatically from one country to another. The target audience for advertising may be illiterate—making print ads useless. Commercial television may not be available. If it is, governments may place severe limits on the type of advertising permitted or when ads can be shown. Radio broadcasts in a market area may not be in the target market's language. Cultural, social, and behavioral influences may limit what type of advertising messages can be communicated. Advertising agencies who know a nation's unique advertising environment may be less than helpful.

International dimensions may also have a significant impact on sales promotion alternatives. For example, in countries with a large number of very small retailers some types of trade promotion are difficult, or even impossible, to manage. A typical Japanese grocery retailer with only 200 square feet of space, for example, doesn't have room for *any* special end-of-aisle displays. Consumer promotions may be affected too. Polish consumers, for example, are skeptical about product samples; they don't have a lot of experience with sampling and they figure that if it's free something's amiss. In some developing nations samples can't be distributed through the mail—because they're routinely stolen from mailboxes before they ever get to the target customer. Similarly, coupons won't work unless consumers can redeem them, and in some regions there are no facilitators to help with that effort. Similarly, some countries ban consumer sweepstakes—because they see it as a form of gambling.

Throughout this chapter we'll consider a number of these international promotion issues, but we'll focus on the array of choices available in the United States and other advanced, market-directed economies.[2]

THE IMPORTANCE OF ADVERTISING

Total spending is big—and growing internationally

As an economy grows, advertising becomes more important—because more consumers have income and advertising can get results. But good advertising results cost money. And spending on advertising is significant. In 1946, U.S. advertising spending was slightly more than $3 billion. By 1982, it was $66 billion—and by 1995 it reached about $160 billion.

Advertising spending per capita in other countries is typically much lower than in the U.S. Although exact and up-to-date figures aren't available, all other nations combined spend only about 25 percent more than the United States alone—and roughly half of that spending takes place in Europe. Even in Japan's developed economy, advertising spending (for 1993) was less than $31 billion. Lower media costs account for part of the difference in spending. Traditionally, however, there has just been less use of advertising in other countries. That's beginning to change. During the last decade, the rate of advertising spending in many parts of the world has increased even more rapidly than in the United States.[3]

Most advertisers aren't really spending that much

While total spending on advertising seems high, especially in the United States, it represents a small portion of what people pay for the goods and services they buy. U.S. corporations spend an average of only about 2.5 percent of their sales dollars on advertising. Worldwide, the percentage is even smaller.

Exhibit 16–2 shows, however, that advertising spending as a percent of sales dollars varies significantly across product categories. Producers of consumer products generally spend a larger percent than firms that produce business products. For example, U.S. beverage companies spend 7.5 percent, and companies that make toys and games spend a whopping 16.4 percent. At the other extreme, companies that sell plastics to manufacturers spend only about 0.8 percent on advertising. Some business products companies—those that depend on personal selling—may spend less than 1/10 of 1 percent.

In general, the percent is smaller for retailers (and wholesalers) than for producers. Kmart and JC Penney spend about 3 percent, but many retailers and wholesalers spend 1 percent or less.

Individual firms may spend more or less than others in the industry—depending on the role of advertising in their promotion blend and marketing mix.

Of course, percentages don't tell the whole story. Nissan, which spends less than 1 percent of sales on advertising, is among the top 50 advertisers worldwide. The really big spenders are very important to the advertising industry because they account for a very large share of total advertising spending. For example, in

EXHIBIT 16–2   Advertising Spending as Percent of Sales for Illustrative Product Categories

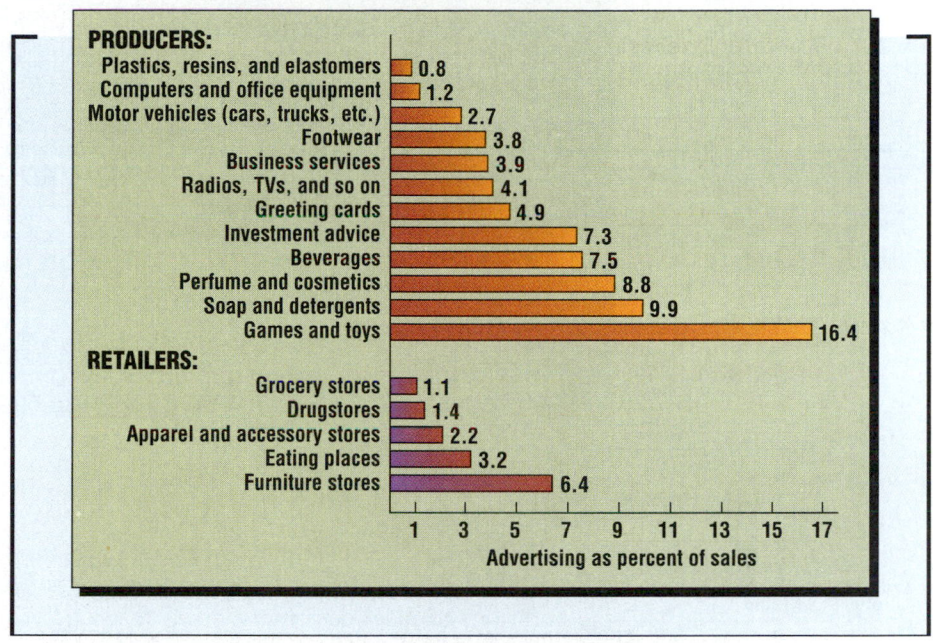

the United States, the top 100 advertisers (many of which are based in other countries) typically account for about 25 percent of all advertising spending.[4]

You can see that advertising is important in certain markets—especially final consumer markets. Nevertheless, in total, advertising costs much less than personal selling and sales promotion.

Advertising doesn't employ that many people

While total advertising expenditures are large, the advertising industry itself employs relatively few people. The major expense is for media time and space. In the United States, the largest share of this—23 percent—goes for newspaper space. That reflects the importance of local advertising by retailers. Television (including cable) takes about 22 percent of the total and direct mail about 20 percent. The shares for radio (7 percent) and magazines (5 percent) are much smaller.[5]

Many students hope for a glamorous job in advertising, but there are fewer jobs in advertising than you might think. Even in the United States, with the highest advertising spending of any nation, only about 500,000 people work directly in the advertising industry. This includes all people who help create or sell advertising or advertising media—advertising people in radio and television stations, newspapers, and magazines; those in advertising agencies; and those working for retailers, wholesalers, and producers. Advertising agencies employ only about half of all these people.[6]

ADVERTISING OBJECTIVES ARE A STRATEGY DECISION

Advertising objectives must be specific

Every ad and every advertising campaign should have clearly defined objectives. These should grow out of the firm's overall marketing strategy—and the jobs assigned to advertising. It isn't enough for the marketing manager to say—

Many nonprofit organizations—including Mothers Against Drunk Driving—rely on marketing to help achieve their objectives.

"Promote the product." The marketing manager must decide exactly what advertising should do.

Advertising objectives should be more specific than personal selling objectives. One of the advantages of personal selling is that salespeople can shift their presentations to meet customers' needs. Each ad, however, is a specific communication. It must be effective not just for one customer but for thousands—or millions—of them.

The marketing manager sets the overall direction

The marketing manager might give the advertising manager one or more of the following specific objectives—along with the budget to accomplish them:

1. Help introduce new products to specific target markets.
2. Help position the firm's brand or marketing mix by informing and persuading target customers or middlemen about its benefits.
3. Help obtain desirable outlets and tell customers where they can buy a product.
4. Provide ongoing contact with target customers—even when a salesperson isn't available.
5. Prepare the way for salespeople by presenting the company's name and the merits of its products.
6. Get immediate buying action.
7. Help to maintain relationships with satisfied customers and confirm their purchase decisions.

If you want half the market, say so!

The objectives listed above are not as specific as they could be. If a marketing manager really wants specific results, they should be clearly stated. A general objective is: "To help expand market share." This could be rephrased more specifically: "To increase shelf space in our cooperating retail outlets by 25 percent during the next three months."

Once the marketing manager sets the overall objectives, the advertising manager should set specific objectives for each ad—as well as a whole advertising campaign. Without specific objectives, the creative people who develop individual ads may pursue their own objectives. They might set some vague

EXHIBIT 16–3 Examples of Different Types of Advertising over Adoption Process Stages

Awareness	Interest	Evaluation and trial	Decision	Confirmation
Teaser campaigns Pioneering ads Jingles and slogans Announcements	Informative or descriptive ads Image/celebrity ads Demonstration of benefits	Competitive ads Persuasive copy Comparative ads Testimonials	Direct-action retail ads Point-of-purchase ads Price deal offers	Reminder ads Informative "why" ads

objective—like promote the product—and then create ads that win advertising industry artistic awards but fail to achieve the desired results.

Objectives guide implementation too

The specific objectives obviously affect implementation. Advertising that might be right for encouraging consumers to switch from a competing brand might be all wrong for appealing to established customers with whom a firm already has a good relationship. Similarly, an ad that appeals to opinion leaders might not be what's needed to get repeat customers back into a retail store. As Exhibit 16–3 shows, the type of advertising that achieves objectives for one stage of the adoption process may be off target for another. For example, most advertising for cameras in the United States, Germany, and Japan focuses on foolproof pictures or state-of-the-art design because most consumers in these countries already own *some* camera. In Africa, where only about 20 percent of the population owns a camera, ads must sell the whole concept of picture-taking.

With new products, most of the target market may have to be brought through the early stages of the adoption process. The advertising manager may use teaser campaigns—along with informative ads. For more established products, advertising's job might be to build brand preference—as well as help purchasers confirm their decisions.

OBJECTIVES DETERMINE THE KINDS OF ADVERTISING NEEDED

The advertising objectives largely determine which of two basic types of advertising to use—product or institutional.

Product advertising tries to sell a product. It may be aimed at final users or channel members.

Institutional advertising tries to promote an organization's image, reputation, or ideas—rather than a specific product. Its basic objective is to develop goodwill or improve an organization's relations with various groups—not only customers but also current and prospective channel members, suppliers, shareholders, employees, and the general public. Dow, for example, appeals to college grads and other potential employees with image-oriented ads that proclaim "Dow lets you do great things." The British government, one of the top 50 advertisers in the world, uses institutional advertising to promote England as a place to do business.

Product advertising— know us, like us, remember us

Product advertising falls into three categories: pioneering, competitive, and reminder advertising.

Hitachi's attention-getting institutional ad is effective in promoting the company's name and image, rather than trying to sell just one of its many specific product lines.

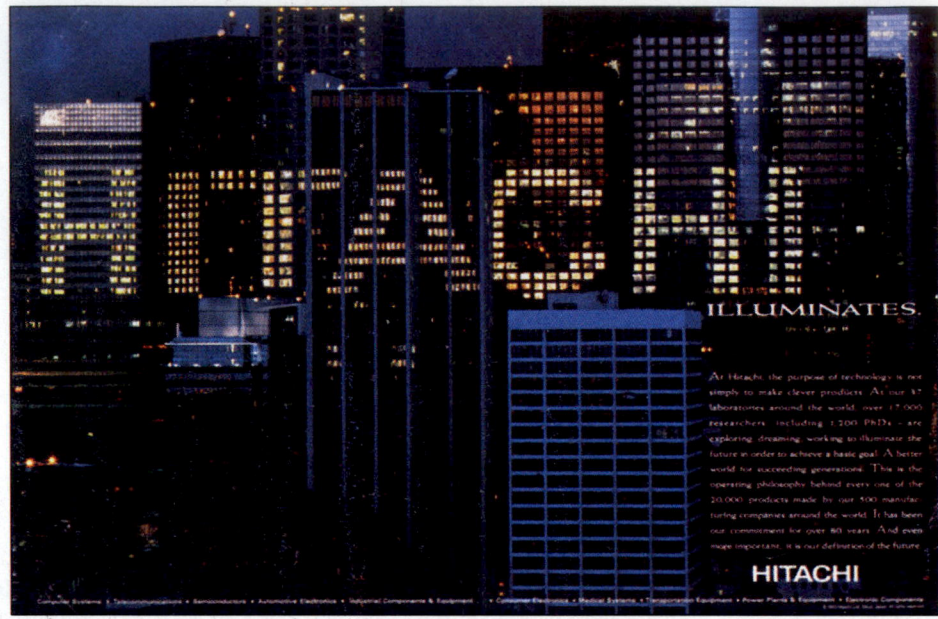

ILLUMINATES.

At Hitachi, the purpose of technology is not simply to make clever products. At our 37 laboratories around the world, over 17,000 researchers, including 1,200 PhDs, are exploring, dreaming, working to illuminate the future in order to achieve a basic goal: A better world for succeeding generations. This is the operating philosophy behind every one of the 20,000 products made by our 500 manufacturing companies around the world. It has been our commitment for over 80 years. And even more important, it is our definition of the future.

HITACHI

Pioneering advertising—builds primary demand

Pioneering advertising tries to develop primary demand for a product category rather than demand for a specific brand. Pioneering advertising is usually done in the early stages of the product life cycle; it informs potential customers about the new product and helps turn them into adopters. When Merrell Dow Pharmaceutical introduced a prescription drug to help smokers break the habit, it did pioneering advertising to inform both doctors and smokers about its breakthrough. The ad didn't even mention the name of the drug. Instead it informed smokers who wanted to quit that doctors could now help them overcome their nicotine dependence. Later, as other firms put similar drugs on the market, Merrell Dow turned to competitive advertising.

Competitive advertising—emphasizes selective demand

Competitive advertising tries to develop selective demand for a specific brand. A firm is forced into competitive advertising as the product life cycle moves along—to hold its own against competitors. The United Fruit Company gave up a 20-year pioneering effort to promote bananas in favor of promoting its own Chiquita brand. The reason was simple. While United Fruit was single-handedly promoting bananas, it slowly lost market share to competitors. It launched its competitive advertising campaign to avoid further losses.

Competitive advertising may be either direct or indirect. The **direct type** aims for immediate buying action. The **indirect type** points out product advantages to affect future buying decisions.

Most of Delta Airlines' advertising is of the competitive variety. Much of it tries for immediate sales—so the ads are the direct type with prices, timetables, and phone numbers to call for reservations. Some of its ads are the indirect type. They focus on the quality of service and number of cities served—and suggest you mention Delta's name the next time you talk to your travel agent.

Comparative ads make direct comparisons with other brands using actual product names. For example, the Betty Crocker ad shows that Duncan Hines muffins are smaller. The Advil ad touts its superiority over aspirin, Extra-Strength Tylenol, and naproxen sodium (which is the main ingredient in Procter & Gamble's Aleve painkiller).

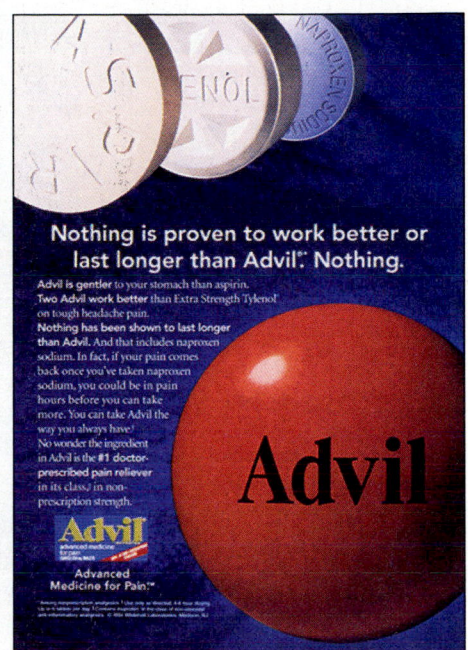

Comparative advertising is even rougher. **Comparative advertising** means making specific brand comparisons—using actual product names. A recent comparative ad for Advil shows pictures of competing pain relievers and the ad copy makes specific superiority claims that it is longer lasting and easier on the stomach. In the same vein, MCI and AT&T battle it out in TV ads—each claiming that their long-distance services are the better value.

Many countries forbid comparative advertising, but that situation is changing. For example, Japan banned comparative advertising until about seven years ago, when the restrictions were relaxed. Japan's move followed an earlier change in the United States. The Federal Trade Commission decided to encourage comparative ads, after banning them for years—because it thought that lifting the ban would increase competition and provide consumers with more useful information. But this approach led to legal as well as ethical problems—and some advertisers and their agencies now back away from comparative advertising even in countries where it is allowed.

In the United States, superiority claims are supposed to be supported by research evidence—but the guidelines aren't clear. Some firms just keep running tests until they get the results they want. Others talk about minor differences that don't reflect a product's overall benefits. Some comparative ads leave consumers confused—or even angry if the product they're using is criticized. Comparative ads can also backfire by calling attention to competing products that consumers had not previously considered.[7]

Comparative advertising may be a can of worms that some advertisers wish they hadn't opened. But comparative ads seem to attract attention. So some advertisers will probably continue using this approach—at least in countries that allow it.[8]

Sunkist uses reminder advertising in Canada and other countries where the brand name is already well established.

Reminder advertising—reinforces a favorable relationship

Reminder advertising tries to keep the product's name before the public. It may be useful when the product has achieved brand preference or insistence— perhaps in the market maturity or sales decline stages. It is used primarily to reinforce previous promotion. Here, the advertiser may use soft-sell ads that just mention or show the name—as a reminder. Sunkist, for example, often relies on reminder ads because most consumers already know the brand name and—after years of promotion—associate it with high product quality.

Institutional advertising—remember our name

Institutional advertising usually focuses on the name and prestige of an organization or industry. It may seek to inform, persuade, or remind.

Large companies with several divisions sometimes use a persuading kind of institutional advertising to link the divisions in customers' minds. Many Japanese firms—like Hitachi—emphasize institutional advertising, in part because they often use the company name as a brand name.

Companies sometimes rely on institutional advertising to present the company in a favorable light—perhaps to overcome image problems. Ads for an oil company, for example, might highlight its concern for the environment.

Some organizations use institutional advertising to advocate a specific cause or idea. Insurance companies and organizations like Mothers Against Drunk Driving, for example, use these advocacy ads to encourage people not to drink and drive.[9]

COORDINATING ADVERTISING EFFORTS WITH COOPERATIVE RELATIONSHIPS

Vertical cooperation— advertising allowances, cooperative advertising

Sometimes a producer knows that a promotion job or advertising job should be done but finds that it can be done more effectively or more economically by someone further along in the channel. Alternatively, a large retail chain may approach manufacturers with a catalog or program—and tell them how much it will cost to participate. In either case, the producer may offer **advertising allowances**—price reductions to firms further along in the channel to encourage them to advertise or otherwise promote the firm's products locally.

Cooperative advertising involves middlemen and producers sharing in the cost of ads. This helps wholesalers and retailers compete in their local markets. It also helps the producer get more promotion for the advertising dollar because media usually give local advertisers lower rates than national or international firms. In addition, a retailer or wholesaler who is paying a share of the cost is more likely to follow through.

Integrated communications from cooperative relationships

Coordination and integration of ad messages in the channel is another reason for cooperative advertising. One big, well-planned, integrated advertising effort is often better than many different—perhaps inconsistent—local efforts. Many franchise operations like the idea of communicating with one voice. KFC, for example, encourages its franchises to use a common advertising program. Before, many developed their own local ads—with themes like "Eight clucks for four bucks"—that didn't fit with the company's overall marketing strategy.

Producers often get this coordination—and reduce local middlemen costs—by providing a master of an ad on a videotape, cassette tape, or printed sheets. The middlemen add their identification before turning the ad over to local media.

However, allowances and support materials alone don't ensure cooperation. When channel members don't agree with the advertising strategy, it can be a serious source of conflict. For example, Benetton, the Italian sportswear company, wanted its "United Colors" ad campaign to be controversial. Pictures showed a dying AIDS victim and a torn, bloody uniform from the war in Bosnia. Most Europeans—including many of Benetton's retailers–franchisees—saw the ads as a tasteless attempt to exploit suffering. To protest the ads, a group of German franchisees stopped paying their franchise fees and sued Benetton for damages. This is an extreme example, but even in routine situations a marketing manager should consider the likely reaction of other channel members before implementing any advertising program.[10]

? Ethical concerns may arise

Ethical issues sometimes arise concerning advertising allowance programs. For example, a retailer may run one producer's ad to draw customers to the store but then sell them another brand. Is this unethical? Some producers think it is—that the retailer is intentionally misusing the money and switching customers to brands that pay the retailer a higher profit margin. A different view is that retailers are obligated to the producer to run the ad—but obligated to consumers to sell them what they want, no matter whose brand it may be. A producer can often avoid the problem with a strategy decision—by setting the allowance amount as a percent of the retailer's *actual purchases*. That way, a retailer who doesn't produce sales doesn't get the allowance.

Sometimes a retailer takes advertising allowance money but doesn't run the ads at all. Some producers close their eyes to this problem because they don't know what to do about intense competition from other suppliers for the retailer's attention. But there are also legal and ethical problems with that response. Basically, the allowance may have become a disguised price concession that results in price discrimination, which is illegal in the United States. Some firms pull back from cooperative advertising to avoid these problems. Smart producers insist on proof that the advertising was really done.

Horizontal cooperation— promotes different firms

Sometimes two or more firms with complementary products join together in a common advertising effort. Joint ads encourage travelers to stay at a Hyatt Hotel and handle the expenses with an American Express card. Retailers in the same shopping center often share the costs of promotion efforts. They might buy full-page newspaper ads listing the individual stores or promoting sale days. Generally, the objective is the same as in vertical cooperation—to get more for the advertising dollar.[11]

CHOOSING THE "BEST" MEDIUM—HOW TO DELIVER THE MESSAGE

What is the best advertising medium? There is no simple answer to this question. Effectiveness depends on how well the medium fits with the rest of a marketing strategy—that is, it depends on (1) your promotion objectives, (2) what target markets you want to reach, (3) the funds available for advertising, and (4) the nature of the media—including whom they *reach*, with what *frequency*, with what *impact*, and at what *cost.*

Exhibit 16–4 shows some pros and cons of major kinds of media—and some typical costs. However, some of the advantages noted in this table may not apply in all markets. In less-developed nations, for example, newspapers may *not* be timely. Placing an ad may require a long lead time if only a limited number of pages are available for ads. Direct mail may not be a flexible choice in a country with a weak postal system or high rate of illiteracy. Similarly, TV audiences are often less selective and targeted, but a special-interest cable TV show may reach a very specific audience.[12]

Specify promotion objectives

Before you can choose the best medium, you have to decide on your promotion objectives. If the objective is to increase interest and that requires demonstrating product benefits, TV may be the best alternative. If the objective is to inform—telling a long story with precise detail—and if pictures are needed, then print media—including magazines and newspapers—may be better. For example, Jockey switched its advertising to magazines from television when it decided to show the variety of colors, patterns, and styles of its men's briefs. Jockey felt that it was too hard to show this in a 30-second TV spot. Further,

EXHIBIT 16–4 Relative Size and Costs, and Advantages and Disadvantages of Major Kinds of Media

Kinds of Media	Sales Volume–1993 ($ billions)	Typical Costs–1993	Advantages	Disadvantages
Newspaper	32.0	$30,674 for one-page weekday, *Baltimore Sun*	Flexible, timely, local market	May be expensive, short life, no "pass-along"
Television	30.6	$4,300 for a 30-second spot, prime time, Baltimore	Demonstrations, good attention, wide reach	Expensive in total, "clutter," less-selective audience
Direct mail	27.3	$105/1,000 for listing of 110,000 female executives	Selected audience, flexible, can personalize	Relatively expensive per contact, "junk mail"—hard to retain attention
Radio	9.5	$350–$400 for one minute drive time, Baltimore	Wide reach, segmented audience, inexpensive	Weak attention, many different rates, short exposure
Magazine	7.4	$147,000 for one-page, 4-color in *Time*	Very targeted, good detail, good "pass-along"	Inflexible, long lead times
Outdoor	1.1	$4,500 (painted) for prime billboard, 30- to 60-day showings, Baltimore	Flexible, repeat exposure, inexpensive	"Mass market," very short exposure

Advertising managers are always looking for cost-effective media that will get the message to the target market. In Eastern Europe, where traditional media are less available, Campbell's looks for other alternatives, like space in this bus shelter.

Jockey felt that there were problems with modeling men's underwear on television. However, Jockey might have stayed with TV if it had been targeting consumers in France or Brazil—where nudity in TV ads is common.[13]

Match your market with the media

To guarantee good media selection, the advertiser first must *clearly* specify its target market—a necessary step for all marketing strategy planning. Then the advertiser can choose media that are heard, read, or seen by those target customers.

The media available in a country may limit the choices. In less-developed nations, for example, radio is often the only way to reach a broad-based market of poor consumers who can't read or afford television.

In most cases, however, the major problem is to select media that effectively reach the target audience. Most of the major media use marketing research to develop profiles of the people who buy their publications—or live in their broadcasting area. Generally, media research focuses on demographic characteristics. But the research seldom includes information on the segmenting dimensions specific to the product-markets that are important to *each* different advertiser. Research also can't be definite about who actually reads each page or sees or hears each show.

In some countries the problem is even worse because the media don't provide any information, or they provide audience profiles that make the media seem more attractive than they are.

Another problem is that the audience for media that *do* reach your target market may also include people who are *not* in the target group. But *you pay for the whole audience the media delivers*—including those who aren't potential customers. For example, Delta Faucet, a faucet manufacturer that wanted its ads to reach plumbers, placed ads on ESPN's Saturday college football telecasts. Research showed that many plumbers watched the ESPN games. Yet, plumbers are only a very small portion of the total college football audience—and the size of the total audience determined the cost of the advertising time. The cost of reaching the real target market goes up fastest when the irrelevant audience is very large. Ads during the last Olympics, for example, cost between $250,000 and $350,000 for 30 seconds. The Olympics reach a very large audience, but it is also very diverse. Research suggests that many of the firms that sponsor ads on these big-audience shows would have gotten more bang for the buck by placing ads on shows that reached more targeted audiences.[14]

Because it is so difficult to evaluate alternative media, some media analysts focus on objective measures—such as cost per thousand of audience size or circulation. But advertisers preoccupied with keeping these costs down may ignore the relevant segmenting dimensions—and slip into mass marketing. The media buyer may look only at the relatively low cost of mass media when a more specialized medium might be a much better buy. Its audience might have more interest in the product—or more money to spend—or more willingness to buy. Gillette Co. buys advertising time on cable TV—especially MTV—to increase its market penetration with teenagers and young adults, who are more willing to try new products.

Some media help zero in on specific target markets

Today the major media direct more attention to reaching smaller, more defined target markets. The most obvious evidence of this is in the growth of spending on direct-mail advertising to consumers listed in a database. However, other major media are becoming more targeted as well.

National print media may offer specialized editions. *Time* magazine, for example, offers not only several regional and metropolitan editions but also special editions for college students, educators, doctors, and business managers. Magazines like *Newsweek*, France's *Paris Match International*, and Germany's *Wirtschaftwoche* provide international editions.

Large metro newspapers often have several editions to cater to city and suburban areas. Where these outlying areas are not adequately covered, however, suburban newspapers are prospering—catering to the desire for local news.

Many magazines serve only special-interest groups—such as fishermen, soap opera fans, new parents, professional groups, and personal computer users. In fact, the most profitable magazines seem to be the ones aimed at clearly defined markets. Many specialty magazines also have international editions that help marketers reach consumers with similar interests in different parts of the world. *PC Magazine*, for example, offers European and Japanese editions.

There are trade magazines in many fields—such as chemical engineering, furniture retailing, electrical wholesaling, farming, and the aerospace market. *Standard Rate and Data* provides a guide to the thousands of magazines now available in the United States. Similar guides exist in most other countries.

Radio has become a more specialized medium. Some stations cater to particular ethnic and racial groups—such as Hispanics, African-Americans, or French Canadians. Others aim at specific target markets with rock, country, or classical music. Stations that play golden oldies have been popping up around the United States to appeal to the baby-boomer crowd.

Cable TV channels—like MTV, Cable News Network (CNN), Nickelodeon, and ESPN—also target specific audiences. ESPN, for example, has an audience heavily weighted toward affluent, male viewers. MTV appeals most strongly to affluent, young viewers 25 to 34 years old. British Sky Broadcasting does a good job of reaching homemakers with young children.

By advertising in specialized media, a marketer can often zero in on a specific target market. Consumers who read *Bike* magazine, for example, are likely to be interested in information about helmets.

Infomercials—long commercials that are broadcast with a TV show format—give a glimpse of how targeted cable TV will become when consumers have access to hundreds—or perhaps even thousands—of TV channels. With so many alternative channels competing for consumer attention, most channels will succeed only if they offer programs and commercials that are very specific to the interests and needs of smaller, more homogeneous target markets. Consumers will be able to seek out—or avoid—channels that offer information about products that interest them.

Specialized media are small—but gaining

The *major* advertising media listed in Exhibit 16–4 attract the vast majority of advertising media budgets. But advertising specialists always look for cost-effective new media that will help advertisers reach their target markets. For example, one company successfully sells space for signs on bike racks that it places in front of 7-Eleven stores. In Eastern Europe, where major media are still limited, companies like Campbell's pay to put ads on bus shelters. Hotels and auto rental companies buy space on advertising boards placed in the restrooms on airplanes.

In recent years, these specialized media have gained in popularity. One reason is that they get the mass-selling message to the target market close to the point of purchase. They also offer the advantage of making an advertiser's message stand out from the usual advertising clutter in the mass media. For example, Actmedia sells advertising space on little message boards that hang on shopping carts and shelves in grocery stores and drugstores. These ads reach target customers in the store, where 80 percent of the purchase decisions are made. Other advertising specialists offer special in-store radio and TV advertising and ads on grocery bags.[15]

Most marketing managers who serve local markets view Yellow Pages advertising as a "must buy"—because it usually reaches customers when they are ready to buy.

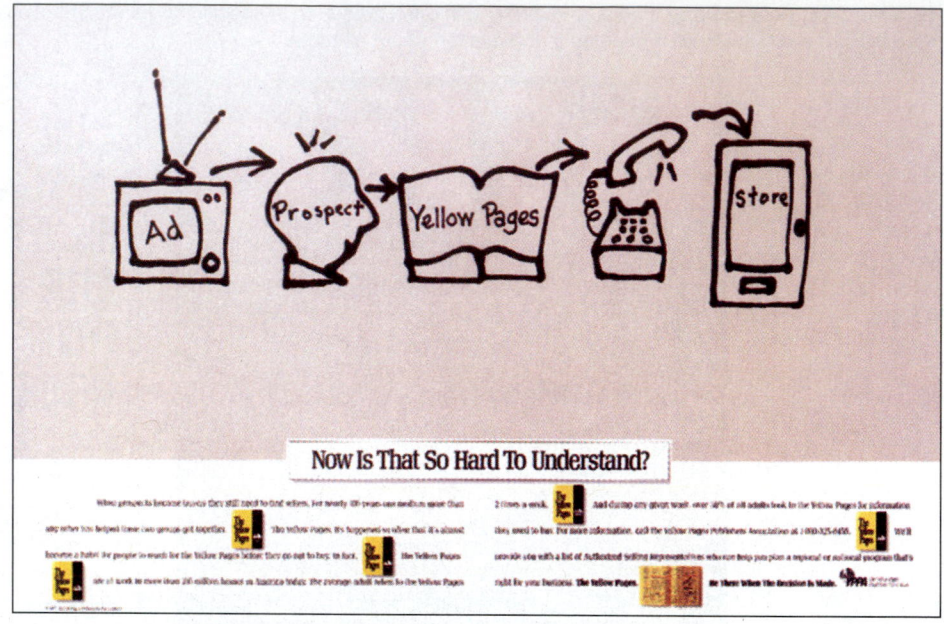

There are too many specialized media to go into all of them in detail here. But all of them require the same type of strategy decisions as the more typical mass media.

"Must buys" may use up available funds

Selecting which media to use is still pretty much an art. The media buyer may start with a budgeted amount and try to buy the best blend to reach the target audience.

Some media are obvious "must buys"—such as *the* local newspaper for a retailer in a small or medium-sized town. Most firms serving local markets view a Yellow Pages listing as a must buy. These ads may even use up the available funds. If not, the media buyer must compare the relative advantages and disadvantages of alternatives—and select a media *blend* that helps achieve the promotion objectives, given the available budget.

For many firms—even national advertisers—the high cost of television may eliminate it from the media blend. The average cost just to produce a national TV ad is now about $250,000—and a big impact ad can easily cost twice that. In the United States, a 30-second commercial on a popular prime-time show, like "Seinfeld," is well over $300,000. The price goes up rapidly for "big event" shows that attract the largest audiences. A minute of advertising on a recent Super Bowl cost sponsors nearly $2.5 million.[16]

Because TV advertising costs so much, many firms are moving away from television—especially the networks—and experimenting with combinations of other media. Very targeted media, like direct-mail advertising, are growing rapidly as a result of this shift. But an even bigger media revolution is brewing—and it has the potential to radically change the nature and role of advertising.

Interactive media and the information highway

Advances in information technology are impacting every aspect of communication—and advertising communication is no exception. Satellite feeds instantly send radio and TV ads around the world. Computerized systems print individual consumers' names in the middle of magazine ads. New switching systems allow a cable TV company to route different ads to different households. Customer databases target direct-mail advertising.

As significant as such advances are, they mainly make it more efficient for advertisers to do what they have always done: send one-way communications to some target customers. More radical changes—based on interactive media that allow each different customer to get very different messages and to respond in different ways—are coming.

For years, advertisers have eagerly anticipated the widespread availability of interactive cable systems—in part because of publicity surrounding Time Warner's joint venture with U.S. West to develop interactive cable systems. Interactive cable will let consumers instantly respond to TV ads, perhaps by pushing a button on a special box that connects the TV set, phone, and computer to incoming cable TV or telephone lines. One button might signal a request for more detailed information, or perhaps place an order for the product. These systems are beginning to come on-line in some areas.

Some companies aren't waiting for interactive cable. They're experimenting with interactive ads using multimedia computer networks that offer the same basic capabilities. For example, Fidelity Investments pays about $27,000 a month for five linked "electronic pages" of exposure on the Prodigy network. Even McDonald's is in the act. It pushes fast food on the America Online network; users can even download a McDonald's coloring book.

The potential impact on advertising of interactive media and two-way communications is huge. But, as with other innovations, the diffusion of interactive advertising will take time. No one can yet be certain how it will develop. As an advertising manager for Toyota put it, "There's a hell of a future for interactive advertising, only no one knows when the future starts."[17]

PLANNING THE "BEST" MESSAGE—WHAT TO COMMUNICATE

Specifying the copy thrust

Once you decide *how* the messages will reach the target audience, you have to decide on the **copy thrust**—what the words and illustrations should communicate. This decision should flow from the promotion objectives—and the specific jobs assigned to advertising.

Carrying out the copy thrust is the job of advertising specialists. But the advertising manager and the marketing manager need to understand the process to be sure that the job is done well.

There are few tried-and-true rules in message construction, but behavioral research can help. Recall our discussion of the communication process and common frames of reference in Chapter 14. The concepts of needs, learning, and perception discussed in Chapter 7 apply here too. We know, for example, that consumers have a fantastic ability to tune out messages or ideas that don't interest them. How much of the daily newspaper do you actually see as you page through it? We don't see everything the advertisers want us to see—or learn all they want us to learn. How can an advertiser be more effective?

Let AIDA help guide message planning

Basically, the overall marketing strategy should determine *what* the message should say. Then management judgment—perhaps aided by marketing research—can help decide how to encode this content so it will be decoded as intended.

As a guide to message planning, we can use the AIDA concept: getting Attention, holding Interest, arousing Desire, and obtaining Action.

Target Stores uses attention-getting pop-up ads to encourage consumers to visit its new stores. To reach consumers in a store's market area, the ads are distributed as free-standing inserts in local Sunday papers.

Getting attention

Getting attention is an ad's first job. If an ad doesn't get attention, it doesn't matter how many people see or hear it. Many readers leaf through magazines and newspapers without paying attention to any of the ads. Many listeners or viewers do chores—or get snacks—during radio and TV commercials. When watching a program on videotape, they may zap past the commercial with a flick of the fast forward button.

Many attention-getting devices are available. A large headline, newsy or shocking statements, attractive models, babies, animals, special effects—anything different or eye-catching—may do the trick. However, the attention-getting device can't detract from—and hopefully should lead to—the next step, holding interest.

Holding interest

Holding interest is more difficult. A humorous ad, an unusual video effect, or a clever photo may get your attention—but once you've seen it, then what? You may pause to appreciate it, but if there is no relation between what got your attention and the marketing mix, you'll move on.

The behavioral sciences give advertisers some insight about how to hold interest. The tone and language of the ad must fit with the experiences and attitudes of the target customers—and their reference groups. As a result, many advertisers develop ads that relate to specific moods and emotions. They hope that the good feeling about the ad (and the whole marketing mix) will stick—even if the specific details of the copy thrust are forgotten.

To hold interest, informative ads need to speak the target customer's language. Persuasive ads must provide evidence that convinces the customer. For example, TV ads often demonstrate a product's benefits.

Layouts for print ads should look right to the customer. Print illustrations and

Billboards are good for getting attention with a simple copy thrust.

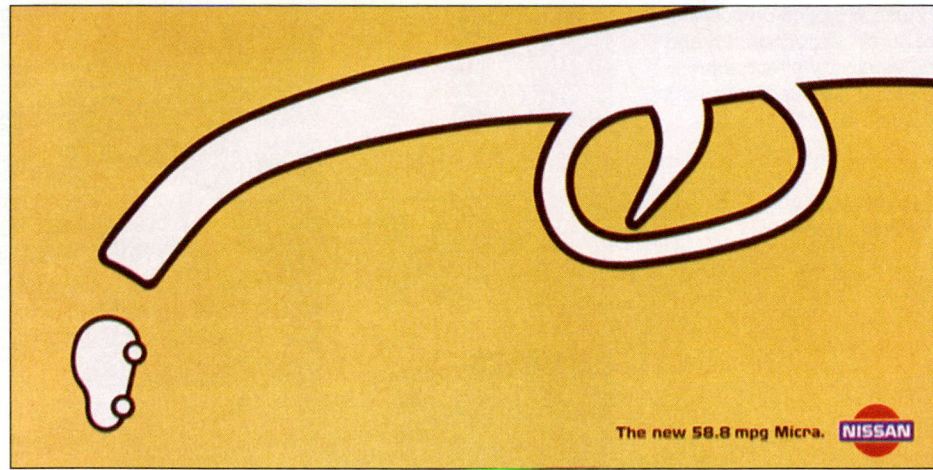

The new 58.8 mpg Micra. NISSAN

copy should be arranged to encourage the eye to move smoothly through the ad—perhaps from a headline that starts in the upper left-hand corner to the illustration or body copy in the middle and finally to the company or brand name ("signature") at the lower right-hand corner. If all of the elements of the ad work together as a whole, they will help to hold interest and build recall.[18]

Arousing desire

Arousing desire to own or use a particular product is one of an ad's most difficult jobs. The advertiser must communicate with the customer. To do this effectively, the advertiser must understand how target customers think, behave, and make decisions. Then the ad must convince customers that the product can meet their needs. Testimonials may persuade a consumer that other people—with similar needs—have purchased the product and liked it. Product comparisons may highlight the advantages of a particular brand.

Some experts feel that an ad should focus on one *unique selling proposition* that aims at an important unsatisfied need. They discourage the typical approach of trying to tell the whole story in a single ad. Telling the whole story is the job of the whole promotion blend—not one ad.

If consumers see many different competing brands as essentially the same, focusing on a unique selling proposition may be particularly important. This can help set the brand apart—and position it as especially effective in meeting the needs of the target market. For example, consumers who wear dentures are especially concerned about dentures not coming loose. So, print ads for Seabond denture fixative use a humorous approach and pictures to focus on Seabond's holding power. Focusing on a unique selling proposition makes the most sense when a brand really does have a comparative advantage on an *important* benefit. That reduces the likelihood of competitors imitating the same idea.

An ad may also have the objective—especially during the market growth and market maturity stages—of supplying words customers can use to rationalize their desire to buy. Although products may satisfy certain emotional needs, many consumers find it necessary to justify their purchases on some economic or rational basis. Snickers candy bar ads helped ease the guilt of calorie-conscious snackers by assuring them that "Snickers satisfies you when you need an afternoon energy break."

A unique selling proposition can help to position a brand as especially effective in meeting the needs of a target market.

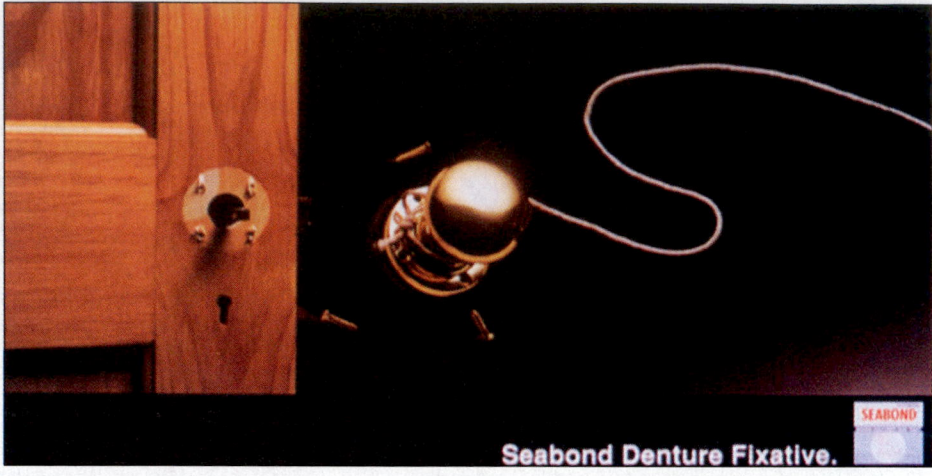

Seabond Denture Fixative.

Obtaining action

Getting action is the final requirement—and not an easy one. From communication research, we now know that prospective customers must be led beyond considering how the product *might* fit into their lives—to actually trying it or letting the company's sales rep come in and demonstrate it.

Direct-response ads can sometimes help promote action by encouraging interested consumers to do *something* that is less risky or demanding than actually making a purchase. For example, an ad that includes a toll-free telephone number might prompt some consumers who are not yet ready to buy at least to call for more information. Then follow-up brochures or a telephone salesperson can provide additional information and attempt to prompt another action—perhaps a visit to a store or a "satisfaction guaranteed" trial period. This approach seeks to get action one step at a time, where the first action suggested provides a "foot in the door" for subsequent communication efforts.

Whether or not some direct-response approach is used, to communicate more effectively ads might emphasize strongly felt customer needs. Careful research on attitudes in the target market may help uncover such strongly felt *unsatisfied* needs. Appealing to important needs can get more action—and also provide the kind of information buyers need to confirm their decisions. Post-purchase dissonance may set in—and obtaining confirmation may be one of the important advertising objectives. Some customers seem to read more advertising *after* a purchase than before. The ad may reassure them about the correctness of their decision—and also supply the words they use to tell others about the product.

Can global messages work?

During the 1980s, many international consumer products firms tried to use one global advertising message all around the world. Of course, they translated the message or made other minor adjustments—but the focus was one global copy thrust. Some did it because it looked like it would save the cost of developing different ads for different countries. Others did it because they felt their customers' basic needs were the same, even if they lived in different countries. Some just did it because it was fashionable to "go global."

This approach worked for some firms. Coca-Cola and Gillette, for example, feel that the needs their products serve are very similar for all consumers. They focus on the similarities among consumers who make up their target market rather

GILLETTE'S MEDIUM-CLOSE SHAVE IN IRAN

Gillette faces sharp competition from other razor producers in most parts of the world. But the situation it faced in Iran was even more prickly. Gillette wanted to introduce its Contour razor with a series of TV ads. Gillette used TV in other countries because it was the best medium for demonstrating the advantages of the Contour razor. And the cost was right; a one-minute ad on Iranian TV cost only $1,000. But TV ads turned out to be impossible as a first step. Since the 1980 Iranian revolution, the Ministry of Guidance, which controls advertising in Iran, prohibited Iran's two TV channels from advertising foreign products. In fact, until 1990 the ministry did not allow any TV advertising, even for local products.

The Ministry of Guidance wasn't Gillette's only obstacle. The Islamic religion discourages its followers from shaving. On the other hand, many Iranians *do* shave—and Gillette figured that people who shave need razors.

Gillette turned to Mormohamad Fathi, head of an Iranian advertising agency, for help. He thought a practical first step would be to try to find a medium that would accept advertising for Gillette's Blue II, a less expensive razor than the Contour. Fathi took a Blue II ad from one Tehran newspaper to another, but they repeatedly turned him down. Fathi thought it was a good omen when he finally found a newspaper advertising manager without a beard—but the man still needed persuading. Fathi explained to him, "Shaving is not just for your face. If you have a car accident and someone has to shave your head, Gillette Blue II is the best." Using this argument, the newspaper's ad manager consulted his clergyman, who gave him permission to take the ad.

Once over that hurdle, other papers followed, and before long Gillette ads appeared regularly in Iranian print media. That helped pave the way for Fathi to plaster Gillette posters on buses all over Tehran. He also handed out hundreds of free samples—to encourage consumers to try the razor and to build repeat sales. Fathi is persistent. With sales momentum building, you can bet it won't be long before Gillette's demonstration ads are showing in Iran's movie theaters.[19]

than the differences. However, most firms who use this approach experience terrible results. They may save money by developing fewer ads, but they lose sales because they don't develop advertising messages—and whole marketing mixes—aimed at specific target markets. They're just trying to appeal to a global "mass market."

Combining smaller market segments into a single, large target market makes sense if the different segments can be served with a single marketing mix. But when that is not the case, the marketing manager should treat them as different target markets—and develop different marketing mixes for each target.[20]

ADVERTISING AGENCIES OFTEN DO THE WORK

An advertising manager manages a company's advertising effort. Many advertising managers—especially those working for large retailers—have their own advertising departments that plan specific advertising campaigns and carry out the details. Others turn over much of the advertising work to specialists—the advertising agencies.

Ad agencies are specialists

Advertising agencies are specialists in planning and handling mass-selling details for advertisers. Agencies play a useful role—because they are independent of the advertiser and have an outside viewpoint. They bring experience to an individual client's problems because they work for many other clients. Further, as specialists they can often do the job more economically than a company's own department.

Some full-service agencies handle any activities related to advertising. They may even handle overall marketing strategy planning—as well as marketing research, product and package development, and sales promotion. Some agencies make good marketing partners—and almost assume the role of the firm's marketing department. In these situations, the relationship between the agency and the company is very close.

Some agencies don't offer a full line of services. *Media buying services* specialize in selecting media to fit a firm's marketing strategy. They are used when a firm wants to schedule a number of ads—perhaps in different media—and needs help finding the blend that will deliver what it needs at the lowest cost. Similarly, creative specialists just create ads. These agencies handle the artistic elements of advertising but leave media planning, research, and related services to others.

The biggest agencies handle much of the advertising

The vast majority of advertising agencies are small—with 10 or fewer employees. But the largest agencies account for most of the billings.

Recently, some big agencies merged—creating mega-agencies with worldwide networks. Exhibit 16–5 shows a list of 10 of the largest agency networks and examples of some of the products they advertise. Although their headquarters are located in different nations, they have offices worldwide. The move toward international marketing is a key reason behind the mergers.

Before the mergers, marketers in one country often had difficulty finding a capable, full-service agency in the country where they wanted to advertise. The mergers combined the strengths of the individual agencies. The mega-agency can offer varied services—wherever in the world a marketing manager needs them. This may be especially important for managers in large corporations—like Toyota,

EXHIBIT 16–5 Top-10 Advertising Agency Supergroups and Examples of Products They Advertise

Supergroup	Headquarters	Worldwide Gross Income 1993 ($ millions)	Products
WPP Group	London	$2,633.6	American Express, Schick Tracer, 7-Eleven, Jaguar, Sprint
Interpublic Group of Companies	New York	2,078.5	Taster's Choice, Maybelline, Buick, Del Monte, L'Oreal
Omnicom Group	New York	1,876.0	Pepsi, Du Pont Stainmaster, Gillette, Frito-Lay, Bud Light
Dentsu	Tokyo	1,403.2	Japan Air Lines, Shiseido, Best Western
Saatchi & Saatchi	London/New York	1,355.1	Toyota, British Airways, Johnson & Johnson, Tylenol, Wendy's
Young & Rubicam	New York	1,008.9	Lincoln-Mercury, Andersen Consulting, Colgate-Palmolive, KFC, Kraft
Euro RSCG Worldwide	Paris (Neuilly)	864.8	France Telecom, MCI, Volvo, Old Spice, Wonder bread
Grey Advertising	New York	765.7	Gerber, Iberia, International Olympic Committee, Jif, Dannon
Hakuhodo	Tokyo	667.8	Canon, NEC, Nissan
Foote, Cone & Belding Communications	Chicago	633.7	Levi's, Taco Bell, Bell Atlantic Yellow Pages, Coors Brewing, Clorox

Renault, Unilever, NEC, Phillips, Procter & Gamble, Nestlé, and Coca-Cola—who advertise worldwide.[21]

In spite of the growth of these very large agencies, smaller agencies will continue to play an important role. The really big agencies are less interested in smaller accounts. Smaller agencies will continue to appeal to customers who want more personal attention and a close relationship that is more attuned to their marketing needs.

It's easy to fire an ad agency

An advertiser is usually free to cancel the relationship at any time. This gives the advertiser extreme flexibility. If an agency isn't doing a good job, the client can shop around for a new one. However, a decision to terminate the relationship with an agency shouldn't be taken lightly. Too many marketing managers just use their advertising agency as a scapegoat. Whenever anything goes wrong, they blame the agency. While agency-swapping is common, in some countries, like Brazil, it's tougher for a firm to dump its agency.

Are they paid too much?

Traditionally, most U.S. advertising agencies are paid a commission of about 15 percent on media and production costs. This arrangement evolved because media usually have two prices: one for national advertisers and a lower rate for local advertisers, such as local retailers. The advertising agency gets a 15 percent commission on national rates—but not on local rates. This makes it worthwhile for producers and national middlemen to use agencies. National advertisers have to pay the full media rate anyway, so it makes sense to let the agency experts do the work—and earn their commission. Local retailers—allowed the lower media rate—seldom use agencies. Even large retail chains may do most of their advertising in local markets where they have stores: Toys "R" Us, for example, uses local newspapers for most of its ads.

There is growing resistance to the idea of paying agencies the same way regardless of the work performed or *the results achieved*. The commission approach also makes it hard for agencies to be completely objective about inexpensive media—or promotion campaigns that use little space or time. Much of the opposition to the traditional commission system comes from very large consumer products advertisers. They spend the most on media ads, and they think a 15 percent fee is often too high—especially when an expensive ad campaign doesn't produce the desired results. Not all agencies are satisfied with the present arrangement either. Some would like to charge additional fees as their costs rise and advertisers demand more services.

Firms that need a lot of service but spend relatively little on media—including most producers of business products—favor a fixed commission system. These are the firms the agencies would like to—and sometimes do—charge additional fees.

Some firms pay the agency based on results

A number of advertisers now "grade" the work done by their agencies—and the agencies' pay depends on the grade. For example, General Foods lowered its basic commission to about 13 percent. However, the company pays the agency a bonus of about 3 percent on campaigns that earn an A rating. If the agency only earns a B, it loses the bonus. If it earns a C, it must improve fast—or GF removes the account.

Variations on this approach are becoming common. For example, Carnation directly links its agency's compensation with how well its ads score in market research tests. Gillette and Lorillard use a sliding scale, and the percentage of compensation declines with increased advertising volume. And some agencies develop their own plans in which they guarantee to achieve the results expected or give the advertiser a partial refund. These agencies realize that the advertising service they provide for their business customers is *their* product—and providing a guarantee helps to differentiate the quality of the service.

An advantage of this approach is that it forces the advertiser and agency to agree on very specific objectives for their ads—and what they expect to achieve. Yet many ad agencies dislike the idea of being so closely scrutinized by clients—or having to negotiate what they're paid. But if the current trends continue, they may have to get used to it.[22]

Conflicts between ad agencies and clients

The creative people in ad agencies and their more business-oriented clients often disagree. Some creative people are production-oriented. They create an ad they like themselves—or that will win artistic approval within their industry—and are less concerned about how well it fits into the rest of the client's marketing mix.

You can see why this creates conflict. The advertiser's product managers or brand managers may be personally responsible for the success of particular products—and feel that they have some right to direct and even veto the work of the creative agency people. Because the advertiser is paying the bills, the agency often loses these confrontations.

? Ethical conflicts may arise

Ad agencies usually work closely with their clients, and they often have access to confidential information. This can create ethical conflicts if an agency is working with two or more competing clients. Most agencies are very sensitive to the potential problems and work hard to keep people and information from competing accounts completely separated. But many advertisers don't think that's enough—and they don't want to risk a problem. They refuse to work with an agency that handles any competing accounts, even when they're handled in different offices. For example, a top executive for the Budweiser brand ended a 79-year relationship with an agency when one of the agency's subsidiaries accepted an assignment to buy media space for a competing brand of beer.

This potential conflict of interest in handling competing products has been a problem for the big international mega-agencies. Saatchi & Saatchi, for example, gained over $300 million in billings through its mergers but then quickly lost $462 million in billings when old clients departed because Saatchi's new clients—at one of its offices around the world—included competitors.[23]

MEASURING ADVERTISING EFFECTIVENESS IS NOT EASY

Success depends on the total marketing mix

It would be convenient if we could measure the results of advertising by looking at sales. Certainly some breakthrough ads do have a very direct effect on a company's sales—and the advertising literature is filled with success stories that "prove" advertising increases sales. Similarly, market research firms like Information Resources can sometimes compare sales levels before and after—or during—the period of an ad campaign. Yet, we usually can't measure advertising success just by looking at sales. The total marketing mix—not just promotion generally or advertising specifically—is responsible for the sales result. And sales results are also affected by what competitors do and by other changes in the external marketing environment. Only with direct-response advertising can a company make a direct link between advertising and sales results. Then, if an ad doesn't produce immediate results, it's considered a failure.

Research and testing can improve the odds

Ideally, advertisers should pretest advertising before it runs—rather than relying solely on their own guesses about how good an ad will be. The judgment of creative people or advertising experts may not help much. They often judge only on the basis of originality—or cleverness—of the copy and illustrations.

Many progressive advertisers now demand laboratory or market tests to evaluate an ad's effectiveness. Sometimes laboratory-type devices that measure skin moisture or eye reaction are used to gauge consumer responses. In addition, researchers often try to evaluate consumers' reactions to an advertising concept—or to parts of ads—before the ad is finalized. American Express used focus group interviews to get reactions to a series of possible TV ads. The company wanted the ads to convey the idea that younger people could qualify for its credit cards—but it still wanted to present a prestige image. The agency prepared picture boards presenting different approaches—as well as specific copy. Four of six possible ads failed to communicate the message to the focus groups. One idea that seemed to be effective became the basis for an ad that was tested again before being launched on TV.[24]

In addition, split runs on cable TV systems in test markets are proving to be an important approach for testing ads in a normal viewing environment. Scanner sales data from retailers in those test markets can provide an estimate of how an ad is likely to affect sales. This approach provides marketing managers with a powerful new tool—and it will become even more powerful in the future as more cable systems and telephone companies add new interactive technology that allows viewers to provide immediate feedback to an ad as it appears on the TV.

Hindsight may lead to foresight

After ads run, researchers may try to measure how much consumers recall about specific products or ads. Inquiries from customers may be used to measure the effectiveness of particular ads. The response to radio or television commercials—or magazine readership—can be estimated using various survey methods to check the size and composition of audiences (the Nielsen and Starch reports are examples).

While advertising research methods aren't foolproof, they're far better than relying on judgment by advertising "experts." Until more effective advertising research tools are developed, the present methods—carefully defining specific advertising objectives, choosing media and messages to accomplish these objectives, testing plans, and then evaluating the results of actual ads—seem to be most productive.[25]

HOW TO AVOID UNFAIR ADVERTISING

Government agencies may say what is fair

In most countries, the government takes an active role in deciding what kinds of advertising are allowable, fair, and appropriate. For example, France and Japan limit the use of cartoon characters in advertising to children, and Sweden and Canada ban *any* advertising targeted directly at children. In Switzerland, an advertiser cannot use an actor to represent a consumer. New Zealand and Switzerland limit political ads on TV. In the United States, print ads must be identified so they aren't confused with editorial matter; in other countries ads and editorial copy can be intermixed. Most countries limit the number and length of commercials on broadcast media. Until recently, an Italian TV ad could be shown only 10 times a year.

What is seen as positioning in one country may be viewed as unfair or deceptive in another. For example, in many countries Pepsi advertises its cola as "the choice of the new generation." Japan's Fair Trade Committee doesn't allow it—because right now Pepsi is not "the choice." Similarly, Hungary's Economic Competition Council fined Unilever $25,000 for running an ad that claimed that its OMO detergent removed stains better than ordinary detergent. The Council said the ad was unfair because Hungarian consumers would interpret the phrase "ordinary detergent" as a reference to a locally produced detergent.[26]

Differences in rules mean that a marketing manager may face very specific limits in different countries, and local experts may be required to ensure that a firm doesn't waste money developing advertising programs that will never be shown—or which consumers will think are deceptive.

FTC controls unfair practices in the United States

In the United States, the Federal Trade Commission (FTC) has the power to control unfair or deceptive business practices—including deceptive advertising. The FTC has been policing deceptive advertising for many years. And it may be getting results now that advertising agencies as well as advertisers must share equal responsibility for false, misleading, or unfair ads.

This is a serious matter. If the FTC decides that a particular practice is unfair or deceptive, it has the power to require affirmative disclosures—such as the health warnings on cigarettes—or **corrective advertising**—ads to correct deceptive advertising. The FTC has not required much corrective advertising recently, but that may be because several of its earlier actions got a lot of attention. For example, the FTC forced Listerine to spend millions of dollars on advertising to

A newspaper ad for Badedas shower gel had to overcome several obstacles in Malaysia. In this Islamic country, the ad couldn't show a person bathing and could only show the model's face. The model was of mixed race to appeal to the country's varied ethnicity.

"correct" earlier ads that claimed the mouthwash helped prevent colds. The FTC concluded that Listerine could not prove its claim. The possibility of large financial penalties and/or the need to pay for corrective ads has caused more agencies and advertisers to stay well within the law—rather than just along the edge.[27]

When the FTC found fewer outright deceptive ads in national campaigns, the agency moved more aggressively against what it felt to be other "unfair" practices. Some in the FTC felt it was unfair to target advertising at children. Others thought a case could be made against promotion that "encourages materialism"—by persuading consumers to buy things that they otherwise wouldn't. An FTC lawyer created a stir by criticizing electric hair dryers. His feeling was "that if you wait 15 minutes, your hair gets dry anyway." And there were questions about whether food and drug advertising should be controlled to protect vulnerable groups, such as the aged, poor, or less-educated. For example, some critics argue that ads for high-calorie foods are a cause of obesity among low-income women.

Not everyone agreed with this thrust, however. Congress specifically limits FTC rule making to advertising that is *deceptive* rather than *unfair*. Note, however, that while the FTC is prohibited from using unfairness in a rule affecting a whole industry, unfairness can still be used against an individual company. So advertisers *do* have to worry about being unfair![28]

What is unfair or deceptive is changing

What constitutes unfair and deceptive advertising is a difficult question and one marketing managers will have to wrestle with for years. Sometimes the law provides guidelines, but in most cases the marketing manager must make personal judgments as well. The social and political environment is changing worldwide. Practices considered acceptable some years ago are now questioned—or considered deceptive. Saying or even implying that your product is best may be viewed as deceptive.

A 1988 revision of the Lanham Act brought new attention to this area in the United States. It prohibits advertisers from misrepresenting the qualities or characteristics of "another person's goods, services, or commercial activities." This means companies that believe that their brand names were unfairly tarnished in another company's comparative ads are protected by federal law. By contrast, the earlier federal law only prohibited an advertiser from misrepresenting its own products.

Supporting ad claims is a fuzzy area

Companies get no clear guidelines about how much research support they need to back up their ad claims. Unfortunately, there are many ways to lie with statistics, and unethical and/or desperate advertisers of me-too products try many of them. It only takes one such competitor in an industry to cause major shifts in market share—and affect the nature of competition in that market. As an old cliché says: One bad apple can spoil a whole barrel.

Most advertisers have good intentions and aren't trying to compete unfairly or deceive consumers. Clear guidelines on research support might eliminate much unfair or deceptive advertising. Those in favor of self-regulation are well aware of this. This is why they organize and work cooperatively with the government—and probably will continue to do so.[29]

Self-regulation works some of the time

Some industry groups make efforts at self-regulation. But most of these groups fail because they lack the power to enforce their guidelines. One exception in the United States is the National Advertising Division (NAD) of the Council of

Better Business Bureaus. It helped shape the guidelines that many advertisers follow. In addition, the NAD encourages consumers, advertisers, and government agencies to complain about questionable advertising. If a complaint seems justified, the NAD asks the advertiser for proof of the claims it has made. The NAD makes its findings public—and its decisions are reviewed by a larger group representing different groups of advertisers and consumers. Most firms comply when asked to discontinue problem ads.

In the long run, the best way to avoid criticisms of being unfair and deceptive is to stop the typical production-oriented effort to differentiate me-too product offerings with promotion. A little puffing is acceptable—and probably always will be. But advertisers should avoid trying to pass off me-too products as really new or better. Some advertising agencies already refuse such jobs.

SALES PROMOTION—DO SOMETHING DIFFERENT TO STIMULATE CHANGE

The nature of sales promotion

Sales promotion refers to those promotion activities—other than advertising, publicity, and personal selling—that stimulate interest, trial, or purchase by final customers or others in the channel. Exhibit 14–2 shows examples of typical sales promotions targeted at final customers, channel members, or a firm's own employees.

Sales promotion is generally used to complement the other promotion methods. While advertising campaigns and sales force strategy decisions tend to have longer-term effects, a particular sales promotion activity usually lasts for only a limited time period. Sales promotion can often be implemented quickly—and get sales results sooner than advertising. Further, sales promotion objectives usually focus on prompting some short-term action. For a middleman, such an action might be a decision to stock a product, provide a special display space, or give the product special emphasis in selling efforts to final customers. For a consumer, the desired action might be to try a new product, switch from another brand, buy more of a product, or perhaps buy earlier than would otherwise be the case. The desired action by an employee might be a special effort to satisfy customers or more emphasis on selling a certain product.

Sales promotion spending is growing

Sales promotion involves so many different types of activities that it is difficult to estimate accurately how much is spent in total. There is general consensus, however, that the total spending on sales promotion exceeds spending on advertising. It's likely that sales promotion costs exceed $160 billion a year.

Spending on sales promotion has grown rapidly. Companies that sell frequently purchased consumer products—especially staples such as food products, health and beauty aids, and household cleaning products—have been the source of much of that increased spending. There are several reasons why these firms have been shifting their promotion blends to put more emphasis on sales promotion.[30]

One basic reason for increased use of sales promotion by consumer products firms is that they are generally competing in mature markets. There's only so much soap, cereal, and deodorant that consumers want to buy—regardless of how many different brands there are vying for their attention and dollars. There's also only so much shelf space that retailers will allocate to a particular product category.

The competitive situation is intensified by the growth of large, powerful retail chains. They have put more emphasis on their own dealer brands and also demanded more sales promotion support for the manufacturer brands they do carry.

Sales promotion at the point of purchase can be very targeted at potential customers and increase the likelihood of prompting action.

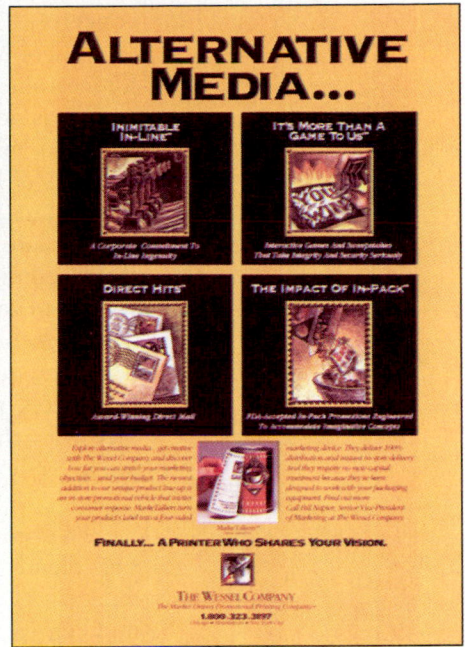

Perhaps in part because of this competition, many consumers have become more price sensitive. Many sales promotions—like coupons—have the effect of lowering the prices consumers pay. So sales promotion has been effective as a tool to overcome consumer price resistance.

Changes in technology have also made sales promotion more efficient. For example, with scanners at retail checkout counters, it's possible to instantly pinpoint a customer who is the target for a particular coupon. If a customer buys a bottle of Kraft salad dressing, Kraft can have the retailer's computerized cash register print out a coupon—on the spot—to encourage the customer to buy Kraft again the next time. Alternatively, a competitor might target that customer with a coupon to encourage brand switching.

The growth of sales promotion has also been fostered by the availability of more consultants, ad agencies, and specialists who help plan and implement sales promotion programs. Segmented Marketing Services (SMS) is a good example. SMS has developed a number of creative ways to help consumer packaged goods producers distribute free product samples to hard-to-reach African-American and Hispanic consumers in major urban areas.

Of course, the basic reason for the growth of spending on sales promotion is that it can be very effective if it is properly done. But there are problems in the sales promotion area.

PROBLEMS IN MANAGING SALES PROMOTION

Does sales promotion erode brand loyalty?

Some experts think that marketing managers—especially those who deal with consumer packaged goods—put too much emphasis on sales promotions. They argue that the effect of most sales promotion is temporary and that money spent on advertising and personal selling helps the firm more over the long term. Their view is that most sales promotions don't help develop close relationships with consumers and instead erode brand loyalty. Let's take a closer look at these concerns.

There *is* heavy use of sales promotion in mature markets where competition for customers and attention from middlemen is fierce. Moreover, if the total market is not growing, sales promotions may just encourage "deal-prone" customers (and middlemen) to switch back and forth among brands. Here, all the expense of the sales promotions and the swapping around of customers simply contributes to lower profits for everyone. It also increase the prices that consumers pay because it increases selling costs—and ultimately it is consumers who pay for those selling costs.

However, it's important to see that once a marketing manager is in this situation there may be little choice other than to continue. At the mature stage of the product life cycle, frequent sales promotions may be needed just to offset the effects of competitors' promotions. The only escape from this competitive rat race is for the marketing manager to seek new opportunities—with a strategy that doesn't rely solely on short-term sales promotions for competitive advantage.

There are alternatives

Procter & Gamble is a company that has changed its strategy—and promotion blend—to decrease its reliance on trade promotion. P&G has dramatically reduced its use of sales promotion targeted at middlemen. Instead, it is offering middlemen lower prices on many of its products and supporting those products with more advertising and promotion to final consumers. P&G believes that this approach will build its brand equity, serve consumers better, and lead to smoother-running relationships in its channels. Not all retailers are happy with P&G's changes. However, given the serious concerns about the impact of trade promotion on brand loyalty, many other producers are likely to follow P&G's lead.

Firms are also experimenting with other approaches. For example, some reimburse middlemen for promotion effort in proportion to their sales to final consumers. Thus, their focus is on supporting middlemen who actually increase sales to final consumers—which can be quite different from just directing sales promotion dollars to middlemen who simply make the product available. Making the product available is a means to an end, but if making it available—without producing sales—is all that is accomplished, the sales promotion effort doesn't make sense.[31]

Sales promotion is hard to manage

Another problem in the sales promotion area is that it is easy to make big, costly mistakes. Because sales promotion includes a wide variety of activities—each of which may be custom-designed and used only once—it's difficult for the typical company to develop skill in this area. Mistakes caused by lack of experience can be very costly too. One promotion sponsored jointly by Polaroid and Trans World Airlines (TWA) proved to be a disaster. The promotion offered a coupon worth 25 percent off the price of any TWA ticket with the purchase of a $20 Polaroid camera. The companies intended to appeal to vacationers who take pictures when they travel. Instead, travel agents bought up many of the cameras. For the price of the $20 camera, they made an extra 25 percent on every TWA ticket they sold. And big companies bought thousands of the cameras to save on overseas travel expenses. This is not an isolated example. Such problems are common.[32]

Not a sideline for amateurs

Sales promotion mistakes are likely to be worse when a company has no sales promotion manager. If the personal selling or advertising managers are responsible for sales promotion, they often treat it as a "stepchild." They allocate money to sales promotion if there is any "left over"—or if a crisis develops. Many companies—even some large ones—don't have a separate budget for sales promotion or even know what it costs in total.

Making sales promotion work is a learned skill—not a sideline for amateurs. That's why specialists in sales promotion have developed—both inside larger firms and as outside consultants. Some of these people are real experts—and are willing to take over the whole sales promotion job. But it's the marketing manager's responsibility to set sales promotion objectives and policies that will fit in with the rest of each marketing strategy.[33]

Earlier, we noted that sales promotion can be aimed at final consumers or users, channel members, and company employees. Let's look at some of the sales promotion tools used for these different target receivers—and what objectives they are expected to accomplish.

DIFFERENT TYPES OF SALES PROMOTION FOR DIFFERENT TARGETS

Sales promotion for final consumers or users

Much of the sales promotion aimed at final consumers or users tries to increase demand—perhaps temporarily—or speed up the time of purchase. Such promotion might involve developing materials to be displayed in retailers' stores—including banners, sample packages, calendars, and various point-of-purchase materials. The sales promotion people also might develop special displays for supermarkets. They might be responsible for "sweepstakes" contests as well as for coupons designed to get customers to buy a product by a certain date. Each year, about 325 billion coupons are distributed. That's over 1,300 coupons for every man, woman, and child in America![34]

All of these sales promotion efforts are aimed at specific objectives. For example, if customers already have a favorite brand, it may be hard to get them to try anything new. Or it may take a while for them to become accustomed to a different product. A free trial-size bottle of mouthwash might be just what it takes to get cautious consumers to try—and like—the new product. Such samples might be distributed house to house, by mail, at stores, or attached to other products sold by the firm. In this type of situation, sales of the product might start to pick up as soon as customers try the product and find out that they like it. And sales will continue at the higher level after the promotion is over if satisfied customers make repeat purchases. Thus, the cost of the sales promotion in this situation might be viewed as a long-term investment.

When a product is already established, consumer sales promotion usually focuses on stimulating sales in the short term. For example, after a price-off coupon for a soft drink is distributed, sales might temporarily pick up as customers take advantage of buying at a lower price. They may even consume more of the soft drink than would have otherwise been the case. However, once the coupon period is over, sales would return to the original level or they might even decline for a while. This is what happens if customers use a coupon to "stock up" on a product at the low price. Then it takes them longer than usual to buy the product again.

When the objective of the promotion is focused primarily on producing a short-term increase in sales, it's sensible for the marketing manager to evaluate the cost of the promotion relative to the extra sales expected. If the increase in sales won't at least cover the cost of the promotion, it probably doesn't make sense to do it. Otherwise, the firm is "buying sales" at the cost of reduced profit.

Trade shows are a very important element in the promotion blend for many marketers who target business customers.

Sales promotion directed at industrial customers might use the same kinds of ideas. In addition, the sales promotion people might set up and staff trade show exhibits. Here, attractive models are often used to encourage buyers to look at a firm's product—especially when it is displayed near other similar products in a circuslike atmosphere.

Some industrial sellers give promotion items—pen sets, cigarette lighters, watches, or more expensive items (perhaps with the firm's brand name on them)—to "remind" industrial customers of their products. This is common practice in many industries. But it can be a sensitive area too. Some companies do not allow buyers to take any gift—of any kind—from a supplier. They fear the buyer's judgment may be influenced by the supplier who gives the best promotion items![35]

Sales promotion for middlemen

Sales promotion aimed at middlemen—sometimes called *trade promotion*—stresses price-related matters. The objective may be to encourage middlemen to stock new items, buy in larger quantity, buy early, or stress a product in their own promotion efforts.

The tools used here include price and/or merchandise allowances, promotion allowances, and perhaps sales contests to encourage retailers or wholesalers to sell specific items—or the company's whole line. Offering to send contest winners to Hawaii, for example, may increase sales.

About half of the sales promotion spending targeted at middlemen has the effect of reducing the price that they pay for merchandise from a supplier. Thus, it makes sense to think about trade promotions in the context of other price-related matters. So, we'll go into more detail on different types of trade discounts and allowances in the next chapter.[36]

Sales promotion for own employees

Sales promotion aimed at the company's own sales force might try to encourage getting new customers, selling a new product, or selling the company's whole line. Depending on the objectives, the tools might be contests, bonuses on sales or number of new accounts, and holding sales meetings at fancy resorts to raise everyone's spirits.

Ongoing sales promotion work might also be aimed at the sales force—to help sales management. Sales promotion might be responsible for preparing sales portfolios, videotapes on new products, displays, and other sales aids. Sales promotion people might develop the sales training material that the sales force uses in working with customers and other channel members. They might develop special racks for product displays that the sales rep sells or gives to retailers. In other words, rather than expecting each individual salesperson—or the sales manager—to develop these sales aids, sales promotion might be given this responsibility.

Service-oriented firms, such as hotels or restaurants, now use sales promotions targeted at their employees. Some, for example, give a monthly cash prize for the employee who provides the "best service." And the employee's picture is displayed to give recognition.[37]

CONCLUSION

Theoretically, it may seem simple to develop an advertising campaign. Just pick the media and develop a message. But it's not that easy. Effectiveness depends on using the "best" available medium and the "best" message considering: (1) promotion objectives, (2) the target markets, and (3) the funds available for advertising.

Specific advertising objectives determine what kind of advertising to use—product or institutional. If product advertising is needed, then the particular type must be decided—pioneering, competitive (direct or indirect), or reminder. And advertising allowances and cooperative advertising may be helpful.

Many technical details are involved in mass selling, and specialists—advertising agencies—handle some of these jobs. But specific objectives must be set for them, or their advertising may have little direction and be almost impossible to evaluate.

Effective advertising should affect sales. But the whole marketing mix affects sales—and the results of advertising usually can't be measured by sales changes alone. By contrast, sales promotion tends to be more action-oriented.

Sales promotion spending is big and growing. This approach is especially important in prompting action—by customers, middlemen, or salespeople. There are many different types of sales promotion, and it is a problem area in many firms because it is difficult for a firm to develop expertise with all of the possibilities.

Advertising and sales promotion are often important parts of a promotion blend—but in most blends personal selling also plays an important role. Further, promotion is only a part of the total marketing mix a marketing manager must develop to satisfy target customers. So, to broaden your understanding of the 4Ps and how they fit together, in the next two chapters we'll go into more detail on the role of Price in strategy decisions.

QUESTIONS AND PROBLEMS

1. Identify the strategy decisions a marketing manager must make in the advertising area.

2. Discuss the relation of advertising objectives to marketing strategy planning and the kinds of advertising actually needed. Illustrate.

3. List several media that might be effective for reaching consumers in a developing nation with low per capita income and a high level of illiteracy. Briefly discuss the limitations and advantages of each medium you suggest.

4. Give three examples where advertising to middlemen might be necessary. What are the objective(s) of such advertising?

5. What does it mean to say that "money is invested in advertising"? Is all advertising an investment? Illustrate.

6. Find advertisements to final consumers that illustrate the following types of advertising: (*a*) institutional, (*b*) pioneering, (*c*) competitive, and (*d*) reminder. What objective(s) does each of these ads have? List the needs each ad appeals to.

7. Describe the type of media that might be most suitable for promoting: (*a*) tomato soup, (*b*) greeting cards, (*c*) a business component material, and (*d*) playground equipment. Specify any assumptions necessary to obtain a definite answer.

8. Discuss the use of testimonials in advertising. Which of the four AIDA steps might testimonials accomplish? Are they suitable for all types of products? If not, for which types are they most suitable?

9. Find a magazine ad that you think does a particularly good job of communicating to the target audience. Would the ad communicate well to an audience in another country? Explain your thinking.

10. Johnson & Johnson sells its baby shampoo in many different countries. Do you think baby shampoo would be a good product for Johnson & Johnson to advertise with a single global message? Explain your thinking.

11. Discuss the future of smaller advertising agencies now that many of the largest are merging to form mega-agencies.

12. Does advertising cost too much? How can this be measured?

13. How would your local newspaper be affected if local supermarkets switched their weekly adver-tising and instead used a service that delivered weekly, free-standing ads directly to each home?

14. Is it unfair to advertise to children? Is it unfair to advertise to less-educated or less-experienced people of any age? Is it unfair to advertise for "unnecessary" products? Is it unfair to criticize a competitor's product in an ad?

15. Discuss the factors that have resulted in increased spending on sales promotion by consumer packaged goods firms during the past decade.

16. Discuss some ways that a firm can link its sales promotion activities to its advertising and personal selling efforts—so that all of its promotion efforts result in an integrated effort.

17. Indicate the type of sales promotion that a producer might use in each of the following situations and briefly explain your reasons:

    (a) A firm has developed an improved razor blade and obtained distribution, but customers are not motivated to buy it.

    (b) A competitor is about to do a test market for a new brand and wants to track sales in test market areas to fine tune its marketing mix.

    (c) A big grocery chain won't stock a firm's new popcorn-based snack product because it doesn't think there will be much consumer demand.

18. Why wouldn't a producer of shampoo just lower the price of its product rather than offer consumers a price-off coupon?

19. If sales promotion spending continues to grow—often at the expense of media advertising—how do you think this might affect the rates charged by mass media for advertising time or space? How do you think it might affect advertising agencies?

SUGGESTED CASES

18. Ledges State Bank

19. Leisure World, Inc.

COMPUTER-AIDED PROBLEM

16. Sales Promotion

As a community service, disc jockeys from radio station WMKT formed a basketball team to help raise money for local nonprofit organizations. The host organization finds or fields a competing team and charges $5 admission to the game. Money from ticket sales goes to the nonprofit organization.

Ticket sales were disappointing at recent games—averaging only about 300 people per game. When WMKT's marketing manager, Bruce Miller, heard about the problem, he suggested using sales promotion to improve ticket sales. The PTA for the local high school—the sponsor for the next game—is interested in the idea but is concerned that its budget doesn't include any promotion money. Miller tries to help them by reviewing his idea in more detail.

Specifically, he proposes that the PTA give a free T-shirt (printed with the school name and date of the game) to the first 500 ticket buyers. He thinks the T-shirt giveaway will create a lot of interest. In fact, he says he is almost certain the promotion would help the PTA sell 600 tickets—double the usual number. He speculates that the PTA might even have a sellout of all 900 seats in the school gym. Further, he notes that the T-shirts will more than pay for themselves if the PTA sells 600 tickets.

A local firm that specializes in sales promotion items agrees to supply the shirts and do the printing for $2.40 a shirt—if the PTA places an order for at least 400 shirts.

The PTA thinks the idea is interesting but wants to look at it more closely—to see what will happen if the promotion doesn't increase ticket sales. To help the PTA evaluate the alternatives, Miller sets up a spreadsheet with the relevant information.

a. *Based on the data from the initial spreadsheet, does the T-shirt promotion look like a good idea? Explain your thinking.*

b. *The PTA treasurer worries about the up-front cost of printing the T-shirts and wants to know where they would stand if they ordered the T-shirts and still sold only 300 tickets. He suggests it might be safer to order the minimum number of T-shirts (400). Evaluate his suggestion.*

c. *The president of the PTA thinks the T-shirt promotion will increase sales but wonders if it wouldn't be better just to lower the price. She suggests $2.60 a ticket, which she arrives at by subtracting the $2.40 T-shirt cost from the usual $5.00 ticket price. How many tickets would the PTA have to sell at the lower price to match the money it would make if it used the T-shirt promotion and actually sold 600 tickets? (Hint: Change the selling price in the spreadsheet and then vary the quantity using the What If analysis.)*

For additional questions related to this problem, see Exercise 16–3 in the *Learning Aid for Use with Basic Marketing*, 12th edition.

17

Pricing Objectives and Policies

When You Finish This Chapter, You Should

1. Understand how pricing objectives should guide strategy planning for pricing decisions.

2. Understand choices the marketing manager must make about price flexibility and price levels over the product life cycle.

3. Understand the legality of price level and price flexibility policies.

4. Understand the many possible variations of a price structure, including discounts, allowances, and who pays transportation costs.

5. Understand the important new terms (shown in red).

For years, the Chevy Suburban utility vehicle was a low-price, no-frills, heavy-duty work truck targeted primarily at commercial users. Then changes in the marketing environment presented a new opportunity. To turn the opportunity into profits, marketing managers needed to plan a new strategy for the Suburban—and new price policies were a crucial aspect of the strategy.

In the early 1990s, luxury car sales to the high-income, baby-boomer crowd were growing fast. High-performance BMWs seemed to be the ultimate yuppie status symbol, and new Japanese models, like the Lexus and Infiniti, set a new standard in customer satisfaction. Yet, sales of luxury sedans slowed as affluent consumers looked for other ways to meet their needs. One clear sign of this shift was and is the growth in demand for pickup trucks and fancy utility vehicles—like the Ford Explorer and Jeep Grand Cherokee.

As consumer preferences changed, marketing managers for the Chevy Suburban changed their strategy. The Suburban evolved into an upscale utility vehicle targeted at families who want to haul special cargo—like kids, toys, and pets. And this target market wants to do its hauling in style. So marketing managers for the Suburban have added many luxury features and options—like leather interiors, CD players, and power everything. They have also significantly raised the suggested list price; a fully equipped Suburban costs about $40,000. Suburbans can command that price because no other model is as big, plush, and powerful. In 1995, if a consumer really wanted jumbo-sized luxury, Suburban was the only choice.

Even at such a steep price, the demand for the Suburban was so hot that supply couldn't keep up to it. Yet, GM managers didn't want to build an expensive new factory. They realized that other firms were scrambling to develop competing models that would cut into Suburban's sales and lofty prices. If a new factory turned into excess capacity—and high overhead costs—it would be hard to cut Suburban prices and still make a profit. That risk didn't seem worth it when the profit on each Suburban was about $7,000—much higher than for most cars.

Dealers couldn't get all the Suburbans they could sell, so many dealers sold the ones they could get at a premium of $1,000 or more over the suggested list price. This jacking up of prices irritated many buyers—and some switched to vehicles made by other manufacturers. Yet, there wasn't much that Suburban's marketing managers could do about it. They couldn't make the dealer charge the suggested list price—and it's not legal to charge uncooperative dealers a higher price for the Suburbans that they buy.

As Suburban faces more direct competitors, the marketing strategy will probably need to change again. A lower price may be required—especially if foreign exchange rates shift and give imports a price advantage. Similarly, some features that are now optional may have to be included in the standard price—or the service warranty may need to be extended. Further, the advertising budget may need to be increased; it was cut way back when demand outstripped supply. And some Suburban dealers may face the tough task of trying to woo back customers who walked away when the dealer tried to extract an unreasonable price.[1]

PRICE HAS MANY STRATEGY DIMENSIONS

Price is one of the four major variables a marketing manager controls. Price level decisions are especially important because they affect both the number of sales a firm makes and how much money it earns.

Guided by the company's objectives, marketing managers must develop a set of pricing objectives and policies. They must spell out what price situations the firm will face and how it will handle them. These policies should explain: (1) how flexible prices will be, (2) at what level they will be set over the product life cycle, (3) to whom and when discounts and allowances will be given, and (4) how transportation costs will be handled. See Exhibit 17–1. These Price-related strategy decision areas are the focus of this chapter. In the next chapter, we will discuss how specific prices are set—consistent with the firm's pricing objectives and policies and its whole marketing strategy.

It's not easy to define price in real-life situations because prices reflect many dimensions. People who don't realize this can make big mistakes.

To build store traffic, A&P's Farmer Jack grocery stores rely heavily on weekly price-off specials targeted at value-conscious shoppers; A&P's Super Fresh stores offer regular customers a Bonus Savings Club frequent shopper program—to help build and retain customer loyalty.

EXHIBIT 17–1   Strategy Planning for Price

Suppose you've been saving to buy a new car and you see in an ad that the base price for the new-year model has been dropped to $9,494—5 percent lower than the previous year. At first this might seem like a real bargain. However, your view of this deal might change if you found out you also had to pay a $400 transportation charge—and an extra $480 for an extended service warranty. The price might look even less attractive if you discovered the options you wanted—air conditioning, power windows, and an AM-FM radio—cost $1,200 more than the previous year. The sales tax on all of this might come as an unpleasant surprise too. Further, how would you feel if you bought the car anyway and then learned that a friend who just bought the exact same model had negotiated a much lower price?[2]

The price equation: price equals something

This example emphasizes that when a seller quotes a price, it is related to *some* assortment of goods and services. So **Price** is what is charged for "something." Of course, price may be called different things in different settings. Colleges charge tuition. Landlords collect rent. Motels post a room rate. Banks ask for interest when they loan money. Transportation companies have fares. Doctors, lawyers, and consultants set fees. Employees want a wage. People may call it different things, but *any business transaction in our modern economy can be thought of as an exchange of money—the money being the Price—for something.*

The something can be a physical product in various stages of completion, with or without supporting services, with or without quality guarantees, and so on. Or it could be a pure service—dry cleaning, a lawyer's advice, or insurance on your car.

The nature and extent of this something determines the amount of money exchanged. Some customers pay list price. Others obtain large discounts or allowances because something is *not* provided. Exhibit 17–2 summarizes some possible variations for consumers or users and Exhibit 17–3 does the same for channel members. These variations are discussed more fully below. But here it should be clear that Price has many dimensions.

EXHIBIT 17–2   Price as Seen by Consumers or Users

Price	Equals	Something

List price
Less: **Discounts:**
  Quantity
  Seasonal
  Cash
  Temporary sales
Less: **Allowances:**
  Trade-ins
  Damaged goods
Less: **Rebate and coupon value**
Plus: **Taxes**
	equals	**Product:**
		  Physical good
		  Service
		  Assurance of quality
		  Repair facilities
		  Packaging
		  Credit
		  Warranty
		Place of delivery or when available

EXHIBIT 17–3   Price as Seen by Channel Members

Price	Equals	Something

List price
Less: **Discounts**
  Quantity
  Seasonal
  Cash
  Trade or functional
  Temporary "deals"
Less: **Allowances:**
  Damaged goods
  Advertising
  Push money
  Stocking
Plus: **Taxes and tariffs**
	equals	**Product:**
		  Branded—well known
		  Guaranteed
		  Warranted
		  Service—repair facilities
		  Convenient packaging for handling
		Place:
		  Availability—when and where
		Price:
		  Price-level guarantee
		  Sufficient margin to allow chance for profit
		Promotion:
		  Promotion aimed at customers

OBJECTIVES SHOULD GUIDE STRATEGY PLANNING FOR PRICE

Pricing objectives should flow from—and fit in with—company-level and marketing objectives. Pricing objectives should be *explicitly stated* because they have a direct effect on pricing policies as well as the methods used to set prices. Exhibit 17–4 shows the various types of pricing objectives we'll discuss.

PROFIT-ORIENTED OBJECTIVES

Target returns provide specific guidelines

A **target return objective** sets a specific level of profit as an objective. Often this amount is stated as a percentage of sales or of capital investment. A large manufacturer like Motorola might aim for a 15 percent return on investment. The target for Safeway and other grocery chains might be a 1 percent return on sales.

A target return objective has administrative advantages in a large company. Performance can be compared against the target. Some companies eliminate divisions—or drop products—that aren't yielding the target rate of return. For example, General Electric sold its small appliance division to Black & Decker because it felt it could earn higher returns in other product-markets.

EXHIBIT 17–4   Possible Pricing Objectives

Some just want satisfactory profits

Some managers aim for only satisfactory returns. They just want returns that ensure the firm's survival and convince stockholders they're doing a good job. Similarly, some small family-run businesses aim for a profit that will provide a comfortable lifestyle.[3]

Many private and public nonprofit organizations set a price level that will just recover costs. In other words, their target return figure is zero. For example, a government agency may charge motorists a toll for using a bridge, but then drop the toll when the cost of the bridge is paid.

Companies that are leaders in their industries—like Alcoa, Du Pont, and General Dynamics—sometimes pursue only satisfactory long-run targets. They are well aware that their activities are in public view. The public—and government officials—expect them to follow policies that are in the public interest when they play the role of price leader or wage setter. Too large a return might invite government action. Similarly, firms that provide critical public services—including many utility and insurance companies, transportation firms, and defense contractors—face public or government agencies that review and approve prices.[4]

But this kind of situation can lead to decisions that are not in the public interest. For example, before imported cars became popular, many GM managers were afraid of making too much profit—so they were not motivated to keep costs and prices low. They thought that lower costs—reflected in lower prices to consumers—might result in an even larger market share—and antitrust action by the government. Then, when low-cost foreign producers entered the U.S. market, GM was not able to quickly reduce costs—or prices.

Profit maximization can be socially responsible

A **profit maximization objective** seeks to get as much profit as possible. It might be stated as a desire to earn a rapid return on investment. Or, more bluntly, to charge all the traffic will bear.

Some politicians want to control the prices of drugs, but that may not be in the public interest if it reduces the incentive for firms to make the big investment required to develop innovative new medicines that people need. That, in turn, would reduce consumer choices.

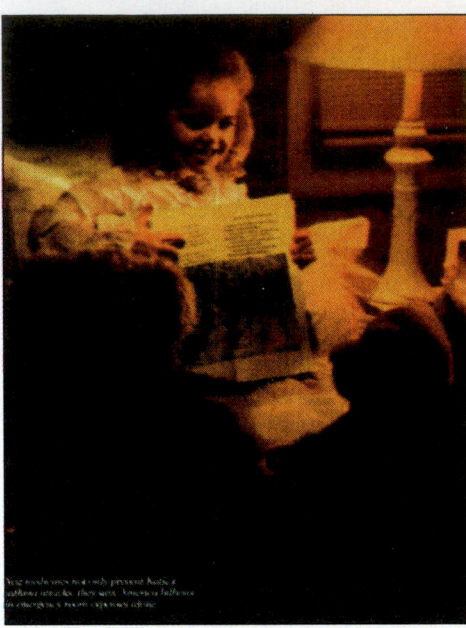

Ask Katie's parents what they think of the asthma drug that's saving her trips to the emergency room.

When asthma medicine can save Katie and her parents from anxious races to the hospital, it's obviously a good thing. What's not so apparent is how dramatically the same drugs reduce healthcare costs.

A study of just one anti-asthma drug showed it reduced emergency room trips by 96%, and hospital admissions by 62%.

As a result, while the cost of Katie's drug over a year's time can be sizable, it's still projected to save America up to $3 billion annually.

America's healthcare crisis calls for this kind of cost-saving power. And new prescription drugs are our best hope for providing it. For more information on how new medicines improve lives and save money, write or call The Pharmaceutical Manufacturers Association, 1100 15th Street, N.W., Box T, Washington, D.C. 20005. 1-800-538-2692.

PHARMACEUTICALS
Saving Lives. Saving Money.

Some people believe that anyone seeking a profit maximization objective will charge high prices—prices that are not in the public interest. However, this point of view is not correct. Pricing to achieve profit maximization doesn't always lead to high prices. Demand and supply *may* bring extremely high prices if competition can't offer good substitutes. But this happens if and only if demand is highly inelastic. If demand is very elastic, profit maximizers may charge relatively low prices. Low prices may expand the size of the market—and result in greater sales and profits. For example, when prices of VCRs were very high, only innovators and wealthy people bought them. When Sony and its competitors lowered prices, nearly everyone bought a VCR. In other words, when demand is elastic, profit maximization may occur at a *lower* price.

Profit maximization objectives can also produce desirable results indirectly. Consumers vote with their purchase dollars for firms that do the right thing. The results of this voting guide other firms in deciding what they should do. If a firm is earning a very large profit, other firms will try to copy or improve on what the company offers. Frequently, this leads to lower prices. IBM sold its original personal computer for about $4,500 in 1981. As Compaq, Dell, and other competitors started to copy IBM, it added more power and features and cut prices. By 1995, customers could buy a personal computer with more than 15 times the power, speed, and data storage for about $1,000, and prices continue to drop.[5]

We saw this process at work in Chapter 10—in the rise and fall of profits during the product life cycle. Contrary to popular belief, a profit maximization objective is often socially desirable.

SALES-ORIENTED OBJECTIVES

A **sales-oriented objective** seeks some level of unit sales, dollar sales, or share of market—*without referring to profit.*

Murray and US Sports have something in common: They both want consumers to know that the price on their quality products makes them a good value.

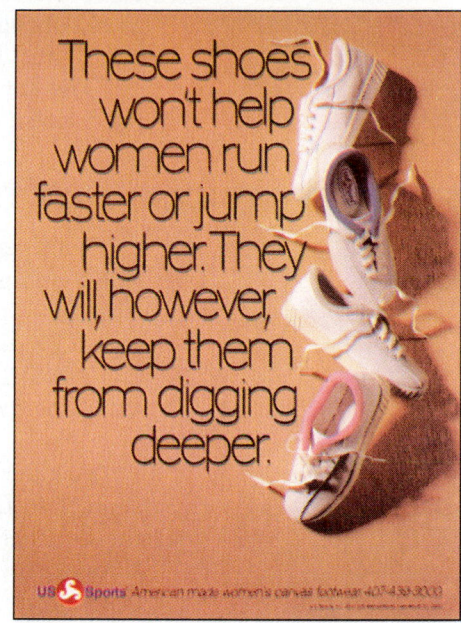

Sales growth doesn't necessarily mean big profits

Some managers are more concerned about sales growth than profits. They think sales growth always leads to more profits. This kind of thinking causes problems when a firm's costs are growing faster than sales—or when managers don't keep track of their costs. Recently, many major corporations have had declining profits in spite of growth in sales. At the extreme, International Harvester kept cutting prices on its tractors—trying to reach its target sales levels in a weak economy—until it had to sell that part of its business. Generally, however, business managers now pay more attention to profits—not just sales.[6]

Managers of some nonprofit organizations set prices to increase market share—precisely because they are *not* trying to earn a profit. For example, many cities set low fares to fill up their buses. Buses cost the same to run empty or full, and there's more benefit when they're full even if the total revenue is no greater.

Market share objectives are popular

Many firms seek to gain a specified share (percent) of a market. A benefit of a market share objective is that it forces a manager to pay attention to what competitors are doing in the market. In addition, it's usually easier to measure a firm's market share than to determine if profits are being maximized. Large consumer packaged goods firms—such as Procter & Gamble, Coca-Cola, and General Foods—often use market share objectives.

Aggressive companies often aim to increase market share—or even to control a market. Sometimes this makes sense. If a company has a large market share, it may have better economies of scale than its competitors. Therefore, if it sells at about the same price as its competitors, it gets more profit from each sale. Or lower costs may allow it to sell at a lower price—and still make a profit.

A company with a longer-run view may decide that increasing market share is a sensible objective when the overall market is growing. The hope is that larger future volume will justify sacrificing some profit in the short run. Companies as diverse as 3M, Coca-Cola, and IBM look at opportunities in Eastern Europe this way.

Of course, objectives aimed at increasing market share have the same limitations as straight sales growth objectives. A larger market share—if gained at too low a price—may lead to profitless "success."

The key point regarding sales-oriented objectives is: Larger sales volume, by itself, doesn't necessarily lead to higher profits.

STATUS QUO PRICING OBJECTIVES

Don't-rock-the-boat objectives

Managers satisfied with their current market share and profits sometime adopt **status quo objectives**—don't-rock-the-*pricing*-boat objectives. Managers may say that they want to stabilize prices, or meet competition, or even avoid competition. This don't-rock-the-boat thinking is most common when the total market is not growing. Maintaining stable prices may discourage price competition and avoid the need for hard decisions.

Or stress nonprice competition instead

A status quo pricing objective may be part of an aggressive overall marketing strategy focusing on **nonprice competition**—aggressive action on one or more of the Ps other than Price. Fast-food chains like McDonald's, Wendy's, and Burger King experienced very profitable growth by sticking to nonprice competition for many years. However, when Taco Bell and others started to take away customers with price-cutting, the other chains also turned to price competition.[7]

MOST FIRMS SET SPECIFIC PRICING POLICIES—TO REACH OBJECTIVES

Specific pricing policies are vital for any firm. Otherwise, the marketing manager has to rethink the marketing strategy every time a customer asks for a price.

Administered prices help achieve objectives

Price policies usually lead to **administered prices**—consciously set prices. In other words, instead of letting daily market forces decide their prices, most firms (including *all* of those in monopolistic competition) set their own prices. They may hold prices steady for long periods of time or change them more frequently if that's what's required to meet objectives.

If a firm doesn't sell directly to final customers, it usually wants to administer both the price it receives from middlemen and the price final customers pay. After all, the price final customers pay will ultimately affect the quantity it sells.

Yet it is often difficult to administer prices throughout the channel. Other channel members may also wish to administer prices to achieve their own objectives. This is what happened to Alcoa, one of the largest aluminum producers. To reduce its excess inventory, Alcoa offered its wholesalers a 30 percent discount off its normal price. Alcoa expected the wholesalers to pass most of the discount along to their customers to stimulate sales throughout the channel. Instead, wholesalers bought *their* aluminum at the lower price but passed on only a small part of the discount to customers. As a result, the quantity Alcoa sold didn't increase much, and it still had excess inventories, while the wholesalers made more profit on the aluminum they did sell.[8]

Some firms don't even try to administer prices. They just meet competition—or worse, mark up their costs with little thought to demand. They act as if they have no choice in selecting a price policy.

American Greeting Cards administers its prices to increase its sales to retailers—and retailers' sales to final consumers. Its Smart Pricing program offers retailers a complete mix of cards at different price levels.

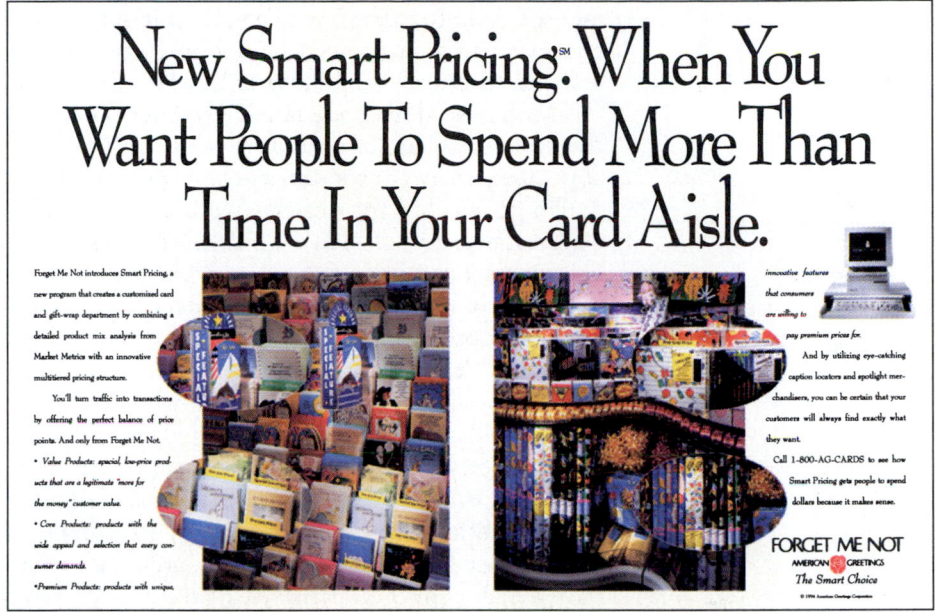

Remember that Price has many dimensions. Managers *do* have many choices. They *should* administer their prices. And they should do it carefully because, ultimately, customers must be willing to pay these prices before a whole marketing mix succeeds. In the rest of this chapter, we'll talk about policies a marketing manager must set to do an effective job of administering Price.[9]

PRICE FLEXIBILITY POLICIES

One of the first decisions a marketing manager has to make is about price flexibility. Should the firm use a one-price or a flexible-price policy?

One-price policy—the same price for everyone

A **one-price policy** means offering the same price to all customers who purchase products under essentially the same conditions and in the same quantities. The majority of U.S. firms use a one-price policy—mainly for administrative convenience and to maintain goodwill among customers.

A one-price policy makes pricing easier. But a marketing manager must be careful to avoid a rigid one-price policy. This can amount to broadcasting a price that competitors can undercut—especially if the price is somewhat high. One reason for the growth of discount houses is that conventional retailers rigidly applied traditional margins—and stuck to them.

Flexible-price policy— different prices for different customers

A **flexible-price policy** means offering the same product and quantities to different customers at different prices. Flexible-price policies often specify a *range* in which the actual price charged must fall.

Flexible pricing is most common in the channels, in direct sales of business products, and at retail for expensive items and homogeneous shopping products. Retail shopkeepers in less-developed economies typically use flexible pricing.

These situations usually involve personal selling—not mass selling. The advantage of flexible pricing is that the salesperson can make price adjustments—considering prices charged by competitors, the relationship with the customer, and the customer's bargaining ability.[10]

Most auto dealers use flexible pricing. The producer suggests a list price, but the dealers bargain for what they can get. Their salespeople negotiate prices every day. Inexperienced consumers—reluctant to bargain—often pay hundreds of dollars more than the dealer is willing to accept. By contrast, however, Saturn dealers have earned high customer-satisfaction ratings by offering haggle-weary consumers a one-price policy.

Flexible pricing does have disadvantages. A customer who finds that others paid lower prices for the same marketing mix will be unhappy. This can cause real conflict in channels. For example, the Winn-Dixie supermarket chain stopped carrying products of some suppliers who refused to give Winn-Dixie the same prices available to chains in other regions of the country.[11]

If buyers learn that negotiating can be in their interest, the time needed for bargaining will increase. This can increase selling costs and reduce profits.

In addition, some sales reps let price-cutting become a habit. This reduces the role of price as a competitive tool—and leads to a lower price level. It can also have a major effect on profit. A small price cut may not seem like much; but keep in mind that all of the revenue that is lost would go to profit. For example, if salespeople for a producer that usually earns profits equal to 15 percent of its sales cut prices by an average of about 5 percent, profits would drop by a third!

PRICE LEVEL POLICIES—OVER THE PRODUCT LIFE CYCLE

When marketing managers administer prices—as most do—they must consciously set a price level policy. As they enter the market, they have to set introductory prices that may have long-run effects. They must consider where the product life cycle is—and how fast it's moving. And they must decide if their prices should be above, below, or somewhere in between relative to the market.

Let's look for a moment at a new product in the market introduction stage of its product life cycle. The price level decision should focus first on the nature of market demand. There are few (or no) direct substitute marketing mixes. And considering the demand curve for this product, a high price may lead to higher profit from each sale, but also to fewer units sold. A lower price might appeal to more potential customers. With this in mind, should the firm set a high or low price?

Skimming pricing— feeling out demand at a high price

A **skimming price policy** tries to sell the top (skim the cream) of a market—the top of the demand curve—at a high price before aiming at more price-sensitive customers. A skimming policy is more attractive if demand is quite inelastic—at least at the upper price ranges.

Skimming may maximize profits in the market introduction stage for an innovation, especially if there is little competition. Competitor analysis may help clarify whether barriers will prevent or discourage competitors from entering.

? Skimming has critics

Some critics argue that firms should not try to maximize profits by using a skimming policy on new products that have important social consequences. A patent-protected, life-saving drug or a genetic technique that increases crop

Skimming may maximize profits in the market introduction stage, but as more firms enter the market, competition typically pushes prices down.

Now UPS delivers for fewer francs, yen or drachmas than our competition.

yields, for example, is likely to have an inelastic demand curve. Yet many of those who need the product may not have the money to buy it. This is a serious concern. However, it's also a serious problem if firms don't have any incentive to take the risks required to develop breakthroughs in the first place.[12]

Price moves down the demand curve

A skimming policy usually involves a slow reduction in price over time. See Exhibit 17–5. Note that as price is reduced, new target markets are probably being sought. So as the price level steps down the demand curve, new Place, Product, and Promotion policies may be needed too.

When Hewlett-Packard (HP) introduced its laser printer for personal computers, it initially set a high price—around $4,000. HP had a good headstart on competitors—and no close substitute was available. HP sold the high-priced printer mainly to computer professionals and business users with serious desktop publishing needs—and distributed them through a select group of authorized HP computer dealers whose salespeople could explain the printer. When other firms entered the market with similar printers, HP added features and lowered its price. It also did more advertising and added mail-order middlemen to reach new target markets. Then, just as competitors were entering the market to go after budget-oriented buyers, HP introduced a new model at a lower price and added office-supply warehouse stores, like Office Depot, to the distribution channel. This is very typical of skimming. It involves dropping prices through a series of marketing strategy changes over the course of the product life cycle.

EXHIBIT 17–5   Alternative Introductory Pricing Policies

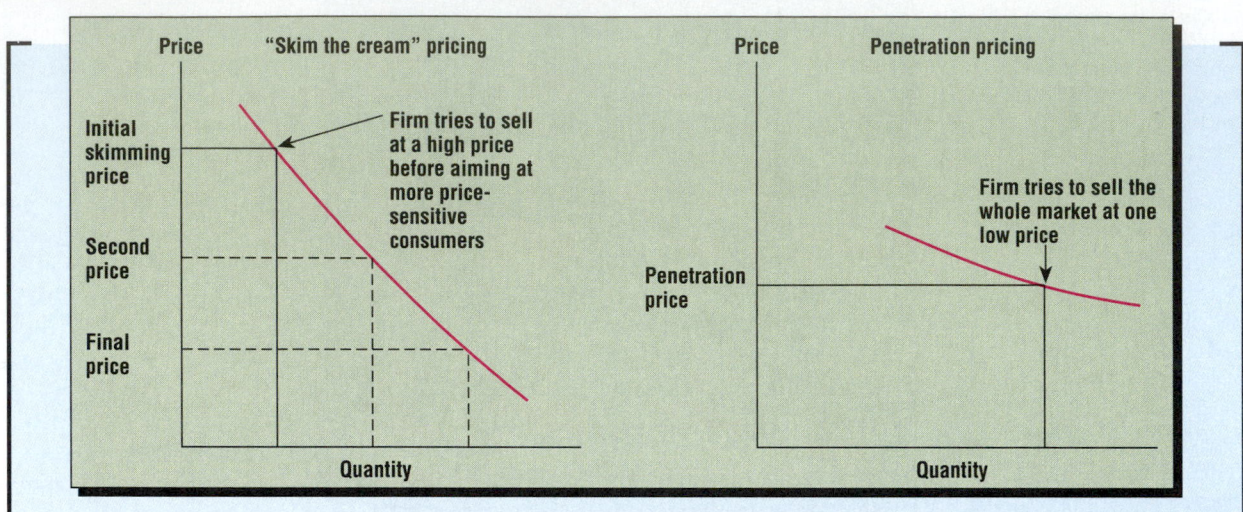

Skimming is also useful when you don't know very much about the shape of the demand curve. It's usually safer to start with a high price that customers can refuse—and then reduce it if necessary.[13]

Penetration pricing—get volume at a low price

A **penetration pricing policy** tries to sell the whole market at one low price. Such an approach might be wise when the elite market—those willing to pay a high price—is small. This is the case when the whole demand curve is fairly elastic. See Exhibit 17–5. A penetration policy is even more attractive if selling larger quantities results in lower costs because of economies of scale. Penetration pricing may be wise if the firm expects strong competition very soon after introduction.

A low penetration price may be called a stay-out price. It discourages competitors from entering the market.

When personal computers became popular, Borland International came out with a complete programming language—including a textbook—for under $50. Business customers had paid thousands of dollars for similar systems for mainframe computers. But Borland felt it could sell to hundreds of thousands of customers—and earn large total profits—by offering a really low price that would attract individual users as well as business firms. A low price helped Borland penetrate the market early. For several years, IBM, Microsoft, and other big companies weren't able—or willing—to compete directly with Borland at that price. When they finally did match Borland's price, Borland already had a large base of very loyal customers who weren't interested in switching to something new.

Introductory price dealing—temporary price cuts

Low prices do attract customers. Therefore, marketers often use **introductory price dealing**—temporary price cuts—to speed new products into a market. Introductory price dealing may be used to get customers to try a new product concept as part of the pioneering effort—or to attract customers to a new brand entry later in the life cycle. However, don't confuse these *temporary* price cuts with low penetration prices. The plan here is to raise prices as soon as the introductory offer is over. By then, hopefully, target customers will have tried the product and decided it was worth buying again at the regular price.

Established competitors often choose not to meet introductory price dealing—as long as the introductory period is not too long or too successful. However, some competitors quickly match introductory price deals with their own short-term sale prices; they want to discourage their established customers from "shopping around."

Meeting competition may be necessary

Regardless of their introductory pricing policy, most firms face competition sooner or later in the product life cycle. When that happens, how high or low a price is may be relative not only to the market demand curve but also to the prices charged by competitors.

The nature of competition usually affects whether companies set their prices below, at, or above competition. The clearest case is pure competition. The market really makes the decision. To offer products above or below the market price is foolish.

Meeting competitors' prices may also be the practical choice in mature markets that are moving toward pure competition. Here, firms typically face downward pressure on both prices and profits. Profit margins are already thin—and for many firms they would disappear or turn into losses at a lower price. A higher price would simply prompt competitors to promote their price advantage.

Similarly, there is little choice in oligopoly situations. Pricing at the market—that is, meeting competition—may be the only sensible policy. To raise prices might lead to a large loss in sales—unless competitors adopt the higher price too. And cutting prices would probably lead to similar reductions by competitors—downward along an inelastic industry demand curve. This can only lead to a decrease in total revenue for the industry and probably for each firm. The major airlines faced these problems recently.

To avoid these problems, each oligopolist may choose a status quo pricing objective—and set its price at the competitive level. Some critics call this pricing behavior conscious parallel action, implying it is unethical and the same as intentional conspiracy among firms. As a practical matter, however, that criticism seems overly harsh. It isn't sensible for firms to ignore their competitors.[14]

There are alternatives in monopolistic competition

In monopolistic competition, there are more pricing options. At one extreme, some firms are clearly above-the-market—they may even brag about it. Tiffany's is well known as one of the most expensive jewelry stores in the world. Other firms emphasize below-the-market prices in their marketing mixes. Prices offered by discounters and mass-merchandisers, such as Wal-Mart and Tesco, illustrate this approach. They may even promote their pricing policy with catchy slogans like "guaranteed lowest prices" or "we'll beat any advertised price."

Above or below what market?

These examples raise an important question. Do these various strategies promote prices that are above or below the market—or are they really different prices for different target markets or different marketing mixes? In setting price level policies, it is important to clearly define the *relevant target market* and *competitors* when making price comparisons.

Perhaps some target customers do see important differences in the product, or in the convenience of location, or in the whole marketing mix. Then what we're talking about are different marketing strategies—not just different price levels.

This attention-getting billboard, on the highway to Tahoe ski resorts, reminds drivers that Reno Air's price isn't just lower than other airlines; it may be less expensive than driving.

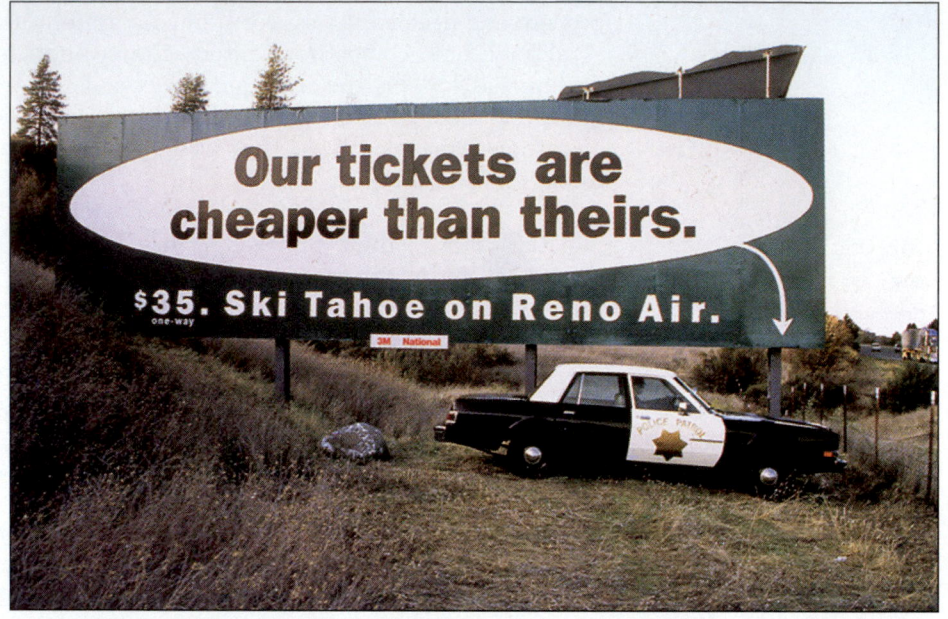

Consider Wal-Mart prices again from this view. Wal-Mart may have lower camera prices than conventional camera retailers, but it offers less help in the store, less selection, and it won't take old cameras in trade. Wal-Mart may be appealing to budget-oriented shoppers who compare prices among different mass-merchandisers. A specialty camera store—appealing to different customers—may not be a direct competitor! Thus, it may be better to think of Wal-Mart's price as part of a different marketing mix for a different target market—not as a below-the-market price.

A camera producer with this point of view might develop a different strategy for the Wal-Mart channel and the specialty store channel. In particular, the producer might offer the specialty store one or more models that are not available to Wal-Mart—to ensure that customers don't view the two stores as direct competitors with price the only difference.

Different price level policies through the channel

When a product is sold to channel members instead of final consumers, the price should be set so that the channel members can cover costs and make a profit. To achieve its objectives, a manufacturer may set different price level policies for different levels in the channel. For example, a producer of a slightly better product might set a price level that is low relative to competitors when selling to retailers, while suggesting an above-the-market retail price. This encourages retailers to carry the product—and to emphasize it in their marketing mix—because it yields higher profits.

The price of money may affect the price level

We've been talking about the price level of a firm's product. But a nation's money also has a price level—what it is worth in some other currency. For example, on March 29, 1995, one U.S. dollar was worth 1.38 German marks. In other words, the exchange rate for the German mark against the U.S. dollar was 1.38. Exhibit 17–6 lists exchange rates for money from several countries over a number of years. From this exhibit you can see that exchange rates change over

EXHIBIT 17–6 Exchange Rates for Various Currencies against the U.S. Dollar over Time

Base Currency	Number of Units of Base Currency per U.S. Dollar*							
	1981	*1983*	*1985*	*1987*	*1989*	*1991*	*1993*	*1995*
German mark	2.26	2.55	2.94	1.80	1.88	1.66	1.65	1.38
Japanese yen	220.63	237.55	238.47	144.60	138.07	134.59	111.08	88.40
French franc	5.44	7.62	8.98	6.01	6.38	5.65	5.67	4.88
Australian dollar	.87	1.11	1.43	1.43	1.26	1.32	1.47	1.38
Canadian dollar	1.20	1.23	1.37	1.33	1.18	1.15	1.29	1.40
British pound	.49	.66	.77	.61	.62	.57	.67	.62

*Units shown are the average for each year 1981–93. For 1995, units shown are for March 29.

time—and sometimes the changes are significant. For example, during 1993, a U.S. dollar was worth, on average, 1.65 German marks; in 1985, the average was 2.94 German marks.

Exchange rate changes can have a significant effect on whether or not a marketing manager's price level has the expected result. As the following example shows, this can be an important factor even for a small firm that sells only in its own local market.

In 1993, the marketing manager for ColorFast—a small firm that mixes and sells special dyes used by textile producers—set a meeting-competition wholesale price at about $100 for a barrel of dye. The wholesalers who distribute her dyes also carried a competing product produced by a German firm. Its wholesale price was also $100, which means that the German firm got about 165 German marks ($100 multiplied times 1.65 marks per dollar) per barrel. However, when the exchange rate for the mark against the dollar fell from 1.65 to 1.38, the German producer got 27 fewer marks for each $100 barrel of dye (165 marks – 138 marks = 27 marks).

Because Colorfast's marketing manager was only selling dye to local customers, she didn't pay any attention to the drop in the exchange rate—at first. However, she did pay attention when the German producer decided to raise its wholesale price to $115 a barrel. At the $115 price, the German firm got about 159 marks per barrel ($115 × 1.38 marks per dollar)—less than it was getting before the exchange rate change. Colorfast's sales increased substantially—at the German competitor's expense—because of the lower Colorfast price. Colorfast's marketing manager concluded that it would probably take a while for the German firm to lower its price, even if the exchange rate went up again. So she decided that she could safely raise her price level by 10 percent—up to $110—and still have a price advantage over the German supplier.[15]

Consumers want value pricing

Sooner or later there's competition in most product-markets. And in today's competitive markets more and more customers are demanding real value. **Value pricing** means setting a fair price level for a marketing mix that really gives customers what they need. Value pricing doesn't necessarily mean cheap if cheap means bare-bones or low-grade. It doesn't mean high prestige either if the prestige is not accompanied by the right quality goods and services. Rather the focus is on the customer's requirements—and the whole strategy.

Toyota is a good example of a firm that has been effective with value pricing. It has different marketing mixes for different target markets. But from the low-price Tercel to the $30,000 Avalon, the Japanese automaker consistently offers better quality and lower prices than its competitors. Among discount retailers, Wal-Mart is a value pricing leader. Its motto, "the low price on the brands you trust," says it all. In the product-market for hosiery, Sara Lee is a value pricer; its L'eggs are priced lower than many dealer brands but it still offers customers the selection, fit, and wear they want.

Value pricing builds relationships—and repeat purchases

These companies deliver on their promises. They try to give the consumer pleasant surprises—like an unexpected service or a useful new feature or environmentally sound packaging—because it builds customer loyalty. They guarantee what they offer—and they return the price if the customer isn't completely satisfied. They avoid unrealistic price levels—prices that are high only because consumers already know the brand name. They build relationships with customers so the customers will be loyal and come back the next time they purchase.[16]

When you stop to think about it, value pricing is simply the best pricing decision for the type of market-oriented strategy planning we've been discussing throughout this whole text. To build profits and customer satisfaction, the whole marketing mix—including the price level—must meet target customers' needs.

MOST PRICE STRUCTURES ARE BUILT AROUND LIST PRICES

Prices start with a list price

Most price structures are built around a base price schedule or price list. **Basic list prices** are the prices final customers or users are normally asked to pay for products. In this book, unless noted otherwise, list price refers to basic list price.

In the next chapter, we discuss how firms set these list prices. For now, however, we'll consider variations from list price—and why they are made.

DISCOUNT POLICIES—REDUCTIONS FROM LIST PRICES

Discounts are reductions from list price given by a seller to buyers who either give up some marketing function or provide the function themselves. Discounts can be useful in marketing strategy planning. In the following discussion, think about what function the buyers are giving up—or providing—when they get each of these discounts.

Quantity discounts encourage volume buying

Quantity discounts are discounts offered to encourage customers to buy in larger amounts. This lets a seller get more of a buyer's business, or shifts some of the storing function to the buyer, or reduces shipping and selling costs—or all of these. Such discounts are of two kinds: cumulative and noncumulative.

Cumulative quantity discounts apply to purchases over a given period—such as a year—and the discount usually increases as the amount purchased increases. Cumulative discounts are intended to encourage *repeat* buying by a single customer by reducing the customer's cost for additional purchases. This is a way to develop closer, ongoing relationships with customers. For example, a Lowe's lumberyard might give a cumulative quantity discount to a building contractor who is not able to buy all of the needed materials at once. Lowe's wants to reward the contractor's patronage—and discourage shopping around. Lowe's knows that its market is very competitive. So the cumulative discount is just part of an effort to build loyalty with the customers it has; the discount is small relative to the cost of constantly trying to attract new customers to replace departures.

JAPANESE CONSUMERS YEN FOR IMPORTED PRODUCTS

For years, U.S. firms have been trying to break into the Japanese market. Most U.S. firms that are there have not had strong sales. However, during the past few years more Japanese consumers have been buying imported products. The main reason is that the rising value of the Japanese yen has resulted in lower prices for imported goods in Japan. For example, in the short period between March and September of 1993 car tire prices declined $9.50, or 11 percent, and the average price for an Apple personal computer dropped $971, or 24 percent. Since 1993 the exchange rate for the yen against the dollar has gone down another 20 percent—leading to even lower prices.

A good way to understand the effect of these changes is to take a closer look at a similar experience—10 years earlier. In 1983, marketing managers for Campbell Soup Company mounted a new effort to enter the Japanese market. They developed corn potage and a line of six other soups in Japanese-style packages. In spite of a good product line, Campbell's salespeople struggled to get shelf space in Japan's small, cramped grocery stores.

Progress was slow. The firm wasn't achieving its market share objective. In fact, Campbell was shipping less soup to Japan than to Albuquerque, New Mexico! In May of 1985, with a meeting-competition retail price of 220 Japanese yen (about 91 cents) per can, Campbell was barely making a profit.

Over the next two years, there was an 89 percent rise in the exchange rate for the Japanese yen against the U.S. dollar. That meant that Campbell made more dollars for each can of soup sold in Japan—and that its profits would increase simply by holding its price level the same. However, Campbell's marketing managers seized the opportunity to be more aggressive in pursuing their market share objective. They lowered the suggested list price of Campbell soup 16 percent—to a price of 185 yen—and kept retailers' profit margins the same. With those changes, sales volume and market share doubled. Moreover, even at the lower price Campbell made the equivalent of $1.30 a can, up nearly 50 percent from the 1985 level. Campbell used the extra money to increase promotion in the Japanese market to help recruit more retailers.[17]

Noncumulative quantity discounts apply only to individual orders. Such discounts encourage larger orders—but do not tie a buyer to the seller after that one purchase. These discounts may be used to discourage small orders, which are expensive to handle. But they are mainly used to encourage bigger orders. Lowe's lumberyard may purchase and resell insulation products made by several competing producers. Owens/Corning might try to encourage Lowe's to stock larger quantities of its insulation by offering a noncumulative quantity discount. The objective would be to encourage Lowe's to push those products to its customers. If the quantity discount is attractive enough, Lowe's might place all of its orders with Corning and not even handle another brand.

Quantity discounts may be based on the dollar value of the entire order, or on the number of units purchased, or on the size of the package purchased. While quantity discounts are usually given as price cuts, sometimes they are given as free or bonus products. Airline frequent flier programs use this approach.

Quantity discounts can be a very useful tool for the marketing manager. Some customers are eager to get them. But marketing managers must use quantity discounts carefully. In business markets, they must offer such discounts to all customers on equal terms—to avoid price discrimination.

Noncumulative discounts sometimes produce unexpected results. If the discount is too big, wholesalers or retailers may buy more than they can possibly sell to their own customers—to get the low price. Then they sell the excess at a low price to whoever will buy it—as long as the buyer doesn't compete in the

Cargill uses a seasonal discount to encourage buyers to stock products earlier than present demand requires.

same market area. These gray-market channels often take customers away from regular channel members, perhaps with a retail price even lower than what most channel members pay. To avoid these problems, a marketing manager must consider the effect of discounts on the whole strategy—not just the effect on sales to a given middleman.

Seasonal discounts— buy sooner

Seasonal discounts are discounts offered to encourage buyers to buy earlier than present demand requires. If used by a manufacturer, this discount tends to shift the storing function further along in the channel. It also tends to even out sales over the year and therefore permit year-round operation. If seasonal discounts are large, they may be passed along to other customers down the channel of distribution. For example, Kyota offers wholesalers a lower price on its garden tillers if they buy in the fall—when sales are slow. The wholesalers can then offer a seasonal discount to retailers—who may try to sell the tillers during a special fall sale.

Service firms that face irregular demand or capacity constraints often use seasonal discounts. For example, AT&T offers a discount for night-time calls when the load of business calls is low. Some tourist attractions—like ski resorts—offer lower weekday rates when attendance would otherwise be down.

Payment terms and cash discounts set payment dates

Most sales to businesses are made on credit. The seller sends a bill (invoice), and the buyer's accounting department processes it for payment. Some firms depend on their suppliers for temporary working capital (credit). Therefore, it is very important for both sides to clearly state the terms of payment—including the availability of cash discounts—and to understand the commonly used payment terms.

Net means that payment for the face value of the invoice is due immediately. These terms are sometimes changed to net 10 or net 30—which means payment is due within 10 or 30 days of the date on the invoice.

Cash discounts are reductions in price to encourage buyers to pay their bills quickly. The terms for a cash discount usually modify the net terms.

2/10, net 30 means the buyer can take a 2 percent discount off the face value of the invoice if the invoice is paid within 10 days. Otherwise, the full face value is due within 30 days. And it usually is stated or understood that an interest charge will be added after the 30-day free-credit period.

Why cash discounts are given and should be evaluated

Smart buyers carefully evaluate cash discounts. A discount of 2/10, net 30 may not look like much at first. But the buyer earns a 2 percent discount for paying the invoice just 20 days sooner than it should be paid anyway. By not taking the discount, the company—in effect—is borrowing at an annual rate of 36 percent. That is, assuming a 360-day year and dividing by 20 days, there are 18 periods during which the company could earn 2 percent—and 18 times 2 equals 36 percent a year.

While the marketing manager can often use a cash discount as a marketing variable, this isn't always true. Purchasing agents who value cash discounts may insist that the marketing manager offer the same discount offered by competitors. In fact, some buyers automatically deduct the traditional cash discount from their invoices regardless of the seller's invoice terms!

Some sellers find themselves in trouble when they don't state exactly when payment is due—or what the penalty will be for late payment. Customers may wait as long as possible to pay the invoice, especially if they are short of cash or if interest rates are high.

Consumers say "charge it"

Credit sales are also important to retailers. Some stores have their own credit systems. But most retailers use credit card services, such as Visa or MasterCard. The retailers pay a percent of the revenue from each credit sale for this service—from 1 to 7 percent depending on the card company and the store's sales volume. For this reason, some retailers offer discounts to consumers who pay cash.

Many consumers like the convenience of credit card buying. But some critics argue that the cards make it too easy for consumers to buy things they really can't afford. Further, because of high interest charges, credit card buying can increase the total costs to consumers.[18]

Trade discounts often are set by tradition

A **trade (functional) discount** is a list price reduction given to channel members for the job they are going to do.

A manufacturer, for example, might allow retailers a 30 percent trade discount from the suggested retail list price to cover the cost of the retailing function and their profit. Similarly, the manufacturer might allow wholesalers a *chain* discount of 30 percent and 10 percent off the suggested retail price. In this case, the wholesalers would be expected to pass the 30 percent discount on to retailers.

Trade discounts might seem to offer manufacturers or wholesalers great flexibility in varying a marketing mix. In fact, however, customary trade discounts can be so well established in the channel that the manager has to accept them as fixed when setting prices.

Low prices help attract customers, but a marketing manager who constantly uses temporary sales to adjust the price level probably has not done a good job setting the normal price.

Special sales reduce list prices—temporarily

A **sale price** is a temporary discount from the list price. Sale price discounts encourage immediate buying. In other words, to get the sale price, customers give up the convenience of buying when they want to buy—and instead buy when the seller wants to sell.

Special sales provide a marketing manager with a quick way to respond to changing market conditions—without changing the basic marketing strategy. For example, a retailer might use a sale to help clear extra inventory or to meet a competing store's price. Or a producer might offer a middleman a special deal—in addition to the normal trade discount—that makes it more profitable for the middleman to push the product. Retailers often pass some of the savings along to consumers.

In recent years, sale prices and deals have become much more common. Some retailers who had an occasional sale a few years ago now have weekly sales. And for some consumer convenience products, the majority of purchases by middlemen involve some sort of deal. At first it may seem that consumers benefit from all this. But that may not be the case. Prices that change constantly may confuse customers and increase selling costs.

To avoid these problems, some firms that sell consumer convenience products offer **everyday low pricing**—setting a low list price rather than relying on a high list price that frequently changes with various discounts or allowances. Many grocery stores use this approach. And some producers, including P&G, are now using it with some product lines.

Sale prices should be used carefully, consistent with well-thought-out pricing objectives and policies. A marketing manager who constantly uses temporary sales to adjust the price level probably has not done a good job setting the normal price.[19]

ALLOWANCE POLICIES—OFF LIST PRICES

Allowances—like discounts—are given to final consumers, customers, or channel members for doing something or accepting less of something.

**Advertising allowances—
something for something**

Advertising allowances are price reductions given to firms in the channel to encourage them to advertise or otherwise promote the supplier's products locally. For example, General Electric gave an allowance (1.5 percent of sales) to its wholesalers of housewares and radios. They, in turn, were expected to spend the allowance on local advertising.

**Stocking allowances—get
attention and shelf space**

Stocking allowances—sometimes called slotting allowances—are given to a middleman to get shelf space for a product. For example, a producer might offer a retailer cash or free merchandise to stock a new item. Stocking allowances are a recent development. So far, they're used mainly to prompt supermarket chains to handle new products. Supermarkets don't have enough slots on their shelves to handle all of the available new products. They're more willing to give space to a new product if the supplier will offset their handling costs—like making space in the warehouse, adding information on computer systems, and redesigning store shelves, for example.

Some retailers get allowances that cover more than handling costs. The Shoprite Stores chain in New York City got an $86,000 allowance to stock $172,000 worth of Old Capital Microwave Popcorn. When the popcorn didn't sell well, Shoprite quickly took it off its shelves. With a big stocking allowance, the middleman makes extra profit—even if a new product fails and the producer loses money.

**❓Are stocking
allowances ethical?**

There is much controversy about stocking allowances. Critics say that retailer demands for big stocking allowances slow new product introductions—and make it hard for small producers to compete. Some producers feel that retailers' demands are unethical—just a different form of extortion. Retailers, on the other hand, point out that the fees protect them from producers that simply want to push more and more me-too products onto their shelves. Perhaps the best way for a producer to cope with the problem is to develop new products that offer consumers a real comparative advantage. Then it will benefit everyone in the channel—including retailers—to get the products to the target market.[20]

PMs—push for cash

Push money (or prize money) allowances—sometimes called PMs or spiffs—are given to retailers by manufacturers or wholesalers to pass on to the retailers' sales-clerks for aggressively selling certain items. PM allowances are used for new items, slower-moving items, or higher-margin items. They are often used for pushing furniture, clothing, consumer electronics, and cosmetics. A salesclerk, for example, might earn an additional $5 for each new model Pioneer cassette deck sold.

**Bring in the old, ring up
the new—with trade-ins**

A **trade-in allowance** is a price reduction given for used products when similar new products are bought.

Trade-ins give the marketing manager an easy way to lower the effective price without reducing list price. Proper handling of trade-ins is important when selling durable products. Customers buying machinery, for example, buy long-term satisfaction in terms of more production capacity. If the list price less the trade-in allowance doesn't offer greater satisfaction—as the customer sees it—then no sale will be made.

SOME CUSTOMERS GET EXTRA SOMETHINGS

**Clipping coupons—more
for less**

Many producers and retailers offer discounts (or free items) through coupons distributed in packages, mailings, print ads, or at the store. By presenting a coupon

Retailers are willing to redeem coupons because it increases their sales—and they usually are paid for handling the coupons.

to a retailer, the consumer is given a discount off list price. This is especially common in the consumer packaged goods business—but the use of price-off coupons is growing in other lines of business too.

Retailers are willing to redeem producers' coupons because it increases their sales—and they usually are paid for the trouble of handling the coupon. For example, a retailer who redeems a 50 cents off coupon might be repaid 75 cents. In effect, the coupon increases the functional discount and makes it more attractive to sell the couponed product.

Couponing is so common that firms have been set up to help repay retailers for redeeming manufacturers' coupons. The total dollar amounts involved are so large that crime has become a big problem. Some dishonest retailers have gone to jail for collecting on coupons they redeemed without requiring customers to buy the products.

Cash rebates when you buy

Some producers offer **rebates**—refunds paid to consumers after a purchase. Sometimes the rebate may be very large. Some automakers offer rebates of $500 to $2,500 to promote sales of slow-moving models. Rebates are used on lower-price items too—ranging from Duracell batteries to Paul Masson wines.

Rebates give the producer a way to be certain that final consumers actually get the price reduction. If the rebate amount were just taken off the price charged middlemen, they might not pass the savings along to consumers. In addition, many consumers buy because the price looks lower with the rebate—but then they don't request the refund.[21]

LIST PRICE MAY DEPEND ON GEOGRAPHIC PRICING POLICIES

Retail list prices sometimes include free delivery. Or free delivery may be offered to some customers as an aid to closing the sale. What the retail list price

Many trade promotions basically lower the price a business pays.

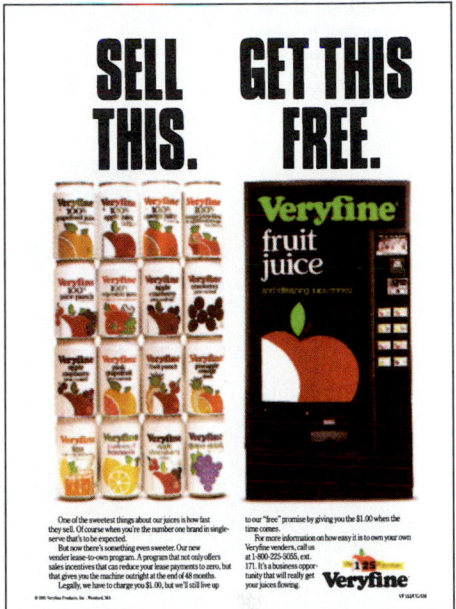

includes (or does not include) may not be formally stated. That way, the retailer can adjust its marketing mix—depending on the customer's needs or bargaining ability.

Deciding who pays the freight charge is more important on sales to business customers than to final consumers because more money is involved. Usually purchase orders specify place, time, method of delivery, freight costs, insurance, handling, and other charges. There are many possible variations for an imaginative marketing manager, and some specialized terms have developed.

F.O.B. pricing is easy

A commonly used transportation term is **F.O.B.**—which means free on board some vehicle at some place. Typically, F.O.B. pricing names the place—often the location of the seller's factory or warehouse—as in F.O.B. Taiwan or F.O.B. mill. This means that the seller pays the cost of loading the products onto some vehicle—usually a truck, railcar, or ship. At the point of loading, title to the products passes to the buyer. Then the buyer pays the freight and takes responsibility for damage in transit—except as covered by the transporting company.

The marketing manager can make variations easily by changing the place named in the F.O.B. description. If a firm wants to pay the freight for the convenience of customers, it can use: F.O.B. delivered or F.O.B. buyer's factory. In this case, title does not pass until the products are delivered. If the seller wants title to pass immediately but is willing to prepay freight (and then include it in the invoice), F.O.B. seller's factory-freight prepaid can be used.

F.O.B. shipping point pricing simplifies the seller's pricing—but it may narrow the market. Since the delivered cost varies depending on the buyer's location, a customer located farther from the seller must pay more and might buy from closer suppliers.

It may be difficult for a firm that operates in many different countries to stick with a one-price policy.

Zone pricing smooths delivered prices

Zone pricing means making an average freight charge to all buyers within specific geographic areas. The seller pays the actual freight charges and bills each customer for an average charge. For example, a company in Canada might divide the United States into seven zones, then bill all customers in the same zone the same amount for freight even though actual shipping costs might vary.

Zone pricing reduces the wide variation in delivered prices that results from an F.O.B. shipping point pricing policy. It also simplifies transportation charges.

Uniform delivered pricing—one price to all

Uniform delivered pricing means making an average freight charge to all buyers. It is a kind of zone pricing—an entire country may be considered as one zone—that includes the average cost of delivery in the price. Uniform delivered pricing is most often used when (1) transportation costs are relatively low and (2) the seller wishes to sell in all geographic areas at one price—perhaps a nationally advertised price.

Freight-absorption pricing—competing on equal grounds in another territory

When all firms in an industry use F.O.B. shipping point pricing, a firm usually competes well near its shipping point but not farther away. As sales reps look for business farther away, delivered prices rise and the firm finds itself priced out of the market.

This problem can be reduced with **freight absorption pricing**—which means absorbing freight cost so that a firm's delivered price meets the nearest competitor's. This amounts to cutting list price to appeal to new market segments.

With freight absorption pricing, the only limit on the size of a firm's territory is the amount of freight cost it is willing to absorb. These absorbed costs cut net return on each sale—but the new business may raise total profit. Some small firms look at international markets this way; they just figure that any profit from export sales is a bonus.

German firms will have new opportunities in a unified Europe, but they may need different geographic pricing policies to expand into new territories.

LEGALITY OF PRICING POLICIES

This chapter discusses the many pricing decisions that must be made. However, as was suggested in Chapter 4, some pricing decisions are limited by government legislation.

The first step to understanding pricing legislation is to know the thinking of legislators and the courts. Ideally, they try to help the economy operate more effectively—in the consumer's interest. In practice, this doesn't always work. But generally their intentions are good. And if we take this view, we get a better idea of the "why" of legislation. This helps us anticipate future rulings. We'll focus on U.S. legislation here, but many other countries have similar pricing laws.[22]

Minimum prices are sometimes controlled

Unfair trade practice acts put a lower limit on prices, especially at the wholesale and retail levels. They have been passed in more than half the states in the United States. Selling below cost in these states is illegal. Wholesalers and retailers are usually required to take a certain minimum percentage markup over their merchandise-plus-transportation costs. The most common markup figures are 6 percent at retail and 2 percent at wholesale.

If a specific wholesaler or retailer can provide conclusive proof that operating costs are lower than the minimum required figure, lower prices may be permitted. But it is nearly impossible to provide satisfactory proof.

Most retailers know enough about their costs to set markups larger than these minimums. The practical effect of these laws is to protect certain limited-line food retailers—such as dairy stores—from the kind of "ruinous" competition supermarkets might offer if they sold milk as a leader—offering it below cost—for a long time.

The United States and most other countries control the minimum price of imported products with antidumping laws. **Dumping** is pricing a product sold in a foreign market below the cost of producing it or at a price lower than in its domestic market. These laws are usually designed to protect the country's domestic producers—and jobs—from foreign competitors, but there is much debate about how well they work.

Even very high prices may be OK

Generally speaking, firms can charge high prices—even outrageously high prices—as long as they don't conspire with their competitors to fix prices, discriminate against some of their customers, or lie.

Of course, there are exceptions. Firms in regulated businesses may need to seek approval for their prices. For example, in the United States, most states regulate automobile insurance rates. Some countries impose more general price controls—to reduce inflation or try to control markets. However, most countries have followed the move toward a market-directed economy. That doesn't mean, however, that there aren't important regulations in the pricing area.

You can't lie about prices

Phony list prices are prices customers are shown to suggest that the price has been discounted from list. Some customers seem more interested in the supposed discount than in the actual price. Most businesses, trade associations, and government agencies consider the use of phony list prices unethical. In the United States, the FTC tries to stop such pricing—using the **Wheeler Lea Amendment**, which bans "unfair or deceptive acts in commerce."[23]

Price fixing is illegal— you can go to jail

Difficulties with pricing—and violations of pricing legislation—usually occur when competing marketing mixes are quite similar. When the success of an entire marketing strategy depends on price, there is pressure (and temptation) to make agreements with competitors (conspire). And **price fixing**—competitors getting together to raise, lower, or stabilize prices—is common and relatively easy. *But it is also completely illegal in the United States.* It is considered "conspiracy" under the Sherman Act and the Federal Trade Commission Act. To discourage price fixing, both companies and individual managers are held responsible. Some executives have already gone to jail!

Price fixing laws in the United States focus on protecting customers who purchase directly from a supplier. For example, a wholesaler could bring action against a producer-supplier for fixing prices. However, retailers or consumers who bought the producer's products from the wholesaler could not bring action. In contrast, many state laws allow "indirect customers" in the channel to sue the price fixer. A 1989 Supreme Court ruling cleared the way for more states to pass this type of law. The expected result will be even tougher penalties for price fixing.[24]

Different countries have different rules concerning price fixing, and this has created problems in international trade. Japan, for example, allows price fixing under certain conditions—especially if it strengthens the position of Japanese producers in world markets.

U.S. antimonopoly laws ban price discrimination unless . . .

Price level and price flexibility policies can lead to price discrimination. The **Robinson-Patman Act** (of 1936) makes illegal any **price discrimination**—selling the same products to different buyers at different prices—*if it injures competition.* The law does permit some price differences—but they must be based on (1) cost differences or (2) the need to meet competition. Both buyers and sellers are considered guilty if they know they're entering into discriminatory agreements. This is a serious matter—price discrimination suits are common.

What does "like grade and quality" mean?

The Robinson-Patman Act allows a marketing manager to charge different prices for similar products if they are *not* of "like grade and quality." But how similar can products be without being considered of like grade and quality? The FTC says that if the physical characteristics of a product are similar, then they are of like grade and quality. A landmark U.S. Supreme Court ruling against the Borden Company upheld the FTC's view. The Court held that a well-known label *alone* does not make a product different from one with an unknown label. The issue was rather clear-cut in the Borden case. The company agreed that the physical characteristics of the canned milk it sold at different prices under different labels were basically the same.

But the FTC's victory in the Borden case was not complete. The U.S. Supreme Court agreed with the FTC in the Borden case with respect to like grade and quality. However, it sent the case back to the U.S. Court of Appeals to determine whether the price difference actually injured competition—which the law also requires. The appeals court found no evidence of injury and further noted that there could be no injury unless Borden's price differential exceeded the "recognized consumer appeal of the Borden label." How to measure "consumer appeal" was not spelled out and may lead to additional suits. Eventually, what the consumer thinks about the product may be the deciding factor. For now, however, producers who want to sell several brands—or dealer brands at lower prices than their main brand—probably should offer physical differences—and differences that are really useful.[25]

Can cost analysis justify price differences?

The Robinson-Patman Act allows price differences if there are cost differences—say, for larger quantity shipments or because middlemen take over some of the physical distribution functions. But justifying cost differences is a difficult job. And the justification must be developed *before* different prices are set. The seller can't wait until a competitor, disgruntled customer, or the FTC brings a charge. At that point, it's too late.[26]

Can you legally meet price cuts?

Under the Robinson-Patman Act, meeting a competitor's price is permitted as a defense in price discrimination cases. A major objective of antimonopoly laws is to protect competition—not competitors. And "meeting competition in good faith" still seems to be legal.

Special promotion allowances might not be allowed

Some firms violate the Robinson-Patman Act by providing push money, advertising allowances, and other promotion aids to some customers and not others. The act prohibits such special allowances—*unless they are made available to all customers on "proportionately equal" terms*.

The need for such a rule is clear—once you try to control price discrimination. Allowances for promotion aid could be granted to retailers or wholesalers without expecting that any promotion actually be done. This plainly is price discrimination in disguise.

The law does cause hardships, however. Sometimes it's difficult to provide allowances on proportionately equal terms to both large and small customers. And it may also be difficult to determine exactly who competing customers are.[27]

How to avoid discriminating

Because price discrimination laws are complicated—and penalties for violations heavy—many business managers deemphasize price as a marketing variable. They follow the safest course by offering few or no quantity discounts—and the same cost-based prices to *all* customers. Perhaps this is *too* conservative a reaction. But when firms consider price differences, they may need a lawyer involved in the discussion!

CONCLUSION

The Price variable offers an alert marketing manager many possibilities for varying marketing mixes. What pricing policies should be used depends on the pricing objectives. We looked at profit-oriented, sales-oriented, and status quo–oriented objectives.

A marketing manager must set policies about price flexibility, price levels over the product life cycle, who will pay the freight, and who will get discounts and allowances. While doing this, the manager should be aware of legislation that affects pricing policies.

In most cases, a marketing manager must set prices—that is, administer prices. Starting with a list price, a variety of discounts and allowances may be offered to adjust for the something being offered in the marketing mix.

Throughout this chapter, we talk about what may be included (or excluded) in the something—and what objectives a firm might set to guide its pricing policies. Price setting itself is not discussed. It will be covered in the next chapter—where we show ways to carry out the various pricing objectives and policies.

QUESTIONS AND PROBLEMS

1. Identify the strategy decisions a marketing manager must make in the Price area. Illustrate your answer for a local retailer.

2. How should the acceptance of a profit-oriented, a sales-oriented, or a status quo–oriented pricing objective affect the development of a company's marketing strategy? Illustrate for each.

3. Distinguish between one-price and flexible-price policies. Which is most appropriate for a hardware store? Why?

4. How would differences in exchange rates between different countries affect a firm's decisions concerning the use of flexible-price policies in different foreign markets?

5. Cite two examples of continuously selling above the market price. Describe the situations.

6. Explain the types of competitive situations that might lead to a meeting-competition pricing policy.

7. What pricing objective(s) is a skimming pricing policy most likely implementing? Is the same true for a penetration pricing policy? Which policy is probably most appropriate for each of the following products: (*a*) a new type of home lawn-sprinkling system, (*b*) a new skin patch drug to help smokers quit, (*c*) a videotape of a best-selling movie, and (*d*) a new children's toy?

8. Would consumers be better off if all nations dropped their antidumping laws? Explain your thinking.

9. How would our marketing system change if manufacturers were required to set fixed prices on *all* products sold at retail and *all* retailers were required to use these prices? Would a manufacturer's marketing mix be easier to develop? What kind of an operation would retailing be in this situation? Would consumers receive more or less service?

10. Is price discrimination involved if a large oil company sells gasoline to taxicab associations for resale to individual taxicab operators for 2½ cents a gallon less than the price charged to retail service stations? What happens if the cab associations resell gasoline not only to taxicab operators but to the general public as well?

11. Do stocking allowances increase or reduce conflict in a channel of distribution? Explain your thinking.

12. Are seasonal discounts appropriate in agricultural businesses (which are certainly seasonal)?

13. What are the effective annual interest rates for the following cash discount terms: (*a*) ⅟10, net 20; (*b*) 1/5, net 10; and (*c*) net 25?

14. Why would a manufacturer offer a rebate instead of lowering the suggested list price?

15. How can a marketing manager change a firm's F.O.B. terms to make an otherwise competitive marketing mix more attractive?

16. What type of geographic pricing policy is most appropriate for the following products (specify any assumptions necessary to obtain a definite answer): (*a*) a chemical by-product, (*b*) nationally advertised candy bars, (*c*) rebuilt auto parts, and (*d*) tricycles?

17. How would a ban on freight absorption (that is, requiring F.O.B factory pricing) affect a producer with substantial economies of scale in production?

SUGGESTED CASES

13. Paper Products Corporation
24. A1 Photo Processors, Inc.

25. Injection Mfg., Inc.

COMPUTER-AIDED PROBLEM

17. Cash Discounts

Joe Tulkin owns Tulkin Wholesale Co. He sells paper, tape, file folders, and other office supplies to about 120 retailers in nearby cities. His average retailer customer spends about $900 a month. When Tulkin started business in 1991, competing wholesalers were giving retailers invoice terms of 3/10, net 30. Tulkin never gave the issue much thought—he just used the same invoice terms when he billed customers. At that time, about half of his customers took the discount. Recently he noticed a change in the way his customers were paying their bills. Checking his records, he found that 90 percent of the retailers were taking the cash discount. With so many retailers taking the cash discount, it seems to have become a price reduction. In addition, Tulkin learned that other wholesalers were changing their invoice terms.

Tulkin decides he should rethink his invoice terms. He knows he could change the percent rate on the cash discount, the number of days the discount is offered, or the number of days before the face amount is due. Changing any of these—or any combination—will change the interest rate at which a buyer is, in effect, borrowing money if he does not take the discount. Tulkin decides that it will be easier to evaluate the effect of different invoice terms if he sets up a spreadsheet to let him change the terms and quickly see the effective interest rate for each change.

  a. With 90 percent of Tulkin's customers now taking the discount, what is the total monthly cash discount amount?

  b. If Tulkin changes his invoice terms to 1/5, net 20, what interest rate is each buyer paying by not taking the cash discount? With these terms, would fewer buyers be likely to take the discount? Why?

  c. Tulkin thinks 10 customers will switch to other wholesalers if he changes his invoice terms to 2/10, net 30, while 60 percent of the remaining customers will take the discount. What interest rate does a buyer pay by not taking this cash discount? For this situation, what will the total gross sales (total invoice) amount be? The total cash discount? The total net sales receipts after the total cash discount? Compare Tulkin's current situation with what will happen if he changes his invoice terms to 2/10, net 30.

For additional questions related to this problem, see Exercise 17–3 in the *Learning Aid for Use with Basic Marketing*, 12th edition.

Appendix B

Marketing Arithmetic

When You Finish This Appendix, You Should

1. Understand the components of an operating statement (profit and loss statement).

2. Know how to compute the stockturn rate.

3. Understand how operating ratios can help analyze a business.

4. Understand how to calculate markups and markdowns.

5. Understand how to calculate return on investment (ROI) and return on assets (ROA).

6. Understand the important new terms (shown in red).

Marketing students must become familiar with the essentials of the language of business. Business people commonly use accounting terms when talking about costs, prices, and profit. And using accounting data is a practical tool in analyzing marketing problems.

THE OPERATING STATEMENT

An **operating statement** is a simple summary of the financial results of a company's operations over a specified period of time. Some beginning students may feel that the operating statement is complex, but as we'll soon see, this really isn't true. *The main purpose of the operating statement is determining the net profit figure—and presenting data to support that figure.* This is why the operating statement is often referred to as the *profit and loss statement.*

Exhibit B–1 shows an operating statement for a wholesale or retail business. The statement is complete and detailed so you will see the framework throughout the discussion, but the amount of detail on an operating statement is *not* standardized. Many companies use financial statements with much less detail than this one. They emphasize clarity and readability rather than detail. To really understand an operating statement, however, you must know about its components.

Only three basic components

The basic components of an operating statement are *sales*—which come from the sale of goods and services; *costs*—which come from the making and selling process; and the balance—called *profit or loss*—which is just the difference between sales and costs. So there are only three basic components in the statement: sales, costs, and profit (or loss). Other items on an operating statement are there only to provide supporting details.

Time period covered may vary

There is no one time period an operating statement covers. Rather, statements are prepared to satisfy the needs of a particular business. This may be at the end of each day or at the end of each week. Usually, however, an operating statement summarizes results for one month, three months, six months, or a full year. Since the time period does vary, this information is included in the heading of the statement as follows:

SMITH COMPANY
Operating Statement
For the (Period) Ended (Date)

Also, see Exhibit B–1.

Management uses of operating statements

Before going on to a more detailed discussion of the components of our operating statement, let's think about some of the uses for such a statement. Exhibit B–1 shows that a lot of information is presented in a clear and concise manner. With this information, a manager can easily find the relation of net sales to the cost of sales, the gross margin, expenses, and net profit. Opening and closing inventory figures are available—as is the amount spent during the period for the purchase of goods for resale. Total expenses are listed to make it easier to compare them with previous statements—and to help control these expenses.

EXHIBIT B–1   An Operating Statement (profit and loss statement)

Smith Company			
Operating Statement			
For the Year Ended December 31, 199X			

Gross sales			$540,000
Less: Returns and allowances			40,000
Net sales			$500,000
Cost of sales:			
Beginning inventory at cost		$ 80,000	
Purchases at billed cost	$310,000		
Less: Purchase discounts	40,000		
Purchases at net cost	270,000		
Plus freight-in	20,000		
Net cost of delivered purchases		290,000	
Cost of products available for sale		370,000	
Less: Ending inventory at cost		70,000	
Cost of sales			300,000
Gross margin (gross profit)			200,000
Expenses:			
Selling expenses:			
Sales salaries	60,000		
Advertising expense	20,000		
Delivery expense	20,000		
Total selling expense		100,000	
Administrative expense:			
Office salaries	30,000		
Office supplies	10,000		
Miscellaneous administrative expense	5,000		
Total administrative expense		45,000	
General expense:			
Rent expense	10,000		
Miscellaneous general expenses	5,000		
Total general expense		15,000	
Total expenses			160,000
Net profit from operation			$ 40,000

All this information is important to a company's managers. Assume that a particular company prepares monthly operating statements. A series of these statements is a valuable tool for directing and controlling the business. By comparing results from one month to the next, managers can uncover unfavorable trends in the sales, costs, or profit areas of the business—and take any needed action.

A skeleton statement gets down to essential details

Let's refer to Exhibit B–1 and begin to analyze this seemingly detailed statement to get first-hand knowledge of the components of the operating statement.

As a first step, suppose we take all the items that have dollar amounts extended to the third, or right-hand, column. Using these items only, the operating statement looks like this:

Gross sales...	$540,000
Less: Returns and allowances......................	40,000
Net sales..	500,000
Less: Cost of sales	300,000
Gross margin	200,000
Less: Total expenses...............................	160,000
Net profits (loss)	$ 40,000

Is this a complete operating statement? The answer is **yes.** This skeleton statement differs from Exhibit B–1 only in supporting detail. All the basic components are included. In fact, the only items we must list to have a complete operating statement are:

Net sales...	$500,000
Less: Costs..	460,000
Net profit (loss)	$ 40,000

These three items are the essentials of an operating statement. All other subdivisions or details are just useful additions.

Meaning of sales

Now let's define the meaning of the terms in the skeleton statement.

The first item is sales. What do we mean by sales? The term **gross sales** is the total amount charged to all customers during some time period. However, there is always some customer dissatisfaction—or just plain errors in ordering and shipping goods. This results in returns and allowances—which reduce gross sales.

A **return** occurs when a customer sends back purchased products. The company either refunds the purchase price or allows the customer dollar credit on other purchases.

An **allowance** occurs when a customer is not satisfied with a purchase for some reason. The company gives a price reduction on the original invoice (bill), but the customer keeps the goods and services.

These refunds and price reductions must be considered when the firm computes its net sales figure for the period. Really, we're only interested in the revenue the company manages to keep. This is **net sales**—the actual sales dollars the company receives. Therefore, all reductions, refunds, cancellations, and so forth made because of returns and allowances—are deducted from the original total (gross sales) to get net sales. This is shown below:

Gross sales..	$540,000
Less: Returns and allowances.......................	40,000
Net sales...	$500,000

Meaning of cost of sales

The next item in the operating statement—**cost of sales**—is the total value (at cost) of the sales during the period. We'll discuss this computation later. Meanwhile, note that after we obtain the cost of sales figure, we subtract it from the net sales figure to get the gross margin.

Meaning of gross margin and expenses

Gross margin (gross profit) is the money left to cover the expenses of selling the products and operating the business. Firms hope that a profit will be left after subtracting these expenses.

Selling expense is commonly the major expense below the gross margin. Note that in Exhibit B–1, **expenses** are all the remaining costs subtracted from the gross margin to get the net profit. The expenses in this case are the selling, administrative, and general expenses. (Note that the cost of purchases and cost of sales are not included in this total expense figure—they were subtracted from net sales earlier to get the gross margin. Note, also, that some accountants refer to cost of sales as cost of goods sold.)

Net profit—at the bottom of the statement—is what the company earned from its operations during a particular period. It is the amount left after the cost of sales and the expenses are subtracted from net sales. *Net sales and net profit are not the same*. Many firms have large sales and no profits—they may even have losses! That's why understanding costs—and controlling them—is important.

DETAILED ANALYSIS OF SECTIONS OF THE OPERATING STATEMENT

Cost of sales for a wholesale or retail company

The cost of sales section includes details that are used to find the cost of sales ($300,000 in our example).

In Exhibit B–1, you can see that beginning and ending inventory, purchases, purchase discounts, and freight-in are all necessary to calculate costs of sales. If we pull the cost of sales section from the operating statement, it looks like this:

Cost of sales:		
Beginning inventory at cost		$ 80,000
Purchases at billed cost...........................	$310,000	
Less: Purchase discounts.......................	40,000	
Purchases at net cost..............................	270,000	
Plus: Freight-in..................................	20,000	
Net cost of delivered purchases		290,000
Cost of goods available for sale		370,000
Less: Ending inventory at cost		70,000
Cost of sales.......................................		$300,000

Cost of sales is the cost value of what is *sold*—not the cost of goods on hand at any given time.

Inventory figures merely show the cost of goods on hand at the beginning and end of the period the statement covers. These figures may be obtained by physically counting goods on hand on these dates—or estimated from perpetual inventory records that show the inventory balance at any given time. The methods used to determine the inventory should be as accurate as possible because these figures affect the cost of sales during the period—and net profit.

The net cost of delivered purchases must include freight charges and purchase discounts received since these items affect the money actually spent to buy goods and bring them to the place of business. A **purchase discount** is a reduction of the original invoice amount for some business reason. For example, a cash discount may be given for prompt payment of the amount due. We subtract the total of such discounts from the original invoice cost of purchases to get the *net* cost of purchases. To this figure we add the freight charges for bringing the goods to the place of business. This gives the net cost of *delivered* purchases. When we add the net cost of delivered purchases to the beginning inventory at cost, we have the total cost of goods available for sale during the period. If we now subtract the ending inventory at cost from the cost of the goods available for sale, we get the cost of sales.

One important point should be noted about cost of sales. The way the value of inventory is calculated varies from one company to another—and can cause big differences in the cost of sales and the operating statement. (See any basic accounting textbook for how the various inventory valuation methods work.)

Cost of sales for a manufacturing company

Exhibit B–1 shows the way the manager of a wholesale or retail business arrives at his cost of sales. Such a business *purchases* finished products and resells them. In a manufacturing company, the purchases section of this operating statement is replaced by a section called cost of production. This section includes purchases of raw materials and parts, direct and indirect labor costs, and factory overhead charges (such as heat, light, and power) that are necessary to produce finished products. The cost of production is added to the beginning finished products inventory to arrive at the cost of products available for sale. Often, a separate cost of production statement is prepared, and only the total cost of production is shown in the operating statement. See Exhibit B–2 for an illustration of the cost of sales section of an operating statement for a manufacturing company.

Expenses

Expenses go below the gross margin. They usually include the costs of selling and the costs of administering the business. They do not include the cost of sales—either purchased or produced.

There is no right method for classifying the expense accounts or arranging them on the operating statement. They can just as easily be arranged alphabetically or according to amount, with the largest placed at the top and so on down the line. In a business of any size, though, it is clearer to group the expenses in some way and use subtotals by groups for analysis and control purposes. This was done in Exhibit B–1.

Summary on operating statements

The statement presented in Exhibit B–1 contains all the major categories in an operating statement—together with a normal amount of supporting detail.

EXHIBIT B–2   Cost of Sales Section of an Operating Statement for a Manufacturing Firm

Cost of sales:			
Finished products inventory (beginning)		$ 20,000	
Cost of production (Schedule 1)		100,000	
Total cost of finished products available for sale . .		120,000	
Less: Finished products inventory (ending)		30,000	
Cost of sales			$ 90,000
Schedule 1, Schedule of cost of production			
Beginning work in process inventory			15,000
Raw materials:			
Beginning raw materials inventory		10,000	
Net cost of delivered purchases		80,000	
Total cost of materials available for use		90,000	
Less: Ending raw materials inventory		15,000	
Cost of materials placed in production		75,000	
Direct labor		20,000	
Manufacturing expenses:			
Indirect labor	$4,000		
Maintenance and repairs	3,000		
Factory supplies	1,000		
Heat, light, and power	2,000		
Total manufacturing expenses		10,000	
Total manufacturing costs			105,000
Total work in process during period			120,000
Less: Ending work in process inventory			20,000
Cost of production			$100,000

Further detail can be added to the statement under any of the major categories without changing the nature of the statement. The amount of detail normally is determined by how the statement will be used. A stockholder may be given a sketchy operating statement—while the one prepared for internal company use may have a lot of detail.

COMPUTING THE STOCKTURN RATE

A detailed operating statement can provide the data needed to compute the **stockturn rate**—a measure of the number of times the average inventory is sold during a year. Note that the stockturn rate is related to the *turnover during a year*—not the length of time covered by a particular operating statement.

The stockturn rate is a very important measure because it shows how rapidly the firm's inventory is moving. Some businesses typically have slower turnover than others. But a drop in turnover in a particular business can be very alarming. It may mean that the firm's assortment of products is no longer as attractive as it was. Also, it may mean that the firm will need more working capital to handle the same volume of sales. Most businesses pay a lot of attention to the stockturn rate—trying to get faster turnover (and lower inventory costs).

Three methods—all basically similar—can be used to compute the stockturn rate. Which method is used depends on the data available. These three methods—which usually give approximately the same results—are shown below.*

(1) $$\frac{\text{Cost of sales}}{\text{Average inventory at cost}}$$

(2) $$\frac{\text{Net sales}}{\text{Average inventory at selling price}}$$

(3) $$\frac{\text{Sales in units}}{\text{Average inventory in units}}$$

Computing the stockturn rate will be illustrated only for Formula 1 since all are similar. The only difference is that the cost figures used in Formula 1 are changed to a selling price or numerical count basis in Formulas 2 and 3. Note: Regardless of the method used, you must have both the numerator and denominator of the formula in the same terms.

If the inventory level varies a lot during the year, you may need detailed information about the inventory level at different times to compute the average inventory. If it stays at about the same level during the year, however, it's easy to get an estimate. For example, using Formula 1, the average inventory at cost is computed by adding the beginning and ending inventories at cost and dividing by 2. This average inventory figure is then divided into the cost of sales (in cost terms) to get the stockturn rate.

For example, suppose that the cost of sales for one year was $1,000,000. Beginning inventory was $250,000 and ending inventory $150,000. Adding the two inventory figures and dividing by 2, we get an average inventory of $200,000. We next divide the cost of sales by the average inventory ($1,000,000 ÷ $200,000) and get a stockturn rate of 5. The stockturn rate is covered further in Chapter 18.

OPERATING RATIOS ANALYZE THE BUSINESS

Many business people use the operating statement to calculate **operating ratios**—the ratios of items on the operating statement to net sales—and compare these ratios from one time period to another. They can also compare their own operating ratios with those of competitors. Such competitive data is often available through trade associations. Each firm may report its results to a trade association, which then distributes summary results to its members. These ratios help managers control their operations. If some expense ratios are rising, for example, those particular costs are singled out for special attention.

Operating ratios are computed by dividing net sales into the various operating statement items that appear below the net sales level in the operating statement. The net sales is used as the denominator in the operating ratio because it shows the sales the firm actually won.

---

*Differences occur because of varied markups and nonhomogeneous product assortments. In an assortment of tires, for example, those with low markups might have sold much better than those with high markups. But with Formula 3, all tires would be treated equally.

We can see the relation of operating ratios to the operating statement if we think of there being another column to the right of the dollar figures in an operating statement. This column contains percentage figures—using net sales as 100 percent. This approach can be seen below:

Gross sales...	$540,000	
Less: Returns and allowances	40,000	
Net sales...	500,000	100%
Cost of sales	300,000	60
Gross margin	200,000	40
Expenses...	160,000	32
Net profit	$ 40,000	8%

The 40 percent ratio of gross margin to net sales in the above example shows that 40 percent of the net sales dollar is available to cover sales expenses and administering the business—and provide a profit. Note that the ratio of expenses to sales added to the ratio of profit to sales equals the 40 percent gross margin ratio. The net profit ratio of 8 percent shows that 8 percent of the net sales dollar is left for profit.

The value of percentage ratios should be obvious. The percentages are easily figured—and much easier to compare than large dollar figures.

Note that because these operating statement categories are interrelated, only a few pieces of information are needed to figure the others. In this case, for example, knowing the gross margin percent and net profit percent makes it possible to figure the expenses and cost of sales percentages. Further, knowing just one dollar amount and the percentages lets you figure all the other dollar amounts.

MARKUPS

A **markup** is the dollar amount added to the cost of sales to get the selling price. The markup usually is similar to the firm's gross margin because the markup amount added onto the unit cost of a product by a retailer or wholesaler is expected to cover the selling and administrative expenses—and to provide a profit.

The markup approach to pricing is discussed in Chapter 18, so it will not be discussed at length here. But a simple example illustrates the idea. If a retailer buys an article that costs $1 when delivered to his store, he must sell it for more than this cost if he hopes to make a profit. So he might add 50 cents onto the cost of the article to cover his selling and other costs and, hopefully, to provide a profit. The 50 cents is the markup.

The 50 cents is also the gross margin or gross profit from that item *if* it is sold. But note that it is *not* the net profit. Selling expenses may amount to 35 cents, 45 cents, or even 55 cents. In other words, there is no guarantee the markup will cover costs. Further, there is no guarantee customers will buy at the marked-up price. This may require markdowns, which are discussed later in this appendix.

Markup conversions

Often it is convenient to use markups as percentages rather than focusing on the actual dollar amounts. But markups can be figured as a percent of cost or selling price. To have some agreement, *markup (percent)* will mean percentage of selling price unless stated otherwise. So the 50-cent markup on the $1.50 selling price is a markup of 33⅓ percent. On the other hand, the 50-cent markup is a 50 percent markup on cost.

Some retailers and wholesalers use markup conversion tables or spreadsheets to easily convert from cost to selling price—depending on the markup on selling price they want. To see the interrelation, look at the two formulas below. They can be used to convert either type of markup to the other.

$$(4) \quad \frac{\text{Percent markup}}{\text{on selling price}} = \frac{\text{Percent markup on cost}}{100\% + \text{Percent markup on cost}}$$

$$(5) \quad \frac{\text{Percent markup}}{\text{on cost}} = \frac{\text{Percent markup on selling price}}{100\% - \text{Percent markup on selling price}}$$

In the previous example, we had a cost of $1, a markup of 50 cents, and a selling price of $1.50. We saw that the markup on selling price was 33⅓ percent—and on cost, it was 50 percent. Let's substitute these percentage figures—in Formulas 4 and 5—to see how to convert from one basis to the other. Assume first of all that we only know the markup on selling price and want to convert to markup on cost. Using Formula 5, we get:

$$\text{Percent markup on cost} = \frac{33\frac{1}{3}\%}{100\% - 33\frac{1}{3}\%} = \frac{33\frac{1}{3}\%}{66\frac{2}{3}\%} = 50\%$$

On the other hand, if we know only the percent markup on cost, we can convert to markup on selling price as follows:

$$\text{Percent markup on selling price} = \frac{50\%}{100\% + 50\%} = \frac{50\%}{150\%} = 33\frac{1}{3}\%$$

These results can be proved and summarized as follows:

Markup $0.50 = 50\%$ of cost, or 33⅓% of selling price
+ Cost $1.00 = 100\%$ of cost, or 66⅔% of selling price
Selling price $1.50 = 150\%$ of cost, or 100% of selling price

It is important to see that only the percentage figures change while the money amounts of cost, markup, and selling price stay the same. Note, too, that when selling price is the base for the calculation (100 percent), then the cost percentage plus the markup percentage equal 100 percent. But when the cost of the product is used as the base figure (100 percent), the selling price percentage must be greater than 100 percent by the markup on cost.

MARKDOWN RATIOS HELP CONTROL RETAIL OPERATIONS

The ratios we discussed above were concerned with figures on the operating statement. Another important ratio—the **markdown ratio**—is a tool many retailers use to measure the efficiency of various departments and their whole business. But note that it is *not directly related to the operating statement*. It requires special calculations.

A **markdown** is a retail price reduction required because customers won't buy some item at the originally marked-up price. This refusal to buy may be due to a variety of reasons—soiling, style changes, fading, damage caused by handling, or an original price that was too high. To get rid of these products, the retailer offers them at a lower price.

Markdowns are generally considered to be due to business errors—perhaps because of poor buying, original markups that are too high, and other reasons. (Note, however, that some retailers use markdowns as a way of doing business rather than a way to correct errors. For example, a store that buys out overstocked fashions from other retailers may start by marking each item with a high price and then reduce the price each week until it sells.) Regardless of the reason, however, markdowns are reductions in the original price—and they are important to managers who want to measure the effectiveness of their operations.

Markdowns are similar to allowances because price reductions are made. Thus, in computing a markdown ratio, markdowns and allowances are usually added together and then divided by net sales. The markdown ratio is computed as follows:

$$\text{Markdown \%} = \frac{\$\,\text{Markdowns} + \$\,\text{Allowances}}{\$\,\text{Net sales}} \times 100$$

The 100 is multiplied by the fraction to get rid of decimal points.

Returns are *not* included when figuring the markdown ratio. Returns are treated as consumer errors—not business errors—and therefore are not included in this measure of business efficiency.

Retailers who use markdown ratios usually keep a record of the amount of markdowns and allowances in each department and then divide the total by the net sales in each department. Over a period of time, these ratios give management one measure of the efficiency of buyers and salespeople in various departments.

It should be stressed again that the markdown ratio is not calculated directly from data on the operating statement since the markdowns take place before the products are sold. In fact, some products may be marked down and still not sold. Even if the marked-down items are not sold, the markdowns—that is, the reevaluations of their value—are included in the calculations in the time period when they are taken.

The markdown ratio is calculated for a whole department (or profit center)—*not* individual items. What we are seeking is a measure of the effectiveness of a whole department—not how well the department did on individual items.

RETURN ON INVESTMENT (ROI) REFLECTS ASSET USE

Another off-the-operating-statement ratio is **return on investment (ROI)**—the ratio of net profit (after taxes) to the investment used to make the net profit, multiplied by 100 to get rid of decimals. Investment is not shown on the operating statement. But it is on the **balance sheet** (statement of financial condition)—another accounting statement—that shows a company's assets, liabilities, and net worth. It may take some digging or special analysis, however, to find the right investment number.

Investment means the dollar resources the firm has invested in a project or business. For example, a new product may require $4 million in new money—for inventory, accounts receivable, promotion, and so on—and its attractiveness may be judged by its likely ROI. If the net profit (after taxes) for this new product is expected to be $1 million in the first year, then the ROI is 25 percent—that is, ($1 million ÷ $4 million) × 100.

There are two ways to figure ROI. The *direct* way is:

$$ROI \ (in \ \%) = \frac{Net \ profit \ (after \ taxes)}{Investment} \times 100$$

The *indirect* way is:

$$ROI \ (in \ \%) = \frac{Net \ profit \ (after \ taxes)}{Sales} \times \frac{Sales}{Investment} \times 100$$

This way is concerned with net profit margin and turnover—that is:

$$ROI \ (in \ \%) = Net \ profit \ margin \times Turnover \times 100$$

This indirect way makes it clearer how to *increase* ROI. There are three ways:

1. Increase profit margin (with lower costs or a higher price).
2. Increase sales.
3. Decrease investment.

Effective marketing strategy planning and implementation can increase profit margins and/or sales. And careful asset management can decrease investment.

ROI is a revealing measure of how well managers are doing. Most companies have alternative uses for their funds. If the returns in a business aren't at least as high as outside uses, then the money probably should be shifted to the more profitable uses.

Some firms borrow more than others to make investments. In other words, they invest less of their own money to acquire assets—what we called investments. If ROI calculations use only the firm's own investment, this gives higher ROI figures to those who borrow a lot—which is called leveraging. To adjust for different borrowing proportions—to make comparisons among projects, departments, divisions, and companies easier—another ratio has come into use. **Return on assets (ROA)** is the ratio of net profit (after taxes) to the assets used to make the net profit—times 100. Both ROI and ROA measures are trying to get at the same thing—how effectively the company is using resources. These measures became increasingly popular as profit rates dropped and it became more obvious that increasing sales volume doesn't necessarily lead to higher profits—or ROI or ROA. Inflation and higher costs for borrowed funds also force more concern for ROI and ROA. Marketers must include these measures in their thinking or top managers are likely to ignore their plans—and requests for financial resources.

QUESTIONS AND PROBLEMS

1. Distinguish between the following pairs of items that appear on operating statements: (*a*) gross sales and net sales, and (*b*) purchases at billed cost and purchases at net cost.

2. How does gross margin differ from gross profit? From net profit?

3. Explain the similarity between markups and gross margin. What connection do markdowns have with the operating statement?

4. Compute the net profit for a company with the following data:

Beginning inventory (cost)	$ 150,000
Purchases at billed cost	330,000
Sales returns and allowances...........	250,000
Rent	60,000
Salaries	400,000
Heat and light.........................	180,000
Ending inventory (cost).................	250,000
Freight cost (inbound)	80,000
Gross sales...........................	1,300,000

5. Construct an operating statement from the following data:

Returns and allowances................	$ 150,000
Expenses..............................	20%
Closing inventory at cost	600,000
Markdowns	2%
Inward transportation..................	30,000
Purchases.............................	1,000,000
Net profit (5%)	300,000

6. Compute net sales and percent of markdowns for the data given below:

Markdowns	$ 40,000
Gross sales...........................	400,000
Returns	32,000
Allowances	48,000

7. (*a*) What percentage markups on cost are equivalent to the following percentage markups on selling price: 20, 37½, 50, and 66⅔? (*b*) What percentage markups on selling price are equivalent to the following percentage markups on cost: 33⅓, 20, 40, and 50?

8. What net sales volume is required to obtain a stockturn rate of 20 times a year on an average inventory at cost of $100,000 with a gross margin of 25 percent?

9. Explain how the general manager of a department store might use the markdown ratios computed for her various departments. Is this a fair measure? Of what?

10. Compare and contrast return on investment (ROI) and return on assets (ROA) measures. Which would be best for a retailer with no bank borrowing or other outside sources of funds, that is, the retailer has put up all the money that the business needs?

18

Price Setting in the Business World

Wal-Mart is growing fast—very fast—and by the year 2000 sales should exceed $200 billion. To put that growth in perspective, Wal-Mart's sales were about $25 billion in 1990; by 1995 they had grown to about $100 billion—or double the sales of its closest competitor, Kmart.

There are many similarities between Wal-Mart and Kmart, but there are also differences. And one of the important differences is that Wal-Mart generally has lower prices. You can see the impact of this price difference most clearly by looking back just a few years to 1991. At that point, sales for both chains were about equal, but Wal-Mart's profits were double Kmart's profits. It's useful to consider how Wal-Mart could earn higher profits when it had about the same total sales as Kmart and at the same time was selling at lower prices.

Part of the answer is that Wal-Mart has more sales volume in each store. Wal-Mart's $300 sales per square foot figure is more than twice the sales per square foot at Kmart. Wal-Mart is getting more sales in each store because it offers lower prices on similar products. That increases demand for its offering. But it also reduces its fixed operating costs as a percentage of sales. On average, that means it can add a smaller markup, still cover its operating expenses, and make a larger profit. And as lower prices pull in more customers, its percent of overhead costs to sales continues to drop—from about 20.2 percent in 1980 to about 17 percent now.

Wal-Mart also has lower costs for the goods it sells. Its buyers are tough in negotiating prices with their suppliers—since they want to be able to offer customers the brands they want at low prices. But Wal-Mart also works closely with producers to reduce costs in the channel. For example, Wal-Mart was one of the first major retailers to insist that all orders be placed by computer; that helps to reduce stock-outs on store shelves and lost sales at the checkout counter.

Even with its lower costs, Wal-Mart isn't content to take the convenient route to price setting by just adding a standard percentage markup on different items. The company was one of the first retailers to install computerized checkout counters that gave managers in every department in every store detailed information about what was selling and what was not. They dropped items that were collecting dust and put even lower prices on the items with the fastest turnover. That further reduced selling costs because it cut inventory carrying costs. At the same time, it increased demand. Wal-Mart also works with vendors to create private-label brands, such as Sam's Choice Cola. Its low price—about 15 percent below what consumers expect to pay for well-known colas—doesn't leave a big profit margin. Yet, when customers come in to buy it they also pick up other—more profitable—products.

Every department manager in every Wal-Mart store has a list of special VPIs (volume producing items). For example, Equate Baby Oil is a VPI in the pharmacy area. Managers and salespeople in the store give VPIs special attention and display space—to get a bigger sales and profit boost.

To continue its growth, Wal-Mart is aggressively developing new superstores, which offer low prices on groceries as well as on Wal-Mart's traditional product lines. The discount stores that Wal-Mart has already converted to superstores are generating sales increases of about 30 to 50 percent. Further, Wal-Mart is taking its low-price approach to other countries—ranging from Mexico to Hong Kong.[1]

PRICE SETTING IS A KEY STRATEGY DECISION

In the last chapter, we discussed the idea that pricing objectives and policies should guide pricing decisions. We accepted the idea of a list price and went on to discuss variations from list. Now, we'll see how the basic list price is set in the first place—based on information about costs, demand, and profit margins. See Exhibit 18–1.

EXHIBIT 18–1 Key Factors That Influence Price Setting

Many firms set a price by just adding a standard markup to the average cost of the products they sell. But this is changing. More managers are realizing that they should set prices by evaluating the effect of a price decision not only on profit margin for a given item but also on demand and therefore on sales volume and costs. In Wal-Mart's very competitive markets, this approach often leads to low prices that increase profits *and* at the same time reduce customers' costs. For other firms in different market situations, careful price setting leads to a premium price for a marketing mix that offers customers something unique. But these firms commonly focus on setting prices that earn attractive profits—as part of an overall marketing strategy that meets customers' needs.

There are many ways to set list prices. But—for simplicity—they can be reduced to two basic approaches: *cost-oriented* and *demand-oriented* price setting. We will discuss cost-oriented approaches first because they are most common. Also, understanding the problems of relying only on a cost-oriented approach shows why a marketing manager must also consider demand to make good price decisions. Let's begin by looking at how most retailers and wholesalers set cost-oriented prices.

SOME FIRMS JUST USE MARKUPS

Markups guide pricing by middlemen

Some firms—including most retailers and wholesalers—set prices by using a **markup**—a dollar amount added to the cost of products to get the selling price. For example, suppose that a Revco drugstore buys a bottle of Prell shampoo for $1. To make a profit, the drugstore obviously must sell the shampoo for more than $1. If it adds 50 cents to cover operating expenses and provide a profit, we say that the store is marking up the item 50 cents.

Markups, however, usually are stated as percentages rather than dollar amounts. And this is where confusion sometimes arises. Is a markup of 50 cents on a cost of $1 a markup of 50 percent? Or should the markup be figured as a percentage of the selling price—$1.50—and therefore be 33⅓ percent? A clear definition is necessary.

Markup percent is based on selling price—a convenient rule

Unless otherwise stated, **markup (percent)** means percentage of selling price that is added to the cost to get the selling price. So the 50-cent markup on the $1.50 selling price is a markup of 33⅓ percent. Markups are related to selling price for convenience.

There's nothing wrong with the idea of markup on cost. However, to avoid confusion, it's important to state clearly which markup percent you're using.

Managers often want to change a markup on cost to one based on selling price—or vice versa. The calculations used to do this are simple (see the section on markup conversion in Appendix B on marketing arithmetic).[2]

Many use a "standard" markup percent

Many middlemen select a standard markup percent and then apply it to all their products. This makes pricing easier. When you think of the large number of items the average retailer and wholesaler carry—and the small sales volume of any one item—this approach may make sense. Spending the time to find the best price to charge on every item in stock (day to day or week to week) might not pay.

Moreover, different companies in the same line of business often use the same markup percent. There is a reason for this: their operating expenses are usually

Many drugstores carry gardening supplies, such as Ortho insecticides; however, because the turnover on these products is likely to be lower than for many other drugstore items, the drugstore is likely to use a higher markup.

similar. So a standard markup is acceptable as long as it's large enough to cover the firm's operating expenses—and provide a reasonable profit.

Markups are related to gross margins

How does a manager decide on a standard markup in the first place? A standard markup is often set close to the firm's *gross margin*. Managers regularly see gross margins on their operating (profit and loss) statements. The gross margin is the amount left—after subtracting the cost of sales (cost of goods sold) from net sales—to cover the expenses of selling products and operating the business. (See Appendix B on marketing arithmetic—it follows Chapter 17—if you are unfamiliar with these ideas.) Our Revco manager knows that there won't be any profit if the gross margin is not large enough. For this reason, Revco might accept a markup percent on Prell shampoo that is close to the store's usual gross margin percent.

Smart producers pay attention to the gross margins and standard markups of middlemen in their channel. They usually allow trade (functional) discounts similar to the standard markups these middlemen expect.

Markup chain may be used in channel pricing

Different firms in a channel often use different markups. A **markup chain**—the sequence of markups firms use at different levels in a channel—determines the price structure in the whole channel. The markup is figured on the *selling price* at each level of the channel.

For example, Black & Decker's selling price for an electric drill becomes the cost the Ace Hardware wholesaler pays. The wholesaler's selling price becomes the hardware retailer's cost. And this cost plus a retail markup becomes the retail selling price. Each markup should cover the costs of running the business—and leave a profit.

Exhibit 18–2 illustrates the markup chain for an electric drill at each level of the channel system. The production (factory) cost of the drill is $21.60. In this case, the producer takes a 10 percent markup and sells the product for $24. The

EXHIBIT 18–2   Example of a Markup Chain and Channel Pricing

markup is 10 percent of $24 or $2.40. The producer's selling price now becomes the wholesaler's cost—$24. If the wholesaler is used to taking a 20 percent markup on selling price, the markup is $6—and the wholesaler's selling price becomes $30. $30 now becomes the cost for the hardware retailer. And a retailer who is used to a 40 percent markup adds $20, and the retail selling price becomes $50.

High markups don't always mean big profits

Some people—including many traditional retailers—think high markups mean big profits. Often this isn't true. A high markup may result in a price that's too high—a price at which few customers will buy. And you can't earn much if you don't sell much—no matter how high your markup. But many retailers and wholesalers seem more concerned with the size of their markup on a single item than with their total profit. And their high markups may lead to low profits—or even losses.

Lower markups can speed turnover—and the stockturn rate

Some retailers and wholesalers, however, try to speed turnover to increase profit—even if this means reducing their markups. They realize that a business runs up costs over time. If they can sell a much greater amount in the same time period, they may be able to take a lower markup—and still earn higher profits at the end of the period.

An important idea here is the **stockturn rate**—the number of times the average inventory is sold in a year. Various methods of figuring stockturn rates can be used (see the section "Computing the Stockturn Rate" in Appendix B). A low stockturn rate may be bad for profits.

At the very least, a low stockturn increases inventory carrying cost and ties up working capital. If a firm with a stockturn of 1 (once per year) sells products that cost it $100,000, it has that much tied up in inventory all the time. But a stockturn of 5 requires only $20,000 worth of inventory ($100,000 cost ÷ 5 turnovers a year).

Whether a stockturn rate is high or low depends on the industry and the product involved. A NAPA auto parts wholesaler may expect an annual rate of 1—while an A&P store might expect 10 to 12 stockturns for soaps and detergents and 50 to 60 stockturns for fresh fruits and vegetables.

Mass-merchandisers run in fast company

Although some middlemen use the same standard markup percent on all their products, this policy ignores the importance of fast turnover. Mass-merchandisers

This ad for Disney-character jewelry, targeted at retailers, emphasizes faster stockturn, which together with markups impacts profitability.

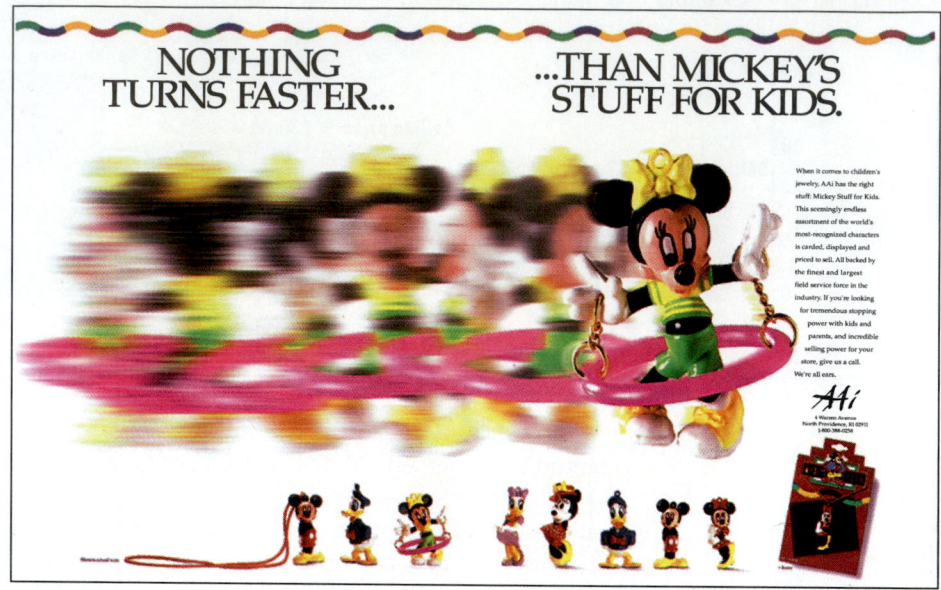

know this. They put low markups on fast-selling items and higher markups on items that sell less frequently. For example, Wal-Mart may put a small markup on fast-selling health and beauty aids (like toothpaste or shampoo) but higher markups on appliances and clothing. Similarly, supermarket operators put low markups on fast-selling items like milk, eggs, and detergents. The markup on these items may be less than half the average markup for all grocery items, but this doesn't mean they're unprofitable. The store earns the small profit per unit more often.

Where does the markup chain start?

Some markups eventually become standard in a trade. Most channel members tend to follow a similar process—adding a certain percentage to the previous price. But who sets price in the first place?

The firm that brands a product is usually the one that sets its basic list price. It may be a large retailer, a large wholesaler, or, most often, the producer.

Some producers just start with a cost per unit figure and add a markup— perhaps a standard markup—to obtain their selling price. Or they may use some rule-of-thumb formula such as:

$$\text{Selling price} = \text{Average production cost per unit} \times 3$$

A producer who uses this approach might develop rules and markups related to its own costs and objectives. Yet even the first step—selecting the appropriate cost per unit to build on—isn't easy. Let's discuss several approaches to see how cost-oriented price setting really works.

AVERAGE-COST PRICING IS COMMON AND CAN BE DANGEROUS

Average-cost pricing means adding a reasonable markup to the average cost of a product. A manager usually finds the average cost per unit by studying past records. Dividing the total cost for the last year by all the units produced and sold in that period gives an estimate of the average cost per unit for the next year. If the cost was $32,000 for all labor and materials and $30,000 for fixed overhead expenses—such as selling expenses, rent, and manager salaries—then the total cost is $62,000. If the company produced 40,000 items in that time period, the average cost is $62,000 divided by 40,000 units, or $1.55 per unit. To get the price, the producer decides how much profit per unit to add to the average cost per unit. If the company considers 45 cents a reasonable profit for each unit, it sets the new price at $2.00. Exhibit 18–3A shows that this approach produces the desired profit—if the company sells 40,000 units.

It does not make allowances for cost variations as output changes

Average-cost pricing is simple. But it can also be dangerous. It's easy to lose money with average-cost pricing. To see why, let's follow this example further.

First, remember that the average cost of $2.00 per unit was based on output of 40,000 units. But if the firm is only able to produce and sell 20,000 units in the next year, it may be in trouble. Twenty thousand units sold at $2.00 each ($1.55 cost plus 45 cents for expected profit) yield a total revenue of only $40,000. The overhead is still fixed at $30,000, and the variable material and labor cost drops by half to $16,000—for a total cost of $46,000. This means a loss of $6,000, or 30 cents a unit. The method that was supposed to allow a profit of 45 cents a unit actually causes a loss of 30 cents a unit! See Exhibit 18–3B.

The basic problem with the average-cost approach is that it doesn't consider cost variations at different levels of output. In a typical situation, costs are high with low output, and then economies of scale set in—the average cost per unit drops as the quantity produced increases. This is why mass production and mass distribution often make sense. It's also why it's important to develop a better understanding of the different types of costs a marketing manager should consider when setting a price.

EXHIBIT 18–3 Results of Average-Cost Pricing

A. Calculation of Planned Profit if 40,000 Items Are Sold		B. Calculation of Actual Profit if Only 20,000 Items Are Sold	
Calculation of costs:		**Calculation of costs:**	
Fixed overhead expenses	$30,000	Fixed overhead expenses	$30,000
Labor and materials ($.80 a unit)	32,000	Labor and materials ($.80 a unit)	16,000
Total costs	$62,000	Total costs	$46,000
"Planned" profit	18,000		
Total costs and planned profit	$80,000		
Calculation of profit (or loss):		**Calculation of profit (or loss):**	
Actual unit sales × price ($2.00*)	$80,000	Actual unit sales × price ($2.00*)	$40,000
Minus: total costs	62,000	Minus: total costs	46,000
Profit (loss)	$18,000	Profit (loss)	($6,000)
Result:		**Result:**	
Planned profit of $18,000 is earned if 40,000 items are sold at $2.00 each.		Planned profit of $18,000 is not earned. Instead, $6,000 loss results if 20,000 items are sold at $2.00 each.	

*Calculation of "reasonable" price: $\dfrac{\text{Expected total costs and planned profit}}{\text{Planned number of items to be sold}} = \dfrac{\$80,000}{40,000} = \$2.00$

ARE WOMEN CONSUMERS BEING TAKEN TO THE CLEANERS?

Women have complained for years that they pay more than men for clothes alterations, dry cleaning, shirt laundering, and haircuts. For example, a laundry might charge $2.25 to launder a woman's white cotton shirt and charge only $1.25 for an identical shirt delivered by a man. Studies confirm that such differences in pricing for men and women are common. For example, a 1994 survey by a state agency in California found that of 25 randomly chosen dry cleaners, 64 percent charged more to launder women's cotton shirts than men's; 28 percent charged more to dry clean women's suits. And 40 percent of 25 hair salons surveyed charged more for basic women's haircuts.

Some consumers feel that such differences in pricing are unethical. Critics argue that firms are discriminating against women by arbitrarily charging them higher prices.

Not everyone shares this view. A spokesperson for an association of launderers and cleaners says that "the automated equipment we use fits a certain range of standardized shirts. A lot of women's blouses have different kinds of trim, different kinds of buttons, and lots of braid work, and it all has to be hand-finished. If it involves hand-finishing, we charge more." In other words, some cleaners charge more for doing women's blouses because the average cost is higher than the average cost for men's shirts. Of course, the cost of cleaning and ironing any specific shirt may not be higher or lower than the average.

There are no federal laws to regulate the prices that dry cleaners, hair salons, or tailors charge. However, city and state politicians in several areas have proposed ordinances that prohibit such discriminatory pricing based on gender. Still, most experts argue that such laws are unnecessary. After all, customers who don't like a particular cleaner's rates are free to visit a competitor who may charge less.

Many firms face the problem of how to set prices when the costs are different to serve different customers. For example, poor, inner-city consumers often pay higher prices for food. But inner-city retailers also face higher average costs for facilities, shoplifting, and insurance. Some firms don't like to charge different consumers different prices, but they also don't want to charge everyone a higher average price—to cover the expense of serving high-cost customers.[3]

MARKETING MANAGER MUST CONSIDER VARIOUS KINDS OF COSTS

Average-cost pricing may lead to losses because there are a variety of costs—and each changes in a *different* way as output changes. Any pricing method that uses cost must consider these changes. To understand why, we need to define six types of costs.

There are three kinds of total cost

1. **Total fixed cost** is the sum of those costs that are fixed in total—no matter how much is produced. Among these fixed costs are rent, depreciation, managers' salaries, property taxes, and insurance. Such costs stay the same even if production stops temporarily.

2. **Total variable cost**, on the other hand, is the sum of those changing expenses that are closely related to output—expenses for parts, wages, packaging materials, outgoing freight, and sales commissions.

   At zero output, total variable cost is zero. As output increases, so do variable costs. If Wrangler doubles its output of jeans in a year, its total cost for denim cloth also (roughly) doubles.

3. **Total cost** is the sum of total fixed and total variable costs. Changes in total cost depend on variations in total variable cost—since total fixed cost stays the same.

Average fixed costs are lower when a larger quantity is produced.

There are three kinds of average cost

The pricing manager usually is more interested in cost per unit than total cost because prices are usually quoted per unit.

1. **Average cost** (per unit) is obtained by dividing total cost by the related quantity (that is, the total quantity that causes the total cost).
2. **Average fixed cost** (per unit) is obtained by dividing total fixed cost by the related quantity.
3. **Average variable cost** (per unit) is obtained by dividing total variable cost by the related quantity.

An example shows cost relations

A good way to get a feel for these different types of costs is to extend our average-cost pricing example (Exhibit 18–3A). Exhibit 18–4 shows the six types of cost and how they vary at different levels of output. The line for 40,000 units is highlighted because that was the expected level of sales in our average-cost pricing example. For simplicity, we assume that average variable cost is the same for each unit. Notice, however, that total variable cost increases when quantity increases.

Exhibit 18–5 shows the three average cost curves from Exhibit 18–4. Notice that average fixed cost goes down steadily as the quantity increases. Although the average variable cost remains the same, average cost decreases continually too. This is because average fixed cost is decreasing. With these relations in mind, let's reconsider the problem with average-cost pricing.

Ignoring demand is the major weakness of average-cost pricing

Average-cost pricing works well if the firm actually sells the quantity it used to set the average-cost price. Losses may result, however, if actual sales are much lower than expected. On the other hand, if sales are much higher than expected, then profits may be very good. But this will only happen by luck—because the firm's demand is much larger than expected.

EXHIBIT 18–4 Cost Structure of a Firm

Quantity (Q)	Total Fixed Costs (TFC)	Average Fixed Costs (AFC)	Average Variable Costs (AVC)	Total Variable Costs (TVC)	Total Cost (TC)	Average Cost (AC)
0	$30,000	—	—	—	$ 30,000	—
10,000	30,000	$3.00	$0.80	$ 8,000	38,000	$3.80
20,000	30,000	1.50	0.80	16,000	46,000	2.30
30,000	30,000	1.00	0.80	24,000	54,000	1.80
40,000	30,000	0.75	0.80	32,000	62,000	1.55
50,000	30,000	0.60	0.80	40,000	70,000	1.40
60,000	30,000	0.50	0.80	48,000	78,000	1.30
70,000	30,000	0.43	0.80	56,000	86,000	1.23
80,000	30,000	0.38	0.80	64,000	94,000	1.18
90,000	30,000	0.33	0.80	72,000	102,000	1.13
100,000	30,000	0.30	0.80	80,000	110,000	1.10

$$\begin{bmatrix} 110,000 \ (TC) \\ -80,000 \ (TVC) \\ \hline 30,000 \ (TFC) \end{bmatrix}$$
$$(Q)100,000\overline{)\ \begin{matrix} 0.30 \ (AFC) \\ 30,000 \ (TFC) \end{matrix}}$$
$$\begin{bmatrix} 0.80 \ (AVC) \end{bmatrix}$$
$$\begin{bmatrix} 100,000(Q) \\ \times 0.80 \ (AVC) \\ \hline 80,000 \ (TVC) \end{bmatrix}$$
$$\begin{bmatrix} 30,000 \ (TFC) \\ +80,000 \ (TVC) \\ \hline 110,000 \ (TC) \end{bmatrix}$$
$$(Q)100,000\overline{)\ \begin{matrix} 1.10 (AC) \\ 110,000 \ (TC) \end{matrix}}$$

To use average-cost pricing, a marketing manager must make *some* estimate of the quantity to be sold in the coming period. Without a quantity estimate, it isn't possible to compute average cost. But unless this quantity is related to price—that is, unless the firm's demand curve is considered—the marketing manager may set a price that doesn't even cover a firm's total cost! You saw this happen in Exhibit 18–3B, when the firm's price of $2.00 resulted in demand for only 20,000 units—and a loss of $6,000. The demand curve is still important even if management doesn't take time to think about it. For example, Exhibit 18–6 shows the demand curve for the firm we're discussing. This demand curve shows *why* the firm lost money when it tried to use average-cost pricing. At the $2.00 price, quantity demanded is only 20,000. With this demand curve and the costs in Exhibit 18–4, the firm will incur a loss whether management sets the price at a high $3 or a low $1.20. At $3, the firm will sell only 10,000 units for a total revenue of $30,000. But total cost will be $38,000—for a loss of $8,000. At the $1.20 price, it will sell 60,000 units—at a loss of $6,000. However, the curve suggests that at a price of $1.65 consumers will demand about 40,000 units, producing a profit of about $4,000.

In short, average-cost pricing is simple in theory—but often fails in practice. In stable situations, prices set by this method may yield profits—but not necessarily *maximum* profits. And note that such cost-based prices may be higher than a price that would be more profitable for the firm—as shown in Exhibit 18–6. When demand conditions are changing, average-cost pricing is even more risky.

Exhibit 18–7 summarizes the relationships discussed above. Cost-oriented pricing requires an estimate of the total number of units to be sold. That estimate determines the *average* fixed cost per unit and thus the average total cost. Then the firm adds the desired profit per unit to the average total cost to get the

EXHIBIT 18–5 Typical Shape of Cost (per unit) Curves when AVC Is Assumed Constant per Unit

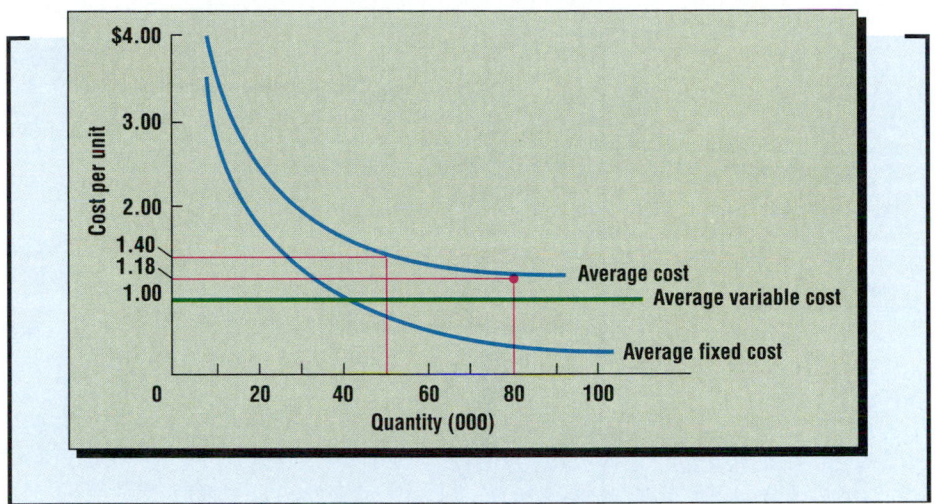

EXHIBIT 18–6 Evaluation of Various Prices along a Firm's Demand Curve

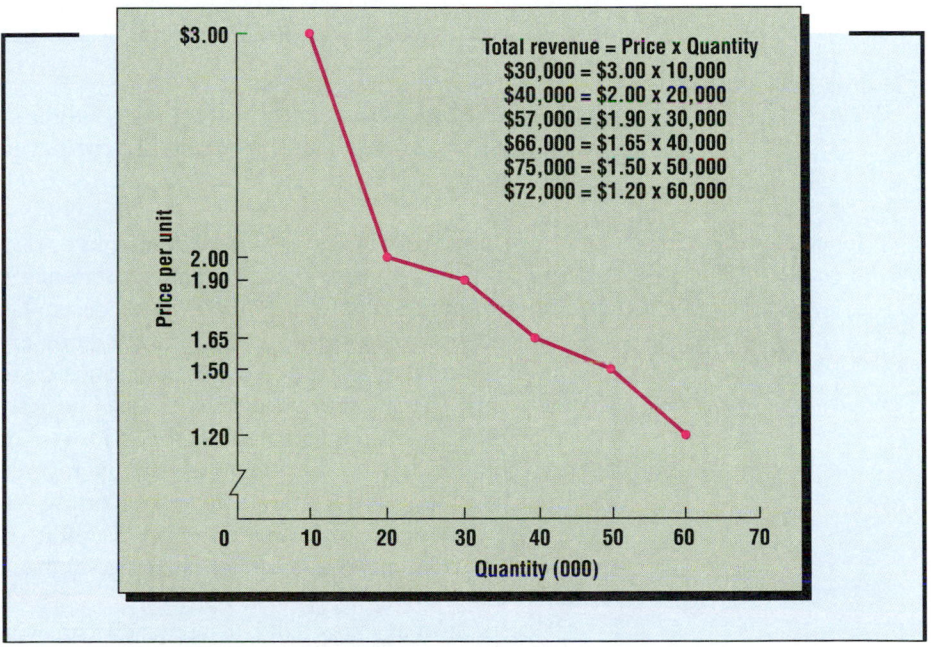

cost-oriented selling price. How customers react to that price determines the actual quantity the firm will be able to sell. But that quantity may not be the quantity used to compute the average cost! Further, the quantity the firm actually sells (times price) determines total revenue (and total profit or loss). A decision

EXHIBIT 18–7 Summary of Relationships among Quantity, Cost, and Price Using Cost-Oriented Pricing

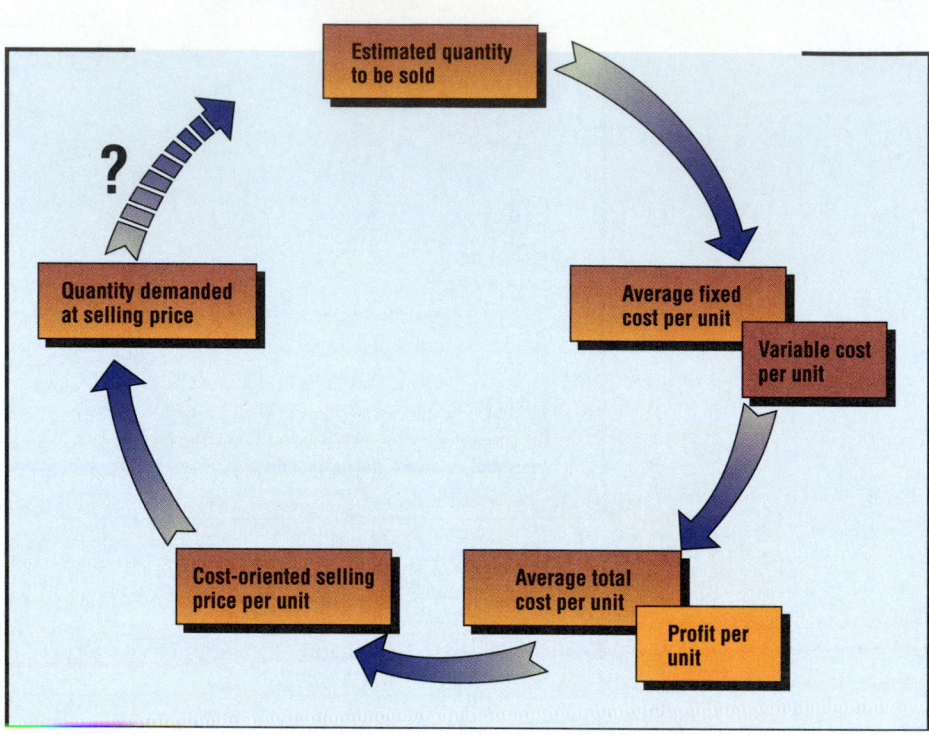

made in one area affects each of the others—directly or indirectly. Average-cost pricing does not consider these effects.[4] A manager who forgets this can make serious pricing mistakes.

Experience curve pricing is even riskier

In recent years, some aggressive firms have used a variation of average-cost pricing called experience curve pricing. **Experience curve pricing** is average-cost pricing using an estimate of *future* average costs. This approach is based on the observation that over time—as an industry gains experience in certain kinds of production—managers learn new ways to reduce costs. The effect of such learning on costs varies in different businesses. Studies suggest that costs decrease about 15 to 20 percent each time cumulative production volume (experience) doubles—at least in some industries. So some firms set average-cost prices where they expect costs to be when products are sold in the future—not where costs actually are when the strategy is set. This approach is more common in rapidly growing markets (such as in the electronics business) because cumulative production volume (experience) grows faster.

If costs drop as expected, this approach can work fairly well. But it has the same risks as regular average-cost pricing—unless demand is included in the price setting. This means the price setter has to estimate what quantity will be sold to be able to read the right price from the experience-based average-cost curve.[5]

Don't ignore competitors' costs

Another danger of average-cost pricing is that it ignores competitors' costs and prices. Just as the price of a firm's own product influences demand, the price of available substitutes may impact demand. We saw this operate in our Wal-Mart case at the start of this chapter. By finding ways to cut costs, Wal-Mart was able to offer prices lower than competitors' and still make an attractive profit. Given a choice between Wal-Mart's low prices and higher prices for similar products at nearby stores, many consumers buy from Wal-Mart.

SOME FIRMS ADD A TARGET RETURN TO COST

Target return pricing scores sometimes

Target return pricing—adding a target return to the cost of a product—has become popular in recent years. With this approach, the price setter seeks to earn (1) a percentage return (say, 10 percent per year) on the investment or (2) a specific total dollar return.

This method is a variation of the average-cost method since the desired target return is added into total cost. As a simple example, if a company had $180,000 invested and wanted to make a 10 percent return on investment, it would add $18,000 to its annual total costs in setting prices.

This approach has the same weakness as other average-cost pricing methods. If the quantity actually sold is less than the quantity used to set the price, then the company doesn't earn its target return—even though the target return seems to be part of the price structure. In fact, we already saw this in Exhibit 18–3. Remember that we added $18,000 as an expected profit—or target return. But the return was much lower when the expected quantity was not sold. (It could be higher too—but only if the quantity sold is much larger than expected.) Target return pricing clearly does not guarantee that a firm will hit the target.

Hitting the target in the long run

Managers in some larger firms, who want to achieve a long-run target return objective, use another cost-oriented pricing approach—**long-run target return pricing**—adding a long-run average target return to the cost of a product. Instead of estimating the quantity they expect to produce in any one year, they assume that during several years' time their plants will produce at, say, 80 percent of capacity. They use this quantity when setting their prices.

Companies that take this longer-run view assume that there will be recession years when sales drop below 80 percent of capacity. For example, Owens/Corning Fiberglas sells insulation. In years when there is little construction, output is low, and the firm does not earn the target return. But the company also has good years when it sells more insulation and exceeds the target return. Over the long run, Owens/Corning managers expect to achieve the target return. And sometimes they're right—depending on how accurately they estimate demand!

BREAK-EVEN ANALYSIS CAN EVALUATE POSSIBLE PRICES

Some price setters use break-even analysis in their pricing. **Break-even analysis** evaluates whether the firm will be able to break even—that is, cover all its costs—with a particular price. This is important because a firm must cover all costs in the long run or there is not much point being in business. This method focuses on the **break-even point (BEP)**—the quantity where the firm's total cost will just equal its total revenue.

Break-even charts help find the BEP

To help understand how break-even analysis works, look at Exhibit 18–8, an example of the typical break-even chart. *The chart is based on a particular selling price*—in this case $1.20 a unit. The chart has lines that show total costs (total

EXHIBIT 18–8 Break-Even Chart for a Particular Situation

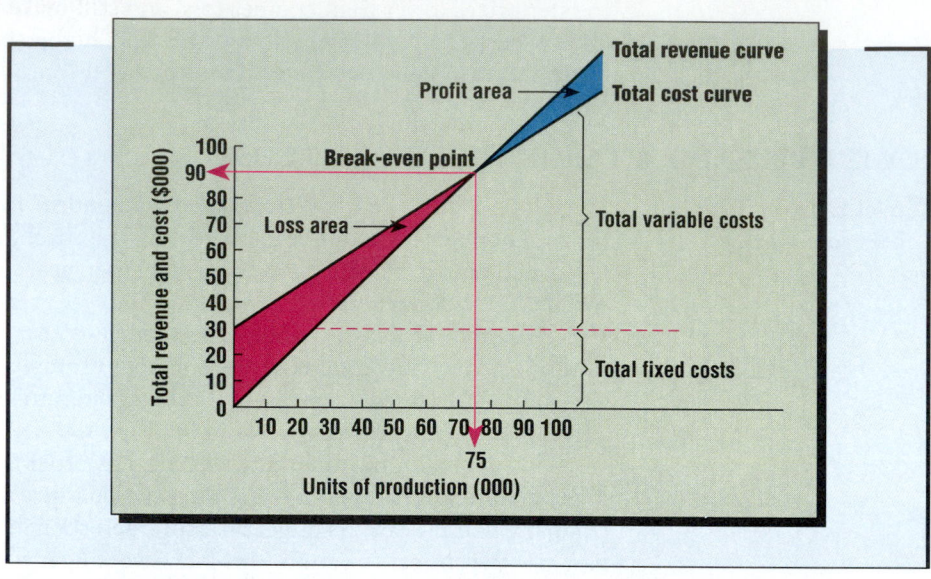

variable plus total fixed costs) and total revenues at different levels of production. The break-even point on the chart is at 75,000 units—where the total cost and total revenue lines intersect. At that production level, total cost and total revenue are the same—$90,000.

This chart also shows some typical assumptions made to simplify break-even analysis. Note that the total revenue curve is assumed to be a straight line. This means that each extra unit sold adds the same amount to total revenue. Stated differently, this assumes that *any quantity can be sold at the same price*. For this chart, we are assuming a selling price of $1.20 a unit. You can see that if the firm sells the break-even quantity of 75,000 at $1.20 each, it will earn a total revenue of $90,000.

In addition, the total cost curve in the chart is assumed to be a straight line. This means that average variable cost (AVC) is the same at different levels of output. For Exhibit 18–8, the AVC is 80 cents per unit.

The difference between the total revenue and total cost at a given quantity is the profit—or loss! The chart shows that below the break-even point, total cost is higher than total revenue—and the firm incurs a loss. The firm would make a profit above the break-even point. However, the firm would only reach the break-even point, or get beyond it into the profit area, *if* it could sell at least 75,000 units at the $1.20 price.

Break-even analysis can be very helpful—if used properly—so let's look at this approach more closely.

How to compute a break-even point

A break-even chart is an easy-to-understand visual aid, but it's also useful to be able to compute the break-even point.

The BEP, in units, can be found by dividing total fixed costs (TFC) by the **fixed-cost (FC) contribution per unit**—the assumed selling price per unit minus the variable cost per unit. This can be stated as a simple formula:

$$\text{BEP (in units)} = \frac{\text{Total fixed cost}}{\text{Fixed-cost contribution per unit}}$$

This formula makes sense when we think about it. To break even, we must cover total fixed costs. Therefore, we must figure the contribution each unit will make to covering the total fixed costs (after paying for the variable costs to produce the item). When we divide this per-unit contribution into the total fixed costs that must be covered, we have the BEP (in units).

To illustrate the formula, let's use the cost and price information in Exhibit 18–8. The price per unit is $1.20. The average variable cost per unit is 80 cents. So the FC contribution per unit is 40 cents ($1.20 – 80 cents). The total fixed cost is $30,000 (see Exhibit 18–8). Substituting in the formula:

$$BEP = \frac{\$30,000}{.40} = 75,000 \text{ units}$$

From this you can see that if this firm sells 75,000 units, it will exactly cover all its fixed and variable costs. If it sells even one more unit, it will begin to show a profit—in this case, 40 cents per unit. Note that once the fixed costs are covered, the part of revenue formerly going to cover fixed costs is now *all profit.*

BEP can be stated in dollars too

The BEP can also be figured in dollars. The easiest way is to compute the BEP in units and then multiply by the assumed per-unit price. If you multiply the selling price ($1.20) by the BEP in units (75,000) you get $90,000—the BEP in dollars.

Each possible price has its own break-even point

Often it's useful to compute the break-even point for each of several possible prices and then compare the BEP for each price to likely demand at that price. The marketing manager can quickly reject some price possibilities when the expected quantity demanded at a given price is way below the break-even point for that price.

A target profit can be included

So far in our discussion of BEP we've focused on the quantity at which total revenue equals total cost—where profit is zero. We can also vary this approach to see what quantity is required to earn a certain level of profit. The analysis is the same as described above for the break-even point in units, but the amount of target profit is added to the total fixed cost. Then, when we divide the total fixed cost plus profit figure by the contribution from each unit, we get the quantity that will earn the target profit.

Break-even analysis shows the effect of cutting costs

Break-even analysis makes it clear why managers must constantly look for effective new ways to get jobs done at lower costs. For example, if a manager can reduce the firm's total fixed costs—perhaps by using computer systems to cut out excess inventory carrying costs—the break-even point will be lower and profits will start to build sooner. Similarly, if the variable cost to produce and sell an item can be reduced, the fixed-cost contribution per unit increases; that too lowers the break-even point and profit accumulates faster for each product sold beyond the break-even point.

Break-even analysis is helpful—but not a pricing solution

Break-even analysis is helpful for evaluating alternatives. It is also popular because it's easy to use. Yet break-even analysis is too often misunderstood. Beyond the BEP, profits seem to be growing continually. And the graph—with its straight-line total revenue curve—makes it seem that any quantity can be sold at the assumed price. But this usually isn't true. It is the same as assuming a perfectly horizontal demand curve at that price. In fact, most managers face down-sloping demand situations. And their total revenue curves do *not* keep going up.

The firm and costs we discussed in the average-cost pricing example earlier in this chapter illustrate this point. You can confirm from Exhibit 18–4 that the total fixed cost ($30,000) and average variable cost (80 cents) for that firm are the same ones shown in the break-even chart (Exhibit 18–8). So this break-even chart is the one we would draw for that firm assuming a price of $1.20 a unit. But the demand curve for that case showed that the firm could only sell 60,000 units at a price of $1.20. So that firm would never reach the 75,000 unit break-even point at a $1.20 price. It would only sell 60,000 units, and it would lose $6,000! A firm with a different demand curve—say, one where the firm could sell 80,000 units at a price of $1.20—would in fact break even at 75,000 units.

Break-even analysis is a useful tool for analyzing costs. But it is a cost-oriented approach and suffers the same limitation as other cost-oriented approaches. Specifically, it does not consider the effect of price on the quantity that consumers will want—that is, the demand curve.

So to really zero in on the most profitable price, marketers are better off estimating the demand curve itself and then using marginal analysis, which we'll discuss next.[6]

Marketing managers know that the price of an item will affect the quantity sold.

MARGINAL ANALYSIS CONSIDERS BOTH COSTS AND DEMAND

Our examples of cost-oriented pricing approaches show that a marketing manager—and anyone else involved in setting a price—must really understand how costs vary at different sales quantities. However, the examples also show that it's not enough just to understand costs. The price setter should also consider demand. The challenge is to consider both demand and costs at the same time because the price decision usually affects both costs and revenue—and they determine profit.

Marginal analysis—helps find the best price

The best pricing tool marketers have for looking at costs and revenue (demand) at the same time is marginal analysis. **Marginal analysis** focuses on the change in total revenue and total cost from selling one more unit to find the most profitable price and quantity. Marginal analysis doesn't just seek a price that will result in *some* profit. It seeks the price that *maximizes* profits. This objective makes sense. If you know how to make the biggest profit, you can always adjust to pursue other objectives—while knowing how much profit you're giving up!

Marginal analysis when demand curves slope down

We'll focus on the many situations in which demand curves are down-sloping, especially monopolistic competition.[7] In these situations, the firm has carved out a market niche for itself—and does have a pricing decision to make. We'll also briefly discuss the special case of oligopoly. We won't deal with pure or nearly pure competition. In that situation, marketing managers have little difficulty with the pricing decision. They don't have much choice except to use the market price.

In monopolistic competition, the firm faces a down-sloping demand curve. The price setter must pick a specific price on that curve—and generally will offer that price to all potential buyers (to avoid price discrimination under the Robinson-Patman Act) for the life of the plan. The marketer can hope to increase sales volume by lowering the price. But all customers—even those who might be willing to pay more—pay this lower price. Even though the quantity has increased, the total revenue may decrease. Therefore, a manager should consider the effect of alternative prices on total revenue (and profit). The way to do this is to look at marginal revenue.

Marginal revenue can be negative

Marginal revenue is the change in total revenue that results from the sale of one more unit of a product. When the demand curve is down-sloping, this extra unit can be sold only by reducing the price of *all* items.

Exhibit 18–9 shows the relationship between price, quantity, total revenue, and marginal revenue in a situation with a straight-line, down-sloping demand curve.

The firm in this example can sell four units for a total revenue of $420 or five units for $460. Thus the marginal revenue for the fifth unit is $460 − $420 or $40. Considering only revenue, it would be desirable to sell this extra unit. But will revenue continue to rise if the firm sells more units at lower prices? No! Exhibit 18-9 shows that negative marginal revenues occur at lower price levels. Obviously, this is not good for the firm! (Note: The total revenue obtained if price is cut may still be positive, but the marginal revenue—the extra revenue gained—may be positive or negative.)

Marginal revenue curve and demand curve are different

The marginal revenue curve is always below a down-sloping demand curve because the price of each last unit must be lower to sell more. You can see this in Exhibit 18–10 where we plot the data from Exhibit 18–9. The fact that the demand

EXHIBIT 18−9   Marginal Revenue and Price

(1) Quantity Q	(2) Price P	(3) Total Revenue (1) × (2) = TR	(4) Marginal Revenue MR
0	$150	$ 0	
1	140	140	$140
2	130	260	120
3	117	351	91
4	105	420	69
5	92	460	40
6	79	474	14
7	66	462	−12
8	53	424	−38
9	42	378	−46
10	31	310	−68

EXHIBIT 18−10   A Plotting of the Demand and Marginal Revenue Data in Exhibit 18−9

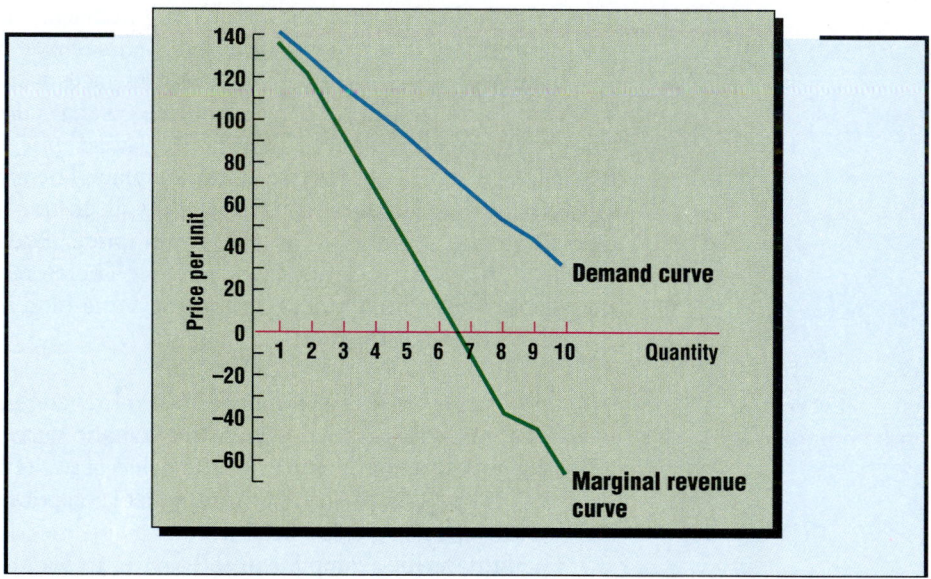

curve and the marginal revenue curves are different in monopolistic competition is very important. We will use both curves to find the best price and quantity.

As we've already seen, various kinds of costs behave differently. Further, there is an important kind of cost similar to marginal revenue: marginal cost. This cost is vital to marginal analysis.

Marginal cost is the change in total cost that results from producing one more unit. If it costs $275 to produce 9 units of a product and $280 to produce 10 units, then marginal cost is $5 for the 10th unit. In other words, marginal cost—

Marginal cost—the cost of one more unit

EXHIBIT 18–11 Cost Structure for Individual Firm (fill in the missing numbers)

(1) Quantity Q	(2) Total Fixed Cost TFC	(3) Average Fixed Cost AFC	(4) Total Variable Cost TVC	(5) Average Variable Cost AVC	(6) Total Cost (TFC + TVC = TC) TC	(7) Average Cost (AC = TC ÷ Q) AC	(8) Marginal Cost (per unit) MC
0	$200	$ 0	$ 0	$ 0	$200	Infinity	
1	200	200	96	96	296	$296	$ 96
2	200	100	116	58	316	___	20
3	200	___	___	___	331	110.33	___
4	200	50	___	___	344	___	___
5	200	40	155	31	___	71	11
6	200	___	168	___	___	61.33	13
7	___	___	183	___	___	___	15
8	___	___	223	___	___	___	___
9	___	___	307	___	507	56.33	___
10	___	20	510	51	710	71	$203

contrasted to average cost per unit—is the additional cost of producing one more *specific unit*; average cost is the average for *all units*.

Cost structure example

Exhibit 18–11 shows how these costs can vary for a typical firm. *Fill in the missing numbers in this exhibit.* Notice that variable cost no longer is assumed constant per unit in Exhibit 18–11. Here we use the more realistic assumption that variable costs will go down for a while and then rise.

Exhibit 18–11 illustrates three important points. *First,* total fixed costs do not change over the entire range of output—but total variable costs increase continually as more and more units are produced. Therefore, total costs—the sum of total fixed costs and total variable costs—will increase as total quantity increases.

Second, average costs will decrease—for a while—as quantity produced increases. Remember that average costs are the sum of average fixed costs and average variable costs—and here average fixed costs are going down because total fixed costs are divided by more and more units as output increases. For example, given a total fixed cost of $200, at a production level of four units, the average fixed cost is $50. At a production level of five units, the average fixed cost is $40.

Third, average costs in this table start rising for the last two units because average variable costs are increasing faster than average fixed costs are decreasing. The firm may be forced to use less efficient facilities and workers, go into overtime work, or pay higher prices for the materials it needs. This turn-up of the average cost curve is common after economies of scale run out.

The marginal cost of just one more is important

The marginal cost column in Exhibit 18–11 is the most important cost column for our purposes. It shows what each extra unit costs. This suggests the *minimum* extra revenue we would like to get for that additional unit. Like average cost, marginal cost drops—but it begins to rise again at a lower level of output than average cost does.

Marginal cost starts to increase at five units. This can be seen in Exhibit 18–12—which shows the behavior of the average cost, average variable cost, and

EXHIBIT 18–12   Per-Unit Cost Curves (for data in Exhibit 18–11)

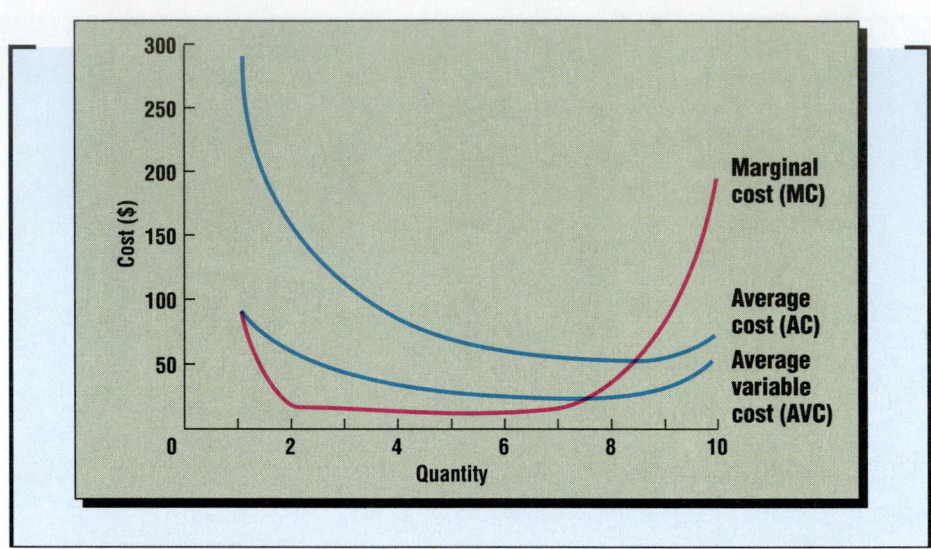

marginal cost curves. Note that the marginal cost curve intersects the average variable cost and average cost curves from below *at their low points,* and then rises rapidly. This is how this curve typically behaves.

How to find the most profitable price and the quantity to produce

Since a manager must choose only *one* price level (for a time period), the question is which price to choose. This price determines the quantity that will be sold. To maximize profit, a manager should be willing to sell more units if the marginal revenue from selling them is at least equal to the marginal cost of the extra units. From this we get the following **rule for maximizing profit**: The highest profit is earned at the price where marginal cost is just less than or equal to marginal revenue.*

This optimal price is *not* found on the marginal revenue curve. This profit-maximizing selling price is found by referring to the demand curve—which shows what price customers are willing to pay for the optimum quantity.

To make sure you understand the method for finding this optimal price, study the following example carefully. To make doubly sure that this approach is fully explained, we will calculate the most profitable price and quantity using total revenue and total cost curves first and then show that you will get the same answer with marginal curves. This will give you a check on the method—as well as help you see how the marginal revenue–marginal cost method works.

Profit maximization with total revenue and total cost curves

Exhibit 18–13 provides data on total revenue, total cost, and total profit for a firm. Exhibit 18–14 graphs the total revenue, total cost, and total profit relationships. The highest point on the total profit curve is at a quantity of six units. This is also the quantity where we find the greatest vertical distance

---

*This rule applies in the typical situations where the curves are shaped similarly to those discussed here. Technically, however, we should add the following to the rule for maximizing profit: The marginal cost must be increasing, or decreasing at a lesser rate than marginal revenue.

EXHIBIT 18–13 Revenue, Cost, and Profit for an Individual Firm

(1) Quantity Q	(2) Price P	(3) Total Revenue TR	(4) Total Cost TC	(5) Profit (TR − TC)	(6) Marginal Revenue MR	(7) Marginal Cost MC	(8) Marginal Profit (MR − MC)
0	$150	$ 0	$200	$−200			
1	140	140	296	−156	$140	$96	$+ 44
2	130	260	316	− 56	120	20	+100
3	117	351	331	+ 20	91	15	+ 76
4	105	420	344	+ 76	69	13	+ 56
5	92	460	355	+105	40	11	+ 29
6	79	474	368	+106	14	13	+ 1
7	66	462	383	+ 79	− 12	15	− 27
8	53	424	423	+ 1	− 38	40	− 78
9	42	378	507	−129	− 46	84	−130
10	31	310	710	−400	− 68	203	−271

between the TR curve and the TC curve. Exhibit 18–13 shows that a price of $79 will result in selling six units, so $79 is the price that leads to the highest profit.

A price lower than $79 would result in a higher sales volume. But you can see that the total profit curve declines beyond a quantity of 6 units. So a profit-maximizing marketing manager would not be interested in setting a lower price.

Profit maximization using marginal curves

Now we can apply the rule for maximizing profit using marginal curves. We again find that $79 is the best price and that 6 is the best quantity. See Exhibit 18–15, which graphs the marginal revenue and marginal cost data from Exhibit 18–13.

In Exhibit 18–15, the intersection of the marginal cost and marginal revenue curves occurs at a quantity of six. This is the most profitable quantity. But the best price must be obtained by going up to the demand curve and then over to the vertical axis—*not* by going from the intersection of MR and MC over to the vertical axis. Again, the best price is $79.

The graphic solution is supported by the data in Exhibit 18–13. At a price of $79 and a quantity of six, marginal revenue equals $14, and marginal cost is $13. There is a profit margin of $1—suggesting that it might be profitable to offer seven rather than six units. This is not the case, however. The marginal cost of the seventh unit is $15, while its marginal revenue is actually negative. Lowering the price to $66 to sell seven units (instead of only six) will reduce total profit by $27.

It is important to realize that *total* profit is *not* near zero when marginal revenue (MR) equals marginal cost (MC). **Marginal profit**—the extra profit on the last unit—is near zero. But that is exactly why the quantity obtained at the MR-MC intersection is the most profitable. Marginal analysis shows that when the firm is finding the best price to charge, it should lower the price—to increase the quantity it will sell—as long as the last unit it sells will yield *extra* profits.

Again, the marketing manager must choose only *one* price. Marginal analysis is useful in helping to set the best price to charge for all that will be sold. It might help to think of the demand curve as an if-then curve—*if* a price is selected, *then*

EXHIBIT 18–14   Graphic Determination of the Output Giving the Greatest Total Profit for a Firm

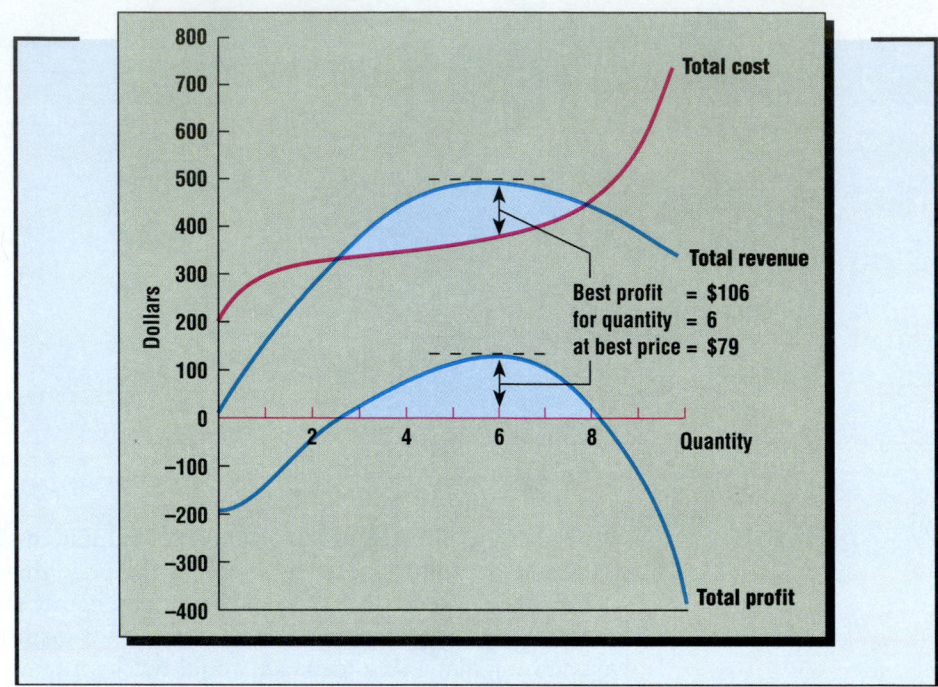

its related quantity will be sold. Before the marketing manager sets the actual price, all these *if-then* combinations can be evaluated for profitability. But once the price level is set, the results will follow—that is, the related quantity will be sold.

A profit range is reassuring

We've been trying to find the most profitable price and quantity. But in a changing world, this is difficult. Fortunately, this best point is surrounded by a profitable range.

Note that in Exhibit 18–14, there are two break-even points rather than a single point, which was the case when we were discussing break-even analysis. The second break-even point falls farther to the right because total costs turn up and total revenue turns down.

These two break-even points are important. They show the range of profitable operations. Although marginal analysis seeks the price that gives the *maximum* profit, we know that this point is an ideal rather than a realistic possibility. So it's essential that you know there is a *range of profit* around the optimum—it isn't just a single point. This means that pursuing the most profitable price is a wise approach.

How to lose less, if you must

The marginal analysis approach to finding the most profitable price will also find the price that will be *least unprofitable* when market conditions are so poor that the firm must operate at a loss.

If sales are slow, the firm may even have to consider closing. But a marketing manager might have something to say about that. A key point here is that most fixed costs will continue even if the firm stops its operations. Some fixed costs may

EXHIBIT 18–15   Alternate Determination of the Most Profitable Output and Price for a Firm

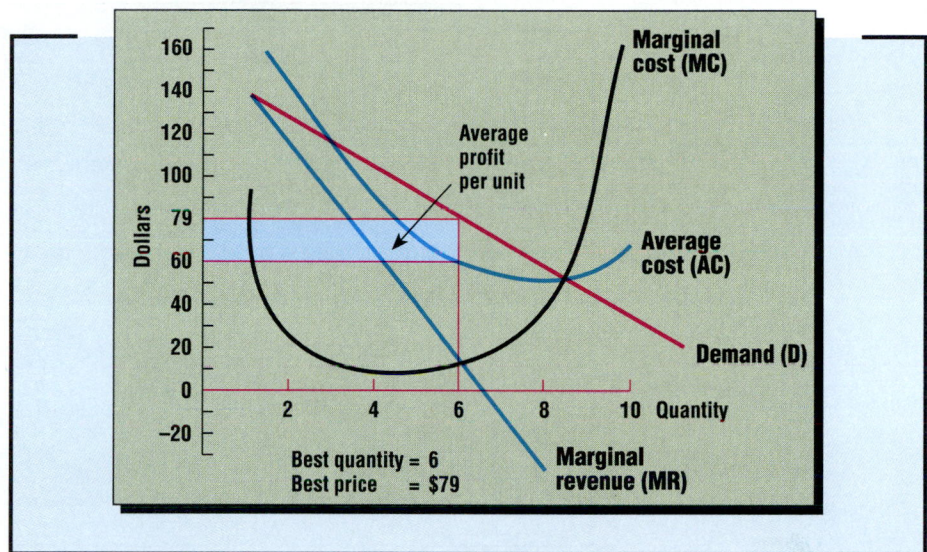

even involve items that are so "sunk" in the business that they cannot be sold for anything near the cost shown on the company's records. An unsuccessful company's special-purpose buildings and machines may be worthless to anyone else. So fixed costs may be irrelevant to a decision about closing the business.

Marginal costs are another matter. If the firm can recover the marginal cost of the last unit (or, more generally, the variable cost of the units being considered), it may want to continue operating. The extra income would help pay the fixed costs and reduce the firm's losses. If it can't meet marginal costs, it should stop operations temporarily or go out of business. The exceptions involve social or humanitarian considerations—or the fact that the marginal costs of closing temporarily are high and stronger demand is expected *soon*. But if marginal costs can be covered in the short run—even though all fixed costs cannot—the firm should stay in operation.

Marginal analysis helps get the most in pure competition

Marketing managers caught in pure competition can also apply marginal methods. They don't have a price decision to make since the demand curve is flat. (Note: This means that the marginal revenue curve is flat at the same level.) But they do have output decisions. They can use the marginal revenue curve, therefore, with their own unique marginal cost curve to determine the most profitable (or least unprofitable) output level. See Exhibit 18–16. And this approach leads to a different (and more profitable) output than the lowest average-cost decision favored by some commonsense managers. Note in Exhibit 18–16 that the quantity associated with the lowest average cost is not the most profitable quantity.

Marginal analysis applies in oligopoly too

In Chapter 17, we noted that marketing managers who compete in oligopoly situations often just set a price that meets what competitors charge. Marginal analysis helps us understand this situation better.

EXHIBIT 18–16 Finding the Most Profitable (or least unprofitable) Price and Quantity in Pure Competition (in the short run)

Exhibit 18–17 shows a demand curve and marginal revenue curve typical of what a marketing manager in an oligopoly situation faces. The demand curve is kinked, and the current market price is at the kink. The dashed part of the marginal revenue line in Exhibit 18–17 shows that marginal revenue drops sharply at the kinked point. This is a technical but important matter. It helps explain why prices are relatively "sticky" at the kinked point.

Even if costs change (and each firm's supply curve moves up or down), the marginal cost curve is still likely to cross the marginal revenue curve someplace along the drop in the marginal revenue curve. In this case, even though costs are changing—and there may seem to be a reason for changing the price—setting the price at the level of the kink maximizes profit!

A price leader usually sets the price

Most of the firms in an oligopoly are aware of the economics of their situation—at least intuitively. Usually, a **price leader** sets a price for all to follow—perhaps to maximize profits or to get a certain target return on investment—and (without any collusion) other members of the industry follow. The price leader is usually the firm with the lowest costs. That may give it more flexibility than competitors. This price may be maintained for a long time—or at least as long as all members of the industry continue to make a reasonable profit. Sometimes, however, a price leader tries to lower the price, and a competitor lowers it even further. This can lead to price wars—at least temporarily. You sometimes see this in competition between major airlines. But price wars in oligopoly tend to be very unprofitable for each firm and the whole industry—so they usually pass fairly quickly.

A rough demand estimate is better than none

Marginal analysis is a flexible and useful tool for marketing managers. Some managers don't take advantage of it because they think it's just not practical to try to determine the exact shape of the demand curve. But that view misses the point of marginal analysis.

EXHIBIT 18–17   Marginal Revenue Drops Fast in an Oligopoly

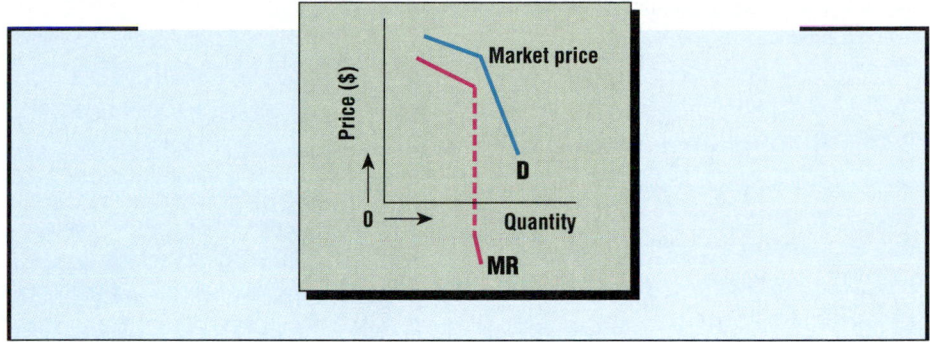

Marginal analysis encourages managers to think very carefully about what they *do know* about costs and demand. Only rarely is either type of information exact. So in practical applications the focus of marginal analysis is not on finding the precise price that will maximize profit. Rather, the focus is on getting an estimate of how profit might vary across a *range of relevant prices*. Further, a number of practical demand-oriented approaches can help a marketing manager do a better job of understanding the likely shape of the demand curve for a target market. We'll discuss these approaches next.

DEMAND-ORIENTED APPROACHES FOR SETTING PRICES

Value in use pricing—how much will the customer save?

Organizational buyers think about how a purchase will affect their total costs. Many marketers who aim at business markets keep this in mind when estimating demand and setting prices. They use **value in use pricing**—which means setting prices that will capture some of what customers will save by substituting the firm's product for the one currently being used.

For example, a producer of computer-controlled machines used to assemble cars knows that his machine doesn't just replace a standard machine. It also reduces labor costs, quality control costs, and—after the car is sold—costs of warranty repairs. The potential savings (value in use) might be different for different customers—because they have different operations, costs, and the like. The marketer can estimate what each auto producer will save by using the machine—and then set a price that makes it less expensive for the auto producer to buy the computerized machine than to stick with the old methods. The number of customers who have different levels of potential savings also provides some idea about the shape of the demand curve.[8]

Customers may have reference prices

Some people don't devote much thought to what they pay for the products they buy—including some frequently purchased goods and services. But most consumers have a **reference price**—the price they expect to pay—for many of the products they purchase. And different customers may have different reference prices for the same basic type of purchase. For example, a person who really enjoys reading might have a higher reference price for a popular paperback book than another person who is only an occasional reader. Marketing research can sometimes identify different segments with different reference prices.[9]

Value in use pricing considers what a customer will save by buying a product.

You'll save enough with Philips SL to buy an SL from a different manufacturer.

Philips Lighting

PHILIPS

Leader pricing—make it low to attract customers

Leader pricing means setting some very low prices—real bargains—to get customers into retail stores. The idea is not to sell large quantities of the leader items but to get customers into the store to buy other products.[10] Certain products are picked for their promotion value and priced low—but above cost. In food stores, the leader prices are the "specials" that are advertised regularly to give an image of low prices. Leader items are usually well-known, widely used items that customers don't stock heavily—milk, butter, eggs, or coffee—but on which they will recognize a real price cut. In other words, leader pricing is normally used with products for which consumers do have a specific reference price.

Leader pricing may try to appeal to customers who normally shop elsewhere. But it can backfire if customers buy only the low-price leaders. To avoid hurting profits, managers often select leader items that aren't directly competitive with major lines—as when bargain-priced recording tape is the leader for a stereo equipment store.

Bait pricing—offer a steal, but sell under protest

Bait pricing is setting some very low prices to attract customers—but trying to sell more expensive models or brands once the customer is in the store. For example, a furniture store may advertise a color TV for $199. But once bargain hunters come to the store, salesclerks point out the disadvantages of the low-price TV and try to convince them to trade up to a better (and more expensive) set. Bait pricing is something like leader pricing. But here the seller *doesn't* plan to sell many at the low price.

If bait pricing is successful, the demand for higher-quality products expands. This approach may be a sensible part of a strategy to trade-up customers. And customers may be well-served if—once in the store—they find a higher-priced product offers better value, perhaps because its features are better suited to their needs. But bait pricing is also criticized as unethical.

If the price of a product is set higher than the target market's reference price, there is not likely to be much demand.

AT $79 IT'S SEXY.
AT $320 IT'S OBSCENE.

Designer clothing 40-70% off, every day. 5th Ave. & 18th St., Madison Ave. & 44th St.
DAFFY'S
CLOTHES THAT WILL MAKE YOU, NOT BREAK YOU.™

Is bait pricing ethical?

Extremely aggressive and sometimes dishonest bait-pricing advertising has given this method a bad reputation. Some stores make it very difficult to buy the bait item. The Federal Trade Commission considers this type of bait pricing a deceptive act and has banned its use in interstate commerce. Even Sears, one of the nation's most trusted retail chains, has been criticized for bait-and-switch pricing. But some unethical retailers who operate only within one state continue to advertise bait prices on products they won't sell.

Psychological pricing—some prices just seem right

Psychological pricing means setting prices that have special appeal to target customers. Some people think there are whole ranges of prices that potential customers see as the same. So price cuts in these ranges do not increase the quantity sold. But just below this range, customers may buy more. Then, at even lower prices, the quantity demanded stays the same again—and so on. Exhibit 18–18 shows the kind of demand curve that leads to psychological pricing. Vertical drops mark the price ranges that customers see as the same. Pricing research shows that there *are* such demand curves.[11]

Odd-even pricing is setting prices that end in certain numbers. For example, products selling below $50 often end in the number 5 or the number 9—such as 49 cents or $24.95. Prices for higher-priced products are often $1 or $2 below the next even dollar figure—such as $99 rather than $100.

Some marketers use odd-even pricing because they think consumers react better to these prices—perhaps seeing them as "substantially" lower than the next highest even price. Marketers using these prices seem to assume that they have a rather jagged demand curve—that slightly higher prices will substantially reduce the quantity demanded. Long ago, some retailers used odd-even prices to force their clerks to make change. Then the clerks had to record the sale and could not pocket the money. Today, however, it's not always clear why firms use these prices—or whether they really work. Perhaps it's done simply because everyone else does it.[12]

Prestige pricing indicates quality

Prestige pricing is setting a rather high price to suggest high quality or high status. Some target customers want the best, so they will buy at a high price. But if the price seems cheap, they worry about quality and don't buy.[13] Prestige pricing is most common for luxury products—such as furs, jewelry, and perfume.

EXHIBIT 18–18
Demand Curve when Psychological
Pricing Is Appropriate

EXHIBIT 18–19
Demand Curve Showing a Prestige
Pricing Situation

It is also common in service industries—where the customer can't see the product in advance and relies on price to judge its quality. Target customers who respond to prestige pricing give the marketing manager an unusual demand curve. Instead of a normal down-sloping curve, the curve goes down for a while and then bends back to the left again. See Exhibit 18–19.

Price lining—a few prices cover the field

Price lining is setting a few price levels for a product line and then marking all items at these prices. This approach assumes that customers have a certain reference price in mind that they expect to pay for a product. For example, most neckties are priced between $10 and $40. In price lining, there are only a few prices within this range. Ties will not be priced at $10.00, $10.50, $11.00, and so on. They might be priced at four levels—$10, $20, $30, and $40.

Price lining has advantages other than just matching prices to what consumers expect to pay. The main advantage is simplicity—for both clerks and customers. It is less confusing than having many prices. Some customers may consider items in only one price class. Their big decision, then, is which item(s) to choose at that price.

For retailers, price lining has several advantages. Sales may increase because (1) they can offer a bigger variety in each price class and (2) it's easier to get customers to make decisions within one price class. Stock planning is simpler because demand is larger at the relatively few prices. Price lining can also reduce costs because inventory needs are lower.

Demand-backward pricing

Demand-backward pricing is setting an acceptable final consumer price and working backward to what a producer can charge. It is commonly used by producers of final consumer products—especially shopping products, such as women's and children's clothing and shoes. It is also used for toys or gifts for which customers will spend a specific amount—because they are seeking a $5 or a $10 gift. Here a reverse cost-plus pricing process is used. This method has been called market-minus pricing.

The producer starts with the retail (reference) price for a particular item and then works backward—subtracting the typical margins that channel members expect. This gives the approximate price the producer can charge. Then, the average or planned marketing expenses can be subtracted from this price to find how much can be spent producing the item. Candy companies do this. They alter the size of the candy bar to keep the bar at the expected price.

Prestige pricing is most common for luxury products such as furs, jewelry, and perfume.

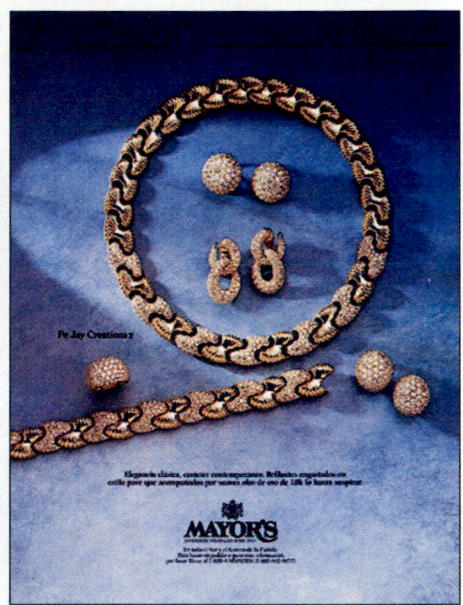

Demand estimates are needed for demand-backward pricing to be successful. The quantity that will be demanded affects production costs—that is, where the firm will be on its average cost curve. Also, since competitors can be expected to make the best product possible, it is important to know customer needs to set the best amount to spend on manufacturing costs. By increasing costs a little, the product may be so improved in consumers' eyes that the firm will sell many more units. But if consumers only want novelty, additional quality may not increase the quantity demanded—and shouldn't be offered.

PRICING A FULL LINE

Our emphasis has been—and will continue to be—on the problem of pricing an individual product mainly because this makes our discussion clearer. But most marketing managers are responsible for more than one product. In fact, their "product" may be the whole company line! So we'll discuss this matter briefly.

Full-line pricing— market- or firm-oriented?

Full-line pricing is setting prices for a whole line of products. How to do this depends on which of two basic situations a firm is facing.

In one case, all products in the company's line are aimed at the same general target market, which makes it important for all prices to be related. For example, a producer of TV sets can offer several price and quality levels to give its target customers some choice. The different prices should appear reasonable when the target customers are evaluating them.

In the other case, the different products in the line are aimed at entirely different target markets so there doesn't have to be any relation between the various prices. A chemical producer of a wide variety of products with several target markets, for example, probably should price each product separately.

Demand-backward pricing starts with the retail price for a particular item and then works backward—subtracting the typical margins that channel members expect.

Cost is not much help in full-line pricing

The marketing manager must try to recover all costs on the whole line—perhaps by pricing quite low on competitive items and much higher on less competitive items. Estimating costs for each product is a big problem because there is no single right way to assign a company's fixed costs to each of the products. Further, if any cost-oriented pricing method is carried through without considering demand, it can lead to very unrealistic prices. To avoid mistakes, the marketing manager should judge demand for the whole line as well as demand for each individual product in each target market.

As an aid to full-line pricing, marketing managers can assemble directly variable costs on the many items in the line to calculate a price floor. To this floor they can add a reasonable markup based on the quality of the product, the strength of the demand for the product, and the degree of competition. But finally, the image projected by the full line must be evaluated.

Complementary product pricing

Complementary product pricing is setting prices on several products as a group. This may lead to one product being priced very low so that the profits from another product will increase—and increase the product group's total profits. A new Gillette shaver, for example, may be priced low to sell the blades, which must be replaced regularly.

Complementary product pricing differs from full-line pricing because different production facilities may be involved—so there's no cost allocation problem. Instead, the problem is really understanding the target market and the demand curves for each of the complementary products. Then, various combinations of prices can be tried to see what set will be best for reaching the company's pricing objectives.

Product-bundle pricing—one price for several products

A firm that offers its target market several different products may use **product-bundle pricing**—setting one price for a set of products. Firms that use product-bundle pricing usually set the overall price so that it's cheaper for the customer to buy the products at the same time than separately. Drugstores sometimes bundle the cost of a roll of film and the cost of the processing. A bank may offer a product-bundle price for a safe-deposit box, travelers checks, and a savings account. Bundling encourages customers to spend more and buy products that they might not otherwise buy—because the "added cost" of the extras is not as high as it would normally be.

Most firms that use product-bundle pricing also set individual prices for the unbundled products. This may increase demand by attracting customers who want one item in a product assortment but don't want the extras. Many firms treat services this way. A software company may have a product-bundle price for its software and access to a toll-free telephone assistance service. However, customers who don't need help can pay a lower price and get just the software.[14]

BID PRICING AND NEGOTIATED PRICING DEPEND HEAVILY ON COSTS

A new price for every job

Bid pricing means offering a specific price for each possible job rather than setting a price that applies for all customers. Building contractors, for example, must bid on possible projects. And many companies selling services (like cleaning or data processing) must submit bids for jobs they would like to have.

The big problem in bid pricing is estimating all the costs that will apply to each job. This may sound easy, but a complicated bid may involve thousands of cost components. Further, management must include an overhead charge and a charge for profit.

Sometimes it isn't even possible to figure out costs in advance. This may lead to a contract where the customer agrees to pay the supplier's total cost plus an agreed-on profit figure (say, 10 percent of costs or a dollar amount)—after the job is finished.

Ethical issues in cost-plus bid pricing

Some unethical sellers give bid prices based on cost-plus contracts a bad reputation by faking their records to make costs seem higher than they really are. In other cases, there may be honest debate about what costs should be allowed.

Demand must be considered too

Competition must be considered when adding in overhead and profit for a bid price. Usually, the customer will get several bids and accept the lowest one. So unthinking addition of typical overhead and profit rates should be avoided. Some bidders use the same overhead and profit rates on all jobs—regardless of competition—and then are surprised when they don't get some jobs.

Because bidding can be expensive, a marketing manager may want to be selective about which jobs to bid on and choose those where she feels she has the greatest chance of success. Firms can spend thousands—or even millions—of dollars just developing bids for large business or government customers.[15]

Sometimes bids are negotiated

Some buying situations (including much government buying) require the use of bids—and the purchasing agent must take the lowest bid. In other cases, however, the customer asks for bids and then singles out the company that submits the *most attractive* bid—not necessarily the lowest—for further bargaining.

Negotiated prices—what will a specific customer pay?

The list price or bidding price the seller would like to charge is sometimes only the *starting point* for discussions with individual customers. What a customer will buy—if the customer buys at all—depends on the **negotiated price**, a price set based on bargaining between the buyer and seller.

As with simple bid pricing, negotiated pricing is most common in situations where the marketing mix is adjusted for each customer—so bargaining may involve the whole marketing mix, not just the price level. For example, a firm that produces machine tools used by other manufacturers to make their products might use this approach. Each customer may need custom-designed machines and different types of installation service. Through the bargaining process, the seller tries to determine what aspects of the marketing mix are most important to the customer. For one customer, selling price may be most important. There the seller might try to find ways to reduce costs of other elements of the marketing mix—consistent with the customer's needs—in order to earn a profit. Another customer might want more of some other element of the marketing mix—like more technical help after the sale—and be less sensitive to price.

Sellers must know their costs to negotiate prices effectively. However, negotiated pricing *is* a demand-oriented approach. Here, the seller is very carefully analyzing a particular customer's position on a demand curve—or on different possible demand curves based on different offerings—rather than the overall demand curve for a group of customers. This is a challenging job, and the details are beyond the scope of this book. However, the techniques for supply and demand analysis we've been discussing apply here as they do with other price setting approaches.

CONCLUSION

In this chapter, we discussed various approaches to price setting. Generally, retailers and wholesalers use markups. Some just use the same markups for all their items. Others find that varying the markups increases turnover and profit. In other words, they consider demand and competition!

Many firms use average-cost pricing to help set their prices. But this approach sometimes ignores demand completely. A more realistic approach to average-cost pricing requires a sales forecast—maybe just assuming that sales in the next period will be roughly the same as in the last period. This approach *does* enable the marketing manager to set a price—but the price may or may not cover all costs and earn the desired profit.

Break-even analysis is useful for evaluating possible prices. It provides a rough-and-ready tool for eliminating unworkable prices. But management must estimate demand to evaluate the chance of reaching these possible break-even points.

Marginal analysis is a useful tool for finding the most profitable price—and the quantity to produce. The most profitable quantity is found at the intersection of the marginal revenue and marginal cost curves. To determine the most profitable price, a manager takes the most profitable quantity to the firm's demand curve to find the price target customers will be willing to pay for this quantity.

The major difficulty with demand-oriented pricing is estimating the demand curve. But experienced managers—aided perhaps by marketing research—can estimate the nature of demand for their products. Such estimates are useful—even if they aren't exact. They get you thinking in the right ballpark. Sometimes, when all you need is a decision about raising or lowering price, even rough demand estimates can be very revealing. Further, a firm's demand curve does not cease to exist simply because it's ignored. Some information is better than none at all. And it appears that some marketers do consider demand in their pricing. We see this with value in use pricing, leader pricing, bait pricing, odd-even pricing, psychological pricing, full-line pricing, and even bid pricing.

Throughout the book, we stress that firms must consider the customer before they do anything. This certainly applies to pricing. It means that when managers are setting a price, they have to consider what customers will be willing to pay. This isn't always easy. But it's nice to know that there is a profit range around the best price. Therefore, even rough estimates about what potential customers will buy at various prices will probably lead to a better price than mechanical use of traditional markups or cost-oriented formulas.

While our focus in this chapter is on price setting, it's clear that pricing decisions must consider the cost of offering the whole marketing mix. Smart marketers don't just accept costs as a given. Target marketers always look for ways to be more efficient—to reduce costs while improving what they offer customers. Improved coordination of physical distribution, for example, may improve customer service and reduce costs. Carefully defined target markets may make promotion spending more efficient. Products that really meet customers' needs reduce costly new-product failures. Channel members can shift and share functions—so that the cost of performing needed marketing activities is as low as possible. Marketers should set prices based on demand as well as on costs. But creative marketers look for ways to reduce costs—because costs affect profit.[16]

QUESTIONS AND PROBLEMS

1. Why do many department stores seek a markup of about 40 percent when some discount houses operate on a 20 percent markup?

2. A producer distributed its riding lawn mowers through wholesalers and retailers. The retail selling price was $800, and the manufacturing cost to the company was $312. The retail markup was 35 percent and the wholesale markup 20 percent. (*a*) What was the cost to the wholesaler? To the retailer? (*b*) What percentage markup did the producer take?

3. Relate the concept of stock turnover to the growth of mass-merchandising. Use a simple example in your answer.

4. If total fixed costs are $200,000 and total variable costs are $100,000 at the output of 20,000 units, what are the probable total fixed costs and total variable costs at an output of 10,000 units? What are the average fixed costs, average variable costs, and average costs at these two output levels? Explain what additional information you would want to determine what price should be charged.

5. Explain how experience curve pricing differs from average-cost pricing.

6. Construct an example showing that mechanical use of a very large or a very small markup might still lead to unprofitable operation while some intermediate price would be profitable. Draw a graph and show the break-even point(s).

7. The Davis Company's fixed costs for the year are estimated at $200,000. Its product sells for $250. The variable cost per unit is $200. Sales for the coming year are expected to reach $1,250,000. What is the break-even point? Expected profit? If sales are forecast at only $875,000, should the Davis Company shut down operations? Why?

8. Distinguish among price, marginal revenue, and average revenue (where average revenue is total revenue divided by the quantity sold).

9. Draw a graph showing a demand and supply situation where marginal analysis correctly indicates that the firm should continue producing even though the profit and loss statement shows a loss.

10. Discuss the idea of drawing separate demand curves for different market segments. It seems logical because each target market should have its own marketing mix. But won't this lead to

many demand curves and possible prices? And what will this mean with respect to functional discounts and varying prices in the marketplace? Will it be legal? Will it be practical?

11. Nicor Company is having a profitable year. Its only product sells to wholesalers for 80 cents a can. Its managers feel that a 60 percent gross margin should be maintained. Its manufacturing costs consist of: material, 50 percent of cost; labor, 40 percent of cost; and overhead, 10 percent of cost. Both material and labor costs increased 10 percent since last year. Determine the new price per can based on its present pricing method. Is it wise to stick with a 60 percent margin if a price increase would mean lost customers? Answer using graphs and MC-MR analysis. Show a situation where it would be most profitable to (*a*) raise price, (*b*) leave price alone, (*c*) reduce price.

12. How does a prestige pricing policy fit into a marketing mix? Would exclusive distribution be necessary?

13. Cite a local example of odd-even pricing and evaluate whether it makes sense.

14. Cite a local example of psychological pricing and evaluate whether it makes sense.

15. Distinguish between leader pricing and bait pricing. What do they have in common? How can their use affect a marketing mix?

16. Is a full-line pricing policy available only to producers? Cite local examples of full-line pricing. Why is full-line pricing important?

SUGGESTED CASES

23. Wire Solutions, Inc.
27. Electrotech, Inc.

31. Hendrix Chevrolet, Inc.

COMPUTER-AIDED PROBLEM

18. **Break-Even/Profit Analysis**

This problem lets you see the dynamics of break-even analysis. The starting values (costs, revenues, etc.) for this problem are from the break-even analysis example in this chapter (see Exhibit 18–8).

The first column computes a break-even point. You can change costs and prices to figure new break-even points (in units and dollars). The second column goes further. There you can specify target profit level, and the unit and dollar sales needed to achieve your target profit level will be computed. You can also estimate possible sales quantities and the program will compute costs, sales, and profits. Use this spreadsheet to answer the following questions.

a. *Vary the selling price between $1.00 and $1.40. Prepare a table showing how the break-even point (in units and dollars) changes at the different price levels.*

b. *If you hope to earn a target profit of $15,000, how many units would you have to sell? What would total cost be? Total sales dollars? (Note: Use the right-hand ["profit analysis"] column in the spreadsheet.)*

c. *Using the "profit analysis" column (column 2), allow your estimate of the sale quantity to vary between 64,000 and 96,000. Prepare a table that shows, for each quantity level, what happens to total cost, average cost per unit, and profit. Explain why average cost changes as it does over the different quantity values.*

For additional questions related to this problem, see Exercise 18–5 in the *Learning Aid for Use with Basic Marketing*, 12th edition.

19

Developing Innovative Marketing Plans

When You Finish This Chapter, You Should

1. Know the content of and differences among strategies, marketing plans, and a marketing program.

2. Know how to use S.W.O.T. analysis and other planning approaches to zero in on a marketing strategy that fits the firm's objectives and resources and meets customers' needs.

3. Understand why the product classes and typical mixes are a good starting point for planning.

4. Understand the basic forecasting approaches and why they are used to evaluate the profitability of potential strategies.

5. Know what is involved in preparing a marketing plan, including estimates of costs and revenue and specification of other time-related details.

6. Understand the different ways a firm can plan to become involved in international marketing.

7. Understand the important new terms (shown in red).

By the summer of 1995 Packard Bell—not IBM or Compaq or one of the other pioneers of the personal computer movement—had become the number one marketer of computers. As the PC market matured, a producer who wanted growth had to shift its focus to a new target market—to the final consumers rather than the business users. And Packard Bell was well positioned in this

battle as it had focused on distributing its well-equipped models through consumer electronics chains and other mass-merchandisers. In this environment, many experts felt that only the largest producers with big economies of scale would survive. That put real pressure on Michael Dell—and Dell Computer Corp.—to identify a profitable new strategy.

As a freshman in college, Michael Dell started buying and reselling computers from his dorm room. When he saw how big the opportunity was, he developed a marketing plan and worked to implement it. Over time he added innovative new strategies to reach new target markets—and in the process he built Dell Computer Corp. into a profitable business that earns top customer satisfaction ratings.

When Dell started, the typical marketing mix for PCs emphasized distribution through computer stores that sold to business users and some

final consumers. The quality of the dealers' machines and service didn't always justify the high prices they charged. Moreover, dealers often couldn't give customers the combination of features they wanted from machines they had in stock, and repairs could be a hassle. Dell decided there was a large target market of price-conscious customers who would respond to a different marketing mix. He used direct-response advertising in computer magazines—and customers called a toll-free number to order a computer with the exact features they wanted. Dell used UPS to quickly ship orders directly to the customer. Prices were low, too—because the direct channel held down costs. It also kept Dell in constant contact with customers. Dell also implemented the plan well—with constant improvements—to make good on its promise of reliable machines and superior service. For example, Dell pioneered a system of guaranteed on-site service—within 24 hours. Dell also offers ongoing training programs so all employees work together to "please, not just satisfy" customers.

Dell also developed new strategies to reach new markets. For example, Dell put money into R&D specifically focused on creating the powerful machines that business customers said they wanted. And in 1987 Dell added a direct sales force to call on government and corporate buyers—because they expected in-person selling. The machines that these customers bought to run their corporate networks offered big profit margins.

Dell also realized that there were big opportunities in Europe. Many other firms moved into that market by exporting, but Dell set up its own operations there—because that was a way to control its direct approach. Dell knew it would be a challenge to win over skeptical European buyers. They had never bought big-ticket items such as PCs through the mail. Yet Dell's marketing mix delighted European customers, and in less than five years annual sales in Europe grew to $240 million—40 percent of Dell's revenue.

In late 1989, Dell broke with its tradition and added indirect distribution through office supply superstores. These superstores were becoming an important new channel for reaching small- and medium-sized businesses.

In the 1990s, other firms—including IBM and Compaq—are imitating Dell's direct-order approach and cutting prices deeply. And other giant consumer electronics firms—like Sony—are likely to enter the computer market now that differences between computers and their other home-entertainment products begin to blur. In this frantic competition, Dell now faces slim profit margins and limited growth. Clearly, its future will depend on careful strategy planning. But perhaps Dell can continue to find new ways to satisfy customers' PC-related needs—or even identify new, higher-growth opportunities to pursue.[1]

MARKETING PLANNING PROCESS IS MORE THAN ASSEMBLING THE FOUR Ps

The Dell case shows that developing a successful marketing strategy is a creative process. But it is also a logical process. And the logic that leads to a sound strategy may need to change as the market environment and target customers change.

Even so, strategy planning is guided by basic principles. The marketing concept emphasizes that all of a firm's activities should focus on its target markets. Further, a firm should try to find a competitive advantage in meeting the needs of some target market(s) that it can satisfy very well. The target market(s) should be large enough to support the firm's efforts—and yield a profit. And, ideally, the strategy should take advantage of trends in the external market, not buck them.

As we explained in Chapter 2, a marketing *strategy* consists of a target market and a marketing mix; it is a "big picture" of what a firm will do in some target market. A marketing *plan* includes the time-related details—including expected costs and revenues—for that strategy. In most firms, the marketing manager must ultimately combine the different marketing plans into an overall marketing *program*.

In this chapter, we'll develop these ideas further. We'll start with a review of the many variables that must be considered in the marketing strategy planning process, and we'll highlight some of the key ways a marketing manager can identify the right blend of the marketing mix for an innovative strategy. Then we'll discuss how these ideas come together in a marketing plan.

We'll also discuss ways to forecast target market potential and sales, which is important not only in evaluating opportunities but also in developing the time-related details for a plan. Of course, plans must ultimately be blended into an

Consolidated Freightways plans and develops different marketing mixes—including different services, promotion, and pricing—for different target markets around the world.

overall program—and we'll suggest ways to approach that task. Planning strategies for international markets presents some special challenges, so we'll conclude the chapter by describing the different ways a marketer can address these challenges.

BLENDING THE FOUR Ps TAKES UNDERSTANDING OF A TARGET MARKET

Marketing strategy planning process brings focus to efforts

Developing a good marketing strategy and turning the strategy into a marketing plan requires blending the ideas we've discussed throughout this text. Exhibit 19–1 provides a broad overview of the major areas we've been talking about. Now we must integrate ideas about these different areas to narrow down to logical marketing mixes, marketing strategies, marketing plans—and a marketing program.

As suggested in Exhibit 19–1, developing an effective marketing strategy involves a process of narrowing down to a specific target market and marketing mix that represent a real opportunity. This narrowing down process requires a thorough understanding of the market. That understanding is enhanced by careful analysis of customers' needs, current or prospective competitors, and the firm's own objectives and resources. Similarly, favorable or unfavorable factors and trends in the external market environment may make a potential opportunity more or less attractive.

There are usually more different strategy possibilities than a firm can pursue. Each possible strategy usually has a number of different potential advantages and disadvantages. This can make it difficult to zero in on the best target market and marketing mix. However, as we discussed in Chapter 4, developing a set of specific qualitative and quantitative screening criteria—to define what business and markets the firm wants to compete in—can help eliminate potential strategies that are not well suited for the firm.

EXHIBIT 19–1   Overview of Marketing Strategy Planning Process

Another useful aid for zeroing in on a feasible strategy is *S.W.O.T. analysis*—which identifies and lists the firm's strengths and weaknesses and its opportunities and threats. S.W.O.T. is simply an abbreviation for the first letters of the words *strengths*, *weaknesses*, *opportunities*, and *threats*. A good S.W.O.T. analysis helps the manager focus on a strategy that takes advantage of the firm's opportunities and strengths while avoiding its weaknesses and threats to its success. These can be compared with the pros and cons of strategies that are considered. For example, if a firm is considering a strategy that focuses on a target market that is already being served by several strong competitors, success will usually hinge on some sort of competitive advantage. Such a competitive advantage might be based on a better marketing mix—perhaps an innovative new product, improved distribution, more effective promotion, or a better price. Just offering a marketing mix that is like what is available from competitors usually doesn't provide a competitive advantage—or any real basis for the firm to position or differentiate its marketing mix as better for customers.

Marketing mix flows from target market dimensions

Ideally, the ingredients of a good marketing mix flow logically from all the relevant dimensions of a target market. The market definition and segmenting approaches we discussed in Chapter 3 help the marketing manager identify which dimensions are qualifying and which are determining in customers' choices.

Marketing managers at Oscar Mayer realized that busy working parents wanted a no-hassle lunch for their kids and that the kids wanted some variety. So marketing managers at Oscar Mayer developed a marketing mix that includes the new line of ready-to-eat Lunchables to appeal to kids and attention-getting promotion to inform the parents.

Product benefits must match needs. If and how customers search for information helps to define the promotion blend. Demographic dimensions reveal where customers are located and if they have the income to buy. Where customers shop for or buy products helps define channel alternatives. The value of the whole marketing mix and the urgency of customer needs, combined with an understanding of what customers see as substitute ways of meeting needs, help companies estimate price sensitivity.

It would seem that if we fully understand the needs and attitudes of a target market, then combining the four Ps should be easy. Yet there are three important gaps in this line of reasoning: (1) We don't always know as much as we would like to about the needs and attitudes of our target markets. (2) Competitors are also trying to satisfy these or similar needs—and their efforts may force a firm to shift its marketing mix. (3) The other dimensions of the marketing environment may be changing—which may require more changes in marketing mixes. These points warrant further consideration.

Product classes suggest typical marketing mixes

Even if you don't or can't know all you would like to about a potential target market, you usually know enough to decide whether the product is a consumer product or a business product—and which product class is most relevant (Exhibit 9–3 summarizes the product classes).

Identifying the proper product class helps because it suggests how a typical product should be distributed and promoted. So if you don't know as much as you'd like about potential customers' needs and attitudes, at least knowing how *they* would view the company's product can give you a head start on developing a marketing mix. A convenience product, for example, usually needs more intensive distribution and the producer usually takes on more responsibility for promotion.

QUICK METAL STRATEGY PLANNING FASTENS ON CUSTOMER NEEDS—AND PROFITS

Loctite Corporation, a producer of industrial supplies, used careful strategy planning to launch Quick Metal—a puttylike adhesive for repairing worn machine parts. Loctite chemists had developed similar products in the past. But managers paid little attention to developing a *complete marketing strategy*—and sales had been poor.

Before creating Quick Metal, Loctite identified some attractive target customers. Research showed that production people were eager to try any product that helped get broken machines back into production. Quick Metal was developed to meet the needs of this target market. Ads appealed to such needs with copy promising that Quick Metal "keeps machinery running until the new parts arrive." Channel members also received attention. During the introduction stage, sales reps made frequent phone calls

and sales visits to the nearly 700 wholesalers who handle Loctite products. Loctite awarded cash prices to those selling the most Quick Metal.

A tube of Quick Metal was priced at $17.75—about twice the price (and profit margin) of competing products. But Loctite's customers weren't concerned about price. They responded to a quality product that could keep their production lines operating.

Based on past experience, some estimated that a typical product for this market might reach sales of $300,000 a year. But Loctite didn't rely on a typical strategy. Instead the company offered a carefully targeted marketing mix to meet the needs of a *specific* target market. It sold 100,000 tubes the first week—and within seven months sales exceeded $2.2 million. Loctite's careful planning paid off in an immediate market success—and high profits.[2]

A specialty product needs a clear brand identity—which may require a positioning effort. A new unsought product will need a mix that leads customers through the adoption process.

It's reassuring to see that product classes do summarize some of what you would like to know about target markets and what marketing mixes are relevant. After all, what others have done in similar situations must have satisfied someone—and that can serve as a guide. Beyond this, you need judgment or perhaps some marketing research. In this way, you can use past experience—while not relying on that experience blindly.

Typical is not necessarily right

The typical marketing mix for a given product class is not necessarily right for all situations. Some very profitable marketing mixes depart from the typical—to satisfy some target markets better.

A marketing manager may have to develop a mix that is *not* typical because of various market realities—including special characteristics of the product or target market, the competitive environment, and each firm's capabilities and limitations. In fact, it is often through differentiation of the firm's product and/or other elements of the marketing mix that the marketing manager can offer target customers unique value.

Superior mixes may be breakthrough opportunities

When marketing managers fully understand their target markets, they may be able to develop marketing mixes that are superior to competitors' mixes. Such understanding may provide breakthrough opportunities. Taking advantage of these opportunities can lead to large sales—and profitable growth. This is why we stress the importance of looking for breakthrough opportunities rather than just trying to imitate competitors' offerings.

NutraSweet built its original success on an innovative product that met consumers' needs. But the strategy NutraSweet's marketing managers planned involved more than a good product. The typical marketing strategy for firms that supply ingredients to food and soft-drink companies emphasized personal selling to producers. In contrast, NutraSweet's marketing managers used mass selling to promote their brand name and red swirl logo directly to consumers.

They also persuaded producers who used the ingredient to feature the NutraSweet brand name prominently on containers and in ads. In addition, because there was little direct competition, they used a profitable skimming approach to pricing—and charged different producer-customers different prices depending on the value NutraSweet added to their product. Now that NutraSweet's patent has expired, competitors will face a challenge entering the market because it will take a huge marketing effort—and a high promotion budget—to offset consumers' familiarity with the NutraSweet name.[3]

Inferior mixes are easy to reject

Just as some mixes are superior, some mixes are clearly inferior—or unsuitable. For example, a national TV advertising campaign might make sense for a large company—but it might be completely out of the question for a small manufacturer that only has the resources to start offering a new product in a limited geographic area.

Marketing manager must blend the four Ps

Exhibit 19–2 reviews the major marketing strategy decision areas organized by the four Ps. Each of these requires careful decision making. Yet, marketing planning involves much more than just independent decisions and assembling the parts into a marketing mix. The four Ps must be creatively *blended*—so the firm develops the best mix for its target market. In other words, each decision must fit well as part of a logical whole to work well with all of the others.

Throughout the text, we've given the job of integrating the four Ps strategy decisions to the marketing manager. Now you should see the need for this

EXHIBIT 19–2   Strategy Decision Areas Organized by the Four Ps

Product	Place	Promotion	Price
Physical good	Objectives	Objectives	Objectives
Service	Channel type	Promotion blend	Flexibility
Features	Market exposure	Salespeople	Level over
Quality level	Kinds of	Kind	product life
Accessories	middlemen	Number	cycle
Installation	Kinds and	Selection	Geographic terms
Instructions	locations of	Training	Discounts
Warranty	stores	Motivation	Allowances
Product lines	How to handle	Advertising	
Packaging	transporting	Targets	
Branding	and storing	Kinds of ads	
	Service levels	Media type	
	Recruiting	Copy thrust	
	middlemen	Prepared by	
	Managing	whom	
	channels	Sales promotion	
		Publicity	

Intel could plan a marketing strategy—and forecast likely sales—for its Pentium processors based on the stage in the product life cycle and the experience it had with its earlier 386 and 486 processors.

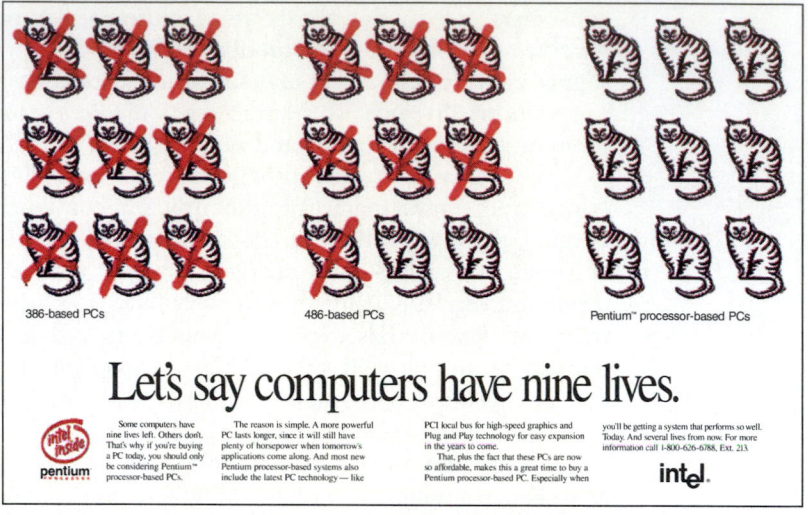

integrating role. It is easy for specialists to focus on their own areas and expect the rest of the company to work for or around them. This is especially true in larger firms—where specialists are needed—just because the size of the whole marketing job is too big for one person. Yet, the ideas of the product manager, advertising manager, sales manager, and physical distribution manager may have to be adjusted to improve the whole mix. It's critical that each marketing mix decision work well with all of the others. A breakdown in any one decision area may doom the whole strategy to failure.

Product life cycle guides planning

Careful consideration of where a firm's offering fits in the product life cycle can also be a big help in evaluating the best marketing mix. Exhibit 19–3 summarizes how marketing mix variables typically change over the product life cycle. This exhibit is a good review of many topics we've discussed throughout the text. Certainly, the pioneering effort required for a really new product concept is different from the job of taking market share away from an established competitor late in the market growth stage.

Further, when you're thinking about the product life cycle, don't forget that markets change continually. This means you must plan strategies that can adjust to changing conditions. The original marketing plan for a new marketing strategy may even include details about what adjustments in the marketing mix or target market will be required as the nature of competition and the adoption process evolve.[4]

FORECASTING TARGET MARKET POTENTIAL AND SALES

Effective strategy planning—and developing a marketing plan—require estimates of future sales, costs, and profits. Without such information, it's hard to know if a strategy is potentially profitable.

The marketing manager's estimates of sales, costs, and profits are usually based on a forecast (estimate) of target **market potential**—what a whole market segment might buy—and a **sales forecast**—an estimate of how much an industry or firm

EXHIBIT 19–3   Typical Changes in Marketing Variables over the Product Life Cycle

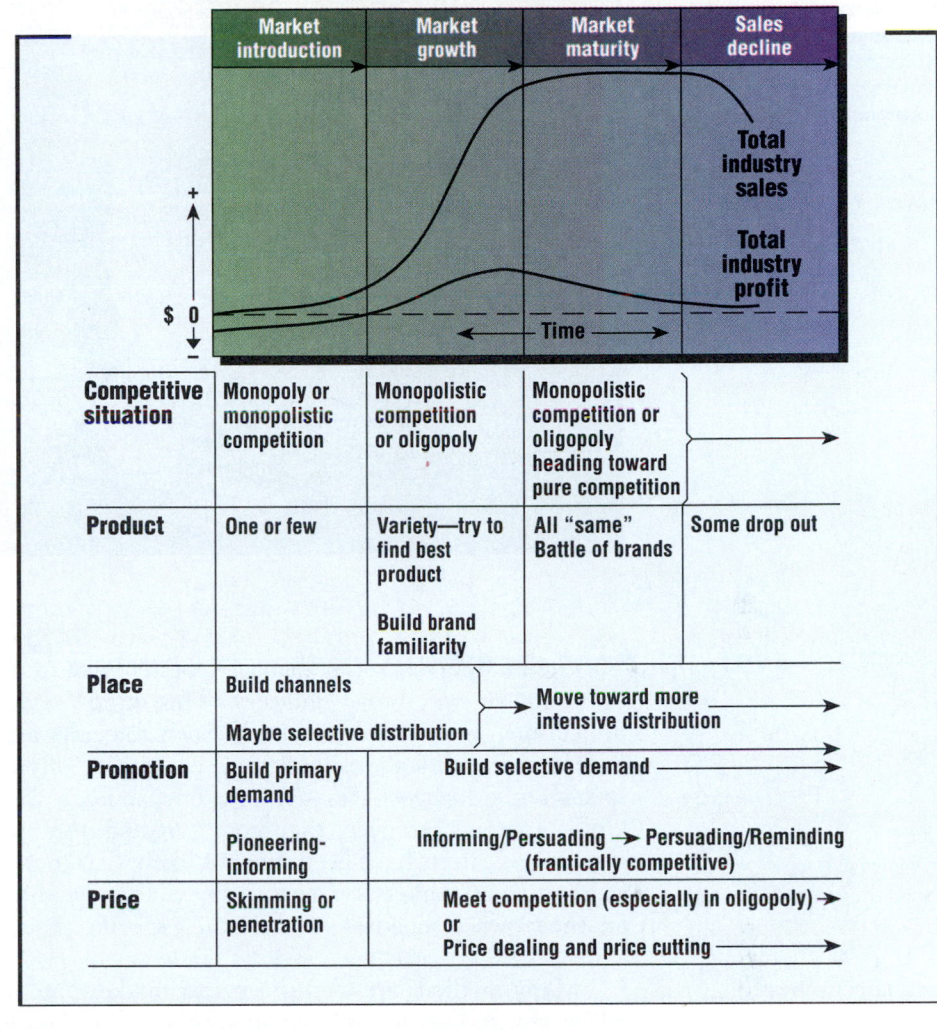

	Market introduction	Market growth	Market maturity	Sales decline
Competitive situation	Monopoly or monopolistic competition	Monopolistic competition or oligopoly	Monopolistic competition or oligopoly heading toward pure competition	
Product	One or few	Variety—try to find best product Build brand familiarity	All "same" Battle of brands	Some drop out
Place	Build channels Maybe selective distribution	Move toward more intensive distribution		
Promotion	Build primary demand Pioneering-informing	Build selective demand Informing/Persuading → Persuading/Reminding (frantically competitive)		
Price	Skimming or penetration	Meet competition (especially in oligopoly) → or Price dealing and price cutting		

hopes to sell to a market segment. Usually we must first try to judge market potential before we can estimate what share a particular firm may be able to win with its particular marketing mix.

Three levels of forecast are useful

We're interested in forecasting the potential in specific market segments. To do this, it helps to make three levels of forecasts.

Some economic conditions affect the entire global economy. Others may influence only one country or a particular industry. And some may affect only one company or one product's sales potential. For this reason, a common approach to forecasting is to:

1. Develop a *national income forecast* (for each country in which the firm operates) and use this to:
2. Develop an *industry sales forecast*, which then is used to:
3. Develop *specific company* and *product forecasts*.

Marketing managers for Genentech work together to develop a sales forecast, which they need to prepare a marketing plan for their new biotechnology product.

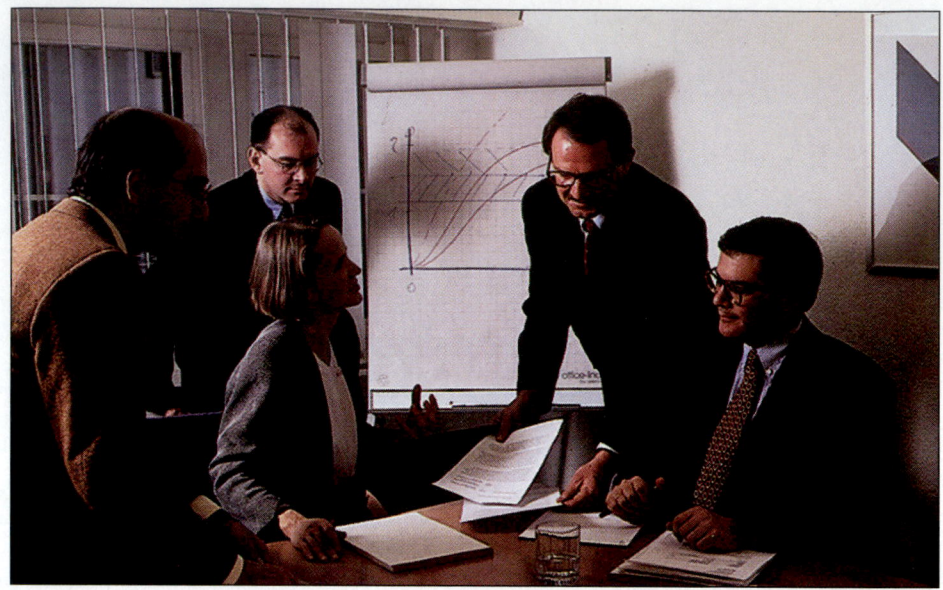

Generally, a marketing manager doesn't have to make forecasts for a national economy or the broad industry. This kind of forecasting—basically trend projecting—is a specialty in itself. Such forecasts are available in business and government publications, and large companies often have their own technical specialists. Managers can use just one source's forecast or combine several. Unfortunately, however, the more targeted the marketing manager's earlier segmenting efforts have been, the less likely that industry forecasts will match the firm's product-markets. So managers have to move directly to estimating potential for their own companies—and for their specific products.

Two approaches to forecasting

Many methods are used to forecast market potential and sales, but they can all be grouped into two basic approaches: (1) extending past behavior and (2) predicting future behavior. The large number of methods may seem confusing at first, but this variety has an advantage. Forecasts are so important that managers often develop forecasts in two or three different ways and then compare the differences before preparing a final forecast.

Extending past behavior can miss important turning points

When we forecast for existing products, we usually have some past data to go on. The basic approach—called **trend extension**—extends past experience into the future. With existing products, for example, the past trend of actual sales may be extended into the future. See Exhibit 19–4.

Ideally, when extending past sales behavior, we should decide why sales vary. This is the difficult and time-consuming part of sales forecasting. Usually we can gather a lot of data about the product or market—or about changes in the marketing environment. But unless we know the *reason* for past sales variations, it's hard to predict in what direction—and by how much—sales will move. Graphing the data and statistical techniques—including correlation and regression analysis—can be useful here. (These techniques, which are beyond our scope, are discussed in beginning statistics courses.)

EXHIBIT 19–4   Straight-Line Trend Projection—Extends Past Sales into the Future

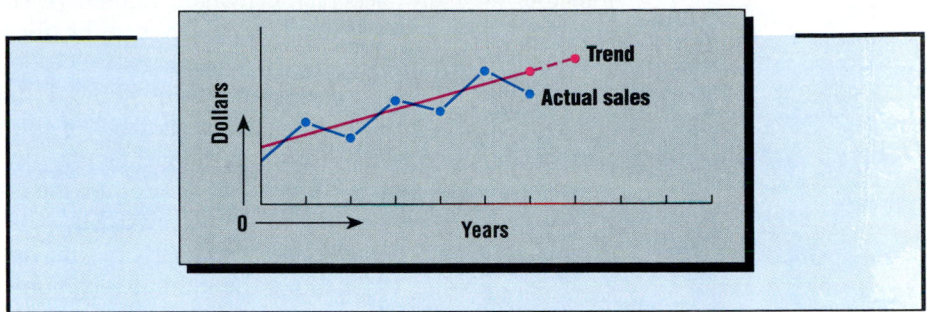

Once we know why sales vary, we can usually develop a specific forecast. Sales may be moving directly up as population grows, for example. So we can just estimate how population is expected to grow and project the impact on sales.

The weakness of the trend extension method is that it assumes past conditions will continue unchanged into the future. In fact, the future isn't always like the past. For example, for years the trend in sales of disposable diapers moved closely with the number of new births. However, as the number of women in the workforce increased and as more women returned to jobs after babies were born, use of disposable diapers increased, and the trend changed. As in this example, trend extension estimates will be wrong whenever big changes occur. For this reason—although they may extend past behavior for one estimate—most managers look for another way to help them forecast sharp market changes.

Predicting future behavior takes judgment

When we try to predict what will happen in the future—instead of just extending the past—we have to use other methods and add a bit more judgment. Some of these methods (to be discussed later) include juries of executive opinion, salespeople's estimates, surveys, panels, and market tests.

FORECASTING COMPANY AND PRODUCT SALES BY EXTENDING PAST BEHAVIOR

Past sales can be extended

At the very least, a marketing manager ought to know what the firm's present markets look like—and what it has sold to them in the past. A detailed sales analysis—for products and geographic areas—helps to project future results.

Just extending past sales into the future may not seem like much of a forecasting method. But it's better than just assuming that next year's total sales will be the same as this year's.

Factor method includes more than time

A simple extension of past sales gives one forecast. But it's usually desirable to tie future sales to something more than the passage of time.

The factor method tries to do this. The **factor method** tries to forecast sales by finding a relation between the company's sales and some other factor (or factors). The basic formula is: something (past sales, industry sales, etc.) *times* some factor *equals* sales forecast. A **factor** is a variable that shows the relation of some other variable to the item being forecast. For instance, in our example above, both the birthrate and the number of working mothers are factors related to sales of disposable diapers.

A bread producer example

The following example—about a bread producer—shows how firms can make forecasts for many geographic market segments—using the factor method and available data. This general approach can be useful for any firm—producer, wholesaler, or retailer.

Analysis of past sales relationships showed that the bread manufacturer regularly sold one-tenth of 1 percent (0.001) of the total retail food sales in its various target markets. This is a single factor. By using this single factor, a manager could estimate the producer's sales for the coming period by multiplying a forecast of expected retail food sales by 0.001.

Sales & Marketing Management magazine makes retail food sales estimates each year. Exhibit 19–5 shows the kind of geographically detailed data available.

Let's carry this bread example further—using the data in Exhibit 19–5 for Hartford County in Connecticut. Hartford's food sales were $1,822,561,000 for the previous year. By simply accepting last year's food sales as an estimate of next year's sales—and multiplying the food sales estimate for Hartford by the 0.001 factor (the firm's usual share of food purchases in such markets), the manager would have an estimate of next year's bread sales in Hartford. That is, last year's food sales estimate ($1,822,561,000) times 0.001 equals this year's bread sales estimate of $1,822,561.

Factor method can use several factors

The factor method is not limited to just one factor; several factors can be used together. For example, *Sales & Marketing Management* regularly gives a "buying power index" (BPI) as a measure of the potential in different geographic areas. See Exhibit 19–5. This index considers (1) the population in a market, (2) the market's income, and (3) retail sales in that market. The BPI for the Hartford, Connecticut, metro area, for example, is 0.5230—that is, Hartford accounts for 0.5230 percent of the total U.S. buying power. This means that consumers who live in Hartford have higher than average buying power. We know this because Hartford accounts for about 0.4374 percent of the U.S. population, so its buying power is about 19 percent higher than average relative to other cities that size.

Using several factors rather than only one uses more information. And in the case of the BPI, it gives a single measure of a market's potential. Rather than falling back to using population only, or income only, or trying to develop a special index, the BPI can be used in the same way that we used the 0.001 factor in the bread example.

Producers of business products can use several factors too

Exhibit 19–6 shows how a marketing manager for a firm that makes corrugated fiber boxes used several factors to estimate the sales potential in a particular geographic area. The manager started with trade association data on the value of shipments (sales) by all fiber box suppliers to firms in particular industries (column 1). The trade association estimates were for the *national* market. Note, however, that they were grouped by standard industrial classification (SIC) code industry groups. As we discussed in Chapter 8, data on business markets is often organized by SIC codes. That makes it possible to combine different types of data, which is what the manager did here.

Specifically, the manager divided the trade association estimates by government data on the number of people employed in each industry SIC group (column 2). The result, shown in column 3, is simply an estimate of the value of boxes used per employee in each industry group. For example, furniture and fixture manufacturers buy an average of $245 worth of boxes per employee.

EXHIBIT 19–5 Sample of Pages from *Sales & Marketing Management's* Survey of Buying Power

CONNECTICUT

POPULATION

S&MM ESTIMATES: 12/31/92

RETAIL SALES BY STORE GROUP

METRO AREA County City	Total Population (Thou-sands)	% Of U.S.	Median Age Of Pop.	% of Pop. by Age Group 18-24 Years	25-34 Years	35-49 Years	50 & Over	House-holds Thou-sands)	Total Retail Sales ($000)	Food ($000)	Eating & Drinking Places ($000)	General Mdse. ($000)	Furniture/ Furnish. Appliance ($000)	Auto-motive ($000)	Drug ($000)
HARTFORD	**1,123.3**	**.4374**	**34.9**	**10.5**	**16.9**	**23.0**	**26.8**	**424.2**	**9,781,727**	**1,822,561**	**1,097,526**	**1,030,816**	**504,698**	**1,777,626**	**388,044**
Hartford	848.5	.3304	35.2	10.0	16.8	22.6	27.8	323.8	7,788,546	1,361,656	882,372	894,258	436,486	1,372,817	316,152
Bristol	60.4	.0235	34.1	10.0	19.3	21.3	26.9	23.9	697,634	132,058	41,711	90,615	18,292	244,586	25,041
East Hartford. . . .	50.2	.0196	36.1	10.0	18.4	20.6	31.1	20.2	630,905	82,047	63,608	33,784	20,506	155,079	17,076
Enfield	45.4	.0177	33.7	9.7	20.0	21.4	25.9	16.0	580,168	99,811	49,132	102,993	30,423	79,676	16,778
• Hartford	139.2	.0542	28.9	14.8	18.6	18.5	20.2	51.2	813,865	87,012	170,878	94,389	42,847	127,859	47,252
Manchester.	51.4	.0200	35.2	9.3	18.5	22.2	28.1	20.7	688,929	135,544	49,601	94,282	31,491	140,374	18,590
New Britain	75.2	.0293	33.2	13.1	18.8	17.6	29.0	30.0	382,923	87,274	39,479	18,764	11,844	96,162	22,962
West Hartford . . .	59.9	.0233	41.0	8.1	12.7	22.0	37.5	23.8	747,775	140,595	69,260	130,817	57,274	76,328	28,066
Middlesex	144.9	.0564	35.4	9.7	17.3	24.6	26.2	55.5	1,219,903	265,517	111,825	87,057	45,984	247,056	43,180
• Middletown. . . .	43.3	.0169	32.1	15.2	21.2	20.3	23.5	17.1	383,136	62,424	31,411	36,242	11,625	83,953	14,628
Tolland	129.9	.0506	32.0	15.3	16.8	24.3	20.8	44.9	773,278	195,388	103,329	49,501	22,228	157,753	28,712
SUBURBAN TOTAL . .	940.8	.3663	36.0	9.7	16.4	23.8	28.0	355.9	8,584,726	1,673,125	895,237	900,185	450,226	1,565,814	326,164

EFFECTIVE BUYING INCOME

S&MM ESTIMATES: 12/31/92

METRO AREA County City	Total EBI ($000)	Median Hsld. EBI	% of Hslds. by EBI Group: (A) $10,000-$19,999 (B) $20,000-$34,999 (C) $35,000-$49,999 (D) $50,000 & Over A	B	C	D	Buying Power Index
HARTFORD	**22,429,933**	**45,367**	**10.4**	**18.4**	**19.4**	**44.0**	**.5230**
Hartford	16,981,205	44,521	10.8	18.6	18.8	43.2	.4017
Bristol	1,099,328	42,272	11.2	20.9	21.6	39.3	.0294
East Hartford. . . .	891,850	40,536	11.8	22.0	22.1	36.4	.0249
Enfield	816,560	48,593	8.7	16.6	22.2	47.8	.0228
• Hartford	1,676,134	25,176	19.0	23.5	16.7	18.8	.0447
Manchester.	1,023,305	43,970	9.9	21.6	22.0	40.9	.0276
New Britain	1,195,080	33,370	16.1	25.0	20.1	27.3	.0270
West Hartford . . .	1,653,481	53,276	8.6	15.4	17.3	53.3	.0372
Middlesex	3,125,974	49,087	8.7	17.5	19.9	48.8	.0697
• Middletown. . . .	857,462	42,829	10.8	20.2	22.2	39.1	.0202
Tolland	2,322,754	46,225	9.5	18.6	21.8	44.3	.0516
SUBURBAN TOTAL . .	19,896,337	48,410	9.1	17.7	19.5	47.9	.4581

EFFECTIVE BUYING INCOME

METRO AREA County City	Total EBI ($000)	Median Hsld. EBI	% of Hslds. by EBI Group: (A) $10,000-$19,999 (B) $20,000-$34,999 (C) $35,000-$49,999 (D) $50,000 & Over A	B	C	D	Buying Power Index
NEW LONDON–NORWICH	**4,463,108**	**40,491**	**11.4**	**22.8**	**21.2**	**36.9**	**.1082**
New London	4,463,108	40,491	11.4	22.8	21.2	36.9	.1082
Groton (town)	738,101	36,983	11.6	28.8	23.6	30.1	.0181
• New London	397,937	29,202	16.8	28.8	18.1	21.4	.0128
• Norwich	583,680	32,239	16.3	26.3	18.9	26.3	.0165
SUBURBAN TOTAL . . .	3,481,491	44,409	9.5	21.1	22.1	41.8	.0789
OTHER COUNTIES							
Litchfield	3,506,466	44,259	10.5	19.6	21.6	41.5	.0785
Windham	1,599,619	36,852	14.1	23.4	21.9	30.8	.0399
TOTAL METRO COUNTIES .	**63,497,886**	**45,897**	**10.4**	**18.2**	**18.4**	**45.0**	**1.4620**
TOTAL STATE	**68,603,971**	**45,458**	**10.6**	**18.4**	**18.7**	**44.3**	**1.5804**

Then the manager multiplied the value per employee number by the number of people employed in each industry group in the target county (column 4). This results in an estimate of the market potential for each industry group (column 5) in that county. For example, since there are 616 people in this county who work in furniture and fixture companies, the sales potential in that industry is only about $151,000 (616 employees × $245 per employee). The sum of the estimates for specific industries is the total market potential in that county.

EXHIBIT 19–6 Estimated Market for Corrugated and Solid Fiber Boxes for Industry Groups, Phoenix, Arizona, Metropolitan Statistical Area

		National Data			Maricopa County	
		(1)	(2)	(3)	(4)	(5)
SIC Code	Major Industry Group	Value of Box Shipments by End Use ($000)*	Employment by Industry Group†	Value of Shipments per Employee by Industry Group (1÷2) ($)	Employment by Industry Group†	Estimated Sales in This Market (3×4) ($000)
20	Food and kindred products	$586,164	1,578,305	$371	4,973	$1,845
25	Furniture and fixtures	89,341	364,166	245	616	151
32	Stone, clay, and glass products	226,621	548,058	413	1,612	666
33	Primary metal industries	19,611	1,168,110	16	2,889	46
34	Fabricated metal products	130,743	1,062,096	123	2,422	298
35	Machinery (except electrical)	58,834	1,445,558	40	5,568	228
36	Electrical machinery, equipment, and supplies	119,848	1,405,382	85	6,502	553
					Total	$3,787

*Based on data reported in *Fiber Box Industry Statistics*, Fiber Box Association.

†U.S. Bureau of the Census, *County Business Patterns*.

A firm thinking of going into that market would have to estimate the share it could get with its own marketing mix in order to get its sales forecast. This approach could be used county by county to estimate the potential in many geographic target markets. It could also aid management's control job. If the firm is already in this industry, it can compare its actual sales (by SIC code) with the potential to see how it's doing. If its typical market share is 10 percent of the market—and it has only 2 to 5 percent of the market in various SIC submarkets—then it may need to change its marketing mix.

Times series and leading series may help estimate a fluctuating future

Not all past economic or sales behavior can be neatly extended with a straight line or some manipulation. Economic activity has ups and downs, and other uncontrollable factors change. To cope with such variation, statisticians have developed time series analysis techniques. **Time series** are historical records of the fluctuations in economic variables. We can't give a detailed discussion of these techniques here, but note that there *are* techniques to handle daily, weekly, monthly, seasonal, and annual variations.[5]

All forecasters dream of finding an accurate **leading series**—a time series that changes in the same direction *but ahead of* the series to be forecast. For example, car producers watch trends in the "Index of Consumer Sentiment," which is based on regular surveys of consumers' attitudes about their likely future financial security. People are less likely to buy a car or other big-ticket item if they are worried about their future income. As this suggests, a drop in the index usually "leads" a drop in car sales. It is important that there be some logical relation between the leading series and what is being forecast.

No single series has yet been found that leads GNP—or other national figures. Lacking such a series, forecasters develop **indices**—statistical combinations of several time series—in an effort to find some time series that will lead the series they're trying to forecast. Government agencies publish some indices of this type. And business publications—like *Business Week* and *The London Financial Times*—publish their own indices.

PREDICTING FUTURE BEHAVIOR CALLS FOR MORE JUDGMENT AND SOME OPINIONS

These past-extending methods use quantitative data—projecting past experience into the future and assuming that the future will be like the past. But this is risky in competitive markets. Usually, it's desirable to add some judgment to other forecasts before making the final forecast yourself.

Jury of executive opinion adds judgment

One of the oldest and simplest methods of forecasting—the **jury of executive opinion**—combines the opinions of experienced executives—perhaps from marketing, production, finance, purchasing, and top management. Each executive estimates market potential and sales for the *coming years*. Then they try to work out a consensus.

The main advantage of the jury approach is that it can be done quickly and easily. On the other hand, the results may not be very good. There may be too much extending of the past. Some of the executives may have little contact with outside market influences. But their estimates could point to major shifts in customer demand or competition.

Estimates from salespeople can help too

Using salespeople's estimates to forecast is like the jury approach. But salespeople are more likely than home office managers to be familiar with customer reactions—and what competitors are doing. Their estimates are especially useful in some business markets where the few customers may be well known to the salespeople. But this approach may be useful in any type of market. Good retail clerks have a feel for their markets—their opinions shouldn't be ignored.

However, managers who use estimates from salespeople should be aware of the limitations. For example, new salespeople may not know much about their markets. Even experienced salespeople may not be aware of possible changes in the economic climate or the firm's other environments. And if salespeople think the manager is going to use the estimates to set sales quotas, the estimates may be low!

Surveys, panels, and market tests

Special surveys of final buyers, retailers, and/or wholesalers can show what's happening in different market segments. Some firms use panels of stores—or final consumers—to keep track of buying behavior and to decide when just extending past behavior isn't enough.

Surveys are sometimes combined with market tests when the company wants to estimate customers' reactions to possible changes in its marketing mix. A market test might show that a product increased its share of the market by 10 percent when its price was dropped 1 cent below competition. But this extra business might be quickly lost if the price were increased 1 cent above competition. Such market experiments help the marketing manager make good estimates of future sales when one or more of the four Ps is changed.

Accuracy depends on the marketing mix

Forecasting can help a marketing manager estimate the size of possible market opportunities. But the accuracy of any sales forecast depends on whether the firm selects and implements a marketing mix that turns these opportunities into sales and profits.[6]

A marketing plan spells out the detailed costs of different marketing activities in the strategy. For example, Microsoft's plan for its Money software product might include estimates of the cost of each ad as well as the cost of the whole promotion blend.

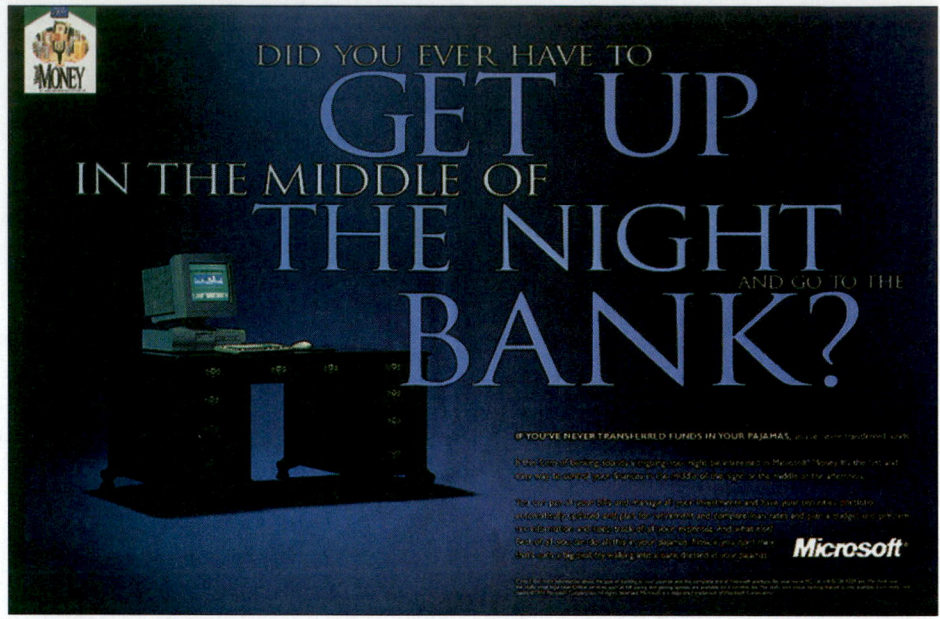

ANALYSIS OF COSTS AND SALES CAN GUIDE PLANNING

Once a manager has narrowed down to a few reasonable marketing mixes—and the relevant forecasts—comparing the sales, costs, and profitability of the different alternatives helps in selecting the marketing mix the firm will implement.

Estimate the cost of each activity

Estimating the costs of the marketing activities for a strategy may be easy or hard depending on the situation. Sometimes the accounting department can help with information about what average costs for similar activities have been in the past. Or, sometimes estimates of competitors' costs—perhaps pulled out of annual reports—can provide some guidance. However, in general the best approach for estimating costs is to use the task method. We recommended this approach in Chapter 14 when we focused on promotion costs and budgets. However, the same ideas apply to any area of marketing activity. The estimated cost and budget for each activity is based on the job to be done—perhaps the number of salespeople needed to call on new customers or the amount of inventory required to provide some distribution customer service level. The costs of these individual tasks are then totaled—to determine how much should be budgeted for the overall plan. With this detailed approach, the firm can subsequently assemble its overall marketing budget directly from individual plans—rather than just relying on historical patterns or ratios.

Compare the profitability of alternative strategies

Once costs and revenue for possible strategies are estimated, it makes sense to compare them with respect to overall profitability. Exhibit 19–7 shows such a comparison for a small appliance currently selling for $15—Mix A in the example. Here, the marketing manager simply estimates the costs and likely results of four reasonable alternatives. And, assuming profit is the objective *and* there are adequate resources to consider each of the alternatives, marketing Mix C is obviously the best alternative.

EXHIBIT 19–7 Comparing the Estimated Sales, Costs, and Profits of Four "Reasonable" Alternative Marketing Mixes*

Marketing Mix	Price	Selling Cost	Advertising Cost	Total Units	Sales	Total Cost	Total Profit
A	$15	$20,000	$ 5,000	5,000	$ 75,000	$ 70,000	$ 5,000
B	15	20,000	20,000	7,000	105,000	95,000	10,000
C	20	30,000	30,000	7,000	140,000	115,000	25,000
D	25	40,000	40,000	5,000	125,000	125,000	0

*For the same target market, assuming product costs per unit are $5 and fixed (overhead) costs are $20,000.

Spreadsheet analysis speeds through calculations

Comparing the alternatives in Exhibit 19–7 is quite simple. But sometimes marketing managers need much more detail to evaluate a plan. Hundreds of calculations may be required to see how specific marketing resources relate to expected outcomes—like total costs, expected sales, and profit. To make that part of the planning job simpler and faster, marketing managers often use spreadsheet analysis. With **spreadsheet analysis**, costs, sales, and other information related to a problem are organized into a data table—a spreadsheet—to show how changing the value of one or more of the numbers affects the other numbers. This is possible because the relationships among the variables are programmed in the computer software. Lotus 1-2-3, Excel, Supercalc, and Appleworks are examples of well-known spreadsheet programs. If you've been working the computer-aided problems in this book, you're already familiar with spreadsheet analysis. Even if you haven't, the basic idea is not complicated.

A spreadsheet helps answer "what if" questions

Spreadsheet analysis allows the marketing manager to evaluate what-if type questions. For example, a marketing manager might be interested in the question "What if I charge a higher price and the number of units sold stays the same? What will happen to profit?" To look at how a spreadsheet program might be used to help answer this what-if question, let's take a closer look at Mix C in Exhibit 19–7.

The manager might set up the data in this table as a computer spreadsheet. The table involves a number of relationships. For example, price times total units equals sales; and total cost equals selling cost plus advertising cost plus overhead cost plus total product costs (7,000 units × $5 per unit). If these relationships are programmed in the spreadsheet, a marketing manager can ask questions like: "What if I raise the price to $20.20 and still sell 7,000 units? What will happen to profit?" To get the answer, all the manager needs to do is type the new price in the spreadsheet and the program computes the new profit—$26,400.

In addition, the manager may also want to do many what-if analyses—for example, to see how sales and profit change over a range of prices. Computerized spreadsheet analysis does this quickly and easily. For example, if the manager wants to see what happens to total revenue as the price varies between some minimum (say, $19.80) and a maximum (say, $20.20), the program can show the total revenue and profit for a number of price levels in the range from $19.80 to $20.20. See Exhibit 19–8.

In a problem like this, the marketing manager might be able to do the same calculations quickly by hand. But with more complicated problems the spreadsheet program can be a big help—making it very convenient to more carefully analyze different alternatives.

EXHIBIT 19–8 A Spreadsheet Analysis Showing How a Change in Price Affects Sales and Profit (based on Marketing Mix C from Exhibit 19–7)

Price	Selling Cost	Advertising Cost	Total Units	Sales	Total Cost	Total Profit
$19.80	$30,000	$30,000	7,000	$138,600	$115,000	$23,600
19.90	30,000	30,000	7,000	139,300	115,000	24,300
20.00	30,000	30,000	7,000	140,000	115,000	25,000
20.10	30,000	30,000	7,000	140,700	115,000	25,700
20.20	30,000	30,000	7,000	141,400	115,000	26,400

THE MARKETING PLAN BRINGS ALL THE DETAILS TOGETHER

Marketing plan provides a blueprint for implementation

Once the manager has selected the target market, decided on the (integrated) marketing mix to meet that target market's needs, and developed estimates of the costs and revenue for that strategy, it's time to put it all together in the marketing plan. The plan basically serves as a "blueprint" for what the firm will do.

Exhibit 19–9, on pages 610–611, provides a summary outline of the different sections of a complete marketing plan. You can see that this outline is basically an abridged overview of the topics we've covered throughout the text—and highlighted in this chapter. Thus, you can "flesh out" your thinking for any portion of a marketing plan by reviewing the section of the book where that topic is discussed in more detail.

Marketing plan spells out the timing of the strategy

Some time schedule is implicit in any strategy. A marketing plan simply spells out this time period—and the time-related details. Usually, we think in terms of some reasonable length of time—such as six months, a year, or a few years. But it might be only a month or two in some cases—especially when rapid changes in fashion or technology are important. Or a strategy might be implemented over several years—perhaps the length of a product life cycle or at least the early stages of the product's life.

Although the outline in Exhibit 19–9 does not explicitly show a place for the time frame for the plan or the specific costs for each decision area, these should be included in the plan—along with expected estimates of sales and profit—so that the plan can be compared with *actual performance* in the future. In other words, the plan not only makes it clear to everyone what is to be accomplished and how—but it also provides a basis for the control process after the plan is implemented.

Flowcharts help set time-related details for the plan

Figuring out and planning the time-related details and schedules for all of the activities in the marketing plan can be a challenge—especially if the plan involves a big start-from-scratch effort. To do a better job in this area, many managers have turned to flowcharting techniques such as CPM (critical path method) or PERT (program evaluation and review technique). These methods were originally developed as part of the U.S. space program (NASA) to ensure that the various contractors and subcontractors stayed on schedule—and reached their goals as planned. PERT, CPM, and other similar project management approaches are even more popular now since inexpensive programs for personal computers make them easier and faster to use. Updating is easier too.

This Arrow Co. ad drives home the idea that its line of golf fashions is different from those typically offered by other companies.
Source: Client—Arrow Shirts, agency—Mandelbaum Mooney Ashley; photo by John Gipe.

The computer programs develop detailed flowcharts to show which marketing activities must be done in sequence and which can be done concurrently. These charts also show the time needed for various activities. Totaling the time allotments along the various chart paths shows the most critical (the longest) path—as well as the best starting and ending dates for the various activities.

Flowcharting is not really complicated. Basically, it requires that all the activities—which have to be performed anyway—be identified ahead of time and their probable duration and sequence shown on one diagram. (It uses nothing more than addition and subtraction.) Working with such information should be part of the planning function anyway. Then the chart can be used later to guide implementation and control.[7]

A complete plan spells out the reasons for decisions

The plan outline shown in Exhibit 19–9 is quite complete. It doesn't just provide information about marketing mix decisions—it also includes information about customers (including segmenting dimensions), competitors' strategies, other aspects of the marketing environment, and the company's objectives and resources. This material provides important background relevant to the "why" of the marketing mix and target market decisions.

Too often, managers do not include this information; their plans just lay out the details of the target market and the marketing mix strategy decisions. This shortcut approach is more common when the plan is really just an update of a strategy that has been in place for some time. However, that approach can be risky.

Managers too often make the mistake of casually updating plans in minor ways—perhaps just changing some costs or sales forecasts—but otherwise just sticking with what was done in the past. A big problem with this approach is that it's easy to lose sight of why those strategy decisions were made in the first place.

EXHIBIT 19–9 Summary Outline of Different Sections of Marketing Plan

Name of Product-Market

Major screening criteria relevant to product-market opportunity selected
    Quantitative (ROI, profitability, risk level, etc.)
    Qualitative (nature of business preferred, social responsibility, etc.)
    Major constraints

Customer Analysis (organizational or final consumer)

Possible segmenting dimensions (customer needs, other characteristics)
    Identification of qualifying dimensions and determining dimensions
Identification of target market(s) (one or more specific segments)
    Operational characteristics (demographics, geographic locations, etc.)
    Potential size (number of people, dollar purchase potential, etc.) and likely growth
Key psychological and social influences on buying purchase
Type of buying situation
Nature of relationship with customers

Competitor Analysis

Nature of current/likely competition
Current and prospective competitors (and/or rivals)
    Current strategies and likely responses to plan
Competitive barriers to overcome and sources of potential competitive advantage

Analysis of Other Aspects of External Market Environment (favorable and unfavorable factors and trends)

Economic environment
Technological environment
Political and legal environment
Cultural and social environment

Company Analysis

Company objectives and overall marketing objectives
Company resources
S.W.O.T.: Identification of major *s*trengths, *w*eaknesses, *o*pportunities, and *t*hreats (based on above analyses of company resources, customers, competitors, and other aspects of external market environment)

Marketing Information Requirements

Marketing research needs (with respect to customers, marketing mix effectiveness, external environment, etc.)
Secondary data and primary data needs
Marketing information system needs

Product

Product class (type of consumer or business product)
Current product life-cycle stage
New-product development requirements (people, dollars, time, etc.)
    Product liability, safety, and social responsibility considerations
Specification of core physical good and/or service
    Features, quality, etc.
Supporting customer service(s) needed
Warranty (what is covered, timing, who will support, etc.)
Branding (manufacturer versus dealer, family brand versus individual brand, etc.)
Packaging
    Promotion needs
    Protection needs
Cultural sensitivity of product
Fit with product line

(continued)

Place

Objectives
  Degree of market exposure required
  Distribution customer service level required
Type of channel (direct, indirect)
  Other channel members and/or facilitators required
    Type/number of wholesalers (agent, merchant, etc.)
    Type/number of retailers
  How discrepancies and separations will be handled
  How marketing functions are to be shared
Coordination needed in channel
  Information requirements (EDI, etc.)
Transportation requirements
Inventory requirements
Facilities required (warehousing, distribution centers, etc.)
Reverse channels (for returns, recalls, etc.)

Promotion

Objectives
Major message theme(s) for integrated marketing communications (desired "positioning")
Promotion blend
  Advertising (type, media, copy thrust, etc.)
  Personal selling (type and number of salespeople, how compensated, how effort will be allocated, etc.)
  Sales promotion (for channel members, customers, employees)
  Publicity
Mix of push and pull required

Price

Nature of demand (price sensitivity, elasticity)
Demand and cost analyses
Markup chain in channel
Price flexibility
Price level(s) (under what conditions)
Adjustments to list price (geographic terms, discounts, allowances, etc.)

Special Implementation Problems to Be Overcome

People required
Other resources required

Control

Marketing information system needs
Criterion measures comparison with objectives (customer satisfaction, sales, cost, performance analysis, etc.)

Forecasts and Estimates

Costs (all elements in plan, over time)
Sales (by market, over time, etc.)
Estimated operating statement (*pro forma*)

Timing

Specific sequence of activities and events, etc.
Likely changes over the product life cycle

When the market situation changes, the original reasons may no longer apply. Yet, if the logic for those strategy decisions is not retained, it's easy to miss changes taking place that should result in a plan being reconsidered. For example, a plan that was established in the growth stage of the product life cycle may have been very successful for a number of years. But, a marketing manager can't be complacent and assume that success will continue forever. When market maturity hits the firm may be in for big trouble—unless the basic strategy and plan are modified. If a plan spells out the details of the market analysis and logic for the marketing mix and target market selected, then it is a simple matter to routinely check and update it. Remember: The idea is for all of the analysis and strategy decisions to fit together as an integrated whole. Thus, as some of the elements of the plan or marketing environment change, the whole plan may need a fresh approach.

COMPANIES PLAN AND IMPLEMENT WHOLE MARKETING PROGRAMS

Several plans make a program

Most companies implement more than one marketing plan at the same time. A *marketing program* blends all a firm's marketing plans into one big plan.

When the various plans in the company's program are different, managers may be less concerned with how well the plans fit together—except as they compete for the firm's usually limited financial resources.

When the plans are more similar, however, the same sales force may be expected to carry out several plans. Or the firm's advertising department may develop the publicity and advertising for several plans. In these cases, product managers try to get enough of the common resources, say, salespeople's time, for their own plans.

Since a company's resources are usually limited, the marketing manager must make hard choices. You can't launch plans to pursue every promising opportunity. Instead, limited resources force you to choose among alternative plans—while you develop the program.

Finding the best program requires judgment

How do you find the best program? There is no one best way to compare various plans. Managers usually rely on evaluation tools like those discussed in Chapter 4. Even so, much management judgment is usually required. Some calculations are helpful too. If a five-year planning horizon seems realistic for the firm's markets, managers can compare expected profits over the five-year period for each plan.

Assuming the company has a profit-oriented objective, managers can evaluate the more profitable plans first—in terms of both potential profit and resources required. They also need to evaluate a plan's impact on the entire program. One profitable-looking alternative might be a poor first choice if it eats up all the company's resources—and sidetracks several plans that together would be more profitable and spread the risks.

Some juggling among the various plans—comparing profitability versus resources needed and available—moves the company toward the most profitable program. This is another area where spreadsheet analysis can help the manager evaluate a large number of alternatives.[8]

PLANNING FOR INVOLVEMENT IN INTERNATIONAL MARKETING

When developing a plan for international markets, marketing managers must decide how involved the firm will be. We will discuss six basic kinds of

Inexpensive computer programs for personal computers make it easier for marketing managers to plan and implement marketing programs.

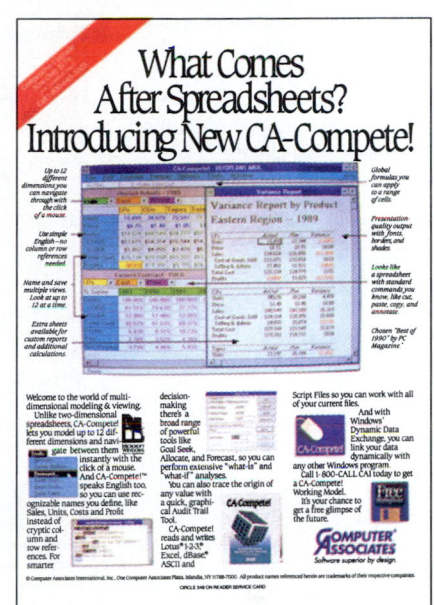

involvement: exporting, licensing, contract manufacturing, management contracting, joint venturing, and wholly owned subsidiaries.

Exporting often comes first

Some companies get into international marketing just by **exporting**—selling some of what the firm produces to foreign markets. Some firms start exporting just to get rid of surplus output. For others, exporting comes from a real effort to look for new opportunities.

Some firms try exporting without doing much planning. They don't change the product—or even the service or instruction manuals! As a result, some early efforts are not very satisfying—to buyers or sellers. When Toyota first exported cars to the United States, the effort was a failure. Americans just weren't interested in the Toyota model that sold well in Japan. Toyota tried again three years later with a new design—and a new marketing mix. Obviously, Toyota's second effort was a real success.[9]

Specialists can help develop the plan

Exporting does require knowledge about the foreign market. But managers who don't have enough knowledge to plan the details of a program can often get expert help from middlemen specialists. As we discussed in Chapter 13, export agents can handle the paperwork as products are shipped outside the country. Then agents or merchant wholesalers can handle the importing details. Even large producers with many foreign operations turn to international middlemen for some products or markets. Such middlemen know how to handle the sometimes confusing formalities and specialized functions. A manager trying to develop a plan alone can make a small mistake that ties products up at national borders for days—or months.[10]

Exporting doesn't have to involve permanent relationships. Of course, channel relationships take time to build and shouldn't be treated lightly—sales reps' contacts in foreign countries are investments. But it's relatively easy to cut back on these relationships—or even drop them—if the plan doesn't work.

AIG, an international financial services firm, relies on local managers who understand their own markets to develop marketing plans that meet the needs of local clients.

WHEREVER YOU DO BUSINESS AROUND THE WORLD, WE'RE PART OF THE LOCAL FABRIC. *At the AIG Companies, our business takes us from the canyons of Wall Street to the marketplaces of East Asia to the bazaars of the Middle East. But there's more to being global providers of insurance than just being a long way from home. AIG traces its roots* to Shanghai in 1919, and today our network stretches across 130 countries and jurisdictions. We hire local managers who understand the business practices and needs of their own markets. If you're a multinational company doing business in today's fast-changing world, you need our unique global reach and global experience. **AIG** WORLD LEADERS IN INSURANCE AND FINANCIAL SERVICES. American International Group, Inc., Dept. A, 70 Pine Street, New York, NY 10270.

Some firms, on the other hand, plan more formal and permanent relationships with nationals in foreign countries. The relationships might involve licensing, contract manufacturing, management contracting, and joint venturing.

Licensing is an easy way

Licensing is a relatively easy way to enter foreign markets. **Licensing** means selling the right to use some process, trademark, patent, or other right for a fee or royalty. The licensee takes most of the risk because it must invest some capital to use the right. Further, the licensee usually does most of the planning for the markets it is licensed to serve. If good partners are available, this can be an effective way to enter a market. Gerber entered the Japanese baby food market this way but still exports to other countries.[11]

Contract manufacturing takes care of the production problems

Contract manufacturing means turning over production to others while retaining the marketing process. Sears used this approach when it opened stores in Latin America and Spain. This approach doesn't make it any easier to plan the marketing program, but it may make it a lot easier to implement.

For example, this approach can be especially desirable where labor relations are difficult or where there are problems obtaining supplies or government cooperation. Growing nationalistic feelings may make this approach more attractive in the future.

Management contracting sells know-how

Management contracting means the seller provides only management skills—others own the production and distribution facilities. Some mines and oil refineries are operated this way—and Hilton operates hotels all over the world for local owners. This is a relatively low-risk approach to international marketing. The company makes no commitment to fixed facilities—which can be taken over or damaged in riots or wars. If conditions get too bad, key management people can fly off on the next plane—and leave the nationals to manage the operation.

Joint venturing is more involved

Joint venturing means a domestic firm entering into a partnership with a foreign firm. As with any partnership, there can be honest disagreements over objectives—for example, how much profit is desired and how fast it should be paid out—as well as operating policies. Where a close working relationship can be developed—perhaps based on one firm's technical and marketing know-how and the foreign partner's knowledge of the market and political connections—this approach can be very attractive to both parties.

In some situations, a joint venture is the only type of involvement possible. For example, IBM wanted to increase its 2 percent share of the $1 billion a year that business customers in Brazil spent on data processing services. But a Brazilian law severely limited expansion by foreign computer companies. To grow, IBM had to develop a joint venture with a Brazilian firm. Because of Brazilian laws, IBM could own only a 30 percent interest in the joint venture. But IBM decided it was better to have a 30 percent share of a business—and be able to pursue new market opportunities—than to stand by and watch competitors take the market.[12]

A joint venture usually requires a big commitment from both parties—and they both must agree on a joint plan. When the relationship doesn't work out well, the ensuing nightmare can make the manager wish that the venture had been planned as a wholly owned operation. But the terms of the joint venture may block this for years.[13]

Wholly owned subsidiaries give more control

When a firm thinks a foreign market looks really promising, it may want to take the final step. A **wholly owned subsidiary** is a separate firm—owned by a parent company. This gives the firm complete control of the marketing plan and operations, and also helps a foreign branch work more easily with the rest of the company. If a firm has too much capacity in a country with low production costs, for example, it can move some production there from other plants and then export to countries with higher production costs.

Multinational corporations evolve to meet the challenge

As firms become more involved in international marketing, some begin to see themselves as worldwide businesses that transcend national boundaries. These **multinational corporations** have a direct investment in several countries and run their businesses depending on the choices available anywhere in the world. Well-known U.S.-based multinational firms include Coca-Cola, Eastman Kodak, Warner-Lambert, Pfizer, Anaconda, Goodyear, Ford, IBM, and ITT. They regularly earn over a third of their total sales or profits abroad. And well-known foreign-based multinationals—such as Nestlé, Shell (Royal Dutch Shell), Unilever, Sony, and Honda—have well-accepted brands all around the world.

These multinational operations no longer just export or import. They hire local workers and build local plants. They have relationships with local businesses and politicians. These powerful organizations learn to plan marketing strategies that deal with nationalistic feelings and typical border barriers—treating them simply as part of the marketing environment. We don't yet have one world politically—but business is moving in that direction. We may have to develop new kinds of corporations and laws to govern multinational operations. In the future, it will make less and less sense for business and politics to be limited by national boundaries.

Planning for international markets

Usually marketing managers must plan the firm's overall marketing program so it's flexible enough to be adapted for differences in different countries. When

Multinational corporations, like 3M, often bring together marketing managers from different countries to plan strategies for a new product, like the medical instrument shown here.

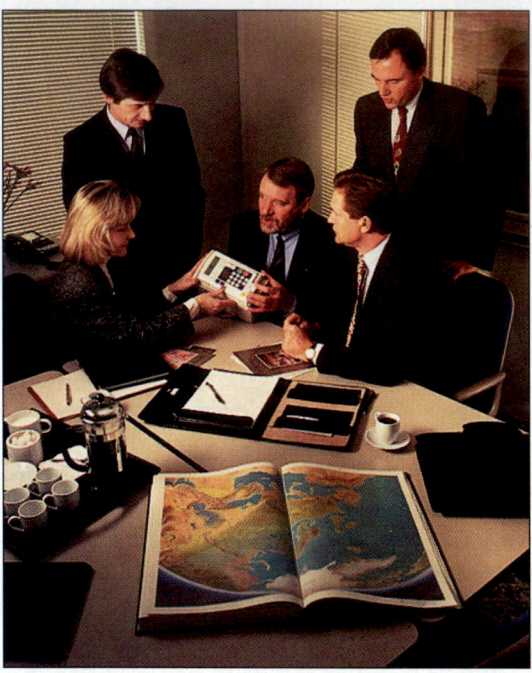

the differences are significant, top management should delegate a great deal of responsibility for strategy planning to local managers (or even middlemen). In many cases, it's not possible to develop a detailed plan without a "local feel." In extreme cases, local managers may not even be able to fully explain some parts of their plans because they're based on subtle cultural differences. Then plans must be judged only by their results. The organizational setup should give these managers a great deal of freedom in their planning—but ensure tight control against the plans they develop. Top management can simply insist that managers stick to their budgets and meet the plans that they themselves create. When a firm reaches this stage, it is being managed like a well-organized domestic corporation—which insists that its managers (of divisions and territories) meet their own plans so that the whole company's program works as intended.[14]

CONCLUSION

In this chapter, we stressed the importance of developing whole marketing mixes—not just developing policies for the individual four Ps and hoping they will fit together into some logical whole. The marketing manager is responsible for developing a workable blend—integrating all of a firm's efforts into a coordinated whole that makes effective use of the firm's resources and guides it toward its objectives.

As a starting place for developing new marketing mixes, a marketing manager can use the product classes that have served as a thread through this text. Even if the manager can't fully describe the needs and attitudes of target markets, it is usually possible to select the appropriate product class for a particular product. This, in turn, will help set Place and Promotion policies. It may also clarify what type of marketing mix is typical for the product. However, just doing what is typical may not give a firm any competitive advantage. Creative strategies are often the ones that identify new and better ways of uniquely giving the target customers what they want or need. Similarly, seeing where a firm's offering fits in the product life cycle helps to clarify how current marketing mixes are likely to change in the future.

Developing and evaluating marketing strategies and plans usually requires that the manager use some approach to forecasting. We talked about two basic approaches to forecasting market potential and sales: (1) extending past behavior and (2) predicting future behavior. The most common approach is to extend past behavior into the future. This gives reasonably good results if market conditions are fairly stable. Methods here include extension of past sales data and the factor method. We saw that projecting the past into the future is risky when big market changes are likely. To make up for this possible weakness, marketers predict future behavior using their own experience and judgment. They also bring in the judgment of others—using the jury of executive opinion method and salespeople's estimates. And they may use surveys, panels, and market tests. Of course, any sales forecast depends on the marketing mix the firm actually selects.

Once forecasts of the expected sales—and estimates of the associated costs—for possible strategies are available, alternatives can be compared on potential profitability. Spreadsheet analysis software is an important tool for such comparisons. In the same vein, project planning approaches, such as CPM and PERT, can help the marketing manager do a better job in planning the time-related details for the strategy that is selected.

Throughout the text, we've emphasized the importance of marketing strategy planning. In this chapter, we went on to show that the marketing manager must develop a marketing plan for carrying out each strategy and then merge a set of plans into a marketing program.

Finally, we discussed different approaches that are helpful in planning strategies to enter international markets. The different approaches have different strengths and weaknesses.

So far, our emphasis has been planning. In the next chapter, we move on to discuss the management jobs of implementation and control. Our focus will be on implementation that continuously improves and does a better job of meeting customers' needs—and on timely control that results in improved implementation and strategies while there's still time to do something about it.

QUESTIONS AND PROBLEMS

1. Distinguish clearly between a marketing strategy, a marketing plan, and a marketing program.

2. Discuss how a marketing manager could go about choosing among several possible marketing plans, given that choices must be made because of limited resources. Would the job be easier in the consumer product or in the business product area? Why?

3. Explain how understanding the product classes can help a marketing manager develop a marketing strategy for a really new product that is unlike anything currently available.

4. Distinguish between competitive marketing mixes and superior mixes that lead to break-through opportunities.

5. Explain the difference between a forecast of market potential and a sales forecast.

6. Suggest a plausible explanation for sales fluctuations for (a) bicycles, (b) ice cream, (c) lawn mowers, (d) tennis rackets, (e) oats, (f) disposable diapers, and (g) latex for rubber-based paint.

7. Explain the factor method of forecasting. Illustrate your answer.

8. Based on data in Exhibit 19–5, discuss the relative market potential of the city of Bristol, Connecticut, and the city of West Hartford, Connecticut, for: (a) prepared cereals, (b) automobiles, and (c) furniture.

9. Why is spreadsheet analysis a popular tool for marketing strategy planning?

10. In your own words, explain how a flowcharting technique such as PERT or CPM can help a marketing manager develop a better marketing plan.

11. Why should a complete marketing plan include details concerning the reasons for the marketing strategy decisions and not just the marketing activities central to the four Ps?

12. Consider how the marketing manager's job becomes more complex when it's necessary to develop and plan *several* strategies as part of a marketing program. Be sure to discuss how the manager might have to handle different strategies at different stages in the product life cycle. To make your discussion more concrete, consider the job of a marketing manager for a sporting products manufacturer.

13. How would marketing planning be different for a firm that has entered foreign marketing with a joint venture and a firm that has set up a wholly owned subsidiary?

14. How can a firm set the details of its marketing plan when it has little information about a foreign market it wants to enter?

SUGGESTED CASES

17. Gulf Coast Safe Water, Inc.
27. Electrotech, Inc.
31. Hendrix Chevrolet, Inc.

32. Inhome Medical, Inc.
33. Lever, Ltd.
35. Alumux Mfg. Co.

COMPUTER-AIDED PROBLEM

19. Comparing Marketing Mixes

Amna Rao is a marketing manager who is looking for new market opportunities that use her firm's current resources. Her firm has been making plastic packages for producers of CDs, panty hose, and other products—but sales have dropped because these customers are switching away from plastic packages. She is considering the possibility of producing and marketing a new consumer product—sunglasses that float. Consumers in focus group interviews say they might be interested in buying floating sunglasses for when they're at the pool, on a boat, fishing, or otherwise near the water. So Rao is doing some rough comparisons of the likely costs and profitability of possible marketing mixes to reach her target market.

She is considering the likely outcomes with two possible marketing mixes. One marketing mix (Mix A) involves selling the sunglasses through discount stores. This mix would involve a plain frame with a simple finish, and the unit production cost would be $5.00. She knows she will have to pay for some consumer advertising to stimulate interest in the product. But personal selling costs would probably be quite low since she would need only one salesperson to call on some retail chains that would make large orders.

An alternative approach (Mix B) would focus on selling the glasses as an impulse product through snack bars at swimming pools and the beach. Selling to the large number of small snackbars would require more personal selling expense. The personal selling would need to be supported with direct-mail advertising to the snack-shop owners. However, the direct-mail ads would be less expensive than advertising to final consumers. To support a higher impulse purchase price in this channel, she would use a more stylish (and somewhat more costly to produce) finish on the sunglasses. She thinks she would sell a smaller quantity through this channel but the snack bars would be willing to pay a higher wholesale price.

To get a better idea of the likely profit and break-even levels for the two different mixes, Rao has developed a spreadsheet based on her estimates of likely sales and costs. She wants to make the biggest profit possible from this new product, but at present she does face one basic limitation: The owner of the company is not willing to invest in new equipment, and with the present equipment *the firm cannot produce more than 300,000 pairs of glasses a year.*

a. *After considering the initial spreadsheet, for both marketing mixes, evaluate the effects of sales volume being 10 percent less than expected. Discuss the implications of your analysis.*

b. *Rao thinks her sales estimates are realistic for the two marketing mixes, but she is not certain what the implications would be if demand is greater than she expects. Discuss this issue and illustrate your conclusions with a specific analysis of your choice based on the spreadsheet.*

c. *Rao feels that the more costly finish for glasses in Mix B would be attractive to impulse buyers, but she also thinks that many of these prospects would buy the product even if the firm offered the lower-cost finish she is considering for Mix A. In that case, the unit production cost for Mix B would be the same as for Mix A. How high would sales have to be with Mix B and the lower unit production cost to make a profit of at least $107,000? If the lower-cost marketing mix was as likely to achieve this level of sales as the original plan for Mix B was to achieve sales of 50,000 units, which of the two variations would you recommend? Give your reasons.*

For additional questions related to this problem, see Exercise 19–3 in the *Learning Aid for Use with Basic Marketing*, 12th edition.

20

Implementing and Controlling Marketing Plans: Evolution and Revolution

Marketing managers at Kmart were implementing a long-range plan to change the company from a no-frills discount store to a retailer of quality, brand-name products. For example, they developed a new advertising campaign to promote their upgraded home furnishings and apparel lines. They put point-of-sale scanners in all the stores—so they could more quickly analyze sales, costs, and profit in different stores and product lines. They also added many new stores in areas where they weren't reaching their target customers.

At first the plan seemed to be working well—and the company was posting healthy gains in both sales and profits. By the next year, however, problems surfaced. Total sales were up 3.9 percent, but sales analysis showed that most of the increase came from new stores. In fact, sales at existing stores grew only .2 percent. That meant that performance at the old stores was not up to par.

Some Kmart managers worried that competition from Wal-Mart's new stores in Kmart's markets might be the problem. Further analysis showed that sales fell off even at Kmart stores that were not near a competing store. To help isolate the problem, Kmart managers broke down total sales by product lines for different types of stores. Their analysis showed that a major problem area was poor performance on important seasonal items—such as patio furniture and gardening products. The analysis could not explain *why* sales for these products were poor, but Kmart's managers thought a likely reason was that the spring weather had been much cooler than usual. There wasn't much that they could do about that. On the other hand, performance analysis revealed that a downward trend existed in the performance of many older, smaller stores. To better understand the problem, Kmart did research and found that consumers wanted bigger stores with more selection, wider aisles, and better lighting. A Kmart executive said that the analysis made it clear that "Kmart had not been changing as rapidly as the consumer had." To be competitive, Kmart needed to further refine its strategy. In addition to adding new stores in new market areas, it needed to do more to expand and refurbish current stores. Some small stores had to be closed and replaced—because there wasn't room to expand.

It takes time and money to remodel old facilities and build new ones. But Kmart moved along with its revised plan because sales analysis showed that refurbished stores were generating more sales and profit than before. And Kmart also worked to open more stores internationally. While that plan was being implemented, Kmart continued to make other changes too. For example, Kmart needed to improve its inventory reorder system. Consumers too often found that Kmart was out of stock on items they wanted. Many experts felt that was because Kmart had left the job of keeping the right inventory to individual store managers. By contrast, Wal-Mart had invested in the latest in computer technologies to make that part of the implementation job go smoothly. And Wal-Mart's excellent implementation was winning customer loyalty.[1]

GOOD PLANS SET THE FRAMEWORK FOR IMPLEMENTATION AND CONTROL

Our primary emphasis in this book is on the strategy planning part of the marketing manager's job. There's a good reason for this focus. The "one-time" strategy decisions—those that decide what business the company is in and the strategies it will follow—set the firm on a course either toward profitable opportunities or, alternatively, toward costly failure. If a marketing manager makes an error with these basic decisions, there may never be a second chance to set things straight. In contrast, if good strategies and plans are developed, the marketing manager—and everyone else in the organization—knows *what* needs to be done. Thus, good marketing plans set the framework for effective implementation and control.

Implementation puts plans into operation—and control provides feedback

Even so, developing a potentially profitable plan does not ensure either satisfied customers or profit for the firm. Achieving the outcomes envisioned in the plan requires that the whole marketing management process work well. As you learned in Chapter 2, the marketing management process includes not only marketing strategy planning but also implementation and control. See Exhibit 2–5. In fact, in today's highly competitive markets customer satisfaction often hinges on skillful implementation. Further, the ongoing success of the firm is often dependent on **control**—the feedback process that helps the marketing manager learn (1) how ongoing plans and implementation are working and (2) how to plan for the future.

We discussed some specific opportunities and challenges with respect to implementation and control as we introduced each of the marketing strategy decision areas. In this chapter, we'll go into more depth on concepts and how-to approaches for making implementation and control more effective. We'll start with a discussion of how dramatic improvements in information technology are resulting in changes in implementation and control—and in the whole strategy planning process. For many firms, these changes are critically important. They offer revolutionary new ways to meet customer needs. Next, we'll highlight some of the new approaches, including total quality management, that are improving marketing implementation. Then, we'll explain how marketing managers use control-related tools—such as sales and performance analysis—to improve the quality of planning and implementation decisions. We'll conclude with a discussion of what a marketing audit is, and why it is sometimes necessary.

SPEED UP INFORMATION FOR BETTER IMPLEMENTATION AND CONTROL

Feedback improves the marketing management process

Not long ago, marketing managers planned their strategies and put them into action—but then it usually took a long time before they got feedback to know if the strategy and implementation were really working as intended. For example, a

Special characteristics of the product or target market must be considered in planning and implementing the marketing mix.

When you've got a very short time to sell a lot of product, you want a magazine that works immediately.

Holidays. New product launches. Sales events. Anytime you haven't got weeks or months to wait for your advertising to work, consider Parade. It reaches its entire audience in hours. Which means your ad reaches all your prospects precisely when you want to sell, precisely when they want to buy.

PARADE

81 million readers in just 48 hours.

marketing manager might not have much feedback on what was happening with sales, expenses, and profits until financial summaries were available—and that sometimes took months or even longer. Further, summary data wasn't very useful in pinpointing which specific aspects of the plan were working and which weren't. In that environment, the feedback was so general and took so long that there often wasn't anything the manager could do about a problem except start over.

That situation has now changed dramatically in many types of business. In Chapter 5, we discussed how firms use marketing information systems to track sales and cost details day by day and week by week. Throughout the book you've seen examples of how marketers get more information faster and use it quickly to improve a strategy or its implementation. For example, scanner data from a consumer panel can provide a marketing manager with almost immediate feedback on whether or not a new consumer product is selling at the expected level in each specific store and whether or not it is actually selling to the intended target market rather than some other group.

Fast feedback can be a competitive advantage

Marketing managers who can get faster feedback on their decisions can often take advantage of it to develop a competitive advantage. They can quickly fine tune a smooth-running implementation to make it work even better. If there are potential problems, they can often spot them early—and keep them from turning into big problems.

For example, a manager who gets detailed daily reports that compare actual sales results in different cities with sales forecasts in the plan is able to see very quickly if there is a problem in a specific city. Then, the manager can track down the cause of the problem. If sales are going slowly because the new salesperson in that city is inexperienced, then the sales manager might immediately spend more time working with that rep. On the other hand, if the problem is that a chain of retail stores in that particular city isn't willing to allocate much shelf space for the firm's product, then the salesperson might need to develop a special analysis to show the buyers for that specific chain how the product could improve the chain's profit.

When information is slow coming in and there is less detail, making implementation changes is usually more difficult. By the time the need for a change is obvious, a bigger change is required for it to have any effect.

The basic strategy planning concepts we've emphasized throughout the text are enduring and will always be at the heart of marketing. Yet, the fast pace that is now possible in getting information for control is resulting in fundamental changes in how many managers work, make decisions, plan, and implement their plans. Managers who can quickly adjust the details of their efforts to better solve customer problems or respond to changes in the market can do a better job for their firms—because they can make certain that their plans are really performing as expected.

The marketing manager must take charge

Fast feedback can improve implementation and control. And computers now take the drudgery out of analyzing data. But this kind of analysis is not possible unless the data is in machine-processable form—so it can be sorted and analyzed quickly. Here, the creative marketing manager plays a crucial role by insisting that the necessary data be collected. If the data he or she wants to analyze is not captured as it comes in, information will be difficult—if not impossible—to get later.

A marketing manager may need many different types of information to improve implementation efforts or develop new strategies. In the past, this has often caused delays—even if the information was in a machine-processable form. In a large company, for example, it could take days or even weeks for a marketing manager to find out how to get needed information from another department. Imagine how long it could take for a marketing manager to get needed sales data from sales offices in different countries around the world.

New information technologies offer speed and detail

New approaches for electronic communication help solve these problems. For example, many companies are using fiber optic telephone lines or satellite transmission systems to *immediately* transfer data from a computer at one location to another. A sales manager with a portable computer can use a regular telephone to pull data off the firm's mainframe computer. And marketing managers working at different locations on different aspects of a strategy can use electronic mail to communicate through networks that link their computers for easy data transfer. The Internet, a computer network that links thousands of other computer networks worldwide, even makes it possible for a manager to work at a computer on the other side of the world as if he or she were sitting in front of it.

This type of electronic pipeline makes data available instantly. A report—such as one that summarizes sales by product, salesperson, or type of customer—that in the past was done once a month now might be done weekly or even daily. The computer software can even be programmed to search for and "flag" results that indicate a problem of some sort. Then the manager can allocate more time to resolving that particular problem.

Of course, many firms don't consider or use these types of approaches. But they are becoming much more common—especially as more marketing managers find that they are losing out to more nimble competitors who get information more quickly and adjust their implementation and strategies more often.[2]

Firms that can find creative ways to implement their strategies are often able to do a better job of building strong relationships with their customers.

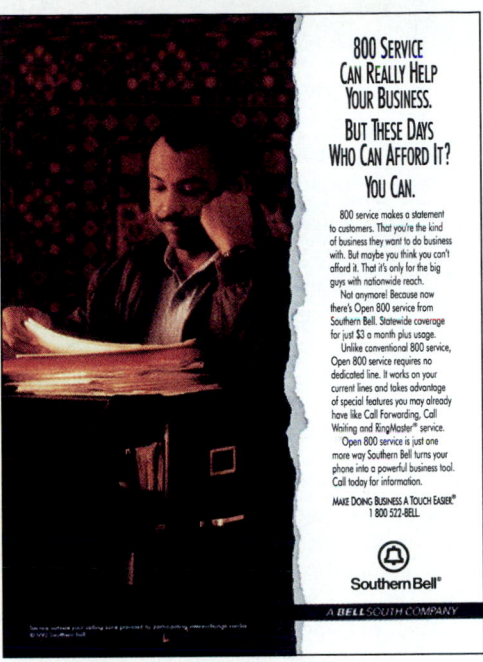

EFFECTIVE IMPLEMENTATION MEANS THAT PLANS WORK AS INTENDED

When a marketing manager has developed a good marketing plan, the challenge of implementing it often involves hundreds—or thousands—of operational decisions and activities. In a small company, these may all be handled by a few people, or even by a single person. In a large corporation, literally hundreds of different people may be involved in implementation. That may require a massive amount of careful coordination and communication. Either way, when operational decisions and activities are executed well customers get what is intended. And if the original plan is good customers will be satisfied and come back again the next time the need arises. However, even a great plan can leave customers unhappy—and switching to someone else's offering—if implementation is poor.

Good implementation builds relationships with customers

Implementation is especially critical in mature and highly competitive markets. When several firms are all following basically the same strategy—quickly imitating competitors' ideas—customers are often won or lost based on differences in the quality of implementation. Consider the rental car business. Hertz has a strategy that targets business travelers with a choice of quality cars, convenient reservations, fast pick-up and drop-off, availability at most major airports, and a premium price. Hertz is extremely successful with that strategy even though there is little to prevent other companies from trying the same approach. But a major part of Hertz's success is due to implementation. Customers keep coming back because the Hertz service is both reliable and pain-free.

When a Hertz "Gold" customer calls to make a reservation, the company already has the standard information about that customer in a computer database. At the airport, the customer skips over the line at the Hertz counter and instead just picks up an already-completed rental contract and goes straight to the Hertz bus. The driver gets the customer's name and radios ahead to have someone start

PILLSBURY RINGS IN SATISFIED CUSTOMERS

There are thousands of ways that a plan or its implementation can go astray. The consumer's box of laundry detergent may be missing the measuring scoop. The VCR's instructions may be very clear about how to record a program but not explain how to hook the VCR to a consumer's cable box. Left unresolved, implementation glitches like these might result in dissatisfied customers. So most producers now have toll-free telephone lines to help customers with questions and complaints.

Pillsbury's line is typical. Some calls involve a question or praise, but about a third are complaints. For example, one caller reported that a cake mix had a funny taste. The service rep asked the caller for a code number on the box and—after keying it in on her computer—found that the box of mix was 6 years old. Perhaps the consumer forgot it in her pantry, or perhaps it was lost in some retailer's storeroom.

Either way, the Pillsbury rep apologized and sent a coupon for a free replacement box.

The calls can also provide important feedback. For example, soon after Pillsbury introduced Funfetti cake mix with bits of edible confetti, callers began complaining that the confetti packet was missing from their box. A check of the manufacturing line showed the confetti packets were too light to alert weight scales when they were missing from the boxes. After the firm changed to a foil package the complaints stopped.

Toll-free lines probably don't win new customers. But they do help a firm keep its current customers. Further, one study found that callers who had their complaints resolved on average told five people about the help they got. Yet, there is also a risk. Those who weren't satisfied told twice as many people.[3]

the specific car that customer will drive. That way the air conditioner or heater is already doing its job when the bus driver delivers the customer right to the parking slot for his or her car. Customers are certain they're at the right place because there's an electronic sign beside each car with the customer's name on it. Making all of this work—day in and day out, customer after customer—isn't easy. But Hertz has set up systems to make it all easier because that's what it takes to implement its plan—and to keep customers loyal.[4]

Implementation deals with internal or external matters

As the Hertz example illustrates, marketing implementation usually involves decisions and activities related to both internal and external matters. Figuring out how the correct car will end up in the right parking slot, how the Hertz bus driver will contact the office, and who will coordinate getting the message to the person that starts the car are all internal matters. They are invisible to the customer—as long as they work as planned. On the other hand, some implementation issues are external and involve the customer. For example, the contract must be completed correctly and be in the right spot when the rental customer comes to pick it up, and someone needs to have filled the car with gas and cleaned it.

Implementation has its own objectives

Whether implementation decisions and activities are internal or external, they all must be consistent with the objectives of the overall strategy and with the other details of the plan. However, there are also three general objectives that apply to all implementation efforts. Other things equal, the manager wants to get each implementation job done:

Better.

Faster.

At lower cost.

EXHIBIT 20–1   Examples of Approaches to Overcome Specific Marketing Implementation Problems

Marketing Mix Decision Area	Operational Problem	Implementation Approach
Product	Develop design of a new product as rapidly as possible without errors	Use 3-D computer-aided design software
	Pretest consumer response to different versions of a label	Prepare sample labels with desktop publishing software
Place	Coordinate inventory levels with middlemen to avoid stock-outs	Use bar code scanner and computerized reorder system
	Get franchisee's inputs and cooperation on a new program	Set up a televideo conference
Promotion	Quickly distribute TV ad to local stations in many different markets	Distribute final video version of the ad via satellite link
	Answer final consumers' questions about how to use a product	Put a toll-free telephone number on product label
Price	Identify frequent customers for a quantity discount	Create a "favored customer" club with an ID card
	Figure out if price sensitivity impacts demand for a product; make it easier for customers to compare prices	Show unit prices (for example, per oz.) on shelf markers

The ideal of doing things better, faster, and at lower cost is easy to accept. But in practice implementation is often complicated by trade-offs among the three objectives. For example, doing a job better may take longer or cost more.

So, just as a marketing manager should constantly look for new strategy opportunities, it's important to be creative in looking for better solutions to implementation problems. That may require finding ways to better coordinate the efforts of the different people involved, setting up standard operating procedures to deal with recurring problems, or juggling priorities to deal with the unexpected. When the Hertz bus driver is sick, someone still has to be there to pick up the customers and deliver them to their cars.

Implementation requires innovation too

Sometimes the implementation effort can be improved by approaching the task in a new or different way. Exhibit 20–1 shows some of the ways that firms are using information technology to improve specific implementation jobs. Note that some of the examples in Exhibit 20–1 focus on internal matters and some on external, customer-oriented matters.

While finding new approaches helps with some implementation problems, getting better implementation often depends on being vigilant in improving what the firm and its people are already doing. So, let's take a closer look at some important ways that managers can improve the quality of their implementation efforts.[5]

BUILDING QUALITY INTO THE IMPLEMENTATION EFFORT

As we've seen on previous occasions throughout this book, even people with the best intentions sometimes lapse into a production orientation. When the pressure's on to get a job done, they forget about satisfying the customer—let alone consider working together! When the product manager is screaming for a budget report, the accountant may view a customer's concerns about a billing error as something a salesperson can smooth over—alone.

Total quality management meets customer requirements

There are many different ways to improve implementation in each of the four Ps decision areas, but here we will focus on total quality management, which you can use to improve *any* implementation effort. With **total quality management (TQM)**, everyone in the organization is concerned about quality, throughout all of the firm's activities, to better serve customer needs.

In Chapter 9 we explained that product quality means the ability of a product to satisfy a customer's needs or requirements. Now we'll expand that idea and think about the quality of the whole marketing mix and how it is implemented—to meet customer requirements.

Total quality management is not just for factories

Most of the early attention in quality management focused on reducing defects in goods produced in factories. Reliable goods are important, but there's usually a lot more to marketing implementation than that. Yet if we start by considering product defects, you'll see how the total quality management idea has evolved and how it applies to implementing a marketing program.

At one time most firms assumed defects were an inevitable part of mass production. They assumed the cost of replacing defective parts or goods was just a cost of doing business—an insignificant one compared to the advantages of mass production. However, many firms were forced to rethink this assumption when Japanese producers of cars, electronics, and cameras showed that defects weren't inevitable. And their success in taking customers away from established competitors made it clear that the cost of defects wasn't just the cost of replacement!

Having dissatisfied customers is costly

From the customer's point of view, getting a defective product and having to complain about it is a big headache. The customer can't use the defective product and suffers the inconvenience of waiting for someone to fix the problem—if *someone* gets around to it. That erodes goodwill and leaves customers dissatisfied. The big cost of poor quality is the cost of lost customers.

Much to the surprise of some production-oriented managers, the Japanese experience showed that it is less expensive to do something right the first time than to pay to do it poorly and *then* pay again to fix problems. And quality wasn't just a matter of adding more assembly-line inspections. Products had to be designed to meet customer needs from the start. One defective part in 10,000 may not seem like much, but if that part keeps a completed car from cranking at the end of the automaker's production line, finding the problem is a costly nightmare.

Firms that adopted TQM methods to reduce manufacturing defects soon used the same approaches to overcome many other implementation problems. Their success brought attention to what is possible with TQM—whether the implementation problem concerns unreliable delivery schedules, poor customer service, advertising that appears on the wrong TV show, or salespeople who can't answer customers' questions.

Getting a handle on doing things right—the first time

The idea of doing things right the first time seems obvious, but it's easier said than done. Problems always come up, and it's not always clear what isn't being done as well as it could be. Most people tend to ignore problems that don't pose an immediate crisis. But firms that adopt TQM always look for ways to improve

Because continuous improvement hinges on employee involvement and communication, Dana Commercial Credit displays all suggestions for improvements where everyone can see them.

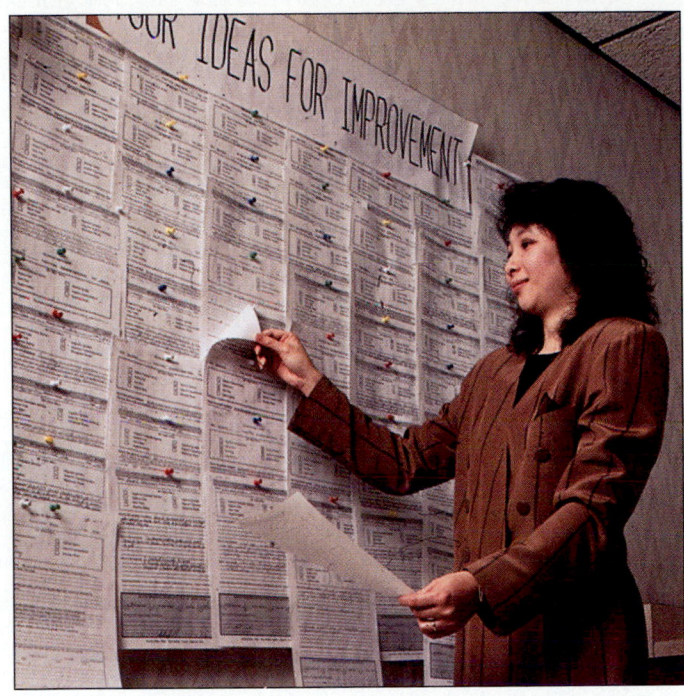

implementation with **continuous improvement**—a commitment to constantly make things better one step at a time. Once you accept the idea that there *may* be a better way to do something and you look for it, you may just find it! The place to start is to clearly define "defects" in the implementation process—from the customers' point of view.

Things gone right and things gone wrong

Managers who use the TQM approach think of quality improvement as a sorting process—a sorting out of things gone right and things gone wrong. The sorting process calls for detailed measurements related to a problem. Then managers use a set of statistical tools to analyze the measurements and identify the problem areas that are the best candidates for fixing. The statistical details are beyond our focus here, but it's useful to get a feel for how managers use the tools.

Starting with customer needs

Let's consider the case of a restaurant that does well during the evening hours but wants to improve its lunch business. The restaurant develops a strategy that targets local business people with an attractive luncheon buffet. The restaurant decides on a buffet because research shows that target customers want a choice of good healthy food and are willing to pay reasonable prices for it—as long as they can eat quickly and get back to work on time.

As the restaurant implements its new strategy, the manager wants a measure of how things are going. So she encourages customers to fill out comment cards that ask "How did we do today?" After several months of operation, things seem to be going reasonably well—although business is not as brisk as it was at first. The manager reads the comment cards and divides the ones with complaints into categories—to count up different reasons why customers weren't satisfied.

EXHIBIT 20–2 Pareto Chart Showing Frequency of Different Complaints

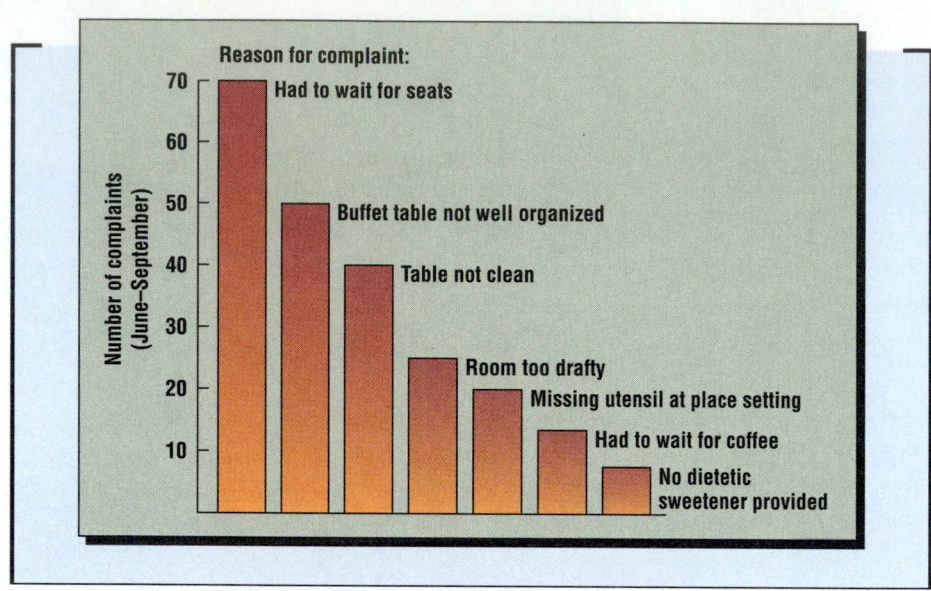

Slay the dragons first

Then the manager creates a graph showing a frequency distribution for the different types of complaints. Quality people call this a **Pareto chart**—a graph that shows the number of times a problem cause occurs, with problem causes ordered from most frequent to least frequent. The manager's Pareto chart, shown in Exhibit 20–2, reveals that customers complain most frequently that they have to wait for a seat. There were other common complaints—the buffet was not well organized, the table was not clean, and so on. However, the first complaint is much more common than the next most frequent.

This type of pattern is typical. The worst problems often occur over and over again. This focuses the manager's attention on which implementation problem to fix first. A rule of quality management is to slay the dragons first—which simply means start with the biggest problem. After removing that problem, the battle moves on to the next most frequent problem. If you do this *continuously*, you solve a lot of problems—and you don't just satisfy customers, you delight them.

Figure out why things go wrong

So far, our manager has only identified the problem. To solve it, she creates a **fishbone diagram**—a visual aid that helps organize cause-and-effect relationships for "things gone wrong."

Our restaurant manager, for example, discovers that customers wait to be seated because tables aren't cleared soon enough. In fact, the Pareto chart (Exhibit 20–2) shows that customers also complain frequently about tables not being clean. So the two implementation problems may be related.

The manager's fishbone diagram (Exhibit 20–3) summarizes the various causes for tables not being cleaned quickly. There are different basic categories of causes—restaurant policy, procedures, people problems, and the physical environment. With this overview of different ways the service operation is going wrong, the manager can decide what to fix. She establishes different formal measures. For example, she counts how frequently different causes delay customers from being seated. She finds that the cashier's faulty credit card machine holds up check

EXHIBIT 20–3   Fishbone Diagram Showing Cause and Effect for "Why Tables Are Not Cleared Quickly"

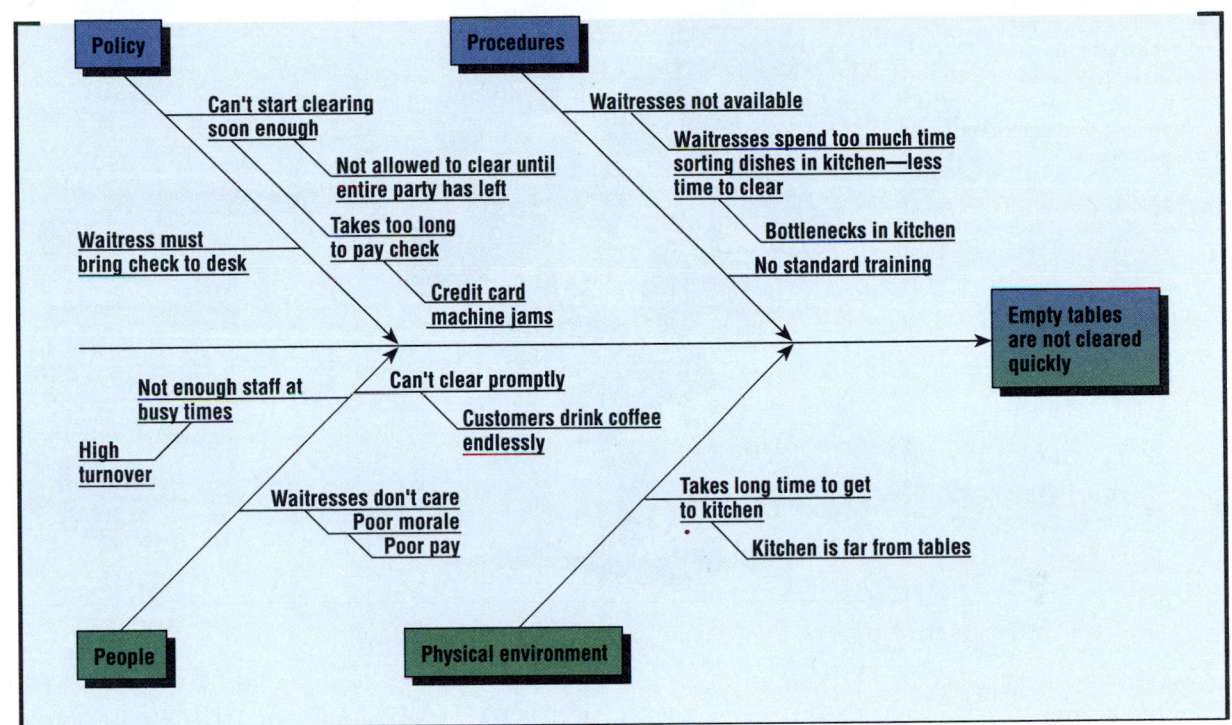

processing. The fishbone diagram shows that restaurant policy is to clear the table after the entire party leaves. But customers have to wait at their tables while the staff deals with the jammed credit card machine, and cleaning is delayed. With the credit card machine replaced, the staff can clear the tables sooner—and because they're not so hurried they do a better cleaning job. Two dragons are on the way to being slayed!

Our case shows that people in different areas of the restaurant affect customer satisfaction. The waitperson couldn't do what was needed to satisfy customers because the cashier had trouble with the credit card machine. The TQM approach helps everyone see—and understand—how their job affects what others do—and the customer's satisfaction.[6]

Building quality into services

The restaurant case illustrates how a firm can improve implementation with TQM approaches. We used a service example because providing customer service is often a difficult area of implementation. Recently, marketers in service businesses have been paying a lot of attention to improving service quality.

But some people seem to forget that almost every firm must implement service quality as part of its plan—whether its product is primarily a service, primarily a physical good, or a blend of both. For example, a manufacturer of ball bearings isn't just providing wholesalers or producers with round pieces of steel. Customers need information about deliveries, they need orders filled properly, and they may have questions to ask the firm's accountant, receptionist, or engineers. Because almost every firm must manage the service it provides customers, let's focus on some of the special concerns of implementing quality service.

SCT markets computer systems that empower employees with the information they need to do a better job implementing and controlling marketing plans.

Train people and empower them to serve

Quality gurus like to say that the firm has only one job: to give customers exactly what they want, when they want it, and where they want it. Marketing managers have been saying that for some time too. But customer service is hard to implement because the server is inseparable from the service. A person doing a specific service job may perform one specific task correctly but still annoy the customer in a host of other ways. Customers will not be satisfied if employees are rude or inattentive—even if they "solve the customer's problem." There are two keys to improving how people implement quality service: (1) training and (2) empowerment.

Firms that commit to customer satisfaction realize that all employees who have any contact with customers need training—many firms see 40 hours a year of training as a minimum. Simply showing customer-contact employees around the rest of the business—so that they learn how their contribution fits in the total effort—can be very effective. Good training usually includes role-playing on handling different types of customer requests and problems. This is not just sales training! A rental car attendant who is rude when a customer is trying to turn in a car may leave the customer dissatisfied—even if the rental car was perfect. How employees treat a customer is as important as whether they perform the task correctly.

Companies can't afford an army of managers to inspect how each employee implements a strategy—and such a system usually doesn't work anyway. Quality cannot be "inspected in." It must come from the people who do the service jobs. So firms that commit to service quality empower employees to satisfy customers' needs. **Empowerment** means giving employees the authority to correct a problem without first checking with management. At a Guest Quarters hotel, an empowered room-service employee knows it's OK to run across the street to buy the specific mineral water a guest requests. In the new Saturn car manufacturing plant, employees can stop the assembly line to correct a problem rather than passing it down the line. At Upton's clothing stores, a salesclerk can make an immediate price adjustment if there's a flaw in an item the customer wants.

Manage expectations—with good communication

The implementation effort sometimes leaves customers dissatisfied because they expect much more than it is possible for the firm to deliver. Some firms react to this by shrugging their shoulders and faulting customers for being unreasonable. Research in the service quality area, however, suggests that the problems often go away if marketers clearly communicate what they are offering. Customers are satisfied when the service matches their expectations, and careful communication leads to reasonable expectations.

Customers often tolerate a delay and remain satisfied with the service when they are given a full explanation. Most airline passengers seethe at the announcement of a takeoff delay but are happy to wait if they know the delay is caused by a thunderstorm high over the airport.

Separate the routine and plan for the special

Implementation usually involves some routine services and some that require special attention. Customer satisfaction increases when the two types of service encounters are separated. For example, banks set up special windows for commercial deposits and supermarkets have cash-only lines. In developing the marketing plan, it's important to analyze the types of service customers will need and plan for both types of situations. In some cases, completely different strategies may be required.

Increasingly, firms try to use computers and other equipment to handle routine services. ATMs are quick and convenient for dispensing cash. American Airlines' Dial a Flight system allows customers to use a touchtone phone to check fares, schedules, and arrival times—without the need for an operator.

Firms that study special service requests can use training so that even unusual customer requests become routine to the staff. Every day, hotel guests lose their keys, bank customers run out of checks, and supermarket shoppers leave their wallets at home. A well-run service operation anticipates these special events so service providers can respond in a way that satisfies customers' needs.

Managers lead the quality effort

Quality implementation—whether in a service activity or in another activity—doesn't just happen by itself. Managers must show that they are committed to doing things right to satisfy customers—and that quality is everyone's job. Without top-level support, some people won't get beyond their business as usual attitude—and TQM won't work. The top executive at American Express had his board of directors give him the title Chief Quality Officer so that everyone in the company would know he was personally involved in the TQM effort.

Getting a return on quality is important

While the cost of poor quality is lost customers, keep in mind that the type of quality efforts we've been discussing also result in costs. It takes time and energy to keep records, analyze the details of implementation efforts, and search for ways to reduce whatever type of defects might appear. It's important to find the right balance between quality in the implementation effort and what it costs to achieve.

Marketing managers who lose sight of that balance have often created quality programs that cost more than they're worth. It's easy to fall into the trap of

As a multinational corporation, Motorola has earned high marks in implementing its marketing plans so that its customers get the quality they want—wherever they may be around the globe.

running up *unnecessary costs* trying to improve some facet of implementation that really isn't that important to customers, customer satisfaction, or customer retention. When that happens, customers may still be satisfied, but the firm can't make a profit because of the extra costs. In other words, there isn't a financial return on the money spent to improve the quality of the implementation effort. Remember that getting everyone to work together to satisfy customers should be the route to profits. If the firm is spending money on quality efforts that don't really contribute to customer satisfaction—or that cost more to provide than customers will ultimately be willing to pay for—then someone has lost sight of the marketing concept.

As this suggests, TQM is not a "cure-all." Further, it is not the only method for improving marketing implementation, but it is an important approach. Some firms don't yet use TQM; they may be missing an opportunity. Other firms apply some quality methods—but act like they are the private property of a handful of "quality specialists" who want to control things. That's not good either. Everyone must own a TQM effort—and keep a balanced view of how it improves customer satisfaction and what it costs.

As more marketing managers see the benefits of TQM, it will become a more important part of marketing thinking, especially marketing implementation. And when managers really understand implementation, they can do a better job developing strategies and plans in the first place.[7]

CONTROL PROVIDES FEEDBACK TO IMPROVE PLANS AND IMPLEMENTATION

Keeping a firmer hand on the controls

We've said that computers and other types of information technology are speeding up the flow of feedback and prompting a revolution by allowing managers to improve plans and implementation quickly and continuously. On the other hand, the basic questions that a modern marketing manager wants to answer to make better implementation and strategy decisions are pretty similar to what they've always been.

A good manager wants to know: which products' sales are highest and why, which products are profitable, what is selling where, and how much the marketing process is costing. Managers need to know what's happening—in detail—to improve the bottom line.

Unfortunately, traditional accounting reports are usually too general to be much help in answering these questions. A company may be showing a profit, while 80 percent of its business comes from only 20 percent of its products—or customers. The other 80 percent may be unprofitable. But without special analyses, managers won't know it. This 80/20 relationship is fairly common—and it is often referred to as the *80/20 rule*.

What happened with Ben & Jerry's Peace Pops premium ice cream bars is a good example. The initial plan called for intensive distribution of boxes of Peace Pops in supermarket freezer cases—to compete with competitors like Dove Bar and Häagen-Dazs. But after six months total sales were 50 percent lower than expected. However, detailed sales analysis by package and channel revealed a bright spot: individual Peace Pops were selling very well in local delis. After further work to better understand the reasons for this focused success, Ben & Jerry's marketing people realized that most of their target customers saw the premium-price Peace Pop as an impulse product—rather than as a staple they were willing to heap into a shopping cart. So Ben & Jerry's revised the strategy to better reach impulse buyers—at convenience stores. Within a year, the revised strategy worked. Sales increased 60 percent, and sales analysis showed that 70 percent of the sales were at convenience stores.[8]

As the Ben & Jerry's example shows, it *is* possible for marketing managers to get detailed information about how marketing plans are working—but only if they ask for and help develop the necessary data. In this section, we'll discuss the kinds of information that can be available and how to use it. The techniques are not really complicated. They basically require only simple arithmetic—and of course a computer can quickly and easily take care of that when a large volume of sorting, adding, and subtracting is required.

SALES ANALYSIS SHOWS WHAT'S HAPPENING

Sales analysis—a detailed breakdown of a company's sales records—can be very informative—especially the first time it's done. Detailed data can keep marketing executives in touch with what's happening in the market. In addition, routine sales analyses prepared each week, month, or year may show trends—and allow managers to check their hypotheses and assumptions.[9]

Some managers resist sales analysis—or any analysis for that matter—because they don't appreciate how valuable it can be. One top executive in a large firm made no attempt to analyze company sales—even by geographic area. When asked why, the executive replied: "Why should we? We're making money!"

But today's profit is no guarantee that you'll make money tomorrow. In fact, ignoring sales analysis can lead not only to poor sales forecasting but to poor decisions in general. One manufacturer did much national advertising on the assumption that the firm was selling all over the country. But a simple sales analysis showed that most present customers were located within a 250-mile radius of the factory! In other words, the firm didn't know who and where its customers were—and it wasted most of the money it spent on national advertising.

But a marketing manager must ask for it

Detailed sales analysis is only possible if a manager asks for the data. Valuable sales information is often buried—perhaps on sales invoices or in billing records on an accountant's computer.

Today, with computers and organized marketing information systems, effective sales analysis can be done easily and at relatively small cost—if marketing managers decide they want it done. In fact, the desired information can be obtained as a by-product of basic billing and accounts receivable procedures. The manager simply must make sure the company captures identifying information—on important dimensions such as territory, sales reps, and so forth. Then, computers can easily run sales analyses and simple trend projections.

What to ask for varies

There is no one best way to analyze sales data. Several breakdowns may be useful—depending on the nature of the company and product and what dimensions are relevant. Typical breakdowns include:

1. Geographic region—country, state, county, city, sales rep's territory.
2. Product, package size, grade, or color.
3. Customer size.
4. Customer type or class of trade.
5. Price or discount class.
6. Method of sale—mail, telephone, or direct sales.
7. Financial arrangement—cash or charge.
8. Size of order.
9. Commission class.

Too much data can drown a manager

While some sales analysis is better than none—or better than getting data too late for action—sales breakdowns that are too detailed can drown a manager in

---

Information Resources, Inc., developed the DataServer Analyzer Software illustrated here to make it easy to do sales analysis and produce graphs that make it easy to "see" patterns that might otherwise be hidden in a table of numbers.

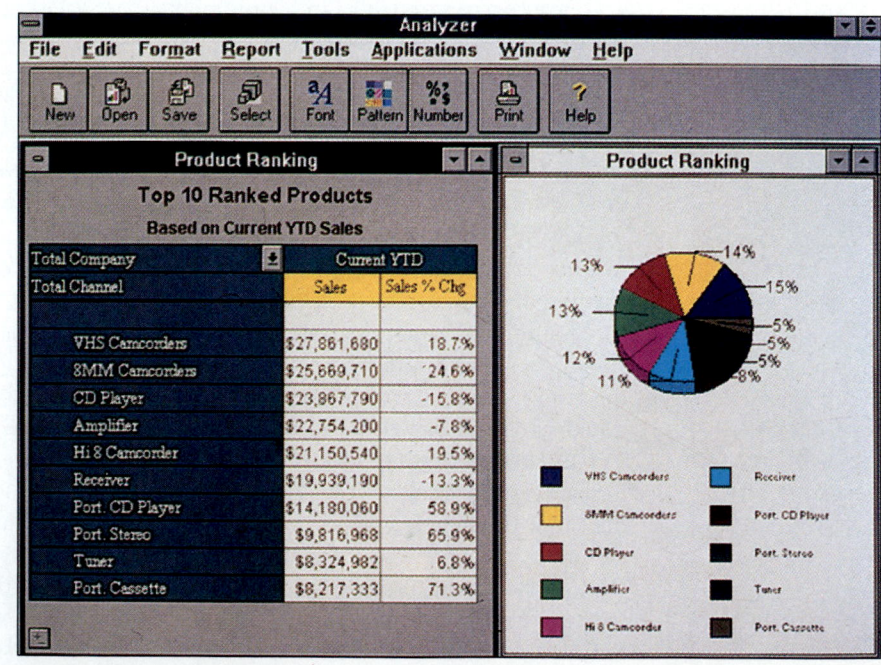

reports. Computers can print over 1,500 lines per minute—faster than any manager can read. So wise managers only ask for breakdowns that will help them make decisions. Further, they use computer programs that draw graphs and figures to make it easy to see patterns that otherwise might be hidden in a 1-inch thick computer printout. But to avoid coping with mountains of data—much of which may be irrelevant—most managers move on to *performance analysis*.

PERFORMANCE ANALYSIS LOOKS FOR DIFFERENCES

Numbers are compared

Performance analysis looks for exceptions or variations from planned performance. In simple sales analysis, the figures are merely listed or graphed—they aren't compared against standards. In performance analysis, managers make comparisons. They might compare one territory against another, against the same territory's performance last year, or against expected performance.

The purpose of performance analysis is to improve operations. The salesperson, territory, or other factors showing poor performance can be identified—and singled out for detailed analysis and corrective action. Or outstanding performances can be analyzed to see if the successes can be explained and made the general rule.

Performance analysis doesn't have to be limited to sales. Other data can be analyzed too. This data may include miles traveled, number of calls made, number of orders, or the cost of various tasks.

A performance analysis can be quite revealing—as shown in the following example.

Straight performance analysis—an illustration

A manufacturer of business products sells to wholesalers through five sales reps—each serving a separate territory. Total net sales for the year amount to $2,386,000. Sales force compensation and expenses come to $198,000, yielding a direct-selling expense ratio of 8.3 percent—that is, $198,000 ÷ $2,386,000 × 100.

This information—taken from a profit and loss statement—is interesting, but it doesn't explain what's happening from one territory to another. To get a clearer picture, the manager compares the sales results with other data *from each territory*. See Exhibits 20–4 and 20–5. Keep in mind that exhibits like these and others that follow in this chapter are now very easy to generate. Popular computer programs like Lotus 1-2-3 and dBASE IV make it easy to apply the ideas discussed here, even on inexpensive desktop computers.

EXHIBIT 20–4 Comparative Performance of Sales Reps

Sales Area	Total Calls	Total Orders	Order–Call Ratio	Sales by Sales Rep	Average Sales Rep Order	Total Customers
A	1,900	1,140	60.0%	$912,000	$800	195
B	1,500	1,000	66.7	720,000	720	160
C	1,400	700	50.0	560,000	800	140
D	1,030	279	27.1	132,000	478	60
E	820	165	20.1	62,000	374	50
Total	6,650	3,284	49.3%	$2,386,000	$634	605

EXHIBIT 20–5 Comparative Cost of Sales Reps

Sales Area	Annual Compensation	Expense Payments	Total Sales Rep Cost	Sales Produced	Cost–Sales Ratio
A	$22,800	$11,200	$34,000	$912,000	3.7%
B	21,600	14,400	36,000	720,000	5.0
C	20,400	11,600	32,000	560,000	5.7
D	19,200	24,800	44,000	132,000	33.3
E	20,000	32,000	52,000	62,000	83.8
Total	$104,000	$94,000	$198,000	$2,386,000	8.3%

The reps in sales areas D and E aren't doing well. Sales are low and marketing costs are high. Perhaps more aggressive sales reps could do a better job, but the number of customers suggests that sales potential might be low. Perhaps the whole plan needs revision.

The figures themselves, of course, don't provide the answers. But they do reveal the areas that need improvement. This is the main value of performance analysis. It's up to management to find the remedy—either by revising or changing the marketing plan.

PERFORMANCE INDEXES SIMPLIFY HUMAN ANALYSIS

Comparing against "what ought to have happened"

With a straight performance analysis, the marketing manager can evaluate the variations among sales reps to try to explain the "why." But this takes time. And poor performances are sometimes due to problems that bare sales figures don't reveal. Some uncontrollable factors in a particular territory—tougher competitors or ineffective middlemen—may lower the sales potential. Or a territory just may not have much potential.

To get a better check on performance effectiveness, the marketing manager compares what did happen with what ought to have happened. This involves the use of performance indexes.

A performance index is like a batting average

When a manager sets standards—that is, quantitative measures of what ought to happen—it's relatively simple to compute a **performance index**—a number like a baseball batting average that shows the relation of one value to another.

Baseball batting averages are computed by dividing the actual number of hits by the number of times at bat (the possible number of times the batter could have had a hit) and then multiplying the result by 100 to get rid of decimal points. A sales performance index is computed the same way—by dividing actual sales by expected sales for the area (or sales rep, product, etc.) and then multiplying by 100. If a sales rep is batting 82 percent, the index is 82.

A simple example shows where the problem is

We show how to compute a performance index in the following example, which assumes that population is an effective measure of sales potential.

In Exhibit 20–6, the population of the United States is broken down by region as a percent of the total population. The regions are Northeastern, Southern, Midwestern, and Western.

EXHIBIT 20–6 Development of a Measure of Sales Performances (by region)

Regions	(1) Population as Percent of United States	(2) Expected Distribution of Sales Based on Population	(3) Actual Sales	(4) Performance Index
Northeastern	20	$ 200,000	$ 210,000	105
Southern	25	250,000	250,000	100
Midwestern	35	350,000	420,000	120
Western	20	200,000	120,000	60
Total	100	$1,000,000	$1,000,000	

A firm already has $1 million in sales—and now wants to evaluate performance in each region. Column 2 shows the actual sales of $1 million broken down in proportion to the population in the four regions. This is what sales *should* be if population were a good measure of future performance. Column 3 in Exhibit 20–6 shows the actual sales for the year for each region. Column 4 shows measures of performance (performance indexes)—Column 3 ÷ Column 2 × 100.

The Western region isn't doing as well as expected. It has 20 percent of the total population—and expected sales (based on population) are $200,000. Actual sales, however, are only $120,000. This means that the Western region's performance index is only 60—(120,000 ÷ 200,000) × 100—because actual sales are much lower than expected on the basis of population. If population is a good basis for measuring expected sales (an important *if*), the poor sales performance should be analyzed further. Perhaps sales reps in the Western region aren't working as hard as they should. Perhaps promotion there isn't as effective as elsewhere. Or competitive products may have entered the market.

Whatever the cause, it's clear that performance analysis does not solve problems. Managers do that. But performance analysis does point out potential problems—and it does this well.

A SERIES OF PERFORMANCE ANALYSES MAY FIND THE REAL PROBLEM

Performance analysis helps a marketing manager see if the firm's marketing plans are working properly—and, if they aren't, it can lead to problem solving. But a marketing manager may need a series of performance analyses, as shown in the following example.

To get a feel for how performance analysis can be part of a problem-solving process, follow this example carefully—one exhibit at a time. Try to anticipate the marketing manager's decision.

The case of Stereo, Inc.   Stereo's sales manager finds that sales for the Pacific Coast region are $130,000 below the quota of $14,500,000 (that is, actual sales are $14,370,000) for the January through June period. The quota is based on forecast sales of the various types of stereo equipment the company sells. Specifically, the quota is based on forecasts for each product type in each store in each sales rep's territory.

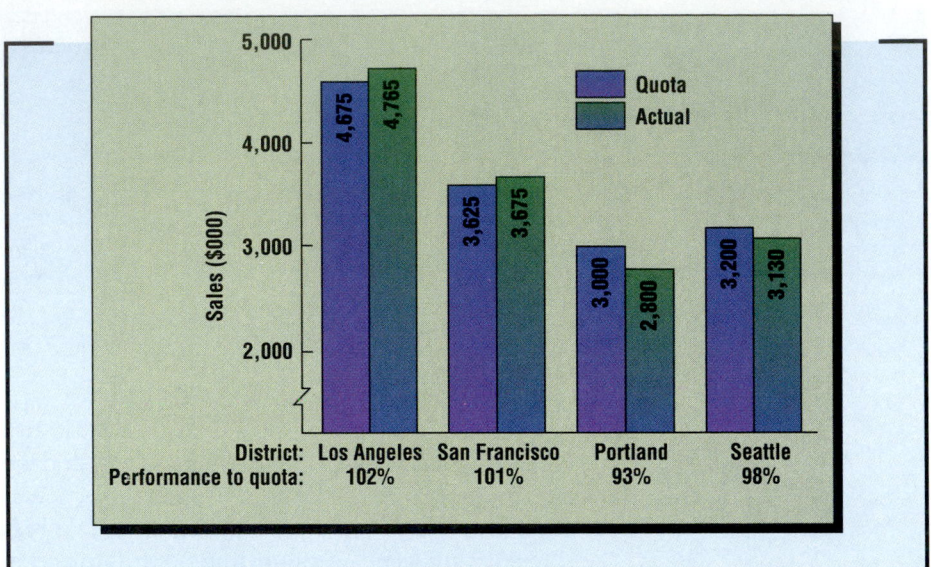

EXHIBIT 20-7 Sales Performance—Pacific Coast Region, January–June ($000)

Pam Dexter, the sales manager, thinks this difference isn't too large (1.52 percent) and is inclined to forget the matter—especially since forecasts usually err to some extent. But she thinks about sending a letter to all sales reps and district supervisors in the region—a letter aimed at stimulating sales effort.

Exhibit 20–7 shows the overall picture of Stereo's sales on the Pacific Coast. What do you think the manager should do?

The Portland district has the poorest performance—but it isn't too bad. Before writing a "let's get with it" letter to Portland and then relaxing, the sales manager decides to analyze the performance of the four sales reps in the Portland district. Exhibit 20–8 shows a breakdown of the Portland figures by sales rep. What conclusion or action do you suggest now?

Since Shanna Smith previously was the top sales rep, the sales manager wonders if Smith is having trouble with some of her larger customers. Before making a drastic move, she obtains an analysis of Smith's sales to the five largest customers. See Exhibit 20–9. What action could the sales manager take now? Should Smith be fired?

Smith's sales in all the large stores are down significantly—although her sales in many small stores are holding up well. Smith's problem seems to be general. Perhaps she just isn't working. Before calling her, the sales manager decides to look at Smith's sales of the four major products. Exhibit 20–10 shows Smith's sales. What action is indicated now?

Smith is having real trouble with portable cassette players. Was the problem Smith or the players?

Further analysis by product for the whole region shows that everyone on the Pacific Coast is having trouble with portable players because a regional competitor is cutting prices. But higher sales on other products hid this fact. Since portable player sales are doing all right nationally, the problem is only now showing up. You can see that this is the *major* problem.

EXHIBIT 20–8   Sales Performance—Portland District, January–June ($000)

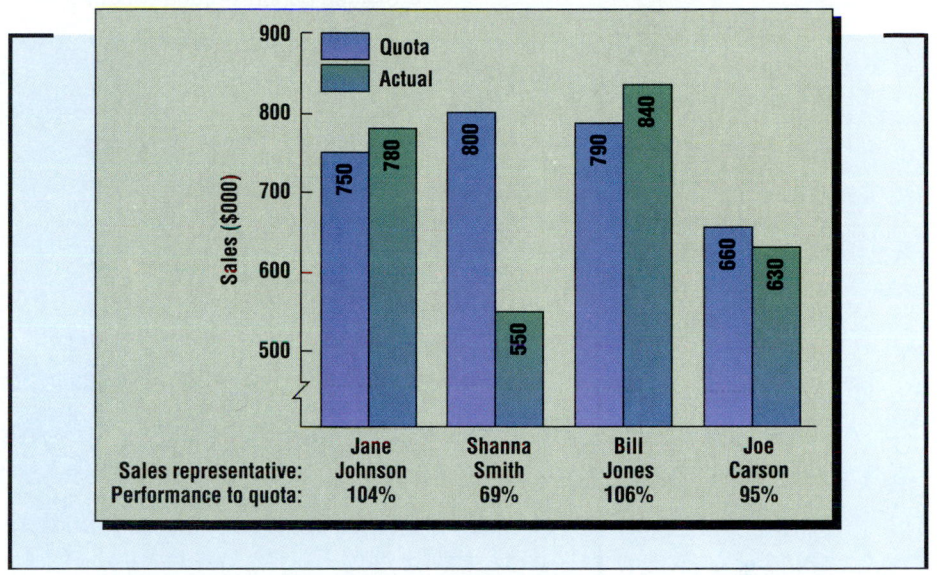

EXHIBIT 20–9   Sales Performance—Selected Stores of Shanna Smith in Portland District, January–June ($000)

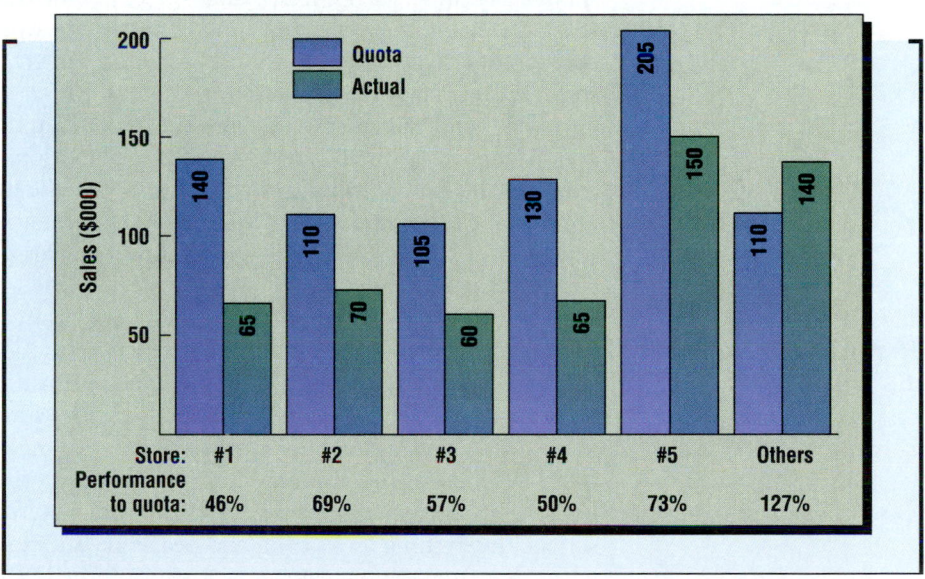

Since overall company sales are fairly good, many sales managers wouldn't bother with this analysis. Some might trace the problem to Smith. But, without detailed sales records and performance analysis, they might assume that Smith—rather than business conditions or aggressive competition—is at fault. And Smith herself might not be able to pinpoint what's happening.

EXHIBIT 20–10 Sales Performance by Product for Shanna Smith in Portland District, January–June ($000)

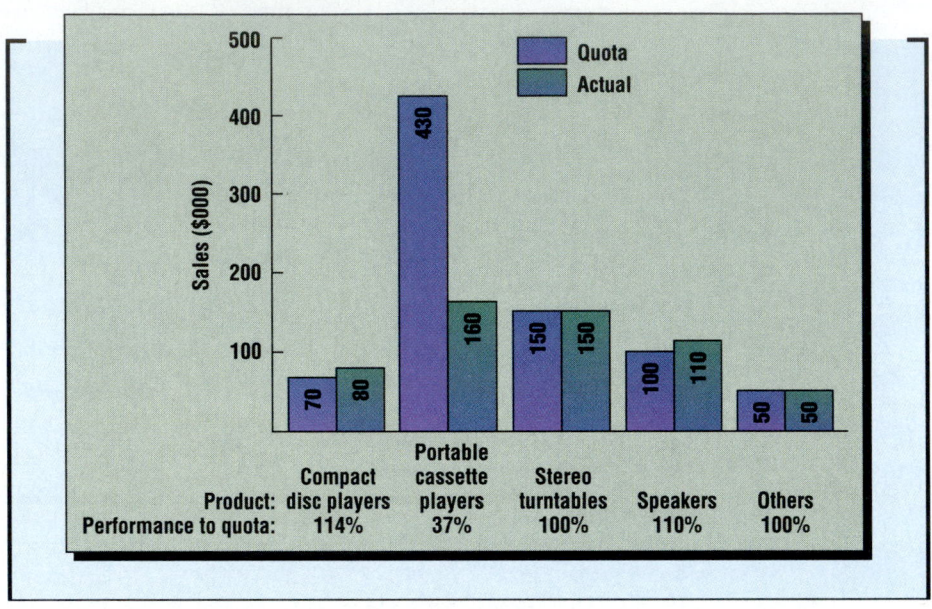

Product:	Compact disc players	Portable cassette players	Stereo turntables	Speakers	Others
Performance to quota:	114%	37%	100%	110%	100%

Quota / Actual values shown on bars: 70/80, 430/160, 150/150, 100/110, 50/50

Stay home and use the computer

This case shows that total figures can be deceiving. Marketing managers should not jump on the first plane—or reach for the phone—until they have all the facts. Even worse than rushing to the scene would be a rash judgment based on incomplete information. Some students want to fire Smith after they see the store-by-store data (Exhibit 20–9).

The home office should have the records and facilities to isolate problem areas—then rely on the field staff for explanations and help with locating the exact problem. Continuing detailed analysis usually gives better insights into problems, as this case shows. With computers, managers can obtain information routinely and in great detail—*provided they ask for it.*

The iceberg principle— 90 percent is below the surface

One of the most interesting conclusions from the Stereo illustration is the **iceberg principle**—much good information is hidden in summary data. Icebergs show only about 10 percent of their mass above water level. The other 90 percent is below water level—and not directly below either. The submerged portion almost seems to search out ships that come too near.

The same is true of much business and marketing data. Since total sales may be large and company activities varied, problems in one area may hide below the surface. Everything looks calm and peaceful. But closer analysis may reveal jagged edges that can severely damage or even sink the business. The 90:10 ratio—or the 80/20 rule we mentioned earlier—must not be ignored. Averaging and summarizing data are helpful, but be sure summaries don't hide more than they reveal.

MARKETING COST ANALYSIS—CONTROLLING COSTS TOO

So far we've emphasized sales analysis. But sales come at a cost. And costs can and should be analyzed and controlled too. You can see why in the case of

Watanake Packaging, Ltd. (WPL). WPL developed a new strategy to target the packaging needs of producers of high-tech electronic equipment. WPL designed unique Styrofoam inserts to protect electronic equipment during shipping. It assigned order getters to develop new accounts and recruited agent middlemen to develop overseas markets. The whole marketing mix was well received—and the firm's skimming price led to good profits. But over time competing suppliers entered the market. When marketing managers at WPL analyzed costs, they realized their once-successful strategy was slipping. Personal selling expense as a percent of sales had doubled because it took longer to find and sell new accounts. It was costly to design special products for the many customers who purchased only small quantities. Profit margins were falling too because of increased price competition. In contrast, the analysis showed that sales of ordinary cardboard shipping boxes for agricultural products were very profitable. So WPL stopped calling on *small* electronics firms—and developed a new plan to build the firm's share of the less glamorous—but more profitable—cardboard box business.

Marketing costs have a purpose

Detailed cost analysis is very useful in understanding production costs—but much less is done with *marketing cost analysis*.[10] One reason is that many accountants show little interest in their firm's marketing process—or they don't understand the different marketing activities. They just treat marketing as overhead and forget about it.

In the next chapter, when we discuss the relationship between marketing and accounting in more detail, we'll explain how some accountants and marketing managers are working together to address this problem. For now, however, you should see that careful analysis of most marketing costs shows that the money is spent for a specific purpose—for example, to develop or promote a particular product or to serve particular customers.

Let's reconsider Exhibit 20–5 from this perspective. It shows that the company's spending on sales compensation and sales expenses varies by salesperson and market area. By breaking out and comparing the costs of different sales reps, the marketing manager has a much better idea of what it is costing to implement the strategy in each sales area. In this example, it's clear that the sales reps in sales areas D and especially E are not only falling short in sales, but also that their costs are high relative to other reps who are getting more results. The table shows that the difference isn't due to annual compensation; that's lower. Rather, these reps have expenses that are two or three times the average. The smaller number of total customers in these sales areas (Exhibit 20–4) might explain the lower levels of sales, but it probably doesn't explain the higher expenses. Perhaps the customers are more spread out and require more travel to reach. Here again, the cost analysis doesn't explain *why* the results are as they are—but it does direct the manager's attention to a specific area that needs attention. A more detailed breakdown of costs may help pinpoint the specific cause.

Allocate costs to specific customers and products

Because marketing costs have a purpose, it usually makes sense to allocate costs to specific market segments—or customers—or to specific products. In some situations, companies allocate costs directly to the various geographical market segments they serve. This may let managers directly analyze the profitability of the firm's target markets. In other cases, companies allocate costs to specific customers or specific products—and then add these costs for market segments depending on how much of which products each customer buys.

Should all costs be allocated?

So far we've discussed general principles. But allocating costs is tricky. Some costs are likely to be fixed for the near future—regardless of what decision is made. And some costs are likely to be *common* to several products or customers—making allocation difficult.

Two basic approaches to handling this allocating problem are possible—the full-cost approach and the contribution-margin approach.

Full-cost approach—everything costs something

In the **full-cost approach**, all costs are allocated to products, customers, or other categories. Even fixed costs and common costs are allocated in some way. Because all costs are allocated, we can subtract costs from sales and find the profitability of various customers, products, and so on. This *is* of interest to some managers.

The full-cost approach requires that difficult-to-allocate costs be split on some basis. Here the managers assume that the work done for those costs is equally beneficial to customers, to products, or to whatever group they are allocated. Sometimes this allocation is done mechanically. But often logic can support the allocation—if we accept the idea that marketing costs are incurred for a purpose. For example, advertising costs not directly related to specific customers or products might be allocated to *all* customers based on their purchases—on the theory that advertising helps bring in the sales. We'll go into more detail on allocating costs in the next chapter.

Contribution margin—ignores some costs to get results

When we use the **contribution-margin approach**, all costs are not allocated in *all* situations. Why?

When we compare various alternatives, it may be more meaningful to consider only the costs directly related to specific alternatives. Variable costs are relevant here.

The contribution-margin approach focuses attention on variable costs—rather than on total costs. Total costs may include some fixed costs that do not change in the short run and can safely be ignored or some common costs that are more difficult to allocate.[11]

The two approaches can lead to different decisions

The difference between the full-cost approach and the contribution-margin approach is important. The two approaches may suggest different decisions, as we'll see in the following example.

Full-cost example

Exhibit 20–11 shows a profit and loss statement—using the full-cost approach—for a department store with three operating departments. (These could be market segments or customers or products.)

The administrative expenses—which are the only fixed costs in this case—have been allocated to departments based on the sales volume of each department. This is a typical method of allocation. In this case, some managers argued that Department 1 was clearly unprofitable—and should be eliminated—because it showed a net loss of $500. Were they right?

To find out, see Exhibit 20–12, which shows what would happen if Department 1 were eliminated.

Several facts become clear right away. The overall profit of the store would be reduced if Department 1 were dropped. Fixed costs of $3,000—now being charged to Department 1—would have to be allocated to the other departments. This would reduce net profit by $2,500, since Department 1 previously covered $2,500

EXHIBIT 20–11   Profit and Loss Statement by Department

	Totals	Dept. 1	Dept. 2	Dept.3
Sales	$100,000	$50,000	$30,000	$20,000
Cost of sales	80,000	45,000	25,000	10,000
Gross margin	20,000	5,000	5,000	10,000
Other expenses				
Selling expenses	5,000	2,500	1,500	1,000
Administrative expenses	6,000	3,000	1,800	1,200
Total other expenses	11,000	5,500	3,300	2,200
Net profit or (loss)	9,000	(500)	1,700	7,800

EXHIBIT 20–12   Profit and Loss Statement by Department if Department 1 Were Eliminated

	Totals	Dept. 2	Dept.3
Sales	$50,000	$30,000	$20,000
Cost of sales	35,000	25,000	10,000
Gross margin	15,000	5,000	10,000
Other expenses			
Selling expenses	2,500	1,500	1,000
Administrative expenses	6,000	3,600	2,400
Total other expenses	8,500	5,100	3,400
Net profit or (loss)	6,500	(100)	6,600

of the $3,000 in fixed costs. Such shifting of costs would then make Department 2 unprofitable!

Contribution-margin example

Exhibit 20–13 shows a contribution-margin income statement for the same department store. Note that each department has a positive contribution margin. Here the Department 1 contribution of $2,500 stands out better. This actually is the amount that would be lost if Department 1 were dropped. (Our example assumes that the fixed administrative expenses are *truly* fixed—that none of them would be eliminated if this department were dropped.)

A contribution-margin income statement shows the contribution of each department more clearly—including its contribution to both fixed costs and profit. As long as a department has some contribution-margin—and as long as there is no better use for the resources it uses—the department should be retained.

Contribution-margin versus full-cost—choose your side

Using the full-cost approach often leads to arguments within a company. Any method of allocation can make some products or customers appear less profitable. For example, it's logical to assign all common advertising costs to customers based on their purchases. But this approach can be criticized on the grounds that it may make large-volume customers appear less profitable than they really are—

EXHIBIT 20–13 Contribution-Margin Statement by Departments

	Totals	Dept. 1	Dept. 2	Dept. 3
Sales	$100,000	$50,000	$30,000	$20,000
Variable costs				
Cost of sales	80,000	45,000	25,000	10,000
Selling expenses	5,000	2,500	1,500	1,000
Total variable costs	85,000	47,500	26,500	11,000
Contribution margin	15,000	2,500	3,500	9,000
Fixed costs				
Administrative expenses	6,000			
Net profit	9,000			

especially if the marketing mix aimed at the larger customers emphasizes price more than advertising.

Those in the company who want the smaller customers to look more profitable usually argue *for* this allocation method on the grounds that general advertising helps build good customers because it affects the overall image of the company and its products.

Arguments over allocation methods can be deadly serious. The method used may reflect on the performance of various managers—and it may affect their salaries and bonuses. Product managers, for example, are especially interested in how the various fixed and common costs are allocated to their products. Each, in turn, might like to have costs shifted to others' products.

Arbitrary allocation of costs also may have a direct impact on sales reps' morale. If they see their variable costs loaded with additional common or fixed costs over which they have no control, they may ask, What's the use?

To avoid these problems, firms often use the contribution-margin approach. It's especially useful for evaluating alternatives—and for showing operating managers and salespeople how they're doing. The contribution-margin approach shows what they've actually contributed to covering general overhead and profit.

Top management, on the other hand, often finds full-cost analysis more useful. In the long run, some products, departments, or customers must pay for the fixed costs. Full-cost analysis has its place too.

PLANNING AND CONTROL COMBINED

We've been treating sales and cost analyses separately up to this point. But management often combines them to keep a running check on its activities—to be sure the plans are working—and to see when and where new strategies are needed.

Sales + Costs + Everybody helps = $163,000

Let's see how this works at Cindy's Fashions, a typical apparel retailer.

This firm netted $155,000 last year. Cindy Reve, the owner, expects no basic change in competition and slightly better local business conditions. So she sets this year's profit objective at $163,000—an increase of about 5 percent.

Next she develops tentative plans to show how she can make this higher profit. She estimates the sales volumes, gross margins, and expenses—broken

EXHIBIT 20–14   Planning and Control Chart for Cindy's Fashions

| | Contribution to Store | | | | | Store Expense | Operating Profit | Cumulative Operating Profit |
	Dept. A	Dept. B	Dept. C	Dept. D*	Total			
January								
Planned	27,000	9,000	4,000	−1,000	39,000	24,000	15,000	15,000
Actual								
Variation								
February								
Planned	20,000	6,500	2,500	−1,000	28,000	24,000	4,000	19,000
Actual								
Variation								
November								
Planned	32,000	7,500	2,500	0	42,000	24,000	18,000	106,500
Actual								
Variation								
December								
Planned	63,000	12,500	4,000	9,000	88,500	32,000	56,500	163,000
Actual								
Variation								
Total								
Planned	316,000	70,000	69,000	−4,000	453,000	288,000	163,000	163,000
Actual								
Variation								

*The objective of minus $4,000 for this department was established on the same basis as the objectives for the other departments—that is, it represents the same percentage gain over last year, when Department D's loss was $4,200. Plans call for discontinuance of the department unless it shows marked improvement by the end of the year.

down by months and by departments in her store—that she would need to net $163,000.

Exhibit 20–14 is a planning and control chart Reve developed to show the contribution each department should make each month. At the bottom of Exhibit 20–14, the plan for the year is summarized. Note that space is provided to insert the actual performance and a measure of variation. So this chart can be used to do both planning and control.

Exhibit 20–14 shows that Reve is focusing on the monthly contribution to overhead and profit by each department. The purpose of monthly estimates is to get more frequent feedback and allow faster adjustment of plans. Generally, the shorter the planning and control period, the easier it is to correct problems before they become emergencies.

In this example, Reve uses a modified contribution-margin approach—some of the fixed costs can be allocated logically to particular departments. On this chart, the balance left after direct fixed and variable costs are charged to departments is called Contribution to Store. The idea is that each department will contribute to covering *general* store expenses—such as top-management salaries and holiday decorations—and to net profits.

In Exhibit 20–14, we see that the whole operation is brought together when Reve computes the monthly operating profit. She totals the contribution from each of the four departments then subtracts general store expenses to obtain the operating profit for each month.

As time passes, Reve can compare actual sales with what's projected. If actual sales were less than projected, corrective action could take either of two courses: improving implementation efforts or developing new, more realistic strategies.

THE MARKETING AUDIT

While crises pop, planning and control must go on

The analyses we've discussed so far are designed to help a firm plan and control its operations. They can help a marketing manager do a better job. Often, however, the control process tends to look at only a few critical elements—such as sales variations by product in different territories. It misses such things as the effectiveness of present and possible marketing strategies and mixes.

The marketing manager usually is responsible for day-to-day implementing as well as planning and control—and may not have the time to evaluate the effectiveness of the firm's efforts. Sometimes, crises pop up in several places at the same time. Attention must focus on adjusting marketing mixes—or on shifting strategies in the short run.

To make sure that the whole marketing program is evaluated *regularly*, not just in times of crisis, marketing specialists developed the marketing audit. A marketing audit is similar to an accounting audit or a personnel audit, which businesses have used for some time.

The **marketing audit** is a systematic, critical, and unbiased review and appraisal of the basic objectives and policies of the marketing function—and of the organization, methods, procedures, and people employed to implement the policies.[12]

A marketing audit requires a detailed look at the company's current marketing plans to see if they are still the best plans the firm can offer. Customers' needs and attitudes change—and competitors continually develop new and better plans. Plans more than a year or two old may be out-of-date—or even obsolete. Sometimes, marketing managers are so close to the trees that they can't see the forest. An outsider can help the firm see whether it really focuses on some unsatisfied needs and offers appropriate marketing mixes. Basically, the auditor uses our strategy planning framework. But instead of developing plans, the auditor works backward—and evaluates the plans being implemented. The auditor also evaluates the quality of the effort—looking at who is doing what and how well. This means interviewing customers, competitors, channel members, and employees. A marketing audit can be a big job. But if it helps ensure that the company's strategies are on the right track—and being implemented properly—it can be well worth the effort.

An audit shouldn't be necessary—but often it is

A marketing audit takes a big view of the business—and it evaluates the whole marketing program. It might be done by a separate department within the company—perhaps by a marketing controller. But to get both expert and objective evaluation, it's probably better to use an outside organization such as a marketing consulting firm. For example, Copernicus—a marketing strategy consulting and research firm in Westport, Connecticut—has developed an in-depth procedure and routinely conducts marketing audits for a number of major firms.

Ideally, a marketing audit should not be necessary. Good managers do their very best in planning, implementing, and control—and should continually evaluate the effectiveness of the operation.

In practice, however, managers often become identified with certain strategies—and pursue them blindly—when other strategies might be more effective. Since an outside view can give needed perspective, marketing audits may be more common in the future.

CONCLUSION

In this chapter, we've focused on the important role of implementation and control in satisfying customers and the firm's ongoing success. We explained how improvements in information technology are playing a critical role in revolutionizing these areas. Managers should seek new and creative ways to improve implementation, which can often give a firm a competitive advantage in building stronger relationships with customers, even in highly competitive mature markets.

We also went into some detail on how total quality management can help the firm get the type of implementation it needs—implementation that continuously improves and does a better job of meeting customers' needs and at lower cost.

A marketing program must also be controlled. Good control helps the marketing manager locate and correct weak spots—and at the same time find strengths that may be applied throughout the marketing program. Control works hand in hand with planning.

Simple sales analysis just gives a picture of what happened. But when sales forecasts or other data showing expected results are brought into the analysis, we can evaluate performance—using performance indexes.

Cost analysis also can be useful. There are two basic approaches to cost analysis—full-cost and contribution-margin. Using the full-cost approach, all costs are allocated in some way. Using the contribution-margin approach, only the variable costs are allocated. Both methods have their advantages and special uses.

Ideally, the marketing manager should arrange for a constant flow of data that can be analyzed routinely—preferably by computer—to help control present plans and plan new strategies. A marketing audit can help this ongoing effort. Either a separate department within the company or an outside organization may conduct this audit.

QUESTIONS AND PROBLEMS

1. Give an example of how a firm has used information technology to improve its marketing implementation and do a better job of meeting your needs.

2. Should marketing managers leave it to the computer experts to develop reports that the marketing manager will use to improve implementation and control? Why or why not?

3. Give an example of a firm that has a competitive advantage because of the excellent job it does with implementation activities that directly impact customer satisfaction. Explain why you think your example is a good one.

4. What are the major advantages of total quality management as an approach for improving implementation of marketing plans? What limitations can you think of?

5. Various breakdowns can be used for sales analysis depending on the nature of the company and its products. Describe a situation (one for each) where each of the following breakdowns would yield useful information. Explain why.

   a. By geographic region.
   b. By product.
   c. By customer.
   d. By size of order.
   e. By size of sales rep commission on each product or product group.

6. Distinguish between a sales analysis and a performance analysis.

7. Carefully explain what the iceberg principle should mean to the marketing manager.

8. Explain the meaning of the comparative performance and comparative cost data in Exhibits 20–4 and 20–5. Why does it appear that eliminating sales areas D and E would be profitable?

9. Most sales forecasting is subject to some error (perhaps 5 to 10 percent). Should we then expect variations in sales performance of 5 to 10 percent above or below quota? If so, how should we treat such variations in evaluating performance?

10. Why is there controversy between the advocates of the full-cost and the contribution-margin approaches to cost analysis?

11. The June profit and loss statement for the Browning Company is shown. If competitive conditions make price increases impossible—and management has cut costs as much as possible—should the Browning Company stop selling to hospitals and schools? Why?

Browning Company Statement

	Retailers	Hospitals and Schools	Total
Sales			
80,000 units at $0.70	$56,000		$56,000
20,000 units at $0.60		$12,000	12,000
Total	56,000	12,000	68,000
Cost of sales	40,000	10,000	50,000
Gross margin	16,000	2,000	18,000
Sales and administrative expenses			
Variable	6,000	1,500	7,500
Fixed	5,600	900	6,500
Total	11,600	2,400	14,000
Net profit (loss)	$ 4,400	$ (400)	$ 4,000

12. Explain why a marketing audit might be desirable—even in a well-run company. Who or what kind of an organization would be best to conduct a marketing audit? Would a marketing research firm be good? Would the present CPA firms be most suitable? Why?

SUGGESTED CASES

34. Huntoon & Balbiera, P.C.

36. Romano's Take-Out, Inc.

COMPUTER-AIDED PROBLEM

20. **Marketing Cost Analysis**

This problem emphasizes the differences between the full-cost approach and contribution-margin approach to marketing cost analysis.

Tapco, Inc., currently sells two products. Sales commissions and unit costs vary with the quantity of each product sold. With the full-cost approach, Tapco's administrative and advertising costs are allocated to each product based on its share of total sales dollars. Details of Tapco's costs and other data are given in the spreadsheet. The first column shows a cost analysis based on the full-cost approach. The second column shows an analysis based on the contribution-margin approach.

a. If the number of Product A units sold were to increase by 1,000 units, what would happen to the allocated administrative expense for Product A? How would the change in sales of Product A affect the allocated administrative expense for Product B? Briefly discuss why the changes you observe might

cause conflict between the product managers of the two different products.

b. What would happen to total profits if Tapco stopped selling Product A but continued to sell 4,000 units of Product B? What happens to total profits if the firm stops selling Product B but continues to sell 5,000 units of Product A? (Hint: To stop selling a product means that the quantity sold would be zero.)

c. If the firm dropped Product B and increased the price of Product A by $2.00, what quantity of Product A would it have to sell to earn a total profit as large as it was originally earning with both products? (Hint: Change values in the spreadsheet to reflect the changes the firm is considering, and then use the What If analysis to vary the quantity of Product A sold and display what happens to total profit.)

For additional questions related to this problem, see Exercise 20–3 in the *Learning Aid for Use with Basic Marketing*, 12th edition.

21

Managing Marketing's Link with Other Functional Areas

When You Finish This Chapter, You Should

1. Understand why turning a marketing plan into a profitable business requires money, information, people, and a way to get or produce goods and services.

2. Understand the ways that marketing strategy decisions may need to be adjusted in light of available financing.

3. Understand how a firm can implement and expand a marketing plan using internally generated cash flow.

4. Understand how different aspects of production capacity and flexibility should be coordinated with marketing strategy planning.

5. Understand the ways that the location and cost of production affect marketing strategy planning.

6. Know how marketing managers and accountants can work together to improve analysis of the costs and profitability of specific products and customers.

7. Know some of the human resource issues that a marketer should consider when planning a strategy and implementing a plan.

8. Understand the important new terms (shown in red).

Illinois Tool Works (ITW) produces and sells a large array of products—ranging from nuts, bolts, screws, nails, and plastic fasteners to sophisticated equipment. You've probably never heard of ITW, but its fasteners are hidden inside or attached to appliances, to cars, and many other products you buy. One key to ITW's success is that it is fast and creative in identifying target markets with their specific needs, and then developing products—actually whole marketing mixes—and implementing its plans to meet the target market's needs. Another key to ITW's success is that managers from different areas—such as production, finance, accounting, and human resources—work closely with the marketing people to be certain that the firm can really deliver on the marketing ideas.

Some competing firms make the mistake of defining their markets in terms of the products they've always produced (for example, the "screw market" or the "bolt market"). By contrast, ITW defines markets in terms of customer needs. And often ITW finds that what a customer needs is not a screw or a bolt but something entirely new. Of course, ITW recognizes that this approach requires more than a marketing plan. It often requires new resources—new production capabilities, money to put the plan into operation, and people with new skills.

For example, a firm that produces life jackets needed a better way to fasten them. So ITW had its R&D people develop just the right product—for this customer—a very durable, safety-rated plastic buckle. And ITW had the money to set up new production facilities for the buckle because its other established products were producing profits that ITW could reinvest. With production capacity in place, ITW targeted marketing mixes at other firms with similar needs. Today, millions of ITW buckles are used not only in life jackets but also in backpacks, luggage, bicycle helmets, and many types of leisure clothing. Adding special buckles for these different markets quickly contributed to profits because most of the major fixed costs had already been covered.

ITW has developed many other innovative products and marketing mixes focused on the needs of specific market segments. For example, ITW makes Kiwi-Lok, a nylon fastener that New Zealand farmers use to secure their kiwi plants. It's not a fluke that ITW saw this put it, unusual fastening need. As one ITW executive "We try to sell where our competitors aren't"— one reason why ITW now serves customers from operations in more than 35 countries. Although ITW is a large company, it is able to stay in close contact with its customers because all of its businesses are locally managed.

ITW organizes all of its activities—including how it sets up its factories—to adjust to the needs of distinct target markets. ITW serves large-volume segments with "focused factories" that concentrate on quickly producing large quantities of a single product line at a low cost. It handles limited production for small segments in special "batches" on equipment dedicated to short runs. This flexible approach helps ITW fill customers' orders faster than competitors— which is yet another reason for the company's success.[1]

MARKETING IN THE BROADER CONTEXT

The marketing concept says that everyone in a firm should work together to satisfy customer needs at a profit. Once a marketing strategy has been developed—and turned into a marketing plan—the blueprint for what needs to be done is in place. So, throughout the text we've developed concepts and how-to approaches relevant to marketing strategy planning, implementation, and control.

From the outset, we've emphasized that what is a good marketing strategy— selection of a target market and a marketing mix to meet target customers' needs—depends on the fit with the specific firm and its market environment— what it's able to do and what it wants to do. In Chapters 3 and 4 we discussed how a firm's resources and objectives might allow it to pursue some opportunities and not others.

Now that you have a better idea about how the marketing decisions fit together into an integrated strategy, we'll broaden our focus to take a closer look at some of the most important ways that marketing links to other functional areas. As the ITW case shows, turning a strategy into a profitable business requires more than a marketing plan—it also requires money, people, and other resources—such as production capacity.

Cross-functional links affect strategy planning

In this chapter we will continue to look at management issues from the view of a marketing manager. Thus the emphasis is not on the technical details of other functional areas but rather on the most important ways that relationships with other areas impact choices among strategy decisions we've discussed throughout the text. In other words, learning about these cross-functional linkages will improve your ability to develop marketing strategies and plans that really work.

Implementing a marketing plan usually requires a financial investment—so we'll start with a discussion of financial issues. We'll consider both money required to start up a new plan and the ongoing money that may be needed to meet expenses. Then, we'll look at production and operations. We've already explained how marketing can make economies of scale in production possible, but here we'll go into more detail on how available production capacity, production flexibility, and operating issues impact marketing planning. We'll also take a closer look at how accounting people and marketing managers work together to get a better handle on marketing costs. Marketers sometimes get so focused on sales that they forget that profits depend on both revenues and costs. We'll conclude with a

GE Capital helps firms get the money they need to implement their marketing plans—but it also can give them help in making production, information systems, and other functional areas more efficient and effective.

discussion of human resource issues—because it's people who put plans into action. New marketing strategies often upset the standard ways of doing things, and without everyone's wholehearted cooperation change is difficult.

How important the linkages with production, finance, accounting, and human resources are for the marketing manager depends on the situation. In an entrepreneurial start-up, the same person may be making all of the decisions and handling everything. In a small but established company that is trying to expand, the challenges may be different. And in a big company with many different specialists, the linkages may be much more complicated.

Cross-functional challenges are greatest with new efforts

Our emphasis will be on new efforts. When a new strategy involves only a minor modification to a plan that the firm is already implementing successfully, specialists in different areas usually have a pretty good idea of how their activities link to other areas. However, when a potential strategy involves a more significant change—like the development and introduction of a totally new product idea or a big reorganization of the firm's sales force or channel systems—understanding the links between the different functional areas is usually much more critical.

You can't expand, add new capabilities, or bring on people to handle new marketing activities if you can't pay the cost. You can't market a product you can't get or produce. And you can't implement your plan if there are not enough people with the right skills available.

THE FINANCE FUNCTION: MONEY TO IMPLEMENT MARKETING PLANS

Chief financial officer handles money matters

Bright marketing ideas for new ways to satisfy customer needs don't go very far if there isn't enough money to put a plan into operation. Finding and allocating **capital**—the money invested in a firm—is usually handled by a firm's chief financial officer. Entrepreneurs and others who own their own companies may handle this job themselves or may get help from outside financial specialists and consultants. In most firms, however, there is a separate manager who handles financial matters and works with the chief executive to make major finance decisions.

Good communication between a marketing manager and the firm's finance manager is critical. They must work together to ensure that marketing plans are realistic and that the firm can successfully implement them with the money that is or will be available. Further, a successful strategy should ultimately generate profit. The financial manager needs to know how much money to expect—and when to expect it—to be able to plan for how it will be used.

Opportunities compete for capital and budgets

Within an organization, different possible opportunities compete for capital. There's usually not enough money to do everything, so strategies that are inconsistent with the firm's financial objectives and resources are not likely to be funded. It's often best for the marketing manager to use relevant financial measures as quantitative screening criteria when evaluating various alternatives in the first place.

Marketing plans that *are* funded usually must work within a budget constraint. Ideally, the marketing manager should have some inputs on what that budget is—to get the marketing tasks done. But, it isn't practical to develop a plan and budget that require money that simply isn't available.

As a result, at least some important marketing strategy decisions may need to be adjusted—either in the short or long term—to work within the available budget. For example, a marketing manager might prefer to have control over the selling effort for a new product by hiring new people for a separate sales force. However, if there isn't enough money available for salesperson salaries and benefits as well as for travel and other selling expenses, then the best alternative might be to start with manufacturers' agents. They work for a commission and aren't paid until after they generate a sale—and some sales revenue. Then, as the market develops and the plan becomes profitable there may be both the money and a good reason—perhaps lower cost or better control—to expand the firm's own sales force.

Working capital pays for short-term expenses

Finance managers usually think about two different uses of capital. First, capital may be required to pay for investments in facilities, equipment, and other "fixed assets." These installations are usually purchased and then used, and depreciated, over a number of years. In addition, a firm needs **working capital**—money to pay for short-term expenses such as employee salaries, advertising, marketing research, inventory storing costs, and what the firm owes suppliers. A firm usually must pay for these ongoing expenses as they occur—and often that's before it gets revenue for the goods and services it sells. As a result there is usually a continuing need for working capital.

It's also useful for a marketing manager who is developing a plan to think about likely capital needs in this same way. In general, the more ambitious the plan, the greater the amount of capital that is needed. Capital is usually a critical resource when a plan calls for rapid growth—especially if the growth calls for expensive new facilities. Clearly, a plan to build a chain of 15 hotels requires more money for buildings and equipment—as well as more money for salaries, food, and supplies—than a plan for a single hotel. Such a plan might require that the firm borrow money from a commercial lender. In contrast, a plan that simply calls for improving the service in an existing hotel—perhaps by adding several people to handle room service—would require much less money. In fact, increased food sales from room service might quickly generate more than enough earnings to pay for the added people.

Capital comes from internal or external sources

As these examples imply, there are a number of different possible sources of capital. However, it's useful to boil them down to two categories: *external sources*, such as loans or sales of stocks or bonds, and *internal sources*, such as cash accumulated from the firm's profits. A firm usually seeks outside funding in advance of when it is needed to invest in a new strategy. Internally generated profits may be accumulated and used in the same way, but often internal money is used as it becomes available. In other words, with internally generated funding a firm's marketing program may be expected to "pay its own way."

The timing of when financing is available has an important effect on marketing strategy planning, so we'll look at this topic in more detail. We'll start by looking at external sources of funds.

External funding— investors expect a return

While a firm might like to fund its marketing program from rapid growth in its own profits, that is not always possible. New companies often don't have enough money to start that way. An established company with some capital may not have as much as it needs to make long-term investments in factories or other facilities and still have enough working capital for the routine expenses of implementing a plan. Getting started may also involve losses—perhaps for several years—before earnings come in. In these circumstances, the firm may need to turn to one of several sources of external capital.

A firm may be able to raise money by selling stock—a share in the ownership of a company. Stock sales may be public or private, and the buyers may be individuals, including a firm's own employees, or institutional investors (such as a pension fund or venture capital firm).

People that own stock in a firm want a good return on their investment. That can happen if the company pays owners of its stock a regular dividend. It also happens if the value of the stock goes up over time. Neither is likely if the firm isn't consistently earning profits. Further, the value of a firm's stock typically doesn't increase unless its profits are *growing*. This is one reason that marketing managers are always looking for profitable new growth opportunities. Profits can also improve by being more efficient—getting the marketing jobs done at lower cost, doing a better job holding onto customers, and the like—but continued growth in profits usually requires that a firm pursue new market opportunities. Ultimately, a firm that doesn't have a successful (or at least promising) marketing strategy can't attract and keep investors.

Investors' time horizon is important

The time horizon for profit and growth that investors have in mind can be very important to the marketing manager. If investors are patient and willing to wait for a new strategy to become profitable, a marketing manager may have the luxury of developing a plan that will be very profitable in the long run even if it racks up short-term losses. Many Japanese firms take this approach. However, most marketing managers face intense pressure to develop plans that will generate profits quickly; there's more risk for investors if potential profits are off in the future.

Trying to develop a plan that produces profit in the short term and also positions the firm for long-run success isn't always the ideal. For example, a low penetration price for a new product may help both to prevent competition and to build a large, loyal base of customers who will be repeat purchasers long into the future. Yet, a skimming price may be better for profits in the short term. Even so, the marketing manager's plans and program must take the investors' time horizon into consideration. Unhappy investors can—and often do—demand new management or put their money somewhere else. In that situation a firm—or a marketing manager—that fails in the short term may find out that there is no long run!

Forecasts may become an ethical issue

Both individual and institutional investors usually want detailed information about a firm and its plans before they invest money in the firm's stock. This information is usually provided by the firm's financial people, but financial estimates don't mean much unless they're based on realistic estimates of demand, revenue, and marketing expenses. The marketing manager is usually the one who must provide that information. A marketing manager who is optimistic about the potential of a marketing plan may be hesitant to lay out the potential limitations of a plan or its forecasts—especially if the full story might scare off needed investors. However, this is an important ethical issue. While investors know that there is always some uncertainty in forecasts, they have a right to information that is as accurate as possible. Put another way, just as a marketing manager shouldn't mislead a buyer of the firm's products, it's not appropriate to mislead investors who are "buying into" the firm's marketing plan.

Debt financing involves an interest cost

Rather than sell stock, some firms prefer **debt financing**—borrowing money based on a promise to repay the loan, usually within a fixed time period and with a specific interest charge. This might involve a loan from a commercial bank or the use of corporate bonds. People or institutions that loan the money typically do not get an ownership share in the company, and they are usually even less willing to take a risk than are investors who buy stock.

Most commercial banks are conservative. There's an element of truth in the old adage that "a bank is only likely to make a loan to a company that really doesn't need one." That excludes many firms—including most new ones—that don't have some valuable assets to put up as a guarantee that the lender will get its money. Investors who buy a firm's bonds are also very concerned about security—but they often don't have a legal right to some specific assets if the firm goes bankrupt or can't repay the borrowed money and interest when it's due. In general, the greater the risk that the borrower takes on to provide the loan the greater the interest rate charge will be.

Interest expense may impact prices

When a firm needs to borrow a large amount of money to fund its plans the cost of borrowing the money can be a real financial burden—especially if the money is to be repaid over time rather than in a lump sum after a plan is already profitable. Just as a firm's selling price must cover all of the marketing expenses and the other costs of doing business before profits begin to accumulate, it must also cover the interest charge on borrowed money. The impact of interest charges on prices can be significant. For example, the spread between the prices charged by fast-growing, efficient supermarket chains and individual grocery stores would be even greater if the chains weren't paying big interest charges on loans to fund new facilities.

Some banks work aggressively to attract business customers who want loans, but most commercial lenders like to avoid risk and making loans that are not secured with assets.

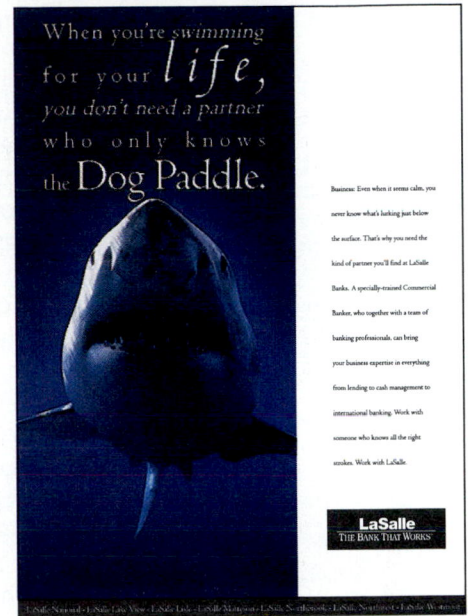

While the cost of borrowing money can be high, it may still make sense if the money is used to implement a marketing plan that earns an even greater return. In that way, the firm "leverages" the borrowed money to make a profit. Even so, there are often advantages if a firm can pay for its plans with internally generated capital.[2]

Winning strategies generate capital

A company with a successful marketing strategy has its own internal source of funds—profits that become cash in the bank!

For example, the building-supply company, Home Depot, reported a profit of just over $600 million from running its businesses in 1994. The company only paid out about 11 percent of that money as dividends to its stockholders. The stockholders like it that way because Home Depot used the remaining half a billion dollars to open 126 new stores.[3]

Reinvesting cash generated from operations is usually less expensive than borrowing money because no interest expense is involved. So, internal financing often helps a firm earn more profit than a competitor that is operating on borrowed money—even if the internally financed company is selling at a lower price.

Expanding profits may support expanded plan

Firms that don't want the expense of borrowed money or that can't get external funding often start with a less costly strategy and a plan to expand it as quickly as is allowed by earnings. Consider the case of Sorrell Ridge, a small company that wanted to compete with the jams and jellies of big competitors like Welch's and Smuckers. Sorrell Ridge started small with a strategy that focused on a better product—"spreadable fruit" with no sugar added—that was targeted at health-conscious consumers. After paying to update its production facilities, Sorrell Ridge didn't have much working capital to pay for promotion and other marketing expenses. So, it turned to health food wholesalers and retailers to give the product a promotion push in the channel. As profits from the health food channel started to grow, Sorrell Ridge used some of the money for local TV and print ads in big cities in the Northeast. The ads increased consumer demand for Sorrell Ridge's spreads and helped get shelf space from supermarkets in that region. Success from selling through supermarkets in the Northeast generated more volume and profit, which provided Sorrell Ridge with the financial base to enter the big California market. The big supermarket chains there wouldn't consider carrying a new fruit spread without a lot of trade promotion—including hefty stocking allowances. Sorrell Ridge had the money to pay for a coupon program to stimulate consumer trial, but that didn't leave enough money for the stocking allowance. However, the marketing manager had a creative idea that involved giving retailers the stocking allowance in the form of a credit against future purchases—rather than cash "up front." With a plan for that blend of trade and consumer promotion in place, one of the best food brokers in California agreed to take on the line. And the expansion into the new large market resulted in fast and profitable growth.[4]

As the Sorrell Ridge case shows, a firm with limited resources can sometimes develop a plan that allows for growth through internally generated money. On the other hand, a company with a mature product that has limited growth potential can invest the earnings from that product in developing a new opportunity that is more profitable. Lotus Development, the software company, is a good example. It used profits from its Lotus 1-2-3 spreadsheet, which faced tough competition from Microsoft's Excel, to fund the development of Lotus Notes, an innovative product for the fast-growing segment of computer users who want an easy way to communicate with other members of their work group.

Cash flow looks at when money will be available

A marketing manager who wants to plan strategies based on the expected flow of internal funding needs a good idea of how much cash will be available. A **cash flow statement** is a financial report that forecasts how much cash will be available after paying expenses. The amount that's available isn't always just the "bottom line" or net profit figure shown on the firm's operating statement. Some expenses, like depreciation of facilities and equipment, are subtracted from revenues for tax and accounting purposes but do not actually involve writing a check. In other words, depreciation is a "non-cash" expense. So, in determining cash flow, marketing managers and their finance manager colleagues often look at a company's earnings *before* subtracting out these expenses. Similarly, they may look at earnings before taxes as certain types of reinvestment result in a reduction in taxes.[5]

Adjusting the strategy to money that's available

Most firms rely on a combination of internal and external capital. An adequate overall amount of capital makes it possible to expand more rapidly or to implement a more ambitious plan from the outset. However, when a marketing manager must rely—at least in part—on internally generated funds to make a strategy self-supporting, that may need to be considered in selecting between alternative strategies or in specific marketing mix decisions for a given strategy.

Improve return of current investment

When finances are tight, it's sensible to look for stategy alternatives that help get a better return on money that's already invested. A firm that sells diagnostic equipment to hospitals might look for another related product for its current salespeople to sell while calling on the same customers. Similarly, a firm that has

Newly formed companies in the Ukraine and other areas of Eastern Europe often have very limited working capital. The factory where these people work didn't have enough cash to pay them in rubles, so instead it paid them in what the firm produces: pots and pans.

a successful domestic product might look for new international markets where little or no modification of the product would be required. A firm that is constantly fighting to rewin customers might be better off with a program that offers loyal customers a discount; the increase in the number of customers served might more than offset the lost revenue per sale. Any increase in revenue and profit contribution that the strategy generates—without increasing fixed costs and capital invested—increases profit and the firm's return on investment.

Market mix decisions affect capital needed

Strategy decisions within each of the marketing mix areas often have significantly different capital requirements. In the product area, for example, new product development for a product that is closely related to a firm's existing line is usually less costly than venturing into a totally new area. And a brand extension or product that uses a family brand name may require less up-front advertising and promotion expense to establish consumer awareness. But, offering more models, package sizes, flavors, or colors of a product will almost certainly increase front-end capital needs and increase costs.

Place decisions often have significant financial implications—depending on how responsibilities are shifted and shared in the channel. Indirect distribution usually requires less investment capital than direct approaches. Merchant wholesalers and retailers who pay for products when they purchase them—and who pay the costs of carrying inventory—help a producer's cash flow. Similarly, agent middlemen may take on much of the selling effort with a lower investment than would be required were the firm to do it alone. Working with intermediaries and facilitators—like public warehousers and transportation firms—may help reduce the capital requirements for logistics facilities. Expanding into new market areas that can be served from an existing distribution center may result in greater economies of scale without increased investment.

Similarly, capital requirements are less when intermediaries take on much of the responsibility for promotion in the channel. Wholesalers and retailers have less incentive to do promotion when the firm uses intensive distribution; intensive distribution is also likely to require a bigger front-end investment in personal selling.

Promotion blends that focus on stimulating consumer pull usually require a big front-end investment in advertising and consumer promotions. For example, it's not unusual for a consumer packaged goods producer to spend half of a new product's first-year sales revenue on advertising. Thus, it may be less risky for a firm with limited capital to put more emphasis on a strategy that relies on push rather than pull.

Of course, when a marketing manager is looking at how different strategy decisions relate to the firm's financial situation, they can't be considered separately. It's the financial impact of the whole strategy that must be considered. However, a strategy that might potentially produce the greatest profit or the fastest return on investment may not be best—or even sensible—if it isn't feasible given the firm's financial situation.

PRODUCTION MUST BE COORDINATED WITH THE MARKETING PLAN

Production capacity takes many forms

You know that being able to produce a product doesn't necessarily mean there's a market for it—or that you can sell it at a profit. On the other hand, if a firm is going to sell a product—whether it's a good or a service or combination of the two—*somebody* has to be able to produce it. So in screening product-market opportunities, a marketing manager needs to have a realistic understanding of what is involved in turning a product concept into something the firm can really deliver. If a firm is going to pursue an opportunity, it's also critical that there be effective coordination between marketing planning and **production capacity**—the ability to produce a certain quantity and quality of specific goods or services.

Different aspects of production capacity may be important in different situations. A firm may have the ability to easily or quickly produce some types of products but not others. For those it can currently produce, it may only be able to handle limited quantities without a major investment in new facilities, equipment, or people. Alternatively, it may have—and be paying for—more capacity than it can use. It may be able to produce only one product at a time—or it may be able to produce many different products. We'll consider these variations in more depth because different aspects of production capacity have different impacts on marketing planning.[6]

Use excess capacity to improve profits

If a firm has unused production capacity, it's sensible for a marketing manager to try to identify new markets or new products that make more effective use of that investment. For example, a company that produces rubber floor mats for automobiles might be able to add a similar line of floor mats for pickup trucks. Expanded production might result in lower costs and better profits for the mats the firm was already producing—because of economies of scale. In addition, revenue and profit contribution from the new products could improve the return on investment the firm had already made.

If a firm's production capacity is flexible, many different marketing opportunities might be possible. For example, in light of growing consumer interest in fancy pickup trucks, the marketing manager for the firm just mentioned might see even better profit potential in rubber pickup-truck bed liners than in floor mats. Opportunities further away from its current markets might be relevant too. For example, there might be better growth and profits in static-electricity-free mats for computer and telecommunications equipment than for auto accessories.

Excess capacity may be a safety net

While excess capacity can be costly, it can also serve as a "safety net" if demand suddenly picks up. For example, many firms that make products for the construction industry faced costly excess capacity during the late 1980s and early 1990s. However, many of those firms were glad that they had that capacity when residential construction started to boom in 1993. Whether excess capacity is a wasteful cost or a safety net for handling unexpected demand depends on the opportunity costs and likelihood of the two situations.

Or it may be a signal of problems

While it makes sense for a marketing manager to understand the firm's current production capacity, there's a hazard in too quickly screening out any other opportunities. Excess capacity may exist because the market for what a firm can produce never really materialized or has moved into long-term decline. Excess capacity may also indicate that there's too much competition—with many other firms all fighting for the same fixed demand. In situations like these, rather than struggling to find minor improvements in capacity use it might be better for the marketing manager to lead the firm toward other—more profitable—alternatives.

Slow adjustments result in stock-outs

Another aspect of flexibility concerns how quickly and easily a firm can adjust the quantity of a product it produces. This can be an especially important consideration when demand is uncertain—as is often the case when the marketing manager is planning a new strategy. If a new marketing mix is more successful than expected, demand can quickly outstrip supply. This happened to RJR Nabisco when it developed fat-free Snackwell chocolate cookies. Health-conscious "chocoholics" responded so enthusiastically to promotion that the cookies were quickly out of stock at most supermarkets. Because the cookies required a special production line, it was a long time before stock-outs could be routinely replenished.[7]

Scarce supply wastes marketing effort

This kind of problem can be serious. Carefully planned promotion spending is wasted if advertising and other promotions can't be put on hold until supply catches up to demand. Further, consumers and channel members may quickly become frustrated by stock-outs. More nimble competitors may get a window of opportunity to introduce an imitation product. By the time the original innovator is able to increase production, consumers may already be loyal to the other brand.

Staged distribution may match capacity

Problems of matching supply and demand are likely to be greatest when a marketing plan calls for quick expansion into many different market areas all at once. That's one reason many marketing managers plan a regional roll out of new product innovations. Similarly, initial distribution may focus on certain types of channels—say, drugstores alone rather than drugstores and supermarkets. Experience with the early stages of the implementation effort can help the marketing manager determine how much promotion effort is required to generate sales in the distribution channel, but not stock out. Conversely, if sales from these initial efforts are developing more slowly than expected, it may be possible to speed up the move into other market areas or new types of channels.

When Kellogg's introduced Rice Krispies Treats Cereal, production couldn't keep up with the unexpectedly high demand. So, Kellogg's used advertising to tell consumers and retailers about the shortages and to ask them to be patient.

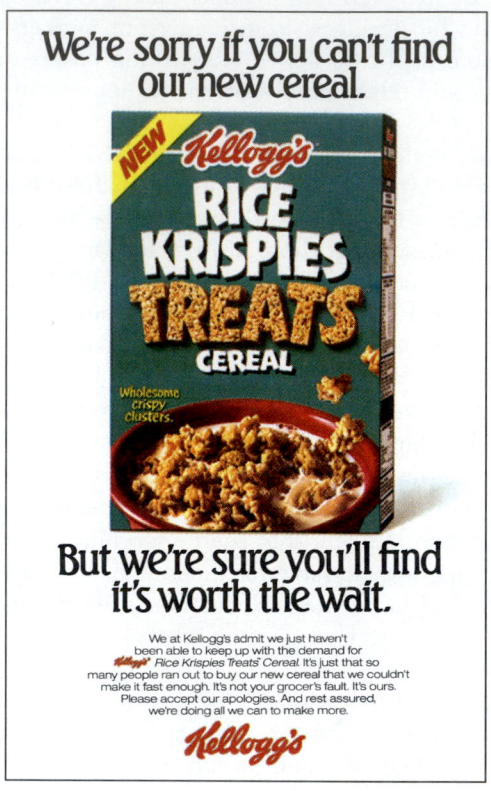

Virtual corporations may not make anything at all

Just because a firm doesn't have the capability to produce a product itself doesn't mean that a potential opportunity should be ignored. A profitable concept may justify investment in new production capabilities. Alternatively, an increasing number of firms have found that they can satisfy customers and build profits without doing any production "in house." Instead, they look for capable suppliers to produce a product that meets the specs laid out in the firm's marketing plan. At the extreme, a firm may even act like a **virtual corporation**—where the firm is primarily a coordinator—with a good marketing concept.

Consider the case of Calvin Klein fashions. At one time Calvin Klein was a large manufacturer of underwear and jeans. However, the company was better at analyzing markets, designing fashions, and marketing them than it was at production. So, the firm sold its factories and arranged for other companies to make the products that carry the Calvin Klein brand.[8]

While out-sourcing production may increase a firm's flexibility in some ways, it often has disadvantages. Costs are often higher and it may be difficult—or even impossible—to control quality. Similarly, product availability may be unpredictable. If several firms are involved in producing the final product, coordination and logistics problems may arise.

A company with a line of accessories for bicycle riders faced this problem when it decided to introduce a plastic water bottle. Its other products were metal, so it turned to outside suppliers to produce the bottles. However, getting the job done required three suppliers. One made the plastic bottles, another printed the colorful designs on them, and the third attached a clip to hold the bottle to a bike.

BALDOR ELECTRIC POWERS PAST WORLDWIDE COMPETITION

Baldor Electric Company manufactures and markets a variety of electric motors. About a decade ago, Baldor and many companies like it faced a real threat. There was a big slump in the demand for electric motors. Even worse, producers in Japan, South Korea, and Taiwan began pumping out low-cost commodity-type motors from automated factories. Some big U.S. firms, including Westinghouse (which had originally developed the electric motor), got out of the business altogether. Others, like General Electric and Emerson Electric, tried to compete by moving production offshore to reduce costs.

This tough situation prompted marketing managers at Baldor to rethink their marketing strategies. Rather than trying to compete with motors that were like those available from many other suppliers, they focused on specific target markets and their special needs. For example, Baldor developed special motors to run heart pumps in hospitals, lint-proof motors

for textile plants, and even a 500 horsepower unit for rolling steel. None of these motors is a big seller. Rather, Baldor's strategy takes advantage of quality and flexibility in production. In fact, Baldor adjusts so much of its production to suit special demands that on average it only produces 50 units of any given motor. However, that doesn't mean that Baldor is settling for lower sales or profits. To the contrary, its net sales grew from less than $150 million in 1983 to over $350 million in 1993—and products introduced in the last five years account for over 25 percent of the total. Baldor is also increasing its share of the global market for electric motors by expanding its distribution and market share in 55 countries outside the U.S. Because Baldor's marketing mix offers target customers something special, they are already interested when the Baldor salesperson calls—and Baldor can command a premium price. The whole marketing program has led to record-breaking profits.[9]

Moving the product from one specialist to another added costs, and whenever one supplier hit a snag all of the others were affected. The firm was constantly struggling to fill orders on time—and too often was losing the battle. In light of these problems, as soon as the bottle proved to be profitable, the firm decided to invest in its own production facilities. With its own production, it could be faster and more flexible in responding to special requests from the large retailers who handle its products.[10]

Design flexibility into operations

Because production flexibility can give a firm a competitive advantage in meeting a target market's needs better or faster, many firms are trying to design more flexibility into their operations. In fact, without flexible production systems it may not be possible for a firm to provide business customers with the just-in-time delivery service or rapid response replenishment of inventories that they want and expect.

Similarly, a firm that uses EDI or some other type of computerized reorder system—to find out immediately when a sale is made further down the channel of distribution—may not be able to take advantage of the information if it can't do anything about it until weeks or months later.

Producing to order requires flexibility too

By contrast, flexible manufacturing systems may make it possible for a firm to better respond to customer needs. For example, this was an advantage of Dell Computer's telephone order approach. Most other computer firms produced large quantities of standard models of computers and then shipped them to dealers for resale. If the dealer didn't have the right model in stock, it often took weeks to get it. Dell's approach was different. It allowed customers to order whatever computer

This woman is being measured by a fit consultant at a Levi's retail store; the Levi's factory will use the measurements to custom-produce a personal pair of jeans for her.

configuration they wanted—then the parts were assembled to match the order. For a small fee, Dell would even install software packages that the customer bought with the computer. This approach reduced the costs of finished goods inventories, constantly matched output to customer needs, and kept everyone at Dell focused on satisfying each and every customer.[11]

Mass customization— serves individual needs

Of course, automobile companies, producers of specialized machine tools, and other types of manufacturers—as well as many service firms—have been creating products based on specific orders from individual customers for a long time. However, a wide variety of companies are now looking for innovative ways to serve smaller segments of customers by using **mass customization**—tailoring the principles of mass production to meet the unique needs of individual customers.

Note that using the principles of mass production is not the same thing as trying to appeal to everyone in some mass market. With the mass-customization approach, a firm may still focus on certain market segments within a broad product-market. However, in serving individuals within those target segments it tries to get a competitive advantage by finding a low-cost way to give each customer more or better choices.

The changes that are coming with mass-customization are illustrated by Levi's Personal Pair personalized jeans program for women, which is now being tested in select Levi's stores. With this program, a woman goes to a participating retail store and is carefully measured by a trained fit consultant. These measurements are entered into a computer that generates the number of prototype trial jean with these measurements. The customer tries on that prototype for fit; if necessary, other prototypes or modifications of measurements may be tried. When the customer is satisfied, the customer's measurements are sent via computer to the Levi's factory, where sewing operators construct the jeans. In about three weeks, the jeans are ready at the store, or they can be shipped directly to the customer via express mail. The customer's measurements are kept in a database to make it easy to place future orders—perhaps in a different color, finish, or style.

Of course, not every firm will be able to adjust its offering to each individual customer, but advances in communications and computer-controlled production may offer a host of possibilities for marketing managers—and firms—who look for better ways to meet the unique needs of individual customers.[12]

Batched production requires inventories

If it is expensive for a firm to switch from producing one product (or product line) to another, it may have no alternative but to produce in large batches and maintain large inventories. Then it can supply demand from inventory while it is producing some other product. However, this approach requires careful planning of where in the channel inventories will be held. A firm that must pay the costs of carrying extra inventory to avoid stock-outs may not be able to compete with a firm that has more flexible production.

Where products are produced matters

A marketing manager also needs to carefully consider the marketing implications of where products are produced. It often does make sense for a firm to produce where it can produce most economically, if the cost of transporting and storing products to match demand doesn't offset the savings. On the other hand, production in areas distant from customers can make the distribution job much more complicated.

Off-shore operations may complicate marketing

As an interesting example, consider the marketing implications of Hanes' decision to use off-shore production for many of its men's underwear products. Hanes sells more underwear through big mass-merchandiser chains—like Wal-Mart, Target, and Kmart—than through any other type of retail outlet. Buyers for these chains put constant pressure on Hanes to find ways to cut prices. One key to cutting prices without killing profit margins is to cut production costs. Because labor costs are a large part of Hanes' cost of goods sold, it has little alternative but to move production to countries where hourly labor costs are much lower than in the U.S. That's why much of the sewing work on Hanes underwear is done in facilities throughout the Caribbean Islands.

However, the only practical way to transport the bulky and inexpensive finished products back to the U.S. market is by boat. Boats are slow, and clearing customs can add further delays. In fact, Hanes had to beef up security at its facilities to prevent drug smugglers from gaining access to its bulk shipping cases.

At the port, the bulk cases of underwear must be handled again and broken down into quantities and assortments for shipping to the retailers' distribution centers. And at the distribution centers the cases need to be grouped with other products going to a specific store. All of these steps are necessary to meet customers' needs at the final point of consumption, but they also make it difficult to quickly adjust supply when there is an unexpected shift in demand.

Hanes' off-shore production also makes other aspects of its marketing plan more difficult to implement. For example, as part of a special promotion to spark Christmas gift giving, a Hanes product manager wanted to put three-pairs of underwear in a special gift box. However, there were delays getting the special packaging to the distant factories, and when the underwear was packaged in the boxes the bulk shipping cases wouldn't hold the standard quantity of underwear.

Of course, any changes in operational routines required to implement a firm's marketing plan can cause unexpected surprises. However, when overseas production is involved the ripple effect of any such problems is likely to be bigger.[13]

? Some critics object to overseas production

Marketing managers must be aware of and sensitive to criticisms that may arise concerning overseas production. Some of these concerns relate to nationalism. But other issues are sometimes at stake.

While low-cost overseas labor may reduce costs and prices for domestic consumers, some critics argue that the costs are only lower because the work is handled in countries with lower workplace safety standards and fewer employee protections. At the extreme, some firms have been boycotted for relying on low-cost Chinese labor; the boycotters charged that Chinese suppliers were using political prisoners as slave labor.

Marketing managers can't ignore such concerns. Just as a firm has a social responsibility in the country where it sells products, it also has a social responsibility to the people who produce its products. However, it makes sense to consider the standard of living in that country. Pay or safety standards that seem low by standards of the developed nations may make it possible for workers in an undeveloped nation to have a better, healthier life.[14]

Service firms may transfer some tasks

Firms that produce services often must locate near their customers. However, some service firms are finding ways to reduce the cost of some of their production work with **task transfer**—using telecommunications to move service operations to places where there are pools of skilled workers. For example, NationsBank puts its automatic teller machines and branch offices where they're convenient for customers, but many of the programmers who do its "back room" computer work are in India. Computer specialists in India earn lower wages than in the U.S., and it's easy and inexpensive to routinely transfer the data they prepare over worldwide networks. Similarly, one U.S. insurance company processes policy renewals in Ireland.

On the other hand, sometimes the decision to expand into a distant market requires moving production closer to that location. For example, import or export tariffs and quotas may make it impossible for an internationally oriented firm to compete if it doesn't have local production facilities. Similarly, some products are very expensive to ship long distances. That may give local firms a big cost—and price—advantage.

Price must cover production costs

In Chapter 18, we introduced the behavior of various cost curves and how they fit—along with demand curves—into the pricing puzzle. Production costs are usually an important component of the overall costs that must be considered in pricing, so a marketing manager needs to have a reasonable understanding of the costs associated with production—especially when product features called for in the marketing plan drive costs.

Cut costs that don't add value for customers

A marketing manager who is well informed in this area can play an important role in working with production people to decide which costs are necessary—to add value that meets customer needs—and which are just added expense with little real benefit. For example, a software firm was providing a very detailed instruction book along with the disks in its distribution package. The book was running up costs and causing delays because it needed to be changed and reprinted every time the firm came out with a new version of its software. The marketing manager realized that most of the detail in the book wasn't necessary. When users of the software had a problem, they didn't want to search for the book but instead wanted the information on the computer screen. Providing the updated information on the disk was faster and cheaper than printing the books. Further, packaging costs were lower without the book. And as icing on the cake, customers were more satisfied with the on-line help than they had been with the book.

In a situation like this, it is easy to identify specific costs associated with the production job. However, often it's difficult to get a good handle on all of the costs associated with a product (or customer) without help from the firm's accountants.

ACCOUNTING DATA CAN HELP IN UNDERSTANDING COSTS AND PROFIT

Accounting data that helps managers track where costs and profits are coming from is an important aid for strategy decisions. Unfortunately, accounting statements that are prepared for tax purposes and for outside investors often aren't helpful for managers who need to make decisions about marketing strategy.

Understanding profitability depends on being able to identify the specific costs of different goods and services. You saw this in the last chapter when two basic approaches to handling costs—the full-cost approach and the contribution-margin approach—resulted in different views of profitability. At that point, however, we didn't go into any detail about how marketing managers and accountants can work together to get a better understanding of costs—especially how to allocate costs that seem to be *common* to several products or customers—making allocation of costs difficult. In recent years, some accountants have devoted more attention to approaches to this problem and given it the name "activity-based accounting." In spite of the new name, the basic ideas behind marketing cost analysis were developed years ago by a marketing specialist.[15]

Marketing cost analysis usually requires a new way of classifying accounting data. Instead of using the type of accounts typically used for financial analysis, we have to use functional accounts.

Natural versus functional accounts— what is the purpose?

Natural accounts are the categories to which various costs are charged in the normal financial accounting cycle. These accounts include salaries, wages, Social Security, taxes, supplies, raw materials, auto, gas and oil expenses, advertising, and others. These accounts are called natural because they have the names of their expense categories.

However, factories don't use this approach to cost analysis—and it's not the one we will use. In the factory, **functional accounts** show the *purpose* for which expenditures are made. Factory functional accounts include shearing, milling, grinding, floor cleaning, maintenance, and so on. Factory cost accounting records are organized so that managers can determine the cost of particular products or jobs and their likely contribution to profit.

Marketing jobs are done for specific purposes too. With some planning, the costs of marketing can also be assigned to specific categories—such as customers and products. Then their profitability can be calculated.

First, get costs into functional accounts

The first step in marketing cost analysis is to reclassify all the dollar cost entries in the natural accounts into functional cost accounts. For example, the many cost items in the natural *salary* account may be allocated to functional accounts with the following names: storing, inventory control, order assembly, packing and shipping, transporting, selling, advertising, order entry, billing, credit extension, and accounts receivable. The same is true for rent, depreciation, heat, light, power, and other natural accounts.

When top executives at Timken Company decided to streamline administrative procedures and reduce operating costs, teams of managers from different functional areas worked to identify the costs of specific activities and how they could be reduced.

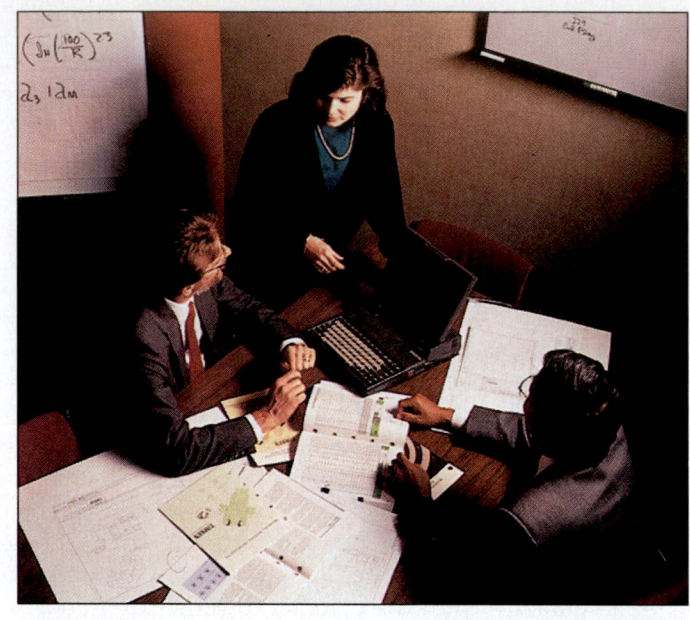

The way natural account amounts are shifted to functional accounts depends on the firm's method of operation. It may require time studies, space measurements, actual counts, and managers' estimates.

Then reallocate to evaluate profitability of profit centers

The next step is to reallocate the functional costs to those items—or customers or market segments—for which the amounts were spent. The most common reallocation of functional costs is to products and customers. After these costs are allocated, the detailed totals can be combined in any way desired—for example, by product or customer class, region, and so on.

The costs allocated to the functional accounts equal, in total, those in the natural accounts. They're just organized differently. But instead of being used only to show *total* company profits, the costs can now be used to calculate the profitability of territories, products, customers, salespeople, price classes, order sizes, distribution methods, sales methods, or any other breakdown desired. Each unit can be treated as a profit center.

Cost analysis helps track down the loser

The following example illustrates these ideas. This case is simplified—and the numbers are small—so you can follow each step. However, you can use the same basic approach in more complicated situations.

In this case, the usual financial accounting approach—with natural accounts—shows that the company made a profit of $938 last month (Exhibit 21–1). But such a profit and loss statement doesn't show the profitability of the company's three customers. So the managers decide to use marketing cost analysis because they want to know whether a change in the marketing mix will improve profit.

First, we distribute the costs in the five natural accounts to four functional accounts—sales, packaging, advertising, and billing and collection (see Exhibit 21–2)—according to the functional reason for the expenses. Specifically, $1,000 of the total salary cost is for sales reps who seldom even come into the office since

EXHIBIT 21–1   Profit and Loss Statement, One Month

Sales		$17,000
Cost of sales		11,900
Gross margin		5,100
Expenses:		
Salaries	$2,500	
Rent	500	
Wrapping supplies	1,012	
Stationery and stamps	50	
Office equipment	100	
		4,162
Net profit		$ 938

their job is to call on customers; $900 of the salary cost is for packaging labor; and $600 is for office help. Assume that the office force split its time about evenly between addressing advertising material and billing and collection. So we split the $600 evenly into these two functional accounts.

The $500 for rent is for the entire building. But the company uses 80 percent of its floor space for packaging and 20 percent for the office. Thus $400 is allocated to the packaging account. We divide the remaining $100 evenly between the advertising and billing accounts because these functions use the office space about equally. Stationery, stamps, and office equipment charges are allocated equally to the latter two accounts for the same reason. Charges for wrapping supplies are allocated to the packaging account because these supplies are used in packaging. In another situation, different allocations and even different accounts may be sensible—but these work here.

Allocating functional cost to customers

Now we can calculate the profitability of the company's three customers. But we need more information before we can allocate these functional accounts to customers or products. It is presented in Exhibit 21–3. Exhibit 21–3 shows that the company's three products vary in cost, selling price, and sales volume. The products also have different sizes, and the packaging costs aren't related to the

EXHIBIT 21–2   Spreading Natural Accounts to Functional Accounts

		Functional Accounts			
Natural Accounts		Sales	Packaging	Advertising	Billing and Collection
Salaries	$2,500	$1,000	$900	$300	$300
Rent	500		400	50	50
Wrapping supplies	1,012		1,012		
Stationery and stamps	50			25	25
Office equipment	100			50	50
Total	$4,162	$1,000	$2,312	$425	$425

EXHIBIT 21–3   Basic Data for Cost and Profit Analysis Example

Products	Cost/Unit	Selling Price/Unit	Number of Units Sold in Period	Sales Volume in Period	Relative "Bulk" per Unit	Packaging "Units"
A	$ 7	$ 10	1,000	$10,000	1	1,000
B	35	50	100	5,000	3	300
C	140	200	10	2,000	6	60
			1,110	$17,000		1,360

Customers	Number of Sales Calls in Period	Number of Orders Placed in Period	Number of Each Product Ordered in Period		
			A	B	C
Smith	30	30	900	30	0
Jones	40	3	90	30	3
Brown	30	1	10	40	7
Total	100	34	1,000	100	10

selling price. So when packaging costs are allocated to products, size must be considered. We can do this by computing a new measure—a packaging unit—that is used to allocate the costs in the packaging account. Packaging units adjust for relative size and the number of each type of product sold. For example, Product C is six times larger than A. While the company sells only 10 units of Product C, it is bulky and requires 10 times 6, or 60 packaging units. So we must allocate more of the costs in the packaging account to each unit of Product C.

Exhibit 21–3 also shows that the three customers require different amounts of sales effort, place different numbers of orders, and buy different product combinations.

Jones seems to require more sales calls. Smith places many orders that must be processed in the office—with increased billing expense. Brown placed only one order—for 70 percent of the sales of high-valued Product C.

Exhibit 21–4 shows the computations for allocating the functional amounts to the three customers. There were 100 sales calls in the period. Assuming that all

EXHIBIT 21–4   Functional Cost Account Allocations

Sales calls	$1,000/100 calls	=	$10/call
Billing	$425/34 orders	=	$12.50/order
Packaging units costs	$2,312/1,360 packaging units	=	$1.70/packaging unit or $1.70 for Product A $5.10 for Product B $10.20 for Product C
Advertising	$425/10 units of C	=	$42.50/unit of C

EXHIBIT 21–5 Profit and Loss Statement for Customers

	Smith		Jones		Brown	Whole Company
Sales						
A	$9,000		$900		$100	
B	1,500		1,500		2,000	
C			600		1,400	
Total sales		$10,500		$3,000	$3,500	$17,000
Cost of sales						
A	6,300		630		70	
B	1,050		1,050		1,400	
C			420		980	
Total cost of sales		7,350		2,100	2,450	11,900
Gross margin		3,150		900	1,050	5,100
Expenses						
Sales calls ($10 each)	300		400.00		300.00	
Order costs ($12.50 each)	375		37.50		12.50	
Packaging costs						
A	1,530		153.00		17.00	
B	153		153.00		204.00	
C			30.60		71.40	
Advertising			127.50		297.50	
		2,358		901.60	902.40	4,162
Net profit (or loss)		$792		$(1.60)	$147.60	$938

calls took the same amount of time, we can figure the average cost per call by dividing the $1,000 sales cost by 100 calls—giving an average cost of $10. We use similar reasoning to break down the billing and packaging account totals. Advertising during this period was for the benefit of Product C only—so we split this cost among the units of C sold.

Calculating profit and loss for each customer

Now we can compute a profit and loss statement for each customer. Exhibit 21–5 shows how each customer's purchases and costs are combined to prepare a statement for each customer. The sum of each of the four major components (sales, cost of sales, expenses, and profit) is the same as on the original statement (Exhibit 21–1)—all we've done is rearrange and rename the data.

For example, Smith bought 900 units of A at $10 each and 300 units of B at $50 each—for the respective sales totals ($9,000 and $1,500) shown in Exhibit 21–5. We compute cost of sales in the same way. Expenses require various calculations. Thirty sales calls cost $300—30 × $10 each. Smith placed 30 orders at an average cost of $12.50 each for a total ordering cost of $375. Total packaging costs amounted to $1,530 for A (900 units purchased × $1.70 per unit) and $153

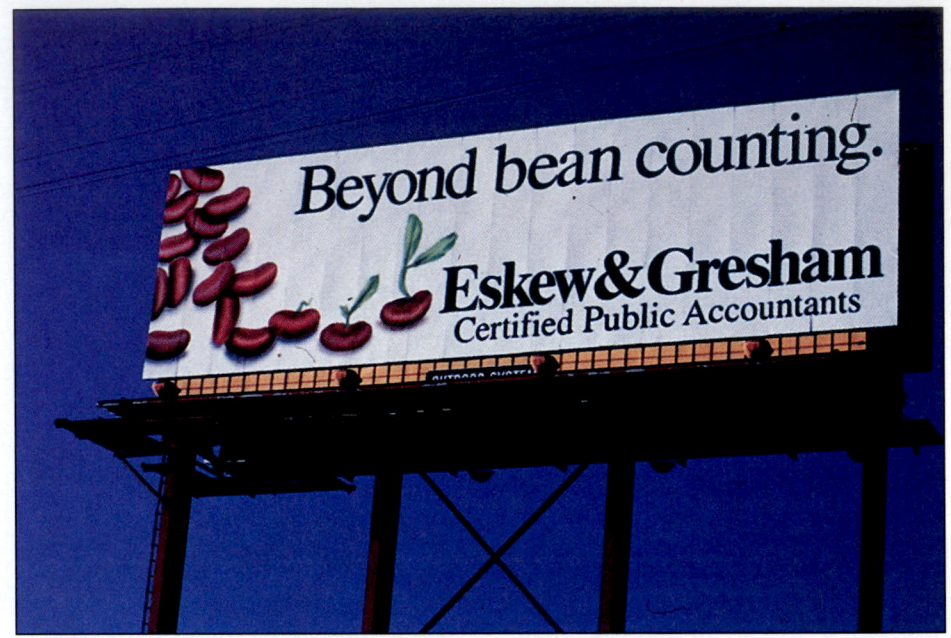

for B (30 units purchased × $5.10 per unit). There were no packaging costs for C because Smith didn't buy any of Product C. Neither were any advertising costs charged to Smith—all advertising costs were spent promoting Product C, which Smith didn't buy.

Analyzing the results

We now see that Smith was the most profitable customer, yielding over 75 percent of the net profit.

This analysis shows that Brown was profitable too—but not as profitable as Smith because Smith bought three times as much. Jones was unprofitable. Jones didn't buy very much and received one-third more sales calls.

The iceberg principle is operating again here. Although the company as a whole is profitable, customer Jones is not. But before dropping Jones, the marketing manager should study the figures and the marketing plan very carefully. Perhaps Jones should be called on less frequently. Or maybe Jones will grow into a profitable account. Now the firm is at least covering some fixed costs by selling to Jones. Dropping this customer may only shift those fixed costs to the other two customers—making them look less attractive. (See the discussion on contribution margin in Chapter 20.)

The marketing manager may also want to analyze the advertising costs against results—since a heavy advertising expense is charged against each unit of Product C. Perhaps the whole marketing plan should be revised.

Cost analysis is not performance analysis

Such a cost analysis is not a performance analysis, of course. If the marketing manager budgeted costs to various jobs, it would be possible to extend this analysis to a performance analysis. This would be logical—and desirable—but many companies have not yet moved in this direction.

Now that more accounting and marketing information is routinely available on computers—and software to analyze it is easier to use—many managers are seizing the opportunity to do marketing cost and performance analysis—just like factory cost accounting systems develop detailed cost estimates for products. These changes also mean that more managers are able to compare marketing cost and performance figures with "expected" figures to evaluate and control their marketing plans.

PEOPLE PUT PLANS INTO ACTION

People are an important resource

The best marketing strategy in the world may fail if the right people aren't available to implement the plan. Large firms usually have a separate human resources department staffed by specialists who work with others in the firm to ensure that good people are available to do jobs that need to be done. A small firm may not have a separate department—but somebody (perhaps the owner or other managers) must deal with people-management matters—like recruiting and hiring new employees, deciding how people will be compensated, and what to do when a job is not being performed well or is no longer necessary. Human resource issues are often critically important both in a marketing manager's choice among different possible marketing opportunities and in the actual implementation of marketing plans.

You've already learned about some of the human resource issues that are important to a marketing manager. For example, in Chapter 15 when we reviewed strategy decisions in the personal selling area we discussed a number of sales management issues—including selection, training, supervision, motivation, and compensation. Similarly, when we discussed total quality management in the previous chapter we discussed why training and empowerment for service providers are often critical in achieving service quality and in satisfying customers.

In this section, we'll briefly reconsider these issues, but from a broader perspective: How and why they need to be considered in planning new strategies and implementing plans—especially plans that involve change. For example, change is likely to occur when a firm's sales are growing and when it is expanding its marketing efforts—to go after new markets or to introduce and promote new products.

New strategies usually require people changes

New strategies often involve new and different ways of doing things. Even if such changes are required to ensure that the firm will survive and make a profit, changes often upset the status quo and long-established vested interests of current employees. A production manager who has spent a career becoming an expert in producing fine wood furniture may not like the idea of switching to an assemble-it-yourself line—even if that's what customers want. A senior sales rep with a well-established territory may not want to work hard at developing new accounts for a new product. When the market maturity stage of the product life cycle hits, a finance manager who looked like a hero during the profitable growth stage may not see that the picnic is over—and that profit growth will resume only if the firm takes some risk and invests in a new product concept.

As these examples suggest, many of the people affected by a new strategy may not be under the control of the marketing manager. And acting alone the marketing manager may not be the "change agent" who can instantly turn everyone in the organization into an enthusiastic supporter of the plan. However, if the marketing manager doesn't think about how a new strategy will affect

Martin Marietta's ad uses the headline, "There's no telling where the next Fortune 500 leaders will come from," and the copy suggests that it may be from one of these kids from Anchorage, Alaska. That may be, but a marketing manager usually has to have a clearer idea who is going to be available to help implement a new marketing program.

There's no telling where the next Fortune 500 leaders will come from.

people—and how what people do will affect the success of the strategy—even the best strategy may fail.

Communication helps promote change

Communication is an important consideration here. The marketing manager must find ways to communicate with others in the organization to explain the new strategy, what needs to happen, and why. You can't expect people to pull together in an organizationwide effort if they don't know what's going on. Such communication might be handled in meetings, memos, casual discussions, internal newsletters—or any number of other ways—depending on the situation. However, the communication should occur. At a minimum, the marketing manager needs to have clear communication with the human resources manager—or with other managers—who will participate in preparing the firm's personnel for a change.

Rapid growth strains human resources

When zeroing in on a marketing strategy or developing a marketing plan, a pragmatic marketing manager must take a realistic look at how quickly the firm's personnel can get geared up for the plan—or whether it will be possible to get people who can. Sometimes a firm simply can't change or grow as fast from a people standpoint as the market might allow.

Firms that are expecting or experiencing rapid growth face special challenges in getting enough qualified people to do what needs to be done. A fast-growing retail chain like Home Depot that opens many new stores doesn't just need money for new land and buildings and inventory. It also needs new store managers, assistant managers, sales clerks, customer service people, advertising managers, computer operators, and even maintenance people. Not all of these jobs are likely to be filled by internal promotions, so at least some of the "new blood" have to learn about the culture of the company, its customers, and its products at the same time they are learning the nuts and bolts of performing their jobs well. Hiring people and getting them up to speed takes time and energy.

Allow time for training and other changes

Training may be especially important in situations like this, but training—like other organizational changes—takes time. A marketing manager who wants to reorganize the firm's sale force so that salespeople are assigned to specific customers rather than by specific product line may have a great idea, but it can't be implemented overnight. A salesperson who is supposed to be a specialist in meeting the needs of a certain customer won't be able to do a very good job if all he or she knows about is the specific product that was previously the focus. Even if nothing else were involved, the plan would need to include time for the training to take place.

Each change may result in several others

That may sound simple, but keep in mind that the changes may not stop there. A change in how sales territories and assignments are structured is likely to require changes in compensation. Someone needs to figure out the specifics of the new compensation system, and accountants need time to adjust their computer programs to make certain that the salespeople actually get paid. Similarly, the changes in the sales force are likely to require changes in the structure of sales management assignments.

Our objective with this example is not just to list all of the specific changes that might be required for this specific strategy decision, but rather to highlight the more general point that changing people usually takes time—and only so much change can be absorbed effectively in a limited period.

Plan time for changes from the outset

A marketing manager who ignores the "ripple effects" of a change in strategy may later expect everyone else in the organization to bend over backwards, work overtime, and otherwise do everything possible to meet a schedule that was put together with little, or no, forethought. Certainly there are cases of heroic efforts by people in organizations to turn someone's vision into a reality. Yet, it's more typical for such a plan to fall behind schedule, to run up unnecessary costs, or to just plain fail. Marketing managers who work that way are likely to be criticized for "not having the time to do it right the first time, but having the time to do it over again."

Cutbacks need human resource plans too

If rapidly expanding marketing efforts involve human resource challenges, decisions to drop products, channels of distribution, or even certain types of customers can be even more traumatic. In these situations, people always worry that *someone* will lose his or her job—and that isn't easy.

Dropping products or making other changes that would result in a cutback on people doing certain jobs must be planned very carefully—and with a good dose of humanity. To the extent possible, it's important to plan a phase-out period so that people can make other plans. During the last decade, too many firms downsized (or, as some people call it, "rightsized") so rapidly that long-time loyal employees who had made valuable contributions to the firm and its customers were simply left to their own devices. If a phase-out is carefully planned—considering not only the implications for production facilities and contracts with outside firms, but also the people inside—it may be possible to develop strategies that will create exciting new jobs for those who would otherwise be displaced.[16]

Marketing pumps life into an organization

This line of thinking highlights again that marketing is the heart that pumps the lifeblood through an organization. Marketing managers who create profitable marketing strategies and implement them well create a need for a firm's production workers, accountants, finance managers, lawyers and—yes—even its human resources people. In this chapter we've talked about marketing links with those other functions, but when you get down to brass tacks organizations and the various departments within them consist of *individuals*. If the marketing manager makes good strategy decisions—ones that lead to satisfied customers and profits—each of the individuals in the organization has a chance to prosper and grow.

CONCLUSION

Even when everyone in an entire company embraces the marketing concept, coordinating marketing strategies and plans with other functional areas is a challenge. Yet, it's a challenge that marketing managers must address. It doesn't make sense to select a strategy that the firm couldn't implement. And implementing new plans usually requires money, people, and a way to produce goods or services the firm will sell.

Cooperation between the marketing manager and the finance people helps to ensure that there's enough money available for the initial one-time investments and ongoing working capital needed to implement a marketing plan. If money comes from outside investors, the marketing manager may need to develop a strategy that satisfies them as well as customers. If the money available is limited, the strategy may need to be scaled back in various ways, or the marketing manager may need to find creative ways to phase in a strategy over time so that it generates enough cash flow to "pay its own way."

There also needs to be close coordination between a firm's production specialists and the marketing plan. To get that coordination, the marketing manager needs to consider the firm's production capacity when evaluating alternative strategies. And flexibility in production may allow the firm to pursue different strategies at the same time—or to switch strategies more easily when new opportunities develop.

Figuring out the profitability of a strategy, product, or customer often requires a real understanding of costs—production costs, marketing costs, and other costs that may accumulate. Traditional accounting reports are often not very useful in pinpointing these costs. However, marketing managers and accountants are now working together to get more accurate cost information—by developing functional accounts rather than just relying on natural accounts typically used for financial analysis.

Money, facilities, and information are all important in developing a successful strategy, but most strategies are implemented by people. So a marketing manager must also be concerned with the availability and skills of the firm's people—its human resources. New marketing strategies may upset established ways of doing things. So, plans need to be clearly communicated so that everyone knows what to expect. Further, plans need to take into consideration the time—and effort—that will be required to get people up to speed on the new jobs they will be expected to do.

Making the strategic planning decisions that concern how a firm is going to use its overall resources—from marketing, production, finance, and other areas—is the responsibility of the chief executive officer, not the marketing manager. Further, the marketing manager usually can't dictate what a manager in some other department should do. However, it is sensible for the marketing manager to make recommendations on these matters. And marketing strategies and plans that the marketing manager recommends are more likely to be accepted—and then successfully implemented—if the links between marketing and other functional areas have been carefully considered from the outset.

QUESTIONS AND PROBLEMS

1. Identify some of the ways that a firm can raise money to support a new marketing plan. Give the advantages and limitations—from a marketing manager's perspective—of each approach.

2. An entrepreneur, who started a chain of auto service centers to do fast oil changes, wants to quickly expand by building new facilities in new markets but doesn't have enough capital. His financial advisor suggested that he might be able to get around the financial constraint—and still grow rapidly—if he franchised his idea. That way the franchisees would invest to build their own centers, but fees from the franchise agreement would also provide cash flow to build more company-owned outlets. Do you think this is a good idea? Why or why not?

3. Explain, in your own words, why investors in a firm's stock might be interested in a firm's marketing manager developing a new growth-oriented strategy. Would it be just as good, from the investors' standpoint, for the manager to just maintain the same level of profits? Why or why not?

4. A woman with extensive experience in home health care and a good marketing plan has approached a bank for a loan, most of which she has explained she intends to "invest in advertising designed to recruit part-time nurses and to attract home-care patients for her firm's services." Other than the furniture in her leased office space, she has few assets. Is the bank likely to loan her the money? Why?

5. Could the idea of mass customization be used by a publisher of college textbooks to allow differ-ent instructors to order customized teaching materials—perhaps even unique books made up of chapters from a number of different existing books? What do you think would be the major advantages and disadvantages of this approach?

6. Give examples of two different ways that a firm's production capacity might influence a marketing manager's choice of a marketing strategy.

7. Is a small company's flexibility increased or decreased by turning to outside suppliers to produce the products it sells? Explain your thinking.

8. Explain how a marketing manager's sales forecast for a new marketing plan might be used by:
   a. A financial manager.
   b. An accountant.
   c. A production manager.
   d. A human resources manager.

9. Explain the difference between natural accounts and functional accounts.

10. Could the approaches to cost allocation that we discussed in this chapter apply to a firm—like a travel agency—that produces only services? Explain your thinking.

11. What types of human resource issues does a marketing manager face when planning to expand sales operations from a branch office in a new overseas market? Are the problems any different than they would be in a new domestic market?

SUGGESTED CASES

17. Gulf Coast Safe Water, Inc.

36. Romano's Take-Out, Inc.

22

Ethical Marketing in a Consumer-Oriented World: Appraisal and Challenges

When You Finish This Chapter, You Should

1. Understand why marketing must be evaluated differently at the micro and macro levels.

2. Understand why the text argues that micro-marketing costs too much.

3. Understand why the text argues that macro-marketing does not cost too much.

4. Know some of the challenges marketers face as they work to develop ethical marketing strategies that serve consumers' needs.

More than ever, the macro-marketing systems of the world are interconnected. The collapse of communism and the worldwide drive toward market-directed economies are dramatic evidence that consumer-citizens want freedom and choices—not only in politics but in markets. The centrally planned economies simply weren't able to meet needs.

Although there's much talk about the world as a global village, we're not there yet. Someone in a *real* village on the plains of Kenya may be able to try a cellular phone or watch a TV and get a glimpse of the quality of life that consumers in the advanced Western economies enjoy, but for that person it doesn't seem real. What is real is the struggle to meet the basic physical needs of life—to survive starvation, malnutrition, and epidemic-carrying water. The plight of consumers doesn't seem quite as severe in the fragile and emerging democracies, like those in Eastern Europe. But the vast majority of citizen-consumers in those societies can only wonder if they'll ever have choices among a wide variety of goods and services—and the income to buy them—that most consumers take for granted in the United States, Canada, Western Europe, Australia, and a few other advanced economies.[1]

The challenges faced by consumers—and marketing managers—in the advanced econo-

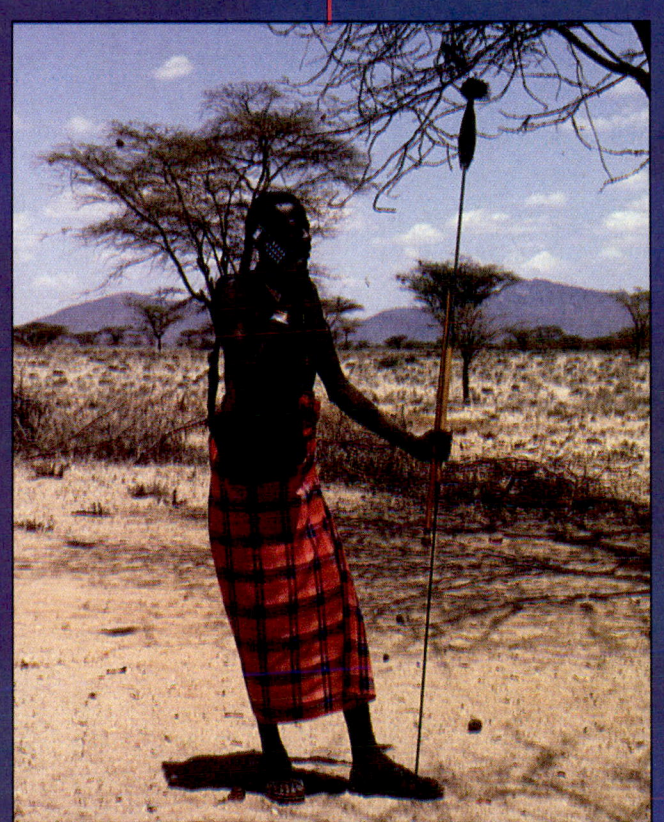

mies seem minor by contrast. When we worry about products being available, we're more likely thinking about instant gratification. We expect the corner convenience store to have a nice selection of frozen gourmet dinners that we can prepare in minutes in a microwave oven. Or perhaps that's too much of a hassle. After all, Domino's will deliver a pizza in less than 30 minutes. And McDonald's has our Egg McMuffins ready when we pull up at the drive-thru at 7 in the morning. We want supermarkets and drugstores handy. And we expect everything from fresh tropical fruits to camera batteries to brand-name fashions to be available when—and where—we want them. In a relative sense, few of the world's consumers can expect so much—and get so much of what they expect. All of this has a price, of course—and we, as consumers, pay the bill.[2]

When you think about these contrasts, it's not hard to decide which set of consumers is better off. But are we making a straw man comparison? Is the first situation one extreme, with the system in the United States and similar societies just as extreme—only in a different way? Would we be better off if we didn't put quite so much emphasis on marketing? Do we need so many brands of products? Does all the money spent on advertising really help consumers? Do middlemen just add to the price consumers pay? More generally, does marketing serve society well? In other words, does marketing cost too much? This is a fundamental question. Some people feel strongly that marketing *does* cost too much—that it's a waste of resources we could better use elsewhere.

Now that you have a better understanding of what marketing is all about—and how the marketing manager contributes to the *macro-marketing process*—you should be able to decide whether marketing costs too much. That's what this chapter is about.

Your answer is very important. It will affect your own business career and the economy in which you live.

Do car producers, for example, produce lower-quality cars than they could? Do produc-

ers of food and drug products spend too much money advertising trivial differences between their brands? Should they stop trying to brand their products at all—and instead sell generics at lower prices? Does marketing encourage us to want too much of the wrong products? Are there too many retailers and wholesalers—all taking "too big" markups? Some critics of marketing would answer Yes! to *all* these important questions. Such critics believe we should change our political and legal environments—and the world in which you live and work. Do you agree? Or are you fairly satisfied with the way our system works? How will you vote on your consumer ballot?

HOW SHOULD MARKETING BE EVALUATED?

We must evaluate at two levels

As we saw in Chapter 1, it's useful to distinguish between two levels of marketing: the *micro* level (how individual firms run) and the *macro* level (how the whole system works). Some complaints against marketing are aimed at only one of these levels at a time. In other cases, the criticism *seems* to be directed to one level—but actually is aimed at the other. Some critics of specific ads, for example, probably wouldn't be satisfied with *any* advertising. When evaluating marketing, we must treat each of these levels separately.

Nation's objectives affect evaluation

Different nations have different social and economic objectives. Dictatorships, for example, may be mainly concerned with satisfying the needs of society as seen by the political elite. In a socialist state, the objective might be to satisfy society's needs as defined by government planners. In a society that has recently broken the chains of communism, the objective may be to make the transition to a market-directed economy as quickly as possible—before there are more revolts.

Consumer satisfaction is the objective in the United States

In the United States, *the basic objective of our market-directed economic system has been to satisfy consumer needs as they—the consumers—see them.* This objective implies that political freedom and economic freedom go hand in hand—and that citizens in a free society have the right to live as they choose. The majority of American consumers would be unwilling to give up the freedom of choice they now enjoy. The same can be said for Canada, Great Britain, and most other countries in the European community. However, for focus we will concentrate on marketing as it exists in American society.

The lifestyle of a middle-class, urban family in Russia (on left) is a stark contrast to the lifestyle of a middle-class family in the U.S. (on right).

Therefore, let's try to evaluate the operation of marketing in the American economy—where the present objective is to satisfy consumer needs *as consumers see them*. This is the essence of our system. The business firm that ignores this fact is asking for trouble.

CAN CONSUMER SATISFACTION BE MEASURED?

Since consumer satisfaction is our objective, marketing's effectiveness must be measured by *how well* it satisfies consumers. Unfortunately, consumer satisfaction is hard to define—and even harder to measure.

Satisfaction depends on individual aspirations

There have been various efforts to measure overall consumer satisfaction not only in the United States but also in other countries. However, measuring consumer satisfaction is difficult because satisfaction depends on your level of aspiration or expectation. Less prosperous consumers begin to expect more out of an economy as they see the higher living standards of others. Also, aspiration levels tend to rise with repeated successes—and fall with failures. Products considered satisfactory one day may not be satisfactory the next day, or vice versa. A few years ago, most of us were more than satisfied with a 19-inch color TV that pulled in three or four channels. But once you've watched one of the newer large-screen models and enjoyed all the options possible with a cable hook-up or VCR, that old TV is never the same again. And when high-definition TVs become readily available, today's most satisfying units won't seem quite so acceptable. So consumer satisfaction is a highly personal concept—and looking at the "average" satisfaction of a whole society does not provide a reliable standard for evaluating macro-marketing effectiveness.[3]

Measuring macro-marketing must be subjective

If the objective of macro-marketing is maximizing consumer satisfaction, then we must measure total satisfaction—of everyone. But there's no good way to measure aggregate consumer satisfaction. At a minimum, some consumers are more satisfied than others. So our evaluation of macro-marketing effectiveness has to be subjective.

Probably the supreme test is whether the macro-marketing system satisfies enough individual consumer-citizens so that they vote—at the ballot box—to keep it running. So far, we've done so in the United States.

Measuring micro-marketing can be less subjective

Measuring micro-marketing effectiveness is also difficult, but it can be done. Individual business firms can and should try to measure how well their marketing mixes satisfy their customers (or why they fail). In fact, most large firms now have some type of ongoing effort to determine whether they're satisfying their target markets. Many large and small firms measure customer satisfaction with attitude research studies. For example, the J. D. Power marketing research firm is well known for its studies of consumer satisfaction with different makes of automobiles and computers. Other widely used methods include unsolicited consumer responses (usually complaints), opinions of middlemen and salespeople, market test results, and profits. Of course, customers may be very satisfied about some aspects of what a firm is doing, but dissatisfied about other dimensions of performance.[4]

In our market-directed system, it's up to each customer to decide how effectively individual firms satisfy his or her needs. Usually, customers will buy more of the products that satisfy them—and they'll do it repeatedly. That's why firms that develop really satisfying marketing mixes are able to develop profitable long-term relationships with the customers that they serve. Because efficient marketing plans can increase profits, profits can be used as a rough measure of a firm's efficiency in satisfying customers. Nonprofit organizations have a different bottom line, but they too will fail if they don't satisfy supporters and get the resources they need to continue to operate.

Evaluating marketing effectiveness is difficult—but not impossible

Because it's hard to measure consumer satisfaction—and, therefore, the effectiveness of micro- and macro-marketing—it's easy to see why opinions differ. If the objective of the economy is clearly defined, however—and the argument is stripped of emotion—the big questions about marketing effectiveness probably *can* be answered.

In this chapter, we argue that micro-marketing (how individual firms and channels operate) frequently *does* cost too much but that macro-marketing (how the whole marketing system operates) *does not* cost too much, *given the present objective of the American economy—consumer satisfaction.* Don't accept this position as *the* answer—but rather as a point of view. In the end, you'll have to make your own judgment.[5]

MICRO-MARKETING OFTEN *DOES* COST TOO MUCH

Throughout the text, we've explored what marketing managers could or should do to help their firms do a better job of satisfying customers—while achieving company objectives. Many firms implement highly successful marketing programs, but others are still too production-oriented and inefficient. For customers of these latter firms, micro-marketing often does cost too much.

Research shows that many consumers are not satisfied. But you know that already. All of us have had experiences when we weren't satisfied—when some firm didn't deliver on its promises. And the problem is much bigger than some marketers want to believe. Research suggests that the majority of consumer complaints are never reported. Worse, many complaints that are reported never get fully resolved.

The failure rate is high

Further evidence that too many firms are too production-oriented—and not nearly as efficient as they could be—is the fact that so many new products fail. New and old businesses—even ones that in the past were leaders in their markets—fail regularly too.

Generally speaking, marketing inefficiencies are due to one or more of three reasons:

1. Lack of interest in—or understanding of—the sometimes fickle customer.
2. Improper blending of the four Ps—caused in part by overemphasis on internal problems as contrasted with a customer orientation.
3. Lack of understanding of—or adjustment to—the marketing environment, especially what competitors do.

The high cost of poor marketing mixes

Perhaps lack of concern for the customer is most noticeable in the ways the four Ps are sometimes combined—or forced—into a marketing mix. This can happen in many ways.

Too many firms develop a new product to satisfy some manager's pet idea—not to meet the needs of certain target customers. Or they see another company with a successful product and try to jump into the market with another me-too imitation—without even thinking about the competition they'll encounter. Often they don't worry about quality. In fact, until very recently, most U.S. manufacturers lacked *any* quality control procedures even in the production of goods or services. The idea of using total quality management to implement marketing plans to meet customers' requirements was foreign.

Some marketing managers don't pay attention to getting needed support from middlemen. Too many producers don't even consider the possibility that a big retail chain may see better value for its customers—and greater profit potential—in someone else's product.

Firms often ignore demand and set prices on a cost-plus basis. While margins are fairly definite, managers can only predict volume. So they choose high margins—which may lead to high prices and reduced volume.

If a product is poorly designed—or if a firm uses inadequate channels or pricing that isn't competitive—it's easy to see why promotion may be costly. Aggressive spending on promotion doesn't make up for the other types of mistakes.

Top-management decisions on company objectives may increase the cost of marketing unnecessarily. Seeking sales growth for growth's sake, for example, often leads to too much spending for promotion and poor profits on what is sold.

Another sign of failure is the inability of firms to identify new target markets and new opportunities. A new marketing mix that isn't offered doesn't fail—but the lost opportunity can be significant for both a firm and society. Too many managers seize on whatever strategy seems easiest rather than seeking really new ways to satisfy customers.

Micro-marketing does cost too much—but things are changing

For reasons like these, marketing does cost too much in many firms. Despite much publicity, the marketing concept is not really applied in many places.

But not all firms and marketers deserve criticism. More of them *are* becoming customer-oriented. And many are paying more attention to market-oriented planning to carry out the marketing concept more effectively. Throughout the text, we've highlighted firms and strategies that are making a difference. The successes of innovative firms—like Wal-Mart, 3M, Toys "R" Us, Toddler University, ITW, McKesson Drug Co., and Rubbermaid—do not go unnoticed. Yes they make some mistakes. That's human—and marketing is a human enterprise. But they have also showed the results that market-oriented strategy planning can produce.

Another encouraging sign is the end of the idea that anybody can run a business successfully. This never was true. Today, the growing complexity of business draws more and more professionals—not only business managers but computer and communications specialists, psychologists, statisticians, and economists.

Managers who adopt the marketing concept as a way of business life do a better job. They look for target market opportunities and carefully blend the elements of the marketing mix to meet their customers' needs. As more of these managers rise in business, we can look forward to much lower micro-marketing costs—and strategies that do a better job of satisfying customer needs.

MACRO-MARKETING DOES NOT COST TOO MUCH

Many critics of marketing take aim at the macro-marketing system. They think (1) advertising—and promotion in general—are socially undesirable and (2) the macro-marketing system causes poor use of resources, limits income and employment, and leads to an unfair distribution of income. Most of these complaints imply that some micro-marketing activities should not be permitted— and, because they are, our macro-marketing system does a poor job. Let's look at some of these positions to help you form your own opinion.

Micro-efforts help the economy grow

Some critics feel that marketing helps create monopoly or at least monopolistic competition. Further, they think this leads to higher prices, restricted output, and reduction in national income and employment.

It's true that firms in a market-directed economy try to carve out separate monopolistic markets for themselves with new products. But consumers do have a choice. They don't *have* to buy the new product unless they think it's a better value. The old products are still available. In fact, to meet the new competition, prices of the old products usually drop. And that makes them even more available.

Over several years, the innovator's profits may rise—but rising profits also encourage further innovation by competitors. This leads to new investments— which contribute to economic growth and higher levels of national income and employment. Around the world, many countries failed to achieve their potential for economic growth under centrally planned systems because this type of profit incentive didn't exist.

Increased profits also attract competition. Profits then begin to drop as new competitors enter the market and begin producing somewhat similar products. (Recall the rise and fall of industry profit during the product life cycle.)

Is advertising a waste of resources?

Advertising is the most criticized of all micro-marketing activities. Indeed, many ads *are* annoying, insulting, misleading, and downright ineffective. This is one reason why micro-marketing often does cost too much. However, advertising can also make both the micro- and macro-marketing processes work better.

Advertising is an economical way to inform large numbers of potential customers about a firm's products. Provided that a product satisfies customer needs, advertising can increase demand for the product—resulting in economies of scale in manufacturing, distribution, and sales. Because these economies may

Marketing stimulates innovation and the development of new ways to meet customers' needs.

more than offset advertising costs, advertising can actually *lower* prices to the consumer.[6]

At the macro level, the increased demand brought about by advertising gives producers a faster return on their investment. This, in turn, stimulates further investment, encourages innovation, creates jobs, raises personal incomes, and generates economic growth.

Does marketing make people buy things they don't need?

From our discussion so far, it seems that micro-marketing activities aimed at satisfying consumer needs do *not* lead to improper use of resources. Giving individuals what they want, after all, is the purpose of our market-directed economic system. However, some critics feel that most firms—especially large corporations—don't really cater to the needs and wants of the consumer. They think such firms use clever ads to persuade consumers to buy whatever the firms want to sell.

Historian Arnold Toynbee, for example, felt that American firms manipulated consumers into buying products that aren't necessary to satisfy "the minimum material requirements of life." Toynbee saw American firms as mainly trying to fulfill "unwanted demand"—demand created by advertising—rather than "genuine wants." He defined genuine wants as "wants that we become aware of spontaneously, without having to be told by Madison Avenue that we want something that we should never have thought of wanting if we had been left in peace to find out our wants for ourselves."[7]

What are the minimum requirements of life?

One problem with this line of reasoning is how to determine the minimum material requirements of life. Does this mean that people should go back to living in caves or log cabins? Which products consumed today are unnecessary—and should not be produced?

Should Chinese consumers be allowed to decide what needs are important and what products should be available—or should those decisions be made by government planners?

Obviously, we have to make some value judgments to answer such questions—and few of us share the same values. One critic suggested that Americans could and should do without such items as pets, newspaper comic strips, second family cars, motorcycles, snowmobiles, campers, recreational boats and planes, aerosol products, pop and beer cans, and hats.[8] You may agree with some of these. But who should determine minimum material requirements of life—consumers or critics?

Consumers are not puppets

The idea that firms can manipulate consumers to buy anything the company chooses to produce simply isn't true. A consumer who buys a soft drink that tastes terrible won't buy another can of that brand—regardless of how much it's advertised. In fact, many new products fail the test of the market. Not even large corporations are assured of success every time they launch a new product. Consider, for example, the dismal fate of products such as Ford's Edsel, Du Pont's Corfam, Campbell's Red Kettle Soups, and RCA's computers. And if powerful corporations know some way to get people to buy products against their will, would General Motors have recently tallied the biggest loss in history?

Needs and wants change

Consumer needs and wants change constantly. Few of us would care to live the way our grandparents lived when they were our age—let alone like the pioneers who traveled to unknown destinations in covered wagons. Marketing's job is not just to satisfy consumer wants as they exist at any particular point in time. Rather, marketing must keep looking for new—and better—ways to serve consumers.[9]

Does marketing make people materialistic?

There is no doubt that marketing caters to materialistic values. However, people disagree as to whether marketing creates these values—or simply appeals to values already there.

Even in the most primitive societies, people want to accumulate possessions. In fact, in some tribal villages, social status is measured by how many goats or sheep a person owns. Further, the tendency for ancient pharaohs and kings to surround themselves with wealth and treasures can hardly be attributed to the persuasive powers of advertising agencies!

The idea that marketers create and serve "false tastes"—as defined by individual critics—was answered by a well-known economist who said:

> The marketplace responds to the tastes of consumers with the goods and services that are salable, whether the tastes are elevated or depraved. It is unfair to criticize the marketplace for fulfilling these desires . . . it is like blaming waiters in restaurants for obesity.[10]

Marketing reflects our own values

Experts who study materialism seem to agree that—in the short run—marketing reflects social values, while—in the long run—it enhances and reinforces them. One expert pointed out that consumers vote for what they want in the marketplace and in the polling place. To say that what they choose is wrong, he said, is to criticize the basic idea of free choice and democracy.[11]

Products do improve the quality of life

More is not always better. The quality of life can't be measured just in terms of quantities of material goods. But when we view products as the means to an end—rather than the end itself—they *do* make it possible to satisfy higher-level needs. Microwave ovens, for example, greatly reduced the amount of time and effort people must spend preparing meals—leaving them free to pursue other interests. And more dependable cars expanded people's geographic horizons—affecting where they can live and work and play.

Consumers ask for it, consumers pay for it

The monopolistic competition typical of our economy results from customer preferences—*not* manipulation of markets by business. Monopolistic competition may seem costly at times when we look at micro-level situations. But if the role of the marketing system is to serve consumers, then the cost of whatever goods and services they demand cannot be considered too high. It's just the cost of serving consumers the way they want to be served.

Not all needs are met

Some critics argue that our macro-marketing system is flawed because it does not provide solutions to important problems, such as questions about how to help the homeless, the uneducated, dependent children, minorities who have suffered discrimination, the elderly poor, and the sick. Many of these people do live in dire circumstances. But is that the result of a market-directed system?

There is no doubt that many firms focus their effort on people who can pay for what they have to offer. But as the forces of competition drive down prices, more people are able to afford more of what they need. And the matching of supply and demand stimulates economic growth, creates jobs, and spreads income among more people. In other words, a market-directed economy makes efficient use of resources. However, it can't guarantee that government aid programs are

Colgate is concerned not only with profit but also with social responsibility; its dental vans offer free dental screenings to children in inner-city communities.

effective. It doesn't ensure that all voters and politicians agree on which problems should be solved first—or how taxes should be set and allocated. It can't eliminate the possibility of a child being ignored.

These are important societal issues. But they are not the result of a market-directed system. Citizen-consumers in a democratic society assign some responsibilities to business and some to government. Most people in business share the concern that government too often does not do an effective job in addressing these problems. Many firms are working to identify and contribute solutions. But ultimately consumer-citizens vote in the ballot box for how to deal with these concerns—just as they vote with their dollars for which firms to support. As more managers in the public sector understand and apply marketing concepts, we should be able to do a better job meeting the needs of all people.

CHALLENGES FACING MARKETERS

We've said that our macro-marketing system does *not* cost too much—given the present objective of our economy. But we admit that the performance of many business firms leaves a lot to be desired. This presents a challenge to serious-minded students and marketers. What needs to be done—if anything?

We need better performance at the micro level

Some business executives seem to feel that they should be completely free in a market-directed economy. They don't understand that ours is a market-directed system—and that they must serve the needs of consumer-citizens. Instead, they focus on their own internal problems—and don't satisfy consumers very well.

We need better market-oriented planning

Many firms are still production-oriented. Some hardly plan at all, and others simply extend one year's plans into the next. Progressive firms are beginning to realize that this doesn't work in our fast-changing markets. Market-oriented

As more private and public nonprofit organizations adopt the marketing concept, they should be able to do a better job of meeting the needs of those they serve.

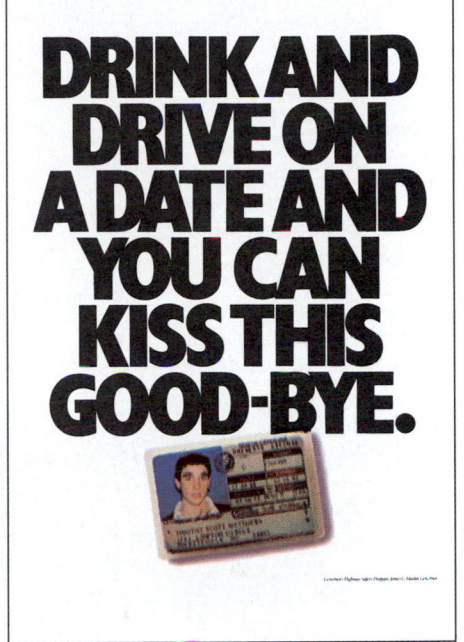

strategy planning is becoming more important in many companies. Firms are paying more attention to changes in the market—including trends in the marketing environment—and how marketing strategies need to be adapted to consider these changes. Exhibit 22–1 lists some of the trends and changes we've discussed throughout this text.

We need continuous improvement

Good marketing strategy planning needs to focus on a specific target market and a marketing mix to meet its needs. The basic frameworks and ideas about how to do that haven't changed as much as the long list in Exhibit 22–1 seems to suggest. At the same time, thinking about all these changes highlights the fact that marketing is dynamic. Marketing managers must constantly evaluate their strategies to be sure they're not being left in the dust by competitors who see new and better ways of doing things.

It's crazy for a marketing manager to constantly change a strategy that's working well. But too many managers fail to see or plan for needed changes. They're afraid to do anything different and adhere to the idea that "if it ain't broke, don't fix it." But a firm can't always wait until a problem becomes completely obvious to do something about it. When customers move on and profits disappear, it may be too late to fix the problem. Marketing managers who take the lead in finding innovative new markets and approaches get a competitive advantage.

Most of the changes and trends summarized in Exhibit 22–1 are having a positive effect on how marketers serve society. Whether it's because marketers are applying new technologies to solve old marketing problems or applying classic marketing concepts to new kinds of opportunities, consumers are better off. And this ongoing improvement is self-directing. As consumers shift their support to firms that do meet their needs, laggard businesses are forced to either improve or get out of the way.

Communication Technologies

Computer-to-computer data exchange
Satellite communications
Fax machine transmissions
Cable television
Telemarketing
Cellular phones and E-mail

Role of Computerization

Personal computers and laptops
Spreadsheet analysis
Computer networks
Checkout scanners
Bar codes for tracking inventory
Computer-to-computer ordering (EDI)

Marketing Research

Growth of marketing information systems
Decision support systems
Single source data
People meters
Use of scanner data
Easy-to-use statistical packages

Demographic Patterns

Aging of the baby boomers
Slowdown in U.S. population growth
Growth of ethnic submarkets
Geographic shifts in population
Slower real income growth in U.S.

Business and Organizational Customers

Closer buyer–seller relationships
Just-in-time inventory systems
More single-vendor sourcing

Product Area

More attention to innovation/new-product development
Faster new-product development
Computer-aided package/product design
Market-driven focus on research and development
More attention to quality and quality control
More attention to services
Advances in packaging
Extending established family brand names to new products

Channels and Logistics

More vertical market systems
Larger, more powerful retail chains
More conflict between producers/chains
More attention to physical distribution service
Better inventory control
Automated warehouses
Integrated distribution centers
More competition among transportation companies
Coordination of logistics in the channel

Channels and Logistics *(continued)*

Growing role of airfreight
Growth of mass-merchandising
Catolog, TV retailing

Sales Promotion

Increased promotion to middlemen
Event sponsorships
Greater use of coupons
Stocking allowances

Personal Selling

Automated order-taking
Use of laptop computers
More specialization
    Major accounts
    Telemarketing
    Team selling

Mass Selling

More targeted mass media
    Specialty publications
    Cable, satellite TV
    Specialty media, especially in-store
Shorter TV commercials
Larger advertising agencies
Changing agency compensation
Growth of direct-response advertising
Shrinking percentage of total promotion budgets

Pricing

Value pricing
Less reliance on traditional markups by middlemen
Overuse of sales and deals on consumer products
Bigger differences in functional discounts
More attention to exchange rate effects
Focus on higher stockturn at lower margins

International Marketing

Collapse of communism worldwide
More international market development
New and different competitors—at home and abroad
Need to adjust to unfamiliar markets, cultures
Widely spread markets
Changing trading restrictions (NAFTA, GATT, tariffs, quotas, etc.)
More attention to exporting by small firms
Growth of multinational corporations

General

Less regulation of business
More attention to marketing ethics
Shift of emphasis away from diversification
More attention to profitability, not just sales
Greater attention to competitive advantage
Implementation of total quality management
Greater attention to environmental issues

We need to welcome international competition

Increasingly, marketing managers face global competition. Some managers hate that thought. Worldwide competition creates even more pressure on marketing managers to figure out what it takes to gain a competitive advantage—both at home and in foreign markets. But with the challenge comes opportunities. The forces of competition in and among market-directed economies will help speed the diffusion of marketing advances to consumers everywhere. As macro-marketing systems improve worldwide, more consumers will have income to buy products—wherever in the world the products come from.

Marketers can't afford to bury their heads in the sand and hope that international competition will go away. Rather, they must realize that it is part of today's marketing environment—and they must do marketing strategy planning that rises to the challenges it poses.

May need more social responsibility

Good business managers put themselves in the consumer's position. A useful rule to follow might be: Do unto others as you would have others do unto you. In practice, this means developing satisfying marketing mixes for specific target markets. It may mean building in more quality or more safety. The consumer's long-run satisfaction should be considered too. How will the product hold up in use? What about service guarantees? While trying to serve the needs of some target market, does the marketing strategy disregard the rights and needs of other consumers—or create problems that will be left for future generations?

Short-sighted, production-oriented approaches undoubtedly won't work in the future. Tougher competition—from companies at home and abroad—may force old-style production-oriented business managers to change their thinking—just to survive.

The environment is everyone's need

Marketers need to work harder and smarter at finding ways to satisfy consumer needs without sacrificing the current or future environment. All consumers need the environment—whether they realize it yet or not. We are only beginning to understand the consequences of the environmental damage that's already been done. Acid rain, depletion of the ozone layer, and toxic waste in water supplies—to mention but a few current environmental problems—have catastrophic effects. Many top executives now say that preserving and protecting the environment will be one of the major challenges—if not *the* major challenge—of business firms in the next decade.

In the past, most firms didn't pass the cost of environmental damage on to consumers in the prices that they paid. Pollution was a hidden and unmeasured cost for most companies. That is changing rapidly. Firms are already paying billions of dollars to correct problems—including problems created years ago. The government isn't accepting the excuse that "nobody knew it was a big problem." Consider yourself warned: Business people who fail to anticipate the coming public backlash on this issue put their careers and businesses at risk!

May need attention to consumer privacy

While focusing on consumers' needs, marketers also must be sensitive to other consumer concerns. Today, sophisticated marketing research methods and new technologies make it easier to abuse consumers' rights to privacy. For example, credit card records—which reveal much about consumers' purchases and private lives—are routinely computerized and sold to anybody who pays for the list.

Most consumers don't realize how much data about their personal lives—some of it incorrect but treated as fact—is collected and available. A simple

ARE ELECTRIC CAR LAWS A HIGHLY CHARGED PROBLEM?

In a free market, business firms usually decide what to sell based on customer demand. When government planners try to dictate what products they should sell, problems usually arise. Electric vehicles (EVs) are not likely to be an exception.

California passed a law that 2 percent of the major car producers' sales (about 40,000 units) must have zero emissions by 1998. By 2001, the hurdle is 5 percent of sales. Other states may pass similar laws. At present, EVs are the only way for car producers to meet the zero emissions requirement. But, that doesn't mean that it will be easy for automakers to sell the EVs—or that consumers will be satisfied with what the automakers can provide.

An EV can only go about 100 miles before its batteries run down; then it takes 8 hours for a recharge. That makes an EV unsuitable for emergencies, vacation trips, or even for many commuters. The cost of owning an EV is also high—perhaps double the cost of a regular car. Marketing research shows that few consumers are willing to pay a premium price for a limited-use vehicle, even if it does help with pollution.

It's also not clear what the pollution impact of the EVs will really be. They might help reduce emissions in the congested Los Angeles basin. However, LA's pollution problems may just be shoved off on other people. Rather than producing pollution at the tailpipe, an EV soils the air at the power plant that produces the electricity to charge its batteries.

The California agency that came up with this idea thinks the law is "visionary" and will create a market and give producers the incentive to develop batteries that are stronger and less expensive. Yet, firms haven't yet had a breakthrough—and there isn't one in sight. Costs are likely to continue to be sky-high.

Given those costs, EVs have sold in other parts of the world—there are 25,000 in Europe—only with the support of government subsidies. No one's proposing government subsidies in the U.S. market. Thus, most experts think that to get sales in California the auto firms will need to set a price that is much lower than cost. That will cut into profits immediately, but sooner or later it will result in consumers paying higher prices for other cars. Japanese car makers face an even more complicated problem. If they sell at a price below cost to get the required EV sales, they may be in violation of antidumping laws.[12]

computer billing error may land consumers on a computer bad-credit list—without their knowledge. Marketing managers should use technology responsibly to improve the quality of life—not disrupt it.

Need to rethink some present laws

One of the advantages of a market-directed economic system is that it operates automatically. But in our version of this system, consumer-citizens provide certain constraints (laws), which can be modified at any time. Managers who ignore consumer attitudes must realize that their actions may cause new restraints.

Before piling on too many new rules, however, we should review the ones we have. Some of them may need to be changed—and others may need to be enforced more carefully. Antitrust laws, for example, are often applied to protect competitors from each other—when they were really intended to encourage competition.

On the other hand, U.S. antitrust laws were originally developed with the idea that all firms competing in a market would be on a level playing field. That is no longer always true. For example, in many markets individual U.S. firms compete with foreign firms whose governments urge them to cooperate with each other. Such foreign firms don't see each other as competitors; rather they see U.S. firms—as a group—as the competitors.

Socially responsible marketing managers are concerned about the environmental impact of their products. Ford, for example, assembles cars with parts that can be recycled. The toy in this German ad was made from recycled auto parts and the headline says "I was a car."

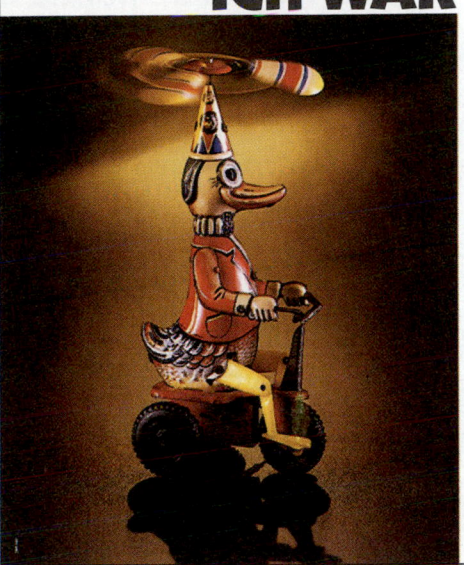

ICH WAR EIN AUTO.

Ford-Automobile sind in hohem Maße aus wiederverwertbaren Teilen gefertigt. Da kann es vorkommen, daß manche dieser Teile in einem völlig anderen Produkt wieder auftauchen.

Wichtiger ist uns jedoch die umfassende und sinnvolle Wiederverwendung aller eingesetzten Werkstoffe im Automobilbau. Deshalb untersucht Ford in einer Pilot-Demontageanlage die optimale Zerlegung von Altfahrzeugen.

Mit den dort gewonnenen Erkenntnissen verbessern wir ständig die Recyclingfähigkeit neuer Ford-Modelle. So können wir bereits seit Oktober 1991 die kostenlose Rücknahme aller ab diesem Zeitpunkt vom Band gelaufenen Fahrzeuge der Escort-/Orion-Baureihe garantieren.

Wenn Sie mehr über Recycling oder andere umweltentlastende Maßnahmen beim Produktionsprozeß bei Ford wissen möchten, rufen Sie uns einfach an: 0130 42 42.

FORD. BEI UNS DREHT SICH ALLES UM SIE.

Laws should affect top managers

Strict enforcement of present laws could have far-reaching results if more price fixers, fraudulent or deceptive advertisers, and others who violate existing laws—thus affecting the performance of the macro-marketing system—were sent to jail or given heavy fines. A quick change in attitudes might occur if unethical top managers—those who plan strategy—were prosecuted, instead of the salespeople or advertisers expected to deliver on weak or undifferentiated strategies.

In other words, if the government made it clear that it was serious about improving the performance of our economic system, much could be achieved within the present system—*without* adding new constraints.

Laws merely define minimal ethical standards

As we discussed ethical issues in marketing throughout the text, we emphasized that a marketing manager doesn't face an ethical dilemma about complying with laws and regulations. Whether a marketer is operating in his or her own country or in a foreign nation, the legal environment sets the *minimal* standards of ethical behavior as defined by a society. In addition, the American Marketing Association's code of ethics (Exhibit 2–4) provides a checklist of basic guidelines that a marketing manager should observe. But marketing managers constantly face ethical issues where there are no clearly defined answers. Every marketing manager should be aware of this and make a personal commitment to carefully evaluate the ethical consequences of marketing strategy decisions.

On the other hand, our marketing system is designed to encourage firms to compete aggressively as long as they do it in a fair way. New and better ways of serving customers and society give a firm a competitive advantage—at least for some period of time. This is how we move forward as a society. Innovative new marketing strategies *do* sometimes cause problems for those who have a vested interest in the old ways. Some people try to portray anything that disrupts their own personal interest as unethical. But protecting the status quo is not by itself an appropriate ethical standard. To the contrary, our society's most basic ethical charge to marketers is to find new and better ways to serve society's needs.

Alfatec si candida: "A fare pulizia in Italia non ci deve pensare solo la magistratura."

Perché Alfatec vende tanti aspirapolvere.

Need socially responsible consumers

We've stressed that marketers should act responsibly—but consumers have responsibilities too.[13] Some consumers abuse policies about returning goods, change price tags in self-service stores, and expect attractive surroundings and courteous, well-trained sales and service people—*and* want discount prices. Some are downright abusive to salespeople. Others think nothing of ripping off businesses because "they're rich." Shoplifting is a major problem for most retailers—and honest consumers pay for the cost of shoplifting in higher prices.

Americans tend to perform their dual role of consumer-citizens with a split personality. We often behave one way as consumers—then take the opposite position at the ballot box. For example, we cover our beaches and parks with garbage and litter, while urging our legislators to take stiff action to curb pollution. We protest sex and violence in the media—and then flock to see the latest R- or X-rated movies. Parents complain about advertising aimed at children—then use TV as a Saturday morning babysitter.

Consumers share the responsibility for preserving an effective macro-marketing system. And they should take this responsibility seriously.

Let's face it, there's a wealth of information already available to aid consumer decision making. The consumerism movement has encouraged nutritional labeling, open dating, unit pricing, truth-in-lending, plain-language contracts and warranties, and so on. And government agencies publish many consumer buying guides, as do organizations such as Consumers Union. Yet the majority of consumers continue to ignore most of this information.

HOW FAR SHOULD THE MARKETING CONCEPT GO?

Our macro-marketing system is built on the assumption that we are trying to satisfy consumers. But how far should the marketing concept be allowed to go?

Consumers have social responsibilities too.

Should marketing managers limit consumers' freedom of choice?

Achieving a better macro-marketing system is certainly a desirable objective. But what part should a marketer play in deciding what products to offer?

This is extremely important, because some marketing managers—especially those in large corporations—can have an impact far larger than they do in their roles as consumer-citizens. For example, should they refuse to produce hazardous products—like skis or motorcycles—even though such products are in strong demand? Should they install safety devices that increase costs—but that customers don't want?

These are difficult questions to answer. Some things marketing managers do clearly benefit both the firm and consumers because they lower costs and/or improve consumers' options. But other choices may actually reduce consumer choice and conflict with a desire to improve the effectiveness of our macro-marketing system.

Consumer-citizens should vote on the changes

It seems fair to suggest, therefore, that marketing managers should be expected to improve and expand the range of goods and services they make available to consumers—always trying to better satisfy their needs and preferences. This is the job we've assigned to business.

If pursuing this objective makes excessive demands on scarce resources—or has an unacceptable ecological effect—then consumer-citizens have the responsibility to vote for laws restricting individual firms that are trying to satisfy consumers' needs. This is the role that we, as consumers, have assigned to the government—to ensure that the macro-marketing system works effectively.

It is important to recognize that some *seemingly minor* modifications in our present system *might* result in very big, unintended problems. Allowing some government agency to prohibit the sale of products for seemingly good reasons could lead to major changes we never expected. (Bicycles, for example, are a very hazardous consumer product. Should they continue to be sold?) Clearly, such government actions could seriously reduce consumers' present rights to freedom of choice—including "bad" choices.[14]

We, as consumer-citizens, should be careful to distinguish between proposed changes designed simply to modify our system and those designed to change it—perhaps drastically. In either case, we should have the opportunity to make the decision (through elected representatives). This decision should not be left in the hands of a few well-placed managers or government planners.

Marketing people may be even more necessary in the future

Regardless of the changes consumer-citizens may enact, we will need some kind of a marketing system in the future. Further, if satisfying more subtle needs—such as for the good life—becomes our objective, it could be even more important to have market-oriented firms. We may have to define not only an individual's needs, but also society's needs—perhaps for a better neighborhood or more enriching social experiences, and so on. As we go beyond tangible physical goods into more sophisticated need-satisfying blends of goods and services, the trial-and-error approach of the typical production-oriented manager will become even less acceptable.

CONCLUSION

Macro-marketing does *not* cost too much. Consumers have assigned business the role of satisfying their needs. Customers find it satisfactory—and even desirable—to permit businesses to cater to them and even to stimulate wants. As long as consumers are satisfied, macro-marketing will not cost too much—and business firms will be permitted to continue as profit-making entities.

But business exists at the consumer's discretion. It's mainly by satisfying the consumer that a particular firm—and our economic system—can justify its existence and hope to keep operating.

In carrying out this role—granted by consumers—business firms are not always as effective as they could be. Many business managers don't understand the marketing concept—or the role that marketing plays in our way of life. They seem to feel that business has a God-given right to operate as it chooses. And they proceed in their typical production-oriented ways. Further, many managers have had little or no training in business management—and are not as competent as they should be. Others fail to adjust to the changes taking place around them. And a few dishonest or unethical managers can do a great deal of damage before consumer-citizens take steps to stop them. As a result, micro-marketing often *does* cost too much. But the situation is improving. More business train-

ing is now available, and more competent people are being attracted to marketing and business generally. Clearly, *you* have a role to play in improving marketing activities in the future.

Marketing has new challenges to face in the future. *Our* consumers may have to settle for a lower standard of living. Resource shortages, slower population growth, and a larger number of elderly—with a smaller proportion of the population in the work force—may all combine to reduce our income growth. This may force consumers to shift their consumption patterns—and politicians to change some of the rules governing business. Even our present market-directed system may be threatened.

To keep our system working effectively, individual firms should implement the marketing concept in a more efficient, ethical, and socially responsible way. At the same time, we—as consumers—should consume goods and services in an intelligent and socially responsible way. Further, we have the responsibility to vote and ensure that we get the kind of macro-marketing system we want. What kind do you want? What should you do to ensure that fellow consumer-citizens will vote for your system? Is your system likely to satisfy you as well as another macro-marketing system? You don't have to answer these questions right now—but your answers will affect the future you'll live in and how satisfied you'll be.

QUESTIONS AND PROBLEMS

1. Explain why marketing must be evaluated at two levels. What criteria should be used to evaluate each level of marketing? Defend your answer. Explain why your criteria are better than alternative criteria.

2. Discuss the merits of various economic system objectives. Is the objective of the American economic system sensible? Could it achieve more consumer satisfaction if sociologists—or public officials—determined how to satisfy the needs of lower-income or less-educated consumers? If so, what education or income level should be required before an individual is granted free choice?

3. Should the objective of our economy be maximum efficiency? If your answer is yes, efficiency in what? If not, what should the objective be?

4. Discuss the conflict of interests among production, finance, accounting, and marketing executives. How does this conflict affect the operation of an individual firm? The economic system? Why does this conflict exist?

5. Why does adoption of the marketing concept encourage a firm to operate more efficiently? Be specific about the impact of the marketing concept on the various departments of a firm.

6. In the short run, competition sometimes leads to inefficiency in the operation of our economic system. Many people argue for monopoly in order to eliminate this inefficiency. Discuss this solution.

7. How would officially granted monopolies affect the operation of our economic system? Consider the effect on allocation of resources, the level of income and employment, and the distribution of income. Is the effect any different if a firm obtains a monopoly by winning out in a competitive market?

8. Comment on the following statement: "Ultimately, the high cost of marketing is due only to consumers."

9. How far should the marketing concept go? How should we decide this issue?

10. Should marketing managers, or business managers in general, refrain from producing profitable products that some target customers want but that may not be in their long-run interest? Should firms be expected to produce "good" but less profitable products? What if such products break even? What if they are unprofitable but the company makes other profitable products—so on balance it still makes some profit? What criteria are you using for each of your answers?

11. Should a marketing manager or a business refuse to produce an "energy-gobbling" appliance that some consumers are demanding? Should a firm install an expensive safety device that will increase costs but that customers don't want? Are the same principles involved in both these questions? Explain.

12. Discuss how one or more of the trends or changes shown in Exhibit 22–1 are affecting marketing strategy planning for a specific firm that serves the market where you live.

13. Discuss how slower economic growth or no economic growth would affect your college community—in particular, its marketing institutions.

SUGGESTED CASES

27. Electrotech, Inc.
28. TMC, Inc.
29. Castings Supply, Inc.

30. DeLuxe Foods, Ltd.
33. Lever, Ltd.

Career Planning in Marketing

When You Finish This Appendix, You Should

1. Know that there is a job—or a career—for you in marketing.

2. Know that marketing jobs can be rewarding, pay well, and offer opportunities for growth.

3. Understand the difference between "people-oriented" and "thing-oriented" jobs.

4. Know about the many marketing jobs you can choose from.

One of the hardest jobs facing most college students is the choice of a career. Of course, we can't make this decision for you. You must be the judge of your own objectives, interests, and abilities. Only you can decide what career *you* should pursue. However, you owe it to yourself to at least consider the possibility of a career in marketing.

THERE'S A PLACE IN MARKETING FOR YOU

We're happy to tell you that many opportunities are available in marketing. There's a place in marketing for everyone—from a service provider in a fast-food restaurant to a vice president of marketing in a large company such as Microsoft or Procter & Gamble. The opportunities range widely—so it will help to be more specific. In the following pages, we'll discuss (1) the typical pay for different marketing jobs, (2) setting your own objectives and evaluating your interests and abilities, and (3) the kinds of jobs available in marketing.

MARKETING JOBS CAN PAY WELL

There are many interesting and challenging jobs for those with marketing training. Fortunately, marketing jobs open to college-level students do pay well! At the time this book went to press, marketing undergraduates were being offered starting salaries ranging from about $15,000 to $36,000 a year. Of course, these figures are extremes. Starting salaries can vary considerably—depending on your background, experience, and location. But many jobs are in the $22,000–$26,000 range.

Starting salaries in marketing compare favorably with many other fields. They are lower than those in such fields as computer science and engineering where college graduates are currently in very high demand. But there is even better opportunity for personal growth, variety, and income in many marketing positions. *The American Almanac of Jobs and Salaries* ranks the median income of marketers number 10 in a list of 125 professions. Marketing also supplies about 50 percent of the people who achieve senior management ranks.

How far and fast your career and income rises above the starting level, however, depends on many factors—including your willingness to work, how well you get along with people, and your individual abilities. But most of all, it depends on *getting results*—individually and through other people. And this is where many marketing jobs offer the newcomer great opportunities. It is possible to show initiative, ability, and judgment in marketing jobs. And some young people move up very rapidly in marketing. Some even end up at the top in large companies—or as owners of their own businesses.

Marketing is often the route to the top

Marketing is where the action is! In the final analysis, a firm's success or failure depends on the effectiveness of its marketing program. This doesn't mean the other functional areas aren't important. It merely reflects the fact that a firm won't have much need for accountants, finance people, production managers, and so on if it can't successfully meet customers' needs and sell its products.

Because marketing is so vital to a firm's survival, many companies look for people with training and experience in marketing when filling key executive positions. In general, chief executive officers for the nation's largest corporations are more likely to have backgrounds in marketing and distribution than in other fields such as production, finance, and engineering.

EXHIBIT C–1   Organizing Your Own Personal Marketing Strategy Planning

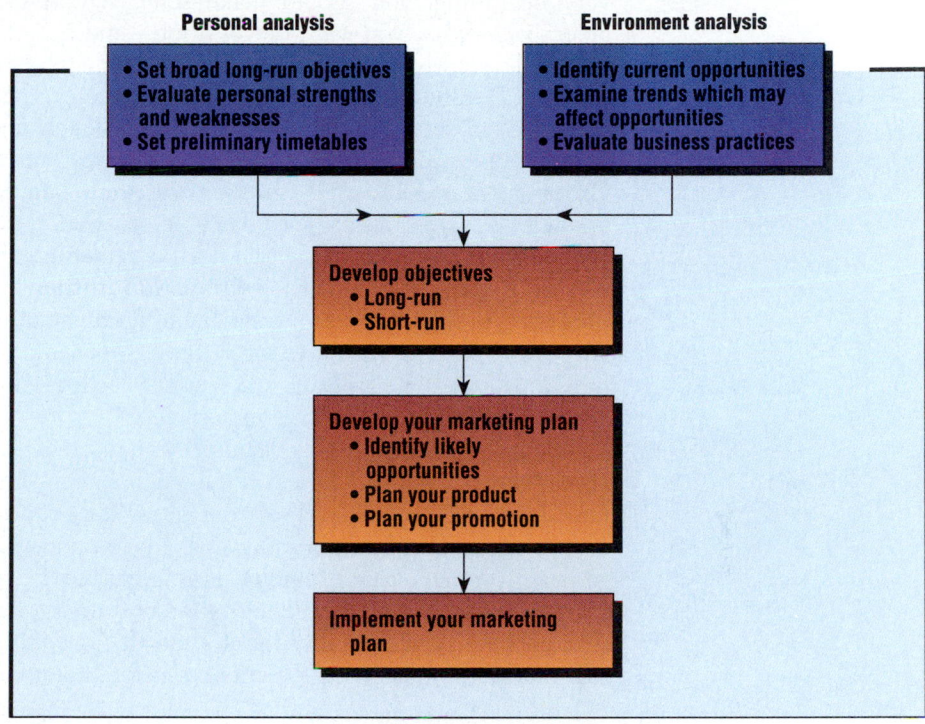

DEVELOP YOUR OWN PERSONAL MARKETING STRATEGY

Now that you know there are many opportunities in marketing, your problem is matching the opportunities to your own personal objectives and strengths. Basically the problem is a marketing problem: developing a marketing strategy to sell a product—yourself—to potential employers. Just as in planning strategies for products, developing your own strategy takes careful thought. Exhibit C–1 shows how you can organize your own strategy planning. This exhibit shows that you should evaluate yourself first—a personal analysis—and then analyze the environment for opportunities. This will help you sharpen your own long- and short-run objectives—which will lead to developing a strategy. And, finally, you should start implementing your own personal marketing strategy. These ideas are explained more fully below.

CONDUCT YOUR OWN PERSONAL ANALYSIS

You are the Product you are going to include in your own marketing plan. So first you have to decide what your long-run objectives are—what you want to do, how hard you want to work, and how quickly you want to reach your objectives. Be honest with yourself—or you will eventually face frustration. Evaluate your own personal strengths and weaknesses—and decide what factors may become the key to your success. Finally, as part of your personal analysis, set some preliminary timetables to guide your strategy planning and implementation efforts. Let's spell this out in detail.

Set broad long-run objectives

Strategy planning requires much trial-and-error decision making. But at the very beginning, you should make some tentative decisions about your own objectives—what you want out of a job—and out of life. At the very least, you should decide whether you are just looking for a job—or whether you want to build a career. Beyond this, do you want the position to be personally satisfying—or is the financial return enough? And just how much financial return do you need? Some people work only to support themselves and their leisure-time activities. Others work to support themselves and their families. These people seek only financial rewards from a job. They try to find job opportunities that provide adequate financial returns but aren't too demanding of their time or effort.

Other people look first for satisfaction in their job—and they seek opportunities for career advancement. Financial rewards may be important too, but these are used only as measures of success. In the extreme, the career-oriented individual may be willing to sacrifice a lot—including leisure and social activities—to achieve success in a career.

Once you've tentatively decided these matters, then you can get more serious about whether you should seek a job—or a career—in marketing. If you decide to pursue a career, you should set your broad long-run objectives to achieve it. For example, one long-run objective might be to pursue a career in marketing management (or marketing research). This might require more academic training than you planned—as well as a different kind of training. If your objective is to get a job that pays well, on the other hand, then this calls for a different kind of training and different kinds of job experiences before completing your academic work.

Evaluate personal strengths and weaknesses

What kind of a job is right for you?

Because of the great variety of marketing jobs, it's hard to generalize about what aptitudes you should have to pursue a career in marketing. Different jobs attract people with various interests and abilities. We'll give you some guidelines about what kinds of interests and abilities marketers should have. However, if you're completely lost about your own interests and abilities, see your campus career counselor and take some vocational aptitude and interest tests. These tests will help you to compare yourself with people who are now working in various career positions. They will *not* tell you what you should do, but they can help—especially in eliminating possibilities you are less interested in and/or less able to do well in.

Are you "people-oriented" or "thing-oriented"?

One of the first things you need to decide is whether you are basically "people-oriented" or "thing-oriented." This is a very important decision. A people-oriented person might be very unhappy in an inventory management job, for example, while a thing-oriented person might be miserable in a personal selling or retail management job that involves a lot of customer contact.

Marketing has both people-oriented and thing-oriented jobs. People-oriented jobs are primarily in the promotion area—where company representatives must make contact with potential customers. This may be direct personal selling or customer service activities—for example, in technical service or installation and repair. Thing-oriented jobs focus more on creative activities and analyzing data—as in advertising and marketing research—or on organizing and scheduling work—as in operating warehouses, transportation agencies, or the back-end of retailers.

People-oriented jobs tend to pay more, in part because such jobs are more likely to affect sales—the lifeblood of any business. Thing-oriented jobs, on the other hand, are often seen as cost-generators rather than sales-generators. Taking a big view of the whole company's operations, the thing-oriented jobs are certainly necessary—but without sales no one is needed to do them.

Thing-oriented jobs are usually done at a company's facilities. Further, especially in lower-level jobs, the amount of work to be done—and even the nature of the work—may be spelled out quite clearly. The time it takes to design questionnaires and tabulate results, for example, can be estimated with reasonable accuracy. Similarly, running a warehouse, totaling inventories, scheduling outgoing shipments, and so on are more like production operations. It's fairly easy to measure an employee's effectiveness and productivity in a thing-oriented job. At least, time spent can be used to measure an employee's contribution.

A sales rep, on the other hand, might spend all weekend thinking and planning how to make a half-hour sales presentation on Monday. For what should the sales rep be compensated—the half-hour presentation, all of the planning and thinking that went into it, or the results? Typically, sales reps are rewarded for their sales results—and this helps account for the sometimes extremely high salaries paid to effective order getters. At the same time, some people-oriented jobs can be routinized and are lower paid. For example, salesclerks in some retail stores are paid at or near the minimum wage.

Managers needed for both kinds of jobs

Here we have oversimplified deliberately to emphasize the differences among types of jobs. Actually, of course, there are many variations between the two extremes. Some sales reps must do a great deal of analytical work before they make a presentation. Similarly, some marketing researchers must be extremely people-sensitive to get potential customers to reveal their true feelings. But the division is still useful because it focuses on the primary emphasis in different kinds of jobs.

Managers are needed for the people in both kinds of jobs. Managing others requires a blend of both people and analytical skills—but people skills may be the more important of the two. Therefore, people-oriented persons are often promoted into managerial positions more quickly.

What will differentiate your Product?

After deciding whether you're generally people-oriented or thing-oriented, you're ready for the next step—trying to identify your specific strengths (to be built on) and weaknesses (to be avoided or remedied). It is important to be as specific as possible so you can develop a better marketing plan. For example, if you decide you are more people-oriented, are you more skilled in verbal *or* written communication? Or if you are more thing-oriented, what specific analytical or technical skills do you have? Are you good at working with numbers, solving complex problems, or coming to the root of a problem? Other possible strengths include past experience (career-related or otherwise), academic performance, an outgoing personality, enthusiasm, drive, motivation, and so on.

It is important to see that your plan should build on your strengths. An employer will be hiring you to do something—so promote yourself as someone who is able to do something *well*. In other words, find your competitive advantage in your unique strengths—and then communicate these unique things about *you* and what you can do.

While trying to identify strengths, you also must realize that you may have some important weaknesses—depending on your objectives. If you are seeking a career that requires technical skills, for example, then you need to get these skills.

Or if you are seeking a career that requires independence and self-confidence, then you should try to develop these characteristics in yourself—or change your objectives.

Set some timetables

At this point in your strategy planning process, set some timetables to organize your thinking and the rest of your planning. You need to make some decisions at this point to be sure you see where you're going. You might simply focus on getting your first job, or you might decide to work on two marketing plans: (1) a short-run plan to get your first job and (2) a longer-run plan—perhaps a five-year plan—to show how you're going to accomplish your long-run objectives. People who are basically job-oriented may get away with only a short-run plan—just drifting from one opportunity to another as their own objectives and opportunities change. But those interested in careers need a longer-run plan. Otherwise, they may find themselves pursuing attractive first job opportunities that satisfy short-run objectives—but quickly leave them frustrated when they realize that they can't achieve their long-run objectives without additional training or other experiences that require starting over again on a new career path.

ENVIRONMENT ANALYSIS

Strategy planning is a matching process. For your own strategy planning, this means matching yourself to career opportunities. So let's look at opportunities available in the marketing environment. (The same approach applies, of course, in the whole business area.) Exhibit C–2 shows some of the possibilities and salary ranges. Keep in mind that the salary ranges in Exhibit C–2 are rough estimates. Salaries for a particular job often vary depending on a variety of factors, including company size and geographic area. In recent years *Advertising Age* has been publishing an annual survey of salary levels for different marketing and advertising jobs—with breakdowns by company size and other factors.[1]

Identifying current opportunities in marketing

Because of the wide range of opportunities in marketing, it's helpful to narrow your possibilities. After deciding on your own objectives, strengths, and weaknesses, think about where in the marketing system you might like to work. Would you like to work for manufacturers, or wholesalers, or retailers? Or does it really matter? Do you want to be involved with consumer products or business products? By analyzing your feelings about these possibilities, you can begin to zero in on the kind of job and the functional area that might interest you most.

One simple way to get a better idea of the kinds of jobs available in marketing is to review the chapters of this text—this time with an eye for job opportunities rather than new concepts. The following paragraphs contain brief descriptions of job areas that marketing graduates are often interested in with references to specific chapters in the text. Some, as noted below, offer good starting opportunities, while others do not. While reading these paragraphs, keep your own objectives, interests, and strengths in mind.

Marketing manager (Chapter 2)

This is usually not an entry-level job, although aggressive students may move quickly into this role in smaller companies.

EXHIBIT C–2   Some Career Paths and Salary Ranges

Marketing research opportunities (Chapter 5)

There are entry-level opportunities at all levels in the channel (but especially in large firms where more formal marketing research is done) and in advertising agencies and marketing research firms. Quantitative and behavioral science skills are extremely important in marketing research, so some firms prefer to hire statistics or psychology graduates rather than business graduates. But there still are many opportunities in marketing research for marketing graduates, especially if they have some experience in working with computers and statistical software. A recent graduate might begin in a training program—conducting interviews or summarizing open-ended answers from questionnaires—before being promoted to a position as an analyst, assistant project manager, and subsequent management positions.

Customer or market analyst (Chapters 3 and 5)

Opportunities as consumer analysts and market analysts are commonly found in large companies, marketing research organizations, and advertising agencies. Beginners start in thing-oriented jobs until their judgment and people-oriented skills are tested. The job may involve collecting or analyzing secondary data or preparation of reports and plans. Because knowledge of statistics, computers software, and/or behavioral sciences is very important, marketing graduates often find themselves competing with majors in fields such as psychology, sociology, statistics, and computer science. Graduates who have courses in marketing *and* one or more of these areas may have the best opportunities.

Purchasing agent/buyer (Chapter 8)

Entry level opportunities are commonly found in large companies. Beginners start as trainees or assistant buyers under the supervision of experienced buyers. That's good preparation for a promotion to more responsibility.

Product planner (Chapter 10)

This is usually not an entry-level position. Instead, people with experience on the technical side of the business and/or in sales might be moved into new-product development as they demonstrate judgment and analytical skills.

Product/brand manager (Chapters 9 and 10)

Many multiproduct firms have brand or product managers handling individual products—in effect, managing each product as a separate business. Some firms hire marketing graduates as assistant brand or product managers, although larger firms typically recruit MBAs for these jobs. Most firms prefer that recent college graduates spend some time in the field doing sales work before moving into brand or product management positions.

Packaging specialists (Chapter 9)

Packaging manufacturers tend to hire and train interested people from various backgrounds—there is little formal academic training in packaging. There are many sales opportunities in this field—and with training, interested people can become specialists fairly quickly in this growing area.

Distribution channel management (Chapter 11)

This work is typically handled or directed by sales managers—and therefore is not an entry-level position.

Physical distribution opportunities (Chapter 12)

There are many sales opportunities with physical distribution specialists—but there are also many thing-oriented jobs involving traffic management, warehousing, and materials handling. Here, training in accounting, finance, and quantitative methods could be very useful. These kinds of jobs are available at all levels in the channels of distribution.

Retailing opportunities (Chapter 13)

Most entry-level marketing positions in retailing involve some kind of sales work, although that is changing now as large retail chains recruit graduates for management training programs. Retailing positions tend to offer lower than average starting salaries—but they often provide opportunities for very rapid advancement. In a fast-growing chain, results-oriented people can move up very quickly. Most retailers require new employees to have some selling experience before managing others—or buying. A typical marketing graduate can expect to do some sales work and manage one or several departments before advancing to a store management position—or to a staff position that might involve buying, advertising, location analysis, and so on.

Wholesaling opportunities (Chapter 13)

Entry level jobs with merchant wholesalers typically fall into one of two categories. The first is in the logistics area—working with transportation management, inventory control, distribution customer service, and related activities. The other category usually involves personal selling and customer support. Agent wholesalers typically focus on selling, and entry level jobs often start out with order-taking responsibilities that grow into order-getting responsibilities.

Personal sales opportunities (Chapter 15)

Most of the job opportunities—especially entry-level jobs—are in personal selling. This might be order-getting, order-taking, or missionary selling. Many students are reluctant to get into personal selling—but this field offers benefits that are hard to match in any other field. These include the opportunity to earn extremely high salaries and commissions—quickly—a chance to develop your self-confidence and resourcefulness, an opportunity to work with minimal supervision—almost to the point of being your own boss—and a chance to acquire product and customer knowledge that many firms consider necessary for a successful career in product/brand management, sales management, and marketing management. Many salespeople spend their entire careers in selling—preferring the freedom and earning potential that go with a sales job over the headaches and sometimes lower salaries of sales management positions.

Advertising opportunities (Chapter 16)

Job opportunities are varied in this area—and highly competitive. And because the ability to communicate and knowledge of the behavioral sciences are important, marketing graduates often find themselves competing with majors from fields such as English, journalism, psychology, and sociology. There are thing-oriented jobs such as copywriting, media buying, art, and so on. Competition for these jobs is very intense—and they go to people with a track record. So the entry level positions are as assistant to a copywriter, media buyer, or art director. There are also people-oriented positions involving work with clients—which are probably of more interest to marketing graduates. This is a glamorous, but small and extremely competitive industry where young people can rise very rapidly—but they can also be as easily displaced by new bright young people. Entry-level salaries in advertising are typically low. There are sometimes good opportunities to get started in advertising with a retail chain that prepares its advertising internally. Another way to get more experience with advertising is to take a sales job with one of the media. Selling advertising space in a newspaper or for a magazine may not seem as glamorous as developing TV ads, but media salespeople help their customers solve promotion problems—and get experience dealing with both the business and creative side of advertising.

Sales promotion opportunities (Chapters 14 and 16)

There are not many entry-level positions in this area. Creativity and judgment are required, and it is difficult for an inexperienced person to demonstrate these skills. A beginner would probably move from sales or advertising jobs into sales promotion.

Pricing opportunities (Chapters 17 and 18)

Pricing is generally handled by experienced executives, so there are no entry-level opportunities here. However, in a few large companies and in some consulting firms there are opportunities as pricing analysts for marketing graduates who have quantitative skills. These people work as assistants to higher-level executives and collect and analyze information about competitors' prices and costs as well as the firm's own costs. Thus, being able to work with accounting numbers and having computer spreadsheet skills is often important in these jobs. However, sometimes the route to these jobs is through experience in marketing research or product management.

Credit management opportunities

Specialists in credit have a continuing need for employees who are interested in evaluating customers' credit ratings and ensuring that money gets collected. Both people skills and thing skills can be useful here. Entry positions normally involve a training program—and then working under the supervision of others until your judgment and abilities are tested.

International marketing opportunities

Many marketing students are intrigued with the adventure and foreign travel promised by careers in international marketing. Some firms hire recent college graduates for positions in international marketing, but more often these positions go to MBA graduates. However, that is changing as more and more firms are pursuing international markets. It's an advantage in seeking an international marketing job to know a second language and to know about the culture of countries where you would like to work. Your college may have courses or international exchange programs that would help in these areas. Graduates aiming for a career in international marketing usually must spend time mastering the firm's domestic marketing operations before being sent abroad. So a good way to start is to focus on firms that are already involved in international marketing, or who are planning to move in that direction soon.

Customer relations/consumer affairs opportunities (Chapters 14 and 22)

Most firms are becoming more concerned about their relations with customers and the general public. Employees in this kind of work, however, usually have held various positions with the firm before doing customer relations.

Study trends that may affect your opportunities

A strategy planner should always be evaluating the future because it's easier to go along with trends than to buck them. This means you should watch for political, technical, or economic changes that might open—or close—career opportunities.

If you can spot a trend early, you may be able to prepare yourself to take advantage of it as part of your long-run strategy planning. Other trends might mean you should avoid certain career options. For example, rapid technological changes in computers and communications are likely to lead to major changes in retailing and advertising—as well as in personal selling. Cable television, telephone selling, and direct-mail selling may reduce the need for routine order takers—while increasing the need for higher-level order getters. More targeted and imaginative sales presentations for delivery by mail, phone, or even the Internet may be needed. The retailers who survive may need a better understanding of their target markets. And they may need to be supported by wholesalers and manufacturers who can plan targeted promotions that make economic sense. This will require a better understanding of the production and physical distribution side of business—as well as the financial side. And this means better training in accounting, finance, inventory control, and so on. So plan your personal strategy with such trends in mind.

Evaluate business practices

Finally, you need to know how businesses really operate—and the kind of training required for various jobs. We've already seen that there are many opportunities in marketing—but not all jobs are open to everyone, and not all jobs are entry-level jobs. Positions such as marketing manager, brand manager, and sales manager are higher rungs on the marketing career ladder. They become available only when you have a few years of experience and have shown leadership and judgment. Some positions require more education than others. So take a hard look at your long-run objectives—and then see what degree you may need for the kinds of opportunities you might like.

DEVELOP OBJECTIVES

Once you've done a personal analysis and environment analysis—identifying your personal interests, your strengths and weaknesses, and the opportunities in the environment—define your short-run and long-run objectives more specifically.

Develop long-run objectives

Your long-run objectives should clearly state what you want to do—and what you will do for potential employers. You might be as specific as indicating the exact career area you want to pursue over the next 5 to 10 years. For example, your long-run objective might be to apply a set of marketing research and marketing management tools to the food manufacturing industry—with the objective of becoming director of marketing research in a small food manufacturing company.

Your long-run objectives should be realistic and attainable. They should be objectives you have thought about and for which you think you have the necessary skills (or the capabilities to develop those skills) as well as the motivation to reach the objectives.

Develop short-run objectives

To achieve your long-run objective(s), you should develop one or more short-run objectives. These should spell out what is needed to reach your long-run objective(s). For example, you might need to develop a variety of marketing research skills *and* marketing management skills—because both are needed to reach the longer-run objective. Or you might need an entry-level position in marketing research for a large food manufacturer—to gain experience and background. An even shorter-run objective might be to take the academic courses that are necessary to get that desired entry-level job. In this example, you would probably need a minimum of an undergraduate degree in marketing—with an emphasis on marketing research. (Note that, given the longer-run objective of managerial responsibility, a business degree would probably be better than a degree in statistics or psychology.)

DEVELOPING YOUR MARKETING PLAN

Now that you've developed your objectives, move on to developing your own personal marketing plan. This means zeroing in on likely opportunities and developing a specific marketing strategy for these opportunities. Let's talk about that now.

Identify likely opportunities

An important step in strategy planning is identifying potentially attractive opportunities. Depending on where you are in your academic training, this can vary all the way from preliminary exploration to making detailed lists of companies that offer the kinds of jobs that interest you. If you're just getting started, talk to your school's career counselors and placement officers about the kinds of jobs being offered to your school's graduates. Your marketing instructors can help you be more realistic about ways you can match your training, abilities, and interests to job opportunities. Also, it helps to read business publications such as *Business Week, Fortune, The Wall Street Journal,* and *Advertising Age. Applications in Basic Marketing*, which comes shrinkwrapped with this text, provides reprints of recent articles from these publications. If you are interested in opportunities in a particular industry, check at your library to see if there are trade publications that can bring you up to speed on the marketing issues in that area. Your library may also have an on-line service to make it easier to search for articles about specific companies or industries.

Don't overlook the business sections of your local newspapers to keep in touch with marketing developments in your area. And take advantage of any opportunity to talk with marketers directly. Ask them what they're doing—and what satisfactions they find in their jobs. Also, if your college has a marketing club, join it and participate actively in the club's programs. It will help you meet marketers and students with serious interest in the field. Some may have had interesting job experiences and can provide you with leads on part-time jobs or exciting career opportunities.

If you're far along in your present academic training, list companies that you know something about or are willing to investigate—trying to match your skills and interests with possible opportunities. Narrow your list to a few companies you might like to work for.

If you have trouble narrowing down to specific companies, make a list of your personal interest areas—sports, travel, reading, music, or whatever. Think about the companies that compete in markets related to these interests. Often your own knowledge about these areas—and interest in them—can give you a competitive advantage in getting a job. This helps you focus on companies that serve needs you think are important or interesting.

Then do some research on these companies. Find out how they are organized, their product lines, and their overall strategies. Try to get clear job descriptions for the kinds of positions you're seeking. Match these job descriptions against your understanding of these jobs and your objectives. Jobs with similar titles may offer very different opportunities. By researching job positions and companies in depth, you should begin to have a feel for where you would be comfortable as an employee. This will help you narrow your target market of possible employers to perhaps five firms. For example, you may decide that your target market for an entry position is large corporations with: (1) in-depth training programs, (2) a wide product line, and (3) a wide variety of marketing jobs that will enable you to get a range of experiences and responsibilities within the same company.

Planning your Product

Just like any strategy planner, you must decide what Product features are necessary to appeal to your target market. Identify which credentials are mandatory—and which are optional. For example, is your present academic program enough, or will you need more training? Also, identify what technical skills are needed—such as computer programming or accounting. Further, are there any business experiences or extracurricular activities that might help make your Product more attractive to employers? This might involve active participation in college organizations or work experience—either on the job or in internships.

Planning your promotion

Once you identify target companies and develop a Product you hope will be attractive to them, you have to tell these potential customers about your Product. You can write directly to prospective employers—sending a carefully developed résumé that reflects your strategy planning. Or you can visit them in person (with your résumé). Many colleges run well-organized interviewing services. Seek their advice early in your strategy planning effort.

IMPLEMENTING YOUR MARKETING PLAN

When you complete your personal marketing plan, you have to implement it—starting with working to accomplish your short-run objectives. If, as part of your plan, you decide that you need specific outside experience, then arrange to get it. This may mean taking a low-paying job—or even volunteering to work in political organizations or volunteer organizations where you can get that kind of experience. If you decide that you need skills you can learn in academic courses, plan to take these courses. Similarly, if you don't have a good understanding of your opportunities, then learn as much as you can about possible jobs by talking to professors, taking advanced courses, and talking to business people. And, of course, trends and opportunities can change—so continue to read business publications, talk with professionals in your areas of interest, and be sure that the planning you've done still makes sense.

Strategy planning must adapt to the environment. If the environment changes or your personal objectives change, you have to develop a new plan. This is an ongoing process—and you may never be completely satisfied with your strategy planning. But even trying will make you look much more impressive when you begin your job interviews. Remember, while all employers would like to hire a Superman or a Wonder Woman, they are also impressed with candidates who know what they want to do and are looking for a place where they can fit in—and make a contribution. So planning a personal strategy and implementing it almost guarantee you'll do a better job of career planning and this will help ensure that you reach your own objectives—whatever they are.

Whether or not you decide to pursue a marketing career, the authors wish you the best of luck in your search for a challenging and rewarding career—wherever your interests and abilities may take you.

Video
Cases

This edition of *Basic Marketing* includes two different types of marketing cases: the five special video cases in this section and the 36 traditional cases in the next section. All of the cases offer you the opportunity to evaluate marketing concepts at work in a variety of real-world situations. However, the video cases add a multimedia dimension because we have produced a special video to accompany each of the written cases. The videos are available to professors who adopt *Basic Marketing* for use in their courses. (These case-based videos are in addition to 18 other video segments we have custom produced and made available to instructors for possible use with other parts of the text.)

The videos bring to life many of the issues considered in each case. However, you can read and analyze the written case descriptions even if there is not time or opportunity to view the video. Either way, you'll find the case interesting—and closely tied to the important concepts you've studied in the text.

The set of questions at the end of each case will get you started in thinking about the marketing issues in the case. Further, we provide instructors with a number of suggestions on using the video cases—both for group discussion in class or individual assignments. Thus, as is also true with the traditional cases in the next section, the video cases can be used in many different ways and sequences. You can analyze all of the cases, or only a subset. In fact, the same case can be analyzed several times for different purposes. As your understanding of marketing deepens throughout the course, you'll "see" many more of the marketing issues considered in each case.

1 Marketing in the Hardwood Industry*

Logs cut from hardwood forests are an important raw material used by many domestic and foreign producers. Unlike pine and other softwoods, which are used mostly for general construction, the demand for oak, black walnut, black cherry, white ash, maple, and other hardwoods derives from the consumer demand for high-value products such as hardwood furniture, cabinets, flooring, millwork, and moldings. When properly finished, hardwoods offer a finish that is both durable and beautiful. The wood is also very strong, so even pieces that do not have a perfect appearance are well suited for making frames of chairs, sofas, and other furniture that are covered up with various upholstery materials.

Hardwood forests cover many of the rural areas of the eastern United States—areas where there is often little other industry. Thus, the forest products industry is potentially important to economic development—and to the employment and quality of life of people who live and work in these areas.

Unfortunately, that potential for economic development is not always achieved. A key reason for this is that many of the firms that harvest the logs are not focusing on any particular target market or customers. Rather, they just see the market opportunity in terms of the products they have always produced: hardwood logs or perhaps "green" roughsawn lumber cut from the logs. Thus, they are selling a commodity to distant customers who view logs from one supplier as like all of the others on the market. There is nearly perfect competition in these commodity markets, and buyers just want to purchase the wood at the lowest price.

As a consequence of this production-oriented, commodity approach, the hardwood produced in rural regions of the U.S. has usually been shipped to other regions—including foreign countries—before the wood is processed into intermediate and finished products. When the wood is sold and shipped out of the region as an unfinished commodity, the profit opportunities—and associated employment—relevant to the secondary processing are exported as well.

Historically, in this commodity-market environment, successful producers were those who could operate with the lowest total cost. The major cost areas are for the raw material (lumber) itself, labor, any processing that is done, transportation, and, of course, any marketing-related expenses. Small and medium-sized suppliers are at an inherent disadvantage in this competitive, cost-oriented environment. They cannot achieve economies of scale because they can't spread their overhead expenses over a larger number of units produced. As a result, there

is little way for them to obtain a competitive advantage in production or distribution.

Some hardwood producers, including some smaller ones, were able to improve sales and profits—from both the U.S. and international markets—by differentiating their offerings with higher-quality products. For example, firms that worked to keep lumber dry and clean were better able to meet the needs of some customers. Further, some customers appreciated supplier firms that did a good job of sorting and grading different types of woods. And some suppliers focused on supplying species of wood that were desirable but less-readily available.

In spite of such efforts, in the past most hardwood from U.S. producers was just sold as a commodity in a very competitive market. However, some people in the hardwood industry are applying marketing concepts to help change this situation. They are focusing attention on ways to expand the market for existing hardwood products and also trying to identify markets with specific needs so that they can increase the value added to the hardwood lumber—by producing finished or semiprocessed products—before it is shipped out of the region where the trees are cut.

These efforts are having an effect. For example, an increasing number of customers want to buy kiln-dried boards rather than green lumber that isn't immediately ready to use for their own production purposes. So, many firms that cut and sell hardwood are taking the step of adding value to their product by doing the kiln-drying process. By doing this processing in the rural areas close to where the logs are cut, local people have more job opportunities and more income. There is also less wasted expense in shipping the kiln-dried boards rather than the rough logs.

However, adding kiln-dried lumber is just one way to meet customer needs that were not previously being satisfied. U.S. hardwood suppliers are also seeking to identify other value-added opportunities. They are asking basic questions like: What are the needs of different customers in the broad product-market for hardwood? Who are these customers and where are they located? What kind of hardwood products—beyond the commodity lumber we've sold in the past—do they want? What are the opportunities to differentiate what we sell and add more value to our product by doing processing that meets the needs of specific target segments? How do we go about finding the answers to these questions?

One opportunity for expanding both the market and value-added product opportunities lies in the area of international exports. Prior to 1980, many firms that supplied hardwood ignored the export market. Domestic demand was sufficiently large to sustain growth and profitability. However, as domestic demand softened and the competition grew more intense, U.S. suppliers began to rethink entry into the international marketplace. In

---

*This case and the script for the accompanying video were prepared by Thomas G. Ponzurick and James P. Armstrong.

the last decade, efforts to market hardwood products to foreign markets have expanded significantly and the value of the hardwood products exported has increased substantially.

Despite some recent success, there is still a vital need for more U.S. suppliers to adopt the marketing concept, especially in targeting the export marketplace. Currently, international buyers are focusing most of their attention on the higher-grade hardwood products. But growth of sales and profits from exporting will depend on the U.S. industry's ability to find markets for more of their available product inventory—including lower grades and species of hardwoods. In fact, finding markets for value-added products may be the best way to improve sales of the lower grades and species. This would not only result in more efficient and more profitable use of the hardwood resources, but it could also reduce costs by improving economies of scale in production.

However, the question that should be uppermost in marketers' minds is what do these customers want in the way of hardwood products? To answer this question, one must first determine the needs of these international buyers. In the case of U.S. hardwood suppliers, Canadian buyers are currently the largest market for these products.

Most of the Canadian firms that import U.S. hardwood to Canada are concentrated in a few geographic areas; over 75 percent are located in either Ontario or Quebec. Much of the imported lumber is purchased by Canadian manufacturers who use it to produce their own products—including furniture, cabinets, hardwood flooring, and molding and millwork for the construction industry. However, these customers account for only about 31 percent of U.S. imports. Canadian wholesalers—especially brokers and agents—account for more than half of the Canadian hardwood lumber purchased from U.S. sources. Many of these middlemen specialize in international sales. In fact, nearly 20 percent of all U.S. hardwood lumber imported to Canada is subsequently resold and exported to Europe—usually after some value-adding activities such as grading, sorting, repackaging, or additional product processing.

Red oak, hard maple, and white oak are the principal hardwood species that Canadian customers are importing from the United States. However, there are also markets for some species of lesser value—including soft maple and yellow poplar.

All types of lumber are graded according to quality, and this grading is important to Canadian buyers who have different hardwood needs. About 70 percent of the total volume of hardwood lumber purchased by Canadian firms is the higher-quality Number 1 Common grade or better. The other 30 percent of lumber imported is graded as Number 2 Common or lower. Firms that purchase the lower grades of lumber are mostly flooring manufacturers, furniture manufacturers, and brokers.

Marketing research studies indicate that Canadian hardwood lumber buyers are *relatively* satisfied with the quality of goods and services now being provided by U.S. suppliers. However, the research reveals that suppliers could enhance their customer satisfaction and their competitive advantage by improving their product quality through more accurate grading and reporting of moisture content as well as by providing cleaner and straighter lumber. Buyers would also like to see better distribution customer service from U.S. suppliers. This includes making supplies of lumber more reliable and reducing order-cycle time—that is, the time from when a customer orders lumber until it is delivered. And, of course, organizational buyers are always interested in competitive pricing.

Importantly, the research also shows that over one-third of the firms that import hardwood lumber from the United States are potentially interested in purchasing finished hardwood parts from U.S. suppliers. Examples in the area of finished hardwood parts include parts for making furniture, doors, and stairways or railings. Organizations showing an interest in these finished products include importers, export brokers, and manufacturers of various hardwood products. These research results indicate that there *may* be a good opportunity for U.S. suppliers of hardwood products to custom-produce such parts for specific customers. Yet, it is still unknown how substantial this opportunity might be, how eager Canadian buyers might be to purchase value-added finished hardwood products, and at what prices. To begin to answer those questions, U.S. suppliers need to determine the types and specifications of the finished hardwood products desired by individual buyers. That will require that supplier firms do more marketing research or have more direct personal selling contact with buyers for specific firms than has been typical in the past. Alternatively, working with these customers may require closer relationships—partnerships—with middlemen who can help producers with some of the required marketing functions.

It appears that U.S. hardwood firms face a variety of possible opportunities to expand sales and improve profits. Export markets, including Canada, appear to offer greater potential than has in the past been captured. Further, some of the opportunities are ones that focus on the value-added products that have the potential to foster economic development in rural areas of the U.S. where such activities have in the past been limited. However, just having access to hardwood forests alone isn't enough to turn these opportunities into profitable business. Developing international markets for value-added hardwood products requires that individual supplier firms develop specific marketing strategies. They need to identify specific target markets and understand their unique needs and buying behavior. They also need to get beyond production-oriented thinking and develop whole marketing mixes to serve their target customers. That means figuring out what type of goods and services to offer. It also means making decisions about how to price specific offerings—because a firm that is doing something unique for these customers won't just face perfect competition and a price that is set by the market. A firm that does a good job with this marketing strategy planning has the potential to satisfy some target customers very well—and in the process to get a sustainable competitive advantage. And, of course, as more firms do that they will not only make better profits but also contribute to the economic development of the areas in which they operate.

1. Why is it important for firms that produce and supply hardwood to adopt the marketing concept?

2. What are some of the reasons for a firm that supplies hardwood to focus on identifying target markets with needs for specific value-added products rather than just selling roughsawn logs in a commodity market?

3. In what ways does marketing strategy planning need to be different for hardwood suppliers who focus on specific target markets than for firms that just sell logs or green lumber in the commodity market?

4. What are some of the important marketing mix variables that a supplier of hardwood can control to do a better job of meeting customer needs?

5. What are some of the potential target markets for U.S. hardwood suppliers in the Canadian export market? Which marketing mix variables are likely to be most important to the target markets you have identified?

❷ Harley-Davidson Motor Company*

Somewhat like the mythical phoenix, which arose from its own ashes, Harley-Davidson has staged a remarkable business comeback—from the brink of bankruptcy in 1981 to more worldwide demand than it can satisfy in the 1990s.

It all began in 1903 when Bill Harley and the three Davidson brothers started the company because they thought there was a market for a motor-driven bicycle. Their first model featured a 3.9-horsepower engine and a single-belt drive. They sold only three of those cycles.

*This case and the script for the accompanying video were prepared by Phillip B. Niffenegger.

However, by 1908, when they introduced a 7-horsepower, 45-degree V-twin engine—the first of its kind—sales were up to 150 units.

Harley continued to prosper and grow until 1933, when the Depression cut sales to 6,000 units. However, during world War II Harley kept busy supplying bikes for the troops, and then after the war the company introduced its classic Hydra-Glide model. When the Indian Motorcycle Company went out of business in 1953, Harley was left as the sole manufacturer of motorcycles in the U.S.

Throughout the 1960s the only serious competition that Harley faced came from imported British bikes—with brand names like BSA, Triumph, and Norton. But by the 1970s, the competitive environment changed. Japanese producers entered the U.S. market and quickly built a following for their light- and mediumweight cycles—the weak point in Harley's product line. Honda's ad campaign—with its "You meet the nicest people on a Honda" slogan—attacked Harley's bad-boy image and helped expand the market as it pulled in a new type of motorcycle rider.

In 1969, AMF (American Machine and Foundry) acquired Harley-Davidson hoping to take advantage of the growing market. And AMF's timing was good. By 1974, total U.S. motorcycle sales soared to 1.1 million as the key owner group of 14- to 24-year-olds rose from 27 to 41 million—and eager buyers gave Harley a 78 percent share of the heavyweight market.

Yet, as AMF nearly tripled the output of Harleys in the 1970s, the founding families lost control of product quality. Harley's reputation suffered as its bikes became less dependable and more prone to oil leaks and breakdowns. And sales slipped fast as Japanese competitors stole Harley's customers by introducing heavyweight cycles that were more reliable and technically sophisticated.

By 1980, Harley's share of the market for heavyweight cycles had dwindled to only 30 percent—and the company was facing financial ruin. However, a 1981 leveraged buyout of the firm by a group of Harley executives marked a turning point—and the beginning of a new strategy and multifaceted comeback plan.

First they attacked the quality problems that had resulted in lost customers. With a loan of $100 million they improved Harley's facilities and production processes. They also adopted statistical controls and employee involvement programs to improve quality. And they designed quality into their product line by creating cycles powered with a new V-twin engine developed for improved reliability. At the same time, management brought costs under control by downsizing the organization, cutting executive salaries and perks, and developing closer relationships and contracts with fewer suppliers. Further, they cut inventory expense by copying their Japanese competitors' just-in-time delivery approach.

Harley also worked to strengthen relations in the distribution channel and the quality of its dealers. For example, the company worked with dealers to modernize their showrooms and service facilities and to improve sales training.

In 1983, Harley charged its Japanese competitors with dumping cycles at predatory prices that were below cost. And, in response to a request from Harley's management, the U.S. government imposed a five-year tariff of 49 percent on imported motorcycles. The tariffs gave Harley a significant price advantage over Japanese producers.

Harley's sales improved quickly as all of these changes took effect. By 1987, its share of the big bike segment was up to 45 percent. In fact, Harley was strong enough that it asked the government to drop the protective tariffs a year early.

To build closer relationships with customers, Harley executives started a Harley Owners Group (H.O.G.). Local H.O.G. clubs across the U.S. have proved to be very popular. The company keeps H.O.G. members involved with a *Harley* magazine and by sponsoring weekend rallies around the country—often coupled with free concerts featuring groups like ZZ Top. To stay in closer touch with their customers, Harley executives circulate among bikers at the rallies and solicit their suggestions and complaints.

The local H.O.G.s now have over 250,000 owner-members. Harley's marketing research shows that a typical Harley owner is 38 years old and has a household income of $53,000. Sixty percent are married, about 30 percent have a college degree, and most (95 percent) are male. A surprising number are affluent professionals—doctors, lawyers, and the like. In fact, the Harley owners in this segment are nicknamed the "Rubbies"—short for rich urban bikers. The Rubbies view their Harleys and the weekend H.O.G. events as a way to express their individuality and as an escape from weekday pressures. To reinforce these attitudes, Harley advertising focuses not just on its cycles but on the whole Harley lifestyle.

Harley has also been aggressive in expanding overseas—especially in the big Japanese and European markets. In fact, about 30 percent of Harley's total production is exported. To promote export growth, the company encourages overseas H.O.G.s, publishes *Harley* magazine in foreign languages, and stages beer and band fests that are adapted to the local culture.

With all of these changes in marketing strategy, Harley's sales rose steadily and by 1992 it had a 63 percent share of the superheavyweight category. However, in 1993 and 1994 there was more demand than Harley could supply and Harley's share actually dropped slightly (to 56 percent). Even now most dealers sell out their allocation of cycles by 6 months into the year. As a result, customers face a waiting list to buy one of the pricey bikes—which sell in the $6,000–$19,000 range in the U.S. market.

Despite pressure from dealers to increase the number of Harleys available to sell, Richard Teerlink—Harley-Davidson's CEO—has allowed only modest production increases at the two U.S. plants and he has refused to open overseas plants. He maintains that limited production is necessary to keep quality high, and he is determined that Harley not repeat the mistakes of the late 1970s when Harley got sloppy with success and allowed quality and customer satisfaction to slip. Further, some observers think that the deliberate shortage of Harleys helps to maintain their exclusive image and high prices. It may also make buying a bike a better investment for customers; if an owner keeps a bike long enough, its resale value is often greater than the original price.

The combination of eager customers and high prices helps explain why Harley continues to rack up successive years of double digit increases in sales and profits. In 1994, sales of 95,800 units resulted in profits of $163 million—a far cry from Harley's brush with bankruptcy in 1980.

Harley and its dealers are now putting more emphasis on sales of parts and accessories—because many owners want to express their individuality by customizing their bikes. These lines represent over 20 percent of the motorcycle division revenues. Part of the revenue comes from Harley's MotorClothes apparel line. Each year the firm sells millions of garments bearing the famous Harley trademark—and nonbikers make nearly 70 percent of those purchases.

1. How has Harley adjusted its marketing mix to meet the needs of its target customers? Be specific and consider both the nature of the target market and Harley's strategy decisions with respect to each of the 4 Ps.

2. How have various aspects of the external market environment affected Harley's strategy planning over the years?

3. Japanese motorcycle companies still lead in sales of motorcycles in the light- and mediumweight category. Should Harley develop a new strategy—concurrent with what it's already doing—to compete better in that market? Explain your logic.

4. What challenges do you think Harley faces as it moves to increase sales in international markets? How can it best address these challenges?

5. Should Harley increase its production capacity so that it can supply its dealers with more cycles and reduce the time customers must wait to get a new cycle? Explain your thinking.

3   Briggs & Stratton Corporation*

Briggs & Stratton is the world's largest producer of air-cooled gasoline engines for outdoor power equipment, mainly for lawn mowers. The company designs, manufactures, markets, and services these products—which are sold as components to original equipment manufacturers (OEMs) in 85 countries.

Steve Briggs and Harry Stratton started the company in 1909 to produce a six-cylinder, two-cycle engine similar to one Briggs had developed a few years earlier as an engineering student in college. The engine turned out to be too expensive to mass produce, so the partners turned their attention to designing and producing electrical parts for automobiles—including switches, starters, and regulators.

Later B&S acquired the patent for the Motor Wheel—a gasoline engine designed to fit on a bicycle. It was a market success and ultimately proved to be a good way to power several other types of vehicles. In some parts of Asia it was even used on rickshas.

To build on the success of the Motor Wheel, B&S looked for new markets for engines. Its search led to the development of a stationary utility engine for use on such products as garden cultivators and reel-type mowers. Before utility companies brought electricity to rural parts of the U.S., these B&S engines even powered refrigerators, milking machines, and elevators.

After World War II, the booming U.S. economy, the shift of population to the suburbs, and the growth of leisure time prompted new consumer interest in lawn and garden equipment. B&S saw this growth opportunity and shifted its focus to producing motors for the lawn mower manufacturers who served that market. But, B&S didn't just try to push engines it was already producing.

At that time, most power mowers used two-cycle engines; their light weight made mowers easy to push. However, two-cycles weren't reliable and needed a mix of gas and oil—which was inconvenient for consumers. Four-cycle engines like the ones B&S produced were very reliable, but they were made from cast iron and very heavy. Marketing people at B&S realized that consumers wanted *both* reliability and light weight, so the firm designed a new lawn mower engine from aluminum alloy.

Over time, the Briggs & Stratton name has become almost synonymous with the lawn mower. Top producers such as Toro, Snapper, and John Deere proudly proclaim in their ads that their mowers are powered by a Briggs & Stratton engine. In fact, Briggs & Stratton is often the most prominent brand name on the mower, even though the engine is just a component. The Briggs & Stratton name helps sell the mowers because it means quality,

reliability, and performance to consumers. Because of this reputation—and consumer demand—many retailers won't sell a mower unless it uses a Briggs & Stratton motor.

Early in the 1980s B&S faced a serious competitive threat. A shift in international exchange rates made Japanese products less expensive in the U.S. and other parts of the world. This gave Japanese motorcycle producers a pricing edge to expand into the market for small engines. Because B&S was the leading producer of small engines, any competitive inroads would be at its expense.

Marketers at B&S realized that to keep competitors from carving up its market they would need to fine tune the firm's offerings for specific market segments. A starting point for that effort was to develop new product lines—actually, whole marketing strategies—for each type of need rather than just trying to get economies of scale by serving bigger but heterogeneous product-markets. B&S invested $250 million to develop carefully targeted new products, build new plants, and develop new processes to improve quality and reduce costs.

B&S' new-product development effort for specific segments cut short the Japanese invasion—and increased customer satisfaction and brand loyalty. That put B&S in a better position to deal with another change—a big shift in the channel of distribution for lawn mowers. In the past, most consumers bought lawn mowers from independent lawn and garden equipment dealers. However, over time mass-merchandisers have taken away almost all of that business. In fact, five of the largest retail chains now account for half of all the lawn mowers sold in the U.S.—and about 80 percent of B&S' lawn and garden equipment sales are through mass-merchandisers.

This concentration of purchasing power has given the big retail chains new clout in the channel of distribution. Retail buyers pressure lawn mower producers to keep costs and prices low; and the producers in turn expect B&S to keep its prices in check. While this has probably reduced the price premium that the B&S brand commands, it hasn't eliminated it. Retailers know that consumers want lawn mowers with B&S engines. So brand loyalty by final consumers gives B&S an advantage in negotiations with its producer-customers. Even so, the squeeze on profit margins throughout the channel—and intense competition—mean that B&S must continue to find better ways to meet customers' needs if it is to maximize market share and earn attractive profits. And for B&S developing innovative new products has long been the key to meeting needs better. Its skill in this arena is illustrated by its success in developing a 4-horsepower motor to fill a gap in its product line.

In 1993 B&S had four main lines of lawn mower engines. B&S' Classic 3.5-horsepower (HP) engine was at the low end of the price range and it was found on mowers priced at about $99. As the name implies, this

*This case and the script for the accompanying video were prepared by Roger C. Schoenfeldt.

reliable model has been popular for many years. If a customer wanted a bit more power and a mower that took less pulling effort to start, B&S' 3.75-HP Sprint engine was available on mowers that sell for about $119. For consumers who wanted an easy-starting engine that quietly conquered even the thickest grass, the Quantum 5.0 HP Plus line was the choice—on a mower that cost from $160 up to $500. Finally, B&S offered a top-of-the-line Diamond Plus model with about 6.0 HP, unique European styling, and all the "bells and whistles." A customer who had to ask how much it cost probably couldn't afford it.

In spite of multiple models in each of these lines, B&S did not have a good 4-HP mower engine. Yet, there was a clear market for one. B&S' main competitor, Tecumseh, proved that. Its 4-HP engine was a market leader. And B&S needed to develop a new engine if it wanted to compete for the segment of customers who wanted a 4.0-HP engine. To take customers away from Tecumseh, B&S marketers knew they needed to develop a cost-effective engine that was better than the Tecumseh model on all operating and performance criteria. Research also showed that styling was becoming an important purchase criteria for many customers—perhaps because that was the one difference in engines that consumers could see while shopping.

Although they had a clear idea of what the market wanted, marketing managers at B&S faced a real challenge. Creating a superior new engine wouldn't do much good if lawn mower producers and retailers didn't know about it, and *the* time and place to introduce an important new lawn and garden product was at a big, national trade show that was less than a year away. If they missed that date, they'd effectively lose a year. So getting the new product to market fast—without making costly mistakes—was critical.

To speed up development and also reduce costs, B&S designers created a contemporary, aerodynamic look with a computer-aided design (CAD) system; the tooling of the parts—direct from the computer drawings—was very fast. Further, B&S engineers used standard parts from other B&S engines when they could. This helped to control costs, reduce development time, cut inventory requirements, and later would make after-the-sale service easier and faster. As a result of efforts like these, the new product went from the concept stage to production in about 9 months—in time for the trade show deadline.

While the new product team was developing the engine, B&S marketing people had other work to do. To emphasize the new engine's distinct identity, they used an individual brand name, Quattro. This word, though spelled differently, means four in Spanish. They also developed promotional materials to use at the trade show, and started work on ads and other cooperative promotional materials so they would be ready for producers and retailers to use when the Quattro started to appear on lawn mowers in retail stores.

The B&S salespeople also started to call on their top OEM customers. Besides explaining the advantages of the new Quattro motor and answering questions, they provided hundreds of sample motors. That made it possible for the producers to get a head start in creating prototypes of new mowers to show their retailer-customers. And, since the retailers have a big influence on the producer's purchase decisions, B&S salespeople also promoted the features of the new motor—and the pull appeal of the Briggs & Stratton name—to retail buyers.

The salespeople also explained the benefits of the B&S cooperative advertising arrangements and how they work. B&S provides cooperative advertising allowances and materials to all of its OEM customers and to the retailers who sell their products.

As a result of all this front-end planning, the Quattro got off to a very successful start. In fact, customer reaction to the new engine's sleek appearance, power, and reliablity was so strong that demand was double what B&S had forecast. By mid-1995, the company was hard-pressed to keep up with demand.

That's one reason that during the first year B&S decided to focus the marketing effort for the Quattro primarily on the U.S. market. It didn't make sense to spend money promoting the product in foreign markets if supply would be limited. However, exports account for 21 percent of all B&S engine and parts sales, and the Quattro isn't likely to be an exception to that pattern. When the time comes for the Quattro's international rollout some changes in the domestic marketing strategies may be required. For example, while lawn and garden equipment is important in nations with developed economies, in less-developed countries the Quattro is likely to be used for other types of applications—in agricultural, marine, and other commerical markets.

1. Are there any disadvantages to Briggs & Stratton's decision to hold off introducing its new Quattro engine in international markets? Explain your thinking.

2. What are the marketing implications for Briggs & Stratton of the fact that the U.S. market for lawn mowers is in the market maturity stage?

3. Given that engines are such an important component in manufacturing lawn mowers, would it make sense for Briggs & Stratton to develop and market its own line of mowers? Explain your thinking.

4. Given B&S' ability to compete well with Japanese motorcycle producers when they tried to take market share away from Briggs & Stratton's small engines, would it make sense for Briggs & Stratton to produce a small

motorcycle—or perhaps a motorscooter—to market in India and other countries where incomes are low but demand for personal transportation is increasing? Explain your thinking.

 ### 4   Papa John's International, Inc.*

From humble beginnings in a converted broom closet in the back of a Jeffersonville, Indiana, tavern in 1984, Papa John's has become America's fastest growing pizza chain.

Founder John Schnatter was just 21 years old in early 1984 when he began his first pizza venture. As a teenager, he had learned much about the art of creating a good pie through various jobs at a number of pizzerias. After graduating from Ball State University, John managed Mick's Lounge, a bar co-owned by his father in their hometown of Jeffersonville, Indiana. The bar was on the brink of bankruptcy. John implemented several pricing and marketing changes and began offering fresh pizza as an additional source of revenue.

"One night, I got a sledge hammer and tore down the closet to make an 8-foot by 10-foot kitchen, basically just enough for an oven," recalls Schnatter. The new product addition worked well. With an initial investment of $1,600 for equipment and ingredients, he pounded out enough pizzas to save the lounge.

With bigger profits in mind, John leased a nearby storefront in 1985, which became the first Papa John's, and by the following year he had sold the first franchise.

Then, as now, the goal was to offer a high-quality pizza, priced to be an excellent value.

CEO John and his brother Chuck (senior vice president) are of German-Irish descent and they like their pizza "with a sweeter sauce than most, I guess," says Chuck. They feel the most important element of a good pizza is the crust, so theirs is made with "a thinner, rather than a bready crust." And the pizzas are made with fresh dough, real mozzarella cheese, and sauce from fresh tomatoes, not concentrate.

To keep its profits up, Papa John's also follows a number of cost-containment approaches. Through its wholly-owned commissary system (PJ Food Service) Papa John's supplies fresh pizza dough, as well as food and paper products, to each restaurant twice weekly. Besides enabling the company to closely monitor and control product quality and consistency, Papa John's benefits from volume purchase discounts on the food and paper products. The four regional commissaries now in place will allow Papa John's to serve a total of 1,200 restaurants in

the 20 states in which the company and its franchisees now operate.

A focused menu also allows Papa John's to maintain quality and control costs. It's limited to pizza, bread sticks, cheese sticks, and canned soft drinks. However, Papa John's provides a buttery "special garlic sauce"—for dipping pizza crust—and two pepperoncini peppers with each pie to help give the perception of added value. Unlike its major competitors who have added items like buffalo wings and new types of pizza, Papa John's is determined to continue its simplified menu. Says CEO Schnatter, "We will not be adding more menu items. We feel that if we do what we do better—and better than anyone else—then we will maximize profits." Adds company president J. Daniel Holland, "We've learned that if you're willing to do it right and do it *consistently* right and not lose your focus, you can be successful, no matter *how many* players are in a particular market."

Another cost-containment effort involves minimizing site costs. Most new Papa John's restaurants are built into existing buildings (in retail strip developments, for example) rather than in new freestanding structures. And by emphasizing delivery and take-out sales rather than sit-down dining, the average size is kept down to 1,200 to 1,500 square feet (no dough-making machines required). "Pull In, Pull Out" is the norm in Papa John's. The red, green, and white decor emphasizes cleanliness more than coziness; there is no enticement to linger.

Both the company and its franchisees purchase equipment packages from the company's J-Town Equipment Division—which provides a cost-effective means of opening a restaurant. As a result, a new Papa John's restaurant can be capitalized for $125,000 to $150,000, which makes it easier to earn an attractive return on investment.

Finally, the employee training and incentive programs are structured to exemplify the Japanese-like principle of continuous improvement. All store managers and supervisors are required to complete a two-week training program at one of eight regional training centers. Store managers are trained and certified at every store position: order-taking, dough-slapping, pizza-topping, routing, and delivery. The company provides an on-site training crew three days before and after the opening of a franchisee's first two restaurants, and ongoing supervision through company-employed franchise consultants. An employee stock purchase plan is also in place; employees who have been with the company a year are awarded options to buy shares of the company's common stock. The company policy states, "We feel there is no limit to what can be accomplished when the right people are put in the right environment. We are dedicated to constant and never-ending improvement." Adds CEO Schnatter, "It's like playing sports: Do you want an occasional excellent

---

*This case and the script for the accompanying video were prepared by Phillip B. Niffenegger.

game, or a *game of excellence* every day? We strive for excellence every day."

Papa John's is headquartered in Louisville, a 15-minute drive from its broom closet beginnings. Its growth strategy is to cluster company-owned restaurants in regional markets, from Louisville to Orlando and Atlanta, which allows it to take advantage of distribution efficiencies from its commissaries in those areas. Targeted regional ad campaigns are run to maximize consumer awareness, with expansion taking place to fill in the circles surrounding the core markets and avoid cannibalization of existing restaurant sales.

So far the strategy has worked well. In 1994, sales were up 81 percent to $89.2 million, with profits increasing 77 percent from 1993 to $7.2 million. Sales in the 133 company-owned restaurants were up to $670,000 (from $653,000 in 1993), about $200,000 above the average for Domino's and 10 percent over Pizza Hut's. The company and its franchisees have aggressive plans to open 525 new restaurants during 1995 and 1996. Meanwhile, Domino's profits for 1994 were up by 15 percent (to $31 million) while Pizza Hut's fell by 21 percent for the year.

Nonetheless, Schnatter is determined to avoid potential problems of overexpansion: "We'll build them one at a time; and, as long as we can do them and do them well, we'll continue to grow. And, if we can't, then we'll stop at that point and make sure we're building the company properly."

1. What factors account for Papa John's strong growth rate?
2. What are the potential advantages and disadvantages of Papa John's working with both company-owned restaurants and franchisees?
3. Should Papa John's follow the lead of Pizza Hut and Domino's and expand its menu as a way of attracting additional customers? Why or why not?

5 Jewish Hospital*

The year was 1987, and health care providers were faced with rapidly changing competitive and regulatory environments. These market forces prompted senior managers at Louisville, Kentucky's Jewish Hospital to issue a "call to accountability" to the various departments within their organization. That is, all parts of the organization participated in a cost-benefit analysis that required them to prove that they contributed more to the organization than they took from it.

This call to accountability led to a change in direction for Jewish Hospital's marketing activities. The hospital had traditionally used a centralized approach in which one department was responsible for the marketing activities of the various operating units. The new approach recognizes that the hospital has various product lines (e.g., heart care, outpatient care, organ transplantation, and hand and microsurgery)—and a manager is responsible for each product line. These managers are responsible for their lines' marketing activities, revenue, expenses, and profits.

The need to develop marketing programs that are specific to each product line led to discussions between the hospital's top management and Doe-Anderson advertising agency of Louisville. Together, they developed a financially accountable, integrated approach to each product line's marketing communications program. The four guidelines described below were established for each program.

First, each program would have clear-cut objectives. Jewish Hospital's heart care services was the first of the product lines to be promoted under the new approach. The objective of the heart care communications program was to reestablish Jewish Hospital as the number one heart hospital in the Louisville market area. Initially, outcomes would be measured in terms of the percentage of the population who considered Jewish Hospital to be the leading provider of heart care.

Second, advertising would focus on specific product lines and be presented in a public service–type format. For example, one 30-second heart care advertisement showed a shooting-range target with a human silhouette and a heart located in the center of the silhouette's chest. Viewers heard the sound of gun shots and saw bullet holes appear in the heart as they were given the admonition, "When chest pain strikes, get to the Emergency Heart Center at Jewish Hospital immediately to minimize damage to your heart . . . because ignoring chest pain is like playing with a loaded gun."

Most marketing communications contained direct response mechanisms. A broadcast entitled "The Heart Special" was one part of the communications program that generated a particularly large number of responses from potential patients. This one-hour television program was broadcast during prime viewing time on two separate occasions. And each broadcast generated over 6,000 telephone calls! "The Heart Special" provided information about the risk factors for a heart attack, the early warning signs of a heart attack, and procedures to follow should a heart attack occur. Testimonials and slice-of-life vignettes presented throughout the program underscored

---

*This case and the script for the accompanying video were prepared by W. Glynn Mangold. He would like to thank Mr. David Fleming, senior vice president of Jewish Hospital Healthcare Services, for providing information in the case and for his constructive suggestions during its preparation.

the need for those experiencing the early warning signs of a heart attack to seek help. Telephone numbers were presented on-screen and viewers were invited to call with questions or to receive additional information. The telephone bank, staffed by doctors and nurses, was shown to viewers in a format similar to those often used in telethons for public TV or other nonprofit organizations.

Third, Jewish Hospital's integrated communications program provided opportunities for personal contact between hospital personnel and potential patients. Thousands of personal contacts were made at the hospital's Health Information Centers. These centers, strategically located in various high-traffic shopping malls in the Louisville metropolitan area, were staffed by registered nurses who provided a variety of services to visitors. For example, a visitor to a Health Information Center could have his or her blood pressure checked, cholesterol screened, or could use the center's library to access material about the treatment of diabetes. Seminars on various medical topics were also provided by physicians and other health professionals. For instance, a cardiologist might discuss the risk factors for a heart attack and the ways to reduce susceptibility to heart attacks.

Finally the integrated communications program achieved financial accountability through a database-oriented patient tracking system. This system enabled management to track all patient encounters from the point at which the patient had initial contact with the hospital. For example, a point of initial contact may have been a visit to a Health Information Center, a telephone call made in response to "The Heart Special," a visit to the emergency room, or an admission into the hospital. The following example of a fictitious patient illustrates how the patient tracking system monitors patient contact and provides evidence about the effectiveness of the marketing effort:

1. Mr. Smith, whose father and grandfather died of heart attacks at early ages, watched "The Heart Special" on television. He called the telephone number provided during the program to request more information about the early warning signs of a heart attack. The information was immediately mailed to the address he provided.

2. A couple of weeks later, Mr. Smith noticed one of Jewish Hospital's Health Information Centers at a mall where he shops. Remembering "The Heart Special" and the literature he requested, he stopped in to have his blood pressure checked. While there, he gave his name and address to the staff and briefly talked with a nurse about the need to reduce the level of fat in his diet.

3. Mr. Smith's awareness of the early warning signs of a heart attack and the need to monitor his cardiac health were periodically reinforced by Jewish Hospital's television advertisements. The advertising that featured the target with a human silhouette and bullet holes that appeared in the chest seemed particularly poignant to Mr. Smith.

4. Several months later, Mr. Smith experienced some chest pain while working in his garden. He immediately sought treatment at Jewish Hospital's emergency room.

5. After an initial examination, Mr. Smith was admitted to the hospital and, a few days later, received bypass surgery for his heart condition. Mr. Smith's medical insurance paid for his $30,000 hospital bill.

If Mr. Smith had been a real person, the patient tracking system would have provided Jewish Hospital's management with valuable insight about the effectiveness of its communications program. For example, the system would have indicated that the first point of contact occurred in response to "The Heart Special." His visit to the Health Information Center would have also been recorded. Such information provides management with strong evidence about the ability of "The Heart Special" and the Health Information Centers to attract cardiac patients to Jewish Hospital.

Although our fictitious Mr. Smith benefited from the television advertisements he saw, he did not contact the hospital in response to those advertisements. That is why the information provided by the patient tracking system was supplemented with patient interviews during the first six months of the heart care communications program. The patient interviews indicated that television advertising was by far the most effective media for bringing patients into the hospital. During those interviews, numerous patients indicated that Jewish Hospital's advertising had saved their lives by prompting them to go to the Emergency Heart Center when they experienced the symptoms of a heart attack. In fact, each of the media used by the Emergency Heart Center (television, radio, newspaper, magazine, and billboards) was credited with saving at least one person's life!

By 1993, Jewish Hospital was the 16th largest heart center in the United States! This success is attributable to the high quality of service provided by Jewish Hospital's physicians, nurses, and other medical personnel. But it can also be largely attributed to the hospital's financially accountable, integrated marketing communications program. The number of open heart surgeries conducted at Jewish Hospital increased significantly between 1990 and 1994, and another substantial increase was forecast for 1995.

The program also enhanced the hospital's image among consumers. Survey research showed that the percent of people who considered Jewish Hospital to be the best provider of heart care increased substantially between 1990 and 1995. The percent of people who considered Jewish Hospital's major competitor to be the best provider decreased significantly during the same period.

1. What are the major strengths of Jewish Hospital's integrated, financially accountable marketing communications program?

2. What are the weaknesses or limitations of Jewish Hospital's integrated, financially accountable marketing communications program?

3. Jewish Hospital is also the home of a world-renowned team of hand surgeons. How would Jewish Hospital go about developing a similar program for hand surgery? What types of integrated marketing communications might be used in such a program?

Cases

Guide to the Use of These Cases

Cases can be used in many ways. And the same case can be analyzed several times for different purposes.

"Suggested cases" are listed at the end of most chapters, but these cases can also be used later in the text. The main criterion for the order of these cases is the amount of technical vocabulary—or text principles—that are needed to read the case meaningfully. The first cases are "easiest" in this regard. This is why an early case can easily be used two or three times—with different emphasis. Some early cases might require some consideration of Product and Price, for example, and might be used twice, perhaps regarding product planning and, later, pricing. In contrast, later cases, which focus more on Price, might be treated more effectively *after* the Price chapters are covered.

In some of the cases, we have disguised certain information—such as names or proprietary financial data—at the request of the people or firms involved in the case. However, such changes do not alter the basic substantive problems you will be analyzing in a case.

1 McDonald's "Seniors" Restaurant

Patty Maloney is manager of a McDonald's restaurant in a city with many "seniors." She has noticed that some senior citizens have become not just regular patrons—but patrons who come for breakfast and stay on until about 3 PM. Many of these older customers were attracted initially by a monthly breakfast special for people aged 55 and older. The meal costs $1.99, and refills of coffee are free. Every fourth Monday, between 100 and 150 seniors jam Patty's McDonald's for the special offer. But now almost as many of them are coming every day—turning the fast-food restaurant into a meeting place. They sit for hours with a cup of coffee, chatting with friends. On most days, as many as 100 will stay from one to four hours.

Patty's employees have been very friendly to the seniors, calling them by their first names and visiting with them each day. In fact, Patty's McDonald's is a happy place—with her employees developing close relationships with the seniors. Some employees have even visited customers who have been hospitalized. "You know," Patty says, "I really get attached to the customers. They're like my family. I really care about these people." They are all "friends" and being friendly with the customers is a part of McDonald's corporate philosophy.

These older customers are an orderly group—and very friendly to anyone who comes in. Further, they are neater than most customers, and carefully clean up their tables before they leave. Nevertheless, Patty is beginning to wonder if anything should be done about her growing "nonfast-food" clientele. There's no crowding problem yet during the time when the seniors like to come. But if the size of the senior citizen group continues to grow, crowding could become a problem. Further, Patty is concerned that her restaurant might come to be known as an "old people's" restaurant—which might discourage some younger customers. And if customers felt the restaurant was crowded, some might feel that they wouldn't get fast service. On the other hand, a place that seems busy might be seen as "a good place to go" and a "friendly place."

Patty also worries about the image she is projecting. McDonald's is a fast-food restaurant, and normally customers are expected to eat and run. Will allowing people to stay and visit change the whole concept? In the extreme, Patty's McDonald's might become more like a European-style restaurant where the customers are never rushed—and feel very comfortable about lingering over coffee for an hour or two! Patty knows that the amount her senior customers spend is similar to the average customer's purchase—but the seniors do use the facilities for a much longer time. However, most of the older customers leave McDonald's by 11:30—before the noon crowd comes in.

Patty is also concerned about another possibility. If catering to seniors is OK, then should she do even more with this age group? In particular, she is considering offering bingo games during the slow morning hours—9 AM to 11 AM. Bingo is popular with some seniors, and this could be a new revenue source—beyond the extra food and drink purchases that probably would result. She figures she could charge $5 per person for the two-hour period and run it with two underutilized employees. The prizes would be coupons for purchases at her store (to keep it legal) and would amount to about two-thirds of the bingo receipts (at retail prices). The party room area of her McDonald's would be perfect for this use and could hold up to 150 people.

Evaluate Patty Maloney's current strategy regarding senior citizens. Does this strategy improve this McDonald's image? What should she do about the senior citizen market— that is, should she encourage, ignore, or discourage her seniors? What should she do about the bingo idea? Explain.

2 Agricom, Inc.

It is 1995, and Dan Martin, newly elected president of Agricom, Inc., faces a severe decline in profits. Agricom, Inc., is a 127-year-old California-based food processor. Its multiproduct lines are widely accepted under the Agricom brand. The company and its subsidiaries prepare, package, and sell canned and frozen foods—including fruits, vegetables, pickles, and condiments. Agricom, which operates more than 30 processing plants in the United States, is one of the largest U.S. food processors— with annual sales (in 1994) of about $650 million.

Until 1993, Agricom was a subsidiary of a major midwestern food processor, and many of the present managers came from the parent company. Agricom's last president recently said: "The influence of our old parent company is still with us. As long as new products look like they will increase the company's sales volume, they are produced. Traditionally, there has been little, if any, attention paid to margins. We are well aware that profits will come through good products produced in large volume."

Fred Lynch, a 25-year employee and now production manager, agrees with the multiproduct-line policy. As he puts it: "Volume comes from satisfying needs. We will can or freeze any vegetable or fruit we think consumers might want." Fred Lynch also admits that much of the expansion in product lines was encouraged by economics. The typical plants in the industry are not fully used. By adding new products to use this excess capacity, costs are spread over greater volume. So the production department is always looking for new ways to make more effective use of its present facilities.

The wide expansion of product lines, coupled with Agricom's line-forcing policy, has resulted in 88 percent of the firm's sales coming from supermarket chain stores—such as Safeway, Kroger, and A&P. Smaller stores are generally not willing to accept the Agricom policy—which requires that any store wanting to carry its brand name must be willing to carry all 65 items in the line. Fred Lynch explains, "We know that only large stores can afford to stock all our products. But the large stores are the volume! We give consumers the choice of any Agricom product they want, and the result is maximum sales." Many small retailers have complained about Agricom's policy, but they have been ignored because they are considered too small in potential sales volume per store to be of any significance.

In 1995, a stockholders' revolt over low profits (in 1994, they were only $500,000) resulted in Agricom's president and two of its five directors being removed. Dan Martin, an accountant from the company's outside auditing firm, was brought in as president. One of the first things he focused on was the variable and low levels of profits in the past several years. A comparison of Agricom's results with comparable operations of some large competitors supported his concern. In the past 13 years, Agricom's closest competitors had an average profit return on shareholder's investment of 6 to 12 percent, while Agricom averaged only 2.5 percent. Further, Agricom's sales volume, $650 million in 1994, has not increased much from the 1976 level (after adjusting for inflation)—while operating costs have soared upward. Profits for the firm were about $8 million in 1976. The closest Agricom has come since then is about $6 million—in 1984. The outgoing president blamed his failure on an inefficient sales department. He said, "Our sales department has deteriorated. I can't exactly put my finger on it, but the overall quality of salespeople has dropped, and morale is bad. The team just didn't perform." When Dan Martin confronted Jose Lopez—the vice president of sales—with this charge, his reply was, "It's not our fault. I think the company made a key mistake after World War II. It expanded horizontally—by increasing its number of product offerings—while major competitors were expanding vertically, growing their own raw materials and making all of their packing materials. They can control quality and make profits in manufacturing that can be used in promotion. I lost some of my best people from frustration. We just aren't competitive enough to reach the market the way we should with a comparable product and price."

In further conversation with Jose Lopez, Dan Martin learned more about the nature of Agricom's market. Although all the firms in the food processing industry advertise heavily, the size of the market for most processed foods hasn't grown much for many years. Further, most consumers are pressed for time and aren't very selective. If they can't find the brand of food they are looking for, they'll pick up another brand rather than go to some other store. No company in the industry has much effect on the price at which its products are sold. Chain store buyers are very knowledgeable about prices and special promotions available from all the competing suppliers, and they are quick to play one supplier against another to keep the price low. Basically, they have a price they are willing to pay—and they won't exceed it. However, the chains will charge any price they wish on a given brand sold at retail. (That is, a 48-can case of beans might be purchased from any supplier for $18.10, no matter whose product it is. Generally, the shelf price for each is no more than a few pennies different, but chain stores occasionally attract customers by placing a well-known brand on sale.)

Besides insisting that processors meet price points, as for the canned beans, some chains require price allowances if special locations or displays are desired. They also carry nonadvertised brands and/or their own brands at lower price—to offer better value to their customers. And most will willingly accept producers' cents-off coupons—which are offered by Agricom as well as most of the other major producers of full lines.

At this point, Dan Martin is trying to decide why Agricom, Inc., isn't as profitable as it once was. And he is puzzled about why some competitors are putting products on the market with low potential sales volume. (For example, one major competitor recently introduced a line of exotic foreign vegetables with gourmet sauces.) And others have been offering frozen dinners or entrees with vegetables for several years. Apparently, Agricom's managers considered trying such products several years ago but decided against it because of the small potential sales volumes and the likely high costs of new-product development and promotion.

Evaluate Agricom's present situation. What would you advise Dan Martin to do to improve Agricom's profits? Explain why.

3 Gerber Products Company

Andrea Kelly, president of Kelly Research, Inc., wants to develop a research proposal for Gerber Products Company's CEO, David Johnson, who is seriously looking for new product-market opportunities that might make sense for Gerber. David Johnson has just cleaned out some weak diversification efforts—including trucking, furniture, and toy ventures—that tended to take the company away from its core baby food business. Now he is looking for new opportunities close to the food business. But Mr. Johnson has also made it clear that Gerber may want to move beyond baby foods because only about 4 percent of U.S. households have babies—and the baby food market is *very* competitive.

Mr. Johnson (according to trade press articles) would like new ideas for "premium-quality, value-added products in niche markets." It might be possible, for example, to extend the sales of its baby food products to adults (in general) and/or senior citizens. Some of its current chunky food items are intended for older tots and might be attractive to some adults. They are no-salt, easy-to-chew items. But care may be needed in expanding into these markets. Gerber had troubles in the 1970s with some products that were intended for adult tastes—one was beef stroganoff in a baby food jar. Yet Mr. Johnson now wonders, "How come we can't develop food products that target everyone over the toddler age?"

Recent Gerber product offerings include a line of applesauce-based fruit cups, bottled water, and shelf-stable homogenized milk. All three of these seem to fit with Gerber's growth plans—offering more premium-quality, value-added products to niche markets. Further growth efforts might include products that will enable the company to get enough experience to understand a market area and be able to pursue joint ventures or acquisitions. This might include activities other than food, or at least baby food—which has become almost a commodity business. The feeling of some Gerber executives is that "opportunities must be better elsewhere—in niches that haven't been worked as hard as baby food." Some market possibilities that have been mentioned in the food-oriented trade press for a company like Gerber are: canned or frozen food items for restaurants, military commissaries, gourmet food stores, or specialty departments in chain food stores.

Mr. Johnson's background includes not only domestic but international marketing with major companies that sell cleaning products, health and beauty aids, drug products, and baked goods. So it is likely that he will be willing to consider going quite far from baby foods. And given that Gerber is a major U.S. food processor—with sales over $1 billion—it is clear the company has the production, distribution, and financial resources to consider a good-sized product-market opportunity. But are there any attractive new opportunities—or must Gerber simply copy someone else's earlier developments?

Andrea Kelly wants to develop a research proposal to find and evaluate some new opportunities for Gerber. But she wants to narrow the scope of the search somewhat so she doesn't seem to be "fishing in the whole ocean." She also wants to suggest some attractive-sounding possibilities to catch Mr. Johnson's attention. So she is asking her staff for ideas—to make her proposal more attractive.

Explain how Andrea Kelly should go about selecting possible "attractive opportunities." Suggest five product-market opportunities that might make sense for Gerber Products Company, and explain why.

4 Galloway Carpet Service, Inc.

Jane Galloway is getting desperate about her new business. She's not sure she can make a go of it—and she really wants to stay in her hometown of Petoskey, Michigan, a beautiful summer resort area along the eastern shore of Lake Michigan. The area's permanent population of 10,000 more than triples in the summer months and doubles at times during the winter skiing and snowmobiling season.

Jane spent seven years in the Navy after high school graduation, returning home in June 1994. She decided to go into business for herself because she couldn't find a good job in the Petoskey area. She set up Galloway Carpet Service, Inc. She thought that her savings would allow her to start the business without borrowing any money. Her estimates of required expenditures were: $9,000 for a used panel truck, $625 for a steam-cleaning machine adaptable to carpets and furniture, $400 for a heavy-duty commercial vacuum cleaner, $50 for special brushes and attachments, $100 for the initial supply of cleaning fluids and compounds, and $200 for insurance and other incidental expenses. This total of $10,375 still left Jane with about $3,000 in savings to cover living expenses while getting started.

One of the reasons Jane chose the cleaning business was her previous work experience. From the time she was 16, Jane had worked part-time for Joel Bullard. Mr. Bullard operates the only successful complete (carpet, furniture, walls, etc.) cleaning company in Petoskey. (There is one other cleaning company in Petoskey, but it is rumored to be near bankruptcy.)

Mr. Bullard prides himself on quality work and has a loyal clientele. Specializing in residential carpet cleaning and furniture care, Bullard has built a strong customer franchise. For 40 years, Bullard's major source of new business—besides retailer recommendations—has been satisfied customers who tell friends about his quality service. He is so highly thought of that the leading carpet and furniture stores in Petoskey always recommend Bullard for preventive maintenance in quality carpet and furniture care. Often Bullard is given the keys to the area's finest homes for months at a time—when owners are out of town and want his services. Bullard's customers are so loyal, in fact, that Vita-Clean—a national household carpet-cleaning franchise—found it impossible to compete with him. Even price-cutting was not an effective weapon against Mr. Bullard.

Jane Galloway thought that she knew the business as well as Mr. Bullard—having worked for him many years. Jane was anxious to reach her $60,000-per-year sales objective because she thought this would provide her with a comfortable living in Petoskey. While aware of cleaning opportunities in businesses such as office buildings and motels, Jane felt that the sales volume available there was small because most businesses had their own cleaning staffs. As Jane saw it, her only opportunity was direct competition with Mr. Bullard.

To get started, Jane spent $1,000 to advertise her business in the local newspaper. With this money she bought two large announcement ads and 52 weeks of daily ads in the classified section—listed under Miscellaneous Residential Services. She painted a sign on her truck and waited for business to take off.

Jane had a few customers and was able to gross about $150 a week. Of course, she had expected much more. These customers were usually Bullard regulars who, for one reason or another (usually stains, spills, or house guests), weren't able to wait the two weeks until Bullard could work them in. While these people agreed that Jane's work was of the same quality as Mr. Bullard's, they preferred Bullard's "quality care" image. Sometimes Jane did get more work than she could handle. This happened during April and May—when seasonal businesses were preparing for summer openings and owners of summer homes and condos were ready to "open the cottage." The same rush occurred in September and October—as many of these places were being closed for the winter. During these months, Jane was able to gross about $130 to $150 a day—working 10 hours.

Toward the end of her discouraging first year in business, Jane Galloway is thinking about quitting. While she hates to think about leaving Petoskey, she can't see any way of making a living there in the carpet and furniture-cleaning business. Mr. Bullard seems to have dominated the market—except in the rush seasons and for people who need emergency cleaning. And the resort housing market is not growing very fast, so there is little hope of a big increase in potential customers.

Evaluate Jane Galloway's strategy planning for her new business. Why wasn't she able to reach her objective of $60,000? What should Jane do now? Explain.

5 Union Chemical Company

Kim Lu, a chemist in Union Chemical's polymer resins laboratory, is trying to decide how hard to fight for the new product he has developed. Lu's job is to find new, more profitable applications for the company's present resin products—and his current efforts are running into unexpected problems.

During the last four years, Lu has been under heavy pressure from his managers to come up with an idea that will open up new markets for the company's foamed polystyrene.

Two years ago, Lu developed the "foamed-dome concept"—a method of using foamed polystyrene to make dome-shaped roofs and other structures. He described the

procedure for making domes as follows: The construction of a foamed dome involves the use of a specially designed machine that bends, places, and bonds pieces of plastic foam together into a predetermined dome shape. In forming a dome, the machine head is mounted on a boom, which swings around a pivot like the hands of a clock, laying and bonding layer upon layer of foam board in a rising spherical form.

According to Lu, polystyrene foamed boards have several advantages:

1. Foam board is stiff—but can be formed or bonded to itself by heat alone.
2. Foam board is extremely lightweight and easy to handle. It has good structural rigidity.
3. Foam board has excellent and permanent insulating characteristics. (In fact, the major use for foam board is as an insulator.)
4. Foam board provides an excellent base on which to apply a variety of surface finishes, such as a readily available concrete-based stucco that is durable and inexpensive.

Using his good selling abilities, Lu easily convinced his managers that his idea has potential.

According to a preliminary study by the marketing research department, the following were areas of construction that could be served by the domes:

1. Bulk storage.
2. Cold storage.
3. Educational construction.
4. Covers for industrial tanks.
5. Light commercial construction.
6. Planetariums.
7. Recreational construction (such as a golf course starter house).

The marketing research study focused on uses for existing dome structures. Most of the existing domes are made of cement-based materials. The study showed that large savings would result from using foam boards—due to the reduction of construction time.

Because of the new technology involved, the company decided to do its own contracting (at least for the first four to five years). Lu thought this was necessary to make sure that no mistakes were made by inexperienced contractor crews. (For example, if not applied properly, the plastic may burn.)

After building a few domes in the United States to demonstrate the concept, Lu contacted some leading U.S. architects. Reactions were as follows:

"It's very interesting, but we're not sure the fire marshall of Chicago would ever give his OK."

"Your tests show that foamed domes can be protected against fires, but there are no *good* tests for unconventional building materials as far as I am concerned."

"I like the idea, but foam board does not have the impact resistance of cement."

"We design a lot of recreational facilities, and kids will find a way of poking holes in the foam."

"Building codes in our area are written for wood and cement structures. Maybe we'd be interested if the codes change."

After this unexpected reaction, management didn't know what to do. Lu still thinks they should go ahead with the project. He wants to build several more demonstration projects in the United States and at least three each in Europe and Japan to expose the concept in the global market. He thinks architects outside the United States may be more receptive to really new ideas. Further, he says, it takes time for potential users to "see" and accept new ideas. He is sure that more exposure to more people will speed acceptance. And he is convinced that a few reports of well-constructed domes in leading trade papers and magazines will go a long way toward selling the idea. He is working on getting such reports right now. But his managers aren't sure they want to OK spending more money on "his" project. His immediate boss is supportive, but the rest of the review board is less sure about more demonstration projects or going ahead at all—just in the United States or in global markets.

Evaluate how Union Chemical got into the present situation. What should Kim Lu do? What should Lu's managers do? Explain.

6 Inland Steel Company

Inland Steel Company is one of the major producers of wide-flange beams in the United States. The other major producer is the U.S. Steel Corporation (now USX). A few small and lower-cost firms compete and have tended to push prices lower in a flat construction market. Typically, all interested competitors charge the same delivered price, which varies some depending on how far the customer is from either of the two major producers. In other words, local prices are higher in more remote geographic markets.

Wide-flange beams are one of the principal steel products used in construction. They are the modern version of what are commonly known as I-beams. U.S. Steel rolls a full range of wide flanges from 6 to 36 inches. Inland entered the field about 30 years ago—when it converted an existing mill to produce this product. Inland's mill is limited to flanges up to 24 inches, however. At the time of the conversion, Inland felt that

customer usage of sizes over 24 inches was likely to be small. In the past few years, however, there has been a definite trend toward the larger and heavier sections.

The beams produced by the various competitors are almost identical—since customers buy according to standard dimensional and physical-property specifications. In the smaller size range, there are a number of competitors. But above 14 inches, only U.S. Steel and Inland compete. Above 24 inches, U.S. Steel has no competition.

All the steel companies sell these beams through their own sales forces. The customer for these beams is called a structural fabricator. This fabricator typically buys unshaped beams and other steel products from the mills and shapes them according to the specifications of each customer. The fabricator sells to the contractor or owner of the structure being built.

The structural fabricator usually must sell on a competitive-bid basis. The bidding is done on the plans and specifications prepared by an architectural or structural engineering firm—and forwarded to him by the contractor who wants the bid. Although thousands of structural fabricators compete in the U.S., relatively few account for the majority of wide-flange tonnage in the various geographical regions. Since the price is the same from all producers, they typically buy beams on the basis of availability (i.e., availability to meet production schedules) and performance (i.e., reliability in meeting the promised delivery schedule).

Several years ago, Inland's production schedulers saw that they were going to have an excess of hot-rolled plate capacity in the near future. At the same time, a new production technique allowed a steel company to weld three plates together into a section with the same dimensional and physical properties and almost the same cross section as a rolled wide-flange beam. This development appeared to offer two advantages to Inland: (1) It would enable Inland to use some of the excess plate capacity. (2) Larger sizes of wide-flange beams could be offered. Cost analysts showed that by using a fully depreciated plate mill and the new welding process it would be possible to produce and sell larger wide-flange beams at competitive prices—that is, at the same price charged by U.S. Steel.

Inland's managers were excited about the possibilities—because customers usually appreciate having a second source of supply. Also, the new approach would allow the production of up to a 60-inch flange. With a little imagination, these larger sizes might offer a significant breakthrough for the construction industry.

Inland decided to go ahead with the new project. As the production capacity was converted, the salespeople were kept well informed of the progress. They, in turn, promoted this new capability to their customers—emphasizing that soon they would be able to offer a full range of beam products. Inland sent several general information letters to a broad mailing list but did not advertise. The market development section of the sales department was very busy explaining the new possibilities of the process to fabricators—at engineering trade associations and shows.

When the new production line was finally ready to go, the market reaction was disappointing: No orders came in and none were expected. In general, customers were wary of the new product. The structural fabricators felt they couldn't use it without the approval of their customers—because it would involve deviating from the specified rolled sections. And as long as they could still get the rolled section, why make the extra effort for something unfamiliar—especially with no price advantage. The salespeople were also bothered with a very common question: How can you take plate that you sell for about $460 per ton and make a product that you can sell for $470? This question came up frequently and tended to divert the whole discussion to the cost of production—rather than to the way the new product might be used.

Evaluate Inland's situation. What should Inland do?

 ## 7 Pillsbury's Häagen-Dazs

Carol Hodgman is the newly hired ice cream product-market manager for the United States for Häagen-Dazs'—the market leader in the U.S. super premium ice cream market. The company has seen its sales continue to grow during the 1980s and early 1990s, but the markets are facing significant change and very aggressive competition. Ms. Hodgman is now responsible for Häagen-Dazs' ice cream strategy planning for the United States.

Other product-market managers are responsible for Europe, Japan, and other global markets—where very rapid growth is expected, following on what happened (and happens) in the United States. Therefore, Ms. Hodgman will be expected to focus only on the United States while knowing that "everyone" will be watching her (and the United States) for clues about what may happen elsewhere.

Sales growth in super premium ice cream is slowing down in the United States, in part because of competition from other products, such as lower-calorie yogurts and ice milk. Some producers' sales, including Häagen-Dazs', are continuing to grow at attractive rates—10 to 50 percent a year. But other U.S. super premium producers are reporting flat sales—and some are going out of business.

There is also evidence that some Americans are becoming more concerned with diet and health and reducing or even eliminating super desserts. And "dessert junkies" who want to indulge without too much guilt are turning to low-fat frozen yogurt and low-calorie ice milk. This has encouraged some super premium ice cream

competitors to offer these products too. Pillsbury's Häagen-Dazs, International Dairy Queen, Inc., and Baskin and Robbins are selling frozen yogurt. And Kraft, Inc., which makes Frusen Glädjé, and Dreyer's Grand Ice Cream, Inc., are among many other ice cream makers who are promoting gourmet versions of ice milk. Some producers are even seeking government approval to call such ice milk "light ice cream."

Most ice cream products are considered economy and regular brands—priced at $2 to $3 a half gallon. But the higher priced—and higher profit—super premium products provided most of the growth in the ice cream market in the 1980s. The super premium ice cream category accounted for about 12 percent of total ice cream sales ($7 billion) in 1990 compared to almost 5 percent in 1980. Super premium ice cream, with more than 14 percent butterfat (economy ice cream has a minimum of 10 percent) is the "ultimate" ice cream product—rich, indulgent, and fashionable. It retails for $2 to $2.50 a *pint*, or $8 to $10 a half gallon.

The rapid growth of the U.S. super premium market seems to be over, as more and more consumers become concerned about fat and cholesterol (and ice cream is high in cholesterol). Some of the super premium producers remain optimistic, however. Häagen-Dazs, for example, feels that because "people like to make every calorie count—they want wonderful food." But other competitors are more concerned because they see many close competitors going out of business. The easy availability of super premium ice cream in supermarkets has hurt some competitors who sell through ice cream stores, which specialize in take-out cones, sundaes, and small containers of ice cream.

Many U.S. ice cream producers have turned to frozen yogurt for growth. A fad in the 1970s, frozen yogurt went into a long slump because many people didn't like the tart taste. But now the product has been reformulated and is winning customers. The difference is that today's frozen yogurt tastes more like ice cream.

The yogurt market leader, TCBY Enterprises, Inc., which had sales of only about $2 million in 1983, has risen to over $120 million in sales. U.S. yogurt makers are using aggressive promotion against ice cream. TCBY ads preach: "Say goodbye to high calories—say goodbye to ice cream" and "All the pleasure, none of the guilt." And the ads for its nonfat frozen yogurt emphasize: "Say goodbye to fat and high calories with the great taste of TCBY Nonfat Frozen Yogurt."

Baskin Robbins has introduced yogurt in many of its U.S. stores and has even changed its name to Baskin Robbins Ice Cream and Yogurt. Häagen-Dazs also offers yogurt in most of its stores.

A new threat to super premium ice cream comes from ice milk. Traditionally, ice milk was an economical product for families on a budget. The butterfat content was at the low end of the 2 to 7 percent range. And, in part because of this, it was dense, gummy, stringy, and had a coarse texture. But the new "gourmet" ice milk products taste better due to 6 to 7 percent butterfat, less air content, and improved processing. And they still have only about half the calories of ice cream. Some U.S. producers of these products find their sales increasing nicely. Dreyer's, for example, is experiencing rapid growth of its Dreyer's Light, which retails for about $4.50 a half gallon.

Other ice cream producers, including Häagen-Dazs, have been saying they are not planning to offer ice milk—under any name. These firms feel their brands stand for high quality and the best ingredients and they do not want to offer a cheap product. As one marketing manager put it, "Ice milk is a failure, and that is why some producers are trying to reposition it as light ice cream."

Evaluate what is happening in the ice cream market, especially regarding the apparent leveling off of the super premium ice cream market and the possible growth of the ice milk market. Should Carol Hodgman plan to have Häagen-Dazs offer an ice milk product in the near future—either under the Häagen-Dazs brand or another brand? Why?

8 Maria's Place

Maria Forlenza, the owner of Maria's Place, is reviewing the slow growth of her restaurant. She's also thinking about the future and wondering if she should change her strategy. In particular, she is wondering if she should join a fast-food or family restaurant franchise chain. Several are located near her, but there are many franchisors without local restaurants. She has heard that with help from the franchisors, some of these places gross $500,000 to $1 million a year. Of course, she would have to follow someone else's strategy—and thereby lose her independence, which she doesn't like to think about. But those sales figures do sound good, and she has also heard that the return to the owner-manager (including salary) can be over $100,000 per year.

Maria's Place is a fairly large restaurant—about 2,000 square feet—located in the center of a small shopping center completed early in 1993. In addition to Maria's restaurant, other businesses in the shopping center include a supermarket, a beauty shop, a liquor store, a hardware-variety store, and a video rental store. Ample parking space is available.

The shopping center is located in a residential section of a growing suburb in the East—along a heavily traveled major traffic route. The nearby population is mostly middle-income Italian-American families.

Maria's sells mainly full-course "home-cooked" Italian-style dinners (no bar) at moderate prices. Maria's

is owned and managed by Maria Forlenza. She graduated from a local high school and a nearby university and has lived in this town with her husband and two children for many years. She has been self-employed in the restaurant business since her graduation from college in 1972. Her most recent venture—before opening Maria's—was a large restaurant that she operated successfully with her brother from 1983 to 1989. In 1989, Maria sold out her share because of illness. Following her recovery, Maria was anxious for something to do and opened the present restaurant in April 1993. Maria feels her plans for the business and her opening were well thought out. When she was ready to start her new restaurant, she looked at several possible locations before finally deciding on the present one. Maria explained: "I looked everywhere, but here I particularly noticed the heavy traffic when I first looked at it. This is the crossroads for practically every main road statewide. So obviously the potential is here."

Having decided on the location, Maria signed a 10-year lease with option to renew for 10 more years, and then eagerly attacked the problem of outfitting the almost empty store space in the newly constructed building. She tiled the floor, put in walls of surfwood, installed plumbing and electrical fixtures and an extra washroom, and purchased the necessary restaurant equipment. All this cost $100,000—which came from her own cash savings. She then spent an additional $1,500 for glassware, $2,000 for an initial food stock, and $2,125 to advertise Maria's Place's opening in the local newspaper. The paper serves the whole metro area, so the $2,125 bought only three quarter-page ads. These expenditures also came from her own personal savings. Next she hired five waitresses at $175 a week and one chef at $350 a week. Then, with $24,000 cash reserve for the business, she was ready to open. (Her husband—a high school teacher—was willing to support the family until the restaurant caught on.) Reflecting her sound business sense, Maria knew she would need a substantial cash reserve to fall back on until the business got on its feet. She expected this to take about one year. She had no expectations of getting rich overnight.

The restaurant opened in April and by August had a weekly gross revenue of only $1,800. Maria was a little discouraged with this, but she was still able to meet all her operating expenses without investing any new money in the business. By September business was still slow, and Maria had to invest an additional $2,000 in the business just to survive.

Business had not improved in November, and Maria stepped up her advertising—hoping this would help. In December, she spent $800 of her cash reserve for radio advertising—10 late-evening spots on a news program at a station that aims at middle-income America. Maria also spent $1,100 more during the next several weeks for some metro newspaper ads.

By April 1994, the situation had begun to improve, and by June her weekly gross was up to between $2,100 and $2,300. By March 1995, the weekly gross had risen to about $2,800. Maria increased the working hours of her staff six to seven hours a week—and added another cook to handle the increasing number of customers. Maria was more optimistic for the future because she was finally doing a little better than breaking even. Her full-time involvement seemed to be paying off. She had not put any new money into the business since the summer of 1994 and expected business to continue to rise. She had not yet taken any salary for herself, even though she had built up a small surplus of about $6,000. Instead, she planned to put in a bigger air-conditioning system at a cost of $4,000—and was also planning to use what salary she might have taken for herself to hire two new waitresses to handle the growing volume of business. And she saw that if business increased much more she would have to add another cook.

Evaluate Maria's past and present marketing strategy. What should she do now? Should she seriously consider joining a franchise chain?

9 Mountain View Lodge

Jack Roth is trying to decide whether he should make some minor changes in the way he operates his Mountain View Lodge or if he should join either the Days Inn or Holiday Inn motel chains. Some decision must be made soon because his present operation is losing money. But joining either of the chains will require fairly substantial changes, including new capital investment if he goes with Holiday Inn.

Jack bought the recently completed 60-room motel two years ago after leaving a successful career as a production manager for a large producer of industrial machinery. He was looking for an interesting opportunity that would be less demanding than the production manager job. The Mountain View is located at the edge of a very small town near a rapidly expanding resort area and about one-half mile off an interstate highway. It is 10 miles from the tourist area, with several nationally franchised full-service resort motels suitable for "destination" vacations. There is a Best Western, a Ramada Inn, and a Hilton Inn, as well as many "mom and pop" and limited-service, lower-price motels in the tourist area. The interstate highway near the Mountain View carries a great deal of traffic since the resort area is between several major metropolitan areas. No development has taken place around the turnoff from the interstate highway. The only promotion for the tourist area along the interstate highway is two large signs near the turnoffs. They show the popular name for the area and that the area is only 10 miles to the west. These signs are maintained by the

tourist area's Tourist Bureau. In addition, the state transportation department maintains several small signs showing (by symbols) that near this turnoff one can find gas, food, and lodging. Jack does not have any signs advertising Mountain View except the two on his property. He has been relying on people finding his motel as they go toward the resort area.

Initially, Jack was very pleased with his purchase. He had traveled a lot himself and stayed in many different hotels and motels—so he had some definite ideas about what travelers wanted. He felt that a relatively plain but modern room with a comfortable bed, standard bath facilities, and free cable TV would appeal to most customers. Further, Jack thought a swimming pool or any other nonrevenue-producing additions were not necessary. And he felt a restaurant would be a greater management problem than the benefits it would offer. However, after many customers commented about the lack of convenient breakfast facilities, Jack served a free continental breakfast of coffee, juice, and rolls in a room next to the registration desk.

Day-to-day operations went fairly smoothly in the first two years, in part because Jack and his wife handled registration and office duties—as well as general management. During the first year of operation, occupancy began to stabilize around 55 percent of capacity. But according to industry figures, this was far below the average of 68 percent for his classification—motels without restaurants.

After two years of operation, Jack was concerned because his occupancy rates continued to be below average. He decided to look for ways to increase both occupancy rate and profitability—and still maintain his independence.

Jack wanted to avoid direct competition with the full-service resort motels. He stressed a price appeal in his signs and brochures—and was quite proud of the fact that he had been able to avoid all the "unnecessary expenses" of the full-service resort motels. As a result, Jack was able to offer lodging at a very modest price—about 40 percent below the full-service hotels and comparable to the lowest-priced resort area motels. The customers who stayed at Mountain View said they found it quite acceptable. But he was troubled by what seemed to be a large number of people driving into his parking lot, looking around, and not coming in to register.

Jack was particularly interested in the results of a recent study by the regional tourist bureau. This study revealed the following information about area vacationers:

1. 68 percent of the visitors to the area are young couples and older couples without children.
2. 40 percent of the visitors plan their vacations and reserve rooms more than 60 days in advance.
3. 66 percent of the visitors stay more than three days in the area and at the same location.

4. 78 percent of the visitors indicated that recreational facilities were important in their choice of accommodations.

5. 13 percent of the visitors had family incomes of less than $24,000 per year.

6. 38 percent of the visitors indicated that it was their first visit to the area.

After much thought, Jack began to seriously consider affiliating with a national motel chain in hopes of attracting more customers and maybe protecting his motel from the increasing competition. There were constant rumors that more motels were being planned for the area. After some investigating, he focused on two national chain possibilities: Days Inn and Holiday Inn. Neither had affiliates in the area.

Days Inn of America, Inc., is an Atlanta-based chain of economy lodgings. It has been growing rapidly—and is willing to take on new franchisees. A major advantage of Days Inn is that it would not require a major capital investment by Jack. The firm is targeting people interested in lower-priced motels—in particular, senior citizens, the military, school sports teams, educators, and business travelers. In contrast, Holiday Inn would probably require Jack to upgrade some of his facilities, including adding a swimming pool. The total new capital investment would be between $300,000 and $500,000 depending on how fancy he got. But then Jack would be able to charge higher prices—perhaps $75 per day on the average, rather than the $45 per day per room he's charging now.

The major advantages of going with either of these national chains would be their central reservation system—and their national names. Both companies offer toll-free reservation lines—nationwide—which produce about 40 percent of all bookings in affiliated motels.

A major difference between the two national chains is their method of promotion. Days Inn uses little TV advertising and less print advertising than Holiday Inn. Instead, Days Inn emphasizes sales promotions. In a recent campaign, for example, Blue Bonnet margarine users could exchange proof-of-purchase seals for a free night at a Days Inn. This tie-in led to the Days Inn system *selling* an additional 10,000 rooms. Further, Days Inn operates a September Days Club for over 300,000 senior citizens who receive such benefits as discount rates and a quarterly travel magazine. This club accounts for about 10 percent of the chain's room revenues.

Both firms charge 8 percent of gross room revenues for belonging to their chain—to cover the costs of the reservation service and national promotion. This amount is payable monthly. In addition, franchise members must agree to maintain their facilities—and make repairs and improvements as required. Failure to maintain facilities can result in losing the franchise. Periodic inspections are conducted as part of supervising the whole chain and helping the members operate more effectively.

Evaluate Jack Roth's present strategy. What should he do? Explain.

10 Fulton's Ice Arena

Matt O'Keefe, the manager of Fulton's Ice Arena, is trying to decide what strategies to use to increase profits.

Fulton's Ice Arena is an ice-skating rink with a conventional hockey rink surface (85 feet × 200 feet). It is the only indoor ice rink in a northern U.S. city of about 450,000. The city's recreation department operates some outdoor rinks in the winter, but they don't offer regular ice-skating programs because of weather variability.

Matt runs a successful hockey program that is more than breaking even—but this is about all he can expect if he only offers hockey. To try to increase his profits, Matt is trying to expand and improve his public skating program. With such a program, he could have as many as 700 people in a public session at one time, instead of limiting the use of the ice to 12 to 24 hockey players per hour. While the receipts from hockey can be as high as $175 an hour (plus concession sales), the receipts from a two-hour public skating session—charging $4 per person—could yield up to $2,800 for a two-hour period (plus much higher concession sales). The potential revenue from such large public skating sessions could make Fulton's Ice Arena a really profitable operation. But, unfortunately, just scheduling public sessions doesn't mean that a large number will come. In fact, only a few prime times seem likely: Friday and Saturday evenings and Saturday and Sunday afternoons.

Matt has included 14 public skating sessions in his ice schedule, but so far they haven't attracted as many people as he hoped. In total, they only generate a little more revenue than if the times were sold for hockey use. Offsetting this extra revenue are extra costs. More staff people are needed to handle a public skating session—guards, a ticket seller, skate rental, and more concession help. So the net revenue from either use is about the same. He could cancel some of the less attractive public sessions—like the noon-time daily sessions, which have very low attendance—and make the average attendance figures look a lot better. But he feels that if he is going to offer public skating he must have a reasonable selection of times. He does recognize, however, that the different public skating sessions do seem to attract different people and, really, different kinds of people.

The Saturday and Sunday afternoon public skating sessions have been the most successful—with an average of 200 people attending during the winter season. Typically, this is a "kid-sitting" session. More than half of the patrons are young children who have been dropped off by their parents for several hours, but there are also some family groups.

In general, the kids and the families have a good time—and a fairly loyal group comes every Saturday and/or Sunday during the winter season. In the spring and fall, however, attendance drops about in half, depending on how nice the weather is. (Matt schedules no public sessions in the summer—focusing instead on hockey clinics and figure skating.)

The Friday and Saturday evening public sessions are a big disappointment. The sessions run from 8 until 10—a time when he had hoped to attract teenagers and young adult couples. At $4 per person, plus $1 for skate rental, this would be an economical date. In fact, Matt has seen quite a few young couples—and some keep coming back. But he also sees a surprising number of 8-to-12-year-olds who have been dropped off by their parents. The younger kids tend to race around the rink playing tag. This affects the whole atmosphere—making it less appealing for dating couples and older patrons.

Matt has been hoping to develop a teenage and young-adult market for a "social activity"—adapting the format used by roller-skating rinks. Their public skating sessions feature a variety of couples-only and group games as well as individual skating to dance music. Turning ice-skating sessions into such social activities is not common, however, although industry rumors suggest that a few ice-rink operators have had success with the roller-skating format. Seemingly, the ice-skating sessions are viewed as active recreation, offering exercise and/or a sports experience.

Matt installed some soft lights to try to change the evening atmosphere. The music was selected to encourage people to skate to the beat and couples to skate together. Some people complained about the "old" music; but it was "danceable," and some skaters really liked it. For a few sessions, Matt even tried to have some couples-only skates. The couples liked it, but this format was strongly resisted by the young boys who felt that they had paid their money and there was no reason why they should be kicked off the ice. Matt also tried to attract more young people and especially couples by bringing in a local rock radio station disk jockey to broadcast from Fulton's Ice Arena—playing music and advertising the Friday and Saturday evening public sessions. But this had no effect on attendance—which varies from 50 to 100 per two-hour session during the winter.

Matt seriously considered the possibility of limiting the Friday and Saturday evening sessions to people age 13 and over—to try to change the environment. He knew it would take time to change people's attitudes. But when he counted the customers, he realized this would be risky. More than a quarter of his customers on an average weekend night appear to be 12 or under. This means that he would have to make a serious commitment to building the teenage and young-adult market. And, so far, his efforts haven't been successful. He has already invested over $3,000 in lighting changes and over $9,000 promoting the sessions over the rock music radio station—with very disappointing results. Although the station's sales rep said they reached teenagers all over town, an on-air offer for a free skating session did not get a single response!

Some days, Matt feels it's hopeless. Maybe he should accept that most public ice-skating sessions are a mixed bag. Or maybe he should just sell the time to hockey groups. Still he keeps hoping that something can be done to improve weekend evening public skating attendance, because the upside potential is so good. And the Saturday and Sunday afternoon sessions are pretty good money-makers.

Evaluate Fulton's Ice Arena's situation. What should Matt O'Keefe do? Why?

⑪ Runners World

Tamara Lang, owner of the Runners World, is trying to decide what she should do with her retail store and how committed she should be to her current target market.

Tamara is 36 years old, and she started her Runners World retail store in 1984 when she was only 24 years old. She was a nationally ranked runner herself—and felt that the growing interest in jogging offered real potential for a store that provided serious runners with the shoes and advice they needed. The jogging boom helped to quickly turn Runners World into a profitable business—and Tamara made a very good return on her investment for the first five or six years. However, sales flattened out as more and more people found that jogging was hard work—and hard on the body, especially the knees. For the past three years, sales have slowly declined and Tamara has dabbled in various changes to try to recover her lost profitability.

From 1984 until 1990, Tamara emphasized Nike shoes, which were well accepted and seen as top quality. At that time, Nike's aggressive promotion and quality shoes resulted in a positive image that made it possible to get a $5 to $7 per pair premium for Nike shoes. Good volume and good margins resulted in attractive profits for Tamara Lang.

Committing so heavily to Nike seemed like a good idea when its quality was up and the name was good. But in the late 1980s Nike quality began to slip. It hurt not only Nike but retailers such as Tamara who were heavily committed to the Nike line. Now Nike has gotten its house in order again, and it has worked hard at developing other kinds of athletic shoes, including walking shoes,

shoes for aerobic exercise, basketball shoes, tennis shoes, and cross-trainers.

While Nike was making these changes and emphasizing engineering function, a number of other firms started to focus on fashion and style in their shoe lines. In addition, with this shift more and more consumers—including many who don't really do any serious exercise—were just buying running shoes as their day-to-day casual shoes. As a result, many department stores, discount stores, and regular shoe stores put more emphasis on athletic shoes in their product assortment.

All of the change has forced Tamara to reconsider the emphasis in her store and to question what she should do. As growth in sales of running shoes started to flatten out, Tamara was initially able to keep profits up by adding a line of running accessories for both men and women. Her current customers seemed to be a ready market for a carefully selected line of ankle weights, warm-up suits, athletic bras, T-shirts, and water bottles. These items offered good margins and helped with profits. However, as the number of serious runners declined, sales of these items dropped off as well and Tamara and her salespeople found that they were "pushing" products that other customers didn't want. Further, many of the sporting goods stores in the Runners World market area started to offer similar items—often at lower prices.

Tamara also tried adding specialized shoes for other types of athletic activities—like shoes for serious walkers and for aerobic exercise. She was hopeful that some of the past runners would be interested in high-quality shoes designed specifically for walking or other types of exercise. However, demand for these shoes hasn't been strong and keeping a varied line in stock—without fast turnover—is an expensive proposition.

For the past few years traffic in the store has continued to drop. In addition, an increasing number of the customers who come in the store to browse do only that—and leave without buying anything. From discussions with many of these shoppers, Tamara is pretty certain that they're more interested in style, fashion, and economy than in the high-quality shoes designed for specific athletic activities that she carries. For example, a number of customers who came in looking for "walking shoes" left quickly when they realized that Tamara's walking shoes were in the $60 and up range.

Part of the problem is that a number of retail chains offer lower-cost and lower-quality versions of similar shoes as well as related fashion apparel. Even Wal-Mart has expanded its assortment of athletic shoes—and it offers rock-bottom prices. Other chains, like Lady Foot Locker, have focused their promotion and product lines on specific target markets.

Tamara is not certain what to do. Although sales have dropped, she is still making a reasonable profit and has a relatively good base of repeat customers—primarily serious runners. She worries that she'll lose their loyalty if she shifts the store further away from her running "niche" toward fashion and casual wear. Even a change in the name of the store—to pull in more customers who are not runners—might have a serious impact on her current customers.

An important question that Tamara is debating is whether there really is a big enough market in her area for serious athletic shoes. Further, is there a market for the Nike version of these shoes that tend to emphasize function over fashion? She has already added shoes from other companies to provide customers with more choices, including some lower-priced ones. She is trying to decide if there is anything else she can do to better promote her current store and product line, or if she should think about changing her strategy in a more dramatic way. At a minimum, that would involve retraining her current salespeople and perhaps hiring more fashion-oriented salespeople.

She thinks that a small shift in emphasis probably won't make much of a difference. Actually, that's what she's tried already. But a real shift in emphasis would require that Tamara make some hard decisions about her target market and her whole marketing mix. She's got some flexibility—it's not like she's a manufacturer of shoes with a big investment in a factory that can't be changed. On the other hand, she's not certain she's ready for a big change—especially a change that would mean starting over again from scratch. She started Runners World because she was interested in running—and felt she had something special to offer. Now, she worries that she's just clutching at straws without a real sense of purpose—or any obvious competitive advantage. She also knows that she is already much more successful than she ever dreamed when she started her business—and in her heart she wonders if she wasn't just spoiled by growth that came fast and easy at the start.

Evaluate Tamara Lang's present strategy. Evaluate the alternative strategies she is considering. What should she do? Why?

 Dow

Tiffany Chin, a new product manager for Dow, must decide what to do with a new engine cooling system product that is not doing well compared to the company's other cooling system products. Dow is one of the large chemical companies in the United States—making a wide line of organic and inorganic chemicals and plastics. Technical research has played a vital role in the company's growth.

Recently, one of Dow's researchers developed a new engine cooling system product—EC-301. Much time and money was spent on the technical phase, involving various experiments concerned with the quality of the new product. Then Tiffany Chin took over and has been trying to develop a strategy for the product.

The engine coolant commonly used now is ethylene glycol. If it leaks into the crankcase oil, it forms a thick, pasty sludge that can cause bearing damage, cylinder scoring, or a dozen other costly and time-consuming troubles for both the operator and the owner of heavy-duty engines.

Dow researchers believed that the new product—EC-301—would be very valuable to the owners of heavy-duty diesel and gasoline trucks—as well as other heavy-equipment owners. Chemically, EC-301 uses a propanol base—instead of the conventional glycol and alcohol bases. It cannot prevent leakage, but if it does get into the crankcase, it won't cause serious problems.

The suggested list price of EC-301 is $22 per gallon—more than twice the price of regular coolants. The higher price was set because of higher production costs and to obtain a "premium" for making a better engine coolant.

At first, Chin thought she had two attractive markets for EC-301: (1) the manufacturers of heavy-duty trucks and (2) the users of heavy-duty trucks. Dow sales reps have made numerous calls. So far neither type of customer has shown much interest, and the sales reps' sales manager is discouraging any more calls for EC-301. He feels there are more profitable uses for their time. The truck manufacturer prospects are reluctant to show interest in the product until it has been proven in actual use. The buyers for construction companies and other users of heavy-duty trucks have also been hesitant. Some say the suggested price is far too high for the advantages offered. Others don't understand what is wrong with the present coolants—and refuse to talk any more about paying extra for just another me-too product.

Explain what has happened so far. What should Tiffany Chin do? Why?

13 Paper Products Corporation*

Mary Miller, marketing manager for Paper Products Corporation, must decide whether she should permit her largest customer to buy some of Paper Products' commonly used file folders under the customer's brand rather than Paper Products' own FILEX brand. She is afraid that if she refuses, this customer—Natcom, Inc.—will go to another file folder producer and Paper Products will lose this business.

---

*Adapted from a case written by Professor Hardy, University of Western Ontario, Canada.

Natcom, Inc., is a major distributor of office supplies and has already managed to put its own brand on more than 45 large-selling office supply products. It distributes these products—as well as the branded products of many manufacturers—through its nationwide distribution network, which includes 150 retail stores. Now Tom Lupe, vice president of marketing for Natcom, is seeking a line of file folders similar in quality to Paper Products' FILEX brand, which now has over 60 percent of the market.

This is not the first time that Natcom has asked Paper Products to produce a file folder line for Natcom. On both previous occasions, Mary Miller turned down the requests and Natcom continued to buy. In fact, Natcom not only continued to buy the file folders but also the rest of Paper Products' lines. And total sales continued to grow. Natcom accounts for about 30 percent of Mary Miller's business. And FILEX brand file folders account for about 35 percent of this volume.

Paper Products has consistently refused such dealer-branding requests—as a matter of corporate policy. This policy was set some years ago because of a desire (1) to avoid excessive dependence on any one customer and (2) to sell its own brands so that its success is dependent on the quality of its products rather than just a low price. The policy developed from a concern that if it started making products under other customers' brands, those customers could shop around for a low price and the business would be very fickle. At the time the policy was set, Mary Miller realized that it might cost Paper Products some business. But it was felt wise nevertheless—to be better able to control the firm's future.

Paper Products Corporation has been in business 28 years and now has a sales volume of $40 million. Its primary products are file folders, file markers and labels, and a variety of indexing systems. Paper Products offers such a wide range of size, color, and type that no competition can match it in its part of the market. About 40 percent of Paper Products' file folder business is in specialized lines such as files for oversized blueprint and engineer drawings; see-through files for medical markets; and greaseproof and waterproof files for marine, oil field, and other hazardous environmental markets. Paper Products' competitors are mostly small paper converters. But excess capacity in the industry is substantial, and these converters are always hungry for orders and willing to cut price. Further, the raw materials for the FILEX line of file folders are readily available.

Paper Products' distribution system consists of 10 regional stationery suppliers (40 percent of total sales), Natcom, Inc. (30 percent), and more than 40 local stationers who have wholesale and retail operations (30 percent). The 10 regional stationers each have about six branches, while the local stationers each have one wholesale and three or four retail locations. The regional suppliers sell directly to large corporations and to some retailers. In contrast, Natcom's main volume comes from retail sales to small businesses and walk-in customers in its 150 retail stores.

Mary Miller has a real concern about the future of the local stationers' business. Some are seriously discussing the formation of buying groups to obtain volume discounts from vendors and thus compete more effectively with Natcom's 150 retail stores, the large regionals, and the superstore chains, which are spreading rapidly. These chains—e.g., Staples, Office World, Office Max, and Office Square—operate stores of 16,000 to 20,000 square feet (i.e., large stores compared to the usual office supply stores) and let customers wheel through high-stacked shelves to supermarketlike checkout counters. These chains generate $5 million to $15 million in annual business—stressing convenience, wide selection, and much lower prices than the typical office supply retailers. They buy directly from manufacturers such as Paper Products, bypassing wholesalers like Natcom. It is likely that growing pressure from these chains is causing Natcom to renew its proposal to buy a file line with its own name.

None of Mary's other accounts is nearly as effective in retailing as Natcom—which has developed a good reputation in every major city in the country. Natcom's profits have been the highest in the industry. Further, its brands are almost as well known as those of some key producers—and its expansion plans are aggressive. And now, these plans are being pressured by the fast-growing superstores—which are already knocking out many local stationers.

Mary is sure that Paper Products' brands are well entrenched in the market, despite the fact that most available money has been devoted to new-product development rather than promotion of existing brands. But Mary is concerned that if Natcom brands its own file folders it will sell them at a discount and may even bring the whole market price level down. Across all the lines of file folders, Mary is averaging a 35 percent gross margin, but the commonly used file folders sought by Natcom are averaging only a 20 percent gross margin. And cutting this margin further does not look very attractive to Mary.

Mary is not sure whether Natcom will continue to sell Paper Products' FILEX brand of folders along with Natcom's own file folders if Natcom is able to find a source of supply. Natcom's history has been to sell its own brand and a major brand side by side, especially if the major brand offers high quality and has strong brand recognition.

Mary is having a really hard time deciding what to do about the existing branding policy. Paper Products has excess capacity and could easily handle the Natcom business. And she fears that if she turns down this business, Natcom will just go elsewhere and its own brand will cut into Paper Products' existing sales at Natcom

stores. Further, what makes Natcom's offer especially attractive is that Paper Products' variable manufacturing costs would be quite low in relation to any price charged to Natcom—that is, there are substantial economies of scale, so the "extra" business could be very profitable—if Mary doesn't consider the possible impact on the FILEX line. This Natcom business will be easy to get, but it will require a major change in policy, which Mary will have to sell to Bob Butcher, Paper Products' president. This may not be easy. Bob is primarily interested in developing new and better products so the company can avoid the "commodity end of the business."

Evaluate Paper Products' current strategy. What should Mary Miller do about Natcom's offer? Explain.

14 Multimedia Technology, Inc.

Rich Monash, manager of Multimedia Technology, Inc., is looking for ways to increase profits. But he's turning cautious after the poor results of his last effort—during the previous Christmas season. Multimedia Technology, Inc. (MT), is located along a busy cross-town street about 2 miles from the downtown of a metropolitan area of 1 million and near a large university. It sells a wide variety of products used for its different types of multimedia presentations. Its lines include high-quality still cameras and video cameras, color scanners for use with computers, and projection equipment—including 35-mm slide projectors, overhead projectors, and electronic projectors that produce large-screen versions of computer output. Most of the sales of this specialized equipment are made to area school boards for classroom use, to industry for use in research and sales, and to the university for use in research and instruction.

Multimedia Technology (MT) also offers a good selection of production-quality videotapes (including hard-to-get betacam and S-VHS tapes), specialized supplies (such as the acetates used with full-color computer printers), video and audio editing equipment, and a specialized video editing service. Instead of just duplicating videos on a mass production basis, MT gives each video editing job individual attention—to add an audio track or incorporate computer graphics as requested by a customer. This service is really appreciated by local firms that need help producing high-quality videos, for example, for training or sales applications.

To encourage the school and industrial trade, MT offers a graphics consultation service. If a customer wants to create a video or computerized presentation, professional advice is readily available. In support of this free service, MT carries a full line of computer software for multimedia presentations and graphics work.

MT has four full-time store clerks and two outside sales reps. The sales reps call on business firms, attend trade shows, make presentations for schools, and help both present and potential customers in their use and choice of multimedia materials. Most purchases are delivered by the sales reps or the store's delivery truck. Many orders come in by phone or mail.

The people who make most of the over-the-counter purchases are (1) serious amateurs and (2) some professionals who prepare videos or computerized presentation materials on a fee basis. MT gives price discounts of up to 25 percent of the suggested retail price to customers who buy more than $2,000 worth of goods per year. Most regular customers qualify for the discount.

In recent years, many amateurs have been buying relatively lightweight and inexpensive video cameras to capture family events and "memories." Frequently, the buyer is a first-time mother or father who wants to record the early development of a new baby. MT has not offered the lower-priced and lower-quality models such buyers commonly want. But Rich Monash knew that lots of such video cameras were bought and felt that there ought to be a good opportunity to expand sales during the Christmas gift-giving season. Therefore, he planned a special pre-Christmas sale of two of the most popular brands of video cameras and discounted the prices to competitive discount store levels—about $600 for one and $900 for the other. To promote the sale, he posted large signs in the store windows and ran ads in a Christmas gift-suggestion edition of the local newspaper. This edition appeared each Wednesday during the four weeks before Christmas. At these prices and with this promotion, Rich hoped to sell at least 100 cameras. However, when the Christmas returns were in, total sales were five cameras. Rich was extremely disappointed with these results—especially because trade experts suggested that sales of video cameras in these price and quality ranges were up 200 percent over last year—during the Christmas selling season.

Evaluate what Multimedia Technology is doing and what happened with the special promotion. What should Rich Monash do to increase sales and profits?

15 Kazwell, Inc.

Karen Zito, owner of Kazwell, Inc., is deciding whether to take on a new line. She is very concerned, however, because although she wants more lines she feels that something is wrong with her latest possibility.

Karen Zito graduated from a large midwestern university in 1991 with a BS in business. She worked selling cellular telephones for a year. Then Karen decided to go into business for herself and formed Kazwell, Inc. Looking for opportunities, Karen placed several ads in her local newspaper in Columbus, Ohio, announcing that she was interested in becoming a sales representative in the area.

She was quite pleased to receive a number of responses. Eventually, she became the sales representative in the Columbus area for three local computer software producers: Accto Company, which produces accounting-related software; Saleco, Inc., a producer of sales management software; and Invo, Inc., a producer of inventory control software. All of these companies were relatively small—and were represented in other areas by other sales representatives like Karen Zito.

Karen's main job was to call on possible customers. Once she made a sale, she would send the order to the respective producer, who would ship the programs directly to the customer. The producer would bill the customer, and Zito would receive a commission varying from 5 to 10 percent of the dollar value of the sale. Zito was expected to pay her own expenses. And the producers would handle any user questions—using 800 numbers for out-of-town calls.

Zito called on anyone in the Columbus area who might use the products she sold. At first, her job was relatively easy, and sales came quickly because she had little competition. Many national companies offer similar products, but at that time they were not well represented in the Columbus area.

In 1993, Zito sold $250,000 worth of Accto software, earning a 10 percent commission; $100,000 worth of Saleco software, also earning a 10 percent commission; and $200,000 worth of Invo software, earning a 5 percent commission. She was encouraged with her progress and looked forward to expanding sales in the future. She was especially optimistic because she had achieved these sales volumes without overtaxing herself. In fact, she felt she was operating at about 60 percent of her capacity and could easily take on new lines. So she began looking for other products she could sell in the Columbus area. A manufacturer of small lift trucks had recently approached her, but Karen wasn't too enthusiastic about this offer because the commission was only 2 percent on potential annual sales of $150,000.

Now Karen Zito is faced with another decision. The owner of the Metclean Company, also in Columbus, has made what looks like an attractive offer. She called on Metclean to see if the firm might be interested in buying her accounting software. The owner didn't want the software, but he was very impressed with Karen. After two long discussions, he asked if she would like to help Metclean solve its current problem. Metclean is having trouble with marketing and the owner would like Karen Zito to take over the whole marketing effort.

Metclean produces solvents used to make coatings for metal products. It sells mainly to industrial customers in the mid-Ohio area and faces many competitors selling essentially the same products and charging the same low prices. Metclean is a small manufacturer. Last year's sales were $400,000. It could handle at least four times this sales volume with ease—and is willing to expand to increase sales—its main objective in the short run. Metclean's owner is offering Karen a 12 percent commission on all sales if she will take charge of their pricing, advertising, and sales efforts. Karen is flattered by the offer, but she is a little worried because the job might require a great deal more traveling than she is doing now. For one thing, she would have to call on new potential customers in mid-Ohio, and she might have to travel up to 200 miles around Columbus to expand the solvent business. Further, she realizes that she is being asked to do more than just sell. But she did have marketing courses in college, and thinks the new opportunity might be challenging.

Evaluate Karen Zito's current strategy and how the proposed solvent line fits in with what she is doing now. What should she do? Why?

16 Blackburn Company

Frank Blackburn, owner of Blackburn Company, feels his business is threatened by a tough new competitor. And now Frank must decide quickly about an offer that may save his business.

Frank Blackburn has been a sales rep for lumber mills for about 20 years. He started selling in a clothing store but gave it up after two years to work in a lumberyard because the future looked much better in the building materials industry. After drifting from one job to another, Frank finally settled down and worked his way up to manager of a large wholesale building materials distribution warehouse in Buffalo, New York. In 1975, he formed Blackburn Company and went into business for himself, selling carload lots of lumber to lumberyards in western New York and Pennsylvania.

Frank works with five large lumber mills on the West Coast. They notify him when a carload of lumber is available to be shipped, specifying the grade, condition, and number of each size board in the shipment. Frank isn't the only person selling for these mills—but he is the only one in his area. He isn't required to take any particular number of carloads per month—but once he tells a mill he wants a particular shipment, title passes to him and he has to sell it to someone. Frank's main function is to find a buyer, buy the lumber from the mill as it's being shipped, and have the railroad divert the car to the buyer.

Having been in this business for 20 years, Frank knows all of the lumberyard buyers in his area very well—and is on good working terms with them. He does most of his business over the telephone from his small office, but he tries to see each of the buyers about once a month. He has been marking up the lumber between 4

and 6 percent—the standard markup, depending on the grades and mix in each car—and has been able to make a good living for himself and his family. The going prices are widely publicized in trade publications, so the buyers can easily check to be sure Frank's prices are competitive.

In the last few years, a number of Frank's lumberyard customers have gone out of business—and others have lost sales. The problem is competition from several national home-improvement chains that have moved into Frank's market area. These chains buy lumber in large quantities direct from a mill, and their low prices are taking some customers away from the traditional lumberyards. Some customers think the quality of the lumber is not quite as good at the big chains, and some stick with the lumberyards out of loyalty. However, if it weren't for a boom in the construction market—helping to make up for lost market share—Frank's profits would have taken an even bigger hit.

Six months ago, things got worse. An aggressive young salesman set up in the same business, covering about the same area but representing different lumber mills. This new salesman charges about the same prices as Frank but undersells him once or twice a week in order to get the sale. Many lumber buyers—feeling the price competition from the big chains and realizing that they are dealing with a homogeneous product—seem to be willing to buy from the lowest-cost source. This has hurt Frank financially and personally—because even some of his old friends are willing to buy from the new competitor if the price is lower. The near-term outlook seems dark, since Frank doubts that there is enough business to support two firms like his, especially if the markup gets shaved any closer. Now they seem to be splitting the shrinking business about equally—as the newcomer keeps shaving his markup.

A week ago, Frank was called on by Mr. Talbott of Bear Mfg. Co., a large manufacturer of windows and accessories. Bear doesn't sell to the big chains, and instead distributes its line only through independent lumberyards. Talbott knows that Frank is well acquainted with the local lumberyards and wants him to become Bear's exclusive distributor (sales rep) of residential windows and accessories in his area. Talbott gave Frank several brochures on the Bear product lines. He also explained Bear's new support program, which will help train and support Frank and interested lumberyards on how to sell the higher markup accessories. Talbott explained that this program will help Frank and interested lumberyards differentiate themselves in this very competitive market.

Most residential windows of specified grades are basically "commodities" that are sold on the basis of price and availability, although some premium and very low-end windows are sold also. The national home-improvement chains usually stock and sell only the standard sizes. Most independent lumberyards do not stock windows because there are so many possible sizes. Instead, the lumberyards custom order from the stock sizes each factory offers. Stock sizes are not set by industry standards; they vary from factory to factory, and some offer more sizes. Most factories can deliver these custom orders in two to six weeks—which is usually adequate to satisfy contractors who buy and install them according to architectural plans. This part of the residential window business is well established, and most lumberyards buy from several different window manufacturers—to ensure sources of supply in case of strikes, plant fires, and so on. How the business is split depends on price and the personality and persuasiveness of the sales reps. And, given that prices are usually similar, the sales rep–customer relationship can be quite important.

Bear Mfg. Co. gives more choice that just about any supplier. It offers many variations in ⅛-inch increments—to cater to remodelers who must adjust to many situations. One reason Talbott has approached Frank Blackburn is because of Frank's many years in the business. But the other reason is that Bear is aggressively trying to expand—relying on its made-to-order windows, a full line of accessories, and a newly developed factory support system to help differentiate it from the many other window manufacturers.

To give Frank a quick big picture of the opportunity he is offering, Talbott explained the window market as follows:

1. For commercial construction, the usual building code ventilation requirements are satisfied with mechanical ventilation. So the windows do not have to operate to permit natural ventilation. They are usually made with heavy-grade aluminum framing. Typically, a distributor furnishes and installs the windows. As part of its service, the distributor provides considerable technical support, including engineered drawings and diagrams, to the owners, architects, and/or contractors.

2. For residential construction, on the other hand, windows must be operable to provide ventilation. Residential windows are usually made of wood, frequently with light-gauge aluminum or vinyl on the exterior. The national chains get some volume with standard size windows, but lumberyards are the most common source of supply for contractors in Frank's area. These lumberyards do not provide any technical support or engineered drawings. A few residential window manufacturers do have their own sales centers in selected geographic areas, which provide a full range of support and engineering services, but none are anywhere near Frank's area.

Bear Mfg. Co. feels a big opportunity exists in the commercial building repair and rehabilitation market—sometimes called the retrofit market—for a crossover of residential windows to commercial applications, and it has designed some accessories and a factory support program to help lumberyards get this "commercial" business. For applications such as nursing homes and dormitories (which must meet commercial codes), the wood interior of a residential window is desired, but the owners and architects are accustomed to commercial grades and building systems. And in some older facilities, the windows may have to provide supplemental ventilation for a deficient mechanical system. So, what is needed is a combination of the residential *operable* window with a heavy-gauge commercial exterior "frame" that is easy to specify and install. And this is what Bear Mfg. Co. is offering with a combination of its basic windows and easily adjustable accessory frames. Two other residential window manufacturers offer a similar solution, but neither has pushed its products aggressively and neither offers technical support to lumberyards or trains sales reps like Frank to do the necessary job. Talbott feels this could be a unique opportunity for Frank.

The sales commission on residential windows would be about 5 percent of sales. Bear Mfg. Co. would do the billing and collecting. By getting just 20 to 30 percent of his lumberyards' residential window business, Frank could earn about half of his current income. But the real upside would come from increasing his residential window share. To do this, Frank would have to help the lumberyards get a lot more (and more profitable) business by invading the commercial market with residential windows and the bigger markup accessories needed for this market. Frank would also earn a 20 percent commission on the accessories—adding to his profit potential.

Frank is somewhat excited about the opportunity because the retrofit market is growing. And owners and architects are seeking ways of reducing costs (which Bear's approach does—over usual commercial approaches). But he is also concerned that a lot of sales effort will be needed to introduce this new idea. He is not afraid of work, but he is concerned about his financial survival.

Frank thinks he has three choices:

1. Take Talbott's offer and sell both products.
2. Take the offer and drop lumber sales.
3. Stay strictly with lumber and forget the offer.

Talbott is expecting an answer within one week, so Frank has to decide soon.

Evaluate Frank Blackburn's current strategy and how the present offer fits in. What should he do now? Why?

17 Gulf Coast Safe Water, Inc.*

John Davidson established his company, Gulf Coast Safe Water, Inc. (Gulf Coast), to market a product designed to purify drinking water. The product, branded as the PURITY II Naturalizer Water Unit, is produced by Environmental Control, Inc., a corporation that focuses primarily on water purification and filtering products for industrial markets.

Gulf Coast Safe Water is a small but growing business. Davidson started the business with initial capital of only $20,000—which came from his savings and loans from several relatives. Davidson manages the company himself. He has a secretary and six full-time salespeople. In addition, he employs two college students part-time; they make telephone calls to prospect for customers and set up appointments for a salesperson to demonstrate the unit in the consumer's home. By holding spending to a minimum, Davidson has kept the firm's monthly operating budget at only $4,500—and most of that goes for rent, his secretary's salary, and other necessities like computer supplies and telephone bills.

The PURITY II system uses a reverse osmosis purification process. Reverse osmosis is the most effective technology known for improving drinking water. The device is certified by the Environmental Protection Agency to reduce levels of most foreign substances, including mercury, rust, sediment, arsenic, lead, phosphate, bacteria, and most insecticides.

Each PURITY II unit consists of a high-quality 1 micron sediment removal cartridge, a carbon filter, a sediment filter, a housing, a faucet, and mounting hardware. The compact system fits under a kitchen sink or a wet bar sink. A Gulf Coast salesperson can typically install the PURITY II in about a half hour. Installation involves attaching the unit to the cold-water supply line, drilling a hole in the sink, and fastening the special faucet. It works equally well with water from a municipal system or well water and it can purify up to 15 gallons daily. Gulf Coast sells the PURITY II to consumers for $395, which includes installation.

The system has no movable parts or electrical connections and it has no internal metal parts that will corrode or rust. However, the system does use a set of filters that must be replaced after about two years. Gulf Coast sells the replacement filters for $80. Taking into consideration the cost of the filters, the system provides water at a cost of approximately $.05 per gallon for the average family.

There are two major benefits from using the PURITY II system. First, water treated by this system tastes better. Blind taste tests confirm that most consumers can tell the difference between water treated with the PURITY II and ordinary tapwater. Consequently, the unit improves the taste of coffee, tea, frozen juices, ice cubes, mixed drinks, soup, and vegetables cooked in water. Perhaps more important, the PURITY II's ability to remove potentially harmful foreign matter makes the product of special interest to people who are concerned about health and the safety of the water they consume.

The number of people with those concerns is growing. In spite of increased efforts to protect the environment and water supplies, there are many problems. Hundreds of new chemical compounds—ranging from insecticides to industrial chemicals to commercial cleaning agents—are put into use each year. Some of the residue from chemicals and toxic waste eventually enters water supply sources. Further, floods and hurricanes have damaged or completely shut down water treatment facilities in some cities. Problems like these have led to rumors of possible epidemics of such dread diseases as cholera and typhoid—and more than one city has recently experienced near-panic buying of bottled water.

Given these problems and the need for pure water, Davidson believes that the market potential for the PURITY II system is very large. Residences, both single family and apartment, are one obvious target. The unit is also suitable for use in boats and recreational vehicles; in fact, the PURITY II is standard equipment on several upscale RVs. And it can be used in taverns and restaurants, in institutions such as schools and hospitals, and in commercial and industrial buildings.

There are several competing ways for customers to solve the problem of getting pure water. Some purchase bottled water. Companies such as Ozarka deliver water monthly for an average price of $.60 per gallon. The best type of bottled water is distilled water; it is absolutely pure because it is produced by the process of evaporation. However, it may be too pure. The distilling process removes needed elements such as calcium and phosphate—and there is some evidence that removing these trace elements contributes to heart disease. In fact, some health-action groups recommend that consumers not drink distilled water.

A second way to obtain pure water is to use some system to treat tapwater. PURITY II is one such system. Another system uses an ion exchange process that replaces ions of harmful substances like iron and mercury with ions that are not harmful. Ion exchange is somewhat less expensive than the PURITY II process, but it is not well suited for residential use because bacteria can build up before the water is used. In addition, there are a number of other filtering and softening systems. In general, these are less expensive and less reliable than the PURITY II. For example, water softeners remove minerals but do not remove bacteria or germs.

---

*The original version of this case was developed by Professor Ben Enis of the University of Southern California, and it is adapted for use here with his permission.

Davidson's first year with his young company has gone quite well. Customers who have purchased the system like it, and there appear to be several ways to expand the business and increase profits. For example, so far he has had little time to make sales calls on potential commercial and institutional users or residential builders. He also sees other possibilities such as expanding his promotion effort or targeting consumers in a broader geographic area.

At present, Gulf Coast distributes the PURITY II in the 13-county Gulf Coast region of Texas. Because of the Robinson-Patman Act, the manufacturer cannot grant an exclusive distributorship. However, Gulf Coast is currently the only PURITY II distributor in this region. In addition, Gulf Coast has the right of first refusal to set up distributorships in other areas of Texas. The manufacturer has indicated that it might even give Gulf Coast distribution rights in a large section of northern Mexico.

The agreement with the manufacturer allows Gulf Coast to distribute the product to retailers, including hardware stores, plumbing supply dealers, and the like. Davidson has not yet pursued this channel, but a PURITY II distributor in Florida reported some limited success selling the system to retailers at a wholesale price of $275. Retailers for this type of product typically expect a markup of about 33 percent of their selling price.

Environmental Control, Inc., ships the PURITY II units directly from its warehouse to the Gulf Coast office via UPS. The manufacturer's $200 per unit selling price includes the cost of shipping. Gulf Coast only needs to keep a few units on hand because the manufacturer accepts faxed orders and then ships immediately—so delivery never takes more than a few days. Further, the units are small enough to inventory in the backroom of the Gulf Coast sales office. Several of the easy-to-handle units will fit in the trunk of a salesperson's car.

Davidson is thinking about recruiting additional salespeople. Finding capable people has not been a problem so far. However, there has already been some turnover, and one of the current salespeople is complaining that the compensation is not high enough. Davidson pays salespeople on a straight commission basis. A salesperson who develops his or her own prospects gets $100 per sale; the commission is $80 per unit on sales leads generated by the company's telemarketing people. For most salespeople, the mix of sales is about half and half. Gulf Coast pays the students who make the telephone contacts $4 per appointment set up and $10 per unit sold from an appointment.

An average Gulf Coast salesperson can easily sell 20 units per month. However, Davidson believes that a really effective and well-prepared salesperson can sell much more, perhaps 40 units per month.

Gulf Coast and its salespeople get good promotion support from Environmental Control, Inc. For example,

Environmental Control supplies sales training manuals and sales presentation flip charts. The materials are also well done, in part because Environment Control's promotion manager previously worked for Electrolux vacuum cleaners, which are sold in a similar way. The company also supplies print copy for magazine and newspaper advertising, and tapes of commercials for radio and television. Thus, all Gulf Coast has to do is buy media space or time. In addition, Environmental Control furnishes each salesperson with a portable demonstration unit, and the company recently gave Gulf Coast three units to be placed in models of condominium apartments.

Davidson has worked long hours to get his company going, but he realizes that he has to find time to think about how his strategy is working and to plan for the future.

Evaluate John Davidson's current marketing strategy for Gulf Coast Safe Water. How do you think he's doing so far, and what should he do next? Why?

18 Ledges State Bank

Tom Nason isn't having much luck convincing his father that their bank needs the new look and image he is proposing.

Tom Nason was recently appointed director of marketing by his father Bob Nason, long-time president of the Ledges State Bank. Tom is a recent marketing graduate of the nearby state college. He worked in the bank during summer vacations, but this is his first full-time job.

The Ledges State Bank is a profitable, family-run business located in Ledges—the county seat. The town itself has a population of only 15,000, but it serves suburbanites and farmers as far away as 20 miles. About 10 miles east is a metropolitan area of 350,000—to which many in the Ledges area commute. Banking competition is quite strong there. But Ledges has only one other downtown full-service bank—of about the same size—and two small limited-service branches of two metro banks on the main highway going east. The Ledges State Bank has been quite profitable, last year earning about $400,000—or 1 percent of assets—a profit margin that would look very attractive to big-city bankers.

Ledges State Bank has prospered over the years by emphasizing its friendly, small-town atmosphere. The employees are all local residents and are trained to be friendly with all customers—greeting them on a first-name basis. Even Tom's father tries to know all the customers personally and often comes out of his office to talk with them. The bank has followed a conservative policy—for example, insisting on 25 percent down payments on homes and relatively short maturities on loans.

The interest rates charged are competitive or slightly higher than in the nearby city, but they are similar to those charged by the other full-service bank in town. In fact, the two local banks seem to be following more or less the same approach—friendly, small-town service. Since they both have fairly convenient downtown locations, Tom feels that the two banks will continue to share the business equally unless some change is made.

Tom has an idea that he thinks will attract a greater share of the local business. At a recent luncheon meeting with his father, he presented his plan and was disappointed when it wasn't enthusiastically received. Nevertheless, he has continued to push the idea.

Basically, Tom wants to differentiate the bank by promoting a new look and image. His proposal is to try to get all the people in town to think of the bank as "The Friendly Bank." And Tom wants to paint the inside and outside of the bank in current designers' colors (e.g., pastels) and have all the bank's advertising and printed materials refer to "The Friendly Bank" campaign. The bank would give away pastel shopping bags, offer pastel deposit slips, mail out pastel interest checks, advertise on pastel billboards, and have pastel stationery for the bank's correspondence. The friendly bank message would be printed on all of these items. And all the employees will be trained to be even more friendly to everyone. Tom knows that his proposal is different for a conservative bank. But that's exactly why he thinks it will work. He wants people to notice his bank instead of just assuming that both banks are alike. He is sure that after the initial surprise, the local people will think even more positively about Ledges State Bank. Its reputation is very good now, but he would like it to be recognized as different. Tom feels that this will help attract a larger share of new residents and businesses. Further, he hopes that his "The Friendly Bank" campaign will cause people to talk about Ledges State Bank—and given that word-of-mouth comments are likely to be positive, the bank might win a bigger share of the present business.

Bob Nason is less excited about his son's proposal. He thinks the bank has done very well under his direction—and he is concerned about changing a good thing. He worries that some of the older townspeople and farmers who are loyal customers will question the integrity of the bank. His initial request to Tom was to come up with some way of differentiating the bank without offending present customers. Further, Bob Nason thinks that Tom is talking about an important change that will be hard to undo once the decision is made. On the plus side, Bob agrees that the proposal will make the bank appear quite different from its competitor. Further, people are continuing to move into the Ledges area, and he wants an increasing share of this business.

Evaluate Ledges State Bank's situation and Tom's proposal. What should the bank do to increase its market share?

19 Leisure World, Inc.

Ben Huang, owner of Leisure World, Inc., is worried about his business' future. He has tried various strategies for two years now, and he's still barely breaking even.

Two years ago, Ben Huang bought the inventory, supplies, equipment, and business of Leisure World—located on the edge of Sacramento, California. The business is in an older building along a major highway leading out of town—several miles from any body of water. The previous owner had sales of about $400,000 a year—but was just breaking even. For this reason—plus the desire to retire to southern California—the owner sold to Ben for roughly the value of the inventory.

Leisure World had been selling two well-known brands of small pleasure boats, a leading outboard motor, two brands of snowmobiles and jet-skis, and a line of trailer and pickup-truck campers. The total inventory was valued at $150,000—and Ben used all of his own savings and borrowed some from two friends to buy the inventory and the business. At the same time, he took over the lease on the building—so he was able to begin operations immediately.

Ben had never operated a business of his own before, but he was sure that he would be able to do well. He had worked in a variety of jobs—as a used-car salesman, an auto repair man, and a jack-of-all-trades in the maintenance departments of several local businesses.

Soon after starting his business, Ben hired his friend, Larry, who had a similar background. Together, they handle all selling and setup work on new sales and do maintenance work as needed. Sometimes the two are extremely busy—at the peaks of each sport season. Then both sales and maintenance keep them going up to 16 hours a day. At these times it's difficult to have both new and repaired equipment available as soon as customers want it. At other times, however, Ben and Larry have almost nothing to do.

Ben usually charges the prices suggested by the various manufacturers—except at the end of a weather season when he is willing to make deals to clear the inventory. He is annoyed that some of his competitors sell mainly on a price basis—offering 10 to 30 percent off a manufacturer's suggested list prices—even at the beginning of a season! Ben doesn't want to get into that kind of business, however. He hopes to build a loyal following based on friendship and personal service. Further, he doesn't think he really has to cut price because all of his lines are exclusive for his store. No stores within a 10-mile radius carry any of his brands, although nearby retailers offer many brands of similar products.

To try to build a favorable image for his company, Ben occasionally places ads in local papers and buys some radio spots. The basic theme of this advertising is that Leisure World is a friendly, service-oriented place to buy the equipment needed for the current season. Sometimes he mentions the brand names he carries, but generally Ben tries to build an image for concerned, friendly service—both in new sales and repairs—stressing, "We do it right the first time." He chose this approach because, although he has exclusives on the brands he carries, there generally are 10 to 15 different manufacturers' products being sold in the area in each product category—and most of the products are quite similar. Ben feels that this similarity among competing products almost forces him to try to differentiate himself on the basis of his own store's services.

The first year's operation wasn't profitable. In fact, after paying minimal salaries to Larry and himself, the business just about broke even. Ben made no return on his $150,000 investment.

In hopes of improving profitability, Ben jumped at a chance to add a line of lawn mowers, tractors, and trimmers as he was starting into his second year of business. This line was offered by a well-known equipment manufacturer who wanted to expand into the Sacramento area. The equipment is similar to that offered by other lawn equipment manufacturers. The manufacturer's willingness to do some local advertising and to provide some point-of-purchase displays appealed to Ben. And he also liked the idea that customers probably would want this equipment sometime earlier than boats and other summer items. So he thought he could handle this business without interfering with his other peak selling seasons.

It's two years since Ben bought Leisure World—and he's still only breaking even. Sales have increased a little, but costs have gone up too because he had to hire some part-time help. The lawn equipment helped to expand sales—as he had expected—but unfortunately, it did not increase profits as he had hoped. Ben needed part-time helpers to handle this business—in part because the manufacturer's advertising had generated a lot of sales inquiries. Relatively few inquiries resulted in sales, however, because many people seemed to be shopping for deals. So Ben may have even lost money handling the new line. But he hesitates to give it up because he doesn't want to lose that sales volume, and the manufacturer's sales rep has been most encouraging—assuring Ben that things will get better and that his company will be glad to continue its promotion support during the coming year.

Ben is now considering the offer of a mountain bike producer that has not been represented in the area. The bikes have become very popular with students and serious bikers in the last several years. The manufacturer's sales rep says industry sales are still growing (but not as fast as in the first two to three years) and probably will grow for many more years. The sales rep has praised Ben's service orientation and says this could help him sell lots of bikes because many mountain bikers are serious about buying a quality bike and then keeping it serviced. He says Ben's

business approach would be a natural fit with bike customers' needs and attitudes. As a special inducement to get Ben to take on the line, the sales rep says Ben will not have to pay for the initial inventory of bikes, accessories, and repair parts for 90 days. And, of course, the company will supply the usual promotion aids and a special advertising allowance of $10,000 to help introduce the line to Sacramento. Ben kind of likes the idea of carrying mountain bikes because he has one himself and knows that they do require some service year-round. But he also knows that the proposed bikes are very similar in price and quality to the ones now being offered by the bike shops in town. These bike shops are service rather than price-oriented, and Ben feels that they are doing a good job on service—so, he is concerned with how he could be "different."

Evaluate Ben Huang's overall strategy(ies) and the mountain bike proposal. What should he do now?

20 Globe Chemical, Inc.

Globe Chemical, Inc., is a multinational producer of various chemicals and plastics with plants in the United States, England, France, and Germany. It is run from its headquarters in New Jersey.

Gerry Mason is marketing manager of Globe's international plastics business. Gerry is reconsidering his promotion approach. He is evaluating what kind of promotion—and how much—should be directed to car producers and to other major plastics customers worldwide. Currently, Gerry has one salesperson who devotes most of his time to the U.S. car industry. This man is based in the Detroit area and focuses on the Big Three—GM, Ford, Chrysler—as well as the various firms that mold plastics to produce parts to supply the car industry. This approach worked well when relatively little plastic was used in each car *and* the auto producers did all of the designing themselves and then sent out specifications for very price-oriented competitive bidding. But now the whole product planning and buying system is changing—and, of course, foreign producers with facilities in the U.S. are much more important.

How the present system works can be illustrated in terms of Ford's "program management" approach—which it originally tested and refined in the 1980s on its Taurus-Sable project.

Instead of the old five-year process of creating a new automobile in sequential steps, the new system is a team approach. Under the old system, product planners would come up with a general concept and then expect the design team to give it artistic form. Next engineering would develop the specifications and pass them on to manufacturing and suppliers. There was little communication between the groups—and no overall project responsibility.

Under the new program management approach, representatives from all the various functions—planning, design, engineering, purchasing, marketing, and manufacturing—work together. In fact, representatives from key suppliers are usually involved from the outset. The whole team takes final responsibility for a car. Because all of the departments are involved from the start, problems are resolved as the project moves on—before they cause a crisis. Manufacturing, for example, can suggest changes in design that will result in higher productivity—or better quality.

In the Taurus-Sable project, Ford engineers followed the Japanese lead and did some reverse engineering of their own. They dismantled several competitors' cars, piece by piece, looking for ideas they could copy or improve. This helped them learn how the parts were assembled—and how they were designed. Further, Ford engineers carefully analyzed over 50 similar cars to find the best parts of each. The Audi had the best accelerator-pedal feel, and Toyota Supra was best for fuel-gauge accuracy. Eventually, Ford incorporated almost all of the best features into its Taurus–Sable.

In addition to reverse engineering, Ford researchers conducted the largest series of market studies the company had ever done. This led to the inclusion of additional features, such as easier-to-read gauges, oil dipsticks painted a bright yellow for faster identification, and a net in the trunk to hold grocery bags upright.

Ford also asked assembly-line workers for suggestions before the car was designed—and then incorporated their ideas into the new car. All bolts had the same-size head, for example, so workers didn't have to switch from one wrench to another.

Finally, Ford included its best suppliers as part of the program management effort. Instead of turning to a supplier after the car's design was completed, the Ford team signed long-term contracts with suppliers—and invited them to participate in product planning.

This project was so successful that most other vehicles are now developed with this approach. And Ford is not alone in the effort. Chrysler, for example, used a very similar team approach to develop its popular "cab-forward" series, including the Concorde and Intrepid. And major firms in most other industries are using similar approaches. A major outgrowth of this effort has been a trend by these producers to develop closer working relationships with a smaller number of suppliers.

For example, the suppliers selected for the Taurus project were major suppliers who had already demonstrated a serious commitment to the car industry. They had not only the facilities but also the technical and professional managerial staff who could understand—and become part of—the program management approach.

Ford expected these major suppliers to join in its total quality management push and to be able to provide just-in-time delivery systems. Ford dropped suppliers whose primary sales technique was to entertain buyers and then submit bids on standard specifications.

Because many firms have moved to these team-oriented approaches and developed closer working relationships with a subset of their previous suppliers, Gerry Mason is trying to determine if Globe's present effort is still appropriate. Gerry's strategy has focused primarily on responding to inquiries and bringing in Globe technical people as the situation seems to require. Potential customers with technical questions are sometimes referred to other customers already using the materials or to a Globe plant—to be sure that all questions are answered. But basically, all producer-customers are treated more or less alike. The sales rep makes calls and tries to find good business wherever he can.

Each Globe sales rep usually has a geographic area. If an area like Detroit needs more than one rep, each may specialize in one or several similar industries. But Globe uses the same basic approach—call on present users of plastic products and try to find opportunities for getting a share (or bigger share) of existing purchases or new applications. The sales reps are supposed to be primarily order getters rather than technical specialists. Technical help can be brought in when the customer wants it.

Gerry sees that some of his major competitors—including General Electric and Dow Chemical—are becoming more aggressive. They are seeking to affect specifications and product design from the start, rather than after a product design is completed. This takes a lot more effort and resources, but Gerry thinks it may get better results. A major problem he sees, however, is that he may have to drastically change the nature of Globe's promotion. Instead of focusing primarily on buyers and responding to questions, it may be necessary to try to contact *all* the multiple buying influences and not only answer their questions but help them understand what questions to raise—and help answer them. Such a process may even require more technically trained sales reps. In fact, it may require that people from Globe's other departments—engineering, manufacturing, R&D, and distribution—get actively involved in discussions with their counterparts in customer firms.

While Gerry doesn't want to miss the boat if changes are needed, he also doesn't want to go off the deep end. After all, many of the firm's customers don't seem to want Globe to do anything very different from what it's been doing. In fact, some say that they're very satisfied with their current supply arrangements and really have no interest in investing in a close relationship with a single supplier.

Contrast Ford Motor Company's previous approach to designing and producing cars to its program management approach, especially as it might affect suppliers' promotion efforts. Given that many other major producers have moved in the program management direction, what promotion effort should Gerry Mason develop for Globe? Should every producer in every geographic area be treated alike—regardless of size? Explain.

21 Boynton Wire and Cable, Inc.

Jack Meister, vice president of marketing for Boynton Wire and Cable, Inc., is deciding how to organize and train his sales force—and what to do about Tom Brogs.

At its plant in Pittsburgh, Pennsylvania, Boynton Wire and Cable, Inc., produces wire cable—ranging from ½ inch to 4 inches in diameter. Boynton sells across the United States and Canada. Customers include firms that use cranes and various other overhead lifts in their own operations—ski resorts and amusement parks, for example. The company's main customers, however, are cement plants, railroad and boat yards, heavy-equipment manufacturers, mining operations, construction companies, and steel manufacturers.

Boynton employs its own sales specialists to call on and try to sell the buyers of potential users. All of Boynton's sales reps are engineers who go through an extensive training program covering the different applications, product strengths, and other technical details concerning wire rope and cable. Then they are assigned their own district—the size depending on the number of potential customers. They are paid a good salary plus generous travel expenses—with small bonuses and prizes to reward special efforts.

Tom Brogs went to work for Boynton in 1965, immediately after receiving a civil engineering degree from the University of Wisconsin. After going through the training program, he took over as the only company rep in the Illinois district. His job was to call on and give technical help to present customers of wire cable. He was also expected to call on new customers, especially when inquiries came in. But his main activities were to: (1) service present customers and supply the technical assistance needed to use cable in the most efficient and safe manner, (2) handle complaints, and (3) provide evaluation reports to customers' management regarding their use of cabling.

Tom Brogs soon became Boynton's outstanding representative. His exceptional ability to handle customer complaints and provide technical assistance was noted by many of the firm's customers. This helped Tom bring in more sales dollars per customer and more in total from present customers than any other rep. He also brought in many new customers—mostly heavy equipment manufacturers in northern Illinois. Over the years, his sales have been about twice the sales rep average, and always at least 20 percent higher than the next best rep—even though each district is supposed to have about the same sales potential.

Tom's success established Illinois as Boynton's largest-volume district. Although the company's sales in Illinois have not continued to grow as fast in the last few years because Tom seems to have found most of the possible applications and won a good share for Boynton, the replacement market has been steady and profitable. This fact is mainly due to Tom Brogs. As one of the purchasing managers for a large machinery manufacturer mentioned, "When Tom makes a recommendation regarding use of our equipment and cabling, even if it is a competitor's cable we are using, we are sure it's for the best of our company. Last week, for example, a cable of one of his competitors broke, and we were going to give him a contract. He told us it was not a defective cable that caused the break, but rather the way we were using it. He told us how it should be used and what we needed to do to correct our operation. We took his advice and gave him the contract as well!"

Four years ago, Boynton introduced a unique and newly patented wire sling device for holding cable groupings together. The sling makes operations around the cable much safer—and its use could reduce both injuries and lost-time costs due to accidents. The slings are expensive—and the profit margin is high. Boynton urged all its representatives to push the sling, but the only sales rep to sell the sling with any success was Tom Brogs. Eighty percent of his customers are currently using the wire sling. In other areas, sling sales are disappointing.

As a result of Tom's success, Jack Meister is now considering forming a separate department for sling sales and putting Tom Brogs in charge. His duties would include traveling to the various sales districts and training other representatives to sell the sling. The Illinois district would be handled by a new rep.

Evaluate Jack Meister's strategy(ies). What should he do about Tom Brogs—and his sales force? Explain.

Comfort Furniture Store

Jean Mead, owner of Comfort Furniture Store, is discouraged with her salespeople and is even thinking about hiring some new blood. Ms. Mead has been running Comfort Furniture Store for 10 years and has slowly built the sales to $3.5 million a year. Her store is located on the outskirts of a growing city of 275,000 population. This is basically a factory city, and she has deliberately selected blue-collar workers as her target market. She carries some higher-priced furniture lines but emphasizes budget combinations and easy credit terms.

TABLE 1

In shopping for furniture I found (find) that	Demographic Groups			
	Group A	Group B	Group C	Group D
I looked at furniture in many stores before I made a purchase.	78%	72%	52%	50%
I went (am going) to only one store and bought (buy) what I found (find) there.	2	5	10	11
To make my purchase I went (am going) back to one of the stores I shopped in previously.	63	59	27	20
I looked (am looking) at furniture in no more than three stores and made (will make) my purchase in one of these.	20	25	40	45
I like a lot of help in selecting the right furniture.	27	33	62	69
I like a very friendly salesperson.	23	28	69	67

Ms. Mead is concerned that she may have reached the limit of her sales growth—her sales have not been increasing during the last two years even though total furniture sales have been increasing in the city as new people move in. Her newspaper advertising seems to attract her target customers, but many of these people come in, shop around, and leave. Some of them come back—but most do not. She thinks her product selections are very suitable for her target market and is concerned that her salespeople don't close more sales with potential customers. She has discussed this matter several times with her 10 salespeople. Her staff feels they should treat customers the way they personally want to be treated. They argue that their role is to answer questions and be helpful when asked—not to make suggestions or help customers make decisions. They think this would be too "hard sell."

Ms. Mead says their behavior is interpreted as indifference by the customers attracted to the store by her advertising. She has tried to convince her salespeople that customers must be treated on an individual basis—and that some customers need more help in looking and deciding than others. Moreover, Ms. Mead is convinced that some customers would appreciate more help and suggestions than the salespeople themselves might want. To support her views, she showed her staff the data from a trade-association study of furniture store customers (Tables 1 and 2). She tried to explain the differences in demographic groups, and pointed out that her store was definitely trying to aim at specific people. She argued that they (the salespeople) should cater to the needs and attitudes of their customers—and think less about how they would like to be treated themselves. Further, Ms. Mead announced that she is considering changing the sales compensation plan or hiring new blood if the present employees can't do a better job. Currently, the sales reps are paid $20,000 per year plus a 5 percent commission on sales.

TABLE 2   The Sample Design

Demographic Status
Upper class (Group A); 13% of sample This group consisted of managers, proprietors, or executives of large businesses; professionals, including doctors, lawyers, engineers, college professors and school administrators, and research personnel and sales personnel, including managers, executives, and upper-income salespeople above level of clerks. *Family income over $40,000*
Middle class (Group B); 37% of sample Group B consists of white-collar workers, including clerical, secretarial, salesclerks, bookkeepers, etc. It also includes school teachers, social workers, semiprofessionals, proprietors or managers of small businesses; industrial foremen, and other supervisory personnel. *Family income between $20,000 and $50,000*
Lower middle class (Group C); 36% of sample Skilled workers and semiskilled technicians were in this category along with custodians, elevator operators, telephone linemen, factory operatives, construction workers, and some domestic and personal service employees. *Family income between $10,000 and $40,000. No one in this group had above a high school education.*
Lower class (Group D); 14% of sample Nonskilled employees, day laborers. It also includes some factory operatives and domestic and service people. *Family income under $18,000. None had completed high school; some had only grade school education.*

Contrast Ms. Mead's strategy and thoughts about her salespeople with their apparent view of her strategy and especially their role in it. What should she do now? Explain.

23 Wire Solutions, Inc.

Myra Martinez, marketing manager of consumer products for Wire Solutions, Inc., is trying to set a price for her most promising new product—a space-saving shoe rack suitable for small homes or apartments.

Wire Solutions, Inc.—located in Ft. Worth, Texas—is a custom producer of industrial wire products. The company has a lot of experience bending wire into many shapes—and also can chrome- or gold-plate finished products. The company was started 13 years ago and has slowly built its sales volume to $3.2 million a year. Just one year ago, Myra Martinez was appointed marketing manager of the consumer products division. It is her responsibility to develop this division as a producer and marketer of the company's own branded products—as distinguished from custom orders, which the industrial division produces for others.

Ms. Martinez has been working on a number of different product ideas for almost a year now and has developed several designs for CD holders, cassette holders, plate holders, doll stands, collapsible book ends, and other such products. Her most promising product is a shoe rack for crowded homes and apartments. The wire rack attaches to the inside of a closet door and holds 8 pairs of shoes.

The rack is very similar to one the industrial division produced for a number of years for another company. That company sold the shoe rack and hundreds of other related items out of its "products for organizing and storing" mail-order catalog. Managers at Wire Solutions were surprised by the high sales volume the catalog company achieved with the rack. In fact, that is what interested Wire Solutions in the consumer market—and led to the development of the separate consumer products division.

Ms. Martinez has sold hundreds of the shoe racks to various local hardware, grocery, and general merchandise stores and wholesalers on a trial basis, but each time she has negotiated a price—and no firm policy has been set. Now she must determine what price to set on the shoe rack—which she plans to push aggressively wherever she can. Actually, she hasn't decided on exactly which channels of distribution to use. But trials in the local area have been encouraging, and, as noted above, the experience in the industrial division suggests that there is a large market for this type of product. The manufacturing cost on this product—when made in reasonable quantities—is approximately $1.40 if it is painted black and $1.80 if it is chromed. Similar products have been selling at retail in

the $4.95 to $9.95 range. The sales and administrative overhead to be charged to the division will amount to $90,000 a year. This will include Ms. Martinez's salary and some office expenses. She expects that a number of other products will be developed in the near future. But for the coming year, she hopes the shoe rack will account for about half the consumer products division's sales volume.

Evaluate Myra Martinez's strategy planning so far. What should she do now? What price should she set for the shoe rack? Explain.

24 A1 Photo Processors, Inc.

Kevin Masters, marketing manager of A1 Photo Processors, is faced with price-cutting and wants to fight fire with fire. But his boss feels that they should promote harder to retailers and/or final consumers and maybe add mini-minilabs in some stores to combat the minilab competition.

A1 Photo Processors, Inc., is one of the three major Colorado-based photofinishers—each with annual sales of about $8 million. A1 has company-owned plants in five cities in Colorado and western Kansas. They are located in Boulder, Pueblo, Denver, and Colorado Springs, Colorado, and Hays, Kansas.

A1 does all of its own black-and-white processing. While it has color-processing capability, A1 finds it more economical to have most color film processed by the regional Kodak processing plant. The color film processed by A1 is either off-brand film—or special work done for professional photographers. A1 has always given its customers fast, quality service. All pictures—including those processed by Kodak—can be returned within three days of receipt by A1.

A1's major customers are drugstores, camera stores, grocery stores, and any other retail outlets that offer photofinishing to consumers. These retailers insert film rolls, cartridges, negatives, and so on, into separate bags—marking on the outside the kind of work to be done. The customer gets a receipt but seldom sees the bag into which the film has been placed. The bag has the retailer's name on it—not A1's.

Each processing plant has a small retail outlet for drop-in customers who live near the plant. This is a minor part of A1's business.

The company also does direct-mail photofinishing within the state of Colorado. The Denver plant processes direct-mail orders from consumers. All film received is handled in the same way as the other retail business.

A breakdown of the dollar volume by type of business is shown in Table 1 on page 740.

All retail prices are set by local competition—and all major competitors charge the same prices. A1 sets a retail

TABLE 1

Type of Business	Percent of Dollar Volume
Sales to retail outlets	80%
Direct-mail sales	17
Retail walk-in sales	3
	100%

TABLE 2

Monthly Dollar Volume (12-month average)	Discount (2/10, net 30)
$ 0–100	33⅓%
$ 101–500	40
$ 501–$1,000	45
$1,001+	50

list price and offers each retailer a trade discount based on the volume of business generated. Table 2 shows the pricing schedule used by each of the major competitors in the Colorado-Kansas market.

All direct-mail processing for final consumers is priced at 33⅓ percent discount off the usual store price. But this is done under the Mountain Prints name—not the A1 name—to avoid complaints from retailer customers. Retail walk-in accounts are charged the full list price for all services.

Retail stores offering photofinishing are served by A1's own sales force. Each processing plant has at least three people servicing accounts. Their duties include daily visits to all present accounts to pick up and deliver all photofinishing work. The reps are not expected to call on possible new accounts. However, it is their responsibility to make daily trips to nearby bus terminals to drop off color film to be processed by Kodak and pick up color slides or prints from Kodak; buses run all day, so they're usually faster than using UPS.

Since the final consumer does not come in contact with A1, it has not advertised its retail store servicing business to final consumers. Similarly, possible retailer accounts are not called on or advertised to—except that A1 Photo Processors is listed under "Photofinishing: Wholesale" in the Yellow Pages of all telephone books in cities and towns served by the five plants. Any phone inquiries are followed up by the nearest sales rep.

The direct-mail business—under the Mountain Prints name—is generated by regular ads in the Sunday pictorial sections of newspapers serving Pueblo, Denver, Colorado Springs, and Boulder. These ads usually stress low price, fast service, and fine quality. Mailers are provided for consumers to send to the plant. Some people in the company feel this part of the business might have great potential if pursued more aggressively.

A1's president, Mr. Zang, is worried about the loss of a number of retail accounts in the $501 to $1,000 monthly sales volume range (see Table 2). He has been with the company since its beginning—and has always stressed quality and rapid delivery of the finished products. Demanding that all plants produce the finest quality, Mr. Zang personally conducts periodic quality tests of each plant through the direct-mail service. Plant managers are advised of any slips in quality.

To find out what is causing the loss in retail accounts, Mr. Zang is reviewing sales reps' reports and talking to employees. In their weekly reports, A1's sales reps report a major threat to the company—price-cutting. Speedpro, Inc.—a competitor of equal size that offers the same services as A1—is offering an additional 5 percent trade discount in each sales volume category. This really makes a difference at some stores—because these retailers think that all the major processors do an equally good job. Further, they note, consumers apparently feel that the quality is acceptable because no complaints have been heard so far.

A1 has faced price-cutting before—but never by an equally well-established company. Mr. Zang can't understand why these retailer customers would leave A1 because A1 is offering higher quality and the price difference is not that large. Mr. Zang thinks the sales reps should sell quality a lot harder. He is also considering a radio or TV campaign to consumers to persuade them to demand A1's quality service from their favorite retailer. Mr. Zang is convinced that consumers demanding quality will force retailers to stay with—or return to—A1 Photo Processors. He says: "If we can't get the business by convincing the retailer of our fine quality, we'll get it by convincing the consumer."

Mr. Zang also feels that Kevin Masters should seriously consider the pros and cons of offering A1's customers the opportunity of installing a mini-minilab in their stores—to serve customers who want immediate processing of color film into color prints. Many consumers have gone to one-hour minilab operators in the last decade. In fact, over 30 percent of photofinishing work is now done by such operators—companies like Fotomart and Moto Photo, which are often located in shopping centers. Over 15,000 such minilabs are in operation and they have taken almost all of the growth in photofinishing in recent years. Some retail chains—especially drugstores and mass-merchandisers—have even put in their own one-hour minilab operations.

As a result, A1 and similar operators have seen flat or declining sales and increasingly aggressive sales efforts as they fight for market share. Mr. Zang feels the development of more or less self-service mini-minilabs, which can process and print a roll of color film in about 30 minutes, may help A1 succeed in this increasingly competitive market. Mr. Zang is thinking of installing one of these $35,000 machines in every logical retail store willing to operate the service along with A1's present three-day photo service. The machines are the size of a small office copier, and the whole system requires as little as 18 square feet. The machines need no plumbing hookup and little monitoring after a few hours of training (which probably could be done by the sales reps who already call on the stores). Installing these machines in A1's larger volume stores might win back some of the 30 percent of the market using minilabs—without cutting much into the three-day customer business.

Kevin Masters, the marketing manager, disagrees with Mr. Zang regarding the price-cutting problem. Kevin thinks A1 ought to at least meet the price cut or cut prices up to another 5 percent wherever Speedpro has taken an A1 account. This would do two things: (1) get the business back and (2) signal that continued price-cutting will be met by still deeper price cuts. Further, he says: "If Speedpro doesn't get the message, we ought to go after a few of their big accounts with 10 percent discounts. That ought to shape them up."

With respect to installing mini-minilabs, Kevin Masters has serious reservations. His sales reps might have to become service reps and lose their effectiveness as sales reps. Also, that might slow up the pick-up and delivery activity and cause the three-day system to slip into a four-day cycle—which could open A1 accounts to three-day supplier competitors—a disaster! Also, he worries that the stores would have little incentive to promote the use of the machines because it is not their $35,000 machine! Finally, most of A1's stores—being in outlying areas—don't compete with shopping centers so they have not really felt the impact of the minilabs. But offering an in-store minilab might result in a large shift in business and loss of the present system's production economies of scale. Further, more investment will be required, but it probably won't be possible to raise the retail price much (if at all—the one-hour minilab operators usually meet the market price).

Evaluate A1's present and proposed strategies. What should it do now? Explain.

25 Injection Mfg., Inc.

Al Kelman, the marketing manager of Injection Mfg., Inc., wants to increase sales by adding sales reps rather than playing with price. That's how Al describes what Henry Kelman, his father and Injection's president, is suggesting. Henry is not sure what to do either. But he does want to increase sales, so something new is needed.

Injection Mfg., Inc.—of Long Beach, California—is a leading producer in the plastic forming machinery industry. It has patents covering over 200 variations, but Injection's customers seldom buy more than 30 different types in a year. The machines are sold to plastic forming manufacturers to increase production capacity or replace old equipment.

Established in 1952, the company has enjoyed a steady growth to its present position with annual sales of $50 million.

Twelve U.S. firms compete in the U.S. plastic forming machinery market. Several Japanese, German, and Swedish firms compete in the global market, but the Kelmans have not seen much of them on the West Coast. Apparently the foreign firms rely on manufacturers' agents, who have not provided an ongoing presence. They don't follow up on inquiries, and their record for service on the few sales they have made on the East Coast is not good. So the Kelmans are not worried about them right now.

Each of the 12 U.S. competitors is about the same size and manufactures basically similar machinery. Each has tended to specialize in its own geographic area. None has exported much because of high labor costs in the United States. Six of the competitors are located in the East, four in the Midwest, and two—including Injection—on the West Coast. The other West Coast firm is in Tacoma, Washington. All of the competitors offer similar prices and sell F.O.B. their factories. Demand has been fairly strong in recent years. As a result, all of the competitors have been satisfied to sell in their geographic areas and avoid price-cutting. In fact, price-cutting is not a popular idea in this industry. About 20 years ago, one firm tried to win more business and found that others immediately met the price cut—but industry sales (in units) did not increase at all. Within a few years, prices returned to their earlier level, and since then competition has tended to focus on promotion and avoid price.

Injection's promotion depends mainly on six company sales reps, who cover the West Coast. In total, these reps cost about $660,000 per year, including salary, bonuses, supervision, travel, and entertaining. When the sales reps are close to making a sale, they are supported by two sales engineers—at a cost of about $120,000 per year per engineer. Injection does some advertising in trade journals—less than $50,000—and occasionally uses direct mailings. But the main promotion emphasis is on personal selling. Any personal contact outside the West Coast market is handled by manufacturers' agents who are paid 4 percent on sales—but sales are very infrequent.

Henry Kelman is not satisfied with the present situation. Industry sales have leveled off and so have Injection's sales—although the firm continues to hold its share of the market. Henry would like to find a way to compete more effectively in the other regions because he sees great potential outside of the West Coast.

Competitors and buyers agree that Injection is the top-quality producer in the industry. Its machines have generally been somewhat superior to others in terms of reliability, durability, and productive capacity. The difference, however, usually has not been great enough to justify a higher price—because the others are able to do the necessary job—unless an Injection sales rep convinces the customer that the extra quality will improve the customer's product and lead to fewer production line breakdowns. The sales rep also tries to sell Injection's better sales engineers and technical service people—and sometimes is successful. But if a buyer is only interested in comparing delivered prices for basic machines—the usual case—Injection's price must be competitive to get the business. In short, if such a buyer has a choice between Injection's and another machine *at the same price*, Injection will usually win the business in its part of the West Coast market. But it's clear that Injection's price has to be at least competitive in such cases.

The average plastic forming machine sells for about $220,000, F.O.B. shipping point. Shipping costs within any of the three major regions average about $4,000—but another $3,000 must be added on shipments between the West Coast and the Midwest (either way) and another $3,000 between the Midwest and the East.

Henry Kelman is thinking about expanding sales by absorbing the extra $3,000 to $6,000 in freight cost that occurs if a midwestern or eastern customer buys from his West Coast location. By doing this, he would not be cutting price in those markets but rather reducing his net return. He thinks that his competitors would not see this as price competition—and therefore would not resort to cutting prices themselves.

Al Kelman, the marketing manager, disagrees. Al thinks that the proposed freight absorption plan would stimulate price competition in the Midwest and East—and perhaps on the West Coast. He proposes instead that Injection hire some sales reps to work the Midwest and Eastern regions—selling quality—rather than relying on the manufacturers' agents. He argues that two additional sales reps in each of these regions would not increase costs too much—and might greatly increase the sales from these markets over that brought in by the agents. With this plan, there would be no need to absorb the freight and risk disrupting the status quo. Adding more of Injection's own sales reps is especially important, he argues, because competition in the Midwest and East is somewhat hotter than on the West Coast—due to the number of competitors (including foreign competitors) in those regions. A lot of expensive entertaining, for ex-

ample, seems to be required just to be considered as a potential supplier. In contrast, the situation has been rather quiet in the West—because only two firms are sharing this market and each is working harder near its home base. The eastern and midwestern competitors don't send any sales reps to the West Coast—and if they have any manufacturers' agents, they haven't gotten any business in recent years.

Henry Kelman agrees that his son has a point, but industry sales are leveling off and Henry wants to increase sales. Further, he thinks the competitive situation may change drastically in the near future anyway, as global competitors get more aggressive and some possible new production methods and machines become more competitive with existing ones. He would rather be a leader in anything that is likely to happen—rather than a follower. But he is impressed with Al's comments about the greater competitiveness in the other markets and therefore is unsure about what to do.

Evaluate Injection's current strategies. Given Henry Kelman's sales objective, what should Injection Mfg. do? Explain.

26 Valley Packers, Inc.

Jon Dow, president of Valley Packers, Inc., is not sure what he should propose to the board of directors. His recent strategy change isn't working. And Bill Jacobs, Valley's only sales rep (and a board member), is so frustrated that he refuses to continue his discouraging sales efforts. Jacobs wants Jon Dow to hire a sales force or *something*.

Valley Packers, Inc., is a long-time processor in the highly seasonal vegetable canning industry. Valley packs and sells canned beans, peas, carrots, corn, peas and carrots mixed, and kidney beans. It sells mainly through food brokers to merchant wholesalers, supermarket chains (such as Kroger, Safeway, A&P, and Jewel), cooperatives, and other outlets—mostly in the Chicago area. Of less importance, by volume, are sales to local institutions, grocery stores, and supermarkets—and sales of dented canned goods at low prices to walk-in customers.

Valley is located in Wisconsin's Devil's River Valley. The company has more than $28 million in sales annually (exact sales data is not published by the closely held corporation). Plants are located in strategic places along the valley—with main offices in Riverside. The Valley brand is used only on canned goods sold in the local market. Most of the goods are sold and shipped under a retailer's label or a broker's/wholesaler's label.

Valley is well known for the consistent quality of its product offerings. And it's always willing to offer competitive prices. Strong channel relations were built by Valley's former Chairman of the Board and Chief Executive Officer Fritz Allshouse. Mr. Allshouse—who owns controlling interest in the firm—worked the Chicago area as the company's sales rep in its earlier years, before he took over from his father as president in 1965. Allshouse was an ambitious and hard-working top manager—the firm prospered under his direction. He became well known within the canned food processing industry for technical/product innovations.

During the off-canning season, Mr. Allshouse traveled widely. In the course of his travels, he arranged several important business deals. His 1975 and 1987 trips resulted in the following two events: (1) inexpensive pineapple was imported from Formosa and sold by Valley—primarily to expand the product line, and (2) a technically advanced continuous process cooker (65 feet high) was imported from England and installed at one of the Valley plants in February–March 1990. It was the first of its kind in the United States and cut processing time sharply.

Mr. Allshouse retired in 1994 and named his son-in-law, 35-year-old Jon Dow, as his successor. Mr. Dow is intelligent and hard working. He was concerned primarily with the company's financial matters and only recently with marketing problems. During his seven years as financial director, the firm received its highest credit rating—and was able to borrow working capital ($5 million to meet seasonal can and wage requirements) at the lowest rate ever.

The fact that the firm isn't unionized allows some competitive advantage. However, changes in minimum wage laws have increased costs. And these and other rising costs have squeezed profit margins. This led to the recent closing of two plants—as they became less efficient to operate. Valley expanded capacity of the remaining two plants (especially warehouse facilities) so they could operate more profitably with maximum use of existing processing equipment.

Shortly after Mr. Allshouse's retirement, Jon Dow reviewed the company's situation with his managers. He pointed to narrowing profit margins, debts contracted for new plant and equipment, and an increasingly competitive environment. Even considering the temporary labor-saving competitive advantage of the new cooker system, there seemed to be no way to improve the status quo unless the firm could sell direct—as it does in the local market—thereby eliminating the food brokers' 5 percent commission on sales. This was the plan decided on, and Bill Jacobs was given the new sales job. An inside sales clerk was retained to handle incoming orders.

Bill Jacobs, the only full-time outside sales rep for the firm, lives in Riverside. Other top managers do some selling—but not much. Being a nephew of Mr. Allshouse, Bill Jacobs is also a member of the board of directors. He is well qualified in technical matters and has a college degree in food chemistry. Although Bill Jacobs formerly did call on some important customers with the brokers' sales reps, he is not well known in the industry or even by Valley's usual customers.

It is now five months later. Bill Jacobs is not doing very well. He has made several selling trips and hundreds of telephone calls with discouraging results. He is unwilling to continue sales efforts on his own. There seem to be too many potential customers for one person to reach. And much negotiating, wining, and dining seems to be needed—certainly more than he can or wants to do.

Jacobs insists that Valley hire a sales force to continue the present way of operating. Sales are down in comparison both to expectations and to the previous year's results. Some regular supermarket chain customers have stopped buying—though basic consumer demand has not changed. Further, buyers for some supermarket chains that might be potential new customers have demanded quantity guarantees much larger than Valley Packers can supply. Expanding supply would be difficult in the short run—because the firm typically must contract with growers to ensure supplies of the type and quality they normally offer.

Mr. Allshouse, still the controlling stockholder, has asked for a special meeting of the board in two weeks to discuss the present situation.

Evaluate Valley's past and current strategy planning. What should Jon Dow tell Mr. Allshouse? What should Valley do now?

27 Electrotech, Inc.

Amy Wilson is trying to decide whether to leave her present job to buy into another business and be part of top management.

Wilson is now a sales rep for a plastics components manufacturer. She calls mostly on large industrial accounts—such as refrigerator manufacturers—who might need large quantities of custom-made products like door liners. She is on a straight salary of $35,000 per year, plus expenses and a company car. She expects some salary increases but doesn't see much long-run opportunity with this company.

As a result, she is seriously considering changing jobs and investing $40,000 in Electrotech, Inc.—an established Chicago (Illinois) thermoplastic molder (manufacturer). Mr. Hanson, the present owner, is nearing retirement and has not trained anyone to take over the business. He has agreed to sell the business to Steve Plunkett, a lawyer, who has invited Amy Wilson to invest

TABLE 1 Electrotech, Inc., Statement of Financial Conditions, December 31, 199x

Assets			Liabilities and Net Worth		
Case		$ 13,000	Liabilities:		
Accounts receivable		55,000	Accounts payable		$ 70,000
Building	$225,000		Notes payable—7 years (machinery)		194,000
Less: depreciation	75,000				
		150,000			
Machinery	1,400,000		Net worth:		
Less: depreciation	450,000		Capital stock		900,000
		950,000	Retained earnings		4,000
Total assets		$1,168,000	Total liabilities and net worth		$1,168,000

and become the sales manager. Steve Plunkett has agreed to match Wilson's current salary plus expenses, plus a bonus of 2 percent of profits. However, she must invest to become part of the new company. She will get a 5 percent interest in the business for the necessary $40,000 investment—almost all of her savings.

Electrotech, Inc., is well established—and last year had sales of $2.2 million but zero profits (after paying Mr. Hanson a salary of $40,000). In terms of sales, cost of materials was 46 percent; direct labor, 13 percent; indirect factory labor, 15 percent; factory overhead, 13 percent; and sales overhead and general expenses, 13 percent. The company has not been making any profit for several years—but has been continually adding new machines to replace those made obsolete by technological developments. The machinery is well maintained and modern, but most of it is similar to that used by its many competitors. Most of the machines in the industry are standard. Special products are made by using specially made dies with these machines.

Sales have been split—about two-thirds custom-molded products (that is, made to the specification of other producers or merchandising concerns) and the balance proprietary items (such as housewares and game items, like poker chips and cribbage sets). The housewares are copies of articles developed by others—and indicate neither originality nor style. Mr. Hanson is in charge of selling the proprietary items, which are distributed through any available wholesale channels. The custom-molded products are sold through two full-time sales reps—who receive a 10 percent commission on individual orders up to $20,000 and then 3 percent above that level—and also by three manufacturers' reps who get the same commissions.

The company seems to be in fairly good financial condition—at least as far as book value is concerned. The $40,000 investment will buy almost $60,000 in assets—and ongoing operations should pay off the seven-year

note. See Table 1. Steve Plunkett thinks that—with new management—the company has a good chance to make big profits. He expects to make some economies in the production process—because he feels most production operations can be improved. He plans to keep custom-molding sales at approximately the present $1.4 million level. His new strategy will try to increase the proprietary sales volume from $800,000 to $2 million a year. Amy Wilson is expected to be a big help here because of her sales experience. This will bring the firm up to about capacity level—but it will mean adding additional employees and costs. The major advantage of expanding sales will be spreading overhead.

Some of the products proposed by Steve Plunkett for expanding proprietary sales are listed below.

New products for consideration:
Safety helmets for cyclists.
Water bottles for cyclists.
School lunch boxes.
Toolboxes.
Closet organizer/storage boxes for toys.
Short legs for furniture.
Step-on garbage cans without liners.
Outside house shutters and siding.
Importing and distributing foreign housewares.

Electrotech faces heavy competition from many other similar companies. Further, most retailers expect a wide margin—sometimes 50 to 60 percent of retail selling price. Even so, manufacturing costs are low enough so Electrotech can spend some money for promotion while still keeping the price competitive. Apparently, many customers are willing to pay for novel new products—if they see them in stores. And Wilson isn't worried too much by tough competition. She sees plenty of that in her present job. And she does like the idea of being an "owner and sales manager."

Evaluate Electrotech's situation and Steve Plunkett's strategy. What should Amy Wilson do? Why?

28 TMC, Inc.

Tony Kenny, president and marketing manager of Tool Manufacturing Company, Inc., is deciding what strategy—or strategies—to pursue.

Tool Manufacturing Company (TMC) is a manufacturer of industrial cutting tools. These tools include such items as lathe blades, drill press bits, and various other cutting edges used in the operation of large metal cutting, boring, or stamping machines. Tony Kenny takes great pride in the fact that his company—whose $5.2 million in sales in 1995 is small by industry standards—is recognized as a producer of a top-quality line of cutting tools.

Competition in the cutting-tool industry is intense. TMC competes not only with the original machine manufacturers but also with many other larger domestic and foreign manufacturers offering cutting tools as one of their many different product lines. This has had the effect, over the years, of standardizing the price, specifications, and, in turn, the quality of the competing products of all manufacturers. It has also led to fairly low prices on standard items.

About a year ago, Tony was tiring of the financial pressure of competing with larger companies enjoying economies of scale. At the same time, he noted that more and more potential cutting-tool customers were turning to small tool-and-die shops because of specialized needs that could not be met by the mass production firms. Tony thought perhaps he should consider some basic strategy changes. Although he was unwilling to become strictly a custom producer, he thought that the recent trend toward buying customized cutting edges suggested new markets might be developing—markets too small for the large, multiproduct-line companies to serve profitably but large enough to earn a good profit for a flexible company of TMC's size.

Tony hired a marketing research company, Holl Associates, to study the feasibility of serving these markets. The initial results were encouraging. It was estimated that TMC might increase sales by 65 percent and profits by 90 percent by serving the emerging markets. This research showed that there are many large users of standard cutting tools who buy directly from large cutting-tool manufacturers (domestic or foreign) or wholesalers who represent these manufacturers. This is the bulk of the cutting-tool business (in terms of units sold and sales dollars). But there are also many smaller

users all over the United States who buy in small but regular quantities. And some of these needs are becoming more specialized. That is, a special cutting tool may make a machine and/or worker much more productive, perhaps eliminating several steps with time-consuming setups. This is the area that the research company sees as potentially attractive.

Next, Tony had the sales manager hire two technically oriented market researchers (at a total cost of $60,000 each per year, including travel expenses) to maintain continuous contact with potential cutting-tool customers. The researchers were supposed to identify any present—or future—needs that might exist in enough cases to make it possible to profitably produce a specialized product. The researchers were not to take orders or sell TMC's products to the potential customers. Tony felt that only through this policy could these researchers talk to the right people.

The initial feedback from the market researchers was most encouraging. Many firms (large and small) had special needs—although it often was necessary to talk to the shop foreman or individual machine operators to find these needs. Most operators were making do with the tools available. Either they didn't know customizing was possible or doubted that their supervisors would do anything about it if they suggested that a more specialized tool would increase productivity. But these operators were encouraging because they said that it would be easier to persuade supervisors to order specialized tools if the tools were already produced and in stock than if they had to be custom-made. So Tony decided to continually add high-quality products to meet the ever-changing, specialized needs of users of cutting tools and edges.

TMC's potential customers for specialized tools are located all over the United States. The average sale per customer is likely to be less than $500, but the sale will be repeated several times within a year. Because of the widespread market and the small order size, Tony doesn't think that selling direct—as is done by small custom shops—is practical. At the present time, TMC sells 90 percent of its regular output through a large industrial wholesaler—National Mill Supplies, Inc.—which serves the area east of the Mississippi River and carries a very complete line of industrial supplies (to "meet every industrial need"). Each of National's sales reps sells over 10,000 items from a 910-page catalog. National Mill Supplies, although very large and well known, is having trouble moving cutting tools. National is losing sales of cutting tools in some cities to newer wholesalers specializing in the cutting-tool industry. The new wholesalers are able to give more technical help to potential customers and therefore better service. National's president is convinced that the newer, less-experienced concerns will either realize that a substantial profit margin can't be maintained along with their aggressive strategies or they will eventually go broke trying to overspecialize.

From Tony's standpoint, the present wholesaler has a good reputation and has served TMC well in the past. National Mill Supplies has been of great help in holding down Tony's inventory costs—by increasing the inventory in National's 35 branch locations. Although Tony has received several complaints about the lack of technical assistance given by National's sales reps—as well as their lack of knowledge about TMC's new special products—he feels that the present wholesaler is providing the best service it can. All its sales reps have been told about the new products at a special training session, and a new page has been added to the catalog they carry with them. So regarding the complaints, Tony says: "The usual things you hear when you're in business."

Tony thinks there are more urgent problems than a few complaints. Profits are declining, and sales of the new cutting tools are not nearly as high as forecast—even though all research reports indicate that the company's new products meet the intended markets' needs perfectly. The high costs involved in producing small quantities of special products and in adding the market research team—together with lower-than-expected sales—have significantly reduced TMC's profits. Tony is wondering whether it is wise to continue to try to cater to the needs of many specific target markets when the results are this discouraging. He also is considering increasing advertising expenditures in the hope that customers will pull the new products through the channel.

Evaluate TMC's situation and Tony Kenny's present strategy. What should he do now?

29. Castings Supply, Inc.

Rick Moore, marketing manager for Castings Supply, Inc., is trying to figure out how to explain to his boss why a proposed new product line doesn't make sense for them. Rick is sure it's wrong for Castings Supply, Inc.—but isn't able to explain why.

Castings Supply, Inc., is a producer of malleable iron castings for automobile and aircraft manufacturers—and a variety of other users of castings. Last year's sales of castings amounted to over $70 million.

Castings Supply also produces about 30 percent of all the original equipment bumper jacks installed in new U.S.-made automobiles each year. This is a very price-competitive business, but Castings Supply has been able to obtain its large market share with frequent personal contact between the company's executives and its customers—supported by very close cooperation between the company's engineering department and its customers' buy-

ers. This has been extremely important because the wide variety of models and model changes frequently requires alterations in the specifications of the bumper jacks. All of Castings Supply's bumper jacks are sold directly to the automobile manufacturers. No attempt has been made to sell bumper jacks to final consumers through hardware and automotive channels—although they are available through the manufacturers' automobile dealers.

Tim Owen, Castings Supply's production manager, now wants to begin producing hydraulic garage jacks for sale through automobile-parts wholesalers to retail auto parts stores. Owen saw a variety of hydraulic garage jacks at a recent automotive show—and knew immediately that his plant could produce these products. This especially interested him because of the possibility of using excess capacity—now that auto sales are down. Further, he says "jacks are jacks," and the company would merely be broadening its product line by introducing hydraulic garage jacks. (Note: Hydraulic garage jacks are larger than bumper jacks and are intended for use in or around a garage. They are too big to carry in a car's trunk.)

As Tim Owen became more enthusiastic about the idea, he found that Castings Supply's engineering department already had a design that appeared to be at least comparable to the products now offered on the market. None of these products have any patent protection. Further, Owen says that the company would be able to produce a product that is better made than the competitive products (smoother castings, etc.)—although he agrees that most customers probably wouldn't notice the difference. The production department estimates that the cost of producing a hydraulic garage jack comparable to those currently offered by competitors would be about $48 per unit.

Rick Moore, the marketing manager, has just received a memo from Bill Borne, the company president, explaining the production department's enthusiasm for broadening Castings Supply's present jack line into hydraulic jacks. Bill Borne seems enthusiastic about the idea too, noting that it would be a way to make fuller use of the company's resources and increase its sales. Borne's memo asks for Rick's reaction, but Bill Borne already seems sold on the idea.

Given Borne's enthusiasm, Rick Moore isn't sure how to respond. He's trying to develop a good explanation of why he isn't excited about the proposal. The firm's six sales reps are already overworked with their current accounts. And Rick couldn't possibly promote this new line himself—he's already helping other reps make calls and serving as sales manager. So it would be necessary to hire someone to promote the line. And this sales manager would probably have to recruit manufacturers' agents (who probably will want 10 to 15 percent commission on sales) to sell to automotive wholesalers who would stock the jack and sell to the auto parts retailers. The wholesalers will probably expect trade discounts of about 20 percent, trade show exhibits, some national advertising, and sales promotion help (catalog sheets, mailers, and point-of-purchase displays). Further, Rick Moore sees that Castings Supply's billing and collection system will have to be expanded because many more customers will be involved. It will also be necessary to keep track of agent commissions and accounts receivable.

Auto parts retailers are currently selling similar hydraulic garage jacks for about $99. Rick Moore has learned that such retailers typically expect a trade discount of about 35 percent off the suggested list price for their auto parts.

All things considered, Rick Moore feels that the proposed hydraulic jack line is not very closely related to the company's present emphasis. He has already indicated his lack of enthusiasm to Tim Owen, but this made little difference in Tim's thinking. Now it's clear that Rick will have to convince the president or he will soon be responsible for selling hydraulic jacks.

Contrast Castings Supply, Inc.'s current strategy and the proposed strategy. What should Rick Moore say to Bill Borne to persuade him to change his mind? Or should he just plan to sell hydraulic jacks? Explain.

30 Deluxe Foods, Ltd.*

Jessica Walters, marketing manager of Deluxe Foods, Ltd.—a Canadian company—is being urged to approve the creation of a separate marketing plan for Quebec. This would be a major policy change because Deluxe Foods' international parent is trying to move toward a global strategy for the whole firm and Jessica has been supporting Canadawide planning.

Jessica Walters has been the marketing manager of Deluxe Foods, Ltd., for the last four years—since she arrived from international headquarters in Minneapolis. Deluxe Foods, Ltd.—headquartered in Toronto—is a subsidiary of a large U.S.-based consumer packaged-food company with worldwide sales of more than $2 billion in 1994. Its Canadian sales are just over $350 million—with the Quebec and Ontario markets accounting for 69 percent of the company's Canadian sales.

The company's product line includes such items as cake mixes, puddings, pie fillings, pancakes, prepared foods, and frozen dinners. The company has successfully introduced at least six new products every year for the last five years. Products from Deluxe Foods are known for their high quality and enjoy much brand preference throughout Canada—including the province of Quebec.

*This case was adapted from one written by Professor Roberta Tamilia, University of Windsor, Canada.

TABLE 1 Per Capital Consumption Index, Province of Quebec (Canada = 100)

Cake mixes	107	Soft drinks	126
Pancakes	87	Pie fillings	118
Puddings	114	Frozen dinners	79
Salad dressings	85	Prepared packaged foods	83
Molasses	132	Cookies	123

The company's sales have risen every year since Jessica Walters took over as marketing manager. In fact, the company's market share has increased steadily in each of the product categories in which it competes. The Quebec market has closely followed the national trend except that, in the past two years, total sales growth in that market began to lag.

According to Mrs. Walters, a big advantage of Deluxe Foods over its competitors is the ability to coordinate all phases of the food business from Toronto. For this reason, Mrs. Walters meets at least once a month with her product managers—to discuss developments in local markets that might affect marketing plans. While each manager is free to make suggestions—and even to suggest major changes—Jessica Walters has the responsibility of giving final approval for all plans.

One of the product managers, Marie LeMans, expressed great concern at the last monthly meeting about the poor performance of some of the company's products in the Quebec market. While a broad range of possible reasons—ranging from inflation and the threat of job losses to politics—were reviewed to try to explain the situation, Ms. LeMans insisted that it was due to a basic lack of understanding of that market. She felt not enough managerial time and money had been spent on the Quebec market—in part because of the current emphasis on developing all-Canada plans on the way to having one global strategy.

Marie LeMans felt the current marketing approach to the Quebec market should be reevaluated because an inappropriate marketing plan may be responsible for the sales slowdown. After all, she said, "80 percent of the market is French-speaking. It's in the best interest of the company to treat that market as being separate and distinct from the rest of Canada."

Marie LeMans supported her position by showing that Quebec's per capita consumption of many product categories (in which the firm competes) is above the national average (Table 1). Research projects conducted by Deluxe Foods also support the "separate and distinct" argument. Over the years, the firm has found many French-English differences in brand attitudes, lifestyles, usage rates, and so on.

Ms. LeMans argued that the company should develop a unique Quebec marketing plan for some or all of its brands. She specifically suggested that the French-language advertising plan for a particular brand be developed independently of the plan for English Canada. Currently, the Toronto agency assigned to the brand just translates its English-language ads for the French market. Jessica Walters pointed out that the present advertising approach assured Deluxe Foods of a uniform brand image across Canada. Marie LeMans said she knew what the agency was doing, and that straight translation into Canadian French might not communicate the same brand image. The discussion that followed suggested that a different brand image might be needed in the French market if the company wanted to stop the brand's decline in sales.

The managers also discussed the food distribution system in Quebec. The major supermarket chains have their lowest market share in that province. Independents are strongest there—the "mom and pop" food stores fast disappearing outside Quebec remain alive and well in the province. Traditionally, these stores have stocked a higher proportion (than supermarkets) of their shelf space with national brands—an advantage for Deluxe Foods.

Finally, various issues related to discount policies, pricing structure, sales promotion, and cooperative advertising were discussed. All of this suggested that things were different in Quebec—and that future marketing plans should reflect these differences to a greater extent than they do now.

After the meeting, Jessica Walters stayed in her office to think about the situation. Although she agreed with the basic idea that the Quebec market was in many ways different, she wasn't sure how far the company should go in recognizing this fact. She knew that regional differences in food tastes and brand purchases existed not only in Quebec but in other parts of Canada as well. But people are people, after all, with far more similarities than differences, so a Canadian and eventually a global strategy makes some sense too.

Jessica Walters was afraid that giving special status to one region might conflict with top management's objective of achieving standardization whenever possible—one global strategy for Canada, on the way to one worldwide global strategy. She was also worried about the long-term effect of such a policy change on costs, organizational structure, and brand image. Still, enough product managers had expressed their concern over the years about the Quebec market to make her wonder if she shouldn't modify the current approach. Perhaps they could experiment with a few brands—and just in Quebec. She could cite the language difference as the reason for trying Quebec rather than any of the other provinces. But Mrs. Walters realizes that any change of policy could be seen as the beginning of more change, and what would Minneapolis think? Could she explain it successfully there?

Evaluate Deluxe Foods, Ltd.'s present strategy. What should Jessica Walters do now? Explain.

31 Hendrix Chevrolet, Inc.

Bob Hendrix owns Hendrix Chevrolet, Inc., a Chevrolet/Nissan dealership in suburban Dallas, Texas. Bob is seriously considering moving into a proposed auto mall—a large display and selling area for 10 to 15 auto dealers, none handling the same car brands. This mall will be a few miles away from his current location but easily available to his present customers and quite convenient to many more potential customers. He can consider moving now because the lease on his current location will be up in one year. He is sure he can renew the lease for another five years, but he feels the building owner is likely to want to raise the lease terms so his total fixed costs will be about $100,000 more per year than his current fixed costs of $650,000 per year. Moving to the new mall will probably increase his total fixed costs to about $1.1 million per year. Further, fixed costs—wherever he is—will probably continue to rise with inflation. But he doesn't see this as a major problem. Car prices tend to rise at about the same rate as inflation, so these rising revenues and costs tend to offset each other.

Bob Hendrix is considering moving to an auto mall because he feels this is the future trend. Already, about 200 such malls operate in the United States. And the number should double in the next 5 to 10 years because they do seem to increase sales per dealership. Some dealers in auto malls have reported sales increases of as much as 30 percent over what they were doing in their former locations outside the mall. The auto mall concept seems to be a continuing evolution from isolated car dealerships to car dealer strips along major traffic arteries to more customer-oriented clusters of dealerships that make it easier for customers to shop.

Bob is considering moving to a mall because of the growing number of competing brands and the desire of some consumers to shop more conveniently. Over 30 different brands of cars and 15 brands of trucks compete in the U.S. market—not including specialty cars such as Ferarri and Rolls-Royce. Increasing competition is already taking its toll on some domestic and foreign car dealers as they have to take less profit on each sale. For example, even owners of luxury car franchises such as Infiniti, Porsche, and Acura are having troubles, and some have moved into malls. Dealer ranks have thinned considerably too. Once there were 50,000 dealerships in the

United States. Now, there are less than half that number—and failures are reported all the time. Recently, some dealers tried to become "megadealers" operating in several markets, but this did not work too well because they could not achieve economies of scale. Now owners of multiple dealerships seem to be going to malls to reduce their overhead and promotion costs. And if customers begin to go to these malls, then this may be *the* place to be—even for a dealer with only one or two auto franchises. That's the position that Bob Hendrix is in—with his Chevrolet and Nissan franchises. And he wonders if he should become well positioned in a mall before it is too late.

Bob Hendrix's dealership is now selling between 550 and 700 new and used cars per year—at an average price of about $16,000. With careful management, he is grossing about $1,100 per car. This $1,100 is not all net profit, however. It must go toward covering his fixed costs of about $650,000 per year. So if he sells more than 650 cars he will more than cover his fixed costs and make a profit. Obviously, the more cars he sells beyond 650, the bigger the profit—assuming he controls his costs. So he is thinking that moving to a mall might increase his sales and therefore lead to a larger profit. A major question is whether he is likely to sell enough extra cars in a mall to help pay for the increase in fixed costs. He is also concerned about how his Chevrolet products will stand up against all of the other cars when consumers can more easily shop around and compare. Right now, Bob has some loyal customers who regularly buy from him because of his seasoned, helpful sales force *and* his dependable repair shop. But he worries that making it easy for these customers to compare other cars might lead to brand switching or put greater pressure on price to keep some of his "loyal" customers.

Another of Bob's concerns is whether the Big Three car manufacturers will discourage dealers from going into auto malls. Now these auto manufacturers do not encourage dealers to go into a supermarket setting. Instead, they prefer their dealers to devote their full energies to one brand in a free-standing location. But as real estate prices rise, it becomes more and more difficult to insist on free-standing dealerships in all markets—and still have profitable dealerships. The rising number of bankruptcies or dealerships in financial difficulties has caused the manufacturers to be more relaxed about insisting on a free-standing location. Chevrolet and Nissan seem to be accepting this change, so this is not Bob's main concern right now.

Adding to the competitiveness in the U.S. auto market—which is Bob's biggest concern—is the increasing aggressiveness of foreign auto importers as well as Japanese-owned U.S. car producers like Honda. As they increase their penetration on the East and West Coasts,

they are moving into the center of the United States. As they set up more dealers in this area, the competition is likely to become even more intense. In Texas, imports account for over 25 percent of the market, but this share will probably rise in the future. And Bob wants to be able to survive in this increasingly competitive market. That is why he added the Nissan franchise recently—to give his sales reps more to sell and increase his chances for making a profit.

Evaluate Bob Hendrix's present and possible new strategy. What should Bob Hendrix do? Why?

32 Inhome Medical, Inc.

Jackie Johnson, executive director of Inhome Medical, Inc., is trying to clarify her strategies. She's sure some changes are needed, but she's less sure about how *much* change is needed and/or whether it can be handled by her people.

Inhome Medical, Inc. (IM), is a nonprofit organization that has been operating—with varying degrees of success—for 25 years, offering nursing services in clients' homes. Some of its funding comes from the local United Way—to provide emergency nursing services for those who can't afford to pay. The balance of the revenues—about 90 percent of the $2.2 million annual budget—comes from charges made directly to the client or to third-party payers—including insurance companies, health maintenance organizations (HMOs), and the federal government—for Medicare or Medicaid services.

Jackie Johnson has been executive director of IM for two years. She has developed a well-functioning organization able to meet most requests for service that come from some local doctors and from the discharge officers at local hospitals. Some business also comes by self-referral—the client finds the IM name in the Yellow Pages of the local phone directory.

The last two years have been a rebuilding time—because the previous director had personnel problems. This led to a weakening of the agency's image with the local referring agencies. Now the image is more positive, but Jackie is not completely satisfied with the situation. By definition, Inhome Medical is a nonprofit organization. But it still must cover all its costs: payroll, rent payments, phone expenses, and so on—including Jackie's own salary. She can see that while IM is growing slightly and is now breaking even, it doesn't have much of a cash cushion to fall back on if (1) the demand for IM nursing services declines, (2) the government changes its rules about paying for IM's kind of nursing services—either cutting back what it will pay for or reducing the amount it will pay for specific services, or (3) new competitors enter the market. In fact, the last possibility concerns Jackie greatly. Some hospitals—squeezed for revenue— are expanding into home health care, especially nursing services as patients are being released earlier from hospitals because of payment limits set by government guidelines. For-profit organizations (e.g., Kelly Home Care Services) are expanding around the country to provide a complete line of home health care services—including nursing services of the kind offered by IM. These for-profit organizations appear to be efficiently run—offering good service at competitive and sometimes even lower prices than some nonprofit organizations. And they seem to be doing this at a profit—which suggests that it would be possible for these for-profit companies to lower their prices if nonprofit organizations try to compete on price.

Jackie is considering whether she should ask her board of directors to let her offer a complete line of home health care services—that is, move beyond just nursing services into what she calls "care and comfort" services.

Currently, IM is primarily concerned with providing professional nursing care in the home. But IM nurses are much too expensive for routine home health care activities—helping fix meals, bathing and dressing patients, and other care and comfort activities. The full cost of a nurse to IM (including benefits and overhead) is about $65 per hour. But, a registered nurse is not needed for care and comfort services. All that is required is someone who can get along with all kinds of people and is willing to do this kind of work. Generally, any mature person can be trained fairly quickly to do the job— following the instructions and under the general supervision of a physician, a nurse, or family members. The full cost of aides is $8 to $15 per hour for short visits—and as low as $65 per 24 hours for a live-in aide who has room and board supplied by the client.

The demand for all kinds of home health care services seems to be growing. With more dual career families and more single-parent households, there isn't anyone in the family to take over home health care when the need arises—due to emergencies or long-term disabilities. And with people living longer, there are more single-survivor family situations where there is no one nearby to take care of the needs of these older people. But often some family members—or third-party payers such as the government or insurers—are willing to pay for some home health care services. Now Jackie occasionally recommends other agencies, or suggests one or another of three women who have been doing care and comfort work on their own—part-time. But with growing demand, Jackie wonders if IM should get into this business—hiring aides as needed.

Jackie is concerned that a new, full-service home health care organization may come into her market and provide both nursing services *and* less-skilled home care

and comfort services. This has happened already in two nearby but somewhat larger cities. Jackie fears that this might be more appealing than IM to the local hospitals and other referrers. In other words, she can see the possibility of losing nursing service business if IM does not begin to offer a complete home health care service. This would cause real problems for IM—because overhead costs are more or less fixed. A loss in revenue of as little as 10 percent would require some cutbacks— perhaps laying off some nurses or secretaries, giving up part of the office, and so on.

Another reason for expanding beyond nursing services—using paraprofessionals and relatively unskilled personnel—is to offer a better service to present customers *and* make more effective use of the computer systems and organization structure that she has developed over the last two years. Jackie estimates that the administrative and office capabilities could handle twice as many clients without straining the system. It would be necessary to add some clerical help—if the expansion were quite large—as well as expanding the hours when the switchboard is open. But these increases in overhead would be minor compared to the present proportion of total revenue that goes to covering overhead. In other words, additional clients or more work for some clients could increase revenue and ensure the survival of IM, provide a cushion to cover the normal fluctuations in demand, and ensure more job security for the administrative personnel.

Further, Jackie thinks that if IM were successful in expanding its services—and therefore could generate some surplus—it could extend services to those who aren't now able to pay. Jackie says one of the worst parts of her job is refusing service to clients whose third-party benefits have run out or who, for whatever reason, can no longer afford to pay. She is uncomfortable about having to cut off service, but she must schedule her nurses to provide revenue-producing services if she's going to meet the payroll every two weeks. By expanding to provide more services, she might be able to keep serving more of these nonpaying clients. This possibility excites Jackie because her nurse's training has instilled a deep desire to serve people—whether they can pay or not. This continual need to cut off service because people can't pay has been at the root of many disagreements—and even arguments—between the nurses serving the clients and Jackie, as executive director and representative of the board of directors.

Jackie knows that expanding into care and comfort services won't be easy. Some decisions would be needed about relative pay levels for nurses, paraprofessionals, and aides. IM would also have to set prices for these different services and tell the present customers and referral agencies about the expanded services.

These problems aren't bothering Jackie too much, however—she thinks she can handle them. She is sure that care and comfort services are in demand and could be supplied at competitive prices.

Her primary concern is whether this is the right thing for Inhome Medical—basically a nursing organization—to do. IM's whole history has been oriented to supplying *nurses' services*. Nurses are dedicated professionals who bring high standards to any job they undertake. The question is whether IM should offer less-professional services. Inevitably, some of the aides will not be as dedicated as the nurses might like them to be. And this could reflect unfavorably on the nurse image. At a minimum, she would need to set up some sort of training program for the aides. As Jackie worries about the future of IM—and her own future—it seems that there are no easy answers.

Evaluate IM's present strategy. What should Jackie Johnson do? Explain.

33 Lever, Ltd.*

Joe Hall is product manager for Guard Deodorant Soap. He was just transferred to Lever, Ltd., a Canadian subsidiary of Lever Group, Inc., from world headquarters in New York. Joe is anxious to make a good impression because he is hoping to transfer to Lever's London office. He is working on developing and securing management

*Adapted from a case prepared by Daniel Aronchick, who at the time of its preparation was marketing manager at Thomas J. Lipton, Limited.

approval of next year's marketing plan for Guard. His first job is submitting a draft marketing plan to Sarah Long—his recently appointed group product manager—who is responsible for several such plans from product managers like Joe.

Joe's marketing plan is the single most important document he will produce on this assignment. This annual marketing plan does three main things:

1. It reviews the brand's performance in the past year, assesses the competitive situation, and highlights problems and opportunities for the brand.
2. It spells out marketing strategies and the plan for the coming year.
3. Finally, and most importantly, the marketing plan sets out the brand's sales objectives and advertising/promotion budget requirements.

In preparing this marketing plan, Joe gathered the information in Table 1.

Joe was somewhat surprised at the significant regional differences in the bar soap market:

a. The underdevelopment of the deodorant bar segment in Quebec with a corresponding overdevelopment of the beauty bar segment. But some past research suggested that this is due to cultural factors—English-speaking people have been more interested than others in cleaning, deodorizing, and disinfecting. A similar pattern is seen in most European countries, where the adoption of deodorant soaps has been slower

TABLE 1 Past 12-month Share of Bar Soap Market (percent)

	Maritimes	Quebec	Ontario	Manitoba/Saskatchewan	Alberta	British Columbia
Deodorant segment						
Zest	21.3%	14.2%	24.5%	31.2%	30.4%	25.5%
Dial	10.4	5.1	12.8	16.1	17.2	14.3
Lifebuoy	4.2	3.1	1.2	6.4	5.8	4.2
Guard	2.1	5.6	1.0	4.2	4.2	2.1
Beauty bar segment						
Camay	6.2	12.3	7.0	4.1	4.0	5.1
Lux	6.1	11.2	7.7	5.0	6.9	5.0
Dove	5.5	8.0	6.6	6.3	6.2	4.2
Lower-priced bars						
Ivory	11.2	6.5	12.4	5.3	5.2	9.0
Sunlight	6.1	3.2	8.2	4.2	4.1	8.0
All others (including stores' own brands)	26.9	30.8	18.6	17.2	16.0	22.6
Total bar soap market	100.0	100.0	100.0	100.0	100.0	100.0

TABLE 2 Standard Cases of 3-Ounce Bars Consumed per 1,000 People in 12 Months

	Maritimes	Quebec	Ontario	Manitoba/ Saskatchewan	Alberta	British Columbia
Guard	4.1	10.9	1.9	8.1	4.1	6.2
Sales index	66	175	31	131	131	100

TABLE 3 Usage Results (in percent)

	Maritimes	Quebec	Ontario	Manitoba/ Saskatchewan	Alberta	British Columbia
Respondents aware of Guard	20%	58%	28%	30%	32%	16%
Respondents ever trying Guard	3	18	2	8	6	4

than in North America. For similar reasons, the perfumed soap share is highest in French-speaking Quebec.

b. The overdevelopment of synthetic bars in the Prairies. These bars, primarily in the deodorant segment, lather better in the hard water of the Prairies. Nonsynthetic bars lather very poorly in hard-water areas—and leave a soap film.

c. The overdevelopment of the "all-other" segment in Quebec. This segment, consisting of smaller brands, fares better in Quebec where 43 percent of the grocery trade is done by independent stores. Conversely, large chain grocery stores dominate in Ontario and the Prairies.

Joe's brand, Guard, is a highly perfumed deodorant bar. His business is relatively weak in the key Ontario market. To confirm this share data, Joe calculated consumption of Guard per thousand people in each region (see Table 2).

These differences are especially interesting since per capita sales of all bar soap products are roughly equal in all provinces.

A consumer attitude and usage research study was conducted approximately a year ago. This study revealed that consumer "top of mind" awareness of the Guard brand differed greatly across Canada. This was true despite the even—by population—expenditure of advertising funds in past years. Also, trial of Guard was low in the Maritimes, Ontario, and British Columbia (see Table 3).

The attitude portion of the research revealed that consumers who had heard of Guard were aware that its deodorant protection came mainly from a high fragrance level. This was the main selling point in the copy, and it was well communicated by Guard's advertising. The other important finding was that consumers who had tried

Guard were satisfied with the product. About 70 percent of those trying Guard had repurchased the product at least twice.

Joe has also discovered that bar soap competition is especially intense in Ontario. It is Canada's largest market, and many competitors seem to want a share of it. The chain stores are also quite aggressive in promotion and pricing—offering specials, in-store coupons, and so on. They want to move goods. And because of this, two key Ontario chains have put Guard on their pending delisting sheets. These chains, which control about half the grocery volume in Ontario, are dissatisfied with how slowly Guard is moving off the shelves.

Now Joe feels he is ready to set a key part of the brand's marketing plan for next year: how to allocate the advertising/sales promotion budget by region.

Guard's present advertising/sales promotion budget is 20 percent of sales. With forecast sales of $4 million, this would amount to an $800,000 expenditure. Traditionally such funds have been allocated in proportion to population (see Table 4).

Joe feels he should spend more heavily in Ontario where the grocery chain delisting problem exists. Last year, 36 percent of Guard's budget was allocated to Ontario, which accounted for only 12 percent of Guard's sales. Joe wants to increase Ontario spending to 48 percent of the total budget by taking funds evenly from all other areas. Joe expects this will increase business in the key Ontario market, which has over a third of Canada's population, because it is a big increase and will help Guard "out-shout" the many other competitors who are promoting heavily.

Joe presented this idea to Sarah, his newly appointed group product manager. Sarah strongly disagrees. She has also been reviewing Guard's business and feels that

TABLE 4 Allocation of Advertising/Sales Promotion Budget, by Population

	Maritimes	Quebec	Ontario	Manitoba/ Saskatchewan	Alberta	British Columbia	Canada
Percent of population	10%	27%	36%	8%	8%	11%	100%
Possible allocation of budget based on population (in 000s)	$80	$216	$288	$64	$64	$88	$800
Percent of Guard business at present	7%	51%	12%	11%	11%	8%	100%

promotion funds have historically been misallocated. It is her strong belief that, to use her words: "A brand should spend where its business is." Sarah believes that the first priority in allocating funds regionally is to support the areas of strength. She suggested to Joe that there may be more business to be had in the brand's strong areas, Quebec and the Prairies, than in chasing sales in Ontario. The needs and attitudes toward Guard, as well as competitive pressures, may vary a lot among the provinces. Therefore, Sarah suggested that spending for Guard in the coming year be proportional to the brand's sales by region rather than to regional population.

Joe is convinced this is wrong, particularly in light of the Ontario situation. He asked Sarah how the Ontario market should be handled. Sarah said that the conservative way to build business in Ontario is to invest incremental promotion funds. However, before these incremental funds are invested, a test of this Ontario investment proposition should be conducted. Sarah recommended that some of the Ontario money should be used to conduct an investment-spending market test in a small area or town in Ontario for 12 months. This will enable Joe to see if the incremental spending results in higher sales and profits—profits large enough to justify higher spending. In other words, an investment payout should be assured before spending any extra money in Ontario. Similarly, Sarah would do the same kind of test in Quebec—to see if more money should go there.

Joe feels this approach would be a waste of time and unduly cautious, given the importance of the Ontario market and the likely delistings in two key chains.

Evaluate the present strategy for Guard and Joe's and Sarah's proposed strategies. How should the promotion money be allocated? Should investment-spending market tests be run first? Why? Explain.

34 Huntoon & Balbiera P.C.

The partners of Huntoon & Balbiera are having a serious discussion about what the firm should do in the near future.

Huntoon & Balbiera P.C. (H&B) is a large regional certified public accounting firm based in Grand Rapids, Michigan—with branch offices in Lansing and Detroit. Huntoon & Balbiera has nine partners and a professional staff of approximately 105 accountants. Gross service billings for the fiscal year ending June 30, 1995, were $6.9 million. Financial data for 1993, 1994, and 1995 are presented in Table 1.

H&B's professional services include auditing, tax preparation, and bookkeeping. Its client base includes municipal governments (cities, villages, and townships), manufacturing companies, professional organizations (attorneys, doctors, and dentists), and various other small businesses. A good share of revenue comes from the firm's municipal practice. Table 1 gives H&B's gross revenue by service area and client industry for 1993, 1994, and 1995.

At the monthly partners' meeting held in July 1995, Pat Hogan, the firm's managing partner (CEO), expressed concern about the future of the firm's municipal practice. Hogan's presentation to his partners appears below:

> Although our firm is considered to be a leader in municipal auditing in our geographic area, I am concerned that as municipals attempt to cut their

TABLE 1 Fiscal Year Ending June 30

	1995	1994	1993
Gross billings	$6,900,000	$6,400,000	$5,800,000
Gross billings by service area:			
Auditing	3,100,000	3,200,000	2,750,000
Tax preparation	1,990,000	1,830,000	1,780,000
Bookkeeping	1,090,000	745,000	660,000
Other	720,000	625,000	610,000
Gross billings by client industry:			
Municipal	3,214,000	3,300,000	2,908,000
Manufacturing	2,089,000	1,880,000	1,706,000
Professional	1,355,000	1,140,000	1,108,000
Other	242,000	80,000	78,000

operating costs, they will solicit competitive bids from other public accounting firms to perform their annual audits. Due to the fact that the local offices of most of the Big Six firms* in our area concentrate their practice in the manufacturing industry—which typically has December 31 fiscal year-ends—they have "available" staff during the summer months.

Therefore, they can afford to low-ball competitive bids to keep their staffs busy and benefit from on-the-job training provided by municipal clientele. I am concerned that we may begin to lose clients in our most established and profitable practice area.†

Ann Yost, a senior partner in the firm and the partner in charge of the firm's municipal practice, was the first to respond to Pat Hogan's concern.

Pat, we all recognize the potential threat of being underbid for our municipal work by our Big Six competitors. However, H&B is a recognized leader in municipal auditing in Michigan, and we have much more local experience than our competitors. Furthermore, it is a fact that we offer a superior level of service to our clients—which goes beyond the services normally expected during an audit to include consulting on financial and other operating issues. Many of our less sophisticated clients depend on our nonaudit consulting assistance. Therefore, I believe, we have been successful in differentiating our services from our competitors. In many recent situations, H&B was selected over a field of as many as 10 competitors even though our proposed prices were much higher than those of our competitors.

The partners at the meeting agreed with Ann Yost's comments. However, even though H&B had many success stories regarding its ability to retain its municipal clients—despite being underbid—it had lost three large municipal clients during the past year. Ann Yost was asked to comment on the loss of those clients. She explained that the lost clients were larger municipalities with a lot of in-house financial expertise—and therefore less dependent on H&B's consulting assistance. As a result, H&B's service differentiation went largely unnoticed. Ann explained that the larger, more sophisticated municipals regard audits as a necessary evil and usually select the low-cost reputable bidder.

Pat Hogan then requested ideas and discussion from the other partners at the meeting. One partner, Joe Reid, suggested that H&B should protect itself by diversifying. Specifically, he felt a substantial practice development effort should be directed toward manufacturing. He reasoned that since manufacturing work would occur during H&B's off-season, H&B could afford to price very low to gain new manufacturing clients. This strategy would also help to counter (and possibly discourage) Big Six competitors' low-ball pricing for municipals.

Another partner, Bob LaMott, suggested that "if we have consulting skills, we ought to promote them more, instead of hoping that the clients will notice and come to appreciate us. Further, maybe we ought to be more aggressive in calling on smaller potential clients."

Another partner, John Smith, agreed with LaMott but wanted to go further. He suggested that they recognize that there are at least two types of municipal customers and that two (at least) different strategies be implemented, including lower prices for auditing only for larger municipal customers and/or higher prices for smaller customers who are buying consulting too. This caused a big uproar from some who said this would lead to price-cutting of professional services and H&B didn't want to be price cutters: "One price for all is the professional way."

However, another partner, Megan Cullen, agreed with John Smith and suggested they go even further—pricing consulting services separately. In fact, she suggested that the partners consider setting up a separate department for consulting—like the Big Six have done. This can be very profitable business. But it is a different kind of business and eventually may require different kinds of people and a different organization. For now, however, it may be desirable to appoint a manager for consulting services— with a budget—to be sure it gets proper attention. This suggestion too caused serious disagreement. Some of the partners knew that having a separate consulting arm had led to major conflicts in some firms. The main problem seemed to be that the consultants brought in more profit than the auditors, but the auditors controlled the partnership and did not properly reward the successful consultants—at least as they saw it!

Pat Hogan thanked everyone for their comments and charged them with thinking hard about the firm's future before coming to a one-day retreat (in two weeks) to continue this discussion and come to some conclusions.

Evaluate Huntoon & Balbiera's situation. What strategy(ies) should the partners select? Why?

35 Alumux Mfg. Co.*

Ed Mackey, newly hired VP of Marketing for Alumux Mfg. Co., is reviewing the firm's international distribution arrangements because they don't seem to be very well

---

*The "Big Six" firms are a group of the six largest public accounting firms in the United States. They maintain offices in almost every major U.S. city. Until recently, these firms were known as the "Big Eight," but after several mergers they have come to be known as the "Big Six."

†Organizations with December fiscal year-ends require audit work to be performed during the fall and in January and February. Those with June 30 fiscal year-ends require auditing during the summer months.

---

*Adapted from a case written by Professor Peter Banting, McMaster University, Canada.

thought out. He is not sure if anything is wrong, but he feels that the company should follow a global strategy rather than continuing its current policies.

Alumux, based in Atlanta, Georgia, produces finished aluminum products such as aluminum ladders, umbrella-type clothes racks, scaffolding, and patio tables and chairs that fold flat. Sales in 1994 reached $25 million—primarily to U.S. customers.

In 1990, Alumux decided to try foreign markets. The sales manager, Ruth Ways, believed the growing affluence of European workers would help the company's products gain market acceptance quickly. As a personal goal she wanted to develop at least some distribution relationships before the 1992 target for forming the European Union.

Ruth's first step in investigating foreign markets was to join a trade mission to Europe—a tour organized by the U.S. Department of Commerce. This trade mission visited Italy, Germany, Denmark, Holland, France, and England. During this trip, Ruth was officially introduced to leading buyers for department store chains, import houses, wholesalers, and buying groups. The two-week trip convinced Ruth that there was ample buying power to make exporting a profitable opportunity.

On her return to Atlanta, Ruth's next step was to obtain credit references for the firms she considered potential distributors. To those who were judged creditworthy, she sent letters expressing interest and samples, brochures, prices, and other relevant information.

The first orders were from a French wholesaler. Sales in this market totaled $70,000 in 1991. Similar success was achieved in Germany and England. Italy, on the other hand, did not produce any sales. Ruth felt the semiluxury nature of the company's products and the lower incomes in Italy encouraged a "making do" attitude rather than the purchase of goods and services that would make life easier.

In the United States, Alumux distributes through fairly aggressive and well-organized merchant hardware distributors and buying groups, such as cooperative and voluntary hardware chains, who have taken over much of the strategy planning for cooperating producers and retailers. In its foreign markets, however, there is no recognizable pattern. Channel systems vary from country to country. To avoid mixing channels of distribution, Alumux has only one account in each country. The chosen distributor is the exclusive distributor.

In France, Alumux distributes through a wholesaler based in Paris. This wholesaler has five salespeople covering the country. The firm specializes in small housewares and has contacts with leading buying groups, wholesalers, and department stores. Ruth is impressed with the firm's aggressiveness and knowledge of merchandising techniques.

In Germany, Alumux sells to a Hamburg-based buying group for hardware wholesalers throughout the country.

Ruth felt this group would provide excellent coverage of the market because of its extensive distribution network.

In Denmark, Alumux's line is sold to a buying group representing a chain of hardware retailers. This group recently expanded to include retailers in Sweden, Finland, and Norway. Together this group purchases goods for about 500 hardware retailers. The buying power of Scandinavians is quite high, and it is expected that Alumux's products will prove very successful there.

In the United Kingdom, Alumux uses an importer-distributor, who both buys on his own account and acts as a sales agent. This firm sells to department stores and hardware wholesalers. This firm has not done very well overall, but it has done very well with Alumux's line of patio tables and chairs.

Australia is handled by an importer who operates a chain of discount houses. It heard about Alumux from a United Kingdom contact. After much correspondence, this firm discovered it could land aluminum patio furniture in Melbourne at prices competitive with Japanese imports. So it started ordering because it wanted to cut prices in a high-priced garden furniture market.

The Argentina market is handled by an American who came to the United States from Buenos Aires in search of new lines. Alumux attributes success in Argentina to the efforts of this aggressive and capable agent. He has built a sizable trade in aluminum ladders.

In Trinidad and Jamaica, Alumux's products are handled by traders who carry such diversified lines as insurance, apples, plums, and fish. They have been successful in selling aluminum ladders. This business grew out of inquiries sent to the U.S. Department of Commerce, which Ruth Ways followed up by mail.

Ruth Ways' export policies for Alumux are as follows:

1. Product: No product modifications will be made in selling to foreign customers. This may be considered later after a substantial sales volume develops.

2. Price: The company does not publish suggested list prices. Distributors add their own markup to their landed costs. Supply prices will be kept as low as possible. This is accomplished by: (a) removing advertising expenses and other strictly domestic overhead charges from price calculations, (b) finding the most economical packages for shipping (smallest volume per unit), and (c) bargaining with carriers to obtain the lowest shipping rates possible.

3. Promotion: The firm does no advertising in foreign markets. Brochures and sales literature already being used in the United States are supplied to foreign distributors. Alumux will continue to promote its products by

participating in overseas trade shows. These are handled by the sales manager. All inquiries are forwarded to the firm's distributor in that country.

4. Distribution: New distributors will be contacted through foreign trade shows. Ruth Ways considers large distributors desirable. She feels, however, that they are not as receptive as smaller distributors to a new, unestablished product line. Therefore, she prefers to appoint small distributors. Larger distributors may be appointed after the company has gained a strong consumer franchise in a country.

5. Financing: Alumux sees no need to provide financial help to distributors. The company views its major contribution as providing good products at the lowest possible prices.

6. Marketing and planning assistance: Ruth Ways feels that foreign distributors know their own markets best. Therefore, they are best equipped to plan for themselves.

7. Selection of foreign markets: The evaluation of foreign market opportunities for the company's products is based primarily on disposable income and lifestyle patterns. For example, Ruth fails to see any market in North Africa for Alumux's products, which she thinks are of a semiluxury nature. She thinks that cheaper products such as wood ladders (often homemade) are preferred to prefabricated aluminum ladders in regions such as North Africa and Southern Europe. Argentina, on the other hand, she thinks is a more highly industrialized market with luxury tastes. Thus, Ruth sees Alumux's products as better suited for more highly industrialized and affluent societies.

Evaluate Alumux's present foreign markets strategies. Should it develop a global strategy? What strategy or strategies should Ed Mackey (the new VP of Marketing) develop? Explain.

36 Romano's Take-Out, Inc.

Angelina Cello, manager of the Romano's Take-Out store in Flint, Michigan, is trying to develop a plan for the "sick" store she just took over.

Romano's Take-Out, Inc. (RT), is an owner-managed pizza take-out and delivery business with three stores located in Ann Arbor, Southfield, and Flint, Michigan. RT's business comes from telephone or walk-in orders. Each RT store prepares its own pizzas. In addition to pizzas, RT also sells and delivers a limited selection of soft drinks.

RT's Ann Arbor store has been very successful. Much of the store's success may be due to being close to the University of Michigan campus—with more than 35,000 students. Most of these students live within five miles of RT's Ann Arbor store.

The Southfield store has been moderately successful. It serves mostly residential customers in the Southfield area—a largely residential suburb of Detroit. Recently, the store advertised—using direct-mail flyers—to several office buildings within three miles of the store. The flyers described RT's willingness and ability to cater large orders for office parties, business luncheons, and so on. The promotion was quite successful. With this new program and RT's solid residential base of customers in Southfield, improved profitability at the Southfield location seems assured.

RT's Flint location has had mixed results during the last three years. The Flint store has been obtaining only about half of its orders from residential delivery requests. The Flint store's new manager, Angelina Cello, believes the problem with residential pizza delivery in Flint is due to the location of residential neighborhoods in the area. Flint has several large industrial plants (mostly auto industry related) located throughout the city. Small, mostly factory-worker neighborhoods are distributed in between the various plant sites. As a result, RT's store location can serve only two or three of these neighborhoods on one delivery run. Competition is also relevant. RT has several aggressive competitors who advertise heavily, distribute cents-off coupons, and offer 2-for-1 deals. This aggressive competition is probably why RT's residential sales leveled off in the last year or so. And this competitive pressure seems likely to continue as some of this competition comes from aggressive national chains that are fighting for market share and squeezing little firms like Romano's Take-Out. For now, anyway, Angelina feels she knows how to meet this competition and hold onto the present sales level.

Most of the Flint store's upside potential seems to be in serving the large industrial plants. Many of these plants work two or three shifts—five days a week. During each work shift, workers are allowed one half-hour lunch break—which usually occurs at 11 AM, 8 PM, or 2:30 AM (depending on the shift).

Generally, a customer will call from a plant about 30 minutes before a scheduled lunch break and order several (5 to 10) pizzas for a work group. RT may receive many orders of this size from the same plant (i.e., from different groups of workers). The plant business is very profitable for several reasons. First, a large number of pizzas can be delivered at the same time to the same location, saving transportation costs. Second, plant orders usually involve many different toppings (double cheese, pepperoni, mushrooms, hamburger) on each pizza. This results in $11

TABLE 1 Practical Capacities and Sales Potential of Current Equipment and Personnel

	11 AM Break	8 PM Break	2:30 AM Break	Daily Totals
Current capacity (pizzas)	48	48	48	144
Average selling price per unit	$ 12.50	$ 12.50	$ 12.50	$ 12.50
Sales potential	$600	$600	$600	$1,800
Variable cost (approximately 40 percent of selling price)*	240	240	240	720
Contribution margin of pizzas	360	360	360	1,080
Beverage sales (2 medium-sized beverages per pizza ordered at 75¢ a piece)†	72	72	72	216
Cost of beverages (30% per beverage)	22	22	22	66
Contribution margin of beverages	50	50	50	150
Total contribution of pizza and beverages	$410	$410	$410	$1,230

*The variable cost estimate of 40% of sales includes variable costs of delivery to plant locations.

†Amounts shown are not physical capacities (there is almost unlimited physical capacity), but potential sales volume is constrained by number of pizzas that can be sold.

to $14 revenue per pizza. The delivery drivers also like delivering plant orders because the tips are usually $1 to $2 per pizza.

Despite the profitability of the plant orders, several factors make it difficult to serve the plant market. RT's store is located 5 to 8 minutes from most of the plant sites, so RT's staff must prepare the orders within 20 to 25 minutes after it receives the telephone order. Often, inadequate staff and/or oven capacity means it is impossible to get all the orders heated at the same time.

Generally, plant workers will wait as long as 10 minutes past the start of their lunch break before ordering from various vending trucks that arrive at the plant sites during lunch breaks. (Currently, no other pizza delivery stores are in good positions to serve most plant locations and/or have chosen to compete.) But there have been a few instances when workers refused to pay for pizzas that were only five minutes late! Worse yet, if the same work group gets a couple of late orders, they are lost as future customers. Angelina Cello believes that the inconsistent profitability of the Flint store is partly the result of such lost customers.

In an effort to rebuild the plant delivery business, Angelina is considering various methods to ensure prompt customer delivery. She thinks that potential demand during lunch breaks is significantly above RT's present capacity. Angelina also knows that if she tries to satisfy all phone orders on some peak days, she won't be able to provide prompt service—and may lose more plant customers.

Angelina has outlined three alternatives that may win back some of the plant business for the Flint store. She has developed these alternatives to discuss with RT's owner. Each alternative is briefly described below:

TABLE 2 Capacity and Demand for Plant Customer Market

	Estimated Daily Demand	Current Daily Capacity	Proposed Daily Capacity
Pizza units (1 pizza)	320	144	300

Alternative 1: Determine practical capacities during peak volume periods using existing equipment and personnel. Accept orders only up to that capacity and politely decline orders beyond. This approach will ensure prompt customer service and high product quality. It will also minimize losses resulting from customers' rejection of late deliveries. Financial analysis of this alternative—shown in Table 1—indicates that a potential daily contribution to profit of $1,230 could result if this alternative is implemented successfully. This would be profit before promotion costs, overhead, and net profit (or loss). Note: Any alternative will require several thousand dollars to reinform potential plant customers that Romano's Take-Out has improved its service and "wants your business."

Alternative 2: Add additional equipment (one oven and one delivery car) and hire additional staff to handle peak loads. This approach would ensure timely customer delivery and high product quality—as well as provide additional capacity to handle unmet demand. Table 2 is a conservative estimate of potential daily demand for plant orders compared to current capacity and proposed in-

TABLE 3 Cost of Required Additional Assets

	Cost	Estimated Useful Life	Salvage Value	Annual Depreciation*	Daily Depreciation†
Delivery car (equipped with pizza warmer)	$11,000	5 years	$1,000	$2,000	$5.71
Pizza oven	$20,000	8 years	$2,000	$2,250	$6.43

*Annual depreciation is calculated on a straight-line basis.

†Daily depreciation assumes a 350-day (plant production) year. All variable expenses related to each piece of equipment (e.g., utilities, gas, oil) are included in the variable cost of a pizza.

creased capacity. Table 3 gives the cost of acquiring the additional equipment and relevant information related to depreciation and fixed costs.

Using this alternative, the following additional pizza preparation and delivery personnel costs would be required:

	Hours Required	Cost per Hour	Total Additional Daily Cost
Delivery Personnel	6	6	$36.00
Preparation personnel	8	6	48.00
			$84.00

The addition of even more equipment and personnel to handle all unmet demand was not considered in this alternative because the current store is not large enough.

Alternative 3: Add additional equipment and personnel as described in alternative 2, but move to a new location that would reduce delivery lead times to two to five minutes. This move would probably allow RT to handle all unmet demand—because the reduction in delivery time will provide for additional oven time. In fact, RT might have excess capacity using this approach.

A suitable store is available near about the same number of residential customers (including many of the store's current residential customers). The available store is slightly larger than needed. And the rent is higher. Relevant cost information on the proposed store appears below:

Additional rental expense of proposed store over current store	$ 1,600 per year
Cost of moving to new store (one-time cost)	$16,000

Angelina Cello presented the three alternatives to RT's owner—Romano Marino. Romano was pleased that Angelina had done her homework. He decided that Angelina should make the final decision on what to do (in part because she had a profit-sharing agreement with Romano) and offered the following comments and concerns:

1. Romano agreed that the plant market was extremely sensitive to delivery timing. Product quality and pricing, although important, were of less importance.

2. He agreed that plant demand estimates were conservative. "In fact they may be 10 to 30 percent low."

3. Romano expressed concern that under alternative 2, and especially under alternative 3, much of the store's capacity would go unused over 80 percent of the time.

4. He was also concerned that RT's store had a bad reputation with plant customers because the prior store manager was not sensitive to timely plant delivery. So Romano suggested that Angelina develop a promotion plan to improve RT's reputation in the plants and be sure everyone knows that RT has improved its delivery service.

Evaluate Angelina's possible strategies for the Flint store's plant market. What should Angelina do? Why? Suggest possible promotion plans for your preferred strategy.

Computer-Aided Problems

Guide to the Use of the Computer-Aided Problems

COMPUTER-AIDED PROBLEM SOLVING

Marketing managers are problem solvers who must make many decisions. Solving problems and making good decisions usually involve analysis of marketing information. Such information is often expressed in numbers. For example, a marketing manager needs to know how many customers are in the target market—how many units of a product will be sold at a certain price—to estimate how much profit a company is likely to earn with a marketing strategy. Marketing managers also analyze marketing-related costs—to help control their marketing plans.

Many marketing managers now use personal computers to help them analyze information. The speed of computer calculations means that managers can look at a problem from many different angles. They can see how a change in one aspect of the plan may affect the rest of the plan.

The computer can only take a manager so far. It can help keep track of the numbers and speed through tedious calculations. But the manager is the one who puts it all together. It takes skill to decide what the information means.

The computer-aided problems at the end of each chapter in this text—and the accompanying computer program that you will use to solve them—were specially developed by the authors to help you develop this skill. The computer program is named PLUS—an abbreviation for Professional Learning Units Systems. PLUS is similar to other programs that marketing managers use to analyze decisions—but it is easier to use. Master diskettes in both DOS and Windows formats with the computer program and all of the problems are available to instructors from the publisher.

Most of the problems are short descriptions of decisions faced by marketing managers. Each description includes information to help make the decision. The information for each problem is in the PLUS computer program. There are several questions for you to answer to each problem. The *Learning Aid for Use with Basic Marketing* includes additional exercises related to each problem. Although you will use the computer program to do an analysis, most problems ask you to indicate what decision you would make—and why. Thus, in these problems—as in the marketing manager's job—the computer program is just a tool to help you make better decisions.

Each of the problems focuses on one or more of the marketing decision areas discussed in that chapter. The earlier problems require less marketing knowledge and are simpler in terms of the analysis involved. The later problems build on the principles already covered in the text. The problems can be used in many ways. And the same problem can be analyzed several times for different purposes. While it is not necessary to do all of the problems or to do them in a particular order, you will probably want to start with the first problem. This practice problem is simpler than the others. In fact, you could do the calculations quite easily without a computer. But this problem will help you see how the program works—and how it can help you solve the more complicated problems that come later.

SPREADSHEET ANALYSIS OF MARKETING PROBLEMS

Marketing managers often use spreadsheet analysis to evaluate their alternatives—and the PLUS program does computerized spreadsheet analysis. In spreadsheet analysis, costs, revenue, and other data related to a marketing problem are organized into a data table—a spreadsheet. Spreadsheet analysis allows you to change the value of one or more of the variables in the data table—to see how each change affects the value of other variables. This is possible because the relationships among the variables are programmed into the computer. Let's look at an overly simple example.

You are a marketing manager interested in the total revenue that will result from a particular marketing strategy. You are considering selling your product at $10.00 per unit. You expect to sell 100 units. In our PLUS analysis, this problem might be shown in a (very simple) spreadsheet that looks like this:

Variable	Value
Selling price	$ 10.00
Units sold	100
Total revenue	$1,000.00

There is only one basic relationship in this spreadsheet: total revenue is equal to the selling price multiplied by the number of units sold. If that relationship has been programmed into the computer (as it is in these problems), you can change the selling price or the number of units you expect to sell, and the program will compute the new value for total revenue.

But now you can ask questions like: "What if I raise the price to $10.40 and still sell 100 units? What will happen to total revenue?" To get the answer, all you have to do is enter the new price in the spreadsheet, and the program will compute the total revenue for you.

You may also want to do many What If analyses—for example, to see how total revenue changes over a range of prices. Computerized spreadsheet analysis allows you to do this quickly and easily. For example, if you want to see what happens to total revenue as you vary the price between some minimum value (say, $8.00) and a maximum value (say, $12.00), the program will provide a What If analysis showing total revenue for 11 different prices in the range from $8.00 to $12.00.

In a problem like this—with easy numbers and a simple relationship between the variables—the spreadsheet does not do that much work for you. You could do it in your head. But with more complicated problems, the spreadsheet program can be a big help—making it very convenient to more carefully analyze different alternatives or situations.

USING THE PLUS PROGRAM

Don't worry. You don't have to know about computers to use the PLUS program! It was designed to be easy to learn and use. Instructions appear on the screen when you need them, and the program will give you more detailed "help" information whenever you need it. Feel free to try things out. A mistake won't hurt anything! If you try something that isn't useful at that point in the program, the computer will beep at you or display a message. In that case, just check the message and do what it says—or use the help feature and try again! Help is available whenever you need it by pressing H in the DOS version or by clicking on the Help button in the Windows version. So you may want to go ahead and install the program and try the practice problem now—especially if you've used a computer before.

BOTH DOS AND WINDOWS VERSIONS ARE EASY TO USE

The PLUS program is available from the publisher in two popular formats—DOS and Windows. Both versions are easy to use. Your instructor can give you information about which version(s) of the software are available to you or where you can use it. For example, one or both versions of the program may already be loaded and available in the computer lab at your school. Or, your instructor may tell you how you can make your own copy of the program.

Both versions of the software are easy to use and specifically designed for the computer-aided problems, so which version is "best" depends mainly on the computing situation at your school. Or, if you will be using it somewhere else, it may depend on your computer experience and the computer on which you will be using the software. In general, if you don't have much (or any) previous computer experience, you may want to stick with the DOS version; it will work on almost any IBM-compatible computer and doesn't assume any experience in using a mouse or the Windows operating system. On the other hand, if you have used other Windows programs in the past and prefer using a mouse over using the keyboard, you'll probably like the newer Windows version. As detailed below, the Windows version requires a computer with more memory.

Hardware/software requirements

DOS version: The DOS version of the PLUS computer program is designed to work on IBM personal computers (microcomputers) and other true IBM-compatible microcomputers with at least 256K of memory and Microsoft DOS version 2.0 or higher. Almost all IBM computers have this much memory. But you don't have to know how much memory your computer has. The program will tell you if your computer doesn't have enough memory to make the program work. Some problems will work with less memory than others; even if your computer has less than 256K of memory, the program will work if the computer has enough memory for the problem you're working on. The software operates faster if it is run from a hard drive, but a hard drive is not necessary and the DOS version can be run from the floppy disk. You control the DOS version by pressing keys on the keyboard; in other words, your computer does not need to have a mouse. If the computer does have a mouse, it simply isn't used for the DOS version of PLUS.

Windows version: The Windows version of the PLUS computer program is designed to work on IBM personal computers and other true IBM-compatible microcomputers with at least 2 MB of memory. For PLUSWIN to run, Microsoft ® Windows™ 3.1 must already be installed and set up on your computer. Unlike the DOS version of PLUS, the Windows version cannot be run from a floppy disk; rather, it must first be installed on the computer's hard drive before you can run it.

EXHIBIT 1 The Problem Selection Screen for the DOS Version of the PLUS Computer Program

```
                    P L U S – Problem Selection

            1.   Revenue, Cost, and Profit Relationships
            2.   Target Marketing
            3.   Segmenting Customers
            4.   Competitor Analysis
            5.   Marketing Research
            6.   Demographic Analysis
            7.   Selective Processes
            8.   Vendor Analysis
            9.   Branding Decision
           10.   Growth Stage Competition
           11.   Intensive vs. Selective Distribution
           12.   Total Distribution Cost
           13.   Selecting Channel Intermediaries
           14.   Selecting a Communications Channel
           15.   Sales Compensation
         ↓ 16.   Sales Promotion

     ┌──────────────────────────────────────────────────────┐
     │ Use the arrow keys to highlight the desired problem.  Press  P  to │
     │ "Work the highlighted Problem."   Press the  H  key if you need Help. │
     ├──────────────────────────────────────────────────────┤
     │ Highlight Down   Highlight Up    Work Highlighted Problem    Help    Quit │
     │ Use  PgDn  or  PgUp  key to see more of problem list │
     └──────────────────────────────────────────────────────┘
```

While the DOS and Windows versions of the program are very similar, some of the specifics of installing and using the versions differ. Thus, the rest of these instructions are divided into two parts—one for the DOS version and one for the Windows version. *You don't need to read both parts.* If you will be using the DOS version, read the next section. However, if you will be using the Windows version, skip to the section titled "Installing and Using the Windows Version" on page 777.

INSTALLING AND USING THE DOS VERSION OF PLUS

Typically, all you need to do to start the PLUS software is put the disk in the disk drive, make that drive the default drive, and type PLUS and press return. For example, if you put the disk in the A: drive you type

A: <enter>

at the DOS prompt to make A: the default drive, and then you type

PLUS <enter>

to start the program. However, if the software has been set up for your use on a computer with a hard drive or in

a computer lab, the person who has set it up will give you instructions on starting it.

If you want to install the program on the hard drive of your own personal computer, place the disk in the A drive and, at the A: > prompt, type **install** <Enter>. Then, simply follow the instructions displayed on your screen. Once the software is installed on your hard drive, make the subdirectory of the hard drive where the PLUS software is installed the default directory. For example, the install procedure puts the software on the C: drive in the subdirectory with the name \BMSPREAD; you would set that as the default drive by typing

C:\BMSPREAD <enter>

at the DOS prompt. Then, to start the program you simply type

PLUS <enter>

at the DOS prompt.

If your computer does not have a color monitor, the highlighting may not show on your screen. In that case, just press Q to exit the program. Then start the software over again by typing

PLUS NOCOLOR <enter>

at the DOS prompt. That should correct the problem.

Start at the problem selection screen

When you use the program, the first screen displayed is the Title Screen. By pressing any key, you will move on to the Problem Selection Screen—the real starting point of the program. The Problem Selection Screen (see Exhibit 1) shows a list of problems. The problem at the top of the list will be highlighted. In the menu box at the bottom of the screen, you will see the phrase "Work Highlighted **P**roblem," and the letter P will be highlighted. If you want to work the problem highlighted on the list, simply press the P key, and the program will display a short description of the problem you selected. The questions for each problem appear in this book—so have this book with you at the computer when you're actually doing the problem.

If you want to work another problem on the list—instead of the highlighted one—look again at the menu box at the bottom of the Problem Selection Screen. You will see the phrase "Highlight **D**own" with the letter D highlighted and "Highlight **U**p" with the letter U highlighted. Press the letter D to move the highlighting down to the next problem on the list. Pressing the U key will move the highlighting up the list of problems.

Most personal computers have special keys labeled with left, right, up, and down arrows. You can also use these special arrow keys to move up or down the problem list. If you've never used a computer, you will probably find it useful to look at Exhibit 2. It provides a labeled drawing of a typical keyboard—and briefly explains the purpose of the special keys. It also shows the normal location of the arrow keys and other keys mentioned in these instructions.

On the Problem Selection Screen, you will also see a small down-pointing arrow near the bottom of the list of problems. You will see an arrow like this on other screen displays as well. The arrow means that additional information is available—but won't all fit on the screen at the same time. For example, on the Problem Selection Screen the down-pointing arrow means that the list of problems continues beyond what you see on the screen. To bring the additional information onto the screen—continue to press the D key (to move highlighting **D**own). Similarly, you will sometimes see a small up-pointing arrow on the screen. When this appears, you can use the U key ("Highlight **U**p") to move back to the top of the information. The special keys marked PgDn (which stands for "Page Down") and PgUp (which stands for "Page Up") can also be used when the down arrow or up arrow appears on a screen. The best way to see what they do is to try them out when a small arrow appears on the screen.

Moving to the problem description and spreadsheet screens

Once you select a problem from the Problem Selection Screen, a Problem Description Screen will appear. This gives a brief description of that problem. Then you can continue to the Spreadsheet Screen for that problem by following the menu box instructions. The spreadsheet displays the starting values for the problem.

Each spreadsheet consists of one or two columns of numbers. Each column and row is labeled. Look at the row and column labels carefully to see what variable is represented by the value (number) in the spreadsheet. Study the layout of the spreadsheet and get a feel for how it organizes the information from the printed problem description in this text. You will see that some of the values in the spreadsheet are marked with an asterisk (*). These are usually values related to the decision variables in the problem you are solving. *You can change any value (number) marked with an asterisk.* When you make a change, the rest of the values (numbers) in that column are recalculated to show how a change in the value of one variable affects the others.

Making changes in values is easy. When the Spreadsheet Screen appears, you will see that one of the values in the spreadsheet is highlighted. As on the Problem Selection Screen, think of the highlighting as a pointer that shows where you are in the spreadsheet. Use the D key to move **D**own, the U key to move **U**p, the R key to move **R**ight, and the L key to move **L**eft until you are highlighting the value you want to change. (Note: You can also use the up, down, left, and right arrow keys to move around on the screen.)

When you have highlighted the value (number) you want to change, just type in your new number. This number will show in the menu box at the bottom of the screen as you type. When you are finished typing the number, press the enter key and the other values in the spreadsheet will be recalculated to show the effect of your new value. (Note: The enter key is much like a "carriage return" key on a typewriter. It is usually larger than other keys and is located on the right side of the keyboard. Usually, a bent arrow is printed on the enter key (Exhibit 2 shows the normal location of the enter key).

When you are typing numbers into the PLUS program, you type the numbers and the decimal point as you would on a typewriter. For example, a price of $1,000.50 would be typed as 1000.50 or just 1000.5—*using the number keys on the top row of the keyboard* and the period key for the decimal point. *Do not type in the dollar sign or the commas to indicate thousands.* Be careful not to type the letters o or l (lowercase L) instead of the numbers 0 or 1.

Typing percent values is a possible point of confusion since there are different ways to think about a percent. For example, 10½ percent might be represented by 10.5 or .105. To avoid confusion, the program always expects you to enter percents using the first approach, which is the way percents are discussed in the problems. Thus, if you want to enter the value for 10½ percent, you would type 10.5.

EXHIBIT 2   Diagram of a Typical Keyboard for an IBM-Compatible Computer

Press PgUp key to view additional text when an up-pointing arrow appears on the screen.

Press PgDn key to view additional text when a down-pointing arrow appears on the screen.

Use number keys to type numbers for spreadsheet and what if analysis.

Press backspace key to erase typing errors.

Press space bar to select highlighted value to vary, or to select (or unselect) value(s) to display.

Use period key to type a decimal point in a number.

Press enter key when you are finished typing a number.

Press right arrow key to move highlighting to right column on spreadsheet.

Press up arrow key to move highlighting up on the screen.

Press down arrow key to move highlighting down on the screen.

Press left arrow key to move highlighting to left column on spreadsheet.

To help prevent errors, a set of permitted values is programmed into the computer for each problem. For example, you cannot accidentally type a letter when the computer program expects a number. Or, if you type a number that is outside of the permitted range, the program will display a message in the menu box. Just read the message—to see what range of values are permitted—and then use the backspace key to erase what you have typed. (Note: The backspace key is usually toward the right side of the top row of the keyboard—along with the number keys—and it is usually marked with a left-pointing bold arrow. See Exhibit 2.) After you use the backspace key to erase what you typed earlier, retype a new number that is in the permitted range—and then press the enter key to recompute the spreadsheet.

For example, if you try to type −10.00 as the price of a product, the menu box might display a message that you can only enter a value greater than 1 and less than 20 for that variable. (It doesn't make sense to set the price as a negative number!) You could then backspace to erase what you typed, type in a new value, and finally press the enter key.

Remember that a value stays changed until you change it again. Some of the questions that accompany the problems ask you to evaluate results associated with different sets of values. It's good practice to check that you have entered all the correct values on a spreadsheet before interpreting the results.

In addition to changing values (numbers) in the spreadsheet itself, the selections in the menu box have other uses. If you press the O key for "**O**utput to printer," the current spreadsheet will be printed. (Before you press the O key, make sure that your computer has a printer, that it is plugged into both power and the computer, that it is turned on, and that the paper is loaded where you want it to start printing. The first time you use the printer, the program will ask you to type in your name. That way, each printout will have your name at the top.)

The menu box may also show the phrase "Select another **P**roblem," with the letter P highlighted. If you press the P key, you will be returned to the Problem Selection Screen. Similarly, you may see the phrase "Do What If" with the letter W highlighted. If you press the W key, you will see a new screen that starts a What If analysis.

What If analysis

The What If part of the program allows you to study in more detail the effect of changing the value of a particular variable. It systematically changes the value of a variable—and displays the effect that variable has on other variables. As before, all you have to do is follow the instructions in the menu box at the bottom of the screen. You could do the same thing "manually" at the Spreadsheet Screen—by entering a value for a variable, checking the effect on other variables, and then repeating the process over and over again. But the manual approach is time-consuming and requires you to keep track of the results after each change. A What If analysis does all this very quickly and presents the results on the screen.

Now let's go through the What If analysis part of the PLUS program step-by-step. The menu box will remind you what to do, and you can press the H key (for help) to get additional detail while you're using the program. You start a What If analysis by pressing the W key when "Do What If" is an option in the menu box. The Select Value to Vary Screen will appear. It shows the values for those variables you can change (ones marked with an asterisk on the original Spreadsheet Screen). One value on the Select Value to Vary Screen will be highlighted. As with other screens, you can use the D, U, R, or L keys (or the up, down, right, or left arrow keys) to "move" the highlighting to some other variable. When the value (number) you want to change is highlighted, simply press the space bar (the long key across the bottom center of the keyboard). The letter V will appear beside that value—to remind you what variable you have selected to vary.

The menu box at the bottom of the screen will then prompt you to type in a new minimum value for that variable. It will also show a suggested minimum value. This suggested minimum value is usually 20 percent smaller than the value from the initial spreadsheet. If you press the enter key at this point, this suggested value will be used as the minimum value in the analysis. You might want to do this your first time through to get some quick results. Later, you can type in your own minimum value the same way you do in the Spreadsheet Screen. Remember that you can use the backspace key to correct any errors. Press the enter key when you are finished typing.

Next you will be prompted to provide the largest value for the analysis. Here again, you can accept the program's suggested maximum value by pressing the enter key. Or, if you wish, you can type in your own value.

After you enter the minimum and maximum values for the variable you want to change, the screen will change to the Select Values to Display Screen. You will be prompted to select the variables for which you want summary results to be displayed. Typically, you will want to display the results (computed values) for variables that will be affected by the variable you select to vary. Remember the example we used earlier. If you specified that price was going to vary, you might want to display total revenue—to see how it changes at different price levels.

You select a variable to display in the same way you select the variable you are going to change. Use the arrow keys to move from one value (number) to another. The highlighting moves to show you where you are. If you want the values of the highlighted variable to appear in the results table, press the space bar. The letter D will appear beside that value—as a reminder of the variable you selected to be displayed. If you change your mind, you can press the space bar again to "unselect" the highlighted value. The D will disappear—and that variable will not be displayed in the results table.

You can use this approach to select up to three variables to be displayed as the output of a What If analysis. When you have completed this step, you will see a V beside the variable you chose to vary and a D beside one, two, or three variables that you want to display.

Now you can let the computer take over. In the menu box at the bottom of the screen, you will see the phrase "**A**nalyze & display data," and the letter A will be highlighted. If you press the A key, the results of the What If analysis will appear on the screen. Each row in the first column of the table will show a different value for the variable you wanted to vary. The minimum value you specified will be in the first row. The maximum value will be in the bottom row. Evenly spaced values between the minimum and maximum will be in the middle rows. The other column(s) show the calculated "results" for the values you selected to display. Each column of values is labeled at the top to identify the column and row from the spreadsheet. The row portion of the label is a short version of the label from the spreadsheet. The results are based on the values that were on the Spreadsheet Screen when you started the What If analysis—except for the value you selected to vary.

At this point you will want to study the results of your analysis. As with the Spreadsheet Screen, you can output a printed copy of the results. The menu box shows other possibilities. For example, if you press the C key to Continue with the What If analysis, the Select Value to Vary Screen will reappear. The screen will show the values you selected in the previous analysis. The value you varied before will be highlighted. You can select the same value again by pressing the space bar, or highlight and select another value. If you want to display the values you selected before, press the A key (Analyze & display data). Or you can "Clear" those selections by pressing the C key, and then you can highlight and select new values to display.

At any point in the What If analysis, you can return to the Spreadsheet Screen. From there you can make additional changes in the values in the spreadsheet, do a new What If analysis, or select another problem to work. Or, if your computer has the right equipment, you can look at (and print) a graph of values on the What If Display Screen.

Viewing a graph of your results

You can create a graph of values on the What If Display Screen by pressing the G key (for **G**raph Data). The horizontal axis for the graph will be the variable in the first column of the display. The vertical axis is based on the column that is highlighted when you press the G key. Before you press the G key, you can use the right arrow key (or the R key for **R**ight) to change which column is highlighted and will be graphed. From the Graph View Screen, you can print the graph, or you can go back and select other values to vary or select another column to graph. Or you can go back to the Spreadsheet Screen.

For the Graph Data feature to work properly, your computer must be equipped with the correct type of graphics display (monitor) and printer. If you press G for **G**raph Data and your computer does not have the correct type of graphics monitor, the Graph View Screen will not appear and instead you will see a message indicating that your computer can't display the type of graphs produced by the PLUS program. For a graph to print properly, your printer must be 100 percent compatible with IBM graphics standards. That means, for example, that graphs for the DOS version of PLUS will not print properly on most Hewlett-Packard printers, including the HP Laserjet series of printers.

What to do next

The section titled "Some Tips on Using the PLUS Program"—which starts on page 781, gives additional tips on using the PLUS program. You will probably want to look through it after you have done some work with the practice problem. For now, however, you're probably tired of reading instructions. So work a problem or two. It's easier and faster to use the program than to read about it! Give it a try, and don't be afraid to experiment. If you have problems, remember that the *Help* option is available when you need it.

This completes the instructions for the DOS version of the program—so you can skip the material that follows—it focuses on the Windows version.

INSTALLING AND USING THE WINDOWS VERSION

(Note: you should read this section only if you will be using the Windows version of the software.)

The Windows version of the PLUS software follows conventions that are standard to all Windows programs, and as a result there are usually several different ways to accomplish the same task. For example, you typically use a mouse to "move around" in the program and select options, but you can usually do the same thing by using the keyboard. In these instructions we'll explain how the key Windows conventions apply in the context of the PLUS software, but we'll focus primarily on using the mouse. However, if you want more general information about using Windows software you may want to review the documentation and tutorial that comes with the Windows operating system.

Installing the software

The Windows version of the PLUS software must be installed to the computer's hard drive before it will run. Place the setup disk for the Windows version of PLUS in your A: drive. From the Windows Program Manager (the screen you usually see when you start Windows), select the File option from the menu at the top of the screen. You can do this by pressing the alt-key and the F key at the same time, or by moving the mouse until the cursor is over the word File and then clicking the mouse (that is, press the left key). Then, from the menu that appears, select the Run option using the same approach. In the prompt window that appears, type **a:\setup** and click the mouse on the Ok button. The installation program will copy the program to a subdirectory on your hard drive and create a Program Group icon in your Program Manager to use in starting the program. Simply double click on the PLUS icon to start the program.

Let's use the first problem in the PLUS program to illustrate how the program works.

Start by selecting a problem

When you start the program, the first screen displayed is the Title Screen. Move the mouse so that the cursor (which appears on your screen as an arrow) is over the image of the Basic Marketing text, and quickly press and release the left button on the mouse. This process of using the mouse to position the cursor and then pressing and releasing the left bottom is called "clicking." In these instructions, we'll refer to this often. For example, we'll say things like "click on help." Sometimes we'll tell you to "double click," which simply means to click the mouse twice in quick succession.

When you click on the image on the title page, you will move to the Name Entry box. Type in your name and press enter or click on Ok. This takes you to the Problem Selection window—the real starting point of the program. The Problem Selection window (see Exhibit 3) shows a list of problems, two "bars" at the top of the screen with information, and an instruction box at the bottom of the screen. You'll see similar bars and instruction boxes on other screens, so we'll discuss them briefly before getting to the problem selection list.

The title bar at the very top of the screen shows the name of the program and features three "control boxes." As with any Windows program, if you double click on the control box on the left side of the title bar, you'll immediately exit the program and return to the Program Manager. Or, if you want to run some other Windows program while you are still working with PLUS (perhaps a word processor to make notes concerning your answers for one of the computer-aided problems), you can click on the control box with the down-pointing arrow on the right-hand side of the title bar. Clicking that control box returns you to the Windows Program Manager and creates an icon (symbol) that represents the PLUS program—without actually shutting down the program. Then, when you're ready, you can instantly return to where you left off in the PLUS program by double clicking on the icon. You may never use these features, but they're ready if you need them.

Under the title bar there is a menu bar. On the left side of the menu bar you'll see labels for two options: File and Help. If you click on the Help option, you'll get more information about using the PLUS software—starting with information about what to do at the current screen. You can also search for help on other topics. Alternatively, if you click on the File option, a drop-down menu allows you to exit the program by clicking on the label for the Exit option.

Rather than clicking to select an option, you can select an option on the menu bar by pressing the alt key and holding it while you also press the key for the letter that is underlined in the option label. For example, pressing the alt key and the H key at the same time activates the Help option.

As you use the PLUS program, you'll see that different options appear at different points during your work. Simply select the one(s) you want by clicking on the option label or by pressing—at the same time—the alt key and the underlined letter in the option name. And, if you want a brief reminder about what to do next,

you're likely to find it displayed in the instruction box at the bottom of the screen.

Now, let's take a closer look at the problem list; there's one problem for each of the first 20 chapters in this text. One problem is highlighted. To work that problem, just double click on it or press the enter key. If you want to work some other problem, double click its name on the list. Alternatively, as explained in the instruction box at the bottom of the screen, you can use the up or down arrow keys to highlight the new problem and then press the enter key.

From the problem selection to the problem description and spreadsheet

Once you select a problem, there is a slight delay and then the Problem Description window appears. This window is a convenient reminder of the problem description found in this text. (The questions for each problem are in this book, so have your book with you at the computer when you're actually doing an assigned problem.)

There is usually more text than fits in the Problem Description window at one time. You can scroll the rest of the text onto the screen by using the up or down arrow keys or the special PgUp or PgDn keys. If you prefer, you can use your mouse to scroll the text. Note that there is a *scroll bar* along the right-hand edge of the Problem Description window; there are arrows at the top and bottom of the scroll bar and between the arrows there is a scroll box. To move text up or down in the window, click on either the scroll bar's up or down arrow. For continuous scrolling, position the cursor over the arrow and hold the button on the mouse down rather than clicking it; when you release the button the scrolling stops. To move up or down more quickly, position the mouse over the scroll box, press and hold the button on your mouse, and move the mouse up or down. This allows the mouse to "drag" the scroll box, which moves text up or down in the window. Release the button to stop dragging and scrolling.

At other points in the PLUS program, you will see a scroll bar like this one whenever there is more information than can be displayed in the window at one time. For example, you will usually see a scroll bar when help information is on the screen. You can use the approaches described above in working with any scroll bar.

After you have reviewed the Problem Description, move on to the spreadsheet window for that problem by clicking the "Continue to Spreadsheet" button at the bottom center of the description window. (Remember, as with other options, you can also select this option by pressing the alt key and the C key at the same time, because C is the underlined letter in the option label.)

EXHIBIT 3   Problem Selection Screen for the Windows Version of PLUS

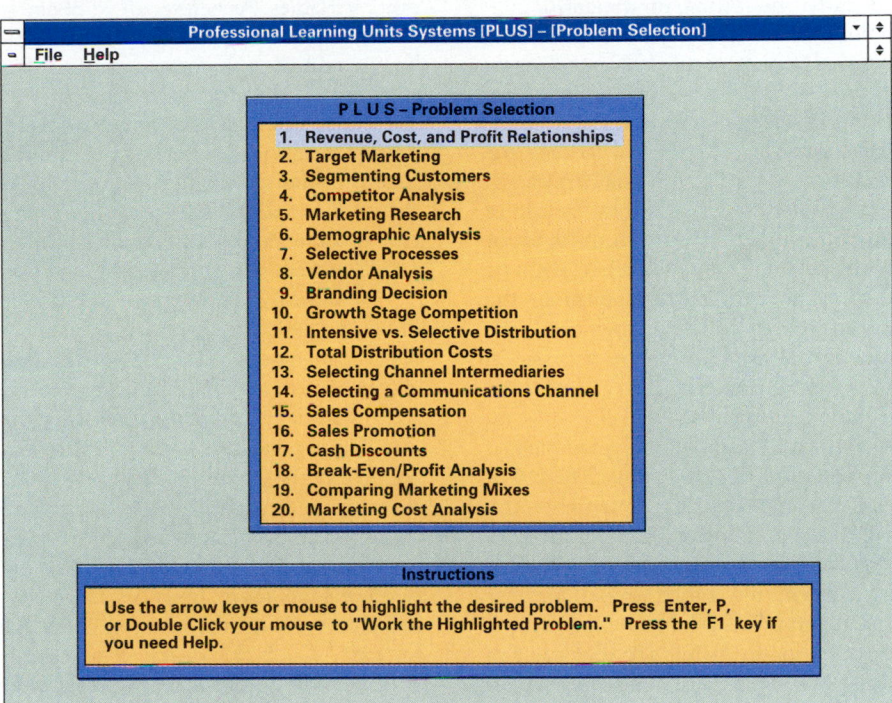

Professional Learning Units Systems [PLUS] – [Problem Selection]

File   Help

P L U S – Problem Selection

1. Revenue, Cost, and Profit Relationships
2. Target Marketing
3. Segmenting Customers
4. Competitor Analysis
5. Marketing Research
6. Demographic Analysis
7. Selective Processes
8. Vendor Analysis
9. Branding Decision
10. Growth Stage Competition
11. Intensive vs. Selective Distribution
12. Total Distribution Costs
13. Selecting Channel Intermediaries
14. Selecting a Communications Channel
15. Sales Compensation
16. Sales Promotion
17. Cash Discounts
18. Break-Even/Profit Analysis
19. Comparing Marketing Mixes
20. Marketing Cost Analysis

Instructions

Use the arrow keys or mouse to highlight the desired problem. Press Enter, P, or Double Click your mouse to "Work the Highlighted Problem." Press the F1 key if you need Help.

Each spreadsheet consists of one or two columns of numbers. Each column and row is labeled. Look at the row and column labels carefully to see what variable is represented by the value (number) in the spreadsheet. Study the layout of the spreadsheet, and get a feel for how it organizes the information from the problem description. The spreadsheet displays the starting values for the problem. You will see that some of the values in the spreadsheet appear in a highlighted box. These are usually values related to the decision variables in the problem you are solving. *You can change any value (number) that appears in one of these boxes.* When you make a change, the rest of the values (numbers) in that column are recalculated to show how a change in the value of one variable affects the others.

Making changes in values is easy. When the spreadsheet first appears, your cursor appears as a free-floating arrow; however, when you pass the cursor over the box for the value that you want to change, the cursor changes to the shape of an "I beam." When you click on the value in that box you can change it. Or, to move the cursor to a value in a different box, just click on that box. Note: Rather than using the mouse, you can also use the tab key to move to the next box, or you can use the combination

of the shift key and the tab key to move backwards to a previous box.

When you have selected the box with the value (number) you want to change, there are different ways to type in your new number. A good approach is to position the I-beam cursor before the first digit, and while holding the mouse button drag the cursor across all of the digits in the number. This will highlight the entire number. Then, simply type in the new number and the old one will be replaced. Alternatively, you can use other keys to "edit" the number. For example, you can use the backspace key to "erase" digits to the left of the I-beam cursor; similarly, you can use the Del key to erase digits to the right of the cursor. Or, you can use the arrow keys to move the cursor to the point where you want to change part of a number. Then you just type in your change. You may want to experiment to see which of these "editing" approaches you like the best.

When you are finished typing the new number, press the enter key and the other values in the spreadsheet will be recalculated to show the effect of your new value. Similarly, the other numbers will recalculate if you click on a different box after you have entered a number.

When you are typing numbers into the PLUS program, you'll probably find it most convenient to type the numbers and the decimal point with the keys on the main part of the keyboard (rather than those on the cursor control pad). For example, a price of one thousand dollars and 50 cents would be typed as 1000.50 or just 1000.5 —*using the number keys on the top row of the keyboard* and the period key for the decimal point. *Do not type in the dollar sign or the commas to indicate thousands.* Be careful not to type the letters o or l (lower case L) instead of the numbers 0 or 1.

Typing percent values is a possible point of confusion—since there are different ways to think about a percent. For example, "ten and a half" percent might be represented by 10.5 or .105. To avoid confusion, the program always expects you to enter percents using the first approach—which is the way percents are discussed in the problems. Thus, if you want to enter the value for ten and a half percent you would type 10.5.

To help prevent errors, each problem is programmed with a set of permitted values for each boxed field. For example, you cannot accidentally type a letter when the computer program expects a number. Further, the program won't allow you to enter a new value for a variable that is outside of a permitted range of values. For example, if you try to type -10.00 as the price of a product, a message might appear to tell you that you can only enter a value that is greater than 1 and less than 20 for that variable. (It doesn't make sense to set the price as a negative number!) If an error message appears, read it to see what range of values is permitted—and then click on the Qk button to return to the spreadsheet. Then, retype a new number that is in the permitted range, and press the enter key to recompute the spreadsheet.

Remember that a value on the spreadsheet stays changed until you change it again. Some of the questions that accompany the problems ask you to evaluate results associated with different sets of values. It's good practice to check that you have entered all the correct values on a spreadsheet before interpreting the results.

In addition to changing values (numbers) on the spreadsheet itself, there are other options on the spreadsheet menu bar. If you click on the Print option, the current spreadsheet will be printed—assuming of course that a printer is properly hooked up to your computer and that it is configured for Windows. Before you select the Print option, make sure that the printer is turned on and loaded with paper.

There are also options to go back and review the problem description or to select another problem. Similarly, you will see the What-If option. If you click on the What-If option (or press the alt key and the W key) a new window will appear that starts a What If analysis.

What If Analysis

The What If part of the program allows you to study in more detail the effect of changing the value of a particular variable. It systematically changes the value of a variable—and displays the effect that variable has on other variables. As before, all you have to do is follow the instructions in the menu box at the bottom of the screen. You could do the same thing "manually" at the spreadsheet—by entering a value for a variable, checking the effect on other variables, and then repeating the process over and over again. But the manual approach is time-consuming and requires you to keep track of the results after each change. A What If analysis does all this very quickly and presents the results in a summary table on the screen; you can also print or graph the results.

Now, let's go through the What If analysis part of the PLUS program step-by-step. Remember that you don't have to memorize this. The instruction box will remind you what to do or you can click on the Help option to get additional detail while you are using the program.

When you start a What If analysis by clicking that option on the menu bar, the appearance of the spreadsheet changes slightly. As before, values for those variables that you can change appear in a highlight box—and the values are the same as they were on the spreadsheet. Beside each of them, however, there is a check box that is in a column under the letter V; the V stands for "Variable to Vary." Click the check box beside the value of the variable you want to vary—and when you do an X appears in the box. You can only select one variable to vary at a time. So, if you click on one variable and then later want to vary some other variable, click on the variable with the X again to unselect it before clicking on your new selection.

When you select a value to vary, a range window will open and show you a "suggested" minimum value and maximum value for the range over which the variable may vary. The suggested minimum value is usually 20 percent smaller than the value from the initial spreadsheet, and the maximum value is 20 percent larger. To get some quick results, you may want to accept these suggested values. If you click on the Qk button at this point, these suggested values will be used as the minimum and maximum values for the What if analysis. However, before you click on the Qk option, you can type in your own minimum value and maximum value. To do that, you can use any of the same approaches as entering new values in the spreadsheet.

After you have entered the minimum and maximum values for the variable you want to change, you select the variables that you want to display in the results of the What If analysis. Typically, you will want to display the results (computed values) for variables that will be affected by the variable you select to vary. Remember the example we used earlier. If you had specified that price was going to vary, you might want to display total revenue—to see how it changes at different price levels.

You select a variable to display in the same way that you select the variable you are going to vary. Any variable that you can display in the What If results table has a check box beside it under the letter D. When you click on the check box beside the value (number) you want to display, an X appears in the box as a reminder of the variable you selected to be displayed. If you change your mind, you can click on the box again to "unselect" it. The X in the box will disappear—and that variable will not be displayed in the Results Table.

You can use this approach to select up to three variables to be displayed in the results table for a What If analysis. When you have completed this step, you will see an X in the box beside the variable you chose to vary, and and X in the check box(es) beside the one, two, or three variables that you want to display.

Now you can let the computer take over. On the menu bar at the top of the What If screen you will see an option for the Results Table. If you click on that option, the results of the What If analysis will appear on the screen. Each row in the first column of the Results Table will show a different value for the variable you wanted to vary. The minimum value you specified will be in the first row. The maximum value will be in the bottom row. Evenly spaced values between the minimum and maximum will be in the middle rows. The other column(s) show the calculated "results" for the values you selected to display. Each column of values is labeled at the top to identify the column and row from the spreadsheet. The row portion of the label is a short version of the label from the spreadsheet. The results are based on the values that were in the spreadsheet when you started the What If analysis—except for the value you selected to vary.

At this point you will want to study the results of your analysis. You can also print a copy of the Results Table by selecting the Print option on the menu bar. The menu bar also shows other possibilities. For example, if you select the Return to What If option the What If window will reappear. Xs in the check boxes will show the values you selected in the previous analysis. You can use that same variable to vary (and minimum and maximum range) again, or you can unselect a variable and select another one. Similarly, you can clear the Xs for all of your previous selections by clicking on the Clear option on the menu bar.

At any point in the What If analysis, you can return to the Spreadsheet by clicking on the Return to Spreadsheet option button. From there you can make additional changes in the values in the spreadsheet, do a new What If analysis, or select another problem to work. Or, you can look at (and print) a graph of values in the What If Results Table.

Viewing a graph of your results

You can create a graph of values in the Results Table by clicking the Graph option on the Results Table menu bar. The horizontal axis for the graph will be the variable in the first column of the display. The vertical axis is based on the column that is selected when you select the Graph option. Before you select the Graph option, click on the bullet button over the column that you want to graph. When the graph is displayed, you can select the Print option to print a copy or you can Close the graph and then go back and select other values to vary or select another column to graph. Or, you can go back to the spreadsheet.

What to do next

The next section gives additional tips on the PLUS program. You will probably want to look through it after you have done some work with the practice problem. For now, however, you're probably tired of reading instructions. So work a problem or two. It's easier and faster to use the program than to read about it! Give it a try, and don't be afraid to experiment. If you have problems, remember that the Help option is available when you need it.

SOME TIPS ON USING THE PLUS PROGRAM

Resetting the spreadsheet to the initial values

The initial spreadsheet for each problem gives the starting values for the problem. While working a problem, you will often change one or more of the starting values to a new number. A changed value stays in effect—unless you change it again. This is a handy feature. But after you make several changes, you may not be able to remember the starting values. There is a simple solution—you can return to the Problem Selection Screen, highlight the problem again, and press the enter key. The spreadsheet will appear with the original set of starting values.

Checking the computer's calculations

Some values appear in the spreadsheet as whole numbers, and others appear with one or more digits to the right of a decimal point. For example, dollar values usually have two digits to the right of the decimal point—indicating how many cents are involved. A value indicating, say, number of customers, however, will appear as a whole number.

When you are doing arithmetic by hand (or with a calculator) you sometimes have to make decisions about how much detail is necessary. For example, if you divide 13 by 3 the answer is 4.33, 4.333, 4.3333, 4.33333, or perhaps 4.333333, depending on how important it is to be precise. Usually we round off the number to keep things manageable. Similarly, computers usually display results after rounding off the numbers. This has the potential to create confusion and seeming inaccuracy when many calculations are involved. If the computer uses a lot of detail in its calculations and then displays intermediate results after rounding off, the numbers may appear to be inconsistent. To illustrate this, let's extend the example above. If you multiply 4.33 times 2640, you get 11431.20. But if you multiply 4.333 by 2640, you get 11439.12. To make it easier for you to check relationships between the values on a spreadsheet, the PLUS program does not use a lot of "hidden detail" in calculations. If it rounds off a number to display it in the spreadsheet, the rounded number is used in subsequent calculations. It would be easy for the computer to keep track of all of the detail in its calculations—but that would make it harder for you to check the results yourself. If you check the results on a spreadsheet with "outside" calculations and find that your numbers are close but do not match exactly, it is probably because you are making different decisions about rounding than were programmed into the spreadsheet.

A warning that you've made an error

The PLUS program was designed and tested to be easy to use and error free. In fact, it is programmed to help prevent the user from making typing errors. But, it is impossible to anticipate every possible combination of numbers that you might enter—and some combinations of numbers can cause problems. For example, a certain combination of numbers might result in an instruction for the computer to divide a number by zero—which is a mathematical impossibility! When a problem of this sort occurs, the word ERROR will appear in the spreadsheet (or in the What If results) instead of a number. If this happens, you should recheck the numbers in the spreadsheet and redo the analysis—to make certain that the numbers you typed in were what you intended. That should straighten out the problem in almost every case. Yet, with any computer program there can be hidden bugs that only surface in unusual situations—or on certain computers. Thus, if you think you have found a bug, we would like to know so that we can track down the source of the difficulty.

Notes

Chapter 1

1. Eric H. Shaw, "A Review of Empirical Studies of Aggregate Marketing Costs and Productivity in the United States," *Journal of the Academy of Marketing Science*, Fall 1990, pp. 285–92; Christopher H. Lovelock and Charles B. Weinberg, *Marketing for Public and Nonprofit Managers* (New York: John Wiley & Sons, 1984).

2. Gregory D. Upah and Richard E. Wokutch, "Assessing Social Impacts of New Products: An Attempt to Operationalize the Macromarketing Concept," *Journal of Public Policy and Marketing* 4 (1985), pp. 166–78.

3. Malcolm P. McNair, "Marketing and the Social Challenge of Our Times," in *A New Measure of Responsibility for Marketing*, ed. Keith Cox and Ben M. Enis (Chicago: American Marketing Association, 1968).

4. An American Marketing Association committee developed a similar—but more complicated—definition of marketing: "Marketing is the process of planning and executing conception, pricing, promotion, and distribution of ideas, goods, and services to create exchanges that satisfy individual and organizational objectives." See *Marketing News*, March 1, 1985, p. 1. See also Ernest F. Cooke, C. L. Abercrombie, and J. Michael Rayburn, "Problems with the AMA's New Definition of Marketing Offer Opportunity to Develop an Even Better Definition," *Marketing Educator*, Spring 1986, p. 1ff.; O. C. Ferrell and George H. Lucas, Jr., "An Evaluation of Progress in the Development of a Definition of Marketing," *Journal of the Academy of Marketing Science*, Fall 1987, pp. 12–23.

5. George Fisk, "Editor's Working Definition of Macromarketing," *Journal of Macromarketing* 2, no. 1 (1982), pp. 3–4; Shelby D. Hunt and John J. Burnett, "The Macromarketing/Micromarketing Dichotomy: A Taxonomical Model," *Journal of Marketing*, Summer 1982, pp. 11–26; J. F. Grashof and A. Kelman, *Introduction to Macro-Marketing* (Columbus, OH: Grid, 1973).

6. For a more complete discussion of this topic see Y. H. Furuhashi and E. J. McCarthy, *Social Issues of Marketing in the American Economy* (Columbus, OH: Grid, 1971), pp. 4–6.

7. Stanislaw Gajewski, "Consumer Behavior in Economics of Shortage," *Journal of Business Research*, January 1992, pp. 5–10; Krystyna Iwinska-Knop, "Distribution as a Barrier to Application of Marketing in the Centrally Planned Economy (Case Study of Poland)," *Journal of Business Research*, January 1992, pp. 19–26; "Russia's New Capitalism," *Business Week*, October 10, 1994, pp. 68–80; "They're Better Rich than Red," *Newsweek*, August 23, 1993, pp. 34–36; "In Russia, Wealth Glimmers amid Poverty," *USA Today*, August 23, 1993, p. 7A; "In Capitalist Moscow, Young Business Grads Reap Money and Envy," *The Wall Street Journal*, August 2, 1993, p. A1ff.; "Russia: The Final Frontier," *Adweek*, March 29, 1993, pp. 26–35; "Despite Their Woes, Russians Somehow Find Ways to Cope," *The Wall Street Journal*, January 29, 1993, p. A1ff.; "The New Russia: Special Report," *Time*, December 7, 1992, pp. 32–69; "A Taste of Capitalism at Russian Collective Brings Chaos and Strife," *The Wall Street Journal*, November 27, 1992, p. A1ff.; "Success Story: This Russian Plant Actually Makes Stuff," *The Wall Street Journal*, October 27, 1992, p. A1ff.; "Project Capitalism," *Business Week*, September 28, 1992, pp. 104–8; "Arise, Comrades, Cast Off Your Chains and Go Get a Coke," *Brandweek*, July 20, 1992, pp. 22–24; "Russians Learn Caveats of a Free Market," *The Wall Street Journal*, July 2, 1992, p. A4; "Instead of MTV, Russian Kids Watch Their Profit Margins," *The Wall Street Journal*, June 25, 1992, p. A1ff.; "The Battle against the Bottlenecks," *Newsweek*, January 27, 1992, p. 31; "Businesses Learn How to Skip Old Laws," *USA Today*, November 5, 1991, p. 1Bff.; "As Socialism Wanes, a Soviet Family Waits in Line, and Worries," *The Wall Street Journal*, October 22, 1991, p. A1ff.

8. Victor V. Cordell, "Effects of Public Policy on Marketing," *Journal of Macromarketing*, Spring 1993, pp. 20–32; James M. Carman and Robert G. Harris, "Public Regulation of Marketing Activity, Part III: A Typology of Regulatory Failures and Implications for Marketing and Public Policy," *Journal of Macromarketing*, Spring 1986, pp. 51–64; Venkatakrishna V. Bellur et al., "Strategic Adaptations to Price Controls: The Case of Indian Drug Industry," *Journal of the Academy of Marketing Science*, Winter/Spring 1985, pp. 143–59.

9. Charles R. Taylor and Glenn S. Omura, "An Evaluation of Alternative Paradigms of Marketing and Economic Development, Part 1," *Journal of Macromarketing*, Fall 1994, pp. 6–20; Van R. Wood and Scott J. Vitell, "Marketing and Economic Development: Review, Synthesis and Evaluation," *Journal of Macromarketing* 6, no. 1 (1986), pp. 28–48; Robert W. Nason and Phillip D. White, "The Visions of Charles C. Slater: Social Consequences of Marketing," *Journal of Macromarketing* 1, no. 2 (1981), pp. 4–18; Franklin S. Houston and Jule B. Gassenheimer, "Marketing and Exchange," *Journal of Marketing*, October 1987, pp. 3–18; Suzanne Hosley and Chow Hou Wee, "Marketing and Economic Development: Focusing on the Less Developed Countries," *Journal of Macromarketing*, Spring 1988, pp. 43–53.

10. "The Big Rise," *Fortune*, May 30, 1994, pp. 74–90; "Eastern Europe Hung in Red Tape," *USA Today*, May 12, 1994, p. 1Bff.; "As Capitalism Takes Root, Dreams Grow among Many Poles," *The Wall Street Journal*, May 18, 1992, p. A1ff.

11. John S. McClenahen, "The Third World Challenge," *Industry Week*, May 28, 1984, pp. 90–95.

12. "Exports: 'This Show Has Legs,' " *Business Week*, September 19, 1994, pp. 48–49; "Japan's Imports Rise, and U.S. Companies Are Gaining New Sales," *The Wall Street Journal*, April 15, 1994, p. A1ff.; "King of the Hill," *The Raleigh News & Observer*, March 13, 1994, p. 1Fff.; "U.S. Exporters Keep On Rolling," *Fortune*, June 14, 1993, pp. 130–31; "U.S. Service Exports Are Growing

Rapidly, but Almost Unnoticed," *The Wall Street Journal*, April 21, 1993, p. A1ff.; "Many U.S. Companies Expect Strong Exports Despite Talk of Slump," *The Wall Street Journal*, January 18, 1993, p. A1ff.; "Exports: Ship 'Em Out," *Fortune*, Special Issue (The New American Century), Spring/Summer 1991, p. 58; Christopher M. Korth, "Managerial Barriers to U.S. Exports," *Business Horizons*, March/April 1991, pp. 18–26.

13. "Facing Reality in Japan Trade," *Business Week*, October 10, 1994, pp. 58–59; "China's Gates Swing Open," *Business Week*, June 13, 1994, pp. 52–53; "U.S. Firms Favor China Trade," *USA Today*, May 23, 1994, p. 3B; "Clinton Likely to Renew China Trade Status," *USA Today*, May 19, 1994, p. 10A; "Tough Talk: Are the U.S. and Japan Headed for a Trade War?" *Business Week*, February 28, 1994, pp. 26–31; "No Winners in Japanese Trade War," *USA Today*, February 16, 1994, p. 13A; "BMW, Mercedes, Rolls-Royce—Could This Be Russia?" *Business Week*, August 2, 1993, p. 40; "Rethinking Japan: The New, Harder Line toward Tokyo," *Business Week*, August 7, 1989, pp. 44–52.

14. Peter W. Liesch, "Government-Mandated Countertrade in Australia: Some International Marketing Implications," *Industrial Marketing Management*, October 1994, pp. 299–306; Sam C. Okoroafo, "Implementing International Countertrade: A Dyadic Approach," *Industrial Marketing Management*, July 1994, pp. 229–34; Aspy P. Palia and Heon Deok Yoon, "Countertrade Practices in Korea," *Industrial Marketing Management*, July 1994, pp. 205–14; Aspy P. Palia, "Countertrade Practices in Japan," *Industrial Marketing Management*, May 1993, pp. 125–32; Abla M. Abdel-Latif and Jeffrey B. Nugent, "Countertrade as Trade Creation and Trade Diversion," *Contemporary Economic Policy*, January 1994, pp. 1–11; "Barter Exchanges: Gateway to a Cashless Society," *Omni*, May 1993, p. 12; "Why Countertrade Is Getting Hot," *Fortune*, June 29, 1992, p. 25; Aspy P. Palia and Oded Shenkar, "Countertrade Practices in China," *Industrial Marketing Management* 20, no. 1 (1991), pp. 57–66.

15. "Who Stands to Win, Lose under Trade Treaty," *USA Today*, December 1, 1994, p. 4B; "Agreement Potentially Worth Billions," *USA Today*, November 30, 1994, p. 1Aff.; "GATT Weaves through Heart of Textile Country," *USA Today*, November 25, 1994, p. 6A; "What's Next after GATT's Victory?" *Fortune*, January 10, 1994, p. 66ff.; "Trade Pact Is Set by 117 Nations, Slashing Tariffs, Subsidies Globally," *The Wall Street Journal*, December 16, 1993, p. A3ff.; "Uruguay Talks Settle Key Issues," *USA Today*, December 15, 1993, p. 1Bff.; "After Years of Talks, GATT Is at Last Ready to Sign Off on a Pact," *The Wall Street Journal*, December 15, 1993, p. A1ff.; "Firms Far and Wide Are Looking to GATT for Competitive Edge," *The Wall Street Journal*, December 7, 1993, p. A1ff.

16. William McInnes, "A Conceptual Approach to Marketing," in *Theory in Marketing*, second series, ed. Reavis Cox, Wroe Alderson, and Stanley J. Shapiro (Burr Ridge, IL: Richard D. Irwin, 1964), pp. 51–67.

17. *1990 Annual Report*, Tandem; "The New Germany's Glowing Future," *Fortune*, December 3, 1990, pp. 146–54; "Berlin Tries to Raze Its Great Divide," *Insight*, October 15, 1990, pp. 8–17; "West Brands Rain on East's Parade," *Advertising Age*, October 1, 1990, p. 15ff.; "Speeding over the Bumps," *Time*, July 30, 1990, pp. 30–31; "A New Germany," *Newsweek*, July 9, 1990, pp. 28–36; "One Germany," *Business Week*, April 2, 1990, pp. 46–54.

18. Reed Moyer, *Macro Marketing: A Social Perspective* (New York: John Wiley & Sons, 1972), pp. 3–5; see also Roger A. Layton, "Measures of Structural Change in Macromarketing Systems," *Journal of Macromarketing*, Spring 1989, pp. 5–15.

19. For a discussion of some criticisms of advertising, see Banwari Mittal, "Public Assessment of TV Advertising: Faint Praise and Harsh Criticism," *Journal of Advertising Research*, January/February 1994, pp. 35–53; Richard W. Pollay and Banwari Mittal, "Here's the Beef: Factors, Determinants, and Segments in Consumer Criticism of Advertising," *Journal of Marketing*, July 1993, pp. 99–114. For a discussion of ethical issues in marketing, see Anusorn Singhapakdi et al., "The Perceived Importance of Ethics and Social Responsibility on Organizational Effectiveness: A Survey of Marketers," *Journal of the Academy of Marketing Science*, Spring 1995, pp. 49–56; Ishmael P. Akaah and Daulatram Lund, "The Influence of Personal and Organizational Values on Marketing Professionals' Ethical Behavior," *Journal of Business Ethics*, June 1994, pp. 417–30; Anusorn Singhapakdi and Scott J. Vitell, "Personal and Professional Values Underlying the Ethical Judgments of Marketers," *Journal of Business Ethics*, July 1993, pp. 525–34; Donald P. Robin and R. Eric Reidenbach, "Searching for a Place to Stand: Toward a Workable Ethical Philosophy for Marketing," *Journal of Public Policy & Marketing*, Spring 1993, pp. 97–105; Donelson R. Forsyth, "Judging the Morality of Business Practices: The Influence of Personal Moral Philosophies," *Journal of Business Ethics*, May 1992, pp. 461–70; Robert W. Armstrong, "An Empirical Investigation of International Marketing Ethics: Problems Encountered by Australian Firms," *Journal of Business Ethics*, March 1992, pp. 161–72; "Can You Afford to Be Ethical?" *Inc.*, September 1992, p. 17; "The New Crisis in Business Ethics," *Fortune*, April 20, 1992, pp. 167–76.

Chapter 2

1. "A Star Is Born," *Fortune*, Special Issue, Autumn/Winter 1993, pp. 44–47; "B&D Retools with Quantum," *Brandweek*, July 5, 1993, p. 4; *1993 Annual Report*, Black & Decker; "New Selling Tool: The Acura Concept," *Fortune*, February 24, 1992, pp. 88–89.

2. R. W. Ruekert, "Developing a Market Orientation: An Organizational Strategy Perspective," *International Journal of Research in Marketing*, August 1992, pp. 225–46; J. David Lichtenthal and David T. Wilson, "Becoming Market Oriented," *Journal of Business Research*, May 1992, pp. 191–208; Bernard J. Jaworski and Ajay K. Kohli, "Market Orientation: Antecedents and Consequences," *Journal of Marketing*, July 1993, pp. 53–70; Stanley F. Slater and John C. Narver, "Market Orientation, Customer Value, and Superior Performance," *Business Horizons*, March–April 1994, pp. 22–28; Caron H. St. John and Ernest H. Hall, Jr., "The Interdependency between Marketing and Manufacturing," *Industrial Marketing Management* 20, no. 3 (1991), pp. 223–30. For an early example of how the marketing revolution affected one firm, see Robert J. Keith, "The Marketing Revolution," *Journal of Marketing*, January 1960, pp. 35–38. For an overview of some of Procter & Gamble's recent marketing efforts, see "P&G's New Analgesic Promises Pain for Over-the-Counter Rivals," *The Wall Street Journal*, June 16, 1994, p. B9; "Procter & Gamble Hits Back," *Business Week*, July 19, 1993, pp. 20–22;

"Procter & Gamble's Prescription for the Future," *Brandweek*, July 20, 1992, pp. 14–19; "P&G Rewrites the Marketing Rules," *Fortune*, November 6, 1989, pp. 34–36ff.; "Stalking the New Consumer," *Business Week*, August 28, 1989, pp. 54–62; "The Marketing Revolution at Procter & Gamble," *Business Week*, July 25, 1988, pp. 72–73ff. See also Adrian J. Slywotzky and Benson P. Shapiro, "Leveraging to Beat the Odds: The New Marketing Mind-Set," *Harvard Business Review*, September–October 1993, pp. 97–107; Frederick E. Webster, Jr., "The Changing Role of Marketing in the Corporation," *Journal of Marketing*, October 1992, pp. 1–17; Thomas Masiello, "Developing Market Responsiveness throughout Your Company," *Industrial Marketing Management*, May 1988, pp. 85–94; Franklin S. Houston, "The Marketing Concept: What It Is and What It Is Not," *Journal of Marketing*, April 1986, pp. 81–87; George S. Day, "The Capabilities of Market-Driven Organizations, *Journal of Marketing*, October 1994, pp. 37–52; Eugene W. Anderson, Claes Fornell, and Donald R. Lehmann, "Customer Satisfaction, Market Share, and Profitability: Findings from Sweden," *Journal of Marketing*, July 1994, pp. 53–66.

3. For more on the marketing concept in the banking industry, see "Shopping List: Car Loan, Canned Corn," *USA Today*, July 20, 1994, p. 6B; "Banks Profit by Sweet-Talking Overdue Payers," *The Wall Street Journal*, June 27, 1994, p. B1ff.; "Bank Helps Homeless Veterans by Letting Them Open Accounts," *The Wall Street Journal*, June 23, 1994, p. B1ff.; "Banks Bag Profits with Supermarket Branches," *The Wall Street Journal*, May 20, 1994, p. B1ff.; "Corporate Banking, Given Up for Dead, Is Reinventing Itself," *The Wall Street Journal*, January 31, 1994, p. A1ff.; "Banks Push Insurance, Public May Profit," *The Wall Street Journal*, October 5, 1993, p. B1ff.; "Banks Court Disenchanted Customers," *The Wall Street Journal*, August 30, 1993, p. B1; "Banks Discover the Consumer," *Fortune*, February 12, 1990, pp. 96–104; "Making Change for a Segmented Market, Banks Package Services to Woo Target Groups," *The Wall Street Journal*, November 2, 1989, p. B1ff. For more on the marketing concept and the legal profession, see Madeline Johnson, Khalil Yazdi, and Betsy D. Gelb, "Attorney Advertising and Changes in the Demand for Wills," *Journal of Advertising*, March 1993, pp. 35–46; "Mixed Verdict: Prepaid Legal Services Draw Plenty of Customers and Criticism," *The Wall Street Journal*, August 6, 1991, p. B1ff.; " 'I Love My Lawyer' Ads May Spread to More States," *The Wall Street Journal*, December 7, 1990, p. B1ff.; F. G. Crane, Carolyn Meacher, and T. K. Clarke, "Lawyers' Attitudes towards Legal Services Advertising in Canada," *International Journal of Advertising* 8, no. 1 (1989), pp. 71–78. For more on the marketing concept and the accounting profession, see "Big Accounting Firms, Striving to Cut Costs, Irritate Small Clients," *The Wall Street Journal*, April 21, 1994, p. A1ff.; "Coopers & Lybrand TV Ads Paint Inspirational Image for Accounting," *The Wall Street Journal*, January 3, 1994, p. 12; "Ad Campaigns Multiply at Big Accounting Firms," *Advertising Age*, October 11, 1993, p. 10; "Accountants Struggle as Marketers," *The Wall Street Journal*, July 10, 1989, p. B1. For more on the marketing concept and the academic community, see "Fortress Academia Sells Security," *The Wall Street Journal*, October 25, 1993, p. B1ff.; "Business Schools Revamp to Win Students," *The Wall Street Journal*, August 21, 1991, p. B1ff.; "Ailing College Treats Student as Customer, and Soon Is Thriving," *The Wall Street Journal*, July 17, 1991, p. A1ff. For more on the marketing concept and the medical profession, see E. O.

Teisberg, M. E. Porter, and G. B. Brown, "Making Competition in Health Care Work," *Harvard Business Review*, July–August 1994, p. 131ff.; William A. Schaffer, "Physician Advertising in the United States Since 1980," *International Journal of Advertising* 8, no. 1 (1989), pp. 25–34; "Pediatric Centers Spring Up to Provide Off-Hour Care, *The Wall Street Journal*, February 13, 1989, p. B1. For more on other service industries, see "KinderCare Learning Centers: New Lessons in Customer Service," *Fortune*, September 20, 1993, pp. 79–80; "Marketing-Minded Child-Care Centers Become More than 9-to-5 Baby Sitters," *The Wall Street Journal*, June 18, 1990, p. B1; Gary D. Hailey, "The Federal Trade Commission, the Supreme Court and Restrictions on Professional Advertising," *International Journal of Advertising* 8, no. 1 (1989), pp. 1–16; Betsy D. Gelb, Samuel V. Smith, and Gabriel M. Gelb, "Service Marketing Lessons from the Professionals," *Business Horizons*, September–October 1988, pp. 29–34; Valarie A. Zeithaml, A. Parasuraman, and Leonard L. Berry, "Problems and Strategies in Services Marketing," *Journal of Marketing*, Spring 1985, pp. 33–46; Paul N. Bloom, "Effective Marketing for Professional Services," *Harvard Business Review*, September–October 1984, pp. 102–10.

4. "Why Some Customers Are More Equal than Others," *Fortune*, September 19, 1994, pp. 215–24; "Firm Takes Season Rush in Stride," *USA Today*, December 17, 1993, p. 1Aff.; "How to Get Closer to Your Customers," *Business Week*, Enterprise 1993, pp. 42–45; "Companies That Serve You Best," *Fortune*, May 31, 1993, pp. 74–88; "Finding New Ways to Sell More," *Fortune*, July 27, 1992, pp. 100–3; "Relationships: Six Steps to Success," *Sales & Marketing Management*, April 1992, pp. 50–58; "King Customer," *Business Week*, March 12, 1990, pp. 88–94; "Here's the Maine Store for the Great Outdoors," *The Blade* (Toledo, Ohio), August 26, 1990; "L. L. Bean Scales Back Expansion Goals to Ensure Pride in Its Service Is Valid," *The Wall Street Journal*, July 31, 1989, p. B3; "Training at L. L. Bean," *TRAINING, The Magazine of Human Resources Development*, October 1988; "Using the Old (L. L.) Bean," *The Reader's Digest*, June 1986.

5. William G. Bowen, "When a Business Leader Joins a Nonprofit Board," *Harvard Business Review*, September–October 1994, pp. 38–44; "Charities Draw Younger Donors with Hip Events and Door Prizes," *The Wall Street Journal*, April 25, 1994, p. B1; "With Coffers Less Full, Big Companies Alter Their Gifts to Charities," *The Wall Street Journal*, November 26, 1993, p. A1ff.; "Nonprofits Dig into Databases for Big Donors," *The Wall Street Journal*, September 8, 1992, p. B1ff.; "Marketing Comes to an Aging YMCA," *Adweek's Marketing Week*, January 14, 1991, p. 35; Larry C. Giunipero, William Crittenden, and Vicky Crittenden, "Industrial Marketing in NonProfit Organizations," *Industrial Marketing Management*, August 1990, p. 279; Jeffrey A. Barach, "Applying Marketing Principles to Social Causes," *Business Horizons*, July/August 1984, pp. 65–69; C. Scott Greene and Paul Miesing, "Public Policy, Technology, and Ethics: Marketing Decisions for NASA's Space Shuttle," *Journal of Marketing*, Summer 1984, pp. 56–67; Alan R. Andreasen, "Nonprofits: Check Your Attention to Customers," *Harvard Business Review*, May–June 1982, pp. 105–10.

6. "CFC-Span: Refrigerant's Reign Nears an End," *USA Today*, August 22, 1994, p. 5B; "Who Scores Best on the Environment," *Fortune*, July 26, 1993, pp. 114–22; "Quick, Save the Ozone," *Business Week*, May 17, 1993, pp. 78–79; "Air-Conditioner Firms

Put Chill on Plans to Phase Out Use of Chlorofluorocarbons," *The Wall Street Journal*, May 10, 1993, p. B1ff.; *1993 Annual Report*, Du Pont. See also Alan R. Andreasen, "Social Marketing: Its Definition and Domain," *Journal of Public Policy & Marketing*, Spring 1994, pp. 108–14.

7. Edward J. O'Boyle and Lyndon E. Dawson, Jr., "The American Marketing Association Code of Ethics: Instructions for Marketers," *Journal of Business Ethics*, December 1992, pp. 921–30; Ellen J. Kennedy and Leigh Lawton, "Ethics and Services Marketing," *Journal of Business Ethics*, October 1993, pp. 785–96; "A Matter of Ethics," *Industry Week*, March 16, 1992, pp. 57–62; Michael R. Hyman, Robert Skipper, and Richard Tansey, "Ethical Codes Are Not Enough," *Business Horizons*, March/April 1990, pp. 15–22; Alan J. Dubinsky and Barbara Loken, "Analyzing Ethical Decision Making in Marketing," *Journal of Business Research*, September 1989, pp. 83–108; John Tsalikis and David J. Fritzsche, "Business Ethics: A Literature Review with a Focus on Marketing Ethics," *Journal of Business Ethics*, September 1989, pp. 695–702; G. R. Laczniak, R. F. Lusch, and P. E. Murphy, "Social Marketing: Its Ethical Dimensions," *Journal of Marketing*, Spring 1979, pp. 29–36.

8. Mary Anne Raymond and Hiram C. Barksdale, "Corporate Strategic Planning and Corporate Marketing: Toward an Interface," *Business Horizons*, September/October 1989, pp. 41–48; George S. Day, "Marketing's Contribution to the Strategy Dialogue," *Journal of the Academy of Marketing Science*, Fall 1992, pp. 323–30; Joel E. Ross and Ronnie Silverblatt, "Developing the Strategic Plan," *Industrial Marketing Management*, May 1987, pp. 103–8; P. Rajan Varadarajan and Terry Clark, "Delineating the Scope of Corporate, Business, and Marketing Strategy," *Journal of Business Research*, October–November 1994, pp. 93–106.

9. "Broderbund: Identify a Need, Turn a Profit," *Fortune*, November 30, 1992, pp. 78–79.

10. "Designing a New Hospital? Let Malls Be Your Muse," *The Wall Street Journal*, August 1, 1994, p. B1ff.; "Offering Aerobics, Karate, Aquatics, Hospitals Stress Business of 'Wellness,' " *The Wall Street Journal*, August 9, 1993, p. B1ff.

11. "Genesco Names New Executive of Children's Footwear Division," *Press Release*, Genesco, July 15, 1994; "Toddler University Ends Up in Westport," *Westport News*, March 8, 1991, p. A13; "Whiz Kid," *Connecticut*, August 1989, pp. 56–57; "Toddlers' Shoes Fit This Entrepreneur Well," *The Advocate and Greenwich Times*, June 25, 1989; "The Young and the Restless," *Children's Business*, May 1989, p. 29; "Making the Grade," *Young Fashions Magazine*, February 1989; "At Toddler University, the Chairman Is Getting A's," *Business Week*, January 16, 1989, p. 61.

12. Orville C. Walker, Jr., and Robert W. Ruekert, "Marketing's Role in the Implementation of Business Strategies: A Critical Review and Conceptual Framework," *Journal of Marketing*, July 1987, pp. 15–33; Thomas V. Bonoma, "A Model of Marketing Implementation," *1984 AMA Educators' Proceedings* (Chicago: American Marketing Association, 1984), pp. 185–89; Kevin Romer and Doris C. Van Doren, "Implementing Marketing in a High-Tech Business," *Industrial Marketing Management*, August 1993, pp. 177–86.

13. *1993 Annual Report*, Gillette Company.

14. "Swatch Adds Metal Watch," *Advertising Age*, November 7, 1994, p. 60; Benetton Readies Watch Campaign," *Brandweek*, August 8, 1994, p. 5; "Indiglo Watch Lights Up Better Times for Timex," *Brandweek*, April 25, 1994, pp. 30–32; "Seiko Show the Way to Cocka-Doodle-Doo It," *Advertising Age*, April 25, 1994, p. 62; "Seiko, Wittnauer Point to Quality," *Advertising Age*, April 11, 1994, p. 12; "At Timex, They're Positively Glowing," *Business Week*, July 12, 1993; "Swiss Watchmaker Mondaine Builds Timepieces with Ecological Touch," *The Wall Street Journal*, June 25, 1993, p. B5C; "Swatch Readies Telecom Push," *Brandweek*, April 5, 1993, p. 4; "And If It Matters, They Also Tell Time," *The Wall Street Journal*, September 20, 1991, p. B1; "High Time for Timex," *Adweek's Marketing Week*, July 29, 1991, p. 24; "Swatch Says It's Time to Reach Older Crowd," *The Wall Street Journal*, July 2, 1990, p. B1; "Watchmakers Put Emphasis on Technology," *Advertising Age*, April 3, 1989, p. 28; "Timex, Swatch Push Fashion," *Advertising Age*, July 18, 1988, p. 4.

Chapter 3

1. "New Strategies for the New Export Boom," *Fortune*, August 22, 1994, pp. 124–32.

2. George S. Day and Robin Wensley, "Assessing Advantage: A Framework for Diagnosing Competitive Superiority," *Journal of Marketing*, April 1988, pp. 1–20; Kevin P. Coyne, "Sustainable Competitive Advantage—What It Is, What It Isn't," *Business Horizons*, January/February 1986, pp. 54–61; Michael E. Porter, *Competitive Advantage—Creating and Sustaining Superior Performance* (New York: Free Press, MacMillan, 1986).

3. For more on Visa, see "The Makeover of American Express," *USA Today*, October 24, 1994, p. 3B; "Merchants' Ire Flares over Fees on Credit Cards," *The Wall Street Journal*, October 11, 1993, p. B1ff.; "Visa Volleys for Market Share," *Business Week*, September 27, 1993, p. 46; "Credit Cards Bag Grocery Sales," *Advertising Age*, January 4, 1993, p. 12; "Visa, MasterCard Make Inroads Wooing American Express's Corporate Clients," *The Wall Street Journal*, July 3, 1991, p. B1ff. For more on MCI, see "How AT&T Finally Found Its True Calling," *Advertising Age*, January 20, 1995, p. 3ff.; "Fighting for Customers Gets Louder," *USA Today*, January 9, 1995, p. 1Bff.; "All Those Long-Distance Discounts Are Sweet, but . . . ," *Business Week*, September 19, 1994, pp. 66–67; "Drama Drives MCI Ads," *Advertising Age*, September 12, 1994, p. 1ff. For more on McDonald's, see "McDonald's Conquers the World," *Fortune*, October 17, 1994, pp. 103–16; "Working on the Chain Gang," *Brandweek*, September 19, 1994, pp. 45–52; "McDonald's Shaking Marketing, Agencies," *Advertising Age*, September 19, 1994, p. 4; *1993 Annual Report*, McDonald's Corporation; "Burger Wars Fought with Salads, Pizza," *USA Today*, June 16, 1992, p. 1Bff.; "Soviet McDonald's Tastes Success," *USA Today*, November 22, 1991, p. 8B; "McDonald's Beats Lenin 3 to 1," *Fortune*, December 17, 1990, p. 11; "McRisky," *Business Week*, October 21, 1991, pp. 114–22; "McLifestyle," *Adweek's Marketing Week*, September 16, 1991, pp. 4–5. For more on Microsoft, see "What Bill Gates Really Wants," *Fortune*, January 16, 1995, pp. 35–63; "Bill Gates' Vision of Microsoft in Every Home," *Advertising Age*, December 19, 1994, pp. 14–15; "Microsoft's New World," *Advertising Age*, November 14, 1994, p. 1ff.; "Is Microsoft Too Powerful?" *Business Week*, March 1, 1993, pp. 82–90. For more on ski resorts, see "Bikers Give Ski Resorts Summertime Lift," *The Wall Street Journal*, July 7, 1994, p. B1ff. For more on Blockbuster, see "Blockbuster Thinks Big in Videogames," *Advertising Age*, January 10, 1994, p. 1ff.; "New Kid on the Block, Buster," *Newsweek*, January 11, 1993, p. 48; "Blockbuster Moves to Enter Record

Business," *The Wall Street Journal*, October 20, 1992, p. B1ff.; "They Don't Call It Blockbuster for Nothing," *Business Week*, October 19, 1992, pp. 113–14. For more on Coleman, see "Growing to Match Its Brand Name," *Fortune*, June 13, 1994, p. 114; "Coleman's Familiar Name Is Both Help and Hindrance," *The Wall Street Journal*, May 17, 1990, p. B2.

4. "The Little Guys Are Making It Big Overseas," *Business Week*, February 27, 1989, pp. 94–96.

5. "American Greeting, Hallmark's Cards Will Send an Earful," *The Wall Street Journal*, November 5, 1993, p. B10B; "Old-Fashioned Sentiments Go High-Tech," *The Wall Street Journal*, November 9, 1992, p. B1ff.; "Congratulations on Your Big Earnings Increase," *Business Week*, August 17, 1992, p. 58; "Love Story Has a Lucrative Twist," *USA Today*, February 13, 1992, p. 6B; "Selling Greeting Cards Is No Valentine," *Adweek*, December 9, 1991, p. 10; "Hallmark Cards Get Personal," *Advertising Age*, September 9, 1991, p. 14; "Inside Hallmark's Love Machine," *The Wall Street Journal*, February 14, 1990, p. B1ff.

6. George S. Day, A. D. Shocker, and R. K. Srivastava, "Customer-Oriented Approaches to Identifying Product-Markets," *Journal of Marketing*, Fall 1979, pp. 8–19; Rajendra K. Srivastava, Mark I. Alpert, and Allan D. Shocker, "A Customer-Oriented Approach for Determining Market Structures," *Journal of Marketing*, Spring 1984, pp. 32–45.

7. "Tapping into Cheerleading," *Adweek's Marketing Week*, March 2, 1992, p. 17.

8. "The Riches in Market Niches," *Fortune*, April 27, 1987, pp. 227–30; Robert E. Linneman and John L. Stanton, Jr., "Mining for Niches," *Business Horizons*, May–June 1992, pp. 43–51; Michael E. Raynor, "The Pitfalls of Niche Marketing," *The Journal of Business Strategy*, March/April 1992, pp. 29–32.

9. Terry Elrod and Russell S. Winer, "An Empirical Evaluation of Aggregation Approaches for Developing Market Segments," *Journal of Marketing*, Fall 1982, pp. 32–34; Frederick W. Winter, "A Cost-Benefit Approach to Market Segmentation," *Journal of Marketing*, Fall 1979, pp. 103–11; Andrew Hilton, "Mythology, Markets, and the Emerging Europe," *Harvard Business Review*, November–December 1992, pp. 50–127.

10. James W. Harvey, "Benefit Segmentation for Fund Raisers," *Journal of the Academy of Marketing Science*, Winter 1990, pp. 77–86; Dianne S. P. Cermak, Karen Maru File, and Russ Alan Prince, "A Benefit Segmentation of the Major Donor Market," *Journal of Business Research*, February 1994, pp. 121–30; Robert L. Armacost and Jamshid C. Hosseini, "Identification of Determinant Attributes Using the Analytic Hierarchy Process," *Journal of the Academy of Marketing Science*, Fall 1994, pp. 383–92; Ajay S. Sukhdial, Goutam Chakraborty, and Eric K. Steger, "Measuring Values Can Sharpen Segmentation in the Luxury Auto Market," *Journal of Advertising Research*, January/February 1995, pp. 9–24; Joel S. Dubow, "Occasion-Based vs. User-Based Benefit Segmentation, A Case Study," *Journal of Advertising Research*, March/April 1992, pp. 11–19; Susan Mitchell, "Birds of a Feather," *American Demographics*, February 1995, pp. 32–39; Steven A. Sinclair and Edward C. Stalling, "How to Identify Differences between Market Segments with Attribute Analysis," *Industrial Marketing Management*, February 1990, pp. 31–40; Peter R. Dickson and James L. Ginter, "Market Segmentation, Product Differentiation, and Marketing Strategy," *Journal of Marketing*, April 1987, pp. 1–10; Russell I. Haley, "Benefit Segmentation—

20 Years Later," *Journal of Consumer Marketing* 1, no. 2 (1984), pp. 5–14.

11. Richard W. Pollay, Jung S. Lee, and David Carter-Whitney, "Separate, but Not Equal: Racial Segmentation in Cigarette Advertising," *Journal of Advertising*, March 1992, pp. 45–58; "Young Drinkers Do Shots in Potent New Flavors," *The Wall Street Journal*, May 13, 1994, p. B1ff.; "Fighting and Switching," *Newsweek*, March 21, 1994, pp. 52–53; "U.S. Aid Plan for Poor Helps Big Food Firms," *The Wall Street Journal*, March 29, 1991, p. B1ff.; "Molson Ice Ads Raise Hackles of Regulators," *The Wall Street Journal*, February 25, 1994, p. B1ff.; Suzeanne Benet, Robert E. Pitts, and Michael LaTour, "The Appropriateness of Fear Appeal Use for Health Care Marketing to the Elderly: Is It OK to Scare Granny?" *Journal of Business Ethics*, January 1993, pp. 45–56; "New Converse Shoe Named Run 'N Gun Is Angering Critics," *The Wall Street Journal*, February 8, 1993, p. B5; " 'Black Death' Becomes 'Black Hat' so that Vodka Can Stay on Shelves," *The Wall Street Journal*, May 12, 1992, p. B6; "Malt Liquor Makers Find Lucrative Market in the Urban Young," *The Wall Street Journal*, March 9, 1992, p. A1ff.; "Malt Advertising that Touts Firepower Comes under Attack by U.S. Officials," *The Wall Street Journal*, July 1, 1991, p. B1ff.; "Sneaker Makers Face Scrutiny from PUSH," *The Wall Street Journal*, July 19, 1990, p. B1; "Don't Blame Sneakers for Inner-City Crime," *Adweek's Marketing Week*, May 7, 1990, p. 65.

12. Jerry Wind, Paul E. Green, Douglas Shifflet, and Marsha Scarbrough, "Courtyard by Marriott: Designing a Hotel Facility with Consumer-Based Marketing Models," *Interfaces*, January–February 1989, pp. 25–47. See also "Can the Savoy Cut Costs and Be the Savoy?" *The Wall Street Journal*, October 25, 1994, p. B1ff.; "Trying to Keep Guests Home for Breakfast," *The Wall Street Journal*, October 5, 1994, p. B1; "Vacationing Families Head Downtown to Welcoming Arms of Business Hotels," *The Wall Street Journal*, June 13, 1994, p. B1ff.; "Hotels Turn Guest Rooms into Well-Stocked Offices," *The Wall Street Journal*, September 20, 1993, p. B1ff.; "Hotels: Home, Home on the Road," *USA Today*, April 13, 1993, pp. 1E–12E; "Lodging Chain to Give Older Guests a Choice," *The Wall Street Journal*, February 19, 1993, p. B1; "Travelers Find a Home on the Road," *USA Today*, January 19, 1993, p. 9E; *1993 Annual Report*, Marriott Corporation; "Band-Aids Replace Bourbon in Minibars," *The Wall Street Journal*, November 25, 1992, p. B1ff.; "Hotel Recovery Will Be a Late Arrival," *The Wall Street Journal*, July 27, 1992, p. B1ff.; "Limited-Service Chains Offer Enough to Thrive," *The Wall Street Journal*, July 27, 1992, p. B1.

13. Kristiaan Helsen, Kamel Jedidi, and Wayne S. DeSarbo, "A New Approach to Country Segmentation Utilizing Multinational Diffusion Patterns," *Journal of Marketing*, October 1993, pp. 60–71; Russell Abratt, "Market Segmentation Practices of Industrial Marketers," *Industrial Marketing Management*, May 1993, pp. 79–84; Sally Dibb and Lyndon Simkin, "Implementation Problems in Industrial Market Segmentation," *Industrial Marketing Management*, February 1994, pp. 55–64; Rodney L. Griffith and Louis G. Pol, "Segmenting Industrial Markets," *Industrial Marketing Management*, February 1994, pp. 39–46; Jay L. Laughlin and Charles R. Taylor, "An Approach to Industrial Market Segmentation," *Industrial Marketing Management* 20, no. 2 (1991), pp. 127–36; V. Kasturi Rangan, Rowland T. Moriarty, and Gordon S. Swartz, "Segmenting Customers in Mature Industrial Markets,"

Journal of Marketing, October 1992, pp. 72–82; Herbert E. Brown, Ramesh Shivashankar, and Roger W. Brucker, "Requirements Driven Market Segmentation," *Industrial Marketing Management*, May 1989, pp. 105–12; Cornelis A. de Kluyver and David B. Whitlark, "Benefit Segmentation for Industrial Products," *Industrial Marketing Management*, November 1986, pp. 273–86.

14. Girish Punj and David W. Stewart, "Cluster Analysis in Marketing Research: Review and Suggestions for Application," *Journal of Marketing Research*, May 1983, pp. 134–48; Fernando Robles and Ravi Sarathy, "Segmenting the Computer Aircraft Market with Cluster Analysis," *Industrial Marketing Management*, February 1986, pp. 1–12.

15. Donna K. Hoffman and William D. Perreault, Jr., "Market Research: Consumer Preference and Perception," in *Multidimensional Scaling: History, Theory and Applications*, ed. F. W. Young and R. M. Hamer (Hillsdale, NJ: Erlbaum Associates, 1987).

16. David A. Aaker and J. Gary Shansby, "Positioning Your Product," *Business Horizons*, May/June 1982, pp. 56–62; Al Ries and Jack Trout, *Positioning: The Battle for Your Mind* (New York: McGraw-Hill, 1981), p. 53. For some current examples of positioning, see "From the Horse's Mouth: Try a Little Hoof Fix on Your Nails," *The Wall Street Journal*, July 29, 1994, p. B1ff.; "Campbell's New Ad Campaign Is Stirring Up Dormant Soup Sales," *The Wall Street Journal*, March 17, 1994, p. B5; Hans Muhlbacher, Angelika Dreher, and Angelika Gabriel-Ritter, "MIPS-Managing Industrial Positioning Strategies," *Industrial Marketing Management*, October 1994, pp. 287–98; "Campbell Shifts Familiar Slogan to Back Burner," *The Wall Street Journal*, September 9, 1993, p. B1ff.; "Snack Time? Give Me My Cereal Bowl!" *Brandweek*, May 3, 1993, pp. 24–26; "Chew on This: Wrigley's Extra Tackles Tooth Decay," *Advertising Age*, December 21, 1992, p. 30; "Lure of a Lovelier Smile Prompts a Rush to Buy Do-It-Yourself Teeth Whiteners," *The Wall Street Journal*, July 6, 1992, pp. 13–14.

Chapter 4

1. "Plastic vs. Steel Rages in Day-Care Playgrounds," *The Wall Street Journal*, August 5, 1994, p. B1; "America's Most Admired Company," *Fortune*, February 7, 1994, pp. 50–54; *1993 Annual Report*, Rubbermaid; "Thriving in a Lame Economy," *Fortune*, October 5, 1992, pp. 44–54; "Rubbermaid Turns Up Plenty of Profit in the Mundane," *The Wall Street Journal*, March 27, 1992, p. B4; "The Art of Rubbermaid," *Adweek's Marketing Week*, March 16, 1992, pp. 22–25; "At Rubbermaid, Little Things Mean a Lot," *Business Week*, November 11, 1991, p. 126; "Little Tikes with a Grown-Up Dilemma," *Adweek's Marketing Week*, September 10, 1991, pp. 18–19.

2. See Peter F. Drucker, *Management: Tasks, Responsibilities, Practices, and Plans* (New York: Harper & Row, 1973).

3. This point of view is discussed at much greater length in a classic article by T. Levitt, "Marketing Myopia," *Harvard Business Review*, September–October 1975, p. 1ff. See also David J. Morris, Jr., "The Railroad and Movie Industries: Were They Myopic?" *Journal of the Academy of Marketing Science*, Fall 1990, pp. 279–84.

4. "Why Inflation Is Not Inevitable," *Fortune*, September 12, 1988, pp. 117–24.

5. "Reichhold Chemicals: Now the Emphasis Is on Profits Rather than Volume," *Business Week*, June 20, 1983, pp. 178–79;

Carolyn Y. Woo, "Market-Share Leadership—Not Always So Good," *Harvard Business Review*, January–February 1984, pp. 50–55; Robert Jacobson and David A. Aaker, "Is Market Share All that It's Cracked Up to Be?" *Journal of Marketing*, Fall 1985, pp. 11–22.

6. "Harley-Davidson's U-Turn," *USA Today*, March 2, 1990, p. 1Bff.; "How Harley Beat Back the Japanese," *Fortune*, September 25, 1989, pp. 155–64.

7. "No Air Bags for Passengers; Ford Stores 3,000 Lincolns," *Automotive News*, March 26, 1990, p. 1ff.; "TRW Says Air-Bag Supply OK Despite Factory Explosions," *Automotive News*, August 7, 1989, p. 4.

8. "Still Battling the Ozone Stigma," *Adweek's Marketing Week*, March 16, 1992, pp. 18–19. For more on the competitive environment, see "Firms Analyze Rivals to Help Fix Themselves," *The Wall Street Journal*, May 3, 1994, p. B1ff.; Klaus Brockhoff, "Competitor Technology Intelligence in German Companies," *Industrial Marketing Management* 20, no. 2 (1991), pp. 91–98; John L. Haverty and Myroslaw J. Kyj, "What Happens When New Competitors Enter an Industry," *Industrial Marketing Management* 20, no. 1 (1991), pp. 73–80; Arch G. Woodside and Elizabeth J. Wilson, "Diagnosing Customer Comparisons of Competitors' Marketing Mix Strategies," *Journal of Business Research*, October–November 1994, pp. 133–44; James F. Moore, "Predators and Prey: A New Ecology of Competition," *Harvard Business Review*, May–June 1993, pp. 75–86; Anita M. McGahan, "Industry Structure and Competitive Advantage," *Harvard Business Review*, November–December 1994, pp. 115–27; David W. Cravens and Shannon H. Shipp, "Market-Driven Strategies for Competitive Advantage," *Business Horizons*, January/February 1991, pp. 53–61; William W. Keep, Glenn S. Omura, and Roger J. Calantone, "What Managers Should Know about Their Competitors' Patented Technologies," *Industrial Marketing Management*, July 1994, pp. 257–64; Fahri Karakaya and Michael J. Stahl, "Barriers to Entry and Market Entry Decisions in Consumer and Industrial Goods Markets," *Journal of Marketing*, April 1989, pp. 80–91.

9. *Kao* (Cambridge, MA: Harvard Business School, 1984).

10. "P&G Wins Lawsuit, Loses Market," *Advertising Age*, September 18, 1989, p. 72; Shaker A. Zahra, "Unethical Practices in Competitive Analysis: Patterns, Causes and Effects," *Journal of Business Ethics*, January 1994, pp. 53–62.

11. "Most U.S. Companies Are Innocents Abroad," *Business Week*, November 16, 1987, pp. 168–69.

12. Paul Coomes, "Recession Winners and Losers," *American Demographics*, October 1992, p. 62; "We're #1 and It Hurts," *Time*, October 24, 1994, pp. 50–56; "Currency Hits Post-War Low against Yen," *USA Today*, June 22, 1994, p. 1Bff.; "Biggest Show of Force in a Decade Halts Slide of the Dollar—for Now," *The Wall Street Journal*, May 5, 1994, p. A1ff.; "Price Rises Are Small, so Are Raises," *USA Today*, March 17, 1994, p. 1Bff.; "Price Index Overstates Inflation," *USA Today*, January 14, 1994, p. 1Bff.; "Can't Get Enough of that Super-Yen," *Business Week*, October 4, 1993, p. 50; "Demand for Wood Leads to Building Panic," *USA Today*, March 17, 1993, p. 1Bff.; "The Global Economy: Can You Compete?" (Special Report), *Business Week*, December 17, 1990, pp. 60–93; "Markets of the World Unite," *Fortune*, July 30, 1990, pp. 101–20.

13. "The Digital Factory," *Fortune*, November 14, 1994, pp. 92–110; "Making Sense of the Internet," *Newsweek*, October

24, 1994, pp. 46–49; "Technology Has Travelers under Seige," *USA Today*, October 14, 1994, p. 1Bff.; "Video Conference Calls Change Business," *The Wall Street Journal*, October 12, 1994, p. B1ff.; "High-Tech Edge Gives U.S. Firms Global Lead in Computer Networks," *The Wall Street Journal*, September 9, 1994, p. A1ff.; "Battle for the Soul of the Internet," *Time*, July 25, 1994, pp. 50–56; "Waking Up to the New Economy," *Fortune*, June 17, 1994, pp. 36–46; "The Productivity Payoff Arrives," *Fortune*, June 27, 1994, pp. 79–84; "Speech Recognition Gets Cheaper and Smarter," *The Wall Street Journal*, June 6, 1994, p. B1ff.; "High-Tech Gurus Develop Cheap Networks of Chips to Control Array of Tasks," *The Wall Street Journal*, May 20, 1994, p. B1ff.; "The Interactive Future," *The Wall Street Journal*, May 18, 1994, p. B1ff.; "They've Got the Whole World on a Chip," *Business Week*, April 25, 1994, pp. 132–35; "The Learning Revolution," *Business Week*, February 28, 1994, pp. 80–88; "Technological Gains Are Cutting Costs, and Jobs, in Services," *The Wall Street Journal*, February 24, 1994, p. A1ff.; "Info Highway Needs Bait to Lure Traffic," *USA Today*, February 17, 1994, p. 1Bff.; "The Race to Rewire America," *Fortune*, April 19, 1993, pp. 42–61; "Take a Trip into the Future on the Electronic Superhighway," *Time*, April 12, 1993, pp. 50–58; "Publishers Deliver Reams of Data on CDs," *The Wall Street Journal*, February 22, 1993, p. B4; "Telephone Service Seems on the Brink of Huge Innovations," *The Wall Street Journal*, February 10, 1993, p. A1ff.; "Prime Time for Videoconferences," *Fortune*, December 28, 1992, pp. 90–95; "Virtual Reality," *Business Week*, October 5, 1992, pp. 97–105; "Your Digital Future," *Business Week*, September 7, 1992, pp. 56–64; "Phones that Will Work Anywhere," *Fortune*, August 24, 1992, pp. 100–12; "From Technology to Market—First," *Fortune*, March 23, 1992, p. 108; "The Videophone Era May Finally Be Near, Bring Big Changes," *The Wall Street Journal*, March 10, 1992, p. A1ff.; "Get Smart: Everyday Products Will Soon Come with Built-In Intelligence," *The Wall Street Journal*, October 21, 1991, p. R18; Noel Capon and Rashi Glazer, "Marketing and Technology: A Strategic Coalignment," *Journal of Marketing*, July 1987, pp. 1–14. For more on privacy, see "Systems Let You Pay from the Fast Lane," *USA Today*, June 30, 1993, p. 1Aff.; "Who's Reading Your Screen?" *Time*, January 18, 1993, p. 46; "Technology Has No Conscience," *USA Today*, September 18, 1992, p. 1Aff.; "Debate Mounts over Disclosure of Driver Data," *The Wall Street Journal*, August 25, 1992, p. B1ff.; "Nowhere to Hide," *Time*, November 11, 1991, pp. 34–40.

14. Michael G. Harvey, " 'Buy American': Economic Concept or Political Slogan?" *Business Horizons*, May–June 1993, pp. 40–46; Hans B. Thorelli and Aleksandra E. Glowacka, "Willingness of American Industrial Buyers to Source Internationally," *Journal of Business Research*, January 1995, pp. 21–30; "Now Marketers in Japan Stress the Local Angle," *The Wall Street Journal*, February 23, 1994, p. B1ff.; "Made in America Becomes a Boast in Europe," *The Wall Street Journal*, January 19, 1994, p. B1ff.; "Car Makers Roll Out Ads to Influence National Mood," *Adweek*, February 8, 1993, p. 58; "More Made-in-the-USA Claims Show Up," *The Wall Street Journal*, January 5, 1993, p. B5; " 'Made in USA' Tells Nike: Come Home," *Advertising Age*, October 26, 1992, p. 3ff.

15. For more on NAFTA, see "Worst Fears of Free Trade Have Cooled," *USA Today*, November 25, 1994, p. 1Bff.; "NAFTA," *The Wall Street Journal*, October 28, 1994, pp. R1–13; Kent Jones, "NAFTA Chapter 19: Is There Hope for Bilateral Dispute Resolution of Unfair Trade Law Decisions?" *Journal of Public Policy & Marketing*, Fall 1994, pp. 300–6; "Border Crossings," *Business Week*, November 22, 1993, pp. 40–42; "House Approves NAFTA, Providing President with Crucial Victory," *The Wall Street Journal*, November 18, 1993, p. A1ff.; "Mexicans Anticipate Passage of Trade Pact Will Lift Economy," *The Wall Street Journal*, April 20, 1993, p. A1ff.; "How NAFTA Will Help America," *Fortune*, April 19, 1993, pp. 95–102; "World Business," *The Wall Street Journal*, September 24, 1992, pp. R1–22; "Megamarket," *Time*, August 10, 1992, pp. 43–44; Paul A. Dion and Peter M. Banting, "What Industrial Marketers Can Expect From U.S.–Canadian Free Trade," *Industrial Marketing Management*, February 1990, pp. 77–80. For more on EU, see "Europe: Unification for the Favored Few," *Business Week*, September 19, 1994, p. 54; "World Business," *The Wall Street Journal*, September 30, 1994, pp. R1–24; "European Shoppers Save Money by Making Cross-Border Treks," *The Wall Street Journal*, May 2, 1994, p. B5A; "No One Ever Said It Would Be Easy," *Time*, March 1, 1993, p. 32ff.; "Europe's Borders Fade and People and Goods Can Move more Freely," *The Wall Street Journal*, May 18, 1993, p. A1ff.; "Europe Looks Ahead to Hard Choices," *Fortune*, December 14, 1992, pp. 144–53; "EC's Woes Could Choke U.S. Recovery," *USA Today*, November 27, 1992, p. 1Bff.; "French Vote Leaves Europeans Scrambling to Salvage Unity Plan," *The Wall Street Journal*, September 21, 1992, p. A1ff.; "Currencies in Turmoil, Europe Faces Chaos at a Time of Unity," *The Wall Street Journal*, September 17, 1992, p. A1ff.; "10,000 New EC Rules," *Business Week*, September 7, 1992, pp. 48–50; "Europe 1992: More Unity than You Think," *Fortune*, August 24, 1992, pp. 136–42; "They Speak German, Eat French Food, but Fear Maastricht," *The Wall Street Journal*, June 26, 1992, p. A1ff.; "European Unity Plan Receives Big Setback in Danes' Referendum," *The Wall Street Journal*, June 3, 1992, p. A1ff.; "EC Is Swamped by Would-Be Members," *The Wall Street Journal*, May 13, 1992, p. A10; Andrew I. Millington and Brian T. Bayliss, "Non-Tariff Barriers and U.K. Investment in the European Community," *Journal of International Business Studies*, Fourth Quarter 1991, pp. 695–710; Alan Wolfe, "The Single European Market: National or Euro-Brands?" *International Journal of Advertising* 10, no. 1 (1991), pp. 49–58; Jack G. Kaikati, "Opportunities for Smaller U.S. Industrial Firms in Europe," *Industrial Marketing Management*, November 1990, pp. 339–48. See also James M. Higgins and Timo Santalainen, "Strategies for Europe 1992," *Business Horizons*, July/August 1989, pp. 54–58.

16. "Artais Finds Smallness Isn't Handicap in Global Market," *The Wall Street Journal*, June 23, 1994, p. B2.

17. Roger Swagler, "Evolution and Applications of the Term Consumerism: Theme and Variations," *Journal of Consumer Affairs*, Winter 1994, pp. 347–60; Alan Morrison, "The Role of Litigation in Consumer Protection," *The Journal of Consumer Affairs*, Winter 1991, pp. 209–20; "Educating the Customer," *American Demographics*, September 1991, pp. 44–47; William K. Darley and Denise M. Johnson, "Cross-National Comparison of Consumer Attitudes toward Consumerism in Four Developing Countries," *Journal of Consumer Affairs*, Summer 1993, pp. 37–54; "Nader Suits Up to Strike Back against 'Slapps,' " *The Wall Street Journal*, July 9, 1991, p. B1ff.; "The Resurrection of Ralph Nader," *Fortune*, May 22, 1989, pp. 106–16; "Attorneys General Flex Their Muscles: State Officials Join Forces to Press Consumer and Antitrust Concerns," *The Wall Street Journal*, July 13, 1988, p. 25.

18. "What Led Beech-Nut Down the Road to Disgrace," *Business Week*, February 22, 1988, pp. 124–28. See also Louis W. Stern and Thomas L. Eovaldi, *Legal Aspects of Marketing Strategy: Antitrust and Consumer Protection Issues* (Englewood Cliffs, NJ: Prentice Hall, 1984); Gregory T. Gundlach and Jakki J. Mohr, "Collaborative Relationships: Legal Limits and Antitrust Considerations," *Journal of Public Policy & Marketing*, Fall 1992, pp. 101–14.

19. "Clinton's Regulators Zero In on Companies with Renewed Fervor," *The Wall Street Journal*, October 19, 1994, p. A1ff.; "Toddlers Taking Many Drugs, Mostly Untested," *The Wall Street Journal*, October 5, 1994, p. B1ff.; "New Label Law May Help Consumers Decipher Just How Domestic a Car Is," *The Wall Street Journal*, October 3, 1994, p. B5A; "FCC Chief to Pave Way for Next Era," *USA Today*, August 18, 1994, p. 1Bff.; "Clean-Air Deadlines Pull 'Clunker' Vehicles into Inspection Lines," *The Wall Street Journal*, August 17, 1994, p. A1ff.; "Government Learns Humility," *Fortune*, June 27, 1994, pp. 64–65; "Pre-Emptive Strike," *The Wall Street Journal*, May 20, 1994, p. R6; "New Rules Pave Way for Cleaner Cars," *USA Today*, December 6, 1993, p. 1Bff.; "Strong Medicine," *Business Week*, September 6, 1993, pp. 20–21; "FTC Broadens Trust Powers with Old Law," *The Wall Street Journal*, September 30, 1992, p. B1ff.; "Getting Tougher with Toxics," *Industry Week*, February 17, 1992, pp. 46–51; "Labels We Can Live By," *Newsweek*, November 18, 1991, p. 90; "Large Food Companies Express Relief at FDA's Truth-in-Labeling Proposals," *The Wall Street Journal*, November 7, 1991, p. B9; Joseph C. Miller and Michael D. Hutt, "Assessing Societal Effects of Product Regulations: Toward An Analytic Framework," in *1983 American Marketing Association Educators' Proceedings*, ed. P. E. Murphy et al. (Chicago: American Marketing Association, 1983), pp. 364–68.

20. John Tsalikis and Osita Nwachukwu, "A Comparison of Nigerian to American Views of Bribery and Extortion in International Commerce," *Journal of Business Ethics*, February 1991, pp. 85–98; "Marketing Law: A Marketer's Guide to Alphabet Soup," *Business Marketing*, January 1990, pp. 56–68; Ray O. Werner, "Marketing and the Supreme Court in Transition, 1982–1984," *Journal of Marketing*, Summer 1985, pp. 97–105; Ray O. Werner, "Marketing and the United States Supreme Court, 1975–1981," *Journal of Marketing*, Spring 1982, pp. 73–81; Dorothy Cohen, "Trademark Strategy," *Journal of Marketing*, January 1986, pp. 61–74; A. R. Beckenstein, H. L. Gabel, and Karlene Roberts, "An Executive's Guide to Antitrust Compliance," *Harvard Business Review*, September–October 1983, pp. 94–102.

21. "America's Vanishing Housewife," *Adweek's Marketing Week*, June 24, 1991, pp. 28–29. For more on firms targeting women, see "High-Tech Marketers Try to Attract Women without Causing Offense," *The Wall Street Journal*, March 17, 1994, p. B1ff.; "Fitness Firms Catch Up to Female Market," *USA Today*, February 9, 1993, p. 1Bff.; "Women Are the New Focus of a PC Maker," *The Wall Street Journal*, October 7, 1993, p. B1ff.; "Nike Has Women in Mind," *Advertising Age*, January 4, 1993, p. 36; "Wall Street Courts Women with Pitch They Have Different Financial Needs," *The Wall Street Journal*, June 12, 1992, p. C1ff.; "BMW Tailors for Women," *Brandweek*, April 11, 1994, p. 4; "In the Fast Lane," *Brandweek*, July 5, 1993, pp. 21–24.

22. "Home Front," *Advertising Age*, September 19, 1994, p. 1ff.; "Narrowcast in Past, Women Earn Revised Role in Advertising," *Advertising Age*, October 4, 1993, p. S1ff.; "Stay-at-Home Moms Are Fashionable Again in Many Communities," *The Wall Street Journal*, July 23, 1993, p. A1ff.; "Women Change Places," *American Demographics*, November 1992, pp. 46–51; "Marketplace: Women," *Adweek*, June 22, 1992, pp. 31–38; "Farewell, at Last, to Bimbo Campaigns?" *The Wall Street Journal*, January 31, 1992, p. B2.

23. Frank R. Bacon, Jr., and Thomas W. Butler, Jr., *Planned Innovation*, rev. ed. (Ann Arbor: Institute of Science and Technology, University of Michigan, 1980).

24. Paul F. Anderson, "Marketing, Strategic Planning and the Theory of the Firm," *Journal of Marketing*, Spring 1982, pp. 15–26; George S. Day, "Analytical Approaches to Strategic Market Planning," in *Review of Marketing 1981*, ed. Ben M. Enis and Kenneth J. Roering (Chicago: American Marketing Association, 1981), pp. 89–105; Ronnie Silverblatt and Pradeep Korgaonkar, "Strategic Market Planning in a Turbulent Business Environment," *Journal of Business Research*, August 1987, pp. 339–58.

25. *1993 Annual Report*, Sara Lee; *1993 Annual Report*, Philip Morris; Richard N. Cardozo and David K. Smith, Jr., "Applying Financial Portfolio Theory to Product Portfolio Decisions: An Empirical Study," *Journal of Marketing*, Spring 1983, pp. 110–19; Yoram Wind, Vijay Mahajan, and Donald J. Swire, "An Empirical Comparison of Standardized Portfolio Models," *Journal of Marketing*, Spring 1983, pp. 89–99; Philippe Haspeslagh, "Portfolio Planning: Uses and Limits," *Harvard Business Review*, January–February 1982, pp. 58–73; Samuel Rabino and Arnold Wright, "Applying Financial Portfolio and Multiple Criteria Approaches to Product Line Decisions," *Industrial Marketing Management*, October 1984, pp. 233–40.

26. Keith B. Murray and Edward T. Popper, "Competing under Regulatory Uncertainty: A U.S. Perspective on Advertising in the Emerging European Market," *Journal of Macromarketing*, Fall 1992, pp. 38–54; "Inside Russia—Business Most Unusual," *UPS International Update*, Spring 1994, p. 1ff.; "Freighted with Difficulties," *The Wall Street Journal*, December 10, 1993, p. R4; "The Trick to Selling in Europe," *Fortune*, September 20, 1993, p. 82; "Japan Begins to Open the Door to Foreigners, a Little," *Brandweek*, August 2, 1993, pp. 14–16; "Russia Snickers after Mars Invades," *The Wall Street Journal*, July 13, 1993, p. B1ff.; "Enticed by Visions of Enormous Numbers, More Western Marketers Move into China," *The Wall Street Journal*, July 12, 1993, p. B1ff.; "We Got the Achtung, Baby!" *Brandweek*, January 18, 1993, pp. 22–26; "BSN Finds Eastern Europe Expansion Hard to Swallow," *The Wall Street Journal*, January 5, 1993, p. B4; "Making It in Mother Russia," *Newsweek*, October 19, 1992, p. 52; "U.S. Firms Take Chances in South Korea," *The Wall Street Journal*, June 15, 1992, p. B1ff.; "Bargain Hunting Catches On in Japan, Boosting the Fortunes of Discount Stores," *The Wall Street Journal*, May 19, 1992, p. B1ff.; "Soviet Breakup Stymies Foreign Firms," *The Wall Street Journal*, January 23, 1992, p. B1ff.; "Some Americans Take the Steppes in Stride," *The Wall Street Journal*, January 23, 1992, p. B1ff.; "Some U.S. Firms Profit in Booming Far East Despite Mighty Japan," *The Wall Street Journal*, January 8, 1992, p. A1ff.; "Korean Black Market Stymies U.S. Firms," *The Wall Street Journal*, July 19, 1991, p. B1ff.; "How 3M, by Tiptoeing into Foreign Markets, Became a Big Exporter," *The Wall Street Journal*, March 29, 1991, p. A1ff.; Thomas W. Shreeve, "Be Prepared for Political Changes Abroad," *Harvard Business Review*, July–August 1984, pp. 111–18; Victor H. Frank, Jr., "Living with Price Control Abroad," *Harvard Business Review*, March–April

1984, pp. 137–42; Michael G. Harvey and James T. Rothe, "The Foreign Corrupt Practices Act: The Good, the Bad and the Future," in *1983 American Marketing Association Educators' Proceedings*, ed. P. E. Murphy et al. (Chicago: American Marketing Association, 1983), pp. 374–79.

27. "Lessons Learned beyond the Lira," *Going Global—Italy* (supplement to *Inc.*), 1994; "What Makes Italy Easier?" *Going Global—Italy* (supplement to *Inc.*), 1994; "Jean Cloning," *Brandweek*, May 30, 1994, pp. 15–22; "Double Entendre: The Life and the Life of Pepsi Max," *Brandweek*, April 18, 1994, p. 40; "Eurofizz," *Fortune*, March 22, 1993, p. 15; "Global Ad Campaigns, after Many Missteps, Finally Pay Dividends," *The Wall Street Journal*, August 27, 1992, p. A1ff.; Kamran Kashani, "Beware the Pitfalls of Global Marketing," *Harvard Business Review*, September–October 1989, pp. 91–98; "How to Go Global—and Why," *Fortune*, August 28, 1989, pp. 70–76; "Coke to Use 'Can't Beat the Feeling' as World-Wide Marketing Theme," *The Wall Street Journal*, December 12, 1988, p. 35; "Marketers Turn Sour on Global Sales Pitch Harvard Guru Makes," *The Wall Street Journal*, May 12, 1988, p. 1ff.; John A. Quelch and E. J. Hoff, "Customizing Global Marketing," *Harvard Business Review*, May–June 1986, pp. 59–68.

Chapter 5

1. *1993 Annual Report*, U.S. Shoe; "'SuperOpticals' Edge Out the Corner Optician," *Adweek's Marketing Week*, October 1, 1990, p. 36; "LensCrafters Takes the High Road," *Adweek's Marketing Week*, April 30, 1990, pp. 26–27; "The Big Battle over Eyewear," *The New York Times*, November 26, 1989, sec. 6, p. 4.

2. *1993 Annual Report*, PepsiCo; "In the Chips: At Frito-Lay, the Consumer Is an Obsession," *The Wall Street Journal*, March 22, 1991, pp. B1–2; "Frito-Lay Adds High-Tech Crunch," *American Demographics*, March 1991, pp. 18–20; "Frito-Lay Bets Big with Multigrain Chips," *The Wall Street Journal*, February 28, 1991, p. B1ff.; "What the Scanner Knows about You," *Fortune*, December 3, 1990, pp. 51–52; "Hand-Held Computers Help Field Staff Cut Paper Work and Harvest More Data," *The Wall Street Journal*, January 30, 1990, p. B1ff.; "Frito-Lay Shortens Its Business Cycle," *Fortune*, January 15, 1990, p. 11; *1990 Annual Report*, PepsiCo.

3. John T. Mentzer and Nimish Gandhi, "Expert Systems in Marketing: Guidelines for Development," *Journal of the Academy of Marketing Science*, Winter 1992, pp. 73–80; William D. Perreault, Jr., "The Shifting Paradigm in Marketing Research," *Journal of the Academy of Marketing Science*, Fall 1992, pp. 367–76; J. M. McCann, W. G. Lahti, and J. Hill, "The Brand Manager's Assistant: A Knowledge-Based System Approach to Brand Management," *International Journal of Research in Marketing*, April 1991, pp. 51–74; A. A. Mitchell, J. E. Russo, and D. R. Wittink, "Issues in the Development and Use of Expert Systems for Marketing Decisions," *International Journal of Research in Marketing*, April 1991, pp. 41–50; "Marketers Increase Their Use of Decision Support Systems," *Marketing News*, May 22, 1989, p. 29; Thomas H. Davenport, Michael Hammer, and Tauno J. Metsisto, "How Executives Can Shape Their Company's Information Systems," *Harvard Business Review*, March–April 1989, pp. 130–34.

4. Susan Krafft, "How to Sell an Information System to Your Boss," *American Demographics*, February 1994, p. 54; Nancy J.

Merritt and Cecile Bouchy, "Are Microcomputers Replacing Mainframes in Marketing Research Firms?" *Journal of the Academy of Marketing Science*, Winter 1992, pp. 81–86; Michael R. Czinkota, "International Information Needs for U.S. Competitiveness," *Business Horizons*, November/December, 1991, pp. 86–91; Lawrence B. Chonko, John F. Tanner, Jr., and Ellen Reid Smith, "The Sales Force's Role in International Marketing Research and Marketing Information Systems," *Journal of Personal Selling and Sales Management*, Winter 1991, pp. 69–80; Alfred C. Holden, "How to Locate and Communicate with Overseas Customers," *Industrial Marketing Management* 20, no. 3 (1991), pp. 161–68; Naresh K. Malhotra, Armen Tashchian, and Essam Mahmoud, "The Integration of Microcomputers in Marketing Research and Decision Making," *Journal of the Academy of Marketing Science*, Summer 1987, pp. 69–82; Martin D. J. Buss, "Managing International Information Systems," *Harvard Business Review*, September–October 1982, pp. 153–62.

5. "A Potent New Tool for Selling: Database Marketing," *Business Week*, September 5, 1994, pp. 56–62; "They Know Where You Live—and How You Buy," *Business Week*, February 7, 1994, p. 89; "Marketers Mine Their Corporate Databases," *The Wall Street Journal*, June 14, 1993, p. B4; "More Market Researchers Swear by PCs," *The Wall Street Journal*, March 15, 1993, p. B5; "What's the Best Source of Market Research?" *Inc.*, June 1992, p. 108; "Focusing on Customers' Needs and Motivations," *Business Marketing*, March 1991, pp. 41–43; James M. Sinkula, "Perceived Characteristics, Organizational Factors, and the Utilization of External Market Research Suppliers," *Journal of Business Research*, August 1990, pp. 1–18; Bruce Stern and Scott Dawson, "How to Select a Market Research Firm," *American Demographics*, March 1989, p. 44.

6. For a discussion of ethical issues in marketing research, see "How 'Tactical Research' Muddied Diaper Debate: A Case," *The Wall Street Journal*, May 17, 1994, p. B1ff.; "Studies Galore Support Products and Positions, but Are They Reliable?" *The Wall Street Journal*, November 14, 1991, p. A1ff.; Stephen B. Castleberry, Warren French, and Barbara A. Carlin, "The Ethical Framework of Advertising and Marketing Research Practitioners: A Moral Development Perspective," *Journal of Advertising*, June 1993, pp. 39–46; Joel N. Axelrod, "Politics and Poker: Deception and Self-Deception in Marketing Research," *Journal of Advertising Research*, November/December 1992, p. 79; Ishmael P. Akaah, "Attitudes of Marketing Professionals toward Ethics in Marketing Research: A Cross-National Comparison," *Journal of Business Ethics*, January 1990, pp. 45–54. For more details on doing marketing research, see Harper W. Boyd, Jr., Ralph Westfall, and Stanley F. Stasch, *Marketing Research: Text and Cases* (Burr Ridge, IL: Richard D. Irwin, 1993). See also Christine Moorman, Rohit Deshpande, and Gerald Zaltman, "Factors Affecting Trust in Market Research Relationships," *Journal of Marketing*, January 1993, pp. 81–101; Stephen W. McDaniel and Roberto Solano-Mendez, "Should Marketing Researchers Be Certified?" *Journal of Advertising Research*, July/August 1993, pp. 20–31.

7. "The 'Bloodbath' in Market Research," *Business Week*, February 11, 1991, pp. 72–74; "Why Products Fail," *Adweek's Marketing Week*, November 5, 1990, pp. 20–25; Bickley Townsend, "Market Research that Matters," *American Demographics*, August 1992, p. 58.

8. For a discussion of European secondary data, see "The New Europeans," *The Economist*, November 16, 1991, pp. 65–66;

"Reaching the Real Europe," *American Demographics*, October 1990, pp. 38–43ff. An excellent review of commercially available secondary data may be found in Donald R. Lehmann, *Marketing Research and Analysis*, 3rd ed. (Burr Ridge, IL: Richard D. Irwin, 1988), pp. 231–72. See also Staff of *American Demographics*, "The Best 100 Sources for Marketing Information," *American Demographics*, January 1995, p. 21; Jackson Morton, "Census on the Internet," *American Demographics*, March 1995, p. 52; Katherine S. Chiang, "How to Find Online Information," *American Demographics*, September 1993, p. 52; Dowell Myers, "How to Use Local Census Data," *American Demographics*, June 1993, p. 52.

9. "The Irresistible Customer Questionnaire," *Inc.*, November 1994, pp. 97–99; Jeffrey Durgee, "Richer Findings from Qualitative Research," *Journal of Advertising Research*, August–September 1986, pp. 36–44; Kathleen M. Wallace, "The Use and Value of Qualitative Research Studies," *Industrial Marketing Management*, August 1984, pp. 181–86. For more on focus groups see William J. McDonald, "Focus Group Research Dynamics and Reporting: An Examination of Research Objectives and Moderator Influences," *Journal of the Academy of Marketing Science*, Spring 1993, pp. 161; "Old Market Research Tricks No Match for New Technology," *The Wall Street Journal*, November 1, 1994, p. B1ff.; "Focus Groups Meeting in Cyberspace," *The Wall Street Journal*, February 4, 1994, p. B1; "Nickelodeon Puts Kids Online," *American Demographics*, The 1994 Directory, pp. 16–17; "Focus Groups Key to Reaching Kids," *Advertising Age*, February 10, 1992, p. S1ff.; Joe L. Welch, "Researching Marketing Problems and Opportunities with Focus Groups," *Industrial Marketing Management*, November 1985, pp. 245–54.

10. "Selling Sibelius Isn't Easy," *American Demographics*, The 1994 Directory, pp. 24–25; "Symphony Strikes a Note for Research as It Prepares to Launch a New Season," *Marketing News*, August 29, 1988, p. 12.

11. "How Researchers Can Win Friends and Influence Politicians," *American Demographics*, August 1993, p. 9; Frederick Wiseman and Maryann Billington, "Comment on a Standard Definition of Response Rates," *Journal of Marketing Research*, August 1984, pp. 336–38; Jolene M. Struebbe, Jerome B. Kernan, and Thomas J. Grogan, "The Refusal Problem in Telephone Surveys," *Journal of Advertising Research*, June–July 1986, pp. 29–38.

12. Tyzoon T. Tyebjee, "Telephone Survey Methods: The State of the Art," *Journal of Marketing*, Summer 1979, pp. 68–77; Nicolaos E. Synodinos and Jerry M. Brennan, "Computer Interactive Interviewing in Survey Research," *Psychology and Marketing*, Summer 1988, pp. 117–38; A. Dianne Schmidley, "How to Overcome Bias in a Telephone Survey," *American Demographics*, November 1986, pp. 50–51.

13. "Call It Worldpool," *Business Week*, November 28, 1994, pp. 98–99; "The Gold Mine of Data in Customer Service," *Business Week*, March 21, 1994, pp. 113–14; "How to Listen to Consumers," *Fortune*, January 11, 1993, pp. 77–79; *1993 Annual Report*, Whirlpool.

14. For more detail on observational approaches, see Stephen J. Grove and Raymond P. Fisk, "Observational Data Collection Methods for Services Marketing: An Overview," *Journal of the Academy of Marketing Science*, Summer 1992, pp. 217–24; "High-Tech Coupons and Kiosks," *Inc.*, October 1994, p. 33;

"More U.S. Grocers Turning to ECR to Cut Waste," *Marketing News*, September 12, 1994, p. 3; "Coupon Clippers, Save Your Scissors," *Business Week*, June 20, 1994, pp. 164–66; "Targeted Discounts Scrap Paper Coupons," *Advertising Age*, June 13, 1994, p. 40; Magid M. Abraham and Leonard M. Lodish, "An Implemented System for Improving Promotion Productivity Using Store Scanner Data," *Marketing Science*, Summer 1993, pp. 248–69; "The Nitty-Gritty of ECR Systems: How One Company Makes It Pay," *Advertising Age*, May 2, 1994, pp. S1ff.; "James Bond Hits the Supermarket: Stores Snoop on Shoppers' Habits to Boost Sales," *The Wall Street Journal*, August 25, 1993, p. B1ff.; "Nielsen's Study, 'Wake-Up Calls' to Homes Spark TV Controversy," *The Wall Street Journal*, December 23, 1992, p. B8; Peter J. Danaher and Terence W. Beed, "A Coincidental Survey of People Meter Panelists: Comparing What People Say with What They Do," *Journal of Advertising Research*, January/February 1993, p. 86; "Nielsen Rival to Unveil New 'Peoplemeter,'" *The Wall Street Journal*, December 4, 1992, p. B8; J. Bayer and R. Harter, "'Miner,' 'Manager,' and 'Researcher': Three Modes of Analysis of Scanner Data," *International Journal of Research in Marketing*, April 1991, pp. 17–28; "Using Hidden Eyes to Mind the Store," *Insight*, February 25, 1991, p. 50.

15. "Ads Awaken to Fathers' New Role in Family Life," *Advertising Age*, January 10, 1994, p. S8; "AT&T's Secret Multimedia Trials Offer Clues to Capturing Interactive Audiences," *The Wall Street Journal*, July 28, 1993, p. B1ff.; "Experimenting in the U.K.: Phone, Cable Deals Let U.S. Test Future," *USA Today*, June 28, 1993, p. 1Bff.; "America's Next Test Market? Singapore," *Adweek's Marketing Week*, February 4, 1991, p. 22; Alan G. Sawyer, Parker M. Worthing, and Paul E. Fendak, "The Role of Laboratory Experiments to Test Marketing Strategies," *Journal of Marketing*, Summer 1979, pp. 60–67; "Bar Wars: Hershey Bites Mars," *Fortune*, July 8, 1985, pp. 52–57.

16. "Special Report: Research," *Advertising Age*, November 28, 1994, pp. 27–30; "Amid Share Slump, Market Researcher Plays 'Patch-Up,'" *The Wall Street Journal*, April 25, 1994, p. B4; "Spy Service to Transport Rival Ads on TV for Lickety-Split Response," *The Wall Street Journal*, December 2, 1993, p. B6; "Nielsen in Turmoil," *Advertising Age*, November 15, 1993, pp. 21–24; "Rivals Duel Bitterly for Job of Supplying Market Information," *The Wall Street Journal*, November 15, 1993, p. A1ff.; "Special Report: Research," *Advertising Age*, October 18, 1993, pp. S1–6; *1993 Annual Report*, Information Resources; *1993 Annual Report*, A. C. Nielsen; "Nielsen vs. IRI: Battle of the Research Titans," *Advertising Age*, October 12, 1992, p. 1ff.; "Special Report: Research," *Advertising Age*, June 22, 1992, pp. S1–6; "Researchers Rev Up," *Advertising Age*, January 13, 1992, p. 34; "More Power to J. D. Power," *Fortune*, May 18, 1992, pp. 103–6; "J. D. Power Keeps Raising the Chinning Bar," *Adweek*, September 9, 1991, p. 17.

17. For more detail on data analysis techniques, see Naresh Malhotra, *Marketing Research: An Applied Orientation* (New York: Prentice Hall, 1993) or other current marketing research texts.

18. See John G. Keane, "Questionable Statistics," *American Demographics*, June 1985, pp. 18–21. Detailed treatment of confidence intervals is beyond the scope of this text, but this topic is covered in most marketing research texts, such as Donald R. Lehmann, *Marketing Research and Analysis*, 3rd ed. (Burr Ridge, IL: Richard D. Irwin, 1988).

19. E. Jerome McCarthy et al., *Basic Marketing: A Managerial Approach*, 1st Australasian ed. (Burr Ridge, IL: Richard D. Irwin, 1994), pp. 128–29.

20. "GM Seeks Revival of Buick and Olds," *The Wall Street Journal*, April 12, 1988, p. 37.

21. Alan R. Andreasen, "Cost-Conscious Marketing Research," *Harvard Business Review*, July–August 1983, pp. 74–81; A. Parasuraman, "Research's Place in the Marketing Budget," *Business Horizons*, March/April 1983, pp. 25–29; Jack J. Honomichl, "Point of View: Why Marketing Information Should Have Top Executive Status," *Journal of Advertising Research*, November/December 1994, pp. 61–66; James M. Sinkula, "Market Information Processing and Organizational Learning," *Journal of Marketing*, January 1994, pp. 35–45; Jim Bessen, "Riding the Marketing Information Wave," *Harvard Business Review*, September–October 1993, pp. 150–61; Danny N. Bellenger, "The Marketing Manager's View of Marketing Research," *Business Horizons* June 1979, pp. 59–65.

Chapter 6

1. "Citicorp: Capturing the Global Consumer," *Fortune*, December 13, 1993, pp. 166–67; "Citicorp Seeks Niche among Rich in Japan," *The Wall Street Journal*, November 1, 1993, p. B1ff.; *1993 Annual Report*, Citicorp; "For Citibank, There's No Place Like Asia," *Business Week*, March 30, 1992, pp. 66–69; "Citibank Assumes a Starring Role in Asia," *The Wall Street Journal*, August 2, 1990, p. A8; "Citicorp Strives to Be McDonald's and Coke of Consumer Banking," *The Wall Street Journal*, August 9, 1989, p. A1ff.

2. "Retailers Aim Straight at Teens," *Advertising Age*, September 5, 1994, p. 1ff.; "Teens, the Most Global Market of All," *Fortune*, May 16, 1994, pp. 90–97; "Teens, Here Comes the Biggest Wave Yet," *Business Week*, April 11, 1994, pp. 76–86: "Special Report: Marketing to Teens," *Advertising Age*, August 23, 1993, pp. S1–11; "Marketplace: Teens," *Adweek*, June 15, 1992, pp. 64–71.

3. Based on U.S. Census data, including "World Population Profile: 1994," United Nations statistical data, *Rand McNally 1995 Commercial Atlas and Marketing Guide* (Skokie, IL: Rand McNally, 1995), and *The World Market Atlas* (New York: Business International Corp., 1992).

4. Based on U.S. Census data, United Nations statistical data, and PC Globe Maps 'N' Facts software (Novato, CA: Broderbund, 1993); "More Power to Women, Fewer Mouths to Feed," *Time*, September 26, 1994, pp. 64–65; "Body Politics: Population Wars," *Newsweek*, September 12, 1994, pp. 22–27; "Too Many People?" *Business Week*, August 29, 1994, pp. 64–66; "Population: Frightening Forecast," *USA Today*, July 18, 1994, p. 7A; "Population Growing at a Furious Rate," *USA Today*, July 18, 1994, p. 1Aff.; "Superpowers Lose Population Momentum," *The Wall Street Journal*, April 23, 1990, p. B1; James V. Koch, "An Economic Profile of the Pacific Rim," *Business Horizons*, March/April 1989, pp. 18–25.

5. U.S. Bureau of the Census, Reports WP/94 and WP/94-DD, *World Population Profile: 1994* (Washington, DC: U.S. Government Printing Office, 1994); U.S. Bureau of the Census, *Statistical Abstract of the United States 1994* (Washington, DC: U.S. Government Printing Office, 1994), pp. 850–52; PC Globe Maps 'N' Facts software (Novato, CA: Broderbund, 1993); "The World Economy," *Fortune*, July 25, 1994, pp. 118–26; "Where the

Global Action Is," *Fortune*, Special Issue, Autumn/Winter 1993, pp. 63–65; "The New Global Consumer," *Fortune*, Special Issue, Autumn/Winter 1993, pp. 68–77; "Megacities," *Time*, January 11, 1993, pp. 28–38; "The Global Economy: Can You Compete?" (Special Report), *Business Week*, December 17, 1990, pp. 60–93.

6. Raj Aggarwal, "The Strategic Challenge of the Evolving Global Economy," *Business Horizons*, July/August 1987, pp. 38–44; J. S. Hill and R. R. Still, "Adapting Products to LDC Tastes," *Harvard Business Review*, March/April 1984, pp. 92–101; James M. Hulbert, William K. Brant, and Raimar Richers, "Marketing Planning in the Multinational Subsidiary: Practices and Problems," *Journal of Marketing*, Summer 1980, pp. 7–16.

7. "As a Global Marketer Coke Excels by Being Tough and Consistent," *The Wall Street Journal*, December 19, 1989, p. A1ff.; "American Home Infant-Formula Giveaway to End," *The Wall Street Journal*, February 4, 1991, p. B1ff.; "Three Small Businesses Profit by Taking On the World," *The Wall Street Journal*, November 8, 1990, p. B2.

8. "The Lowdown on Literacy," *American Demographics*, June 1994, p. 6; Lee D. Dahringer and Hans Muhlbacher, *International Marketing: A Global Perspective* (Reading, MA: Addison-Wesley, 1991), p. 182; Philip R. Cateora, *International Marketing* (Burr Ridge, IL: Richard D. Irwin, 1990), pp. 387–90, 468–70; Hana Noor Al-Deen, "Literacy and Information Content of Magazine Advertising: USA versus Saudi Arabia," *International Journal of Advertising* 10, no. 3 (1991), pp. 251–58.

9. Based on U.S. Census data and "States of the Future," *American Demographics*, October 1994, pp. 36–43; "Retirees Seek the Good Life Far from Florida," *The Wall Street Journal*, August 8, 1994, p. B1ff.; "America's Heartland: The Midwest's New Role in the Global Economy," *Business Week*, July 11, 1994, pp. 116–24; "The Geography of an Emerging America," *Fortune*, June 27, 1994, pp. 88–94; "Californians Flood In and Tension Is Rising in Small Towns in Utah," *The Wall Street Journal*, January 29, 1994, p. A1ff.; "Census Bureau Lifts Population Forecast, Citing Fertility, Immigration, Longevity," *The Wall Street Journal*, December 4, 1992, p. B1ff.; "American Diversity," *American Demographics* (supplement), July 1991; "More than It Grows, the Population Flows," *The Wall Street Journal*, March 2, 1990, p. B1.

10. Based on U.S. Census data and "A Slow Fade for the Echo Boom," *American Demographics*, July 1994, p. 15; "The Baby Boomlet May End with a Blizzard," *American Demographics*, March 1994, p. 16; "The Baby Boomlet Is for Real," *Fortune*, February 10, 1992, pp. 101–4; "Wooing Boomers' Babies," *Advertising Age*, July 22, 1991, p. 3ff.; "Why Birth Rates Have Turned Up in the U.S. and Europe," *Business Week*, February 11, 1991, p. 16.

11. For more on baby boomers, see U.S. Census data and William R. Swinyard and Heikki J. Rinne, "The Six Shopping Worlds of Baby Boomers," *Business Horizons*, September–October 1994, pp. 64–69; Campbell Gibson, "The Four Baby Booms," *American Demographics*, November 1993, pp. 36–43; "Home Hair-Color Sales Get Boost as Baby Boomers Battle Aging," *The Wall Street Journal*, February 3, 1994, p. B7; "CBS Radio Retunes to Rock-and-Roll Hits of the '70s," *The Wall Street Journal*, December 30, 1993, p. B2; "The Master Trend," *American Demographics*, October 1993, pp. 28–37; "Baby Boomers Settle Down and Slow the Pace of Change," *USA Today*, June 24, 1993, p. A1A; "Aging Boomers Are New Target for Maybelline," *The Wall Street Journal*, April 13, 1994, p. B1ff.; "Lee Aims at Bigger Targets: Pudgy

People," *The Wall Street Journal*, January 27, 1993, p. B7; "Old Rockers Never Die—They Just Switch to CDs," *Business Week*, August 17, 1992, p. 54; "Baby Boomers May Seek Age-Friendly Stores," *The Wall Street Journal*, July 1, 1992, p. B1.

12. For more on the changing nature of families, see "Cool Pad, Fab Food, One Catch: Mom Lives There Too," *The Wall Street Journal*, September 12, 1994, p. A1ff.; "How Small a Household," *American Demographics*, August 1994, p. 59; "The Art of Flying Solo," *Newsweek*, March 1, 1993, pp. 70–73; "It's OK to Be Single, but Marriage Still Is a Touted Possibility," *The Wall Street Journal*, February 3, 1993, p. A1ff.; "More Eateries Hop to Serve Tables for One," *USA Today*, October 7, 1992, p. 6D; "Census Data May Make Ads More Single-Minded," *Advertising Age*, July 20, 1992, p. 2; Diane M. McConocha, Shirlee A. Tully, and Carl H. Walther, "Household Money Management: Recognizing Nontraditional Couples," *Journal of Consumer Affairs*, Winter 1993, pp. 258–83; "Where Have All the Families Gone?" *Business Week*, June 29, 1992, pp. 90–91; "Where the Growth Is among Households," *The Wall Street Journal*, October 28, 1991, p. B1; "Home Alone—with $660 Billion," *Business Week*, July 29, 1991, pp. 76–77; Martha Farnsworth Riche, "The Future of the Family," *American Demographics*, March 1991, pp. 44–46; Pamela L. Kiecker, Shelby D. Hunt, and Lawrence B. Chonko, "Gender, Income Differences, and Marketing: Examining the 'Earnings Gap' in Three Areas of Marketing," *Journal of the Academy of Marketing Science*, Spring 1991, pp. 77–82.

13. Based on U.S. Census data and "The Rural Rebound," *American Demographics*, May 1994, pp. 24–29; "Beliefs Bound to the Land Hold Firm as Times Change," *Insight*, December 7, 1987, pp. 10–11.

14. Based on U.S. Census data and "Census: City Growth Booming," *USA Today*, December 18, 1991, p. 3A; Joel Garreau, "Edge Cities: Life on the New Frontier," *American Demographics*, September 1991, pp. 24–53; "America's Megamarkets," *American Demographics*, June 1991, p. 59; Joe Schwartz and Thomas Exter, "This World Is Flat," *American Demographics*, April 1991, pp. 34–39; Gary Gappert, "The Future of Urban Environments: Implications for the Business Community," *Business Horizons*, November–December 1993, pp. 70–74; Richard L. Forstall, "Going to Town," *American Demographics*, May 1993, pp. 42–47; Jan Larson, "Density Is Destiny," *American Demographics*, February 1993, pp. 38–43; "The MSA Mess," *American Demographics*, January 1989, pp. 53–56.

15. "Going Where the Grass Is Greener," *Brandweek*, August 22, 1994, pp. 20–21; "Census Finds Fewer People Are on the Move," *The Wall Street Journal*, November 17, 1992, p. A5; "Mobility of U.S. Society Turns Small Cities into Giants," *The Wall Street Journal*, February 8, 1991, p. B1ff.; "Americans on the Move," *American Demographics*, June 1990, pp. 46–49; James R. Lumpkin and James B. Hunt, "Mobility as an Influence on Retail Patronage Behavior of the Elderly: Testing Conventional Wisdom," *Journal of the Academy of Marketing Science*, Winter 1989, pp. 1–12; Michael R. Hyman, "Long-Distance Geographic Mobility and Retailing Attitudes and Behaviors: An Update," *Journal of Retailing*, Summer 1987, pp. 187–208.

16. " 'Hi' Road to Success," *Advertising Age*, September 12, 1994, p. 58; "No Hola Here, No Generation X: Chrysler Steers Neon to Yuppies South of Border," *Advertising Age*, July 18, 1994, p. 123; "Detroit Moves to Woo Blacks," *Advertising Age*, April 11, 1994, p. 10; "Chrysler Directs Neon Campaign at Generation X," *The*

Wall Street Journal, August 27, 1993, p. B1ff.; "Neon May Be a Bright Light for Chrysler," *The Wall Street Journal*, April 23, 1993, p. B1ff.

17. Based on U.S. Census data and "Children Get Poorer; Nation Gets Richer," *USA Today*, November 14, 1994, p. 1Aff.; "Inequality," *Business Week*, August 15, 1994, pp. 78–83; "Minimum-Wage Jobs Give Many Americans Only a Miserable Life," *The Wall Street Journal*, November 12, 1993, p. A1ff.; "The Economic Crisis of Urban America," *Business Week*, May 18, 1992, pp. 38–47; "Apartheid, American Style," *Newsweek*, March 23, 1992, p. 61; "The Middle Class Boom of the 1980s," *The Wall Street Journal*, March 12, 1992, p. A10; Greg J. Duncan, Timothy M. Smeeding, and Willard Rodgers, "The Incredible Shrinking Middle Class," *American Demographics*, May 1992, pp. 34–39; "The 'Fortunate Fifth' Fallacy," *The Wall Street Journal*, January 28, 1992, p. A14; S. K. List, "Inconspicuous Consumption," *American Demographics*, December 1992, p. 58; "A Class Structure that Won't Stay Put," *The Wall Street Journal*, November 20, 1991, p. A16; Jan Larson, "Reaching Downscale Markets," *American Demographics*, November 1991, pp. 38–40ff.; "What Happened to the American Dream?" *Business Week*, August 19, 1991, pp. 80–85; "Why the Middle Class Is Anxious," *Fortune*, May 21, 1990, pp. 106–12; "The Rich Are Different from One Another," *The Wall Street Journal*, November 12, 1990, p. B1; "The New Middle Class: How It Lives," *Fortune*, August 13, 1990, pp. 104–13.

18. "Nutrament, Debunked as a 'Fitness' Drink, Is Reborn in the Slums," *The Wall Street Journal*, November 2, 1994, p. B1ff.; "Some Mortgage Firms Neglect Black Areas More than Banks Do," *The Wall Street Journal*, August 9, 1994, p. A1ff.; "A Marketing Giant Uses Its Sales Prowess to Profit on Poverty," *The Wall Street Journal*, September 22, 1993, p. A1ff.; "Poor to Receive Nicotine Patch from Cyanamid," *The Wall Street Journal*, February 23, 1993, p. B1ff.; "Merck's 'River Blindness' Gift Hits Snags," *The Wall Street Journal*, September 23, 1992, p. B1ff.; "Breakthrough in Birth Control May Elude Poor," *The Wall Street Journal*, March 4, 1991, p. B1ff.

19. U.S. Department of Labor, *Consumer Expenditure Survey 1993* (Washington, DC: U.S. Government Printing Office, 1994), Table 1201; "What Is a Luxury? It Depends," *American Demographics*, July 1993, pp. 13–15; Cheryl Russell and Thomas G. Exter, "Mad Money," *American Demographics*, July 1993, pp. 26–32; Gail DeWeese and Marjorie J. T. Norton, "Impact of Married Women's Employment on Individual Household Member Expenditures for Clothing," *Journal of Consumer Affairs*, Winter 1991, pp. 235–57; Margaret Ambry, "The Age of Spending," *American Demographics*, November 1990, pp. 16–23ff.; "What Does It Take to Get Along?" *American Demographics*, May 1990, pp. 36–39.

20. Margaret K. Ambry, "Receipts from a Marriage," *American Demographics*, February 1993, pp. 30–37; "A Snapshot of Younger Lifestage Group Purchases," *American Demographics*, November 9, 1992, p. 28; "How Spending Changes during Middle Age," *The Wall Street Journal*, January 14, 1992, p. B1; "How the Average American Gets By," *Fortune*, October 21, 1991, pp. 52–64; "Here Come the Brides," *American Demographics*, June 1990, p. 4; "Feathering the Empty Nest," *American Demographics*, June 1990, p. 8; Patrick E. Murphy and William A. Staples, "A Modernized Family Life Cycle," *Journal of Consumer Research*, June 1979, pp. 12–22.

21. Paula M. DeWitt, "Breaking Up Is Hard to Do," *American Demographics*, October 1992, pp. 52–61; "Marital Bust," *American Demographics*, June 1994, p. 59; Paula M. DeWitt, "The Second Time Around," *American Demographics*, November 1992, pp. 60–63; "Breaking the Divorce Cycle," *Newsweek*, January 13, 1992, pp. 48–53; "Marrying Age Higher than Ever Before," *USA Today*, June 7, 1991, p. 1D; " 'I Do' Is Repeat Refrain for Half of Newlyweds," *USA Today*, February 15, 1991, p. 1A; Jan Larson, "Understanding Stepfamilies," *American Demographics*, July 1992, pp. 36–41.

22. For more on teens, see U.S. Census data and "Squeaky Clean Teens," *American Demographics*, January 1995, p. 42; "Oh Mom, Those Jeans Are, Like, So Five Minutes Ago," *Business Week*, September 5, 1994, p. 36; "Kids Get the Clothes, Mom Gets the Bill," *The Wall Street Journal*, August 26, 1994, p. B1; "Teenagers: The Lessons that 'Junky Jobs' Teach," *The Wall Street Journal*, July 13, 1994, p. B1; "Why Teens Have Less Green," *American Demographics*, July 1994, p. 9; "Will Teens Buy It?" *Time*, May 30, 1994, pp. 50–51; "Coke to Generation X: You're OK, Drink OK," *Advertising Age*, April 25, 1994, p. 58; "New Magazines for New Cliques of Teens," *The Wall Street Journal*, March 14, 1994, p. B1ff.; "You Just Can't Talk to These Kids," *Business Week*, April 19, 1993, pp. 104–5; "13 Going on 21," *Adweek's Marketing Week*, March 11, 1991, pp. 17–22.

23. "Spreading the Word with Bigger Street Signs," *USA Today*, December 29, 1994, p. 6A; "Wanted: Six Bedrooms, Seven Baths for Empty Nesters," *The Wall Street Journal*, October 17, 1994, p. B1ff.; David B. Wolfe, "Targeting the Mature Mind," *American Demographics*, March 1994, pp. 32–37; Diane Crispell and William H. Frey, "American Maturity," *American Demographics*, March 1993, pp. 31–43; C. D. Schewe and A. L. Balazs, "Role Transitions in Older Adults: A Marketing Opportunity," *Psychology & Marketing*, March/April 1992, pp. 85–100; Charles F. Longino, Jr., "Myths of an Aging America," *American Demographics*, August 1994, pp. 36–45; George P. Moschis, Anil Mathur, and Ruth Belk Smith, "Older Consumers' Orientations toward Age-Based Marketing Stimuli," *Journal of the Academy of Marketing Science*, Summer 1993, pp. 195–206; "The Economics of Aging," *Business Week*, September 12, 1994, pp. 60–68; "United, AmEx Put Seniors in New Class," *Advertising Age*, June 27, 1994, p. 52; Louis Pol, Michael May, and Frank Hartranft, "Eight Stages of Aging," *American Demographics*, August 1992, pp. 54–57; "Travel Agents Target Grandma and Grandpa," *The Wall Street Journal*, June 17, 1994, p. B1; "Special Report: The Mature Market," *Advertising Age*, November 16, 1992, pp. S1–8; "Three Strategies for Reaching Older Consumers in the 1990s," *Adweek's Marketing Week*, December 3, 1990, pp. 30–31; Ellen Day et al., "Reaching the Senior Citizen Market(s)," *Journal of Advertising Research*, December 1987–January 1988, pp. 23–30.

24. For an overview of ethnic populations in the U.S., see "Marketers Pay Attention! Ethnics Comprise 25% of the U.S.," *Brandweek*, July 18, 1994, pp. 26–33; "Should the Census Be Less Black and White?" *Business Week*, July 4, 1994, p. 40; Gabrielle Sandor, "The 'Other' Americans," *American Demographics*, June 1994, pp. 36–42; "In Living Color," *Small World*, February 1994, pp. 21–25; "America: Still a Melting Pot?" *Newsweek*, August 9, 1993, pp. 16–25; "Sentiment Sours as Rate of Arrival Rises," *USA Today*, July 14, 1993, p. 1Aff.; Samia El-Badry, "The Arab-American Market," *American Demographics*, January 1994, pp. 22–33; "Immigration," *USA Today*, July 14, 1993, p. 6A; Scott Koslow, Prem N. Shamdasani, and Ellen E. Touchstone, "Exploring Language Effects in Ethnic Advertising: A Sociolinguistic Perspective," *Journal of Consumer Research*, March 1994, pp. 575–85; "The Immigrants," *Business Week*, July 13, 1992, pp. 114–22; "Ethnics Gain Market Clout," *Advertising Age*, August 5, 1991, pp. 3ff. For more on the African-American market, see U.S. Census data and "Heritage and Tradition Are Changing the Face of Today's Toys," *Discount Store News*, February 6, 1995, p. 77; William P. O'Hare and William H. Frey, "Booming, Suburban, and Black," *American Demographics*, September 1992, pp. 30–39; Eugene Morris, "The Difference in Black and White," *American Demographics*, January 1993, pp. 44–51; "Detroit Moves to Woo Blacks," *Advertising Age*, April 11, 1994, p. 10; "Full-Color Press," *The Raleigh News & Observer*, January 23, 1994, p. 1Fff.; "A 'Street-Smart' KFC Woos Black Consumers," *The Wall Street Journal*, December 6, 1993, p. B1; "Random Harvest," *Adweek*, May 17, 1993, p. 30; "Mining the Non-White Markets," *Brandweek*, April 12, 1993, pp. 29–32; "Marketers Miss Out by Alienating Blacks," *The Wall Street Journal*, April 9, 1993, p. B3; "Data Gap," *The Wall Street Journal*, February 19, 1993, p. R18; Eugene Morris, "The Difference in Black and White," *American Demographics*, January 1993, pp. 44–49; "Buying Black," *Time*, August 31, 1992, pp. 52–53; "Waking Up to a Major Market," *Business Week*, March 23, 1992, pp. 72–73; "Black Middle Class Debates Merits of Cities and Suburbs," *The Wall Street Journal*, August 6, 1991, p. B1ff.; "Special Report: Marketing to African-Americans," *Advertising Age*, July 1, 1991; "Six Myths about Black Consumers," *Adweek's Marketing Week*, May 6, 1991, pp. 16–19; Peter K. Tat and David Bejou, "Examining Black Consumer Motives for Coupon Usage," *Journal of Advertising Research*, March/April 1994, pp. 29–35; "The Black Middle Class," *Business Week*, March 14, 1988, pp. 62–70. For more on the Hispanic market, see U.S. Census data and "Special Report: Marketing to Hispanics," *Advertising Age*, January 23, 1995, pp. 29–37; Francis J. Mulhern and Jerome D. Williams, "A Comparative Analysis of Shopping Behavior in Hispanic and Non-Hispanic Market Areas," *Journal of Retailing*, Fall 1994, pp. 231–52; Patricia Braus, "What Does 'Hispanic' Mean?" *American Demographics*, June 1993, pp. 46–51; "Run to the Supermart and Pick Me Up Some Cactus," *Business Week*, June 20, 1994, pp. 70–71; William H. Frey and William P. O'Hare, "Vivan los Suburbios!" *American Demographics*, April 1993, pp. 30–37; "Listening to Their Latin Beat," *Newsweek*, March 28, 1994, pp. 42–43; Naveen Donthu and Joseph Cherian, "Impact of Strength of Ethnic Identification on Hispanic Shopping Behavior," *Journal of Retailing*, Winter 1994, pp. 383–96; Morton Winsberg, "Specific Hispanics," *American Demographics*, February 1994, pp. 44–53; "Special Report: Marketing to Hispanics," *Advertising Age*, January 24, 1994, pp. S1–10; "Radio Stations Gain by Going after Hispanics," *The Wall Street Journal*, July 14, 1993, p. B1ff.; "The Largest Minority," *American Demographics*, February 1993, p. 59; "One-Quarter of Hispanics Move Every Year," *American Demographics*, April 1992, p. 12; "Hispanic Growth Booms," *USA Today*, February 6, 1991, p. 1Aff. For more on the Asian-American market, see U.S. Census data and "Two English-Speaking Magazines Target Affluent Asian-Americans," *The Wall Street Journal*, October 1, 1993, p. A5A; Charles R. Taylor and Ju Yung Lee, "Not in *Vogue*: Portrayals of Asian Americans in Magazine Advertising," *Journal of Public Policy & Marketing*, Fall 1994, pp. 239–45; "Taking the Pulse of

Asian-Americans," *Adweek's Marketing Week*, August 12, 1991, p. 32; William P. O'Hare, William H. Frey, and Dan Fost, "Asians in the Suburbs," *American Demographics*, May 1994, pp. 32–39; Wei-Na Lee and David K. Tse, "Changing Media Consumption in a New Home: Acculturation Patterns among Hong Kong Immigrants to Canada," *Journal of Advertising*, March 1994, pp. 57–70; "Suddenly, Asian-Americans Are a Marketer's Dream," *Business Week*, June 17, 1991, pp. 54–55.

Chapter 7

1. "Why Do We Work?" *Fortune*, December 26, 1994, pp. 196–204; "Volvo, Saturn Cultivate Their Cult Following," *Advertising Age*, March 28, 1994, p. S12; "Latter-Day Easy Riders Boost Sales," *USA Today*, November 17, 1993, p. 1Bff.; "100,000 Converge to Pay Homage," *USA Today*, June 10, 1993, p. 1Aff.; "The Rumble Heard Round the World," *Business Week*, May 24, 1993, pp. 58–60; *1993 Annual Report*, Harley-Davidson; "Put to the Test," *Adweek*, December 7, 1992, pp. 28–32; "Yuppies Help Fuel Demand," *USA Today*, July 22, 1991, p. 1Bff.; "After Nearly Stalling, Harley-Davidson Finds New Crowd of Riders," *The Wall Street Journal*, August 31, 1990, p. A1ff.

2. K. H. Chung, *Motivational Theories and Practices* (Columbus, OH: Grid, 1977), pp. 40–43; A. H. Maslow, *Motivation and Personality* (New York: Harper & Row, 1970). See also M. Joseph Sirgy, "A Social Cognition Model of Consumer Problem Recognition," *Journal of the Academy of Marketing Science*, Winter 1987, pp. 53–61.

3. "What Works for One Works for All," *Business Week*, April 20, 1992, pp. 112–13.

4. Frances K. McSweeney and Calvin Bierley, "Recent Developments in Classical Conditioning," *Journal of Consumer Research*, September 1984, pp. 619–31; Walter R. Nord and J. Paul Peter, "A Behavior Modification Perspective on Marketing," *Journal of Marketing*, Spring 1980, pp. 36–47; Scott A. Hawkins and Stephen J. Hoch, "Low-Involvement Learning: Memory without Evaluation," *Journal of Consumer Research*, September 1992, pp. 212–25; James R. Bettman, "Memory Factors in Consumer Choice: A Review," *Journal of Marketing*, Spring 1979, pp. 37–53; Richard Weijo and Leigh Lawton, "Message Repetition, Experience and Motivation," *Psychology and Marketing*, Fall 1986, pp. 165–80.

5. "Color Nuprin's Success Yellow," *Advertising Age*, October 31, 1988, p. 28.

6. For just a few references, see Alvin A. Achenbaum, "Advertising Doesn't Manipulate Consumers," *Journal of Advertising Research*, April 1972, pp. 3–14; Sharon E. Beatty and Lynn R. Kahle, "Alternate Hierarchies of the Attitude-Behavior Relationship: The Impact of Brand Commitment and Habit," *Journal of the Academy of Marketing Science*, Summer 1988, pp. 1–10; B. L. Bayus and S. Gupta, "An Empirical Analysis of Consumer Durable Replacement Intentions," *International Journal of Research in Marketing*, August 1992, pp. 257–68; Calvin P. Duncan and Richard W. Olshavsky, "External Search: The Role of Consumer Beliefs," *Journal of Marketing Research*, February 1982, pp. 32–43; M. Joseph Sirgy, "Self-Concept in Consumer Behavior: A Critical Review," *Journal of Consumer Research*, December 1982, pp. 287–300.

7. "Will the British Warm Up to Iced Tea? Some Big Marketers Are Counting on It," *The Wall Street Journal*, August 22, 1994,

p. B1ff.; "Taiwan Soft Drink Sales Break for Tea," *The Wall Street Journal*, July 29, 1994, p. A7B.

8. "Restaurants See 'Health-Mex' as Hot Cuisine," *The Wall Street Journal*, August 9, 1994, p. B1ff.; "Buttering Up Customers for Margarine," *The Wall Street Journal*, June 7, 1994, p. B1ff.; "Candy-Crammed or Free of Fat, Frozen Yogurt Is Selling like Hot Cakes," *The Wall Street Journal*, June 2, 1994, p. B1ff.; "Oreo, Ritz Join Nabisco's Low-Fat Feast," *Advertising Age*, April 4, 1994, p. 3ff.; "Slim-Fast Ads Use Brooke Shields to Appeal to the Low-Fat Dieter," *The Wall Street Journal*, January 10, 1994, p. B5; "The King of Cream Returns: Häagen-Dazs's Creator Goes Low Fat," *Newsweek*, November 1, 1993, p. 48; "Three Diet Firms Settle False-Ad Case; Two Others Vow to Fight FTC Charges," *The Wall Street Journal*, October 1, 1993, p. B5; " 'Light' Foods Are Having Heavy Going," *The Wall Street Journal*, March 9, 1993, p. B1ff.; "FTC Is Cracking Down on Misleading Ads," *The Wall Street Journal*, February 4, 1991, p. B6.

9. "Men Are Taking a Cotton to Wrinkle-Free Pants," *USA Today*, June 16, 1994, p. 5D; " 'Wrinkle-Free' Shirts Don't Live Up to the Name," *The Wall Street Journal*, May 11, 1994, p. B1ff.; Valarie A. Zeithaml, Leonard L. Berry, and A. Parasuraman, "The Nature and Determinants of Customer Expectations of Service," *Journal of the Academy of Marketing Science*, Winter 1993, pp. 1–12; Scott W. Kelley and Mark A. Davis, "Antecedents to Customer Expectations for Service Recovery," *Journal of the Academy of Marketing Science*, Winter 1994, pp. 52–61; R. Kenneth Teas, "Expectations, Performance Evaluation, and Consumers' Perceptions of Quality," *Journal of Marketing*, October 1993, pp. 18–34.

10. Harold H. Kassarjian and Mary Jane Sheffet, "Personality and Consumer Behavior: An Update," in *Perspectives in Consumer Behavior*, ed. H. Kassarjian and T. Robertson (Glenview, IL: Scott, Foresman, 1981), p. 160; Raymond L. Horton, *Buyer Behavior: A Decision Making Approach* (Columbus, OH: Charles E. Merrill, 1984).

11. "Lifestyle Study: Who We Are, How We Live, What We Think," *Advertising Age*, January 20, 1992, pp. 16–18; Robert A. Mittelstaedt, "Economics, Psychology, and the Literature of the Subdiscipline of Consumer Behavior," *Journal of the Academy of Marketing Science*, Fall 1990, pp. 303–12; Martha Farnsworth Riche, "Psychographics for the 1990s," *American Demographics*, July 1989, pp. 24–31; W. D. Wells, "Psychographics: A Critical Review," *Journal of Marketing Research*, May 1975, pp. 196–213.

12. Judith Waldrop, "Markets with Attitude," *American Demographics*, July 1994, pp. 22–33; "New VALS 2 Takes Psychological Route," *Advertising Age*, February 13, 1989, p. 24; Lynn R. Kahle, Sharon E. Beatty, and Pamela Homer, "Alternative Measurement Approaches to Consumer Values: The List of Values (LOV) and Values and Life Styles (VALS)," *Journal of Consumer Research*, December 1986, pp. 405–10.

13. For more on kids' influence in purchase decisions, see "Dial, Lever Eye Baby Boomlet," *Brandweek*, September 19, 1994, p. 1ff.; Sharon E. Betty and Salil Talpade, "Adolescent Influence in Family Decision Making: A Replication with Extension," *Journal of Consumer Research*, September 1994, pp. 332–41; "Playing with Their Food," *Advertising Age*, September 12, 1994, p. 23; "Food Firms Concoct Dino Nuggets, Gaudy Yogurt to Attract Kids," *The Wall Street Journal*, April 12, 1994, p. B1ff.; "Hasbro Bets Muppets Will Be Cereal Killers," *Brandweek*, February 14, 1994, p. 1ff.;

"Special Report: Marketing to Kids," *Advertising Age*, February 14, 1994, pp. S1–14; Horst Stipp, "New Ways to Reach Children," *American Demographics*, August 1993, pp. 50–56; "War Stories from the Sandbox: What Kids Say," *Brandweek*, July 5, 1993, pp. 26–32; James U. McNeal and Chyon-Hwa Yeh, "Born to Shop," *American Demographics*, June 1993, pp. 34–39; "Special Report: Marketing to Kids," *Advertising Age*, February 8, 1993, pp. S1–24; "Special Report: Marketing to Parents," *Advertising Age*, July 27, 1992, pp. 28–30; "Getting 'Em While They're Young," *Business Week*, September 9, 1991, pp. 94–95; James McNeal, "Children as Customers," *American Demographics*, September 1990, pp. 36–39. For more on men's influence, see "Guys Show Their Muscle as Buyers of Groceries," *Advertising Age*, July 11, 1994, p. 29; "The Daddy Track," *The Raleigh News & Observer*, April 17, 1994, p. 17Aff.; John B. Ford, Michael S. LaTour, and Tony L. Henthorne, "Perception of Marital Roles in Purchase Decision Processes: A Cross-Cultural Study," *Journal of the Academy of Marketing Science*, Spring 1995, pp. 120–31; Ugur Yavas, Emin Babakus, and Nejdet Delener, "Family Purchasing Roles in Saudi Arabia: Perspectives from Saudi Wives," *Journal of Business Research*, September 1994, pp. 75–86; Rosemary Polegato and Judith L. Zaichkowsky, "Family Food Shopping: Strategies Used by Husbands and Wives," *Journal of Consumer Affairs*, Winter 1994, pp. 278–99; "From Choices to Checkout, the Genders Behave Very Differently in Supermarkets," *The Wall Street Journal*, March 22, 1994, p. B1ff.; "Mr. Mom Goes Mainstream," *American Demographics*, March 1994, p. 59; "As More Men Become 'Trailing Spouses,' Firms Help Them Cope," *The Wall Street Journal*, April 13, 1993, p. A1ff.; "White Male Paranoia," *Newsweek*, March 29, 1993, pp. 48–53; "Real Men Buy Paper Towels, Too," *Business Week*, November 9, 1992, pp. 75–76; "Marketplace: Men," *Adweek*, June 19, 1992, pp. 33–38; "Special Report: Marketing to Men," *Advertising Age*, April 15, 1991, pp. S1–12. For more on women's influence, see "Woman's Work Is Never Done," *Newsweek*, July 31, 1989, p. 65; W. Keith Bryant, "Durables and Wives' Employment Yet Again," *Journal of Consumer Research*, June 1988, pp. 37–47; "The Lasting Changes Brought by Women Workers," *Business Week*, March 15, 1982, pp. 59–67; Michael D. Reilly, "Working Wives and Convenience Consumption," *Journal of Consumer Research*, March 1982, pp. 407–18. For more on family decision making, see Robert Boutilier, "Pulling the Family's Strings," *American Demographics*, August 1993, pp. 44–48; Ellen R. Foxman, Patriya S. Tansuhaj, and Karin M. Ekstrom, "Adolescents' Influence in Family Purchase Decisions: A Socialization Perspective," *Journal of Business Research*, March 1989, pp. 159–72; C. Lackman and J. M. Lanasa, "Family Decision-Making Theory: An Overview and Assessment," *Psychology & Marketing*, March/April 1993, pp. 81–94; Thomas C. O'Guinn, Ronald J. Faber, and Giovann Imperia, "Subcultural Influences on Family Decision Making," *Psychology and Marketing*, Winter 1986, pp. 305–18.

14. "Class in America," *Fortune*, February 7, 1994, pp. 114–26; Greg J. Duncan, Timothy M. Smeeding, and Willard Rodgers, "The Incredible Shrinking Middle Class," *American Demographics*, May 1992, pp. 34–38; Dennis L. Rosen and Richard W. Olshavsky, "The Dual Role of Informational Social Influence: Implications for Marketing Management," *Journal of Business Research*, April 1987, pp. 123–44; Jeffrey D. Ford and Elwood A. Ellis, "A Reexamination of Group Influence on Member Brand Preference," *Journal of Marketing Research*, February 1980,

pp. 125–32; Oswald A. J. Mascarenhas and Mary A. Higby, "Peer, Parent, and Media Influences in Teen Apparel Shopping," *Journal of the Academy of Marketing Science*, Winter 1993, pp. 53–58; George P. Moschis, "Social Comparison and Informal Group Influence," *Journal of Marketing Research*, August 1976, pp. 237–44; Terry L. Childers and Akshay R. Rao, "The Influence of Familial and Peer-Based Reference Groups on Consumer Decisions," *Journal of Consumer Research*, September 1992, pp. 198–211; Basil G. Englis and Michael R. Solomon, "To Be and Not to Be: Lifestyle Imagery, Reference Groups, and the Clustering of America," *Journal of Advertising*, Spring 1995, pp. 13–28.

15. "Survey: If You Must Know, Just Ask One of These Men," *Marketing News*, August 19, 1991, p. 13; James H. Myers and Thomas S. Robertson, "Dimensions of Option Leadership," *Journal of Marketing Research*, February 1972, pp. 41–46; Charles W. King and John O. Summers, "Overlap of Opinion Leadership across Consumer Product Categories," *Journal of Marketing Research*, February 1970, pp. 43–50.

16. "After Early Stumbles, P&G Is Making Inroads Oversees," *The Wall Street Journal*, February 6, 1989, p. B1; R. Mead, "Where Is the Culture of Thailand?" *International Journal of Research in Marketing*, September 1994, pp. 401–04.

17. Grant McCracken, "Culture and Consumption: A Theoretical Account of the Structure and Movement of the Cultural Meaning of Consumer Goods," *Journal of Consumer Research*, June 1986, pp. 71–84; A. Suerdem, "Social De(re)construction of Mass Culture: Making (non)Sense of Consumer Behavior," *International Journal of Research in Marketing*, September 1994, pp. 423–44; Walter A. Henry, "Cultural Values Do Correlate with Consumer Behavior," *Journal of Marketing Research*, May 1976, pp. 121–27. See also Lynn R. Kahle, "The Nine Nations of North America and the Value Basis of Geographic Segmentation," *Journal of Marketing*, April 1986, pp. 37–47.

18. Russell W. Belk, "Situational Variables and Consumer Behavior," *Journal of Consumer Research* 2 (1975), pp. 157–64; John F. Sherry, Jr., "Gift Giving in Anthropological Perspective," *Journal of Consumer Research*, September 1983, pp. 157–68; C. Whan Park, Easwar S. Iyer, and Daniel C. Smith, "The Effects of Situational Factors on In-Store Grocery Shopping Behavior: The Role of Store Environment and Time Available for Shopping," *Journal of Consumer Research*, March 1989, pp. 422–33; Mary T. Curren and Katrin R. Harich, "Consumers' Mood States: The Mitigating Influence of Personal Relevance on Product Evaluations," *Psychology & Marketing*, March/April 1994, pp. 91–108.

19. Adapted and updated from James H. Myers and William H. Reynolds, *Consumer Behavior and Marketing Management* (Boston: Houghton Mifflin, 1967), p. 49. See also Judith Lynne Zaichkowsky, "Consumer Behavior: Yesterday, Today, and Tomorrow," *Business Horizons*, May/June 1991, pp. 51–58.

20. Wayne D. Hoyer, "An Examination of Consumer Decision Making for a Common Repeat Purchase Product," *Journal of Consumer Research*, December 1984, pp. 822–29; James R. Bettman, *An Information Processing Theory of Consumer Choice* (Reading, MA: Addison-Wesley, 1979); Richard W. Olshavsky and Donald H. Granbois, "Consumer Decision Making—Fact or Fiction?" *Journal of Consumer Research*, September 1979, pp. 93–100.

21. Raj Arora, "Consumer Involvement—What It Offers to Advertising Strategy," *International Journal of Advertising* 4, no. 2 (1985), pp. 119–30; J. Brock Smith and Julia M. Bristor, "Uncertainty Orientation: Explaining Differences in Purchase Involvement and External Search," *Psychology & Marketing,* November/December 1994, pp. 587–608; P. G. Patterson, "Expectations and Product Performance as Determinants of Satisfaction for a High-Involvement Purchase," *Psychology & Marketing,* September/October 1993, p. 449; Don R. Rahtz and David L. Moore, "Product Class Involvement and Purchase Intent," *Psychology and Marketing,* Summer 1989, pp. 113–28; James D. Gill, Sanford Grossbart, and Russell N. Laczniak, "Influence of the Involvement, Commitment, and Familiarity on Brand Beliefs and Attitudes of Viewers Exposed to Alternative Ad Claims," *Journal of Advertising* 17, no. 2 (1988), pp. 33–43; Marsha L. Richins and Peter H. Bloch, "After the New Wears Off: The Temporal Context of Product Involvement," *Journal of Consumer Research,* September 1986, pp. 280–85.

22. Adapted from E. M. Rogers with F. Shoemaker, *Communication of Innovation: A Cross Cultural Approach* (New York: Free Press, 1968).

23. "3M's Aggressive New Consumer Drive," *Business Week,* July 16, 1984, pp. 114–22.

24. William Cunnings and Mark Venkatesan, "Cognitive Dissonance and Consumer Behavior: A Review of the Evidence," *Journal of Marketing Research,* August 1976, pp. 303–8; Sarah Fisher Gardial et al., "Comparing Consumers' Recall of Prepurchase and Postpurchase Product Evaluation Experience," *Journal of Consumer Research,* March 1994, pp. 548–60.

25. Robert M. March, *The Honourable Customer: Marketing and Selling to the Japanese in the 1990s* (Melbourne, Victoria, Australia: Longman Professional, 1990); Robert Gottliebsen, "Japan's Stark Choices," *Business Review Weekly,* October 16, 1992.

Chapter 8

1. *1993 Annual Report,* Toyota; "Japanese Auto Makers Help U.S. Suppliers Become More Efficient," *The Wall Street Journal,* September 9, 1991, p. A1ff.; David L. Blenkhorn and A. Hamid Noori, "What It Takes to Supply Japanese OEMs," *Industrial Marketing Management,* February, 1990, pp. 21–30.

2. "Purchasing's New Muscle," *Fortune,* February 20, 1995, pp. 75–83; Ravi Venkatesan, "Strategic Sourcing: To Make or Not To Make," *Harvard Business Review,* November–December 1992, pp. 98–108.

3. Robert D. McWilliams, Earl Naumann, and Stan Scott, "Determining Buying Center Size," *Industrial Marketing Management,* February 1992, pp. 43–50; Herbert E. Brown and Roger W. Brucker, "Charting the Industrial Buying Stream, " *Industrial Marketing Management,* February 1990, pp. 55–62; Robert J. Thomas, "Industrial Market Segmentation on Buying Center Purchase Responsibilities," *Journal of the Academy of Marketing Science,* Summer 1989, pp. 243–52; Ajay Kohli, "Determinants of Influence in Organizational Buying: A Contingency Approach," *Journal of Marketing,* July 1989, pp. 50–65; Melvin R. Mattson, "How to Determine the Composition and Influence of a Buying Center," *Industrial Marketing Management,* August 1988, pp. 205–14; Donald L. McCabe, "Buying Group Structure: Constriction at the Top," *Journal of Marketing,* October 1987, pp. 89–98; W. E. Patton III,

Christopher P. Puto, and Ronald H. King, "Which Buying Decisions Are Made by Individuals and Not by Groups?" *Industrial Marketing Management,* May 1986, pp. 129–38.

4. M. Bixby Cooper, Cornelia Dröge, and Patricia J. Daugherty, "How Buyers and Operations Personnel Evaluate Service," *Industrial Marketing Management* 20, no. 1 (1991), pp. 81–90; Richard Germain and Cornelia Dröge, "Wholesale Operations and Vendor Evaluation," *Journal of Business Research,* September 1990, pp. 119–30; James F. Wolter, Frank R. Bacon, Dale R. Duhan, and R. Dale Wilson, "How Designers and Buyers Evaluate Products," *Industrial Marketing Management* 18, no. 2 (1989), pp. 81–90; Jim Shaw, Joe Giglierano, and Jeff Kallis, "Marketing Complex Technical Products: The Importance of Intangible Attributes," *Industrial Marketing Management* 18, no. 1 (1989), pp. 45–54; "Shaping Up Your Suppliers," *Fortune,* April 10, 1989, pp. 116–22.

5. Richard F. Beltramini, "Exploring the Effectiveness of Business Gifts: A Controlled Field Experiment," *Journal of the Academy of Marketing Science,* Winter 1992, pp. 87–92; I. Fredrick Trawick, John E. Swan, Gail W. McGee, and David R. Rink, "Influence of Buyer Ethics and Salesperson Behavior on Intention to Choose a Supplier," *Journal of the Academy of Marketing Science,* Winter 1991, pp. 17–24; Michael J. Dorsch and Scott W. Kelley, "An Investigation into the Intentions of Purchasing Executives to Reciprocate Vendor Gifts," *Journal of the Academy of Marketing Science,* Fall 1994, pp. 315–27; J. A. Badenhorst, "Unethical Behaviour in Procurement: A Perspective on Causes and Solutions," *Journal of Business Ethics,* September 1994, pp. 739–46; Laura B. Forker, "Purchasing Professionals in State Government: How Ethical Are They?" *Journal of Business Ethics,* November 1990, pp. 903–10; "New Jolt for Nynex: Bawdy 'Conventions' of Buyers, Suppliers," *The Wall Street Journal,* July 12, 1990, p. A1ff.; "Vendors' Gifts Pose Problems for Purchasers," *The Wall Street Journal,* June 26, 1989, p. B1ff.; Minette E. Drumwright, "Socially Responsible Organizational Buying: Environmental Concern as a Noneconomic Buying Criterion," *Journal of Marketing,* July 1994, pp. 1–19; Monroe Murphy Bird, "Gift-Giving and Gift-Taking in Industrial Companies," *Industrial Marketing Management* 18, no. 2 (1989), pp. 91–94.

6. Michele D. Bunn, "Taxonomy of Buying Decision Approaches," *Journal of Marketing,* January 1993, pp. 38–56; A. Ben Oumlil and Alvin J. Williams, "Market-Driven Procurement," *Industrial Marketing Management* 18, no. 4 (1989), pp. 289–92; Vithala R. Rao and Edward W. McLaughlin, "Modeling the Decision to Add New Products by Channel Intermediaries," *Journal of Marketing,* January 1989, pp. 80–88; Peter Banting et al., "Similarities in Industrial Procurement across Four Countries," *Industrial Marketing Management,* May 1985, pp. 133–44; Raydel Tullous and J. Michael Munson, "Organizational Purchasing Analysis for Sales Management," *Journal of Personal Selling & Sales Management,* Spring 1992, pp. 15–26; Ellen Day and Hiram C. Barksdale, Jr., "How Firms Select Professional Services," *Industrial Marketing Management,* May 1992, pp. 85–92; Edward F. Fern and James R. Brown, "The Industrial/Consumer Marketing Dichotomy: A Case of Insufficient Justification," *Journal of Marketing,* Spring 1984, pp. 68–77.

7. Richard E. Plank et al., "The Impact of Computer Usage by Purchasing," *Industrial Marketing Management,* August 1992, pp. 243–48; John W. Henke, Jr., A. Richard Krachenberg, and Thomas F. Lyons, "Competing against an In-House Supplier," *Industrial Marketing Management* 18, no. 3 (1989), pp. 147–54.

8. "On-Line Service Offers Fast Lane to Small Businesses," *The Wall Street Journal*, October 11, 1994, p. B2; "The New Race for Intelligence," *Fortune*, November 2, 1992, pp. 104–7; John R. G. Jenkins, "Consumer Media as an Information Source for Industrial Products: A Study," *Industrial Marketing Management*, February 1990, pp. 81–86; Barbara Kline and Janet Wagner, "Information Sources and Retailer Buyer Decision-Making: The Effect of Product-Specific Buying Experience," *Journal of Retailing*, Spring 1994, p. 75; H. Michael Hayes and Steven W. Hartley, "How Buyers View Industrial Salespeople," *Industrial Marketing Management* 18, no. 2 (1989), pp. 73–80; Barbara C. Perdue, "The Size and Composition of the Buying Firm's Negotiation Team in Rebuys of Component Parts," *Journal of the Academy of Marketing Science*, Spring 1989, pp. 121–28; Rowland T. Moriarty, Jr., and Robert E. Spekman, "An Empirical Investigation of the Information Sources Used during the Industrial Buying Process," *Journal of Marketing Research*, May 1984, pp. 137–47; Joseph A. Bellizzi and Phillip McVey, "How Valid Is the Buy-Grid Model?" *Industrial Marketing Management*, February 1983, pp. 57–62.

9. "The New Golden Rule of Business," *Fortune*, February 21, 1994, pp. 60–64.

10. Much of the discussion in this section is based on research reported in Joseph P. Cannon and William D. Perreault, Jr., "Buyer-Seller Relationships in Business Markets," Working Paper, Center for Relationship Marketing, Goizueta Business School, Emory University, Atlanta, GA, June 1994.

11. "Purchasing's New Muscle," *Fortune*, February 20, 1995, pp. 75–83.

12. "The New Golden Rule of Business," *Fortune*, February 21, 1994, pp. 60–64.

13. Sang-Lin Han, David T. Wilson, and Shirish P. Dant, "Buyer-Supplier Relationships Today," *Industrial Marketing Management*, November 1993, pp. 331–38; Allan J. Magrath and Kenneth G. Hardy, "Building Customer Partnerships," *Business Horizons*, January–February 1994, pp. 24–28; Paul Dion, Debbie Easterling, and Shirley Jo Miller, "What Is Really Necessary in Successful Buyer/Seller Relationships?" *Industrial Marketing Management*, January 1995, pp. 1–10; "The Auto Industry Meets the New Economy," *Fortune*, September 5, 1994, pp. 52–60; Jean Perrien, Pierre Filiatrault, and Line Ricard, "The Implementation of Relationship Marketing in Commercial Banking," *Industrial Marketing Management*, May 1993, pp. 141–48; "Hardball Is Still GM's Game," *Business Week*, August 8, 1994, p. 26; "Big Customers' Late Bills Choke Small Suppliers," *The Wall Street Journal*, June 22, 1994, p. B1; Marvin W. Tucker and David A. Davis, "Key Ingredients for Successful Implementation of Just-in-Time: A System for All Business Sizes," May–June 1993, pp. 59–65; Jon Hawes, "To Know Me Is to Trust Me," *Industrial Marketing Management*, July 1994, pp. 215–20; Patricia E. Moody, "Customer Supplier Integration: Why Being an Excellent Customer Counts," *Business Horizons*, July–August 1992, pp. 52–57; "Relationships: Six Steps to Success," *Sales and Marketing Management*, April 1992, pp. 50–58; "Learning from Japan," *Business Week*, January 27, 1992, pp. 52–60; "Suppliers Struggle to Improve Quality as Big Firms Slash Their Vendor Rolls," *The Wall Street Journal*, August 16, 1991, p. B1ff.; "Broken Promises," *Inc.*, July 1991, pp. 25–27; "Close Ties with Suppliers Can Pay for Small Firms," *The Wall Street Journal*, April 3, 1991, p. B1; "Service Enables Nuts-and-Bolts Supplier to Be More than the Sum of Its Parts," *The Wall Street Journal*, November 16, 1990,

p. B1ff.; Manohar U. Kalwani and Narakesari Narayandas, "Long-Term Manufacturer-Supplier Relationships: Do They Pay Off for Supplier Firms?" *Journal of Marketing*, January 1995, pp. 1–16. For more on JIT, see Paul A. Dion, Peter M. Banting, and Loretta M. Hasey, "The Impact of JIT on Industrial Marketers," *Industrial Marketing Management*, February 1990, pp. 41–46.

14. "Polaroid Corp. Is Selling Its Technique for Limiting Supplier Price Increases," *The Wall Street Journal*, February 13, 1985, p. 36. For other examples, see "Making Honda Parts, Ohio Company Finds, Can Be Road to Ruin," *The Wall Street Journal*, October 5, 1990, p. A1ff.; "Toshiba Official Finds Giving Work to Firms in U.S. Can Be Tricky," *The Wall Street Journal*, March 20, 1987, p. 1ff.

15. Madhav N. Segal, "Implications of Single vs. Multiple Buying Sources," *Industrial Marketing Management*, August 1989, pp. 163–78; Cathy Owens Swift, "Preferences for Single Sourcing and Supplier Selection," *Journal of Business Research*, February 1995, pp. 105–12; Christopher P. Puto, Wesley E. Patton III, and Ronald H. King, "Risk Handling Strategies in Industrial Vendor Selection Decisions," *Journal of Marketing*, Winter 1985, pp. 89–98.

16. "You Buy My Widgets, I'll Buy Your Debt," *Business Week*, August 1, 1988, p. 85; Robert E. Weigand, "The Problems of Managing Reciprocity," *California Management Review*, Fall 1973, pp. 40–48.

17. U.S. Bureau of the Census, *Statistical Abstract of the United States 1994* (Washington, DC: U.S. Government Printing Office, 1994); U.S. Bureau of the Census, *County Business Patterns 1992, United States* (Washington, DC: U.S. Government Printing Office, 1994); U.S. Bureau of the Census, *1987 Census of Manufacturers, Subject Series, Establishment and Firm Size* (Washington, DC: U.S. Government Printing Office, 1991); Stanley J. Paliwoda and Andrea J. Bonaccorsi, "Trends in Procurement Strategies within the European Aircraft Industry," *Industrial Marketing Management*, July 1994, pp. 235–44; "Looking to Lure Suppliers, USX Plays Up a Town, " *The Wall Street Journal*, August 17, 1989, p. B1; Tomasz Domanski and Elzbieta Guzek, "Industrial Buying Behavior: The Case of Poland," *Journal of Business Research*, January 1992, pp. 11–18.

18. For more detail, see "SIC: The System Explained," *Sales and Marketing Management*, April 22, 1985, pp. 52–113; "Enhancement of SIC System Being Developed," *Marketing News Collegiate Edition*, May 1988, p. 4.

19. U.S. Bureau of the Census, *Statistical Abstract of the United States 1994* (Washington, DC: U.S. Government Printing Office, 1994); U.S. Bureau of the Census, *County Business Patterns 1992, United States* (Washington, DC: U.S. Government Printing Office, 1994); *1993 Annual Report*, Canon; "Can Anyone Duplicate Canon's Personal Copiers' Success?" *Marketing and Media Decisions*, Special Issue, Spring 1985, pp. 97–101.

20. *1993 Annual Report*, Super Valu.

21. *1993 Annual Report*, Safeway; *1993 Annual Report*, Food Lion; *1993 Annual Report*, Winn-Dixie; *1993 Annual Report*, A&P; Daulatram B. Lund, "Retail Scanner Checkout System: How Buying Committees Functioned," *Industrial Marketing Management* 18, no. 3 (1989), pp. 179–86; Janet Wagner, Richard Ettenson, and Jean Parrish, "Vendor Selection among Retail Buyers: An Analysis by Merchandise Division," *Journal of Retailing*, Spring 1989, pp. 58–79.

22. "There's Life after Selling PCS, McKesson Chief Vows," *The Wall Street Journal*, July 12, 1994, p. B4; "And the Next Juicy Plum May Be . . . McKesson," *Business Week*, February 28, 1994, p. 36; *1993 Annual Report*, McKesson; "Who's Winning the Information Revolution," *Fortune*, November 30, 1992, pp. 110–17; "A High-Tech Rx for Profits," *Fortune*, March 23, 1992, pp. 106–7; "For Drug Distributors, Information Is the Rx for Survival," *Business Week*, October 14, 1985, p. 116; Robert E. Spekman and Wesley J. Johnston, "Relationship Management: Managing the Selling and the Buying Interface," *Journal of Business Research*, December 1986, pp. 519–32.

23. "Create Open-to-Buy Plans the Easy Way," *Retail Control*, December 1984, pp. 21–31.

24. Based on U.S. Census data and "Young Firm Sells Old Indian Formula to Fight Fires," *The Wall Street Journal*, June 1, 1994, p. B2; "How Not to Buy 300,000 Personal Computers," *Business Week*, March 8, 1993, p. 36; "How Do You Chase a $17 Billion Market? With Everything You've Got," *Business Week*, November 23, 1987, pp. 120–22; M. Edward Goretsky, "When to Bid for Government Contracts," *Industrial Marketing Management*, February 1987, pp. 25–34; Lambros Laios and Evangelos Xideas, "An Investigation into the Structure of the Purchasing Function of State-Controlled Enterprises," *Journal of Business Research*, January 1994, pp. 13–22; Warren H. Suss, "How to Sell to Uncle Sam," *Harvard Business Review*, November–December 1984, pp. 136–44.

25. Michael G. Harvey and James T. Rothe, "The Foreign Corrupt Practices Act: The Good, the Bad and the Future," in *1983 American Marketing Association Educators' Proceedings*, ed. P. E. Murphy et al. (Chicago: American Marketing Association, 1983), pp. 374–79. See also Massoud M. Saghafi, Fanis Varvoglis, and Tomas Vega, "Why U.S. Firms Don't Buy from Latin American Companies," *Industrial Marketing Management* 20, no. 3 (1991), pp. 207–14; Peter Banting, Jozsef Beracs, and Andrew Gross, "The Industrial Buying Process in Capitalist and Socialist Countries," *Industrial Marketing Management* 20, no. 2 (1991), pp. 105–14.

Chapter 9

1. "The Eclipse of Mars," *Fortune*, November 28, 1994, pp. 82–92; "Russians Quick to Embrace Ads as Comrades," *Advertising Age International*, June 20, 1994, p. I19; "In Moscow, the Attack of the Killer Brands," *Business Week*, January 10, 1994, p. 40; "Russia Snickers after Mars Invades," *The Wall Street Journal*, July 13, 1993, p. B1ff.; "In Pursuit of the Elusive Euroconsumer," *The Wall Street Journal*, April 23, 1992, p. B1ff.

2. Joseph M. Juran, "Made In U.S.A.: A Renaissance in Quality," *Harvard Business Review*, July–August 1993, pp. 42–53; "Measuring Quality Perception of America's Top Brands," *Brandweek*, April 4, 1994, pp. 24–26; "Quality Woes Are Spreading Like a Rash," *USA Today*, March 18, 1994, p. 1Bff.; Neil A. Morgan and Nigel F. Piercy, "Market-Led Quality," *Industrial Marketing Management*, May 1992, pp. 111–18; "Gurus of Quality Are Gaining Clout," *The Wall Street Journal*, November 27, 1990, p. B1ff.; H. Michael Hayes, "ISO9000: The New Strategic Consideration," *Business Horizons*, May–June 1994, pp. 52–60; John R. Hauser and Don Clausing, "The House of Quality," *Harvard Business Review*, May–June 1988, pp. 63–73; Y. K. Shetty, "Product Quality and Competitive Strategy," *Business Horizons*, May–June 1987, pp. 46–52.

3. *1993 Annual Report*, MCI; *1993 Annual Report*, Merrill Lynch; "Policies Are High-Risk, Not Practices," *USA Today*, September 15, 1994, p. 1Bff.; "Service Is Everybody's Business," *Fortune*, June 27, 1994, pp. 48–60; "Service Providers Try to Make the Mundane Bearable," *The Wall Street Journal*, July 13, 1993, p. B2; Mary Jo Bitner, Bernard H. Booms, and Lois A. Mohr, "Critical Service Encounters: The Employee's Viewpoint," *Journal of Marketing*, October 1994, pp. 95–106; Leonard L. Berry, A. Parasuraman, and Valarie A. Zeithaml, "The Service-Quality Puzzle," *Business Horizons*, September/October 1988, pp. 35–43; Shirley Taylor, "Waiting for Service: The Relationship between Delays and Evaluations of Service," *Journal of Marketing*, April 1994, pp. 56–69; Leonard L. Berry, "Services Marketing Is Different," in Christopher H. Lovelock, *Services Marketing* (Englewood Cliffs, NJ: Prentice Hall, 1984), pp. 29–37.

4. *1993 Annual Report*, Sara Lee; *1993 Annual Report*, Avis; *1993 Annual Report*, CPC International; J. B. Mason and M. L. Mayer, "Empirical Observations of Consumer Behavior as Related to Goods Classification and Retail Strategy," *Journal of Retailing*, Fall 1972, pp. 17–31; Edward M. Tauber, "Why Do People Shop?" *Journal of Marketing*, October 1972, pp. 46–49; Christopher H. Lovelock, "Classifying Services to Gain Strategic Marketing Insights," *Journal of Marketing*, Summer 1983, pp. 9–20.

5. Dennis W. Rook, "The Buying Impulse," *Journal of Consumer Research*, September 1987, pp. 189–99; Cathy J. Cobb and Wayne D. Hoyer, "Planned versus Impulse Purchase Behavior," *Journal of Retailing*, Winter 1986, pp. 384–409.

6. William S. Bishop, John L. Graham, and Michael H. Jones, "Volatility of Derived Demand in Industrial Markets and Its Management Implications," *Journal of Marketing*, Fall 1984, pp. 95–103.

7. William B. Wagner and Patricia K. Hall, "Equipment Lease Accounting in Industrial Marketing Strategy," *Industrial Marketing Management* 20, no. 4 (1991), pp. 305–10; Robert S. Eckley, "Caterpillar's Ordeal: Foreign Competition in Capital Goods," *Business Horizons*, March/April 1989, pp. 80–86; M. Manley, "To Buy or Not to Buy," *Inc.*, November 1987, pp. 189–90.

8. P. Matthyssens and W. Faes, "OEM Buying Process for New Components: Purchasing and Marketing Implications," *Industrial Marketing Management*, August 1985, pp. 145–57; Paul A. Herbig and Frederick Palumbo, "Serving the Aftermarket in Japan and the United States," *Industrial Marketing Management*, November 1993, pp. 339–46; Ralph W. Jackson and Philip D. Cooper, "Unique Aspects of Marketing Industrial Services," *Industrial Marketing Management*, May 1988, pp. 111–18.

9. Ruth H. Krieger and Jack R. Meredith, "Emergency and Routine MRO Part Buying," *Industrial Marketing Management*, November 1985, pp. 277–82; Warren A. French et al., "MRO Parts Service in the Machine Tool Industry," *Industrial Marketing Management*, November 1985, pp. 283–88.

10. For more on Rice Krispies Treats cereal, see "Special Report: Brand in Demand," *Advertising Age*, February 7, 1994, pp. S1–10; "Kellogg to Consumers: Please Bear with Us," *Advertising Age*, March 29, 1993, p. 44. For more on brand extensions, see A. Rangaswamy, R. R. Burke, and T. A. Oliva, "Brand Equity and the Extendibility of Brand Names," *International Journal of Research in Marketing*, March 1993, pp. 61–76; Barbara Loken and Deborah Roedder John, "Diluting Brand Beliefs: When Do Brand Extensions Have a Negative Impact?" *Journal of Marketing*, July

1993, pp. 71–84; Daniel C. Smith, "Brand Extensions and Advertising Efficiency: What Can and Cannot Be Expected," *Journal of Advertising Research*, November/December 1992, pp. 11–21; "Milky Way Spread Takes on Reese's," *Brandweek*, July 18, 1994, p. 12; "Painkillers Are About to O.D.," *Business Week*, April 11, 1994, pp. 54–55; "Nabisco to Bring Top Cookie Brands to Breakfast Line," *The Wall Street Journal*, Febraury 23, 1994, p. B5; "Multiple Varieties of Established Brands Muddle Consumers, Make Retailers Mad," *The Wall Street Journal*, January 24, 1992, p. B1ff. For more on the importance of branding, see Kevin Lane Keller, "Conceptualizing, Measuring, and Managing Customer-Based Brand Equity," *Journal of Marketing*, January 1993, pp. 1–22; "Rx for Profitable Switch to OTC: Brand before Others Join the Fray," *Brandweek*, September 12, 1994, pp. 30–32; "Coca-Cola Shows that Top-Brand Fizz," *Advertising Age*, July 11, 1994, p. 3; "FedEx Delivers Faster Name," *USA Today*, June 24, 1994, p. 1B; "What's in a Brand Name? Nothing Inherent to Start," *Brandweek*, February 7, 1994, p. 16; "Computers: They're No Commodity," *The Wall Street Journal*, October 15, 1993, p. B1; "Brands: It's Thrive or Die," *Fortune*, August 23, 1993, pp. 52–56; "Who Said Brands Are Dead?" *Brandweek*, August 9, 1993, pp. 20–33; David Shipley and Paul Howard, "Brand-Naming Industrial Products," *Industrial Marketing Management*, February 1993, p. 59.

11. "More Firms Turn to Translation Experts to Avoid Costly Embarrassing Mistakes," *The Wall Street Journal*, January 13, 1977, p. 32.

12. Itamar Simonson, "Trademark Infringement from the Buyer Perspective: Conceptual Analysis and Measurement Implications," *Journal of Public Policy & Marketing*, Fall 1994, pp. 181–99; "Asian Trademark Litigation Continues," *The Wall Street Journal*, February 16, 1994, p. B8; "Trademark Laws Don't Cover Color Alone," *The Wall Street Journal*, January 5, 1994, p. B8; "Picking Pitchy Names Is Getting Trickier as Trademark Applications Proliferate," *The Wall Street Journal*, January 14, 1992, p. B1ff.

13. "The Risks Are Rising in China," *Fortune*, March 6, 1995, pp. 179–80; "Hackers Put Pirated Software on Internet," *The Wall Street Journal*, October 31, 1994, p. B5; "Declaring War on the Pirates," *Business Week*, October 24, 1994, p. 56; Janeen E. Olsen and Kent L. Granzin, "Using Channels Constructs to Explain Dealers' Willingness to Help Manufacturers Combat Counterfeiting," *Journal of Business Research*, June 1993, pp. 147–70; "Copycats on a Hot Tin Roof," *Business Week*, September 19, 1994, p. 43; "A Cookie Maker's Aim Is to Be Famous Once Again," *The Wall Street Journal*, August 16, 1994, p. B2; "Will China Scuttle Its Pirates?" *Business Week*, August 15, 1994, pp. 40–41; "Someone's on the Line," *Time*, August 15, 1994, p. 30; "Fashion Knockoffs Hit Stores before Originals as Designers Seethe," *The Wall Street Journal*, August 8, 1994, p. A1ff.; "Levi Tries to Round Up Counterfeiters," *The Wall Street Journal*, February 19, 1992, p. B1ff.; "The Patent Pirates Are Finally Walking the Plank," *Business Week*, February 17, 1992, pp. 125–27; Ronald F. Bush, Peter H. Block, and Scott Dawson, "Remedies for Product Counterfeiting," *Business Horizons*, January–February 1989, pp. 59–65.

14. "Sunkist, a Pioneer in New Product Promotions," *Advertising Age*, November 9, 1988, p. 22ff. For more on licensing, see "Smokey Bear Wants to Catch Fire," *Advertising Age*, August 15, 1994, p. 43; " 'Lion' Is New King of Licensing Jungle," *Advertising Age*, July 4, 1994, p. 8; "The Mystique of the Brand: Jarred,

Bagged, Boxed, Canned," *Brandweek*, June 27, 1994, p. 25ff.; "E. Europe Surge for Licensed Goods," *Advertising Age*, June 20, 1994, p. 1; "Special Report: Licensing '94," *Brandweek*, June 13, 1994, pp. 29–45; " 'Better Homes' Sprouts at Wal-Mart," *Advertising Age*, November 22, 1993, p. 36; "The 1990 Advertising Age Marketer's Resource to Licensing" (special supplement), *Advertising Age*, May 28, 1990.

15. "Brand Managing's New Accent," *Adweek's Marketing Week*, April 15, 1991, pp. 18–22; "Brand Managers: '90s Dinosaurs?" *Advertising Age*, December 19, 1988, p. 19; "The Marketing Revolution at Procter & Gamble," *Business Week*, July 25, 1988, pp. 72–76; "P&G Widens Power Base—Adds Category Managers," *Advertising Age*, October 12, 1987, p. 1ff.; "P&G Creates New Posts in Latest Step to Alter How Firm Manages Its Brands," *The Wall Street Journal*, October 12, 1987, p. 6.

16. "Drugs: What's in a Name Brand? Less and Less," *Business Week*, December 5, 1988, pp. 172–76; "Ten Years May Be Generic Lifetime," *Advertising Age*, March 23, 1987, p. 76; Brian F. Harris and Roger A. Strang, "Marketing Strategies in the Age of Generics," *Journal of Marketing*, Fall 1985, pp. 70–81.

17. "Big Firms Come Out Fighting, Slow Sales of Private-Label Rivals," *The Wall Street Journal*, July 7, 1994, p. B8; "Exposing the Five Myths of Private Label Brands," *Brandweek*, June 20, 1994, p. 17; R. Sethuraman and J. Mittelstaedt, "Coupons and Private Labels: A Cross-Category Analysis of Grocery Products," *Psychology and Marketing*, November/December 1992, pp. 487–500; "Store-Brand Sales Have Their Ups and Downs as Buying Habits Shift," *The Wall Street Journal*, May 12, 1994, p. B6; "Attack of the Fighting Brands," *Business Week*, May 2, 1994, p. 125; "Brands Fight for Market Share," *USA Today*, April 12, 1994, p. 4B; "Kmart's Private Label Marketing Strategies," *Private Label*, March/April 1994, pp. 70–73; "Wholesalers and Cooperatives Put Private Label Out in Front," *Private Label*, March/April 1994, pp. 66–68; "Brands on the Run," *Adweek*, February 14, 1994, pp. 38–40; "Brand Erosion Potential: Retailers Seek Gains in Private Label," *Chain Store Age Executive*, February 1994, p. 28ff.; "Retailers Hungry for Store Brands," *Advertising Age*, January 11, 1993, p. 20; "Cereal Killers," *Brandweek*, January 11, 1993, pp. 14–18; "More Shoppers Bypass Big-Name Brands and Steer Carts to Private-Label Products," *The Wall Street Journal*, October 20, 1992, p. B1ff.; J. A. Bellizzi et al., "Consumer Perceptions of National, Private, and Generic Brands," *Journal of Retailing* 57 (1981), pp. 56–70.

18. *1993 Annual Report*, Procter & Gamble; "P&G Plans All-Family Pert," *Adweek's Marketing Week*, April 20, 1992, p. 6; "How Innovation at P&G Restored Luster to Washed-Up Pert and Made It No. 1," *The Wall Street Journal*, December 6, 1990, p. B1ff.; "Pert Plus' New Rivals," *Advertising Age*, November 12, 1990, p. 4; "Pert Plus Pops to No. 1," *Advertising Age*, March 19, 1990, p. 3ff.

19. "Film Proves Fitting for Labeling Bottles," *The Wall Street Journal*, October 28, 1994, p. B1; "Bottle Design Overshadows the Can," *The Wall Street Journal*, July 25, 1994, p. B1; "If Your Brand's Number Two, Get with the Package Program," *Brandweek*, June 27, 1994, pp. 26–27; "Wine Is Bottled in More Shapes and Sizes," *The Wall Street Journal*, December 9, 1993, p. B1ff.; "Toothpaste Makers Tout New Packaging," *The Wall Street Journal*, November 10, 1992, p. B1ff.; "Romancing the Package," *Adweek's Marketing Week*, January 21, 1991, pp. 10–14; "Pop-Open

Packages for a Hurried Populace," *The Wall Street Journal*, April 2, 1990, p. B1; "Special Report: Packaging," *Advertising Age*, December 12, 1988, pp. S1–4.

20. Pauline M. Ippolito and Alan D. Mathios, "New Food Labeling Regulations and the Flow of Nutrition Information to Consumers," *Journal of Public Policy & Marketing*, Fall 1993, pp. 188–205; "FTC to Require Food Ads to Follow FDA Guides," *The Wall Street Journal*, May 16, 1994, p. A6; "New Labeling Doesn't Tell All about Nutrition," *The Wall Street Journal*, May 6, 1994, p. B1ff.; Scot Burton and Abhijit Biswas, "Preliminary Assessment of Changes in Labels Required by the Nutrition Labeling and Education Act of 1990," *Journal of Consumer Affairs*, Summer 1993, pp. 127–44; Janet R. Hankin et al., "The Impact of the Alcohol Warning Label on Drinking during Pregnancy," *Journal of Public Policy & Marketing*, Spring 1993, pp. 10–18; Karen L. Graves, "An Evaluation of the Alcohol Warning Label: A Comparison of the United States and Ontario, Canada, in 1990 and 1991," *Journal of Public Policy & Marketing*, Spring 1993, pp. 19–29; "Using Labeling Rules to Pitch a Product," *The Wall Street Journal*, March 25, 1994, p. B1; "Label Law Stirs Up Food Companies," *The Wall Street Journal*, June 2, 1993, p. B1ff.

21. For a discussion of one effort toward social responsibility, see "Record Makers Giving Retailers the Blues," *The Wall Street Journal*, March 16, 1992, p. B1ff. For discussion of another effort, see "Shed the Egg, Spare the Image," *Adweek's Marketing Week*, July 15, 1991, p. 9; "L'eggs Egg Cracks," *Advertising Age*, July 15, 1991, p. 16. For additional discussion, see "New Packaging that's Thriftier! Niftier! and Cooks Your Food!" *Fortune*, September 5, 1994, p. 109; "Dissolvable Bags Destined for Kitchen Use," *The Wall Street Journal*, May 2, 1994, p. B1; "States Debate Solid Waste Bills," *Food Business*, May 6, 1991, pp. 22–23; James H. Barnes, Jr., "Recycling: A Problem in Reverse Logistics," *Journal of Macromarketing* 2, no. 2 (1982), pp. 31–37.

22. Paula Fitzgerald Bone and Robert J. Corey, "Ethical Dilemmas in Packaging: Beliefs of Packaging Professionals," *Journal of Macromarketing*, Spring 1992, pp. 45–54. For more on downsizing, see "Big Trend: Smaller Packaging," *USA Today*, April 1, 1993, p. 1Bff.; "State AGs Attack Downsized Brands," *Advertising Age*, February 18, 1991, p. 1ff.; "Critics Call Cuts in Package Size Deceptive Move," *The Wall Street Journal*, February 5, 1991, p. B1ff. For more discussion on disposable products, see "Disposing of the Green Myth," *Adweek's Marketing Week*, April 13, 1992, pp. 20–21; "The Waste Land," *Adweek*, November 11, 1991, p. 26; "Ridding the Nation of Polystyrene Peanuts," *Adweek's Marketing Week*, October 22, 1990, p. 17.

23. J. E. Russo, "The Value of Unit Price Information," *Journal of Marketing Research*, May 1977, pp. 193–201; David A. Aaker and Gary T. Ford, "Unit Pricing Ten Years Later: A Replication," *Journal of Marketing*, Winter 1983, pp. 118–22.

24. "UPC Registers Retailing Impact," *Advertising Age*, April 7, 1986, p. 3ff.; "Bar Codes: Beyond the Checkout Counter," *Business Week*, April 8, 1985, p. 90; "Bar Codes Are Black-and-White Stripes and Soon They Will Be Read All Over," *The Wall Street Journal*, January 8, 1985, p. 39; Ronald C. Goodstein, "UPC Scanner Pricing Systems: Are They Accurate?" *Journal of Marketing*, April 1994, pp. 20–30; "Firms Line Up to Check Out Bar Codes," *USA Today*, December 4, 1985, pp. B1–2.

25. For more on service guarantees, see "It's Service in a Box from Hewlett-Packard," *Advertising Age*, May 10, 1993, p. 5;

"More Firms Pledge Guaranteed Service," *The Wall Street Journal*, July 17, 1991, p. B1ff.; "Satisfaction Guaranteed for Customers and Crew," *The Wall Street Journal*, January 28, 1991, p. A10. For more on product warranties, see Ellen M. Moore and F. Kelly Shuptrine, "Warranties: Continued Readability Problems after the 1975 Magnuson-Moss Warranty Act," *Journal of Consumer Affairs*, Summer 1993, pp. 23–36; M. A. J. Menezes and I. S. Currim, "An Approach for Determination of Warranty Length," *International Journal of Research in Marketing*, May 1992, pp. 177–96; "Service Dealers Complain about Warranty Business," *The Wall Street Journal*, February 20, 1992, p. B2; "Fine Print Can Make a Guarantee Not So Fine," *The Wall Street Journal*, July 17, 1991, p. B1; Craig A. Kelley and Jeffrey S. Conant, "Extended Warranties: Consumer and Manufacturer Perceptions," *The Journal of Consumer Affairs*, Summer 1991, pp. 68–83; Joshua Lyle Wiener, "Are Warranties Accurate Signals of Product Reliability?" *Journal of Consumer Research*, September 1985, p. 245ff.

Chapter 10

1. "Kodak's New Focus," *Business Week*, January 30, 1995, pp. 62–68; "Photography Companies Focus on Niches," *The Wall Street Journal*, March 12, 1993, p. B1ff.; *1993 Annual Report*, Kodak; "Smile, You're on Compact Disk," *Business Week*, August 10, 1992, p. 26; "Kodak Tries to Prepare for Filmless Era without Inviting Demise of Core Business," *The Wall Street Journal*, April 18, 1991, p. B1ff.; A New Decade Puts Electrons into the Kodak Viewfinder," *Insight*, November 5, 1990, pp. 38–39.

2. George Day, "The Product Life Cycle: Analysis and Applications Issues," *Journal of Marketing*, Fall 1981, pp. 60–67; John E. Swan and David R. Rink, "Fitting Marketing Strategy to Varying Product Life Cycles," *Business Horizons*, January/February 1982, pp. 72–76; Igal Ayal, "International Product Life Cycle: A Reassessment and Product Policy Implications," *Journal of Marketing*, Fall 1981, pp. 91–96; G. David Hughes, "Managing High-Tech Product Cycles," *Academy of Management Executive* 4 (1990), pp. 44–54; Edward T. Popper and Bruce D. Buskirk, "Technology Life Cycles in Industrial Markets," *Industrial Marketing Management*, February 1992, pp. 23–32; Vijay Mahajan, Subhash Sharma, and Robert D. Buzzell, "Assessing the Impact of Competitive Entry on Market Expansion and Incumbent Sales," *Journal of Marketing*, July 1993, pp. 39–52; Roger C. Bennett and Robert G. Cooper, "The Product Life Cycle Trap," *Business Horizons*, September/October 1984, pp. 7–16; Sak Onkvisit and John J. Shaw, "Competition and Product Management: Can the Product Life Cycle Help?" *Business Horizons*, July/August 1986, pp. 51–62; Mary Lambkin and George S. Day, "Evolutionary Processes in Competitive Markets: Beyond the Product Life Cycle," *Journal of Marketing*, July 1989, pp. 4–20.

3. Jorge Alberto Sousa De Vasconcellos, "Key Success Factors in Marketing Mature Products," *Industrial Marketing Management* 20, no. 4 (1991), pp. 263–78; Paul C. N. Michell, Peter Quinn, and Edward Percival, "Marketing Strategies for Mature Industrial Products," *Industrial Marketing Management* 20, no. 3 (1991), pp. 201–6; "Computers Become a Kind of Commodity, to Dismay of Makers," *The Wall Street Journal*, September 5, 1991, p. A1ff.; Peter N. Golder and Gerard J. Tellis, "Pioneer Advantage: Marketing Logic or Marketing Legend?" *Journal of Marketing Research*, May 1993, pp. 158–70; "What Do You Do When Snowmobiles Go on a Steep Slide?" *The Wall Street Journal*,

March 8, 1978, p. 1ff.; "Home Smoke Detectors Fall on Hard Times as Sales Apparently Peaked," *The Wall Street Journal*, April 3, 1980, p. 1; "As Once Bright Market for CAT Scanners Dims, Smaller Makers of the X–Ray Devices Fade Out," *The Wall Street Journal*, May 6, 1980, p. 40.

4. U.S. Bureau of the Census, *Statistical Abstract of the United States 1994* (Washington, DC: U.S. Government Printing Office, 1994), p. 855.

5. "Pepsi, Coke Say They're Loyal to NutraSweet," *The Wall Street Journal*, April 22, 1992, p. B1ff.; "A Sweet Case of the 'Blahs,'" *Advertising Age*, May 27, 1991, p. 3; "NutraSweet Launches New Ads," *Adweek's Marketing Week*, May 20, 1991, p. 6; "NutraSweet Tries Being More of a Sweetie," *Business Week*, April 8, 1991, p. 88; "NutraSweet Rivals Stirring," *Advertising Age*, June 26, 1989, p. 3ff.; "Calories and Cash: Sugar and Its Substitutes Fight for an $8 Billion Market," *Newsweek*, August 26, 1985, p. 54ff.; "Searle Fights to Keep Red-Hot Aspartame Hot for a Long Time," *The Wall Street Journal*, September 18, 1984, p. 1ff.

6. "Rivals Square Off Toe to Toe," *USA Today*, August 24, 1993, p. 1Bff.; "The Patent Pirates Are Finally Walking the Plank," *Business Week*, February 17, 1992, pp. 125–27; "Is It Time to Reinvent the Patent System?" *Business Week*, December 2, 1991, pp. 110–15; Karen Bronikowski, "Speeding New Products to Market," *The Journal of Business Strategy*, September/October 1990, pp. 34–37; "How Managers Can Succeed through Speed," *Fortune*, February 13, 1989, pp. 54–59.

7. "Sony Isn't Mourning the 'Death' of Betamax," *Business Week*, January 25, 1988, p. 37; "Sony to Begin Selling VCRs in VHS Format," *The Wall Street Journal*, January 12, 1988, p. 39; Steven P. Schnaars, "When Entering Growth Markets, Are Pioneers Better than Poachers?" *Business Horizons*, March/April 1986, pp. 27–36; M. Lambkin, "Pioneering New Markets: A Comparison of Market Share Winners and Losers," *International Journal of Research in Marketing*, March 1992, pp. 5–22.

8. "Can the Limited Fix Itself?" *Fortune*, October 17, 1994, pp. 161–72; "Limited Puts 'Weiss Methodology' to Test," *The Wall Street Journal*, August 9, 1993, p. B1ff.; "The Winning Organization," *Fortune*, September 26, 1988, pp. 50–58.

9. Martin G. Letscher, "How to Tell Fads from Trends," *American Demographics*, December 1994, pp. 38–45; "From License Plates to Fashion Plates," *The Wall Street Journal*, September 21, 1994, p. B1ff.; R. E. Goldsmith, J. B. Freiden, and J. C. Kilsheimer, "Social Values and Female Fashion Leadership: A Cross-Cultural Study," *Psychology & Marketing*, September/October 1993, pp. 399–412; "Clothes Make the Man More Comfortable," *USA Today*, September 6, 1994, p. 1Bff.; "Special Report: Fashion Marketing," *Advertising Age*, August 22, 1994, pp. 23–28; "Ninja Turtles, Eat Our Dust," *Newsweek*, August 8, 1994, pp. 34–35; "Fashion Knockoffs Hit Stores before Originals as Designers Seethe," *The Wall Street Journal*, August 8, 1994, p. A1ff.; "Anatomy of a Fad: How Clear Products Were Hot and Then Suddenly Were Not," *The Wall Street Journal*, March 15, 1994, p. B1ff.; "For Complex Times, Simple Footwear," *USA Today*, February 7, 1994, p. 1Dff.; "Why Are Your Kids Beginning to Look like Your Plumber," *The Wall Street Journal*, May 4, 1993, p. A1ff.; "More and More Teens Can't Live without Beepers on Their Belts," *The Wall Street Journal*, December 7, 1992, p. B6; "Seller of Velcro Ball and Mitts Hits Homer," *The Wall Street Journal*, July 9, 1991, p. B1; "The Ultimate Squeeze Play: Girdles Are Back in Style," *Newsweek*, May 13, 1991, p. 63.

10. "Video Games Win Respect as Researchers Adapt Features for Computer Programs," *The Wall Street Journal*, August 29, 1991, p. B1ff.; "Multimedia Goes Mainstream," *Business Marketing*, June 1991, pp. 20–22; "A New Spin on Videodiscs," *Newsweek*, June 5, 1989, pp. 68–69.

11. "Oreo, Ritz Join Nabisco's Low-Fat Feast," *Advertising Age*, April 4, 1994, p. 3ff.; "They're Not Crying in Their Crackers at Nabisco," *Business Week*, August 30, 1993, p. 61; *1993 Annual Report*, RJR Nabisco; "Nabisco Unleashes a New Batch of Teddies," *Adweek's Marketing Week*, September 24, 1990, p. 18.

12. "Ultra-Clean—Retail Cheers Still More P&G Concentrates," *Advertising Age*, August 22, 1994, p. 1ff.; "Detergent Industry Spins into New Cycle," *The Wall Street Journal*, January 5, 1993, p. B1ff.; "P&G Unleashes Flood of New Tide Products," *Advertising Age*, June 16, 1986, p. 3ff.; "P&G's High Tide Sinks Wisk to No. 2," *Advertising Age*, May 26, 1986, p. 88; "P&G Takes Lead with High-Tech Detergent," *Advertising Age*, April 14, 1986, p. 3ff.; "Industry Is Shopping Abroad for Good Ideas to Apply to Products," *The Wall Street Journal*, April 29, 1985, p. 1ff.; "'Good Products Don't Die,' P&G Chairman Declares," *Advertising Age*, November 1, 1976, p. 8.

13. For more on rejuvenating mature products, see "Classic Cheerios and Wheaties Reformulated," *The Wall Street Journal*, August 31, 1994, p. B1ff.; "Cereal Science," *Brandweek*, May 2, 1994, pp. 28–36; "The Famous Brands on Death Row," *New York Times*, November 7, 1993, p. F1ff.; "A Boring Brand Can Be Beautiful," *Fortune*, November 18, 1991, pp. 169–77; Regina Fazio Maruca and Amy L. Halliday, "When New Products and Customer Loyalty Collide," *Harvard Business Review*, November–December 1993, pp. 22–36; Geoffrey L. Gordon, Roger J. Calantone, and C. Anthony di Benedetto, "Mature Markets and Revitalization Strategies: An American Fable," *Business Horizons*, May/June 1991, pp. 39–50; "Teflon Is 50 Years Old, but Du Pont Is Still Finding New Uses for Invention," *The Wall Street Journal*, April 7, 1988, p. 34.

14. "Smart Toothbrush," *Fortune*, November 4, 1991, p. 168; "Toothbrush Makers Hope to Clean Up with Array of 'New, Improved' Products," *The Wall Street Journal*, October 22, 1991, p. B1ff.; "From Making Hearts to Winning Them," *Business Week*, November 16, 1987, pp. 153–56; "Alza Finally Finds a Cure for Losses," *Fortune*, April 28, 1986, p. 80.

15. "Diaper Firms Fight to Stay on the Bottom," *The Wall Street Journal*, March 23, 1993, p. B1ff.; "Multiple Varieties of Established Brands Muddle Consumers, Make Retailers Mad," *The Wall Street Journal*, January 24, 1992, p. B1ff.; "Do Americans Have Too Many Brands?" *Adweek's Marketing Week*, December 9, 1991, pp. 14–15; "Kimberly-Clark Bets, Wins on Innovation," *The Wall Street Journal*, November 22, 1991, p. A5.

16. "Seems the Only Problem with New Products Is that They're New," *Brandweek*, August 22, 1994, pp. 36–40; "Flops: Too Many New Products Fail. Here's Why—and How to Do Better," *Business Week*, August 16, 1993, pp. 76–82; "To Outpace Rivals, More Firms Step Up Spending on New-Product Development," *The Wall Street Journal*, October 28, 1992, p. B1ff.; "New-Product Troubles Have Firms Cutting Back," *The Wall Street Journal*, January 13, 1992, p. B1; G. Dean Kortge and Patrick A. Okonkwo, "Simultaneous New Product Development: Reducing the New Product Failure Rate," *Industrial Marketing Management* 18, no. 4 (1989), pp. 301–6.

17. "Makers of Chicken Tonight Find Many Cooks Say, 'Not Tonight,' " *The Wall Street Journal*, May 17, 1994, p. B1ff.; "Failure of Its Oven Lovin' Cookie Dough Shows Pillsbury Pitfalls of New Products," *The Wall Street Journal*, June 17, 1993, p. B1ff.; "Why Do So Many New Products Fail?" *Brandweek*, October 19, 1992, pp. 14–25; Sharad Sarin and Gour M. Kapur, "Lessons from New Product Failures: Five Case Studies," *Industrial Marketing Management*, November 1990, pp. 301–14; Peter L. Link, "Keys to New Product Success and Failure," *Industrial Marketing Management*, May 1987, pp. 109–18.

18. Joseph T. Vesey, "Time-to-Market: Put Speed in Product Development," *Industrial Marketing Management*, May 1992, pp. 151–58; "Mattel's Wild Race to Market," *Business Week*, February 21, 1994, pp. 62–63; "Giant Goes from Stodgy to Nimble," *USA Today*, May 18, 1994, p. 1Bff.; "How H-P Continues to Grow and Grow," *Fortune*, May 2, 1994, pp. 90–100; "Motorola Illustrates How an Aged Giant Can Remain Vibrant," *The Wall Street Journal*, December 9, 1992, p. A1ff.; "Closing the Innovation Gap," *Fortune*, December 2, 1991, pp. 56–62.

19. Adapted from Frank R. Bacon, Jr., and Thomas W. Butler, Jr., *Planned Innovation*, rev. ed. (Ann Arbor: Institute of Science and Technology, University of Michigan, 1980). See also Linda Rochford, "Generating and Screening New Product Ideas," *Industrial Marketing Management* 20, no. 4 (1991), pp. 287–96; Spencer B. Graves et al., "Improving the Product Development Process," *Hewlett-Packard Journal*, June 1991, pp. 71–76; Milton D. Rosenau, Jr., *Managing the Development of New Products* (New York: Van Nostrand Reinhold, 1993); Robert G. Cooper and Elko J. Kleinschmidt, "New Product Processes at Leading Industrial Firms," *Industrial Marketing Management* 20, no 2 (1991), pp. 137–48; "Task Force for New Products," *Business Marketing*, July 1991, pp. 34–36; Artemis March, "Usability: The New Dimension of Product Design," *Harvard Business Review*, September–October 1994, pp. 144–52; "Product Development: Where Planning and Marketing Meet," *The Journal of Business Strategy*, September/October 1990, pp. 13–17; Massoud M. Saghafi, Ashok Gupta, and Jagdish N. Sheth, "R&D/Marketing Interfaces in the Telecommunications Industry," *Industrial Marketing Management*, February 1990, pp. 87–95; F. Axel Johne and Patricia A. Snelson, "Product Development Approaches in Established Firms," *Industrial Marketing Management*, May 1989, pp. 113–24; Gordon R. Foxall, "User Initiated Product Innovations," *Industrial Marketing Management*, May 1989, pp. 95–104.

20. "Seeing the Future First," *Fortune*, September 5, 1994, pp. 64–70; "Detroit's New Strategy to Beat Back Japanese Is to Copy Their Ideas," *The Wall Street Journal*, October 1, 1992, p. A1ff.; "Getting Hot Ideas from Customers," *Fortune*, May 18, 1992, pp. 86–87; "How to Let Innovation Happen," *Industry Week*, March 16, 1992, p. 43; "Striking Gold with the Explorer," *Adweek's Marketing Week*, January 14, 1991, pp. 20–21; Abbie Griffin and John R. Hauser, "The Voice of the Customer," *Marketing Science*, Winter 1993, pp. 1–27.

21. "U.S. Companies Shop Abroad for Product Ideas," *The Wall Street Journal*, March 14, 1990, p. B1ff.

22. Eric von Hippel, *The Sources of Innovation* (New York: Oxford University Press, 1988).

23. "How a Jury Decided that a Coffee Spill Is Worth $2.9 Million," *The Wall Street Journal*, September 1, 1994, p. A1ff.; Debra L. Scammon and Mary Jane Sheffet, "Market Share Liability: An Analysis Since *Sindel*," *Journal of Public Policy & Marketing*, Spring 1992, pp. 1–11; Paul A. Herbig and James E. Golden, "Innovation and Product Liability," *Industrial Marketing Management*, July 1994, pp. 245–56; Robert N. Mayer and Debra L. Scammon, "Caution: Weak Product Warnings May Be Hazardous to Corporate Health," *Journal of Business Research*, June 1992, pp. 347–60; "Consumers Drive Push for Safer Cars," *USA Today*, August 16, 1994, p. 1Bff.; "Parents Love, Coaches Hate a 'Safer' Baseball," *The Wall Street Journal*, May 24, 1994, p. B1ff.; "Keyboard Users Say Makers Knew of Problems," *The Wall Street Journal*, May 4, 1994, p. B1ff.; Thomas V. Greer, "Product Liability in the European Community: The Legislative History," *Journal of Consumer Affairs*, Summer 1992, pp. 159–76; "States Claim Share of Awards in Liability Suits," *The Wall Street Journal*, March 3, 1993, p. B1ff.; "Breast Implants Raise More Safety Issues," *The Wall Street Journal*, February 4, 1993, p. B1ff.; "Product-Liability Groups Take Up Arms," *The Wall Street Journal*, January 29, 1993, p. B1ff.; "Bungee Jumping's Unencumbered Cord Gets Tangled," *The Wall Street Journal*, August 11, 1992, p. B2; "Toy Maker Faces Dilemma as Water Gun Spurs Violence," *The Wall Street Journal*, June 11, 1992, p. B1ff.; "Consumers Start Telling It to the Judge: They're Challenging Japan's Legal Shields," *Business Week*, March 9, 1992, p. 50; Frances E. Zollers and Ronald G. Cook, "Product Liability Reform: What Happened to the Crisis?" *Business Horizons*, September/October 1990, pp. 47–52; Marisa Manley, "Product Liability: You're More Exposed than You Think," *Harvard Business Review*, September–October 1987, pp. 28–41; Phillip E. Downs and Douglas N. Behrman, "The Products Liability Coordinator: A Partial Solution," *Journal of the Academy of Marketing Science*, Fall 1986, p. 66ff.; Ronald J. Adams and John M. Browning, "Product Liability in Industrial Markets," *Industrial Marketing Management*, November 1986, pp. 265–72.

24. "Want Shelf Space at the Supermarket? Ante Up," *Business Week*, August 7, 1989, pp. 60–61; "Grocer 'Fee' Hampers New-Product Launches," *Advertising Age*, August 3, 1987, p. 1ff.; Frank H. Alpert, Michael A. Kamins, and John L. Graham, "An Examination of Reseller Buyer Attitudes toward Order of Brand Entry," *Journal of Marketing*, July 1992, pp. 25–37.

25. "This Bright Idea Could Make GE a Billion," *Business Week*, December 4, 1989, p. 120.

26. Adapted from Frank R. Bacon, Jr., and Thomas W. Butler, Jr., *Planned Innovation*, rev. ed. (Ann Arbor: Institute of Science and Technology, University of Michigan, 1980).

27. "Secrets of Product Testing," *Fortune*, November 28, 1994, pp. 166–72; "A Smarter Way to Manufacture," *Business Week*, April 30, 1990, pp. 110–17; "Oops! Marketers Blunder Their Way through the 'Herb Decade,' " *Advertising Age*, February 13, 1989, p. 3ff.

28. "Gillette Succeeds as Others Fail by Reinventing Itself," *Brandweek*, May 3, 1993, p. 12; "Gillette Holds Its Edge by Endlessly Searching for a Better Shave," *The Wall Street Journal*, December 10, 1992, p. A1ff.; "How a $4 Razor Ends Up Costing $300 Million," *Business Week*, January 29, 1990, pp. 62–63.

29. "Oops! Marketers Blunder Their Way through the 'Herb Decade,' " *Advertising Age*, February 13, 1989, p. 3ff.

30. "The Company Store: How to Test Market for Fun and Profit," *Inc.*, November 1989, pp. 153–55; "Test Marketing—The Next Generation," *Nielsen Researcher*, no. 3 (1984), pp. 21–23; "Test Marketing Enters a New Era," *Dun's Business Month*, October 1985, p. 86ff.; Steven H. Star and Glen L. Urban, "The Case of the Test Market Toss-Up," *Harvard Business Review*, September–October 1988, pp. 10–27.

31. Peter F. Drucker, "A Prescription for Entrepreneurial Management," *Industry Week*, April 29, 1985, p. 33ff.; Ashok K. Gupta, S. P. Raj, and David Wilemon, "R&D Marketing Dialogue in High-Tech Firms," *Industrial Marketing Management* 14 (1985), pp. 289–300; Linda Rochford and William Rudelius, "How Involving More Functional Areas within a Firm Affects the New Product Process," *Journal of Product Innovation Management* 9, pp. 287–99; John P,.Workman, Jr., "Marketing's Limited Role in New Product Development in One Computer Systems Firm," *Journal of Marketing Research*, November 1993, pp. 405–21; Gloria Barczak and David Wilemon, "Successful New Product Team Leaders," *Industrial Marketing Management*, February 1992, pp. 61–68.

32. "Why to Go for Stretch Targets," *Fortune*, November 14, 1994, pp. 145–58; "The Drought Is Over at 3M," *Business Week*, November 7, 1994, pp. 140–41; *1993 Annual Report*, 3M; "3M Run Scared? Forget about It," *Business Week*, September 16, 1991, p. 59ff.; "How 3M, by Tiptoeing into Foreign Markets, Became a Big Exporter," *The Wall Street Journal*, March 29, 1991, p. A1ff.; "Masters of Innovation," *Business Week*, April 10, 1989, pp. 58–67.

33. Don Frey, "Learning the Ropes: My Life as a Product Champion," *Harvard Business Review*, September/October 1991, pp. 46–57; "Brand Managers: The Buck Stops Here," *Food Business*, May 6, 1991, pp. 33–34; "Brand Managing's New Accent," *Adweek's Marketing Week*, April 15, 1991, pp. 18–22; Manfred F. Maute and William B. Locander, "Innovation as a Socio-Political Process: An Empirical Analysis of Influence Behavior among New Product Managers," *Journal of Business Research*, June 1994, pp. 161–74; V. Kasturi Rangan, Rajiv Lal, and Ernie P. Maier, "Managing Marginal New Products," *Business Horizons*, September–October 1992, pp. 35–42; "P&G Keen Again on Ad Managers," *Advertising Age*, September 25, 1989, p. 6; Robert W. Eckles and Timothy J. Novotny, "Industrial Product Managers: Authority and Responsibility," *Industrial Marketing Management*, May 1984, pp. 71–76; William Theodore Cummings, Donald W. Jackson, Jr., and Lonnie L. Ostrom, "Differences between Industrial and Consumer Product Managers," *Industrial Marketing Management*, August 1984, pp. 171–80.

Chapter 11

1. "Goodyear Expands Just Tires by Converting Full Service Centers," *Discount Store News*, May 16, 1994, p. 6; "Water Fight for Michelin, Goodyear," *Advertising Age*, November 15, 1993, p. 12; "Goodyear Sets Tire Deal," *The Wall Street Journal*, November 2, 1993, p. A5; *1993 Annual Report*, Goodyear; "The Bounce Is Back at Goodyear," *Fortune*, September 7, 1992, pp. 70–72; "Independent Tire Dealers Rebelling against Goodyear," *The Wall Street Journal*, July 8, 1992, p. B2; "The Marvels of High Margins," *Fortune*, May 2, 1994, pp. 73–74; "Goodyear Plans to Sell Its Tires at Sears Stores," *The Wall Street Journal*, March 3, 1992, p. B1ff.; "Tire Makers Are Traveling Bumpy Road as Car Sales Fall, Foreign Firms Expand," *The Wall Street Journal*, September 19, 1990, p. B1ff.; Thomas L. Baker, "Leaders in Selling and Sales Management: An Analysis of the Impact of Sales and Marketing Principles on the Career of Stanley C. Gault," *Journal of Personal Selling & Sales Management*, Spring 1993, pp. 91–94.

2. "It's Becoming a Dogfight for the $15 Billion Pet Supply Market," *The Raleigh News & Observer*, September 25, 1994, p. 5F; "Pet Superstores Collar Customers from Supermarkets, Small Shops," *The Wall Street Journal*, November 18, 1993, p. B12; *1993 Annual Report*, Colgate-Palmolive; "Pet-Food Makers Are Trying to Entice Dog, Cat Owners with Healthier Fare," *The Wall Street Journal*, August 16, 1991, p. B4B; "New Pet Food Scrap in Supermarkets," *Advertising Age*, January 28, 1991, p. 3ff.

3. For a discussion of the advantages and disadvantages of direct channel systems, see "Sears Takes Direct Approach," *Chain Store Age Executive*, March 1994, p. 168ff.; "Direct Sellers Defy Odds, Making PC Books Winners, Too," *Advertising Age*, November 9, 1992, p. S2; Kenneth G. Hardy and Allan J. McGrath, *Marketing Channel Management* (Glenview, IL: Scott, Foresman, 1988). See also David Shipley, Colin Egan, and Scott Edgett, "Meeting Source Selection Criteria: Direct versus Distributor Channels," *Industrial Marketing Management* 20, no. 4 (1991), pp. 297–304; Thomas L. Powers, "Industrial Distribution Options: Trade-Offs to Consider," *Industrial Marketing Management* 18, no. 3 (1989), pp. 155–62.

4. *1988 Direct Selling Industry Survey* (Washington, DC: Direct Selling Association, 1989); Robert A. Peterson, Gerald Albaum, and Nancy M. Ridgway, "Consumers Who Buy from Direct Sales Companies," *Journal of Retailing*, Summer 1989, p. 275ff.

5. Edward L. Nash, *Direct Marketing* (New York: McGraw-Hill, 1986).

6. For a discussion of indirect channel systems, see Louis W. Stern, Adel I. El-Ansary, and James R. Brown, *Management in Marketing Channels* (Englewood Cliffs, NJ: Prentice-Hall, 1994). See also Bert Rosenbloom and Trina L. Larsen, "How Foreign Firms View Their U.S. Distributors," *Industrial Marketing Management*, May 1992, pp. 93–102; Frank Lynn, "The Changing Economics of Industrial Distribution," *Industrial Marketing Management*, November 1992, pp. 355–60; Teresa Jaworska, "Channel Members' Behavior in Industrial Markets in Poland," *Journal of Business Research*, January 1992, pp. 51–56; Donald B. Rosenfield, "Storefront Distribution for Industrial Products," *Harvard Business Review*, July/August 1989, pp. 44–49. For more on middlemen intermediaries and their functions, see Richard Greene, "Wholesaling," *Forbes*, January 2, 1984, pp. 226–28; James D. Hlavacek and Tommy J. McCuistion, "Industrial Distributors—When, Who, and How?" *Harvard Business Review*, January–February 1983, pp. 96–101; Steven Flax, "Wholesalers," *Forbes*, January 4, 1982. See also Geoff Gordon, Roger Calantone, and C. A. di Benedetto, "How Electrical Contractors Choose Distributors," *Industrial Marketing Management* 20, no. 1 (1991), pp. 29–42; Elizabeth J. Wilson and Arch G. Woodside, "Marketing New Products with Distributors," *Industrial Marketing Management*, February 1992, pp. 15–22; W. Benoy et al., "How Industrial Distributors View Distributor-Supplier Partnership Arrangements," *Industrial Marketing Management*, January 1995, pp. 27–36; Donald M. Jackson and Michael F. d'Amico, "Products and Markets Served by Distributors and Agents," *Industrial*

Marketing Management, February 1989, pp. 27–34; Thomas L. Powers, "Switching from Reps to Direct Salespeople," *Industrial Marketing Management*, August 1987, pp. 169–72.

7. For a classic discussion of the discrepancy concepts, see Wroe Alderson, "Factors Governing the Development of Marketing Channels," in *Marketing Channels for Manufactured Goods*, ed. Richard M. Clewett (Burr Ridge, IL: Richard D. Irwin, 1954), pp. 7–9. See also "Distributors: No Endangered Species," *Industry Week*, January 24, 1983, pp. 47–52; "Coke Unveils Compact Dispenser, Hoping to Sell More Soft Drinks in Small Offices," *The Wall Street Journal*, November 17, 1988, p. B1.

8. "More Small Firms Are Turning to Trade Intermediaries," *The Wall Street Journal*, February 2, 1993, p. B2.

9. "For Video Sales, It's a Green Christmas," *The Wall Street Journal*, December 24, 1991, p. B1ff.; "Children's Tapes Help the Sales Market Grow Up," *The Wall Street Journal*, December 24, 1991, p. B1ff.; "After Frantic Growth, Blockbuster Faces Host of Video-Rental Rivals," *The Wall Street Journal*, March 22, 1991, p. A1ff.

10. Robert A. Mittelstaedt and Robert E. Stassen, "Structural Changes in the Phonograph Record Industry and Its Channels of Distribution, 1946–1966," *Journal of Macromarketing*, Spring 1994, pp. 31–44; Arun Sharma and Luis V. Dominquez, "Channel Evolution: A Framework for Analysis," *Journal of the Academy of Marketing Science*, Winter 1992, pp. 1–16; "PC Slump? What PC Slump?" *Business Week*, July 1, 1991, pp. 66–67.

11. "What's Wrong with Selling Used CDs?" *Business Week*, July 26, 1993, p. 38; Rajiv P. Dant and Patrick L. Schul, "Conflict Resolution Processes in Contractual Channels of Distribution," *Journal of Marketing*, January 1992, pp. 38–54.

12. "Making the Middleman an Endangered Species," *Business Week*, June 6, 1994, pp. 114–15; "Twenty-Eight Steps to a Strategic Alliance," *Inc.*, April 1993, pp. 96–104; Jule B. Gassenheimer et al., "Models of Channel Maintenance: What Is the Weaker Party to Do?" *Journal of Business Research*, July 1994, pp. 225–36; *1993 Annual Report*, Wal-Mart; Teresa Jaworska, "Channel Members' Behavior in Industrial Markets in Poland," *Journal of Business Research*, January 1992, pp. 51–56; Gregory T. Gundlach, Ravi S. Achrol, and John T. Mentzer, "The Structure of Commitment in Exchange," *Journal of Marketing*, January 1995, pp. 78–92; Jan B. Heide, "Interorganizational Governance in Marketing Channels," *Journal of Marketing*, January 1994, pp. 71–85; Jean L. Johnson et al., "The Exercise of Interfirm Power and Its Repercussions in U.S.-Japanese Channel Relationships," *Journal of Marketing*, April 1993, pp. 1–10; B. Ramaseshan and Leyland F. Pitt, "Major Industrial Distribution Issues Facing Managers in Australia," *Industrial Marketing Management*, August 1990, pp. 225–34; Gul Butaney and Lawrence H. Wortzell, "Distributor Power versus Manufacturer Power: The Customer Role," *Journal of Marketing*, January 1988, pp. 52–63; Bruce J. Walker, Janet E. Keith, and Donald W. Jackson, Jr., "The Channels Manager: Now, Soon or Never?" *Academy of Marketing Science*, Summer 1985, pp. 82–96.

13. "It's about Control," *Inc.*, August 1994, pp. 25–26; Saul Klein, "A Transaction Cost Explanation of Vertical Control in International Markets," *Journal of the Academy of Marketing Science*, Summer 1989, pp. 253–60; "Beer and Antitrust," *Fortune*, December 9, 1985, pp. 135–36; "Car Megadealers Loosen Detroit's Tight Rein," *The Wall Street Journal*, July 1, 1985, p. 6; Wilke D.

English and Donald A. Michie, "The Impact of Electronic Technology upon the Marketing Channel," *Academy of Marketing Science*, Summer 1985, pp. 57–71; Robert D. Buzzell, "Is Vertical Integration Profitable?" *Harvard Business Review*, January–February 1983, pp. 92–102; Michael Etgar and Aharon Valency, "Determinants of the Use of Contracts in Conventional Marketing Channels," *Journal of Retailing*, Winter 1983, pp. 81–92; "Why Manufacturers Are Doubling as Distributors," *Business Week*, January 17, 1983, p. 41; Louis W. Stern and Torger Reve, "Distribution Channels as Political Economies: A Framework for Comparative Analysis," *Journal of Marketing*, Summer 1980, pp. 52–64.

14. "Esprit's Spirited Style Is Hot Seller," *USA Today*, March 25, 1986, p. B5; "Apparel Firm Makes Profits, Takes Risks by Flouting Tradition," *The Wall Street Journal*, June 11, 1985, p. 1ff.

15. "This Isn't the Legend Acura Dealers Had in Mind," *Business Week*, November 28, 1988, pp. 106–10; "Car Dealers Mull Going Public at Cost of Independence," *The Wall Street Journal*, May 23, 1988, p. 6.

16. "Antitrust Issues and Marketing Channel Strategy" and "Case 1—Continental T.V., Inc., et al. v. GTE Sylvania, Inc.," in *Legal Aspects of Marketing Strategy*, ed. Louis W. Stern and Thomas L. Eovaldi (Englewood Cliffs, NJ: Prentice Hall, 1984), pp. 300–61.

17. *1993 Annual Report*, Reebok; "Reebok's Direct Sales Spark a Retail Revolt," *Adweek's Marketing Week*, December 2, 1991, p. 7. See also James R. Burley, "Territorial Restriction and Distribution Systems: Current Legal Developments," *Journal of Marketing*, October 1975, pp. 52–56; "Justice Takes Aim at Dual Distribution," *Business Week*, July 7, 1980, pp. 24–25; Saul Sands and Robert J. Posch, Jr., "A Checklist of Questions for Firms Considering a Vertical Territorial Distribution Plan," *Journal of Marketing*, Summer 1982, pp. 38–43; Debra L. Scammon and Mary Jane Sheffet, "Legal Issues in Channels Modification Decisions: The Question of Refusals to Deal," *Journal of Public Policy and Marketing* 5 (1986), pp. 82–96.

18. Gary L. Frazier, James D. Gill, and Sudhir H. Kale, "Dealer Dependence Levels and Reciprocal Actions in a Channel of Distribution in a Developing Country," *Journal of Marketing*, January 1989, pp. 50–69; Gregory T. Gundlach and Patrick E. Murphy, "Ethical and Legal Foundations of Relational Marketing Exchanges," *Journal of Marketing*, October 1993, pp. 35–46; Robert A. Robicheaux and James E. Coleman, "The Structure of Marketing Channel Relationships," *Journal of the Academy of Marketing Science*, Winter 1994, pp. 38–51; Brett A. Boyle and F. Robert Dwyer, "Power, Bureaucracy, Influence and Performance: Their Relationships in Industrial Distribution Channels," *Journal of Business Research*, March 1995, pp. 189–200.

19. See, for example, "Turning Trash into Cash," *Traffic Management*, October 1993, pp. 46–48; Harvey Alter, "Cost of Recycling Municipal Solid Waste with and without a Concurrent Beverage Container Deposit Law," *Journal of Consumer Affairs*, Summer 1993, pp. 166–86; James H. Barnes, Jr., "Recycling: A Problem in Reverse Logistics," *Journal of Macromarketing* 2, no. 2 (1982), pp. 31–37.

Chapter 12

1. "Behemoth on a Tear," *Business Week*, October 3, 1994, pp. 54–55; "The Cola Wars Go to College," *Business Week*, September 19, 1994, p. 42; "Coca-Cola Still It in India despite

Fight from Pepsi," *Advertising Age International*, July 18, 1994, p. 12ff.; "Still Discontented after All These Years," *Beverage World*, April 1994, pp. 22–49; "Soda Pop Sales Sparkle at Fountain Outlets," *The Wall Street Journal*, November 18, 1993, p. B1ff.; "Fountain of Growth Found Abroad," *USA Today*, August 16, 1993, p. 1Bff.; "Coke's Soda Fountain for Offices Fizzles, Dashing High Hopes," *The Wall Street Journal*, June 14, 1993, p. A1ff.; "The World's Best Brand," *Fortune*, May 31, 1993, pp. 44–54; "The Real Thing Is Thundering Eastward," *Business Week*, April 13, 1992, pp. 96–98; "Coke Plans 'Real Thing' Global Attack," *Advertising Age*, August 5, 1991, p. 1ff.; "Pressure Grows at Coke as Ads Go Flat," *The Wall Street Journal*, August 2, 1991, p. B1ff.; "In Asia, the Sweet Taste of Success," *Business Week*, November 26, 1990, p. 96; "Coke Gets off Its Can in Europe," *Fortune*, August 13, 1990, pp. 67–73.

2. "Delivering the Goods," *Fortune*, November 28, 1994, pp. 64–78; "More U.S. Grocers Turning to ECR to Cut Waste," *Marketing News*, September 12, 1994, p. 3; "Making the Middleman an Endangered Species," *Business Week*, June 6, 1994, pp. 114–15; "The Nitty-Gritty of ECR Systems: How One Company Makes It Pay," *Advertising Age*, May 2, 1994, pp. S1ff.; "Behind the Tumult at P&G," *Fortune*, March 7, 1994, pp. 74–82; "The Economy's Power Shift," *The Wall Street Journal*, September 24, 1992.

3. "Delivering the Goods," *Fortune*, November 28, 1994, pp. 64–78; Brian F. O'Neil and Jon L. Iveson, "Strategically Managing the Logistics Function," *The Logistics and Transportation Review*, December 1991, pp. 359–78; Lloyd M. Rinehart, M. Bixby Cooper, and George D. Wagenheim, "Furthering the Integration of Marketing and Logistics through Customer Service in the Channel," *Journal of the Academy of Marketing Science*, Winter 1989, pp. 63–72; Patricia J. Daughtery, Robert E. Sabath, and Dale S. Rogers, "Competitive Advantage through Customer Responsiveness," *The Logistics and Transportation Review*, September 1992, pp. 257–72; Philip B. Schary, "A Concept of Customer Service," *The Logistics and Transportation Review*, December 1992, pp. 341–52; Edward A. Morash and John Ozment, "Toward Management of Transportation Service Quality," *The Logistics and Transportation Review*, June 1994, pp. 115–40; Michael H. Morris and Duane L. Davis, "Measuring and Managing Customer Service in Industrial Firms," *Industrial Marketing Management*, November 1992, pp. 343–54; William D. Perreault, Jr., and Frederick A. Russ, "Physical Distribution Service in Industrial Purchase Decisions," *Journal of Marketing*, April 1976, pp. 3–10; Gary L. Frazier, Robert E. Spekman, and Charles R. O'Neal, "Just-In-Time Exchange Relationships in Industrial Markets," *Journal of Marketing*, October 1988, pp. 52–67.

4. Roy D. Shapiro, "Get Leverage from Logistics," *Harvard Business Review*, May–June 1984, pp. 119–26; James E. Morehouse, "Operating in the New Logistics Era," *Harvard Business Review*, September–October 1983, pp. 18–19; Graham Sharman, "The Rediscovery of Logistics," *Harvard Business Review*, September–October 1984, pp. 71–79; see also Goran Persson and Lars-Olof Backman, "Logistics in Eastern Europe," *The Logistics and Transportation Review*, December 1993, pp. 319–28.

5. A. Coskun Samli, Laurence W. Jacobs, and James Wills, "What Presale and Postsale Services Do You Need to Be Competitive," *Industrial Marketing Management*, February 1992, pp. 33–42; R. Mohan Pisharodi, "Preference for Supplier When Supplier and Customer Perceptions of Customer Service Levels

Differ," *The Logistics and Transportation Review*, March 1994, pp. 31–54; Benson P. Shapiro, V. K. Rangan, and J. J. Sviokla, "Staple Yourself to an Order," *Harvard Business Review*, July–August 1992, pp. 113–22; J. B. Fuller, J. O'Conor, and R. Rawlinson, "Tailored Logistics: The Next Advantage," *Harvard Business Review*, May–June 1993, pp. 87–98; John T. Mentzer, Roger Gomes, and Robert E. Krapfel, Jr., "Physical Distribution Service: A Fundamental Marketing Concept?" *Journal of the Academy of Marketing Science*, Winter 1989, pp. 53–62; Frances G. Tucker, "Creative Customer Service Management," *International Journal of Physical Distribution and Materials Management* 13, no. 3 (1983), pp. 34–50; William D. Perreault, Jr., and Frederick R. Russ, "Physical Distribution Service: A Neglected Aspect of Marketing Management," *MSU Business Topics*, Summer 1974, pp. 37–46.

6. Arthur M. Geoffrion, "Better Distribution Planning with Computer Models," *Harvard Business Review*, July–August 1976, pp. 92–99; David P. Herron, "Managing Physical Distribution for Profit," *Harvard Business Review*, May–June 1979, pp. 121–32; "'What If' Help for Management," *Business Week*, January 21, 1980, p. 73.

7. Bernard J. LaLonde and P. H. Zinszer, *Customer Service: Meaning and Measurement* (Chicago: National Council of Distribution Management, 1976).

8. For more detail on deregulation of transportation, see Paul D. Larson, "Transportation Deregulation, JIT, and Inventory Levels," *The Logistics and Transportation Review*, June 1991, pp. 99–112; J. J. Coyle, Edward J. Bardi, and Joseph L. Cavinato, *Transportation* (St. Paul, MN: West, 1986); "Deregulating America," *Business Week*, November 28, 1983; James C. Nelson, "Politics and Economics in Transport Regulation and Deregulation—A Century Perspective of the ICC's Role," *Logistics and Transportation Review*, March 1987, pp. 5–32; Karl M. Ruppentha, "U.S. Airline Deregulation, Winners and Losers," *Logistics and Transportation Review*, March 1987, pp. 65–82.

9. For a more detailed comparison of mode characteristics, see Roger Dale Abshire and Shane R. Premeaux, "Motor Carriers' and Shippers' Perceptions of the Carrier Choice Decision," *The Logistics and Transportation Review*, December 1991, pp. 351–58; Brian J. Gibson, Harry L. Sink, and Ray A. Mundy, "Shipper-Carrier Relationships and Carrier Selection Criteria," *Logistics and Transportation Review*, December 1993, pp. 371–82; Ronald L. Coulter et al., "Freight Transportation Carrier Selection Criteria: Identification of Service Dimensions for Competitive Positioning," *Journal of Business Research*, August 1989, pp. 51–66; Donald J. Bowersox, David L. Closs, and Omar K. Helferich, *Logistical Management* (New York: Macmillan, 1986); Edward L. Fitzsimmons, "Factors Associated with Intramodal Competition Reported by Small Railroads," *Logistics and Transportation Review*, March 1991, pp. 73–90.

10. "High Tech Puts Them Back on Track," *USA Today*, November 2, 1994, p. 1Bff.; "Railroads Face Unfamiliar Problem: Too Little Capacity," *The Wall Street Journal*, May 31, 1994, p. B4; "After Sharp Cost Cuts, Conrail Is Resembling a Growth Company," *The Wall Street Journal*, November 20, 1992, p. A1ff.; "Railroads Getting in Better Shape for the Long Haul," *The Wall Street Journal*, February 26, 1992, p. B4; "Big Rail Is Finally Rounding the Bend," *Business Week*, November 11, 1991, pp. 128–29; Philip G. Laird, "Rail Freight Development in

Australia," *Logistics and Transportation Review*, September 1992, pp. 273–88.

11. "Riding the Data Highway," *Newsweek*, March 21, 1994, pp. 54–55; "Hauling It for Less," *Nation's Business*, January 1994, pp. 46–48; "Truck Cabs Turn into Mobile Offices as Drivers Take on White-Collar Tasks," *The Wall Street Journal*, August 3, 1993, p. B1ff.; "Riding the High-Tech Highway," *Inc.*, March 1993, pp. 72–85; Eiji Shiomi et al., "Physical Distribution and Freight Transportation in the Tokyo Metropolitan Area," *The Logistics and Transportation Review*, December 1993, pp. 335–54.

12. "Can Europe Deliver," *The Wall Street Journal*, September 30, 1994, p. R15ff.; "Modern Network Brings Advantage," *Importing Today*, May/June 1993; "Fragile: Handle with Care," *Financial Times*, June 29, 1993; "Federal Express Finds Its Pioneering Formula Falls Flat Overseas," *The Wall Street Journal*, April 15, 1991, p. A1ff.; "UPS Challenges Leaders in Air Express," *The Wall Street Journal*, December 20, 1990, p. A5; "Federal Express's Battle Overseas," *Fortune*, December 3, 1990, pp. 137–40; Gunna K. Sletmo and Jacques Picard, "International Distribution Policies and the Role of Air Freight," *Journal of Business Logistics* 6, no. 1 (1985), pp. 35–53.

13. K. Raguraman and Claire Chan, "The Development of Sea-Air Intermodal Transportation: An Assessment of Global Trends," *Logistics and Transportation Review*, December 1994, p. 379; "Cargo that Phones Home," *Fortune*, November 15, 1993, p. 143; "Grain Processor Improvises to Stay Afloat," *The Wall Street Journal*, July 21, 1993, p. B1ff.; *1993 Annual Report*, CSX.

14. Joseph T. Kane, "Future Shock Is Now for Freight Forwarders," *Handling and Shipping Management*, October 1983, pp. 65–68; Kant Rao, Richard R. Young, and Judith A. Novick, "Third Party Services in the Logistics of Global Firms," *Logistics and Transportation Review*, December 1993, pp. 363–70; Judith A. Fuerst, "Sorting Out the Middlemen," *Handling and Shipping Management*, March 1985, pp. 46–50.

15. "You Make It, They Distribute It," *Nation's Business*, March 1994, pp. 46–48; C. H. White and R. B. Felder, "Turn Your Truck Fleet into a Profit Center," *Harvard Business Review*, May–June 1983, pp. 14–17.

16. Paul A. Dion, Loretta M. Hasey, Patrick C. Dorin, and Jean Lundin, "Consequences of Inventory Stockouts," *Industrial Marketing Management* 20, no. 1 (1991), pp. 23–28; R. Douglas White, "Streamline Inventory to Better Serve Customers," *Journal of Business Strategy*, March/April 1989, pp. 43–47; David J. Armstrong, "Sharpening Inventory Management," *Harvard Business Review*, November–December 1985, pp. 42–59.

17. "Compaq Borrows Wal-Mart's Idea to Boost Production," *The Wall Street Journal*, June 17, 1994, p. B4; Wade Ferguson, "Buying an Industrial Service Warehouse Space," *Industrial Marketing Management*, February 1983, pp. 63–66; Arnold B. Maltz, "Outsourcing the Warehousing Function: Economics and Strategic Considerations," *Logistics and Transportation Review*, September 1994, pp. 245–66; Patricia J. Daugherty, Dale S. Rogers, and Theodore P. Stank, "Benchmarking: Strategic Implications for Warehousing Firms," *Logistics and Transportation Review*, March 1994, pp. 55–72; G. O. Pattino, "Public Warehousing: Supermarket for Distribution Services," *Handling and Shipping*, March 1977, p. 59.

18. "Scanning the Distribution Horizon," *Foodservice Equipment & Supplies Specialist*, June 1994, pp. 44–52; Kenneth B. Ackerman and Bernard J. LaLonde, "Making Warehousing More Efficient," *Harvard Business Review*, April 1980, pp. 94–102.

19. *1993 Annual Report*, Tyson Foods; "Holly Farms' Marketing Error: The Chicken that Laid an Egg," *The Wall Street Journal*, February 9, 1988, p. 44.

20. *1993 Annual Report*, Clorox; *1991 Annual Report*, Clorox.

21. Faye W. Gilbert, Joyce A. Young, and Charles R. O'Neal, "Buyer-Seller Relationships in Just-in-Time Purchasing Environments," *Journal of Business Research*, February 1994, pp. 111–20; Steve McDaniel, Joseph G. Ormsby, and Alicia B. Gresham, "The Effect of JIT on Distributors," *Industrial Marketing Management*, May 1992, pp. 145–50; "Toy Industry Finds It's Harder and Harder to Pick the Winners," *The Wall Street Journal*, December 21, 1993, p. A1ff.; "Some Manufacturers Drop Efforts to Adopt Japanese Techniques," *The Wall Street Journal*, May 7, 1993, p. A1ff.; "Supermarkets Reorganize Distribution to Help Fight K, Wal and Other Marts," *The Wall Street Journal*, January 19, 1993, p. B8; "Allen-Edmonds Shoe Tries 'Just-in-Time' Production," *The Wall Street Journal*, March 4, 1993, p. B2; Shirley J. Daniel and Wolf D. Reitsperger, "Management Control Systems for J.I.T.: An Empirical Comparison of Japan and the U.S.," *Journal of International Business Studies*, Winter 1991, pp. 603–18; "How to Keep Truckin' in the Age of Just-in-Time Delivery," *Business Week*, December 10, 1990, p. 181; "Firms' Newfound Skill in Managing Inventory May Soften Downturn," *The Wall Street Journal*, November 19, 1990, p. A1ff.; Charles R. O'Neal, "JIT Procurement and Relationship Marketing," *Industrial Marketing Management* 18, no. 1 (1989), pp. 54–64; Prabir K. Bagchi, T. S. Raghumathan, and Edward J. Bardi, "The Implications of Just-in-Time Inventory Policies on Carrier Selection," *Logistics and Transportation Review*, December 1987, pp. 373–84.

22. "Who's Winning the Information Revolution," *Fortune*, November 30, 1992, pp. 110–17; "Circuit City's Wires Are Sizzling," *Business Week*, April 27, 1992, p. 76; "Earning More by Moving Faster," *Fortune*, October 7, 1991, pp. 89–94; "An Electronic Pipeline that's Changing the Way America Does Business," *Business Week*, August 3, 1987, p. 80ff.; Brian Dearing, "The Strategic Benefits of EDI," *Journal of Business Strategy*, January/February 1990, pp. 4–6; Ramon O'Callaghan, Patrick J. Kaufmann, and Benn R. Konsynski, "Adoption Correlates and Share Effects of Electronic Data Interchange Systems in Marketing Channels," *Journal of Marketing*, April 1992, pp. 45–56; Richard Germain, "The Adoption of Logistics Process Technology by Manufacturers," *Journal of Business Research*, May 1993, pp. 51–64; Ned C. Hill and Michael J. Swenson, "Sales Technology Applications: The Impact of Electronic Data Interchange on the Sales Function," *Journal of Personal Selling & Sales Management*, Summer 1994, pp. 79–88; "Computer Finds a Role in Buying and Selling, Reshaping Businesses," *The Wall Street Journal*, March 18, 1987, p. 1ff.

23. "A Smart Cookie at Pepperidge," *Fortune*, December 22, 1986, pp. 67–74.

24. "As Stores Scrimp More and Order Less, Suppliers Take On Greater Risks, Costs," *The Wall Street Journal*, December 10, 1991, p. B1ff.

25. *1993 Annual Report*, Du Pont; *1993 Annual Report*, Matlack; *1993 Annual Report*, Shell; " 'Green Cars' Are Still Far in the Future," *The Wall Street Journal*, January 13, 1992, p. B1ff.; "Conservation Power," *Business Week*, September 16, 1991, pp. 86–91; "On the Road Again and Again and Again: Auto Makers Try to Build Recyclable Car," *The Wall Street Journal*, April 30, 1991, p. B1; "Clean-Air Proposal Eventually May Add as Much as $600 to Car Sticker Prices," *The Wall Street Journal*, October 11, 1990, p. B1ff.; "Shell Pumps Cleaner Gas in 'Dirtiest' Cities in U.S.," *The Wall Street Journal*, April 12, 1990, p. B1ff.; "Clean-Air Legislation Will Cost Americans $21.5 Billion a Year," *The Wall Street Journal*, March 28, 1990, p. A1ff.

26. Maureen E. Lynch, Sharon J. Imada, and James H. Bookbinder, "The Future of Logistics in Canada: A Delphi-Based Forecast," *Logistics and Transportation Review*, March 1994, p. 95; John J. Burbridge, Jr., "Strategic Implications of Logistics Information Systems," *Logistics and Transportation Review*, December 1988, pp. 368–83.

Chapter 13

1. "Searching for the Next Kiwi: Frieda's Branded Produce," *Brandweek*, May 2, 1994, pp. 46–48; "Strange Fruits," *Inc.*, November 1989, pp. 80–90; "The Produce Marketer," *Savvy*, June 1988, pp. 26–28.

2. U.S. Bureau of the Census, *Statistical Abstract of the United States 1994* (Washington, DC: U.S. Government Printing Office, 1994), pp. 780–95; U.S. Bureau of the Census, *County Business Patterns 1992, United States* (Washington, DC: U.S. Government Printing Office, 1994).

3. "Stores Tinker with the Hours They Stay Open," *The Wall Street Journal*, October 28, 1994, p. B1ff.; "All Decked Out, Stores Head Downtown," *The Wall Street Journal*, February 15, 1994, p. B1ff.; William R. Darden and Barry J. Babin, "Exploring the Concept of Affective Quality: Expanding the Concept of Retail Personality," *Journal of Business Research*, February 1994, pp. 101–10; Jeffrey S. Conant, Denise T. Smart, and Roberto Solano-Mendez, "Generic Retailing Types, Distinctive Marketing Competencies, and Competitive Advantage," *Journal of Retailing*, Fall 1993, pp. 254–79; Robert J. Donovan et al., "Store Atmosphere and Purchasing Behavior," *Journal of Retailing*, Fall 1994, p. 283; "Location, Luck, Service Can Make a Store Top Star," *The Wall Street Journal*, February 1, 1993, p. B1. For additional examples on retailers targeting social classes, see John P. Dickson and Douglas L. MacLachlan, "Social Distance and Shopping Behavior," *Journal of the Academy of Marketing Science*, Spring 1990, pp. 153–62; "Penney Moves Upscale in Merchandise but Still Has to Convince Public," *The Wall Street Journal*, June 7, 1990, p. A1ff.; "Selling to the Poor: Retailers that Target Low-Income Shoppers Are Rapidly Growing," *The Wall Street Journal*, June 24, 1985, p. 1ff.

4. "Buoyant Shoppers Boost Specialty Sales," *The Wall Street Journal*, December 15, 1992, p. B1ff.; "Specialty Retailing, a Hot Market, Attracts New Players," *The Wall Street Journal*, April 2, 1987, p. 1.

5. U.S. Bureau of the Census, *County Business Patterns 1992, United States*, pp. 53–54; U.S. Bureau of the Census, *Current Business Reports*, p. 5.

6. "Department Store Frequency Marketing," *Colloquy* 4, no. 3 (1994); "Dillard's Has a Dilly of a Headache," *Business Week*, October 3, 1994, pp. 85–86; "Department Stores Winning Over Teens," *USA Today*, August 17, 1994, p. 6B; "Department Stores, Seemingly Outmoded, Are Perking Up Again," *The Wall Street Journal*, January 4, 1994, p. A1ff.; "Remaking a Dinosaur,"

Newsweek, February 10, 1992, pp. 38–43; Richard A. Rauch, "Retailing's Dinosaurs: Department Stores and Supermarkets," *Business Horizons*, September/October 1991, pp. 21–25; Myron Gable, Susan S. Fiorito, and Martin T. Topol, "The Current Status of Women in Department Store Retailing: 1993," *Journal of Retailing*, Spring 1994, pp. 65–74.

7. David Appel, "The Supermarket: Early Development of an Institutional Innovation," *Journal of Retailing*, Spring 1972, pp. 39–53.

8. "As Big as Kodak Is in Rochester, N.Y., It Still Isn't Wegmans," *The Wall Street Journal*, December 27, 1994, p. A1ff.; "Special Report: Grocery Marketing," *Advertising Age*, May 8, 1989, pp. S1–22; "The Transformation of the Nation's Supermarkets," *New York Times*, September 2, 1984, p. 1ff.

9. "Ahold's Supermarkets 'Go Native' to Succeed in U.S.," *The Wall Street Journal*, October 4, 1994, p. B4; "Supermarkets Mimic Warehouse Clubs," *Advertising Age*, July 12, 1993, p. 20; "Supermarkets Want to Join the Club," *Adweek*, July 5, 1993, p. 10; "Special Report: Grocery Marketing," *Advertising Age*, May 10, 1993, pp. S1–12; "Supermarkets Can Beat Warehouse Clubs, but Not on Price Alone," *Brandweek*, January 4, 1993, p. 25.

10. "Catalog Showrooms Revamp to Keep Their Identity," *Business Week*, Industrial/Technology Edition, June 10, 1985, pp. 117–20; Pradeep K. Korgaonkar, "Consumer Preferences for Catalog Showrooms and Discount Stores," *Journal of Retailing*, Fall 1982, pp. 76–88; "Best Products: Too Much Too Soon at the No. 1 Catalog Showroom," *Business Week*, July 23, 1984, pp. 136–38.

11. "Wal-Mart: The Next Generation," *Discount Store News*, December 5, 1994, pp. 47–113; "Aging Activists Turn, Turn, Turn Attention to Wal-Mart Protests," *The Wall Street Journal*, October 11, 1994, p. A1ff.; "Once Easily Turned Away by Local Foes, Wal-Mart Gets Tough in New England," *The Wall Street Journal*, September 7, 1994, p. B1; "Up against the Wal-Mart," *Time*, August 22, 1994, p. 58; "Kmart's Dowdy Stores Get a Snazzy Face Lift, but Problems Linger," *The Wall Street Journal*, November 5, 1993, p. A1ff.; "The High Cost of Second Best," *Fortune*, July 26, 1993, pp. 99–102; "When Wal-Mart Comes to Town," *Inc.*, July 1993, pp. 76–88.

12. "Wal-Mart's Super Day: 23 Supercenters in 14 States," *Discount Store News*, February 6, 1995, p. 1ff.; "Hypermarkets Seem to Be Big Flop in U.S.," *Advertising Age*, October 4, 1993, p. 20; "When Wal-Mart Starts a Food Fight, It's a Doozy," *Business Week*, June 14, 1993, pp. 92–93; "Hypermarkets: A Sure-Fire Hit Bombs," *The Wall Street Journal*, June 25, 1992, p. B1.

13. "Toys 'R' Us Plans U.S. Refinement, Int'l Expansion," *Discount Store News*, February 6, 1995, pp. 23–32; "Toys 'R' Us Busy Playing Overseas," *USA Today*, November 22, 1994, p. 4B; "After You Win the Fun Begins," *Fortune*, May 2, 1994, p. 76; *1993 Annual Report*, Toys 'R' Us; "Brawls in Toyland," *Business Week*, December 21, 1992, pp. 36–37; "Toys 'R' Us Seeks Global Growth," *Advertisng Age*, March 30, 1992, p. 33; "Breaking into European Markets by Breaking the Rules," *Business Week*, January 20, 1992, pp. 88–89; "Toys 'R' Us Learns Give-and-Take Game in Japan, Sets the Debut for First Store," *The Wall Street Journal*, October 8, 1991, p. A18.

14. "Price/Costco's Spinoff Reflects a Difficult Marriage," *The Wall Street Journal*, July 19, 1994, p. B4; "Why Sam's Wants Businesses to Join the Club," *Business Week*, June 27, 1994, p. 48; "And the Winner Is Still . . . Wal-Mart," *Fortune*, May 2, 1994, pp. 62–70; "Warehouse-Club War Leaves Few Standing, and They Are Bruised," *The Wall Street Journal*, November 18, 1993, p. A1ff.; "Kmart Will Sell 91 Warehouse Clubs to Wal-Mart, Shut Rest of Pace Chain," *The Wall Street Journal*, November 3, 1993, p. A4; "Wal-Mart Sets Sights on Big Customers in Bid to Improve Warehouse-Club Unit," *The Wall Street Journal*, November 2, 1993, p. A5; "Who Shops at the Clubs?" *American Demographics*, October 1993, pp. 25–26.

15. "Category Killer Growth Awes Analysts," *Discount Store News*, November 21, 1994, p. 45; "Small Software Sellers Face King-Size Problem," *Advertising Age*, May 16, 1994, p. S13; "Superstore Sells Every Necessity for Reading, 'Riting, 'Rithmetic," *The Wall Street Journal*, May 16, 1994, p. B1ff.; "This Do-It-Yourself Store Is Really Doing It," *Business Week*, May 2, 1994, p. 108; "Pet Superstores Collar Customers from Supermarkets, Small Shops," *The Wall Street Journal*, November 18, 1993, p. B12; "What's Next Chapter in Bookstore Battle," *Advertising Age*, April 12, 1993, p. 12; "There's No Place like Home Depot," *Nation's Business*, February 1992, pp. 30–35; "This Is a Job for Superstores," *USA Today*, October 8, 1991, p. 4B.

16. "7-Eleven Stores Face Fresh Food Showdown," *Brandweek*, February 28, 1994, p. 1ff.; "Pumping Up at Texaco," *Business Week*, June 7, 1993, pp. 112–13; "Some 7-Elevens Try Selling a New Image," *The Wall Street Journal*, October 25, 1991, p. B1ff.; "Stop N Go's Van Horn Wants to Reinvent the Convenience Store," *The Wall Street Journal*, February 6, 1991, pp. A1ff.

17. "Smokers Take 'em One at a Time," *USA Today*, August 9, 1994, p. 2B; "Push-Button Lover," *The Economist*, November 16, 1991, p. 88; "Machines Start New Fast-Food Era," *USA Today*, July 19, 1991, pp. 1B–2B; "High-Tech Vending Machines Cook Up a New Menu of Hot Fast-Food Entrees," *The Wall Street Journal*, May 13, 1991, p. B1ff.

18. "Spiegel's Book Is a Real Page-Turner," *Business Week*, September 12, 1994, pp. 74–76; "U.S. Catalogers Test International Waters," *The Wall Street Journal*, April 19, 1994, p. B1; C. R. Jasper and P. N. R. Lan, "Apparel Catalog Patronage: Demographic, Lifestyle, and Motivational Factors," *Psychology & Marketing*, July/August 1992, pp. 275–96; "Once Very Hot, Mail-Order PCs Are Cooling Off," *The Wall Street Journal*, December 1, 1993, p. B1ff.; "Why Gateway Is Racing to Answer on the First Ring," *Business Week*, September 13, 1993, pp. 92–94; "Shoppers Seem to Prefer Mail over Mall," *USA Today*, August 12, 1993, p. 4B; "Lands' End Does It. Dell Does It. Why Not Big Blue?" *Brandweek*, July 12, 1993, pp. 22–24; "This Magazine Could Be on Your PC Screen," *Business Week*, June 28, 1993, p. 56; "Extend Your Reach by Catalog Sales," *Nation's Business*, March 1992, pp. 33–37.

19. "QVC Draws Wares from Everywhere," *USA Today*, November 1, 1994, p. 1Dff.; "Battling for Buck$," *Profiles*, November 1994, pp. 49–52; "MTV Home Shopping Picks Model Host," *The Wall Street Journal*, July 18, 1994, p. B5; "TV or Not TV," *Inc.*, June 1994, pp. 63–68; "Purchasing Power," *U.S. News & World Report*, January 31, 1994, pp. 56–59; "Home Shoppers to Be Given Yet Another Service," *The Wall Street Journal*, January 14, 1994, p. B1ff.; "One Viewer Turns into Home Shopper," *USA Today*, December 22, 1993, p. 1Aff.; "TV Shopping Plays Grinch for Retailers," *Advertising Age*, November 29, 1993, p. 1ff.; "TV Shopping Hooks High-Toned Viewers," *The Wall Street Journal*, November 16, 1993, p. B1ff.; "QVC Ads Tout Network over Retailers," *The Wall Street Journal*, October 19, 1993, p. B8;

"Battle Looms for Affluent Home Shoppers," *The Wall Street Journal*, September 26, 1993, p. B1ff.

20. "Kmart Goes On Line with Interactive Shopping," *Discount Store News*, January 16, 1995, p. 3; "Holiday Shopping Comes to Cyberspace," *The Wall Street Journal*, November 18, 1994, p. B5; "It's Getting Crowded On Line," *Business Week*, November 7, 1994, pp. 134–36; "Purists Beware: Ads Have Invaded On-Line Services," *The Wall Street Journal*, August 23, 1994, p. B1ff.; "Computer-Ordering Method Helps Newcomer Blossom," *The Wall Street Journal*, January 22, 1991, p. B2; "Electronic Retailing Filling Niche Needs," *Discount Store News*, December 19, 1988, p. 111.

21. "Stung by Mass Merchandisers, Drugstores Try New Remedies," *The Wall Street Journal*, February 11, 1993, p. B1ff.; "Nabisco Plots Strategy to Sell Oreos with Videos," *Advertising Age*, May 4, 1992, p. 3ff.; "Stores Find Photo Minilabs Quick Way to Process Profit," *Supermarket News*, June 10, 1991, pp. 22–25; Jack M. Cadeaux, "Industry Product Volatility and Retailer Assortments," *Journal of Macromarketing*, Fall 1992, pp. 28–37; "Special Report: Stores Juggle Space, Specialties," *Advertising Age*, October 12, 1987, p. S1ff. For more on how life cycles apply to retailers, see "Rewriting the Rules of Retailing," *New York Times*, October 15, 1990, sec. 3, p. 1ff.; Video Chain Aims to Star as Industry Leader," *USA Today*, July 22, 1988, pp. B1–2; "What Ails Retailing," *Fortune*, January 30, 1989, pp. 61–64; Ronald Savitt, "The 'Wheel of Retailing' and Retail Product Management," *European Journal of Marketing* 18, no. 6/7 (1984), pp. 43–54; Jack G. Kaikati, Rom J. Markin, and Calvin P. Duncan, "The Transformation of Retailing Institutions: Beyond the Wheel of Retailing and Life Cycle Theories," *Journal of Macromarketing* 1, no. 1 (1981), pp. 58–66.

22. "How Did Sears Blow This Gasket?" *Business Week*, June 29, 1992, p. 38; "An Open Letter to Sears Customers," *USA Today*, June 25, 1992, p. 8A; see also John Paul Fraedrich, "The Ethical Behavior of Retail Managers," *Journal of Business Ethics*, March 1993, pp. 207–18.

23. "Retailers Grab Power, Control Marketplace," *Marketing News*, January 16, 1989, pp. 1–2; Dale D. Achabal, John M. Heineke, and Shelby H. McIntyre, "Issues and Perspectives on Retail Productivity," *Journal of Retailing*, Fall 1984, p. 107ff.; Charles A. Ingene, "Scale Economies in American Retailing: A Cross-Industry Comparison," *Journal of Macromarketing* 4, no. 2 (1984), pp. 49–63; "Mom-and-Pop Videotape Shops Are Fading Out," *Business Week*, September 2, 1985, pp. 34–35; Vijay Mahajan, Subhash Sharma, and Roger Kerin, "Assessing Market Penetration Opportunities and Saturation Potential for Multi-Store, Multi-Market Retailers," *Journal of Retailing*, Fall 1988, pp. 315–34.

24. "Forging Ahead with Custom Contracts," *Foodservice Equipment & Supplies Specialist*, June 1994, p. 52; "Manufacturers Start to Spurn Big Discounters," *The Wall Street Journal*, November 30, 1993, p. B1ff.; "CLOUT! More and More, Retail Giants Rule the Marketplace," *Business Week*, December 21, 1992, pp. 66–73.

25. Richard C. Hoffman and John F. Preble, "Franchising into the Twenty-First Century," *Business Horizons*, November–December 1993, pp. 35–43; "Trouble in Franchise Nation," *Fortune*, March 6, 1995, pp. 115–29; "FTC Says Franchisers Fed Clients a Line and Failed to Deliver," *The Wall Street Journal*, May 16, 1994,

p. A1ff.; Dan Fost and Susan Mitchell, "Small Stores with Big Names," *American Demographics*, November 1992, pp. 52–59; Francine Lafontaine and Patrick J. Kaufmann, "The Evolution of Ownership Patterns in Franchise Systems," *Journal of Retailing*, Summer 1994, pp. 97–114; "The Franchise Hall of Fame," *Inc.*, April 1994, pp. 86–95; "Winds of Change in Franchising," *Nation's Business*, January 1994, pp. 49–56; "Franchisers See a Future in East Bloc," *The Wall Street Journal*, June 5, 1990, p. B1ff.; "Avis Hit by Almost Every Obstacle in Franchise Book," *The Wall Street Journal*, May 3, 1990, p. B2.

26. "An Asian Mall in the Great Midwest," *American Demographics*, May 1994, pp. 36–37; "Malls Draw Shoppers with Ferris Wheels and Carousels," *The Wall Street Journal*, June 22, 1994, p. B1ff.; A. Finn, S. McQuitty, and J. Rigby, "Residents' Acceptance and Use of a Mega-Multi-Mall: West Edmonton Mall Evidence," *International Journal of Research in Marketing*, March 1994, pp. 127–44; "What Has the Mall of America Done to Minneapolis?" *American Demographics*, February 1994, pp. 13–15; "Developed to Reinvigorate Downtowns, Many Urban Malls Are Disappointments," *The Wall Street Journal*, November 16, 1992, p. B1ff.; Abhik Roy, "Correlates of Mall Visit Frequency," *Journal of Retailing*, Summer 1994, pp. 139–62; "Special Report: Mega Malls," *Advertising Age*, January 27, 1992, pp. S1–8; "Strip Malls: Plain but Powerful," *American Demographics*, October 1991, pp. 48–51; "Developers of Big Shopping Malls Tutor Faltering Tenants in Retail Techniques," *The Wall Street Journal*, April 24, 1991, p. B1; "Japan Becomes Land of the Rising Mall," *The Wall Street Journal*, February 11, 1991, p. B1ff.; Peter H. Bloch, Nancy M. Ridgway, and Scott A. Dawson, "The Shopping Mall as Consumer Habitat," *Journal of Retailing*, Spring 1994, pp. 23–42; Francesca Turchiano, "The (Un) Malling of America," *American Demographics*, April 1990, pp. 37–39; "Too Many Malls Are Chasing a Shrinking Supply of Shoppers," *Adweek's Marketing Week*, February 5, 1990, pp. 2–3.

27. Saeed Samiee, "Retailing and Channel Considerations in Developing Countries: A Review and Research Propositions," *Journal of Business Research*, June 1993, pp. 103–30; Rolando Arellano, "Informal-Underground Retailers in Less-Developed Countries: An Exploratory Research from a Marketing Point of View," *Journal of Macromarketing*, Fall 1994, pp. 21–35; "Retailers Go Global," *Fortune*, February 20, 1995, pp. 102–8; "Russians Say 'Ja' to Swedish Shops," *Advertising Age*, November 7, 1994, p. 47; "A Different World," *The Wall Street Journal*, October 28, 1994, p. R6; "The Avon Lady of the Amazon," *Business Week*, October 24, 1994, pp. 93–96; "Wal-Mart Is Slowed by Problems of Price and Culture in Mexico," *The Wall Street Journal*, July 29, 1994, p. A1ff.; "A Bargain Basement Called Japan," *Business Week*, June 27, 1994, pp. 42–43; "From Men's Suits to Sake, Discounting Booms in Japan," *Advertising Age International*, March 21, 1994, p. I1ff.; "Penney Pushes Abroad in Unusually Big Way as It Pursues Growth," *The Wall Street Journal*, February 1, 1994, p. A1ff.; "As Discounting Rises in Japan, People Learn to Hunt for Bargains," *The Wall Street Journal*, December 31, 1993, p. A1ff.; "Shop till You Drop Hits Europe," *Business Week*, November 29, 1993, pp. 58–59; "To Succeed in Russia, U.S. Retailer Employs Patience and Local Ally," *The Wall Street Journal*, May 27, 1993, p. A1ff.; "Europe's Smaller Food Shops Face Finis," *The Wall Street Journal*, May 12, 1993, p. B1ff.; Marta Ortiz-Buonafina, "The Evolution of Retail Institutions: A Case Study of the Guatemalan Retail Sector," *Journal of Macromarketing*, Fall 1992, pp. 16–27;

Philip R. Cateora, *International Marketing* (Burr Ridge, IL: Richard D. Irwin, 1990), pp. 586–93.

28. "Hooked Up to the Max," *Time*, September 26, 1994, pp. 58–60; "Peapod's On-Line Grocery Service Checks Out Success," *The Wall Street Journal*, June 30, 1994, p. B2; "With eWorld, Apple Begins an Onslaught of On-Line Services," *The Wall Street Journal*, June 23, 1994, p. B1; "Is Going On-Line Worth the Money?" *Fortune*, June 13, 1994, pp. 104–8; "Will the Information Superhighway Be the Death of Retailing?" *Fortune*, April 18, 1994, pp. 98–110; "Services Slug It Out to Snare New PC Users," *USA Today*, March 21, 1994, p. 1Bff.; "The REAL Home-Shopping Network," *Business Week*, February 21, 1994, p. 85; "New Cyberspace Stores Market Their Software On-Line," *The Wall Street Journal*, January 17, 1994, p. B1ff.; "What Cart? Turn On Your TV to Buy Food," *Advertising Age*, January 10, 1994, p. 1ff.; "Prodigy Unit of IBM, Sears Turns to Cable," *The Wall Street Journal*, June 3, 1993, p. B1ff.

29. "Garment Scanner Could Be a Perfect Fit," *The Wall Street Journal*, September 20, 1994, p. B1ff.; "Do-It-Yourself Grocery Checkout," *The Wall Street Journal*, January 31, 1994, p. B1; "The End of the Line," *Newsweek*, December 13, 1993, p. 73; "Inside Andersen's Army of Advice," *Fortune*, October 4, 1993, pp. 78–86; "21st Century Supermarket Shopping," *Adweek's Marketing Week*, March 9, 1992, p. 9; "What Selling Will Be Like in the '90s," *Fortune*, January 13, 1992, pp. 63–65; "The New Stars of Retailing," *Business Week*, December 16, 1991, pp. 120–22; "Retailers with a Cause," *Newsweek*, December 16, 1991, p. 51; "Shop Talk: What's in Store for Retailers," *The Wall Street Journal*, April 9, 1991, p. B1ff.; "The Little Stores that Could," *Adweek's Marketing Week*, February 4, 1991, pp. 16–17; "Retailing: Who Will Survive," *Business Week*, November 26, 1990, pp. 134–44; Dale D. Achabal and Shelby H. McIntyre, "Guest Editorial: Information Technology Is Reshaping Retailing," *Journal of Retailing*, Winter 1987, pp. 321–25; Leonard L. Berry and Larry G. Greshan, "Relationship Retailing: Transforming Customers into Clients," *Business Horizons*, November/December 1986, pp. 43–47.

30. U.S. Bureau of the Census, *County Business Patterns 1992, United States*, p. 48; "Why Manufacturers Are Doubling as Distributors," *Business Week*, January 17, 1983, p. 41.

31. "Revolution in Japanese Retailing," *Fortune*, February 7, 1994, pp. 143–46; Arieh Goldman, "Evaluating the Performance of the Japanese Distribution System," *Journal of Retailing*, Spring 1992, pp. 11–39; "Japan Begins to Open the Door to Foreigners, a Little," *Brandweek*, August 2, 1993, pp. 14–16.

32. Robert F. Lusch, Deborah S. Coykendall, and James M. Kenderine, *Wholesaling in Transition: An Executive Chart Book* (Norman, OK: Distribution Research Program, University of Oklahoma, 1990).

33. "Direct Marketing: A Modern Marketing Solution," *Directions* (New York: Direct Marketing Association, 1990); "Special Report: Direct Marketing," *Advertising Age*, September 25, 1990, pp. S1–16; Robert F. Lusch, Deborah S. Coykendall, and James M. Kenderine, *Wholesaling in Transition: An Executive Chart Book* (Norman, OK: Distribution Research Program, University of Oklahoma, 1990).

34. "Pecan Industry Finds Getting Organized Is Driving It Nuts," *The Wall Street Journal*, April 1, 1994, p. A1ff.; "Fruit Fight: Independent Growers Challenge Agribusiness Giants," *Insight*, July 29, 1991, pp. 13–19.

35. For more on manufacturers' agents being squeezed, see "Wal-Mart Draws Fire: Reps, Brokers Protest Being Shut Out by New Policy," *Advertising Age*, January 13, 1992, p. 3ff.; Patrick R. Mehr, "Identifying Independent Reps," *Industrial Marketing Management*, November 1992, pp. 319–22; "Independent Sales Reps Are Squeezed by the Recession," *The Wall Street Journal*, December 27, 1991, p. B1. For more discussion on wholesaling abroad, see "Japan Rises to P&G's No. 3 Market," *Advertising Age*, December 10, 1990, p. 42; "P&G Rewrites the Marketing Rules," *Fortune*, November 6, 1989, pp. 34–48; " 'Papa-Mama' Stores in Japan Wield Power to Hold Back Imports," *The Wall Street Journal*, November 14, 1988, p. 1ff.; Yoo S. Yang, Robert P. Leone, and Dana L. Alden, "A Market Expansion Ability Approach to Identify Potential Exporters," *Journal of Marketing*, January 1992, pp. 84–96; "Campbell's Taste of the Japanese Market Is Mm-Mm Good," *Business Week*, March 28, 1988, p. 42; "Brazil Captures a Big Share of the U.S. Shoe Market," *The Wall Street Journal*, August 27, 1985, p. 35; Daniel C. Bello and Ritu Lohtia, "The Export Channel Design: The Use of Foreign Distributors and Agents," *Journal of the Academy of Marketing Science*, Spring 1995, pp. 83–93; Jim Gibbons, "Selling Abroad with Manufacturers' Agents," *Sales & Marketing Management*, September 9, 1985, pp. 67–69; Evelyn A. Thomchick and Lisa Rosenbaum, "The Role of U.S. Export Trading Companies in International Logistics," *Journal of Business Logistics*, September 1984, pp. 85–105.

36. "Computer Wholesalers Face Shakeout and Consolidation," *The Wall Street Journal*, August 26, 1994, p. B4; "Electric Power Brokers Create New Breed of Business," *The Wall Street Journal*, August 2, 1994, p. B4; "Cut Out the Middleman? Never," *Business Week*, January 10, 1994, p. 96; "Existing Distributors Are Being Squeezed by Brewers, Retailers," *The Wall Street Journal*, November 22, 1993, p. A1ff.; "Firms Innovate to Get It for You Wholesale," *The Wall Street Journal*, July 23, 1993, p. B1ff.; "Marketers Shouldn't Give Up on Wholesalers Just Yet," *Brandweek*, July 5, 1993, p. 13; "Steel Service Centers: No More Warehouses," *Industry Week*, February 3, 1992, pp. 36–43; Allan J. Magrath, "The Hidden Clout of Marketing Middlemen," *Journal of Business Strategy*, March/April 1990, pp. 38–41; J. A. Narus and J. C. Anderson, "Turn Your Industrial Distributors into Partners," *Harvard Business Review*, March–April 1986, pp. 66–71; Paul Herbig and Bradley S. O'Hara, "Industrial Distributors in the Twenty-First Century," *Industrial Marketing Management*, July 1994, pp. 199–204.

37. "Cold War: Amana Refrigeration Fights Tiny Distributor," *The Wall Street Journal*, February 26, 1992, p. B2; "Four Strategies Key to Success in Wholesale Distribution Industry," *Marketing News*, March 13, 1989, pp. 22–23. For another example, see "Quickie-Divorce Curbs Sought by Manufacturers' Distributors," *The Wall Street Journal*, July 13, 1987, p. 27; "Merger of Two Bakers Teaches Distributors a Costly Lesson (3-parts)," *The Wall Street Journal*, September 14, 1987, p. 29; October 19, 1987, p. 35; November 11, 1987, p. 33.

Chapter 14

1. "Modems Operandi," *MediaWeek*, June 27, 1994, pp. S12–13.

2. "Cabbage Patch Campaigner Tells Secret," *The Chapel Hill Newspaper*, December 1, 1985, p. D1.

3. "PR Shouldn't Mean 'Poor Relations,' " *Industry Week*, February 3, 1992, p. 51; "Ads Convert Rejection into Free Publicity," *The Wall Street Journal*, July 30, 1990, p. B5; "Wooing Press and Public at Auto Shows," *The Wall Street Journal*, January 8, 1990, p. B1; "Free Association," *Advertising Age*, October 23, 1989, p. 36ff.; Len Kessler, "Get the Most Bang for Your PR Dollars," *Journal of Business Strategy*, May/June 1989, pp. 13–17; "PR on the Offensive," *Advertising Age*, March 13, 1989, p. 20; Thomas H. Bivins, "Ethical Implications of the Relationship of Purpose to Role and Function in Public Relations," *Journal of Business Ethics*, January 1989, pp. 65–74; E. Cameron Williams, "Product Publicity: Low Cost and High Credibility," *Industrial Marketing Management*, November 1988, pp. 355–60; "Despite Ban, Liquor Marketers Finding New Ways to Get Products on Television," *The Wall Street Journal*, March 14, 1988, p. 31.

4. "Eye-Catching Logos All Too Often Leave Fuzzy Images in Minds of Consumers," *The Wall Street Journal*, December 5, 1991, p. B1ff.; Ronald E. Dulek, John S. Fielden, and John S. Hill, "International Communication: An Executive Primer," *Business Horizons*, January/February 1991, pp. 20–25; Tony Meenaghan, "The Role of Sponsorship in the Marketing Communications Mix," *International Journal of Advertising* 10, no. 1 (1991) pp. 35–48; Martin R. Lautman and Shirley Hsieh, "Creative Tactics and the Communication of a 'Good Taste' Message," *Journal of Advertising Research*, July/August 1993, pp. 11–19; Kaylene C. Williams, Rosann L. Spiro, and Leslie M. Fine, "The Customer-Salesperson Dyad: An Interaction/Communication Model and Review," *Journal of Personal Selling and Sales Management*, Summer 1990, pp. 29–44; Susan Mitchell, "How to Talk to Young Adults," *American Demographics*, April 1993, p. 50; Susan M. Petroshius and Kenneth E. Crocker, "An Empirical Analysis of Spokesperson Characteristics on Advertisement and Product Evaluations," *Journal of the Academy of Marketing Science*, Summer 1989, pp. 217–26; David J. Moore, John C. Mowen, and Richard Reardon, "Multiple Sources in Advertising Appeals: When Product Endorsers Are Paid by the Advertising Sponsor," *Journal of the Academy of Marketing Science*, Summer 1994, pp. 234–43; Barbara B. Stern, "A Revised Communications Model for Advertising: Multiple Dimensions of the Source, the Message, and the Recipient," *Journal of Advertising*, June 1994, pp. 5–16; Richard F. Beltramini and Edwin R. Stafford, "Comprehension and Perceived Believability of Seals of Approval Information in Advertising," *Journal of Advertising*, September 1993, pp. 3–14; "High-Tech Hype Reaches New Heights," *The Wall Street Journal*, January 12, 1989, p. B1; "Car Ads Turn to High-Tech Talk—but Does Anybody Understand It?" *The Wall Street Journal*, March 7, 1988, p. 23; Jacob Jacoby and Wayne D. Hoyer, "The Comprehension/Miscomprehension of Print Communication: Selected Findings," *Journal of Consumer Research*, March 1989, pp. 434–43.

5. "Lost in Translation: How to 'Empower Women' in Chinese," *The Wall Street Journal*, September 13, 1994, p. A1ff.; "In World Cup Games, Words Get Lost and Gained in Translation," *The Wall Street Journal*, July 14, 1994, p. B1ff.; "Too Many Computer Names Confuse Too Many Buyers," *The Wall Street Journal*, June 29, 1994, p. B1ff.; "A Sassy Approach to Cosmetics," *Advertising Age*, May 23, 1994, p. 17; "Go Ask Alice," *Adweek*, January 17, 1994, p. 32; "Once Again, Ads Woo Teens with Slang," *The Wall Street Journal*, March 29, 1993, p. B1ff.; "Eastern Europe Poses Obstacles for Ads," *The Wall Street Journal*, July 30, 1992, p. B6; "A Little Bad English Goes a Long Way in Japan's Boutiques,"

The Wall Street Journal, May 20, 1992, p. A1ff.; "How Does Slogan Translate?" *Advertising Age*, October 12, 1987, p. 84.

6. "Collagen Corp.'s Video Uses News Format," *The Wall Street Journal*, March 29, 1994, p. B8; "Totally Hidden Video," *Inside PR*, August 1990, pp. 11–13; " 'News' Videos that Pitch Drugs Provoke Outcry for Regulations," *The Wall Street Journal*, February 8, 1990, p. B6; Thomas H. Bivins, "Public Relations, Professionalism, and the Public Interest," *Journal of Business Ethics*, February 1993, pp. 117–26; Siva K. Balasubramanian, "Beyond Advertising and Publicity: Hybrid Messages and Public Policy Issues," *Journal of Advertising*, December 1994, pp. 47–58.

7. "100 Happy Families Help Chevy Launch," *USA Today*, April 27, 1994, p. 1B; Rebecca Piirto, "The Influentials," *American Demographics*, October 1992, pp. 30–38; "Reaching Influential Buyers," *Inc.*, May 1991, p. 86–88; Jagdip Singh, "Voice, Exit, and Negative Word-of-Mouth Behaviors: An Investigation across Three Service Categories," *Journal of the Academy of Marketing Science*, Winter 1990, pp. 1–16; Jeffrey G. Blodgett, Donald H. Granbois, and Rockney G. Walters, "The Effects of Perceived Justice on Complainants' Negative Word-of-Mouth Behavior and Repatronage Intentions," *Journal of Retailing*, Winter 1993, pp. 399–428; Paula Fitzgerald Bone, "Word–of–Mouth Effects on Short-Term and Long-Term Product Judgments," *Journal of Business Research*, March 1995, pp. 213–24; Bruce MacEvoy, "Change Leaders and the New Media," *American Demographics*, January 1994, pp. 42–49; Jacqueline Johnson Brown and Peter H. Reingen, "Social Ties and Word-of-Mouth Referral Behavior," *Journal of Consumer Research*, December 1987, pp. 350–62; Robin A. Higie, Lawrence F. Feick, and Linda L. Price, "Types and Amount of Word-of-Mouth Communications about Retailers," *Journal of Retailing*, Fall 1987, pp. 260–78.

8. Meera P. Venkatraman, "Opinion Leaders, Adopters, and Communicative Adopters: A Role Analysis," *Psychology and Marketing*, Spring 1989, pp. 51–68; Mary Dee Dickerson and James W. Gentry, "Characteristics of Adopters and Non-Adopters of Home Computers," *Journal of Consumer Research*, September 1983, pp. 225–35; S. Ram and Hyung-Shik Jung, "Innovativeness in Product Usage: A Comparison of Early Adopters and Early Majority," *Psychology & Marketing*, January/February 1994, pp. 57–68; Robert J. Fisher and Linda L. Price, "An Investigation into the Social Context of Early Adoption Behavior," *Journal of Consumer Research*, December 1992, p. 477; Everett M. Rogers and F. Floyd Shoemaker, *Communication of Innovations: A Cross-Cultural Approach* (New York: Free Press, 1971), pp. 203–9.

9. See, for example, "Analgesics See Big Prospects from Arthritis," *Advertising Age*, August 15, 1994, p. 38; "Out of the Lab into the Screening Room," *Brandweek*, April 18, 1994, pp. 30–31; "Branding Fever Strikes among Prescription Drugs," *Advertising Age*, November 22, 1993, p. 12; "New Contraceptive Targets the Pill," *USA Today*, November 15, 1993, p. 3B; "TV Ads Boost Nestle's Infant Formula," *The Wall Street Journal*, March 30, 1993, p. B1ff.; "Drug Ads: A Prescription for Controversy," *Business Week*, January 18, 1993, pp. 58–60; "Nicotine Patch Promotion Blitz Draws Scrutiny," *The Wall Street Journal*, October 19, 1992, p. B1ff.; "Special Report: Health Marketing," *Advertising Age*, August 3, 1992, pp. 18–20; "Kellogg Shifts Strategy to Pull Consumers In," *The Wall Street Journal*, January 22, 1990, p. B1ff.; Alvin A. Achenbaum and F. Kent Mitchel, "Pulling Away from Push Marketing," *Harvard Business Review*, May–June 1987, pp. 38–42; Michael Levy, John Webster, and Roger Kerin,

"Formulating Push Marketing Strategies: A Method and Application," *Journal of Marketing*, Winter 1983, pp. 25–34.

10. "Hershey's Sweet Tooth Starts Aching," *Business Week*, February 7, 1970, pp. 98–104; "Big Chocolate Maker, Beset by Profit Slide, Gets More Aggressive," *The Wall Street Journal*, February 18, 1970, p. 1ff.

11. "Schools Learning New Ad Lessons," *Advertising Age*, February 13, 1995, p. 27; "Pay Attention, Class; Marketers Do," *Advertising Age*, February 13, 1995, p. S8; "A Lesson in Sample Arithmetic," *Advertising Age*, January 2, 1995, p. 22; "A KKR Vehicle Finds Profit and Education a Rich but Uneasy Mix," *The Wall Street Journal*, October 12, 1994, p. A1ff.; "Liked the Lesson, and Loved the Shoes," *The Wall Street Journal*, August 25, 1994, p. B1ff.; "Companies Teach All Sorts of Lessons with Educational Tools They Give Away," *The Wall Street Journal*, April 19, 1994, p. B1ff.; "Firms Learn that Subtle Aid to Schools Can Polish Their Images, Sell Products," *The Wall Street Journal*, March 25, 1991, p. B1ff.; "The Classroom as a Marketing Tool," *Insight*, September 24, 1990, pp. 40–41.

12. "Compensation and Expenses," *Sales & Marketing Management*, June 28, 1993, p. 65; "The Cost of Selling Is Going Up," *Boardroom Reports*, December 15, 1991, p. 15; "An In-House Sales School," *Inc.*, May 1991, pp. 85–86.

13. "Ryder Redraws the Self-Move Map with Service, Convenience," *Brandweek*, January 25, 1993, pp. 34–35; *1993 Annual Report*, Ryder System; *1990 Annual Report*, Ryder System; *Mover's Advantage: The Complete Home Moving Guide & Planning Kit* (Ryder System, October 1990); "At the Echo Awards, It's Not Just Junk Mail Anymore," *Adweek's Marketing Week*, October 29, 1990, pp. 20–21.

14. Albert Schofield, "Alternative Reply Vehicles in Direct-Response Advertising," *Journal of Advertising Research*, September/October 1994, pp. 28–34; "An Untapped Market of 11 Million Homes," *The Wall Street Journal*, September 7, 1994, p. B1; "For Charity Groups, 'Tis a Prime Season for Sending Lots of Direct-Mail Appeals," *The Wall Street Journal*, December 23, 1993, p. B1ff.; "Special Report: Integrated Marketing," *Advertising Age*, November 8, 1993, pp. S1–12; "Special Report: Direct Response," *Advertising Age*, July 12, 1993, pp. S1–8; "Machine Dreams," *Brandweek*, April 26, 1993, pp. 17–24; "Pizza Hut's Perkins Has No Time to Stop," *Brandweek*, January 11, 1993, pp. 20–21; "The Spanish Mails," *Adweek's Marketing Week*, June 22, 1992, pp. 28–29; "The Mail Train," *Adweek's Marketing Week*, May 25, 1992, p. 18; "Now, They're Selling BMWs Door-to-Door—Almost," *Business Week*, May 14, 1990, p. 65; Keith Fletcher, Colin Wheeler, and Julia Wright, "Database Marketing: a Channel, a Medium or a Strategic Approach?" *International Journal of Advertising* 10, no. 2 (1991), pp. 117–28; "Devising Mailing Lists for Every Marketer," *The Wall Street Journal*, May 7, 1991, p. B1; "Warner Tries Target Marketing to Sell Film Lacking Typical Box-Office Appeal," *The Wall Street Journal*, October 3, 1990, p. B1ff.; "Direct Marketing Agency Report," *Advertising Age*, May 21, 1990, pp. S1–10; "Direct Marketing: A Modern Marketing Solution," *Directions* (New York: Direct Marketing Association, 1990); "Special Report: Direct Marketing," *Advertising Age*, September 25, 1990, pp. S1–16; Robert L. Sherman, *Mailing Lists, Information and Privacy* (New York: Prepared for DMA, June 1989); Lindsay Meredith, "Developing and Using a Data Base Marketing System," *Industrial*

Marketing Management 18, no. 4 (1989), pp. 245–58; Rachel Kaplan, "Video on Demand," *American Demographics*, June 1992, pp. 38–45; Gordon Storholm and Hershey Friedman, "Perceived Common Myths and Unethical Practices among Direct Marketing Professionals," *Journal of Business Ethics*, December 1989, pp. 975–80; Steven Miller, "Mine the Direct Marketing Riches in Your Database," *Journal of Business Strategy*, November/December 1989, pp. 33–36; Bob Stone and John Wyman, *Successful Telemarketing* (Lincolnshire, IL: NTC Books, 1986). For more on the privacy issue, see George R. Milne and Mary Ellen Gordon, "Direct Mail Privacy-Efficiency Trade-Offs within an Implied Social Contract Framework," *Journal of Public Policy & Marketing*, Fall 1993, pp. 206–15; "Canadian Privacy Code Shows U.S. the Way," *American Demographics*, September 1993, p. 15; "FTC Takes Aim at Trans Union, TRW Mail Lists," *The Wall Street Journal*, January 13, 1993, p. B1ff.; "As Phone Technology Swiftly Advances, Fears Grow They'll Have Your Number," *The Wall Street Journal*, December 13, 1991, p. B1ff.

15. Kusum L. Ailawadi, Paul W. Farris, and Mark E. Parry, "Share and Growth Are Not Good Predictors of the Advertising and Promotion/Sales Ratio," *Journal of Marketing*, January 1994, pp. 86–97.

16. C. L. Hung and Douglas West, "Advertising Budgeting Methods in Canada, the UK, and the USA," *International Journal of Advertising* 10, no. 3 (1991), pp. 239–50; Pierre Filiatrault and Jean-Charles Chebat, "How Service Firms Set Their Marketing Budgets," *Industrial Marketing Management*, February 1990, pp. 63–68; James E. Lynch and Graham J. Hooley, "Industrial Advertising Budget Approaches in the U.K.," *Industrial Marketing Management* 18, no. 4 (1989), pp. 265–70; "Beat the Budgeting Blues," *Business Marketing*, July 1989, pp. 48–57; Kim P. Corfman and Donald R. Lehmann, "The Prisoner's Dilemma and the Role of Information in Setting Advertising Budgets," *Journal of Advertising*, June 1994, pp. 35–48; Vincent J. Blasko and Charles H. Patti, "The Advertising Budgeting Practices of Industrial Marketers," *Journal of Marketing*, Fall 1984, pp. 104–10; Douglas J. Dalrymple and Hans B. Thorelli, "Sales Force Budgeting," *Business Horizons*, July/August 1984, pp. 31–36; Don Y. Lee, "The Impact of Firms' Risk-Taking Attitudes on Advertising Budgets," *Journal of Business Research*, October–November 1994, pp. 247–56; Peter J. Danaher and Roland T. Rust, "Determining the Optimal Level of Media Spending," *Journal of Advertising Research*, January/February 1994, pp. 28–34.

Chapter 15

1. *1993 Annual Report*, Alcoa; *1993 Annual Report*, Boeing; "A New Way to Wake Up a Giant," *Fortune*, October 22, 1990, pp. 90–103; "Alcoa Tries to Tap Entrepreneurial Spirit," *The Wall Street Journal*, August 1, 1990, p. B2; "O'Neill Recasts Alcoa with His Eyes Fixed on a Decade Ahead," *The Wall Street Journal*, April 9, 1990, p. A1ff.

2. "The Seoul Answer to Selling," *Going Global* (supplement to *Inc.*), March 1994; "AIG Sells Insurance in Shanghai, Testing Service Firms' Role," *The Wall Street Journal*, July 21, 1993, p. A1ff.; "Hungarians Seeking to Find a New Way Find Instead Amway," *The Wall Street Journal*, January 15, 1993, p. A1ff.; "The Secret to Northern's Japanese Success: When in Tokyo . . . ," *Business Week*, July 27, 1992, p. 57; "U.S. Companies in China Find Patience, Persistence and Salesmanship Pay Off," *The Wall Street Journal*, April 3, 1992, p. B1ff.; Paul A. Herbig and Hugh E. Kramer, "Do's and Don'ts of Cross-Cultural Negotiations," *Industrial Marketing Management*, November 1992, pp. 287–98; Alan J. Dubinsky et al., "Differences in Motivational Perceptions among U.S., Japanese, and Korean Sales Personnel," *Journal of Business Research*, June 1994, pp. 175–86; Carl R. Ruthstrom and Ken Matejka, "The Meanings of 'YES' in the Far East," *Industrial Marketing Management*, August 1990, pp. 191–92; John S. Hill and Richard R. Still, "Organizing the Overseas Sales Force—How Multinationals Do It," *Journal of Personal Selling and Sales Management*, Spring 1990, pp. 57–66.

3. Tom Richman, "Seducing the Customer: Dale Ballard's Perfect Selling Machine," *Inc.*, April 1988, pp. 96–104; *1987 Annual Report*, Ballard Medical Products.

4. Thomas R. Wotruba, "The Evolution of Personal Selling," *Journal of Personal Selling and Sales Management*, Summer 1991, pp. 1–12; Douglas M. Lambert, Howard Marmorstein, and Arun Sharma, "Industrial Salespeople as a Source of Market Information," *Industrial Marketing Management*, May 1990, pp. 141–48; Michael J. Morden, "The Salesperson: Clerk, Con Man or Professional?" *Business and Professional Ethics Journal* 8, no. 1 (1989), pp. 3–24; George J. Avlonitis, Kevin A. Boyle, and Athanasios G. Kouremenos, "Matching the Salesmen to the Selling Job," *Industrial Marketing Management*, February 1986, pp. 45–54; Kenneth R. Evans and John L. Schlacter, "The Role of Sales Managers and Salespeople in a Marketing Information System," *Journal of Personal Selling and Sales Management*, November 1985, pp. 49–58; Patrick L. Schul and Brent M. Wren, "The Emerging Role of Women in Industrial Selling: A Decade of Change," *Journal of Marketing*, July 1992, pp. 38–54.

5. "Pushing Doctors to Buy High Tech for the Office," *Business Week*, September 2, 1985, pp. 84–85.

6. "NationsBank Asks Tellers to Branch Out," *The Raleigh News & Observer*, September 12, 1993, p. 1Fff.

7. S. Joe Puri and Pradeep Korgaonkar, "Couple the Buying and Selling Teams," *Industrial Marketing Management* 20, no. 4 (1991), pp. 311–18; "P&G Rolls Out Retailer Sales Teams," *Advertising Age*, May 21, 1990, p. 18; Frank C. Cespedes, Stephen X. Doyle, and Robert J. Freedman, "Teamwork for Today's Selling," *Harvard Business Review*, March–April 1989, pp. 44–59; Mark A. Moon and Gary M. Armstrong, "Selling Teams: A Conceptual Framework and Research Agenda," *Journal of Personal Selling & Sales Management*, Winter 1994, pp. 17–30.

8. John Barrett, "Why Major Account Selling Works," *Industrial Marketing Management*, February 1986, pp. 63–74; Catherine Pardo, Robert Salle, and Robert Spencer, "The Key Accountization of the Firm: A Case Study," *Industrial Marketing Management*, March 1995, pp. 123–34; Thomas R. Wotruba and Stephen B. Castleberry, "Job Analysis and Hiring Practices for National Account Marketing Positions," *Journal of Personal Selling & Sales Management*, Summer 1993, pp. 49–66; Michael J. Swenson and Adilson Parrella, "Sales Technology Applications: Cellular Telephones and the National Sales Force," *Journal of Personal Selling & Sales Management*, Fall 1992, pp. 67–74; Jerome A. Colletti and Gary S. Tubridy, "Effective Major Account Sales Management," *Journal of Personal Selling and Sales Management*, August 1987, pp. 1–10.

9. "Telephone Sales Reps Do Unrewarding Jobs that Few Can Abide," *The Wall Street Journal*, September 9, 1993, p. A1ff.;

"FCC Adopts Rules to Curb Telemarketing," *The Wall Street Journal*, September 18, 1992, p. B1; "Congress' 'Cure' for Junk Calls Faces a Skeptical FCC," *The Wall Street Journal*, May 19, 1992, p. B6; "Telemarketers Take Root in the Country," *The Wall Street Journal*, February 2, 1989, p. B1.

10. "How to Remake Your Sales Force," *Fortune*, May 4, 1992, pp. 98–103; "What Flexible Workers Can Do," *Fortune*, February 13, 1989, pp. 62–64; "Apparel Makers Play Bigger Part on Sales Floor," *The Wall Street Journal*, March 2, 1988, p. 31; David W. Cravens and Raymond W. LaForge, "Salesforce Deployment Analysis," *Industrial Marketing Management*, July 1983, pp. 179–92; Michael S. Herschel, "Effective Sales Territory Development," *Journal of Marketing*, April 1977, pp. 39–43.

11. "Smart Selling: How Companies Are Winning Over the Tougher Customer," *Business Week*, August 3, 1992, pp. 46–52; "Systematizing Salesperson Selection," *Sales and Marketing Management*, February 1992, pp. 65–68; "The Faxable International Sales-Rep Application," *Inc.*, November 1993, pp. 95–97; "The Art of Selling," *Inc.*, June 1993, pp. 72–80; Earl D. Honeycutt, Jr., John B. Ford, and John F. Tanner, Jr., "Who Trains Salespeople? The Role of Sales Trainers and Sales Managers," *Industrial Marketing Management*, February 1994, pp. 65–70; Earl D. Honeycutt, Jr., Tom McCarty, and Vince Howe, "Self-Paced Video Enhanced Training: A Case Study," *Journal of Personal Selling & Sales Management*, Winter 1993, pp. 73–80; Robert C. Eriffmeyer, K. Randall Russ, and Joseph F. Hair, Jr., "Traditional and High-Tech Sales Training Methods," *Industrial Marketing Management*, May 1992, pp. 125–32; Stephen X. Doyle and George Thomas Roth, "The Use of Insight Coaching to Improve Relationship Selling," *Journal of Personal Selling & Sales Management*, Winter 1992, pp. 59–64; Warren S. Martin and Ben H. Collins, "Interactive Video Technology in Sales Training: A Case Study," *Journal of Personal Selling and Sales Management*, Summer 1991, pp. 61–66; Jeffrey K. Sager, "Recruiting and Retaining Committed Salespeople," *Industrial Marketing Management* 20, no. 2 (1991), pp. 99–104; S. Joe Puri, "Where Industrial Sales Training Is Weak," *Industrial Marketing Management*, May 1993, pp. 101–8; Earl B. Honeycutt, Jr., Vince Howe, and Thomas N. Ingram, "Shortcomings of Sales Training Programs," *Industrial Marketing Management*, May 1993, pp. 117–24; Donald B. Guest and Havva J. Meric, "The Fortune 500 Companies Selection Criteria for Promotion to First Level Sales Management: An Empirical Study," *Journal of Personal Selling and Sales Management*, Fall 1989, pp. 47–58; Robert H. Collins, "Sales Training: A Microcomputer-Based Approach," *Journal of Personal Selling and Sales Management*, May 1986, p. 71; Wesley J. Johnston and Martha Cooper, "Analyzing the Industrial Salesforce Selection Process," *Industrial Marketing Management*, April 1981, pp. 139–47.

12. Bradley S. O'Hara, James S. Boles, and Mark W. Johnston, "The Influence of Personal Variables on Salesperson Selling Orientation," *Journal of Personal Selling and Sales Management*, Winter 1991, pp. 61–68; "Fire Up Your Sales Force," *Business Marketing*, July 1990, pp. 52–55; Richard F. Beltramini and Kenneth R. Evans, "Salesperson Motivation to Perform and Job Satisfaction: A Sales Contest Participant Perspective," *Journal of Personal Selling and Sales Management*, August 1988, pp. 35–42; William L. Cron, Alan J. Dubinsky, and Ronald E. Michaels, "The Influence of Career Stages on Components of Salesperson Motivation," *Journal of Marketing*, January 1988, pp. 78–92.

13. "Incentive Pay Isn't Good for Your Company," *Inc.*, September 1994, pp. 23–24; "The Few, the True, the Blue," *Business Week*, May 30, 1994, pp. 124–26; "How to Unite Field and Phone Sales," *Inc.*, July 1992, p. 115; Russell Abratt and Michael R. Smythe, "A Survey of Sales Incentive Programs," *Industrial Marketing Management*, August 1989, pp. 209–14; Thomas R. Wotruba, "The Effect of Goal-Setting on the Performance of Independent Sales Agents in Direct Selling," *Journal of Personal Selling and Sales Management*, Spring 1989, pp. 22–29; William Strahle and Rosann L. Spiro, "Linking Market Share Strategies to Salesforce Objectives, Activities, and Compensation Policies," *Journal of Personal Selling and Sales Management*, August 1986, pp. 11–18.

14. "Companies Sold on the Latest Technology for the Sales Force," *Chicago Tribune*, November 8, 1992, sec. 19, p. 5; "New Software Is Helping Reps Fill Custom Orders without Glitches," *The Wall Street Journal*, August 11, 1992, p. B6; "Salespeople on Road Use Laptops to Keep in Touch," *The Wall Street Journal*, April 25, 1991, p. B1; "If Only Willy Loman Had Used a Laptop," *Business Week*, October 12, 1987, p. 137.

15. David J. Good and Robert W. Stone, "How Sales Quotas Are Developed," *Industrial Marketing Management* 20, no. 1 (1991), pp. 51–56; James W. Gentry, John C. Mowen, and Lori Tasaki, "Salesperson Evaluation: A Systematic Structure for Reducing Judgmental Biases," *Journal of Personal Selling and Sales Management*, Spring 1991, pp. 27–38; William A. Weeks and Lynn R. Kahle, "Salespeople's Time Use and Performance," *Journal of Personal Selling and Sales Management*, Winter 1990, pp. 29–38; Jhinuk Chowdhury, "The Motivational Impact of Sales Quotas on Effort," *Journal of Marketing Research*, February 1993, pp. 28–41; Alan J. Dubinsky, Francis J. Yammarino, and Marvin A. Jolson, "Closeness of Supervision and Salesperson Work Outcomes: An Alternate Perspective," *Journal of Business Research*, March 1994, pp. 225–38; Jeffrey M. Ferguson, Lexis R. Higgins, and Gary R. Phillips, "How to Evaluate and Up-Grade Technical Service," *Industrial Marketing Management*, August 1993, pp. 187–94; David W. Cravens et al., "Behavior-Based and Outcome-Based Salesforce Control Systems," *Journal of Marketing*, October 1993, pp. 47–59; Daniel A. Sauers, James B. Hunt, and Ken Bass, "Behavioral Self-Management as a Supplement to External Sales Force Controls," *Journal of Personal Selling and Sales Management*, Summer 1990, pp. 17–28; Douglas N. Behrman and William D. Perreault, Jr., "A Role Stress Model of the Performance and Satisfaction of Industrial Salespersons," *Journal of Marketing*, Fall 1984, pp. 9–21; Richard T. Hise and Edward L. Reid, "Improving the Performance of the Industrial Sales Force in the 1990s," *Industrial Marketing Management*, October 1994, pp. 273–80; Douglas N. Behrman and William D. Perreault, Jr., "Measuring the Performance of Industrial Salespersons," *Journal of Business Research*, September 1982, pp. 350–70.

16. "Chief Executives Are Increasingly Chief Salesmen," *The Wall Street Journal*, August 6, 1991, p. B1ff.; Joe F. Alexander, Patrick L. Schul, and Emin Babakus, "Analyzing Interpersonal Communications in Industrial Marketing Negotiations," *Journal of the Academy of Marketing Science*, Spring 1991, pp. 129–40.

17. William C. Moncrief et al., "Examining the Roles of Telemarketing in Selling Strategy," *Journal of Personal Selling and Sales Management*, Fall 1989, pp. 1–12; J. David Lichtenthal, Saameer Sikri, and Karl Folk, "Teleprospecting: An Approach for Qualifying Accounts," *Industrial Marketing Management*, February

1989, pp. 11–18; Judith J. Marshall and Harrie Vrendenburg, "Successfully Using Telemarketing in Industrial Sales," *Industrial Marketing Management*, February 1988, pp. 15–22; Eugene M. Johnson and William J. Meiners, "Telemarketing—Trends, Issues, and Opportunities," *Journal of Personal Selling and Sales Management*, November 1987, pp. 65–68.

18. "The New Wave of Sales Automation," *Business Marketing*, June 1991, pp. 12–16; L. Brent Manssen, "Using PCs to Automate and Innovate Marketing Activities," *Industrial Marketing Management*, August 1990, pp. 209–14; Doris C. Van Doren and Thomas A. Stickney, "How to Develop a Database for Sales Leads," *Industrial Marketing Management*, August 1990, pp. 201–8; Al Wedell and Dale Hempeck, "Sales Force Automation: Here and Now," *Journal of Personal Selling and Sales Management*, August 1987, pp. 11–16.

19. For more on sales presentation approaches, see "The 60-Second Sales Pitch," *Inc.*, October 1994, pp. 87–89; L. E. Dawson, Jr., B. Soper, and C. E. Pettijohn, "The Effects of Empathy on Salesperson Effectiveness," *Psychology & Marketing*, July/August 1992, pp. 297–310; Stephen B. Castleberry and C. David Shepherd, "Effective Interpersonal Listening and Personal Selling," *Journal of Personal Selling & Sales Management*, Winter 1993, pp. 35–50; Ray A. DeCormier and David Jobber, "The Counselor Selling Method: Concepts and Constructs," *Journal of Personal Selling & Sales Management*, Fall 1993, pp. 39–60; Morgan P. Miles, Danny R. Arnold, and Henry W. Nash, "Adaptive Communication: The Adaption of the Seller's Interpersonal Style to the Stage of the Dyad's Relationship and the Buyer's Communication Style," *Journal of Personal Selling and Sales Management*, Winter 1990, pp. 21–28; Harish Sujan, Barton A. Weitz, and Nirmalya Kumar, "Learning Orientation, Working Smart, and Effective Selling," *Journal of Marketing*, July 1994, pp. 39–52; Marvin A. Jolson, "Canned Adaptiveness: A New Direction for Modern Salesmanship," *Business Horizons*, January/February 1989, pp. 7–12.

20. For more on pharmaceutical company selling tactics, see "In Marketing of Drugs, Genentech Tests Limits of What Is Acceptable," *The Wall Street Journal*, January 10, 1995, p. A1ff.; "Owing Medco, Merck Takes Drug Marketing the Next Logical Step," *The Wall Street Journal*, May 31, 1994, p. A1ff.; "Pharmacy Chain's Successful Sales Pitch Dismays Some Doctors and Drug Firms," *The Wall Street Journal*, February 26, 1993, p. B1ff. For more on Sears' selling tactics, see "Sears Reinstates Sales Incentives in Some Centers," *The Wall Street Journal*, March 7, 1994, p. B1ff.; "Did Sears Take Other Customers for a Ride?" *Business Week*, August 3, 1992, pp. 24–25; "An Open Letter to Sears Customers," *USA Today*, June 25, 1992, p. 8A; "Sears Is Accused of Billing Fraud at Auto Centers," *The Wall Street Journal*, June 12, 1992, p. B1ff. See also James B. Deconinck, "How Sales Managers Control Unethical Sales Force Behavior," *Journal of Business Ethics*, October 1992, pp. 789–98; Ralph W. Clark and Alice Darnell Lattal, "The Ethics of Sales: Finding an Appropriate Balance," *Business Horizons*, July–August 1993, pp. 66–69; Kenneth C. Schneider and James C. Johnson, "Professionalism and Ethical Standards among Salespeople in a Deregulated Environment: A Case Study of the Trucking Industry," *Journal of Personal Selling & Sales Management*, Winter 1992, pp. 33–44; Alan J. Dubinsky, Marvin A. Jolson, Masaaki Kotabe, and Chae Un Lim, "A Cross-National Investigation of Industrial Salespeople's Ethical Perceptions," *Journal of*

International Business Studies, Winter 1991, pp. 651–70; Anusorn Singhapakdi and Scott J. Vitell, "Analyzing the Ethical Decision Making of Sales Professionals," *Journal of Personal Selling and Sales Management*, Fall 1991, pp. 1–12.

Chapter 16

1. "Grey Poupon Tones Down Tony Image," *The Wall Street Journal*, July 22, 1994, p. B2; "Grey Poupon," *Brandweek*, May 9, 1994, p. 8.

2. "Colgate-Palmolive Is Really Cleaning Up in Poland," *Business Week*, March 15, 1993, pp. 54–56; John L. Graham, Michael A. Kamins, and Djoko S. Oetomo, "Content Analysis of German and Japanese Advertising in Print Media from Indonesia, Spain, and the United States," *Journal of Advertising*, June 1993, pp. 5–16; Bob D. Cutler and Rajshekhar G. Javalgi, "A Cross-Cultural Analysis of the Visual Components of Print Advertising: The United States and the European Community," *Journal of Advertising Research*, January/February 1992, p. 71; Abhijit Biswas, Janeen E. Olsen, and Valerie Carlet, "A Comparison of Print Advertisements from the United States and France," *Journal of Advertising*, December 1992, pp. 73–82; Terence Nevett, "Differences between American and British Television Advertising: Explanations and Implications," *Journal of Advertising*, December 1992, pp. 61–72; Bob D. Cutler and Rajshekhar G. Javalgi, "Comparison of Business-to-Business Advertising: The United States and the United Kingdom," *Industrial Marketing Management*, April 1994, pp. 117–24; Fred Zandpour, Cypress Chang, and Joelle Catalano, "Stories, Symbols, and Straight Talk: A Comparative Analysis of French, Taiwanese, and U.S. TV Commercials," *Journal of Advertising Research*, January/February 1992, pp. 25–38; "Eastern Europe Poses Obstacles for Ads," *The Wall Street Journal*, July 30, 1992, p. B6.

3. "Upbeat Forecasts Keep on Rolling In," *Advertising Age*, December 12, 1994, p. 3; "Overview," *Media Outlook*, September 19, 1994, pp. 4–46; "International Special Report: Top Global Markets," *Advertising Age International*, March 21, 1994, pp. I11–20; Lee D. Dahringer and Hans Muhlbacher, *International Marketing: A Global Perspective* (Reading, MA: Addison-Wesley, 1991), p. 481.

4. "1994 Advertising to Sales Ratios for the 200 Largest Ad Spending Industries," *Advertising Age*, August 8, 1994, p. 38; Kip D. Cassino, "An Advertising Atlas," *American Demographics*, August 1994, pp. 44–55.

5. "Ad Gain of 5.2% in '93 Marks Downturn's End," *Advertising Age*, May 2, 1994, p. 4; "TV Is Advertisers' Big Pick in Europe," *Advertising Age International*, June 21, 1993, p. I19.

6. Exact data on this industry are elusive, but see U.S. Bureau of the Census, *Statistical Abstract of the United States 1994* (Washington, DC: U.S. Government Printing Office, 1994), p. 407; "Number of Jobs in Advertising Declines 3.7%," *The Wall Street Journal*, August 5, 1991, p. B1ff.; "A Blizzard of Pink Slips Chills Adland," *Business Week*, December 10, 1990, pp. 210–12.

7. For more on AT&T, MCI, and Sprint's comparative ads, see "Fighting for Customers Gets Louder," *USA Today*, January 9, 1995, p. 1Bff.; "Discount War Can Be Confusing," *USA Today*, September 23, 1994, p. 1Bff.; "All Those Long-Distance Discounts Are Sweet, but . . . ," *Business Week*, September 19, 1994, pp. 66–67; "Only a Matter of Trust," *Brandweek*, July 25, 1994, pp. 46–48; "The Race Is On," *Brandweek*, May 9, 1994, pp. 223–27; *1993 Annual Report*, MCI, pp. 12–13; "AT&T Tweaks MCI's 'Friends,'" *Advertising Age*, March 2, 1992, p. 4. For other examples of comparative advertising, see "New Ammo for Comparative Ads," *Advertising Age*, February 14, 1994, p. 26; "Comparative Advertising Often Effective," *USA Today*, February 7, 1994, p. 6B; "American Express Opens a Volley on Visa," *The Wall Street Journal*, September 13, 1993, p. B3; "PC Marketers Punch Up Combative Ads," *The Wall Street Journal*, October 21, 1992, p. B1ff.; "Chemical Firms Press Campaigns to Dispel Their 'Bad Guy' Image," *The Wall Street Journal*, September 20, 1988, p. 1ff.; "Spiffing Up the Corporate Image," *Fortune*, July 21, 1986, pp. 68–72.

8. Thomas E. Barry, "Comparative Advertising: What Have We Learned in Two Decades?" *Journal of Advertising Research*, March/April 1993, pp. 19–29; "Prescription Drug Ads Stir New Wave of Court Battles," *The Wall Street Journal*, October 4, 1994, p. B10; "Agencies Feel More Heat on Comparative Claims," *Advertising Age*, August 31, 1992, p. 39; Naveen Donthu, "Comparative Advertising Intensity," *Journal of Advertising Research*, November/December 1992, pp. 53–58; "Comparative TV Ad Reviews Criticized," *The Wall Street Journal*, October 23, 1990, p. B6; William T. Neese and Ronald D. Taylor, "Verbal Strategies for Indirect Comparative Advertising," *Journal of Advertising Research*, March/April 1994, pp. 56–69; Sanjay Putrevu and Kenneth R. Lord, "Comparative and Noncomparative Advertising: Attitudinal Effects under Cognitive and Affective Involvement Conditions," *Journal of Advertising*, June 1994, p. 77; Dhruv Grewal and Larry D. Compeau, "Comparative Price Advertising: Informative or Deceptive?" *Journal of Public Policy & Marketing*, Spring 1992, pp. 52–62.

9. "Cause-Driven Companies' New Cause: Profits," *The Wall Street Journal*, November 8, 1994, p. B1; "Advertisers Try 'Doing Good' to Help Make Sales Do Better," *The Wall Street Journal*, September 2, 1994, p. B8; "Are Good Causes Good Marketing?" *Business Week*, March 21, 1994, pp. 64–66; "Critics See Self-Interest in Lilly's Funding of Ads Telling the Depressed to Get Help," *The Wall Street Journal*, April 15, 1993, p. B1ff.; John K. Ross III, Larry T. Patterson, and Mary Ann Stutts, "Consumer Perceptions of Organizations that Use Cause-Related Marketing," *Journal of the Academy of Marketing Science*, Winter 1992, pp. 93–98.

10. "Store Owners Rip into Benetton," *Advertising Age*, February 6, 1995, p. 1; "Benetton, German Retailers Squabble," *Advertising Age*, February 6, 1995, p. 46; "Benetton Brouhaha," *Advertising Age*, February 17, 1992, p. 62.

11. For more on co-op ads, see "Retailers Open Doors Wide for Co-Op," *Advertising Age*, August 1, 1994, p. 30; "Hard Times Mean Growth for Co-Op Ads," *Advertising Age*, November 12, 1990, p. 24; "Ad Agencies Press Franchisees to Join National Campaigns," *The Wall Street Journal*, January 17, 1985, p. 29. For more on joint promotions, see "Ford, Blockbuster Are Riding Together in Windstar Promo," *Advertising Age*, April 11, 1994, p. 1ff.; "Joint Promotions Spawn Data Swap," *Advertising Age*, October 7, 1991, p. 44; "H&R Block, Excedrin Discover Joint Promotions Can Be Painless," *The Wall Street Journal*, February 28, 1991, p. B3.

12. *Standard Rate and Data*, July and September 1994. For more on the Yellow Pages medium, see "'Sleeping Giant,' the Yellow Pages, Tries to Waken Madison Avenue," *The Wall Street Journal*, August 19, 1993, p. B6; "An Old Industry Finally Grows Up,"

Adweek, August 10, 1992, pp. 30–36. For more on videotapes medium, see "Direct Marketers Press Fast-Forward on Videotape Use," *The Wall Street Journal*, October 31, 1994, p. B8B; "Buick Goes Golfing with Car Shoppers," *Advertising Age*, December 6, 1993, p. 18. For more on the outdoor medium, see Charles R. Taylor and John C. Taylor, "Regulatory Issues in Outdoor Advertising: A Content Analysis of Billboards," *Journal of Public Policy & Marketing*, Spring 1994, pp. 97–107; "More Firms Turn to Skies as New Medium," *The Wall Street Journal*, January 6, 1995, p. B6; "Special Report: Out-of-Home," *Advertising Age*, August 1, 1994, pp. 27–30; "Billboards Gain Respect as Spending Rises," *The Wall Street Journal*, June 27, 1994, p. B8. For more on the radio medium, see Rebecca Piirto, "Why Radio Thrives," *American Demographics*, May 1994, pp. 40–47; Darryl W. Miller and Lawrence J. Marks, "Mental Imagery and Sound Effects in Radio Commercials," *Journal of Advertising*, December 1992, pp. 83–94; "Motel 6 Wins with Network Radio," *Advertising Age*, September 6, 1993, p. R6; "Special Report: Radio," *Advertising Age*, September 14, 1992, pp. 41–43. For more on the newspaper medium, see Lawrence C. Soley and Robert L. Craig, "Advertising Pressures on Newspapers: A Survey," *Journal of Advertising*, December 1992, pp. 1–10; "Newspapers Raise Prices, Pare Staff," *USA Today*, December 5, 1994, p. 1Bff.; "Special Report: Newspapers," *Advertising Age*, April 25, 1994, pp. 35–41; Srini S. Srinivasan, Robert P. Leone, and Francis J. Mulhern, "The Advertising Exposure Effect of Free Standing Inserts," *Journal of Advertising*, Spring 1995, pp. 29–40; "Bound to the Printed Word," *Newsweek*, June 20, 1994, pp. 52–53; "Special Report: Newspapers," *Advertising Age*, October 5, 1992, pp. S1–10. See also Dean M. Krugman and Roland T. Rust, "The Impact of Cable and VCR Penetration on Network Viewing: Assessing the Decade," *Journal of Advertising Research*, January/February 1993, pp. 67–73; Glen J. Nowak, Glen T. Cameron, and Dean M, Krugman, "How Local Advertisers Choose and Use Advertising Media," *Journal of Advertising Research*, November/December 1993, pp. 39–49; "What's Right, What's Wrong with Each Medium," *Business Marketing*, April 1990, pp. 40–47.

13. "Sexy Sony Ad Riles a Network of Women," *The Wall Street Journal*, August 23, 1993, p. B5; "Klein Jeans' Sexy Insert Didn't Spur Sales," *The Wall Street Journal*, May 5, 1992, p. B1ff.; "No Sexy Sales Ads, Please—We're Brits and Swedes," *Fortune*, October 21, 1991, p. 13; "Why Jockey Switched Its Ads from TV to Print," *Business Week*, July 25, 1976, pp. 140–42.

14. "Looking for Mr. Plumber," *MediaWeek*, June 27, 1994, p. 7ff.; "Those Really Big Shows Are Often Disappointing to Those Who Advertise," *The Wall Street Journal*, June 14, 1994, p. B1ff.

15. "The Writing on the Bathroom Wall," *Business Week*, October 31, 1994, p. 8; "Technology Has Travelers under Siege," *USA Today*, October 14, 1994, p. 1Bff.; Alan J. Greco and Linda E. Swayne, "Sales Response of Elderly Consumers to Point-of-Purchase Advertising," *Journal of Advertising Research*, September/October 1992, pp. 43–53; "In-Floor Ads Open Door to Higher Sales," *Advertising Age*, June 27, 1994, p. 53; "Wilma! What Happened to the Plain Old Ad?" *Business Week*, June 6, 1994, pp. 54–58; "Big Brother Is Grocery Shopping with You," *Business Week*, March 29, 1993, p. 60; "Sony's Ad Boldly Goes Where No Ad Has Gone Before," *The Wall Street Journal*, March 3, 1993, p. B1ff.; "'Infomercials' Fill Up Air Time on Cable, Aim for Prime Time," *The Wall Street Journal*, October 22, 1992, p. A1ff.; "Where Should Advertising Be?" *Adweek's Marketing*

Week, May 6, 1991, pp. 26–27; "In-Store Ads Are Getting Harder to Ignore," *The Wall Street Journal*, October 16, 1990, p. B6.

16. "Some Sponsors Pass In-Game Ads," *Advertising Age*, January 23, 1995, p. 8; "Madison Avenue Rates the Ads of '94," *USA Today*, December 29, 1994, p. 1Bff.; "ABC Wins Record Prices for Super Bowl," *The Wall Street Journal*, November 2, 1994, p. B6; "Study Shows Costs of TV Spots," *Advertising Age*, August 1, 1994, p. 32; "Cost to Make TV Ad Nears Quarter-Million," *Advertising Age*, July 4, 1994, p. 3ff.; Darrel D. Muehling and Carl S. Bozman, "An Examination of Factors Influencing Effectiveness of 15-Second Advertisements," *International Journal of Advertising* 9, no. 4 (1990), pp. 331–44.

17. "Purists Beware: Ads Have Invaded On-Line Services," *The Wall Street Journal*, August 23, 1994, p. B1ff.; "Advertisers Anticipate Interactive Media as Ingenious Means to Court Consumers," *The Wall Street Journal*, August 17, 1994, p. B1ff.; "Battle for the Soul of the Internet," *Time*, July 25, 1994, pp. 50–56; "The Interactive Future," *The Wall Street Journal*, May 18, 1994, p. B1ff.; "New Online ADs Scream for Miss Manners," *The Wall Street Journal*, April 12, 1994, p. B9.

18. "Celebrity Endorsements: Women Take the Lead," *USA Today*, October 20, 1994, p. 1Cff.; D. A. Aaker and D. M. Stayman, "Implementing the Concept of Transformational Advertising," *Psychology & Marketing*, May/June 1992, pp. 237–54; Kenneth R. Lord and Robert E. Burnkrant, "Attention versus Distraction: The Interactive Effect of Program Involvement and Attentional Devices on Commercial Processing," *Journal of Advertising*, March 1993, pp. 47–60; Martha Rogers and Kirk H. Smith, "Public Perceptions of Subliminal Advertising: Why Practitioners Shouldn't Ignore This Issue," *Journal of Advertising Research*, March/April 1993, pp. 10–18; Kathryn T. Theus, "Subliminal Advertising and the Psychology of Processing Unconscious Stimuli: A Review of Research," *Psychology & Marketing*, May/June 1994, pp. 271–90; Marc G. Weinberger and Charles S. Gulas, "The Impact of Humor in Advertising," *Journal of Advertising*, December 1992, pp. 35–60; Carolyn A. Lin, "Cultural Differences in Message Strategies: A Comparison between American and Japanese TV Commercials," *Journal of Advertising Research*, July/August 1993, pp. 40–49; Robert Chamblee and Dennis M. Sandler, "Business-to-Business Advertising; Which Layout Style Works Best?" *Journal of Advertising Research*, November/December 1992, pp. 39–46; "Business-to-Business Pitches Lack Pizazz," *The Wall Street Journal*, October 1, 1993, p. B5; "Repetitive Ads Keep Viewer Recall Going," *The Wall Street Journal*, April 7, 1993, p. B5; Prema Nakra, "Zapping Nonsense: Should Television Media Planners Lose Sleep Over It?" *International Journal of Advertising* 10, no. 3 (1991), pp. 217–22; Gary L. Clark, Peter F. Kaminski, and Gene Brown, "The Readability of Advertisements and Articles in Trade Journals," *Industrial Marketing Management*, August 1990, pp. 251–60.

19. "Smooth Talk Wins Gillette Ad Space in Iran," *Advertising Age International*, April 27, 1992, p. I-40; Courtland L. Bovee and William F. Arens, *Contemporary Advertising* (Burr Ridge, IL: Richard D. Irwin, 1992), pp. 671–72; Joshua Levine, "Global Lather," *Forbes*, February 5, 1990, pp. 146, 148; Alison Fahey, "International Ad Effort to Back Gillette Sensor," *Advertising Age*, October 16, 1989, p. 34; "Multinationals Tread Softly while Advertising in Iran," *Advertising Age International*, November 8, 1993, p. I21.

20. "Microsoft Global Image Campaign Is Dizzying without a Hard Sell," *The Wall Street Journal*, November 11, 1994, p. B7; Fred Zandpour et al., "Global Reach and Local Touch: Achieving Cultural Fitness in TV Advertising," *Journal of Advertising Research*, September/October 1994, pp. 35–63; Michael G. Harvey, "A Model to Determine Standardization of the Advertising Process in International Markets," *Journal of Advertising Research*, July/August 1993, pp. 57–64; Barbara Mueller, "Standardization vs. Specialization: An Examination of Westernization in Japanese Advertising," *Journal of Advertising Research*, January/February 1992, pp. 15–24; Dana L. Alden, Wayne D. Hoyer, and Chol Lee, "Identifying Global and Culture-Specific Dimensions of Humor in Advertising: A Multinational Analysis," *Journal of Marketing*, April 1993, pp. 64–75; "International Special Report: Global Media," *Advertising Age International*, July 18, 1994, p. I11–16; Ali Kanso, "International Advertising Strategies: Global Commitment to Local Vision," *Journal of Advertising Research*, January/February 1992, pp. 10–14; "Global Campaigns Don't Work; Multinationals Do," *Advertising Age*, April 18, 1994, p. 23; "Professor Stands by His Theory on Global Advertising," *The Wall Street Journal*, October 13, 1992, p. B10; Theodore Levitt, "The Globalization of Markets," *Harvard Business Review*, May–June 1983, pp. 92–102; Kamran Kashani, "Beware the Pitfalls of Global Marketing," *Harvard Business Review*, September/October 1989, pp. 91–98.

21. "World Brands 1994," *Advertising Age International*, September 19, 1994, pp. I13–26; "Special Issue: Agency Report," *Advertising Age*, April 13, 1994, pp. S1–56; James R. Wills, Jr., "Winning New Business: An Analysis of Advertising Agency Activities," *Journal of Advertising Research*, September/October 1992, pp. 10–17; M. Louise Ripley, "Why Industrial Advertising Is Often Done in House," *Industrial Marketing Management*, November 1992, p. 331–34; "Special Issue: Agency Report," *Advertising Age*, April 13, 1992, pp. S1–44; Alan T. Shao and John S. Hill, "Executing Transnational Advertising Campaigns: Do U.S. Agencies Have the Overseas Talent?" *Journal of Advertising Research*, January/February 1992, pp. 49–58.

22. "Blame-the-Messenger Mentality Leaves Scars on Madison Avenue," *The Wall Street Journal*, November 20, 1991, p. B4; R. Susan Ellis and Lester W. Johnson, "Agency Theory as a Framework for Advertising Agency Compensation Decisions," *Journal of Advertising Research*, September/October 1993, p. 76; Brian Jacobs, "Trends in Media Buying and Selling in Europe and the Effect on the Advertising Agency Business," *International Journal of Advertising* 10, no. 4 (1991), pp. 283–92; Thorolf Helgesen, "Advertising Awards and Advertising Agency Performance Criteria," *Journal of Advertising Research*, July/August 1994, pp. 43–53; "Big Agency, Small Agency: Which One Is Right for Your Business?" *Business Marketing*, May 1991, pp. 13–15; "DDB Needham 'Results' Plan Draws Yawns," *Advertising Age*, April 1, 1991, p. 3ff.; Ali Kanso, "The Use of Advertising Agencies for Foreign Markets: Decentralized Decisions and Localized Approaches?" *International Journal of Advertising* 10, no. 2 (1991), pp. 129–36; Richard Beltramini and Dennis A. Pitta, "Underlying Dimensions and Communications Strategies of the Advertising Agency-Client Relationship," *International Journal of Advertising* 10, no. 2 (1991), pp. 151–60; "Pursuing Results in the Age of Accountability," *Adweek's Marketing Week*, November 19, 1990, pp. 20–22; "More Companies Offer Their Agencies Bonus Plans that Reward Superior Work," *The Wall Street Journal*,

July 26, 1988, p. 37; Michael G. Harvey and J. Paul Rupert, "Selecting an Industrial Advertising Agency," *Industrial Marketing Management*, May 1988, pp. 119–28.

23. "Bowl Postmortem: Tadpoles, Ad Polls," *Advertising Age*, February 6, 1995, p. 44; "Why A-B Bounced Bud," *Advertising Age*, November 21, 1994, p. 1ff.; "Ties that Bind Agency, Client Unravel," *The Wall Street Journal*, November 16, 1994, p. B9; Paul C. N. Mitchell, Harold Cataquet, and Stephen Hague, "Establishing the Causes of Disaffection in Agency-Client Relations," *Journal of Advertising Research*, March/April 1992, pp. 41–48.

24. "Behind the Scenes at an American Express Commercial," *Business Week*, May 20, 1985, pp. 84–88.

25. Karen Whitehill King, John D. Pehrson, and Leonard N. Reid, "Pretesting TV Commercials: Methods, Measures, and Changing Agency Roles," *Journal of Advertising*, September 1993, p. 85; "Researchers Probe Ad Effectiveness Globally," *Marketing News*, August 29, 1994, pp. 6–7; "New David Ogilvy Award Takes Research Out of Hiding," *The Wall Street Journal*, April 13, 1994, p. B8; Mukesh Bhargava, Naveen Donthu, and Rosanne Caron, "Improving the Effectiveness of Outdoor Advertising: Lessons from a Study of 282 Campaigns," *Journal of Advertising Research*, March/April 1994, pp. 46–55; Erik du Plessis, "Recognition versus Recall," *Journal of Advertising Research*, May/June 1994, pp. 75–91; Russell I. Haley, James Staffarone, and Arthur Fox, "The Missing Measures of Copy Testing," *Journal of Advertising Research*, May/June 1994, pp. 46–61; John R. Rossiter and Geoff Eagleson, "Conclusions from the ARF Copy Research Validity Project," *Journal of Advertising Research*, May/June 1994, pp. 19–32; "Loved the Ad. May (or May Not) Buy the Product," *The Wall Street Journal*, April 7, 1994, p. B1ff.; Michael J. Polonsky and David S. Waller, "Does Winning Advertising Awards Pay?: The Australian Experience," *Journal of Advertising Research*, January/February 1995, pp. 25–36; Anthony J. Adams and Margaret H. Blair, "Persuasive Advertising and Sales Accountability: Past Experience and Forward Validation," *Journal of Advertising Research*, March/April 1992, pp. 20–25; George M. Zinkhan, "Rating Industrial Advertisements," *Industrial Marketing Management*, February 1984, pp. 43–48; Lawrence C. Soley, "Copy Length and Industrial Advertising Readership," *Industrial Marketing Management*, August 1986, pp. 245–52; David W. Stewart, "Measures, Methods, and Models in Advertising Research," *Journal of Advertising Research*, June–July 1989, p. 54ff.

26. Steve Lyonski and Michael F. Duffy, "The New Zealand Fair Trading Act of 1986: Deceptive Advertising," *Journal of Consumer Affairs*, Summer 1992, pp. 177–99; "South Koreans Are Offered Naked Truth in Advertising but Some Find It Hurts," *The Wall Street Journal*, May 9, 1994, p. A9C; "TV Is Exploding All over Asia," *Fortune*, January 24, 1994, pp. 98–101; "Drop that Remote! In Britain, Watching TV Can Be a Crime," *The Wall Street Journal*, September 27, 1993, p. A1ff.; "Germany Debates 'Perverse' Ad Rule," *Advertising Age*, September 20, 1993, p. I1ff.; "East Europeans Adjust to Western Ads; Information after Years of Propaganda," *The Wall Street Journal*, July 17, 1993, p. A5B; "Ad Regs a Hot Topic in Spain's Senate," *Advertising Age International*, May 17, 1993, p. I6; "Russia Goes Private: It's Fun, It's Now, It's an Ad on TV," *The Wall Street Journal*, September 23, 1992, p. A1ff.; "Eastern Europe Poses Obstacles for Ads," *The Wall Street Journal*, July 30, 1992, p. B6; "Pepsi Challenges Japanese Taboo as It Ribs Coke," *The Wall Street Journal*, March 6, 1991, p. B1ff.;

Albert Schofield, "International Differences in Advertising Practices: Britain Compared with Other Countries," *International Journal of Advertising* 10, no. 4 (1991), pp. 299–308.

27. "Shoe Companies Charged by FTC with False Ads," *The Wall Street Journal*, September 21, 1994, p. B10; "Gasoline Ads Canceled; Lack of Truth Cited," *The Wall Street Journal*, July 21, 1994, p. B1ff.; "General Nutrition to Pay FTC Penalty of $2.4 Million over False Advertising," *The Wall Street Journal*, April 29, 1994, p. B5; "Eggland's Halts Claims," *The Wall Street Journal*, February 14, 1994, p. B3; Barbara B. Stern, " 'Crafty Advertisers': Literary versus Literal Deceptiveness," *Journal of Public Policy & Marketing*, Spring 1992, pp. 72–81; Joel J. Davis, "Ethics in Advertising Decisionmaking: Implications for Reducing the Incidence of Deceptive Advertising," *Journal of Consumer Affairs*, Winter 1994, pp. 380–402; Jef I. Richards and Ivan L. Preston, "Proving and Disproving Materiality of Deceptive Advertising Claims," *Journal of Public Policy & Marketing*, Fall 1992, pp. 45–56; Mariea Grubbs Hoy and Michael J. Stankey, "Structural Characteristics of Televised Advertising Disclosures: A Comparison with the FTC Clear and Conspicuous Standard," *Journal of Advertising*, June 1993, pp. 47–58.

28. John S. Healey and Harold H. Kassarjian, "Advertising Substantiation and Advertiser Response: A Content Analysis of Magazine Advertisements," *Journal of Marketing*, Winter 1983, pp. 107–17; George M. Zinkhan, "Advertising Ethics: Emerging Methods and Trends," *Journal of Advertising*, September 1994, pp. 1–4; Alexander Simonson and Morris B. Holbrook, "Permissible Puffery versus Actionable Warranty in Advertising and Salestalk: An Empirical Investigation," *Journal of Public Policy & Marketing*, Fall 1993, pp. 216–33.

29. "Joe Camel Gets Reprieve, for Now," *Advertising Age*, June 8, 1994, p. 52; "TV Advertising Aimed at Kids Is Filled with Fat," *The Wall Street Journal*, November 9, 1993, p. B1; Claude R. Martin, Jr., "Ethical Advertising Research Standards: Three Case Studies," *Journal of Advertising*, September 1994, pp. 17–30; William K. Darley and Robert E. Smith, "Advertising Claim Objectivity: Antecedents and Effects," *Journal of Marketing*, October 1993, pp. 100–13; Avery M. Abernethy, "Advertising Clearance Practices of Radio Stations: A Model of Advertising Self-Regulation," *Journal of Advertising*, September 1993, pp. 15–26; Herbert J. Rotfeld, "Power and Limitations of Media Clearance Practices and Advertising Self-Regulation," *Journal of Public Policy & Marketing*, Spring 1992, pp. 87–95.

30. "Special Report: Promotional Marketing," *Advertising Age*, March 21, 1994, pp. S1–14; "Special Report: Sales Promotion," *Advertising Age*, May 4, 1992, pp. 29–36; " 'Recession-Proof' Industry Feels Pinch," *Advertising Age*, April 29, 1991, pp. 31–38; "Special Report: Premiums, Incentives," *Advertising Age*, May 2, 1988, pp. S1–12; "More Marketers Leaving a (Prepaid) Calling Card," *The Wall Street Journal*, July 25, 1994, p. B1; "Beyond the Plastic Swizzle Stick," *Adweek's Marketing Week*, May 13, 1991, p. 20; "Hallmark Gives Away Its Best Cards in an Unusual Promotion," *Adweek's Marketing Week*, July 9, 1990, p. 10; "Audubon Society Hopes Music Videos and Movies Get Its 'Green' Message Out," *The Wall Street Journal*, April 10, 1990, p. B1ff.

31. "Pay for Performance Picking Up Speed," *Advertising Age*, August 9, 1993, p. 19; Donald R. Glover, "Distributor Attitudes toward Manufacturer-Sponsored Promotions," *Industrial Marketing*

Management 20, no. 3 (1991), pp. 241–50; A. S. C. Ehrenberg, Kathy Hammond, and G. J. Goodhardt, "The After-Effects of Price-Related Consumer Promotions," *Journal of Advertising Research*, July/August 1994, pp. 11–21; Jean J. Boddewyn and Monica Leardi, "Sales Promotions: Practice, Regulation and Self-Regulation around the World," *International Journal of Advertising* 8, no. 4 (1989), pp. 363–74; Thomas L. Powers, "Should You Increase Sales Promotion or Add Salespeople?" *Industrial Marketing Management* 18, no. 4 (1989), pp. 259–64.

32. "What's New in Joint Promotions," *New York Times*, March 10, 1985; Henry H. Beam, "Preparing for Promotion Pays Off," *Business Horizons*, January/February 1984, pp. 6–13; P. Rajan Varadarajan, "Horizontal Cooperative Sales Promotion: A Framework for Classification and Additional Perspectives," *Journal of Marketing*, April 1986, pp. 61–73.

33. J. F. Engel, M. R. Warshaw, and T. C. Kinnear, *Promotional Strategy* (Burr Ridge, IL: Richard D. Irwin, 1988).

34. "Coupon Clippers, Save Your Scissors," *Business Week*, June 20, 1994, pp. 164–66; "Awash in Coupons? Some Firms Try to Stem the Tide," *The Wall Street Journal*, May 10, 1994, p. B1ff.; Judy F. Graham, "Increasing Repurchase Rates: A Reappraisal of Coupon Effects," *Psychology & Marketing*, November/December 1994, pp. 533–48; "Paper Coupons Losing Lure in High-Tech Store," *Advertising Age*, March 21, 1994, p. S14; "Hold the Comics, Sports, and Give Me that FSI," *Brandweek*, March 21, 1994, pp. 40–42; A. Krishna and R. W. Shoemaker, "Estimating the Effects of Higher Coupon Face Values on the Timing of Redemptions, the Mix of Coupon Redeemers, and Purchase Quality," *Psychology & Marketing*, November/December 1992, pp. 453–68; "Mattel Steps Up Toy Promotions for Christmas," *The Wall Street Journal*, August 17, 1993, p. B1ff.; "Actmedia Presages New Era in Couponing," *Adweek*, July 12, 1993, p. 16; "Get Ready for Global Coupon Wars," *Adweek's Marketing Week*, July 8, 1991, pp. 20–22; Jamie Howell, "Potential Profitability and Decreased Consumer Welfare through Manufacturers' Cents-Off Coupons," *The Journal of Consumer Affairs*, Summer 1991, pp. 164–84.

35. Brad O'Hare, Fred Palumbo, and Paul Herbig, "Industrial Trade Shows Abroad," *Industrial Marketing Management*, August 1993, pp. 233–38; "Gizmos Get Fancier as Trade Show Opens," *The Wall Street Journal*, May 4, 1993, p. B8; "Marketers Swap More than Goodwill at Trade Show," *Business Marketing*, September 1990, pp. 48–51; "Latest in Corporate Freebies Try to Be Classy instead of Trashy," *The Wall Street Journal*, August 7, 1989, p. B4; Rockney G. Walters, "An Empirical Investigation into Retailer Response to Manufacturer Trade Promotions," *Journal of Retailing*, Summer 1989, pp. 253–72; S. Gopalakrishna and J. D. Williams, "Planning and Performance Assessment of Industrial Trade Shows: An Exploratory Study," *International Journal of Research in Marketing*, August 1992, pp. 207–24; C. M. Sashi and Jim Perretty, "Do Trade Shows Provide Value?" *Industrial Marketing Management*, August 1992, p. 273; Ronald C. Curhan and Robert J. Kopp, "Obtaining Retailer Support for Trade Deals: Key Success Factors," *Journal of Advertising Research*, December 1987–January 1988, pp. 51–60; Donald W. Jackson, Janet E. Keith, and Richard K. Burdick, "The Relative Importance of Various Promotional Elements in Different Industrial Purchase Situations," *Journal of Advertising* 16, no. 4 (1987), pp. 25–33.

36. "Getting Tough on Trade," *Adweek*, April 13, 1992, pp. 20–30; "A Shift in Direction?" *Adweek's Marketing Week*, April 13, 1992, pp. 26–27; "Trade Promos Devour Half of All Marketing $," *Advertising Age*, April 13, 1992, p. 3ff.; Sunil Gupta, "Impact of Sales Promotions on When, What, and How Much to Buy," *Journal of Marketing Research*, November 1988, pp. 342–55; John A. Quelch, "It's Time to Make Trade Promotion More Productive," *Harvard Business Review*, May–June 1983, pp. 130–36.

37. "IBM Is Offering Workers Prizes to Hawk OS/2," *The Wall Street Journal*, March 27, 1992, p. B1ff.; "3M Distributors Go for the Gold," *Business Marketing*, May 1991, p. 49; "Chain Finds Incentives a Hard Sell," *The Wall Street Journal*, July 5, 1990, p. B1ff.; "Rewards for Good Work," *USA Today*, April 8, 1988, p. B1; Joanne Y. Cleaver, "Employee Incentives Rising to Top of Industry," *Advertising Age*, May 5, 1986, p. S1ff.

Chapter 17

1. "Demand in Overdrive for Top Models," *USA Today*, November 18, 1994, p. 1Aff.; "GM Finds It Can't Make Enough of the Models That Make Money," *The Wall Street Journal*, November 7, 1994, p. B1ff.; "GM Packs Practical with Plush," *USA Today*, September 9, 1994, p. 1Bff.; "World War II Workhorse Started Trend," *USA Today*, June 6, 1994, p. 1Bff.

2. "Adding Options Helps Car Firms Increase Prices," *The Wall Street Journal*, December 27, 1993, p. 9ff.; "Car Makers Seek to Mask Price Increases," *The Wall Street Journal*, August 16, 1989, p. B1.

3. Alfred Rappaport, "Executive Incentives versus Corporate Growth," *Harvard Business Review*, July–August 1978, pp. 81–88; David M. Szymanski, Sundar G. Bharadwaj, and P. Rajan Varadarajan, "An Analysis of the Market Share-Profitability Relationship," *Journal of Marketing*, July 1993, pp. 1–18.

4. Pricing "in the public interest" is often an issue in pricing government services; for an interesting example, see "Price Policy on Space Shuttle's Commercial Use Could Launch—or Ground—NASA's Rockets," *The Wall Street Journal*, March 21, 1985, p. 64.

5. "Crashing Prices," *Time*, August 2, 1993, pp. 48–49; "Computer Chaos," *U.S. News & World Report*, July 26, 1993, pp. 46–49; "PC Price War May Break Out, Starting in Fall," *The Wall Street Journal*, July 22, 1994, p. B1ff.; "U.S. Computer Firms, Extending PC Wars, Charge into Japan," *The Wall Street Journal*, March 31, 1993, p. A1ff.; "PC Land's Little Guys Get Slaughtered," *Business Week*, February 15, 1993, pp. 105–6; "Computer Industry Divides into Camps of Winners and Losers," *The Wall Street Journal*, January 27, 1993, p. A1ff.; "Here's a PC for Peanuts," *Newsweek*, January 25, 1993, p. 63.

6. "Harvester Sells Many Trucks below Cost, Citing Need to Maintain Dealer Network," *The Wall Street Journal*, April 19, 1983, p. 8.

7. "Price Wars," *Adweek's Marketing Week*, June 8, 1992, pp. 18–22; "Why the Price Wars Never End," *Fortune*, March 23, 1992, pp. 68–78; "Middle-Price Brands Come under Siege," *The Wall Street Journal*, April 2, 1990, p. B1ff.; "Avis, Sidestepping Price Wars, Focuses on the Drive Itself," *Adweek's Marketing Week*, February 12, 1990, p. 24.

8. "Aluminum Firms Offer Wider Discounts but Price Cuts Stop at Some Distributors," *The Wall Street Journal*, November 16, 1984, p. 50.

9. Michael V. Marn and Robert L. Rosiello, "Managing Price, Gaining Profit," *Harvard Business Review*, September–October 1992, pp. 84–94; Subhash C. Jain and Michael B. Laric, "A Framework for Strategic Industrial Pricing," *Industrial Marketing Management* 8 (1979), pp. 75–80; Peter R. Dickson and Joel E. Urbany, "Retailer Reactions to Competitive Price Changes," *Journal of Retailing*, Spring 1994, pp. 1–22; Mary Karr, "The Case of the Pricing Predicament," *Harvard Business Review*, March–April 1988, pp. 10–23; Saeed Samiee, "Pricing in Marketing Strategies of U.S. and Foreign-Based Companies," *Journal of Business Research*, February 1987, pp. 17–30; Gerard J. Tellis, "Beyond the Many Faces of Price: An Integration of Pricing Strategies," *Journal of Marketing*, October 1986, pp. 146–60.

10. "18-Month-Old Saturn Walking Tall," *USA Today*, February 24, 1992, p. 1B; "Car Hagglers May Still Drive Best Car Deals," *The Wall Street Journal*, October 12, 1994, p. B1ff.; "Flexible Pricing," *Business Week*, December 12, 1977, pp. 78–88; Michael H. Morris, "Separate Prices as a Marketing Tool," *Industrial Marketing Management*, May 1987, pp. 79–86; P. Ronald Stephenson, William L. Cron, and Gary L. Frazier, "Delegating Pricing Authority to the Sales Force: The Effects on Sales and Profit Performance," *Journal of Marketing*, Spring 1979, pp. 21–24.

11. "Squeezin' the Charmin," *Fortune*, January 16, 1989, pp. 11–12; "Grocers Join Winn-Dixie," *Advertising Age*, November 7, 1988, p. 3; "Grocery Chains Pressure Suppliers for Uniform Prices," *The Wall Street Journal*, October 21, 1988, p. B1; "Grocery Chain Dumps Major Package Goods," *Advertising Age*, October 10, 1988, p. 1ff.

12. "Breakthrough in Birth Control May Elude Poor," *The Wall Street Journal*, March 4, 1991, p. B1ff.; "Burroughs Wellcome Reaps Profits, Outrage from Its AIDS Drug," *The Wall Street Journal*, September 15, 1989, p. A1ff.; Richard A. Spinello, "Ethics, Pricing and the Pharmaceutical Industry," *Journal of Business Ethics*, August 1992, pp. 617–26.

13. Alan Reynolds, "A Kind Word for 'Cream Skimming,'" *Harvard Business Review*, November–December 1974, pp. 113–20.

14. Stuart U. Rich, "Price Leadership in the Paper Industry," *Industrial Marketing Management*, April 1983, pp. 101–4; "OPEC Member Offers Discounts to Some amid Downward Pressure on Oil Prices," *The Wall Street Journal*, November 16, 1984, p. 4.

15. 1995 exchange rates are from the March 30, 1995, issue of *The Wall Street Journal*, but they are available on a daily basis. Earlier years' exchange rates are from *Statistical Abstract of the World* (Detroit, MI: Gale Research, 1994), p. 881, and *The World Almanac and Book of Facts 1995* (Mahwah, NJ: Funk & Wagnalls, 1994), p. 122. See also David N. Hyman, *Economics*, 2nd ed. (Burr Ridge, IL: Richard D. Irwin, 1992), pp. 82–83; Timothy A. Luehrman, "Exchange Rate Changes and the Distribution of Industry Value," *Journal of International Business Studies*, Winter 1991, pp. 619–50; James K. Weekly, "Pricing in Foreign Markets: Pitfalls and Opportunities," *Industrial Marketing Management*, May 1992, p. 173.

16. "Makeup Ads Downplay Glamour for Value," *The Wall Street Journal*, June 20, 1994, p. B5; "Value Pricing Kicks Off Model Year," *USA Today*, October 1, 1993, p. 1Bff.; "Value Pricing Comes to Funerals," *USA Today*, July 14, 1993, p. 5B; "Tide, Cheer Join P&G 'Value Pricing' Plan," *Advertising Age*, February 15, 1993, p. 3ff.; "More Stores Switch from Sales to 'Everyday Low Prices,'" *The Wall Street Journal*, November 12, 1992, p. B1ff.;

"For Saturn, Copying Japan Yields Hot Sales but No Profits," *The Wall Street Journal*, October 1, 1992, p. A12; "Value Marketing," *Business Week*, November 11, 1991, pp. 132–40; Louis J. De Rose, "Meet Today's Buying Influences with Value Selling," *Industrial Marketing Management* 20, no. 2 (1991), pp. 87–90.

17. "Can't Get Enough of that Super Yen," *Business Week*, October 4, 1993, p. 50; *1993 Annual Report*, Campbell; *1990 Annual Report*, Campbell; "Campbell's Taste of the Japanese Market Is Mm-Mm Good," *Business Week*, March 28, 1988, p. 42; "Most U.S. Firms Seek Extra Profits in Japan, at the Expense of Sales," *The Wall Street Journal*, May 15, 1987, p. 1ff.

18. K. J. Blois, "Discounts in Business Marketing Management," *Industrial Marketing Management*, April 1994, pp. 93–100; George S. Day and Adrian B. Ryans, "Using Price Discounts for a Competitive Advantage," *Industrial Marketing Management*, February 1988, pp. 1–14; James B. Wilcox et al., "Price Quantity Discounts: Some Implications for Buyers and Sellers," *Journal of Marketing*, July 1987, pp. 60–70; "Collecting Bonus Miles Now a Mania," *USA Today*, November 21, 1994, p. 1Aff.; "Frequent Shopper Programs Ripen," *Advertising Age*, August 6, 1990, p. 21; "Clubs Reward Buyers at Bookstore Chains," *Insight*, March 26, 1990, p. 43; Mark T. Spriggs and John R. Nevin, "The Legal Status of Trade and Functional Price Discounts," *Journal of Public Policy & Marketing*, Spring 1994, pp. 61–75; Judith Waldrop, "The Seasons of Business," *American Demographics*, May 1992, pp. 40–45; "Cash Discounts," *Electrical Wholesaling*, May 1989, pp. 90–96.

19. For more on P&G's everyday low pricing, see "Company Makes Big Cuts to Stay Fit," *USA Today*, July 16, 1993, p. 1Bff.; "The Dumbest Marketing Ploy," *Fortune*, October 5, 1992, pp. 88–94; "P&G Plays Pied Piper on Pricing," *Advertising Age*, March 9, 1992, p. 6; "Not Everyone Loves a Supermarket Special," *Business Week*, February 17, 1992, pp. 64–68; "Stalking the New Consumer," *Business Week*, August 28, 1989, pp. 54–62; "The Marketing Revolution at Procter & Gamble," *Business Week*, July 25, 1988, pp. 72–73ff.; Stephen J. Hoch, Xavier Dreze, and Mary E. Purk, "EDLP, Hi-Lo, and Margin Arithmetic," *Journal of Marketing*, October 1994, pp. 16–27; "The 'Sale' Is Fading as a Retailing Tactic," *The Wall Street Journal*, March 1, 1989, p. B1ff.

20. "Beer Makers Frothing over Plan to Charge for Retail Shelf Space," *The Wall Street Journal*, April 22, 1994, p. B1ff.; "Getting around Slotting Fees," *Food Business*, June 17, 1991, p. 12; "Slotting Fees May Get FTC OK," *Advertising Age*, June 18, 1990, p. 4; "Want Shelf Space at the Supermarket? Ante Up," *Business Week*, August 7, 1989, pp. 60–61.

21. William D. Diamond, "Just What Is a 'Dollar's Worth'? Consumer Reactions to Price Discounts vs. Extra Product Promotions," *Journal of Retailing*, Fall 1992, pp. 254–70; Kenneth A. Hunt and Susan M. Keaveney, "A Process Model of the Effects of Price Promotions on Brand Image," *Psychology & Marketing*, November/December 1994, pp. 511;–32. For more on coupons, see "Awash in Coupons? Some Firms Try to Stem the Tide," *The Wall Street Journal*, May 10, 1994, p. B1ff.; "Coupon Scams Are Clipping Companies," *Business Week*, June 15, 1992, pp. 110–11; "Pious Town Finds Mighty Temptation in Coupon Clipping," *The Wall Street Journal*, February 21, 1992, p. A1ff.; "Coupons Maintain Redeeming Qualities," *Direct Marketing*, December 1991, pp. 25–27; "ActMedia Puts the Coupon on the Shelf," *Adweek's Marketing Week*, January 21, 1991, p. 8. For more on rebates, see

Peter K. Tat, "Rebate Usage: A Motivational Perspective," *Psychology & Marketing*, January/February 1994, pp. 15–26; Abdul Ali, Marvin A. Jolson, and Rene Y. Darmon, "A Model for Optimizing the Refund Value in Rebate Promotions," *Journal of Business Research*, March 1994, pp. 239–46; "Rebate Program Rings Wright Bell," *Advertising Age*, May 21, 1990, p. 44; "Marketers Tighten Rules on Rebate Offers in Effort to Reduce Large Fraud Losses," *The Wall Street Journal*, March 18, 1987, p. 33.

22. For an excellent discussion of laws related to pricing, see Louis W. Stern and Thomas L. Eovaldi, *Legal Aspects of Marketing Strategy: Antitrust and Consumer Protection Issues* (Englewood Cliffs, NJ: Prentice Hall, 1984).

23. For more on dumping, see "Antidumping Laws Keep Out Goods that Pacts Would Ordinarily Let In," *The Wall Street Journal*, February 26, 1993, p. A11. For more on phony list prices, see Larry D. Compeau, Dhruv Grewal, and Diana S. Grewal, "Adjudicating Claims of Deceptive Advertised Reference Prices: The Use of Empirical Evidence," *Journal of Public Policy & Marketing*, Fall 1994, pp. 312–18; Patrick J. Kaufmann, N. Craig Smith, and Gwendolyn K. Ortmeyer, "Deception in Retailer High-Low Pricing: A 'Rule of Reason' Approach," *Journal of Retailing*, Summer 1994, pp. 115–38; John Liefeld and Louise A. Heslop, "Reference Prices and Deception in Newspaper Advertising," *Journal of Consumer Research*, March 1985, pp. 868–76; "States Crack Down on Phony Price-Cutting 'Sales,'" *The Wall Street Journal*, January 30, 1986, p. 1.

24. "U.S. Launches Antitrust Probe of Auto Dealers," *The Wall Street Journal*, October 11, 1994, p. A3; "A White Shoe Firm, a Rock Band and a Threat," *The Wall Street Journal*, July 29, 1994, p. B1ff.; "Gunning for Microsoft," *Business Week*, May 9, 1994, p. 90; Larry L. Miller, Steven P. Schnaars, and Valerie L. Vaccaro, "The Provocative Practice of Price Signaling: Collusion versus Cooperation," *Business Horizons*, July–August 1993, pp. 59–65; "Price-Fixing Charges Put GE and De Beers under Tough Scrutiny," *The Wall Street Journal*, February 22, 1994, p. A1ff.; "Carbon Dioxide Suppliers Are Accused of Price Fixing," *The Wall Street Journal*, November 17, 1993, p. B4; "Predatory Pricing Issue Is Due to Be Taken Up in American Air's Trial," *The Wall Street Journal*, July 12, 1993, p. A1ff.; Mary Jane Sheffet, "The Supreme Court and Predatory Pricing," *Journal of Public Policy & Marketing*, Spring 1994, pp. 163–67; Michael L. Ursic and James G. Helgeson, "Using Price as a Weapon: An Economic and Legal Analysis of Predatory Pricing," *Industrial Marketing Management*, April 1994, pp. 125–32; "Methods of Marketing Infant Formula Land Abbott in Hot Water," *The Wall Street Journal*, May 25, 1993, p. A1ff.; Robert L. Cutts, "Capitalism in Japan: Cartels and Keiretsu," *Harvard Business Review*, July–August 1992, pp. 48–129; Daniel T. Ostas, "Ethics of Contract Pricing," *Journal of Business Ethics*, February 1992, pp. 137–46; "Antitrust Laws Roil World of Healing," *The Wall Street Journal*, May 14, 1993, p. B1ff.; "How Three Companies Allegedly Conspired to Fix Matzo Prices," *The Wall Street Journal*, March 11, 1991, p. A1ff.; "Anti-Discount Policies of Manufacturers Are Penalizing Certain Cut-Price Stores," *The Wall Street Journal*, February 27, 1991, p. B1ff.; "State Attorneys General Battle for Direction of Antitrust Law," *Insight*, February 25, 1991, pp. 40–42; "Court Says Indirect Buyers Can Sue Violators of State Antitrust Laws," *The Wall Street Journal*, April 19, 1989, p. B7. See also Mary Jane Sheffet and Debra L. Scammon, "Resale Price Maintenance: Is It Safe to Suggest Retail

Prices?" *Journal of Marketing*, Fall 1985, pp. 82–91.

25. Morris L. Mayer, Joseph B. Mason, and E. A. Orbeck, "The Borden Case—A Legal Basis for Private Brand Price Discrimination," *MSU Business Topics*, Winter 1970, pp. 56–63.

26. "Is the Cost Defense Workable?" *Journal of Marketing*, January 1965, pp. 37–42; B. J. Linder and Allan H. Savage, "Price Discrimination and Cost Defense—Change Ahead?" *MSU Business Topics*, Summer 1971, pp. 21–26; "Firms Must Prove Injury from Price Bias to Qualify for Damages, High Court Says," *The Wall Street Journal*, May 19, 1981, p. 8.

27. "Booksellers Say Five Publishers Play Favorites," *The Wall Street Journal*, May 27, 1994, p. B1ff.; Joseph P. Vaccaro and Derek W. F. Coward, "Managerial and Legal Implications of Price Haggling: A Sales Manager's Dilemma," *Journal of Personal Selling & Sales Management*, Summer 1993, pp. 79–86; John R. Davidson, "FTC, Robinson-Patman and Cooperative Promotion Activities," *Journal of Marketing*, January 1968, pp. 14–18; L. X. Tarpey, Sr., "Buyer Liability under the Robinson-Patman Act: A Current Appraisal," *Journal of Marketing*, January 1972, pp. 38–42.

Chapter 18

1. "Wal-Mart's Super Day: 23 Supercenters in 14 States," *Discount Store News*, February 6, 1995, p. 1ff.; "Wal-Mart: The Next Generation," *Discount Store News*, December 5, 1994, pp. 47–113; "A Different World," *The Wall Street Journal*, October 28, 1994, p. R6; "Wal-Mart Is Slowed by Problems of Price and Culture in Mexico," *The Wall Street Journal*, July 29, 1994, p. A1ff.; "Retailers Try Every Angle to Lure Buyers," *USA Today*, November 26, 1993, p. 1Bff.; "Wal-Mart Readies Private-Label Laundry Assault," *Advertising Age*, August 30, 1993, p. 1ff.; "Brands Beware, Wal-Mart Adds Giant House Label," *Advertising Age*, April 5, 1993, p. 1ff.; "Manufacturers Get New Set of Rules," *Adweek*, February 15, 1993, p. 10; "Up against the Wall," *Brandweek*, February 8, 1993, p. 1ff.; *1993 Annual Report*, Wal-Mart; *1993 Annual Report*, Kmart; "Wal-Mart's Big Blitz into the Grocery Field Meets Stiff Resistance," *The Wall Street Journal*, October 9, 1992, p. A1ff.; "A Week aboard the Wal-Mart Express," *Fortune*, August 24, 1992, pp. 77–84; "Wal-Mart Expands Sam's Choice Line," *Advertising Age*, April 27, 1992, p. 4; "Pioneer Changed Face of Retailing," *USA Today*, April 6, 1992, pp. 1B–2B; "O.K., So He's Not Sam Walton," *Business Week*, March 16, 1992, pp. 56–58; "Wal-Mart Puts Its Own Spin on Private Label," *Advertising Age*, December 16, 1991, p. 26; "The Sam's Generation?" *Business Week*, November 25, 1991, pp. 36–38; "America's Most Successful Merchant," *Fortune*, September 23, 1991, pp. 46–59; "Is Wal-Mart Unstoppable?" *Fortune*, May 6, 1991, pp. 50–59; "Mr. Sam Stuns Goliath," *Time*, February 25, 1991, pp. 62–63.

2. Marvin A. Jolson, "A Diagrammatic Model for Merchandising Calculations," *Journal of Retailing*, Summer 1975, pp. 3–9.

3. "Women Demand Fair Shear," *U. Magazine*, May 1995, p. 8; "State May Ban Bias in Pricing Hairdos, Wash," *The Wall Street Journal*, May 11, 1994, p. B1ff.; "Blouse-Cleaning Rates Are Unfair, Woman Charges," *The Raleigh News & Observer*, July 7, 1992, p. 3B; "Urban Consumers Pay More and Get Less, and Gap May Widen," *The Wall Street Journal*, July 2, 1992, p. A1ff.

4. Mary L. Hatten, "Don't Get Caught with Your Prices Down: Pricing in Inflationary Times," *Business Horizons*, March 1982, pp. 23–28; "Why Detroit Can't Cut Prices," *Business Week*, March 1, 1982, p. 110; Douglas G. Brooks, "Cost-Oriented Pricing: A Realistic Solution to a Complicated Problem," *Journal of Marketing*, April 1975, pp. 72–74.

5. William W. Alberts, "The Experience Curve Doctrine Reconsidered," *Journal of Marketing*, July 1989, pp. 36–49; George S. Day and David B. Montgomery, "Diagnosing the Experience Curve," *Journal of Marketing*, Spring 1983, pp. 44–58; G. Dean Kortge et al., "Linking Experience, Product Life Cycle, and Learning Curves: Calculating the Perceived Value Price Range," *Industrial Marketing Management*, July 1994, pp. 221–28; Alan R. Beckenstein and H. Landis Gabel, "Experience Curve Pricing Strategy: The Next Target of Antitrust?" *Business Horizons*, September/October 1982, pp. 71–77.

6. G. Dean Kortge, "Inverted Breakeven Analysis for Profitable Marketing Decisions," *Industrial Marketing Management*, October 1984, pp. 219–24; Thomas L. Powers, "Breakeven Analysis with Semifixed Costs," *Industrial Marketing Management*, February 1987, pp. 35–42.

7. Approaches for estimating price-quantity relationships are reviewed in Kent B. Monroe, *Pricing: Making Profitable Decisions* (New York: McGraw-Hill, 1979). For a specific example see Frank D. Jones, "A Survey Technique to Measure Demand under Various Pricing Strategies," *Journal of Marketing*, July 1975, pp. 75–77; or Gordon A. Wyner, Lois H. Benedetti, and Bart M. Trapp, "Measuring the Quantity and Mix of Product Demand," *Journal of Marketing*, Winter 1984, pp. 101–9. See also Michael H. Morris and Mary L. Joyce, "How Marketers Evaluate Price Sensitivity," *Industrial Marketing Management*, May 1988, pp. 169–76.

8. "New Long-Life Bulbs May Lose Brilliance in a Crowded Market," *The Wall Street Journal*, June 2, 1992, p. B4; Benson P. Shapiro and Barbara P. Jackson, "Industrial Pricing to Meet Customer Needs," *Harvard Business Review*, November–December 1978, pp. 119–27; "The Race to the $10 Light Bulb," *Business Week*, May 19, 1980, p. 124; see also Michael H. Morris and Donald A. Fuller, "Pricing an Industrial Service," *Industrial Marketing Management*, May 1989, pp. 139–46.

9. Thomas T. Nagle, *The Strategy and Tactics of Pricing* (Englewood Cliffs, NJ: Prentice-Hall, 1987), pp. 249–55; Abhijit Biswas, Elizabeth J. Wilson, and Jane W. Licata, "Reference Pricing Studies in Marketing: A Synthesis of Research Results," *Journal of Business Research*, July 1993, pp. 239–56; K. N. Rajendran and Gerard J. Tellis, "Contextual and Temporal Components of Reference Price," *Journal of Marketing*, January 1994, pp. 22–34; Daniel S. Putler, "Incorporating Reference Price Effects into a Theory of Consumer Choice," *Marketing Science*, Summer 1992, pp. 287–309; Kristina D. Frankenberger and Ruiming Liu, "Does Consumer Knowledge Affect Consumer Responses to Advertised Reference Price Claims?" *Psychology & Marketing*, May/June 1994, pp. 235–52; Abhijit Biswas, "The Moderating Role of Brand Familiarity in Reference Price Perceptions," *Journal of Business Research*, November 1992, pp. 251–62; Tridib Mazumdar and Kent B. Monroe, "Effects of Inter-Store and In-Store Price Comparison on Price Recall Accuracy and Confidence," *Journal of Retailing*, Spring 1992, pp. 66–89; Donald R. Lichtenstein and William O. Bearden, "Contextual Influences on Perceptions of Merchant-Supplied Reference Prices," *Journal of Consumer Research*, June 1989, pp. 55–66.

10. For an example applied to a high-price item, see "Sale of Mink Coats Strays a Fur Piece from the Expected," *The Wall Street Journal*, March 21, 1980, p. 30.

11. B. P. Shapiro, "The Psychology of Pricing," *Harvard Business Review*, July–August 1968, pp. 14–24; C. Davis Fogg and Kent H. Kohnken, "Price-Cost Planning," *Journal of Marketing*, April 1978, pp. 97–106.

12. Robert M. Schindler and Alan R. Wiman, "Effects of Odd Pricing on Price Recall," *Journal of Business Research*, November 1989, pp. 165–78; "Strategic Mix of Odd, Even Prices Can Lead to Increased Retail Profits," *Marketing News*, March 7, 1980, p. 24.

13. "Special Report: Marketing to the Affluent," *Advertising Age*, October 19, 1987, pp. S1–32; Peter C. Riesz, "Price versus Quality in the Marketplace," *Journal of Retailing*, Winter 1978, pp. 15–28; John J. Wheatly and John S. Y. Chiu, "The Effects of Price, Store Image, and Product and Respondent Characteristics on Perceptions of Quality," *Journal of Marketing Research*, May 1977, pp. 181–86; N. D. French, J. J. Williams, and W. A. Chance, "A Shopping Experiment on Price-Quality Relationships," *Journal of Retailing*, Fall 1972, pp. 3–16; J. Douglas McConnell, "Comment on 'A Major Price-Perceived Quality Study Reexamined,'" *Journal of Marketing Research*, May 1980, pp. 263–64; K. M. Monroe and S. Petroshius, "Buyers' Subjective Perceptions of Price: An Update of the Evidence," in *Perspectives in Consumer Behavior*, ed. T. Robertson and H. Kassarjian (Glenview, IL: Scott, Foresman, 1981), pp. 43–55; G. Dan Kortge and Patrick A. Okonkwo, "Perceived Value Approach to Pricing," *Industrial Marketing Management*, May 1993, pp. 133–40; Valarie A. Zeithaml, "Consumer Perceptions of Price, Quality, and Value: A Means-End Model and Synthesis of Evidence," *Journal of Marketing*, July 1988, pp. 2–22.

14. Thomas T. Nagle, *The Strategy and Tactics of Pricing*, pp. 170–72; Manjit S. Yadav and Kent B. Monroe, "How Buyers Perceive Savings in a Bundle Price: An Examination of a Bundle's Transaction Value," *Journal of Marketing Research*, August 1993, pp. 350–58; Dorothy Paun, "When to Bundle or Unbundle Products," *Industrial Marketing Management*, February 1993, pp. 29–34.

15. Daniel T. Ostas, "Ethics of Contract Pricing," *Journal of Business Ethics*, February 1992, pp. 137–46; J. Steve Davis, "Ethical Problems in Competitive Bidding: The Paradyne Case," *Business and Professional Ethics Journal* 7, no. 2 (1988), pp. 3–26; David T. Levy, "Guaranteed Pricing in Industrial Purchases: Making Use of Markets in Contractual Relations," *Industrial Marketing Management*, October 1994, pp. 307–14; Akintola Akintoye and Martin Skitmore, "Pricing Approaches in the Construction Industry," *Industrial Marketing Management*, November 1992, pp. 311–18; Wayne J. Morse, "Probabilistic Bidding Models: A Synthesis," *Business Horizons*, April 1975, pp. 67–74; Stephen Paranka, "Competitive Bidding Strategy," *Business Horizons*, June 1971, pp. 39–43.

Chapter 19

1. "What's Driving the New PC Shakeout?" *Fortune*, September 19, 1994, pp. 109–22; "Beyond Rock Bottom," *Business Week*, March 14, 1994, pp. 90–92; "Dell Programs New Products, Sales Strategy," *The Wall Street Journal*, August 2, 1993, p. B1ff.; "Dell Computer Goes into the Shop," *Business Week*, July 12, 1993,

pp. 138–40; "For Compaq and Dell, Accent Is on Personal in the Computer Wars," *The Wall Street Journal*, July 2, 1993, p. A1ff.; "Companies that Serve You Best," *Fortune*, May 31, 1993, pp. 74–88; "The Education of Michael Dell," *Business Week*, March 22, 1993, pp. 82–88; "Dell Computer, Battling Large Retailers, to Slip a Superstore in America's Mailbox," *The Wall Street Journal*, September 10, 1992, p. B1ff.; "Smart Selling: How Companies Are Winning over Today's Tougher Customers," *Business Week*, August 3, 1992, pp. 46–52; "Dell Computer Battles Its Rivals with a Lean Machine," *The Wall Street Journal*, March 30, 1992, p. B4; "Breaking into European Markets by Breaking the Rules," *Business Week*, January 20, 1992, pp. 88–89; "Computer Superstores Muscle In," *USA Today*, July 8, 1991, pp. 1B–2B; "Whatever Happened to the Corner Computer Store?" *Business Week*, May 20, 1991, pp. 131–32ff.

2. *1993 Annual Report*, Loctite; "Companies to Watch: Loctite Corporation," *Fortune*, June 19, 1989, p. 148; "Loctite: Home Is Where the Customers Are," *Business Week*, April 13, 1987, p. 63; *1987 Annual Report*, Loctite; "Loctite 'Listens' to the Marketplace," in *The Wall Street Journal on Marketing*, ed. Ronald Alsop and Bill Abrams (New York: Dow Jones & Company, 1986), pp. 281–83.

3. *1993 Annual Report*, Monsanto; "Monsanto Touts New Sugar Substitute as Sweetest Yet," *The Wall Street Journal*, March 29, 1991, p. B1; "NutraSweet Rivals Stirring," *Advertising Age*, June 26, 1989, p. 3ff.; "New Sweeteners Head for the Sugar Bowl," *The Wall Street Journal*, February 6, 1989, p. B1; "NutraSweet Sets Out for Fat-Substitute City," *Business Week*, February 15, 1988, pp. 100–103; "NutraSweet May Develop Its Own Simplesse Brands," *Advertising Age*, February 8, 1988, p. 4ff.; "Marketing NutraSweet in Leaner Times," *The Wall Street Journal*, May 7, 1987, p. 36.

4. John E. Smallwood, "The Product Life Cycle: A Key to Strategic Marketing Planning," *MSU Business Topics*, Winter 1973, pp. 29–35; Richard F. Savach and Laurence A. Thompson, "Resource Allocation within the Product Life Cycle," *MSU Business Topics*, Autumn 1978, pp. 35–44; Peter F. Kaminski and David R. Rink, "PLC: The Missing Link between Physical Distribution and Marketing Planning," *International Journal of Physical Distribution and Materials Management* 14, no. 6 (1984), pp. 77–92.

5. See most basic statistics textbooks under time series analysis.

6. Checking the accuracy of forecasts is a difficult subject. See "Don't Be Trapped by Past Success," *Nation's Business*, March 1992, pp. 52–54; Margaret K. Ambry, "States of the Future," *American Demographics*, October 1994, pp. 36–45; John B. Mahaffie, "Why Forecasts Fail," *American Demographics*, March 1995, pp. 34–41; Richard H. Evans, "Analyzing the Potential of a New Market," *Industrial Marketing Management*, February 1993, pp. 35–40; Shelby H. McIntyre, Dale D. Achabal, and Christopher M. Miller, "Applying Case-Based Reasoning to Forecasting Retail Sales," *Journal of Retailing*, Winter 1993, pp. 372–98; Paul A. Berbig, John Milewicz, and James E. Golden, "The Do's and Don'ts of Sales Forecasting," *Industrial Marketing Management*, February 1993, pp. 49–58; David L. Kendall and Michael T. French, "Forecasting the Potential for New Industrial Products," *Industrial Marketing Management* 20, no. 3 (1991), pp. 177–84; John T. Mentzer and Roger Gomes, "Evaluating a Decision Support Forecasting System," *Industrial Marketing Management* 18, no. 4 (1989), pp. 313–24; James E. Cox, Jr.,

"Approaches for Improving Salespersons' Forecasts," *Industrial Marketing Management* 18, no. 4 (1989), pp. 307–12; Ronald D. Michman, "Why Forecast for the Long Term?" *The Journal of Business Strategy*, September/October 1989, pp. 36–41; F. William Barnett, "Four Steps to Forecast Total Market Demand," *Harvard Business Review*, July–August 1988, pp. 28–40; Robert H. Collins and Rebecca J. Mauritson, "Artificial Intelligence in Sales Forecasting Applications," *Journal of Personal Selling and Sales Management*, May 1987, pp. 77–80; Arthur J. Adams, "Procedures for Revising Management Judgments Forecasts," *Journal of the Academy of Marketing Science*, Fall 1986, pp. 52–57; D. M. Georgoff and R. G. Murdick, "Manager's Guide to Forecasting," *Harvard Business Review*, January–February 1986, pp. 110–20.

7. William Sandy, "Avoid the Breakdowns between Planning and Implementation," *The Journal of Business Strategy*, September/October 1991, pp. 30–33; Michael MacInnis and Louise A. Heslop, "Market Planning in a High-Tech Environment," *Industrial Marketing Management*, May 1990, pp. 107–16; Bay Arinze, "Market Planning with Computer Models: A Case Study in the Software Industry," *Industrial Marketing Management*, May 1990, pp. 117–30; "Marketing Software Review: Project Management Made Easy," *Business Marketing*, February 1989, pp. 20–27.

8. For further discussion on evaluating and selecting alternative plans, see Francis Buttle, "The Marketing Strategy Worksheet—A Practical Planning Tool," *Long Range Planning*, August 1985, pp. 80–88; Douglas A. Schellinck, "Effect of Time on a Marketing Strategy," *Industrial Marketing Management*, April 1983, pp. 83–88; George S. Day and Liam Fahey, "Valuing Market Strategies," *Journal of Marketing*, July 1988, pp. 45–57.

9. Sam C. Okoroafo, "Modes of Entering Foreign Markets," *Industrial Marketing Management* 20, no. 4 (1991), pp. 341–46; Mike Van Horn, "Market-Entry Approaches for the Pacific Rim," *Journal of Business Strategy*, March/April 1990, pp. 14–19; Refik Culpan, "Export Behavior of Firms: Relevance of Firm Size," *Journal of Business Research*, May 1989, pp. 207–18; Anthony C. Koh and Robert A. Robicheaux, "Variations in Export Performance Due to Differences in Export Marketing Strategy: Implications for Industrial Marketers," *Journal of Business Research*, November 1988, pp. 249–58; S. Tamer Cavusgil, Shaoming Zou, and G. M. Naidu, "Product and Promotion Adaptation in Export Ventures: An Empirical Investigation," *Journal of International Business Studies*, third quarter 1993, pp. 479–506; S. Tamer Cavusgil and Jacob Naor, "Firm and Management Characteristics as Discriminators of Export Marketing," *Journal of Business Research*, June 1987, pp. 221–36; Camille P. Schuster and Charles D. Bodkin, "Market Segmentation Practices of Exporting Companies," *Industrial Marketing Management*, May 1987, pp. 95–102.

10. "For U.S. Marketers, the Russian Front Is No Bowl of 'Vishnyas,' " *Adweek's Marketing Week*, March 5, 1990; "Learning the Exporting Ropes," *Business Marketing*, May 1989, pp. 80–85; " 'Papa-Mama' Stores in Japan Wield Power to Hold Back Imports," *The Wall Street Journal*, November 14, 1988, p. A1ff.; Jerry Haar and Marta Ortiz-Buonafina, "The Internationalization Process and Marketing Activities: The Case of Brazilian Export Firms," *Journal of Business Research*, February 1995, pp. 175–82; "U.S. Concerns Trying to Do Business in Japan Face Government, Market, Cultural Barriers," *The Wall Street Journal*, July 8, 1985, p. 16; F. H. Rolf Seringhaus, "Using Trade Missions for Export

Market Entry," *Industrial Marketing Management*, November 1987, pp. 249–56.

11. John A. Quelch, "How to Build a Product Licensing Program," *Harvard Business Review*, May–June 1985, p. 186ff.

12. "The Steel Deal that Could Boost Big Blue in Brazil," *Business Week*, May 19, 1986, p. 66. See also Robert Porter Lynch, "Building Alliances to Penetrate European Markets," *The Journal of Business Strategy*, March/April 1990, pp. 4–9; D. Robert Webster, "International Joint Ventures with Pacific Rim Partners," *Business Horizons*, March/April 1989, pp. 65–71; Kenichi Ohmae, "The Global Logic of Strategic Alliances," *Harvard Business Review*, March/April 1989, pp. 143–54.

13. "Top U.S. Companies Move into Russia," *Fortune*, July 31, 1989, pp. 165–71; "When U.S. Joint Ventures with Japan Go Sour," *Business Week*, July 24, 1989, pp. 30–31; "More Competitors Turn to Cooperation: Joint Ventures Are Encouraged by Government," *The Wall Street Journal*, June 23, 1989, p. B1; Paul Lawrence and Charalambos Vlachoutsicos, "Joint Ventures in Russia: Put the Locals in Charge," *Harvard Business Review*, January–February 1993, pp. 44–55; "Your Rivals Can Be Your Allies," *Fortune*, March 27, 1989, pp. 66–76; "How a German Firm Joined with Soviets to Make Good Shoes," *The Wall Street Journal*, February 14, 1989, p. A1ff.; F. Kingston Berlew, "The Joint Venture—A Way into Foreign Markets," *Harvard Business Review*, July–August 1985, pp. 48–55; Robert B. Reich and Eric D. Mankin, "Joint Ventures with Japan Give Away Our Future," *Harvard Business Review*, March/April 1986, pp. 78–86; D. Robert Webster, "International Joint Ventures with Pacific Rim Partners," *Business Horizons*, March/April 1989, pp. 65–71.

14. "Young Managers Learn Global Skills," *The Wall Street Journal*, March 31, 1992, p. B1; "As Costs of Overseas Assignments Climb, Firms Select Expatriates More Carefully," *The Wall Street Journal*, January 9, 1992, p. B1ff.; Chi-fai Chan and Neil B. Holbert, "Whose Empire Is This, Anyway? Reflections on the Empire State of Multi-National Corporations," *Business Horizons*, July–August 1994, pp. 51–54; Syed H. Akhter and Yusuf A. Choudhry, "Forced Withdrawal from a Country Market: Managing Political Risk," *Business Horizons*, May–June 1993, pp. 47–54; M. Krishna Erramilli and C. P. Rao, "Service Firms' International Entry-Mode Choice: A Modified Transaction-Cost Analysis Approach," *Journal of Marketing*, July 1993, pp. 19–38; "Companies in Europe Seeking Executives Who Can Cross Borders in a Single Bound," *The Wall Street Journal*, January 25, 1991, p. B1ff.; Christopher A. Bartlett, "MNCs: Get Off the Reorganization Merry-Go-Round," *Harvard Business Review*, March–April 1983, pp. 138–46; M. Krishna Erramilli, "Influence of Some External and Internal Environmental Factors on Foreign Market Entry Mode Choice in Service Firms," *Journal of Business Research*, December 1992, pp. 263–76; James M. Hulbert, William K. Brant, and Raimar Richers, "Marketing Planning in the Multinational Subsidiary: Practices and Problems," *Journal of Marketing*, Summer 1980, pp. 7–16.

Chapter 20

1. "Retailers Go Global," *Fortune*, February 20, 1995, pp. 102–8; "Kmart's Dowdy Stores Get a Snazzy Face Lift, but Problems Linger," *The Wall Street Journal*, November 5, 1993, p. B1ff.; "The High Cost of Second Best," *Fortune*, July 26, 1993, pp. 99–102; "Shopping's Big Chill," *U.S. News & World Report*,

July 12, 1993, pp. 44–46; "Kmart's Czech Invasion Lurches Along," *The Wall Street Journal*, June 8, 1993, p. A12; "U.S. Firms Yell Ole to Future in Mexico," *The Wall Street Journal*, March 8, 1993, p. B1ff.; *1993 Annual Report*, Kmart; "The 'New' Kmart Has the Last Laugh," *Adweek's Marketing Week*, February 24, 1992, pp. 26–27; *1991 Annual Report*, Kmart; "Kmart Introduces High-Tech Changes to Make Sales Comeback," *Marketing News*, October 28, 1991, p. 7; "Kmart Corp. Stands Pat Despite Sears' Offensive," *Advertising Age*, June 5, 1989, p. 55; "Kmart's Hyperactive," *Advertising Age*, January 23, 1989, p. 1ff.; "Attention Kmart Shoppers: Style Coming to This Aisle," *The Wall Street Journal*, August 9, 1988, p. 6.

2. Ram Charan, "How Networks Reshape Organizations—For Results," *Harvard Business Review*, September/October 1991, pp. 104–15; "The Personal Computer Finds Its Missing Link," *Business Week*, June 5, 1989, pp. 120–29; "An Electronic Pipeline that's Changing the Way America Does Business," *Business Week*, August 3, 1987, pp. 80–82; "Computer Finds a Role in Buying and Selling, Reshaping Businesses," *The Wall Street Journal*, March 18, 1987, p. 1ff.; "Computers Bringing Changes to Basic Business Documents," *The Wall Street Journal*, March 6, 1987, p. 33; "Networking: Japan's Latest Computer Craze," *Fortune*, July 7, 1986, pp. 94–96; William J. Bruns, Jr., and W. Warren McFarlan, "Information Technology Puts Power in Control Systems," *Harvard Business Review*, September–October 1987, pp. 89–94.

3. "Pillsbury's Telephones Ring with Peeves, Praise," *The Wall Street Journal*, April 20, 1994, p. B1ff.; " 'Do Call Us': More Companies Install 1-800 Phone Lines," *The Wall Street Journal*, April 20, 1994, p. B1ff.; "Your Pet Iguana Swallowed a Staple? Computerized Help Desk Will Try to Help," *The Wall Street Journal*, November 3, 1993, p. B1ff.

4. "How Market Leaders Keep Their Edge," *Fortune*, February 6, 1995, pp. 88–98.

5. Thomas V. Bonoma, "Making Your Marketing Strategy Work," *Harvard Business Review*, March–April 1984, pp. 68–76; Barbara J. Coe, "Key Differentiating Factors and Problems Associated with Implementation of Strategic Market Planning," in *1985 American Marketing Association Educators' Proceedings*, ed. R. F. Lusch et al. (Chicago: American Marketing Association, 1985), pp. 275–81.

6. The restaurant case is adapted from Marie Gaudard, Roland Coates, and Liz Freeman, "Accelerating Improvement," *Quality Progress*, October 1991, pp. 81–88. For more on quality management and control, see "Heath-Care Providers Try Industrial Tactics to Reduce Their Costs," *The Wall Street Journal*, November 3, 1993, p. A1ff.; "TQM: More than a Dying Fad?" *Fortune*, October 18, 1993, pp. 66–72; "Total Quality by Satellite," *Nation's Business*, March 1992, pp. 49–51; "Quality Control from Mars," *The Wall Street Journal*, January 27, 1992, p. A12; "Can American Steel Find Quality?" *Industry Week*, January 20, 1992, pp. 36–39; Charles R. O'Neal and William C. LaFief, "Marketing's Lead Role in Total Quality," *Industrial Marketing Management*, May 1992, pp. 133–44; Sumer Aggarwal, "A Quick Guide to Total Quality Management," *Business Horizons*, May–June 1993, pp. 66–68; Daniel Niven, "When Times Get Tough, What Happens to TQM?" *Harvard Business Review*, May–June 1993, pp. 20–37; Peter Mears, "How to Stop Talking about, and Begin Progress toward, Total Quality Management," *Business Horizons*, May–June 1993, pp. 11–14; "The Quality Imperative," *Business Week*, (special issue), October 25, 1991; "Motorola's Baldrige Award-Winning Ways," *Business Marketing*, September 1991, pp. 14–15; " 'Q' Tips," *CIO*, August 1991, pp. 26–31; "The Fabric of Quality," *CIO*, August 1991, pp. 34–41.

7. Roland T. Rust, Anthony J. Zahorik, and Timothy L. Keiningham, *Return on Quality* (Chicago: Probus, 1994); "Finding, Training & Keeping the Best Service Workers," *Fortune*, October 3, 1994, pp. 110–22; Timothy L. Keiningham, Roland T. Rust, and M. Marshall Weems, "The Bottom Line on Quality," *Financial Executive*, September/October 1994, pp. 50–52; "Pipe Dreams," *Inc.*, August 1994, pp. 64–70; Harvey N. Shycon, "Improved Customer Service: Measuring the Payoff," *The Journal of Business Strategy*, January/February 1992, pp. 13–17; A. Lynn Daniel, "Overcome the Barriers to Superior Customer Service," *The Journal of Business Strategy*, January/February 1992, pp. 18–24; Leonard A. Schlesinger and James L. Heskett, "The Service-Driven Service Company," *Harvard Business Review*, September/October 1991, pp. 71–81; M. P. Singh, "Service as a Marketing Strategy: A Case Study at Reliance Electric," *Industrial Marketing Management*, August 1990, pp. 193–200; "For Computer Makers, Service Is the Soul of the New Machine," *Adweek's Marketing Week*, May 21, 1990, pp. 20–26; James S. Hensel, "Service Quality Improvement and Control: A Customer-Based Approach," *Journal of Business Research*, January 1990, pp. 43–54; Scott W. Kelley, "Developing Customer Orientation among Service Employees," *Journal of the Academy of Marketing Science*, Winter 1992, pp. 27–36; William George, "Internal Marketing and Organizational Behavior: A Partnership in Developing Customer-Conscious Employees at Every Level," *Journal of Business Research*, January 1990, pp. 63–70; Robert Frey, "Empowerment or Else," *Harvard Business Review*, September–October 1993, p. 80; Frank K. Sonnenberg, "Marketing: Service Quality: Forethought, Not Afterthought," *The Journal of Business Strategy*, September/October 1989, pp. 54–58; Glenn DeSouza, "Now Service Businesses Must Manage Quality," *The Journal of Business Strategy*, May/June 1989, pp. 21–25; Christopher Meyer, "How the Right Measures Help Teams Excel," *Harvard Business Review*, May–June 1994, pp. 95–104; Stephen W. Brown and Teresa A. Swartz, "A Gap Analysis of Professional Service Quality," *Journal of Marketing*, April 1989, pp. 92–98.

8. *1993 Annual Report*, Ben & Jerry's; "Ben & Jerry's: Surviving the Big Squeeze," *Food Business*, May 6, 1991, pp. 10–12; "The Peace Pop Puzzle," *Inc.*, March 1990, p. 25; *1990 Annual Report*, Ben & Jerry's. See also William C. Taylor, "Control in an Age of Chaos," *Harvard Business Review*, November–December 1994, pp. 64–90; Bernard J. Jaworski, Vlasis Stathakopoulos, and H. Shanker Krishnan, "Control Combinations in Marketing: Conceptual Framework and Empirical Evidence," *Journal of Marketing*, January 1993, pp. 57–69; Subhash Sharma and Dale D. Achabal, "STEMCOM: An Analytical Model for Marketing Control," *Journal of Marketing*, Spring 1982, pp. 104–13; Sam R. Goodman, *Techniques of Profitability Analysis* (New York: John Wiley & Sons, 1970), especially Chapter 1; Kenneth A. Merchant, "Progressing toward a Theory of Marketing Control: A Comment," *Journal of Marketing*, July 1988, pp. 40–44.

9. Ed Weymes, "A Different Approach to Retail Sales Analysis," *Business Horizons*, March/April 1982, pp. 66–74; D. H. Robertson, "Sales Force Feedback on Competitors' Activities," *Journal of Marketing*, April 1974, pp. 69–71. See also Robert H. Collins, Regan F. Carey, and Rebecca F. Mauritson, "Microcomputer

Applications: Maps on a Micro—Applications in Sales and Marketing Management," *Journal of Personal Selling and Sales Management*, November 1987, p. 83ff.

10. Robin Cooper and Robert S. Kaplan, "Profit Priorities from Activity-Based Costing," *Harvard Business Review*, May/June 1991, pp. 130–37; Douglas M. Lambert and Jay U. Sterling, "What Types of Profitability Reports Do Marketing Managers Receive?" *Industrial Marketing Management*, November 1987, pp. 295–304; Nigel F. Piercy, "The Marketing Budgeting Process: Marketing Management Implications," *Journal of Marketing*, October 1987, pp. 45–59; Michael J. Sandretto, "What Kind of Cost System Do You Need?" *Harvard Business Review*, January–February 1985, pp. 110–18; Patrick M. Dunne and Harry I. Wolk, "Marketing Cost Analysis: A Modularized Contribution Approach," *Journal of Marketing*, July 1977, pp. 83–94; V. H. Kirpalani and Stanley J. Shapiro, "Financial Dimensions of Marketing Management," *Journal of Marketing*, July 1973, pp. 40–47.

11. Technically, a distinction should be made between variable and direct costs, but we will use these terms interchangeably. Similarly, not all costs that are common to several products are fixed costs, and vice versa. But the important point here is to recognize that some costs are fairly easy to allocate, and other costs are not. See Stewart A. Washburn, "Establishing Strategy and Determining Costs in the Pricing Decision," *Business Marketing*, July 1985, pp. 64–78.

12. Leonard L. Berry, Jeffrey S. Conant, and A. Parasuraman, "A Framework for Conducting a Services Marketing Audit," *Journal of the Academy of Marketing Science*, Summer 1991, pp. 255–68; John F. Grashof, "Conducting and Using a Marketing Audit," in *Readings in Basic Marketing*, ed. E. J. McCarthy, J. J. Grashof, and A. A. Brogowicz (Burr Ridge, IL: Richard D. Irwin, 1984); Alice M. Tybout and John R. Hauser, "A Marketing Audit Using a Conceptual Model of Consumer Behavior: Application and Evaluation," *Journal of Marketing*, Summer 1981, pp. 82–101.

Chapter 21

1. "The Ultimate Nuts and Bolts Company," *Fortune*, July 16, 1990, pp. 70–73.

2. Robert C. Pozen, "Institutional Investors: The Reluctant Activists," *Harvard Business Review*, January–February 1994, p. 140; W. Keith Schilit, "The Globalization of Venture Capital," *Business Horizons*, January–February 1992, pp. 17–23; Michael E. Porter, "Capital Disadvantage: America's Failing Capital Investment System," *Harvard Business Review*, September–October 1992, pp. 65–83; Bill Parks, "Rate of Return—The Poison Apple?" *Business Horizons*, May–June 1993, pp. 55–58.

3. *1993 Annual Report*, Home Depot.

4. *Sorrell Ridge: Slotting Allowances* (Cambridge, MA: Harvard Business School, 1988).

5. Amar Bhide, "Bootstrap Finance: The Art of Start-Ups," *Harvard Business Review*, November–December 1992, pp. 109–17; Marv Rubinstein, "Effective Industrial Marketing with a Piggy Bank Budget," *Industrial Marketing Management*, August 1992, pp. 203–14; Amar Bhide, "How Entrepreneurs Craft Strategies that Work," *Harvard Business Review*, March–April 1994, pp. 150–63.

6. Roger S. Schroeder and Michael J. Pesch, "Focusing the Factory: Eight Lessons," *Business Horizons*, September–October

1994, pp. 76–81; James P. Womack and Daniel T. Jones, "From Lean Production to the Lean Enterprise," *Harvard Business Review*, March–April 1994, pp. 93–105; Andrew D. Bartmess, "The Plant Location Puzzle," *Harvard Business Review*, March–April 1994, pp. 20–38; Robert H. Hayes and Gary P. Pisano, "Beyond World-Class: The New Manufacturing Strategy," *Harvard Business Review*, January–February 1994, pp. 77–87; Victoria L. Crittenden, Lorraine R. Gardiner, and Antonie Stam, "Reducing Conflict between Marketing and Manufacturing," *Industrial Marketing Management*, November 1993, pp. 299–310; Paul A. Konijnendijk, "Dependence and Conflict between Production and Sales," *Industrial Marketing Management*, August 1993, pp. 161–68; Kenneth B. Kahn and John T. Mentzer, "Norms That Distinguish between Marketing and Manufacturing," *Journal of Business Research*, June 1994, pp. 111–18; William B. Wagner, "Establishing Supply Service Strategy for Shortage Situations," *Industrial Marketing Management*, December 1994, pp. 393–402; Roger W. Schmenner, "So You Want to Lower Costs?" *Business Horizons*, July–August 1992, pp. 24–28.

7. For more on Nabisco's Snackwell cookies, see "Man Walked on the Moon but Man Can't Make Enough Devil's Food Cookie Cakes," *The Wall Street Journal*, September 26, 1993, p. B1ff.; "They're Not Crying in Their Crackers at Nabisco," *Business Week*, August 30, 1993, p. 61. For more on Rice Krispies Treats cereal, see "Special Report: Brand in Demand," *Advertising Age*, February 7, 1994, pp. S1–10; "Kellogg to Consumers: Please Bear with Us," *Advertising Age*, March 29, 1993, p. 44; see also J. Mahajan et al., "An Exploratory Investigation of the Interdependence between Marketing and Operations Functions in Service Firms," *International Journal of Research in Marketing*, January 1994, pp. 1–16.

8. " 'Virtual' Companies Leave the Manufacturing to Others," *New York Times*, July 17, 1994, sec. 3, p. 5; "Shaken by a Series of Business Setbacks, Calvin Klein Is Redesigning Itself," *The Wall Street Journal*, March 21, 1994, p. B1; "Calvin Klein Inc.: Definitive Pact Is Reached on Sales of Jeans Division," *The Wall Street Journal*, July 15, 1994, p. B4.

9. *1993 Annual Report*, Baldor; "Baldor's Success: Made in the U.S.A.," *Fortune*, July 17, 1989, pp. 101–4; see also Jeen-Su Lim and David A. Reid, "Vital Cross-Functional Linkages with Marketing," *Industrial Marketing Management*, May 1992, pp. 159–66.

10. L. Scott Flaig, "The 'Virtual Enterprise': Your New Model for Success," *Electronic Business*, March 30, 1992, pp. 153–55; William H. Davidow and Michael S. Malone, *The Virtual Corporation* (New York: Harper Collins, 1992).

11. "For Compaq and Dell, Accent Is on Personal in the Computer Wars," *The Wall Street Journal*, July 2, 1993, p. A1ff.; "Dell Computer Goes into the Shop," *Business Week*, July 12, 1993, pp. 138–40; "Companies that Serve You Best," *Fortune*, May 31, 1993, pp. 74–88; "Dell Computer Battles Its Rivals with a Lean Machine," *The Wall Street Journal*, March 30, 1992, p. B4.

12. For more on Levi Strauss's custom-fit jeans for women, see "One Writer's Hunt for the Perfect Jeans," *Fortune*, April 17, 1995, p. 30; "Levi Strauss Sizes the Retail Scene," *Advertising Age*, January 23, 1995, p. 4; B. Joseph Pine II, Bart Victor, and Andrew C. Boynton, "Making Mass Customization Work," *Harvard Business Review*, September–October 1993, pp. 108–21.

13. *Sara Lee: Rapid Response at Hanes Knitware* (Cambridge, MA: Harvard Business School, 1993); see also Edward W. Davis, "Global Outsourcing: Have U.S. Managers Thrown the Baby Out with the Bath Water?" *Business Horizons*, July–August 1992, pp. 58–65.

14. For more on Levi Strauss hiring foreign labor, see "Managing by Values," *Business Week*, August 1, 1994, pp. 46–52; "Working for Mr. Clean Jeans," *U.S. News & World Report*, August 2, 1993, pp. 49–50; Martha Nichols, "Third-World Families at Work: Child Labor or Child Care?" *Harvard Business Review*, January–February 1993, pp. 12–23.

15. Jae K. Shim and Joel G. Siegel, *Modern Cost Management and Analysis* (Hauppauge, NY: Barrons, 1992); John K. Shank and Vijay Govindarajan, *Strategic Cost Management: The New Tool for Competitive Advantage* (New York: Free Press, 1993); Robin Cooper and Robert S. Kaplan, "Profit Priorities from Activity-Based Costing," *Harvard Business Review*, May/June 1991, pp. 130–37; Douglas M. Lambert and Jay U. Sterling, "What Types of Profitability Reports Do Marketing Managers Receive?" *Industrial Marketing Management*, November 1987, pp. 295–304.

16. Myron Glassman and Bruce McAfee, "Integrating the Personnel and Marketing Functions: The Challenge of the 1990s," *Business Horizons*, May–June 1992, pp. 52–59; Madhubalan Viswanathan and Eric M. Olson, "The Implementation of Business Strategies: Implications for the Sales Function," *Journal of Personal Selling & Sales Management*, Winter 1992, pp. 45–58; L. McTier Anderson and James W. Fenton, Jr. "The Light at the End of the HRM Tunnel: Window of Opportunity or an Oncoming Train?" *Business Horizons*, January–February 1993, pp. 72–76; Jeanie Daniel Duck, "Managing Change: The Art of Balancing," *Harvard Business Review*, November–December 1993, pp. 109–18; James R. Emshoff, "How to Increase Employee Loyalty while You Downsize," *Business Horizons*, March–April 1994, pp. 49–57.

Chapter 22

1. "Little Is Common beyond Gender?" *Insight*, December 10, 1990, pp. 48–49; Terry Clark, "Moving Mountains to Market: Reflections on Restructuring the Russian Economy," *Business Horizons*, March–April 1994, pp. 16–21.

2. "Push-Button Age," *Newsweek*, July 9, 1990, pp. 56–57; "After the Beep: The Message Is Convenience Matters Most," *The Wall Street Journal*, September 19, 1989, pp. B1–2; "Design Is Hot in the Cold Business," *Insight*, September 18, 1989, pp. 44–45; Cornelia Dröge et al., "The Consumption Culture and Its Critiques: A Framework for Analysis," *Journal of Macromarketing*, Fall 1993, pp. 32–45; John P. Robinson, "Your Money or Your Time," *American Demographics*, November 1991, pp. 22–26; "Fast-Track Kids Exhaust Their Parents," *The Wall Street Journal*, August 7, 1991, p. B1ff.; John P. Robinson, "The Time Squeeze," *American Demographics*, February 1990, pp. 30–33; "Smart Cards: Pocket Power," *Newsweek*, July 31, 1989, pp. 54–55; "How America Has Run Out of Time," *Time*, April 24, 1989, pp. 58–67; Cheryl Russell, "What's Your Hurry?" *American Demographics*, April 1989, p. 2; Ruth Hamel, "Living in Traffic," *American Demographics*, March 1989, pp. 49–51; "Life in the Express Lane," *Time*, June 16, 1986, p. 64.

3. Claes Fornell, "A National Customer Satisfaction Barometer: The Swedish Experience," *Journal of Marketing*, January 1992, pp. 6–21; John F. Gaski and Michael J. Etzel, "The Index of Consumer Sentiment toward Marketing," *Journal of Marketing,* July 1986, pp. 71–81; Robert B. Woodruff, Ernest R. Cadotte, and Roger L. Jenkins, "Modeling Consumer Satisfaction Processes Using Experience-Based Norms," *Journal of Marketing Research,* August 1983, pp. 297–304; Hiram C. Barksdale et al., "A Cross-National Survey of Consumer Attitudes toward Marketing Practices, Consumerism, and Government Regulations," *Columbia Journal of World Business,* Summer 1982, pp. 71–86; Hiram C. Barksdale and William D. Perreault, Jr., "Can Consumers Be Satisfied?" *MSU Business Topics,* Spring 1980, pp. 19–30.

4. Robert A. Peterson and William R. Wilson, "Measuring Customer Satisfaction: Fact and Artifact," *Journal of the Academy of Marketing Science,* Winter 1992, pp. 61–72; Glenn DeSouza, "Designing a Customer Retention Plan," *Journal of Business Strategy,* March/April 1992, pp. 24–28; Frank V. Cespedes, "Once More: How Do You Improve Customer Service?" *Business Horizons,* March/April 1992, pp. 58–67; Mary C. Gilly, William B. Stevenson, and Laura J. Yale, "Dynamics of Complaint Management in the Service Organization," *Journal of Consumer Affairs,* Winter 1991, pp. 295–322; F. Gouillart and F. Sturdivant, "Spend a Day in the Life of Your Customers," *Harvard Business Review,* January–February 1994, pp. 116–27; C. Dröge and D. Halstead, "Postpurchase Hierarchies of Effects: The Antecedents and Consequences of Satisfaction for Complainers versus Non-Complainers," *International Journal of Research in Marketing,* November 1991, pp. 315–28; Erdener Kaynak, Orsay Kucukemiroglu, and Yavuz Odabasi, "Consumer Complaint Handling in an Advanced Developing Economy: An Empirical Investigation," *Journal of Business Ethics,* November 1992, pp. 813–30; Jagdip Singh, "Industry Characteristics and Consumer Dissatisfaction," *Journal of Consumer Affairs,* Summer 1991, pp. 19–56; Jerry Plymire, "Complaints as Opportunities," *Business Horizons,* March/April 1991, pp. 79–81; Barbara C. Garland and Robert A. Westbrook, "An Exploration of Client Satisfaction in a Nonprofit Context," *Journal of the Academy of Marketing Science,* Fall 1989, pp. 297–304; A. Parasuraman, Valarie A. Zeithaml, and Leonard L. Berry, "SERVQUAL: A Multiple-Item Scale for Measuring Consumer Perceptions of Service Quality," *Journal of Retailing,* Spring 1988, pp. 12–40; "Banks Stress Resolving Complaints to Win Small Customers' Favor," *The Wall Street Journal,* December 8, 1986, p. 31.

5. Kevin J. Clancy and Robert S. Shulman, *Marketing Myths that Are Killing Business: The Cure for Death Wish Marketing* (New York: McGraw-Hill, 1994); "Prof: TV Ads Not as Effective as Price and Promotions," *Marketing News,* March 27, 1989, p. 7; "IRI Research Bolsters Value of Advertising," *Advertising Age,* March 6, 1989, p. 71; "Don't Blame Television, Irate Readers Say," *The Wall Street Journal,* March 1, 1989, p. B6; "Television Ads Ring Up No Sale in Study," *The Wall Street Journal,* February 15, 1989, p. B6. For classic discussions of the problem and mechanics of measuring the efficiency of marketing, see Stanley C. Hollander, "Measuring the Cost and Value of Marketing," *Business Topics,* Summer 1961, pp. 17–26; Reavis Cox, *Distribution in a High-Level Economy* (Englewood Cliffs, NJ: Prentice Hall, 1965).

6. For more on this point, see Robert L. Steiner, "Does Advertising Lower Consumer Prices?" *Journal of Marketing,* October 1973, pp. 19–26; Robert L. Steiner, "Marketing Productivity in Consumer Goods Industries—A Vertical Perspective," *Journal of Marketing,* January 1978, pp. 60–70; see

also Robert B. Archibald, Clyde A. Haulman, and Carlisle E. Moody, Jr., "Quality, Price, Advertising, and Published Quality Ratings," *Journal of Consumer Research,* March 1983, pp. 347–56.

7. Arnold J. Toynbee, *America and World Revolution* (New York: Oxford University Press, 1966), pp. 144–45; see also John Kenneth Galbraith, *Economics and the Public Purpose* (Boston: Houghton Mifflin, 1973), pp. 144–45.

8. Russell J. Tomsen, "Take It Away," *Newsweek,* October 7, 1974, p. 21.

9. J. L. Engledow, "Was Consumer Satisfaction a Pig in a Poke?" *MSU Business Topics,* April 1977, p. 92.

10. "Deregulating America," *Business Week,* November 28, 1983, pp. 80–82; E. T. Grether, "Marketing and Public Policy: A Contemporary View," *Journal of Marketing,* July 1974, pp. 2–7; "Intellectuals Should Re-Examine the Marketplace: It Supports Them, Helps Keep Them Free," *Advertising Age,* January 28, 1963; David A. Heenan, "Congress Rethinks America's Competitiveness," *Business Horizons,* May/June 1989, pp. 11–16; Irvin Grossack and David A. Heenan, "Cooperation, Competition, and Antitrust: Two Views," *Business Horizons,* September/October 1986, pp. 24–28; Donald P. Robin and R. Eric Reidenbach, "Identifying Critical Problems for Mutual Cooperation between the Public and Private Sectors: A Marketing Perspective," *Journal of the Academy of Marketing Science,* Fall 1986, pp. 1–12.

11. Frederick Webster, *Social Aspects of Marketing* (Englewood Cliffs, NJ: Prentice Hall, 1974), p. 32.

12. "California 'Driving Force' in Cleaning Up the Air," *USA Today,* June 3, 1994, p. 9A; "Electric Cars," *Business Week,* May 30, 1994, pp. 104–14; "Why Electric Cars Make No Sense" *Fortune,* July 26, 1993, pp. 126–27.

13. Robert F. Lusch and Gene R. Laczniak, "Macroenvironmental Forces, Marketing Strategy and Business Performance: A Futures Research Approach," *Journal of the Academy of Marketing Science,* Fall 1989, pp. 283–96; "The Community's Persuasive Power," *Insight,* December 12, 1988, pp. 58–59; "Companies as Citizens: Should They Have a Conscience?" *The Wall Street Journal,* February 19, 1987, p. 29; Scott J. Vitell and James Muncy, "Consumer Ethics: An Empirical Investigation of Factors Influencing Ethical Judgments of the Final Consumer," *Journal of Business Ethics,* August 1992, pp. 585–98; John H. Antil, "Socially Responsible Consumers: Profile and Implications for Public Policy," *Journal of Macromarketing* 4, no. 2 (1984), pp. 18–39; John Priddle, "Marketing Ethics, Macromarketing, and the Managerial Perspective Reconsidered," *Journal of Macromarketing,* Fall 1994, pp. 47–62; Bernard Avishai, "What Is Business's Social Compact?" *Harvard Business Review,* January–February 1994, pp. 38–49. For more on privacy, see Paul N. Bloom, George R. Milne, and Robert Adler, "Avoiding Misuse of New Information Technologies: Legal and Societal Considerations," *Journal of Marketing,* January 1994, pp. 98–110; Ellen R. Foxman and Paula Kilcoyne, "Information Technology, Marketing Practice, and Consumer Privacy: Ethical Issues," *Journal of Public Policy & Marketing,* Spring 1993, pp. 106–19; "The $3 Billion Question: Whose Info Is It, Anyway?" *Business Week,* July 4, 1988, pp. 106–7; "Federal Agencies Press Data-Base Firms to Curb Access to 'Sensitive' Information," *The Wall Street Journal,* February 5, 1987, p. 23. For more on shoplifting, see "Indelible Color Guard against Shoplifting," *Insight,* June 25, 1990, p. 46; "Chicago Retailers' 'Sting' Aims to Put Shoplifting Professionals

Out of Business," *The Wall Street Journal*, June 5, 1990, p. B1ff.; Scott Dawson, "Consumer Responses to Electronic Article Surveillance Alarms," *Journal of Retailing*, Fall 1993, pp. 353–62; "Retailers Use Hidden Gadgets, High Alertness to Battle Theft," *Insight*, December 18, 1989, pp. 42–43; Warren A. French, Melvin R. Crask, and Fred H. Mader, "Retailers' Assessment of the Shoplifting Problem," *Journal of Retailing*, Winter 1984, pp. 108–15; Robert E. Wilkes, "Fraudulent Behavior by Consumers," *Journal of Marketing*, October 1978, pp. 67–75. For more on ethics, see Joel J. Davis, "Ethics and Environmental Marketing," *Journal of Business Ethics*, February 1992, pp. 81–88; James A. Muncy and Scott J. Vitell, "Consumer Ethics: An Investigation of the Ethical Beliefs of the Final Consumer," *Journal of Business Research*, June 1992, pp. 297–312; Scott J. Vitell, James R. Lumpkin, and Mohammed Y. A. Rawwas, "Consumer Ethics: An Investigation of the Ethical Beliefs of Elderly Consumers," *Journal of Business Ethics*, May 1991, pp. 365–76; Gene R. Laczniak and Patrick E. Murphy, "Fostering Ethical Marketing Decisions," *Journal of Business Ethics*, April 1991, pp. 259–72; Robert E. Pitts and Robert Allan Cooke, "A Realist View of Marketing Ethics," *Journal of Business Ethics*, April 1991, pp. 243–44; R. Eric Reidenbach, Donald P. Robin, and Lyndon Dawson, "An Application and Extension of a Multidimensional Ethics Scale to Selected Marketing Practices and Marketing Groups," *Journal of the Academy of Marketing Science*, Spring 1991, pp. 83–92; Donald P. Robin and R. Eric Reidenbach, "Social Responsibility, Ethics, and Marketing Strategy: Closing the Gap between Concept and Application," *Journal of Marketing*, January 1987, pp. 44–58.

14. "Green Groups Enter a Dry Season as Movement Matures," *The Wall Street Journal*, October 21, 1994, p. B1ff.; "Leaner Times Test Limits of Movement," *USA Today*, October 19, 1994, p. 1Aff.; Joel J. Davis, "Ethics and Environmental Marketing," *Journal of Business Ethics*, February 1992, pp. 81–88; David Biddle, "Recycling for Profit: The New Green Business Frontier," *Harvard Business Review*, November–December 1993, pp. 145–56; "The Green Movement Sows Demand for Ecofurniture," *The Wall Street Journal*, September 2, 1994, p. B1ff.; "CFC-Span: Refrigerant's Reign Nears an End," *USA Today*, August 22, 1994, p. 5B; "Wal-Mart Turns Green in Kansas," *American Demographics*, December 1993, p. 23; "Who Scores Best on the Environment," *Fortune*, July 26, 1993, pp. 114–22; "Air-Conditioner Firms Put Chill on Plans to Phase Out Use of Chlorofluorocarbons," *The Wall Street Journal*, May 10, 1993, p. B1ff.; "Environmental Price Tags," *Nation's Business*, April 1992, pp. 36–41; "It Doesn't Pay to Go Green When Consumers Are Seeing Red," *Adweek*, March 23, 1992, pp. 32–33; "Pollution Prevention Picks Up Steam," *Industry Week*, February 17, 1992, pp. 36–42; "Reach Out and Prod Someone," *Newsweek*, October 14, 1991, p. 50; "Herman Miller: How Green Is My Factory," *Business Week*, September 16, 1991, pp. 54–56; "The Big Muddle in Green Marketing," *Fortune*, June 3, 1991, pp. 91–100; "The Greening of Detroit," *Business Week*, April 8, 1991, pp. 54–60.

Appendix C

1. "Don't Call Me Slacker!" *Fortune*, December 12, 1994, pp. 180–96; "Special Report: Salary Survey," *Advertising Age*, December 5, 1994, pp. S1–12; "Coke's Move to Retain Goizueta Spotlights a Succession Problem," *The Wall Street Journal*, May 13, 1994, p. A1ff.; "New Job Path: From Cookies to Computers," *The Wall Street Journal*, May 9, 1994, p. B1ff.; "Careers: The Trade Winds Blow," *Brandweek*, August 10, 1992, pp. 12–14.

Illustration Credits

Chapter 1
Exhibits: *P. 16*, 1–2, adapted from Wroe Alderson, "Factors Governing the Development of Marketing Channels," in *Marketing Channels for Manufactured Products*, ed. Richard M. Clewett (Burr Ridge, IL: Richard D. Irwin, 1954), p. 7. *P. 23*, 1–3, adapted from William McInnes, "A Conceptual Approach to Marketing," in *Theory in Marketing*, 2nd ser., ed. Reavis Cox, Wroe Alderson, and Stanley J. Shapiro (Burr Ridge, IL: Richard D. Irwin, 1964), pp. 51–67. *P. 26*, 1–4, model suggested by Professor A. A. Brogowicz, Western Michigan University.

Photos/ads: *P.* © 1994, Kellogg Company. *p. 4*, (left) Courtesy Prince Sports Group, Inc.; (right) Courtesy Dunlop Slazenger Corporation. *p. 7*, Courtesy Ford Motor Company. *p. 9*, (left) Courtesy CPC International; © 1994 Chuck Fishman; (right) Courtesy The Hertz Corporation. *p. 12*, (left) P. LeSegretain/Sygma; (right) Courtesy Chiquita Brands International. *p. 13*, Courtesy Lever Brothers Company. *p. 16*, (left) © Steven Begleiter; (right) Greg Girard/Contact Press Images. *p. 20*, Courtesy Phillips Taiwan Ltd. © Adobe Systems Incorporated. All Right Reserved. Used with express permission. PhotoShop is a trademark of Adobe Systems, Incorporated or its subsidiaries and may be registered in certain jurisdictions. *p. 24*, Agency: Hal Riney & Partners; Art Director: Chris Chaffin; Copywriter: Tony Barlow; Photographer: Bob Mizono. *p. 25*, (left) Courtesy DHL Worldwide Express; (right) Courtesy Claritas.

Chapter 2
Exhibits: *P. 41*, 2–3, adapted from R. F. Vizza, T. E. Chambers, and E. J. Cook, *Adoption of the Marketing Concept—Fact or Fiction* (New York: Sales Executive Club, Inc., 1967), pp. 13–15. *P. 47*, 2–4, adapted from discussions of an American Marketing Association Strategic Planning Committee.

Photos/ads; *P. 33*, Zigy Kaluzny/Gamma Liaison. *p. 39*, Courtesy Bank of America Illinois. *p. 42*, © 1991 Jose Azel/Aurora. *p. 43*, Sharp Hartwig; Creative Director: Cynthia Hartwig. *p. 44*, Scott Wanner/Nawrocki Stock Photo. *P. 51*, (left) © 1994 The Upjohn Company; (right) © 1994 British Airways. *p. 54*, (left and right) courtesy University Brands. *p. 59*, The Clorox Company. *p. 60*, (left) Courtesy Timex Corporation; (right) Agency: AMH Italy; Creative director: Pasquale Barbella; Art Director: Agostino Toscana; Copywriter: Roberta Sollazzi; Photographer: Antonia Capa.

Chapter 3
Exhibits: *P. 84*, 3–2, Igor Ansoff, *Corporate Strategy* (New York, McGraw-Hill, 1965). *P. 111*, 3–15, Russell I. Haley, "Benefit Segmentation: A Decision-Oriented Research Tool," *Journal of Marketing*, July 1968, p. 33.

Photos/ads: *P. 81*, © 1994 Craig Molenhouse. *p. 83*, Courtesy Reebok International Ltd. *p. 86*, Courtesy MasterCard International, Inc. *p. 88*, (left) Courtesy Samsung Electronics America; (right) Courtesy Reynolds Metals Company. *p. 90*, (left) Courtesy Lever Brothers Company; (right) Courtesy Neutrogena Mexico Corporation. *p. 94*, (left and right) Courtesy USAir Group, Inc. *p. 101*, Courtesy Canon USA, Inc. *p. 109*, (left) Courtesy Den-Mat Corporation; (right) courtesy Colgate-Palmolive Company.

Chapter 4
Exhibits: *P. 143*, 4–7, adapted from M. G. Allen, "Strategic Problems Facing Today's Corporate Planner," speech given at the Academy of Management, 36th Annual Meeting, Kansas City, Missouri, 1976.

Photos/ads: *P. 117*, © 1993 Rubbermaid Incorporated, Wooster, Ohio. (Used with permission). *p. 119*, Courtesy British Airways, *p. 123*, Courtesy Spalding Sports Worldwide. *p. 124*, Courtesy Bozell Testa Pella Rossetti, Milan. *p. 131*, Courtesy RR Donnelley & Sons Company. *p. 133*, Courtesy AT&T. *p. 135*, (left) © 1994, Merck & Co., Inc.; (right) © 1994 SEARLE.

p. 145, (left and right) Courtesy Philip Morris Companies. *p. 146*, (left) Courtesy Unisys Corporation; (right) Courtesy Bates South Africa Cape Town.

Chapter 5
Exhibits: *P. 173*, 5–5, adapted from Paul E. Green, Frank J. Carmone, and David P. Wachpress, "On the Analysis of Qualitative Data in Marketing Research," *Journal of Marketing Research*, February 1977, pp. 52–59.

Photos/ads: *P. 151*, © 1994 LensCrafters, Inc., The United States Shoe Corporation, LensCrafters' parent company, is owner of LensCrafters' trademarks and service marks. *p. 152*, (left) Courtesy SAS Institute, Inc.; (right) Courtesy Norand Corporation. *p. 163*, Courtesy Renfro Corporation. *p. 164* © Steve Smith/Onyx. *p. 167*, Courtesy Colgate-Palmolive Company. *p. 169*, (left) © 1989 Jay Brousseau; (right) Courtesy The Great Atlantic & Pacific Tea Company. *p. 170*, (left and right) Courtesy Simmons Company. *p. 171*, (left) Courtesy Carewell Industries, Inc.; (right) Courtesy Nice-Pak Products, Inc. *p. 172*, (left) Courtesy SPSS, Inc.; (right) STSC, Inc. *p. 174*, (left) Courtesy Survey Sampling, Inc.; (right) Courtesy Donnelley Marketing Information Services.

Chapter 6
Exhibits: *Pp. 184–85*, 6–1, map developed by the authors based on data from U.S. Bureau of the Census, Reports WP/94 and WP/94-DD, *World Population Profile: 1994* (Washington, DC: U.S. Government Printing Office, 1994). *Pp. 186–87*, 6–2, table developed by the authors based on data from U.S. Bureau of the Census, Reports WP/94 and WP/94-DD, *World Population Profile: 1994* (Washington, DC: U.S. Government Printing Office, 1994) and U.S. Bureau of the Census, *Statistical Abstract of the United States 1994* (Washington, DC: U.S. Government Printing Office, 1994), pp. 850–52; PC Globe Maps 'N' Facts software (Novato, CA: Broderbund, 1993). *P. 191*, 6–3, map developed by the authors based on data from U.S. Bureau of the Census, *Statistical Abstract of the United States 1994* (Washington, DC: U.S. Government Printing Office, 1994), p. 33, and *Current Population Reports*, Series P25-1111, Table 1, "Total Population of Regions, Divisions, and States: 1990–2020—Series A (Preferred Series)." *P. 193*, 6–4, map developed by the authors based on data from *Current Population Reports*, Series P25-1111, Table 1, "Total Population of Regions, Divisions, and States: 1990–2020—Series A (Preferred Series)." *P. 194*, 6–5, U.S. Bureau of the Census, *Statistical Abstract of the United States 1994* (Washington, DC: U.S. Government Printing Office, 1994), p. 75, and *Current Population Reports*, Series 25-1104, Table 1, "Annual Projections and Components of Change for the United States: 1993 to 2050 (Middle Series), Part A, Total Population." *P. 195*, 6–6, 1980 and 1990 figures from U.S. Bureau of the Census, *Statistical Abstract of the United States 1988*, pp. 13 and 15; 2000 figures from U.S. Bureau of the Census, *Statistical Abstract of the United States 1994*, p. 24. *P. 199*, 6–7, *Current Population Reports*, Series P60, Table F-3, "Race and Hispanic Origin of Householder—Families by Median and Mean Income, 1947–1993" (unpublished table from Income Statistics Branch, Bureau of the Census). *P. 200*, 6–8, *Current Population Reports*, Series P60, Table 15, "Percent Distribution of Families, by Selected Characteristics within Income Quintile and Top 5 Percent in 1993," and Table B-7, "Share of Aggregate Income and Mean Income in 1967 to 1993 Received by Each Fifth and Top 5 Percent of Families, by Race and Hispanic Origin of Householder" (unpublished tables from Income Statistics Branch, Bureau of the Census). *P. 203*, 6–9, *Consumer Expenditure Survey, 1993*, U.S. Department of Labor, 1994, Table 1201. *P. 205*, 6–10, Patrick E. Murphy and William A. Staples, "A Modern Family Life Cycle," *Journal of Consumer Research*, June 1979, p. 17.

Photos/ads: *P. 181*, Mary Beth Camp/Matrix. *p. 183*, Krapit Phanvut/Sipa. *p. 188*, Raghu Rai/Magnum. *p. 196*, Modern Maturity a publication of AARP. *p. 197*, (left and right) Courtesy Strategic Mapping, Inc. *p. 202*,

Courtesy Gouchenour Advertising. *p. 204*, (left) Courtesy MasterCard International, Inc.; (right) Courtesy Sears Roebuck & Co. *p. 207*, Courtesy Don Coleman & Associates. *p. 208*, Reproduced with permission of Southwestern Bell Telephone Company.

Chapter 7

Exhibits: *P. 217*, 7–2, adapted from C. Glenn Walters, *Consumer Behavior*, 3rd ed. (Burr Ridge, IL: Richard D. Irwin, 1979). *P. 224*, 7–5, Joseph T. Plummer, "The Concept and Application of Life-Style Segmentation," *Journal of Marketing*, January 1974, pp. 33–37. *P. 227*, 7–6, adapted from Steven L. Diamond, Thomas S. Robertson, and F. Kent Mitchel, "Consumer Motivation and Behavior," in *Marketing Manager's Handbook*, ed. S. H. Britt and N. F. Guess (Chicago: Dartnell, 1983), p. 239; "Class in America," *Fortune*, February 7, 1994, pp. 114–26; Greg J. Duncan, Timothy M. Smeeding, and Willard Rodgers, "The Incredible Shrinking Middle Class," *American Demographics*, May 1992, pp. 34–38; Richard P. Coleman, "The Continuing Significance of Social Class to Marketing," *Journal of Consumer Research*, December 1983, pp. 265–80; "What Is Happening to the Middle Class?" *American Demographics*, January 1985, pp. 18–25; Donald W. Hendon, Emelda L. Williams, and Douglas E. Huffman, "Social Class System Revisited," *Journal of Business Research*, November 1988, pp. 259–70.

Photos/ads: *P. 213*, Copyright 1995, *USA Today*. Reprinted with permission. *p. 214*, (left) Courtesy Pizza Hut, Inc.; (right) Courtesy McDonald's Corporation; photo by Tom Casalini. *p. 219*, © The Proctor & Gamble Company. Used with permission. *p. 220*, Courtesy 3M. *p. 222*, Courtesy Forsman & Bodenfors. *p. 228*, Courtesy: The Richards Group. *p. 229*, (left) Courtesy Bailey's Nursery; Art Director: Tim Ward; Creative Director/Copywriter/Photographer: Michael LaMonica; (right) Courtesy Ace Hardware Corporation. *p. 232*, (left) Dan Ford Connolly; (right) © 1994, Kellogg Company. *p. 234*, (left) Courtesy PPG Industries, Inc.; (right) Frederick Charles. *p. 236*, (left) Courtesy United Airlines; (right) Courtesy Fogarty Klein & Partners/Houston, Texas.

Chapter 8

Exhibits: *P. 243*, 8–1, *County Business Patterns—United States, 1992; Statistical Abstract of the United States, 1994; Information Please Almanac, 1995* (Boston: Houghton Mifflin, 1994). *P. 252*, 8–5, Rowland T. Moriarty, Jr., and Robert E. Spekman, "An Empirical Investigation of the Information Sources Used during the Industrial Buying Process, *Journal of Marketing Research*, May 1984, pp. 137–47. *P. 261*, 8–7, data adapted from *County Business Patterns—United States, 1992*, and *1987 Census of Manufactures, Subject Series, Establishment and Firm Size, and General Summary. P. 263*, 8–8, adapted from *Standard Industrial Classification Manual, 1987*.

Photos/ads: *P. 241*, Courtesy Toyota Motor Corporation. *p. 244*, Courtesy Hormel Foods. *p. 245*, Courtesy Hercules Incorporated. *p. 247*, (left and right) © Roger Ball Photography. *p. 253*, (left) Courtesy SuperValu Stores, Inc.; (right) © Roger Ball Photography. *p. 254*, Courtesy Uniroyal Chemical Company; Agency: Keller & Company. *p. 256*, (left) © 1994 Chemical Banking Corporation; (right) Courtesy Rockwell International Corporation. *p. 260*, (left) Courtesy JC Penney Company; (right) Courtesy Sears Merchandise Group, Hoffman Estates, Illinois. *p. 262*, Courtesy Lukens Steel Company. *p. 265*, Courtesy Walgreen Company. *p. 267* (left) Courtesy Big Toys; (right) Courtesy Caterpillar Inc.

Chapter 9

Exhibits: *P. 292*, Courtesy The Quaker Oats Company; Reprinted Courtesy Eastman Kodak Company; NESTLE and the NESTLE NEST DEVICE are registered trademarks of Societe des Produits Nestle S. A.; Courtesy Del Monte; Courtesy Rolex Watch USA, Inc.; Courtesy Dole Packaged Food Company; Courtesy Nabisco; Courtesy MasterCard International; Courtesy Boys & Girls Club.

Photos/ads: *P. 273*, Peter Blakely/SABA. *p. 275*, (left) Courtesy Muratec; (right) Courtesy BRIO Corporation 1994. *p. 276*, (left) Reproduced courtesy of the Workrite Uniform Company, Oxnard, California, and its agency, Applied Concepts, Ventura, California; (right) Courtesy The Hertz Corporation. *p. 278*, (left and right) Courtesy Imasco Limited. *p. 279*, (left) Courtesy CPC International; (right) Courtesy CPC International, © 1994 Chuck Fishman. *p. 287*, Courtesy Ryder Trucks Rental, Inc. *p. 290*, (left) Courtesy Rockwell International Corporation; (right) © 1994 Kelly Services, Inc. All rights reserved. *p. 294*, Courtesy CPC International. *p. 297*, (left and right)

Sara Lee Corporation. *p. 301*, (left) Used by permission of Dean's Foods Company. *p. 303*, Courtesy Compaq Computer Corporation.

Chapter 10

Exhibits: *P. 324*, 10–5, adapted from Frank R. Bacon, Jr., and Thomas W. Butler, *Planned Innovation* (Ann Arbor: University of Michigan Institute of Science and Technology, 1980). *P. 326*, 10–6, adapted from Philip Kotler, "What Consumerism Means for Marketers," *Harvard Business Review*, May–June 1972, pp. 55–56.

Photos/ads: *P. 309*, Michael Greenlar/The Image Works. *p. 311*, Courtesy of Sony Corporation. *p. 313*, © 1993 Thermoscan, Inc. *p. 316*, (left) Courtesy M. Hidary & Company; Agency: Marcus Grubard Communications, Inc.; (right) Courtesy of Women's Speciality Retailing Group, A Division of United States Shoe Corporation. *p. 319*, (left) Courtesy Nabisco, Inc., photo by Steven H. Hartman; (right) © Grant Peterson. *p. 321*, Courtesy Du Pont Fluroproducts. *p. 323*, (left and right) Courtesy 3M. *p. 325*, © 1994 Louis Psihoyos/Matrix. *p. 329*, Courtesy The Timken Company. *p. 330*, Courtesy Porsche Cars North America, Inc. *p. 333*, (left) © 1994 Alan Levenson; (right) Michael J. Hruby.

Chapter 11

Exhibits: *P. 348*, 11–2, adapted from D. J. Bowersox and E. J. McCarthy, "Strategic Development of Planned Vertical Marketing Systems," in *Vertical Marketing Systems*, ed. Louis Bucklin (Glenview, IL: Scott, Foresman, 1970).

Photos/ads: *P. 337*, Reproduced with permission from The Goodyear Tire & Rubber Company, Akron, Ohio. *p. 339*, Photo by Caroline Parson/Liasion International, courtesy of GE. *p. 343*, Courtesy Bruno's. *p. 346*, Sunbrella® brand is a registered trademark of Glen Raven Mills, Inc. Agency: Wray Ward Laseter. *p. 349*, (left) Courtesy Nyman; (right) Courtesy Doane Products Company. *p. 351*, (left and right) Courtesy Colgate-Palmolive Company. *p. 352*, (left) Courtesy Libbey Glass, Inc.; (right) Courtesy Oneida Silversmiths. *p. 357*, Courtesy Owens-Corning Fiberglas Corporation.

Chapter 12

Exhibits: *P. 369*, 12–4, adapted from B. J. LaLonde and P. H. Zinzer, *Customer Service: Meaning and Measurement* (Chicago: National Council of Physical Distribution Management, 1976); and D. Phillip Locklin, *Transportation for Management* (Burr Ridge, IL: Richard D. Irwin, 1972. *P. 377*, 12–6, adapted from Louis W. Stern and Adel I. El-Ansary, *Marketing Channels* (Englewood Cliffs, NJ: Prentice Hall, 1977), p. 150.

Photos/ads: *P. 361*, c Arthur Meyerson. All rights reserved. *p. 363*, (left) Courtesy Prince Castle Inc.; (right) Courtesy Americold. *p. 368*, (left) Reuven Kopitchinski; (right) Steve Smith/Onyx. *p. 371*, Courtesy Hyundai Motor America. *p. 372*, (left) Courtesy Litton Industries, Inc.; (right) © Federal Express Corporation. *p. 374*, Courtesy Ryder System, Inc. *p. 378*, (left, center, and right) Mattel distribution center: All photos used with permission of Mattel, Inc. *p. 379*, © Ovak Arsianian. *p. 383*, (left) Photo Courtesy Du Pont, Inc.; (right) Courtesy Matlack, Inc.

Chapter 13

Exhibits: *P. 401*, 13–4, based on data from *1987 Census of Retail Trade, Subject Series, Establishment and Firm Size. P. 405*, 13–6, based on data from *1987 Census of Wholesale Trade, Geographic Area Series, United States.*

Photos/ads: *P. 387*, © Steve Goldstein. *p. 389*, (left and right) Courtesy Eckerd Corporation. *p. 390*, (left) © 1993 Rubbermaid Incorporated. Wooster, Ohio. (Used with permission.); (right) Robert Wallis/JB Pictures. *p. 391*, Courtesy Kauffman Stewart. *p. 397*, Courtesy Compuserv/H&R Block, Inc. *p. 399*, © Alan Levenson. *p. 404*, © John Abbott. *p. 407*, David Barned/ The Stock Market. *p. 408*, © Steve Niedorf. *p. 410*, (left) Courtesy R. C. Steele; (right) Courtesy Cutters Exchange, Inc. *p. 413*, (left) Courtesy T. L. Ashford & Associates; (right) Reprinted courtesy of Computer Associates International, Inc. © copyright Computer Associates International, Inc. All rights reserved. *p. 414* Courtesy SUPERVALU INC.

Photos/ads: *P. 419*, Scott Wanner. *p. 421*, (left) © 1995 Seth Resnick; (right) *Kellogg's Corn Flakes* cereal,® © 1994 Kellogg Company. *p. 423*, Courtesy American Greetings Corporation. *p. 425*, Courtesy Scharbo & Co. *p. 428*, Canon is a registered trademark of Canon, Inc. Reprinted with the express written consent of Canon Computer Systems, Inc. All rights reserved. *p. 431,* Courtesy Roland Corporation. *p. 432,* (left) Courtesy Southwest Airlines.; (right) Courtesy Duraflame, Inc. *p. 434,* Courtesy Du Pont. *p. 439,* Client: Sega of America; Agency: Goodby Berlin & Silverstein; Art Director: Tom Rouston; Copywriter: Taylor Heydman; Photographer: Heimo. *p. 441,* Agency: Ketchum Advertising/San Francisco; Creative Director: Millie Olson; Art Director: Ken Woodward; Copywriter: Suzanne Finnamore; Photographer: Dan Escobar. *p. 442,* Agency: DMB&B/Copenhagen; Art Director: Craig Frank; Copywriter: Phillip Scherrer; Photographer: Hans Ole Madsen.

Chapter 15

Exhibits: *P. 465,* 15–2, exhibit suggested by Professor A. A. Brogowicz, Western Michigan University.

Photos/ads: *P. 447,* Courtesy Alcoa; photo by Robert Feldman. *p. 450,* (left) Photograph courtesy of Glaxo Holdings, p.l.c.; (right) Courtesy ARAMARK. *p. 452,* (left) Courtesy Bridgestone/Firestone; (right) Photo provided by Maytag Corporation; Photographer: Arnold Zann. *p. 455,* Courtesy Catalina Marketing. *p. 457,* Courtesy Hewlett-Packard. *p. 459,* (left) Courtesy Raychem Corporation; (right) Courtesy Alcoa; photo by Robert Feldman. *p. 461,* Courtesy Ross Roy Advertising Agency; (right) Used with permission of Learning International, Inc. *p. 463,* (left) Courtesy Lance; (right) Courtesy BellSouth Corporation. *p. 468,* (left) Courtesy Zenith Data Systems; (right) Courtesy Software Publising Corporation.

Chapter 16

Exhibits: *P. 479,* 16–2, "1994 Advertising to Sales Ratios for the 200 Largest Ad Spending Industries," *Advertising Age,* August 8, 1994, p. 38; Kip D. Cassino, "An Advertising Atlas," *American Demographics,* August 1994, pp. 44–55. *P. 481,* 16–3, adapted from R. J. Lavidge and G. A. Steiner, "A Model for Predictive Measurements of Advertising Effectiveness," *Journal of Marketing,* October 1961, p. 61. *P. 486,* 16–4, cost data from *Standard Rate and Data,* July and September 1994, and sales estimates from "Ad Gain of 5.2% in '93 Marks Downturn's End," *Advertising Age,* May 2, 1994, p. 4; "TV Is Advertisers' Big Pick in Europe," *Advertising Age International,* June 21, 1993, p. I19. *P. 496,* 16–5, based on data from "World Brands 1994," *Advertising Age International,* September 19, 1994, pp. I13–26; "Special Issue: Agency Report," *Advertising Age,* April 13, 1994, pp. S1–56; "World Brands 1993," *Advertising Age International,* September 20, 1993, pp. I1ff.; "Special Issue: Agency Report," *Advertising Age,* April 13, 1992, pp. S1–44; "Special Issue: Agency Report Card," *Adweek,* March 23, 1992; "International: World Brands," *Advertising Age,* September 2, 1991, pp. 25–36.

Photos/ads: *P. 475,* Courtesy Nabisco Foods Group. *p. 476,* Dennis Chamberlin/Black Star. *p. 480,* Mothers Against Drunk Driving; Art Director: Matt Whitfield. *p. 482,* Courtesy Hitachi America Ltd. *p. 483,* (left) © 1994 General Mills, Inc.; (right) © 1994 Whitehall Laboratories. *p. 484,* Client: Sunkist Growers; Agency: Backer Spielvogel Bates, Toronto; Creative Director: Bill Maynard; Art Director: John Terry: Copywriter: Dave Crichton: Photographer: Nigel Dickson. *p. 487,* Wotjek Laski/Sipa Press. *p. 489,* (left) Anne Krause Photography; (right) Courtesy Troy Lee Designs. *p. 490,* Courtesy Yellow Pages Publishers Association. *p. 492,* Courtesy RR Donnelley & Sons Company; photo by Marc Hauser. *p. 493,* Agency: TBWA Holmes Knight Ritchie/London; Art Director-Illustrator: Steve Cheltham; Copywriter: Trevor Beattie. *p. 494,* Courtesy Marshallas Advertising, London. *p. 500,* Agency: Ogilvy & Mather Malaysia; Creative Director: Phil Davison: Copywriter: Alex Lim; Photographer: Adam. *p. 503,* (left) Courtesy Catalina Marketing Corporation; (right) Courtesy The Wessel Company, Inc. *p. 506,* © IDEAS—Canada's Largest Residential Construction Show.

Chapter 17

Exhibits: *P. 525,* 17–6, 1995 exchange rates for various currencies are from the March 30, 1995, issue of *The Wall Street Journal.* Earlier years' exchange rates are from *Statistical Abstract of the World* (Detroit, MI: Gale Research, Inc., 1994), p. 881, and *The World Almanac and Book of Facts 1995* (Malıwah, NJ: Funk and Wagnalls Corp., 1994), p. 122.

Photos/ads: *P. 511,* © 1994 Patty Wood. *p. 512,* (left and right) Courtesy The Great Atlantic & Pacific Tea Company. *p. 516,* Courtesy Pharmaceutical Research and Manufacturers of America. *p. 517,* (left) Courtesy The Murray Manufacturing Company Courtesy Pagano, Schenck & Kay, Inc. *p. 519,* Courtesy American Greetings Corporation. *p. 521,* Courtesy United Parcel Service of America, Inc. *p. 524,* Courtesy Reno Air

Inc. *p. 528,* (top) Courtesy Cargill, Inc. *p. 530,* John R. Dillon. *p. 532,* (left) Courtesy Egg-land's Best, Inc.: (right) Courtesy Beef Industry Council. *p. 533,* (left) Courtesy Broder Brothers; (right) Courtesy Veryfine. *p. 534,* Courtesy The Hertz Corporation. *p. 535,* Courtesy Mercedes Benz.

Chapter 18

Photos/ads: *P. 558,* © 1994 John Harding. *p. 560,* courtesy Accessories Associates Inc. and The Walt Disney Company. *p. 563,* Courtesy Colgate-Palmolive Company. *p. 570,* Courtesy BMW of North America, Inc. *p. 580,* Courtesy Philips Lighting Company. *p. 581,* Courtesy Devito/Verdi, New York. *p. 583,* (left) Courtesy Severin Montres AG; (right) Courtesy Zubi Advertising. *p. 584,* Courtesy Affordable Furniture.

Chapter 19

Exhibits: *P. 603,* 19–5, *Sales and Marketing Management,* August 30, 1993. *P. 604,* 19–6, based on data reported in *Fiber Box Industry Statistics,* Fiber Box Association.

Photos/ads: *P. 591,* Caroline Parson/Gamma Liasion. *p. 593,* Advertisement courtesy of Consolidated Freightways, Inc., Palo Alto, California. *p. 595,* Courtesy Oscar Meyer. *p. 598,* © 1994 Intel Corporation. *p. 600,* Photo courtesy of Genetech, Inc. *p. 606,* Print ad reprinted with permission from Microsoft Corporation. *p. 609,* Client: Arrow Shirts.: Agency: Mandelbaum Mooney Ashley; Photographer: Jon Gipe. *p. 613,* (left) Courtesy Full Spectrum Graphic Design, Santa Rosa; (right) Courtesy Computer Associates International, Inc. *p. 614,* Courtesy of American International Group, Inc. *p. 616,* Courtesy 3M.

Chapter 20

Exhibits: *P. 630,* 20–2, Marie Gaudard, Roland Coates, and Liz Freeman, "Accelerating Improvement," *Quality Progress,* October 1991, pp. 81–88. *P. 631,* 20–3, Marie Gaudard, Roland Coates, and Liz Freeman, "Accelerating Improvement," *Quality Progress,* October 1991, pp. 81–88.

Photos/ads: *P. 621,* Michael J. Hruby. *p. 623,* Created for *Parade* magazine by Warwick Baker & Flore Inc. Reprinted with permission. *p. 625,* (left) Courtesy Marriott Corporation; (right) BellSouth. *p. 629,* Courtesy Dana Corporation. *p. 632,* Courtesy Systems & Computer Technology Corporation. *p. 634,* Courtesy of Motorola, Inc. *p. 636,* Courtesy Information Resources, Inc.

Chapter 21

Photos/ads: *P. 653,* William D. Perreault, Jr. *p. 655,* Courtesy GE Capital; Agency: McCann-Erickson/New York. *p. 659,* (left) Courtesy The Bank of New York; Agency: Ally & Gargano, New York; (right) Courtesy LaSalle National Corporation; Agency: DMB&B, Chicago. *p. 661,* James Hill/Colorific. *p. 664,* ™®®Kellogg Company. *p. 666,* © E. Lee White. *p. 670,* Courtesy The Timken Company. *p. 674,* Courtesy of Eskew & Gresham, PSC Louisville, Kentucky; Design: McCafferty & Co. Advertising; Copy: Mary Anne Vollmer, freelance copywriter. *p. 676,* Courtesy Martin Marietta.

Chapter 22

Exhibits: *P. 692,* 22–1, adapted from discussions of an American Marketing Association Strategic Planning Committee.

Photos/ads: *P. 681,* Sally Weiner Grotta/The Stock Market. *p. 683,* (left) Ed Kashi; (right) Melanie Carr/Zephyr Pictures. *p. 687* (right) Courtesy Hewlett-Packard. *p. 688,* Robin Moyer/*Time Magazine.* *p. 690,* Courtesy Colgate-Palmolive Company. *p. 691,* (left) Courtesy McDaniels, Henry & Sproul, San Francisco; (right) Courtesy The North Carolina Governor's Highway Safety Program. *p. 695,* Courtesy Young & Rubicam Gmbh. *p. 696,* Courtesy STZ, Milan. *p. 697,* Courtesy Sensomatic Corporation: Agency: Daniel & Roberts, Inc.

Appendix C

Exhibits: *P. 707,* C–2, adapted and updated from "Special Report: Salary Survey," *Advertising Age,* December 5, 1994, pp. S1–12; "Careers: The Trade Winds Blow," *Brandweek,* August 10, 1992, pp. 12–14; Lila B. Stair, *Careers in Business: Selecting and Planning Your Career Path* (Burr Ridge, IL: Richard D. Irwin, 1980), and *Northwestern Lindquist-Endicott Report, 1988* (Evanston, IL: Northwestern University, The Placement Center).

Author Index

Aaker, David A., 788 n, 802 n, 818 n
Abbott, John, 832
Abdel-Latif, Abla M., 784 n
Abercrombie, C. L., 783 n
Abernathy, Avery M., 819 n
Abraham, Magid M., 792 n
Abrams, Bill, 824 n
Abratt, Russell, 787 n, 815 n
Abshire, Roger Dale, 807 n
Achabal, Dale D., 810 n, 811 n, 824 n, 826 n
Achenbaum, Alvin A., 796 n, 813 n
Achrol, Ravi S., 806 n
Ackerman, Kenneth B., 808 n
Adams, Anthony J., 819 n
Adams, Arthur J., 824 n
Adams, Ronald J., 804 n
Adler, Robert, 828 n
Aggarwal, Raj, 793 n
Aggarwal, Sumer, 825 n
Ailawadi, Kusum L., 814 n
Akaah, Ishmael P., 784 n, 791 n
Akhter, Syed H., 825 n
Akintoye, Akintola, 823 n
Albaum, Gerald, 805 n
Alberts, William W., 823 n
Al-Deen, Hana Noor, 793 n
Alden, Dana L., 812 n, 818 n
Alderson, Wroe, 784 n, 806 n, 831 n
Alexander, Joe F., 815 n
Ali, Abdul, 822 n
Allen, M. G., 831
Alpert, Frank H., 804 n
Alpert, Mark I., 787 n
Alsop, Ronald, 824 n
Alter, Harvey, 806 n
Ambry, Margaret K., 794 n, 824 n
Anderson, Eugene W., 785 n
Anderson, J. C., 812 n
Anderson, L. McTier, 827 n
Anderson, Paul F., 790 n
Andreasen, Alan R., 785 n, 786 n, 793 n
Ansoff, H. Igor, 831
Antil, John H., 828 n
Appel, David, 809 n
Archibald, Robert B., 828 n
Arellano, Rolando, 811 n
Arens, William F., 818 n
Arinze, Bay, 824 n
Armacost, Robert L., 787 n
Armstrong, David J., 808 n
Armstrong, Gary M., 814 n
Armstrong, James P., 716 n
Armstrong, Robert W., 784 n
Arnold, Danny R., 816 n

Arora, Raj, 798 n
Avishai, Bernard, 828 n
Avlonitis, George J., 814 n
Axelrod, Joel N., 791 n
Ayal, Igal, 802 n
Azel, Jose, 831

Babakus, Emin, 797 n, 815 n
Babin, Barry J., 809 n
Backman, Lars-Olof, 807 n
Bacon, Frank R., Jr., 790 n, 798 n, 804 n, 832
Badenhorst, A., 798 n
Bagchi, Prabir K., 808 n
Baker, Thomas L., 805 n
Balasubramanian, Siva K., 813 n
Balazs, A. L., 795 n
Banting, Peter M., 789 n, 798 n, 799 n, 800 n
Barach, Jeffrey A., 785 n
Barczak, Gloria, 805 n
Bardi, Edward J., 807 n, 808 n
Barksdale, Hiram C., Jr., 786 n, 798 n, 828 n
Barlow, Tony, 831
Barned, David, 832
Barnes, James H., Jr., 802 n, 806 n
Barnett, F. William, 824 n
Barrett, John, 814 n
Barry, Thomas E., 817 n
Bartlett, Christopher A., 825 n
Bartmess, Andrew D., 827 n
Bass, Ken, 815 n
Bayer, J., 792 n
Bayliss, Brian T., 789 n
Bayus, B. L., 796 n
Beam, Henry H., 820 n
Bearden, William O., 823 n
Beattie, Trevor, 833
Beatty, Sharon E., 796 n
Beckenstein, Alan R., 823 n, 790 n
Beed, Terence W., 792 n
Begleiter, Steven, 831
Behrman, Douglas N., 804 n, 815 n
Bejou, David, 795 n
Belk, Russell W., 797 n
Bellenger, Danny N., 793 n
Bellizzi, Joseph A., 799 n, 801 n
Bello, Daniel C., 812 n
Bellur, Venkatakrishna V., 783 n
Beltramini, Richard F., 798 n, 812 n, 815 n, 818 n
Benedetti, Lois H., 823 n
Benet, Suzeanne, 787 n

Bennett, Roger C., 802 n
Benoy, W., 805 n
Beracs, Jozsef, 800 n
Bergig, Paul A., 824 n
Berlew, F. Kingston, 825 n
Berry, Leonard L., 785 n, 796 n, 800 n, 811 n, 826 n, 828 n
Bessen, Jim, 793 n
Bettman, James R., 796 n, 797 n
Bharadwaj, Sundar G., 820 n
Bhargava, Mukesh, 819 n
Bhide, Amar, 826 n
Biddle, David, 829 n
Bierley, Calvin, 796 n
Billington, Maryann, 792 n
Bird, Monroe Murphy, 798 n
Bishop, William S., 800 n
Biswas, Abhijit, 802 n, 816 n, 823 n
Bitner, Mary Jo, 800 n
Bivins, Thomas H., 812 n, 813 n
Blair, Margaret H., 819 n
Blakely, Peter, 832
Blasko, Vincent J., 814 n
Blenkhorn, David L., 798 n
Bloch, Peter H., 798 n, 801 n, 811 n
Blodgett, Jeffrey G., 813 n
Blois, K. J., 821 n
Bloom, Paul N., 785 n, 828 n
Boddewyn, Jean J., 820 n
Bodkin, Charles D., 824 n
Boles, James S., 815 n
Bonaccorsi, Andrea J., 799 n
Bone, Paula Fitzgerald, 802 n, 813 n
Bonoma, Thomas V., 786 n, 825 n
Bookbinder, James H., 809 n
Booms, Bernard H., 800 n
Bouchy, Cecile, 791 n
Boutilier, Robert, 797 n
Bovee, Courtland L., 818 n
Bowen, William G., 785 n
Bowersox, Donald J., 807 n, 832
Boyd, Harper W., Jr., 791 n
Boyle, Brett A., 806 n
Boyle, Kevin A., 814 n
Boynton, Andrew C., 827 n
Bozman, Carl S., 818 n
Brant, William K., 793 n, 825 n
Braus, Patricia, 795 n
Brennan, Jerry M., 792 n
Bristor, Julia M., 798 n
Britt, S. H., 832
Brockhoff, Klaus, 788 n
Brogowicz, A. A., 826 n, 831, 833
Bronikowski, Karen, 803 n

Subject Index

Glossary

Accessories short-lived capital items—tools and equipment used in production or office activities.

Accumulating collecting products from many small producers.

Administered channel systems various channel members informally agree to cooperate with each other.

Administered prices consciously set prices aimed at reaching the firm's objectives.

Adoption curve shows when different groups accept ideas.

Adoption process the steps individuals go through on the way to accepting or rejecting a new idea.

Advertising any *paid* form of nonpersonal presentation of ideas, goods, or services by an identified sponsor.

Advertising agencies specialists in planning and handling mass selling details for advertisers.

Advertising allowances price reductions to firms in the channel to encourage them to advertise or otherwise promote the supplier's products locally.

Advertising managers managers of their company's mass selling effort in television, newspapers, magazines, and other media.

Agent middlemen wholesalers who do not own (take title to) the products they sell.

AIDA model consists of four promotion jobs—(1) to get *Attention*, (2) to hold *Interest*, (3) to arouse *Desire*, and (4) to obtain *Action*.

Allowance (accounting term) occurs when a customer is not satisfied with a purchase for some reason and the seller gives a price reduction on the original invoice (bill), but the customer keeps the goods or services.

Allowances reductions in price given to final consumers, customers, or channel members for doing something or accepting less of something.

Assorting putting together a variety of products to give a target market what it wants.

Attitude a person's point of view toward something.

Auction companies agent middlemen who provide a place where buyers and sellers can come together and complete a transaction.

Automatic vending selling and delivering products through vending machines.

Average cost (per unit) the total cost divided by the related quantity.

Average-cost pricing adding a reasonable markup to the average cost of a product.

Average fixed cost (per unit) the total fixed cost divided by the related quantity.

Average variable cost (per unit) the total variable cost divided by the related quantity.

Bait pricing setting some very low prices to attract customers but trying to sell more expensive models or brands once the customer is in the store.

Balance sheet an accounting statement that shows a company's assets, liabilities, and net worth.

Basic list prices the prices that final customers or users are normally asked to pay for products.

Basic sales tasks *order-getting*, *order-taking*, and *supporting*.

Battle of the brands the competition between dealer brands and manufacturer brands.

Belief a person's opinion about something.

Bid pricing offering a specific price for each possible job rather than setting a price that applies for all customers.

Birthrate the number of babies per 1,000 people.

Brand equity the value of a brand's overall strength in the market.

Brand familiarity how well customers recognize and accept a company's brand.

Brand insistence customers insist on a firm's branded product and are willing to search for it.

Brand managers manage specific products, often taking over the jobs formerly handled by an advertising manager—sometimes called product managers.

Brand name a word, letter, or a group of words or letters.

Brand nonrecognition final customers don't recognize a brand at all—even though middlemen may use the brand name for identification and inventory control.

Brand preference target customers usually choose the brand over other brands, perhaps because of habit or favorable past experience.

Brand recognition customers remember the brand.

Brand rejection the potential customers won't buy a brand—unless its image is changed.

Branding the use of a name, term, symbol, or design—or a combination of these—to identify a product.

Break-even analysis an approach to determine whether the firm will be able to break even—that is, cover all its costs—with a particular price.

Break-even point (BEP) the sales quantity where the firm's total cost will just equal its total revenue.

Breakthrough opportunities opportunities that help innovators develop hard-to-copy marketing strategies that will be very profitable for a long time.

Brokers agent middlemen who specialize in bringing buyers and sellers together.

Bulk-breaking dividing larger quantities into smaller quantities as products get closer to the final market.

Business and organizational customers any buyers who buy for resale or to produce other goods and services.

Business products products meant for use in producing other products.

Buying center all the people who participate in or influence a purchase.

Buying function looking for and evaluating goods and services.

Capital the money invested in a firm.

Capital item a long-lasting product that can be used and depreciated for many years.

Cash-and-carry wholesalers like service wholesalers, except that the customer must pay cash.

Cash discounts reductions in the price to encourage buyers to pay their bills quickly.

Cash flow statement a financial report that forecasts how much cash will be available after paying expenses.

Catalog showroom retailers stores that sell several lines out of a catalog and display showroom with backup inventories.

Central markets convenient place where buyers and sellers can meet one-on-one to exchange goods and services.

Chain store one of several stores owned and managed by the same firm.

Channel captain a manager who helps direct the activities of a whole channel and tries to avoid—or solve—channel conflicts.

Channel of distribution any series of firms or individuals who participate in the flow of goods and services from producer to final user or consumer.

Close the salesperson's request for an order.

Clustering techniques approaches used to try to find similar patterns within sets of data.

Combination export manager a blend of manufacturers' agent and selling agent—handling the entire export function for several producers of similar but noncompeting lines.

Combined target market approach combining two or more submarkets into one larger target market as a basis for one strategy.

Combiners firms that try to increase the size of their target markets by combining two or more segments.

Commission merchants agent middlemen who handle products shipped to them by sellers, complete the sale, and send the money (minus their commission) to each seller.

Communication process a source trying to reach a receiver with a message.

Community shopping centers planned shopping centers that are larger and offer some shopping stores as well as convenience stores.

Comparative advertising advertising that makes specific brand comparisons using actual product names.

Competitive advantage a firm has a marketing mix that the target market sees as better than a competitor's mix.

Competitive advertising advertising that tries to develop selective demand for a specific brand rather than a product category.

Competitive barriers the conditions that may make it difficult, or even impossible, for a firm to compete in a market.

Competitive bids terms of sale offered by different suppliers in response to the buyer's purchase specifications.

Competitive environment the number and types of competitors the marketing manager must face, and how they may behave.

Competitive rivals a firm's closest competitors.

Competitor analysis an organized approach for evaluating the strengths and weaknesses of current or potential competitors' marketing strategies.

Complementary product pricing setting prices on several related products as a group.

Components processed expense items that become part of a finished product.

Concept testing getting reactions from customers about how well a new product idea fits their needs.

Confidence intervals the range on either side of an estimate from a sample that is likely to contain the true value for the whole population.

Conjoint analysis a research technique (sometimes called trade-off analysis) that helps marketing managers determine how important certain elements of the firm's marketing mix are to customers.

Consultative selling approach a type of sales presentation in which the salesperson develops a good understanding of the individual customer's needs before trying to close the sale.

Consumer panel a group of consumers who provide information on a continuing basis.

Consumer Product Safety Act a 1972 law that set up the Consumer Product Safety Commission to encourage more awareness of safety in product design and better quality control.

Consumer products products meant for the final consumer.

Consumer surplus the difference to consumers between the value of a purchase and the price they pay.

Consumerism a social movement that seeks to increase the rights and powers of consumers.

Containerization grouping individual items into an economical shipping quantity and sealing them in protective containers for transit to the final destination.

Continuous improvement a commitment to constantly make things better one step at a time.

Contract manufacturing turning over production to others while retaining the marketing process.

Contractual channel systems various channel members agree by contract to cooperate with each other.

Contribution-margin approach a cost analysis approach in which all costs are not allocated in *all* situations.

Control the feedback process that helps the marketing manager learn (1) how ongoing plans and implementation are working and (2) how to plan for the future.

Convenience (food) stores a convenience-oriented variation of the conventional limited-line food stores.

Convenience products products a consumer needs but isn't willing to spend much time or effort shopping for.

Cooperative advertising middlemen and producers sharing in the cost of ads.

Cooperative chains retailer-sponsored groups, formed by independent retailers, to run their own buying organizations and conduct joint promotion efforts.

Copy thrust what the words and illustrations of an ad should communicate.

Corporate chain store one of several stores owned and managed by the same firm.

Corporate channel systems corporate ownership all along the channel.

Corrective advertising ads to correct deceptive advertising.

Cost of sales total value (at cost) of the sales during the period.

Countertrade a special type of bartering in which products from one country are traded for products from another country.

Cues products, signs, ads, and other stimuli in the environment.

Cultural and social environment affects how and why people live and behave as they do.

Culture the whole set of beliefs, attitudes, and ways of doing things of a reasonably homogeneous set of people.

Cumulative quantity discounts reductions in price for larger purchases over a given period, such as a year.

Customer service level how rapidly and dependably a firm can deliver what customers want.

Dealer brands brands created by middlemen—sometimes referred to as *private brands*.

Debt financing borrowing money based on a promise to repay the loan, usually within a fixed time period and with a specific interest charge.

Decision support system (DSS) a computer program that makes it easy for marketing managers to get and use information *as they are making decisions*.

Decoding the receiver in the communication process translating the message.

Demand-backward pricing setting an acceptable final consumer price and working backward to what a producer can charge.

Demand curve a graph of the relationship between price and quantity demanded in a market—assuming all other things stay the same.

Department stores larger stores that are organized into many separate departments and offer many product lines.

Derived demand demand for business products derives from the demand for final consumer products.

Description (specification) buying buying from a written (or verbal) description of the product.

Determining dimensions the dimensions that actually affect the customer's purchase of a *specific* product or brand in a *product-market*.

Direct marketing direct communication between a seller and an individual customer using a promotion method other than face-to-face personal selling.

Direct type advertising competitive advertising that aims for immediate buying action.

Discount houses stores that sell hard goods (cameras, TVs, appliances) at substantial price cuts.

Discounts reductions from list price given by a seller to buyers, who either give up some marketing function or provide the function themselves.

Discrepancy of assortment the difference between the lines a typical producer makes and the assortment final consumers or users want.

Discrepancy of quantity the difference between the quantity of products it is economical for a producer to make and the quantity final users or consumers normally want.

Discretionary income what is left of disposable income after paying for necessities.

Disposable income   income that is left after taxes.

Dissonance   tension caused by uncertainty about the rightness of a decision.

Distribution center   a special kind of warehouse designed to speed the flow of goods and avoid unnecessary storing costs.

Diversification   moving into totally different lines of business—perhaps entirely unfamiliar products, markets, or even levels in the production-marketing system.

Diversion in transit   allows redirection of railroad carloads already in transit.

Door-to-door selling   going directly to the consumer's home.

Drive   a strong stimulus that encourages action to reduce a need.

Drop-shippers   wholesalers who own (take title to) the products they sell—but do not actually handle, stock, or deliver them.

Dual distribution   when a producer uses several competing channels to reach the same target market—perhaps using several middlemen in addition to selling directly.

Dumping   pricing a product sold in a foreign market below the cost of producing it or at a price lower than in its domestic market.

Early adopters   the second group in the adoption curve to adopt a new product; these people are usually well respected by their peers and often are opinion leaders.

Early majority   a group in the adoption curve that avoids risk and waits to consider a new idea until many early adopters try it—and like it.

Economic and technological environment   affects the way firms—and the whole economy—use resources.

Economic buyers   people who know all the facts and logically compare choices in terms of cost and value received—to get the greatest satisfaction from spending their time and money.

Economic needs   needs concerned with making the best use of a consumer's time and money—as the consumer judges it.

Economic system   the way an economy organizes to use scarce resources to produce goods and services and distribute them for consumption by various people and groups in the society.

Economies of scale   as a company produces larger numbers of a particular product, the cost for each of these products goes down.

Elastic demand   if prices are dropped, the quantity demanded will stretch enough to increase total revenue.

Elastic supply   the quantity supplied does stretch more if the price is raised.

Electronic data interchange (EDI)   an approach that puts information in a standardized format easily shared between different computer systems.

Emergency products   products that are purchased immediately when the need is great.

Empowerment   giving employees the authority to correct a problem without first checking with management.

Empty nesters   people whose children are grown and who are now able to spend their money in other ways.

Encoding   the source in the communication process deciding what it wants to say and translating it into words or symbols that will have the same meaning to the receiver.

Equilibrium point   the quantity and the price sellers are willing to offer are equal to the quantity and price that buyers are willing to accept.

Everyday low pricing   setting a low list price rather than relying on a high list price that frequently changes with various discounts or allowances.

Exclusive distribution   selling through only one middleman in a particular geographic area.

Expectation   an outcome or event that a person anticipates or looks forward to.

Expense item   a product whose total cost is treated as a business expense in the period it's purchased.

Expenses   all the remaining costs that are subtracted from the gross margin to get the net profit.

Experience curve pricing   average-cost pricing using an estimate of *future* average costs.

Experimental method   a research approach in which researchers compare the responses of two or more groups that are similar except on the characteristic being tested.

Export agents   manufacturers' agents who specialize in export trade.

Export brokers   brokers in international marketing.

Export commission houses   brokers in international trade.

Exporting   selling some of what the firm produces to foreign markets.

Extensive problem solving   the type of problem solving consumers use for a completely new or important need—when they put much effort into deciding how to satisfy it.

Facilitators   firms that provide one or more of the marketing functions other than buying or selling.

Factor   a variable that shows the relation of some other variable to the item being forecast.

Factor method   an approach to forecast sales by finding a relation between the company's sales and some other factor (or factors).

Fad   an idea that is fashionable only to certain groups who are enthusiastic about it—but these groups are so fickle that a fad is even more short-lived than a regular fashion.

Family brand a brand name used for several products.

Farm products products grown by farmers, such as oranges, wheat, sugar cane, cattle, poultry, eggs, and milk.

Fashion currently accepted or popular style.

Federal Fair Packaging and Labeling Act a 1966 law requiring that consumer goods be clearly labeled in easy-to-understand terms.

Federal Trade Commission (FTC) federal government agency that polices antimonopoly laws.

Financing provides the necessary cash and credit to produce, transport, store, promote, sell, and buy products.

Fishbone diagram a visual aid that helps organize cause and effect relationships for "things gone wrong."

Fixed-cost (FC) contribution per unit the selling price per unit minus the variable cost per unit.

Flexible-price policy offering the same product and quantities to different customers at different prices.

F.O.B. a transportation term meaning free on board some vehicle at some point.

Focus group interview an interview of 6 to 10 people in an informal group setting.

Foreign Corrupt Practices Act a law passed by the U.S. Congress in 1977 that prohibits U.S. firms from paying bribes to foreign officials.

Form utility provided when someone produces something tangible.

Franchise operation a franchisor develops a good marketing strategy, and the retail franchise holders carry out the strategy in their own units.

Freight absorption pricing absorbing freight cost so that a firm's delivered price meets the nearest competitor's.

Freight forwarders transportation wholesalers who combine the small shipments of many shippers into more economical shipping quantities.

Full-cost approach all costs are allocated to products, customers, or other categories.

Full-line pricing setting prices for a whole line of products.

Functional accounts categories of costs that show the *purpose* for which the expenditures are made.

General Agreement on Tariffs and Trade (GATT) a set of rules governing restrictions on world trade and agreed to by most of the nations of the world.

General merchandise wholesalers service wholesalers who carry a wide variety of nonperishable items such as hardware, electrical supplies, plumbing supplies, furniture, drugs, cosmetics, and automobile equipment.

General stores early retailers who carried anything they could sell in reasonable volume.

Generic market a market with *broadly* similar needs—and sellers offering various and *often diverse* ways of satisfying those needs.

Generic products products that have no brand at all other than identification of their contents and the manufacturer or middleman.

Gross margin (gross profit) the money left to cover the expenses of selling the products and operating the business.

Gross national product (GNP) the total value of goods and services produced in an economy in a year.

Gross sales the total amount charged to all customers during some time period.

Heterogeneous shopping products shopping products the customer sees as different—and wants to inspect for quality and suitability.

Homogeneous shopping products shopping products the customer sees as basically the same—and wants at the lowest price.

Hypermarket a very large store that tries to carry not only foods but all goods and services that the consumer purchases *routinely* (also called superstore).

Hypotheses educated guesses about the relationships between things or about what will happen in the future.

Iceberg principle much good information is hidden in summary data.

Ideal market exposure when a product is available widely enough to satisfy target customers' needs but not exceed them.

Implementation putting marketing plans into operation.

Import agents manufacturers' agents who specialize in import trade.

Import brokers brokers in international marketing.

Import commission houses brokers in international trade.

Impulse products products that are bought quickly as *unplanned* purchases because of a strongly felt need.

Indices statistical combinations of several time series used to find some time series that will lead the series to be forecast.

Indirect type advertising competitive advertising that points out product advantages—to affect future buying decisions.

Individual brands separate brand names used for each product.

Individual product a particular product within a product line.

Inelastic demand although the quantity demanded increases if the price is decreased, the quantity demanded will not stretch enough to avoid a decrease in total revenue.

Inelastic supply the quantity supplied does not stretch much (if at all) if the price is raised.

Innovation the development and spread of new ideas and products.

Innovators the first group to adopt new products.

Inspection buying looking at every item.

Installations important capital items such as buildings, land rights, and major equipment.

Institutional advertising advertising that tries to promote an organization's image, reputation, or ideas—rather than a specific product.

Integrated marketing communications the intentional coordination of every communication from a firm to a target customer to convey a consistent and complete message.

Intensive distribution selling a product through all responsible and suitable wholesalers or retailers who will stock and/or sell the product.

Intermediary a middleman.

Introductory price dealing temporary price cuts to speed new products into a market.

Inventory the amount of goods being stored.

Job description a written statement of what a salesperson is expected to do.

Joint venturing in international marketing, a domestic firm entering into a partnership with a foreign firm.

Jury of executive opinion forecasting by combining the opinions of experienced executives—perhaps from marketing, production, finance, purchasing, and top management.

Just-in-time delivery reliably getting products there *just* before the customer needs them.

Laggards prefer to do things the way they have been done in the past and are very suspicious of new ideas—sometimes called nonadopters—see *adoption curve.*

Lanham Act a 1946 law that spells out what kinds of marks (including brand names) can be protected and the exact method of protecting them.

Late majority a group of adopters who are cautious about new ideas—see *adoption curve.*

Law of diminishing demand if the price of a product is raised, a smaller quantity will be demanded—and if the price of a product is lowered, a greater quantity will be demanded.

Leader pricing setting some very low prices—real bargains—to get customers into retail stores.

Leading series a time series that changes in the same direction *but ahead of* the series to be forecast.

Learning a change in a person's thought processes caused by prior experience.

Licensed brand well-known brand that sellers pay a fee to use.

Licensing selling the right to use some process, trademark, patent, or other right for a fee or royalty.

Lifestyle analysis the analysis of a person's day-to-day pattern of living as expressed in that person's Activities, Interests, and Opinions—sometimes referred to as AIOs or psychographics.

Limited-function wholesalers merchant wholesalers who provide only *some* wholesaling functions.

Limited-line stores stores that specialize in certain lines of related products rather than a wide assortment—sometimes called single-line stores.

Limited problem solving when a consumer is willing to put *some* effort into deciding the best way to satisfy a need.

Logistics the transporting and storing of goods so as to match target customers' needs with a firm's marketing mix—both within individual firms and along a channel of distribution (i.e., another name for physical distribution).

Long-run target return pricing pricing to cover all costs and achieve an average target return over the long run.

Low-involvement purchases purchases that have little importance or relevance for the customer.

Macro-marketing a social process that directs an economy's flow of goods and services from producers to consumers in a way that effectively matches supply and demand and accomplishes the objectives of society.

Magnuson-Moss Act a 1975 law requiring that producers provide a clearly written warranty if they choose to offer any warranty.

Mail-order wholesalers sell out of catalogs that may be distributed widely to smaller industrial customers or retailers.

Major accounts sales force salespeople who sell directly to large accounts such as major retail chain stores.

Management contracting the seller provides only management skills—others own the production and distribution facilities.

Manufacturer brands brands created by producers.

Manufacturers' agents agent middlemen who sell similar products for several noncompeting producers for a commission on what is actually sold.

Manufacturers' sales branches separate warehouses that producers set up away from their factories.

Marginal analysis evaluating the change in total revenue and total cost from selling one more unit to find the most profitable price and quantity.

Marginal cost the change in total cost that results from producing one more unit.

Marginal profit profit on the last unit sold.

Marginal revenue the change in total revenue that results from the sale of one more unit of a product.

Markdown a retail price reduction that is required because customers won't buy some item at the originally marked-up price.

Markdown ratio a tool used by many retailers to measure the efficiency of various departments and their whole business.

Market a group of potential customers with similar needs who are willing to exchange something of value with sellers offering various goods and/or services—that is, ways of satisfying those needs.

Market development trying to increase sales by selling present products in new markets.

Market-directed economic system the individual decisions of the many producers and consumers make the macro-level decisions for the whole economy.

Market growth a stage of the product life cycle when industry sales grow fast—but industry profits rise and then start falling.

Market information function the collection, analysis, and distribution of all the information needed to plan, carry out, and control marketing activities.

Market introduction a stage of the product life cycle when sales are low as a new idea is first introduced to a market.

Market maturity a stage of the product life cycle when industry sales level off—and competition gets tougher.

Market penetration trying to increase sales of a firm's present products in its present markets—usually through a more aggressive marketing mix.

Market potential what a whole market segment might buy.

Market segment a relatively homogeneous group of customers who will respond to a marketing mix in a similar way.

Market segmentation a two-step process of: (1) *naming* broad product-markets and (2) *segmenting* these broad product-markets in order to select target markets and develop suitable marketing mixes.

Marketing audit a systematic, critical, and unbiased review and appraisal of the basic objectives and policies of the marketing function and of the organization, methods, procedures, and people employed to implement the policies.

Marketing company era a time when, in addition to short-run marketing planning, marketing people develop long-range plans—sometimes 10 or more years ahead—and the whole company effort is guided by the marketing concept.

Marketing concept the idea that an organization should aim *all* its efforts at satisfying its *customers*—at a *profit*.

Marketing department era a time when all marketing activities are brought under the control of one department to improve short-run policy planning and to try to integrate the firm's activities.

Marketing ethics the moral standards that guide marketing decisions and actions.

Marketing information system (MIS) an organized way of continually gathering and analyzing data to provide marketing managers with information they need to make decisions.

Marketing management process the process of (1) *planning* marketing activities, (2) directing the *implementation* of the plans, and (3) *controlling* these plans.

Marketing mix the controllable variables that the company puts together to satisfy a target group.

Marketing model a statement of relationships among marketing variables.

Marketing orientation trying to carry out the marketing concept.

Marketing plan a written statement of a marketing strategy *and* the time-related details for carrying out the strategy.

Marketing program blends all of the firm's marketing plans into one big plan.

Marketing research procedures to develop and analyze new information to help marketing managers make decisions.

Marketing research process a five-step application of the scientific method that includes (1) defining the problem, (2) analyzing the situation, (3) getting problem-specific information, (4) interpreting the data, and (5) solving the problem.

Marketing strategy specifies a target market and a related marketing mix.

Markup a dollar amount added to the cost of products to get the selling price.

Markup chain the sequence of markups firms use at different levels in a channel—determining the price structure in the whole channel.

Markup (percent) the percentage of selling price that is added to the cost to get the selling price.

Mass customization tailoring the principles of mass production to meet the unique needs of individual customers.

Mass marketing the typical production-oriented approach that vaguely aims at everyone with the same marketing mix.

Mass-merchandisers large, self-service stores with many departments that emphasize soft goods (housewares, clothing, and fabrics) and selling on lower margins to get faster turnover.

Mass-merchandising concept the idea that retailers should offer low prices to get faster turnover and greater sales volume by appealing to larger numbers.

Mass selling communicating with large numbers of potential customers at the same time.

Merchant wholesalers wholesalers who own (take title to) the products they sell.

Message channel the carrier of the message.

Metropolitan Statistical Area (MSA) an integrated economic and social unit with a large population nucleus.

Micro-macro dilemma what is good for some producers and consumers may not be good for society as a whole.

Micro-marketing performing activities that seek to accomplish an organization's objectives by anticipating customer or client needs and directing a flow of need-satisfying goods and services from producer to customer or client.

Middleman someone who specializes in trade rather than production, sometimes called an intermediary.

Missionary salespeople supporting salespeople who work for producers by calling on their middlemen and their customers.

Modified rebuy the in-between process where some review of the buying situation is done—though not as much as in new-task buying or as little as in straight rebuys.

Monopolistic competition a market situation that develops when a market has (1) different (heterogeneous) products and (2) sellers who feel they do have some competition in this market.

Multinational corporations firms that make a direct investment in several countries and run their businesses depending on the choices available anywhere in the world.

Multiple buying influence several people share in making a purchase decision—perhaps even top management.

Multiple target market approach segmenting the market and choosing two or more segments, then treating each as a separate target market needing a different marketing mix.

Nationalism an emphasis on a country's interests before everything else.

Natural accounts the categories to which various costs are charged in the normal financial accounting cycle.

Natural products products that occur in nature—such as fish and game, timber and maple syrup, and copper, zinc, iron ore, oil, and coal.

Needs the basic forces that motivate a person to do something.

Negotiated contract buying agreeing to a contract that allows for changes in the purchase arrangements.

Negotiated price a price that is set based on bargaining between the buyer and seller.

Neighborhood shopping centers planned shopping centers that consist of several convenience stores.

Net an invoice term meaning that payment for the face value of the invoice is due immediately—also see *cash discounts*.

Net profit what the company earns from its operations during a particular period.

Net sales the actual sales dollars the company receives.

New product a product that is new *in any way* for the company concerned.

New-task buying when an organization has a new need and the buyer wants a great deal of information.

New unsought products products offering really new ideas that potential customers don't know about yet.

Noise any distraction that reduces the effectiveness of the communication process.

Nonadopters prefer to do things the way they have been done in the past and are very suspicious of new ideas— sometimes called laggards—see *adoption curve*.

Noncumulative quantity discounts reductions in price when a customer purchases a larger quantity on an *individual order*.

Non-price competition aggressive action on one or more of the Ps other than Price.

North American Free Trade Agreement (NAFTA) lays out a plan to reshape the rules of trade among the U.S., Canada, and Mexico.

Odd-even pricing setting prices that end in certain numbers.

Oligopoly a special market situation that develops when a market has (1) essentially homogeneous products, (2) relatively few sellers, and (3) fairly inelastic industry demand curves.

One-price policy offering the same price to all customers who purchase products under essentially the same conditions and in the same quantities.

Open to buy a buyer has budgeted funds that he can spend during the current time period.

Operating ratios ratios of items on the operating statement to net sales.

Operating statement a simple summary of the financial results of a company's operations over a specified period of time.

Operational decisions short-run decisions to help implement strategies.

Opinion leader a person who influences others.

Order getters salespeople concerned with establishing relationships with new customers and developing new business.

Order-getting seeking possible buyers with a well-organized sales presentation designed to sell a product, service, or idea.

Order takers salespeople who sell to established customers, complete most transactions, and maintain relationships with their customers.

Order-taking the routine completion of sales made regularly to the target customers.

Packaging   promoting and protecting the product.

Pareto chart   a graph that shows the number of times a problem cause occurs, with problem causes ordered from most frequent to least frequent.

Penetration pricing policy   trying to sell the whole market at one low price.

Perception   how we gather and interpret information from the world around us.

Performance analysis   analysis that looks for exceptions or variations from planned performance.

Performance index   a number that shows the relation of one value to another.

Personal needs   an individual's need for personal satisfaction unrelated to what others think or do.

Personal selling   direct communication between sellers and potential customers, usually in person but sometimes over the telephone.

Phony list prices   misleading prices that customers are shown to suggest that the price they are to pay has been discounted from list.

Physical distribution (PD)   the transporting and storing of goods so as to match target customers' needs with a firm's marketing mix—within individual firms and along a channel of distribution.

Physical distribution (PD) concept   all transporting and storing activities of a business and a channel system should be coordinated as one system—which should seek to minimize the cost of distribution for a given customer service level.

Physiological needs   biological needs such as the need for food, drink, rest, and sex.

Piggyback service   transporting truck trailers or flat-bed trailers carrying containers on railcars to provide both speed and flexibility.

Pioneering advertising   advertising that tries to develop primary demand for a product category rather than demand for a specific brand.

Place   making goods and services available in the right quantities and locations—when customers want them.

Place utility   having the product available *where* the customer wants it.

Planned economic system   government planners decide what and how much is to be produced and distributed by whom, when, to whom, and why.

Planned shopping center   a set of stores planned as a unit to satisfy some market needs.

Pool car service   allows groups of shippers to pool their shipments of like goods into a full railcar.

Population   in marketing research, the total group you are interested in.

Portfolio management   treats alternative products, divisions, or strategic business units (SBUs) as though they are stock investments to be bought and sold using financial criteria.

Positioning   an approach that shows how customers locate proposed and/or present brands in a market.

Possession utility   obtaining a good or service and having the right to use or consume it.

Prepared sales presentation   a memorized presentation that is not adapted to each individual customer.

Prestige pricing   setting a rather high price to suggest high quality or high status.

Price   what is charged for something.

Price discrimination   injuring competition by selling the same products to different buyers at different prices.

Price fixing   competitors illegally getting together to raise, lower, or stabilize prices.

Price leader   a seller who sets a price that all others in the industry follow.

Price lining   setting a few price levels for a product line and then marking all items at these prices.

Primary data   information specifically collected to solve a current problem.

Primary demand   demand for the general product idea, not just the company's own brand.

Private brands   brands created by middlemen—sometimes referred to as dealer brands.

Private warehouses   storing facilities owned or leased by companies for their own use.

Producers' cooperatives   operate almost as full-service wholesalers—with the "profits" going to the cooperative's customer-members.

Product   the need-satisfying offering of a firm.

Product advertising   advertising that tries to sell a specific product.

Product assortment   the set of all product lines and individual products that a firm sells.

Product-bundle pricing   setting one price for a set of products.

Product development   offering new or improved products for present markets.

Product liability   the legal obligation of sellers to pay damages to individuals who are injured by defective or unsafe products.

Product life cycle   the stages a new product idea goes through from beginning to end.

Product line   a set of individual products that are closely related.

Product managers   manage specific products, often taking over the jobs formerly handled by an advertising manager—sometimes called brand managers.

Product-market a market with *very* similar needs—and sellers offering various *close substitute* ways of satisfying those needs.

Production actually *making* goods or *performing* services.

Production capacity the ability to produce a certain quantity and quality of specific goods or services.

Production era a time when a company focuses on production of a few specific products—perhaps because few of these products are available in the market.

Production orientation making whatever products are easy to produce and *then* trying to sell them.

Professional services specialized services that support a firm's operations.

Profit maximization objective an objective to get as much profit as possible.

Promotion communicating information between seller and potential buyer or others in the channel to influence attitudes and behavior.

Prospecting following all the leads in the target market to identify potential customers.

Psychographics the analysis of a person's day-to-day pattern of living as expressed in that person's Activities, Interests, and Opinions—sometimes referred to as AIOs or lifestyle analysis.

Psychological pricing setting prices that have special appeal to target customers.

Public relations communication with noncustomers—including labor, public interest groups, stockholders, and the government.

Public warehouses independent storing facilities.

Publicity any *unpaid* form of nonpersonal presentation of ideas, goods, or services.

Pulling using promotion to get consumers to ask middlemen for the product.

Purchase discount a reduction of the original invoice amount for some business reason.

Purchasing managers buying specialists for their employers.

Pure competition a market situation that develops when a market has (1) homogeneous (similar) products, (2) many buyers and sellers who have full knowledge of the market, and (3) ease of entry for buyers and sellers.

Pure subsistence economy each family unit produces everything it consumes.

Push money (or prize money) allowances allowances (sometimes called PMs or spiffs) given to retailers by manufacturers or wholesalers to pass on to the retailers' salesclerks for aggressively selling certain items.

Pushing using normal promotion effort—personal selling, advertising, and sales promotion—to help sell the whole marketing mix to possible channel members.

Qualifying dimensions the dimensions that are relevant to including a customer type in a product-market.

Qualitative research seeks in-depth, open-ended responses, not yes or no answers.

Quality a product's ability to satisfy a customer's needs or requirements.

Quantitative research seeks structured responses that can be summarized in numbers—like percentages, averages, or other statistics.

Quantity discounts discounts offered to encourage customers to buy in larger amounts.

Quotas the specific quantities of products that can move in or out of a country.

Rack jobbers merchant wholesalers who specialize in nonfood products that are sold through grocery stores and supermarkets—they often display the products on their own wire racks.

Random sampling each member of the research population has the *same* chance of being included in the sample.

Raw materials unprocessed expense items—such as logs, iron ore, wheat, and cotton—that are moved to the next production process with little handling.

Rebates refunds to consumers after a purchase.

Receiver the target of a message in the communication process, usually a potential customer.

Reciprocity trading sales for sales—that is, "if you buy from me, I'll buy from you."

Reference group the people to whom an individual looks when forming attitudes about a particular topic.

Reference price the price a consumer expects to pay.

Regional shopping centers the largest planned shopping centers—they emphasize shopping stores and shopping products.

Regrouping activities adjusting the quantities and/or assortments of products handled at each level in a channel of distribution.

Regularly unsought products products that stay unsought but not unbought forever.

Reinforcement occurs in the learning process when the consumer's response is followed by satisfaction—that is, reduction in the drive.

Reminder advertising advertising to keep the product's name before the public.

Requisition a request to buy something.

Research proposal a plan that specifies what marketing research information will be obtained and how.

Resident buyers independent buying agents who work in central markets for several retailer or wholesaler customers based in outlying areas or other countries.

Response an effort to satisfy a drive.

Response rate the percent of people contacted in a research sample who complete the questionnaire.

Retailing all of the activities involved in the sale of products to final consumers.

Return when a customer sends back purchased products.

Return on assets (ROA) the ratio of net profit (after taxes) to the assets used to make the net profit—multiplied by 100 to get rid of decimals.

Return on investment (ROI) ratio of net profit (after taxes) to the investment used to make the net profit—multiplied by 100 to get rid of decimals.

Reverse channels channels used to retrieve products that customers no longer want.

Risk taking bearing the uncertainties that are part of the marketing process.

Robinson-Patman Act a 1936 law that makes illegal any price discrimination—that is, selling the same products to different buyers at different prices—if it injures competition.

Routinized response behavior when consumers regularly select a particular way of satisfying a need when it occurs.

Rule for maximizing profit the firm should produce that output where marginal cost is just less than or equal to marginal revenue.

Safety needs needs concerned with protection and physical well-being.

Sale price a temporary discount from the list price.

Sales analysis a detailed breakdown of a company's sales records.

Sales decline a stage of the product life cycle when new products replace the old.

Sales era a time when a company emphasizes selling because of increased competition.

Sales forecast an estimate of how much an industry or firm hopes to sell to a market segment.

Sales managers managers concerned with managing personal selling.

Sales-oriented objective an objective to get some level of unit sales, dollar sales, or share of market—without referring to profit.

Sales presentation a salesperson's effort to make a sale or address a customer's problem.

Sales promotion those promotion activities—other than advertising, publicity, and personal selling—that stimulate interest, trial, or purchase by final customers or others in the channel.

Sales promotion managers managers of their company's sales promotion effort.

Sales quota the specific sales or profit objective a salesperson is expected to achieve.

Sales territory a geographic area that is the responsibility of one salesperson or several working together.

Sample a part of the relevant population.

Sampling buying looking at only part of a potential purchase.

Scientific method a decision-making approach that focuses on being objective and orderly in *testing* ideas before accepting them.

Scrambled merchandising retailers carrying any product lines that they think they can sell profitably.

Seasonal discounts discounts offered to encourage buyers to stock earlier than present demand requires.

Secondary data information that has been collected or published already.

Segmenters aim at one or more homogeneous segments and try to develop a different marketing mix for each segment.

Segmenting an aggregating process that clusters people with similar needs into a market segment.

Selective demand demand for a company's own brand rather than a product category.

Selective distribution selling through only those middlemen who will give the product special attention.

Selective exposure our eyes and minds seek out and notice only information that interests us.

Selective perception people screen out or modify ideas, messages, and information that conflict with previously learned attitudes and beliefs.

Selective retention people remember only what they want to remember.

Selling agents agent middlemen who take over the whole marketing job of producers—not just the selling function.

Selling formula approach a sales presentation that starts with a prepared presentation outline—much like the prepared approach—and leads the customer through some logical steps to a final close.

Selling function promoting the product.

Senior citizens people over 65.

Service a deed performed by one party for another.

Service mark those words, symbols, or marks that are legally registered for use by a single company to refer to a service offering.

Service wholesalers merchant wholesalers who provide all the wholesaling functions.

Shopping products products that a customer feels are worth the time and effort to compare with competing products.

Simple trade era a time when families traded or sold their surplus output to local middlemen who resold these goods to other consumers or distant middlemen.

Single-line (or general-line) wholesalers service wholesalers who carry a narrower line of merchandise than general merchandise wholesalers.

Single-line stores stores that specialize in certain lines of related products rather than a wide assortment—sometimes called limited-line stores.

Single target market approach segmenting the market and picking one of the homogeneous segments as the firm's target market.

Situation analysis an informal study of what information is already available in the problem area.

Skimming price policy trying to sell the top of the market—the top of the demand curve—at a high price before aiming at more price-sensitive customers.

Social class a group of people who have approximately equal social position as viewed by others in the society.

Social needs needs concerned with love, friendship, status, and esteem—things that involve a person's interaction with others.

Social responsibility a firm's obligation to improve its positive effects on society and reduce its negative effects.

Sorting separating products into grades and qualities desired by different target markets.

Source the sender of a message.

Specialty products consumer products that the customer really wants and makes a special effort to find.

Specialty shop a type of limited-line store—usually small and with a distinct personality.

Specialty wholesalers service wholesalers who carry a very narrow range of products and offer more information and service than other service wholesalers.

Spreadsheet analysis organizing costs, sales, and other information into a data table to show how changing the value of one or more numbers affects the other numbers.

Standard Industrial Classification (SIC) codes codes used to identify groups of firms in similar lines of business.

Standardization and grading sorting products according to size and quality.

Staples products that are bought often, routinely, and without much thought.

Statistical packages easy-to-use computer programs that analyze data.

Status quo objectives "don't-rock-the-*pricing*-boat" objectives.

Stocking allowances allowances given to middlemen to get shelf space for a product—sometimes called slotting allowances.

Stockturn rate the number of times the average inventory is sold in a year.

Storing the marketing function of holding goods.

Storing function holding goods until customers need them.

Straight rebuy a routine repurchase that may have been made many times before.

Strategic business unit (SBU) an organizational unit (within a larger company) that focuses its efforts on some product-markets and is treated as a separate profit center.

Strategic (management) planning the managerial process of developing and maintaining a match between an organization's resources and its market opportunities.

Substitutes products that offer the buyer a choice.

Supermarket a large store specializing in groceries—with self-service and wide assortments.

Superstore a very large store that tries to carry not only foods, but all goods and services that the consumer purchases *routinely* (also called hypermarket).

Supplies expense items that do not become a part of a finished product.

Supply curve the quantity of products that will be supplied at various possible prices.

Supporting salespeople salespeople who help the order-oriented salespeople—but don't try to get orders themselves.

Target market a fairly homogeneous (similar) group of customers to whom a company wishes to appeal.

Target marketing a marketing mix is tailored to fit some specific target customers.

Target return objective a specific level of profit as an objective.

Target return pricing pricing to cover all costs and achieve a target return.

Tariffs taxes on imported products.

Task method an approach to developing a budget—basing the budget on the job to be done.

Task transfer using telecommunications to move service operations to places where there are pools of skilled workers.

Task utility provided when someone performs a task for someone else—for instance, when a bank handles financial transactions.

Team selling different sales reps working together on a specific account.

Technical specialists supporting salespeople who provide technical assistance to order-oriented salespeople.

Technological base the technical skills and equipment that affect the way an economy's resources are converted to output.

Telemarketing   using the telephone to call on customers or prospects.

Telephone and direct-mail retailing   allows consumers to shop at home—usually placing orders by mail or a toll-free long-distance telephone call and charging the purchase to a credit card.

Time series   historical records of the fluctuations in economic variables.

Time utility   having the product available *when* the customer wants it.

Total cost   the sum of total fixed and total variable costs.

Total cost approach   evaluating each possible PD system and identifying *all* of the costs of each alternative.

Total fixed cost   the sum of those costs that are fixed in total—no matter how much is produced.

Total quality management (TQM)   a management approach in which everyone in the organization is concerned about quality, throughout all of the firm's activities, to better serve customer needs.

Total variable cost   the sum of those changing expenses that are closely related to output—such as expenses for parts, wages, packaging materials, outgoing freight, and sales commissions.

Trade (functional) discount   a list price reduction given to channel members for the job they're going to do.

Trade-in allowance   a price reduction given for used products when similar new products are bought.

Trademark   those words, symbols, or marks that are legally registered for use by a single company.

Trade-off analysis   a research technique (sometimes called conjoint analysis) that helps marketing managers determine how important certain elements of the firm's marketing mix are to target customers.

Traditional channel systems   a channel in which the various channel members make little or no effort to cooperate with each other.

Transporting   the marketing function of moving goods.

Transporting function   the movement of goods from one place to another.

Trend extension   extends past experience to predict the future.

Truck wholesalers   wholesalers who specialize in delivering products that they stock in their own trucks.

2/10, net 30   allows a 2 percent discount off the face value of the invoice if the invoice is paid within 10 days.

Unfair trade practice acts   set a lower limit on prices, especially at the wholesale and retail levels.

Uniform delivered pricing   making an average freight charge to all buyers.

Unit-pricing   placing the price per ounce (or some other standard measure) on or near the product.

Universal functions of marketing   buying, selling, transporting, storing, standardizing and grading, financing, risk taking, and market information.

Universal product code (UPC)   special identifying marks for each product readable by electronic scanners.

Unsought products   products that potential customers don't yet want or know they can buy.

Utility   the power to satisfy human needs.

Validity   the extent to which data measures what it is intended to measure.

Value in use pricing   setting prices that will capture some of what customers will save by substituting the firm's product for the one currently being used.

Value pricing   setting a fair price level for a marketing mix that really gives customers what they need.

Vendor analysis   formal rating of suppliers on all relevant areas of performance.

Vertical integration   acquiring firms at different levels of channel activity.

Vertical marketing systems   channel systems in which the whole channel focuses on the same target market at the end of the channel.

Virtual corporation   the firm is primarily a coordinator—with a good marketing concept—instead of a producer.

Voluntary chains   wholesaler-sponsored groups that work with independent retailers.

Wants   needs that are learned during a person's life.

Warranty   what the seller promises about its product.

Wheeler Lea Amendment   law that controls unfair or deceptive acts in commerce.

Wheel of retailing theory   new types of retailers enter the market as low-status, low-margin, low-price operators and then—if they are successful—evolve into more conventional retailers offering more services—with higher operating costs and higher prices.

Wholesalers   firms whose main function is providing *wholesaling activities*.

Wholesaling   the *activities* of those persons or establishments that sell to retailers and other merchants, and/or to industrial, institutional, and commercial users, but who do not sell in large amounts to final consumers.

Wholly-owned subsidiary   a separate firm owned by a parent company.

Working capital   money a firm needs to pay for short-term expenses.

Zone pricing   making an average freight charge to all buyers within specific geographic areas.

Greenland

Iceland

United States

Canada

St. Pierre and Miquelon

United States

Bermuda

United States

Mexico

Cayman Islands

The Bahamas

Cuba

Turks and Caicos Islands

Dominican Republic

Jamaica

Belize

Haiti

Aruba

See Inset A

Guatemala

El Salvador

Honduras

Nicaragua

Costa Rica

Panama

Netherlands Antilles

Venezuela

Guyana

Suriname

French Guiana

Colombia

Ecuador

Kiribati

Peru

Brazil

Cook Islands

Western Samoa

American Samoa

French Polynesia

Bolivia

Paraguay

Tonga

Argentina

Uruguay

Chile

Inset A

British Virgin Islands

Puerto Rico

Anguilla

Virgin Islands

St. Kitts and Nevis

Antigua and Barbuda

Montserrat

Guadeloupe

Dominica

Martinique

Saint Lucia

Barbados

Saint Vincent and the Grenadines

Grenada

Venezuela

Trinidad and Tobago

| | under 2.0 | | 2.0 to 9.9 |